ABNORMAL CHILD PSYCHOLOGY

ABNORMAL CHILD PSYCHOLOGY

A Developmental Perspective

LINDA WILMSHURST

Routledge
Taylor & Francis Group
New York   London

Routledge
Taylor & Francis Group
270 Madison Avenue
New York, NY 10016

Routledge
Taylor & Francis Group
2 Park Square
Milton Park, Abingdon
Oxon OX14 4RN

Printed in the United States of America on acid-free paper
10 9 8 7 6 5 4 3 2 1

International Standard Book Number-13: 978-0-415-95363-4 (0)

Library of Congress Cataloging-in-Publication Data

Wilmshurst, Linda.
   Abnormal child psychology : a developmental perspective / Linda Wilmshurst.
      p. cm.
   Includes bibliographical references and index.
   ISBN 978-0-415-95363-4 (hardbound : alk. paper)
   1. Child psychopathology. I. Title.

RJ499.W459 2008
618.92'89--dc22   2007048333

Visit the Taylor & Francis Web site at
http://www.taylorandfrancis.com

and the Routledge Web site at
http://www.routledge.com

Contents

List of Figures

List of Tables

Preface

How to Use the Book: Format for Optimum Learning

The book has several features which can help in understanding, remembering, and applying the key concepts presented.

Overall Themes and Learning Objectives

The book is organized around *five recurrent themes* which provide the foundation for understanding abnormal child psychology from a developmental perspective:

1. Normal development typically follows an orderly and predictable path,
2. Maladaptive behaviors represent deviations from the normal path,
3. Maladaptive behavior is represented by a continuum of severity,
4. Individual, interpersonal, contextual, and cultural factors influence deviations in development, and
5. Mental health practitioners can draw on a multiplicity of theoretical perspectives to assist in understanding maladaptive behaviors.

The five themes are consistently applied to each chapter on childhood disorders and provide an organizational framework for approaching variations in child behaviors over the course of development. As a result, learning is facilitated in a format that is predictable, consistent, and meaningful. Learning how the five themes apply to different disorders provides a framework for learning built on analysis, synthesis, and integration of information from three essential bodies of knowledge. Within this context, the overall learning objective is to increase students' appreciation of the complex nature of child and adolescent behaviors, and to emphasize the need to integrate information from three essential sources. The *K–3 Paradigm* is a helpful heuristic (learning tool) for reinforcing the three cornerstones of information that are required to understand the nature of maladaptive behavior:

1. Knowledge of developmental expectations,
2. Knowledge of sources of influence (child characteristics and environmental characteristics), and
3. Knowledge of theoretical models and perspectives.

Pedagological Features

Chapter Outlines and Previews. Each chapter is introduced by a *Chapter Preview* which provides an overview of the material to be covered, the rationale for inclusion, and essential highlights. The outlines provide the organizational format and the previews set the stage for assimilating the information to be presented.

Call Out Boxes. Another important learning tool is the use of *call out boxes.* These boxes are inserted throughout the chapters and draw attention to information for several reasons. Recurrent call out boxes are specifically designed to reinforce key concepts (*Important Distinction, or Consider This*). Other boxes are designed to flag information for later recall (*Memory Bank*), highlight research findings (*Science Talks*), and reinforce information previously addressed (*Recall and Rewind*). Where applicable, call out boxes also address the developmental nature of disorders that may set them apart from adult variations (*Development in Focus*). Other call out boxes have unique headings designed to capture the main idea or create increased interest.

Case Studies. The use of *case studies* (*Case in Point*) is a strategic effort to bring the concepts to life in several important ways. Embodied within the case scenarios, readers will obtain vivid images depicting a variety of symptom presentations for the different disorders discussed. The multiple case studies located at the beginning of each chapter are an essential tool for introducing the disorder on several levels. In these introductory scenarios, characters illustrate how disorders appear at different stages of development, different levels of severity of symptoms and how symptoms may be expressed within different environmental contexts.

Use of Tables and Figures. Integrating information across different sources and perspectives can be a very difficult task, especially for students new to the field of abnormal child psychology. Therefore, whenever possible, complex comparisons are made in tabular form. Information can be available "at a glance" through the use of numerous tables and figures developed to illustrate complex information in graphic form.

Fonts, Highlights, and Glossary of New Terms. The use of bold face and italic font styles are also an important feature to set the text apart and reinforce the learning process. Key concepts are emphasized through the use of bold faced and italicized fonts. Each **new term** introduced is displayed in a consistent font and subsequently included in the *Glossary of New Terms* at the end of the chapter. New terms are added to the Glossary in the order that they appear in the chapter to facilitate recall for terms that were clustered together in the main text.

Summary Review. A synopsis of the main ideas and themes follows the presentation of the main chapter text. Students will have an opportunity to review what they have read in capsular form to provide an overview of the information and a glimpse of the bigger picture.

Components That Challenge Critical Thinking, Increase Self Monitoring, and Improve Student Evaluations. Thought provoking questions (*Consolidate and Communicate*) have been developed to challenge students to process information at a deeper level and to relate the new material to previously learned information. Many of these questions can provide excellent material for class room discussions, home work assignments, or projects for extra credit. In addition, a set of *Multiple Choice Review Questions and Answers* provides an opportunity for students to test their comprehension and recall of important details presented in the chapter and can help students prepare for classroom tests and quizzes.

Important Resources for Instructors

An *Instructor's Manual* is available as a resource to instructors to assist in course development and organization. The manual contains an overview of topics covered in each chapter, suggestions for class demonstrations and activities, and discussion topics to enhance critical thinking. In addition, each chapter contains a list of relevant Internet sites, movies, and media references that can be integrated into the classroom experience to engage students in the learning process and provide a catalyst for discussion, group work, and individual assignments.

A comprehensive set of *PowerPoint Presentation Slides* has been developed to closely follow each chapter, outlining relevant themes, highlighting key points and introducing new terms found in the Glossary. Copies of charts, tables, and figures found in the text are also provided as needed.

Important Information for Students

The author has drawn upon her experience of teaching courses in Abnormal Child Psychology from a developmental perspective to provide answers to questions that students often generate about issues, trends, and controversies. Many of these questions and answers appear in the *call out boxes* that draw attention to *important distinctions* between concepts and probe areas for critical thinking (*Consider This*).

Material in the text is presented in a way that conforms to an important and proven approach to enhancing learning effectiveness and recall for textbook information, the **SQ3R Method** (Martin, 1985; Robinson, 1961). The SQ3R method is named for the five steps involved in the learning process: *survey, question, read, recite, and review.* Each chapter begins with a *survey* preview designed to help organize how the information will be received or encoded. Next, headings provide higher order organizers that can be turned into a *question* by the reader. Students who *read* the material trying to answer the question they have formulated will have a deeper understanding of the content. Recall is also enhanced when students *recite* what they have read prior to going on to the next section. *Recall and Rewind* call out boxes provide opportunities to recite and consolidate information. Finally, the chapter closes with a survey *review* intended to enhance the integration and retention of information in the chapter.

Overview of the Book: How the Book Is Organized

The book is divided into two major sections:

Part 1: The Foundations of Abnormal Child Psychology: A Developmental Perspective;
Part 2: Emotional, Behavioral, and Learning Difficulties in Children and Youth: Their Nature and Their Course.

The major goal of Part 1 is to introduce readers to the study of abnormal child psychology from a developmental perspective, as a unique field of study, with its own history and issues. This introductory section contains five chapters, each of which presents information concerning the historical background, conceptual development, current trends, and contemporary issues in the field of abnormal child psychology. The five chapters in Part 1 include, the following.

In *Chapter 1* historical information about the origins of *clinical child psychology* is discussed, along with roadblocks that delayed recognition of clinical child psychology as a unique field of study. Important roadblocks included the initial denial that children could have "emotional problems," only to be followed by an equally fallacious mindset that children are miniature adults and, as such, had the same disorders requiring the same treatment as adults. In this chapter, five consistent themes are introduced that will be addressed throughout the book. These themes are the cornerstone of understanding child psychopathology. The *first three themes* relate to:

- understanding normal development as predictable and orderly;
- recognition of maladaptive behavior as a deviation from the normal pathway; and
- understanding the continuum of maladaptive behavior ranging from mild developmental deviations to more severe disturbance (mild, moderate, severe).

The *fourth theme* speaks to the contextual influences that shape development for better or worse:

- interactions between child characteristics (temperament, genetics) and environmental characteristics (family, peers, school, community, culture) that influence, predispose, precipitate, and maintain the maladaptive behaviors.

Ultimately, the *fifth theme* addresses:

- theoretical models that assist clinicians to interpret and understand maladaptive behavior from a number of different perspectives.

The focus of *Chapter 2* is on several issues pertinent to clinical decision making regarding children and youth. Some of the topics discussed include distinguishing normal from abnormal behavior and the differences between adult and child psychopathology. Six theoretical models are introduced and discussed as they apply to understanding child psychopathology, including: biological, behavioral, cognitive, psychodynamic, attachment and parenting (family systems), and sociocultural models.

Each model is built on a different set of assumptions about human behavior. Relevant theoretical models will be revisited in chapters 6 through 15, as they pertain to unique perspectives in understanding the various disorders discussed.

Chapter 3 provides an in-depth discussion of the many risks and protective factors that can shape the course of development. The chapter follows Bronfenbrenner's ecological model, which is discussed within a transactional framework (on-going and reciprocal influences). Following a general discussion of risks and protective factors, the chapter focuses on the unique challenges facing children and adolescents from ethnic minority populations (African American, Latinio/Hispanic Americans, Asian American/Pacific Islanders, and American Indian). Cultural competence in the assessment and treatment of minority youth is also addressed.

In *Chapter 4,* the focus is on the unique ethical challenges that children and adolescents pose for professionals in their research and practice (assessment, treatment, and issues of confidentiality). A comparative look at different ethical codes (American Counseling Association, ACA; American Psychological Association, APA; American School Counselors Association, ASCA; and National Association of School Psychologists, NASP) provides a broad overview of the many ethical similarities recognized among these disciplines. This chapter contains information regarding research methods and designs that are particularly well-suited to a developmental psychopathology focus (epidemiological research, longitudinal, cross sectional, and accelerated longitudinal designs) and provides on-going, cumulative, and case-based information to assist in the development of critical thinking skills.

In *Chapter 5,* issues in diagnosis, assessment, and treatment are discussed. Controversial issues include:

- the use of the dimensional versus categorical classification systems with children and youth,

- the reliability of various informants in rating children's problems,
- the complex nature of comorbidity among childhood disorders, and
- the need for increased attention to treatments that are empirically supported.

Part 2: Emotional, Behavioral, and Learning Difficulties in Children and Youth: Their Nature and Their Course

Part 2 presents the most prevalent problems of behavioral, emotional, and learning difficulties facing children and youth today. Problem areas have been grouped to emphasize comorbid features, while at the same time, provide the necessary proximity to highlight differential diagnosis. The focus is on presenting the most relevant and empirically based evidence available concerning disorders that practitioners are most likely to encounter in their work with children and adolescents, on a daily basis. As a result, these chapters provide a more in-depth and comprehensive coverage of commonly occurring abnormal child behaviors than can be found in other texts that sample a wider variety of problems.

Each chapter begins with a multiple case illustration designed to introduce the problem of focus in a way that will enhance understanding on various levels, including the:

- range in severity of the problem (normal behavior, mild developmental variation, moderate and severe manifestations),
- developmental presentations (how the behavior may appear at different developmental ages and in different contexts), and
- how behaviors relate to each of the five themes (as outlined in the beginning of this chapter).

Within this context, the most severe level will be discussed relative to *DSM-IV-TR* (APA, 2000) criteria. Each chapter is presented in a predictable format that provides information about each disorder as it relates to:

- description and associated features,
- developmental issues and trends,
- prevalence,
- etiology (sociocultural model: risk factors and protective factors),
- etiology from various theoretical models (biology, psychodynamic behavioral, attachment and parenting, cognitive),
- assessment (a review of the most reliable assessment instruments available),
- treatment/intervention and prevention (empirically supported treatments), and
- treatment from various perspectives (biology, behavioral, parenting and family, cognitive).

In addition, where applicable, information concerning relevant historical trends in conceptualizing the disorder (e.g., learning disabilities, ADHD) and any other pertinent issues and controversies are also addressed.

Discussions of child disorders include references to both the clinical and educational systems of classification to provide students with an excellent grasp of the similarities and differences between systems in preparation for future work with children in a wide variety of clinical and /or school settings.

IA: Internalizing Problems. As an introduction to the next three chapters, internalizing disorders are discussed from a historical perspective that addresses the concept of negative affectivity and the similarities among problems that share internalizing features. Characteristically, internalizing behaviors are "overcontrolled" behaviors that are often covert and difficult to assess. Depression and anxiety are the two most common internalizing disorders experienced by children and youth. Difficulties inherent in diagnosing somotoform disorders in children are addressed in the introductory passage on internalizing problems. Due to the high prevalence of anxiety problems experienced by children, two chapters have been devoted to a discussion of anxiety in children and youth. The chapter on depression, bipolar disorders, and suicide provides a wealth of information and some of the most recent findings available today.

In *Chapter 6,* anxiety problems and disorders that most likely have onset in early childhood are discussed. These anxious behaviors range from normal worries to fears and phobias, and from general problems (generalized anxiety disorder) to specific concerns (separation anxiety disorder). Early onset anxieties include: fears and phobias, separation anxiety, and generalized anxiety disorder.

In *Chapter 7,* later onset anxiety disorders are discussed, including obsessive compulsive disorder, social phobia, and panic disorder. The chapter also presents contemporary research and trends in the evaluation of post traumatic stress disorder (PTSD) related to child and adolescent trauma and current controversies regarding the appropriateness of *DSM* criteria for diagnosing PTSD in children.

Chapter 8 begins with a historical look at depression and how it was once thought that children were incapable of being depressed. Other topics in this chapter include the nature of symptoms of depression across the developmental spectrum, symptom presentation relative to symptoms manifest by adult populations, major depression and suicide risk, and how to distinguish bipolar disorder from attention deficit disorder. A significant portion of this chapter delves into the controversy and multitude of methods and subtyping that are currently employed to measure, describe, and conceptualize the disorders in children and youth.

IB: Externalizing Problems. Externalizing behaviors, or "undercontrolled" behaviors, are characteristically overt, disturbing to others, and more readily observable than internalizing disorders. The introductory section provides an overview of the various methods that can be used to classify externalizing behaviors (dimensional classification), disruptive behavior disorders (*DSM* categorical system), and emotional disturbance (Educational Classification System, IDEA, 2004). In addition, this section also highlights the many different types of behaviors that have been included in rating scales designed to measure externalizing behaviors in children and youth.

In *Chapter 9,* a developmental perspective of aggression will serve as introduction to an increasing array of aggressive behaviors: problems of conduct, oppositional defiant disorder (ODD), and conduct disorder (CD). Controversy regarding whether ODD and CD are variants (degrees of severity) of the same disorder is addressed, as are topics concerning gender differences in aggressive response.

II: Problems of Attention and Learning. The introductory passage provides the rationale for the clustering of these problems within close proximity and the need to increase awareness of the non-disruptive variant of attention deficit disorder.

Chapter 10 begins with a historical view of how our understanding of attention deficit hyperactive disorder has evolved, conceptually, over the course of time. The remainder of the chapter focuses on a range of contemporary issues and controversies regarding ADHD and its variants.

In *Chapter 11*, the different types of specific learning disabilities are discussed, as well as the recent changes in IDEA 2004 that introduced the option of utilizing *response to intervention* (RTI) as a method of identifying children for educational purposes. Recent biological and cognitive research in areas of nonverbal learning disabilities, developmental dyslexia, and math disability are also discussed.

III: Problems With Onset in Late Childhood or Adolescence. Section III begins with a discussion regarding the impact of the transition to adolescence and how the role of peers and family environment influence changes at this time.

Chapter 12 addresses distinctions between disordered eating and eating disorders. Results of national surveys concerning unhealthy dieting and body dissatisfaction among youth are discussed in relation to age, gender, and ethnic variations. The major eating/feeding disorders with onset in early childhood are discussed, as are the two major forms of eating disorders: anorexia nervosa and bulimia nervosa. The roles of family dynamics and peer influence on high-risk behaviors are also addressed.

In *Chapter 13,* substance related disorders are discussed using data from national surveys that have tracked usage rates for youth from grades 8 through 12, for substances such as: tobacco, alcohol, marijuana, and recent increases in the use of prescription-type drugs, such as Oxycontin. Controversy regarding the *gateway phenomenon* (starter drugs that lead to more serious drug usage) will be addressed. Sections on substance use and substance abuse include information concerning *DSM-IV-TR* criteria and particular challenges posed by youth in the area of treatment.

IV: Intellectual and Developmental Disabilities and Pervasive Developmental Disorders. The rationale for including these topics within close proximity and recent debates surrounding this issue are addressed in the introductory comments.

Chapter 14 is concerned with intellectual and developmental disabilities (mental retardation) and the issues and diagnostic implications based on different systems of classification, such as: *DSM* (2000); the American Association on Intellectual and Developmental Disabilities (AAIDD, 2007) [formerly (American Association of Mental Retardation, AAMR]; and Educational Classification System (IDEA, 2004).

In *Chapter 15*, pervasive developmental disorders are discussed from the less well known (Rett's disorder and child disintegration disorder) to the most controversial: autistic spectrum disorders (autism and Asperger's disorder).

1

The Foundations of Abnormal Child Psychology
A Developmental Perspective

Understanding abnormal child behavior from a developmental perspective requires an appreciation of the science of child psychopathology as it exists today and a recognition of how the discipline has evolved over time. In some ways, it is ironic that developmental psychopathology will always be considered one of the youngest disciplines relative to other psychological fields of study, with its birth dating back only some thirty years ago (1984). Yet in many ways, the science is also blessed with the intensity and energy of youth that has resulted in an explosion of research and theory in the area unsurpassed by many of the most mature of disciplines.

It is the author's firm belief that without an appreciation of the evolutionary nature of progress in the field, and the contexts of development, one cannot hope to understand the complex nature of developmental psychopathology. With this goal in mind, rather than rushing on to the problems themselves, this text, probably more than any other, begins by focusing on the essential core upon which the discipline has been built. Within the spirit of a truly developmental perspective, the study of child psychopathology unfolds from its past to the present and with an eye to the future.

In this part, important concepts will be introduced that will be re-addressed and reinforced throughout the text. Laying the foundation for future discussions, the foundations prepare readers with vital information integrating sources from *history, theory, risk and resilience, cultural diversity, ethical issues, research methods, and issues in diagnosis, assessment, and treatment*. Once students have an appreciation for the breadth and depth of the discipline, they will be able to approach developmental problems with a more focused and intense understanding.

1

Abnormal Child Psychology

Past, Present, and Future

Chapter 1 At-A-Glance

A Brief History of the Origins of Clinical Child Psychology
   Child Advocacy and Clinical Child Psychology: Four Historical Phases
      Recognition of Childhood as a Distinct Period of Development
      Industrialization and the Social Reform Movements (Early 20th Century)
      Building Structures in Support of Social Reform
      Regression in Social Welfare (the 1970s Onward)
   Child Psychopathology as a Unique Discipline: Barriers and Roadblocks
      Nature/Nurture Debate
      The Disease Model of Pathology
      The Shift in Emphasis From Treatment to Identification
      Adult Versus Child Perspective
   Clinical Child Psychology: Focus on Development
      Developmental Psychopathology: The Merging of Two Disciplines
      The Increasing Role of Developmental Contexts
      Trends in Conceptualizing Developmental Change and Maladaptive Influences
      Contemporary Viewpoints Regarding Developmental Change
   Understanding Maladaptive Behaviors From a Developmental Perspective
      Looking Ahead: Applying a Developmental Framework to Understanding
        Aggressive Behaviors
   Five Recurrent Themes
   Introducing the K–3 Paradigm

CHAPTER PREVIEW

This chapter will provide an introduction to abnormal child psychology and will focus on relevant information in the following areas:

1. A Brief History of the Origins of Clinical Child Psychology

The development of abnormal child psychology as a unique area of study has not been without growing pains. The developmental pathway was ridden with roadblocks that delayed recognition of abnormal child psychology, or clinical child psychology, as a unique field of study. Initially, there was a denial that children could have "emotional problems"; later on progress was derailed by the equally fallacious mindset that children were miniature adults and, as such, had "adult" disorders requiring the same "adult" treatment. A look at how our understanding has evolved over time will provide a deeper appreciation of some of the more contemporary issues and concerns.

2. Understanding Maladaptive Behavior: Five Recurrent Themes

The five themes emphasize the importance of conceptualizing maladaptive behavior as an offshoot of normal development and provide the foundation of understanding abnormal behavior from a developmental perspective:

1. Normal development typically follows a predictable and orderly path,
2. Maladaptive behaviors veer off the normal path,
3. Maladaptive behavior is represented by a continuum of severity based on the degree to which behaviors deviate from the normal path,
4. Individual, interpersonal, contextual, and cultural factors influence deviations in development, and
5. There are a number of theoretical models that can serve as a framework to assist in understanding how the behavior developed (precipitating factors) and how it is maintained (maintaining factors).

3. The K–3 Paradigm

Ultimately, the five themes converge in the *K–3 Paradigm*, a heuristic (learning) tool that emphasizes three pivotal areas of knowledge fundamental to understanding abnormal child behavior from a developmental perspective:

1. Knowledge concerning normal development and developmental expectations;
2. Knowledge of the sources of influence (child characteristics and environmental characteristics); and
3. Knowledge of theoretical models.

A Brief History of the Origins of Clinical Child Psychology

There are several important milestones evident in the development and recognition of clinical child psychology as a unique field of study. One such milestone was the founding of the *Journal of Clinical Child Psychology* (JCCP) in 1972 by Gertrude J. Williams, who was the initial editor. Williams had previously been associated with the Child Guidance Clinic at Washington University in St. Louis. Over the course of the next 18 years, JCCP evolved from being a forum for "reflective comments" by concerned child advocates to a peer-reviewed journal that focused on publishing "research, reviews, articles on child advocacy, as well as on training and on professional practice in clinical child psychology" (Routh, Patton, & Sanfilippo, 1991, p. 3). In their review of articles published by JCCP between 1972 and 1989, Routh et al. (1991) noted that the percentage of research articles published increased to over 90% relative to articles devoted to advocacy issues which fell to less than 2%. The authors suggest that these changes likely reflect the increased recognition and emphasis on clinical child psychology courses being offered in undergraduate and graduate psychology programs in major universities across the United States, resulting in prolific academic-research initiatives in the area of clinical child psychology.

Child Advocacy and Clinical Child Psychology: Four Historical Phases

In her review of the historical roots of the child advocacy movement, Culbertson (1991) traces the changing conceptualizations of childhood through four historical phases that parallel changes in underlying economic conditions, social beliefs, and the prevailing political climate. The four phases include recognition of childhood as a specific period of development, the impact of increased industrialization and social reform, formal organizations established to support social reform, and a period of regression that began in the 1970s resulting from children living in dire economic conditions. It is Culbertson's belief that this changing perspective on childhood parallels similar changes evident in the fields of developmental and clinical child psychology. Research in areas of child development and clinical child psychology contributed significantly to the growing body of knowledge about the nature of children's emotional and cognitive capacities and served to inform those involved in the social reform movement and shape the nature of their involvement.

1. Recognition of Childhood as a Distinct Period of Development

In Europe, prior to the 15th century, children as young as 5 and 6 years of age were considered to be miniature adults (Culbertson, 1991). Beginning with the Renaissance, educators and scholars of the 15th century began to view the role of children as being different from adults, although this was primarily reserved for children from the upper classes, since poorer families relied on children to occupy the work force. The nature of childhood and the role of parenting went through several transitions, from an emphasis on the responsibility of parents to educate and fill their child's mental slate with knowledge (17th-century English philosopher John Locke) to a belief that childhood was a period of innocence that should be left alone to unfold naturally (18th-century French philosopher Jacques Rousseau).

In the United States, at the end of the 18th century, children as young as 5 and 6 years of age could still be found working alongside their parents as part of the family economy (farms, shops), as apprentices, or if orphaned, following their master's orders. It wasn't until the 19th century that values and beliefs about individual rights ushered in an era of sentimentality towards childhood, as slavery fell out of favor and humanitarian sensibilities increased. However, even at this time, youth 12 to 18 years of age were not considered as part of childhood. By the mid-19th century, Americans began to follow parenting practices suggested some 2 centuries earlier by John Locke as they assumed greater responsibility for instructing and socializing their children. By the late 19th century, there was a paradigm shift from

> seeing the child as primitive and unredeemed (the early American Calvinist child), to the child as innocent and cherubic expression of God's kingdom (the Victorian child). The innocent child had emerged earlier, in the 18th century, but had fewer immediate social and legislative consequences. It was the change in the values to which children contributed from the economic realm to the emotional realm that made the great difference in the late 19th century. (Fass, 2003, p. 966)

2. Industrialization and the Social Reform Movements (Early 20th Century)

With the advent of increased industrialization, the need to rely on children as a primary source of labor was reduced. At the same time, humanitarian concerns about children in the workforce were gaining increased momentum with the formation of such organizations as the National Child Labor Committee in 1904. With a focus on children's rights and improved access to health care and education, child protection and compulsory education became a reality and ushered in the creation of institutions (hospitals, schools, and clinics) for the provision of child services (Culbertson, 1991).

The shift in focus from child labor to child rights, beliefs in child innocence, and vulnerability resulted in an increased emphasis on adult responsibility in areas of education, shelter, and protection. With a view to the child as the promise for a better future, the discipline of psychology began to take on a prominent role in examining emotional and cognitive child development. Mandates for compulsory education for children who previously had very little exposure to formal learning was a cause for concern and resulted in a new wave of interest that focused on the challenge of teaching children who experienced significant difficulties in learning. In the West, many new immigrant families were faced with adjusting to the economic loss resulting from abolishing child labor, mandatory education, and increased focus on the importance of play on child development and learning (Fass, 2003).

At this time, an American psychologist, Lightner Witmer, returned to the United States having recently received his PhD from the University of Leipzig. Witmer immediately set out to address the learning problems experienced by many of the children by establishing the first psychology clinic to treat children with learning disabilities.

Auspicious Beginnings

Witmer established the first child psychology clinic in 1896 and immediately began to expand the clinic's horizons the following year by offering a summer institute in child psychology. Within the next 10 years, more than 450 children were seen at the clinic.

In 1907, Witmer established a residential school for children who were mentally retarded and launched the first psychological journal, *The Psychological Clinic*. Witmer's methods involved individual diagnostic assessment, followed by prescriptions for remedial tutoring. However, despite his popularity with the public schools, Witmer lost the support of his colleagues because he refused to join the widely popular movement to adopt Terman's revision of the Stanford-Binet tests of intelligence. In addition, Witmer did not subscribe to Sigmund Freud's theories on behavior disorders, further setting him apart from the majority in the field. The following year (1908), Henry Goddard opened the first clinical internship training program at the Vineland Training Program for individuals with mental retardation.

Goddard and Martin Kallikak

Although Henry Goddard was the founding father of the Vineland Training Program for the mentally retarded, his firm beliefs in genetic versus environmental "influence" and negative attitudes about mental retardation did more harm than good. In his fictional portrayal of Martin Kallikak, Goddard traced the lives of Martin's offspring from unions with two very different women. While his union with a barmaid produced children who were characterized as being feeble-minded, prone to alcoholism, and in trouble with the law, his offspring from the union with a "good girl" all became upstanding citizens.

In 1909, G. Stanley Hall, president of the newly formed American Psychological Association (APA), arranged for Freud to lecture at Clark University in Massachusetts. William Healey, an English-born psychiatrist, shared America's enthusiasm for Freud's theories, something which set him even further apart from Witmer, whose popularity continued to wane (Nietzel, Bernstein, & Milich, 1994). In that same year, Healey opened the first *child guidance clinic* in Chicago, called the Juvenile Psychopathic Institute. Freud's theories influenced the tone for this clinic, which was established to prevent and treat child mental illness. In only 8 years time, child clinics had more than quadrupled (from 9 to 42) and could be found in a variety of settings including juvenile institutions, courts, hospitals, schools, and universities. Horn (1984) describes the typical child guidance clinic, at this time, as offering a multidisciplinary team approach (psychiatrist, psychologist, and social worker) to the study and treatment of the "maladjusted child."

Read All About It

An editorial written in the *New York Times* (1926) heralded the arrival of the child guidance clinics at a time when "modern life" had tended to "weaken parental authority and destroy the influence of the home."

Horn also suggests that during this time, there was a shift in focus from emphasizing delinquency as a prime concern to concentrating on the causes of deviant behaviors emanating from problems at school or at home. Child guidance clinics commonly dealt with one of three categories of problems: *socially unacceptable behavior* (e.g., tantrums, lying, fighting), *personality reactions* (e.g., reclusiveness, nervousness), and *problems of habit formation* (e.g., eating and sleeping difficulties). Clinic treatment involved a "three step process of study, diagnosis and therapy" and either used direct treatment or "manipulation" of the environment (according to Horn, 1984). The underlying philosophy of the time was that the source of children's problems could be found in the parents and the family (Horn, p. 27).

3. Building Structures in Support of Social Reform
In 1948, 54 child guidance clinics came together to form the American Association of Psychiatric Clinics for Children (AAPCC). A paradigm shift also occurred during this time, as the role of the child guidance clinic changed from the identification of problem children to training and treatment; a movement that sparked debate over standards, professional roles, and status among proponents of psychiatry, psychology, and social work (Horn, 1989). A similar shift was noted in the child advocacy movement, as the United Nations Declaration on the Rights of the Child (1959) and the White House Conference on Children and Youth (1960) placed emphasis on the underlying infrastructure necessary to support the movement.

Between the early 1950s and late 1970s, increased emphasis was being placed on grounding advocacy issues within the context of "sound child development knowledge" (Joint Commission on Mental Health of Children, 1970, p. 9). The contribution of research efforts in clinical child psychology in establishing the conceptual bases of child advocacy issues had clearly been recognized.

4. Regression in Social Welfare (the 1970s Onward)
It has been suggested that the 1970s ushered in a forth wave in the evolution of child advocacy (Shore, 1987), a regression caused by the increasing rate of children living in poverty in the United States. The issue of child poverty and its relationship to child risk factors will be discussed at length in chapter 3.

Child Psychopathology as a Unique Discipline: Barriers and Roadblocks

Despite increased recognition of the importance of clinics designed to assist children, and the growing popularity of child guidance clinics early in the 20th century, the field of clinical child psychology, or child psychopathology, encountered many difficulties that delayed consideration of child psychopathology as a unique discipline. Child psychopathology was not conceptualized as a unique discipline until the 1970s due to four important obstacles:

1. The nature/nurture debate,
2. The introduction of the disease model of pathology,
3. The shift in emphasis from treatment to identification (the testing movement), and
4. The conceptualization of child problems as similar to adult problems.

1. Nature/Nurture Debate

The *nature-nurture* debate stalled the progress in considering child psychopathology as a unique discipline because energy was diverted into endless arguments and debates concerning whether genetic or environmental influences were primary on child development, adaptation, and change; an argument which had no apparent resolution. The debate had its onset in the 17th century when John Locke, an English philosopher, championed the environmental side of the debate by arguing for the importance of parental nurturing in child rearing. According to Locke, young children begin as a blank slate (*tabula rasa*), and the role of the parent is to become actively engaged in filling the slate by nurturing development. In the 18th century, the French philosopher Jean-Jacques Rousseau openly opposed Locke's environmental stance by arguing that the young child was like a flower that would unfold over time, without interference. Rousseau saw the parent's role as passive and argued for a laissez-faire attitude, suggesting that parents were best to leave the child alone and let nature take its course.

Is It Genetics or Environment? Enquiring Minds Want to Know:

Although most psychologists today appreciate the interaction between genes and the environment, the debate is by no means conclusive.

More recent studies suggest that the picture is far more complex than initially thought. Researchers are finding evidence that the impact of environment and heredity on certain traits changes with age. Furthermore, our own genetic predispositions may not only influence how we respond to the environment, but predict how others respond to us and influence the experiences we choose (Azar, 1997).

---

2. The Disease Model of Pathology

The 20th century ushered in two opposing perspectives on abnormal functioning: the **somatogenic perspective** (abnormality results from physical causes) and the **psychogenic perspective** (illness due to mental or psychological causes). Although the somatogenic perspective dates as far back as Hippocrates' beliefs in the four humors, a renewed interest in linking abnormal functioning to physical or biological causes resulted when Kraepelin (1856–1926) published *Compendium der Psychiatrie* in 1883 wherein he argued that physical ailments, such as fatigue, can cause mental dysfunction. Later, Kraepelin devised a diagnostic system that identified a number of syndromes and linked the symptoms to their physical cause (Kihlstrom, 2002).

At the end of the 18th century, Clifford Beers, a rising businessman and graduate of Yale University, attempted suicide due to his despair and fear of suffering a mental collapse. He chronicled the course of his mental illness in his autobiography, *A Mind that Found Itself* (1908). His recovery became walking proof of the ability to "cure" mental illness; however, his testimony also exposed the abusive conditions existing in psychiatric hospitals at the time. In 1909, Beers established the National Committee for Mental Hygiene in an effort to enlighten society about the disease of mental illness and rally support for treatment and prevention (Levine & Levine, 1992). At this time, a German neurologist, Richard von Krafft-Ebing (1840–1902) discovered that syphilis caused general paresis, a disorder that produced both physical (paralysis) and mental (delusions of grandeur) problems. The rise of the somatogenic perspective or the disease model of mental illness brought with it the hope of a "cure," but it also ushered in stigma and fear of potentially "catching" (transmitted from a carrier) or inheriting the illness. For the next half century, the unfortunate consequence was that out of fear and misunderstanding, many individuals with mental disorders were institutionalized; overcrowding often leading to deplorable conditions.

3. The Shift in Emphasis From Treatment to Identification

During the early part of the 20th century, with the advent of IQ testing, many individuals were diagnosed with mental retardation and placed in residential training schools with the intent of curing their mental retardation. Although there had been growing concern with conditions in institutions that housed the mentally ill, it wasn't until the mid-1960s that attention turned towards the increasing numbers of individuals being identified and placed in state hospitals and training schools for the mentally retarded. At this time, Burton Blatt, a university professor from Boston University, and Fred Kaplan (a friend and photographer), released their exposé of the deplorable conditions they uncovered when they visited four large state schools in northeastern United States (Taylor, 2006).

A Picture Is Worth a Thousand Words

Blatt and Kaplan (1966) published their photographic essay of the deplorable conditions that existed in the back wards of state institutions for the mentally retarded. Their book, *Christmas in Purgatory: A Photographic Essay on Mental Retardation*, revealed graphic illustrations of the overcrowded conditions of the residents, many of whom were either naked or scantily clad. The following year, a version of the story "The tragedy and hope of retarded children," describing conditions of these "human warehouses," was published in *Look Magazine* (Blatt & Mangel, 1967).

The failure of the training schools to "cure" mental retardation resulted in conditions of overcrowding, such as those exposed by Blatt. Widespread trends towards deinstitutionalization also were formative in trends to move students back into their own communities when special education classes were initiated in 1975 with the passing of Public Law 94-142, then called the Education of All Handicapped Children Act (EHA) (Wilmshurst & Brue, 2005). As a result, training schools, initially erected as primarily educational institutions shifted their role to that of custodial living centers for the severely mentally retarded (Biasini, Grupe, Huffman, & Braye, 1999).

Past Roadblocks and Ghosts Revisited

Overcrowding in residential training centers resulted from an emphasis on identification and placement spawned largely from the intelligence-testing movement. However, with the advent of special education, emphasis on the use of intelligence tests for identification and placement became even more pronounced as countless numbers of children were tested to determine whether they qualified for special education services. The tendency to equate "assessment" (a process of evaluation) with "testing" (administering a test, such as an IQ test) had its beginnings in 1910 when Goddard translated the Binet-Simon allowing for many children to be tested for "feeblemindedness." However, some 60 years later, the testing movement was called into question by the famous California case of *Larry P. v. Riles* (1972). The California court ruled that the use of standardized IQ tests on Black children for the purposes of placement in special education programs for the educable mentally retarded (EMR) was unconstitutional unless prior approval was obtained by the court.

*On a more recent note…*School psychologists currently spend about two-thirds of their time performing intellectual assessments or other placement procedures for the purposes of identification and placement of children in special education programs, which has lead some to refer to them as "gatekeepers for special education" (Reschly & Wilson, 1995). Models of in-school consultation and response to intervention (RTI) have been proposed as alternative assessment methods to reduce the volume of intelligence tests given for placement decisions.

---

4. Adult Versus Child Perspective

With the advent of child labor laws and child protection issues, children were no longer considered "little adults" as they had been in the 19th century. However, the clinicians who treated children did so following training procedures that had been based primarily on work with adult patients. Therefore, the need to develop methods more suited to developmental populations was not considered necessary, at this time, since childhood psychopathology was considered to share the same features as adult psychopathology and treated using adult methods (Peterson & Roberts, 1991). Furthermore, according to Horn (1984), the child guidance clinics in the 1920s and 1930s held two opposing views of parents: those who blamed parents for the child's problems and those who believed that a stable family environment was essential to positive mental health. The majority of emphasis in the 1930s was firmly entrenched in linking child problems to adult problems; **maternal overprotection** was thought to cause overly submissive children, while **maternal rejection** was thought to promote overly aggressive children.

Freud's Child

While Freudian theories emphasized the importance of childhood in influencing personality development, psychoanalytic theorists held the viewpoint that children were not capable of experiencing major depression. They reasoned that young children did not have the capability of this experience because they did not yet have a well-developed and internalized superego, a necessary precursor to major depression (Clarizio, 1994). These theorists adhered to these beliefs despite Spitz's (1946) observations of depression in institutionalized infants and early descriptions of depression depicted in child case studies (Bleuler, 1934).

Currently, there is increasing emphasis on understanding the unique variants of child and adolescent psychopathology that exist at different developmental levels. As a result, there is growing discontent with the *Diagnostic and Statistical Manual of Mental Disorders* (DSM-IV-TR: APA, 2000) for diagnostic purposes with children for disorders other than those that appear in the section under the category of Disorders First Evident in Infancy, Childhood, and Adolescence. For example, the majority of criteria for disorders of anxiety (other than separation anxiety), mood disorders, and disorders of substance use and abuse disorders have been based on field trials that have been conducted primarily with adult populations. In particular, there is increasing concern about the lack of diagnostic criteria for infants and toddlers, despite a greater understanding of psychopathology in younger children (Boris, Seanah, Larrieu, Scheeringa, & Heller, 1998; Scheeringa & Zenah, 2001).

Clinical Child Psychology: Focus on Development

The terms *abnormal child psychology*, *clinical child psychology*, and *child psychopathology* can be used interchangeably, as is evident in the wide variety of journal titles available. There has been enormous growth in empirical research concerning child and adolescent psychopathology since the 1970s, and a large number of journals have emerged exclusively devoted to research about child and adolescent clinical concerns (e.g., *Journal of Clinical Child Psychology, Journal of Abnormal Child Psychology, Journal of the American Academy of Child and Adolescent Psychiatry, Journal of Child Psychology and Psychiatry*, etc.). In what now seems like a very logical progression, ground breaking events occurred in the mid-1980s when clinical child concerns were conceptualized within a developmental framework, giving rise to the field of **developmental psychopathology** (Sroufe & Rutter, 1984), an offshoot of developmental psychology, complete with its own journal, *Development and Psychopathology*.

Developmental Psychopathology: The Merging of Two Disciplines

In their ground-breaking article on the "Domain of Developmental Psychopathology," Sroufe and Rutter (1984) discuss the complexities evident in developmental psychopathology which was at that stage of an "emergent" discipline. The discipline, the authors suggest, should be closely "wedded" to the "methods, theories and perspectives of developmental psychology," while regarding "pathology" as "developmental deviations." Within this context, the authors define developmental psychopathology as "the study of the origins and course of individual patterns of behavioral maladaptations" (p. 18).

Developmental Psychopathology vs. Clinical Child Psychology

Sroufe and Rutter (1984) distinguish developmental psychopathology from clinical child psychology which they depict as more static in nature. The developmental psychopathologist's emphasis is on the origins and nature of disordered behaviors and how behavior patterns change over the course of development, "its varying manifestations, precursors and sequelae, and its relation to nondisordered patterns of behavior" (p. 18).

The Increasing Role of Developmental Contexts

Within the framework of developmental psychopathology, atypical child behavior is conceptualized as a deviation from normal development. Since its inception, there has been extensive research devoted to many variations on the theme, including how to incorporate developmental psychopathology as an over-arching approach and how to successfully integrate other theoretical models into a comprehensive understanding of the underlying processes which precipitate and maintain maladaptive behaviors (Wilmshurst, 2003).

With an eye on prevention, increased emphasis has been placed on determining processes which can inhibit or escalate the development of maladaptive behaviors. Research efforts have focused on uncovering **risk factors** which place children in jeopardy for the development of maladaptive behaviors and identifying **protective factors** that can buffer children from harm. At its core, developmental psychopathology focuses on human development as a holistic process which is both interactive and dynamic. The "total child" incorporates, and is the sum total of, multiple levels of biological, social, and psychological processes that act and react in a movement that is hierarchical, **transactional**, and increasingly complex (Cicchetti & Toth, 1998; Cicchetti & White, 1988; Wenar & Kerig, 2000).

Important Distinction

Initially, parent-child interactions were thought to be a one-way system of communication, with the onus placed on a parent's ability to influence child behaviors (Parent → Child). Later, the concept of **bidirectional influence** (Bell, 1968) recognized that child behaviors are equally as likely to influence parenting behaviors (Parent → Child; Child → Parent). The **transactional model** (Sameroff & Chandler, 1975) incorporates influences in development as an ongoing process of bidirectional, reciprocal interactions between the child and the environment, such that changes in either can affect each other in a reciprocal way.

Viewing abnormal child behavior from a developmental perspective, several recurrent themes provide the foundation for understanding the nature of psychopathology in children. The first theme acknowledges that understanding deviation from the norm requires, at the onset:

- *a thorough understanding of normal development and normal expectations* (Theme 1).

Within this model, normal development becomes the yardstick that provides the measure of the severity of pathology, since

- *the degree to which behavior deviates from the norm defines the degree of maladaptive behavior* (Theme 2).

The next theme is a natural progression from the first two themes and emphasizes the importance of recognizing that

- *maladaptive behavior exists on a continuum of severity* (Theme 3).

Therefore, the field of developmental psychopathology has emphasized three of the five themes that provide the foundation for this text on abnormal behavior from a developmental perspective. Viewing behaviors along a developmental continuum provides continuity, because normal and abnormal behaviors stem from the same developmental principles. It is through our understanding of normal behavior (its stages and underlying processes), that a greater appreciation is achieved in understanding how and why abnormal behaviors have developed (Sroufe, 1990).

Trends in Conceptualizing Developmental Change and Maladaptive Influences

Bronfenbrenner's (1979, 1989) **ecological model** is a sociocultural framework that can increase our understanding of how child characteristics and environmental characteristics interact at various levels of influence. Graphically, the model is portrayed as a series of concentric circles with the child occupying the central core. The ecological or sociocultural model is depicted in Figure 1.1.

Within this sociocultural model, *individual characteristics* (genotype, intelligence, temperament, personality), interact with environmental characteristics that exist in the *immediate environment* (family, school, peers), the *prevailing social and economic climate* (socioeconomic status, extended family, neighborhood safety), and *culture, laws and values* (policy, customs). Influences from the immediate environment, or what Bronfenbrenner calls the **microsystem** can be acute or chronic, such as ongoing family conflict or the painful loss of a family member. Influences of the **exosystem**, such as available health services, employment opportunities, or neighborhood safety, can have a significant impact on the growing child for better or worse, as is evident in the different trajectories found for children who are raised in secure homes versus those raised in a more chaotic environment. Finally, subtle influences, exerted by factors in the **macrosystem**, can have a profound impact on children as policy changes may alter future opportunities for growth, or cultural expectations may result in parent and child conflicts as new ways clash with the old. To fully appreciate and understand a child's mental status, it is necessary

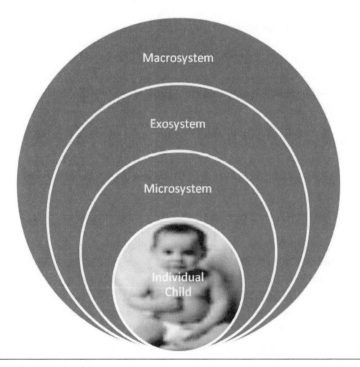

Figure 1.1 Bronfenbrenner's ecological model.

Individual child: Child characteristics, biological, genetic, temperament, IQ

Microsystem: Immediate family, school, peers, community, neighborhood

Exosystem: Extended family, social and economic conditions

Macrosystem: Culture, values, and laws

to not only consider the child, but also the role of contextual variables that serve to *predispose, precipitate,* and *maintain* the disordered behavior.

This interaction is another important and recurrent theme of how *individual, interpersonal, contextual, and cultural factors influence deviations in development* (Theme 4).

Compatibility and Goodness of Fit

A major factor that can contribute to whether influences exert a positive or negative impact is the degree to which communication exists between different members in a child's environment. If the members are not compatible (e.g., mother and father do not communicate effectively, such as in giving the child contradictory messages) then the nature of influence is not cohesive. Bronfenbrenner refers to the communication or interaction between systems as the **mesosystem**. Good communication and sharing similar goals would predict a healthy exchange and more opportunities for success, compared to a mismatch. For example, if there is a communication breakdown between home and school, two immediate environmental influences (microsystems), then the opportunities for successful progress are likely to be seriously compromised. However, if the home and school support a similar agenda, (e.g., compliance with rules, respect for authority, motivation to do well), then the likelihood of success would be predicted to increase.

Contemporary Viewpoints Regarding Developmental Change

Although Bronfenbrenner's **ecological model** provides an excellent beginning for understanding multiple levels of influence, it is important to consider the dual nature of influences that can determine patterns of action and reaction. For instance, an infant who resists his mother's attempts to pick him up may set the stage for the mother being less likely to attempt to hold the infant in the future. Similarly, if a mother continually ignores her child's pleas for attention, the child may withdraw or act up in an attempt to get any form of attention possible. It is within this developing repertoire of responses that the **bidirectional** nature of influences (Bell, 1968), or what Bandura (1985) called **reciprocal determinism**, can be very helpful in understanding the action → reaction paradigm that can result in a wide range of different developmental outcomes.

Never Underestimate the Power of Environmental Influences

Research studies suggest that economically stressed parents of children living in poverty tend to discipline these children more harshly, and inconsistently, while ignoring their children's dependency needs (Dodge, Pettit, & Bates, 1994; McLeod & Shanahan, 1993). Furthermore, prolonged and persistent poverty is significantly more detrimental to the child's social-emotional functioning than transitory financial hardship (Duncan, Brooks-Gunn, & Klebanov, 1994). However, parenting behavior can also serve to buffer children from the effects of poverty (Cowen, Wyman, Work, & Parker, 1990). For example, studies have identified **stress-resilient** children who respond more favorably to parents who were more supportive, less harsh, and more developmentally appropriate and consistent in their discipline.

As theorists' understanding of child development increased, more intricate and advanced models were constructed to capture the complex nature of developmental change. Although Bandura's (1985) model emphasized reciprocal influences, Sameroff wanted to capture the on-going and interactive process of influence and change that occurs as the child continually adapts to his environment and the environment changes as a result. Sameroff's **transactional model** (Sameroff & Chandler, 1975), applied to developmental psychopathology, has provided an increased understanding of the underlying dynamics evident in the development of a given disorder and the different trajectories that can result. By tracing specific pathways, researchers have begun to unravel the influences that can place children at risk for developing disorders and the protective factors that mitigate risk. Though the use of an **ecological transactional model,** Cicchetti and Toth (1998) provide a comprehensive look at the nature and development of depressive disorders in children and youth that would not have been possible without consideration of the diverse and multiple influences that interact to produce depressive outcomes.

Understanding Maladaptive Behaviors From a Developmental Perspective

Looking Ahead: Applying a Developmental Framework to Understanding Aggressive Behaviors

One of the most researched areas of problem behaviors in children concerns the development of aggressive behaviors. There are several reasons for research emphasis in this area, including studies devoted to understanding what is "normal" and what is considered a serious deviation from the "normal" path (e.g., acts of aggression that violate the rights of others or indicate serious rule violations). Aggressive behaviors can be a threat to the safety of others, therefore it is important to know what is "normal" child behavior and what can signal cause for alarm. Research has demonstrated that "early starters" (Aguilar, Sroufe, Egeland, & Carlson, 2000), or those who demonstrate an increasing pattern of aggression in the first 3 years of life, are at greatest risk for continuing to evidence a stable and escalating pattern of aggressive behaviors patterns throughout their lifespan. Therefore, the concept of aggressive behaviors provides an excellent starting point for looking at how problem behaviors are conceptualized and what constitutes behaviors that cross the line into the area of clinically significant variations from normal patterns. The case study below is an example of the types of case presentations that will serve to introduce each of the disorders presented in this text. The cases illustrate various levels of severity and how symptoms can manifest at different developmental levels.

Case in Point: Variations in Aggression

Jerry is easily upset and displays his low tolerance for frustration by throwing his baseball bat into the field when he fails to connect with the ball. When reprimanded by the coach, Jerry throws himself on the ground and begins kicking his feet. Jerry typically has problems coping with emotional upset and he often responds with an intense negative reaction. When asked to remove himself from the playing field, Jerry argues with the coach and refuses to budge.

Sara is angry with Julie. Instead of dealing with her anger directly, Sara waits until that evening and calls all of their mutual friends, saying nasty things about Julie until she rounds up a circle of friends who agree to completely isolate Julie and not talk to her in the morning. The next day, Julie arrives at her locker to find graffiti scribbled in marker across the front and is faced with rejection from her friends for no apparent reason. Sara has been successful in obtaining sweet revenge.

Although George was somewhat oppositional when younger, now his behaviors have escalated out of control. He has been caught stealing CDs from the local music store and he has been truant from school on four occasions in the past month. Rule violations have been a problem at home as well. Not only has he stayed out all night on several occasions, but has been suspected of stealing money from his mother's purse.

In the scenarios just presented, Jerry, Sara, and George all display various levels of aggressive behavior. Viewing these scenarios from a developmental perspective, there are several questions that immediately come to mind that can assist in determining the degree of severity of the problem behaviors. Referring back to the five recurrent themes and the K–3 Paradigm, it becomes essential to first consider what is considered to be "normal" within the context of aggressive behaviors. However, it is not possible to determine what is normal for the children noted above unless we have an idea of where they are developmentally. Therefore, the first obvious question is:

How old are the children in the scenario? Jerry is 8 years of age. For his age level, he has significant problems with emotion regulation and he demonstrates temper tantrums that are more typical of a 2 or 3 year old. He is oppositional and defiant refusing to comply with the coach's requests. Based on the frequency with which these behaviors are demonstrated and the degree to which the behaviors are exhibited in the home environment, a diagnosis of **oppositional defiant disorder (ODD)** is possible. (The diagnostic criteria for ODD according to the *DSM-IV-TR*, APA, 2000, will be addressed in chapter 9.)

Sara is 11 years of age; an age at which retaliatory (getting even) types of aggression are common. Her behavior, although not condoned, does represent a somewhat typical and negative behavior pattern that may be evident in females of middle school age. Sara is displaying **relational aggression**, a predominantly female form of aggression that is directed towards a victim's social relationships with the goal of destroying social ties.

George is also 11 years of age; however, the behaviors that he is engaging in seem to have far more serious consequences. George displays many of the symptoms of **conduct disorder** evident in behaviors that are either serious rule violations or that defy the rights of others. (The diagnostic criteria for conduct disorder will be addressed in chapter 9.) George's behaviors are more consistent with the *covert* (hidden) and *non-destructive* variety, which is less severe than the *overt* and *destructive type* that involves such infractions as property destruction, and intentional cruelty to others or animals.

From a developmental perspective, there are empirical guidelines that provide benchmarks for providing answers to questions about:

- What is normal
- What is a normal variation
- What is a serious deviation from the norm.

We know from longitudinal studies of aggressive behaviors that normally, overt acts of aggression peak in the 2nd year and diminish with age, as children become more socialized (Tremblay et al., 1999). However, not all children follow this preferred path. For some children, like George, overt aggression is a stable pattern of behavior which can persist through middle school and adolescence (Aguilar et al., 2000).

While very young children primarily engage in acts of **instrumental aggression** (I shove you away so I can get a toy), Sara's aggressive behavior is more appropriately labeled as **interpersonal aggression**, or **hostile aggression**, because her intent is to inflict distress on another person. At 11 years of age, typical aggressive patterns are more likely to have a "get even and retaliatory" quality to them, and are more likely to be verbal (name calling, derogatory remarks) than physical. Sara's covert and verbally aggressive behaviors (relational aggression) are more typical of females at this developmental stage. Although the scenario above presents a snap shot in time, there are several clues that hint at the more serious nature of George's aggressive behavior. In order to determine the severity of George's behaviors, we would need more information about the contexts and history of these behaviors. However, to rule out a situational reaction, it would be important to determine if there have been any recent traumatic changes in the family (e.g., parents' separation) or school-social environments (such as victim of bullying). If so, then these conditions might be seen as a ***precipitating factor*** for George's aggression, or acting out behaviors. However, if aggressive behaviors have been ***maintained*** for a much longer duration (e.g., George has *always been difficult to manage*, and he has a *history of noncompliant and defiant responses* at home), then our evaluation of these behaviors takes on a different level of severity.

The above scenarios reinforce the importance of the five underlying themes that are fundamental to understanding maladaptive behaviors from a developmental perspective. Next, we will take a closer look at each of these five themes.

Five Recurrent Themes

The book will stress five consistent themes that can guide the reader and provide a framework for understanding the nature and the development of maladaptive behaviors, thoughts, and feelings.

Theme 1: Normal development typically proceeds slong an orderly and predictable path. Development is cumulative and progressive with age- and stage-related expectations for cognitive, affective, and behavioral outcomes. At each of the ages and developmental stages, there are tasks to be mastered and goals to be fulfilled. Development is a process of qualitative change that provides the background for understanding both the limitations that compromise children's understanding, behaviors, and feelings at various stages and the capacities, or milestones, they are expected to achieve. From our knowledge of developmental expectations, we can assume that unless Sara repeatedly and intensively engages in aggression, her behavior is likely to reflect normal developmental progression.

Familiarity with normal developmental expectations provides an important backdrop for clinical decision-making and evaluation of deviations from the norm. Predominant tasks to be mastered, as well as expected stage-based competencies and limitations, are presented in Table 1.1.

Development in Focus

Although the selection of specific ages to define the beginning or ending of stages can be somewhat arbitrary, this text will use the following stage divisions: Infancy (Birth to 1 year); Toddler (1 to 2-1/2 years); Preschool (2-1/2 to 6 years); School Age (6 to 11 years); Teen or Youth (12+ years).

Theme 2: Maladaptive behaviors represent deviations from the normal path. Although there is a grand plan for developmental progression, and a predicable pattern of stages, there are normal variations, or *individual differences* in the *rate at which these changes take place*. Some children develop more quickly than others and some children meet developmental goals at a much slower pace than the norm. For example, in chapter 13, much of our understanding of mental retardation comes from an appreciation of how cognitive limitations might impact on the rate of learning and the particular challenges that children with these limitations might face in mastering developmental tasks. Behaviorally, some children lag in social and/or emotional skill development,

Table 1.1 Developmental Tasks, Competencies, and Limitations at Each Stage of Development

Age/Stage of Development	Task/Limitations
Infancy *(Birth–1 year)*	Trust vs. Mistrust (Erickson) Secure vs. Insecure Attachment (Bowlby) Differentiation Self and Others Reciprocal Socialization Development of Object Permanence (Piaget: Objects exist when out of sight) First Steps; First Word
Toddler *(1–2-1/2 years)*	Autonomy vs. Shame and Doubt (Erikson) Increased independence, self-assertion, and pride Beginnings of Self Awareness Social Imitation and beginnings of Empathy Beginnings of Self Control Delayed imitation and Symbolic Thought Language increases to 100 words Increase motor skills and exploration
Preschool *(2-1/2–6 years)*	Initiative vs. Guilt (Erickson) Inability to Decenter (Piaget: Logic Bound to Perception; Problems with Appearance-Reality) Egocentric (emotional and physical perspective; one emotion at a time) Increased Emotion Regulation (underregulation vs. over-regulation) Increased need for Rules and Structure Can identify feelings: Guilt and Conscience are evident Emergent anxieties, phobias fears
School age *(6–11 years)*	Industry vs. Inferiority Sense of competence, mastery, and efficacy Concrete Operations (Piaget: no longer limited by appearance, but limited by inability to think in the abstract) Can experience "blends" of emotions (love/hate) Self Concept and Moral Conscience Realistic fears (injury, failure) and irrational fears (mice, nightmares)
Teen years *(12+ years)*	Identity vs. Role Diffusion (Erickson) Abstract reasoning (Piaget) Emotional blends in self and others (ambiguity) Return of Egocentricity (Piaget/Elkind: imaginary audience and personal fable) Self-concept relative to peer acceptance and competence

and these delays may result in poor peer relations, with outcomes of peer rejection or neglect. In our case scenario above, Julie's rejection by her peers may predispose her towards greater social difficulties in the future (Kagan & Snidman, 1999).

In addition to variations in the rate or pace of mastering developmental tasks, developmental deviations may also be evident in the degree to which certain patterns of behaviors, thoughts, or feelings veer off the normal path, or in the course of these abnormal **developmental trajectories or pathways**.

The Tree of Life

Bowlby (1973) used a branching tree to explain the concept of developmental pathways. In this model, the trunk of the tree represents normal development, and the branches represent different pathways that individuals might take in their growth and development. Although this model maintains a positive perspective in that positive choices are always possible, Bowlby does maintain that the choices are constrained by previous choices.

Analogous to a highway with a series of detours, the further off the normal path one deviates, the more difficult it becomes to return to the main road. The concept of pathways is also important because it helps to illustrate two other very important principles of development. The first principle is the concept of **equifinality** which simply stated is the idea that two people can arrive at the same destination using very different roads. The second principle is the concept of **multifinality** or the fact that two people can have very similar risk factors, yet have very different outcomes (or you can start on the same road, but end up in very different destinations).

Important Distinction

The principles of equifinality and multifinality represent different mechanisms for explaining how influences impact outcomes. The principle of equifinality explains how similar symptoms (e.g., depression) can develop from different sources (maternal depression, peer rejection, etc.). Multifinality points to the different outcomes that can result, even if individuals face similar circumstances. For example, two siblings growing up in the same household with a depressed mother may exhibit different outcomes (one may have conduct problems, another may be depressed) or they may demonstrate few atypical symptoms due to protective factors.

Theme 3: Maladaptive behavior is represented by a continuum of severity. Behaviors can diverge from the normal path in mild (symptoms), moderate (syndromes), or severe (disorders) digressions. The extent to which the behavior is deviant requires an understanding of normal expectations. Negativity and power struggles can be anticipated at the toddler stage and again in adolescence; however, severe and persistent noncompliance and defiance across the developmental spectrum is not a normal deviation. In the *Case in Point*, if Jerry's aggressive, defiant, and noncompliant behaviors have longevity and are intense, then we are more concerned about the degree of pathology. Based on the information provided, further investigation would certainly be warranted to determine whether Jerry met DSM criteria for oppositional defiant disorder.

Theme 4: Individual, interpersonal, contextual, and cultural factors influence deviations in development. In order to understand the underlying processes that shape the extent and nature of maladaptive behavior, it is essential to look at the role of *ecological or sociocultural influences* (internal and external) in precipitating and maintaining the behavior patterns.

Although the fourth theme is not unique to child psychology, it is important to understand the degree to which children, by their nature, are embedded in their contexts. Initially, young children are totally dependent on their caregivers. However, even in the initial stages, a subtle exchange of mutual responses between caregiver and child begins to chart the course of development, as a reciprocal pattern of interchanges unfold, each influencing the other.

Recall and Rewind

Bronfenbrenner (1989) conceptualized developmental influences as a series of concentric circles with the child at the inner core. Child characteristics and environmental characteristics interact to produce change, adaptation to change, and further changes.

It is well established that individual factors, such as having a difficult temperament (Rutter, 1990), can place a child at risk for later behavior problems. In charting the course of developmental

Table 1.2 Stages of Development and Ecological Influences

Inner Circle: Child as Individual Internal Influences	Immediate Circle: Family Peers Child in Relationship Reciprocal Influences	Outer Circle: Neighborhood Community Government External Influences	Outermost Circle: Culture of Origin Minority Status External Influences
Biological Make-up	Family and School Context	Social and Economic	Cultural Context
Developmental Stages: All Levels: Infancy Toddler Preschool School Age Teen Years	Family Influence continues through all stages; Peer influences increase with stages	Social and Economic issues Influence all levels of development	Culture influences all levels of development; Increased opportunity for clashes between culture and peer groups as stages increase

pathways and trajectories, we have learned that difficult beginnings can set the stage for insecure attachments (Sroufe, Egeland, & Kreutzer, 1990), maternal rejection, and poor outcomes socially, emotionally, academically, and behaviorally (Cassidy & Mohr, 2001; Lyons-Ruth & Jacobvitz, 1999; Main & Hesse, 1990). Furthermore, theories such as **coercion theory** (Patterson, Reid, & Dishion, 1992) have taught us the importance of linking reciprocal behaviors to family contexts and the interaction of parent and child response patterns that continually recycle negative outcomes. Developmental Stages (Theme 1) and sociocultural influences (Theme 4) provide an initial foundation for understanding adaptive and maladaptive behaviors. The relationship between these two themes can be viewed in Table 1.2.

Memory Bank

Coercion theory, developed by Patterson (1982), provides some insight into the potential causes of aggressive and antisocial behavior in children. The theory suggests that aggressive behaviors are learned through reinforcing events in the social environment. Patterson hypothesized that aggressive behavior develops in children when parents use coercion as the primary mode for controlling their children.

Theme 5: Clinical psychologists can draw on a multiplicity of theoretical perspectives to assist in understanding maladaptive behaviors. Theoretical input from diverse perspectives (psychodynamic, biological, behavioral, cognitive, family systems, parenting/attachment, sociocultural) can provide increased insight and understanding of the nature of maladaptive behaviors and the different pathways that might be involved.

The following exercise will assist in demonstrating the variations in interpretation that might exist among clinicians concerning a young patient who presents with symptoms of depression. The viewpoints presented in Table 1.3 represent a hypothetical view of depression across the spectrum of theoretical viewpoints. Each viewpoint presents a template for understanding the underlying dynamics inherent in the disorder. Each set of questions seeks to obtain answers based on a set of theoretical assumptions. From a *biological* approach, family history of depression is significant, since research has demonstrated that children of depressed mothers are at higher risk for a number of disorders including depression (Hammen, Burge, & Stansbury, 1990; Peterson, Maier, & Seligman, 1993). A *behaviorist* would likely target environmental factors that might be

Table 1.3 Six Theoretical Views of Childhood Depression

Theory	Child Characteristics	Environmental Characteristics
Biomedical Model: Focus on brain and body	Genetic Traits Neurotransmitter Function Chemical Imbalance Temperament/Behavioral Inhibition (wary/ shy)	Familial history of depression
Behavioral Model: Focus on learned behaviors	Depressed behavior is reinforced by attention; or Depressed behaviors serve to drive others away and further alienate	Maternal depression; Caregiver reinforces depressed behaviors Peer rejection; Negative coercive cycles
Cognitive Model: Focus on thoughts and beliefs	Negative thought patterns and attributions; Cognitive triad: helpless, hopeless, and worthless; Learned Helplessness	Maternal depression and modeling of negative parental interactions; Peers reinforce negative thinking in teasing and bullying behaviors
Attachment/Parenting Focus on secure/insecure attachment; Parenting patterns: authoritarian, authoritative, permissive	Insecure attachment; low self-esteem and poor coping ability; Lack of parental support; nurturance	Maternal depression; Parental rejection; inability to soothe; Authoritarian parenting style: high on control low on warmth
Family Systems Focus on family dynamics	Child adopts the role of the "depressed" child	Detouring: family focus on child depression to avoid family problems
Psychodynamic Focus on underlying subconscious conflicts	Depression as anger turned inward, or symbolic loss Subconscious conflict	Parent cold and rejecting
Sociocultural Focus on social networks and social conditions	Poor school relations; Neighborhood safety	Poverty, family stress; lack of community belonging

reinforcing and maintaining the depressed behaviors. For example, depression may be positively reinforced by increased attention from family members or negatively reinforced by a reduction in chores. It may be that the depressed person's behaviors are serving to drive others away and isolation becomes a self-fulfilling prophecy (Lewinsohn, Clarke, Hops, & Andrews, 1990). Depression may also represent mourning of a symbolic loss or anger turned inward, according to *psychodynamic* theories (Bemporad, 1992). A *sociocultural* perspective might look beyond the child's immediate environment to determine factors evident in child's cultural background, neighborhood, or peer associations that might be causing or maintaining the child's sense of depression (Altmann & Gotlib, 1988; Patterson & Capaldi, 1990). A *cognitive* therapist would be interested in how the child is cognitively interpreting the behavior of others. Perhaps the child is overgeneralizing, and considering every slight as a major rejection (Dykman, Horowitz, Abramson, & Usher, 1991; Seligman & Peterson, 1986). A cognitive therapist might want to know if feelings of helplessness are perpetuating the sense of hopelessness and despair. A *family systems therapist* would want to know how family relationships were impacting on the depression (e.g., Do these relationships serve to alleviate or increase feelings of inadequacy and low self-esteem? Are there boundaries and alliances which serve to effectively lock the child out of the family support system?).

Although the above tables and discussion present hypothetical examples concerning the possible influence of theoretical perspectives on symptom presentation and interpretation, there is an increasing appreciation of the need to integrate information from multiple sources and across theoretical perspectives. Recent research has increased our awareness of the complexity of childhood disorders (Kazdin, 1997; Kazdin & Kagan, 1994) and as a result, emphasis has shifted from single factor to multiple factor and interactive explanations for childhood disorders (Cicchetti & Toth, 1998). As a result, contemporary clinicians often draw on several theoretical frameworks in an effort to assess the many factors that may serve to predispose, initiate, and maintain disordered behaviors, with the ultimate goal of targeting these areas for therapeutic interventions.

Introducing the K–3 Paradigm

Ultimately, our understanding of maladaptive behavior in children and adolescence requires the ability to converge the five themes into an overall working paradigm. When theories are integrated with ecological influences and developmental levels, behaviors are understood within a rich contextual presentation. The ultimate goal in understanding patterns of abnormal child behaviors is the ability to bridge theoretical assumptions with developmental contexts and then consider whether this behavior is appropriate or deviant based on the child's development level. This integrated model can be seen in Table 1.4.

Overall learning objective.   Using the K–3 Paradigm, readers will gain an increased appreciation of the complex nature of child and adolescent behaviors and the degree to which these behaviors are maladaptive based on their understanding of the need to integrate information from three key information sources:

1. Knowledge of developmental expectations;
2. Knowledge of sources of influence;
3. Knowledge of theoretical models (Figure 1.2).

Table 1.4   Developmental Stages, Ecological Influences, and Theoretical Perspectives: An Integrated Model

Inner Circle: Child as Individual	Immediate Circle: Family Peers Child in Relationship	Outer Circle: Neighborhood Community Government	Outermost Circle: Culture of Origin Minority Status
Internal Influences	**Reciprocal Influences**	**External Influences**	**External Influences**
Biological Make-up	Family and School Context	Social and Economic	Cultural Context
Developmental Stages:			
All Levels:	Family Influence continues	Social and Economic issues	Culture influences all levels
Infancy	through all stages;	Influence all levels of	of development;
Toddler	Peer influences increase with	development	Increased opportunity for
Preschool	stages		clashes between culture
School Age			and peer groups as stages
Teen Years			increase
Child Centered Theories:	**Relationship Theories:**	**Contextual Theories:**	**Theories:**
Biomedical	Behavioral	Sociocultural	Sociocultural
Physical	Cognitive	Family Systems	
Development	Family Systems		
Behavioral	Attachment-Parenting		
Cognitive			
Psychodynamic			
Personality			

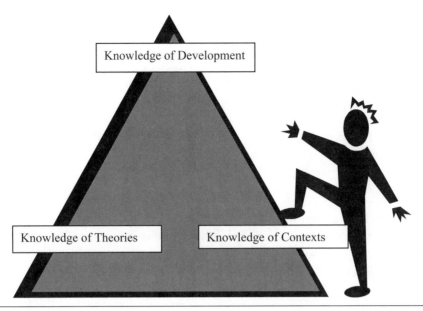

Figure 1.2 The K–3 Paradigm.

CHAPTER SUMMARY AND REVIEW

1. **Historical Background and Organizational Themes**
   a. The reform movement ushered in an era of child protection, as child labor laws were instituted and mandatory education became a reality.
   b. With the advent of the Stanford-Binet Intelligence test, and the new influx of children in the schools, psychologists were preoccupied with intellectual assessments for identification purposes. As a result, unfortunately, many identified as mentally retarded were institutionalized.
   c. In 1909, the first child guidance clinic was established. Twenty years later, there was a shift from focusing on the treatment of delinquent youth to identification of parents as the problem cause. By 1948, 54 child guidance clinics came together to form an association; however, this movement also coincided with a controversial shift in the role of the centers. Rather than focus on the identification of children's problems, the child guidance clinics would become centers for training and research.
   d. Initially, it was thought that children were too young to experience emotions, such as depression; later, the fallacy was that children experienced the same emotions as adults and required the same treatment. Both beliefs deterred recognition of clinical child psychology as a unique field of study.
   e. In 1984, developmental psychopathology emerged as an integrated approach to considering maladaptive behaviors within the context of developmental expectations and norms. Today, there is increasing recognition that maladaptive behavior is a byproduct of ongoing interactions between multiple ecological influences (child, family, peers, school, community, culture).

2. **Five Recurring Themes**
   The book stresses five pivotal themes to understanding maladaptive behaviors:
   - Theme 1: Normal development is orderly and predictable.
   - Theme 2: Maladaptive behaviors are deviations from the normal path.

- Theme 3: The degree of deviation determines the severity along a continuum.
- Theme 4: Developmental change is influenced by child and environmental characteristics (family, peers, community, economics, culture).
- Theme 5: There are a number of theoretical perspectives that can help explain maladaptive behavior.

3. **The K–3 Paradigm**

   Understanding abnormal child behavior requires integrating knowledge from three pivotal areas (K–3 Paradigm): (a) knowledge of normal expectations, (b) knowledge of sources of influence, and (c) knowledge of theoretical models.

Consolidate and Communicate

1. In their article on the domain of developmental psychology, Sroufe and Rutter (1984) discuss how the field of developmental psychopathology differs from the fields of abnormal child psychology and clinical child psychology. The authors suggest several points of distinction, including emphasis on: disordered versus nondisordered behavior, differential diagnosis versus origins and time course, and degree of severity versus diagnosis. Discuss how the position in this article supports or does not support the five themes of this text.

2. Describe some of the possible differences that might be evident at the individual and immediate levels of environment influence for Joey, a preschooler, compared to Sara, who is in Grade 4. Incorporate how different developmental tasks would be evident at both levels and what types of interactions might take place between influences at various levels. In your discussion, demonstrate how an increased rate of interest imposed by the government might impact both of these children at all levels of their world.

3. Six different theoretical frameworks were introduced in this chapter (psychodynamic, biological, behaviorist, cognitive, sociocultural, and attachment-parenting). Explain how each of these theoretical models might explain aggressive behaviors demonstrated by each of the three children referred to in the *Case in Point* (Jerry, George, and Sara).

Chapter Review Questions

1. The precipitating incident that opened the doors for children to attend schools at the end of the 19th century was:
   a. The introduction of the Stanford-Binet
   b. The establishment of the child guidance clinics
   c. The reform movement
   d. Witmer's establishment of learning centers.

2. The arrival of the Stanford-Binet ushered in a new era for psychologists, marked by:
   a. Greater recognition of the role of psychology in treating child disorders
   b. Increased intelligence testing for primarily placement issues
   c. Use of intelligence testing to secure children placements in private schools for the gifted
   d. Greater understanding of the "maladjusted" child

3. In the child guidance clinics, there was a shift in emphasis in the late 1920s and early 1930s from treating children for delinquent behaviors to:
   a. Using clinics for research and training
   b. Using the clinics basically for child care facilities

c. Blaming the parents for the child's problems

d. Developing new testing materials

4. Which of the following was *not* a roadblock to clinical child psychology being recognized as a separate discipline?
    a. Children were seen as miniature adults
    b. The nature/nurture controversy
    c. Denial that children could have "emotional" problems
    d. Establishment of clinical child journals.

5. Which of the following is not one of the five essential themes?
    a. Development proceeds in a unique and unpredictable direction
    b. Maladaptive behaviors represent deviations from the normal path
    c. Adaptive and maladaptive behavior are influenced by child and environmental characteristics
    d. Theoretical perspectives enhance our understanding of maladaptive behaviors

6. In Bronfenbrenner's ecological model, which of the following does not apply?
    a. Family influences are in the immediate environment
    b. The innermost circle represents child characteristics
    c. Cultural influences are not represented
    d. Peer influences are in immediate environment.

7. The theorists Bowbly, Bandura, Sameroff and Chandler, and Cicchetti and Toth all developed models for understanding the relationship between child and environmental characteristics. Which one statement most closely applies to all theories?
    a. Children influence their environments
    b. Environments and communities influence children
    c. The environmental impact of culture influences the child
    d. Children influence their environment, and the environment influences children.

8. Goddard established one of the most prominent training schools for the retarded. In his fictional book, called the *Kallikak Family* (1912), Goddard portrays the mentally retarded as:
    a. Having the ability to rise up in the face of overwhelming odds
    b. Persevering and slow but able to make gains with great effort
    c. Lovingly, in a paternal sense
    d. Feeble-minded and doomed

Glossary of New Terms

somatogenic perspective
psychogenic perspective
developmental psychopathology
risk factors
protective factors
bidirectional influence
transactional model
ecological model
microsystem
exosystem
macrosystem

mesosystem
reciprocal determinism
transactional model
ecological transactional model
relational aggression
instrumental aggression
interpersonal aggression/hostile aggression
developmental trajectories or pathways
equifinality
multifinality
coercion theory

Answers to Multiple Choice Questions:
1. c; 2. b; 3. a; 4. d; 5. a; 6. c; 7. d; 8. d.

2

Understanding Abnormal Development
Theoretical Perspectives

Chapter 2 At-A-Glance

Child Psychopathology and Adult Psychopathology
  Shared Competencies and Skills: Determining Normal From Abnormal Behavior
    The Four Ds: Concepts of Abnormality

Competencies and Skills Unique to Issues of Child Treatment

Trends in Conceptualizing Developmental Change: Theories and Contexts
  The Impact of Theoretical Perspectives
    Biological Theories
    Psychodynamic Theories
    Behavioral Theories
    Cognitive Theories
    Theories of Attachment and Parenting
  Developmental Theories: A Summation
    Integrating Theoretical Perspectives: A Multisystemic Approach
    The Contexts of Development: An Ecological Transactional Framework

---

CHAPTER PREVIEW

This chapter will focus on the complex issue of distinguishing normal from abnormal behaviors and the theoretical perspectives that guide our understanding of child and adolescent psychopathology.

1. **Issues in Clinical Decision Making: Determining Normal From Abnormal Behavior**

Initially, the discussion will focus on the broad challenges facing all clinicians who must distinguish normal from abnormal behavior and how this decision-making process can be guided by the use of the 4 Ds: deviance, dysfunction, distress, and danger. Although clinicians working with adult and child populations share many of the same competencies and expertise, there are several issues unique to clinicians who work with children and adolescents. Child clinicians must also make these decisions in the light of their understanding of which behaviors and interventions are developmentally appropriate.

2. Trends in Conceptualizing Developmental Change: Theories and Perspectives

Theories are hypotheses: a set of assumptions that can guide and enhance our understanding of why behaviors occur and how they are maintained. However, theories can also selectively reduce our capacity to entertain alternative perspectives if our focus is too biased. In this section, we will look at five different theoretical approaches that can enhance our understanding of childhood disorders: biological, psychodynamic, behavioral, cognitive (social cognitive, cognitive behavioral), and family, attachment, and parenting.

3. Integrating Theoretical Perspectives: The Contexts of Development

Contemporary clinicians often integrate assumptions from several theoretical approaches (termed an *eclectic approach*) in their attempt to understand the complex features of childhood disorders. There has been an increased emphasis on verifying the utility of treatment approaches through rigorous empirical research. Using the K–3 Paradigm, the discussion will focus on the need to integrate information about our understanding of child development and theoretical foundations with knowledge about influences in the child's environment. Bronfenbrenner's ecological model will be introduced as a framework for integrating information concerning child characteristics and environmental factors on a number of levels.

Child Psychopathology and Adult Psychopathology

Historically, one of the major roadblocks to recognizing child psychopathology as a unique field of study was the tendency to consider child disorders from an adult perspective. The adult perspective was evident in the description of disorders using adult terms and in the prescription of adult treatments (Peterson & Roberts, 1991). Although there is a common set of professional skills and competencies that form the basis of sound clinical practice, the application of these skill sets to settings that include working with children, rather than adults, can pose unique challenges for some adult-oriented practitioners. For example, a clinician who has considerable expertise in recognizing depression and depressive features in the adult population may encounter difficulty if asked to diagnose whether a 5-year-old has symptoms of depression. In fact, in this situation, if the psychologist was not a "child clinician," it would be most likely that the psychologist would refer the child to a more appropriate source, recognizing the limits of his or her expertise (one of the ethical standards of psychologists).

Initial discussion will focus on skills and competencies that bridge adult and child concerns, while the remainder of the discussion will highlight some unique features of child clinical populations.

Shared Competencies and Skills: Determining Normal From Abnormal Behavior

Clinicians who work with child or adult populations face similar challenges in determining whether a behavior is normal or abnormal. Although all clinicians have a broad understanding of what constitutes "normal" behaviors, *clinical judgments* about abnormality are most consistent among professional colleagues for behaviors that represent the most deviant forms. What about behaviors that are only slightly out of normal range? Should these behaviors also be considered abnormal? In order to address questions of this nature and to assist the decision-making process, clinicians often rely on a number of clinical tools, such as structured interviews and standardized rating scales (e.g., depression inventories) to provide more objective ways of measuring the degree to which behaviors deviate from the norm. Clinicians can also be assisted in their evaluation of normal versus abnormal behavior by applying guidelines to evaluate how the behavior differs from normal behavior in three broad areas: conceptual differences, frequency of occurrence, and pervasiveness across situations.

Conceptually, one way of evaluating a behavior relative to normal expectations is to consider discrepancies from the norm, in four vital areas: **deviance, dysfunction, distress,** and **danger** (Comer, 2001). As part of the overall process of formulating decisions regarding "normal versus abnormal behavior," clinicians will not only evaluate categorically whether the behavior is deviant, dysfunctional, distressing, or dangerous, they will also consider the degree to which the behavior occurs and the magnitude of the impact. To this end, information will be collected to determine the *intensity, duration, and frequency* of the behavior relative to the norm. Furthermore, keeping in perspective how environment can influence behavioral outcomes, emphasis will also be placed on whether a behavior has been noted consistently across various situations, or whether the behavior is specific to a given environmental context (e.g., behavior occurs at home only, not at school or work). Based on the above information, the clinician is guided in decision making about where to place the disordered behavior relative to the norm, along a continuum of mild, moderate, or severe deviation from normal behavior.

The Four Ds: Concepts of Abnormality
Conceptualizing abnormality along a continuum is one way of assisting in the evaluation of whether behaviors are significantly discrepant form the norm.

Deviance. Psychometric instruments are available to assist clinicians in measuring the existence of personality variables, and to obtain information about potential symptoms for a number of disorders. Assessment methods can range from informal interviews or observations to the use of lengthy questionnaires or standardized tests. Classification systems provide clinicians with a framework for determining whether the extent and nature of the symptoms warrant a specific diagnosis (categorical classification system; e.g., *Diagnostic and Statistical Manual of Mental Disorders: DSM*), or the degree of deviance of a behavior along a continuum of normal to abnormal behaviors (empirical classification system; e.g., *Achenbach System of Empirically Based Assessment: ASEBA*). The role of classification systems in child psychpathology will be discussed at greater length in chapter 5. In considering deviant behaviors, several factors must be weighed, including what is considered "normal" in the particular culture or subculture relative to generic norms.

Consider This: Is the Concept of Deviance Universal?

In a movement toward increased global understanding of the concept of "deviance," several articles (Fabrega, 1990; Rogler, 1999) have addressed the need to incorporate cultural variations into our understanding of the concepts of deviance and psychopathology. What may be considered deviant in one culture may not be considered deviant in another. For example, the distinction between externalizing and internalizing problems, which is a common method of classifying child behaviors in Western clinical practice and research, is not as evident in Chinese children. In Chinese children, high rates of comorbidity among academic problems, internalizing disorders, and conduct problems have led some researchers to question the usefulness of such categories as externalizing and internalizing when referring to this population (Chen, Rubin, & Li, 1995).

Deviance and cultural diversity. In response to the movement towards increased cultural awareness and competence, the most recent revision of the DSM (DSM-IV-TR, APA, 2000) has added sections on multicultural disorders and culture-bound syndromes. In addition, sections on cultural factors and cultural reference groups have been embedded into the context of the descriptions for each of the DSM disorders. Although these modifications have no doubt improved the validity of the DSM with respect to recognizing cultural variations in disorder presentation, global concerns persist. One reason for the ongoing concern is the use of two different classification systems worldwide. While the United States follows the DSM system of classification of disorders, many European countries adhere to the ICD-10 Codes published by the World Health Organization (WHO, 1993). For example, although ADHD is the most common childhood disorder reported in the United States (prevalence rates estimated to be between 4–5%), in a recent crosscultural study of prevalence rates, Bird (2002) found that there was wide variability in prevalence rates reported from other countries. Results revealed that prevalence rates for ADHD in Western Europe, China, India, Great Britain, Canada, Japan, Puerto Rico, and New Zealand fell within ranges from less than 1% to more than 20% in these countries. The reason for the wide variation in estimated prevalence rates is suggested to be a result of the different diagnostic classification systems used. The lowest rates were obtained in countries that use the ICD-10 Codes, while the highest rates were associated with the use of the DSM-IV classification system.

A Global Perspective

In countries using the *ICD-10 Codes* (World Health Organization, 1993), ADHD is not generally accepted as a diagnostic term. Instead, the term *Hyperkinetic Disorders* (F90) is used and refers to "a combination of overactive, poorly modulated behavior with marked inattention, lack of persistent task involvement, pervasiveness over situations and persistence over time." This classification of the disorder would be closest to our *DSM* category of ADHD combined type, which would rule out the existence of the diagnostic categories available in the United States: Primarily Hyperactive/Impulsive and Primarily Inattentive Types.

Dysfunction. The degree to which an individual is able to function adequately on a daily basis is another example of normal verses abnormal behavior. Clinicians working with adults might investigate the degree to which having a disorder might compromise employment or family functioning, while child clinicians might be interested in obtaining information from a child's teachers regarding how a child was performing in school academically and socially. Clinicians can be guided in making an appraisal of the degree of *dysfunction* using a number of available measures, such as the Global Assessment of Functioning (DSM, Axis V), which can assist the clinician in reporting an individual's overall functioning level.

It is very possible to have a disorder and yet not have that disorder render an individual dysfunctional. For example, Jonathan's severe phobia of spiders (arachnophobia), although deviant from the norm, may have minimum impact on his daily functioning if he lives in an insect-free environment. However, Jonah, who lives on a farm and has to walk through the woods to get to school, might be incapacitated by the same phobic fears. Similarly, although Wanda and Sally both share a severe phobia of riding elevators, the phobia would cause significant dysfunction for Sally, whose child therapist has an office on the 15th floor of Gold Towers, compared to minimal impact for Wanda, whose therapist resides on the ground floor of a clinic.

Distress.   Another challenging area for evaluation is the level of distress that the disorder causes for an individual and those around them. While adults can be interviewed directly regarding their level of distress, children may have little understanding of their emotions and behaviors and less ability to communicate what they are feeling. Generically, the category of distress can be an illusive concept and difficult to evaluate since some individuals may not be aware of the distress that others are experiencing as a result of their disorder. Hyperactive children or adults in a manic phase may experience minimal distress, but may inadvertently impose a great deal of stress/distress on those in their immediate environment.

Danger.   Historically, clinicians have relied on two broad areas of investigation to determine whether a client is dangerous: questions regarding the client's danger to himself or herself (suicidal intent) and questions directed at whether the client poses a threat or danger to others. Concerns for safety and a duty to protect the client and the public have resulted in the development of the judicial system's response to mental health safety issues in the form of a process called **civil commitment**. Under these proceedings, if concerned individuals (e.g., family members) are unable to persuade a minor to seek help, the family can, with the agreement of a mental health professional, seek an involuntary commitment order. However, the process is more complex when seeking involuntary commitment for adults. In this case, a mental status examination is often ordered, and adults also have the option of legally contesting the commitment order in court.

The duty to protect and the duty to warn can often conflict with other ethical issues such as confidentiality; courts have ruled that clinicians are obligated to inform potential victims of harm, even if this information is confidential (*Tarasoff v. Regents of the University of California*, 17 Cal. 3d 425 [1976]). This ruling also extends to conditions of threats of self harm (Corey, Corey, & Callanan, 1998). Further discussion of the ethical issues surrounding these decisions will be addressed in chapter 4.

Memory Bank: Can Mental Health Professionals Predict Violence? Yes and No.

Studies by Buchanan (1997, 1999) suggest that mental health professionals (psychologists and psychiatrists) demonstrate relatively poor success ratios for making long-term predictions of violence in clinical patients, resulting in more incorrect than correct responses and a bias towards false positives. However, studies do show more promise for mental health professionals in the identification of short-term or more imminent violent threats, since these evaluations are conducted with much higher success ratios (Binder, 1999).

When we consider the concept of danger or risk in relation to child populations, we instinctively think of children as the victims of maltreatment, such as child abuse or neglect, or our mind might turn to thoughts of the risk for self-harm in teenage suicide. However, there has been an increasing tendency to link thoughts of danger with concepts of children and adolescents as the perpetrators, rather than victims, of violence. Reports of aggressive and violent behaviors range from incidents of child bullying on the playground to cases of extreme teenage violence, such as the Columbine shootings in 1999. In addition, we are exposed to increasing press coverage of teen gang activity across the United States and Canada. Recruitment of gang members typically occurs as children enter their teen years, at a time when identity formation is a key facet of their developmental life course (Reiboldt, 2001).

Gang activities have escalated in many areas and have evolved from conflicts of turf protection to increased focus on illegal drug activities and violence that may result in homicide. Currently there are reports of an estimated 4,800 gangs in the United States involving memberships of between 250,000 to 650,000 youth (Gillig & Cingel, 2004).

Competencies and Skills Unique to Issues of Child Treatment

Although mental health professionals working with children face many of the same challenges as professionals working with adults, there are several key features evident in child psychopathology that are unique to working with this population.

RECURRENT THEMES   Child clinicians must have a thorough knowledge of normal development in order to distinguish abnormal variations. *Theme 1: Normal development typically follows an orderly and predictable path* and *Theme 2: Maladaptive behaviors represent deviations from the normal path.* Considering psychopathology from a developmental perspective requires the integration of information from all aspects of development, including biological, cognitive, and social factors. There is a dynamic inter-relationship between the child and his or her world that requires an understanding and evaluation of the interactive and reciprocal nature of these influences (family, peers, school, and neighborhoods) as they shape the course of development. *Theme 4: Individual, interpersonal, contextual, and cultural factors influence deviations in development.*

Although it can be effectively argued that adults face developmental issues across the lifespan which may impact on adult psychopathology, emphasis in these latter stages of development (early, middle, and late adulthood) reflect a slower rate of growth and often depend on consolidation of earlier skill foundations. According to Schaie and his colleagues (Schaie, Willis, Jay, & Chipuer, 1989; Schaie & Willis, 1993) childhood and adolescence represent the **acquisitive stage** of cognitive development where the main developmental task is to amass information which can be applied at later stages of development. Considering the rapid growth in cognitive, physical, social, and emotional development during these early formative years, the need to consider the impact of ages and stages of development on our understanding child psychopathology takes on overwhelming importance.

Understanding child psychopathology from a developmental perspective requires an understanding of the nature of cognitive, social, emotional, and physical competencies, limitations, and task expectations for each stage of development. Knowledge of these developmental sign posts will not only provide a blueprint for understanding the nature of developmental issues but how these issues impact on psychopathology and treatment.

RECURRENT THEMES   *Theme 3: Maladaptive behavior is represented by a continuum of severity.* Having a broad understanding of the types of tasks that normal children are expected to master at each of the developmental stages provides a continuum for evaluation of the degree of deviation that a given behavior is from the norm, given a child's developmental level. Examples of developmental tasks, competencies and limitations can be reviewed in Table 1.1 (Chapter 1).

Memory Bank

Viewing child psychopathology from a developmental perspective will enhance understanding by focusing attention on:

1. Stage-specific symptom presentations (anxiety may appear as fear of the dark at 3 years and nightmares at 10).
2. Normal versus atypical variations (e.g., intentional aggression at 4 years of age is a stable marker for later aggressive behavior).
3. Developmental pathways (e.g., selective mutism at 5 years may resurface as social phobia at 7 or 8 years).

Conceptualizing child psychopathology within a developmental framework requires integrating information from three important sources: (a) theoretical assumptions, (b) environmental contexts, and (c) normal developmental expectations.

 The K–3 Paradigm was introduced in chapter 1 to assist readers in integrating information from the five major themes into an overall working model. The paradigm is an important focal point for emphasizing the three sources noted above:

1. Knowledge of developmental expectations;
2. Knowledge of sources of influence (child characteristics and environmental characteristics); and
3. Knowledge of theoretical models and perspectives.

In their most recent review of contemporary challenges facing developmental psychopathology, Rutter and Sroufe (2000) suggest three important areas of future focus: 1) an increased understanding of causal processes and chain effects that underlay the development of child disorders; 2) how to conceptualize development and the interplay of genetic and environmental influences; and 3) addressing issues of continuity and discontinuity with concepts of normality and psychopathology. We will return to a discussion of these issues and others in chapters 3 and 4.

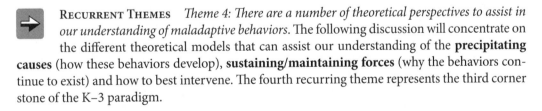 **RECURRENT THEMES** *Theme 4: There are a number of theoretical perspectives to assist in our understanding of maladaptive behaviors.* The following discussion will concentrate on the different theoretical models that can assist our understanding of the **precipitating causes** (how these behaviors develop), **sustaining/maintaining forces** (why the behaviors continue to exist) and how to best intervene. The fourth recurring theme represents the third corner stone of the K–3 paradigm.

Trends in Conceptualizing Developmental Change: Theories and Contexts

The Impact of Theoretical Perspectives

The ability to determine normal from abnormal behavior and select developmentally appropriate child interventions can be guided by information obtained from various theoretical frameworks. A theory is a conceptualization of how events are related. In addition to providing a framework for organizing information to enhance our understanding, theories are also constructed to assist with predicting behavior. However, theories are selective with respect to which observations are emphasized, and which observations are minimized. For example, in describing a given behavior and determining the precipitating and maintaining factors, a behaviorist would emphasize environmental contingencies that serve to reinforce the behavior. Viewing the same behavior from a cognitive perspective, a theorist might attempt to determine what thought processes are responsible for controlling the behavior, while a psychodynamic theorist might try to uncover the unconscious conflicts that are at the root of the behavior. Each model or theory is based upon a given set of assumptions designed to organize the information within a conceptual framework. Therefore different theoretical perspectives can provide the clinician with guidelines concerning expectations for social, emotional, cognitive, physical, and behavioral development over time.

In addition, a therapist's theoretical assumptions will also influence how the disorder is conceptualized, as to potential precipitating and maintaining factors, and guide the course of the treatment focus.

Case in Point

Jordan has been progressively withdrawing from social contact for the past few months. He is lethargic and fatigued and his school work is suffering because he cannot concentrate. Although he had been looking forward to attending high school, he has since lost his motivation to succeed. Jordan's father arranges for a visit to the pediatrician because of symptoms of fatigue, poor ability to concentrate, and recent weight loss. Medical tests are negative and rule out any physical cause for Jordan's symptoms. As a result, the physician recommends Jordan visit a child therapist for depression. The physician suggests four different therapists and recommends a visit to each office to determine which approach the family and Jordan would be most comfortable with: a biological therapist, a family systems therapist, a cognitive behavioral therapist, and a multisystemic therapist.

Dr. Med, a biological therapist, explains Jordan's depression as an inherited family predisposition to mood disorders (an aunt had depression as a teen) and explains the symptoms as resulting from a chemical imbalance. He recommends a trial of Prozac (fluoxetine). Dr. Idea, a cognitive–behaviorist, feels that Jordan's depressed mood results from faulty thinking and his recent rejection by his girlfriend. He recommends cognitive behavioral training aimed at reframing his negative thoughts into more positive alternatives. Dr. Mom, a family systems therapist, feels that Jordan's depression results from changes in family circumstances brought on by his father's loss of job, his mother's return to work for the first time in 15 years, and Jordan's insecurity in making the transition to high school. Dr. Mom recommends that the issues can best be treated by engaging the family in family therapy sessions.

Dr. Eclectic, a multisystemic therapist, suggests that a trial of medication might help, but since Jordon does not present with suicidal ideation, he would like to work with Jordan independently over the next few weeks. He plans to monitor the depression with rating scales to be completed by Jordan, his parents, and teachers. He would like to treat Jordan using cognitive behavioral therapy (CBT), since there is good research support for the use of CBT for teens who have symptoms of depression. He recommends supportive counseling for the parents who are undergoing considerable life changes. He would like to reconvene with the family in one month to discuss Jordan's interim progress and the nature of his future involvement at that time.

In the above case presentation, each therapist responded to Jordan's symptoms in a manner consistent with theoretical assumptions which formed the foundation of his or her understanding of psychopathology.

Consider This: Theories Are Hypotheses About Behavior

Theoretical models can permeate all aspects of clinical decision making. Theory can influence the clinician's questions; the behavior observed; the method of observation and ultimately the conclusions reached. Differing theories can also provide conflicting opinions regarding various aspects of child and adolescent development. Although some theoretical premises have been substantiated by empirical research, other opinions and hypothesis do not have significant research support.

Theoretical assumptions can be found to relate to all facets of human development, including physical, cognitive, behavioral, social, and emotional. The following summary presents a number of basic theoretical assumptions which have been developed to explain normal and abnormal functioning.

Biological Theories

Biological theorists are strong proponents of the "nature" side of the heredity and environment controversy in their consideration of how biological, genetic, and physiological factors contribute to human behavior. Within this context, abnormal behavior would be viewed from a medical perspective and conceptualized as a mental illness (or an illness of the *psyche*) having a number of "**symptoms or a symptom cluster**" that would assist the clinician in making a diagnosis. A biological clinician would look to the *brain* (anatomy or chemical malfunction) or **genetics** to answer questions of probable cause and treatment of the underlying disorder.

How the Brain Can Predict Abnormal Behavior

Brain Anatomy. Historically, scientists were able to understand localization of function in the brain through naturally occurring incidences of brain damage to humans by linking brain injury to subsequent loss of function. Research with animals, using lesions to cut through brain tissue also allowed psychologists to better pinpoint how certain functions, like memory, were impaired when rats with lesions were no longer able to recall where the food pellets were stored in the maze.

Through the advent of modern technology, with techniques such as functional magnetic resonance imagining (fMRI), clinical scientists have begun to unravel the complex functions of the brain. Using fMRI techniques, scientists can map activity levels in the brain and obtain insight regarding how different tasks (concentration, memory, etc.) activate or fail to activate specific areas of the brain in populations with different disorders (attention deficit disorder, schizophrenia, etc.).

Science Talks

As a result of brain imaging studies, we now know that children with ADHD demonstrate reduced activity in the frontal lobes, while brain patterns of dyslexic readers reveal overstimulation of the inferior frontal gyrus (Shaywitz, 1998).

Brain development: Neurons and biochemical activity. Anatomically, it is possible to discuss brain function from different levels: a micro level (how individual brain cells [neurons] develop and transmit messages), or at a macro level (brain structures and functions). Developmentally, neural growth and refinement is very rapid in the first 2 years of life. During this time, less useful neurons die off (*pruned*), making way for new connections to be forged as networks of fibers are developed and send messages to other neurons across the **synapse** (gap between neurons). There are three types of neurons which specialize in transmitting different types of messages: **sensory neurons** (transmitting messages to the five senses); **motor neurons** (transmitting messages of fine and gross motor movements); and **interneurons** (located in the cerebral cortex). During the first 2 years of life, *glial cells*, responsible for **myelination** (a fatty sheath or coating that increases the conductivity of neural impulses), work hard to create more efficient message transmission. The growth and development of neural fibers and myelination is so rapid during this period that the brain, which was 30% of the adult size at birth, grows to 70% its adult size by the second year (Thatcher, Lyon, Rumsey, & Krasnegor, 1996).

Consider This

The rapid growth in brain development that occurs during the first 2 years of life should help us to understand why early intervention programs are so important. The variety and richness of experiences that a toddler is exposed to can influence the number of new neural pathways that are forged during this period of time.

Neurotransmitters. Neurons transmit messages to other neurons by releasing chemicals into the synapse (a space between neurons) that are received by the neighboring neuron. These chemicals are called **neurotransmitters** and they can have a powerful influence on our behaviors. We will be discussing the role of neurotransmitters in greater depth as they relate to each of the childhood disorders. Neurotransmitters send messages to inhibit or activate responses. For example, GABA (gamma-aminobutyric acid) sends a message to inhibit responses; however, when a malfunction occurs, anxiety is often the result. In certain circumstances, abnormal chemical activity (too high or too low levels of a chemical) can cause mental disorders. For example, excess amounts of the neurotransmitter *dopamine* have been linked to schizophrenia, while too little *serotonin* and *norepinephrine* may result in depression.

Endocrine system and hormones. The **endocrine glands** secrete **hormones** into the blood stream. Under certain circumstances (such as stress or depression), the adrenal glands will release the hormone **cortisol** into the system in order to mobilize vital organs in response to a stressful situation, event, or pending threat. The **hypothalamus–pituitary–adrenal** (HPA) system has been implicated in biological explanations for anxiety, stress disorders, and mood disorders.

Brain development: Structures. Developmentally, the **cerebral cortex** is the last structure of the brain to complete its growth which is thought to fully mature by approximately mid to late adolescence. The **frontal lobes** are associated with attention, planning, inhibition of impulses, and behavior regulation. There are four major areas of the brain that have been associated with specific functions: the **Hindbrain, Midbrain, Forebrain,** and the **Cerebral Cortex** (the convoluted mass of gray matter made up of interneurons).

The *Hindbrain* is located just above the spinal cord and houses the **medulla oblongata (medulla)**, *cerebellum,* and parts of the **reticular activating system (RAS)**. The Hindbrain links the spinal cord with the brain, regulates vital functions (heart rate, respiration), and monitors levels of consciousness and arousal (RAS). Damage to the RAS may result in a total loss of consciousness or coma. The **cerebellum** is responsible for several functions, including fine motor movements, some forms of learning, and sensory discrimination. The **tectum** (visual and auditory orientation) and **tegmentum** (movement and arousal) are parts of the *Midbrain*.

The *Forebrain* (located below the cortex) contains the **cerebrum** (consisting of two hemispheres), the **hypothalamus**, and **thalmus**. The cerebrum consists of the **limbic system** and **basal ganglia**. Although one of the main functions of the hypothalmus is to regulate "normal body functions" (such as temperature and metabolism), it can be responsible for activating the pituitary gland to release hormones into the system in times of stress. The thalamus acts as a way station, processing and filtering messages from the sensory neurons and relaying those messages on to the appropriate structures. The limbic system performs a number of functions, involving emotion, learning, memory, and motivation. The limbic system contains the **amygdala** (learning and recall of emotional events, recognition of emotion, e.g., fear), **hippocampus** (storage and recall of new information), and **basal ganglia** (automatic decision making, posture and muscle movement/tone).

The *Cerebral Cortex* (cortex is Latin for "bark") is a convoluted gray mass that covers the brain and consists of many tightly packed interneurons. The **cerebrum** consists of two symmetrical hemispheres (halves) that are separated by a fissure (deep depression) and joined by a strip of neural fibers called the **corpus callosum**. There are four major areas (lobes) found in each of the left and right hemispheres of the brain that are responsible for specific functions: **occipital lobes** (vision), **parietal lobes** (sense of touch, movement, and location of objects/body in space), **frontal lobes** (attention, planing and social skills, abstract reasoning, memory), and **temporal lobes** (auditory discrimination and language; see Figure 2.1).

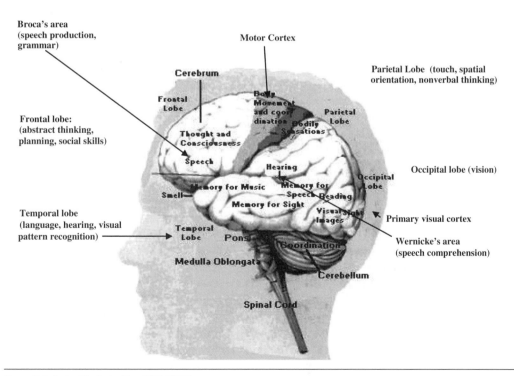

Figure 2.1 Parts of the brain. (From NIMH, 2000.)

Furthermore, function in the brain is lateralized by hemisphere, which for right-handed people would result in verbal functions to be primarily associated with the left hemisphere (language, logic, and motor skill) while nonverbal functions would be associated with the right hemisphere (facial recognition, spatial awareness).

Genetics and heritability.　　Closely tied to a discussion of brain development, anatomy, and chemistry is the concept of genetic inheritance and the extent to which we can inherit abnormalities in brain function or chemistry. But how do we know whether a trait is inherited or learned? In a recent article, Moffitt (2005) has suggested that developmental psychopathology has the potential to be at the leading edge in investigating this gene-environment interplay through the use of experimental designs based on a behavioral–genetic framework, mainly the use of twin and adoption studies. He cites one of the central factors contributing to our lack of progress in the area is our inability to answer questions such as those posed by DiLalla and Gottesman (1991): Does the cycle of violence from abusive parent to aggressive child arise from environmental transmission or genetic transmission?

Read All About It

In 1989, Cathy Spatz Widom published an article summarizing the existing research concerning the *cycle of violence hypothesis*, a hypothesis which supported the notion of the transmission of violence across generations (e.g., abused children become abusive adults). While Widom had conducted an excellent review of the environmental side effects of living in an atmosphere of violence, DiLalla and Gottesman (1991), two behavior geneticists, published a response outlining what they believed to be a crucial missing ingredient in the research to date: namely, the possibility of parents passing on violent tendencies to their children through genetic transmission. They argued that child abuse, and later antisocial behavior, were related by correlation, not causation, since both also shared association to a third factor: genetic risk for antisocial behavior (Koenen, 2005).

According to Moffitt (2002), our inability to answer questions such as the one above stems from our overreliance on correlational methods which do not allow for causal interpretations. Moffit , Caspi, Harrington, and Milne (2002) argue that antisocial behavior in parents is predictive of child abuse and children's future antisocial behavior and that future twin studies need to focus on how violence interacts with genotype to produce negative outcomes in some individuals. Rutter and Sroufe (2000) also emphasize that it is not only understanding the gene-environment interaction that is important for developmental psychopathology, but how these effects carry forward and influence later situations and events in a reciprocal way.

Twin studies and adoption studies.　　Information on genetic transmission has often come from studies of **monozygotic twins (MZ)**, identical twins who share the same DNA (only one ovum was fertilized), compared to **dizygotic twins (DZ)**, fraternal twins who do not share the same DNA (two ovums were fertilized). Comparing MZ twins with DZ twins allows for a study that compares genetic makeup, while controlling for environment. In another variation, MZ twins reared together can be compared to MZ twins reared apart to study the effect of environmental differences or studies of adopted siblings who bring a nonrelated genetic makeup to a different environmental context. Recent longitudinal studies by Caspi, Moffitt, and colleagues (Caspi et al., 2002; Caspi et al., 2003) provide supportive evidence that although child maltreatment does increase the risk of antisocial behavior in adulthood (environmental factors), negative outcomes are dependent upon individual genotype. In their studies, only individuals exposed to child maltreatment who also had low levels of monamine-oxidase (MAOA) were candidates for increased violent behavior as adults. Future research will undoubtedly reflect increased emphasis on determining how specific genetic variants interact with environment factors in the prediction of increased vulnerability for mental disorders.

Genotypes, phenotypes, and endophenotypes. Genetic transmission involves **genotypes** (the genetic material that is not visible), **phenotypes** (visible characteristics, such as hair and eye color), and **endophenotype**s (phenotypical markers or systems that are thought to underlie a given psychological disorder, Gottesman & Gould, 2003). For example, some endophenotypes that have been suggested to align with antisocial behaviors, include frontal lobe hyperarousal, fearlessness, callousness, and negative emotionality (Lahey, Moffitt & Caspi, 2003).

Epigenesis. Recently, emphasis on the genetic and environmental interplay has examined the possibilities of a bidirectional influence. The question now becomes: Can environmental circumstances actually alter genetic makeup? For example, studies have found that certain parenting practices (Meaney, 2001) or exposure to prolonged trauma and abuse (Beers & DeBellis, 2002) can actually alter gene expression in infants and impact on how the brain is genetically wired for hyperresponsiveness to stress.

The role of temperament. Studies have explored genetic transmission of temperamental factors such as activity level and wariness (Plomin, 1994) and the reciprocal impact of early child temperament on child rearing success (e.g., difficult child as a risk factor).

What is temperament? According to Allport (1961), **temperament**, like personality, was a phenomenon "dependent on constitutional makeup and (was) therefore largely heredity in nature" (p. 34). Temperament describes how an individual reacts to emotional stimulation, both in strength and speed of response, and the quality, fluctuation, and prevailing nature of an individual's mood. Within this context, a child who is very outgoing and curious may extend himself or herself out into the world and embrace challenges, while a more timid child may shrink in the face of the unfamiliar. While some personality traits may be learned, research has found evidence that some traits, like wariness/shyness (Kagan, 1992), being inhibited and experiencing negative emotions (Plomin, 1989) may have a hereditary basis. Most behavioral traits are considered to be relatively stable by the end of the infant stage. At this time, parents and caregivers can often describe children based on their individual response style, as being more or less active, fretful, anxious, emotionally reactive or social, than other children.

A Global Perspective

Temperament also differs across cultures. Studies comparing infant temperament across cultures have found that children of non-American cultures have temperaments that differ from American babies. In an early study of cross-cultural influences on temperament, Freedman (1974) found that Chinese American babies, Japanese American babies, and Navajo babies were all calmer than either European American babies or African American babies.

The concept of temperament has evolved over the course of time, and there have been numerous studies developed to investigate the factors involved, the stability of the factors (over time and across situations), and the extent to which factors are heritable or environmentally

Table 2.1 Infant and Child Temperament Characteristics

Trait	Low Level	High Level
Activity Level: Frequency and level of activity		*
Intensity of Response: Response to internal states, situations		*
Distractibility: Ease with which child can be interrupted from task		*
Attention Span and Goal Persistence: Task engagement	*	
Rhythmicity: Regularity of habits, e.g., eating, sleeping, etc.	*	
Adaptability: Ability to adapt to situations over time	*	
Sensory Threshold Amount of stimulation required to produce a response	*	
	Positive	Negative
Approach–Withdrawal: First response to new situation or person	Approach	*Withdraw
Quality of Mood: General frame of mind	Happy/ Pleasant	*Angry/ Irritable/ Anxious

Source: Thomas and Chess, 1977.

influenced. Temperament has been used to explain individual differences in such child areas as activity level, reactivity or emotional intensity, and sociability or withdrawal (Buss & Plomin, 1975; Rothbart, 1981). Thomas and Chess (1977) outlined nine traits that may be used to help define an individual child's temperament. The traits can be ordered on a continuum (e.g., a scale from 1–10) to describe the degree to which certain traits are exhibited by an individual child in areas of: *activity, intensity of response, distractibility, attention span/goal persistence, rhythmicity, adaptability, and sensory threshold.* In addition, a child's ability to *approach versus withdraw* from a novel situation and *overall quality of mood* can be evaluated on a positive or negative level. The list of temperament characteristics developed by Thomas and Chess can be seen in Table 2.1.

Reviewing the traits outlined in Table 2.1 provides greater understanding of how some children may be more difficult to manage than others. While it may be a good thing to have a healthy dose of some traits, like *adaptability* and positive *quality of mood*, children who demonstrate high levels of *activity, intensity, and distractibility* will present more parenting challenges than children who have lower levels of these traits. Similarly, children with low levels of *attention span, rhythmicity, and adaptability* can be more difficult to engage in ongoing tasks and may experience more difficulty shifting between tasks or engaging in self-soothing behaviors (calming themselves). Children who react to low levels of stimulation may become overstimulated in an excitable environment and either act out or retreat in extreme fashions, compared to children who require greater intensity of stimulation to elicit a response. Children who are positive, happy, and approachable are often more popular and at greater social ease than their anxious, timid peers.

Research by Thomas and Chess (1977) concerning these nine traits revealed that about 60% of all children fall into one of three broad categories with the majority having an easy temperament:

1. *Easy temperament*: Adaptable, have well established routines *(rhythmicity),* are socially responsive *(approach),* and positive in their outlook (smiled often).
2. *Difficult child:* Difficulty establishing predictable routines *(rhythmicity),* tendency to respond negatively to new situations *(low adaptability, withdrawal),* and demonstrate inflated responses to highly charged situations, producing such behaviors as tantrums, loud outbursts, and aggression *(intensity, negative mood).*
3. *Slow to warm up child:* Cautious, and can be inhibited in new situations.

The interaction between the child's temperament and that of the parent, known as **goodness of fit** can be instrumental in promoting stability or serve to exacerbate problems.

Science Talks

Patterson, DeBaryshe, and Ramsey (1989) found that children with "difficult temperament traits" who overreact with inflated responses tend to have parents who are themselves highly reactive and punitive. The resulting interactions between parent and child produce what Patterson calls "coercive cycles" and are typified by mutually antagonistic patterns of behavior with the long-term prognosis of children developing aggressive behavior. Scarr and McCartney (1984) have proposed that these types of interactions constitute "evocative" gene–environment interactions.

Buss and Plomin (1975) adopted the Thomas and Chess model to answer questions regarding the continuity of child temperament into adulthood and isolated four broad clusters of traits, including *emotionality, activity, sociability,* and *impulsivity.* Rothbart, Ahadi, and Evans (2000) have investigated the relationship between temperament factors and the **Big Five personality factors** (neuroticism, extraversion, agreeableness, conscientiousness, and openness to experience). The researchers found links between three of the factors and temperament traits, including *negative affectivity* with neuroticism; *effortful control* with conscientiousness; and *surgency* (high pleasure seeking and sociability) with extraversion.

Biological approach: A summation. In defining abnormal behavior, a biological model would seek to determine which parts of the body or brain were malfunctioning, be it genetics, brain chemistry, or brain anatomy. The use of twin studies has been instrumental in providing information concerning the role of genetics in such disorders as autism and schizophrenia. Studies have also revealed that there are greater tendencies for some disorders to run in families, and having a first or second generation family member who had depression, anxiety, or bipolar disorder would place a person a greater risk for a mood disorder. However, the interplay between genetics and environmental influences and the reciprocal manner in which environment can shape the brain and vice versa cannot be underestimated. Refined neurological approaches, such as functional magnetic resonance imaging (fMRI), will continue to influence and add to our understanding of underlying brain based differences in some disorders. Recent investigations of temperament and the Big Five personality factors reveal that some traits evident in childhood can remain stable into adulthood.

Psychodynamic Theories

Psychoanalysis and Freud's psychosexual stages. The psychoanalytic school of thought has had considerable impact on perspectives of child development since the early days of Sigmund Freud (1856–1939). According to Freud, a given personality or **ego** evolves over time as primitive impulses (**id**) come under increasingly greater influence of the **superego** or conscience. Freud described abnormal behaviors in adulthood as **fixations** or **regressions** that had their onset in early stages of development. These **unconscious conflicts** could result from inner turmoil and frustrations due to lack of gratification or overgratification at an earlier stage of development and would manifest or revisit an individual as a symbolic conflict in later life. **Psychosexual stages** were evident in early development and these were related to erogenous zones and gratification: **oral stage** (first year of life), **anal stage** (18 months to 3 years of age), **phallic stage** (3 to 5 years of age), **latency** (school age), and **genital stage** (adolescence). Each stage represented a crucial period that evolved around specific *psychosexual conflicts* that were to be resolved before progressing forward. Unsuccessful attempts to meet these psychosexual challenges could result in unresolved unconscious conflicts that would manifest in the underlying dynamics of certain pathologies.

Toddlers who were subjected to harsh toilet training practices may become fixated at the anal stage of development evident in "anal" personality traits in adulthood (e.g., miserly or stingy disposition and withholding of emotional expression). In the phallic stage, the young child must make the transition from lusting after the parent of the opposite gender (*oedipal complex*) to identifying with the parent of the same gender.

Woven within the fabric of psychodynamic theory is the understanding of the role and nature of **defense mechanisms,** the unconscious ways in which the *ego* tries to defend itself in the wake of demands from the *id* (more primitive pleasure principle) and the *superego* (moral conscience). Developmentally, these defense mechanisms add depth to our understanding of individuals who defend a vulnerable ego through such mechanisms as denial, repression, humor, or sublimation (directing sexual and aggressive energy into acceptable forms, such as karate, soccer, dancing, etc.).

Erik Erikson and psychosocial stages.   Like Freud, Erikson (1902–1994) believed that certain tasks were important at specific developmental stages. However, unlike Freud, who envisioned stages as crises of sexual conflicts that could entrap and fixate or cause its inhabitants to regress to an earlier time, Erikson believed that stages were the threshold to growth and development. At each stage, mastery of the appropriate developmental task or challenge would ensure the necessary preparation to advance to the next developmental level. According to Erikson, individuals do not fixate or regress, but move along a better or worse trajectory. Erikson's **psychosocial stages** provide guidelines about **socioemotional tasks** *or milestones* that children will face at given stages of development. According to Erikson, these tasks produce tension or conflict and failure to successfully master each stage would be predictive of further development along a less advantageous path. Each set of tasks provides a continuum of responses which will ultimately shape the pattern of growth.

Erikson's first developmental task occurs in the 1st year of life and evolves around themes of basic **trust versus mistrust**. The infant develops a sense of trust relative to feelings of security and attachment to caregivers. From the foundation of a secure attachment, the preschooler is free to explore his or her environment and a growing sense of independence, or **autonomy**, develops; or the child may shrink from these experiences due to feelings of **shame** and **self doubt**. The successful school age child masters school-related tasks and welcomes peer socialization, developing a sense of **industry versus inferiority**. In adolescence, amid strong biological and physiological changes, the adolescent must strive to establish his or her individual identity and place or role in society. The degree of the adolescent's success in meeting these challenges will determine the sense of **identity versus role confusion**. Erikson's stages can be reviewed in Table 1.1 (chapter 1).

Psychodynamic interventions and play therapy.   Due to the covert nature of "unconscious" motives, psychodynamic theories have been very difficult to support empirically. However, recent emphasis on empirically based interventions has increased research in the psychodynamic area. One particular area of promise for empirical validation is that of *play therapy*.

With its foundation clearly established in the initial works of Anna Freud (1928) and Melanie Klein (1932), nondirective play therapy gained momentum with Virginia Axline's (1947) account of her play sessions with her client in the popular book: *Dibs in Search of Self* (Axline, 1964). In a recent meta-analysis of 93 controlled outcome studies of play therapy, Bratton, Ray, Rhine, and

Jones (2005) concluded that play therapy is an efficacious form of treatment for children with emotional and behavioral disorders. The authors also found that nondirective play was superior to directive play; treatment was facilitated with length of therapy (up to 35 sessions); and that parent involvement in play therapy also influenced outcomes in a positive direction. Fonagy and Target (1996) provide empirical support for **psychodynamic developmental therapy for children (PDTC)**, a therapeutic approach that integrates psychoanalytic concepts and techniques within a developmental framework. Working through the medium of play, therapists assist severely disturbed children to develop skills in strengthening the self regulation of impulses, enhanced awareness of others, and developing the capacity to play.

More recently, Lefebre-Mcgevna (2007) reviewed the existing literature regarding the etiology, influence of early trauma, and treatment alternatives for **reactive attachment disorder**, **borderline personality disorder,** and **developmental trauma disorder**. Within the discussion, the author considers borderline personality disorder in children to be part of child trauma-based disorders. Lefebre-Mcgevna (2007) has developed a play-based therapeutic approach for young children modeled after **Dialectical Behavior Therapy (DBT)**. The DBT approach has been very successful with adults (Linehan et al., 2001) and is an integrated program that combines cognitive behavioral methods (activities designed to improve social skills and coping with stress) with a psychodynamic emphasis on the therapist–client relationship. Issues regarding the etiology, diagnosis, and treatment of child trauma disorders will be discussed at greater length in chapter 7.

Personality Disorders and the *DSM*

Although Lefebre-Mcgevna (2007) refers to borderline personality disorder in childhood, it is a rare occurrence to diagnose personality disorders in children and adolescents. The *DSM-IV-TR* (APA, 2000) provides the following rationale as to why this is the case: Traits of a personality disorder that appear in childhood will often not persist unchanged into adult life. To diagnose a personality disorder in an individual under 18 years, the features must have been present for at least 1 year. The one exception to this is antisocial personality disorder which cannot be diagnosed in individuals under 18 years of age (p. 687).

As will be discussed in chapter 8, antisocial-type symptoms appearing in youth before 18 years of age would likely be diagnosed as conduct disorder.

Behavioral Theories
According to behaviorists, all human behavior, whether normal or abnormal, develops in response to a prescribed set of learning principles. These principles of learning will predict how behavior can be conditioned in three important ways: **operant conditioning**, **classical conditioning**, and **modeling** or **observational learning**.

Operant conditioning. According to behavioral assumptions of operant behavior, there are two possible explanations for increasing or maintaining behavior: **positive reinforcement** or **negative reinforcement**.

Reinforcements are consequences that have a positive outcome and serve to increase the likelihood that a behavior will be repeated. Associations or contingencies are formed linking the behaviors to these positive consequences.

Consequences are positive if:

1. They *add a benefit* (**positive reinforcement**, e.g., *when your chores are finished you can watch television*), or
2. They *remove a negative* consequence, thereby allowing the individual to *avoid or escape* a negative consequence (**negative reinforcement**, e.g., *if you come home on time, you will not be grounded*).

Important Distinction

The concept of negative reinforcement is more difficult to understand than positive reinforcement because negative reinforcement is often confused with punishment; however, punishments deliver negative consequences and serve to reduce rather than increase behaviors.

Punishments involve consequences that have negative outcomes and serve to decrease the likelihood that a behavior will be repeated.

Consequences are negative if:

1. They *add a negative* consequence (**positive punishment**, e.g., *you are late and you are grounded*), or
2. They *remove a positive* and a penalty is levied (**negative punishment**, e.g., *your assignment is late, you will lose 2 points each day, until it is handed in*).

The positive and negative implications of the reward and punishment paradigm are presented in Table 2.2. Remember that reinforcement always *increases behavior* whether it is positive or negative, and punishment always *decreases behavior* regardless of whether it involves the addition of a negative (positive punishment) or the removal of a positive (negative punishment).

If a behavior ceases to ever be rewarded, or if a behavior is severely punished the response will be the same. That behavior will be eliminated from the repertoire of behaviors because the consequences are either too aversive, or there is no incentive to continue the behavior. The elimination of a behavior under either condition is known as **extinction**.

Behavior is not always what it seems, nor is the concept of what may be rewarding. Consider the following example. A child acts out in class (talking out loud or making silly faces) and the teacher responds by calling out the child's name and asking the child to be quiet. Eventually, the teacher sends the child to the office because the behavior is so distracting to others. However, removal from class may not be the punishment it was intended to be, for two important reasons:

Table 2.2 Reward and Punishment Paradigm

Reinforcement: Behavior Increases	Punishment: Behavior Decreases
Add Positive: (+)	Add Negative (+)
(Positive Reinforcement)	*(Positive Punishment)*
Give reward for good behavior	Punish bad behavior: corporeal punishment, shock, pay a fine
Examples: stickers, candy, money	
Individual acts to obtain reward	Behavior is punished directly
Remove Negative (−)	Remove Positive (−)
(Negative Reinforcement)	*(Negative Punishment)*
Terminology can be confusing.	Punish behavior by removing privileges (telephone, TV, etc.)
Common examples: escape/avoidance	
Individual acts to avoid punishment	Behavior is punished by removing positives

(a) the behavior actually allows the child to *escape/avoid* school work, and

(b) the "office" is a very interesting location where the child can actually receive positive attention from faculty and staff.

In this case, the detention is not a punishment, and is doubly rewarding in the negative sense (negative reinforcement: provides escape from school work) and in the positive sense (positive reinforcement: provides interesting location and attention).

In the above example, the school psychologist can assist the teacher by conducting a **functional behavioral assessment (FBA)** to determine what is causing and sustaining the behavior and develop a **behavioral intervention plan (BIP**; a plan to address increasing compliant and on-task behaviors). A sample behavioral plan will be presented shortly relative to a discussion of Robby in Ms. Strong's class. Prior to reviewing a sample observation and behavior plan, it is important to discuss the concept of how behavior can be categorized relative to the degree to which a behavior is expressed. For example, is the problem one of a **behavioral excess** (too much) or a **behavioral deficit** (too little)? Within this framework, an excessive behavioral pattern can be associated with the **externalizing disorders**, such as oppositional defiant disorder, conduct disorder, which feature behaviors that are excessive and lack behavioral controls. At the other end of the spectrum are the **internalizing disorders** (depression, anxiety, and somatoform disorders) which have the common feature of being behaviors that are overcontrolled and inhibited, such as withdrawal from social contact, or physical responses to mental stressors.

Although individual differences (such as temperament) may account for overall variations in our level of expressiveness, it is very important to develop a behavioral plan that incorporates appropriate developmental expectations, for example, how the behavior is typically manifested, at this point in development, in this type of situation. Therefore, in developing a BIP aimed at increasing a behavior, such as "on-task behavior" or "increased social activity," it will be important to determine not only what is typical for a particular age range, but also the extent to which current behaviors deviate from the norm and how these behaviors are being maintained by the current environmental context.

Recurrent Themes The development of a successful FBA and BIP will rely on the psychologist's knowledge of normal developmental patterns (Theme 1) and how maladaptive behaviors represent deviations from the normal path (Theme 2). Her ability to isolate key environmental contingencies that are sustaining the behavior underlies the importance in identifying how individual, interpersonal, contextual, and cultural factors influence deviations in development (Theme 4).

Case in Point

Rebecca, the school psychologist, is asked to observe Robby, a child in Ms. Strong's Grade 3 classroom. Ms. Strong is concerned about Robby's poor academic progress and his behaviors that are very disruptive to the class routines. Despite numerous warnings, Robby's behavior continues to disrupt the class and is escalating. During her observation, Rebecca charts Robby's behavior by recording the number of times that Robby's behavior is on-task or off-task, and the response to his behaviors by classmates and the teacher. In her observations, Rebecca finds that the teacher is correct in her evaluation that Robby's behavior is disruptive; in fact, he is only on-task for less than one-third of the class time. When he is off-task, he is either out of his seat or chatting to classmates. A sample observational recording protocol is presented in Table 2.3

Table 2.3 Classroom Observation for Robby B.

Time Observed:	9:30–9:55 a.m., Thursday February 19, 2006
Total Observation Time:	25 minutes
Class Activity:	Reading Lesson. Children rotate reading segments of a story out loud, then answer questions asked by the teacher and contribute to ongoing class discussion.
Type of Observation:	Timed Interval: Observe at 60 second intervals. Observe for 20 seconds. Total Observations = 25.

# Obs	On Task Behaviors			Off Task Behaviors			Class Response		Teacher Response	
#	Ask Q Answer Listen	Read	Write	Day Dream	Talk	Move	Attend	Ignore	Attend	Ignore
1				√				√		√
2				√				√	√	
3	√						√		√	
4					√		√			
5					√		√		√	
6						√	√			√
7						√	√		√	
8					Makes Joke √		√		√ Upset	
9		√						√		√
10		√						√		√
11						√		√		√
12						√		√		√
13						Out of Seat	√		√	
14						O of S	√		√ Upset	
15						O of S	√		√ Upset	
16					Talk Back	O of S	√		√ Upset	
17				Stare			√			√
18				Huff			√			√
19		√						√		√
20			√					√		√
21			√							
22						√		√		√
23	√							√		√
24		√								√
25					Talk out		√		√	
Totals	2	4	2	4	5	9	12	11	9	13
%	8%	16%	8%	16%	20%	36%	48%	44%	36%	52%

As a result of her observations, the school psychologist would be able to evaluate the frequency of Robby's off-task behaviors relative to his classmates (observe another student who the teacher feels has average progress and compare incidences of on-task and off-task behavior) and provide insight as to which responses in the classroom (student or teacher attention) may be adding fuel to the fire by reinforcing and causing Robby's behaviors to escalate. Rebecca's observations are part of her FBA. Using information form her observations and teacher interviews, Rebecca is able to provide the following information.

Functional Behavioral Assessment (FBA)

Precipitating Conditions: During reading class, when others are reading or involved in the discussion, Robby engages in off-task behaviors.

Specific Off-task Behaviors	Consequences	Function of Behavior
Robby makes a joke in class	Students laugh	Attention
	Teacher reprimands	Attention
Robby talks back to teacher	Teacher reprimands	Attention
	Office detention	Removal/escape
Robby talks out of turn in class	Students look at him	Attention
	Teacher reprimand	Time out–escape

Based on the above analysis, Rebecca is able to pinpoint a number of specific off task behaviors to target in the BIP (talking out of turn, jokes, talking back). She has also determined that these off-task behaviors are being maintained because Robby is being rewarded by attention and his ability to escape work. Therefore, the psychologist has selected increasing on-task behavior as the goal for Robby's BIP (it is always better to attempt to increase a behavior than decrease a behavior, since positives can be rewarded and maintained). The behaviors to be increased are specified:

1. Robby will remain seated with his eyes focused on the teacher or his work and initiate a response to a prompt within 20 seconds.
2. Robby will raise his hand and wait until permission is given before speaking in class.

Specific rewards and penalties will be stipulated in the **behavioral contract** (a statement of the contingencies and consequences) and will be agreed to and signed by Robby and the teacher. For example, if Robby increases his hand raising and productivity to meet his daily goals, he will be given a coupon to purchase an activity (from the class activity store) to use during free time.

In the above example, exchanging a coupon for a tangible reward (toy) is an example of a **token economy** often used in behavioral programs as incentives to increase behaviors. Children's behaviors can be shaped through **operant conditioning** (increasing behaviors in response to reward, or decreasing behaviors due to punishments), or new behaviors can be acquired through individuals **modeling** what they see, also known as **observational learning**. Observational learning does not have to be immediate and can often occur as a delayed response. Observational learning will be discussed at greater length, shortly.

Classical conditioning. Although the majority of learned behavior occurs through operant conditioning or observational learning, there are situations where behaviors can be conditioned to certain responses by their strength of association to another behavior.

> **Case in Point**
>
> Sara is very afraid of thunderstorms. When she was very young, she and her father were stranded out at sea on an extremely turbulent evening and could not be rescued until the following morning. To this day, Sara responds very badly (anxious, sweaty palms, tremors) when thunder or lightning is very pronounced. Yesterday, the phone rang. Just as Sara went to answer her phone, there was a huge thunderclap and instantaneously, lightning hit the tree beside her house, splitting the tree in two. Ten minutes later, her phone rang again, just as a second clap of thunder and lightning followed. Sara immediately pulled the plug on the phone. The following day, feeling rather foolish, Sara reconnected her phone. However, when the phone rang, she began to tremble and ran to take cover. For Sara, her fear of storms was now inextricably linked to the sound of her phone. A classic case of classical conditioning.

The paradigm of *classical conditioning* can assist our understanding of how *irrational fears* or *phobias* can develop. Although the Russian scientist Pavlov's intent was to study salivation in dogs, his keen observation revealed that dogs salivated not only to the food, but to the sound of the food being prepared. Ultimately, by pairing the sound of a bell with several presentations of food, Pavlov discovered that dogs would salivate to the sound of the bell alone. In Sara's case, fear of thunderstorms was linked to the sound of her telephone and ultimately caused her to fear the ring of the phone. Furthermore, the fear might *generalize* to similar sounds, such as the ringing of a telephone on a movie on the television (**stimulus generalization**). In the case of the loud thunderstorm, the loud noise is the **unconditioned stimulus** and the fear is the **unconditioned response**. However, pairing of the neutral stimulus with the loud thunderstorm can turn a once neutral stimulus (phone ring) into a **conditioned stimulus** that is now capable of eliciting a **conditioned response** of fear. The association between the unconditioned and conditioned stimulus is depicted graphically in Table 2.4.

> **Science Talks: From White Rats to Santa Claus**
>
> In the early attempts to prove that fears could be conditioned, Watson and Raynor used classical conditioning to instill fear of a white rat in little Albert, a young toddler who instinctively showed no fear of the whiter furry rodent. However, after a series of trials presenting a frightening loud noise just prior exposing the rat, Albert eventually became frightened of the rat, by its association to the noise. Ultimately, through *stimulus generalization* (conditioning generalizes to stimuli that resemble the original), Albert became fearful of many fur-like objects, including his mother's fur coat and Santa's white beard. Today, such an experiment would not be considered ethical.

Systematic desensitization (Wolpe, 1958) is a behavioral method developed to assist clients to gradually dissipate their fear or phobia over a number of trials. There are three parts to the program:

1. The development of a **fear hierarchy**, a list of increasingly fearful images or activities related to the fear.
2. Training in **deep relaxation**.
3. Pairing each of the fears in the hierarchy with a relaxation responses until the fear is mastered at each level.

Table 2.4 Classical Conditioning

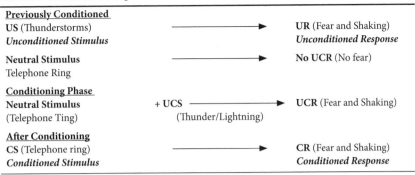

Exposure techniques such as **systematic desensitization** will be discussed at greater length in chapters 6 and 7 when the anxiety disorders and phobias are addressed. Systematic desensitization could be used to assist a young child to conquer school phobia by gradually having the child approach the school yard, while engaging in calming exercises and providing rewards as an increased incentive.

Modeling or observational learning.   A third type of learning involves learning through modeling or observational learning. In their classic experiment on observational learning, Bandura, Roth, and Ross (1963) found that young children who observed an adult reacting aggressively to a "Bobo doll" (inflatable doll with sand feet, like a punching bag) were significantly more likely to abuse the doll when it was their turn to play compared with peers who had not observed the aggressive adult. The experiment was a powerful indicator of the potential role of child exposure to violence, since it was also demonstrated that modeling could be delayed and learned behaviors could be mediated vicariously.

Cognitive Theories

Cognitive theorists are primarily interested in thought processes and how thoughts influence behavior. To the cognitive theorists, behavior is the outcome of thought. Piaget (1896–1980) was a cognitive theorist who attempted to explain how children develop increasingly more sophisticated reasoning abilities over the course of time. According to Piaget, limitations in reasoning ability at some stages of development result in faulty logic and inaccurate assumptions. Cognitive theorists have investigated how faulty assumptions can impact how we perceive others in social relationships and our own self attribution system.

Piaget's stages of cognitive development.   Jean Piaget's theory of **stages of cognitive development** provided psychologists with a framework for developing expectations for child behaviors based on a child's level of cognitive understanding. Piaget's observations of his own children provided the basis for a set of propositions regarding reasoning ability in the developing child. Piaget believed that children are innately curious and that learning is the outcome of a child's interaction with the environment. However, Piaget also believed that "readiness is all" and that children's reasoning was subject to limitations imposed at various stages of development. By acting on their environment, children **assimilate** information into existing structures (**schemas**). Faulty judgements result when the child links new information to old information without changing the level of understanding. When the child is ready, there is an understanding that new information does not fit into an existing schema. This conflict creates tension or a sense of **disequilibrium** which can only be resolved by changing previous ways of understanding (schema) to **accommodate** the new information. The result is movement to a higher level or stage of understanding and a new sense of balance is restored (**equilibrium**).

The developmental tasks that were presented in Table 1.1 reveal the way in which Piaget's stages address cognitive skills across the age span. Piaget reasoned that very young children (ages 2 to 7) function at a **preoperational stage** which is typified by what Piaget called **an inability to decenter.** Focusing on only one dominant visual attribute, children at this stage will erroneously report that there is more liquid in a tall thin glass than a short fat one, even though the child has seen the same amount poured into the two glasses. Unable to consider conflicting information, children will also have difficulty with issues of **appearance and reality**, as well as an inability to take another's point of view due to **egocentrism** or self focus (e.g., the 3-year-old who wants to buy his dad a toy truck for his birthday).

Despite increased competencies, school-aged children are still limited in their thinking by their observations of actual objects and events, which is why Piaget labelled this stage as the **stage of concrete operations**. Piaget reserved the ability to think in the *abstract* for the period of adolescence where the youth's ability to perform tasks requiring hypothetical and deductive reasoning placed then in the **stage of formal operations**.

Science Talks

Piaget's theories were developed and aided by his observations of Swiss children beginning in the 1920s. Although research (Shayer, Demetriou, & Perez, 1986), has demonstrated that the order in which Piaget's stages occur remains fixed across a wide variety of different cultures, there has been greater cultural disparity noted in the ages at which children in different cultures master the various tasks. Research suggests that given the opportunity and training, children who live in cultures that lack formal schooling can be trained to successfully accomplish conservation tasks (Dasen, Ngini, & Lavallee, 1979).

 RECURRENT THEMES   Piaget's theories of cognitive development have assisted greatly in our understanding of how normal cognitive development typically follows an orderly and predictable path (Theme 1).

Social Cognitive Theories

Elkind and personal fables.   A number of theorists have adapted the cognitive framework to social thought and developed theories of social understanding, or **social cognition**. Elkind (1979, 1983) suggests that although egocentrism (self focus) wanes in middle childhood, there is a resurgence in adolescence due to the adolescent's bias to uniqueness in the construction of **personal fables** (Elkind, 1967) and oversensitivity to scrutiny, **imaginary audience** (Elkind & Bowen, 1979). According to Elkind, personal fables often evolve around three common themes: *invulnerability* (absolution from harm), *omnipotence* (sense of heightened authority and knowledge), and *personal uniqueness* (others cannot be expected to understand). While some theorists have suggested that these constructs lay the foundation for faulty risk perception and risk taking behaviors in adolescence (Arnett, 1992), others see personal fables as an adaptive mechanism necessary to provide the adolescent with the sense of agency and drive to complete the process of individuation required at this time (Lapsley, 1993). More recently, Aalsma, Lapsely, and Flannery

(2006) found that omnipotence/narcissism was associated with positive mental health, while invulnerability and personal uniqueness were associated with poorer outcomes, such as anxiety, depression, and suicide ideation.

Case in Point

Lally is a 13-year-old girl who believes that her life is so unique that no one can possibly understand what she feels or thinks. She withdraws to her room regularly to listening to music on her iPod, as she writes volumes in her journal. When her mother tries to coax her out of her room, Lally is convinced that her mother could not possibly understand what she is going through, that in fact, no one could understand what is going on in her life. Lally is demonstrating the quality of *personal uniqueness* as part of her *personal fable*.

Jerzy looks up from his dinner plate during a family meal and immediately stares everyone at the table down, exclaiming, "What are you looking at!" Jerzy often feels that others are staring at him and on a fault-finding mission. This oversensitive perspective is what Elkind referred to as feelings of constantly being on the defensive to observations by *an imaginary audience.*

Bandura and triadic reciprocity.   Albert Bandura's (1977, 1986) studies of young children and modeled aggression led to the development of his concept of **triadic reciprocity** (Bandura, 1977) to explain the dynamics of the interactive forces of the person, behavior, and environment. According to Bandura (1986), "human functioning is explained in terms of a model of triadic reciprocity in which behavior, cognitive and other personal factors, and environmental events all operate as interacting determinants of each other" (p. 18). When Bandura published *Social Foundations of Thought and Action: A Social Cognitive Theory* (1986), he called attention to the shortcomings of linear, mechanistic, and static models that had dominated the field and ushered in an approach that favored a developmental–contextual and dynamically interactive focus (Lerner, 1990).

Bandura's understanding of the social aspects of learning has been instrumental in increasing our awareness of the possible implications of observing the behavior of others. Children's observation and subsequent modeling of adult behavior can have positive (nurturing and empathic caring behaviors) or negative consequences (aggressive responses, e.g., witness to domestic violence). These responses can be immediately observable or can be evident in a delayed response. Bandura's studies of the impact of observed aggression on modeling behavior have gained increased appreciation in modern investigations regarding children who witness domestic violence. For example, when a child demonstrates aggression at school, the social behaviorist may seek to confirm or rule out whether the child may be imitating behaviors observed in the home.

RECURRENT THEMES   Bandura's emphasis on environment and the interaction between the individual and the environment emphasizes the interplay between the individual, interpersonal, contextual, and cultural factors that can influence deviations in development (Theme 4).

Bandura's theories have also been instrumental to our understanding of **self efficacy**. Bandura (1994) defines *self efficacy* as an individual's belief about their own levels of competence, which Bandura feels can permeate an individual's feelings, thoughts, and motivations. According to Bandura, the development of an individual's self efficacy is under four main areas of influence:

1. Mastery experiences (successes increase our sense of efficacy in specific areas);
2. Vicarious experiences (when we identify with someone who succeeds, we see ourselves as also being capable);
3. Social persuasion (having a strong rooting gallery and support system can increase our willingness to attempt challenging experiences); and
4. Stress reduction and reducing negative thought patterns about emotional and physical states.

For each of the areas of positive influence noted above, there are of course negative influences that can serve to undermine an individual's feelings of self efficacy, such as experiencing failure which can warn us of our limitations; observing failed attempts by others who we identify with can lower our expectations for success; unrealistic expectations by others or having too little support from others can undermine our efforts; and experiencing increased levels of stress emotionally and physically can drain us of our resources.

In addition to observational learning, children can also develop their understanding of social relationships in ways that can serve to reinforce poor social skills and faulty problem solving. Studies (Coie, 1985; Coie & Dodge, 1983; Schwartz, Dodge, & Coie, 1993) have demonstrated how children's faulty reasoning about their social relationships can influence inappropriate behavior, whereas cooperative problem solving can serve to enhance more positive social exchanges (Hartup & Laursen, 1993). Dodge, Bates, and Pettit (1990) found that children who were rejected by their peers often exhibited behaviors towards others that were aggressive, argumentative, and retaliatory. In probing why some children responded to seemingly ambiguous situations with negative behaviors, the researchers found that some children act on their faulty interpretations of ambiguous situations as hostile, or a **hostile attribution bias**. Based on this information, treatment for a child who demonstrates aggressive tendencies may require remediation in areas of social cue awareness and the underlying processes which contribute to the development of prosocial behaviors, such as secure attachment, social perspective taking, empathy, and self control.

Consider This

Similar to the concept of equifinality, different social cognitive explanations might be used to explain the same behavior. Aggressive behavior may be seen to develop from observational learning (modeling) or be the result of misinterpretation of social cues, such as a hostile attribution bias (Dodge, Bates, & Pettit, 1990).

Cognitive behavioral theories. The cognitive behavioral approach seeks to understand the link between thinking and behaving. Therefore, the cognitive behavioral therapist focuses on how the child's faulty belief system might contribute to behavior, such as aggression, depression, and anxiety. Cognitive theorists, such as Aaron Beck (1976), have developed theories of how negative and faulty thinking can lead to depression in adults, as well as children and adolescents. While some therapists favor a cognitive or behavioral approach, many combine these two approaches into a more comprehensive model.

Theories of Attachment and Parenting

Attachment Theory

Bowlby and evolution.   Bowlby (1908–1990) developed his theory of attachment based on several influential sources, including Darwin's theory of evolution and adaptation, and Freud's emphasis on early influences in the formation of personality and cognitive structures (**internal working models** that provided the **prototype** for future relationships). Although Bowlby accepted Freud's ideas about internal working models, his view of the child differed significantly from Freud's. While Freud's child was driven to be attached by internal drives such as hunger and drive reduction, Bowlby believed that attachment was related more to adaptation and development. In this way, early experiences shape mental representations that pave the way for how new relationships are perceived.

From an evolutionary perspective, Bowlby's theory of attachment was also influenced by studies of early patterns of animal adaptation that emphasized the need to maintain proximity to the attachment figure, most notably, Lorenz's studies of **imprinting** in baby birds (early following behavior of chicks to an adult to ensure the baby will be fed and protected) and Harlow's studies of rhesus monkeys. Harlow's studies with rhesus monkeys provided significant support to Bowlby's ideas of attachment in that the studies demonstrated that in times of stress, monkeys chose the cloth wire mother as opposed to the wire mother that provided food. The studies were significant in refuting previous claims that attachment formed with caregivers as a result of feeding and demonstrated that security was the significant element in attachment.

Science Talks

In a series of experiments conducted in the 1950s and 1960s under the direction of Harry Harlow (Harlow & Harlow, 1969), rhesus monkeys were separated from their natural mothers shortly after birth and placed in different experimental conditions involving substitute mothers. Some monkeys were raised by two monkey substitutes: a wire monkey who provided food (a bottle) and a wire monkey covered in soft terry cloth. Under these conditions, monkeys did not attach to the wire monkey who provided the food, but instead, spent more time with the cloth monkey and would cling to the cloth monkey if distressed.

Building on these influences, Bowlby believed that infants were genetically wired to make social contact from birth as a strategic method of survival. For Bowlby, early attachments provided the foundation for all future expectations regarding the nature of relationships. Bowlby's (1969) concepts of **reciprocal determinism** have taught us to look at child and caregiver interactions as a bidirectional arrow, and the emphasis on interactive influences was felt in further investigations of attachment behaviors, as well as parenting style. Bowlby's interest in the differential effects of attachment experiences was also influenced by Harlow's findings that some monkeys raised in the artificial conditions became rejecting adults whose infant monkeys responded with an anxious form of attachment.

Ainsworth and the strange situation experiments.   Through her research on early attachment in the **strange situation experiments**, Mary Ainsworth found that different types of attachment patterns predicted unique patterns of behavioral responses.

Science Talks

Mary Ainsworth and colleagues (Ainsworth et al., 1978) devised an experimental design called the **Strange Situation** in order to study the degree of security evident in the mother–child attachment relationship. The laboratory is equipped with one-way observation glass and the infant's behaviors are closely monitored and recorded. Each step in the process provides researchers with additional information about the child's attachment behaviors and attachment pattern. The standardized procedure involves 8 steps during which mother and infant are separated twice.

1. Baby and mother are left in the observational play room to explore toys.
2. A stranger enters the room.
3. After mother talks to the stranger for a brief period, the mother leaves.
4. Shortly afterward, the stranger also leaves and the child is alone.
5. Mother returns to comfort the child.
6. Mother leaves again.
7. Stranger returns and attempts to comfort the child.
8. Mother returns and attempts to comfort the child.

Patterns of attachment. Based on the child's responses to their reunions with their mothers (steps 5 and 8 in the strange situation experiments), researchers classified the child as having one of three attachment patterns:

1. **Secure attachment:** When the caregiver is present, infants in this category are observed to use the caregiver as a secure base for exploration. Other typical behaviors include affective sharing of toys and play, and **social referencing** (looking towards mother for clues as to appropriate behaviors, or for problem solving assistance).
   Reunions: Although the child may respond to mother leaving with distress, he or she is readily comforted when contact resumes. If not distressed, the child can be expected to greet mother's return, often with enthusiasm.
2. **Anxious/Resistant Attachment:** Play is subdued with little exploration, and the child is somewhat wary of the surroundings. The child may protest maternal leaving.
   Reunions: Child may be clingy and distressed and may seek contact and then resist or reject comfort (arching back, pulling away).
3. **Avoidant attachment:** Play is independent and exclusive of maternal involvement. The child may engage stranger in play when caregiver leaves. Readily separates from caregiver (indifference).
   Reunions: Ignores mother when leaving and ignores mother upon her return. Avoids mother completely on second return, however, does not avoid or ignore the stranger.

Later, Main and Weston (1981) added a fourth category:

4. **Disorganized/Disoriented Attachment:** Atypical patterns of play and reunions. Behaviors are contradictory (approach and avoidance) and emotions are volatile. Play may be random and unstructured or repetitive.
   Reunions: No predictable pattern with variations that may include: rocking motions, dazed appearance, and stop and start (incomplete) movements.

Science Talks

In their work with abused and maltreated children, Main and Hesse (1990) have suggested that the disorganized set of responses develop because there is no predictable pattern of separation and reunions in these children's lives. As a result, children do not develop consistent internal working models. Instead, for these children a reunion with an attachment figure simultaneously activates opposing response systems of *approach* (attachment) and *avoidance* (fear) resulting in a disorganized set of responses.

Baumrind and parenting styles.   Baumrind (1991) studied how differences in parenting style can influence child characteristics.

RECURRING THEMES   Parenting style can influence child outcomes directly (individual characteristics, interpersonal relationships) or indirectly (economic hardship, marital problems, cultural factors) in ways that can either protect the child from harm or increase a child's risk for developing deviant behaviors (Theme 4).

A parent's style of interaction with their child, their manner of communication and discipline, and the extent to which the child is allowed to negotiate within the confines of the parent–child relationship, can all have a powerful influence on child development. In her investigation of *parenting styles*, Baumrind (1991) isolated characteristics of parenting approaches that can influence child behaviors and outcomes. The four parenting types are based on indices of parenting practices of control/structure and parent warmth. The resulting grid can be seen in Table 2.5 as parenting styles are seen to reflect characteristics of structure and warmth.

Parenting styles that rate high on *structure* are the **authoritarian** and the **authoritative** parents. Those who rate low on structure are parents who are **permissive** or parents who are **uninvolved**. The main difference between authoritative and authoritarian parents is that while authoritative parents moderate their structure and control with warmth, authoritarian parents impose force in the absence of warmth ("My way or the highway."). As a consequence, children raised in more coercive environments are more likely to demonstrate behaviors that are aggressive and uncooperative relative to their peers raised in authoritative households who demonstrate

Table 2.5 Parenting Style

Parenting Style– Child Characteristics	Acceptance/Involvement	Control/Structure	Autonomy/Independence
Parent: **Authoritative** Child: Self Concept Self Esteem	High Acceptance High Warmth	Consistent/Adaptive	Appropriate
Parent: **Authoritarian** Child: Anxious Hostile	Low Acceptance Low Warmth	Consistent/Coercive	Inappropriate Minimal
Parent: **Permissive** Child: Demanding	High Acceptance High Warmth Overindulgent	Lacking	Inappropriate Excessive
Parent: **Uninvolved** Child: Dependent	Low Acceptance Low Warmth Negligent	Lacking	Indifferent

Source: Baumrind, 1991.

more competence and higher self-esteem. While permissive households provide warmth, children raised in these households are less likely to receive the guidance and modeling available to peers living in more structured households. As a result, permissive children often demonstrate poor sense of individual responsibility, and are often lacking in self-control. Parents who are uninvolved provide little warmth or structure and appear indifferent and self-centered. According to Baumrind, children raised in such an environment may exhibit a number of negative characteristics, including impulsivity, truancy, and be at greater risk for engaging in substance use and delinquent behaviors.

Family Systems Theory. Family Systems Theory represents a multitude of approaches that have the family as the core unit of assessment and intervention. While the majority of theoretical frameworks for evaluating child psychopathology do so from the perspective of individual differences, proponents of family systems theory emphasize the family unit as the main focus of study (Davies & Cicchetti, 2004). Within this framework, the child is seen as a subunit of the family system, similar to other subunits: parent–child, marriage partners, siblings, extended family, etc.

Family Systems Theory recognizes the **identified problem** (e.g., most often the child whose behavior has been identified) and the problem is evaluated within the context of family dynamics as it pertains to systems of communication, alliances, and boundaries.

Boundaries refer to limits set among family members regarding cohesiveness and involvement. Some families have very few limits or have very **loosely** defined limits. In these cases, children are often on the same power level as the adults in the family and often privy to information that is inappropriate for their age level. In other households, children are not allowed to participate in adult conversations and are given few privileges due to limits that are very **rigidly** defined and applied. While some families have a detached (**disengaged**) sense of connection among family members, other families may be overly involved (**enmeshed***)* in each other's lives (Minuchin, 1985). Other concepts of importance to family systems therapy is the need to identify such family characteristics as roles (identified family members who take on the role of clown, rescuer, victim, etc.), rules (unwritten standards and traditions), hierarchy (chain of command), climate (nurturing versus critical), and equilibrium (efforts to maintain the status quo).

Consider This

Recently, some proponents of Family Systems Theory have emphasized the need for greater consideration of the role of initial family stresses (Emery, Fincham, & Cummings, 1992), and child developmental level on therapeutic interventions.

Emery (2001) acknowledges that although supporters of **Behavioral Family Interventions (BFI)** have long acknowledged the dynamics inherent in **coercion theory** (Patterson, Capaldi, & Bank, 1991), their reluctance to consider the impact of current parent stress level, or developmental status has served to significantly reduce the effectiveness of many interventions.

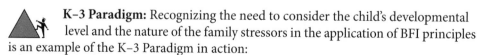 **K–3 Paradigm:** Recognizing the need to consider the child's developmental level and the nature of the family stressors in the application of BFI principles is an example of the K–3 Paradigm in action:

1. Knowledge of development.
2. Knowledge of sources of influence.
3. Knowledge of theoretical perspectives.

Coercion theory was developed to explain the impact of coercive parenting practices on escalating negative behaviors in children. It has long predicted that parents who eventually yield to a child's escalating and demanding behaviors serve to *positively reinforce the child's misbehavior* (child eventually gets what they want) while at the same time receiving *negative reinforcement for their own compliance* (cessation of whining and complaining). Therefore, the parent learns that giving in will stop the demands, while the child learns that increased demands result in parent compliance. Since positive and negative reinforcement serve to strengthen behaviors, parent and child become locked in an escalating and neverending battle. Strict adherence to a BFI plan would dictate that parents change the dynamics of often or occasionally giving in to the child's demands, with a consistent never giving in approach. However, as Emery (2001) points out, there are times when strictly following behavioral guidelines can result in missed opportunities for learning or escalating of stress at vulnerable times. For example, a teenager who attempts to negotiate extending limits (e.g., lobbying for later bedtime or increased allowance) may be very appropriate developmentally, and this exercise may be a necessary precursor to increased autonomy and independence.

Developmental Theories: A Summation

Given the wide range of theoretical viewpoints available, it becomes increasingly clear that clinicians may view any given behavioral response from a variety of different perspectives. It is also evident that while some theories tend to overlap (cognitive/behavioral/social), features of other theories may be more difficult to integrate (biological versus family systems). In many cases, theory influences the direction of the investigator's focus and rationale concerning the causes for a given behavior: e.g., internal/external factors, past/present influences, and individual/interpersonal variables. Returning to our original case presentation of Jordan, whose father was seeking treatment for Jordan's symptoms of depression, it is now possible to provide a more in-depth understanding of how these different viewpoints might generate many different hypotheses and explanations. A hypothetical view of depression across the spectrum of theoretical viewpoints was introduced in chapter 1 (Table 1.3). With an increased level of understanding, revisit Table 1.3 and consider Jordan's case from each of the perspectives presented.

Integrating Theoretical Perspectives: A Multisystemic Approach

There is an increasing appreciation of the need to integrate information from more than one theoretical perspective. There has been a major paradigm shift in understanding childhood disorders resulting from movement away from considering child disorders from an adult perspective to developing an increased awareness of the complex and often unique nature of disorders in childhood and adolescence (Kazdin, 1997; Kazdin & Kagan, 1994). As a result, contemporary clinicians often use an **eclectic approach** (an approach that uses elements from a number of different models) to integrate assumptions from several theoretical frameworks. In addition, there is an increased awareness of the need to link treatment approaches to evidence-based research, such as the growing research support for the use of cognitive behavioral methods in the treatment of depression (Stark, Reynolds, & Kaslow, 1987; Stark, Rouse, & Livingston, 1991), anxiety (Kendall et al., 1992), and obsessive compulsive disorder (Waters, Barrett, & March, 2001).

The K–3 Paradigm: Development, theories, and contexts. Returning to the K–3 Paradigm, up to this point, we have addressed two of the major anchor points of our model: knowledge of normal developmental expectations and knowledge of different theoretical models. One major area remains to be addressed in depth, which is the knowledge of sources of influence, or the contexts of development (Figure 2.2).

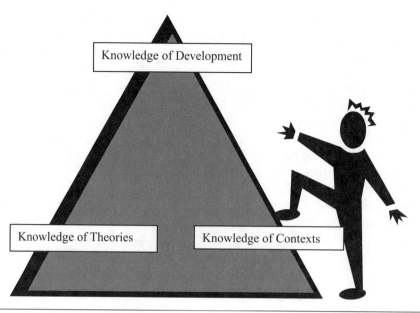

Figure 2.2 The K–3 Paradigm.

The Contexts of Development: An Ecological Transactional Framework

Fully understanding the dynamics involved in child psychopathology also requires consideration of the relationship between the presenting behavior or pathology and the environmental context. The child clinician must examine the impact of **developmental contexts** in *predisposing*, *precipitating*, and *sustaining/maintaining* the behavior in question. While we have a host of theoretical models to choose from to guide our understanding of the development and course of maladaptive behaviors, our comprehension of how these behaviors manifest depends upon our appreciation of the unique way in which environmental influences can shape outcomes for better or worse. Linking mental disorders to developmental contexts requires the need to consider spheres of influence which are inextricably linked to the child's inner world.

Beginning with Bronfenbrenner's ecological model (1979, 1989) as an overarching framework, there is a greater appreciation of how the child's development is influenced, not only by the child's *individual characteristics* (biological context, such as genetic makeup, temperament, intelligence), but the child's *immediate environment/***microsystem** (family, school, peers, community neighborhood), the surrounding *social and economic context/***exosystem** (poverty, divorce, family stress), as well as, *cultural context/***macrosystem**. Therefore, understanding a child's problems requires an understanding of the role of the contextual variables that serve to predispose, precipitate, and maintain the child behaviors over time. The model is a dynamic one with ever-changing roles that can influence players at each and every level in a **transactional** (ongoing system of changes and response to change) and **ecological** manner (contextual influences that can cause and respond to changes at many levels: e.g., individual, immediate, social, cultural). As the child is influenced by his or her environment, the environment also is influenced by the child. Bronfenbrenner's ecological model was presented graphically in chapter 1, Figure 1.1.

Recall and Rewind

Bronfenbrenner used the term **mesosystem** to refer to the indirect effects that can exert a negative or positive influence when parts of the same system interact (microsystem) based on the degree of compatibility and internal coherence. For example, the system can be thrown off-balance if a mother and father give a child conflicting information, or it can be strengthened if messages are consistent and supported.

In the next chapter, using Bronfenbrenner's model as a guide, the role of risks and protective factors will be examined at each level of developmental influence. A major part of the chapter will focus on the macrosystem characteristic of culture, as the unique challenges facing minority youth are explored.

CHAPTER SUMMARY AND REVIEW

1. **Issues in Clinical Decision Making: Determining Normal from Abnormal Behavior**
   a. In determining normal versus abnormal behavior, clinicians often evaluate behaviors relative to a number of criteria, including: the 4 Ds (deviance, dysfunction, distress, danger); the degree to which the behavior occurs (intensity, frequency, duration); and the pervasiveness of the behavior across situations.
   b. Some of the difficulties in determining normal from abnormal behavior are the inherent subjectivity of the process, cultural confounds, and the use of different diagnostic systems for classification (*DSM* versus *ICD-10 Codes*).
   c. Clinicians who work with children and youth have the added difficulty of assessing and diagnosing pathology within a developmental perspective that includes knowledge about what is developmentally appropriate at a given age, and how disorders change throughout the developmental spectrum. Treatments also must be appropriate for the child's developmental level.
   d. Clinicians can be aided in their understanding of child and adolescent disorders by drawing on different theoretical models which seek to explain the etiology, nature, and course of child psychopathology. Models discussed include: biomedical, psychodynamic, behavioral, cognitive, attachment and parenting, family systems theory, and sociocultural models.

2. **Trends in Conceptualizing Developmental Change: Theories and Perspectives**
   a. *Biological* approaches look to the brain (anatomy or chemical malfunction) or heritability in seeking answers to the causes and treatments of psychopathology. Studies of temperament have impacted our understanding of child personality and development.
   b. *Psychodynamic* theories focus on internal drives and unconscious motives in underlying psychopathology and have increased our awareness of the role of defense mechanisms in protecting the ego. We have also gained an appreciation of developmental tasks evident at different psychosocial stages.
   c. *Behavioral* theories provide increased appreciation of how reinforcement and punishment can influence the development and maintenance of adaptive and maladaptive behavior.
   d. *Cognitive* theorists focus on maladaptive thinking as the driving force behind disordered behaviors.

e. Theories of **Attachment and Parenting** illustrate how secure or insecure early *attachment patterns* can provide the basis for internal working models that define how we view relationships later on, while the degree of structure, warmth, and control evident in different *Parenting Styles* can impact of favorable or unfavorable child outcomes.

Evaluating child concerns from a *Family Systems Perspective* allows for a comprehensive look at dynamics among the subsystems (children, siblings, parents) and the role these dynamics play in precipitating and maintaining maladaptive behaviors.

3. **The K–3 Paradigm**

The K–3 Paradigm is a helpful heuristic (learning tool) for reinforcing the three cornerstones of information that are required to understand the nature of maladaptive behavior:

a. Knowledge of developmental expectations,

b. Knowledge of sources of influence (child characteristics and environmental characteristics), and

c. Knowledge of theoretical models and perspectives.

4. **The Contexts of Development: Bronfenbrenner and Ecological Theory**

a. Bronfenbrenner's emphasis on the interaction between child characteristics (biological context) and environmental characteristics (immediate environment, social and economic contexts, and cultural context) were discussed relative to their influences in predisposing, precipitating, and maintaining childhood difficulties.

b. The mesosystem is the interaction/communication effectiveness between two microcosms, such as parent and school, and can increase or be a barrier to a child's success.

c. As an overarching framework, Bronfenbrenner's model assists us in understanding complex layers of influences that shape development and are themselves changed in the process. This dynamic perspective helps to incorporate psychosocial developmental and transactional characteristics in meaningful ways to evaluate behaviors, thoughts, and feelings relative to the social/cultural context in which they have developed.

Consolidate and Communicate

1. Arthur is an 11-year-old boy in Grade 5 who he is having academic problems, especially in math. His mother is also concerned about his behavior at home. Arthur is often argumentative and rarely complies with a request without some fight attached to it. Arguments are especially strong when homework is an issue, and this often evokes another battle with his mother trying to get him to do his homework "now" and Arthur insisting that he will "do it later."

Arthur does not have many friends because he also argues with his peers, and he is usually very upset if he cannot have his own way. As a child clinician, how would you begin to evaluate Arthur's behaviors to determine whether these are "normal or abnormal" using the 4 Ds?

2 Until recently, the concept of danger to children was often thought of in terms of children as the victims of maltreatment or neglect. However, we are increasingly becoming aware of children and youth as perpetrators of violence resulting in the possibilities of danger to themselves or others. Youth gangs are an area of increasing concern. Discuss why teens might be especially vulnerable to recruitment by existing gang members, and how the contexts of development might provide risks or protective factors regarding involvement in gang activity.

3. Using the concept of temperament as a guide, describe how some children may be more difficult to rear than others. How could temperament impact parent–child interactions in a reciprocal way?

Chapter Review Questions

1. Wide variability in reported prevalence rates for ADHD worldwide is suggested to be a result of:
   a. ADHD being largely a North American phenomenon
   b. Different classification systems used by different countries
   c. ADHD occurring largely in male dominated societies
   d. Different rates of prescribed medications

2. Wally does not want to get out of bed. He is feeling very depressed and fatigued. He has called into work for the 5th time this month to report that he is not feeling well and that he will not be coming into work. As a result, Wally will likely be fired. Which of the following best describes the current status of Wally's behavior?
   a. Deviant
   b. Distress
   c. Dysfunction
   d. Danger

3. Research has suggested that mental health professionals:
   a. Excel at making long-term predictions of violent behaviors in clinical populations
   b. Have a poor record of making short-term predictions of imminent violence
   c. Are poor at making both long-term and short-term predictions of violent behavior
   d. Are better at predicting imminent versus long-term violent behaviors

4. In their recent review of contemporary challenges facing developmental psychopathology, Rutter and Sroufe (2000) mentioned all but one of the following. Which did they not Mention?
   a. Increased understanding of the causal processes of developmental disorders
   b. How to conceptualize the interplay between genetic and environmental factors
   c. The role of gender in determining psychopathology
   d. Addressing issues of continuity and discontinuity in normal and abnormal behavior

5. Neurons that relay messages to other neurons are called:
   a. Synaptic neurons
   b. Neurotransmitters
   c. Dendrites
   d. Tectum

6. Brain growth is rapid in the early years. By the second year of life, the brain grows to _____ of the adult brain.
   a. 50%
   b. 30%
   c. 90%
   d. 70%

7. Which of the following statements is true:
   a. Phenotype represents visible genetic material
   b. Genotype refers to genetic material that is not visually apparent
   c. Endophenotypes are markers that underlie a given psychological disorder
   d. All the above are true

8. According to Erickson, the developmental task which the school-aged child faces is:
   a. Trust versus mistrust
   b. Shame versus self doubt
   c. Identify versus role confusion
   d. Industry versus inferiority

9. Internalizing disorders are an example of a behavioral_____, while externalizing disorders are an example of a behavioral_____.
   a. punishment…reinforcement
   b. negative consequence…positive consequence
   c. deficit…excess
   d. operant conditioning…classical conditioning

10. On the playground, Joey is convinced that Ralph is staring at him and furthermore that Ralph is likely to come over and hit him. In truth, Ralph is just looking at a squirrel behind Joey and has no intention of hitting Joey. Social cognitive theorists would be most likely to explain Joey's faulty reasoning as part of a:
    a. Poor upbringing
    b. Hostile attribution bias
    c. Genetic factors
    d. Temperament

Glossary of New Terms

deviance
dysfunction
distress
danger
civil commitment
acquisitive stage
precipitating cause
sustaining/maintaining forces
symptoms/symptom cluster
genetics
synapse
sensory neurons
motor neurons
interneurons
myelination
neurotransmitters
endocrine glands
hormones
cortisol
hypothalamus–pituitary–adrenal (HPA) system
cerebral cortex
frontal lobes
hindbrain
midbrain
forebrain
reticular activating system (RAS)
cerebellum
tectum
tegmentum
cerebrum
hypothalamus

thalamus
limbic system
basal ganglia
amygdale
hippocampus
corpus callosum
occipital lobes
parietal lobes
temporal lobes
monozygotic twins (MZ)
dizygotic twins (DZ)
genotypes
phenotypes
endophenotypes
epigenesis
temperament
difficult child
slow to warm up child
goodness-of-fit
Big Five personality factors
ego
superego
id
fixations
regressions
unconscious conflicts
psychosexual stages: oral, anal, oedipal, latency, genital
defense mechanisms
psychosocial stages: trust vs. mistrust, autonomy vs. shame, industry vs. inferiority, identity vs. role onfusion
psychodynamic developmental therapy for children (PTTC)
reactive attachment disorder
borderline personality disorder
developmental trauma disorder
dialectical behavior therapy (DBT)
operant and classical conditioning
modeling
positive and negative reinforcement
positive and negative punishment
punishment and extinction
behavioral excess/behavioral deficit
functional behavioral assessment (FBA)
behavioral intervention plan (BIP)
token economy
internalizing/externalizing
behavioral contract
observational learning/modeling
unconditioned/conditioned stimulus

stimulus generalization
systematic desensitization
fear hierarchy
deep relaxation
Piaget's stages of cognitive development: preoperational, concrete, formal operations
assimilation/accommodation/equilibrium
schemas
appearance and reality
social cognition
personal fable
imaginary audience
triadic reciprocity
self efficacy
hostile attribution bias
internal working models
prototype
imprinting
reciprocal determinism
strange situation experiments
secure attachment
anxious resistant attachment
avoidant attachment
disorganized/disoriented attachment
parenting styles: authoritarian, authoritative, permissive, uninvolved
identified problem
boundaries: loose, rigid, disengaged, enmeshed
behavioral family interventions (BFI)
coercion theory
microsystem, exosystem, macrosystem, mesosystem
transactional ecological

Answers to Multiple Choice Questions:
1. b; 2. c; 3. d; 4. c; 5. b; 6. d; 7. d; 8. d; 9. c; 10. b.

3

Understanding Abnormal Development
Risks, Protective Factors, and Culturally Diverse Youth

CHAPTER PREVIEW

As development unfolds, the trajectory or course of an individual's life path can be influenced by a number of child characteristics and environmental factors. The process is a transactional one, as reciprocal influences interact and continue to alter the direction and course of development. Some influences can be protective and nurturing, leading to better outcomes. Other influences may act as roadblocks and detours, carrying development further and further away from its normal course. Influences that can alter paths and shape the course of development for better or worse may exist in our own genetic makeup, our family constellation, friends, schooling, neighborhood, and economic conditions. While culture can provide a sense of belonging and heritage, minority youth—especially those who also experience economic hardship—may experience particularly harsh adjustments and transitions between home and school. Some factors that may add to the difficulties of minority youth include a lack of parental education; lack of fit between home and school attitudes and beliefs; and differences in norms and expectations.

1. Risks, Protective Factors, Prevention, and Health Promotion

The initial section of this chapter will concentrate on the interaction between developmental and environmental factors that can place children at greater risk for psychopathology or those that can serve to buffer the child from harm. Placing these risks and protective factors within the contexts of spheres of influence will provide an overarching framework that can greatly enhance our understanding of the complexities that exist in understanding child disorders. The relationship of risks and protective factors to individual and immediate factors (family, peers, school) as well as more distal forces (socioeconomic and cultural influences) will be addressed. Although the major focus of this section is to share information regarding known risks and protective factors, research efforts in proactive areas such as prevention and the promotion of positive mental health are also addressed.

2. Culturally Diverse Youth

Children living in conditions of low socioeconomic status (SES) are at greater risk for negative outcomes (problems of conduct, academics, and social relationships) compared to peers who are not of low SES status. Many ethnic minorities exist in low SES conditions and children who are both impoverished and from an ethnic minority are at increased risk of continuing to live in poverty over time. More than half of Latino children and nearly half of Black children live in single-female households, at or below the poverty line, compared to less than a third of their White peers. The impact of risk factors on minority youth will be reviewed for each of the levels of influence from individual to immediate and ultimately, more global areas of concern.

3. Culturally Diverse Youth From Four Cultural Backgrounds

An in-depth discussion will provide information relevant to minority youth in five areas: background and demographics; family and parenting practices; types and prevalence of mental health issues; and implications for treatment and intervention. Although it is acknowledged that wide variability exists within cultures, the chapter will focus on four minority youth groups: African American, Latino/Hispanic Americans, Asian Americans/ Pacific Islanders, and Native American Indians.

Contexts of Development: Risks and Protective Factors

Developmental contexts represent spheres of influence surrounding the growing child. Based on the nature of the environmental forces, these contexts can erect barriers and obstacles to development (**risk factors**) or provide buffers, shielding the child from potential harm (**protective factors**). Considering risks and protective factors within the context of Bronfenbrenner's (1979) ecological model provides a framework for understanding how child characteristics can interact with environmental characteristics at various levels of influence and, ultimately, how change at any level can result in changes at any or all of the surrounding levels.

Recall and Rewind

Bronfenbrenner's model is depicted as a series of concentric circles with the child and the unique characteristics that define the individual (personality/temperament, intelligence, genetic makeup) at its core. The first circle of influence (**microsystem**) represents the immediate surrounding environment that includes proximal influences such as family, friends, school, and neighborhood. The next wave of influence (**exosystem**) is exerted by more distal forces such as prevailing economical conditions, extended family, or supportive systems such as health care. The outer ring (**macrosystem**) represents influences due to cultural attitudes and laws. Bronfenbrenner also emphasizes the importance of the **mesosystem**, which is the effectiveness of communication and interaction between elements in the microsystem.

The impact of cumulative risks. Adding risk factors can result in a complex process of interactions between and among factors that can produce an increased likelihood of child problems or psychopathology. Sameroff and Fiese (2000) found that adding additional risks at various levels can have a **multiplier effect**. For example, if youth who are socially maladjusted also demonstrate poor school performance, their risk of long-term adjustment problems increases significantly. In his investigation of cumulative risk, Rutter (1979) found that children exposed to two risk factors had a fourfold increase in the likelihood of a disorder, while four risk factors increased the likelihood tenfold. In a more recent study, Herrenkohl, Maguin, and Hill (2000) reported that a 10-year-old exposed to six or more risk factors would be 10 times more likely to commit a violent crime by 18 years of age, compared with a peer who had been exposed to only one risk factor.

Science Talks: Environmental Risks and Outcomes

Atzaba-Poria, Pike, and Deater-Deckard (2004) found that while children with externalizing problems (problems of conduct) were influenced by risks in their microsystem (immediate family, peers), children with internalizing problems (anxiety, depression, somatization) were influenced more by risk factors evident in the exosystem (marital relationship, family hardship) or individual self system. Based on these results, the authors suggest that risks at different ecological levels may produce different trajectories for child outcomes.

Not all children exposed to difficult circumstances develop problem behaviors. Researchers have also investigated child "resilience" in an attempt to explain how positive experiences in early childhood (Luther, Cicchetti, & Becker, 2000; Masten, Hubbard, Gest, Tellegen, Garmezy, & Ramirez, 1999) can provide an anecdote against negative outcomes. An overview of risks and protective factors within the context of Bronfenbrenner's ecological model is available in Table 3.1.

Table 3.1 A Contextual Look at Common Risk and Protective Factors for Behavior Problems and School Failure

Environmental Context	Risk Factors	Protective Factors
Individual Level	Early onset of problems Male Perinatal complications Low birth weight Developmental delays Additional problems Difficult temperament Impulsive/Aggressive	Good social skills Self-efficacy Positive self-concept Intelligence Resilient temperament Social competence (academic achievement)
Immediate Environment **Microsystem** **Family, Peers, School**	*Family* Parenting style/harsh parenting Marital Conflict History of parent pathology; Abusive home Low parent education *Peers* Negative peer influence-models Rejection *School* Poor quality schools High drop out rates Low SES	*Family* Positive parent-child relationship Authoritative style Family cohesion *Peers* Friendship Positive peer influence Peer acceptance *School* Quality schools
Exosystem: Community	Poverty-stricken neighborhood: Less access to health care Less opportunities for recreation Ineffective school policies	Adequate social norms Effective school policies
Macrosystem	Cultural conflicts	Cultural supports
Other	Direct or indirect stressful conditions (any or all levels)	Direct or indirect social support (any or all levels)

Individual Level (Child Characteristics)

Risk factors. The individual child (biological, genetic, temperament) interacts with environmental influences on many levels. Several individual risks have been identified, including gender (male; Rutter, 1979), perinatal complications, developmental delays, chronic physical handicaps (Werner & Smith, 1992), difficult or resistant temperament (Bates, Pettit, Dodge, & Ridge, 1998; Caspi, Henry, McGee, Moffitt, & Silva, 1995), and low birth weight (Breslau, Paneth, & Lucia, 2004). In addition, chromosomal abnormalities (such as Down Syndrome) and genetic vulnerability to certain psychopathologies (schizophrenia, ADHD, learning disabilities, mood disorders, anxiety disorders) can also place children at greater risk.

Development in Focus: *Timing Can be Everything*

Low SES encountered at an early age is a stronger predictor of delinquency in adolescence (Brooks-Gunn & Duncan, 1997; Elder & Rockwell, 1979). Appleyard, Egeland, van Dulmen, and Sroufe (2005) found that risk factors encountered in early childhood (peer relationships, neighborhood ecology, academic achievement) were predictive of problem behaviors in adolescence; however, if these risk factors occurred in middle childhood, they were not predictive of adolescent problems. The authors suggest that *timing of onset of risk factors may be a significant factor in the prediction of later outcomes.*

Protective factors.　Certain child characteristics can also buffer an individual from harm, such as good health, above average intelligence (Williams, Anderson, McGee, & Silva, 1990), positive self-concept, positive temperament, and **social competence** (Garmezy, Masten, & Tellegen, 1984; Rolf, 1972). Social competence includes such factors as academic achievement, ability to relate to others, and engagement in a range of activities. Self-efficacy and high self-esteem have also been linked to increased social competence (Rutter, 1985).

Microsystem: Immediate Environment (Family, Peers, and School)

Risk factors.　Risk factors in the immediate environment can be evident in the **family system** (family dynamics and parenting practices, maternal depression, insecure attachment, parenting style, domestic violence), **peer relations** (peer rejection, negative peer models) **school situation** (quality versus nonquality schools, academic rigor), and **neighborhood** (violent neighborhood, poor access to leisure activities, etc.).

Protective factors.　Protective factors at this level of influence, include having a supportive parent, having successful peer relations, having a supportive person outside the family (teacher, relative, peer), and being involved in extracurricular activities at school (Durlak, 1998).

Family System: Parenting and Attachment.　Research on attachment (Carlson, Cicchetti, Barnett, & Braunwald, 1989; Egeland & Sroufe, 1981) has been instrumental in emphasizing how risk factors can interact to produce different negative outcomes:

1. Child maltreatment and anxious attachment;
2. Physical abuse or emotional unavailability of the parent and anxious/avoidant attachment; or,
3. Poverty/physical neglect resulting in anxious/resistant attachment.

Additional parent/child risk factors that have been identified include: parenting style and use of harsh discipline (Deater-Deckard, Dodge, Bates, & Pettit, 1996); family style (Smets & Hartup, 1988); and parent–child relationship (Shaw, Owens, Vondra, Keenan, & Winslow, 1996).

Other factors in the family system that can influence development negatively include marital discord, overcrowding, paternal criminality, maternal psychiatric disorder (Rutter, 1979), and low parent education (Stevenson, Chen, & Uttal, 1990).

Children who are abused or neglected are one to six times more likely to engage in delinquent activities and one to three times more likely to be incarcerated as adults (Maxfield & Widom, 1996).

On a Positive Note

Although the majority of research in child psychopathology has focused on risk factors, studies of protective factors have identified a number of family factors that can have a positive impact on child outcomes, including: supportive parents, family closeness, adequate rule setting (Werner & Smith, 1992), and support of even one parent in difficult times (Rutter, Cox, Tupling, Berger, & Yule, 1975).

Peer relations. Children who have difficulties in social relationships and act aggressively towards peers are often rejected (Rothbart & Bates, 1998). Youth who experience continued difficulties with peers are at greater risk for longer-term negative outcomes, such as school drop-out, delinquency, and increased incidences of criminal behaviors (Blum, Beuhring, Shew, Bearinger, Sieving, & Resnick, 2000; Parker & Asher, 1987). On the other hand, quality of adolescent friendships (Rae-Grant, Thomas, Offord, & Boyle, 1989) can buffer against family problems in this age group, while peer acceptance and having an extensive network of friends can be a buffer for adverse family conditions at younger age levels, even if a child has a resistant temperament (Criss, Pettit, Bates, Dodge, & Lapp, 2002).

Schooling and education. Lower quality schooling and school drop out are high risk factors for the development of long-term negative outcomes. At-risk toddlers who do not have the benefit of quality child care programs are five times more likely to become chronic juvenile offenders (Schweinhart, Barnes, & Weikart, 1993). Furthermore, children living in poverty are much more likely to experience lower quality teaching and have higher drop out rates. Youths who drop out of school are almost three times as likely to end up in the juvenile justice system compared to high school graduates (Harlow, 2002). On the other hand, being a good student can serve as a protective function and reduce the risk of negative outcomes (Rae-Grant et al., 1989). The potential for negative cycling to occur under conditions of poverty is depicted in Figure 3.1.

Exosystem: Social and Economic Context (Focus on Poverty)

The influences of community and social institutions (such as local government, health care systems, and religious organizations) constitute the exosystem. Social and economic conditions (such as employment conditions, inflation rates, or community atmosphere) can have a profound influence on child-rearing. Communities with highly concentrated poverty levels are often dis-

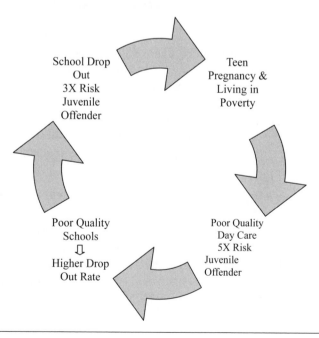

Figure 3.1 The cycle of poverty.

organized and chaotic because residents are either unwilling or too fearful to intervene when youth engage in antisocial behaviors (Sampson, Raudenbush, & Earls, 1997).

Poverty and Child Welfare: The Burden of Poverty Weighs Heavily Upon the Growing Child

The effects of poverty on child development are pervasive and can be seen to impact every aspect of the child including physical, cognitive, social, and emotional health and well-being. "Poverty is the single best predictor of child abuse and neglect" (Center for Disease Control and Prevention [CDC], 2005, p. 149). Children living in poverty are 22 times more likely to be abused or neglected (Maxfield & Widom, 1996).

Memory Bank

According to a recent report by the Children's Defense Fund (CDF; 2005), the number of children living in **poverty** and **extreme poverty** (living below half the poverty level) has increased by 20% between 2000 and 2004. Under conditions of extreme poverty, a family of three would have to survive on less than approximately $7,600 annual income.

Relative to children living in higher income situations, low income children (below 200% of the poverty level) are more likely to

1. Experience only fair or poor health (five times more likely);
2. Have unmet medical needs (three times more likely);
3. Be uninsured and not have seen a medical doctor in over two years; and
4. Miss school at rates more than one-and-a-half times that of other children.

However, despite these daunting statistics, a number of prevention programs have demonstrated that risks can be overcome with long-term and lifetime effects resulting from early prevention programs such as the Perry Preschool Project. In the Perry Preschool Project, children enrolled in the program provided a return on investment of $17 for every $1 invested in the program through gainful employment, and reduction in criminal and negative outcomes (Barnett, 1996).

Investigators have found that economically stressed parents of children living in poverty tend to discipline these children more harshly and inconsistently, while ignoring their children's dependency needs (Dodge, Pettit, & Bates, 1994; McLeod & Shanahan, 1993). Furthermore, prolonged and persistent poverty is significantly more detrimental to the child's social-emotional functioning than transitory financial hardship (Duncan, Brooks-Gunn, & Klebanov, 1994). However, parenting behavior can also serve to buffer children from the effects of poverty (Cowen, Wyman, Work, & Parker, 1990), and in this instance, studies have identified stress-resilient children who identify with parents who were more supportive, less harsh, and more developmentally appropriate and consistent in their discipline.

The impact of living in poverty can have profound influences on other areas of risk. Children who live in poverty often have less opportunities than their advantaged peers and also often experience barriers to their possible involvement in organized recreation due to lack of financial support, issues of transportation, etc. (Jones & Offord, 1989). In addition, those living in poverty also have less access to nutrition and health care (Rogers, 1986).

Macrosystem: Cultural Values and Laws

Although the majority of children living in low socioeconomic conditions are more likely to experience problems with behavior, academics, and social relationships, higher percentages of ethnic minorities live in conditions of low socioeconomic status (Patterson, Kupersmidt, & Vaden, 1990), many ethic minorities exist in low socioeconomic conditions. Children who live in impoverished conditions and are from an ethnic minority are at increased risk of continuing to live in poverty (Wilson & Aponte, 1985). More than half of Latino children and nearly half of Black children living in single female households live in poverty, compared to approximately 3 in 10 White children.

Vigil (2002) has conducted extensive research concerning the formation of street gangs in neighborhoods primarily inhabited by low-income ethnic minorities. Based on his crosscultural investigation of gang formation in Los Angeles, Vigil attributes the formation of gangs as a byproduct of migration and the **multiple marginality** experienced by members of different cultures. Vigil states that gang members often are forced to live in marginal situations and economic conditions and gang membership serves as a source of identity, mutual support, and protection. According to Vigil, cultural repression, ostracism, and economic marginalization provide fertile breeding grounds for spawning gang subcultures. Vigil contends that when traditional sources of social control fail, such as the law, schools, and families, then youth become socialized by the street. Within this context, Vigil states that one should not question why youth deviate from society's norms and values, but rather, why they conform instead to the values and norms of the subculture. According to Vigil, in times of increased stress, poverty, single-parent households, and racism, families become less able to provide support to youth. As a result, youth seek their own "family" and bond with gang members, in ethnically based subcultures such as current gangs in existence of Mexican American, African American, Vietnamese, and Salvadorian origins.

Recall and Rewind

In *A Rainbow of Gangs*, Vigil (2002) attributes gang formation to the breakdown of conventional methods of social control, such as schools, families, and the law. Approximately only half of Black and Latino teens graduate from high school. Drug trafficking, firearms, and gang violence continue to infiltrate high-poverty urban areas. Increase in firearm deaths of children and teens are evident in disproportionate numbers for minorities; death rates for Black males (15 to 19 years) are four times that of their non-Hispanic White peers. Youths who dropout of high school are three times more likely to be incarcerated, compared to peers who graduate (Harlow, 2002).

Contexts of Development: Prevention and Health Promotion

Prevention

Primary, secondary, and tertiary prevention.   Programs are often designed to enhance known protective factors and reduce potential risk factors. Within the context of developmental psychopathology, prevention programs can be viewed along a number of different continuums:

Primary prevention programs are designed to prevent a problem from occurring. An example of a **primary prevention** program would be a prenatal program designed to teach pregnant teens proper nutritional habits in an effort to reduce the number of low birth weight babies.

Secondary prevention is aimed at populations at-risk for developing problems. A program designed to reduce the possibility of developing post traumatic stress responses (anxiety, depression) in children who have been exposed to a natural disaster (hurricane, flood, etc.) is an example of a secondary prevention program. **Tertiary prevention** *programs* target individuals who have existing problems in an effort to prevent the development of more serious consequences (e.g., prevent anxiety symptoms from developing in to general anxiety disorder or specific phobias).

Universal, selective, and indicated prevention. Barrett and Turner (2004) emphasize the importance of articulating the goals of a successful prevention program through a framework that identifies the target audience and the degree and nature of the symptoms. Within their framework, the authors distinguish between **universal prevention**, **selective prevention**, and **indicated prevention**. Each level of intervention parallels the three intervention types noted above: primary prevention targets the universal audience; selective prevention focuses on at risk populations; while indicated prevention targets individuals with preexisting conditions who experience mild to moderate symptoms.

Important Distinction

Barrett and Turner (2004) describe three different types of prevention programs based on the target audience:

Universal Prevention (e.g., school program to prevent violence);
Selective Prevention (e.g., violence prevention program for children at risk of being aggressive);
Indicated Prevention (e.g., violence prevention program developed for aggressive children).

Along the continuum of prevention, **tertiary prevention/indication prevention** is just one step away from an intervention or treatment program and actually may be considered a form of early intervention in some cases. For example, although Barrett, Dadds, and Rapee (1996) initially developed the FRIENDS program as a clinical intervention for children diagnosed with anxiety disorders, they later piloted the program as a school-based early intervention program. Barrett and Turner (2004) note that

> The study represented a combination of indicated prevention and early intervention because it targeted children who were disorder-free but exhibited anxious symptomatology (indicated prevention), as well as children who met the criteria for an anxiety disorder but were in the less severe range (early intervention). (p. 460)

Later in the text, we will revisit the topic of prevention programs and intervention/treatment efforts as they apply to specific childhood disorders, and discuss how these techniques are related to various theoretical models (e.g., psychodynamic, behavioral cognitive, etc.). A number of examples of prevention programs are listed below.

Outcomes of Different Types of Prevention Programs

Primary Prevention/Universal Prevention

While some research programs have demonstrated positive effects of targeting universal audiences, others have reported mixed results. For example, failure to replicate results of an earlier primary prevention program lead Pattison and Lynd-Stevenson (2001) to suggest that lack of significant results (in this case reduction in depression symptoms in adolescents) may have been a function of a *floor effect*, or initial levels of healthy responses in the universal sample that had little room for improvement. Universal programs have been used to target family as well as school environments.

- Cunningham, Brandon, and Frydenberg (1999) found that symptoms of depression were reduced and optimism and self-efficacy increased for adolescents in their program to prevent depression in teens; however, effects were time limited.
- Rice and colleagues (Rice, Herman, & Peterson, 1993; Rice & Meyer, 1994) found that a 16-session program aimed at 7th graders resulted in decreases in negative life events and increase in feelings of self control over school-related problems compared to controls.
- Initial results of studies conducted with primary and secondary school students using the FRIENDS program (Barrett, Johnson, & Turner, 2004) revealed overall reduction in anxiety symptoms that were maintained 12 months later.
- Although observers noted increased prosocial behaviors and reduced aggression after elementary students participated in an anger management program focusing on empathy and emotion regulation, parents and teachers did not confirm these changes (Greenberg, Domitrovich, & Bumbarger, 2001).
- A cognitive problem-solving program (Promoting Alternative Thinking Strategies; PATHS) was found to significantly increase adaptive functioning, understanding of social situations, and effective problem-solving in elementary students which were maintained 2 years later (Greenberg et al., 2001).
- Olweus' (1993) program developed to prevent bullying and victimization is an example of a school-based prevention program that took on epic proportions as it was launched nationally in Norway. The program was successful in reducing bullying and victimization in elementary and middle school by targeting changes at several levels of service: policy changes at an administrative level; behavior management within the classroom (adherence to rules and opportunities for conflict resolution); and at individual and family levels by encouraging home-school communication. In addition to reducing bullying and antisocial behaviors in general (truancy, theft, vandalism), the program also has been successful in increasing student satisfaction with school (Olweus, 1994, 1996).
- Project DARE (Drug Research Resistance Education; Ennett, Tobler, Ringwalt, & Flewelling, 1994) contains a core curriculum of 17 lessons that are provided to children in the 5th grade by uniformed officers. Although immediate effects are positive, most studies have failed to support any differences on drug resistance longer term.

Recall and Rewind

The success of Olweus' program in reducing incidents of bullying and victimization by more than half in the elementary and middle schools of Norway is no doubt attributed to the comprehensive nature of the program. The program follows Bronfenbrenner's ecological model with supports offered at all levels of influence (individual, family, school and educational policy-administration). The **mesosystem** or communication between home and school is seen as one of the cornerstones of the program's success.

Secondary Prevention/Selective Prevention

One major area of secondary prevention is aimed at altering family conditions or parenting practices which may place a child at-risk for developing psychopathology. Developmentally, programs that focus on younger children often include an emphasis on the role of the parent in providing consistency, structure, guidance in emotion regulation, and socialization. With older children and teens, emphasis shifts to parent communication and monitoring of activities and peer influences.

- Beardslee and colleagues (Beardslee et al., 1997; Gladsone & Beardslee, 2000) targeted parental depression as a risk factor for adolescent depression. The program, which focused on strengthening parent support and increasing the child's understanding of the parent illness, resulted in improved parent–child communication and understanding of parental depression and reduced parent guilt.
- Inhibited temperament was targeted as a risk factor by Rapee (2002), who educated parents in the management of child anxiety and encouragement of nonanxious behaviors. Twelve month follow-ups revealed significant reduction of anxious symptoms.
- *Fast Track* (Conduct Problems Prevention Research Group, 1992) is an empirically based program that targets early indicators (1st grade) of conduct problems (e.g., noncompliance, aggression) in all encompassing approach that integrates home and school supports to emphasize structure, consistency, and effective management of child behavior problems.

Tertiary Prevention/Indicated Prevention

For obvious reasons, the majority of preventative initiatives at this level have focused on children and youth with externalizing disorders, such as conduct disorder (CD) or oppositional defiant disorder (ODD). Prevention programs have incorporated parenting and parent–child interactions on several levels.

- Webster-Stratton and colleagues (Webster-Stratton, 1981; Webster-Stratton, Kolpacoff, & Hollinsworth, 1988) have developed a program, the Incredible Years (BASIC), which has been replicated (Scott, Spender, Doolan, Jacobs, & Aspland, 2001; Taylor, Schmidt, Pepler, & Hodgins, 1998) and proven effective in the reduction of aggressive behaviors in younger children.
- The Adolescent Transition Program (ATP; Dishion & Kavanagh, 2000) has provided good initial data on the indicated level of strategies in this three-tiered program involving universal, selected, and indicated populations. Trends also support the use of the program for effective prevention of substance use.

Science Talks

Not all prevention programs are successful. However, some prevention efforts have caused more harm than good. One major violation of the APA ethical code of conduct (APA, 2000) is to cause harm (beneficence and nonmaleficence) and, abiding to this standard, psychologists are ethically responsible to "do no harm." However, sometimes treatment efforts can have **iatrogenic effects** (defined as treatment efforts that cause negative outcomes). In chapter 9, we will discuss in greater detail how at least two efforts to assist youth with emotional and behavioral disorders actually increased their emotional distress. In one program, aggregation of youth with behavioral problems resulted in increased behavioral difficulties (Dishion, McCord, & Poulin, 1999), while in another study, aggregation with peers (residential placement) and removal from the home environment served to exacerbate anxiety in youth with comorbid disorders (Wilmshurst, 2002).

Prevention Programs That Integrate All Levels of Severity

In addition to prevention programs that target specific groups or levels of severity, some programs are multilevel, such as the FRIENDS program discussed earlier, and serve a wider variety of audiences with various degrees of problem symptoms. The following programs are an example of multilevel preventative initiatives:

- Tremblay and colleagues (Tremblay, LeMarquand, & Vitaro, 1999; Tremblay et al., 1992) have combined components of parent training (2- year program modeled after the Oregon Social Learning Program; Patterson, 1982) and social skills training for young boys beginning at 7 years of age. Five years later, results of the Montreal Longitudinal-Experimental Study (McCord, Tremblay, Vitaro, & Desmarais-Gervais, 1994) revealed significant reduction in delinquency and improved academic performance relative to controls.
- The Triple P-Positive Parenting Program developed by Sanders and colleagues (Sanders, Markie-Dadds, Turner, & Ralph, 2004) at the University of Queensland in Brisbane, Australia, is also modeled on the social learning principles from the Oregon Social Learning Program (Patterson, 1982). In addition, the program incorporates findings from empirical studies across a multitude of theoretical perspectives, including: social information processing (Bandura, 1995), developmental psychopathology of risks and protective factors, ecological contexts (community and mental health issues), and applied behavior analysis. The multitiered program offers five levels of intervention of increasing intensity from a universal focus on parent education in areas of child management, and family concerns to indicated preventions designed for more serious problems. One of the most successful aspects of the program is that it targets five developmental stages ranging from infancy to adolescence, while at the same time offering a continuum of preventative services for a variety of target audiences.

 RECURRENT THEMES The Triple P-Positive Parenting Program reinforces all of the recurring themes:

1. Normal development typically follows an orderly and predictable path.
2. Maladaptive behaviors represent deviations from the normal path.
3. Maladaptive behavior is represented by a continuum of severity.
4. Individual, interpersonal, contextual, and cultural factors influence deviations in development.
5. Mental health practitioners can draw on a multiplicity of theoretical perspectives to assist in understanding maladaptive behaviors.

Positive Mental Health Promotion

In addition to efforts directed toward the prevention of mental health issues, contemporary research has also been proactive in areas of ***mental health promotion***. The following studies are examples of the global initiatives that have been launched to promote positive mental health in children and youth.

- In their paper, Byrne, Barry, and Sheridan (2004) discuss the challenges associated with developing and evaluating a universal curriculum-based program to promote positive mental health in adolescents (15–18 years of age) in Ireland. The program, which consists of 13 experiential learning sessions spread over a 2-year span, is designed to improve coping strategies and increase access to supportive networks for youths.

- Vohra (2006) studied the ability to enhance feelings of mental well-being in early and late adolescents in New Delhi, India. Ratings of facilitators, self, peers, parents, and teachers indicated that youth who participated in the Spiritual Values Positive Mental Health Module increased their practice of critical self-analysis, altruism, and forgiveness in their daily living after 5 months in the program.
- Keyes (2006) investigated positive trends in mental health (*flourishing*) and negative trends in mental health (*languishing*) based on responses of 1,234 youth between 12 and 18 years of age to a comprehensive set of subjective well-being items. Results revealed that youth ages 12–14 years of age were most likely to report their status as flourishing (positive mental health) while the most prevalent response for 15–18 year olds was moderate mental health. Increased positive mental health was associated with increases in psychosocial functioning (self-concept, school integration, self-determination), while decreases in mental health were associated with increases in symptoms of depression and problems of conduct.
- Alsma et al. (2006) investigated the degree to which personal fables (omnipotence-narcissism, invulnerability, personal uniqueness) may be indicators of positive adjustment in normal adolescents. Although the researchers found that concepts of personal uniqueness and invulnerability were risk factors for externalizing and internalizing problems, they found that narcissistic omnipotence was actually an indicator of competence and positive adjustment.
- Mental health and its relationship to acculturation styles has also been a focus of recent inquiry. In one study, Constantine, Alleyne, Wallace, and Franklin-Jackson (2006) found that African American adolescent girls who adhered to Africentric cultural values exhibited higher levels of self-esteem and greater life satisfaction compared to their more Caucasian acculturated peers. In her study of Latino acculturation and mental health, Gillespie (2006) reported that Latino college students who adopted a bicultural orientation to acculturation scored higher on indices of psychological well being and lower on measures of anxiety and depression compared to peers who adopted an Anglo oriented acculturation style.

Recall and Rewind

Elkind (1967), a social cognitive theorist, proposed that adolescents revert to cognitive egocentrism to create such personal fables as *personal uniqueness* ("No one is capable of understanding me."), *invulnerability* ("I am incapable of being harmed."), and *omnipotence* ("I know everything.").

Cultural Context and Minority Children: An Overview

Culture, Race, and Ethnicity: An Introduction

The terms **culture**, **race**, and **ethnicity** are often used interchangeably; however, "culture" has the broader meaning referring to the greater social construct. Matsumoto (2000) defines *culture* as a dynamic system of rules (attitudes, values, beliefs, norms, behaviors) developed by a group to insure a group's survival. Although relatively stable (communicated from generation to generation), culture must remain flexible to adapt to changes across time. The word *race* is most often used to refer to physical characteristics associated with different ethic groups, while the term ethnicity is often used when we report differences among minority groups.

> **Important Distinction**
>
> There can be a fine line between *cultural sensitivity* and *cultural stereotyping*. Stuart (2000) cautions that being overly sensitive to an individual's group membership may result in a tendency to lose sight of the person's individuality apart from that group (Stuart, 2000, p. 6).

Ethnicity and Issues in Mental Health

Gibbs and Huang (2001) outline three broad areas in which ethnicity can influence mental health in children and adolescents. Ethnicity can

1. Shape beliefs about what constitutes mental illness;
2. Influence different symptom presentations, reactive patterns, and defensive styles; and
3. Influence whether it is acceptable to seek assistance for mental health issues outside of the family, and whom to consult (elder, priest, minister, herbalist, etc.).

Yet determining "ethnic influences" can be a challenge in a climate of rapidly changing demographics. Currently it is estimated that more than 10% of Americans are foreign born, while approximately one-third of the U. S. population are of minority status. In some states (California, New Mexico, and Hawaii), minorities comprise the majority of the population (Stuart, 2004).

In the past 10 years, there have been several movements to increase awareness of cultural influences in psychopathology. The 4th revision (text version) of the *DSM* (APA, 2000) includes "specific cultural features" for each disorder, as well as guidelines for applying *DSM* diagnoses in a multicultural setting and a glossary of 25 culture-bound syndromes (see Table 3.2 for an example of culture-bound syndromes).

Ethnicity in Context

Bronfenbrenner's ecological system is particularly useful for addressing issues faced by many minority children (Gustavsson & Balgopal, 1990). For some children, problems exist in trying to integrate beliefs held by families with those held by peers or school systems. Conflicts of loyalty and a lack of cohesion between the opposing systems in their life may be pervasive. Children may struggle in their attempts to accommodate diverse systems, behaving differently

Table 3.2 Examples of Some Culture Bound Syndromes

Culture Bound Syndrome: Triggered by	Description	Culture
Amok Insult or Slight	Dissociative episode begins with rumination or brooding and culminates in violent outburst	Malaysia Puerto Rico (*mal de pelea*) Navajo (*iich'aa*)
Sangue dormido	"sleeping blood" Pain, numbness, tremors, paralysis, stroke, heart attack, miscarriage	Portuguese
zar	Dissociative episode, caused by being possessed by a spirit; Can be long-term Episode (shout, laugh, head-banging, weeping) May become withdrawn	Ethiopia, Somalia, Sudan, Middle East

Source: APA, 2000.

in different contexts (family, teachers, and peers). Although minority families may experience similar challenges (e.g., poverty, segregation, racism), variations in cultural beliefs, values, and behavior patterns may influence how parenting practices adapt to meet these challenges (Garcia Coll et al., 1996).

Read All About It

In addition to independent research reports and reports of the Centers for Disease Control and Prevention and Prevention (CDC), interested readers can find a wealth of information in a number of major reports, available on the Internet, including: The World Health Report, 2001—Mental Health: New Understanding, New Hope (WHR; 2001); The State of America's Children, 2005 (Children's Defense Fund: CDF; 2005); and Mental Health: Culture, Race and Ethnicity—A Supplement to Mental Health. A Report to the Surgeon General (U.S. Department of Heath and Human Services [USDHSS, 2001]). The Internet Web site addresses for these documents can be found at the end of this chapter.

Ethnic Minority Children at Risk for Psychopathology

With the advent of globalization, migration, and greater immigration, increased focus has been placed on determining the risks of children in diverse populations. Following an overview, discussion will focus on four minority groups in greater detail.

Individual Child: Birth/Health Issues

Minority and poor children are often disadvantaged due to poor prenatal and childhood health care. Children born to teen mothers are at risk for later delinquency, while low birth weight babies can be at-risk for later educational problems. Black children are twice as likely to be born to a teen mom and are twice as likely to be low birth weight compared to their White peers (Breslau, Paneth, & Lucia, 2004). Furthermore, infants born to Black mothers are more than twice as likely to die in their first year of life compared to those born to White mothers and accounted for almost one-third of all infant deaths in 2002 (Kockanek, Murphy, & Anderson, 2004).

In 1978, there was a nationwide ban on the use of lead-based paint. However, many children living in older houses that contain deteriorating lead paint continue to be exposed to the dangerous levels of lead poisoning that can result in damage to the developing brain. Lead poisoning can also result in problems with behavior, learning, stunted growth, and headaches (U.S. Environmental Protection Agency, 1995). Lead poisoning can be responsible for lowering IQ scores, resulting in cognitive impairments and learning disabilities. From the population of children ranging in ages from 1 to 5 years, high levels of lead were found in the following percentage of the population: White, 7%; Black, 17.4%; and Hispanic, 6.3%. Children in poverty and Black children are also more likely to have asthma than their higher income White or Hispanic peers. Disabling asthma was 66% higher among Black children. The consequences of living with chronic conditions of asthma include increased days of restricted activity and poor school attendance (Newacheck & Halfon, 2000).

Immediate Environment (Family, Peers, Neighborhood, Schools)

Family and parenting practices. There are wide cultural variations in parenting practices, attitudes, and values that can influence child outcomes in a number of ways (Forehand & Kotchick, 1996). Studies have found that cultural background can moderate the impact of parenting practices on child development. The *authoritative parenting style*, a firm and consistent approach that encourages child input into family decision making, seems to produce more positive child outcomes (Baumrind, 1991), especially in middle-class families. However, for families living in conditions of lower SES and inner-city neighborhoods, an authoritarian parenting style, which emphasizes strict adherence to rules and obedience, may serve a protective function, especially in environments that can expose children to risk or danger (McLoyd, 1998). Studies have found that for African American children, the authoritarian parenting style can produce more positive outcomes for both males and females (Baumrind, 1972; Deater-Deckard et al., 1996).

Science Talks

Authoritarian parenting was found to increase self-assertiveness and independence in African American girls (Baumrind, 1972) and to be associated with better outcomes for externalizing problems for African American children from school-age (Deater-Deckard et al., 1996) to adolescence (Lansford, Deater-Deckard, Dodge, Bates, & Pettit, 2004).

Another variable that may be moderated by cultural background is family conflict. Vendlinski, Silk, Criss, Shaw, and Lane (2006) suggest that African American families may engage in more intense and frequent verbal conflicts than European American families, which may increase the African American child's threshold for aggression. In these families, a more firm and authoritarian approach to child rearing may be required. Research has also demonstrated that although *secure attachment* is the preferred attachment mode in North America, the preference is not universal. For example, German mothers value "avoidant attachment" to foster independence (Grossmann, Grossmann, Spangler, Suess, & Unzer, 1985), while the majority of attachment patterns in Japan follow the ambivalent type (child not wanting to separate from parent), which underscores the emphasis on a dependent attachment (Miyake, 1993).

School, education, and neighborhood.   The early years play a formative role in a child's development. The interplay between nature (brain growth and development) and nurture (stimulation, nutrition, and care) can have a profound influence on the first 3 years of life. During these years, stimulation and quality of care can have a significant impact on physical, cognitive, social, and emotion development. Positive social experiences can contribute to the development of emotion regulation, which in turn can have a powerful influence on a child's ability to cope with stress and develop increased behavioral control. However, at a time when early intervention is crucial, children most in need of early intervention or prevention programs may be the least likely to be able to access services for a variety of reasons (transportation, financial problems, etc.), including *expulsion* from preschool.

Read All About It

Shocking news from a study conducted by the Yale University Child Study Center revealed that 6.6% of preschoolers (typically 3 to 4 years of age, although some children turn 5 or 6 while enrolled) were expelled per 1,000 enrolled nationally (Gilliam, 2005). The pre-Kindergarten expulsion rate was 3.2 times the rate of expulsion for students enrolled in K–12 schools. The highest rates of expulsion were for older children with boys four times more likely than girls to be expelled. African American students were twice as likely to be expelled compared to preschoolers of European descent.

Table 3.3 Who Are the Youth in Juvenile Detention (JD)?

- Fifteen thousand children as young as 7 years of age are in JD due to a lack of mental health community resources (Children's Defense Fund: CDF; 2005).
- Seventy-five percent of youth in JD have a diagnosable mental disorder (Teplin, Abram, McClelland, Dulcan, & Meride, 2002).
- Sixty-six percent males and 75% of females in JD have a mental disorder (Teplin et al., 2002).
- Half of males and almost half of females have substance abuse disorder (Teplin et al., 2002).
- Forty percent have disruptive behavior disorders (Teplin et al., 2002)
- Twenty percent females have major depressive disorder (Teplin et al., 2002)
- Over 60% are minority youth from low income families (Poe-Yamagata & Jones, 2000).

Studies of youth in juvenile detention suggest that minority youth are overrepresented in the justice system and underrepresented in the mental health system. Results are summarized in Table 3.3.

Buka, Stichick, Birdthistle, and Earls (2001) conducted a meta-analysis of studies involving youth **exposure to violence (ETV)**. Prevalence of ETV was highest among ethnic minorities (African Americans and Latinos-Latinas), lower SES youth, and those living in inner cities. Although not exclusive to low income neighborhoods, the investigators report that the intensity and severity of violence witnessed by youth is significantly higher in low income areas, as is the risk of subsequently engaging in violent behaviors (Richters, 1993). Repeated exposure to high levels of violence can produce serious risk for developing negative outcomes in all facets of psychological well-being, such as lowered threshold to violence and increased incidence of post traumatic stress disorder (PTSD). Studies of chronic ETV have revealed PTSD symptoms in as many as 27% of African American youth (Fitzpatrick & Boldizar, 1993). In the same study, however, although victims of violence reported higher levels of depressive symptoms than nonvictims, depressive symptoms were negatively related to ETV. The authors suggest that chronic ETV may serve to numb individuals to affective stressors.

Poverty, Childhood, and Minority Status: A Losing Combination

Between 2000 and 2004, minority children were overrepresented among children living in poverty: one in three Black children, almost 1 out of 10 Latino, and more than 1 of out 10 White children were living in poverty in 2004. In circumstances of extreme poverty (living below one-half the poverty level), the percentage increase from 2000 to 2004 was 20.7 % for Black children, 24.9% for Latino children, and 16.5% for White children (CDF, 2005).

Exosystem: Socioeconomic System

Poverty is one of the single best predictors of child risk. Although most reported findings look at broad racial and ethnic groups, Lichter, Quian, and Crowley (2005) found that 9% of White children were living below the poverty line, compared to 33% Black children, 31% Native American children, and 27% Hispanic children. The investigators report Black children's poverty rates, in excess of two-and-a-half times that of their White peers.

Cultural Diversity: Children and Adolescents From Minority Populations

It is important to emphasize that wide variability exists amongst individuals within cultures regarding the extent to which they will adhere to any given set of beliefs. Therefore, although the following discussion will focus on four minority groups in greater detail, it is important to stress the need to balance this knowledge of common cultural background with an understanding of within-culture diversity.

The following discussion will provide information relevant to minority youth in four areas: *background and demographics; family and parenting practices; types and prevalence of mental health issues; and implications for treatment and intervention.* Four major minority groups will be addressed: African American, Latino/Hispanic Americans; Asian Americans/Pacific Islanders, and Native American Indians. The majority of information regarding demographics has been obtained from the Surgeon General's Supplementary Report, Mental Health: Culture, Race and Ethnicity (USDHHS, 2001).

African American Children and Families

Background and demographics.   Approximately 12% of the population in the United States is African American. Diversity within the African American population can be traced to origins in Africa, West Indies, Australia, South America, New Zealand, and the Caribbean. In the United States, the majority of African Americans continue to reside in the southern states. There is wide disparity between income levels among African Americans (McAdoo, 1997), with about 25% earning over $50,000 annually, while another 22% live in poverty. The poverty rate for African Americans is significantly higher than the national rate (13%). Approximately 40% of the homeless population is made up of African Americans.

African American Children and Youth

One in three African American children live in poverty, and those living in conditions of extreme poverty increased 20.7% between 2000 and 2004. Approximately 45% of the foster care population and more than half of all children waiting to be adopted are African American. Infant mortality is twice that of white infants, with Black preschoolers three times more likely to have HIV-AIDS than their White peers (Willis, 1998).

More than half of African Americans (57%) live in inner city areas noted for high crime rates, crowded living, poor employment opportunities, and poor access to mental health facilities. Inner city living is associated with increased risk of homicide, which is the leading cause of death among young African American adults and adolescent males.

Family and parenting practices.   Hill (1998) states that there is a basic lack of understanding and appreciation of Black family functioning because most research efforts tend to divorce family situations from their historical context. Historically, despite racism and oppression, Black families have demonstrated a remarkable ability to survive and preserve their cultural heritage, passed on largely through the oral tradition, such as stories or music. Within European American families "the nuclear family" is at the core, whereas "the African extended family is the African family" (p. 17). Within this perspective, Hill defines Black families as "constellations of households related by blood or marriage or function that provides basic instrumental and expressive functions of the family to members of those networks" (p. 18). Within this constellation are **fictive kin**, who are not related, but who provide a supportive role to the family. Family members are considered immediate family if they reside in the same domain, even if they constitute members from different generations.

Hill (1998) lists four pillars of the Black family that have ensured their continued survival: *strong achievement orientation, flexible family roles, kinship bonds, and strong religious orientation.*

Organized religion is often central to social, civic, and educational activities. Activities such as child care, parenting programs, drug abuse prevention programs, and job-training programs have been routinely housed in community churches (Billingsley, 1992). Flexible family roles have contributed to the resilience of many Black families.

Demographics on Single Family Households

Approximately 55% of African American homes are headed by single females (U.S. Census Bureau, 1999). Many female-headed households require child rearing support from extended family (Taylor, 2000), and approximately one in three households contain elderly heads and younger children.

Although some studies suggest that grandmother-headed households are related to better adjustment outcomes for young children (Smith & Drew, 2002), there is also some support that intergenerational conflict resulting from such arrangements might cancel any positive benefit that might exist (Moore & Brookes-Gunn, 2002). At least one study of African American single-parenting households found that quality of parenting was related to the nature of care experienced by the mother (transmission of generational practices) and level of poverty, rather than due to any coparenting arrangements (Cain & Combs-Orme, 2005).

According to Ogbu (1981), a major goal in the transmission of cultural values from generation to generation is to insure the survival of that culture. Within this context, African Americans have demonstrated their ability to survive despite limited resources and high risk environments. Several studies have focused on developmental concerns regarding children living in impoverished African American families (McCreary & Dancy, 2004; McLoyd, 1990; Spencer, 1990). Cain and Combs-Orme (2005) point out the argument that comparative research that evaluates African American families against European American middle-class standards perpetuates the disregard for diversity among the African American community and serves to minimize the "staggering effects economic deprivation, racism and social stratification on processes and functioning in the African American home" (p. 20).

Parenting in an impoverished African American neighborhood. Jarrett (1998) discusses the impact of contextual and family factors on developmental process and trajectories for African American children growing up in impoverished environments. Following Bronfenbrenner's model, Jarrett characterizes the impoverished neighborhood as providing limited resources, a preponderance of unemployed or marginally employed adults, and poorly resourced schools against a backdrop of high volume drug activity and violence. Despite this dangerous and negative setting, there are also some good quality resources that can be found in libraries, churches, and schools within the community. As a product of their environment, Jarrett outlines how children primarily develop along two potential pathways: *street and nonstreet trajectories.*

Street children. Socialized into their street role at an early age, these children experience accelerated development as they learn from peers how to function and survive on the streets (Moore, 1969; Williams & Kornblum, 1985). Vulnerability to the street path is increased for children whose parents are less competent in seeking out resources, parental management strategies, promoting in-home learning, and who are less protective of their children from street life activity. The path to the street may be direct and unswerving, or may come later, after failure of the nonstreet ways. Many assume adult roles prematurely due to family crises (e.g., parent addiction problem), or parent employment (caring for siblings). Females spend less time on the streets initially, due to domestic responsibilities; however, they tend to increase street time as they mature.

Recall and Rewind

Jarrett (1998) and Vigil (2002) describe similar pathways for street children and gang formation. Both authors relate street socialization to increased tendencies towards crime.

Nonstreet children.   Parents of children who take the more conventional path are more competent in seeking out resources; encourage in-home learning activities; and use child management strategies that protect their children from negative street influences. Parents are more aware of their child's whereabouts and monitor their activities (Furstenberg, 1993; Jarrett, 1992). Parents often have greater access to a support network, such as having kin in more economically advantaged neighborhoods where the child can spend some time, compared to parents of street children who are more isolated. Children reared along the more conventional path develop competencies that are related to more traditional goals, including emphasis on academic achievement, creative efforts, and involvement in team sports. Children on the nonstreet trajectory are better equipped to survive in a conventional world.

Recall and Rewind

Baumrind (1991) reported four different types of parenting styles in her research: *Authoritative* (warm but structured); *Authoritarian* (force in the absence of warmth); *Permissive* (warmth with little structure); and *Uninvolved* (lack of warmth or structure). Most of the positive outcomes for children were initially associated with the Authoritative parenting style.

Authoritative vs. authoritarian parenting style.   A number of studies have confirmed the use of authoritarian practices by African American families (Cain & Coombs-Orme, 2005; Kelley, Power, & Wimbush, 1992). Cain and Coombs-Orme (2005) reported that 67% of their population of African American mothers (regardless of marital status and family structure) condoned the use of "very strict, rigid and authoritarian discipline practices (i.e., hitting, intimidation, pain and belittlement)" (p. 36). However, while some studies support the use of more punitive physical discipline as a deterrent to engaging in high risk behaviors in dangerous neighborhoods (Bradley, 1998; Kelley et al., 1992), others express concern that these practices send a message that condones violence (Raymond, Jones, & Cooke, 1998). However, there is support that in countries where physical discipline is the norm, authoritarian parenting practices are less likely to have an adverse effect on child behavior (Lansford et al., 2005).

In the Eye of the Beholder

Vendlinski, Silk, Shaw, and Lane (2006) found that African American children demonstrated the lowest level of internalizing symptoms in response to high parental conflict over child rearing and low parent openness. This was the reverse of what they found for European American children. The authors suggest that while high parental control may be associated with positive signs of caring and concern for African American children, these same qualities may be interpreted in a negative way (intrusive and rejecting) by European American children.

Table 3.4 Culture Bound Syndromes Associated With Southern U.S., African American, and West African Cultures

Culture Bound Syndrome: Triggered by	Description	Culture
Brain fag Precipitated by school challenges	Difficulties concentrating, thinking, remembering Somatic complaints: head, neck, blurred vision	West Africa
Falling-out or blacking-out	Collapse (may be preceded by dizziness); Eyes are open, but inability to see; Unable to move Similar to conversion disorder	Southern U.S. Caribbean
Rootwork Precipitating cause: Under a spell or hex, witchcraft	Generalized anxiety, gastrointestinal complaints, weakness, dizziness, and paranoia	Southern U.S. African American
Spell	Trance-like state and communication with deceased	Southern US African American

Source: DSM–IV–TR, APA (2000).

Types and Prevalence of Mental Health Issues

Referrals. Although African American youth are overrepresented in special education programs, they are most likely to be referred for service by the juvenile justice or child welfare systems and least likely to be referred by schools (Yeh et al., 2002). It was not certain whether low school referrals resulted from lack of identification of mental health issues or parent lack of acceptance of suggestions from school personnel.

Prevalence rates; psychological and behavioral disorders. As adults, African Americans are least likely to report depression, but are more likely to experience phobias compared to non-Hispanic Whites. Disproportionately high rates of somatization (15%) and schizophrenia (Black males) exist and poorer outcomes are reported. The *DSM-IV-TR* (APA, 2000) lists several culture bound syndromes which may be applicable to African American populations which can be seen in Table 3.4.

Until recently, there have been few studies of eating disorders in African American youth. Although early indications were that eating disorders were relatively rare in African American adolescents (Robinson & Andersen, 1985), contemporary investigations suggest otherwise. In response to the Youth Risk Behavior Survey (YRBS, 2006) conducted by the Centers for Disease Control and Prevention, 27% of African American youth reported body dissatisfaction compared to 23.6% in 1999, while 38.9% admitted to currently engaging in weight loss activities compared to 36.3% in 1999. (The YBRS is discussed at length in chapter 12.) It has been suggested that increases in the desire to lose weight among African American youth may be due to **acculturation** (Striegel-Moore & Smolak, 1997). Support for this theory is evident in at least one study that found African American women attending a predominately White university had higher levels of depression and associated eating problems than those attending a predominately African American university (Ford, 2000).

> ### Memory Bank
>
> *Acculturation* refers to the process of negotiating between a dominant (culture of origin) and less dominant (culture of placement) culture. In moving from a dominant culture to an unknown or lesser known culture, success of the acculturation process would likely be contingent on the number and extent of adjustments required regarding beliefs, values, and practices.

While an early study found that psychiatric hospitalization rates for severe disorders, such as schizophrenia, have been 2 to 3 times higher in Black youth compared to White youth (Myers, 1989), a later study found no significant patterns of disorder prevalence in youth due to race/ethnicity or socioeconomic status (Yee & Sigman, 1998). In adult populations, however, it has been argued that schizophrenia has been overdiagnosed in African American populations (Carter & Neufeld, 1998). African American youth are also more likely to be referred to juvenile justice rather than a treatment facility.

Important Distinction

Weddle and McKenry (1995) express caution that symptoms of suicidal behavior in African American youth may be misinterpreted as acting out, aggressive, and high risk behaviors. However, despite the possibility of underreporting, suicide rates for African American youth (10–14 years old) increased 23% between 1980 and 1995 (Lazear, Doan, & Roggenbaum, 2003).

While the consumption of alcohol is lower in Black youth than White youth, substance abuse in lower income African American youth is more likely to be associated with delinquent behaviors, such as selling drugs, and involve the use of cocaine and heroin. Intravenous drug use and unprotected sex may account for the fact that African American youth make up 55% of all persons aged 13 to 24 years living with HIV/AIDS (CDC, 2004). A CDC study of HIV infection through heterosexual contact (YRBS, 2003) revealed that over 30% of African American males and 5% of African American females reported having sexual intercourse for the first time before age 13. One study found that high rates of teen pregnancy among African American girls was related to high drop-out rates, unemployment, and future welfare use (Rosenheim & Testa, 1992).

Implications for treatment and intervention. African American youth receive less treatment from psychiatric hospitals that are privately funded and are more likely to be found in publicly funded residential treatment centers for emotionally disturbed youth. Angold and colleagues (2002) found that just over one third of youth with a DSM diagnosis had received any mental health service in the previous 3 months. Furthermore, any services received were most likely to be school based due to convenience of access. However, the authors suggest that school-based mental health services might be less than ideal for families whose children are already in special education programs, since these families may be reluctant to obtain services in settings already associated with failure to achieve, high rates of suspensions, and low expectations (Gibbs, 2001).

Latino/Hispanic Americans
Demographics and sociocultural background. The Latino population in the United States is characterized by significant diversity. While Mexican Americans make up the majority of the Hispanic population (66%), the remaining third of the population have origins in Puerto Rico, Cuba, South America, Central America, the Dominican Republic, and Spain. It is estimated that within the next 50 years, the Latino/Hispanic population will represent about one quarter of the population of the United States (Cauce & Domenech-Rodriguez, 2002). The majority of Latinos live in California, Arizona, New Mexico, Colorado, and Texas; however, more recent trends have seen increased growth in Arkansas, North Carolina, Georgia, Nebraska, and Tennessee.

A little more than half of Latinos have completed a high school education, compared with 83% of the U.S. population. Graduation rates among the subgroups vary from a high of 70% (Cuban Americans) to a low of 50% (Mexican Americans). Compared to 13.5% of the American population at or below the poverty line, poverty rates among Hispanic Americans range from a low of 14% (Cuban Americans) to highs between 31% (Puerto Ricans) and 37% (Mexican Americans). Approximately 35% of the Hispanic/Latino population is 19 years of age or younger (Census, 2000).

Memory Bank

The category of Hispanic was originally created to collect data on people belonging to countries of Hispanic origin, including Mexican, Cuban, and Puerto Rican. The term **Latino**, which refers to populations from Latin America, is often used interchangeably with Hispanic.

Family and parenting practices. Although the Hispanic population is very diverse, there are several features of the "family" which are common to many Latino families, including the focus on self-identity related to the family context. Demographically, family size is usually larger in Latino families: 3.7 family members versus 2.97 for White Americans and 3.31 for African American families (U.S. Census Bureau, 2003). Geographically, family members tend to live in close proximity within the community. Extended family members often share housing arrangements, and it is not unusual to find members of different generations residing together and sharing child-care duties (Zinn & Wells, 2000).

The **familia** is at the foundation of the Mexican American community and is a kinship network that supports a mixture of traditional and more contemporary approaches to a strong family orientation. The extended family system incorporates nonfamily members, **compadres** (godparents), who take on a special role during the baptism and provide mutual support. Unlike the individualistic and competitive emphasis found in the nuclear European American family, the collective nature of the Hispanic family network fosters an attitude of cooperation, affiliation, and interdependence among the family members. In many cases, immigrants to the United States remain with relatives for a number of years before they move out into separate quarters within the same community. Children are often at the center of the family (Gonzales, Knight, Morgan-Lopez, Saenz, & Sirolle, 2002).

Early stereotypes of Mexican-origin families discussed the concept of **machismo**, or *an inflated sense of male dominance* as fundamental to the Hispanic family. Contemporary studies have found that, like other families, the patterns are neither male-dominated, nor are they totally egalitarian. Like other families, increased tendencies for women to enter the work force in the United States have shifted the balance of power. However, while women have tended to elevate their position by increased autonomy and economic skills, males continue to occupy low status jobs that may further erode their position of patriarchal authority (Baca Zinn & Pok, 2002).

To an outsider, Mexican American parents may seem less interested in having their children achieve milestones on target and are more accepting of a child's unique patterns of development. Although young children may be treated with more permissiveness, or indulgence, contributing to the family is expected in the later years (duties such as cleaning, cooking, and child-care). Gender roles are traditional and are seen as preparatory for their future roles as mothers and fathers (Ramirez, 2001).

Table 3.5 Culture Bound Syndromes Associated With Latino, Spanish, or Mexican Cultures

Culture Bound Syndrome: Triggered by	Description	Culture
Ataque de nervios Precipitated by stressful life events	Being out of control: trembling; crying, shouting; verbal/physical aggression; dissociative experiences: seizure-like or fainting spells	Latino
Bilis and colera (muina) Precipitated by extreme anger	Acute nervous tension, headache, trembling; screaming, stomachache; severe form can result in loss of consciousness	Latino
Locura Chronic psychosis	Incoherence, agitation, hallucinations, unpredictable and possibly violent	Latino
Mal de ojo (evil eye)	Children are at risk; Crying fits, diarrhea, vomiting, and fever.	Spanish
Nervios Precipitated by stressful life events	Wide range of vague symptoms of stress, including: headaches, tearfulness, irritability, sleep and eating disturbances, trembling, somatic disturbance, etc.	Latino
Susto Precipitated by frightening event	Fright or soul loss; unhappiness and sickness. Resembles PTSD, depression, and somatoform	Latino Mexican

Source: DSM–IV–TR, APA (2000).

Types and Prevalence of Mental Health Issues

Referrals.   Yeh and colleagues (2002) found that Latino youth were underreferred and that mental health issues were underidentified by the school system. Outpatient referrals generated by lay referrals and friends were significantly higher than school identified problems. Latino children, but not adolescents, were the least likely among racial/ethnic groups to be referred for services by child welfare.

Prevalence rates; psychological and behavioral disorders.   Mexican families may be more inclined to seek assistance from natural healers than the medical profession. In the most recent revision of the DSM (APA, 2000), culture-bound syndromes specific to Latino populations have been included in the text revision and a sample can be viewed in Table 3.5.

A Case of Misdiagnosis

In a recent study conducted in California, it was found that Latino American youth were more likely to have been initially diagnosed with a disruptive behavior disorder or a substance abuse disorder by intake workers, despite parent ratings of fewer externalizing and internalizing problems than other ethnic groups. The authors of the study caution that misdiagnoses, at admission, could be based on preconceived notions. Furthermore, they warn that these errors could seriously undermine treatment effectiveness for these youth (Mak & Rosenblatt, 2002).

In another study, also based on Latino youth in California, Yeh and colleagues (2002) found that Latino youth were more likely to be diagnosed with adjustment disorders, anxiety disorders, and psychotic disorders and less likely to be diagnosed with ADHD than their non-Hispanic White (NHW) peers. Furthermore, Latino teens were more likely to receive a diagnosis of a psychotic disorder, and Latino children were more likely to receive a diagnosis of anxiety disorder compared to their NHW peers. Overall, Latino youth demonstrate more anxiety-related and delinquency-related behavior problems, depression, and drug abuse relative to their NHW peers.

Recent investigations have documented an increase in body dissatisfaction among Hispanic youth. According to the YRSB survey conducted in 2005, although overall scores for White youth noted a decline in body dissatisfaction from 32.8% (1991) to 31.5% (2005), Hispanic youth reported a steady increase in body dissatisfaction from 34.9% (1991) to a current rate of 37.1% (2005). Hispanic males reported the highest rate of perceived overweight (10.7%) relative to true weight of all youth surveyed. In 2005, more than 50% of Hispanic youth (51.2 %) were engaged in weight-loss activities relative to 45.6% of the total sample surveyed. In their study of weight loss behaviors, Fitsgibbon, Spring, Avellone, Blackman, Pingitore, and Stolley (1998) found that Hispanic females were more likely to engage in binge-eating episodes than African American or White American females.

There has been increasing investigation of potential links between family acculturation and outcomes for Hispanic children and youth. Intergenerational conflicts regarding traditional values disrupt and weaken family ties. As a result, there is a negative impact in a number of areas, including increased delinquent behavior, association with antisocial peers, increased substance abuse (tobacco, alcohol, drugs), lowered academic performance, depression, and suicide ideation (Gonzales et al., 2002). Hispanic males and females report the highest incidence of suicide attempts of any youth group, with 12.8% of males and 18.9% of females reporting a suicide attempt within the previous 12 months (Lazear, Doan, & Roggenbaum, 2003). Latino men are incarcerated at a rate four times that of NHW males.

Implications for treatment and intervention.   Utilization of mental health services by Hispanics and Latinos is poor (USSDDS, 2001). Less than 1 in 10 contact mental health specialists, and less than 20% contact general health care providers. Estimates of the usage of alternative health care sources range widely, with studies reporting anywhere from 4% to 44% of Mexican Americans consulting a *curandero*, *herbalista*, or other folk healers. Use of alterative remedies seems to be greater than actual consultation with alternative or folk healers, with remedies most likely used to accompany a mainstream care. Approximately 24% of Hispanics with depression and anxiety receive appropriate care, compared to 34% of Whites.

Asian Americans/Pacific Islanders

Background and demographics.   The terms "Asian American" (AA) and "Pacific Islander" (PI) are used to refer to more than 60 different ethnic groups who have emigrated to the United States from Asia, the Pacific Rim, and Pacific Islands. Before 1970, the three most predominant populations of Asian descent in the United States were Japanese, Chinese, and Filipinos. In 1990, by population, the three largest Asian groups were Chinese, Filipinos, and Indo-Chinese (Vietnamese, Cambodian, Hmong, and Laotian; Parke, 2004). There is considerable diversity among this group based on their cultural origins, language, and immigration history. About half of the AA/PI population is located in the West, most notably in California and Hawaii. Most Pacific Islanders are not immigrants because their homelands include areas that have been taken over by the United States (Hawaii, Guam, the Marshall Islands, etc.).

Asian Americans are often referred to as the "model minority," due to their visible success; however, they have also been subjected to anti-immigration sentiment and distinctions between ethnic groups are often blurred (Chan, 1998). In this section, discussion will be restricted to Chinese, Japanese, and to a limited extent, Vietnamese Americans.

Historically, the beliefs, attitudes, and values of the Asian culture have been highly influenced by the philosophies contained in the teachings of **Confucianism**, **Taoism**, and **Buddhism**.

Confucianism provides doctrines regarding the collective good, social harmony, and codes of conduct in the "five virtues" (see Chan, 1998). Most often, Confucian principles are evident in the historical basis for parenting roles in Chinese, Japanese, Korean, and Southeast Asian families (Mirande, 1991).

The Three Teachings

Confucianism teaches a sense of family piety evident in respect for one's parents and elders. Through *Taoism*, meditation, asceticism, and self-discipline, one learns the inner strength that comes from being in balance with nature (yin and yang). *Buddhism* teaches the path to avoidance of human suffering by eliminating earthly desires. The circle of reincarnation (rebirth into suffering) is governed by *karma* (obligations from past lives) and finding *nirvana* (state of peace) is only possible by following the path of Buddha and *dharma* (Buddha's doctrines).

Asian American families have traditionally adhered to a patriarchal structure with the father as head of household. Within this structure, fathers are the authority figures for the family and often distance themselves emotionally from the family (Ishii-Kuntz, 2000). Although Asian women, as a rule, are granted considerable authority and autonomy in their child-rearing role, they are considered to be in a subordinate role to their husbands in matters other than child-rearing (Parke, 2004). Although fathers have been less involved in caretaking activities in the past, women's increasing role in the workplace has resulted in fathers expanding their involvement in the lives of their young children (Kurrien & Vo, 2001).

Chinese Americans. Some Chinese Americans have been in the United States for more than six generations, while others are recent immigrants. In 1882, the Chinese Exclusion Act banned further Chinese immigration and within 40 years was extended to include all Asian immigrants. The act was ultimately repealed in 1943 and a change in immigration policy in 1965 ushered in a second wave of Asian immigration comprised mainly of urban professionals and their families who located primarily in California and New York (Wong, 1995). As new immigrants arrive, they add to the existing communities, or Chinatowns. These towns are often based on a hierarchical structure, as the more wealthy entrepreneurs of old provide employment for the unskilled working class. This situation often results in two distinct classes (Wong, 1995).

Japanese Americans. The Japanese use different words to categorize immigrant generations: **Issei** (first generation arrived early 1900s); **Nisei** (children of the Issei born in the United States); **Sansei** (third generation); **Yonsei** (fourth generation); and **Gosei** (fifth generation). The majority of Japanese Americans settled on the West coast (California and Hawaii). Due to their close proximity, those who settled in Hawaii have maintained a greater extent of their culture than those who remained on the mainland (Nagata, 2001).

Educationally, more than half of Japanese American young adult males and almost half of young adult females have their bachelor's degree or higher. While other Asian groups are increasing in size, Japanese Americans have registered an increasing decline in population.

Vietnamese American. In 1990, the Vietnamese population in the United States numbered more than 600,000 (53% males) making them the sixth largest Asian American group. The majority settled as refugees in California and Texas. Vietnamese refugees are a diverse group, and there are notable differences between those who arrived in the first wave (1975), mainly white-collar or high-ranking military officials, and later arrivals, often known as "boat people," mainly blue-collar workers in sales or service positions.

As refugees, the Vietnamese struggled to maintain the extended family at a time when parents were separated from children and husbands were separated from wives. Under these conditions, the Vietnamese Americans opened their doors to distant relatives and friends, thereby widening their definition of the extended family beyond the prescribed standards for "kin" as set out in Confucianism (Kibria, 1993).

Family and parenting practices. One of the major systems for interpreting cultural differences in behavior is the dimension of **individualism** and **collectivism** (I/C). The I/C dimension reflects the extent to which a given culture fosters the goals of the individual (autonomous, independent) versus the group (connection and cooperation; Hofstede, 1980).

Important Distinction

While families in North America encourage development of the *individual* (competition, independence), Asian families traditionally have been motivated by goals that support the *group* (cooperation and dependency). Given this discrepancy, it is not difficult to understand how conflicts and misunderstandings can create a culture clash.

For Asian Americans, the extended family is an understood obligation and often involves living in multigenerational situations. Vietnamese families are more likely to be involved in extended family living arrangements than any other Asian American group (Kurrien & Vo, 2001). Although typically patriarchal in structure, coparenting is becoming more common as a support structure in Vietnamese families with female family members (e.g., grandmothers and aunts), older siblings, and neighbors playing an increasing role in caregiving arrangements (Kurrien & Vo, 2001). Although possible in any culture, such living or support-giving arrangements in Asian American families can be a particular source of tension and conflict when traditional ways of child rearing clash with more contemporary influences of the "American way" (Brody, Flor, & Nuebaum, 1998).

In North America, adolescence marks a time of increased independence from family and ushering in the creation of a unique identity. However, for Asian American youth, this period can result in extreme pressure and stress resulting from a culture clash that pits the adolescent between his North American self (identifies with peers and school culture) and his traditional heritage evident in family and extended family (Yeh & Huang, 2000). Investigations of the problems facing Asian immigrant youth have provided increased awareness of the unique difficulties that these adolescents face in attempting to adjust to their new surroundings. Yeh (2003) investigated acculturation, adjustment, and mental health symptoms of Asian immigrant Chinese, Korean, and Japanese youth. Results revealed that older students reported more symptoms of mental health stress related to acculturation than younger students. The author suggests that increased demands from family towards familial attachments and obligations with increasing age might result in more obvious culture clash with North American values of autonomy and independence, creating more pressure and conflicts with age.

> **Recall and Rewind**
>
> The degree to which acculturation is successful (negotiating between the culture of origin and the culture of placement) depends on the number and extent of adjustments required regarding beliefs, values, and practices.

While many similarities exist in the parenting practices of Asian families, it is also important to acknowledge the subtle differences that exist in Chinese, Japanese, and Vietnamese families.

Chinese families.   Historically, the Chinese family functioned along prescribed guidelines with privileges assigned to specific roles. The male head of household had unchallenged authority and was responsible for the family's economic status and respect within the community. The mother was responsible for nurturing the childrenm and working outside the home was not encouraged. The first-born male was given preferential treatment, and male children were esteemed relative to females. Contemporary forces have softened rigid adherence to prescribed roles of the past (Huang & Ying, 2001). However, there are unwritten rules regarding communication and a strong cultural emphasis on emotional restraint and not expressing emotions continues to be a valued trait. Piety to family continues to be a significant factor with "shame" and "loss of face" as the ultimate punishment for not maintaining appropriate conduct that might reflect badly on one's family.

Japanese families.   Traditional values were based on the collective good (group rather than individual goals, loyalty, and hierarchical status structure). Japanese concepts of **on** and **giri** focus on the importance of honoring contractual obligations, and **amae** (dependency and love) were the motivating and guiding forces for behaviors (Nagata, 2001). The Japanese American heritage is a collective one which fosters dependency and obligation, rather than independence and confrontation. Avoidance of overtly expressing emotions is similar to Chinese families. Currently, due to the shrinking population of Japanese Americans, more than half of Japanese are married to non-Japanese partners and traditional Japanese values have been influenced accordingly.

Vietnamese families.   Traditionally, Vietnamese families have followed the Confucian principle of the family hierarchy in which young are subordinate to old and women are subordinate to men. However, migration patterns (many young were not accompanied by elders) and opportunities for better education and employment have placed younger Vietnamese in more advantaged positions than their parents or elders. Clashes in cultural expectations are not uncommon (Kibria, 1993), and lack of parental influence has been blamed in part for the growth of Vietnamese youth gangs (Vigil & Yun, 1990).

In a recent study comparing Asian gang members to nongang members in Southern California, Tsunokai (2005) confirmed several findings of earlier investigations, namely that Asian youth joined gangs for reasons similar to other youth gang participants: friendships with existing gang members, the anticipation of camaraderie and fun, and protection and support. Furthermore, similar to findings of Vigil and Yun (1990), Asian youth in gangs reported greater feelings of marginalization and blocked opportunities than nongang members. However, Tsunokai (2005) also found a number of unexpected results. Although gang members were twice as likely to be living below the poverty line compared to nongang members, 24% of gang members' families earned in excess of $50,000 annually. Furthermore, the impoverished tended to come from families of Cambodian, Vietnamese, or Laotian origins. Contrary to theories of gang formation (Vigil,

2002), Tsunokai found no significant between-group differences in perceived parental support or supervision. Of the 28 different gangs represented in the sample, Tsunokai found several gangs with individual members from multiple Asian origins, such as Asian Boyz and Wah Ching, gangs that had Chinese, Japanese, Cambodian, Vietnamese, and Filipino members. Asian youth with low school involvement (lack of participation in clubs) and low school commitment (suspensions, skipping school, time spent studying, GPA) were at greatest risk for future gang membership.

Types and Prevalence of Mental Health Issues

Referrals. There are extremely low rates of utilization of mental health services for Asian Americans. In one study, only 17% of those who were experiencing problems sought out treatment, and then only under the most severe crisis conditions did this occur. Reliance on alternative health care methods, language barriers, and shame and stigma have all been associated with low rate of usage of mental health services (USDHHS, 2001).

Prevalence rates; psychological and behavioral disorders. Historically, given cultural tendencies to refrain from overt emotional expression, coupled with the sentiment of Asians as the "model minority," knowledge of the mental health needs of the Asian and Pacific Islanders has been limited. Culture-bound syndromes DSM-IV-TR (APA, 2000) which are particularly applicable to AA/PIs are listed in Table 3.6.

Among adult populations, the 1-year prevalence rate for depression among Chinese Americans is between 3% and 7%. Depressive symptoms manifest as somatic complaints in Chinese, relative to other ethnic minorities. Although suicide rates for the majority of Asians is lower than White Americans, Native Hawaiian adolescents have higher suicide rates than any other adolescent group in Hawaii (USDHHS, 2001), and suicide rates for Asian Pacific Islander females (15–24) are consistently the highest in that age group in the country (Lazear et al., 2003). Rates for depression among school-aged girls (Grades 5–12) were highest for Asian Americans (30%), compared with 27% (Hispanic), 22% (non-Hispanic Whites), and 17% (African Americans). One study of the correlates of suicidal behaviors in Asian American youth found that suicide could be predicted by the interaction of acculturation and parent–child conflict. Lau, Jernewall, Zane, and Myers (2002) found that compared to their more acculturated Asian peers, Asian youth who were less acculturated were at increased risk for suicide attempts under conditions of parent–child conflict.

Asian/Pacific Islander American youth tend to be underrepresented across the range of service sectors reviewed (McCabe et al., 1999). In California, however, Asian/Pacific Islander Americans were present at rates comparable to other minority groups in alcohol/drug treatment sectors and juvenile justice. McCabe and colleagues conclude that within the community investigated (San Diego County), Asian/Pacific Islander American youth did demonstrate difficulties in their treatment for alcohol/drug abuse and involvement with the juvenile justice system; however, they did not surface in data regarding voluntary admission. The authors suggest that because these youth primarily were from Southeast Asia, a history of refugee-related traumas might account for the vulnerability of this particular population relative to other Asian/Pacific youth studied previously. Recently, studies have investigated differences between Southeast Asian and Chinese immigrant youth. Ngo and Le (2007) found that among Southeast Asian youth, Cambodian and Laotian youth reported the highest levels of stress, with physical abuse predictive of serious violence among Southeast Asian but not Chinese youth. In this study, social support surfaced as a protective factor, while increased acculturation, intergenerational/intercultural conflict, and individualism (versus collectivism) increased the risk for acts of serious violence among youth.

Table 3.6 Culture Bound Syndromes Associated With Asian Cultures

Culture Bound Syndrome: Triggered by	Description	Culture
Qi-gong psychotic reaction Precipitated by involvement in folk health practices	Acute psychotic, paranoid, or delusional response	Chinese
Taijin kyofusho	Phobia regarding body (appearance, odor, expression) causing intense fear of humiliation Symptoms similar to social phobia DSM	Japan
Hwa-byung Precipitated by suppressing anger	Anger syndrome Insomnia, fatigue, panic, fear of death, depression, anorexia, palpitations, lump in throat, body aches	Korean
Shenjing shuairuo	"Neurasthenia" Physical and mental fatigue (memory loss, pain, concentration problems) Gastrointestinal problems, irritability, excitability Symptoms very similar to DSM mood or anxiety disorder	Chinese
Shin-byung	Anxiety and somatic complaints Possession by ancestral spirits	Korean

Source: DSM–IV–TR, APA (2000).

Spencer and Le (2006) found that the refugee process for Southeast Asians can be transmitted through the children of refugees (Vietnamese youth) and increase the likelihood of serious violent acts when mediated by peer delinquency and parental engagement.

The influence of culture on substance use may also differ for Southeast Asian youth. In one study of 31 drug-involved youth living in low income neighborhoods, pervasive marijuana use was found to be the normal coping mechanism for stress emanating from their home and community environments (Lee & Kirkpatrick, 2005). Furthermore, marijuana use was considered to be part of their alternative ghetto lifestyle evolving around music (rap) and youth crime.

Implications for treatment. Minimal data exist about treatment effects, and low rates of usage for Asian Americans compounds the problem. Yeh, Eastman, and Cheung (1994) examined the effects of ethnic match of counselor on the outcomes of Asian Americans and found that having an ethnic match between counselor and client was less important for younger children compared with adolescents. However, other family members are frequently involved in child treatment issues. Yeh, Takeuchi, and Sue (1994) reported that children and adolescents who attended ethnic-specific centers utilized more services and had better outcomes at discharge. Given the increasing diversity recognized in research among Asian youth (e.g., Southeast Asian vs. Chinese), it is also imperative that treatment resources reflect these cultural variations in the services offered.

American Indian (AI)/Alaskan Native (AN) Children and Families
Background and demographics. The American Indian population (also known as Native American) in the United States (including Alaska Native communities) was recently assessed at 4.3 million, which is 1.5% of the total U.S. population (Ogunwole, 2006). However, due to their relatively small numbers and rural living, they have been described as one of the least visible minority groups (Taylor, 2002). The native population is extremely diverse with more than 561 officially recognized tribes. The largest tribal grouping is the Cherokee, which represent almost one third of the entire AI population; while the largest Alaska Native tribal grouping is the Eskimo,

which is slightly less than half the AN population. There are more than 200 different languages spoken among the various AI/AN tribes; however, more than half of Alaskan Eskimos speak either Inuit or Yup'ik (Ogunwole, 2006).

Important Distinction

In the U.S. population at large, 12.4% are 65 years of age or older. But among AI/NA, only 5.6% make it to 65 years of age. While 25% of the U.S. population is under 18 years of age, almost 33% of AI/NA are below 18 years. The median age of AI-NA is 28.5 years compared to 35.4 years for the United States at large.

Although the majority of Native Americans (80%) have lived on reservations in the past, currently only 20% (including Eskimos and Aleuts) continue to live on the reservations, with AI/NA accounting for 8% of the total population of the homeless. Dispersed and dwindling in population, less are able to take advantage of federally funded programs of care, most of which require a one-quarter blood relationship to American Indian descent for eligibility (LaFramboise & Graff Low, 2001). However, future projections predict that persons with one-half blood or more will decline continuously, while those with one-quarter to one-half Indian blood will increase, basically due to marriages to non-Indian partners. Throughout this transition, there is much speculation regarding the degree to which Indians will abandon their cultural heritage along the way (Yellowbird & Snipp, 2002).

Education and employment are issues that set the AI/NA population significantly apart from the national averages. Approximately 80% of the U.S. population graduate high school, compared to 71% of AI/NA youth. About 11% of AI/NA receive at least a bachelor's degree, compared to 24.4 % of the total U.S. population. Twice as many AI/NA are unemployed compared to White Americans. More than one fourth live in poverty, which is more than double that of other U.S. residents. In the criminal justice system, 4% of all inmates are Native American.

Family and parenting practices. The American Indian family supports a "collective" rather than "individualistic" perspective, where members are interdependent. However, unlike the emphasis on fostering dependence versus independence seen in Asian cultures, the Native American culture also places a high degree of value on individual qualities of independence and autonomy. However, Joe and Malach (1998) suggest that wide variations in acculturation may account for much of the diversity; while some communities become Americanized, others focus on preserving their traditional heritage.

Acculturation and Adaptation

Miller (1979) identified four different classifications of "adaptation" to White city culture: **traditional** (retain the Indian values); **transitional** (shift and adaptation to white urban ways); **bicultural** (retain Indian values but adapt to white city ends when needed); and **marginal** (those whose practices are blurred in a hybrid of both cultures). Bicultural families were the most successful at adaptation, while the marginal families continued to remain on the fringe with no clear alliance to city or reservation life.

NA households are less likely to contain married couples today (45% of households) compared to the U.S. norm (52.5%), and are much more likely to be female-led households with no spouse present (20.7%) or male-led households with no spouse present (7.5%), than comparable single-spousal U.S. households nationwide (female householder 11.8%; male householder 4.1%; Ogunwole, 2006).

From a collective perspective, involvement can often extend from the family to the tribe as a whole. Historically, elders have been seen as the purveyors of wisdom and tend to pass down the Indian ways and tradition through storytelling in the oral tradition (LaFramboise & Graff Low, 2001). However, given the poor social, health, and economic conditions, AI/AN elderly populations are the lowest in the country with only 5.6% of the population 65 years or above.

Time Passages

While European American (EA) parents tend to focus on developmental milestones as the yardstick for measuring a child's progress, relative to other children of the same age, AI/AN parents tend to celebrate a child's *accomplishments*, viewing time as the harbinger of important events: "time of first smile, first laugh, first steps, or first attempts at using language" (LaFromboise & Graff Low, 2001, p. 119). In this regard, AI/AN parents focus on the of natural unfolding of the child (much like philosopher, Rousseau) and do not pressure children to conform to rigid timelines. From this perspective, early accomplishments are a reason to celebrate "readiness" as the master of performance (Everett, Proctor, & Carmell, 1983).

Among the traditional tribal values are concepts that differ significantly from white European American concepts, including **time, cooperation, leadership, and harmony with nature** (Yellowbird & Snipp, 2002).

Socialization among tribal members occurs within an atmosphere of respect for authority and quiet behavior evident in having good listening skills. Children often demonstrate this quiet, passive response to their learning environments (Yellowbird & Snipp, 2002). Often communication is indirect, rather than direct, and occurs whether the action is a positive (reward) or negative (punishment) event. Indirect communication serves to protect the immediate family members from having to punish a family member directly (protects family bonds), while at the same time serves to insulate the family from direct rewards for accomplishments (insures family's humility). Communication often flows through a chain of family and kin until the message reaches the intended recipient. Messages worthy of celebration make their way to the "town crier," who will announce the event to the community (LaFramboise & Graff Low, 2001).

In matters of child discipline, physical punishment is limited due to the ongoing respect for the autonomy of the child and respect for individual ways. Although parents may seem permissive and passive when a child does not follow a parent's order, there are direct consequences of violation of traditional cultural norms. Elders often take the role of disciplinarian and teacher (LaFramboise & Graff Low, 2001).

Types and Prevalence of Mental Health Issues

Referrals.   Access to mental health resources is through Indian Health Service (IHS) clinics; however, only 20% of NA populations live on the reservations where the majority of the clinics are located. There is little known about usage rates of services in this population. Referrals and treatment for NA children and youth are more likely to occur, especially for Cherokee children, through the Juvenile Justice system (Ogunwole, 2006). There has been increased concern about the transition from youth to young adulthood in this population and the lack of resources that are available to bridge this important period of development (Fox, Becker-Green, Gault, & Simmons, 2005).

Prevalence rates; psychological and behavioral disorders.   Although no large-scale epidemiological studies are currently available for NA populations, one smaller longitudinal study found that the lifetime prevalence of mental disorders in NA to be as high as 70% (USDHHS, 2001).

Consider This

The surgeon general's supplementary report (USDSHSS, 2001) noted that 50% of adolescents in a juvenile justice facility of a Northern Plains reservation had a substance abuse or mental health disorder.

Recent reports have found higher rates of substance abuse in AI/AN populations than any other minority group. In addition, evidence of tobacco usage, binge drinking, and illicit drug use were also reported to be higher than all other minority groups (National Survey on Drug Use and Health [NSDUH], 2003). As a comparable, the rates reported for substance use among youth (12–17) from diverse ethnic backgrounds is presented in Figures 3.2a and 3.2b. Twice as many AI/NA youth reported the use of cigarettes, heavy alcohol, and illicit drugs compared to other youth in the U.S. population.

In a recent study of substance use among minority youth, Mosher, Rotolo, Phillips, Krupski, and Stark (2004) report that Native Americans are more likely to use inhalants than any other racial/ethnic group and that inhalant use was mediated by risk factors associated with increased family and school problems. The researchers also found that inhalants and other drugs were significant predictors of problem behaviors (parent attachment, parents' drug use, and friends' drug use) and problem behaviors were more common among Native American males than any other demographic category. In this study, the authors found that deviant behavior, although associated with any drug use, was most strongly associated with inhalant use.

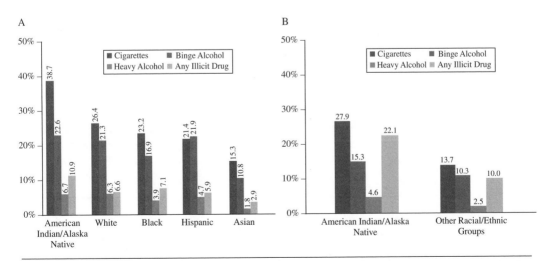

Figure 3.2 A. Percentages of persons aged 12 or older reporting past month substance use, by race/ethnicity: Annual averages based on 1999, 2000, and 2001 NHSDAs. B. Percentages of youth aged 12 to 17 reporting substance use, by race/ethnicity: Annual averages based on 1999, 2000, and 2001 NHSDAs. *Source:* From the National Household Survey on Drug Abuse, Report May 16, 2003 http://www.oas.samhsa.gov/2k3/AmIndians/AmIndians.htm (Retrieved, Jan. 1, 2007).

The rate of violent victimization among this population is in excess of two times the national average. Almost one quarter of the population (22%) suffer from symptoms of PTSD compared to 8% of the population at large (USDHHS, 2001). Sixty-four percent of Native American suicides were committed by youth between 15 and 24 years of age (Lazear et al., 2003).

Action and Reaction: The High Cost of Living on the Edge

In 2001, significantly more AI/AN youth (grades 9–12) reported being threatened or injured with a weapon on school property (15.25%), compared to other youth in the United States (8.9 %). While 11.6% of AI/NA youth reported carrying a weapon to school in 1999, this number increased to 16.4% in 2001. Comparable percentages in the U.S. population were 6.9% (1999) and 6.4% (2001; YRBS, Centers for Disease Control and Prevention, 1999, 2001).

It has been reported that 50% of adolescents in a Juvenile Justice facility of a Northern Plains reservation had a substance abuse or mental health disorder and many were found to have multiple disorders (USDHHS, 2001). The NSDUH (2002, 2003) report stresses the high levels of risk factors among AI/AN youth and the lower levels of protective factors compared to youth of other ethnic groups.

Treatment and intervention.   The most recent revision of the DSM (DSM-IV-TR: APA, 2000) includes culture bound syndromes that have been associated with AI/AN and Eskimo populations. A sample of these syndromes is presented in Table 3.7.

In their study of Native American youth, Clifford and Mills (2002) report several issues that are pertinent to assisting youth in the transition from adolescence to young adulthood and recommend several avenues to improve culturally appropriate services, including the inclusion of alternative and traditional healers in treatment efforts. The authors emphasize that participants in their study indicated that

> Community—which for AI/AN…often comprises the nuclear family, extended family, and other community members—is a common and integral thread highly valued within Native cultures. Native children are taught to be part of their intercultural communities in an interdependent manner. In contrast, mainstream culture, with is predominant emphasis on individual independence, can at times be incongruent with values held in Native communities. (p. 4)

Within this context, positive interventions for AI/NA youth must recognize underlying issues such as self-esteem and anxiety (M. J. Taylor, 2000), the dual nature of peer influence as problematic or supportive (Beauvais, Wayman, Jumper-Thurman, Plested, & Helm, 2002), inclu-

Table 3.7 Culture Bound Syndromes Associated With Native Indian/American Eskimo Cultures

Culture Bound Syndrome: Triggered by	Description	Culture
Ghost Sickness	Preoccupation with death and deceased; Nightmares, weakness, loss of appetite, anxiety, hallucinations, fainting, confusion, suffocation.	American Indian
pibloktoq	Abrupt dissociative episode (30 minutes) where individual may damage possessions, shout obscenities, and perform irrational or dangerous behaviors. Followed by seizures and coma (12 hours).	Eskimo communities

Source: DSM–IV–TR, APA (2000).

sion of traditional tribal values and spirituality (Gilgun, 2002), and the need to treat potential underlying drug and alcohol abuse (Guilmet, Whited, Dorpat, & Pijanowski, 1998). A recent study investigating ethnic differences in treatment initiation and retention for adolescents entering treatment for chemical dependency in private managed care found that Native American youth had the lowest odds of any ethnic/racial group of returning after intake, despite having the greatest severity of problems (Campbell, Weisner, & Sterling, 2006). As a result, the authors emphasize the need to identify and address barriers to utilization and increased cultural competency especially for Native Americans.

Despite the need to focus on unique programs and treatments that address specific ethnic/racial concerns, it is equally important to determine common features that mediate developmental trajectories across ethnic/racial groups. Walls, Whitbeck, Hoyt, and Johnson (2007) examined the influence of substance use by female caretakers on early onset alcohol use among Native American youth. Results demonstrated that

> Consistent with coercion theory, coercive parenting was positively related to youth alcohol use and parental monitoring was negatively associated with youth alcohol use. There was also evidence of direct modeling of drinking behavior. Social learning and coercion theory both operate to some degree to explain the risk of early onset adolescent alcohol use among Native American youth. (p. 460)

The finding that caretaker characteristics (alcohol-use parenting style) can influence early onset drinking behaviors in Native American youth (as opposed to other influences, such as peer influence), was important because findings parallel results obtained in non-Native families and set the stage for the use of preexisting family based approaches to intervention based on principles of social learning and coercion theory. In an example of research informing policy, the study supports Mail and Heurtin-Roberts' (2002) emphasis on the need to adapt and apply information obtained from promising non-Indian-based research on drug intervention/prevention to strategies for use with Native Indian populations.

Cultural Competence in the Assessment and Treatment of Minority Youth

Cultural competence. Sue (2006) suggests that *cultural competenc*e is more than just an understanding of a different cultural perspective; it is a *process* of understanding another culture through the development of knowledge and specific skills. One of the key factors in the acquisition process is **dynamic sizing**, which is the ability to determine where a cultural characteristic begins and where a stereotype ends. This ability requires an appreciation of the culture and the flexibility to see how individuality is reflected within that culture in order to understand the uniqueness of the individual's responses to his or her particular life situation. *Culture-specific expertise* includes knowledge of the culture, its history, and effective treatments for this group, which is part of the process of gaining cultural competency.

Culturally Competent Assessment

The National Association of School Psychologists (NASP) suggests six domains of culturally competent service delivery (Rogers et al., 1999). The five areas include:

1. legal and ethical issues,
2. school culture and educational policy,
3. psycho-educational assessment,

4. working with interpreters, and
5. research.

Under the topic of assessment, the NASP paper suggests several key considerations when working with **culturally and linguistically diverse (CLD)** students. It is important to evaluate how the student's educational history, SES, acculturation, and language acquisition may impact test scores.

Important Distinction

After 2 to 3 years, a student may be expected to acquire basic **interpersonal communication skills (BICS)** or social communication. However, the language necessary to perform adequately for curriculum-based content (reading, writing)—**cognitive, academic language proficiency skills (CALPS)**—requires from 5–7 years to develop (Cummins, 1984).

Tests that are not available in bilingual versions cannot be considered valid when administered directly by an interpreter. The use of a trained interpreter can, however, be very helpful in obtaining assessment information about the child's developmental history. Several factors should be considered when using interpreters to obtain family information. It is important that the interpreter not only be proficient in the language (including dialect) but have an understanding of the available resources in the community (Lynch, 1998). Professionally, the interpreter must also translate information accurately without altering, omitting, or adding information and be aware of the cultural message to the extent that he or she can provide a bridge between the two cultures. The interpreter can also be a valuable ally in guiding the pacing of the interview (Lynch, 1998).

Caution: Family Members as Interpreters

The use of older siblings as family interpreters may seem customary to many families. However, this can be especially problematic by placing a psychological burden on these siblings and engaging them in a family process that may be conflicted and ultimately finding them enmeshed in issues over which they have no control (e.g., sibling welfare; Lynch, 1998).

Clinical experience also suggests other subtle cultural influences that might impact on the actual testing situation and influence overall performance, including *time, response styles (verbal/nonverbal), family privacy versus disclosure, and level of acculturation.*

Time. In different cultures, time can have a *past orientation* (traditions, elders), *present orientation* (in reality/now), *or future orientation* (planning and emphasis on youth). Sattler (2001) suggests that while European American groups have a predominantly future orientation and handle time in a way that is not flexible, this is not the way that other ethnic groups respond. African Americans and Native Americans have a present time orientation. However, while African Americans handle time in the rhythm of relationships, Native Americans handle time as flexible. Hispanic Americans have a past–present orientation and handle time in a relaxed manner. Asian Americans have a past–present concept of time and handle time as a reflection of the eternal (Sattler, 2001, p. 638).

Response styles.   Displays of emotion and eye contact are also subject to different ethnic interpretations. In some cultures, eye contact is seen as a sign of respect (e.g., "Look at me when I am talking to you."); however, Native Americans and some Asian Americans interpret eye contact as a lack of respect (Sue, 1990). Other subtle factors that may result in misinterpretation of responses include the use of silence as a form of respect rather than a reluctance to respond (Asian Americans and Native Americans) or the use of vague and indirect communication as a means of buffering the message (Asian Americans, Native Americans, and some Hispanic Americans), as opposed to the use of direct questions which might be interpreted as invasive (Sue, 1990).

MyPersonalSpace.com...munication

There is wide cultural diversity in what is considered a violation of personal space. Hispanics and African Americans favor close proximity to their discussant, while European Americans value personal distance and space. Given these parameters, it might be easy to misinterpret violation of one's personal space by another as an act of aggression, or feel shunned by someone who tries to retreat into their own comfort zone (Sue, 1990).

Family privacy versus disclosure also differs among ethnic groups.   While some groups are very forthcoming about disclosing intimate details, others (e.g., Asian Americans) consider discussion of family information with an outsider to be inappropriate. Therefore, mental health professionals may find some families reluctant to respond to interview questions and questionnaires in order to protect the family from stigma and loss of respect (Kumaabe, Nishida, & Hepworth, 1985).

Level of acculturation.   As already discussed, some families may be further along the continuum of acculturation than others, which will also influence the degree to which they continue to evidence traditional ethnic values, beliefs, and interactive style.

Culture in Focus

Clinical experience suggests that there are many subtle ways that ethnic diversity can influence the assessment process. When giving timed tests to children of different ethnic groups, in general, European American (EA) children will be more competitive and strive to "beat the clock," while children from other ethnic groups may be penalized by not regarding time as an important construct. Parents from some ethnic minorities may not arrive at meetings "on time" because they do not adhere to rigid schedules in the same manner that EA families are programmed to respond.

Culturally Competent Treatment

Many of the factors already discussed regarding assessment will also impact the treatment process. There are several documents available to assist in developing greater cultural competence, including the National Mental Health Information Center (NMHIC; 1996); NASP (Rogers et al., 1999); APA Guidelines for Providers of Psychological Services to Ethnic, Linguistic and Culturally Diverse Populations; and SAMHSA's National Mental Health Information Center: Cultural Competence in Serving Children and Adolescents with Mental Health Problems.

Although Sue's (2006) recent article on cultural competency does not directly address child and adolescent services, the suggestions for increasing treatment effectiveness are equally valuable for treatment and intervention with children, youth, and families. In the article, Sue suggests 10 steps to increasing the effectiveness of therapy with minority populations:

1. *Self-awareness and stimulus value.* The first step in the process is to become self-aware of any prejudices, biases, or stereotypes that the therapist brings to the therapeutic situation and to recognize how personal features (age, gender, ethnicity) might impact the therapeutic relationship in a negative way based on the client's cultural disposition.

2. *Assessment of the client.* At this juncture, the therapist should conduct a thorough assessment of the client's demographics relative to country of origin, family structure, and any other information that will assist in determining the level of acculturation, and any prior negative minority group experiences (prejudice, racism) that might carry over into the therapy sessions. Placing the client's characteristics within such a perspective can provide further insight, not only into the nature of the problem, but potentially alert the therapist to the goodness of fit between client and therapist.

3. *Pretherapy intervention.* Recognizing that the client may be unfamiliar with Western psychology and psychiatry, Sue recommends **pretherapy intervention** as an important third step. At this stage, the therapist focuses on ensuring that the client is comfortable in the process by explaining the nature of the intervention, roles of client and therapist, and issues of confidentiality. Of particular importance in working with children, youth, and families are the 5th and 6th steps in the process.

4. *Hypothesizing and testing hypotheses.* At this step, the therapist develops hypotheses regarding whether the client's attitudes and behaviors reflect his or her cultural background or whether behaviors are a response to the therapeutic process. Sue suggests that it may be necessary to contact a client's friends or family to verify hypotheses (e.g., is the client improving in the manner that he or she claims to be).

5. *Attending to credibility and gift giving.* This step addresses issues of credibility (both personal and professional) and the benefits that the client can "take away" from the therapy session, such as reduced anxiety or feeling less depressed.

6. *Understanding the nature of discomfort and resistance.* Therapists may also find themselves blocked at this step. Families may resist recommendations and not implement intervention plans as requested, which may be due to having a different value system. For example, asking a family to develop clear guideline for a child may run counter to a family value that supports indirect communication. Ultimately, in the final step of the process, the therapist must be willing to consult with those who have expertise and can help as a resource or in assessing the success of the intervention.

7. *Understanding the client's perspective.* A key ingredient in the therapeutic process is the need for therapists to gain an understanding of how clients interpret the problem through their cultural perspective. Especially salient questions at this point include: How does the client conceptualize the mental health problem? How are problems of this nature dealt with culturally? And what are the client's goals for treatment? Responses to these questions can enlighten the therapist regarding the degree of disparity between the client's concept of problem–resolution and the more traditional Western approaches.

8. *Strategy or plan for intervention.* Sue suggests that it is imperative for the therapist to learn as much as possible about the culture and client characteristics prior to initiating therapy.

9. *Assessment of services.* At the end of each session, Sue emphasizes the need to ask the cli-

ent leading questions regarding the session to clarify the client's level of comfort with the process and the client's understanding of the treatment plan.

10. *Willingness to consult.* Above all, the therapist should recognize the limits of his or her cultural competency and seek outside resources to supplement and support the therapeutic process.

Clinician, Know Thyself

According to Sue (2006), credibility can involve personal or science-based skepticism. Self-awareness that a very young therapist or female therapist may not appear credible to some cultures where elders or males are valued is a critical step to understanding what might undermine the therapeutic process.

CHAPTER SUMMARY AND REVIEW

1. **Developmental Contexts: Risks and Protective Factors**
   a. Bronfenbrenner's ecological model was discussed as it relates to each level of influence: *individual level* (child characteristics), *immediate level/microsystem* (child's immediate environment: parents, peers, school), *socioeconomic level/exosystem* (social and financial context), and *macrosystem* (values and culture).
   b. Risk factors and protective factors can be identified at each level of Bronfenbrenner's system.
   c. Cumulative risks can have a *multiplier effect.*
2. **Prevention and Promotion of Positive Mental Health**
   Prevention programs are primarily developed based on known risk factors and protective factors and can be applied along a continuum of severity to target audiences that are universal (primary prevention), or comprised of at-risk youth (secondary prevention and selective prevention), or in an effort to prevent problems from becoming even more severe (tertiary prevention/indication prevention). Studies that focus on positive mental health take a proactive approach to investigating those factors that are associated with well-being, positive sense of self, and enhanced coping skills.
3. **Cultural Diversity, Minority Youth, and Accelerated Risks**
   Youth in ethnic minorities have increased risk for living in poverty, being exposed to higher s of violence, and engaging in higher rates of substance abuse.
4. **African American Youth**
   More than half (57%) live in inner city areas and as many as 27% experience symptoms of post traumatic stress disorder (PTSD) as a result of exposure to violence. One third lives in poverty and they represent 40% of the nation's homeless. Youth are more likely to be referred to juvenile justice than a treatment facility. Suicide rates among youth increased 23% from 1980 to 1995.
5. **Latino/Hispanic American Youth**
   The rate of seeking help from professionals among Latino/Hispanic populations is extremely low. Less than 10% seek help from mental health professionals. Yet males and females report suicide attempt rates among the highest of any youth group, with 12.8% of males and 18.9% of females reporting a suicide attempt with a 12-month period.
6. **Asian Americans/Pacific Islanders**
   Suicide rates for Asian Pacific Islander females (15–24 years) are the highest of any youth

in that age group, while rates for depression (30%) among school aged girls (Grades 5–12) was highest overall for Asian Americans.

7. **American Indian (AI)/Alaskan Native (AN)**
   Compared to White Americans, approximately twice as many AI individuals are un-employed, and represent 8% of the nation's homeless. Substance abuse is highest in this population, relative to other ethnic groups, for consumption of cigarettes, binge-alcohol, heavy alcohol, and use of any illicit drug.

Consolidate and Communicate

1. Poverty and ethnicity intersect on a number of different levels. Given your understanding of the theories of child development, select one theory and demonstrate how poverty might influence development on levels depicted by Bronfenbrenner's model.

2. While an authoritative parenting style has been associated with increased positive child outcomes in many environments, the use of authoritarian parenting practices has been demonstrated to be most effective in African American families living in difficult circum-stances. Discuss and support.

3. The drive for independence and identity formation in adolescence might be particularly difficult for youth from Asian American families. Discuss this statement relative to concerns from youth in other ethnic environments.

4. Among minority youth, NA/AI youth, evidence the highest rates of substance use and abuse. In a population that has less longevity than most (only 5.6% live to be 65 years of age compared to 12.4% of U.S. population), discuss the long-term implications of substance abuse and shortened lifespan for NA/AI youth.

5. Studies of health promotion that have focused on mental health and acculturation styles suggest that youth who are more flexible and incorporate a bicultural orientation to ac-culturation and who retain some of their African American or Latino heritage rather than adopt an Anglo-oriented style score higher on indices of well-being and lower on measure of anxiety and depression. Discuss these findings based on your understanding of some of the challenges facing youth in diverse cultures.

Chapter Review Questions

1. With respect to cumulative risks, Rutter (1979) found that:
   a. Children exposed to two risk factors had a fourfold increase in the likelihood of a dis-order
   b. Exposure to four risk factors increased the likelihood of a disorder by 10 times the amount
   c. Each additional risk factor added 20 times the risk
   d. Both a and b are correct

2. Atzaba-Poria, Pike, and Deater-Deckard (2004) found that children with:
   a. Internalizing problems were most influenced by risk factors in the microsystem
   b. Externalizing problems were most influenced by risk factors in the immediate environ-ment
   c. Internalizing problems were most influenced by risk factors in the exosystem
   d. Externalizing problems were most influenced by risk factors in the macrosystem

3. According to Bronfenbrenner, the mesosystem:
   a. Is the same as the microsystem

    b. Refers to the level of communication between members in the microsystem

    c. Includes the laws, values, and customs

    d. Includes the workforce and community

4. Problems with peers can place youth at increased risk for:

    a. School drop ou.

    b. Criminal behavior

    c. Delinquency

    d. All of the above

5. Which of the following is FALSE regarding poverty?

    a. Prolonged and persistent poverty is significantly more detrimental than transitory hardship

    b. Children in poverty are not disadvantaged in their access to recreation

    c. Children living in poverty have less access to health and nutrition

    d. Children living in poverty are 22 times more likely to be abused or neglected

6. The word _____ is most often used to refer to the physical characteristics associated with different groups.

    a. Culture

    b. Ethnicity

    c. Minority

    d. Race

7. Lead poisoning can result in problems with:

    a. Hearing

    b. Stunted growth

    c. Feeding

    d. Increased weight

8. Studies have found that African American children living in poor neighborhoods respond best to:

    a. Permissive parenting

    b. Authoritative parenting

    c. Authoritarian parenting

    d. Insistent parenting

9. Which of the following is TRUE regarding youth who experience high levels of exposure to violence (ETV)?

    a. The prevalence of ETV is lowest among minority youth

    b. ETV can result in heightened threshold for subsequent violence

    c. ETV can result in increased incidence of post traumatic stress disorder

    d. ETV can result in increased levels of depressed symptoms

10. Which of the following is TRUE regarding utilization of mental health services?

    a. Only approximately half of Hispanics and Latinos seek mental health specialists

    b. Less than 1 in 10 Hispanics contact mental health specialists

    c. Less than 5% contact general health care providers

    d. Approximately 80% consult a *curandero*, *herbalista*, or other folk healer

Glossary of New Terms

multiplier effect

social competence

poverty

extreme poverty
multiple marginality
primary prevention
secondary prevention
tertiary prevention
universal prevention
selective prevention
indicated prevention
iatrogenic effects
culture
race
ethnicity
exposure to violence (ETV)
fictive kin
acculturation
familia
compadres
machismo
Confucianism
Taoism
Buddhism
Individualism/collectivism
Nisei, Sansei, Yonsei, Gosei
On, Amae/Giri
traditional, transitional, bicultural, marginal
dynamic sizing
culturally and linguistically diverse (CLD)
basic interpersonal communication skills (BICS)
cognitive, academic language proficiency skills (CALPS)
pretherapy intervention

Internet Web Site Links for Reports on Children and Mental Health

Centers for Disease Control and Prevention. http://www.cdc.gov/

Children's Defense Fund. (2005). *The state of America's children, 2005.* Retrieved from http://www.childrensdefense.org/site/PageServer?pagename=research_publications

U.S. Department of Health and Human Services. (2001). *Mental health: Culture, race and ethnicity—A supplement to mental health.* A report to the Surgeon General. Retrieved from http://www.surgeongeneral.gov/library/mentalhealth/cre/

World Health Report, The. (2001). *The World Health Report, 2001: Mental health: New understanding, new hope.* Retrieved rom http://www.who.int/whr/2001/en/

Answers to Multiple Choice Questions:
1. d; 2. b; 3. b; 4. d; 5. b; 6. d; 7. b; 8. c; 9. c; 10. b.

4

Developmental Considerations in Research and Practice

Ethical Issues and Research Methods

CHAPTER PREVIEW

A. Ethical Issues in Providing Mental Health Services to Children and Youth

Professionals who provide mental health services to children, youth, and their families are governed in their actions by ethical standards and codes of conduct specific to their profession, yet have many guidelines in common. Initially, we will take a comparative look across disciplines before concentrating on the latest revision of ethical standards established by the American Psychological Association (APA, 2002). Some of the more challenging aspects of the code include how to apply the code when working with minors (children and youth).

1. General Principles and Ethical Standards

There are five general principles or "aspirational" goals and 10 standards of conduct that apply to a wide variety of psychological roles.

2. Standards of the Ethical Code Particularly Relevant to Working With Children and Youth

The latest revision (APA, 2002) not only recognizes the need to obtain a child's or adolescent's assent to participate in research (as well as treatment and assessment), Standard 3.01(b) now demands that participation also consider the child's "best interest," which includes informed knowledge of procedures and risks, in language that can be understood by the child. Standard 8.02 deals with issues of informed consent applicable to research specifically and covers all aspects of research including community intervention programs.

3. Contemporary Issues in Assent and Consent

Several issues are at the forefront of research aimed at answering some of the most difficult questions raised by the code, including:

1. How do you determine whether a child is competent to provide assent?
2. What does "competent" to assent really mean?
3. How to protect the welfare of the child, while at the same time protecting his/her right to engage in the decision-making process?

B. Research Methods in Child Psychopathology

Research methods particularly suited to studies of child psychopathology often represent a hybrid of methods borrowed from developmental and clinical research paradigms. The three primary models of conducting quantitative research include *descriptive research, correlational research,* and *experimental research.* Given the nature of the population, it is often necessary to conduct research that is quasi-experimental by the use of a wait list control to avoid ethical conflicts of withholding treatment from a control group. *Longitudinal research* can be very informative for child psychopathology as well as *epidemiological research*, a special form of correlational research that lends understanding to changing trends in disorder incidence or prevalence. The potential role of qualitative research in child psychopathology is also addressed.

Ethical Considerations in Research and Practice

Ethical Standards and Codes of Conduct

Children and youth in need of services from mental health professionals may interact with a number of professionals from various disciplines in a variety of settings, such as schools, clinics, and treatment centers. Each of these professionals is guided and monitored in their practice by ethical principles and professional standards that have been developed by the particular professional organization that oversees that profession. The following summary will provide a brief description of some of the professional codes and standards that mental health practitioners are governed by in their practice of working with children and youth. Although the primary focus in this text will be on the Ethical Code developed by the American Psychological Association (APA), the intention is to introduce information concerning other professional codes to develop an awareness of the similarities that exist across a number of mental health professions.

The Ethical Principles of Psychologists and Code of Conduct (APA, 2002)

The major governing body responsible for monitoring psychologists in their scientific, educational, and professional activities is the American Psychological Association (APA). The APA is responsible for the development, revision, and monitoring of the *Ethical Principles of Psychologists and Code of Conduct* (hereafter noted simply as the *Ethics Code*) that primarily consists of *five General Principles (A–E)*, and 10 specific *Ethical Standards*. The Ethics Code is intended to guide psychologists in their professional decision making and in the standards they uphold in their professional conduct. The most recent revision of the Ethics Code was in 2002, and it officially went into practice in June, 2003.

General principles. The five general guidelines represent the highest level of ethical standards. The General Principles are not enforceable rules; however, they are to be held as "aspirational" goals to inspire psychologists to strive towards these ideals of professionalism and moral integrity. The General Principles include:

> Principle A: **Beneficence and Nonmaleficence** (do no harm).
> Principle B: **Fidelity and Responsibility** (Establish relationships of trust; abide by professional and scientific responsibilities to society; and uphold professional standards of conduct).
> Principle C: **Integrity** (promote accuracy, honesty, and truthfulness).
> Principle D: **Justice** (recognize fairness, guard against bias, and recognize and practice within the limits of their competence).
> Principle E: **Respect for the People's Rights and Dignity** (respect rights to confidentiality, privacy and self-determination; respect right of cultural, individual, and role differences).

Ethical standards. The 10 standards represent rules of conduct that apply to a wide variety of psychological roles (clinical, counseling, school psychology) and applied practices (research, education, test construction and design, administrative or supervising capacities). Each standard is comprised of a number of subsections that expand upon the area discussed:

Standard 1:   Resolving Ethical Issues
Standard 2:   Competence
Standard 3:   Human Relations
Standard 4:   Privacy and Confidentiality
Standard 5:   Advertising and Other Public Statements
Standard 6:   Keeping Records and Fees
Standard 7:   Education and Training
Standard 8:   Research and Publication
Standard 9:   Assessment
Standard 10: Therapy

Although it is beyond the scope of this text to engage in an in-depth review of the entire Ethics Code, readers are encouraged to visit the APA Web site where the Ethics Code can be seen in its entirety (http://www.apa.org/ethics/code2002.html). We will, however, explore a number of the standards at greater length, later on in this chapter and throughout relevant areas of the text.

APA code of ethics and other professional bodies.   Other professionals working with children and youth in schools and mental health settings also adhere to Ethical Principles and standards developed by their own professional organizations, such as the *American Counseling Association* (ACA; 1995); *the National Association of School Psychologists* (NASP; 2000); and *the American School Counselors Association* (ASCA; 1998). The major features of the codes of ethics and standards for the APA, ACA, NASP, and ASCA are presented in Table 4.1. Although each of these codes was developed to guide a specific professional interest and intent, many similarities exist among these ethical codes.

Ethical Principles are developed to assist practitioners to conduct their services according to professional guidelines and to assist them in making consistent ethical decisions and choices. In reviewing the Ethical Codes presented in Table 4.1, it becomes apparent that these codes have several guiding principles in common, including: Beneficience and Nonmalficence, Fidelity, and Justice/Competence.

In addition to the guiding principles, ethics codes also provide rules for standards of practice. A review of the standards in Table 4.1 reveals that each of the Ethical Codes provides a similar set of standards, or rules of conduct, to guide professionals in several areas including establishing and maintaining professional relationships, addressing issues of confidentiality, professional record keeping, and conducting research, therapy, and assessments.

Codes of Ethics and the Law

In the United States, there are two separate legal systems: **criminal law** and **civil law**. Criminal actions—or possibly aiding and abetting criminal actions such as assault and battery, homicide, and theft—will be subject to government prosecution in a criminal trial. Noncriminal offenses fall under the umbrella of civil law and are subject to individual/nongovernmental prosecution.

The majority of mental health laws and statues which apply to mental health practitioners fall within the realm of civil law. Statutory law and case law also are commonly encountered by members of the mental health profession. While **statutes** refer to laws which have been enacted at local, state, or federal levels, **case law** is reserved for those precedent-setting cases that have served to drive the legal decision making process.

Ethical guidelines, because they are not laws, are not legally binding. The APA states that the Code of Ethics, in and of itself, is not intended to determine civil liability in a given court action,

Table 4.1 Ethical Principles and Codes of Ethical Conduct

American Psychological Association (APA, 2003)	American Counseling Association (ACA, 1995)	National Association of School Psychologists (NASP, 2000)
General Principles	**Guide to Ethical Decision Making— Moral Principles (1996)**	**Principles for Professional Ethics— General Principles** (Preamble)
• Beneficence and Nonmalficence • Fidelity and Responsibility • Integrity • Justice • Respect for Rights and Dignity	• Autonomy • Nonmaleficence • Beneficence • Justice • Fidelity	• Advocacy • Nonmaleficence • Competency • Professional Relationships
Ethical Standards	**Code of Ethics and Standards of Practice**	**Professional Practice General Principles**
• Resolving Ethical Issues • Competence • Human Relations • Privacy and Confidentiality • Advertising/Public Statements • Record Keeping/Fees • Education/Training • Research/Publications • Assessment • Therapy	• The Counseling Relationship • Confidentiality • Professional Responsibility • Relationships with other professionals • Evaluation, Assessment, Interpretation • Teaching, Training, Supervision • Research and Publications • Resolving Ethical Issues	• Advocacy • Service Delivery • Assessment and Intervention • Reporting Data and Conference Results • Use of Materials and Technology • Research Publication and Presentation • Independent Practice
American School Counselor Association (ASCA, 1998) **Ethical Standards (1998) Basic Tenants: Each person has** • Right to Self-direction and Self-development • Right of Choice and Responsibility for goals reached • Right to Privacy		
Ethical Practices • Responsibilities to Students • Responsibilities to Parents • Responsibilities to School and Community • Responsibility to Self • Multicultural Skills • Professionalism	**Include** Confidentiality, Dual Relationships, Competency Conduct and Maintenance of Standards	

in contract settlement, or in defining legal consequences. However, the professional bodies do monitor and sanction violations of their members. Although a professional body such as the APA may sanction its members for violation of the Ethics Code, it can also inform other professional groups or state and federal associations of non-APA members who violate the Ethics Code.

State laws are not consistent across the United States, therefore, Bricklin (2001) cautions psychologists to be very familiar with state laws and in particular how these laws might conflict with Ethical Principles. Bricklin also notes that there are two ways in which ethics violations can ultimately result in violations of the law: **malpractice suits** (e.g., those involving negligence or sexual psychologist–client relations) and *violations of state licensing laws* which might result in loss of license to practice.

Know Your State Laws

There are a number of very important questions that psychologists working with children and youth need to inquire about their state laws, including:

1. **What is the age of majority in this state?** Currently in the United States, the age of majority ranges from 18 years of age (34 states) to 21 years (Mississippi, Washington, DC, and New York), while Canada is approximately divided in half between 18 and 19 years of age.
2. **Who is the custodial parent; what are custodial versus noncustodial rights?** If parents are divorced or in litigation, who, according to state law, is the "legal guardian?" This is crucial to determining who can provide consent for a child's involvement in assessment, treatment, or research and will likely also impact on issues of confidentiality and release of information concerning the child's reports.
3. **How does the state mandate the duty to report?** States differ in the time lines between alleged and reported abuse and in the penalties levied for failure to report. For example, in Minnesota, reported abuse must have occurred within the 3 years preceding the disclosure, while in Florida, failure to report abuse is considered a misdemeanor of the first degree (subject to 1 year imprisonment or $1,000 fine).

In one discussion of *Ethics Rounds*, Behnke and Kinscherff (2002) provide an example of a dilemma faced by a psychologist concerning whether to report a young adult client's disclosure of sexual molestation by a family member that occurred when the girl was a young teenager. The client does not want the information revealed due to the impact it would have on her family. The family member no longer lives in the vicinity and the client just wants to put the situation behind her and deal with it in therapy. In this situation, the psychologist will have to decide whether the state law mandates the disclosure (if so, the psychologist is mandated to report). If not, she may still report the abuse if the state law concludes that she is legally permitted to disclose confidential information without her client's permission. If the law was on her side, then the psychologist would have to weigh her concern regarding the perpetrator possibly harming another young girl in the future versus her concern for her client's emotional well being and cohesiveness with her family. In this case, the dilemma of *Beneficence* and *Maleficence* (do no harm) becomes a very real and disturbing dilemma.

Ethics and Ethical Dilemmas

The first Standard (Standard 1) of the Ethical Code is concerned with *resolving ethical issues*. Ethical Principles serve as guidelines for ethical decision making and become very important when practitioners are faced with ethical challenges, such as encountering **ethical dilemmas**. Practitioners may face situations where an employer may not be totally supportive of the psychologist's Ethical Code. Ethical dilemmas can also occur when two or more Ethical Principles are in conflict with one another. It is during these times that professionals must depend upon the Ethical Code for guidance and weigh the principles to determine which decision is the morally and ethically correct response. The decision making becomes even more difficult and complex when a child or youth is involved in the dilemma. An example of such a dilemma is presented in the following *Case in Point*.

Case in Point

A psychologist is providing therapy for a 15-year-old girl who is in a conflicted relationship with her father, her only parent. The psychologist has discussed the limits of confidentiality ahead of time with the girl and her father, and the father has agreed that in the best interest of clinical rapport, he will not ask for intimate details of her therapy sessions. As a result, the 15-year-old has disclosed that she has used marijuana on occasion and that she also has been to party where Ecstasy is available, although she has never tried it. The father has found what he believes to be marijuana paraphernalia in his daughter's bedroom under her bed. He now has a change of heart and confronts the psychologist demanding to know if his daughter has disclosed that she has smoked marijuana. In this example of an ethical dilemma, the therapist is caught trying to balance a client's rights to Autonomy (a client's right for self-direction) and Fidelity (maintain relationships of trust) with the principle of Beneficience (benefit) and Nonmalficence (do no harm). In this case, the therapist must face a number of ethically challenging questions, including "Who is the client?"

Over the years, several surveys have been conducted to determine the most common areas of ethical difficulties. Results of a survey of APA psychologists conducted by Pope and Vetter (1992) revealed that, at that time, the largest percentage of ethical challenges (18%) were reported in the area of **confidentiality**, with 17% of the respondents reporting ethical quandaries resulting from **dual or conflictual relationships**. Within the realm of confidentiality, issues of boundaries of confidentiality in situations when multiple caregivers or clients were involved and mandatory reporting of abuse surfaced as particular areas of difficulty. Professionals can be presented with a unique and complex set of ethical concerns in attempting to apply the Ethical Principles and Standards of Practice when working with minors. In the vast majority of cases, parents or legal guardians of children under 18 years of age (or given age of majority in the practicing state or province) are responsible for signing releases of information and/or obtaining or releasing reports pertaining to a child's medical or educational records. However, ethical issues can often result, especially when working with parents and adolescents regarding the limits of confidentiality. Clinicians working with adolescents and older children should always define the limits of confidentiality at the onset of the therapeutic relationship and outline the ethical duties to report any indications of harm to self or others, or reports of abuse. However, the limits of confidentiality with respect to parent access to other information discussed during therapy sessions may be far more difficult to address.

Although a therapeutic rule of thumb is to discuss and negotiate rules of confidentiality and issues of privacy prior to beginning therapeutic sessions, parents can and do change their minds. Parents who seek therapeutic resources for older children and adolescents often can be persuaded that, initially, the clinician's ability to establish a trusting relationship with the youth may require withholding the content of their private sessions from the parents. In most cases, over time, the youth can be encouraged to share private thoughts and feelings with parents in order to improve their relationship.

Standards of the Ethical Code Particularly Relevant to Children and Youth

Applying the Ethical Code to specific situations can present a challenge, especially in situations that overlap legal and ethical concerns. This challenge can become even more pronounced when the client is a child or adolescent. At this time, we will look at a number of standards that are particularly relevant for psychologists working with children and youth.

Ethical Issues in Assessment, Treatment, and Conducting Research With Children

Issues of Informed Consent and Assent: APA Ethics Code and Standards (2002)
As introduced in the opening chapter case study, there is a difference between informed **consent** and **assent**. Although a legal guardian may provide *consent* for the assessment, treatment, or research participation for his or her child, the child must also provide *assent* (*voluntary willingness to participate*) in order for the assessment to be completed. The issues of consent and assent have been debated for some time and as a result, the revised APA Ethics Code and Standards (2002) now address these issues. (The following review follows Fisher [2004] except where noted.)

Adults and Guardians Providing Consent, and Those With Adult Legal Status
Issues of informed consent were initially found in Standard 6.11 (APA, 1992) which addressed issues of Informed Consent to Research. However, the Ethical Code (APA, 2002) now houses a new section (Section 3:10) that specifically addresses *informed consent pertinent to all psychological activities*. Readers in this section are directed to also see Standard 8.02 (*Informed Consent to Research*); Standard 9.03 (*Informed Consent for Assessments*); and Standard 10.1 (*Informed Consent to Therapy*). One important part of this section (Section 3.10a) addresses the role of informed consent for adults, guardians, and those with adult legal status. Although assent is primarily reserved for those children and youth who are under the age of majority, there are specific conditions where minors can have adult legal status. Minors who have adult status can fall within one of two categories:

- **Emancipated minors:** Youth who have not achieved the age of majority of the state (usually 18 years of age) but who have achieved adult status by assuming adult responsibilities (marriage, membership in the armed services, financially self-supportive);
- **Mature minor:** Youth who have not achieved state age requirements for adulthood but who, according to state law, may receive certain adult treatment privileges (e.g., deemed appropriate to provide consent for their own treatment for drug abuse or sexually transmitted diseases).

With respect to proving consent for participation in research, it seems that an emancipated minor can provide consent for participation in research in the majority of cases, although this is not certain for every situation. However, the implication for mature minors is even less clear. Researchers whose work might involve mature minors (e.g., investigators conducting research on youth receiving treatment for sexually transmitted diseases) are urged to take caution in determining what the state might consider appropriate regarding permission for research participation.

Know Your State Law

State laws also differ in their ages of granting *emancipated minor* status. In California, it is possible to be considered an emancipated minor as young as 14 years of age. In New Mexico, the status can be granted at 16 years of age. Furthermore, not all states (e.g., New York) have statutes relating to emancipated minors and make decisions case by case.

Informed consent and communication (language and culture). In Standard 3.10a the importance of appropriateness of language is addressed, a topic that is significant for those working with children and adolescence, but also for all persons whose first language may not be English. In this case, the Standard is clear that psychologists must provide an explanation in a language that is *appropriate to the individual's level of understanding*, and include:

1. A description of the research project, procedures, assessments, and treatments;
2. Statements of participants' rights (assessment and treatment); and
3. Information that is compatible with the individual's level of education, experience, and language use, providing appropriate translations (language, sign language) when appropriate.

Cases where English is not the first language. Families from other cultures often require interpreters to assist in disseminating information. There has been an increasing emphasis on practices that are culturally sound, and to this end, there have been several papers generated to provide guidelines for professionals in developing greater cultural competence (National Mental Health Information Center [NMHIC], 1996; NASP, 1999; APA Guidelines for Providers of Psychological Services to Ethnic, Linguistic and Culturally Diverse Populations). In particular, the use of interpreters has been an area of high interest. Lynch (1998) emphasizes that interpreters should be professionally trained and cautions against the use of family members as interpreters. Other important reasons for not having children or adolescents serve as interpreters are that the information might be misinterpreted or might result in shifting the balance in delicate parent/child relationships (Fisher et al., 2002). The APA revised codes (Standard 2.05 and 9.03c) introduce much needed guidelines for the use of interpreters and provide direction and standards for competency in *communication* (guardian's preferred language at an appropriate level that the guardian can understand) and *professionalism* (training in matters of confidentiality).

Informed consent and passive permission for participation. According to Standard 3.10b, the psychologist is in violation of the code because he or she did not obtain *"active permission"* from the guardian. In addition, attempts to obtain passive permission often serve to alienate parents and older students who feel that they have been duped by a technique that assumes that the majority of parents would give the consent, and provides subtle coercion for parents who may have otherwise dissented.

Case in Point

An educational psychologist wants to study the effect of oral versus silent reading on the comprehension of students in Grade 3. In order to obtain permission for student involvement, the psychologist sends letters home to the parents of the Grade 3 children, asking for parents to respond, only if they *do not* give permission for their child's participation in the study. Is the psychologist following ethical procedure?

Documentation of informed consent. Standard 3.10d of the revised Code of Ethics (APA, 2002) states that psychologists must document that informed consent or assent has been obtained. (This usually involves signed consent, unless the guardian is illiterate or the assent is from a very young child.) When a signature is not possible, the psychologist should document a file note about the obtained permission in their records.

Informed assent.   Although the previous version of the APA Ethics Code (1992) recognized the need to obtain a child's or adolescent's **assent** or preference to participate (agreement to participate or withdraw based on their understanding of the nature and purpose of the research), the most recent revision (Standard 3.10b) also emphasizes the researcher's need to consider not only the child's preferences, but also whether the participation is in the *"child's best interest."* This additional stipulation is meant to protect the child if dissent would result in deprivation of services that could be considered to be in the child's best therapeutic interest. The APA Ethics Code (2002) also serves to protect the child's right to *"informed assent,"* emphasizing the need for the researcher to provide an *appropriate explanation* that takes into account the child's ability to understand, read, or interpret information provided (e.g., developmental level, reading ability, or emotional status).

With the introduction of the *child's best interests* into the Standard, researchers and practitioners are reminded of the need to scrutinize those situations when research is conducted concerning children or juveniles in treatment centers or detention, if placement in these situations has resulted from maltreatment or hostile environments. In these cases, obtaining permission from guardians may actually place the child at risk of harm, or result in a violation of a child or adolescents privacy rights. According to Standard 3.10b, psychologists who act in the *best interests of the child,* in such situations, may be obligated to take steps to insure that the rights of children and adolescents are protected by seeking permission from appropriate, court appointed guardians. In cases of child custody, foster care, and juvenile detainees, determining who has legal responsibility to give consent is a critical matter, especially in situations where transfers of legal authority and responsibility change over time.

APA and Informed Consent Standards Directly Applicable to Research

In the current Ethical Code (APA, 2002), issues of informed consent that apply most directly to clinical research can be found in Standards 8.02a (an expanded version of the 1991 version) and a new standard, Standard 8.02b, specifically addressing issues faced by psychologists conducting research (behavioral, psychosocial, biomedical psychopharmacological) or research involving community intervention.

Significant emphasis has been placed on providing children, youth, and their legal guardians with sufficient information to make an informed decision regarding their participation in a research program, including the purpose, procedures, risks and benefits, and any compensation involved. Nowhere is this more evident than regarding research on intervention. Psychologists who now conduct research involving intervention are required not only to disclose the experimental nature of the intervention, but to do so by outlining: (a) the ways in which this intervention differs from other forms of treatment, such as hospital-based or practitioner-based therapeutic intervention; (b) the experimental purpose of the research is to determine if the intervention works, or is better than some other treatment; (c) the risks and benefits of both the experimental and control condition; and (d) how children and youth will be assigned to each condition.

The APA standards also make it abundantly clear that researchers must inform potential participants that involvement is voluntary and that refusal to participate or subsequent withdrawal will not result in adverse effects or endanger their current services in the facility if they are currently receiving services. Researchers must also inform potential participants and their legal guardians of alternative services that are available, if they currently are not receiving services and decline involvement in the research program.

Contemporary Issues in Assent and Consent

Although the APA Ethical Codes and Standards (APA, 2002) have addressed many questions previously not evident in earlier versions of the code concerning issues of assent and consent when working with children and youth in research and treatment, a number of important issues remain:

1. How do you determine whether a child is competent to provide assent to research or therapeutic intervention?
2. What does "competent" to assent really mean?
3. How do you protect the welfare of children and youth, while at the same time promote their rights to participate in the decision-making process (Fisher, 2004).

Children's Competence for Assent and Consent

Miller, Drotar, and Kodish (2004) conducted a comprehensive review of research to investigate methodologies that researchers were currently using to measure children's competence to provide informed consent or assent in treatment and research. Miller and colleagues found that a lack of standard and operational definitions for **competence** rendered their meta-analysis difficult.

Issues in defining competence.   Several factors contribute to problems in defining competence, in general, and particularly competence in children:

1. Legal vs. psychological concepts of competence;
2. Static versus fluid concepts of competence;
3. Trait versus contextual concepts of competence; and
4. Issues of assent versus consent.

Legal versus psychological definitions.   While legal definitions of competence favor categorical (competent vs. not competent) and age-based criteria (e.g., 18 years of age), psychological definitions have focused more on competence as problem-solving and decision-making skills and how these skills relate to developmental level, gender, prior experience, and intellectual functioning.

Trait versus contextual approach.   Although competence has been readily associated with a trait approach, e.g., "reasoning ability," Miller et al. (2004) suggest that it is less common to focus on the contextual factors that may be instrumental in shaping a child's decisions, namely: implicit or explicit messages from parents, teachers, researchers–clinicians; family and cultural beliefs about research and treatment; and involvement, or lack of parent involvement, in the decision-making process. This is especially true when one considers children's ability to understand the concept of **voluntariness**.

Science Talks

Young children and even older children in some cultures may have a diminished capacity to understand their right to *voluntariness* (awareness that you can participate or withdraw voluntarily). Abramovitch, Freedman, Henry, and Van Brunschot (1995) examined understanding of the "right to withdraw" in 121 healthy 5- to 10-year-olds. When asked if they would like to stop participating in the study, 7 stopped. However, in the elaborated condition, when the examiner added, "and I won't be angry if you stop," twice as many children stopped. In another study, Abramovitch, Freedman, Thoden, and Nikolich (1991) questioned whether children thought that their parents would be mad if they stopped: 22% of the younger children (8–9 year olds) and 18% of the older children (10–11 year olds) felt that their parents would be mad if they stopped.

Static versus fluid concepts of competence.   Treatments that have a long-term focus, or research that is longitudinal in nature, should consider informed consent and competence as an ongoing process that changes developmentally. As such, informed consent or assent should be revisited during the course of the participation to insure adequate understanding (Fisher, 2004).

Conceptual Issues in Child Decision Making

1. Who should make the decision? (Kodish, 2003).   Issues of "autonomy versus best interest of the child" have sparked debate regarding the extent to which children should be involved in the decision-making process. While advocates suggest that increased ability to be involved can be advantageous by increasing a child's sense of control (Weithorn, 1987), it is also possible that decision making might be too stressful or cause conflict if the child does not share the parent's position.

2. What factors should be considered in the decision making process?   Miller et al. (2004) propose a multidimensional model of participation that considers a child's *understanding, reasoning,* and *voluntariness* in evaluating competence. In this model, the authors consider *predisposing factors* (such as cognitive development, family beliefs about child autonomy, and beliefs about treatment and research) as the context within which the issues of competency exist. Next, *child factors* (preference for participation, emotional state, cognitive and health functioning), *parent/ research/clinician factors* (facilitate/support understanding and communication; coercive influences if any), and *situational factors* (time constraints, etc.) are entered into the model. Taken together, these factors and influences will predict the *child's competence to participate in the decision making process* (understanding, reasoning, and voluntariness).

3. How should the decision be made?   Fisher (2004) suggests a model of decision making that builds on the relationships between all participants in the research or treatment program in a *hierarchical decision-making paradigm*, which includes:

a. A research review board that decides whether the risks–benefits justify the clinical study; if yes, then proceed to next step.
b. A parent who decides whether the risks/benefits are warranted given their unique child's characteristics; if yes, then proceed to next step.
c. Child is permitted (APA Ethical Standards) to decide whether he or she wants to participate, given his or her understanding of the risks/benefits.

This paradigm provides opportunities for parent–child discussion and support and creates an environment that increases understanding, minimizes stress, optimizes input of both parents and children in the process, and insures all concerns are adequately addressed.... Parental permission and developmentally fitted assent procedures that protect child and adolescent welfare and promote their maturing autonomy are thus essential to an informed-consent ethic of respect and care. (Fisher, 2004, p. 839)

Summation

Thus far, we have discussed Standards of the Ethics Code that are primarily concerned with issues of informed consent and assent, ethical dilemmas, and mandated duty to report, as these issues relate to the provision of psychological services for children and youth. In chapter 4, we will return to the Ethics Code with particular emphasis on Standards (9 and 10) that are directly related to ethical decisions that are involved in the assessment and treatment process.

Research Methods in Child Psychopathology

Research Methods: An Introduction

The process of conducting psychological research invariably begins with the investigation of some line of inquiry based on a researcher's observations, beliefs, and previous information. Within the domain of clinical psychology, most questions focus on the nature, course, assessment, and treatment of disordered behaviors. For the scientist, questions can be answered through the use of research methods designed to uncover what is known and test how various individual characteristics and environmental characteristics can influence thoughts, behaviors, or feelings. The case study that introduces this section, *Case in Point* (*ME: Main Example*), will be used repeatedly throughout this section to illustrate several of the concepts discussed regarding research procedures, methods, and experimental design.

Case in Point (ME)

A researcher is interested in investigating whether violent video games increase aggressive behaviors in young males. For his study, he has recruited 80 boys who range in age from 8 to 10 years. He randomly assigns the boys to one of three groups: Aggressive Video Action Game (AVAG); Nonaggressive Video Action Game (NAVAG); and a Control Condition (Computer Solitaire Card Game). Prior to participating in the experimental conditions, each child is asked to make up a story to describe what is happening in five pictures that portray children in ambiguous social interactions (Picture Set A). Children tell their stories about the pictures to an observer who captures the story-telling sessions on video/audio tape. The observer prompts the storyteller in the following manner: *"Tell me what is happening in this picture? What do you think caused this to happen? What do you think will happen next? How will the story end?"* After the storytelling segment, each child participates in a 15 minute computer session (AVAG, NAVAG, or Control Condition). At the end of the computer session, children are presented with five more pictures (Picture Set B) and asked once again, to make up a story about the picture in response to the same prompts given in the initial session. The presentation of the pictures is counterbalanced, such that half the children receive Picture Set A first, and half the children receive Picture Set B first. The experimental design is presented in Table 4.2.

Table 4.2 Sample Experimental Design

Research Question: Does viewing violent video games increase aggressive interpretation of ambiguous information?

Group	Pretest Time 1	Experimental Condition	Posttest
Experimental Group (AVAG)	Half Picture Set A Half Picture Set B	Aggressive Video Action Game (AVAG)	Half Picture Set B Half Picture Set A
Experimental Group (NAVG)	Half Picture Set A Half Picture Set B	Nonaggressive Video Action Game (NAVG)	Half Picture Set B Half Picture Set A
Control Group	Half Picture Set A Half Picture Set B	Video Solitaire	Half Picture Set B Half Picture Set A

In the *Case in Point (ME)*, the researcher's interest in aggressive behaviors in children has prompted her to investigate whether participation in violent video games might serve to increase aggressive responses in some children. Although the investigation began with a research question or hypothesis, the study that has been developed to test this hypothesis is the result of careful planning and going through several stages to ensure that the hypothesis will be tested in a scientific manner that is unbiased and objective. The development of a research plan involves a number of prescribed stages which are outlined below.

Initial Steps in the Development of a Research Plan

1. The Hypothesis or Research Question

The investigation often begins with a research question or **hypothesis**, which is a proposed explanation for the relationship between conditions or events based on a researcher's theoretical framework. In this case, the researcher begins by asking the following question: *Does watching violent video games increase aggressive behavior in children?* There are many ways that this question can be investigated, depending on the theoretical framework of the researcher. Within a biological framework, a researcher may monitor violent video game participation by looking at possible elevation in levels of the hormone testosterone (Dabbs & Morris, 1990) or lowering of levels of DBH which converts dopamine to noradrenaline (Quay, 1986), both of which have been linked genetically to sensation seeking and aggressive behaviors in some children. However, this researcher's social cognitive underpinnings have led her to develop a research plan that investigates how aggressive responses might influence social perception in ambiguous situations (responses to pictures) in much the same way that takes place when young children are aggressive due to a *hostile attribution bias* (tendencies noted in some children to view ambiguous situations as having hostile intent).

Because the hypothesis represents a set of testable assumptions, the next stage is to identify the *procedures* that will be used in order to put these assumptions to the test, in a way that is objective, systematic, and without bias.

2. Procedures

The scientific method. Researchers strive to obtain credible and unbiased information by using scientific and objective measures. The **scientific method** is based upon the goals of seeking scientific truths in four areas: *describe, predict, control,* and *understand*. For clinical psychologists, the four objectives of the scientific method would be to *describe* (*the underlying mental processes or behaviors*), in order to *predict* (*the precipitating causes of the disorder*), to better *understand* and *control* (*the disorder through the development of appropriate intervention and treatment plans*).

In our example, the researcher is interested in *describing* the relationship between violent video game participation and aggressive behaviors through the medium of social perception (the possible interpretation of ambiguous social interactions in a hostile manner), in order to *predict* whether violent video games may increase aggressive responses. This information may lead to a better *understanding* of the influence of video game watching on behavior and ultimately result in greater *control* of negative outcomes. As will be discussed at the end of this chapter, research of this nature can provide information that may actually result in changes in social policy: in this case, possibly restricting access or putting warning labels on violent video games.

The scientific method has been developed to reduce error and increase generalization of scientific results across studies based on the principles of increasing the maximum level of objectivity while reducing any bias to a minimum.

Standardization and operational definitions. Other procedures that are important in maintaining objectivity and reducing bias include the use of **standardized procedures** and **operational definitions**. Some examples of standardized procedures include the use of program manuals (such as Multi Systemic Therapy: MST), following strict guidelines for the administration of test questions (such as the *Weschler Intelligence Scale for Children* [*WISC-IV*]), and adhering to strict experimental timelines and protocols. In the case study example, each child participating in the study is asked the identical set of questions concerning the social interaction pictures. Operational definitions are crucial to the success of measuring behavioral outcomes, such as ensuring that multiple raters are recording the same range of behaviors in the required behavioral categories (e.g., What constitutes aggressive behavior?). In the study example, operational definitions would be an integral part of the scoring key developed to evaluate responses that would qualify as incidences of verbal (e.g., name calling, teasing, threatening) or physical (e.g., hitting, punching, tripping, slapping) aggression.

Confounding variables and biases. There are several levels of influence that can undermine the objectivity of research responses and hence, outcomes, when investigating attitudes of children, youth, and families. In chapter 3, we discussed several ways that clinical bias or cultural bias can result in underreporting or overreporting of disordered behaviors in children from some ethnic groups. In chapter 12, we will look at the impact of the mass media on body dissatisfaction among youth. Influences such as culture, mass media, and family values can influence an individual's perception of themselves and their world, and distort what is real (perception/reality distinction), thereby altering the outcomes of a research investigation. The integrity of research findings can also be undermined by **confounding variables**; these variables are **extraneous variables** which are not of interest to the researcher. However, their presence may influence the behavior being studied and compromise research outcomes if not properly controlled. In our example study, if some of the children in the study watched a lot of aggressive television programs prior to participating in the study, while others had restricted television viewing in their homes, those who were exposed to more violence may behave differently, regardless of the nature of the video game they view in the study. We will revisit confounds and how researchers can attempt to reduce this type of interference later in this section in our discussion of experimental controls.

In addition to confounding variables, there are also several types of **biases** that may also distort perceptions and responses of those involved in a research study. A number of common biases are listed below.

- **Personal biases:** Biases that may distort one's perceptions and responses due to personal beliefs, past history, or attitudes. Social cognitive biases, such as **belief perseverance**—the tendency to hold one to one's beliefs despite evidence to the contrary—and **confirmation bias**, which is the tendency to seek out information to support one's beliefs, are two related biases that can also influence research outcomes.

- **Observer bias:** Perceptions can become bias if we distort what we observe due to our own internal motives or expectations whether these are conscious or not.
- **Expectancy bias:** Researchers who are not conscious of this bias could unknowingly influence the direction of a subject's response by subtly providing signals regarding the expected response (e.g., eyes gaze towards a correct answer). This effect, termed the **Pygmalion effect** by Rosen and Jacobson (1968/1992), was dramatically displayed in their study that investigated the influence of teacher expectations on student performance. As part of the experiment, children were assessed and teachers were erroneously informed that a select group of students would be expected to bloom in that academic year. Retesting at the conclusion of the school year revealed that those students labeled as "bloomers" actually increased their performance dramatically compared to students who were not identified, thus confirming the hypothesis that teacher expectations had become a **self-fulfilling prophecy**.
- **Participant bias:** Merely having the knowledge that one is participating in a study itself can alter performance through the power of suggestion, an effect sometimes called the **placebo bias** or the **Hawthorne effect**. In order to control for the placebo bias, some studies—often drug trial studies—will use a placebo or sugar pill to allow for a comparison between groups who are actually getting the drug (treatment) and those who believe they are being treated, but are not actually receiving treatment (placebo group).

Participants may also alter responses in order to conform to expectations of **social desirability** (*being a good subject*), or **demand characteristics**, which occur when a subject believes they have figured out what hypothesis the study is testing and then act in accordance to confirm the hypothesis.

Science Talks

The birthplace of the *Hawthorne effect* was the Western Electric Plant in Hawthorne, Illinois, where researchers investigated factors affecting work productivity in a small sample of female workers who participated in the Relay Assembly experiment over a 10-year period (1924–1933). Results revealed that despite negative changes to working conditions (e.g., increased work hours, decreased lunch time), the small group of females increased their productivity because they knew they were being studied, an effect later called the Hawthorne effect.

---

3. The Study Sample and Variables

Having ensured that the hypothesis under investigation will be evaluated in an objective and unbiased manner, the researcher's focus turns to selecting the subjects and defining the variables to be tested. In the *Case in Point* (*ME*), children make up the **population** of interest for the researcher. The population refers to the entire set of individuals under 18 years of age. As a result of this investigation, the researcher hopes to be able to answer questions about the major hypothesis that could generalize to the population as a whole. The next task is to select a **sample**, a **subset** of the population that will participate in the study. In the sample case, the researcher has selected 80 boys who range in age from 8 to 10 years of age. We are not given any additional information about this sample, and as a result cannot comment on the degree to which the sample is a **representative sample**, or the degree to which the sample is characteristic of all 8- to 10-year-old boys. In order to make this decision, we would need demographic information about the sample and population at-large which might include such information as parent education, ethnicity, household income, single- versus two-parent families, etc.

The next step is to define the **variable** of interest which is the behavior that the researcher has hypothesized will change as a result of experimental manipulation. The variables in our example study include:

- The **independent variable (IV)** that is manipulated by the researcher, in this case the type of video game the child is exposed to; and
- The **dependent variable (DV)** or the behavior that is measured and expected to change as a result of the researcher's manipulation of the IV, which in the example is the number of aggressive responses the child makes when describing what is happening in the social interaction pictures.

4. Selection of Research Methods and Research Design

The researcher can choose among three types of research methods: *descriptive research, correlational research,* and *experimental research.* An overview of these three methods is presented in Table 4.3.

Table 4.3 Research Methods: A Comparative Look

Research Method	Goal	Data Collection and Analysis	Benefits and Limitations
Quantitative Methods			
Descriptive Research Survey Naturalistic Observation Case Study	Describes psychological processes as they exist	**Descriptive Statistics** Frequency distribution and Measures of central tendency	**Benefits** Quick access to data (survey) Ecological validity (naturalistic observation); In-depth analysis (case study) **Limitations** Lack of rigor and control Risk low generalizability (case study); Cannot imply causation
Correlational Research Existing data (census, etc.) Descriptive methods (case study, survey, naturalistic observation) Epidemiological Studies	Describe how variables are related Prevalence and incidence rates of disorders	**Correlation Coefficient:** *Pearson's r* Quantify the strength (−1 to +1) and direction (positive or negative) relationship between variables	**Benefits** High external validity can generalize across populations (survey) **Limitation** Low internal validity: cannot imply causation
Experimental Research **Scientific Experimental Method**	Manipulate variables to determine causative relationships	**Rigor and control** Random assignment; Control and experimental groups Inferential Statistics	**Benefits** High internal validity can determine causation **Limitation** Low external validity; Low ecological validity

Descriptive Research: Goals and Research Methods

The goal of *descriptive research* is to examine the degree that mental processes (attitudes, thoughts) or behaviors exist and how these processes or behaviors are distributed in a sample, relative to "normal expectations."

Descriptive Research: Data Collection and Analysis

Data collection. Researchers can use several different methods to collect descriptive data:

- *Survey* (telephone or in person; verbal or paper and pencil);
- *Naturalistic observation* (e.g., observe mothers and children interacting at a mall, or watching children with peers in a park-like setting); and
- *Case study* (e.g., in-depth analysis and observation of parent–child interactions on a case by case or small group basis).

Because researchers interested in child psychopathology must attend to the clinical and developmental features of their population, they often use a blend of research methods typically found in either clinical or developmental studies. Descriptive methods that are particularly suited to child populations include **naturalistic observation** and the **case study** method.

Data analysis. Once the data is collected, the researcher can then apply a number of descriptive statistics to assist in understanding the results. Descriptive statistics are measures of central tendency that depict how scores cluster around the "average" score, or how scores are distributed around the "average" score. For example, I interview 22 single moms to determine the number of child problems they encounter from a list of 10 problem behaviors and obtain the following results which appear in the frequency table noted in Table 4.4.

Based on my survey, I can calculate the following **measures of central tendency**:

- **Mean:** Single parents interviewed in my sample reported an average of 1.95 (43/22) problem child behaviors, per parent.
- **Median:** The median represents the midpoint of the distribution. Approximately, half of the parents reported 2 or more behaviors, and half reported 2 or less behaviors. We have

Table 4.4 Frequency Table for Number of Behaviors Reported by Single Parents

Number of Problem Behaviors	Total Number Parents = 22		Total Problem Behaviors
	Tally	Frequency (f)	
0	I I I I	4	0
1	H+H I	6	6
2	H+H	5	10
3	I I I	3	9
4	I I	2	8
5	I I	2	10
			Total 43

Mean = 1.95 behaviors
Standard Deviation: 1.56

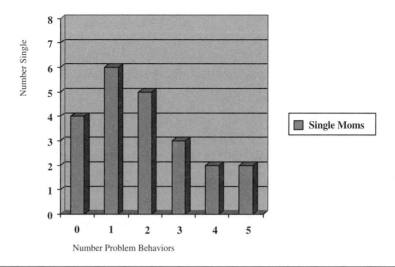

Figure 4.1 Problem behaviors noted by single moms.

22 scores ranging from 0 to 5 (number of behaviors). Because there is an even number we consider the 2 middle numbers (in our distribution, they are both 2). Therefore, our midpoint is 2 behaviors.

- **Mode:** The most frequently reported number of behavior problems in our example is 1 behavior (six parents interviewed reported one behavior problem).

If the Mean, Median, and Mode are all the same number (which they are not in this case), then my distribution would resemble a normal distribution which has the most frequently reported scores in the centre of the distribution. However, when we look at Figure 4.1, we see that the midpoint is not the middle of our distribution, and that the highest concentration of scores is at the lower end (actually, 68% of our single mothers reported two or less problem behaviors). While descriptive statistics can provide an initial picture of what our attitudes or behaviors might look like relative to the norm, we often require more powerful research methods to find out how these scores relate to other attitudes and behaviors, and whether these relationships are statistically significant.

Descriptive Research: Benefits and Limitations

Surveys provide quick access to information and results can provide an initial introduction to exploring questions for future research. Limitations of the survey method include a potential for a biased sample (only those who are willing to be surveyed are included), and survey data is based on self-report, which may also be biased and/or inaccurate. The benefits of *naturalistic observation* versus observing interactions in a laboratory (***analogue studies***) are the realism and ecological validity evident in the naturalistic surroundings. However, limitations are evident in the sacrifice of controls that can accompany a more structured laboratory observation. *Case studies* provide a rich source of information for processing in-depth analysis. However, limitations of this method are inherent in the relatively high risk of low generalizability of results to a larger sample.

Correlational Method: Goals and Research Methods

A researcher is interested in whether child behavior problems are related to marital status and he interviews single- and two-parent families to obtain his data. Because our researcher is interested in investigating the association or **correlation** between two variables (in this case marital status and behavior problems), he has selected a research method that will allow him to make inferences about the relationship of marital status and behavior problems based on the patterns that emerge in the analysis of data. He may also have been able to access this data from existing information such as a data bank that includes all clients serviced in the clinic. When the focus of the investigation concerns the relationship among a set of variables (e.g., age, gender, aggression, leisure habits, parenting style, marital status, problem behaviors, etc.), it is referred to as the **correlational method**. If, on the other hand, the researcher is interested in probing how a change in one variable may *cause* change in another variable (e.g., whether one style of parenting can cause more problem behaviors), then the more rigorous standards of an **experimental method** will be required. The experimental method will be discussed shortly.

While the goal of descriptive research is to determine the nature of existing variables, such as attitudes or behaviors, the goal of correlational research is to determine the nature of the relationship among variables.

Memory Bank

Remember that a variable is anything (attitude, behavior, etc.) that varies. The two most common types of variables are:

Continuous Variables: Variables that vary along a continuum, such as severity of behavior (aggression, depression).

Categorical Variables: Variables that exist in an "all-or-none" fashion, or variables relegated to discrete categories, such as male versus female, married versus single.

Some variables can be either continuous or categorical depending on how they are classified. For example, age is a variable that can be represented as a *continuous variable* or *categorical variable*. In the *Case in Point* (*ME*), the researcher was interested in the behaviors of boys 8–10 years of age, and his study allows for an examination of possible developmental changes over the span of 3 years, since age is a *continuous variable*. However, age can be a *categorical variable* if the researcher chooses to group subjects on the bases of different age groups, e.g., comparing the responses of younger children (ages 5–9 years) versus older children (ages 10–14 years). In the latter example, age is a *categorical variable* because age is grouped into two categories: younger versus older children.

Correlational Research: Data Collection and Analysis

Data collection.   Researchers can use several different *methods* to collect information for the purposes of correlational research, depending on the nature of the research question. Data can be extracted from preexisting information (e.g., census reports, crime reports), or collected in the same way that information was amassed for more descriptive purposes (e.g., survey naturalistic observation, case study).

Naturalistic observation and case study method.   When a laboratory study is neither possible nor desired, the researcher may choose to observe children in their natural environment, such as in their homes or on the playground, in order to document naturally occurring behaviors. This method can be used in research or clinical practice. Unlike an experimental design (which will be discussed shortly), the emphasis in a correlational research design is not on controlling the environment but rather in systematically controlling how behaviors are defined (*operationalized*) and the methods used to record the observations.

Word of Caution

Some problems that may interfere with reliability of observed data include observer bias, observer drift, poor categories for coding, and central tendency (tendencies to pick the middle category more frequently when rating behaviors).

Data Analysis

Comparing data within or between populations.   With a focus on the relationship among variables, researchers may search within their sample to see how certain characteristics are related (e.g., single parents and child behavior problems), or they may chose to compare how characteristics of one sample compares to another sample (e.g., how behavior problems of children from single-parent families compare to children raised in two-parent families).

Statistical analysis will yield a **correlation coefficient** (*Pearson's r*) which will indicate both the degree of relatedness (which can range from −1.00 to +1.00) and the direction of the relationship: **positive correlation** or **negative correlation**. A correlation coefficient of 0 would indicate a **zero order correlation** or no relationship between the variables (e.g., eye color and academic difficulties).

Case in Point

Dr. Scope finds that teacher ratings of behavior problems correlate negatively (−.70) with academic grades and positively (+.60) with school suspensions. Furthermore, results reveal that behavior problems and school suspensions correlate positively (+.65). *Can Dr. Scope conclude that behavior problems cause lower academic grades?*

In the *Case in Point* above, teachers' ratings for behavior problems revealed a strong negative relationship to academic grades and a moderately high positive relationship to school suspensions. This relationship would indicate that as behavior problems increased, school suspensions increased (*positive relationship*) while academic grades decreased (*negative relationship*). Can Dr. Scope conclude that behavior problems cause lower grades? On the surface, one might be tempted to link behavior problems to academic problems in a causal way. However, while the correlational method does provide information about whether the variables are related, the kind of relationship the variables share (positive or negative), and the strength of the relationship, it does not provide any information about which variable influences are which and never implies causation. The reason for this is that statistically, the variables can be related for any of the following three reasons, which cannot be determined based on correlation alone:

1. Behavior problems causes (influence) academic problems (e.g., A → B).
2. Academic problems cause (influence) behavior problems (e.g., B → A).
3. School suspensions or some other third factor related factor cause behavior problems and academic problems (e.g., C → both A and B).

In the third example, both behavior problems and academic problems may be related to yet a third factor (e.g., school suspensions). If children are removed from school due to behavior problems, then they are not in a continuous learning environment and as such, can be expected to have periods of time where learning is interrupted, resulting in lower academic grades. However, in order to prove a causal link, research using the experimental method would be required.

Important Distinction

Signs indicate the *type* of relationship
   Positive (+) correlations indicate that when A increases, B increases (in our example: behavior problems and school suspensions are positive correlations).
   Negative (–) correlations indicate that when A increases, B decreases (in our example: behavior problems increase as academic grades decrease).
Numbers indicate the *strength* of the relationship.
   When strength *increases,* the further the number is away from zero.
   When strength *decreases,* the closer the number is to zero.
   For example: –.8 is stronger than + .2

Data collection, analysis, and internal and external validity.   Studies that use a correlational method rely on statistical *measures of association,* which are statistical procedures that measure the strength and type of relationship that exists between variables. The most commonly used correlation coefficient is the **Pearson's r**, a descriptive statistic used to calculate data measured on either an interval scale or a ratio scale.

Validity refers to the strength of the study conclusions and inferences. **Validity** addresses the question of how convincing the results of an investigation are, in terms of the internal study controls and the degree to which we can generalize our findings to the population at large. In other words, are the results we have obtained a true indication of what exists in reality? Through the use of correlational research methods, researchers can study a wide variety of variables across large sample numbers. Strength of numbers provides the potential for *high* **external validity** because we can generalize our results across a large portion of the population. However, there is a price to pay for casting such a wide net. As has already been discussed, correlational research only allows inferences about the relatedness of the variables in the most general of terms. The inability to draw conclusions about causation results in this research method scoring *low on* **internal validity**.

Correlational Methods Adapted to Studies of Clinical Populations

Epidemiological studies.   One form of correlational research that is of particular importance to clinical studies is the area of **epidemiological** investigations. Information from these studies inform clinicians about the rates (*incidence rates and prevalence rates*) that disorders are present.

Staggering Statistics

According to the Methodology for Epidemiology of Mental Disorders in Children (MECA) study, 21% of all children (9 to 17 years of age) living in the United States met the minimum criteria for a mental or addictive disorder, while 11% were found to be significantly functionally impaired (Shaffer et al., 1996).

Epidemiological studies can be very important because they can serve as a monitoring device for tracking whether certain disordered behaviors are on the increase or decline. Several methods are available for tracking the number of reported cases.

Incidence rates.   Studies that report the *number of new cases* of a disorder within a given time frame (e.g., number of new cases in a year) report incident rates. An example would be to track the number of cases of PTSD among children living in the greater New York area before and after the terrorist attack of Sept. 11, 2001. In this example, the researcher would be interested in determining whether rates increased significantly during this period.

Prevalence rates.   These rates refer to the *total number of cases* in the population within a given time frame. For example, it is estimated that 20% of all children in the United States have sufficient symptoms to be diagnosed with a mental disorder and in need of treatment, according to the *DSM*.

Life time prevalence rate.   This number refers to the percentage expectancy that one might be diagnosed with a given disorder *over the course of a lifetime*.

Memory Bank

It is important to consider the population under investigation and the research questions when reviewing studies that include *"incident/prevalence rates."* For example, rates may vary widely depending on whether studies are reporting rates for clinical populations, normative populations, or partial clinical populations (day treatment programs). Other important considerations include how the disorder was assessed (assessment method used), as well as the method of classification employed (*DSM–III, DSM IV, DSM IVTR; ICD-10 Codes*).

Correlational Research: Benefits and Limitations

The benefits of the correlational method are evident in the use of this method to quantify the strength of relatedness between variables and determine the type of the relationship (positive or negative). In addition to the limitations evident in the survey, case study, and natural observation methods already discussed, the major limitation of the correlational method is its inability to verify which variable influences which variable and the inability to determine any causal relationship between the variables studied. In order to establish the existence of a cause-and-effect relationship between variables, rigorous controls are required that can only be achieved through the use of the experimental method.

Memory Bank

Correlation does **not** imply causation. While early researchers found a positive correlation between single parenthood (variable A) and child maladaptive behavior (variable B), later research confirmed that a third factor (poverty) was directly related to both maladaptive behavior and single parenthood. Single parenthood and poverty cooccurred, as did single parenthood and maladaptive behavior, but poverty (variable C) was the underlying cause of the association (C → both A and B).

The Experimental Method: Goals and Research Methods

The experimental method demands the most rigorous of research designs because it has at its core the ability to determine quantitatively which conditions or variables can actually cause changes in other conditions or variables. Using this research method, investigators can test a number of hypotheses and ultimately reject those hypotheses that are not statistically sound, and verify those that have causative implications. Investigators are able to achieve this level of sophistication in their analyses by manipulating the variables in question (under controlled conditions) in order to systematically support explanations while ruling out other explanations.

Recall and Rewind

Remember that the variable being manipulated is called the *independent variable (IV)*; the variables that are being held constant are called the *extraneous variables* to avoid possible confounds; and the variable being measured is the *dependent variable*.

Experimental Research: Data Collection and Analysis

Data collection.   There are several types of independent variables that investigators can manipulate. Researchers who use independent variables that are **situational variables** will seek to alter something in the environment, such as comparing the influence of different classroom settings (small group, large group) on academic performance. In our initial research, *Case in Point (ME)*, the investigator was interested in the impact of video game violence on children's aggressive responses. In this case, exposure to different types of video games (violent or nonviolent) is a situational independent variable. Clinical studies that investigate the efficacy of different treatment conditions on behavioral outcomes are also manipulating situational variables. Independent variables can also be represented by **task variables** (assigning different tasks to different students to determine which task is the most difficult), or **instructional variables** (e.g., altering the instructions to read aloud or read silently to determine the impact on reading comprehension).

Experimental and control groups.   In many clinically oriented studies, treatment effects are studied by comparing two groups of subjects: a group of subjects who receive a given treatment *(experimental group)* and a group of subjects who do not receive the treatment *(control group)*.

In the study example (*Case in Point, ME*) there were two experimental groups and one control group:

Experimental Group 1:	Aggressive Video Action Game (AVAG)
Experimental Group 2:	Nonaggressive Video Action Game (NAVAG)
Control Group:	Computer solitaire

The researcher equated the computer access time across all three groups; however, while Groups 1 and 2 were exposed to video action games (violent versus nonviolent), the control group spent the same amount of time in a solitaire video card game (nonaction video control).

Experimental Research Designs

Researchers using the experimental method have a number of different research designs they can draw from, including: the **between subject design; the within subject design**; and the **ABA design**, also referred to as **the ABAB–reversal**.

Between-subject design. In this design, different groups of subjects are assigned to an **experimental condition** (exposed to treatment or condition, or to **the control group**, no exposure condition). The *Case in Point* (ME) study is an example of a between-subject design. The advantages of using the between-subject design is that each subject is exposed to the experimental conditions in the same way and for the first time, so carry-over or practice effects are minimal. However, the limitation of this design is that greater emphasis is placed on having equivalent or matched groups to insure that both groups begin at the same level regarding the variable to be measured (e.g., aggressive behavior) prior to the investigation. The two most common methods of developing equivalent groups include **random assignment** and **matching**.

Random assignment is one of the most important ways of assigning subjects to experimental groups that is without inherent bias. Subjects are randomly assigned to either the *experimental group* (group where the variable–treatment is manipulated to test the variable effect) or the *control group* (group not exposed to the variable–treatment) in such a way that every participant has an equal likelihood of being assigned to either group. The separation of subjects into these groups allows the investigator to compare outcomes for the experimental group with outcomes for the control group. For obvious reasons, increased controls are obtained in studies that take place in laboratories (analogue studies) compared to those that are generated in more naturalistic environments (playground).

In some cases it is not possible to randomly assign subjects to groups. This can occur when there are too few subjects, or in clinical studies where it might appear unethical to have a "no treatment" control group, or when subjects have a preexisting condition that is under investigation (e.g., child abuse). In order to test treatment versus no treatment for youth with depression, the researcher might provide a treatment program for one group of youth, while the second group is in a holding pattern waiting for the start of their treatment program. In this way the researcher can compare those who received the initial treatment sessions with those who are in a **wait-list control** condition, without actually depriving the second group (control group) of treatment. If a researcher wanted to investigate the impact of depressed mothers on males and females, the participants would be matched on the majority of variables (age, demographics, maternal education, number of siblings, etc.) in order to control for confounds.

Within-subject designs. When subjects act as their own control group, then the design is a within-subject design. Suppose I want to measure a variety of instructional techniques for improving memory. If I were to use a between-subjects design, I could have three different groups of children use three different memory strategies and then compare the group performances: Verbal group (VE), Visual group (VI), Motor group (M). Or, I could provide each subject with three parallel tasks with instructions to code the information into memory using verbal, visual, or motor activities. In the latter case, I am using a within-subject design. The difficulty with this design is the need to control for confounds due to the particular sequence in which the tasks are performed, in order to control for **practice effects** (ability improves as familiarity with the task increases) or **fatigue effects** (performance is better initially but tapers off due to fatigue or distractibility). In order to control for these effects, it would be important to counterbalance the presentation of the tasks across my subjects, such that equal numbers of participants were given the tasks in the same order. Given that my study has three tasks, then, if I were to completely counterbalance the order of the presentation among my subjects, I would require six different sequences for task presentation:

VE VI M	VE M VI
VI M VE	VI VE M
M VE VI	M VI VE

Memory Bank

Counterbalancing can also be important in other situations, such as the **Case in Point (ME)** study in the introduction to this section. In that case, although it was a *between-subject design*, the researcher counterbalanced the presentation of the pictures sets, such that half the children received Picture Set A first, and half the children received Picture Set B first.

ABA Design or ABAB–Reversal

Single subject experiment.   In some interventions, the child can serve as their own control by using behavior prior to intervention (A) as the baseline. In this type of approach, the treatment (independent variable) is manipulated, and then behavior after treatment (B) is compared to behavior sampled prior to intervention. In the following *Case in Point,* the **ABAB–reversal design** is illustrated.

Case in Point

The school psychologist is asked to observe Matthew to record the percentage of time he is engaged in on-task behaviors prior to the introduction of medication and after medication is introduced. Observations are recorded for 3 days prior to medication. On these days, Matthew's on-task behavior is evident for 20% of the time when he should be engaged in independent seatwork (Condition A). Medication is introduced and Matthew is again observed over 3 days, and during this period, Matthew is engaged in on-task behavior for 45% of the time (Condition B). The psychologist wants to make sure that there are no other factors contributing to the recent increase in on-task behavior (e.g., Matthew is trying to impress a new little girl in the classroom, or parents have threatened to take away his new bike if his grades do not improve). In order to rule out the possibility of contributing factors other than medication, Matthew is taken off medication for the following 3 days. During this time, his on-task behavior returns to 20% (Condition A). Medication is reintroduced for the next 3 days and on-task behavior increases to 50% of the time (Condition B).

In the ABAB design presented, Matthew's baseline behavior serves as the benchmark to determine whether treatment (medication) improves productivity in the classroom (on-task behavior). In order to determine whether the improvement is related to medication and not some other extraneous factor, medication is removed. Under this condition, behavior returns to premedication levels. When medication is added, behavior improves once again. The psychologist is now more confident in his report to the physician that the medication is responsible for the improved on-task behavior.

Data analysis and statistical methods.   In experimental methods, hypothesis testing occurs in what might seem to some like an odd manner. For example, in our *Case in Point (ME)* study, although the researcher sets out to investigate whether participation in violent video games will influence aggressive responses in children, she actually must make the assumption that there will be no difference in the level of aggressive responses between the different experimental groups. The assumption of no difference is called the **null hypothesis** (statement of null or no difference between groups) and is represented by the symbol, H_0. In order to prove that there is a difference between the two groups in their level of aggressive responses as a result of their participation in the violent video game condition, the researcher must have sufficient data to be able to reject the null hypothesis and accept the **alternate hypothesis** (symbolized as H_1).

Inferential statistics.   Statistical analysis of experimental data, unlike the descriptive or correlational methods described so far, requires more sophisticated approaches that enable the researcher to make inferences from the study outcomes that can apply to the population-at-large. Even though our researcher (*Case in Point ME*) has limited her sample to 80 boys between the ages of 8 and 10, ultimately it would be her hopes that results from the study could have far reaching implications concerning the future use of violent video games by children. **Inferential statistics** allow for a comparison of outcomes in terms of probabilities that reflect **confidence levels** which are reported as **alpha levels** (a). Basically, the alpha level provides an index of the confidence that there is a statistical difference between the experimental groups and that this level is high enough to support rejecting the null hypothesis and accepting the alternate hypothesis. Typically, an alpha level of .05 (95% confidence), .01 (99% confidence), and .001 are quoted.

Experimental method: Validity and reliability.   In the *Case in Point* (*ME*) study, the control group serves as a measure of "computer time" to rule out any possible link between time spent on the computer and subsequent tendencies to interpret ambiguous situations as aggressive versus nonaggressive. The control group is the part of the research sample that receives no treatment (in this case, no exposure to active video games). The current study can be said to have good *internal validity*, because the researcher has included a control group (no treatment, computer exposure alone), in addition to the experimental groups (random assignment to conditions of nonaggressive action vs. aggressive action video games). Given the experimental controls (random assignment, matched groups age, gender, SES) it is highly likely that the researcher would be able to make a cause-and-effect link between type of action video game observed and subsequent interpretation of ambiguous social situations. One criticism of the study might be that the measure of interpretation of social situations (storytelling in response to pictures of ambiguous social situations) might lack **ecological validity**. In other words, does a child's response to pictures really predict what would happen in real life? Would interpretation of videotaped scenarios or real-life situations staged by actors provide a better index of social interpretation? In this study design, one question might be: Has the researcher obtained *high internal validity* at the expense of *ecological validity* (*validity of more reality-based contexts*)?

Issues of *internal validity* would also concern:

1. The method used to classify the action video games (aggressive versus nonaggressive action video games); and
2. The rating system used to score storytelling for aggressive versus nonaggressive content (*interrater reliability*; controls for *experimenter bias* [e.g., was the observer/rater of story content aware of the experimental group affiliation, or was the rater *blind/unaware* of group affiliation]).

Questions of internal validity all address the degree to which the study's internal controls are successful in minimizing any potential internal confounds. In examining a study's *external validity*, we address the degree to which results of the study can be generalized to the population at large. In other words, how comfortable would we be in generalizing these results from the laboratory setting to the general population of all children? One way to increase the external validity of the study would be to **replicate** the study with another group of 8- to 10-year-old males. Obtaining the same results for a similar group would increase our confidence in the application of findings to the general population of 8- to 10-year-old males. But would we be certain that results would be similar for 12- to 15-year-old males, or 8- to 10-year-old females? In order to address these questions, additional research would be required (e.g., replicate the study with different age groups and females).

Analogue versus community-based research.   Until very recently, research in child psychopathology had been primarily based on **analogue studies** with minimal research effort directed towards a study of the efficacy of **community-based** outpatient treatments (Weisz, Weiss, Han, Granger, & Morton, 1995). Furthermore, the few studies that did exist which investigated treatment effectiveness at a community level, such as Residential Treatment Centers (Blotcky, Dimperio, & Gottlet, 1984), and/or family preservation programs suffered from a lack of experimental controls (Littell & Schuerman, 1995). However, improved research methods—such as the use of clinical trials, for example—improved controls, and the introduction of measures of treatment fidelity and manualized treatment protocols have established that providing clinical services within the community can be an effective alternative to out-of home placements for youth with severe emotional and behavioral problems (Chamberlain & Reid, 1998; Henggeler & Borduin, 1990; Huey, Henggeler, Brondino, & Pickerel, 2000; Schoenwald, Ward, Henggeler, & Rowland, 2000; Wilmshurst, 2002).

Quasi-experimental design.   Because of the possibility of negative consequences and high premiums placed on ethical concerns of placing experimental groups in jeopardy, randomized placement is often difficult to achieve and often not advised in working with clinical populations. Rather than use randomized placement, the researcher might opt for a quasi-experimental design that employed a **matched control group**. For example, a researcher believes that many inner-city children are deprived of participating in athletic programs, which can be a known protective factor against school drop-out rates. In order to investigate the role of poverty on child involvement in athletic programs, the researcher might identify a group of children who are impoverished and then match these children to a group of children with the same demographics and characteristics (age, gender, birth order, etc.) who are not impoverished (*matched control group*). The next step might be to determine access to athletic programs available for children in these two groups. Researchers could then determine whether impoverished children lack access to organized athletic programs compared to children who are not impoverished. Ultimately, the researcher might improve access to organized athletics for one group of impoverished children (provide transportation and funds) and compare school drop-out rates to a matched sample of impoverished children who do not have access to athletic programs (*matched control group*). This second group of children might be those that are on the wait-list to join athletic programs in the future. In that case, the group would be referred to as the **wait-list control group**.

Memory Bank

In the above example, the establishment of a *wait-list control group* provides the researcher with an opportunity of comparing children who receive treatment (in this case access to organized athletics) to a group of children who are not yet receiving treatment. In this way, the researcher does not have to be faced with the ethical dilemma of providing treatment to one group while depriving another group of children from receiving treatment. The use of the wait-list control group is common in child-treatment studies.

In recent years, there has been increased interest in establishing treatments for children and adolescents that have an empirically-based foundation and in determining whether certain types of treatments might be linked to different types of problems. In 1995, the Task Force on Promotion and Dissemination of Psychological Procedures established by the APA produced a report on empirically validated psychological treatments and suggested a 3-tiered hierarchy for evaluating treatment efficacy: **well-established treatments, probably efficacious treatments, and experimental treatments**. Probably efficacious treatments were those which demonstrated that the treatment was superior to a wait-list control group.

Clinical Child Research: Developmental Considerations

Maladaptive Behavior Over Time

In the introductory chapter, five themes were introduced that emphasize the importance of conceptualizing maladaptive behavior as an offshoot of normal development.

RECURRENT THEMES   Recall that *normal development typically follows an orderly and predictable path* (*Theme 1*) and *maladaptive behaviors represent deviations from the normal path* (*Theme 2*). Furthermore, *maladaptive behavior is represented by a continuum of severity* (*Theme 3*) and there are *a wide range of individual, interpersonal, contextual, and cultural factors that can influence deviations in development* (*Theme 4*).

Clinical child research often seeks to uncover influences that can alter the trajectory of this pathway, as *individual characteristics* *(temperament, heredity)* evolve, shape, and are shaped by *environmental characteristics* *(family, peers, economics, and culture)*. Although development charts a predictable course of maturation (emotionally, physically, and mentally), there can be a wide band of individual variations within the range.

Within a developmental context, studies of child psychopathology often seek to determine *developmental pathways* that can be predictive of maladaptive outcomes or pathways that can serve to buffer a child from harm. Maturation is also crucial to understanding how symptoms of maladaptive behavior manifest at different stages of development (Sroufe, Egeland, & Kreutzer, 1990). For example, at early ages a very young child may demonstrate *instrumental aggression* as she pushes another child off a tricycle because she wants to ride it, whereas *hostile aggression* might be evident in an 8 year old who punches a child or threatens to punch a child if lunch money is not forfeited. Development pathways also require and understanding of *equifinality* (many roads can lead to the same destination; e.g., depression) and *multifinality* (similar roads can lead to different outcomes).

Important Distinction

Sara and John both exhibit symptoms of depression. Sara's depression results from having moved several times and being unable to connect to peers in her new environment. John's depression is due to his parent's divorce. Sara and John are examples of the principle of *equifinality* (both suffer from depression, but the precipitating cause differs). John and his brother are both experiencing the divorce of their parents; however, John reacts by becoming depressed, while his brother Earl decides to pour his energy into academics and wins a scholarship to college (*multifinality*).

Table 4.5 Experimental Design: The Study of Development Over Time

Experimental Design	Subjects	Design	Benefits/Limitations
Longitudinal	60 Grade 3 Children (30 boys; 30 girls)	Collect Social Status and Academic Grades: Time 1: Grade 3 Time 2: Grade 6 Time 3: Grade 9	**Benefits:** Same sample over course of development **Limitation:** **Time:** 6 years **Attrition:** loss subjects
Cross Sectional	60 Children: 20 Grade 3 20 Grade 6 20 Grade 9	Collect Social Status and Academic Grades: Time 1: Grade 3, 6, 9	**Benefits:** time (1 year) **Limitations:** not same subjects Cohort effects
Accelerated Longitudinal	60 Children: 20 Grade 3 20 Grade 6 20 Grade 9	Collect Social Status and Academic Grades: Time 1: Grade 3, 6, 9 Time 2: (3 years later) Grades 6, 9	**Benefits:** time (3 years) Follow two groups over time; Can compare within and between groups **Limitation:** Cohort effects

Development and Research Design

There are a number of research designs that are particularly suited to the study of developmental psychopathology, including: **longitudinal, cross sectional,** and **accelerated longitudinal designs**. The following *Case in Point* will help to illustrate how the various research designs can be used to study similar phenomena. The three methods for addressing the research question are presented in Table 4.5.

Case in Point

A researcher wants to study whether child social status (*popular, neglected, rejected*) is a relatively consistent trait and whether social status is related to academic success. He is most interested in whether social status in Grade 3 remains consistent through middle school and high school and whether social status can be related to academic success during these same time periods.

The researcher uses a **sociometric survey** to obtain an index of social status for each child in the study. The teachers of the Grade 3 children administer a series of oral questions to the children and ask them to answer by indicating the names of children in the classroom. For example, "Write down the name of the classmate you would most like to go to a party with. Who would you like to play with? Who do you not want to come to your party? Who is mean?" Responses for sociometric surveys are collected in Grade 3, Grade 6, and Grade 9. Academic scores are obtained from a standardized scholastic test that is given to all students in grades 3, 6, and 9. GPA scores are also collected for those grades.

While the **longitudinal study** provides a rich data base for investigating individual change over time, there are obvious limitations in potential loss of subjects over time (**subject attrition**), the potential cost of the research program, and the length of overall time to obtain the data. The **cross sectional** approach speeds up the process by using different subjects (matched for similar demographics) at the three different time periods (children enrolled in grades 3, 6, 9). Limitations are the loss of information about developmental pathways and the introduction of **cohort effects**, a confound that exists because different groups of children are exposed to different historical events that may impact their results. (For example, if a major hurricane devastated the area, the impact would be different for children who were 8 years of age in Grade 3 compared to youth who were 15 years of age in Grade 9.) One method that attempts to satisfy the desire to follow a set of children over time and yet reduce the overall time required is the **accelerated longitudinal design** (a hybrid design that combines elements of the longitudinal and cross sectional approaches). Applying this design to the longitudinal study above, the researcher would require only 3 years to collect data, compared to 6 years required for the longitudinal approach.

Qualitative Research

A discussion of research designs and methods available for child psychopathology would not be complete without addressing **qualitative research** methods. While the methods discussed so far serve to illustrate how data has traditionally been collected and analyzed to provide support for conclusions based on objective and numerical (quantitative) data, in recent years there has been increasing emphasis placed on the value of qualitative analysis. Rather than support conclusions with numerical data, qualitative analysis strives to unravel the *experiential* aspect of a situation that often cannot be captured in relying totally on a numbers approach (Krahn & Eisert, 2000). Qualitative research is grounded in the study of anthropology and history and is focused on a rich understanding of process and the meanings that people have developed about their world. Rather than looking at numerical patterns, qualitative research focuses on patterns in subject responses gleaned through interviews or running diaries collected by researchers who want a more in-depth understanding of underlying processes that may help to explain how and why attitudes and behaviors exist. For example, in their evaluation of current programs for fathers, the National Center on Fathers and Families (NCFF: http://www.ncoff.gse.upenn.edu) suggested several ways that qualitative research could benefit outcomes for programs designed to increase responsible parenting, including:

1. Filling in knowledge gaps regarding life situations of fathers and the ability of programs to affect positive change;
2. Building on previous qualitative information about "absent fathers";
3. Further defining the demographics of "absent fathers";
4. Better understanding of "fatherhood" as it relates to community, culture, and local context;
5. Better understanding of multiple perspectives on fatherhood issues (father, mother, child); and
6. Constructive evaluation of existing programs and grass-roots models not amenable to empirical investigation (e.g., random assignment).

Comparison of Quantitative and Qualitative Research

The nature of the questions that researchers seek to answer will dictate whether they choose a qualitative or quantitative method (Stanovich, 2000). Researchers who seek to answer questions about causal relationships, or who want to clarify how variables are related, will likely select quantitative methods that will allow them to support or reject their outcomes or predictions based on theoretical assumptions. On the other hand, if the basis of inquiry is to better understand the meaning of "living in the situation," qualitative researchers will evaluate the patterns in responses that affirm or conflict with underlying philosophical perspectives and potentially integrate the information into the development of new formulations (Creswell, 2003). While

Table 4.6 Comparison of Quantitative and Qualitative Methods

	Quantitative Methods	Qualitative Methods
Description	Research that seeks to describe existing variables, or manipulate variables to determine causative effects Hypothesis testing	Research that seeks to describe psychological processes as experienced by individuals in the situation Hypothesis generating
Data and Analysis	The relationships between variables are measured by using descriptive statistics (measures of central tendency, correlational analysis) or higher powered inferential statistics (analysis of variance) to determine mathematical significance of results	Data collection as notes on observations, transcripts of interviews, and other anecdotal information Analysis of underlying patterns and themes
Rigor and controls	Experimental method uses random assignment	Targets individuals to observe and interview to gain in-depth understanding of person in situation
Benefits and Limitations	**Benefit** Can prove/disprove hypothesis (e.g., Is treatment program effective?); Can test for generalizability **Limitation** Loss of information about "individual experience"	**Benefit** Rich information about individual and psychological processes in given situation **Limitation** May have limited generalizability Cannot prove/disprove hypothesis

the optimum participant in a quantitative initiative is by random selection, those conducting qualitative research will target those individuals who are in the context that they are studying to obtain interviews and observations to explore the dynamics of the individual in the situation (e.g., interview students with learning disabilities to obtain information about how they view their programs and obtain their perspectives on educational outcomes). A summary of the comparative features of qualitative and quantitative research is presented in Table 4.6. Ultimately, by integrating both methods, researchers can use qualitative methods to generate new hypotheses that can be empirically tested using more conventional quantitative methods.

Developmental Research and Issues in Advocacy

In a recent article entitled, *Between a Rock and a Soft Place: Developmental Research and the Child Advocacy Process,* Grisso and Steinberg (2005) discuss the challenges that face researchers who are compelled to conduct research about issues of child welfare and social change. The objectivity and lack of bias necessary to produce research outcomes that can potentially influence and change child welfare laws fall on the responsibility of the scientist who

> in order to truly advocate for children, must proceed to design their studies as if they do not care whether their beliefs and intuitions about what is best for children are borne out by their research. They must formulate their hypotheses on the basis of existing developmental research findings and relevant theories, constructing their research methods as though they hope to prove themselves wrong. (Grisso & Steinberg, 2006, p. 4)

Since 1997, Grisso and colleagues (2003) have been investigating whether juveniles were at greater risk for being found incompetent to stand trial than adults. The study, an applied developmental research effort, was developed using principles of developmental psychology with a focus on addressing the question of competence in a way that would provide important information for policy makers in the future. According to Grisso and Steinberg (2006), it was crucial as researchers that they were consciously aware of their role as scientists at each step along the way, since they did not want to "stack the deck towards finding juveniles less competent," and were aware that their "choices at several points in the data analysis could influence their results…and could affect study findings" (p. 5). Since the focus of their study was on the developmental and cognitive capacities of youth to participate in their own defense (competence to stand trial), the authors were able to side step the issue regarding whether juveniles should be tried as adults and thereby concentrate on the facts that needed to be considered by policy makers. Furthermore, they decided not to release the findings of their study to the public until their manuscript was submitted to a scholarly journal and the research method, results, and interpretation had been subjected to peer review. Having taken all the necessary precautions, the authors were then able to disseminate credible research evidence concerning the incapacities of youth to defend themselves in court, and several states are now in the process of changing their legislation as a result.

CHAPTER SUMMARY AND REVIEW

1. **Ethical Issues in Providing Mental Health Services to Children and Youth**
   Professionals such as psychologists and mental health counselors are guided in their professional practice by ethical standards and codes of conduct. The latest revision by the American Psychological Association (APA, 2000) contains five general principles or "aspirational" goals, and 10 standards of conduct that apply to a wide variety of psychological roles. Ethical guidelines are not laws; however, a governing body, such as the APA, does have the right to sanction members for violations of the Ethical Code. Psychologists rely upon the standards to assist in resolving ethical dilemmas they may face in their practice.
   a. Issues of Informed Consent and Assent
      The latest revision (APA, 2000) of the Ethical Code addresses informed consent across all potential situations (research, assessment, therapy) and how this consent applies to minors with adult legal status (emancipated minors, mature minors). Standard 3.01(b) now addresses that consent–assent to participation also consider the child's *best interest,* which includes informed knowledge of experimental procedures; experimental nature of intervention; risks and benefits of experimental and control group; and how children will be assigned to each condition. Information must be provided in language that can be understood by the child. Standard 8.02 deals with issues of informed consent applicable to research specifically and covers all aspects of research including community intervention programs.
   b. Contemporary Issues in Assent and Consent
      Researchers evaluating how investigators determine "competence" to provide informed consent among participants revealed no consistent definition for competence across studies due to a wide variety of perspectives on how competence was approached (e.g., legal [age based] vs. conceptual approach [problem solving]). Other issues included whether children understand the concept of *voluntariness* (that they have a right to refuse), and the need to consider competence as fluid rather than static, especially in longer term research or treatment programs. Fisher (2004) suggests a hierarchical decision-making paradigm that includes input from all concerned parties, including research review board, parent, and child.
2. **Research Methods in Child Psychopathology**
   The three primary models of quantitative research were discussed, including, *descriptive research, correlational research,* and *experimental research.*

a. *Descriptive research methods* (survey, case study, naturalistic observation) can provide an impression of the extent and nature of an existing variable (attitude, behavior) in a rather efficient way. This method is particularly well suited for gathering information about the frequency of behavior(s) in a given population, measures of central tendency (mean, median, mode), and the general distribution of the sample.

b. *Correlational research methods* are well suited to researchers who are interested in determining how existing variables relate to other existing variables. Results determine the nature (positive or negative) and strength of the relationship between the variables.

c. *The experimental method* is the gold standard of research methods which allows the researcher to manipulate the variables under controlled conditions to determine whether the independent variable causes a change in the dependent variable and thereby either confirming or rejecting the research hypothesis. This method relies on rigorous controls such as random assignment to control and experimental groups. Quasi-experimental designs may use a wait-list control to avoid ethical conflicts of withholding treatment from a control group.

d. Other research forms particularly well suited to a study of child psychopathology include *longitudinal research, epidemiological research* (incidence or prevalence), and *ABAB or single subject reversal designs*. The potential contribution of **qualitative research** to studies of child psychopathology was also addressed. The chapter concluded with a discussion of the particular challenges that researchers face when conducting applied developmental research in areas of child advocacy.

Consolidate and Communicate

1. The importance of knowing your state laws cannot be overemphasized. Answer the following questions about your home state or the state that your current academic institution is in.

a. What is the age of majority in this state?

b. Does the state have a statue relating to emancipated minors, and if so, what is the age for granting someone emancipated minor status?

c. If parents are divorced, or in litigation, who according to state law, is the legal guardian?

d. In cases or suspected child abuse or neglect, how does the state mandate the duty to report? What is the reported time-line between the alleged and reported abuse? What are the fines and penalties levied for failure to report?

2. Reread the *Case in Point* concerning the psychologist who is providing therapy for the 15-year-old girl. What are the ethical dilemmas that exist for this psychologist? Given the case information, which of the five general guidelines are important for the psychologist to consider in order to solve the dilemma? Who is the client and how does that impact the decision-making process?

3. Recall the following study from our discussion of the experimental method: A researcher wants to test the hypothesis that playing aggressive action video games will increase a child's tendencies to interpret ambiguous situations in a more hostile and aggressive way.
   Subjects: 80 boys (8–10 years of age)
   Experimental Groups: Random assignment to one of three groups:
   a. Aggressive Video Action Game (AVAG);
   b. Nonaggressive Video Action Game (NAVAG), and
   c. Control Condition (computer solitaire card game).

Experimental Design
Precondition: (Pretest)
Each child is asked to make up a story to describe what is happening in five pictures that portray children in ambiguous social interactions (Picture Set #A).
Experimental Condition: (15-minute session)
a. AVAG
b. NAVAG
c. Control Condition
Postcondition: Posttest
Each child is asked to make up a story to describe what is happening in five pictures that portray children in ambiguous social interactions (Picture Set #B).
Long-Term Follow-up (2 weeks poststudy)
Each child is asked to make up a story to describe what is happening in five pictures that portray children in ambiguous social interactions (Picture Set #A).
You are on the Research with Human Subjects Committee at Kid University and have just received the study proposal for the research program outlined above. Given the APA ethical guidelines for research with children, describe how you would request that the child's *best interest* be protected in the above study. How would you deal with the issues of child assent and informed consent? Do you see any possible ethical violations that might exist in the study as outlined? What are they and how could you correct for them?

4. Do girls who are encouraged to play with more masculine toys develop more independent skills in later life? How would a researcher approach the above research question using the following research methods:
   a. Descriptive Research
   b. Correlational Research
   c. Experimental Method
   d. Qualitative Research Methods

Chapter Review Questions

1. Which of the following is NOT one of the five general principles (APA, 2002)?
   a. Beneficence and Nonmaleficence
   b. Integrity
   c. Liberty
   d. Justice
2. The majority of mental health laws and statutes fall within the parameters of:
   a. state law
   b. federal law
   c. criminal law
   d. civil law
3. Surveys conducted to determine the most common areas of ethical difficulties among psychologists have found that the largest number of ethical challenges are reported in which of the following areas?
   a. confidentiality
   b. dual or conflicted relationships
   c. sexual relationships with clients
   d. fees and fee collecting

4. Which of the following statements is FALSE concerning an emancipated minor?
   a. can achieve adult status if they can prove that they are enrolled full time at an academic institution
   b. achieve adult status if they are in the armed services
   c. can achieve adult status if they are financially self-supportive
   d. can achieve adult status upon proof of marriage

5. When asked if they would like to stop participating in a study, of 151 children, only 7 actually stopped participating. However, when the researchers added the comments, "[A]nd I won't be angry if you stop," how many of the children quit under this expanded condition?
   a. none
   b. 24
   c. 5
   d. 14

6. The authors used the results of this study to support the concept of children's lack of understanding of:
   a. fluid competence
   b. traits versus contexts
   c. voluntariness
   d. legal versus psychological definitions

7. John is studying the impact of age on child comprehension of time. To this end, he selects younger children (under 10 years of age) and older children (11 years and older). In this situation, age is a _____ variable.
   a. contiguous
   b. categorical
   c. contextual
   d. continuous

8. A researcher is studying whether allowing pets into a residential treatment center can improve outcomes for children with behavioral problems. There are 10 children in the residential program. Half have pets and are allowed to let these pets stay with them during the course of their treatment. Two months later, all five of the children with pets are released from treatment due to a significant improvement in their behaviors. All five children without pets are recommended for further treatment. When interviewed by the local news station, the researcher states emphatically that pet therapy was 100% effective in improved behavior in all children who had pets in the program. What is wrong with this statement?
   a. It was only 50% effective because only half the children had pets.
   b. The researcher did not randomly select the dogs.
   c. Pet therapy is not a legitimate therapeutic approach.
   d. The relationship between pets and improved behavior was positive but not causative.

9. The percentage expectancy that one might be diagnosed with a disorder over one's lifespan is called:
   a. prevalence rate
   b. incidence rate
   c. life-time prevalence rate
   d. life-time incidence rate

10. I am interested in knowing whether the time of day spent studying is more important than the actually number of hours spent studying. To this end, I have three experimental groups, all studying for 4 hours but at different times throughout the day (morning, afternoon, evening). My sample of university students is randomly assigned to one of three groups

and they are all provided with materials to study for a test. In this study, the independent variable is:

a. hours studied
b. material studied
c. time of day studied
d. none, this is not an example of the experimental method

Glossary of New Terms

beneficence and nonmaleficence
fidelity and responsibility
integrity
justice
respect for rights and dignity
criminal law
civil law
statutes
case law
malpractice suits
ethical dilemmas
confidentiality
dual or conflicted relationships
consent and assent
emancipated minors
mature minor
competence
voluntariness
hypothesis
scientific method
standardized procedures
operational definitions
confounding variables
extraneous variables
personal biases
belief perseverance
confirmation bias
observer bias
expectancy bias
Pygmalion effect
self-fulfilling prophecy
participant bias
placebo bias
Hawthorne effect
demand characteristics
social desirability
population
sample
representative sample
variable

independent variable (IV)
dependent variable (DV)
descriptive research
case study
naturalistic observation
descriptive statistics
measures of central tendency (mean, median, mode)
correlational research
continuous and categorical variables
correlational coefficient
positive correlation
negative correlation
zero order correlation
Pearson's r
internal and external validity
epidemiological studies
incidence, prevalence, life time prevalence
experimental method
situational variables
task variables
instructional variables
between-subject design
within-subject design
ABA or ABAB reversal design
null hypothesis
alternate hypothesis
inferential statistics
confidence levels
alpha level
ecological validity
analogue versus community based
random assignment
matched control group
wait-list control group
well established treatments
probably efficacious treatments
longitudinal
cross sectional
accelerated longitudinal
quasi-experimental design
single-subject experiment
longitudinal method
attrition
cohort effects
qualitative research
accelerated longitudinal design
quantitative and qualitative research

Answers to Multiple Choice Questions:
1. c; 2. d; 3. a; 4. a; 5. d; 6. c; 7.b; 8. d; 9. c; 10. c.

5

Issues in Diagnosis, Assessment, and Treatment

Chapter 5 At-A-Glance

Issues in Clinical Decision Making
  Goals of Diagnosis and Assessment: Case Formulation

The Nature of the Problem: Diagnosis and Problem Identification
  Issues in Diagnosis: Systems of Classification
    Categorical Classification: The *DSM*
    Empirical Classification or Dimensional Classification
    Categorical Versus Dimensional Classification: A Summation

The Nature of the Problem: Assessment and Problem Evaluation
  Issues in Child Assessment: Ethical Issues
    Informed Consent and Assent
    Test Security, Scoring, Interpretation, and Release of Test Data
  The Assessment Process and Methods of Assessment
    Goals of Assessment: Evidence-Based Assessments
    Assessment Methods
    Trends in the Assessment of Personality and Psychopathology

The Nature of the Problem: Intervention and Problem Treatment
  Issues in Child Treatment and Intervention
    Issues of Effectiveness and Specificity
    Developmental Issues in Treatment and Intervention
    Goals of Treatment: Evidence-Based Treatments

CHAPTER PREVIEW

Despite controversy concerning how childhood disorders should be classified or conceptualized, it is generally agreed that terms such as *assessment* and *diagnosis* should be thought of as a *process* rather than a specific outcome. In this chapter, issues and trends are discussed as they relate to the *diagnosis* (classification), *assessment* (investigation), and *treatment* of childhood disorders. The major goals of diagnosis and assessment are to develop a case formulation based on the definition of the problem (classification), the evaluation of the problem (assessment), and ultimately plan the course of treatment based on the diagnosis and assessment. Case formulation is an on-going and fluid process where assessments serve to refine the diagnosis and guide the development of the treatment plan.

A. Diagnosis and Problem Identification (Classification)

There are two major systems of classification that clinicians can use for diagnostic purposes: the *categorical system* and the *dimensional system*. Although the categorical system has been widely adopted in North America for the diagnosis of adult disorders, there is considerable controversy as to whether this system or the dimensional system best meets the diagnostic needs of children who demonstrate behavioral, social, or emotional problems.

1. Categorical Classification: *DSM–IV–TR* (2000)

Although the American Psychiatric Association (APA) included only two childhood disorders in its initial version of the *DSM* (*Diagnostic and Statistical Manual of Mental Disorders*: *DSM–I*, 1952), the current version (*DSM–IV–TR*, 2000) includes more than 20 disorders listed under *Disorders Usually First Diagnosed in Infancy, Childhood, or Adolescence*. Despite the increased emphasis on childhood disorders and the benefits of this classification system (wide acceptance and communication ease), there have been many criticisms of this system's portability for the diagnosis of childhood disorders (lack of developmental focus and mutual exclusivity versus comorbidity of disorders).

2. Empirical Classification Systems

The empirical or dimensional system lends itself more readily to a discussion of problem behaviors as symptoms that cluster along a continuum, such as externalizing and internalizing behaviors. Developmentally, this system affords the benefit of considering the extent to which behaviors deviate from the norm and provides ease of access to multirater perspectives regarding the behaviors. Limitations are evident in potential informant bias (attributions and perspectives) and susceptibility of informants to outside influences.

B. Assessment and Problem Evaluation

1. Ethical Issues

Given the child's age, obtaining informed consent for assessment will include obtaining consent from the child's parent or guardian; however, it will also include the need to obtain a child's *assent* (willingness) to participate in the assessment process. Ethical issues are discussed as they relate to consent, test security, and the release of test data.

2. Goals of Assessment

Recent emphasis on *evidence-based assessments* has called for a paradigm shift from solely evaluating the reliability or validity of assessment instruments to increased focus on the *clinical utility* of the assessment process or the ability to link assessment to intervention and treatment outcomes. Using a three-stage model of case formulation, the goals of assessment are discussed as they relate to *problem identification, problem interpretation, and treatment formulation*. Methods of assessment that may be valuable in obtaining information at each stage are also discussed.

3. Assessment Methods

Initial methods of data gathering can include *interviews* (*unstructured, semistructured, structured*) and *direct observation* (*narrative, event recording, interval recording*). The utility of the *functional behavioral assessment (FBA)* will be discussed as it relates to direct observation. The use of multirater scales, such as behavioral rating scales, is discussed and three of the most commonly used scales are introduced. Trends in the types of assessments used by clinicians over the years are discussed, and some of the more popular instruments—developed specifically for use with children and adolescents—are briefly reviewed.

C. Intervention and Treatment

1. Issues of Effectiveness and Specificity

This section addresses whether treatment is generally effective and whether some specific treatments are better suited to specific types of problems.

2. Developmental Issues

Several concerns have been raised regarding the degree to which treatment programs are developmentally appropriate. Several developmental considerations are presented for clinicians to consider in treatment planning and for researchers to factor into future research programs. Guidelines provided for how to better match treatment programs to developmental level and clinical needs.

3. Goals for Evidence-Based Treatments

The need for increased emphasis on evidence-based treatment programs and programs that are community rather than laboratory based is also addressed.

Issues in Clinical Decision Making

Case in Point

Ericka was 8½ years of age when she came to A Child's Place, a clinic providing assessment and intervention for children and youth with serious behavioral and emotional problems. In many ways, Ericka was a walking contradiction. When she came through the door, she was hanging onto her grandmother's arm, as if it were a lifeline. Her gait was awkward, her voice whiney, and her articulation was poor. Within minutes, she dropped her grandmother's arm and ran over to the toy section, initially choosing a stuffed animal but quickly abandoning it in favor of a LEGO set. Ericka became totally absorbed playing with the LEGOS and ignored everything else, including her grandmother's request to put the LEGOS away and meet the therapist. Eventually, with encouragement and praise, Ericka joined her grandmother and the therapist. Ericka's interactions with the adults, her immaturity, and drawings were all suggestive of a child several years younger (more typical of a toddler 2 or 3 years of age). When executing her drawings, Ericka held the crayon with her entire fist, not having developed the more typical tripod grip for her age. Her drawing of a person was very primitive and consisted of a circle for a head, two eyes, and a mouth (smiley face) with the arms extending out from the head.

Formal assessment was attempted (*Wechsler Intelligence Scale for Children: WISC–IV*; *Academic Functioning*); however, Ericka became increasing distressed, uncooperative, and distracted when she did not know the answers. In response to many items, Ericka just kept repeating: "boring, boring" in a sing-song refrain. Even if she did know the answers, she often refused to respond on the first attempt. When she did respond, her answers were very concrete (when asked to describe a clock, she pointed to one on the wall), or tangential and random (when asked to describe a cow, Ericka talked about her visit to the farm and picking corn).

At one point, Ericka called the therapist "Stupid!" and on another occasion a "no-brain head!" When her pencil fell on the floor, Ericka crawled under the table and refused to come out, saying, *"Catch me if you can…I'm the gingerbread man!"* Her attempts to control, manipulate, and test the limits increased in proportion to her frustration and lack of success.

> Although the formal assessment results were of questionable validity, her Full-Scale IQ was in the Borderline Range (range 73 to 83) with academic functioning at a beginning Kindergarten level. Ericka's grandmother provided the therapist with significant information about the family history and completed several questionnaires and behavioral-rating scales.

In the above *Case in Point,* the therapist must meet the challenge of answering a number of very important questions:

1. What are the primary clinical characteristics that best describe Ericka's problems?
2. What is the best way to obtain information and conduct an in-depth evaluation of the problem?
3. What are the most important, relevant, and appropriate interventions for Ericka, given the nature of her problem, her developmental age, and her level of cognitive functioning?

The three questions (Kronenberger & Meyer, 2001) provide a framework for clinical decision making regarding critical issues in the diagnosis, assessment, and treatment of childhood disorders. As was discussed to some extent previously in chapters 2 and 4, the theoretical perspective of the clinician will undoubtedly influence how each of the questions is addressed. For example, a biological psychologist would be curious about whether Ericka's family history is positive for psychopathology due to increasing evidence of the genetic risk of transmission of some disorders. A family systems therapist would be very interested in the family dynamics and especially why the grandmother has custody of Ericka. A behaviorist would be very interested in uncovering the factors that serve to maintain Ericka's controlling behaviors, while a cognitive psychologist would be concerned about how her immaturities and concrete thinking may undermine her ability to adapt and cope with stressors in her environment. Despite these differences, all clinicians would be very interested in probing the nature of individual and environmental factors that influence Ericka's emotional and behavioral problems, for better or worse.

Goals of Diagnosis and Assessment: Case Formulation

The assessment of mental functioning in childhood can have several key goals. According to the Surgeon General's Report on Children and Mental Health (2000), one of the major goals of child **assessment** should be to discern unique functional characteristics of the individual child and to diagnose signs and symptom presentations that are suggestive of specific mental disorders. Within this framework, the purpose of **diagnosis** is to classify the problem within the context of other known behavioral clusters or disorders to draw on clinical knowledge regarding potential etiology, course, and treatment alternatives. A primary goal of the assessment process is to develop a **case formulation** (or **hypothesis**) concerning the underlying influences that **precipitate** (cause) and **maintain** the maladaptive behavior, including the impact of environmental influences such as family, school, and community. A case formulation will assist in developing a better understanding of:

1. The nature of the problem;
2. How the behavior came to be (*precipitating factors*); and,
3. Why the behavior is continuing (*maintaining factors*).

Case formulation is a particularly good approach to use within a developmental psychopathology framework (Shirk & Russell, 1996) because it focuses on *underlying processes* that are at work on an internal (child characteristics) and external (environmental factors) basis and can be adapted as these dynamics change over the course of time. In order to develop an appropriate case formulation, however, there will be several questions that should be addressed, including:

- *What is the nature and extent of the problem?* and
- *If there are multiple problems, which problem is the most important to consider in the treatment plan?*

Case in Point

Arnold and Tommy both present with high levels of anxiety. Using a case formulation approach, however, the clinician discovers that the developmental pathway leading to the manifestation of the disorder is vastly different for each boy (*equifinality*). Arnold, who was initially a very outgoing child, has developed many symptoms of anxiety and depression resulting from a history of child abuse that began approximately 3 years ago. On the other hand, Tommy has always been a very timid and fearful child. As a toddler, he was described as having a very wary temperament, was fearful of strangers, and rarely ventured outside of his back yard. Although both boys are anxious, given the differences in the *precipitating causes*, it is most likely that differential treatment plans would be recommended.

Wilmshurst (2003) presents a three-stage model of case formulation that can provide a useful organizational framework for a discussion of diagnosis and assessment. The three stages of case formulation include:

1. Problem identification, clarification, and classification;
2. Problem interpretation and understanding through problem evaluation; and
3. Treatment formulation (pp. 10–13).

Important Distinction

The terms **assessment** and **diagnosis** can be used to refer to an *on-going process* of investigation or the *outcome* of the investigation. For example, when a clinician refers to an **assessment**, the reference might be to:

1. *assessment as a process* of gathering information, hypothesis testing, and problem-solving required to develop a *case formulation* (a statement about the nature of the problem and the conditions that precipitate and maintain the disorder); or
2. *assessment as the methods, instruments used* (structured or unstructured interviews, psychometric evaluation or personality inventories, etc.) to obtain the information or *outcome/results*.

Similarly, the term **diagnosis** can be used to refer to:

1. *diagnosis as a process* of data gathering and hypothesis generating that refines our understanding of the nature of a given disorder, and allows us to rule out possibilities that do not apply (*differential diagnosis*); or
2. *diagnosis as the outcome* of the clinical decision-making process that results in the classification/categorization of the disorder within an organizational framework (e.g., mood disorder, anxiety) that provides access to information regarding potential etiology, prognosis, and treatment alternatives.

The Nature of the Problem: Diagnosis and Problem Identification

In Stage one of the case formulation model presented, the goal is to define the problem and determine the nature of the problem. At this stage, the clinician will formulate a **provisional diagnosis** or hypothesis concerning the main clinical features of the underlying problem. It is important to understand that considerable hypothesis testing may be required and that often Step 1 will be reinitiated if Step 2 rules out an initial impression. For example, in the *Case in Point,* Ericka's therapist may have initially thought that Ericka's low level of cognitive functioning might be a precipitating cause for her behaviors; however, after obtaining a case history, information about severe abuse and neglect in the formative years may result in a change in hypothesis. Could Ericka's behaviors signal symptoms of *Post Traumatic Stress Disorder (PTSD)?* Further assessment (Step 2) would be needed in order to confirm or rule out this potential diagnosis. The therapist might also want to rule out *Attention Deficit Hyperactivity Disorder (ADHD)*, in this case make a **differential diagnosis** between these two disorders, or to determine if there are any other **comorbid** (cooccurring) disorders. If the therapist learns that the mother's abusive behaviors were due to drug addiction and a diagnosis of bipolar disorder, then she may want to look for any symptoms of aggressive and erratic behaviors that might indicate the possibility that Ericka is also at risk for bipolar disorder.

Mash and Wolfe (2002) suggest three goals of assessment: *diagnosis, prognosis,* and *treatment planning.* Although few clinicians would disagree with these goals, there can be wide variation among theorists and clinicians as to how each of the goals is to be conceptualized. In order to address issues relevant to all three areas, the chapter will focus on current issues and trends in areas of *diagnosis* (how to categorize or classify childhood disorders), *assessment* (what should be assessed and how assessment should be conducted), and *treatment* (what interventions are most appropriate given the child's problem and developmental level).

Clinician as Expert

Contrary to our idealistic portrait of the *all-knowing clinician,* research has shown that clinical judgments can actually reflect underlying personal biases towards such areas as gender, socioeconomic status, race, and age (Baker & Bell, 1999; Von Bergen, Soper, Rosenthal, Cox, & Fullerton, 1999). In addition, clinicians can disagree with respect to patient diagnosis. Although manuals such as the *DSM* provide lists of symptom criteria, clinicians are required to interpret the nature and extent to which these symptoms exist and whether their existence results in "abnormal" versus "normal" behavior. Even mechanisms that can be used to assist decision making, such as the 4Ds discussed in chapter 2 *(deviance, dysfunction, distress, danger),* are themselves somewhat subjective.

Issues in Diagnosis: Systems of Classification

Some of the major issues that are relevant to a discussion of the diagnosis of child disorders include addressing the different types of classification systems that are available for evaluating childhood psychopathology and the appropriateness of different systems of classification as they apply to child psychopathology. There are two primary diagnostic systems that are currently used to classify child disorders in North America: the **categorical system** used by the *Diagnostic and Statistical Manual of Mental Disorders* (*DSM–IV–TR*, APA, 2000); and the **empirical or dimensional system** used by such instruments as the *Achenbach System of Empirically Based Assessment* (*ASEBA;* Achenbach & Rescorla, 2001).

Although most clinicians would agree that a major goal of child assessment is to determine the nature of the child's presenting behavior relative to the realm of adaptive or maladaptive behaviors, the way that the behavior is classified may vary depending on the classification system used. Although the fundamental goal of these classification systems is to provide an overall organizational framework for understanding disorders, the systems differ in terms of:

1. How the systems were developed;
2. How the disorders are conceptualized; and
3. The methods used by each system to determine how a disorder is classified.

A point worth noting at this juncture, however, is that classification of childhood disorders often involves yet another classification system for purposes of determining eligibility for special education services. The educational classification system uses many of the same disorder categories (e.g., learning disability, mental retardation, emotional disturbance) found in the *DSM* and dimensional system; however, the goal of the classification system under the *Individuals with Disabilities Education Improvement Act* (IDEA, 2004) is to determine whether the disorders impact on educational goals and whether a child with disabilities will require special education and related services in order to receive an appropriate education. We will talk more about the differences between IDEA categories and clinical categories as each of the different disorders is introduced and discussed throughout this text.

Categorical Classification: The *DSM*

Historical background and theoretical orientation.   In North America, the most common classification system is the **Diagnostic and Statistical Manual of Mental Disorders** (*DSM–IV–TR*, APA, 2000) developed by the American Psychiatric Association. The *DSM–IV–TR* is the most recent revision (APA, 2000) and updates the original *DSM–IV* (1994). The letters *TR* in the most recent version stand for *text revision* to acknowledge the addition of information from more recent empirical investigations that were added, while retaining the original categories of classification.

The *DSM* was originally published in 1952. Initially, the *DSM–I* (1952) was strongly influenced by the theoretical underpinnings of Adolf Meyer's psychobiological approach. However, by the third revision (*DSM–III*, 1980), the goal of neutralizing classification criteria was evident in the introduction of the multiaxial approach that required clinicians to evaluate a client's presenting problem on each of five axes (see Table 5.1 for indicators of the five axes).

A conscientious effort was made to link criteria to empirical rather than theoretical foundations. Clinicians use the *DSM* to make diagnoses based on clinical evaluations of symptom presentations relative to required criteria developed as a result of field trials. The *DSM* criteria were developed to aid in promoting clarity of communication and uniformity of diagnoses among mental health professionals; facilitate research, and serve as educational tools for teaching students of psychopathology.

Memory Bank

The *categorical* approach adopted by the *DSM* classifies a disorder as present or absent (mutually exclusive) based on a decision as to whether the minimal number of symptoms (criteria) are evident to warrant a given diagnosis.

Table 5.1 *DSM–IV–TR* Multiaxial Assessment

Axis Number	Title	Description
Axis I	Clinical Disorders Other Focus of Attention	Name of the Disorder(s); if more than one, principle disorder is named first
Axis II	Personality Disorder(s) Mental Retardation	Life-long disorders; if more than one, principal diagnosis, or reason for visit should be indicated
Axis III	General Medical Conditions	Name medical conditions that may be relevant to understanding of disorder or treatment, e.g., a person may have an adjustment disorder with depressed mood or depression on Axis I, that is the direct result of a medical diagnosis of life threatening illness.
Axis IV	Psychosocial and Environment Problems	Environmental conditions evident that may impact the diagnosis, treatment, and prognosis are reported here. Examples include: primary support group (family problems, divorce, separation), social support (loss of friend, no friends), educational problems (school problems or lack of education), occupational problems (job loss, job stress), housing problems (safety, security), economic problems (poverty), problems with access to health care (no transportation), legal problems (incarceration, probation), other (natural disaster).
Axis V	Global Assessment of Functioning (GAF)	Clinician completes the GAF Scale. Score ranges from 0 (Inability to meet minimal standards) to 100 (Superior functioning). Scale is comprised of two components (symptom severity and functioning level on job, socially or in school) rated at 10-point intervals. Often the GAF level is reported at intake and at discharge.

Source: DSM–IV–TR, APA (2000).

Over time, increased knowledge of disorders and insight from empirical investigations have altered how a number of disorders have been conceptualized in different versions of the *DSM*. Nowhere is this more evident then in the area of childhood disorders. Recall that developmental psychopathology is a relatively new field of clinical psychology. At its inception, the *DSM* (*DSM–I*) considered only two childhood disorders: *Adjustment Reaction and Childhood Schizophrenia* (APA,1952). The latest revision (*DSM–IV–TR*) contains more than 20 disorders under the category of **Disorders Usually first Diagnosed in Infancy, Childhood, or Adolescence.** This particular section of the *DSM* contains 10 subcategories, including:

1. Mental retardation
2. Learning disorders
3. Motor skills disorder
4. Communication disorders
5. Pervasive developmental disorders,
6. Attention deficit and disruptive behavior disorders
7. Feeding and eating disorders of Infancy or early childhood
8. Tic disorders
9. Elimination disorders, and
10. Other disorders of infancy, childhood, or adolescence (separation anxiety disorder, selective mutism, reactive attachment disorder, stereotypic movement disorder, and disorders NOS [or not otherwise specified]).

In addition, the *DSM* has updated descriptions of many other disorders throughout the manual to include specific culture, age, and gender features to indicate how these disorders manifest in childhood or adolescence (e.g., mood disorders, anxiety disorders, panic and post traumatic stress disorder, eating disorders, sleep disorders, etc.).

Benefits of the categorical system (*DSM*) for use with child and adolescent disorders. Although the *DSM* does not operationally define mental disorders or comment on specific assessment procedures, there are a number of structured and semistructure interviews and rating scales that have been developed modeled on *DSM* criteria. The instruments are available in Table 5.2.

Some benefits of using the *DSM* classification system include:

- Wide usage across North America;
- Facilitates communication with other professionals around issues of diagnosis and treatment;
- A common system of classification can assist continuity of research efforts;
- Mulitaxial structure eases documentation of primary and secondary diagnoses, medical complications, psychosocial status (risks and protective factors), and global assessment of functioning.

The latest version (*DSM–IV-TR*) also represents a substantial improvement in documenting specific disorder features that recognize the influence of culture, age, and gender on the nature of symptom presentation. Finally, the manual provides extensive information on the nature of the disorder (prevalence, familial patterns), its course, and helpful guidelines for making differential diagnoses. The majority of insurance companies rely on *DSM* classification to determine the nature and course of treatment allowed under various policy claims.

Table 5.2 Diagnostic Interview Schedules and Inventories

Structured/Semi Structured Interviews:	Ages	Child Version	Adult Version
Anxiety Disorders Interview Schedule for DSM–IV: ADIS for DSM–IV: C/P (Silverman & Albano, 1996; Silverman, Saavedra, & Pina, 2001).	7–16 years	Yes	Yes
Diagnostic Interview Schedule for Children Version IV (NIMH DISC–IV; Shafer, Fisher, Lucas, Dulcan, & Schwab-Stone, 2000).	9–17 years	Yes	Yes
Schedule for Affective Disorders and Schizophrenia for School-Age Children (K–SADS; Ambrosini, 2000).	6–18 years	Yes	Yes
Early Childhood Inventory-4 norms manual (Gadow & Sprafkin, 1998c).	3–6 years	No	Parent and Teacher
The Children's Symptom Inventory 4 (CSI–4; Gadow & Sprafkin, 1998b).	5–12 years	No	Parent and Teacher
Adolescent Symptom Inventory–4 (Gadow & Sprafkin, 1998a).	11–19 years	No	Parent and Teacher
Youth's Inventory–4 (Gadow & Sprafkin, 1999).	11–19 years	Yes	No
Rating Scales with DSM–IV Scales			
Achenbach System of Empirically Based Assessment (ASEBA; 2001)		No	
Child Behavior Checklist/Teacher Report Form	1-1/2–5 6–18	No	Parent/Teacher
Youth Self-Report	11–18	Yes	
Conners' Rating Scales (Conners, 1997)			
Conners' Parent and Teacher Rating Scales	3–17 years	No	Parent/Teacher
Conners-Wells Adolescent Self-Report	12–17 years	Yes	No

Limitations of the categorical approach (*DSM*) for child and adolescent populations. The *DSM* cites several self-limiting features of a categorical approach that divides mental disorders into categories or types, based on sets of criteria of defining features. Issues of comorbidity are especially pertinent in cases of child and adolescent psychopathology where there are high rates of comorbidity (cooccurring disorders).

Important Distinction

The categorical system readily lends itself to *medical disorders* that have clear boundaries and remain mutually exclusive. However, *mental health disorders* often share symptoms (comorbidity), are not mutually exclusive (e.g., an individual can be diagnosed with both anxiety and depression), and have boundaries that are less clear and tend to overlap.

The *DSM* does not address limitations of the system relative to child or adolescent populations: however, there are four important issues that the *DSM* does not address that have particular significance for child and adolescent populations:

1. High rates of comorbidity of child disorders;
2. Developmental features of disorders;
3. Symptom severity and number of symptoms required as criteria for diagnoses at different developmental levels; and
4. Appropriateness of criteria for developmental populations that have been generated from field trials with primarily adult populations.

Degree of Severity...to a Degree

Although clinicians using the *DSM* categorical approach can refer to symptom severity by the use of *mild, moderate,* and *severe* qualifiers (depending on the number of symptoms matched), these ranges are only established once the minimum symptom criteria is met. That is to say, a disorder would be classified as mild, if and only if the child met the minimal criteria for the diagnosis.

Symptoms often manifest differently at different developmental levels (e.g., depression in preschoolers will look different than in school-aged children or adolescents). The *DSM* does not really address this problem other than recognizing that symptoms in childhood may differ from adulthood. The homogeneity of symptoms does not take into consideration the weight of some symptoms relative to others (e.g., in ADHD all symptoms are created equal). For example, a child may have five severe symptoms of a disorder that requires six symptoms for diagnosis, and thereby might be excluded from treatment. On the other hand, a child with six of the milder symptoms may qualify for treatment under that diagnostic category.

An attempt to adapt the categorical classification system for children and adolescents can be found in the **DSM–PC Child and Adolescent Version** (American Academy of Pediatrics, 1996), which was developed to assist primary care clinicians and is the collaborative project of the American Academy of Pediatrics (AAP) and American Psychiatric Association (APA). The classification system improves upon existing *DSM* criteria by adding possible symptom presentations at various developmental stages and levels of severity. Although this version of the *DSM* is far better suited to pediatric populations, diagnostic decision making still depends upon whether symptoms are present or absent. Information for child populations is often obtained from more than one respondent (e.g., parent, teacher, child).

Important Distinction

Achenbach (1995) suggests that the forced choice format of the *DSM* limits combining data from multiple informants, which can be an integral part of child assessment, and does not give due consideration to the informant's threshold for responding.

Studies have reported a significant amount of overlap among three of the most commonly occurring disorders, the disruptive behavior disorders (conduct disorder, oppositional defiant disorder), and attention deficit hyperactivity disorder (McConaughy & Achenbach, 1993; Wilmshurst, 2002). As such, many children would require multiple diagnoses. In addition, the categorical system also supports the premise that normal and abnormal behavior are two discrete entities, a framework which also poses problems for those who are more attuned to the continuity evident in a developmental psychopathology orientation. Based on the above limitations, some clinicians prefer to use a dimensional classification system that allows for evaluation of behavior patterns along a continuum ranging form adaptive to maladaptive functioning.

Science Talks

Bird, Gould, and Staghezza (1992) investigated the differential effects of multiple informants (parents and children) in their ratings of behaviors on the Diagnostic Interview Schedule for Children (DISC). When rating *externalizing behaviors* such as oppositional defiant disorder or attention deficit hyperactivity disorder, parents' predictions were more valid than youth self-ratings. However, when rating *internalizing* behaviors such as separation anxiety, overanxious disorder, and dysthymic disorder (depression), youth self-ratings were as good a predictor as those of their parents.

Empirical Classification or Dimensional Classification

Historical background and theoretical orientation. The **dimensional classification** system is sometimes referred to as the *empirical classification system*, since the system was derived from empirical evidence (statistical analysis of normal vs. clinical populations). The dimensional classification system provides a framework for discussing behaviors in terms of **symptom clusters, patterns, or syndromes** based on comparisons of those behaviors noted in clinical populations relative to normal populations. In this way, behaviors can be viewed on a continuum as they deviate further and further away from the normal range.

The system readily lends itself to obtaining information from multiple informants (parents, teachers, and children) who complete rating scales to indicate the extent to which a given behavior exists (e.g., often, seldom, never). Currently, several behavioral rating scales exist that have been derived through empirical methods (factor analysis).

The Achenbach System of Empirically-Based Assessment (ASEBA; Achenbach & Rescorla 2001). The ASEBA is a set of parallel rating scales that can be completed by parents (*Child Behavior Checklist* [*CBCL*], 2001, 6–18 yrs.), teachers (*Teacher Rating Form* [*TRF*], 2001), and youth between 11 and 18 years of age (*Youth Self-Report* [*YSR*], 2001). The ASEBA has been used widely as an assessment instrument and in clinical research. The current CBCL scales replace earlier versions of the scale (Achenbach, 1991) and are based on behavioral data obtained from almost

5,000 children from two subject samples: a **nonclinical sample** (children from across the United States, England, and Australia who had never been referred for behavioral/emotional concerns in the previous 12 months); and a **clinical sample** of children receiving mental health services from 20 outpatient and inpatient facilities. Based on the results of this investigation, norms for the scale were established for behavioral categories, clinical cutoff scores, and *T*-scores. In addition to the syndrome scales, it is also possible to obtain scores for three broad-band scales measuring overall *Internalizing, Externalizing,* and *Total Problems.*

The most recent revision of the ASEBA represents a departure from the previous versions of the scales with the addition of a series of *DSM*-oriented scales that allow information to be scored based on *DSM* criteria. This trend to incorporate *DSM*-oriented scales, as well as syndrome scales, is also evident in the most recent revision of the Conners scales (1998). Three of the more common behavioral rating scales will be reviewed when we discuss *Methods of Assessment* later in this chapter.

Memory Bank

Psychologists use norm-based measures that have derived scores based on the normal curve or the normal frequency distribution, A normal distribution is a hypothetical symmetrical distribution of scores (see Figure 5.1). Depending on the nature of your investigation, you might be interested in the distribution of **standard scores, T scores, or percentile ranks**. Intelligence test scores (and in some cases, standardized academic scores) are measured using standard scores that have a mean of 100 and a standard deviation of 15. These scores will be discussed at greater length in later chapters. The majority of clinical scales are expressed as measures of *T scores* that have a mean of 50 and a standard deviation of 10. Children who score above a *T* score of 70 on a clinical scale are said to be within the **clinical range** (equivalent to the 98th percentile) and considered to have serious problems in need of treatment. Children who score between 65 and 69 on the ASEBA or 1-1/2 standard deviations beyond the mean (93rd to 97th percentile) are in the **borderline clinical range**. Children in the borderline range would be considered **at-risk** for developing more serious problems (see Figure 5.1 for a graphic display).

Benefits of the dimensional classification system for use with child and adolescent populations. Factor analysis supports evidence that many behaviors can be represented along an *internalizing/externalizing continuum.* In other words, behaviors cluster around "acting out" or externalizing behaviors (disruptive behaviors such as aggression, delinquent or rule breaking behaviors, hyperactivity) or "acting in" as internalizing behaviors (anxiety, depression, somatic complaints, withdrawal).

Important Distinction

In the past, these two end points of the behavioral continuum have also been referred to as **undercontrolled** versus **overcontrolled** (Achenbach & Edelbrock, 1978) and as **behavior excess** (externalizing) or **behavior deficit** (internalizing).

Research has demonstrated high rates of comorbidity among the externalizing disorders (Spitzer, Davies, & Barkley, 1990; Biederman, Newcorn, & Sprich, 1991; McConaughy & Achenbach, 1993), as well as among the internalizing disorders, such as anxiety and depression

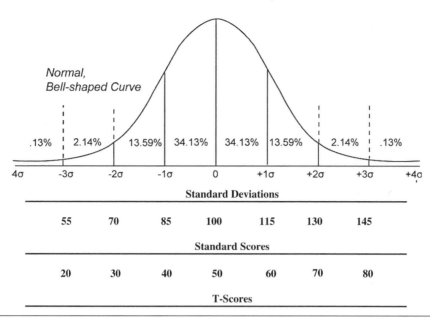

Figure 5.1 Percentage of cases under portions of the Normal Curve.

(Kovacs, Paulauskas, Gatsonis, & Richards, 1988; Zoccolillio, 1992; McConaughy & Skiba, 1993). More recently, investigators have found that some children demonstrate comorbid internalizing and externalizing problems (Angold, Costello, & Erkanli, 1999; McConaughy & Skiba, 1993; Wilmshurst, 2002). In one study of children with severe emotional disabilities (SED), Wilmshurst (2002) found that 74% of the children who tested in the clinical range for externalizing problems also demonstrated clinical levels for internalizing problems. Furthermore, 47% of the children who participated in the study demonstrated a comorbid cluster of four disorders, including *oppositional defiant disorder* (ODD), *attention deficit hyperactivity disorder* (ADHD), *conduct disorder* (CD), and *depression*. Other categories that have been used (primarily educational classification) to designate child problems include terms such as **emotional and behavioral disorders (EBD)** or **severe emotional disorders (SED).** However, many investigators have been critical of the usefulness of such broad categorical labels for youth, arguing instead that emphasis should be placed on determining subgroups of troubled youth within these populations and potentially matching these subgroups to specific treatment interventions and outcomes (Kershaw & Songua-Barke, 1998; Rosenblatt & Furlong, 1998; Walrath, Nicherson, Crowel, & Leaf, 1998).

Science Talks

Support for the need to better identify *subsets* of troubled youth was demonstrated in one study of youth with severe behavior problems and numerous other comoribid disorders. Results revealed that a small subset of the population who had elevated pretreatment levels for anxiety (anxiety plus conduct problems) actually became worse after treatment (anxiety levels were even more elevated) if they were assigned to the residential treatment instead of the home-based alternative (Wilmshurst, 2002).

The majority of rating scales used by child clinicians have been standardized on normative and clinical populations. These scales are relatively easy to use and score, and provide information on the reliability validity and standardization of the samples. Most of the rating scales can be scored by computer programs that generate graphic profiles and an interpretive report. Information provided by the majority of rating scales can include:

- a profile of individual responses
- the distribution of externalizing and internalizing behaviors, relative to the norm
- a quantitative analysis of the degree to which these behavior clusters or syndromes deviate from the norm
- whether the behavior is within the clinical, borderline, or normal range.

Having information about a profile of behaviors can assist clinicians to interpret whether behaviors focus in one specific area (e.g., conduct problems) or whether problems result from more complex and comorbid influences (e.g., depression and conduct problems, anxiety and conduct problems, etc.).

Limitations of the Dimensional Classification System for Use With Child and Adolescent Disorders
Informant characteristics. There are several issues regarding the use of rating scales in general. When asked to complete a rating scale, respondents are often asked to indicate the frequency that a behavior occurs (e.g., often, sometimes, never). However, ratings can be subject to outside influences as presented in the next *Case in Point.*

Although the benefit of including multiple informants has been recognized (Achenbach, Howell, McConaughy, & Stanger, 1995), problems in interpretation may be evident, especially when information is not consistent across raters. In their landmark investigation of 119 studies, Achenbach, McConaughy, and Howell (1987) found wide discrepancies in ratings of social, emotional, and behavioral disorders depending on who provided the information (parent, teacher, child); a finding that has been replicated several times since. According to Achenbach and colleagues (1987), variations in the informant ratings are likely attributed to the different contextual situations in which these informants have interacted with the child and hence provide different observations of behavior.

Case in Point

If you think about any rating scale or survey that you have completed in the past (e.g., a course evaluation or a survey about your television viewing habits), consider what circumstances might have influenced how you completed that form or responded to a telemarketer. For example, your *mental state* (happy, sad, angry) and your *life circumstances* (fight with a partner; just got fired from your job; just got promoted) can influence how you assign your ratings. One of the first concerns with rating scales is the reliability of the rater's perception, which is subject to outside influences.

In their comprehensive review of the literature concerning informant discrepancies, De Los Reyes and Kazdin (2005) suggest that although cross-situational factors might explain some of the variability in informant discrepancies, it is also important to consider:

1. The different perspectives and attributions that observers have about the child; and
2. The different perspective and attribution that the child has about himself or herself.

The authors highlight several ways that discrepant information can impact the assessment, classification, and treatment of childhood disorders. (Information presented follows the context from De Los Reyes and Kazdin, 2005.) The authors contend that what we know about prevalence rates for disorders, comorbidity, and correlates or risks varies widely between studies due to the nature of the informant. Furthermore, **treatment plans** are often compromised because of a lack of consensus among multiple informants regarding:

- the specific nature of the target problem (two thirds of the time) and
- failure to agree on a main treatment goal (one third of the time).

Ultimately the authors propose a theoretical framework, the **Attribution Bias Context Model (ABC Model)** to assist in the analysis and interpretation of information from discrepant respondents. The model is based on sociocognitive research and theory that relies heavily on theoretical assumptions inherent in the **actor–observer phenomenon.**

Memory Bank

The *actor–observer phenomenon* (Jones & Nisbett, 1972) describes a fundamental tendency in human nature to attribute negative behaviors in others to their personal nature (internal/dispositional) and to attribute our own negative behaviors to outside influences. For example, if someone cuts in line ahead of me, I attribute that to their internal characteristics (e.g., the person is a "jerk"). However, if I cut in line in the supermarket, I would attribute this behavior to external causes (e.g., "I need to get home fast to let the dogs out."). Subsequent investigations have noted that the actor–observer phenomenon occurs primarily in individualistic and competitive societies like those found in North America, compared to collective and cooperative societies, such as those found in Asia.

The ABC Model (De Los Reyes & Kazdin, 2005) suggests that discrepancies in **attributions** and **perspectives** of different informants in clinical settings may influence their perceptions of:

- the causes of behaviors,
- which behaviors should be the focus of treatment, and
- whether treatment is required.

Informants' attributions.   In keeping with the actor–observer phenomenon, the ABC model predicts that observers will attribute negative behaviors (e.g., aggression) to internal causes (child has conduct problem), while actors (in this case the child) will attribute negative behaviors to external causes (kids tease him so he hits back).

Informants' perspectives.   Consistent with their belief that the problem resides within the child, observers are more likely to retrieve memories of negative behaviors that support this perspective and see the behavior as needing treatment. Conversely, the child will retrieve memories consistent with his own perspective (teasing was the cause of the behavior) and consequently, he will not see the need for treatment. The authors also comment that children may underreport negative behaviors during a clinical assessment to either avoid treatment or present themselves to others in a more positive light.

Science Talks: What Influences Ratings

Achenbach, McConaughy, and Howell (1987) found that raters who come from similar settings tend to be more similar in their ratings of the same child (e.g., teacher vs. teacher ratings) than raters from different settings (e.g., parent vs. teacher ratings). Raters also tend to have more agreement in their ratings of younger children (6–11 years) compared to older children and for externalizing behaviors versus more covert internalizing behaviors (Offord, Boyle, & Racine, 1989). Gender also exerts an influence. Female adolescents tend to disclose more problems than their masculine peers (Stanger & Lewis, 1993), while parents and teachers rate males as having more behavior problems at all ages than their female peers. On the other hand, adolescent males—especially those who are rated high in emotional disturbance—rate themselves as having adequate social skills and few problem behaviors (Versi, 1995).

Syndrome scales and composite scales. In addition to rater reliability issues, Drotar, Stein, and Perrin (1995) caution that since the Composite Scales (Externalizing, Internalizing, and Total Problems) have much higher reliability (.89) than the individual subscale scores, that composite scale scores should be used to support diagnostic or treatment decisions.

Categorical Versus Dimensional Classification: A Summation

In summary, there are mixed benefits and limitations to the use of each of the classification systems. While the dimensional system seems particularly well suited to the study of developmental psychopathology, proponents of the *DSM* classification system call for increased rigor of classification in research on child treatment (Ollendick & King, 2004). Rather than engage in endless debate as to which is the superior system, Rubio-Stipec, Walker, and Murphy (2002) suggest adopting a system that recognizes the best of both worlds: using a dichotomous measure of whether or not a child meets diagnostic criteria (*DSM*) and using syndrome scales that can add to our knowledge of the dimensional characteristics. A comparison of the dimensional and categorical systems is summarized in Table 5.3.

The Nature of the Problem: Assessment and Problem Evaluation

Goal of the assessment process. Within the case formulation model discussed earlier (Wilmshurst, 2003), although assessment is an on-going process, at Stage 2 the emphasis is on problem evaluation to confirm or reject hypotheses or diagnoses suggested at Stage 1. Remember that Stage 1 and Stage 2 can reiterate a number of times with assessment results continually refining diagnostic impressions. Recall that the three steps in case formulation involve:

1. Problem identification, clarification, and classification;
2. Problem interpretation and understanding through problem evaluation; and
3. Treatment formulation (pp. 10–13).

At this stage of the case formulation process, the goal is to evaluate the problem to confirm or reject potential hypotheses and diagnoses. At a clinical level, both the diagnosis and the assessment/evaluation require an understanding of the nature and course of normal development and what the expectations are for a child at this stage of development.

Table 5.3 Comparison of Categorical and Dimensional Classification Systems

Categorical System (DSM)	Dimensional Classification System (ASEBA; BASC; Conners)
Classification and Conceptualization	**Classification and Conceptualization**
Data obtained	*Data Obtained*
Observation and interview (parent and child);	Multiple informants complete rating scales;
Structured and Semistructured Interviews (NIMH DISC–IV; K–SADS; CSI–4);	Profiles are generated based on ratings and level of severity relative to normal age-based expectations
Information compared to criteria required by DSM symptom lists	
Characteristics	*Characteristics*
Diagnostic categories as mutually exclusive;	Continuum of normal/abnormal; continuous
Disorders as distinct/discrete set of homogenous symptom clusters	Syndromes of cooccuring problems
Disorder either present or absent	Two Broad-Band behavioral dimensions:
Multiaxial approach	Externalizing and Internalizing
	Research-Based
	Statistical Model (Factor Analysis)
Judgment derived	*Judgment derived*
Qualitative analysis	Quantitative analysis
Strengths	**Strengths**
Wide spread usage among professionals in clinical practice and research:	Behaviors can be readily compared to peers at the same developmental level;
Can be required by insurance and clinical trials; requirement; clinical trials (research)	Lends itself to developmental continuum (degree of deviation from norm);
Multiaxial approach provides contextual information;	Degree of severity empirically determined
Availability of information on disorder characteristics and course;	Can statistically measure change resulting from clinical intervention (pre/post administration);
Facilitates communication	Use of multiple informants (parent/teachers)
	Quantitative rating system;
	Syndromes can be comorbid
Weaknesses	**Weaknesses**
Subjective judgment	Not universally accepted (e.g., insurance companies);
Dichotomous (yes or no decision)	Disparities ratings from multiple informants can be difficult to reconcile;
Mutually exclusivity difficult for populations with comorbid disorders (child/adolescent);	Self-ratings subject to bias, project good impression
Developmental presentations given little consideration;	Reliability and Validity issues
Reliability and Validity issues	

Recall and Rewind

As you will recall, the goal of the *assessment process* is to gather information to assist in developing a *case formulation* that will aid in better understanding of:

1. The nature of the problem;
2. How the behavior came to be (*precipitating factors*); and
3. Why the behavior is continuing (*maintaining factors*).

 RECURRENT THEMES In order to identify a problem area and evaluate the validity of the suspected diagnosis it is crucial that clinicians have a firm grasp of the first four of five important and recurring themes:

1. Normal development typically follows an orderly and predictable path.
2. Maladaptive behaviors represent deviations from the normal path.
3. Maladaptive behavior is represented by a continuum of severity.
4. Individual, interpersonal, contextual, and cultural factors influence deviations in development.

Furthermore, it is imperative that clinicians are consciously aware of any potential theoretical bias that may be inherent in shaping their case formulations from a particular theoretical influence (*Theme 5:* Mental health practitioners can draw on a multiplicity of theoretical perspectives to assist in understanding maladaptive behaviors).

As part of the evaluation process, it is also important to gain insight into relevant information about the child's developmental and medical history, family dynamics, and school environment. Major questions at this stage focus on evaluating the nature of the child's problem and pinpointing the problem in more specific terms.

Issues in Child Assessment: Ethical Issues

Informed Consent and Assent

In Section 9.03 of the Ethics Code (APA, 2002), guidelines for obtaining informed consent discussed in section 3.10 are elaborated as they apply specifically to issues of assessment. Ethically, psychologists must obtain informed consent for assessment in all but three conditions:

1. Testing that is mandated by law;
2. Testing that is routinely administered (education, job application); or
3. If the assessment is to determine decision making capacity (issues of competency).

Important Distinction: Assent vs. Consent

When assessment involves a child, even if the guardian provides consent to assessment, if the child does not provide **assent** by being unwilling to participate, then the psychologist would interpret this as the child not providing assent and discontinue the assessment attempt at that time.

Recall and Rewind

Informed consent is discussed in section 3.10 of the Ethics Code (APA, 2002). Part (b) of this section is of particular importance to those working with children because it addresses the psychologist's ethical obligations to obtain consent from those who are legally incapable of giving consent. Under these conditions, the psychologist must:

1. Provide an appropriate explanation;
2. Seek the individual's assent;
3. Consider the person's preferences and best interests; and
4. Obtain appropriate permission from a legally authorized person (http://www.apa.org/ethics/code2002.html).

For persons with questionable capacity to understand (which might be very likely in the case of younger children), psychologists must describe the nature and purpose of the assessment in language that is reasonably understandable. If an interpreter is necessary, every effort must be made to protect the confidentiality of assessment results and test security.

Test Security, Scoring, Interpretation, and Release of Test Data

Historically, there have been a number of controversial issues concerning what should be released and to whom. With the advent of computer scoring and computer-generated reports, there have been questions regarding who is responsible for interpretation and dissemination of test results. The term *test data* in this section of the Ethics Code refers to *all forms of subject responses*, including: *raw and scaled scores, individual responses to test items or stimuli,* and *even the psychologist's notes about the individual's behavior during the assessment.* When requested by the client/patient, the psychologist must release the test data to the client or others the client has requested that the test data be released to. However, the psychologist may withhold test data from release (provided it is not regulated by law) to protect a client/patient from harm, misuse, or misinterpretation.

Case in Point

A psychologist is conducting an assessment of an adolescent who is referred due to symptoms of anxiety, depression, and low scholastic performance. As part of the assessment battery, the psychologist administers the Thematic Apperception Test (TAT), a projective instrument that requires the teen to create a story for each of 20 ambiguous pictures presented. Responses to the TAT reveal a repetitive theme of fear and intimidation from her father and her concerns of disappointing him. As a result of the assessment, the psychologist is recommending therapy to improve the girl's sense of self and enhance her feelings of self-worth. The psychologist summarizes the findings of her assessment in a report and sits down with the parents to explain her results. Unsatisfied with the psychology assessment report, the father demands to see the *test data,* especially the stories that the teen generated to the TAT. **Question:** *Should the psychologist release the test data to the father, or should she withhold the TAT stories to protect the teen?*

Also under Section 9 are ethical standards cautioning against the use of obsolete tests and outdated test results in the clinical decision making process. Regardless of whether the assessment or components of the assessment are computer generated, or obtained through scoring and interpretation services (automated or otherwise), the psychologist is responsible for explaining these results to the client.

The Assessment Process and Methods of Assessment

Goals of Assessment: Evidence-Based Assessment

In this section we will look at a number of different assessment methods and instruments that are available to child clinicians. Until recently, the primary focus of empirical research about assessment instruments has traditionally investigated the **validity** and **reliability** of the assessment instruments. The **Mental Measurements Yearbook** (The Buros Institute of Mental Measurements) has provided more than 65 years of information, critical analyses, and reviews to consumers regarding assessment instruments that are commercially available to clinicians. Currently, the **Mental Measurements Yearbook Data Base** is a common electronic service available on the majority of university and college library Web sites. For example, when inputting the ASEBA (Achenbach & Rescorla, 2001) into the database at Elon University, a 7-page review was retrieved that provided information about the system (*description*), development and technical properties (*validity and reliability data*), commentary (*critical review*), and overall summary. The overall review suggested that "[t]he [ASEBA] scales are supported by a solid research base and are technically sound, both from test development and psychometric perspectives" (Elon University online library database, Mental Measurements Yearbook, p. 3; retrieved August 25, 2007).

While establishing the reliability and validity of assessment instruments will always remain a priority, recently efforts have also stressed the importance of validating the **clinical utility** of assessment instruments. In other words, to what extent do assessment results inform clinical decision making regarding appropriate intervention and treatment strategies?

A note about evidence-based assessments.   In 2005, the *Journal of Clinical Child and Adolescent Psychology* devoted an entire volume (Volume 34(3)) to the topic of evidence-based assessment, approximately 8 years after a similar series of articles appeared on evidence-based treatments for children and youth (*Journal of Clinical Child Psychology*, 1998). In the lead paper, Mash and Hunsley (2005) suggest that although assessment methods are frequently evaluated regarding their reliability and validity as **psychometric instruments**, minimal attention has been directed towards evaluation of *the role of assessment* in intervention and treatment outcomes. The focus of this series of articles was to outline evidence-based assessment procedures that not only adhere to psychometric reliability and validity standards, but also evaluate instruments based on their clinical utility. The authors suggest one important aspect of **clinical utility** is to

> provide psychologists with the kinds of information that can be used in ways that will make a meaningful difference in relation to diagnostic accuracy, case formulation considerations and treatment outcomes. (p. 365)

The authors highlight six potential reasons for conducting assessments with children, including:

1. *Diagnosis* and case formulation,
2. *Screening* (identification of at-risk children),
3. *Prognosis* (prediction of course of disorder),
4. *Treatment* planning and design (target identified problems),
5. *Monitoring* of treatment (tracking symptom change), and
6. *Treatment evaluation* (pre/post assessment, consumer satisfaction). (p. 366)

There has been an increasing trend towards disorder-specific assessment, and less emphasis on a generic test battery. Obvious reasons for more specific assessment include cost and time effectiveness. However, Mash and Hunsley (2005) warn that at times it may be necessary to conceptualize *specificity as a process* whereby the clinician may need to begin at a more general level (e.g., nonspecific referrals) and gradually narrow down the focus over a series of assessment sessions. Also, as discussed earlier, some children may not meet criteria for a specific disorder but are nonetheless impaired enough in a number of areas of functioning to warrant treatment.

Throughout the remainder of the text, as each disorder is presented, specific information about evidence-based assessments and treatments will be introduced and discussed relative to each particular disorder. The remainder of this section will focus on more generic issues and instruments available for the assessment of problems and disorders in children and youth.

Assessment Methods

Clinicians have access to a number of prescribed assessment methods and instruments that can assist in gathering information in ways that are objective, reliable, and valid. The following discussion will provide a summary of some of the more common assessment methods developed for children and adolescents and the type of information that these assessment instruments provide.

Interviews.   The goal of the **clinical assessment interview** is to obtain information about the nature and extent of the child's problem. Information from the interview can guide the clinician in the selection of further types of assessment instruments that may be required and in the types of interventions or treatments that may be recommended. Children rarely self-refer, so clinical interviews may be initially conducted with a child's parents to obtain relevant information about medical and developmental history, as well as the parent's perception of the problem. Clinical interviews are also often conducted with a child's teachers to better understand the social or academic features of a child's difficulties from the teacher's perspective. In the initial stages of an assessment, the child is often engaged in an interview that serves as a **rapport-building** exercise to set the child at ease, and to provide information about what the child can expect to encounter during the assessment sessions, as well as obtain information about the child's perceptions of the problem.

The actual format of the clinical assessment interview can vary widely with respect to structure and can be **unstructured, semistructured, or structured**.

Unstructured interviews.   Clinicians may use an informal information gathering session in order to obtain greater insight into the general nature of the concerns and to get an initial impression of the nature and severity of the problem. It may be that a child's "problem" is a normal behavior that is anticipated at a given developmental stage (e.g., toddler who repeatedly says "no" to a parent's requests; a rebellious teenager), and that reassurance from the clinician is all that is required. However, parents might indicate other behaviors that may signal to the clinician that a more in-depth interview is required.

Semistructured interview.   Clinicians who use a semistructured type of interview have an agenda that they want to follow but also want to allow for flexibility within the interview process. The *Semistructured Clinical Interview for Children and Adolescents* (SCICA; McConaughy & Achenbach, 2001) is an example of a semistructured interview that actually provides a mechanism whereby ratings can be assigned to responses such that a profile can be constructed to reflect a range of responses within different behavioral categories (e.g., anxious/depressed, aggression behavior, family problems, etc.). The semistructured interview often contains a series of open-ended questions that explore different aspects of functioning. Sattler (2002) provides a variety of examples of interviews that would be appropriate for children of different ages, parents, and teachers. Some of the categories sampled on the semistructured interviews for children include questions relating to such topics as: school, home, interests, friends, fears/worries, and the child's perception of the problem. Parent-oriented questionnaires include topics relevant to family and sibling relationships, developmental history, and parent perception of the problem.

One specific type of semistructured interview called the **mental status exam** has traditionally been given in a hospital setting by a mental health practitioner or psychiatrist when questions are raised as to a given patient's mental capacity on intake. The exam covers such areas as awareness and orientation (*time and place*), attention span, judgment and insight, thought content and processes, memory, mood, and appearance (Robinson, 2000). A mental status exam might be conducted for a child who appears disoriented, dazed, or out of touch with his or her surroundings. Sattler (2002) provides an example of a mental status evaluation for an older child or adolescent that includes such topics as general orientation (time, place, and person), recent and remote memory, immediate memory, insight and judgment, reading, writing, spelling, and arithmetic calculation (p. 495).

Structured interviews.   Increased structure may be desirable for those who require information about specific symptoms and syndromes that might assist in making a diagnosis. Because these questions look to rule out competing disorders (*differential diagnosis*), questions may be of the yes/no variety. Examples of structured interviews were provided in the discussion of interviews that are modeled on *DSM*-relevant criteria. The interview schedules have versions available for parents and older children and are available in Table 5.2.

Observations.   As was discussed earlier, behaviors such as anxiety can appear similar in different individuals; however, the causes—or functions—of the behaviors can be very different. Yet, uncovering the underlying cause(s) of behavior can be very difficult, especially when working with children who may have limited verbal skills or insight regarding what drives their behaviors. Similar to the interview, observation can provide significant insight into problem behavior, and, like the interview, observations can range from unstructured anecdotal clinic notes regarding behaviors observed during an assessment to highly structured and detailed observations conducted in a specific setting. There are three different methods of observing and recording behaviors that can provide very different types of information. A summary of the types of responses recorded, the application, advantages, and disadvantages of each method is presented in Table 5.4.

Narrative.   Observations that are recorded on an *anecdotal basis* or through compiling a *running record* of events that occur surrounding a behavior fall within the category of **narrative responses**. One popular use of the narrative recording technique is the **functional behavioral assessment (FBA)**. A functional behavioral assessment is an approach that incorporates a variety of techniques and strategies to "identify biological, social, affective, and environmental factors that initiate, sustain, or end the behavior in question" (Center for Effective Collaboration & Practice; http://www.cecp.air.org/fba/default.asp). The FBA approach is a type of case formulation, since the observer attempts to uncover the function of the behavior by determining the underlying motivation to *"avoid"* (escape) or *"get"* something (the root of all behavior to a functional analyst).

The FBA approach has gained increasing attention within the educational system and has been documented in both IDEA and IDEA 2004 as the prescribed method for determining the cause of problem behavior and developing intervention plans (**Behavioral Intervention Plan: BIP**) for students whose problem behaviors are a concern. For example, if it is determined through a FBA that a student's disruptive behavior is reinforced by peer and teacher attention, then an intervention plan is developed to teach the child alternative and more appropriate behaviors that will serve the *same function* (increased attention) and replace the inappropriate behavior. The approach is sometimes called the ABC approach because it serves to isolate the antecedents, behaviors, and consequences of behavior.

Event recording.   When the behavior to be observed is a discrete behavior (such as hand raising, or amount of time it takes a child to begin a task after teacher request), then documenting whether a behavior occurs or not (**event recording**) can be a simple matter of adding a tally to a recording sheet. This method of recording is best used for low frequency behaviors.

Table 5.4 Observational Recording Methods: Applications, Advantages, and Disadvantages

Recording		Application	Advantages
Narrative Recording Describe behaviors	**Types** *Anecdotal* Record everything *Running Record* Describe behaviors as they are occurring	Used to develop hypotheses. Once you have an idea of what is going on, then you can be more specific in observing in the next stage	General impressions; Sequences of behaviors are maintained (may be helpful in establishing antecedents and consequences **Disadvantages** Lack of focus; time consuming Difficult to quantify
Event Recording **Focus** on specific **discrete** behaviors	*Behavior* Behavior occurs or not *Duration* Length of time (e.g., on-task) *Intensity* Push, shove, hit *Lapsed Time* How much time lapsed between Request → comply	**Discrete Behaviors** (begin and end) e.g., hand raise; talk out **Data** Can use frequency count (tally sheet); Percentage of time or responses	**Advantages** Good for low frequency behaviors (e.g., hand raising); Many behaviors can be observed at once Frequency/change over time **Disadvantages** You get no information about why behavior occurred
Interval Recording Establish time interval for observation, e.g., observe every minute (e.g., 8:01) for 20 seconds, record response and then look up again at 8:02	*Time Sampling* Behaviors listed on coding sheet; during 20-second observations, record whether behavior(s) occurs or not during that time interval (1, 0); At end of observation period can tally # times behavior (s) occur during the observation period	**Continuous Behavior** e.g., playing, on-task behavior Stipulate that playing must be observed for 15 out of 20 seconds being observed **Data** number of intervals of target behavior observed	**Advantages** Can have more than one observer collecting date and then check interobserver agreements Specific Behaviors; # behaviors **Disadvantages** Little info about quality of behavior (good playing, not good playing) Ignores frequency of behavior events (can't talk about behavior count); Wastes much time if using this for low frequency behaviors, e.g., hand raising.

Interval recording. If I want to measure a continuous behavior, such as on-task behavior, I would likely use an **interval recording** procedure. An example would be to observe a child for a 20-minute class period, observing and recording behavior, using the following schedule. Every minute on the minute, I look up and watch for a 20-second interval. If the child is engaged in the task for the entire 20-second period, I give him a checkmark under on-task behavior. If he is not engaged for the entire 20-second observation, then I place a check mark on alternate behaviors I have listed, such as talking, staring into space, looking inside desk, walking around, etc. At the end of 20 minutes I should have 20 observations recorded on my record sheet. (*For an example of an interval recording observation sheet, please review the chart presented in chapter 2, Table 2.3.*)

Behavioral rating scales and multirater scales. Depending on the age of the child, clinicians can use a variety of assessment instruments to gain a deeper appreciation of the nature of the problem, including behavior rating scales and personality assessments (inventories and projective assessments). We have already reviewed a number of the benefits and limitations of ratings scales in our discussion of the dimensional classification system. Despite concerns about the use of rating scales, these instruments are used widely because they can provide norm-referenced data about how a child views themselves or is viewed by others along a number of internalizing and externalizing dimensions, as well as provide indices of their self-concept or social competency. As can be anticipated, self-report scales are difficult to validate and administer at young ages; consequently, the majority of these rating scales have been developed for use with children who are in their early teens, although the BASC2 can be administered to children as young as 8 years of age. As will become readily apparent, ratings scales can provide an index of functioning across several different areas and allow for a comparative look at an individual's strengths and weaknesses.

Achenbach System of Empirically Based Assessment (ASEBA; Achenbach & Recorla, 2001). This most recent revision of the Achenbach scales includes updated versions of the original three scales: *Child Behavior Checklist, Teacher's Report Form,* and *Youth Self-Report* (available for youth 11 years or older) in what Achenbach refers to as "an integrated system of multi-informant assessment." The various rater forms and age ranges for the ASEBA are available in Table 5.5.

Table 5.5 Three Common Behavioral Rating Scales for Use With Children and Adolescents

Achenbach System of Empirically Based Assessment (ASEBA, 2001)	Rater/Age in years	Sample of Areas Rated
Child Behavior Checklist CBCL	Parent/1-1/2–5 Parent/6–18	**Syndrome Scales** Internalizing, (anxiety, depression, somatic) Externalizing (rule breaking, aggressive) and total problems
Teacher Report Form TRF	Teacher, Caregiver/1-1/2– 5	Other problems: Social, Thought, Attention
Youth Self-Report	Teacher/6–18 Youth/11–18	*DSM* **Oriented Scales** Affective, anxiety, somatic ADHD, ODD, CD*
Conners' Rating Scales (Conners, 1997)	**Rater/Age in years**	**Sample of Areas Rated**
Conners' Parent Rating Scale (CPRS–R) Conners' Teacher Rating Scale (CTRS–R) Conners–Wells'	Parent/3–17 Teacher/3–17	**Subscales** Oppositional, conduct problems, anxious/shy, perfectionism, social problems, psychosomatic global index: Impusivity/emotional lability *DSM–IV* **Symptom Scales (ADHD)** Inattentive Hyperactive/impulsive
Conners–Wells' Adolescent Self-Report Scale (CASS; Conners, 1997)	Youth/12–17	Youth scale *also* adds: Problems: Family, emotional and anger control
Behavior Assessment System for Children (BASC-2; Reynolds & Kamphaus, 2004)	**Rater/Age in years**	**Sample of Areas Rated**
Parent Rating Scale (PRS)	Parent/2–5 6–11 12–21	**Composite Scales** Adaptive skills Behavioral symptoms index
Teacher Rating Scale (TRS)	Teacher/2–5 6–11 12–21	Externalizing Internalizing School problems
Self-Report of Personality (SRP)	Child 8–11 12–17 18–21	Composite scores based on information from numerous *Primary (depression, learning problems, somatization, etc.)* and *Content Scales (anger control, resiliency, etc.)*

Sources: The Achenbach System of Empirically Based Assessment (ASEBA; Achenbach & Rescorla, 2001); The Behavior Assessment System for Children (BASC; Reynolds & Kamphaus, 1992); and The Conners Rating Scales–Revised (CRS–R: Conners, 1997).
*ADHD (attention deficity hyperactivity disorder), ODD (oppositional defiant disorder), CD (conduct disorder)

The ASEBA scales yield profiles for eight *syndrome scales*:

- Anxious/depressed
- Withdrawn/depressed
- Somatic complaints
- Social problems
- Thought problems
- Attention problems
- Rule-breaking behavior
- Aggressive behavior

In addition to the syndrome scales, there are also scores provided for the **composite scales**: Internalizing, Externalizing, and Total Problems. Informants respond to questions (*113 questions on the parent and teacher version; 112 questions on the youth form*) using a 3-point scale to indicate whether the statement is *not true* (0 points), *somewhat or sometimes true* (1 point), or *very true or often true* (2 points).

Important Distinction

The revised ASEBA (2001) changed the previous syndromes of *Anxious/Depressed* and *Withdrawn* into *Anxious/Depressed* and *Withdrawn/Depressed* to address potentially different features of these two syndromes with respect to the concept of negative affectivity. (The concept of negative affectivity will be addressed at greater length when the Internalizing Disorders are discussed.)

Another important change was the addition of a set of **DSM-Oriented Scales** that were developed by a panel of clinicians who rated the items based on their consistency with the *DSM* categories and results yielded six *DSM-Oriented Scales*:

- Affective problems
- Anxiety problems
- Somatic complaints
- Attention deficit/hyperactivity problems
- Oppositional defiant problems
- Conduct problems

Behavior Assessment System for Children (BASC–2; Reynolds & Kamphaus, 2004). The recent revision (BASC–2) replaces the original version (1992) and is available in multirater format. Age ranges are available in Table 5.5. The child self-report begins at 8 years of age. The scales consist of five broad band, and a number of narrow band scales from the *Primary Scales and Content* areas. The five broad band scales include:

- Externalizing (*hyperactivity, aggression, conduct problems*)
- Internalizing (*anxiety, depression, somatization*)
- School Problems (*attention problems, learning problems*)
- Behavioral Symptoms Index (*atypicality, withdrawal*)

- Adaptive Skills (*adaptability, social skills, leadership, study skills, functional communication*)

Raters respond to items based on a 4-point scale to indicate frequency of behavior from *Never, Sometimes, Often, or Always*. The BASC–2 was normed based on data collected from 375 testing sites with representative samples of populations of children receiving special assistance and those not receiving assistance (*parent form* N = 4,800; *teacher form* N = 4,650; *child self-report form* N = 3,400).

Conners' Rating Scales (Conners, 1998). The revised Conners' scales are based on data collected from representative community samples in the United States and Canada between 1993 and 1996. Rating forms come in long and short versions with a self-report scale, *Conners–Wells Adolescent Self Report Scale* (CASS: long and short versions) for adolescents 12 to 17 years of age. The scales were revised to align the scales with the *DSM–IV* criteria for ADHD; update and increase the sample; and to include a self-report scale for adolescents. A list of the scale categories is available in Table 5.5.

Science Talks: How Has the Use of Psychological Testing Measures Changed Over the Past 20 Years?

Cashel (2002) surveyed 162 child and adolescent psychologists regarding assessment instruments most commonly used in a variety of settings, including hospitals, outpatient clinics, private practice, and school-based settings. Results from that study revealed psychologists spent more than one quarter of their time (27.3%) conducting assessments, and that the nature of the assessment battery used did not change much based on a comparison with survey results obtained some 20 years earlier.

In their study of 647 practicing school psychologists, Shapiro and Heick (2004) found that the most frequently employed assessment method was the use of parent/teacher (75.7%) and student/self (67%) behavior rating scales and/or checklists.

Trends in the Assessment of Personality and Psychopathology

In their survey of more than 400 members of the APA, Watkins, Campbell, Nieberding, and Hallmark (1995) found that clinical psychologists tend to rely upon a select battery of assessment instruments, and, furthermore that procedures, for the most part, have remained relatively consistent across time (several decades). Results from the Shapiro and Heick (2004) survey of practicing school psychologists (Figure 5.2) are based on the frequency rate for the number of assessment measures used in the past 10 cases referred for social/behavioral and/or emotional problems.

Although the assessment of intelligence continued to be the most prevalent area of assessment (84%) for school psychologists, interviews, behavioral rating scales, and observation were frequently used methods of information gathering (67–75.5%). Of note was the fact that more than half of those surveyed (52.7%) reported the use of projective measures as part of their assessment battery. However, contrary to findings of Watkins and colleagues (1995) who reported a consistency of assessment methods across decades, Shapiro and Heick (2004) report a substantial increase in the usage of behavior rating scales and continued reduction in the use of projective methods compared to surveys conducted 10 to 15 years earlier (Hutton, Dubes, & Muir, 1992).

Assessment	Percentage
Student Interview	69.5%
Parent-Teacher Rating Scales	75.5%
Child Self-Rating	67%
Direct Observation	69%
Intelligence	84%
Achievement	63%
Projectives	52.7%

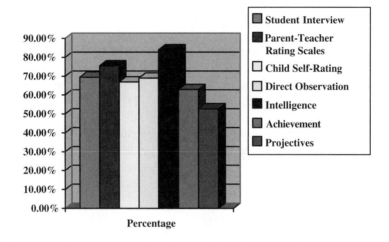

Figure 5.2 Frequency of assessment methods used by practicing school psychologists (Shapiro & Heick, 2004).

In addition to multirater instruments that evaluate emotional and behavioral responses from a variety of perspectives, there are several instruments that have been developed specifically for children and adolescents to assess their perception of their own psychopathology and emotional status. The majority of personality instruments tend to be rather lengthy, contain a large number of response items, and, as a result, may take much longer to administer than behavioral rating scales. The following is a list of some of the more commonly used instruments for assessment of personality.

Adolescent Psychopathology Scale: (APS; Reynolds, 1998). The APS is suitable for youth 12 to 19 years of age and contains 346 items; however, a shortened version, *Adolescent Psychopathology Scale-Short Form* (APS–SF; Reynolds, 2000), is available with 115 items. In addition to the scales noted in Table 5.6, three composite scores are available for overall internalizing, externalizing, and personality disorder. Validity is enhanced through the use of scales to measure such response indicators as lie response tendencies and response consistency. Youth are asked to rate the frequency with which they have experienced a given thought, feeling, or behavior (Never, Almost Never, Sometimes, Nearly All the Time) over a given time interval (e.g., within the past 6 months, within the past year, etc.).

Personality Inventory for Youth (PIY; Lachar & Gruber, 1995). The PIY is a 270-item instrument which is suitable for youth 10 to 18 years of age. Unlike the majority of behavior rating scales, this personality inventory uses a True/False rather than a *Likert-type response* format. In addition to clinical scales listed in Table 5.4, the PIY also provides scales that evaluate response validity, consistency, and defensiveness. One of the clinical scales, *Family Dysfunction,* can be a helpful resource for learning more about family dynamics, such as marital conflict, parent maladjustment, and the nature of parent–child conflict. A parallel parent version of the scale, *Personality Inventory for Children, 2nd ed.* (PIC–2; Wirt, Lachar, Seat, & Broen, 2001), is also available for parents of children and youth ages 5 to 19 years.

Shorter version inventories for screening.   In addition to the rather lengthy and extensive personality inventories discussed, there are two brief, albeit psychometrically sound, instruments available that can provide valuable information and a good start point for further evaluation.

Reynolds Adolescent Adjustment Screening Inventory (RAASI; Reynolds, 2001).   The RAASI contains only 32 items (Likert-type scale 0–3) and provides scores for scales outlined in Table 5.5. Despite the small number of items, the instrument has good reliability and validity based on data standardized on both school based and clinical samples.

Beck Youth Inventories of Emotional and Social Impairment, 2nd ed. (BYI; Beck, Beck, & Jolly, 2005).   The inventory is comprised of 20-item scales for each of five categories (see Table 5.5). The inventories were conormed based on a standardized sample of youth in the United States stratified to match the U.S. census. Scores on the individual scales can be compared using the same *T*-score metric.

Projective tests.   Unlike structured questionnaires or behavior rating scales, **projective tests** require responses to vague and ambiguous stimuli. A clinician may ask a child to describe inkblots (Rorschach Test), create stories to illustrate what is happening in pictures (Thematic Apperception Test; Child Apperception Test), or to fill in the missing words in a statement or to create an ending to an incomplete sentence (Sentence Completion Tests). Clinicians may also engage children in open-ended tasks such as executing drawings of people (Draw a Person Test), shapes (Bender Gestalt), or situations (Kinetic Family Drawing; Kinetic School Drawing; House Tree Person). With adult populations, projective measures are primarily used by psychodynamic therapists to gain access to repressed thoughts and unconscious conflicts that may be at the core of deep-seated client problems (Sugarman & Kanner, 2000).

Clinicians from a variety of therapeutic models may use projective tests with children to access information that may be otherwise unavailable due to a child's limited insight into their own emotional difficulties. In the majority of cases, projective measures are only one of many types of assessment instruments (called the **test battery**) that make up the total assessment process. A number of recent studies have confirmed the continued use of projective measures with child and adolescent populations by clinicians in both managed care (Cashel, 2002) and school settings (Hojnoski, Morrison, Brown, & Matthews, 2006), although other researchers (Shapiro & Heick, 2004) report a more recent trend to reduced usage of these measures among school psychologists. However, despite controversy and debate regarding the utility and validity of projective measures, and a warning that projective measures should only be used "in the earliest stages" of investigation (Knoff, 2002, p. 1299), projective measures continue to be used by many child clinicians. Responses from a random sample of 500 practicing school psychologists (Hojnoski et al., 2006) revealed that the most frequently used projective measures include the *sentence completion test* (60.7%), the *Bender Gestalt Test* (49%), the *House–tree–person* (43.5%), and the

Kinetic family drawing (41.3%). Those measures used by less than 20% of psychologists included TAT, Rorshach, and CAT.

Memory Bank

Hojnoski et al. (2006) report that psychologists found projective measures most useful in the diagnostic process and least useful in treatment planning. Of note was the finding that projective measures were used by school psychologists to assist in making important educational decisions (such as eligibility determination and intervention planning) despite the fact that there is no reported validity of these measures being used in this way.

Finally, in their recent article on the diagnosis and treatment of childhood mood disorders, McClure, Kubiszyn, and Kaslow (2002) suggest that in the wake of inadequacies in developmental sensitivity and well-validated instruments, clinicians may find a rich data source concerning the child's internal life through the use of projective techniques, such as drawings, sentence completion, thematic cards, or mutual story telling (p. 131). However, Hunsley, Lee, and Wood (2003) argue that projective measures fail to meet scientific standards of psychological tests, as recommended by the APA. The debate continues.

The Nature of the Problem: Intervention and Problem Treatment

Once the psychologist has confirmed a diagnosis of the child's problem based on the assessment findings, the next stage in the process is to devise a **treatment plan**. The treatment plan addresses the areas that require intervention and the particular treatment method selected to improve the child's **prognosis** (prediction for future success). An important component of developing a treatment plan is to insure that the plan is monitored regularly to determine whether interventions are successful, and to alter the plan as needed. In the area of child treatment, a key factor to consider is whether the treatment is developmentally appropriate.

Issues in Child Treatment and Intervention

Although there are some issues regarding treatment formulation that can generalize to treatment concerns for all cases (e.g., are treatments more effective than no treatment, and are some treatments more effective for certain problems), other issues are specific to developmental populations. There are several important questions that child clinicians should ask regarding the degree to which treatment formulation is developmentally appropriate.

Issues of Effectiveness and Specificity
General effectiveness of treatment for childhood disorders. Initial investigations of child treatment programs focused on treatment effectiveness relative to no treatment and results indicated that treatment was more effective than no treatment or placebos (Weisz & Weiss, 1993). Later investigations focused on more specific treatment effects and determined that positive outcomes were strongest when specific problems were targeted, behavioral versus nonbehavioral interventions were used, and when the subjects of treatment were adolescent girls (Weisz, Weiss, Han, Granger, & Morton, 1995). Although these findings shed more light on the specificity of treatment outcomes, the authors expressed concern about the generalizability of these findings in real life, since the majority of studies were conducted in laboratory settings.

Specificity of treatment: Are some treatments more effective for certain problems? Increasingly, researchers have focused their investigations on the impact of particular treatment approaches for specific treatment problems. One approach that has proven successful for hard-to-treat adolescent populations is Multisystemic Therapy (MST). The MST approach has worked well for adolescents with substance abuse problems (Henggeler, Melton, & Smith, 1990) and those with serious emotional disturbance (Schoenwald, Ward, Henggeler, & Rowland, 2000). Barkley (1997) has also demonstrated the efficacy of multimodal programs that combine components of parent awareness (education) with psychosocial (behavior and contingency management) and pharmacological supports for the treatment of children with ADHD. Specific treatment programs that have been identified for the treatment of specific problems will be discussed in the chapters related to each specific problem (e.g., anxiety reduction: Kendall et al., 1992; disruptive disorders: Spaccarelli, Cotler, & Penman, 1992).

 The K–3 Paradigm, introduced in chapter 1, can be helpful in illustrating the critical components necessary to developing intervention plans for children and youth that are appropriate developmentally, target relevant individual and environmental characteristics, and are based on sound theoretical foundations. In this way, treatment formulation utilizes information from three essential sources:

1. Knowledge of developmental expectations;
2. Knowledge of sources of influence (child characteristics and environmental characteristics); and
3. Knowledge of theoretical models and perspectives.

Despite increased emphasis on the need to focus on evidence or empirically-based treatments (EBTs), several conceptual difficulties exist in the area of treatment research:

*   how to measure treatment success (Strupp, 1989, 1996);
*   how to measure improvement (Jacobson, Roberts, Berns, & McGlinchey, 1999);
*   how to account for variations among complex problems in therapy;
*   how to account of variations in therapist approach within disciplines;
*   how to measure treatment fidelity (Huey, Hennenger, Brondino, & Pickrel, 2000);
*   how to determine use of analogue versus ecological treatments (Weisz et al., 1995).

The answer to the final question, regarding treatment specificity, clearly requires more controlled research, especially in real world situations. Kazdin (1997) has suggested several directions in which future research can benefit our understanding of treatment effectiveness:

*   a study of how processes are related to dysfunction
*   increased specification of treatment
*   inclusion of tests of treatment outcomes, and
*   conduct tests of contextual influences.

Developmental Issues in Treatment and Intervention

In their chapter, Holmbeck, Greenely, and Franks (2004) ask the question: *Are current child and adolescent treatments developmentally oriented* (p. 29)? Their answer is a resounding "No."

Although the authors recognize that several theorists have addressed the issues of developmental variability as it relates to the course of child psychopathology, they admit that there are minimal guidelines anywhere for adapting treatment programs to various developmental levels. Within this context, the authors suggest several developmental factors that can be highly influential in determining the success of a given treatment program. While most clinicians recognize the need to scrutinize cognitive aspects of a treatment program as to developmental level, other areas of child functioning (*behavioral, emotional, social*) have all but been ignored in treatment planning. The authors suggest several guidelines to assist clinicians to improve their understanding of the issues inherent in providing developmentally appropriate treatment planning, including:

- increased understanding of developmental levels, norms, tasks, and milestones;
- increased understanding of what constitutes psychopathology, at a given level of development (*risk factors, equifinality, multifinality, trajectories*), and how specific disorders appear at different levels of development;
- increased understanding of the role of context and context inclusion in therapeutic interventions; and
- increased parent and teacher understanding of development, its nature, and course.

 RECURRENT THEMES Holmbeck and colleagues' (2004) guidelines for designing interventions and treatments which are developmentally appropriate highlight the major developmental themes that have been emphasized throughout this text:

1. Normal development typically follows an orderly and predictable path.
2. Maladaptive behaviors represent deviations from the normal path.
3. Maladaptive behavior is represented by a continuum of severity.
4. Individual, interpersonal, contextual, and cultural factors influence deviations in development.

Furthermore, the authors recommend a number of ways that researchers can enhance addressing developmental concerns. Three of these recommendations are to:

1. Conceptualize the disorder from a developmental perspective.
2. Include measures of developmental moderator variables, such as cognitive–developmental level, motivation, social skills, emotion regulation, and self-control.
3. Evaluate mediator effects, such as developmental level (tasks to be mastered) or level of cognitive appraisal/problem solving (pp. 39–44).

Finally, the authors caution clinicians about the portability of treatment plans across developmental levels, especially cognitive behavioral programs (CBT). Such programs, they argue, may contain higher level thinking skills (such as self-reflective thinking, recursive thought, and metacognition, or thinking about thinking) unavailable to the younger child.

> **Staggering Statistics**
>
> There are more than 400 varieties of treatments available for adults with mental disorders (Comer, 2001). Many of the therapeutic approaches available for adult treatment have been adapted for use with children and adolescents. Methods have been derived from a variety of theoretical frameworks, including psychodynamic (play therapy); ego–supportive; behavioral and cognitive behavioral; interpersonal (social skills); and family systems. In keeping with the emphasis on multimodal assessment, current trends in treatment have also revealed an increased emphasis on the use of combined and multimodal treatment methods (Kazdin, 1996).

Goals of Treatment: Evidence-Based Treatments

Chambless and Hollon (1998) outline the criteria developed to evaluate the degree to which treatment programs can be qualified as evidence-based resulting from the Task Force on Psychological Intervention Guidelines (APA, 1995). The most rigid level of criteria are for programs that qualify as **well-established psychosocial interventions,** and included in the list of criteria is a manualized program that has proven evidence of superiority to another form of treatment in at least two between-group studies conducted by two different research teams. In order to qualify as a **probably efficacious intervention,** a program should meet all the more rigorous criteria with the exception of requiring two independent research teams. The Task Force found significantly more studies that would match the probably efficacious treatment category than the category for well-established psychosocial treatments and a higher percentage of research devoted to the treatment of externalizing disorders (conduct problems, ADHD) than internalizing disorders (anxiety, depression).

In a *Special Issue on Empirically Supported Psychosocial Interventions for Children* appearing in the *Journal of Clinical Child Psychology* (June, 1998), several researchers report the extent to which existing treatment programs match criteria for well-established and probably efficacious interventions for a number of high-frequency problems encountered in children's mental health: depression, anxiety disorders, conduct disorders, ADHD, and autism.

Ollendick and King (2004) address recent trends to investigate the specificity of treatment effectiveness. In their review, the authors not only point out the scarcity of identified empirically supported treatments for some of the most prevalent disorders (anxiety and depression), but also emphasize the need to incorporate more rigorous scientific methods in verifying treatment efficacy, such as randomized clinical trials (RCT) and the use of manualized programs to ensure treatment fidelity. In addition to increased emphasis on community based treatment (real life vs. laboratory based findings) , the authors also highlight the need to expand the breadth of types of treatment evaluated, since the majority of research to date concerns cognitive/behavioral or behavioral treatments, with only marginal attempts to evaluate alternative methods based on psychodynamic or family systems theories.

CHAPTER SUMMARY AND REVIEW

1. **Goals of Diagnosis and Assessment: Case Formulation**
   The goals of developing a case formulation are to identify the problem (diagnosis), evaluate the problem (assessment), and formulate a treatment plan. Throughout the stages of formulation, the process of evaluation (assessment) assists in refining the diagnosis and in

guiding the development of the treatment or intervention. Monitoring is on-going at all stages of case formulation.

2. **Problem Identification: Diagnosis and Classification**
The categorical (*DSM*) and dimensional (empirical) classification systems provide benefits and limitations in their applicability to diagnosis for behavioral, social, or emotional problems of childhood.

a. *Categorical Classification:* DSM–IV–TR *(APA, 2000)*
The categorical system is a mutually exclusive system of classification widely used in North America for adult populations. Children are diagnosed with a disorder if they meet the criteria based on a number of listed symptoms. The most recent revision (*DSM–IV–TR*) contains 20 disorders of childhood and includes increased references to childhood features of other disorders. Benefits include wide acceptance and communication ease; however, the system lacks a developmental focus and issues of disorder comorbidity are more difficult to address using this system.

b. *Empirical Classification Systems*
Derived from comparisons of normal and deviant populations at various age levels, the empirical or dimensional system affords the benefit of considering the extent to which behaviors deviate from the norm and provides ease of access to multirater perspectives.
In addition to sampling a number of behaviors that would not appear in the *DSM* (social problems, family problems), symptom clusters are also available as they relate to overall externalizing and internalizing behaviors. The multirater aspect is a double-edged factor providing the benefit of multiple perspectives, yet, having the limitation of being subject to informant bias (attributions and perspectives) and outside influences.

3. **Assessment and Problem Evaluation**

a. *Ethical Issues*
In addition to obtaining informed parent (guardian) consent for child assessment, clinicians must also obtain a child's **assent** (agreement to willingly participate) in the assessment process. Other ethical issues discussed included test security and the release of test data.

b. *Goals of Assessment*
Although the importance of reliability and validity of test instruments cannot be underrated, recent emphasis on **evidence-based assessments** has called attention to the need to consider the **clinical utility** of assessments, or linking assessment to intervention and treatment outcomes.

c. *Assessment Methods*
In the initial stages, interviews (unstructured, semistructured, structured) and direct observation (narrative, event recording, interval recording) can provide valuable information. A **functional behavioral assessment (FBA)** is one way of structuring observations to provide information that will assist with the development of a **behavioral intervention plan (BIP)**. Several assessment instruments, including multirater scales and individually administered personality inventories can provide increased insight into a child's inner world and the specific nature of the problem in question.

4. **Intervention and Treatment**

a. There are several questions about treatment effectiveness at a general (are treatments more effective than no treatment) and more specific levels (are some treatment more effective than others for specific problems).

b. Although contemporary trends have witnessed increased emphasis in the use of treatment programs that are evidence-based, less focus has been placed on consideration of whether the treatment program is developmentally appropriate. Some of the key developmental factors that should be considered include: how various disorders appear at different developmental levels; potential cognitive and social limitations of the child at various developmental levels; and the need to measure developmental moderator variables prior to implementing a program.

Consolidate and Communicate

1. It has been argued that the *DSM* system of classification is an "all or nothing" way of classifying mental disorders. Discuss this statement and argue the merits and limitations of this system in the classification of a specific disorder (for example, attention deficit hyperactivity disorder or autism).

2. The *DSM* is a multiaxial system of classification. Describe what that statement means and complete a five axis classification for the following case:

   Wally is an 11-year-old boy who scored 65 on a recent IQ test. His mother describes him as outgoing, but often impulsive and not very socially aware. In fact, his mother is concerned that he might walk off with any stranger because he is not aware of the potential danger. His mother is also concerned about his very oppositional way of dealing with every problem. He is continually in trouble with his siblings and annoys them on a repeated basis. His favorite word is "no," and he refuses to do any chores that his mother gives him. He is currently enrolled in a special education class and is currently functioning at about a Grade 2 level academically. His mother sees the benefit of his enrolling in programs like the Special Olympics; however, she has no transportation and cannot afford to purchase the athletic shoes he would need to participate. Wally attends weekly group counseling sessions at the school, held by the school guidance counselor. Progress has been slow due to Wally's lack of compliance and oppositional behavior.

3. A parent completes the Child Behavior Checklist (CBCL), and, based on the parent's ratings, her 12-year-old daughter Emily has clinically significant elevations in the following areas: Externalizing Behaviors, Total Problems, and Aggressive Behaviors. The teacher completes the Teacher Rating Form (TRF) and also finds that Emily has significant Externalizing Problems, Total Problems, Rule Breaking Behaviors, and Aggressive Behaviors. Emily completes the Youth Self-Report form and rates herself as completely normal in all areas. During the interview with the school psychologist, Emily states that she only is acting out because the girls are teasing her and she is fighting back.

   She does not want to go to counseling sessions because it is not her fault. Furthermore, she is not cooperative, and, although parents have consented to assessment, Emily refuses to take part in the assessment.

   Provide an explanation for why ratings on the parent CBCL and TRF are slightly different. Based on the actor–observer phenomenon, provide a rationale for the variations in reporting on the adult (parent/teacher) and youth rating forms. Emily does not want to go to counseling or participate in any assessment; discuss Emily's rights to refusal in terms of ethical concerns.

4. Discuss "clinical elevation" of scores on multirater scales such as the ASEBA and what that means in terms of *T*–score distribution.

5. What are the goals of assessment? Describe how these goals relate to the three stage model of case formulation.

6. A teacher asks you to observe a child in her classroom. The teacher reports that the child is never in his seat and that he always blurts out answers without raising his hand. What would you select as an observational recording method and why? What are the advantages and disadvantages of this method?

Chapter Review Questions

1. Achenbach (1995) addressed the need to clarify term usage. According to Achenbach the term **assessment** might more appropriately refer to _____, while the term **taxonomy** might be reserved for the _____.
   a. diagnosis…assessment
   b. process of data gathering…diagnostic outcome
   c. testing instruments…diagnosis
   d. testing instruments…labels

2. The original *DSM* (1952) contained _____ childhood disorders.
   a. no
   b. one
   c. two
   d. five

3. The current version of the *DSM* (*IV–TR*) includes over _____ childhood disorders.
   a. 20
   b. 50
   c. 30
   d. 10

4. The *DSM* has been criticized for use with child populations because:
   a. forced choice responses do not allow for combining data from multiple informants
   b. comorbidity is problematic
   c. disorders are not considered in developmental context
   d. all of the above

5. A child who obtains a *T* score of 70 on the ASEBA is equivalent to functioning at the:
   a. 90th percentile
   b. 70th percentile
   c. 98th percentile
   d. 30th percentile

6. Studies of multiple raters, have found which of the following to be true:
   a. raters who come from similar settings tend to be more similar in their ratings of children
   b. raters tend to have more agreement in their ratings of older children (11–18 years)
   c. raters tend to have more agreement in their ratings of internalizing behaviors
   d. male adolescents disclose more than females

7. Which of the following is true regarding the actor–observer phenomenon?
   a. the tendency to attribute negative behaviors of others to internal characteristics
   b. the tendency to attribute negative behaviors of self to internal characteristics
   c. the actor–observer phenomenon is universal
   d. the actor–observer phenomenon is most evident in cooperative societies

8. The term *test data* refers to"
   a. raw and scaled scores
   b. psychologist's notes about test behavior
   c. individual responses to test items
   d. all of the above
9. In their discussion of evidence-based assessments, Mash and Hunsley (2005) use the term *clinical utility* to refer to:
   a. reliability of the assessment instrument
   b. the validity of the assessment instrument
   c. relationship of assessment instrument to diagnosis, case formulation, and treatment outcomes
   d. all of the above
10. Which of the following areas would be least likely to be covered as part of a mental status exam?
    a. insight and judgment
    b. life goals
    c. orientation in place and time
    d. recent and remote memory

Glossary of New Terms

assessment
diagnosis
case formulation (hypothesis)
precipitate
maintain
provisional diagnosis
differential diagnosis
comorbid
categorical classification
dimensional classification
Diagnostic & Statistical Manual of Mental Disorders (DSM)
DSM–PC Child and Adolescent Version
symptom clusters, patterns, or syndromes
nonclinical sample
clinical sample
standard scores, *T* scores, percentiles
clinical range
borderline range
at-risk
undercontrolled/overcontrolled
behavior excess/behavior deficit
emotional and behavioral disorders (EBD)
severe emotional disorders (SED)
Attribution Bias Context Model (ABC Model)
treatment plans
actor–observer phenomenon

attributions/perspectives
assent
validity
reliability
mental measurements yearbook
mental measurements database
clinical utility
psychometric instruments
clinical assessment interview
rapport building
unstructured, semistructured, structured interviews
mental status exam
narrative recording
event recording
interval recording
functional behavioral assessment (FBA)
syndrome scales
composite scales
DSM-oriented scales
treatment plans
prognosis
projective measures
test battery
well-established psychosocial interventions
probably efficacious interventions

Answers to Multiple Choice Questions:
1. b; 2. c; 3. a; 4. d; 5. c; 6. a; 7. a; 8. d; 9. c; 10. b.

Part 2
Emotional, Behavioral, and Learning Difficulties in Children and Youth
Their Nature and Their Course

The next 10 chapters focus on the most common and challenging problems facing children, youth, and families today. The chapters are clustered around important themes with the intention of linking disorders with shared features to increase understanding and to assist with differential diagnosis. Beginning with the *internalizing problems* (*section IA*), the wide range of anxiety disorders with likely onset in childhood (chapter 6) and adolescence (chapter 7) are presented. Mood disorders and suicide are discussed in chapter 8. In *section IB* (chapter 9) the focus is on *externalizing problems* (social problems and aggressive behaviors) and the disruptive behavior disorders. The next segment, *section II*, includes chapters (10 and 11) that concentrate on *problems of attention and learning* (i.e., attention deficit hyperactivity disorder and specific learning disabilities). *Problems that are most often evident in late childhood and adolescence* (i.e., eating problems and substance use/abuse) are discussed in *section III* (chapters 12 and 13). The discussion of child and adolescent problems concludes with *section IV*, which devotes two chapters (14 and 15) *to pervasive developmental problems and disorders* (mental retardation and pervasive developmental disorders, such as autism/Asperger's). Each of the problem areas is discussed along a continuum, as it relates to more serious deviations from the norm.

Information about each of the problem areas focuses on a spectrum of behaviors from normal variations to severely disordered behaviors. Discussions follow the developmental characteristics and course of the disorder as it manifests over time. Current theories and issues are addressed. Each problem also features a discussion of common methods of assessment and empirically supported treatments.

IA
Internalizing Problems
An Introduction

This section contains three chapters which are clustered together under the topic of internalizing disorders: anxiety disorders with likely onset in childhood (chapter 6); anxiety disorders with likely onset in adolescence (chapter 7) and mood disorders (chapter 8). Due to the emphasis on developmental course in this volume, anxiety disorders are discussed prior to mood disorders given evidence that in the majority of cases, developmental onset for anxiety is prior to onset for depression and mood disorders (Kovacs & Devlin, 1998).

Section IA At-A-Glance

The Nature of Internalizing Problems
  Prevalence Rates for Internalizing Problems
  Developmental Trends: Issues and Controversies

Negative Affectivity: A Historical Perspective
  The Tripartite Model of Anxiety and Depression
    Affect and Temperament
    Affect and Biochemical Influences
  Somatic Complaints and Somatic Disorders
  Somatoform Disorders
    Hysterical Disorders
    Preoccupation Disorders
    Etiology of Somatoform Disorders in Children and Youth
    Assessment and Treatment

The Nature of Internalizing Problems

As was discussed in chapter 5, one method of classifying child and adolescent problems or disorders is to conceptualize these behaviors along two broadband dimensions: **internalizing** (*overcontrolled*) and **externalizing** (*undercontrolled*) behaviors (Achenbach & Edelbrock,1978; Chicchetti, & Toth, 1991). Internalizing behaviors include a wide variety of symptoms related to problems and syndromes which signify *"problems within the self, such as anxiety, depression, somatic complaints, without known medical cause, and withdrawal from social contact"*

(Achenbach & Rescorla, 2001, p. 93). As will become increasingly evident, internalizing problems can be subtle in their presentation, elusive and difficult to detect compared to the more obvious and observable externalizing behaviors.

Case in Point

The saying *"the squeaky wheel gets the grease"* can often sum-up how children with externalizing problems get more immediate and direct attention than their peers with internalizing problems. For example, it is easy to sympathize with a teacher who is insistent on getting some intervention for Andy compared to Arthur who is withdrawn and does not participate in classroom discussions. Faced with daily interruptions resulting from *angry Andy's* disruptive outbursts, the teacher's concerns for *anxious Arthur* will likely be placed on hold. Although teachers and parents might express concern for Arthur and a desire to enhance his social interactions and participation, their effort may often be derailed and overshadowed by greater concerns about the behaviors of angry Andy whose aggressive outbursts could pose a potential threat to others' safety.

Achenbach and Rescorla (2001) consider *three syndromes scales* under the composite scale for internalizing:

- anxious/depressed
- withdrawn/depressed
- somatic complaints.

The concept of clustering *anxiety, depression, and somatic problems* under the umbrella of internalizing disorders has benefited researchers and clinicians on several levels:

1. High rates of comorbidity among these disorders is often due to shared symptom features which can assist in understanding not only the complex nature of the disorders but also can help to explain developmental pathways and trajectories.
2. When anxiety and depression are viewed in close proximity, it is possible to gain an in-depth appreciation of the complexity and controversies which have existed regarding whether anxiety and depression actually represent two unique disorders, or whether the category of **"negative affectivity"** would better conceptualize the shared features of anxiety and depression.
3. Due to the covert nature of internalizing disorders, clinicians are often faced with unique challenges in the assessment, diagnosis and treatment of these disorders.
4. Internalizing disorders often share similar negative outcomes, such as withdrawal from social relationships, peer neglect, lower levels of self-efficacy, and reduced self-esteem.

Although the *DSM–IV–TR* (APA, 2000) does not specifically refer to internalizing disorders (or externalizing disorders), within the ASEBA system (Achenbach & Rescorla, 2001), three of the *DSM* oriented scales align with symptoms along the internalizing dimension:

- Affective problems
- Anxiety problems
- Somatic problems

> **Memory Bank**
>
> Internalizing disorders (unipolar and bipolar disorder, somatoform disorders, anxiety disorders) all share features of a response to conflict or distress that is manifested in internally oriented symptoms.

Prevalence Rates for Internalizing Problems

Depending on the source, the reader can expect to find wide variations in prevalence rates for the majority of disorders discussed throughout this text, and the internalizing disorders are not an exception in this regard. Prevalence rates will vary based on:

1. whether these numbers represent annual or lifetime prevalence rates
2. whether numbers represent clinical populations or community populations
3. the criteria used to classify the disorders
4. the different assessment instruments used to measure the disorders

A review of the literature reveals some of the following information regarding prevalence rates for internalizing disorders:

- Although the prevalence rates for internalizing disorders in younger children (4–11 years) is similar for boys (7%) and girls (9%), in adolescent populations (12 to 16 years), female prevalence rates (15.7%) were approximately four times higher than male prevalence rates (3.9%) for internalizing disorders (Offord, Boyle, & Racine, 1989);
- Lifetime prevalence during childhood (0–18 years) for major depressive disorder is 9% (Reinherz, Giaconia, Pakiz, & Silverman, 1993);
- As many as 10–15 percent of children and youth will experience symptoms of depression (Smucker, Craighead, Craighead, & Greem, 1986);
- In any one year, 13 percent of children will be diagnosed as having an anxiety disorder (Costello, Angold, Burns, Stangel, Tweed, Erkanli, et al., 1996);
- As high as 25% of clinic children who report headaches have a somatoform disorder, while low energy is acquainted with the disorder in 23% of the population (Garber, Walker, & Seman, 1991).

> **Science Talks**
>
> A recent epidemiological study of children and youth (9 to 16 years of age) revealed approximately 17% demonstrated at least one psychiatric disorder, while 25% of those with a disorder also had a comorbid disorder. Children with a disorder were three times more likely to develop another disorder. Although boys initially had more severe problems than girls, prevalence rates for girls increased in areas of depression, social phobia, and substance use during adolescence. Females were significantly more likely to develop **homotypic patterns** (develop a similar type of disorder within gender) than boys. Female homotypic patterns included: depression, generalized anxiety disorder, and social phobia (Costello, Mustillo, Erkanli, Keeler, & Angold, 2003).

There are high rates of comorbidity among the internalizing disorders and symptom overlap has led to considerable discussion regarding how to best conceptualize these disorders in children and adults. In particular, there has been significant discussion regarding the development of models to understand the impact of **negative affectivity** or negative emotions in determining such emotional states as fear, anxiety and depression (Chorpita, Albano, & Barlow, 1998). Although somatic disorders are a part of the internalizing triad, at this point the discussion will focus primarily on the two areas that have the most documented research support: anxiety and depression/mood disorders.

Development in Focus

A key component in better understanding internalizing disorders is to view the disorders from a developmental perspective. For example, prior to adolescence, symptoms of generalized anxiety and depression often occur together as *"negative affectivity."* There is evidence that anxious-depressed symptoms often outweigh either symptom presentation in isolation (Kronenberger & Meyer, 2000). Developmentally, overlap between these two disorders is supported by research that demonstrates extremely high comorbidity rates for depression and anxiety (60–70%), and evidence of developmental onset of anxiety prior to depression (Kovacs & Devlin, 1998).

Developmental Trends: Issues and Controversies

Based on results of high comorbidity rates and developmental onset, debate has ensued for the past two decades concerning whether anxiety and depression should be conceptualized as distinct diagnostic categories, or whether a broad band notion of *negative affectivity (negative affective states)* might better describe the comorbid nature of symptoms that exist between these two emotional states in developmental populations.

Negative Affectivity: A Historical Perspective

Historically, the concept of negative affectivity had its beginnings when Watson and Clark (1984) questioned the meaningfulness of considering anxiety, depression and neuroticism as separate entities based on the high intercorrelations among these three constructs on adult self report measures. They argued that a broad band measure of *negative affectivity* might be more useful for conceptualizing the inter-related nature of the symptoms.

Science Talks

Researchers tested out the applicability of the broad band nature of negative affectivity in two separate studies with children. Wolfe, Finch, Saylor, Blount, Pallmeyer, and Carek (1987) found that the highest correlations on children's self-report measures were for the depression and anxiety measures, and that teacher reports also confirmed that the children's negative self view corresponded to higher teacher ratings for depression, anxiety, and social withdrawal. Extending these results globally, Ollendick and Yule (1990) launched a study of over 600 British and American school-aged children (8–10 years of age), confirming the notion that depression and anxiety were highly correlated in both populations. Furthermore, they also found that children who reported high levels of anxiety and depression were also significantly more likely to report high levels for fears of negative social evaluation (fear of failure/criticism/oversensitivity).

As a result of increased investigations into the comorbid nature of depression and anxiety, two schools of thought emerged:

1. advocates for a unitary and dimensional view of anxiety and depression based on overlapping symptomology; and
2. proponents of the status quo who supported retention of the unique features of each disorder.

The Tripartite Model of Anxiety and Depression

In 1991, Clark and Watson proposed a model, called the **tripartite model of anxiety and depression**, in which they conceptualized:

- **negative affect** (*emotional distress*) as a common symptom shared by both anxiety and depression,
- **physiological arousal** (*hyperarousal*) a symptom unique to anxiety, and
- **low positive affect** (*anhedonia*) as a feature unique to depression.

Since its inception, the model has inspired numerous investigations and debate. The model is presented in Table IA.1.

One area of associated research has focused on the importance of considering the impact of temperament/personality on affect. In child populations, studies have supported the notion that low positive affect is a feature that can discriminate between children with depressive disorders and anxiety disorders (Lonigan, Carey, & Finch, 1994). Furthermore, the applicability of the tripartite model to adult (Brown, Chorpita, & Barlow, 1998), child (Chorpita, 2002) and clinical child populations (Chorpita, Plummer, & Moffit, 2000) has supported the model's shared association of negative affectivity with anxiety and depression and the uniqueness of low positive affect to depression. In their revised model, an *integrated hierarchical model of anxiety and depression,* Mineka, Watson, and Clark (1998) stress the increased recognition that negative affectivity is a common shared feature for anxiety and depressive disorders, while low positive affect or *anhedonia* is a unique feature of the depressive disorders.

Affect and Temperament

Research evidence suggests that negative affectivity and low positive affect can both be inherited characteristics that are relatively stable across time (Clark, Watson, & Mineka, 1994). One recent investigation found significant correlations between negative temperament and negative affectivity and positive temperament and positive affectivity (Anthony, Lonigan, Hooe, & Phillips, 2002). Factor analysis conducted by Ahadi, Rothbart, and Ye (1993) revealed a three factor temperament/affect solution with two factors resembling *Negative Affect* and *Positive Affect* and a third factor representing *Effortful Control.*

Table IA.1 Tripartite Model of Anxiety and Depression

Negative Affect (*emotional distress*)	⟶	**Anxiety and Depression**
Physiological Arousal (*heightened arousal*)	⟶	**Anxiety**
Low Positive Affect (*loss of pleasure*)	⟶	**Depression**

Source: Clark & Watson, 1991.

In their recent review, Muris and Ollendick (2005) pose the following question:

Why do some children develop psychological problems after being exposed to a negative life event, while others adapt to similar circumstances without developing problems? (p. 271)

Based on their extensive review of the research on temperament and child psychopathology, the authors suggest two potential models to explain how features of temperament and *effortful control* might interact to produce interrnalizing and externalizing behaivors. (The following summary is based on Muris and Ollendick, 2005.) Using the temperament dimension of *emotionality/neuroticism*, as the **reactive component** in the model, it is possible to predict the nature of potential pathology by isolating the lower-order traits of fear (anxiety response), anger/frustration (aggressive response) and sadness (depressed response). The degree to which these responses manifest and the nature of the response will further be moderated by the *regulatory component* of the model, the dimension of *effortful control*, which relates to both **behavioral control** (**behavioral inhibition**) and **attentional control** (*ability to focus and shift attention when needed*). Lack of attentional control has been linked to internalizing disorders, while problems with behavioral inhibition have been more strongly linked with externalizing behaviors. Several studies have supported the notion that high levels of emotionality and low levels of effortful control predict both internalizing and externalizing problems in children (Eisenberg, Pidada, & Liew, 2001; Eisenberg, Zhou, Spinrad, Valkiente, Fabes, & Liew, 2005; Valiente et al., 2003). Research has also demonstrated that children with high emotionality/neuroticism and low efforful control are also significantly bias in their interpretation of threat and cognitive distortions of threat perception (Lonigan, Vasey, Phillips, & Hazen, 2004), which may help explain how psychological problems endure across situations. Muris and Ollendick (2005) suggest two possible explanations for how the *emotionality/neuroticism* and *effortful control model* model might work:

1 effortful control might serve as a moderator either exaserbating or buffering emotional reactivity; or
2 each component might be unique and contribute an "additive" effect.

The authors suggest that further research will be required to better understand the dynamics of the proposed model (See Table IA.2)

Affect and Biochemical Influences

Genetic and environmental factors can influence tendencies to respond to situations with a negative response set. Caspi and colleagues (2003) have found that children with abnormalities

Table IA.2 Temperament: Effortful Control and Emotionality/Neuroticism

---

High emotionality/neuroticism and high effortful control:

Anxiety and Fear ⟶ Effortful Control (buffer) ⟶ Reduce Fear and Response

High emotionality/neuroticism and low effortful control:

Anxiety and Fear ⟶ Low Effortful Control ⟶ Increase Fear and Response

Effortful control and temperament;

Effortful Control ⟶ Lack Behavioral Control ⟶ Externalizing Disorders

Effortful Control ⟶ Lack Attentional control ⟶ Internalizing Behaviors

---

in the 5-HTT gene (responsible for transporting the neurotransmitter serotonin) exhibit more depressive responses to stressful events than peers without the abnormal gene.

Somatic Complaints and Somatic Disorders

There are high rates of comorbidity reported among the internalizing disorders. The third category of symptoms and disorders that cluster in this area are those related to somatic or physical complaints. However, compared to our knowledge of anxiety disorders and mood disorders in children and youth, significantly less is known about the somatization disorders. Somatic complaints and somatization disorders will not be featured in a separate chapter in this text, since the focus is on the most commonly occurring problems and disorders. However, it is possible to share some relevant findings in this area, at this time.

Children often complain of headaches, stomachaches, and pain, yet approximately 20% of visits to the physician result in a report of no physical cause (Robinson, Greene, & Walker, 1988). It has been demonstrated that health care utilization rates for children and youth peak during two key transitional periods: transition to elementary school and junior high school (Schor, 1986). The link between stress and somatic complaints in children and youth has also been demonstrated in studies by Garber, Walker, and Seaman (1991). In their investigations, Garber and colleagues (1991) found that it was possible to predict the nature of the somatic complaints developmentally. Prepubertal children predominantly reported headaches and abdominal pains, while adolescents reported symptoms of muscles aches, pain in the extremities, fatigue, and neurological symptoms (Walker, Garber ,& Greene, 1991).

Somatoform Disorders

Although physical complaints can often be linked to psychosocial stressors, it is rare for children and adolescents to be diagnosed with **Somatoform Disorders** (a serious mental disorder resulting in complaints of numerous physical symptoms that have no medical basis, or if there is an existing medical problem, symptoms are far in excess of what would be anticipated). There are two major categories of Somatoform Disorders listed in the *DSM–IV–TR* (APA, 2000): **hysterical disorders** (which are accompanied **by** an actual loss or change in physical functioning) and the **preoccupation disorders** (with the predominant features of excessive concern regarding physical status or well-being).

Hysterical Disorders

There are four hysterical disorders: somatization disorder, undifferentiated somatizatoin disorder, conversion disorder and pain disorder.

Somatization disorder.   According to the *DSM–IV–TR* (APA, 2000), somatization disorder is diagnosed when an individual presents *eight symptoms* from the following list:

- experience of pain in at least four areas (head, abdomen, back, legs, etc)
- two gastrointestinal symptoms (e.g., nausea, vomiting)
- one sexual symptom (e.g., painful intercourse, loss of sexual interest)
- one pseudoneurological symptom (double vision, paralysis, problems with balance, etc).

The disorder is relatively rare (2% of women; 0.2% of men) and onset is prior to 30 years of age. Since the nature of the symptoms required for a diagnosis is not *developmentally appropriate*, it is not surprising that diagnosis is rare in children and youth.

Undifferentiated somatization disorder. Although somatization disorder is rare in children and youth, a diagnosis of **undifferentiated somatoform disorder** may be more prevalent. This disorder requires:

- one or more physical complaints (from the list for somatization disorder, e.g., fatigue, gastrointestinal problems, etc)
- lasting for at least 6 months
- having no medical cause, and causing
- significant dysfunction.

In at least ones study, 11% of the adolescent population (12 to 17 years of age) sampled from over 1000 adolescents residing in Bremen, Germany satisfied diagnostic criteria for undifferentiated somatoform disorder (Essau, Conradt, & Petermann, 2000). In that sample, the most commonly reported symptoms (lasting at least 6 months) were: headaches (15.5%), lump in the throat (14.4%), and stomach pain (12.4%).

Conversion disorder. **Conversion disorder** is one of the most researched somatoform disorders in children and youth. The disorder epitomizes the dramatic nature of symptom presentation of the *hysterical somatoform disorders*. The symptoms are totally disabling, yet are without any medical basis. Examples of conversion disorder include: hand paralysis (glove anesthesia), foot paralysis (foot anesthesia) blindness, deafness, convulsions (seizures) and loss of balance. According to the *DSM–IV–TR* (APA, 2000) conversion symptoms are most likely to be experienced as seizures or loss of balance in children under ten years of age

Pain disorder (associated with psychological factors). Individuals who suffer significant pain without any apparent medical cause may be experiencing pain disorder. Garber and colleagues (1991) reported that between 10% to 30% of children and adolescents presented with **recurrent abdominal pain** (**RAP**), defined as having three or more episodes of pain within a three month period, without apparent medical cause and resulting in significant distress and dysfunction.

Important Distinction

There is an important distinction between individuals with *somatoform disorders* (who believe they are ill) compared to those who demonstrate **factitious disorders** (intentionally causing oneself to be ill to assume a sick role) or **malingering** (deliberately feigning illness to avoid an unpleasant task, or for secondary gain, such as attention, sympathy).

Preoccupation Disorders

Hypochondriasis. Individuals who have **hypochondriasis** believe that they are seriously ill, yet there is no medical basis for their belief. There is minimal information or research concerning the presence of this disorder in children and adolescents.

Body dysmorphic disorder. The cardinal feature of **body dysmorphic disorder** is a preoccupation with a physical defect or imagined imperfection to the extent that it interferes with normal functioning and causes significant distress. Although adults with the disorder suggest onset in adolescence and developmentally self-conscious awareness in adolescence would support the assumption, there is minimal research evidence to support these claims.

Etiology of Somatoform Disorders in Children and Youth

Based on the limited information available, somatoform disorders tend to occur comorbid with symptoms of anxiety and depression (Essau et al., 1999) and exist in greater numbers in the presence of family characteristics such as, increased emphasis on family illness and maternal depression and anxiety (Garber, Zeman, & Walker, 1990). Risk factors for the development of somatoform disorders in children and youth include: a recent and significant stressor at home or at school (90%); having a family member with a chronic disease; or having a legitimate illness for a period of time (Fritz, Fritsch, & Hagino, 1997; Siegel & Barthel, 1986).

Assessment and Treatment

Given the nature of somatoform disorders, initial assessment often involves a medical professional. Some disorders, such as somatization disorder may take years to diagnose correctly, and involve considerable doctor shopping, since individuals are convinced they are ill. Many of the child behavior rating scales (ASEBA; 2001, Achenbach & Rescorla; BASC2; Reynolds & Kamphaus, 2004; CRPS-RL, 1998) presented in Table 5.5 contain scales that measure somatic complaints. Empirical investigations for the treatment of somatoform disorders in children and youth are rare, although one study reported success for a combined cognitive behavioral program and SSRI regime for adolescents with body dysmorphic disorder (Albertini, Phillips, & Guevrement, 1996).

Glossary of New Terms:

negative affectivity
homotypic patterns
tripartite model
negative affect, low positive affect (anhedonia)
hyperarousal
low positive affect/anhedonia
effortful control
behavioral control (behavioral inhibition)
attentional control
somatoform disorders
hysterical disorders
preoccupation disorders
somatization disorder
undifferentiated somatoform disorder
conversion disorder
recurrent abdominal pain (RAP)
factitious disorders
malingering
hypochondriasis
body dysmorphic disorder

6

Anxiety Disorders With Likely Onset in Childhood

CHAPTER PREVIEW

Negative affectivity is a common thread that is pervasive across the anxiety disorders and depression, especially in childhood. From a developmental perspective, reactive and regulatory aspects of temperament can also be instrumental in determining the different guises that negative affective or anxious responses may assume at different stages of development, in response to different developmental stressors (Muris & Ollendick, 2005).

Due to the extensive nature of anxiety, its comorbidity with other disorders and the large number of different types of anxiety disorders that exist, it seems most reasonable to divide information about these disorders into two related chapters. Although any division among the anxiety disorders will be somewhat arbitrary, for purposes of discussion, this text has adopted a division by likely age of onset. This chapter will focus on a historical review of how anxiety disorders have been conceptualized, the methods and instruments used to assess anxiety, and anxiety disorders most likely to have onset in childhood.

1. Historical Evolutions in the Classification of Anxiety Disorders

Conceptually, both the dimensional (ASEBA, 2001) and categorical systems (*DSM–TR*, 2000) have altered their view of anxiety disorders in children in their most recent revisions compared to earlier versions. In response to recent information on negative affectivity, the ASEBA system now recognizes two syndromes in children and youth: *withdrawn/depressed* (low positive affect) and *anxious/depressed* (negative affectivity). Although the *DSM* (1980) recognized three anxiety disorders of childhood; currently, only separation anxiety disorder remains under the category of disorders first evident n childhood.

2. Assessment and Treatment of Anxiety Disorders

Due to high prevalence rates for anxiety disorders, the majority of broadband instruments, such as the interview schedules and behavioral rating scales discussed in chapter 5, include scales to identify general anxiety symptoms. In addition, a number of syndrome specific scales are introduced. The most common treatments for anxiety disorders rely on behavioral and cognitive behavioral methods.

3. Specific Phobias and Fears

From a developmental perspective, fears are common in childhood and can be predicted to change with age. Phobias occur in approximately 15% of children with anxiety issues and represent an exaggerated and irrational fear or dread of an object or situation. Etiology can be linked to biological, parenting (attachment), and/or behavioral causes. A variety of behavioral exposure treatments are introduced such as systematic desensitization.

4. Separation Anxiety Disorder (SAD)

Intense feelings of anxiety or panic occur in children with SAD when they anticipate separation from their caregiver. These feelings are often accompanied by fears of the caregiver being harmed in their absence. As a result, the vast majority of children with SAD (75%) will refuse to attend school. SAD has been linked to genetic and parenting influences. Cognitive behavioral treatments have been successful.

5. General Anxiety Disorder (GAD)

Children with GAD demonstrate pervasive uncontrollable worries across a wide variety of themes including family, peers, and performance that is accompanied by at least one somatic complaint. In younger children, 70% of those with GAD have comorbid SAD. Causes have been linked to genetics, faulty chemical reactivity, negative information, and parenting practices. Treatments available for SAD are also appropriate for GAD.

Anxiety: A Conceptual Perspective

What Is Anxiety and What Are the Anxiety Disorders?

Barlow (2002) describes an anxious response as a *"future-oriented emotion"* that carries with it feelings of *"uncontrollability and unpredictability"* about a *"potentially aversive event"* (p. 104). As described, *worry* then becomes the *anticipation* of some dreaded event. Since feelings of lack of control and unpredictability cause the worry to escalate, heightened physiological responses also accompany the anxious state. In order to reduce the uncomfortable state of arousal (emotional and physiological) that occurs in the wake of feelings of imminent danger, *avoidance* of situations or events that trigger the anxious response becomes a likely response. Although anxious responses and worry are a normal part of living and can provide inoculation against real threat, anxious responses that are excessive and pervasive can result in the development of a host of avoidant behaviors that can interfere with the course of normal development. Under these conditions, avoidance behaviors can become extreme or dysfunctional as anxiety becomes a disordered behavior.

Anxiety and anxiety disorders represent one of the most common disorders evident in childhood and adolescence. Prevalence rates vary by population (clinical vs. nonclinical) and subtype (general, specific); however, 1-year prevalence rates for anxiety disorders have been estimated to be as high as 13% of the population (Costello, Mustillo, Erkanli, Keeler, & Angold, 1996). Anxiety disorders share features of chronic worry about current or future events, and often involve responses from three levels of reactivity:

1. *Behavioral responses* (often of withdrawal, avoidance, or escape);
2. *Cognitive responses* (evident in negative self-appraisals, or interpretation of events as threatening); and
3. *Physiological arousal* (involuntary responses, such as increased heart rate, breathing, tremors, and muscle tension).

Anxiety Disorders from a Historical Perspective

The Dimensional System of Classification

Prior to the recent revision of the ASEBA (2001), three syndromes were included under the Internalizing dimensions of the Achenbach scales (1991), which included: *Withdrawn, Somatic, and Anxious/Depressed* syndromes. Currently, in the wake of empirical evidence regarding the pervasive nature of negativity affectivity across anxiety and depression and low positive affect unique to depression, the newly revised ASEBA (2001) distinguishes these features in two separate syndromes:

- **Withdrawn/Depressed syndrome** (includes low positive affect/anhedonia)
- **Anxious/Depressed syndrome** (which is more in tune with negative affectivity).

The Somatic Complaints syndrome on the revised ASEBA scale remains the same.

> **Memory Bank**
>
> While the dimensional syndromes were obtained through factor analytic methods, the ASEBA (2001) also provides a *DSM–IV* oriented set of scales, including separate scales for Anxiety and Affective Problems. The *DSM* oriented scales were derived by having experienced practitioners (psychiatrists and psychologists) rate the existing items regarding their consistency (not consistent, consistent, or very consistent) with *DSM* criteria. Items rated as very consistent by 64% of the raters were included in the *DSM*-oriented scales (Achenbach & Rescorla, 2001).

The *DSM* System of Classification

Historically, the *DSM* system has evolved its conceptualization of anxiety disorders in adults and children. The changes in *DSM* classification concerning anxiety disorders in children and adolescents over the past 30 years are summarized in Table 6.1.

The *DSM–III* (APA, 1980) defined three anxiety disorders of childhood: separation anxiety disorder, avoidance disorder, and overanxious disorder. In the early classifications, two of the anxiety disorders were situation specific (separation anxiety disorder, avoidant disorder), while one disorder was pervasive across situations (overanxious disorder).

Table 6.1 Historical Evolution of Anxiety Disorders and the *DSM*

DSM	Year	Category for Child and Adolescent Anxiety	Adult Types that might apply
DSM–II	1968		Overanxious reaction
DSM–III	1980	**Anxiety disorders of childhood and adolescence** Separation anxiety disorder Overanxious disorder Avoidant disorder	Simple phobia Social phobia
DSM–III–R	1987	**Anxiety disorders of childhood or adolescence:** Separation anxiety disorder Avoidant disorder Overanxious disorder	Panic disorder (with or without agoraphobia) Specific phobia Social phobia (social anxiety disorder) Obsessive compulsive disorder General anxiety disorder Post traumatic stress disorder Acute stress disorder
DSM–IV	1994	**Other disorders of infancy, childhood or adolescence:** Separation anxiety disorder	Panic disorder (with or without agoraphobia) Specific phobia Social phobia Obsessive compulsive disorder General anxiety disorder (includes overanxious disorder of dhildhood) Post traumatic stress disorder Acute stress disorder

---

Important Distinction

In the *DSM–III–R* (APA, 1987) pervasive symptoms shared by the anxiety disorders were evident in common symptoms of *worry, concern, avoidance, and somatic complaints* (Bernstein, 1990). In the *DSM–III–R*, a diagnosis of Overanxious Disorder of Childhood required four of the following seven symptoms: *worry about future events; concern about past behavior; concern regarding competence; physical complaints; significant self-onsciousness; continual need for reassurance; and feelings of tension, or an inability to relax.* Currently the *DSM–IV* considers the above symptoms as descriptive features of the disorder rather than diagnostic criteria.

Generalized Anxiety Disorder (GAD) is located within the major section of the *DSM–IV–TR* (APA, 2000) under Anxiety Disorders and includes the previously known category of Overanxious Disorder of Childhood, now called GAD.

Memory Bank

Currently (*DSM–IV–TR*, APA, 2000), only **separation anxiety** remains within the section devoted to disorders with onset in childhood or adolescence. However, Spence's (1997) recent factor–analytic study of the structure of anxiety symptoms (using *DSM–IV* classifications) has verified the existence of six separate, but correlated, forms of anxiety that exist in children:

1. panic–agoraphobia
2. social phobia
3. separation anxiety
4. obsessive compulsive problems
5. generalized anxiety
6. physical fears.

Presently, there are 9 different anxiety disorders recognized in the *DSM–IV–TR* (APA, 2000), including:

1. specific phobias
2. separation anxiety disorder (SAD)
3. generalized anxiety disorder (GAD)
4. obsessive compulsive disorder (OCD)
5. social phobia
6. panic attack (with and without agoraphobia)
7. acute stress disorder
8. post traumatic stress disorder (PTSD)
9. substance-induced anxiety disorders.

While only SAD appears specifically with a childhood onset, the *DSM* does present some characteristics that might be present in child and adolescent populations for the majority of other anxiety disorders. However, criteria and symptom guidelines remain primarily adult based for all anxiety disorders except SAD.

Anxiety Disorders From a Developmental Perspective

Developmentally, the discussion of anxiety disorders in this text will follow the pattern of developmental onset for the disorders in child and adolescent populations. Two chapters will focus on anxiety disorders and anxious behaviors. Disorders with onset primarily in childhood (specific phobias and fears, separation anxiety disorder, general anxiety) will be discussed in chapter 6, while later occurring anxious responses (obsessive compulsive disorder, social phobia, panic disorder with and without agoraphobia, and the stress disorders) will be discussed in chapter 7. Studies of the age of onset of specific anxiety disorders suggest that the earliest forms of anxiety disorders are the *specific phobias* and *separation anxiety disorder (SAD)*, followed by *generalized anxiety disorder (GAD)*, with likely onset within the age range from 8 to 10 years of age. Adolescence is the likely age of onset for *social phobia, panic disorder with or without agoraphobia*, and *obsessive compulsive disorder* (see Saavedra & Silverman, 2002, for a review). Despite different ages of onset, anxiety disorders can be enduring and it is not uncommon to see overlapping anxiety disorders. If a child is diagnosed with an anxiety disorder of any type, the likelihood of having another anxiety disorder is highest for social phobia (46%), followed by simple phobia (34%), and general anxiety disorder (29%; Kendall, Brady, & Verduin, 2001).

Development in Focus

Temperament has been linked to a child's predisposition to developing an anxiety disorder. Parent reports reveal that children with anxiety disorders have a history of difficult temperaments as infants (*crying, fussy, irritable, difficult to soothe*) and experienced more fears as toddlers. In addition, they also experienced more problems adjusting to changes in routines than peers who did not have anxiety disorders (Rapee, 1997).

Developmental Pathways

Prior to a discussion of each of the anxiety disorders individually, it may be very beneficial, initially, to look at the anxiety disorders as an integrated cluster. From this vantage point, Vasey and Dadds (2001) and Ollendick and Vasey (2001) present a transactional model based on factors that *predispose, precipitate, and maintain/ameliorate* the development of anxiety in individuals. Although an in-depth discussion of the model is beyond the scope of this text, a very brief synopsis will be provided as an overarching framework for discussions of anxiety disorders to follow.

Two potential pathways.   Based on their extensive research review, the researchers have isolated two potential pathways: **a cumulative risk pathway** and a **precipitating event pathway**.

Cumulative risk pathway. This pathway results from having a number of *predisposing factors* that place the child at greater risk and exposure to repeated situations that cause anxiety.

Precipitating event pathway. This pathway develops as a *learned response* to an event (e.g., traumatic event; repeated exposure to an event resulting in repeated aversive consequences, or seemingly unrelated to a given event, but may result from prior learning and stimulus generalization). The model is summarized in Table 6.2.

Predisposing factors.   An **inhibited temperament** (emotionality/neuroticism) is one factor that can predispose an individual to negative or anxious reactions. Individuals with an inhibited temperament tend to demonstrate:

Table 6.2 Cumulative Risk and Precipitating Event Models of Anxiety Disorders and Developmental Pathways

Pathway 1: Cumulative Risk Model	Pathway 2: Precipitating Event Model
History: *Child characteristics:* Child has a number of **risk factors** that increased vulnerability to developing an anxiety disorder. Unstable environment, anxious parenting style, anxious attachment, overprotective parenting, genetic risk for anxiety, etc); wary temperament.	**Learned Response:** *Environmental characteristics:* encountering a traumatic event (or repeated **exposure to aversive consequences**, or stimulus generalization) place individual at greater likelihood to react anxiously to "perceived" threat in other situations.
Predisposing Factors: Heredity (genetics), inhibited temperament (emotionality/neuroticism), increased vulnerability to anxiety	**Predisposing Factors:** Parenting style and response to anxious event (e.g., overprotective response style; lack of neighborhood safety); **number and/or intensity** of anxiety provoking events encountered.

Maintaining Factors Across Both Pathways:
1. avoidance of anxiety provoking situations;
2. limited development of competencies (social, emotional, academic);
3. cognitive bias to interpret situations as threatening;
4. negative experiences; and
5. parent/caregiver responses that are either overprotective or overly controlling.

Sources: Vasey & Dadds (2001); Ollendick & Vasey (2001).

- high emotional reactivity,
- bias to interpret situations as threatening, and
- poor effortful control.

Anxiety disorders are also more prevalent among member of families and genetic risk is high. Family dynamics can also escalate anxiety levels and insecure attachment sets the stage for greater anxiety risk.

Maintaining factors.   Anxiety is maintained or exacerbated as a result of **transactional processes** (on-going bidirectional and cumulative series of interactions) that often involve several of the five factors listed in Table 6.2. The five factors include:

1. avoidance behaviors
2. limited development of competencies (social, emotional, academic)
3. cognitive bias to threat
4. exposure to negative experiences
5. parental responses of overprotection or over control.

Parents who encourage avoidance by being overprotective can reinforce their child's feelings of helplessness and fear. As a result, they may limit their child's growth in ways necessary to overcome fears and build needed competencies in social, emotional, and academic areas. The process can be daunting for the parent whose child may increase their fearfulness, as a result, causing the parent to become even more protective in an increasing cycle of negative transactions.

Protective factors.   In their model, Vasey and Dadds (2001) emphasize that not all roads lead to anxiety. Awareness of the five factors that can augment and maintain anxiety can alert one to realizing how each of the five situations above can be reframed to produce the opposite effect, e.g., replace avoidance with encouraging engagement. Throughout this and the following chapter, although the anxiety disorders will be discussed individually, the transactional model proposed by Vasey and colleagues can be very helpful in better understanding the underlying processes and the precipitating and maintaining factors that can strengthen or ameliorate anxious responses.

Assessment of Childhood Anxiety and the Anxiety Disorders

Evidence-Based Assessment of Anxiety

Silverman and Saavedra (2004) conducted a review of the psychometric properties of instruments used in evidence-based treatment research on anxiety and based on their analysis recommend using the *Anxiety Disorders Interview Schedule for DSM–IV: Child and Parent Versions (ADIS for DSM–IV: C/P*; Silverman & Albano, 1996: Silverman et al., 2001) and the *Achenbach Child Behavior Checklist* as a parent rating scale for internalizing disorders such as anxiety and mood.

In their extensive review of methods and instruments that are currently available for the assessment of anxiety in children and youth, Silverman and Ollendick (2005) emphasize the need to address the **clinical utility** of assessment instruments, or how the instruments will serve to inform treatment. (The following discussion follows Silverman & Ollenick, 2005.) The authors emphasize goals for assessment as outlined by Jensen and Haynes (1986), such as screening, diagnoses and identification of symptoms and behaviors, identification of mediating variables, and/or planning and evaluation of treatment outcomes. A summary of some of the common assessment methods outlined in the reports by Silverman and Saavedra (2004) and Silverman and Ollendick (2005) are available in Table 6.3.

For diagnostic purposes, the authors recommend the interview schedule method and the *ADIS* in particular; however, they also discuss the contribution of a variety of self-report instruments (many of which are presented in Table 6.3) in meeting other goals inherent in clinical utility. Although beyond the scope of this text, the report presents several recommendations for future evaluation of assessment instruments based on their ability to provide an identification of maintaining variables, evaluation of treatment outcomes, and other assessment goals. Ultimately, the authors stress the need not only of conducting a **multi-informant assessment**, but also a **multiresponse format** in order to provide better differential diagnosis for symptoms that share negative affective features. Of the many existing instruments, Silverman and Saavedra (2004) recommend three instruments for use in evidence based practice:

1. Revised Children's Manifest Anxiety Scale (RCMAS),
2. Stait-trait Anxiety Inventory for Children (STAIC), and
3. The Fear Survey Schedule for Children—Revised (FSSC–R).

Table 6.3 Common Assessment Instruments for Anxiety Disorders

Self-Report Instruments	Ages	Description
Multidimensional Anxiety Scale for Children (MASC; March, Parker, Sullivan, Stallings, & Conners, 1997)	8–19	39 items. Anxiety across four domains: Physical symptoms, social anxiety, harm avoidance, and separation/panic.
Stait-Trait Anxiety Inventory for Children (STAIC; Spielberger, 1973)	8–15	20 items. Two subcales: Trait anxiety (child characteristics/ chronic); state anxiety (environmental/ transitory)
Revised Children's Manifest Anxiety Scale (RC-MAS; Reynolds & Richmond, 1985).	7–17	37 items. Total anxiety and three domains: Physiological anxiety, worry/oversensitivity, social concerns/concentration.
Fear Survey Schedule for Children—Revised (FSSC–R; Ollendick, 1983)	7 -18	80 Items. Total score and five scales for sear of: Failure and criticism; unknown, danger, and death; medical procedures and small animals.
Trauma Symptom Checklist for Children (TSCC; Briere, 1996)	8–16	54 items. Five clinical subscales: Anxiety, depression, anger, post traumatic stress, and dissociation.
Social Phobia and Anxiety Inventory for Children (Beidel, Turner, & Morris, 1995, 1999)	8–18	26 items. Three subscales: Assertiveness/general cConversation, traditional social encounters and public performance.
Spence Children's Anxiety Scale (Spence, 1998)	7–14	44 items. Symptom scales for: SAD, social phobia, OCD, panic disorder-agoraphobia, GAD and fears of physical injury
Achenbach System of Empirically Based Assessment (ASEBA, Achenbach & Rescorla, 2001).	Youth 11–18 Parent/ Teacher 6–18	102 items: Parent/Teach and Youth parallel forms. Externalizing, internalizing, and total problems. Internalizing scale: anxious/depressed. *DSM*– oriented scales: anxiety problems
Beck Youth Inventories: Anxiety Scale (Beck, Beck, & Jolly, 2005).	7–12	20 Items. One of five scales: Anxiety, depression, disruptive behavior, anger, and self-concept.
Semistructured Interviews		
The Children's Yale–Brown Obsessive Compulsive Scale (Goodman et al., 1989)	Child 7–17 or Parent	10 items. Separate scores obtained for obsessions and compulsions. Ratings based on duration, frequency, interference, and distress.
Anxiety Disorders Interview Schedule for *DSM–IV*: Child and Parent Versions (ADIS for *DSM–IV*: C/P; Silverman & Albano, 1996)	Child 7–16 or Parent	Each *DSM–IV* anxiety disorder rated as to severity and distress, as well as dysfunction (school, peers, family)

Note: SAD = separation anxiety disorder; GAD = general anxiety disorder; OCD = obsessive compulsive disorder

Phobias and Fears

Description and Associated Clinical Features

Fears in childhood are a common occurrence. Developmental studies suggest, however, that the nature of what is feared changes with age, while the actual number of fears declines with age. The nature of children's fears is often related to important cognitive transitions that occur across the developmental spectrum. Although fears are common, it is less common to experience a significant and specific fear that is enduring and debilitating.

Development in Focus

It is often possible to predict common childhood fears based on an understanding of how children think at various stages of development. Fear of strangers peaks at 7–8 months of age, the same time when the infant is gaining greater awareness of their own self as an individual entity. Toddlers' fears often involve fear of toileting activities and fear of personal injury. Preschool children who have significant difficulties with appearance/reality distinctions and who tend to empower inanimate objects with life (animism) can readily turn shadows into monsters. Common fears in preschool children involve imaginary creatures, monsters, fear of the dark, and fear of animals. Furthermore, the emergence of intuitive thought around 4 years of age often results young children's attempts to explain situations/events in a way that may incorporate their fears. For example, at this stage, a young child may explain a bad circumstance (a broken bike, etc.) by believing that wild animals came and broke it apart. Early school-aged children fear environmental elements (thunder and lightning), while middle school children's fears evolve around health issues (dentist) or authority figures (principal, school resource officer). Adolescent fears often include activities that might potentially cause embarrassment in front of peers (public speaking) and global issues such as the potential for catastrophic events.

The *DSM–IV–TR* (APA, 2000) describes **specific phobia** as a *persistent fear* of a definable object, place, or situation *which does not have a reasonable basis*. The resulting fearful and anxious response is significant enough to potentially cause a panic attack. Although the *DSM* states that the person is aware that this fear is unreasonable, often this will not hold true for very young children. The most likely response is avoidance of the feared object/event, or facing it with increased anxiety and evoking of the fear response. Unless the phobia interferes with functioning to a significant degree (social, emotional, academic, family), a diagnosis is not made. In child and adolescent populations (under 18 years of age), the phobia must endure for at least 6 months.

Development in Focus

According to some researchers, it is debatable whether young children experience phobic responses to the extent required to match criteria set out in the DSM for "true phobias." In addition, given the complex nature of negative reactions at this age, it has been suggested that describing these reactions in terms of negative affectivity might be more useful (Kearney, Eisen, & Silverman, 1995).

In phobic responses, the focus of the fear is often the anticipation of harm (e.g., fear of flying would be based on fear of the plane crashing). Exposure to the feared object may elicit significant physiological responses, as in dizziness, shortness of breath, increased heart rate, and even fainting.

Responses of heightened anxiety will increase in proximity to the feared object/situation and abate as the distance increases. Often an element of escape is imminent and inability to escape may result in heightened arousal potentially producing a panic attack. Individuals who have a specific phobia are more likely to have another phobia or other anxiety disorders and mood disorders. The most common types of phobias include:

- Animal type (animals and insects, usually childhood onset)
- Natural environment type (thunder, lightning)

- Blood-injection-injury type
- Situational type (flying, elevators, school)
- Other type (choking, falling, etc.)

Other developmental considerations concerning the onset of fears and phobias are the actual events that take place and the stressors surrounding them. It might be predicted that a young child going to school for the first time might experience symptoms of separation anxiety, or that adolescents who are very sensitive to peer criticism might display symptoms of social phobia. However, when these responses trigger avoidance behaviors (school refusal, social withdrawal) that are uncontrollable and interfere with the course of normal development, then greater concern is warranted as the anxiety takes on more clinical features and behavior becomes more disordered and dysfunctional (Silverman & Ollendick, 2005).

Prevalence

Although as high as 9% of the population in the United States will have symptoms of a specific phobia, less than 30% will seek professional help (*DSM–IV–TR*, APA, 2000). Twice as many females report specific phobias than males. The most common fear in females is fear of animals, while the most common fear in men is fear of heights. One of the most prevalent fears in 9- to 13-year-old children was a fear of spiders (Muris, Merckelbach, Meesters, & Van Lier, 1997). Approximately 15% of children who are referred for anxiety issues present with specific phobias. In addition to number and types of fears changing with age, gender differences have also been noted. One study found that girls reported more intense fears and more overall tendency to be fearful than boys (Silverman & Nelles, 2001), while another study has linked fearfulness in girls to fathers' authoritarian parenting style and mothers' fearfulness (Pickersgill, Valentine, Pincus, & Foustok, 1999).

Lions and Tigers and Bears, Oh My

The children's song "If you go out in the woods today, you're in for a big surprise" was not far off in citing the most common animal fears in children. A survey of 37 Kindergarten children revealed that the most commonly feared animals were bears (18%), tigers (12%), snakes (12%), dogs (12%), and lions (9%). Furthermore, the children reported that the overriding fear was of the animal causing physical harm (being bitten) or injury (Bowd, 1983).

The *DSM* also recognizes phobic responses specific to social situations or performance anxiety (*social phobias*) and those that are reactive to fears of being trapped and unable to escape, such as *panic disorder with agoraphobia*. Given the self-conscious awareness often evident during the adolescent period, it is not surprising to find that onset of social phobia or panic disorder with agoraphobia linked to midadolescence. We will revisit these disorders at length in chapter 7.

Important Distinction

The Phobias (specific, social, and agoraphobia) elicit fear as a response to an imminent and threatening situation or object, while anxiety, as in generalized anxiety disorder (GAD), refers to a more free-floating and nonspecific worry. The *DSM* criteria for the phobias are summarized in Table 6.4.

Table 6.4 Criteria for Specific Phobia

- Persistent unreasonable fear of specific event or object (e.g., heights, animals, sight of blood, receiving an inoculation)
- Exposure to the object or event produces extreme anxiety reaction, which may involve a panic attack. Children may respond by intense crying, tantrums, freezing, and clinging behaviors
- Adults and youth recognize the fear is unreasonable. Young children are not likely to understand this consciously
- Tendency to avoid the situation or object, or else extreme discomfort, distress, and anxiety results
- There is marked distress about having the phobia, or there is marked interference (*avoidance, distress, anxious anticipation*) resulting from the phobia in areas such as employment, school, peer, and family relationships
- Duration of at least 6 months in children and youth under 18 years of age
- Responses are not better accounted for by another disorder, such as obsessive compulsive disorder (OCD), post traumatic stress disorder (PTSD), separation anxiety disorder (SAD), social phobia, or panic disorder with or without agoraphobia
- Specify type of phobia:
  Animal type
  Natural environment type (e.g., heights, storms)
  Blood-injection-injury type
  Situational type (elevators, bridges, enclosed places)
  Other (fear of contamination, fear of clowns, etc.)

Source: APA (2000), pp. 449–450.

Etiology and Theoretical Perspectives

The development of phobias in children and adolescents has been attributed to multiple risk factors including *child characteristics* such as genetic factors and temperament (behavioral inhibition), *environmental characteristics* such as parent psychopathology, and family dynamics (communication styles, parenting practices, and attachment history). However, the specific nature of the phobias often suggests that individual **conditioning experiences** may be the most commonly reported pathway related to the onset and maintenance of phobic reactions (Muris et al., 1998).

Biological and Genetic Components

Studies of twins and families have found several genetic links to the anxiety disorders; however, it is generally agreed that the etiology for specific phobias is better represented by multiple pathways that include *child characteristics* (genetics, temperament) and *environmental characteristics* (family dynamics, exposure to conditioning experiences).

Behavioral Explanations for Phobias

According to behaviorists we learn behaviors in three important ways: **classical conditioning**, **operant conditioning**, and **modeling**. Behaviorists draw upon all three sources when they attempt to modify behavior. However, operant conditioning and modeling are the main sources for behavioral change, while classical conditioning seems to be the most important feature of acquiring irrational fears to situations or objects that are not really dangerous.

Memory Bank

Watson created a conditioned fear in a toddler, little Albert, to a "white furry rat." Although the child initially demonstrated no fear towards the rat, by pairing presentations of the rat with a loud noise (which is inherently fearful to infants and some toddlers), Albert was conditioned to associate the fear he experienced with the rat. Eventually this fear generalized to most white and furry things (e.g., Santa Clause's beard, his mother's fur coat, etc.).

In **classical conditioning**, if a previously innocuous object or situation is paired with a fearful object or event, we can develop a fear by association.

Case in Point

Sally takes showers on a daily basis as part of her morning get-ready-for-work routine. She gives it little thought and often is on auto-pilot planning her daily activities while getting ready. However, on Saturday night Sally is feeling particularly tense and so she goes to the movies. It is oldies night at the movies, and Sally will finally get to see the original version of the classic movie, *Psycho*, which she has never seen. She has also not seen the remake, so she is excited about it. However, Sally nearly jumps out of her skin when she sees the "shower scene" at the Bates Motel. The next day, Sally gets ready for her shower and drawing the shower curtain, immediately triggers visions of the "shower scene" in her head that she cannot escape from. Sally quickly throws back the shower curtain and gets right out of the bathroom, her heart beating very quickly. Sally now is frightened of showers.

The classical conditioning explanation for Sally's conditioned fear of showers is presented in Table 6.5.

At Stage 1, the shower curtain in the apartment is a **neutral stimulus**; it really doesn't elicit any strong emotions. However, at Stage 2, the shower curtain in the movie is an **unconditioned stimulus (UCS)** that does produce the immediate and strong emotion of fear. Because the response occurs naturally without conditioning, it is referred to as the **unconditioned response (UCR)**. At Stage 3, the shower curtain in the apartment is now associated with strong images of the *Psycho* scene and becomes the **conditioned stimulus (CS)** which elicits a **conditioned response (CR)** of fear. So, Sally has developed an irrational fear of showers.

Classical conditioning provides a blueprint for understanding how people can develop phobic responses. If the situation is traumatic enough, the conditioning can occur almost immediately (e.g., being bitten by a dog may result in subsequent fear of all dogs). It is also possible to "de-condition" a fear response, using the same type of classical conditioning paradigm. *If we can learn it...we can unlearn it.* Often behavioral techniques can be used to successfully unlearn or de-condition phobic responses by pairing feared associations with nonfearful images. The process referred to as **systematic desensitization** can be a very successful tool to disentangle fear

Table 6.5 Classical Conditioning

Previously Conditioned		
UCS (Scary Movie) *Unconditioned Stimulus*	⟶	UCR (Fear and Shaking) *Unconditioned Response*
Neutral Stimulus (Shower)	⟶	No UCR (Fear and Shaking)
Conditioning Phase		
Neutral Stimulus (Shower)	+ UCS ⟶ (Psycho Murder Scene)	UCR (Fear and Shaking)
After Conditioning		
CS (Shower Curtain) *Conditioned Stimulus*	⟶	CR (Fear and Shaking) *Conditioned Response*

response associations from their source. There are several variations of this technique which will be discussed shortly, under treatment for phobias.

Another method of acquiring irrational fears is by observing someone else and then reacting to their fear by **modeling** the fear behavior, a response akin to the **contagion effect**. For example, a child may become anxious and fearful by observing a parent's fearful response to a situation or object (Pickersgill et al., 1999). Once a fear is established, patterns of avoidant behaviors may develop and be sustained since avoidance of the object or event alleviates the fear and anxiety. This pattern of behavior is the result of **operant conditioning**. For Sally, staying away from the shower will help to alleviate her anxiety, and this will serve to positively reinforce her avoidant behavior and the avoidant behaviors will likely continue. Sally may also become fearful of taking baths or become fearful of water, as her fears take on a life of their own and associations connect fears to similar situations or objects, a process referred to as **stimulus generalization**.

Memory Bank

The **Law of Effect** (Thorndike), simply stated, is that consequences of behavior are highly influential in establishing whether a given behavior will be repeated or not. Behaviors followed by desirable consequences will be repeated. Behaviors followed by undesirable consequences will be avoided, or dropped from our repertoire.

In order to explain why some phobias are more common than others, some theorists have suggested the notion of **preparedness** based on the fact that some fears seem to have a definite survivor value to them.

Science Talks

Ohman, Erixon, and Lofberg (1975) conducted a series of studies to investigate whether people may have a predisposition to acquire specific fears. In these classic studies, researchers attempted to condition fear in adults to pictures of houses, faces, snakes, and spiders. What they found was that conditioned fears to houses and faces disappeared once shocks were discontinued; however, fear of snakes and spiders remained long after the shocks were terminated.

Parenting and Attachment Theory

According to theories of attachment, insecure attachment can result from a variety of caregiver responses to distressing situations or events. If parents are inconsistent in their responses, are unable to soothe the infant adequately, or are overprotective, the infant does not have an opportunity to internalize and organize information regarding how to respond in a healthy way to distressing circumstances. Throughout the course of development, when faced with stressful situations, children who were insecurely attached as infants have demonstrated poor ability to handle school-based anxiety at 5 years of age (Kendall & Ronan, 1990), and are significantly more likely to develop anxiety disorders as adolescents compared to peers who were securely attached as infants (Warren, Huston, Egeland, & Sroufe, 1997).

Treatment

Participant modeling and **reinforced practice** are two well-established treatments alternatives for children with phobic disorders (Ollendick & King, 1998). Intervention techniques that draw on the principle of modeling take advantage of observational learning using models to demonstrate positive and nonfearful behavior towards the feared object or situation. Models can be live models or models viewed on video taped segments; in addition, models can be adults, peers, or multiple models. Research consistently has demonstrated that actual or *in vivo participation* in the modeling experience is superior to either observing models on film or mentally trying to imagine oneself in a fearful situation, *covert or imaginal participation*. The technique used in reinforced practice is self-explanatory and is based on principles of operant conditioning. When practice in facing a feared situation or object is reinforced positively, anxiety is reduced and behavior becomes more normalized (see Ollendick & King, 1998, for a review).

Several techniques are available for developing *systematic desensitization programs* based on methods initially developed by Wolpe (1958) to de-condition responses of fear. As mentioned earlier, techniques that emphasize actual involvement (**in vivo desensitization**) in the desensitization process are more successful than those that feature **imaginal desensitization techniques**. Based on principles of learning and **successive approximation**, an individual is slowly exposed to the feared object/event on a very gradual basis in such a way as to make initial steps less anxiety provoking and ultimately lead to facing the object/event that is feared and overcoming anxiety/fear associated with the object. Crucial to the development of the desensitization program are two important ingredients:

1. The need to teach the individual methods of deep relaxation; and
2. The development of a fear hierarchy (listing steps from least to most feared aspect of a phobia).

At each step of the program, the individual is exposed to increasingly closer approximations to the object of their fears, while pairing each step with a relaxation response. Since a relaxed state of mind is incompatible with being frightened or highly anxious, ultimately the fear (anxiety) is extinguished. An example of a systematic desensitization program for school phobia is presented in the next *Case in Point*. Depending on the severity of the case, steps may be constructed in more gradual or more abrupt stages. In this case, the effort was made to link Sara to her friends' school-going behavior and to reward this gradually as a positive experience. If Sara did not have a friend at school, then the steps would have taken a different turn.

Systematic desensitization is not limited to pairing a feared response with relaxation training. In one study, researchers used "emotive imagery" and had children pair feared situations with stories they created about how their favorite hero would conquer the fear. In this study, **positive affect** and **child mastery**, rather than muscle relaxation, became the antidote against feelings of fear and anxiety (Lazarus & Abramowitz, 1962).

Case in Point

Shortly after enrolling in the Grade 1 program, Sara missed several weeks of school due to illness. Although fully recovered, the morning routine of getting ready for school would continually result in Sara complaining of stomach pains, trembling, and actually being physically sick to her stomach. Forcing Sara to go to school resulted in her being physically ill in class and having to be sent home. Finally, the school psychologist became involved and worked with Sara's mother to develop a graded hierarchy of events related to school attendance. Sara was taught how to reduce her anxiety level through deep breathing and was rewarded for her ability to do so. Some of the steps in the program included:

1. Drive by school on weekend.
2. Stop at school playground on weekend.
3. Sunday evening, get school materials ready for next day.
4. Monday, put school materials in book bag and place bag near door.
5. Tuesday, walk with school bag out door and to the end of the first street.
6. Wednesday, walk to the next street towards school.
7. Thursday, have a friend from school come to play with Sara after school.
8. Friday, play school with Sara at home and go to meet friend when school is out.
9. Saturday, play with her friend in school yard.
10. Sunday, go to school and walk up the front steps, look through window.
11. Walk with her friend to school.

Separation Anxiety Disorder

Description and Associated Clinical Features

Separation anxiety disorder (SAD) was not recognized as a unique psychological disorder until the 3rd revision of the *DSM* (*DSM–III*; APA, 1980). Although normal stranger anxiety in the infant peaks at approximately 9–10 months of age, and children may experience feelings of homesickness and longing for a parent when they are away from home for the first time (e.g., Kindergarten children beginning school; or summer camp experiences), the form of separation anxiety recognized as a childhood disorder is a far more intense and disabling experience.

Children who experience SAD do so at an intense level which is developmentally inappropriate and for an extended period of time (at least 4-weeks). SAD manifests before 18 years of age, but occurrence prior to age 6 is considered to be **early onset SAD**. In order to avoid separation from the caregiver, children with SAD demonstrate significant impairment in social and academic functioning. The need to remain attached to the caregiver can take the form of actual physical presence or frequent contact calls via telephone to reassure themselves that no harm has come to the caregiver.

According to the *DSM–IV–TR* (APA, 2000), a diagnosis of SAD is expected if excessive worry about separation from the caregiver is demonstrated in *three* from the following list of symptoms:

- anticipation of separation results in excessive distress
- excessive fears of the caregiver succumbing to an accident or harm

- excess worry that an event will trigger separation at some future time
- school refusal
- fearful of being alone without the caregiver or adult substitute
- reluctance to sleep alone or sleep away from home
- nightmares about separation
- repeated physical complaints (headaches, stomachaches)

Due to the extreme nature of SAD, children may experience significant discomfort when asked to perform tasks which require them to leave familiar territory. Physical complaints may also be excessive with pronounced stomach upset that may actually result in vomiting and visits to the physician to determine the need for medical intervention. Given the nature of the disorder, parents often find the child with SAD to be very demanding and intrusive.

Case in Point

Nancy had always been a rather shy and timid girl. As a toddler she never ventured far from her mother's side. Babysitters were not an option because Nancy would sob incessantly at the suggestion and cling to her mother Kathy's leg at the mere thought of her mother leaving. Kathy was concerned, but they rarely had an evening out, due to financial problems, so it really wasn't a major problem. On these occasions, Nancy would stay with her grandmother who acted very much like a mother substitute.

Nancy had a few close friends in the neighborhood but preferred to play in her own yard. When she did go to the neighbor's yard to play, she often ran home to check that her mother was all right. One night Nancy was invited to a sleepover party for her friend Terry's 5th birthday. Nancy was excited about the present and the party, and Kathy even bought Nancy a new Barbie sleeping bag for the event. However, at 8 o'clock that evening the door-bell rang. There was Nancy, sleeping bag in tow, complaining of a headache and bad stomachache. She couldn't stay the night; she had to come home.

Six months later, when Kathy tried to enroll Nancy in Kindergarten, the severity of the problem became dramatically clear. Nancy became violently ill and sick to her stomach the first day of school and had to be picked up and taken home. The second day she was too sick to attend school. Ultimately after seeking medical advice, Kathy's physician recommended professional assistance for Nancy due to her severe and early onset separation anxiety disorder (SAD).

Separation anxiety and school refusal. Although **school refusal** is the most common symptom of children with SAD (75%), only one third of all children who refuse to attend school do so because they have SAD (Black, 1995). Children may refuse to attend school following a period of legitimate absence (e.g., period of illness), following a change of schools (move), or gradually over the course of frequently accumulating absences. School refusal may also signal a fear of legitimate circumstances. For example, a child may refuse to attend school to avoid victimization by the school bully. While cognitive behavioral treatment methods (CBT) can be successful in reducing SAD, children who demonstrate school refusal are more responsive to highly structured behaviorally oriented interventions that use firm guidelines, rules, and expectations about school attendance and provide rewards for mastering progressive steps in the reentry process. However, in cases where symptoms of SAD are more ingrained, systematic desensitization using in vivo exposure can be used to increase gradual separation from the parent.

Memory Bank

There are several techniques that can be used to achieve systematic desensitization: *in vivo exposure* (real life), *imagined exposure, live modeling,* and *vicarious modeling.* In most studies, outcomes for in vivo exposure are superior to imagined exposure. Unlike the progressive exposure of the systematic desensitization technique, *flooding* is a technique which thrusts the child immediately into the fear-producing situation. In the case of school refusal, flooding is often recommended at the onset with immediate placement of the child back into the school environment and school routines. However, prolonged or severe anxiety associated with school refusal may require the use of more gradual desensitization.

Prevalence

According to the *DSM–IV–TR* (APA, 2000), approximately 4% of children and adolescents will be diagnosed with SAD. However, prevalence rates can be as high as 10% in clinical populations. SAD tends to be somewhat more frequent in females than males, and shares comorbidity with GAD, depression, and somatic complaints (Last, 1991). The remission rate of SAD is high, with stressful situations (transitions) causing the symptoms to reappear. SAD may be a precursor to increased risk for later depression and anxiety disorders and for the onset of panic attacks and agoraphobia for females in adulthood (Albano, Chorpita, & Barlow, 1996).

Etiology

Although the exact cause of SAD is unknown, there are several associated features, risks, and protective factors which have been isolated.

Biological Model
The role of biological, genetic, and temperament factors.   Although specific details are lacking at this point, SAD is likely under genetic influence by virtue of being an anxiety disorder. One study found that over 80% of mothers who had children with SAD or GAD presented with a history of anxiety disorders themselves (Last, Hersen, Kazdin, Finkelstein, & Strauss, 1987). One model which has been developed to explain the possible development of panic disorder in children and adolescents might be applied to SAD equally as well (Ollendick, 1998). Within this framework, one possible developmental pathway to panic disorder might involve aspects of the child's temperament (*inhibited*), patterns of attachment to the caregiver (*insecure/anxious*), and internalized responses to stress that become *habitual stress responses* that are evoked when faced with repeated separations. The model also would seem to fit for SAD as well.

Parenting Practices and Behavioral Modeling
Parent overprotectiveness and reinforcement of the child's avoidance behaviors can be an integral component to the maintenance of SAD. Parents who are overly enmeshed with their children

may inadvertently create heightened dependencies and stunt the emotional growth in these children. In some families, maternal depression and family dysfunction may result in the **over parentification** of the child (child assumes the role of the parent) who does not want to leave home for fear that they will not be able to protect the parent. Furthermore, recent research linking parenting style to child psychopathology suggests that children with anxiety disorders may experience heightened anxiety due to feelings of ineffectiveness resulting from parental reliance on authoritarian parenting practices (Hudson & Rapee, 2000).

Treatment

Cognitive behavioral interventions. Cognitive behavioral treatment (CBT) methods have been successful in treating a host of child disorders, and it is not surprising to find CBT also successful in the treatment of SAD (see Ollendick & King, 1998, for a review). The **Coping Cat Program** is suitable for children 7 to 16 years of age, is classified as an "efficacious" CBT treatment program, and has been successful in targeting multiple anxiety disorders, including SAD, GAD, and social phobia (Kendall, 1994; Kendall & Southam-Gerow, 1996). The Coping Cat Program (Kendall, 2000) was initially developed to assist children to reduce anxiety by using child-focused individual CBT but has been successfully adapted to suit a group setting (Flannery-Schroeder & Kendall, 2000). The program consists of 16 to 18 sessions divided equally between the development of coping skills (first half) and the practice of those skills (in both imagined and in vivo conditions). The FEAR acronym is used as a mnemonic device to outline the key points and stages in the process:

F   Feel frightened *(emphasis on the physical symptoms that accompany arousal)?*
E   Expect the worse *(awareness of negative self talk)?*
A   Attitude/Actions that can help *(replace negative with positive coping self-statements).*
R   Results and Rewards *(self-monitoring, evaluation, and self-reward).*

Two other versions of similar shorter programs, Coping Koala and Coping Bear have also been recognized as "efficacious" treatments for multiple anxiety disorders (SAD, GAD, and social phobia) and have been demonstrated effective in individual (Barrett, 1998; Barrett, Dadds, & Rapee, 1996; Manassis et al., 2002) and group versions (Mendlowitz et al., 1999; Muris, Meesters, & van Melick, 2002).

General Anxiety Disorder

Description and Associated Features

Children who experience GAD report pervasive worries about family, friends, school, health, and performance issues. According to the *DSM–IV–TR* (APA, 2000), a diagnosis of GAD in childhood requires that the child demonstrate *excessive worry and anxiety* and experience *difficulty controlling* the worry. The pervasive and nonspecific nature of GAD has often earned the description of **free floating anxiety**. In the adult population, symptoms of excessive worry must be accompanied by at least *three* additional symptoms from the symptom list, *but in children only one item from the symptom list is required*. According to the *DSM*, the excessive worry is a pervasive mood which is evident on more days than not, and in existence for at least 6 months. In addition, the disorder must be responsible for dysfunction in important areas such as school work, social relationships, and family. Children with GAD also must demonstrate *at least one somatic symptom* from the following list:

- restlessness
- ease of fatigue
- irritability
- concentration problems
- muscle tension
- sleep problems

Recent studies have reported significantly higher levels of somatic complaints in parent reports for younger children (9–11) and self-reports for older children (11–13) with GAD (Pimentel & Kendall, 2003).

Memory Bank

Given that somatic symptoms of GAD share many symptom features with ADHD, it is not surprising that many children with GAD can be misdiagnosed as having ADHD. Despite the possibility of misdiagnosis between ADHD and GAD due to symptom overlap, the *DSM* cautions about the potential for overdiagnosis of GAD in children. It is advised that emphasis be placed on conducting *differential diagnosis* to determine whether children's worries might be more appropriately explained by one of the other anxiety disorders: separation anxiety, social phobia, or obsessive compulsive disorder.

According to the *DSM–IV–TR* (APA, 2000) children's worries about performance issues may be pervasive across academic as well as leisure (sports) activities regardless of whether these activities are being evaluated by others or not. As a result, children with GAD may be overly perfectionistic, conforming, and reluctant to engage in activities outside the home, and require excessive reassurance about their performance from others. Thoughts not only focus on their immediate world, but can take on global proportions as they dwell on the possibility of catastrophic events entering their life and loved ones around them.

Children may not hand it assignments in time due to overworking of assignments, and lack of participation in less structured school activities, such as field trips, may also result from vague fears and worries that have little basis in reality. Global issues and health concerns may also be among the worrisome thoughts that plague these children (Strauss, Lease, Last, & Francis, 1988). Due to the vague and pervasive nature of their concerns, these "worriers" often exist below the radar and are described as hard working and conforming by school personnel who rarely refer these children for assessment or treatment (Last, Hersen, Kazdin, Orvaschel, & Perri, 1991).

Case in Point

Initially, Eric's mother thought that it was a good thing that Eric was an excellent writer. His neat printing was a pleasure to read and the teacher would often select his work to be posted as an example. However, Eric's perfectionistic tendencies began to cause problems when multiple erasures became the rule and reworking his notes often continued until he made holes in his papers. He was worried that his answers were not correct either, so even if the letters looked right, he was afraid the answer was wrong. He often neglected to hand in his homework for fear that it was not good enough. Eric's worries were beginning to intrude on his thinking in many different ways.

Today, Eric's teacher is going over the history lesson before they are to write a short passage about George Washington. As usual, Eric's mind drifts off, as a dozen random concerns bombard his thoughts and float into his head. He thinks about his baseball try-outs this weekend; the disasters he watches on television; the break-in three blocks from his home; and about having enough air in his bicycle tires. His teacher catches Eric, yet again, staring off into space.

"Eric…earth to Eric….what are you thinking about?"

"Nothing, mam…just thinking about what to write down."

Eric writes on his paper: "Check bike tires for air."

Eric's teacher recommends his mother take him to the doctor to check out if he has ADHD. After the clinical interview, Eric is diagnosed with having a deneralized anxiety disorder (GAD).

Prevalence

According to the *DSM–IV–TR* (APA, 2000), approximately 2–5 % of the population will be diagnosed with GAD in the course of their lifetime. Studies suggest a relatively early onset for GAD, with reported intake ages between 8–10 years (Last, Perrin, Hersen, & Kazdin, 1992), while outcome risks for developing other anxiety or depressive disorders has been suggested to be as high as in one third of the initial intake population (Last, Perrin, Hersen, & Kazdin, 1996).

Memory Bank

In their study of anxiety disorders, Strauss et al. (1988) found that 70% of the younger sample (5–11 year olds) diagnosed with GAD also had SAD, while 35% had ADHD. Within the older GAD group (adolescent population), Strauss and colleagues found 47% also met the diagnosis for major depressive episode, while 41% also had a specific phobia.

Etiology

Within a developmental framework, it is important to remember the concepts of *equifinality* and *multifinality* in considering the possible pathways which might lead to the onset of GAD in childhood.

Rewind and Recall

Developmental pathways to psychopathology are best understood within the framework of equifinality—several pathways may lead to the same outcome; and multifinality—similar risks may produce different outcomes (Cicchetti & Rogosh, 1996).

Biological Model

The role of biological, genetic, and temperament factors.   Some studies have demonstrated an increased risk in 1st-degree relatives of individuals with GAD, while twin studies have reported as high as 30–40% of etiology may be due to genetic factors (Eley, 1999).

The neurotransmitter Gamma-amniobutyric acid (GABA).   Neurotransmitters are chemicals that carry messages between neurons. Studies have determined that **GABA** carries a message to *inhibit* responses and when the message arrives, the neuron stops firing. According to some researchers, rapid neuron firing influences the anxiety feedback loop to increase states of heightened arousal and excitability in response to fear and anxiety. Eventually, GABA is responsible for sending a cease fire message which reduces excitability and anxiety levels. Although the direct cause is unknown (too little GABA, or too few GABA receptors), studies have suggested that individuals with GAD may have a neurotransmitter malfunction (Lloyd, Fletcher, & Minchin, 1992).

Cognitive Model

Information processing and cognitive biases for emotional information.   Studies have linked emotionality with high threat appraisal, avoidant coping, and increase for adjustment problems (Lengua & Long, 2002). In their discussion of temperament and effortful control, Muris and Ollendick (2005) discuss the relationship between **lack of attentional control** (**effortful control**) and internalizing symptoms which can be characterized by uncontrollable negative thoughts. Anxious individuals anticipate and interpret future events in a negative way, especially when faced with ambiguous situations. However, whereas impulsive children—such as those with oppositional defiant disorder—attend to the hostile features in an aggressive way (evident in **the hostile attribution bias**), anxious children may develop avoidant responses based on their cognitive bias towards interpretation of ambiguous situations in negative ways (Barrett, Rapee, Dadds, & Ryan, 1996; Muris, Luermans, Merckelbach, & Mayer, 2000). In similar situations, adults have been shown to overestimate the potential for threat, danger, and fear, and underestimate their ability to cope (Beck, Emery, & Greenberg, 1996).

Cognitive theorists suggest that early negative experiences and adversity may set the stage for the child internalizing the view of the world as a fearful place (Manassis & Hood, 1998), which may cause anxious children to engage in self-blame more readily and focus on the negative rather than positive aspects of events (Silverman & Ginsburg, 1995). Furthermore, compared to controls, anxious children have increased negative cognitions about events and decreased estimates of their own ability to cope with threat (Bogels & Zigterman, 2000). Studies have shown that although children were able to articulate worries as young as 5 years of age, the nature of the cognitive thought processes became more complex with increasing age. Older children exhibited tendencies to focus on worries about psychological well being, and social approval (Vasey, 1993).

Science Talks

In a study of more than 250 school-aged children (7–12 years), researchers found that the three most common areas of worry were school, health, and personal harm. Although few age-related differences were noted, girls reported more worries than boys (Barrett Rapee, Dadds, & Ryan, 1996).

Parenting Style and Behavioral Modeling

Social learning theorists look to the parenting environment for explanations of the development of GAD. Parents may be highly influential sources for increased anxiety in children or significant factors in the maintenance of anxious responses. The reinforcing power of parental encouragement and support to increase avoidant behaviors was demonstrated in an extension of the above study by Barrett and colleagues (1996). When children were instructed to discuss their responses with their parents, the parents of anxious children were actually instrumental in having their child increase their avoidant responses (Dadds, Barrett, Rapee, & Ryan, 1996).

In their study of anxious parents and children, Cobham, Dadds, and Spence (1998) found that children of anxious parents did not benefit from CBT to reduce anxiety (CBT alone), unless parents were included in the CBT training program (CBT+ Parent Anxiety Management: PAM). However, inclusion of the parent in the PAM program only made a difference if the parent was also anxiety disordered.

Memory Bank

Parents who are overprotective or who are anxious themselves may act to shield the child from perceived threat and thereby reduce the child's opportunity to develop adequate coping skills while reinforcing the child's avoidance tendencies. At least one study has demonstrated that children who were anxiously attached as infants were twice as likely to develop an anxiety disorder in adolescence compared to peers who were securely attached (Warren et al., 1997).

Treatment

In their review of evidence-based treatments for childhood disorders, Ollendick and King (2004) revealed that there has been no well-established treatment identified for the anxiety disorders other than specific phobias, despite the high incidence of these disorders in children and adolescence (GAD, SAD, social phobia). However, they do identify *cognitive behavioral therapy* and *cognitive behavioral therapy combined with family anxiety management* as treatments which are probably efficacious. The Coping Cat program discussed under SAD is also an appropriate treatment for GAD.

In addition to the use of more cognitively oriented tools, such as the use of self-talk and cognitive problem solving techniques, the coping skills program also relies heavily on more behaviorally oriented components such as *imagined* and *in vivo* (real life) exposure to the fear producing situations using systematic desensitization.

Science Talks

The **Coping Cat program** has been demonstrated to be an effective way to reduce anxiety in children in randomized clinical trials of individual CBT training (Kendall, 1994) and more recently in group (Flannery-Schroeder & Kendall, 2000) and family-focused formats (Barrett et al., 1996). Barrett and colleagues (1996) found that for younger children (7–10 years) and females, involvement in the family group CBT program was significantly more effective than CBT alone.

CHAPTER SUMMARY AND REVIEW

1. **Historical Trends in the Classification of Anxiety Disorders**

    Although at one time the *DSM* (*DSM–III–R*, 1987) recognized three anxiety disorders with onset in childhood and adolescence *(separation anxiety disorder, avoidant disorder, and overanxious disorder),* currently only one anxiety disorder with child onset (separation anxiety disorder, SAD) remains in the *DSM–IV–TR* (APA, 2000). All of the remaining anxiety disorders are classified in the *DSM,* at large—generalized anxiety disorder (GAD), obsessive compulsive disorder (OCD), social phobia, panic disorder with and without agoraphobia, and the stress disorders: acute stress and post traumatic stress disorder (PTSD).

    The ASEBA (Achenbach & Rescorla, 2001) revised syndrome scales to better represent concepts of negative affectivity: *anxious/depressed* (negative affectivity) and *withdrawn/depressed* (anhedonia, or low positive affect).

2. **Developmental Trends**

    The nature of fears and worries change over the course of development in response to increased cognitive maturity, as the number of fears decrease with age. Children who experience persistent, uncontrollable fears that are intense and interfere with normal functioning may develop anxiety disorders. Earlier onset disorders include specific phobias, SAD, and GAD. Chronic worry can be evident behaviorally, cognitively, and physiologically (arousal) and avoidance of the anxiety provoking target is a predictable response. There are high levels of comorbidity among the anxiety disorders.

3. **Etiology and Assessment of Anxiety Disorders**

    Temperament, genetics, parenting, and environmental circumstances have all been linked to the etiology of anxiety disorders. Vasey and Dadds (2001) and Vasey and Ollendick suggest two potential pathways: a cumulative risk pathway and a precipitating event pathway, and suggest several factors that can serve to maintain and augment anxious responses in children. Reversing these trends can provide a protective benefit.

    In addition to broad-based assessment instruments that include anxiety scales, a number of syndrome specific scales for the assessment of anxiety in children and youth are revealed. Generally, treatments for anxiety disorders use cognitive behavioral methods.

4. **Specific Phobias**

    Specific phobias represent unreasonable fear and dread of objects or circumstances that interfere with normative functioning (school, work, relationships with peers and family).

    There are several common types of phobias (e.g., fears of animals; nature, such as thunder; blood-injection-injury; etc.). Fears can be learned and treatment methods often involve behavioral programs that involve desensitization to "undo" the conditioned response.

5. **Separation Anxiety Disorder (SAD)**

   Children with SAD experience extreme distress upon separation or anticipated separation from a caregiver, lasting for at least 4 weeks. The result can be panic attacks, fear of being alone, nightmares, and somatic complaints. School refusal is evident in 75% of children with SAD. Approximately 4% of children will be diagnosed with SAD. Etiology has been linked to genetic factors, maternal depression, and overprotective parenting practices. Cognitive behavioral treatment (CBT) programs such as the Coping Cat Program (Kendall, 2000) have been successful for SAD as well as GAD.

6. **Generalized Anxiety Disorder (GAD)**

   Children with GAD experience uncontrollable "free-floating anxiety" that is pervasive and across a wide variety of themes, lasts at least 6 months, and has at least on accompanying somatic symptom. Seventy percent of children with GAD also suffer from SAD. Genetic factors, chemical imbalance (GABA), maladaptive thinking, and parenting practices have all been associated with increased risk for GAD.

Consolidate and Communicate

1. The ASEBA (Achenbach & Rescorla, 2001) revised the syndrome scales to incorporate increasing support for evidence of the existence of negative affectivity in children. Based on your understanding of negative affectivity discussed in the introduction to internalizing disorders just prior to this chapter, answer the following questions:
   a. Should anxiety and depression be considered as two separate disorders in young children? Discuss.
   b. Does the tripartite model of anxiety and depression support or contradict assumptions inherent in the concept of negative affectivity?
   c. What is the relationship between negative affectivity, positive affectivity, and temperament, and how do these concepts relate to effortful control?
   d. Why do some children develop problems after exposure to a negative life event, while others do not? Discuss giving an example of two children with two different trajectories that have witnessed a negative life event.
2. Currently, the *DSM* only includes 1 out of 10 anxiety disorders under disorders first encountered in childhood or adolescence. If you were revising the *DSM*, what anxiety disorders would you include under disorders first encountered in childhood and why?
3. Children are most likely to develop GAD between 8 and 10 years of age. Discuss why this stage of development might be most vulnerable.
4. Vasey, Dadds, and Ollendick have developed a theory that recognizes two potential pathways that can predispose a child to developing an anxiety disorder. Discuss the model as it relates to predisposing, maintaining, and protective factors for the development of anxiety disorders in children.
5. Lilly is a 7-year-old girl who was recently involved in a car accident where she sustained painful injuries to her arm, chest, and jaw. As a result, Lilly will not go into any vehicle. Lilly lives five miles from the nearest school. The only way to get Lilly to school is by some form of transportation. Develop a systematic desensitization program for Lilly and explain how this program might change if *in vivo* versus imaginal methods were used.
6. Approximately 70% of children with GAD also have SAD. Discuss some underlying features that might link these two disorders at such a high rate of comorbidity.

Chapter Review Questions

1. The syndrome scale on the ASEBA (Achenbach & Rescorla, 2001) that most clearly evaluates negative affectivity is:
   a. withdrawn/depressed syndrome
   b. anxious/depressed syndrome
   c. withdrawn
   d. affective problems

2. According to the most recent *DSM* (APA, 2000), there are _____ anxiety disorders listed under *Disorders Usually First Diagnosed in Infancy, Childhood, or Adolescence*.
   a. one
   b. three
   c. five
   d. 10

3. From a developmental perspective, according to research, which of the following disorders is most likely to occur earliest in childhood?
   a. separation anxiety disorder
   b. simple phobia
   c. obsessive compulsive disorder
   d. social phobia

4. Atty's mother is concerned because Atty is very fearful of monsters and is afraid of the dark. You explain to Atty's mother that at Atty's age this is a common fear. How old is Atty?
   a. 7 years old,
   b. 9 years old
   c. 6 years old
   d. 4 years old.

5. Which of the following is not a common type of phobia?
   a. fear of books
   c. fear of heights
   d. fear of thunder
   e. fear of flying

6. Survey of Kindergarten children revealed that the most commonly feared animals were:
   a. mouse
   b. bear
   c. elephant
   d. monkey

7. It is time to feed Buddy, my dog. I go into the laundry room and pour the bag of kibble into the dog dish. Even though Buddy cannot smell the food or taste the food, he runs from the living room and begins to bark in anticipation of being fed. In this situation, after conditioning, the sounds of food preparation (crackling bag, pouring into dog dish) have become the _____ that elicit a _____.
   a. conditioned stimulus…unconditioned response
   b. unconditioned stimulus…conditioned response
   c. conditioned stimulus…conditioned response
   d. neutral stimulus…neutral response

8. Which of the following is FALSE regarding SAD and school refusal?
   a. 75% of children with SAD demonstrate school refusal
   b. only 10% of children who refuse to attend school have SAD

    c. school refusal can occur for many reasons, including school bullying

    d. highly structured behavioral methods are the best intervention for school refusal

9. Coping Cat is a program that was developed by Kendall (2000) and can be effective in the treatment of which of the following?

    a. separation anxiety disorder

    b. generalized anxiety disorder

    c. obsessive compulsive disorder

    d. both a and b

10. General Anxiety Disorder (GAD) is diagnosed in approximately what percent of the general population?

    a. 20%

    b. 2–5%

    c. 7–10%

    d. 12–15%

Glossary of New Terms

withdrawn/depressed syndrome
anxious/depressed syndrome
cumulative risk pathway
precipitating event pathway
inhibited temperament
transactional processes
clinical utility
multi-informant assessment
multi-response format
specific phobia
conditioning experiences
classical conditioning
operant conditioning, modeling
neutral stimulus
unconditioned stimulus (UCS)
unconditioned response (UCR)
conditioned stimulus (CS)
conditioned response (CR)
systematic desensitization
modeling
contagion effect
operant conditioning
stimulus generalization
law of effect
preparedness
participant modeling
reinforced practice
in vivo desensitization
imaginal desensitization
successive approximation

positive affect
child mastery
early onset SAD
school refusal
over parentification
generalized anxiety disorder
Coping Cat program
free floating anxiety
GABA
attentional control
cffortful control
hostile attribution bias

Answers to Multiple Choice Questions:
1. b; 2. a; 3. b; 4. d; 5. a; 6. b;, 7. c; 8. b; 9. d; 10. b.

Etiology
    Biological Model
    Behavioral Model
    Cognitive Behavioral Model
    Parenting Style and Attachment
Treatment

CHAPTER PREVIEW

This chapter will concentrate on anxiety disorders that have onset in later childhood and adolescence, including: obsessive compulsive disorder, social phobia, panic disorder with and without agoraphobia, and the stress disorders (acute stress disorder and posttraumatic stress disorder). Assessment of anxiety disorders was discussed in chapter 6 and the same assessment instruments are appropriate for the later occurring anxiety disorders, and will not be discussed again.

1. Obsessive-Compulsive Disorder (OCD)

Youth with OCD experience intrusive persistent thoughts (obsessions) and are driven to perform compulsive behaviors, such as fears of contamination and handwashing; safety concerns and checking; perfectionism and aligning. OCD is more common in male youth with earlier onset than for females. Youth with OCD are at increased risk for comorbid SAD, ADHD, and Tourette's disorder. Etiology has been linked to genetics, overactivity in particular areas of the brain, and low levels of serotonin. Treatment can involve SSRI medications, behavioral therapy (Rachman's procedure), and CBT.

2. Social Phobia

Excessive fear of performance or social situations linked to anticipated embarrassment is at the basis of social phobia. As a result, situations are often avoided to escape fears (e.g., fears of eating or writing in public). Generalized social phobia (pervasive across situations) is more severe than specific social phobia (e.g., public speaking). Increased risk for social phobia has been found in individuals with an inhibited temperament, those with a bias to interpret threat, individuals who experience negative affectivity. Treatments previously discussed for specific phobia apply, in addition to social skills development.

3. Panic Disorder With and Without Agoraphobia

Panic attacks are an intense anxiety response that can last up to 10 minutes and can be triggered by environmental situations (crowds, heights) or can occur unexpectedly and can last up to 10 minutes and include a wide array of physiological (heart palpitations, sweating), emotional (fear of losing control, going insane), and cognitive (strong need to escape) reactions. Repeated panic attacks can result in a panic disorder which develops from a fear of having a panic attack. Individuals can become homebound (panic disorder with agoraphobia) as a result. Children and youth with panic attacks are 20 times more likely to have a close relative with the disorder. Irregular neurotransmitter activity and oversensitivity to threat/panic have been suggested as causes. Antidepressant medications and CBT are the treatments of choice.

4. The Stress Disorders and Posttraumatic Stress Disorder (PTSD)

Daily stressors are evident at all ages and are moderated by developmental level, gender, and individual characteristics. Increased stress is one of the major negative outcomes of living in poverty. Unlike the other anxiety disorders that represent uncontrollable and pervasive fears resulting from the *perception of threat*, acute and posttraumatic stress disorders represent responses to horrific and catastrophic events that cluster around three central themes: *reexperiencing, avoidance/numbing, and hyperarousal*. Developmentally, although young children can experience PTSD, there is significant concern that the *DSM* diagnostic criteria are inappropriate at younger age levels. It has been suggested that a new disorder, developmental trauma disorder, may better capture the pervasive impact of chronic exposure to trauma in children and adolescents. Explanations for the development of PTSD have included biological (neurological), behavioral and family environment factors. Treatments have mainly focused on methods that incorporate CBT into the process.

Obsessive-Compulsive Disorder

Description and Associated Features

The essential features of **obsessive-compulsive disorder (OCD)** are persistent, recurring, and intrusive **obsessions** (thoughts) and **compulsions** (behaviors) that are significantly time consuming (in excess of an hour) on a daily basis and interfere with normal day to day functioning.

Important Distinction

Obsessions are intrusive thoughts, impulses, or images that are unavoidable, cause significant anxiety/distress and persist, despite attempts to ignore them or neutralize them by performing or engaging in other activities or thoughts.

Compulsions are rigid mental (praying, counting, etc.) or physical (hand washing, ordering) acts driven by obsessions or to avoid rule violation. The acts are performed to reduce distress or to avert some dreaded consequence; however, the acts are in no way connected to the feared consequence in any realistic manner and are excessive.

The *DSM* describes obsessive thoughts, images or impulses as **ego-dystonic** to signify that people are aware of their "alien" (illogical) nature, but are simultaneously aware that no one has planted the thought in their heads (as in a psychotic delusion). Given their cognitive capacity and limitations, younger children would not be expected to recognize the ego-dystonic nature of the disorder.

Developmental Issues and Trends

Normally young children use rituals in play, engage in magical thinking in the preschool years, and also believe in superstitions. A comparison of OCD children with controls revealed that OCD children did not harbor any more superstitious beliefs than their peers (Leonard, Goldberger, & Rapoport, 1990). However, investigations of the nature of normally occurring rituals and superstitions reveals that normal compulsive behaviors peak at the preschool level (2–4 years) and then progressively decline during the late-elementary to middle-school period (8–14 years). However, OCD rituals and compulsions are on a different trajectory, becoming more frequent with increasing age (Zohar & Bruno, 1997).

Studies of the obsessive and compulsive patterns of behaviors in OCD children and youth reveal common clusters for obsessions and compulsions. Obsessions (irrational thoughts) and compulsions (uncontrollable behaviors) often evolve around themes of:

- contamination (*excessive cleaning, hand washing, showering, teeth brushing*)
- safety (*checking doors, locks*)
- preoccupations with orderliness/symmetry (*aligning, obsessive neatness*)
- repetitive rituals (*counting or touching rituals*)
- hoarding or saving (*collect useless objects, rubber bands, paper clips, etc.*)
- compulsive list making (*making, changing lists*)

Development in Focus

While there are many similarities between OCD in children and adults, patterns noted in younger children (8 years of age) has led to the suggestion that OCD in childhood is a unique developmental variation of adult OCD (Geller et al., 1998). In younger children, compulsive rituals are often devoid of obsessive thoughts.

The most commonly reported obsessions in two accounts of children and youth with OCD were fear of contamination (35–52%); aggressive/violent images, including thoughts of harming oneself or familiar others (30–38%); and somatic obsessions (38%). OCD patterns involved repeated rituals (76%), handwashing (62–75%), checking (40–57%), and ordering or straightening (35–62%; Riddle et al., 1990). In the sample observed by Riddle and colleagues, common behaviors of indecisiveness, foreboding, and pathological doubting were also evident. Younger children may engage in compulsive motor symptoms such as walking in a particular design (circle, zigzag) or finger licking (Swedo, Rapoport, Leonard, Leanane, & Cheslow, 1989).

Case in Point

Bobby was referred for psychological assessment due to academic difficulties when he was in the fourth grade. At almost 11 years of age, Bobby had already repeated a grade due to high absenteeism in his early school years. Assessment revealed a wide discrepancy between verbal (average) and performance (borderline) functioning on the intellectual assessment, while academic levels were at least delayed by 2 years. The psychologist noted that Bobby required significant time to complete the written work, due to constant erasures, and that the Bender drawings were seriously overworked.

When Bobby was admitted to a residential program for student's with severe learning disabilities, significant symptoms of separation anxiety emerged. Bobby was extremely distraught, complained of physical distress, and was observed to engage in countless rituals and checking routines: arranging and rearranging family pictures on his night stand; bed sheet straightening; and attempting to engage the residential counselors in lengthy conversations prior to bedtime. Bobby was diagnosed with OCD.

One large sample of OCD children (*n* = 70) reported as many as 85% of children in the study engaged in washing rituals, the most common form of compulsion, which was accompanied in almost half the cases by obsessional fears of contamination (germs, dirt, and environmental toxicity; Swedo et al., 1989). In the same study, almost half (46%) demonstrated checking rituals, while 17% were preoccupied with maintaining symmetry (lining up toys, walking in a prescribed manner, etc.). Children and adolescents are also more likely to engage other family members in their rituals. Rituals can often go undetected and can be performed in secret (Wever & Phillips, 1994). Sometimes, children just "appear slow" at doing their work or homework but could be secretly engaged in counting or tapping rituals. Children may experience embarrassment about the need to perform their repetitive rituals and continue to suffer in silence.

Adolescents often report multiple obsessions and compulsions (Kashani & Orvaschel, 1988). Children with OCD may do poorly in school due to difficulties with concentration, or perfectionistic tendencies to rework, erase, and rewrite homework assignments.

Science Talks

In a recent investigation of functional impairment in 151 children and adolescents diagnosed with OCD, Piacentini, Bergman, Keller, and McCracken (2003) found that almost 50% reported significant OCD-related problems at school, home, and socially. In this study, the two most common areas of school-related problems were concentration and homework. In another study, disorder onset followed a traumatic event in 38–54% of youth with OCD resulting in obsessions and compulsions related to themes of loss, school-related stress, or transition to high school (Geller et al., 1998).

In a study of OCD groups with and without related tic disorders, Hanna et al. (2002) found no difference in the obsessions between the two groups; however, they did find significant between-group differences for the compulsions. Findings revealed that ordering, hoarding, and washing compulsions were significantly more prevalent in children with OCD who had no tic-related history.

Prevalence

Prevalence rates for OCD among children and adolescents have been estimated at least between 2% to 4% with higher numbers when subclinical OCD is reported. Although the prevalence rates for males and females are equivalent in adult populations, OCD is more common in males with childhood onset. The usual onset for OCD is in adolescence or early adulthood; however, child onset is possible. Onset for males (between 6 and 15 years) is earlier than onset for females (between 20 and 29 years). In one study between 30% to 50% of adults with OCD reported onset in childhood or adolescence (Martini, 1995), while in another the rate was as high as 80% (Grados, Labuda, Riddle, & Walkup, 1997).

Memory Bank

Comorbidity rates for OCD are high. Between 5% to 7% of children with OCD will have Tourette's disorder (APA, 2000). In one study, only 26% of juvenile onset OCD had no comorbid disorder. More recent investigations suggest that comorbidity of OCD with the disruptive behavior disorders and ADHD might be as high as 57% in children and 47% in adolescents (Geller et al., 2001). Sudden flare-ups of OCD may be more likely to also share features of separation anxiety disorder (Grados et al., 1997).

Etiology

Biological Model

Biological, genetic, and neurotransmitter. The risk for OCD is higher in first degree biological relatives of parents with OCD or Tourette's disorder. Children who have OCD and a tic-related disorder are more likely to be males, report a wider range of OCD symptoms, and have weaker response to SSRI's as a treatment alternative (Tucker, Leckman, & Scahill 1996). In one study, risk for OCD was as high as 8% in relatives with early onset OCD (Bellodi, Sciuto, Diaferia, Ronchi, & Smeraldi, 1992).

The tricyclic antidepressant, clomipramine (Anafranil), and the SSRI fuoxetine (Prozac) have both been used to successfully reduce symptoms of OCD in many individuals. Since both drugs work to increase **serotonin** activity in the brain, the implication is that OCD symptoms are somehow related to serotonin malfunction.

Studies have also isolated organic causes of OCD in children with postencephalitis states, head injury, and insults to the **basal ganglia** (Grados et al., 1997; Saint-Cyr, Taylor, & Nicholson, 1995).

Science Talks

The **orbital region of the frontal cortex** and the **caudate nuclei** (located in the basal ganglia) are responsible for translating thoughts into actions. The orbital region is especially noted for primitive impulses (sexual, violent) which are normally filtered by the caudate nuclei prior to sending messages on to the **thalamus.** Pet scans have revealed overactivity in these areas in the brains of individuals with OCD compared to controls (Saxena, Brody, & Maidment, 1999).

The neurotransmitter serotonin is further implicated, since low serotonin levels might also contribute to malfunction in relaying messages between these parts of the brain.

Development in Focus

Pediatric autoimmune neuropsychiatric disorder (PANDAS) is a stretococcal infection resulting in abrupt onset of OCD and/or tic disorder. Over a 3-year period, Murphy and Pinchinero (2002) monitored 12 school-aged children with new-onset PANDAS. Severe OCD symptoms demonstrated by this group included hand washing and preoccupation with germs. Antibiotics were effective in treating the throat infections as well as eliminating the OCD symptoms. However, relapse of the throat infection in 50% of the group was accompanied by reoccurrence of OCD symptoms, which were again treated successfully with antibiotics.

Behavioral Model

Despite increasing support for the biological and neurological basis for OCD, behaviorists turn their focus on the resulting behaviors or compulsions. From a behavioral perspective, compulsions can begin by a random association that links the behavior with a reinforcing event or circumstance.

Case in Point

Arthur is next at bat in an important baseball game. While waiting on deck, he rubs his knee with his hand and rolls the cuff on his batting arm. Arthur hits a home run. The next time Arthur is waiting to bat, he performs the same ritual because it helps reduce his anxiety, and he associates the ritual with good luck.

The behaviorists suggest that similar associations can occur between hand-washing rituals and the reduction of anxiety. Since hand washing reduces anxious feelings, it is positively reinforced, and the behavior pattern will be repeated when the person again feels anxious.

Parenting Style and Family Environment

Studies have also investigated the possible role of family factors in the precipitation and maintenance of OCD symptoms. The literature has noted an increasing interest in exploring the role of family influences on negative thought patterns in anxious children. Studies of communication patterns and parenting styles (Hibbs et al., 1991) have found that 82% of children with OCD have families high on **expressed emotion** (high degree of criticism, high degree of overinvolvement), while adolescents with OCD indicate less warmth, support, and closeness in their families compared to controls (Valleni-Basile et al., 1995). Children and adolescents with OCD often involve family members in their rituals.

Development in Focus

At least one study (Cooper, 1996) has demonstrated the devastating effects that child rituals can have on immediate family members. In this investigation, approximately 60% of families noted detrimental effects of OCD behaviors on siblings and increased marital discord. Furthermore, family members reported significant personal distress, depression, and feelings of manipulation (being drawn into the rituals) resulting from the OCD behaviors.

Cognitive Model

The role of maladaptive or dysfunctional thinking in OCD populations has been explored at length by cognitive theorists. According to the cognitive perspective, appraisals of risk (intensity, severity, probability) and personal responsibility for harm are two core cognitive components which serve to drive OCD symptoms (Rachman, 1993; Salkovskis, 1989). It is the combined influence of feelings of inability to control the risk factors (e.g., harm), while simultaneously being responsible for their occurrence (e.g., thoughts about harming) that perpetuate the need to cleanse the thought by repeating compulsive behaviors.

Treatment

Psychopharmacology. Increasing investigations and randomized controlled trials have determined that selective serotonin reuptake inhibitors (SSRIs) can be effective in the treatment of OCD in children and adolescents (McClellan & Werry, 2003). A recent meta-analysis of 12 pediatric studies involving medication treatment versus placebo for OCD found that the tricylclic clomipramine was significantly superior to the SSRIs in alleviating symptoms of OCD; however, given the adverse side effects and the need for close monitoring, the authors suggest that the use of clomipramine be restricted to the more severe cases and/or cases which are not responsive to the SSRIs (Geller, Biederman, & Stewart, 2003).

Development in Focus

Although medication trials have been successful in reducing initial symptoms of OCD, a controlled 12-week trial comparison of the effects of clomipramine versus **exposure and response prevention therapy (ERP)** revealed that while both treatments were effective, ERP was significantly superior to medication in the reduction of OCD symptoms (de Haan, Hoogduin, Buitelaar, & Keijser, 1998). This finding and relapse results from studies where medication was withdrawn (Leonard et al., 1991) have prompted the recommendation that CBT/ERP should be attempted as an initial treatment for the majority of child and adolescent cases with OCD (March, Frances, Carpenter, & Kahn, 1997).

Behavioral Therapy

Exposure and response prevention (ERP).   Behavioral interventions often involve some variation of Rachman's procedure which involves repeated exposure to the anxiety producing situation/object (e.g., contamination/dirt) while simultaneously preventing the compulsive response (e.g., handwashing). Exposure and response prevention commonly takes place in a gradual and systematic way.

Cognitive behavioral therapy (CBT).   Based on a growing body of empirical evidence, the OCD Expert Consensus Guidelines (March et al., 1997) has recommended the use of exposure-based CBT as an alternative to medication for all prepubertal children with OCD and adolescents who exhibit mild to moderate symptoms.

In their review of findings from 11 CBT open-trial studies to date, Barrett, Healy-Farrell, and March (2004) suggest that these studies collectively do provide preliminary evidence for the effectiveness of CBT for OCD, even though they lack inclusion of randomized control group studies at present. The authors also report the results of their controlled treatment outcome trial of **family-based CBT (CBFT)** involving 77 children and adolescents with OCD who were randomly assigned to one of three groups: individual CBFT, group CBFT, and a wait-list control group. Their manualized program (**Focus Program**: Freedom from Obsessions and Compulsions Using Special Tools) included 14 weeks of FBFT protocols with family and sibling involvement and booster sessions delivered over the 12 months following treatment. Components of the program draw on principles of cognitive behavior therapy and exposure and response prevention. The Program is developed to increase skills in disorder awareness (including CBT techniques and anxiety management); actual exposure and response prevention; and relapse prevention. Results revealed pretest to posttest symptom reduction that was clinically and statistically significant for programs delivered individually and in groups.

Social Phobia

Description and Associated Features

According to the *DSM*, **social phobia**, previously called social anxiety disorder, has the central feature of a *pervasive fear of embarrassment,* which often results in avoidance of social or performance situations, or if unable to avoid the circumstances, extreme anxiety due to concerns regarding potential for embarrassment. Facing exposure to a social or performance situation causes an immediate feeling of heightened anxiety and fear and may elicit a panic attack.

Case in Point

Gloria was about to sit down in the cafeteria with her lunch tray when all of a sudden she had an overwhelming fear that her soup would drip from her mouth all over her blouse, embarrassing her in front of her classmates. In middle school this would cause severe embarrassment. She quickly dropped the tray on the table and ran out of the room, her heart pounding. She ran to the nurse's office and felt as if she would surely die. She was sweating and her hands were trembling. After about 10 minutes, the panic attack subsided. Each day after that, Gloria would forget to bring her lunch or lunch money to avoid eating in front of her peers. Eventually, Gloria volunteered to work in the library sorting books during lunch break to avoid the lunch room and to avoid engaging in lunch room chatter, another potential source of embarrassment for her.

Developmental Issues and Trends

Even though the adolescent is aware that the fear is unreasonable (children may not be aware of the unreasonableness of it), they are unable to control it. Fear of embarrassment may be associated with such activities as eating, drinking, or writing in public due to concerns that others may notice their nervous tremors, blushing, problems breathing, or other physical responses to their fear. Although social fears can be common at all ages, a diagnosis of social phobia in children and adolescents requires that the condition must be evident *for at least 6 months* (in individuals under 18 years of age) and significantly interfere with functioning.

Young children who suffer from social phobia may demonstrate their symptoms of refusal to engage in social situations through tantrum behavior, crying, or freezing. According to the *DSM*, in order to be diagnosed with social phobia, two additional symptoms are required:

1. Children must demonstrate normal social responses in familiar situations (with familiar people); and
2. Evidence of social phobia must be pervasive across situations involving both adults and peers. (*DSM*; APA, 2000, p. 456)

Common reactions to social phobia are avoidance behaviors that might be evident in issues of school absenteeism and other escape behaviors such as bypassing the lunch room to retreat to study hall. Somatic complaints may also be evident and escaping might take the form of spending more time in the nurses' office due to feelings of discomfort resulting from physiological arousal. In addition to low self-esteem, there is often an accompanying lack of social skills, or at least a feeling of discomfort in social situations. The *DSM* (APA, 2000) also distinguishes between two adult subtypes of social phobia: a **generalized form of social phobia,** which is pervasive across most social situations; and a more **specific social phobia,** which may be evident in particular situations, e.g., public speaking.

Science Talks

Are there subtypes of social phobia in adolescents? In a recent study conducted by Hoffman, Albano, Heimberg, Tracey, Chorpita, and Barlow (1999), almost half the adolescents in their study endorsed generalized anxiety across all four domains investigated, suggesting that subtypes of social phobia also exist in adolescent populations. Like adults, teens with the *generalized subtype* were more severe and evidenced higher levels of psychopathology. However, unlike adults, more than half the teens rated the *informal speaking category* (talking to other kids, introducing self to others, going to a party) as more fearful than the *formal speaking category* (asking questions in class; giving an oral report). Furthermore, given the nature of adolescent concerns and self-conscious attitudes, such as feelings that everyone is staring at them (e.g., Elkind's concept of the *the imaginary audience*). It is not surprising that onset for social phobia often occurs in adolescence (Beidel et al., 1999).

Is selective mutism an early precursor to social phobia? **Selective mutism** is a disorder listed in the *DSM–IV–TR* under the catgory of *Other Childhood Disorders* (*DSM*, APA, 2000). The main feature of this disorder is a persistent reluctance and failure to speak in certain social situations. Whether this disorder might better be conceptualized as an anxiety disorder, as an early precursor to social phobia, has been the subject of considerable debate. According to more recent reviews and investigations, there is increasing support for the inclusion of selective mutism among the anxiety disorders, especially as a form of social phobia (Krysanski, 2003). However, since social phobia tends to occur in adolescence, while the onset of selective mutism is usually much earlier (4 or 5 years of age), there may be considerable controversy regarding whether selective mutism is eventually conceptualized as an early variant of social phobia, or as a distinct and separate type of anxiety disorder.

Although specific phobias are one of the earliest onset disorders, onset for social phobias tends to be later (corresponding to onset of adolescence). In addition, those who suffer from social phobia tend to have a more severe form of the disorder and are also much more likely to develop depression later on (Last et al., 1992). In addition, youth with social phobia demonstrate increased negative self-talk regarding social and performance competencies then their nonsocial phobic peers (Spence, Donovan, & Brechman-Toussaint, 1999).

Prevalence

In the course of one's lifetime, the likelihood of developing social phobia is estimated to be between 3% and 13% (*DSM–IV–TR*, APA, 2000); however, the expectancy of onset in childhood is considerably lower and estimated to be between 1% and 2% (Beidel et al., 1999). Children who have social phobia often have another comorbid anxiety disorder. In one study of a clinical sample of children with GAD and SAD, more than one fourth (27%) of children with GAD and 5% of children with SAD had social phobia (Bernstein & Borchardt, 1991).

Etiology

Biological Model and Temperament
As with the specific phobias, there has been increased interest in linking inhibited temperament (shyness or wariness) to the subsequent development of a vulnerability towards fears and threats; in this case, in social situations. As has already been discussed, temperament factors *of emotion-*

ality/neuroticism and *effortful control* have been implicated in the etiology of a host of anxiety disorders. The **Behavioral Inhibition System (BIS)** is a brain system that serves the function of alerting individuals to possible threat or punishment and has been implicated in increased levels of anxiety and avoidant behaviors (Gray, 1987, 1991). The BIS system has been likened to the component of negative affectivity relative to the tripartite model (Muris & Ollendick, 2005). Studies of children with behavioral inhibition (Biederman et al., 1993) have found increased risk for anxiety disorders in general and social phobia, in particular, in these children. Genetically, having a relative with social phobia places one at increased risk of developing the disorder (Fryer, Mannuzza, Chapman, Liebowitz, & Klein, 1993).

Treatment

The techniques previously discussed for specific phobias (participant modeling, reinforced practice/contingency management, and systematic desensitization are all appropriate for social phobia). As an adjunctive therapy, inclusion of a **social skills training** component (role play, direct practice and modeling) can also be a very valuable for this population (Francis & Ollendick, 1988; LeCroy, 1994).

Panic Disorder With and Without Agoraphobia

Description and Associated Features

Panic attacks involve an intense set of somatic, emotional, and cognitive symptoms that result from an intense fear/discomfort without a real and imminent danger. The attack is sudden and usually peaks after about 10 minutes. In adults, the symptoms often are confused with a heart attack. Symptoms can include:

- palpitations
- sweating
- trembling
- shortness of breath
- feelings of smothering, dying
- chest pain
- dizziness
- a strong urge to escape
- feelings of loss of control
- fear of going crazy
- a sense of depersonalization.

Panic attacks can be overwhelming and the *DSM requires at least 4 out of a possible 13 symptoms* be present. Panic attacks can be very frightening because they can occur unexpectedly, or they can be triggered by environmental situations or circumstances (e.g., crowds, heights, confined spaces).

Case in Point

Sandra and her mother were shopping for her high school prom dress at the mall on a Saturday afternoon. The mall was very crowded and Sandra was becoming increasingly frustrated with her options. Ultimately, her mother decided to give Sandra some space and return some items she had purchased the week before. She suggested they reconnect in an hour at the food court. When her mother returned, Sandra was nowhere in sight. She waited for about 20 minutes, thinking Sandra was still trying on clothes. However, panic quickly set in. Where was she? She called for Sandra on the "all call" system, but there was still no response. Time was running out. She was getting very frightened and anxious. She ran to her car to get her cell phone to call her husband, but when she opened the door, she found Sandra huddled on the floor in the back seat, looking traumatized. Immediately thinking the worst, her mother was prepared to get the police to track down the perpetrator who tried to kidnap Sandra. However, Sandra confessed that what drove her to seek refuge was not a perpetrator, but her own feelings of panic. Sandra said that she had to "get out of there, at all cost," or else she would surely die. She felt like she was "going crazy" and that she had to run and hide. She could hear her heart pounding in her ears, she couldn't swallow, and she couldn't breathe. Her body began to tremble. It was as if she was losing control and her body was taking over. All she knew was she had to go…quick.

Sandra and her mother are both experiencing the physiological responses of a panic reaction (heightened arousal). However, while Sandra's mother is experiencing a legitimate feeling of panic in response to the fear that her daughter has been abducted, Sandra's responses, in the absence of a reality-based trigger, represent a full-blown panic attack. Panic attacks can be associated with other anxiety disorders which may predispose to having a panic attack in a vulnerable situation (e.g., panic attack when exposed to a specific phobia, or a child with SAD having a panic attack when not being able to return home).

When an individual suffers recurrent or unexpected panic attacks or is preoccupied with fears of having panic attacks, a diagnosis of **panic disorder** is possible. When panic disorder is accompanied by a fear of going out into public places (especially alone) a diagnosis of panic disorder with **agoraphobia** is made. Panic disorder can be diagnosed in the absence of agoraphobia but often they will occur together. On the other hand, agoraphobia, by itself, is not a codable disorder according to the *DSM* unless it occurs in conjunction with panic disorder.

Memory Bank

People who have agoraphobia (Greek for "fear of the marketplace") develop fears of leaving home and going places where they might not be able to escape quickly should a panic attack develop. In its most serious form, people with agoraphobia may become home bound.

Although minimal research exists concerning panic disorder with agoraphobia in children and adolescents, it has been documented that family transmission of the disorder from parent to child can be evident (Last et al., 1991). This form of anxiety can be progressively more restrictive as the person attempts to avoid increased public interaction and becomes increasingly home bound.

The most common symptoms reported in youth experiencing panic attacks involved *nausea, heart palpitation, shortness of breath, shaking, and extremes in temperature (hot/cold flashes)*. Youth diagnosed with panic disorder are also more likely to have symptoms of depression and heightened sensitivity to anxiety (Kearney, Albano, Eisen, Allan, & Barlow, 1997).

Development in Focus

There may a certain level of physical/cognitive maturity required for panic attacks to occur. In one study of sixth- and seventh-grade girls, Hayward, Killen, and Hammer (1992) found that while more than 8% of the physically mature girls reported having a full-blown panic attack, no attacks were reported by the least mature group.

Based on a review of the literature and research, Ollendick (1998) suggests that although panic attacks in adolescents seem to mimic those of adults, younger children may respond differently, and attacks may be more *event related*, rather than come out of the blue. Furthermore, Ollendick's model for the origin of panic attacks suggests that interactions between *temperament* (high distress reactivity and behavioral inhibition) and *attachment issues* (separation distress) may result in some children becoming more vulnerable to panic attacks. Ollendick's proposed model for the development of panic attacks is framed within a behavioral perspective of fear conditioning leading to increased anxiety sensitivity over time.

Prevalence

Onset for panic disorder can be in late teens to early 30s with a lifetime prevalence rate up to 3.5% based on community (as opposed to clinic) sample. This disorder is significantly more common in women, who are twice as likely to have a panic disorder than are men (*DSM-IV-TR*; APA, 2000). Adolescent reports of panic disorder are in keeping with adult prevalence scores; however, prevalence for panic attacks is significantly higher than in adults—as high as 35% to 60%, depending on the study (Hayward, Killen, & Taylor, 1989; King et al., 1997).

Science Talks

King, Ollendick, Mattis, Yang, and Tonge (1997) surveyed more than 600 youth regarding whether they had ever experienced a panic attack. Results revealed that 16% reported at least one panic attack, admitting to having at least 4 of 13 possible symptoms. In the same sample, females reported having a panic attack at twice the rate (21.3%) compared to males (10.8%).

Etiology

According to the *DSM–IV–TR* (APA, 2000), if panic attacks occur before the age of 20, then youth are 20 times more likely to have a first-degree relative who also experiences panic disorder. Twin studies also suggest a genetic link. Although comorbidity rates are high among all anxiety disorders, those who experienced separation anxiety seem to be particulary vulnerable to panic attacks and panic disorder.

Biological Model

Biological, Genetic, and Neurotransmitter Function. There is evidence that irregular activity of the neurotransmitter **norepinephrine** may play a role in the onset of panic attacks. Parts of the brain which might be implicated in panic attacks are the **locus ceruleus**, an area high in norepinephrine usage, which sends messages to the **amygdale**, known to trigger emotional reactions. Stimulation of the locus ceruleus in monkeys will cause a panic reaction (Redmond, 1981).

Cognitive Model

According to cognitive theorists, panic attacks can result from a misinterpretation of bodily sensations. Theorists have suggested several factors which may predispose individuals to maladaptive thinking concerning their bodily sensations. One theory suggests that abnormal functioning of the locus ceruleus in panic prone individuals may lead to overactivity in the *behavioral inhibition system* (*BIS*), resulting in heightened sensitivity to bodily functions, hypervigilence, and overestimations of threat/panic (Gray, 1995).

Treatment

Pharmacological treatment. Further support for the implication of norepinephrine in panic attacks is the success of antidepressant drugs (most of which work to restore appropriate levels of norepinephrine) in alleviating panic attacks. Although little information is known about the medical management of the disorder in youth, at least one study demonstrated success using SSRIs to reduce panic symptoms in children and youth (Renaud, Birmaher, Wassick, & Bridge, 1999). In cases of panic attacks with agoraphobia, antidepressants or benzodiazepines have met with good success (Rickels, Downing, & Schweizer, 1993). However, often treatment of panic disorder with agoraphobia will also require use of *exposure techniques* already mentioned in the discussions of treatment for other phobias.

Cognitive behavioral treatment. The **Panic Control Treatment for Adolescents** (PCT-A; Hoffman & Mattis, 2000) provides a systematic program for helping adolescents to develop skills in key areas to assist in better coping and reducing the risk of future panic attacks. The program includes a *disorder awareness component* (*recognizing inappropriate cognitive appraisals*), educational *awareness regarding hyperventilation*, and a *desensitization component* (*situational exposure to reduce panic responses*). Initial findings suggest that in addition to reducing the number of panic attacks experienced, this program can also be successful in alleviating symptoms of fear, anxiety, and depression, and enhance feelings of self-efficacy. Cognitive behavioral approaches work to correct faulty thought patterns which in the case of panic attack would likely focus on misinterpretation of bodily sensations due to heightened sensitivity. At least one study of the effectiveness of cognitive therapy for panic disorder has demonstrated that cognitive therapy is as successful as antidepressant medication (Zaubler & Katon, 1998).

Stress Disorders: Acute Stress Disorder and Posttraumatic Stress Disorder

Moderating and Mediating Impact of Stressors

The impact of stressors on the etiology and maintenance of internalizing and externalizing disorders in child psychopathology has been the topic of considerable research and theoretical conjecture (Cicchetti & Toth, 1991; Rutter, 1989). Grant, Compass, and Thurm (2006) recently conducted an extensive review of research concerning the moderating and mediating effects of stressors in child psychopathology. (The following discussion follows Grant et al., 2006.)

Variables are considered to be **moderators** if the variable *influences the direction or strength between two variables*. Examples of moderators include:

- age
- gender
- ethnicity
- individual characteristics (cognitions, competence, coping)
- environmental characteristics (family and peer influences)

Variables are considered to be **mediators** if there was a *causal influence between independent and dependent variables*. The majority of studies that test mediational hypotheses are theoretically based studies, the most common of which involve *interpersonal theory* (mental health is disturbed by interpersonal difficulties; Hammen & Rudolph, 1996) or *cognitive theory* (mental health is disturbed by maladaptive thinking). Examples of mediator variables include:

- poverty
- environment-based stressors (stressful life events)
- family-based stressors
- child-based mediators

Some patterns that emerged among studies of **moderator effects** included findings that:

- stressors were reported most frequently in parent reports of younger children and in the self-reports of older children
- girls were more likely to react to stress with internalizing symptoms, while boys were more likely to react with externalizing symptoms
- boys were more likely to respond to stress negatively if the stressor involved poverty, divorce, or abuse
- girls were more likely to respond to stress negatively if the stressor involved violence, or exposure to disaster
- if race was identified as a moderator for stress, it was most common for White youth
- older youth with negative self-thoughts and patterns of negative thinking (attributions) were at greater risk for depression in response to stressors

In addition to negative moderator effects, studies also revealed *protective effects* of some moderators. For example, *social competence* was a protective variable against stressors in preadolescent girls, while *academic competence* was linked with significant protective effects at all ages.

The majority of studies examining the **mediator effects** of stressors have focused on poverty as a variable. Poverty has been studied in relation to environmental, family and child-based mediators with findings indicating link between poverty and psychological symptoms in areas including stressful life events, parent depressed mood, marital conflict, decreased parent nurturance, harsh/inconsistent parenting, disrupted family routines, child characteristics of aggression, and self-esteem.

Posttraumatic stress disorder (PTSD).   Historically, **posttraumatic stress disorder (PTSD)** did not appear in the DSM until the 3rd edition (*DSM–III*: APA, 1980). However, by the time the 3rd edition was revised (*DSM–III*; APA, 1987), there was greater awareness that children and youth could also be vulnerable to developing PTSD. The recognition that PTSD could occur at any age brought with it the need to focus on how symptoms of PTSD manifest in children exposed to extreme stress and psychic trauma (Pynoos, 1990). The next decade ushered in a paradigm shift away from consideration of children's response to trauma as a temporary "adjustment" towards an increasing awareness that the impact of trauma could result in far reaching consequences for development (Yule, 1998). With this trend came the recognition of the biological, psychological, and social ramifications of PTSD in children and youth (Pynoos, 1994).

Case in Point

Marco had just obtained his drivers' license 3 weeks before the accident happened. It was a dark night and the road was slippery. Marco doesn't remember much about the accident, but he does remember his friend Julio's face just before the truck smashed into them. It was a look of horror. He still sees that face most nights when he tries to fall asleep. At other times, he can't seem to wake up. Marco suffered several broken ribs, but they have since healed. He walks around wishing he would have lost an arm or leg, so that he could show others that he too was near death. But no one can see into his head. That is where the damage really is. Marco cannot concentrate, he cannot think, and he tries not to feel. The pain is no longer in his body; it is in his head and heart. He wants it to stop. But he does not know how to make it go away.

Description and Associated Features

In the above case, Marco is faced with the aftermath of a traumatic experience in which he was seriously injured and his friend was killed. He feels helpless because of the accidental nature of the wreck. No doubt, for Marco there is significant **survivor guilt**. Faced with traumatic events of this nature, adults react with intense feelings of fear, horror, or helplessness, which in young children may appear as *disorganized and agitated behaviors* (*DSM–IV–TR*, APA, 2000, p. 467).

Although the **stress disorders** (**acute stress disorder** and **PTSD**) are classified as part of the anxiety disorders (*DSM–IV–TR*, APA, 2000), they differ from the other anxiety disorders in a significant way. While the other anxiety disorders are triggered by *perceptions of threat* that most people would not find disconcerting, the situations or events that trigger the stress disorders would be considered traumatic by anyone exposed to such an event. There are three major components involved in a diagnosis of PTSD, as outlined in the *DSM–IV–TR* (APA, 2000):

1. Identification of the **traumatic event** (criterion A);
2. Identification of a number of symptoms that have developed in response to the traumatic event from among *three symptom clusters* (criteria B, C, and D); and
3. Duration of the disorder (criterion E: in excess of 1 month for PTSD).

The first four criteria are presented in Table 7.1 along with a summary of how symptoms may present somewhat differently in children and adults.

As can be seen in *criterion A* (Table 7.1), the nature of the event is far beyond that which most people would experience in a lifetime and includes such examples as natural disasters, wars, victimization (sexual or physical), terrorist attacks, serious automobile accidents, or being diagnosed with a life-threatening disease. In response to the traumatic event, the *DSM* outlines possible symptoms that may develop within each of three symptom clusters:

Table 7.1 *DSM* Criteria for Posttraumatic Stress Disorder (PTSD) With Child Symptoms

DSM Criteria	Child Symptoms
A. Traumatic event involves *both*: (1) Experience or witness to event(s) of actual or threatened death, or serious injury to self or others; (2) Response intense fear, helplessness, horror	**A. Traumatic event involves *both*:** (1) Experience or witness traumatic event (*what constitutes a traumatic event may differ in adults and children*) (2) Response may appear as disorganized or agitated behavior
B. Reexperiencing of event *(1 or more of following)*: • Recurrent, obtrusive , distressing images, thoughts; • Persistent distressing dreams • Recurring illusions, hallucinations, flashbacks/reliving experience • Intense psychological distress triggered by cues (internal/external) of event • Physiological distress triggered by cues (internal/external) of event	**B. Reexperiencing of event** *(1 or more of following)*: • Response may involve repetitive play about trauma themes • Dreams of monsters, or rescue • Trauma specific reenactment • Distress (psychological/physiological) triggered by stimuli associated with event. *May take the form of stomachaches and headaches*
C. Avoidance of stimuli associated with event and numbing of responsiveness *(3 or more of following)*: • Avoid discussions of event • Avoid activities associated with event • Inability to recall event • Sense of foreshortened future • Detachment and estrangement • Diminished interest in activities • Restricted range of affect	**C. Avoidance of stimuli associated with event and numbing of responsiveness** *(3 or more of following)*: • Avoid discussions of event • Avoid activities associated with event • Inability to recall event • Omen formation (belief in ability to foresee future) • Detachment and estrangement Parent/Teacher report of: • Diminished interest in activities • Restricted range of affect
D. Persistent symptoms increased arousal *(2 or more of following)*: • Difficulty falling/staying asleep • Irritable/anger outbursts • Concentration problems • Hypervigilance • Exaggerated startle response	**D. Persistent symptoms increased arousal** *(2 or more of following)*: • Difficulty falling/staying asleep • Irritable/anger outbursts • Concentration problems • Hypervigilance • Exaggerated startle response
E. Duration Symptoms B, C, D, more than 1 month	**E. Duration** Symptoms B, C, D, more than 1 month
F. Dysfunction Outcome: significant impairment/distress in social/occupational areas	**F. Dysfunction** Outcome: significant impairment/distress in peer relationships, family, and school

Source: DSM–IV–TR, APA (2000).

- Criteria B (*reexperiencing of intrusive thoughts and images*)
- Criteria C (*avoidance and numbing*)
- Criteria D (*hyperarousal*).

For diagnostic purposes, there must be evidence of ***at least six symptoms*** and the symptoms must match the minimal criteria of ***one or more symptoms from cluster B; three or more from cluster C; and two or more from cluster D***. Diagnosis is based on the duration of symptoms (***criteria E***), either ***acute stress disorder*** (symptoms dissipate within a month) or ***posttraumatic stress disorder*** (symptoms may be immediate or delayed, but last at least for a month). Cases of acute stress disorder can develop into PTSD. Because symptoms for the stress disorders are almost identical—with the exception of onset and duration—the remainder of the discussion will be limited to PTSD.

Despite some attempts to address how symptoms in children and youth may differ from adults, there are several reasons for questioning the appropriateness of the *DSM* symptoms in detecting PTSD in children and youth. For one, there were no children or youth in the *DSM–IV* field trial for PTSD (Scheeringa, Wright, Hunt, & Zeanah, 2006). Furthermore, diagnosis of PTSD in children poses a number of challenges that are not evident in adult populations. Difficulties exist at various levels of the diagnostic process, including a definition of what constitutes a traumatic event for children and youth, and how symptoms may present differently at different developmental levels. On the one hand, the child's cognitive and expressive limitations may restrict comprehension of the nature of the traumatic event. On the other hand, the young child's propensity to embellish ordinary events with fantasy overtones, and the tendency to confuse appearance and reality, further complicate the issue. While an event may not be of catastrophic proportions in terms of violence or threat to life, the event may still impact significant trauma on a child, such as incidents of inappropriate sexual touching, or being lost among a sea of strangers in unknown territory. Children and adolescents who experience PTSD can demonstrate a host of symptoms including flashbacks, numbing, avoidance, heightened physiological arousal, and a sense of foreshortened future.

The *DSM–IV–TR* (APA, 2000) describes features of PTSD which may be evident in children. Themes of **recurrent images** and **reexperiencing** may translate into forms of **repetitive play** where the child enacts the traumatic event. Although children may not recognize the nature of their frightening dreams, they may experience dreams of monsters or rescue. Although children may not be able to articulate the nature of flashbacks, they may reenact trauma scenes as if they were recurring all over again in a form of repetitive play. Whereas adults may demonstrate many symptoms of *avoidant behaviors* in their effort to remove themselves from people, events, and situations associated with the trauma in an attempt to *numb their emotional responsiveness*, children are less likely to be aware of these behaviors at a cognitive level. Instead, teachers and parents must be keenly aware of avoidance and withdrawal evident in the behaviors of these children after exposure to a traumatic event. Similarly, loss of interest in activities may be evident only subtly and may go unnoticed in such behaviors as *subdued play, day dreaming,* and *increased retreat into fantasy play*. The third cluster of symptoms, cluster D, includes physiological or vegetative symptoms of **increased agitation and arousal**. Many of these symptoms share many features similar to ADHD, including problems falling or staying asleep; anger or irritable outbursts; problems with concentration or completing tasks; and distractibility. Children may respond with symptoms of **hypervigilence** (on heightened alert) and **startle response** to reminders of the event.

Depending on the nature of the event, some, like Marco in the opening vignette, may develop a sense of increased guilt, or survivor guilt, which can result in feelings of self-blame, responsibility, and pervasive feelings of hopelessness and despair. Other children may respond to feelings hopelessness by developing **magical powers** such as a belief that they can foresee the future (**omen formation**).

Carrion et al. (2002) found that while **emotional numbing** is not a common symptom in childhood PTSD, it was observed at all developmental levels. Furthermore, there is initial evidence to suggest that the process of numbing in children occurs in response to emotional exhaustion from extended experiencing of a hyperarousal state (Weems, Saltzman, Reiss, & Carrion, 2003).

Development in Focus

There is considerable controversy regarding the appropriateness of the *DSM* for diagnosis of childhood symptoms, since the majority of disorders (with the exception of the specific childhood disorders) rely on criteria consistent with adult symptoms. Two clusters of symptoms, emotional numbing and reexperiencing have been evaluated in independent studies to verify their application to PTSD in childhood. Studies have concurred that the most common symptom demonstrated by children is the **reexperiencing** of the traumatic event, either in play or reenactment (Carrion, Weems, Ray, & Reiss, 2002; La Greca, Silverman, Vernberg, & Prinstein, 1996).

Developmental Issues and Trends

Increasing attention has been placed on determining how PTSD is manifested developmentally. Even though there are likely a number of core symptoms of PTSD that would be seen across all age levels, it would be anticipated that there would also be differences in symptom presentations at different stages of development, and most certainly between adult and child populations. In a recent study conducted with 62 children between the ages of 0–18 who were hospitalized with injuries, Scheeringa, Wright, and Hunt (2006) investigated the developmental nature of risk factors, symptom presentation, and parent versus youth self-report. Results of this study revealed that none of the very young children (7 years of age) met the threshold number of symptoms for cluster C, *numbing/avoidance* (three items). In addition, there was a significant discrepancy in symptom presentation for the younger group (0- to 6-year-old group) versus the older group (12- to 18-year-olds).

There is increasing evidence that different symptom clusters for PTSD may be evident at different stages of development (AACAP, 1998). McDermott and Palmer (2002) interviewed more than 2,000 students at varying stages of development (Grades 4–12), 6 months after a bushfire disaster. Developmentally, while those in the youngest (Grades 4, 5, and 6) and oldest groups (Grades 11 and 12) were more prone to developing postdisaster *depressive symptoms,* children of middle-school age (Grades 7, 8, and 9) were most likely to respond with symptoms of *emotional distress.* In their research, Amaya-Jackson and March (1995a) also noted developmental differences in outcomes for PTSD relative to the age of onset of the traumatic event. They found that **earlier onset PTSD** (prior to age 14) was more often associated with developing interpersonal problems, while **later onset PTSD** was predictive of greater academic difficulties.

Characteristics evident in very young children.   For the past decade, Scheeringa and Zeanah (1995) have argued that the *DSM* (APA, 2000) criteria for PTSD are not applicable for diagnosis in very young children and are not developmentally sensitive. For example, despite recognition of a child's limited verbal repertoire, 8 out of a possible 19 symptoms require verbal reports of internal experiences and feelings. More recent investigations (Scheeringa et al., 2006) suggest that symptom presentations, especially in cluster C, can be problematic for children even up to 7 years of age. The authors reason that cognitive shifts that occur after age 7 (concrete operations) and greater neurological maturity and differentiation after that time may be possible explanations for the presence or absence of criterion C symptoms.

Very young children may also demonstrate more generalized fears such as stranger or separation anxiety, avoidance of new situations, sleep disturbance, and may become preoccupied with certain words or symbols that may or may not be related to the trauma. There may also be signs of regression, as in a loss of previously attained skills, such as toilet training (National Center for Posttraumatic Stress Disorder [NCPTSD], 2001).

Characteristics evident in school-age children.   Although few elementary school-aged children may be expected to experience visual flashbacks or amnesia for the traumatic event (Scheeringa & Zeanah, 2001), **time skew** and **omen formation** have been reported. Time skew is evident when children demonstrate faulty recall for the sequence of traumatic events, while omen formation is a belief that they can predict the occurrence of traumatic events. Both responses are developed as a coping response (NCPTSD, 2001). While some children might alter their play or stories to include a happy ending, as an attempt at child mastery, others may engage in continual **repetitive trauma play** (compulsive repetition of some aspect of the traumatic event), which actually can cause increased anxiety and stress (Amaya-Jackson & March, 1995b).

Symptoms are likely to be pervasive at home and at school. At home, children may experience increased sleep problems evident in nightmares, night terrors, problems falling asleep or staying asleep, sleepwalking, and bedwetting (Amaya-Jackson & March, 1995b). As a result, children may demonstrate behavior problems associated with bedtime routines in anticipation of experiencing nightmares or night terrors. Fears of the dark and fears of sleeping alone may also become problematic.

At school, instead of symptoms of numbing and avoidance evident in adults with PTSD, children may demonstrate symptoms of restlessness, poor concentration, hypervigilence, and behavioral problems (Malmquist, 1986). Problem behaviors may be evident as children exposed to traumatic events may engage in increased risk taking behaviors (Pynoos, 1990). Academically, children may encounter difficulties learning and retaining information due to problems with attention and concentration (Amaya-Jackson & March, 1995a), or react with an exaggerated startle response to unusual and unpredictable occurrences such as fire drills (March, Amaya-Jackson, & Pynoos, 1994). Due to the high overlap in symptoms between ADHD and PTSD, it is not surprising that some children with PTSD may be misdiagnosed as having ADHD. In addition, there is also a high rate of comorbidity between PTSD and ADHD, which makes diagnosis even more complex (Cuffe, McCullough, & Pumariega,1994; McLeer, Callaghan, & Henry, 1994).

The American Academy of Child and Adolescent Psychiatry (AACAP, 1997) cautions that some adults (parents and teachers) may underestimate the impact of traumatic events on young children due to their reasoning that children are too young to feel the full emotional impact in a lasting way. Studies of associated features of children who have been traumatized by sexual abuse yield a number of problems that develop as a result, including fears, anxieties, depression, anger, self-destructive behaviors, feelings of isolation, and poor self-esteem (NCPTSD, 2001). In school-aged children, anxiety may often take the form of vague somatic symptoms (generally not feeling well, complaints of stomachaches, headaches, or body aches).

Characteristics evident in adolescence.   As children approach adolescence, symptoms may more closely approximate those of adults; however, there has been the suggestion that adolescents may be especially vulnerable to adverse effects from exposure to a traumatic incident (Pynoos, 1993). During this time, there is increased influence of peers in schools and the neighborhood, and risk factors continue to increase under pressures of peer group influence; adolescent tendencies to engage in risk-taking behaviors can exacerbate stressful consequences. Pynoos (1994) also warns that traumatic consequences at this stage can disrupt the trajectory of normal development with the potential to produce long-range and life-altering effects. Since these years are formative for the development of one's sense of purpose in life and identity formation, the devastation following a traumatic event may cause significant developmental change in a negative way. Adolescents are also more likely than adults or younger children to respond with impulsive and aggressive behaviors, or to reenact the trauma by incorporating aspects of the trauma into their daily life (NCPTSD, 2001).

Risk Factors

There are a number of factors that can increase vulnerability to developing PTSD symptoms following exposure to a traumatic event. Some characteristics which can moderate the likelihood of developing PTSD include:

- the nature of the traumatic event (severity)
- the physical or temporal proximity to the event
- the nature of the impact, personally
- child's age or stage of development
- mental health status
- the manner in which the parent responds to the trauma

The nature of the traumatic event.   As was discussed initially, determining the severity and nature of the traumatic event poses a challenge for child clinicians due to limitations and wide variations in cognitive processing that may influence children's interpretation of traumatic events and their ability to express their feelings and responses to a traumatic event. However, it is generally agreed that the greater the trauma, the greater the likelihood of developing symptoms of PTSD. If the trauma is grief related (death of a family member or friend), the situation can be very complex (Pynoos & Nader, 1993), and involve the combined interaction between trauma and grief responses. The result can be a progressive preoccupation with the traumatic circumstances surrounding the death which will ultimately block both the grieving process and subsequent recovery. In a severe case where the youth feels responsible for the trauma and loss, significant survivor guilt may be present, such as in Marco's case concerning the loss of his friend and his own responsibility for the car accident.

Type I and type II trauma.   Differences also exist regarding whether the trauma resulted from a one-time occurrence (referred to as **type I trauma**), or is the consequence of repeated exposure to traumatic incidents over a lengthy period, as in the case of repeated sexual or physical abuse (referred to as **type II trauma**). Different types of responses might be expected, depending on whether a type I or type II trauma was experienced. It has been suggested that while type I trauma would produce more typical PTSD response patterns (*reexperiencing, avoidance, and hyperarousal*), exposure to type II traumas might elicit more pervasive symptoms of denial, numbing/dissociation and rage (Terr, 1991).

Developmental Trauma Disorder

There has been increasing frustration with the lack of suitability of the *DSM–IV–TR* (APA, 2000) criteria for the diagnosis of PTSD in child populations, especially with respect to children exposed to chronic and prolonged traumatic circumstances. As a result, the National Child Traumatic Stress Network (NCTSN) *DSM V* task force has suggested a new diagnostic category to better capture the pervasive impact and consequences of exposure to **complex trauma** in children. The term complex trauma is used to describe the "experience of multiple, chronic and prolonged, developmentally adverse traumatic events, most often of an interpersonal nature (e.g., sexual or physical abuse, war, community violence) and early-life onset" (van der Kolk, 2005, p. 402). The exposure most often involves the caregiver.

Based on results of a national survey of clinicians involved with traumatized children and extensive research in the area, it has been suggested that children of complex trauma not only suffer from the consequences of exposure to the trauma but the consequences of their adaptation to living in traumatic circumstances (Spinazzola et al., 2005). Furthermore, based on the *DSM–IV* Field Trial conducted between 1992–1994 involving 400 adults and adolescents, researchers found that trauma that is prolonged, occurs at an early age, and is interpersonal in nature, results in psychological effects that are far beyond those contained in PTSD symptomatology and can include "affect dysregulation, aggression against self and others, dissociative symptoms, somatization, and character pathology" (van der Kolk, Rothe, Pelcovitz, Sunday, & Spinazzola, 2005, p. 394–395).

Proximity. In two independent studies, Pynoos (1994) reports that the degree of impact of PTSD was directly related to how close the child was to the traumatic event (physical proximity). However, children can also develop PTSD symptoms by vicarious exposure, such as witnessing domestic or neighborhood violence (Horowitz, Weine, & Jekel, 1995), observing traumatic events on television (Huesmann, Moise-Titus, & Podolski, 2003), or by living in battle-torn countries (Laor, Wolmer, & Cohen, 2001).

The nature of the parent response. While strong parental support is associated with more positive outcomes (Rossman, Bingham, & Emde, 1997), whether the parent was exposed to the event also can contribute to their understanding and support. While parents can minimize PTSD symptoms in their children (Foa, 2000), one would expect that parents who are exposed to the same traumatic event should be more sensitive. However, research shows that if the parent is traumatized as well, they can also be less sensitive to their child's needs. Parents who are overwhelmed and distressed can give less support (Drell, Siegel, & Gaensbauer, 1993).

Memory Bank

In discussing parental reactions to PTSD symptoms in their children, Pynoos (1994) notes that parent reactions can have *two possible effects*: a *positive influence* serving to reassure and calm the child; or a *negative influence* which can serve to exacerbate the emotional climate through emotional contagion.

Other risk factors. Pfefferbaum (1997) suggests several factors that can result in increased vulnerability to PTSD, including repeated exposures to television coverage of the event (e.g.,

World Trade Center collapse; devastation of Hurricane Katrina), previous exposure to trauma, family support, and socioeconomic factors. Studies of adults who were traumatized as children (physically or sexually abused) suggest that they are at greater risk for developing PTSD than adults who were not abused as children. In addition to past history of abuse, or having a mental disorder, studies have also demonstrated increase risk for developing PTSD, as a result of being female, having low self-esteem, or separation from parents prior to age 10 (Davidson, 1993). Furthermore, poorer child outcomes for exposure to trauma were also associated with poverty, parent mental illness, or having a teen parent (Zeanah, Boris, & Larrieu, 1997). Children who are anxious/depressed or who demonstrate symptoms of negative emotionality tend to not only be at greater risk for developing PTSD, but more severe forms of PTSD (Breslau, Davis, Andreski, & Peterson, 1991; Lonigan, Shannon, Saylor, Finch, & Sallee, 1994).

Adolescents who are chemically dependent have been reported to have increased risk for PTSD, up to 5 times the rate of those who are not (Deykin & Buka, 1997).

Moderating and Protective Factors

While the majority of the discussion thus far has focused on factors that can increase the risk of developing PTSD, it is also important to discuss those factors that can moderate or reduce the negative impact. Lower levels of family stress, successful coping with previous stressors, and positive and effective coping styles have all be associated with reduced impact of PTSD symptoms (Martini, 1995). Positive associations and better child outcomes have also been linked to a number of parent (cohesive marital status, higher educational level, psychological well-being) and family characteristics (family support network, and stability; Amaya-Jackson & March, 1995a).

Science Talks

What are the long-term outcomes for children with PTSD? Results from studies of natural disasters (Buffalo Creek Dam collapse, Hurricane Andrew) suggest that symptoms of PTSD are not the temporary responses they were once thought to be. In one study, 7% of children initially exposed to the Buffalo Creek Dam collapse met PTSD criteria 17 years later (Green, 1996).

Prevalence

In view of recent discussions of the suitability of the *DSM* criteria for diagnosing PTSD in children, it is not surprising that estimates of prevalence rates for PTSD in children are difficult to obtain. According to the *DSM* (APA, 2000), adult lifetime prevalence rate for PTSD in a community population is approximately 8%. Rates for children and adolescents vary widely depending on whether the sample is a clinical- or community-based sample. For example, while one study reported an adolescent rate of 6.3% in a community sample from Massachusetts (Giaconia, Reinherz, & Silverman, 1995), rates as high 67% have been reported in a clinical all-female sample (79 females; Horowitz et al., 1995). Although many studies have demonstrated that females are at significantly higher risk (up to 5 times the risk compared to males) for developing PTSD in response to a traumatic event (Breslau et al., 1991), other studies have found that males have higher rates of exposure to trauma (Pfefferbaum, 1997). High rates of PTSD responses are also found in profiles of sexually abused children, with up to as many as 44% meeting criteria for PTSD in one study (McLeer, Deblinger, Henry, & Orvaschel, 1992). Some researchers have argued that prevalence rates may be biased towards females because boys may not present symptoms that would be recognized as clearly as girls and that instruments used to assess PTSD are often directed towards internalizing symptoms (anxiety and depression), while boys may in fact act out their PTSD responses (Ostrov, Offer, & Howard, 1989). According to Pfefferbaum (1997), approximately 6% of children and youth can be expected to meet the criteria for PTSD.

Comorbidity. PTSD, similar to other anxiety disorders, often sets the stage for the development of other comorbid disorders. Depression, anxiety, and substance abuse (Pfefferbaum, 1997) are among the most common comorbid disorders. However, there is research evidence to support the premise that the actual type of comorbid disorder may be predicted by different age-based vulnerabilities (McDermott & Palmer, 2002).

Etiology

Biological Model
Biological, medical, neurotransmitter. When a stressful event occurs, the **hypothalamus** responds setting in motion a series of reactions resulting in the release of chemicals throughout the body, as two important systems are called to action: the **autonomic nervous system (ANS)**, the system that regulates involuntary activities of organs, such as respiration, heart rate, pupil dilation, etc.; and the **endocrine system**, the system of glands that release hormones into the bloodstream. There are two pathways that are responsible for arousal and fear: the **sympathetic nervous system** pathway and the **hypothalamic–pituitary–adrenal (HPA)** pathway (see Figure 7.1).

Sympathetic nervous symptom pathway. The **sympathetic nervous system** works in conjunction with the **parasympathetic system**, both parts of the ANS. When faced with danger, the sympathetic nervous system sends a message to the organs to speed up reactions, either directly through nerve impulses (pupils dilate, heart rate increases), or indirectly, as the adrenal medulla releases the chemicals **epinephrine (adrenaline)** or **norepinephrine (noradrenaline)** into the bloodstream. When the fear subsides, the **parasympathetic system** is activated and is responsible for returning the response levels back to normal (pupils contract, heart rate slows).

Hypothalmic–pituitary–adrenal pathway. In response to danger, the hypothalamus is also responsible for activating the pituitary gland to release a stress hormone, **adrenocorticotropic hormone (ACTH)**, which in turn causes the adrenal glands to release **corticosteroids**, a group of stress hormones, such as **cortisol**. The corticosteroids are responsible for causing increased arousal and fear responses throughout the body, until, the **hippocampus** (part of brain that stores emotional memories) is activated which send the message to return to normal.

Science Talks

Does parenting have an impact on infant cortisol levels? Traumatized infants who demonstrate disorganized/disoriented attachment response patterns demonstrate elevated levels of cortisol when reunited with their caregiver (Spangler & Grossmann, 1999). However, securely attached infants with a timid (wary) temperament actually show reduction in levels of cortisol when reunited with their caregivers (Nachmias, Gunnar, Mangelsdorf, Parritz, & Buss, 1996)

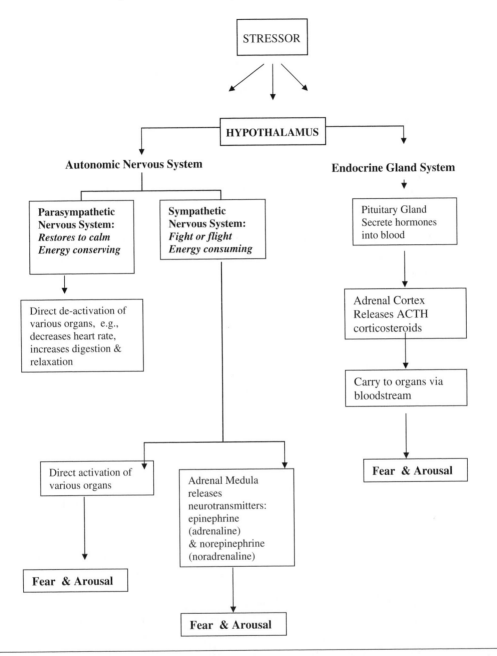

Figure 7.1 Stress activates the hypothalamus and responses proceed along two paths: Direct responses transmitted through the sympathetic nervous system and indirect via the pituitary and adrenal cortex.

There are indications that highly stressful events are related to changes in body- and brain-based chemistry that may alter one's ability to respond to stressful events in the future. Pfefferbaum's (1997) review of the research in the past 10 years provides increasing evidence that these changes can result in dulling the child's **fight or flight** response pattern and produce emotional numbing and dissociative tendencies. In support of this theory is evidence of abnormal activity of the neurotransmitter norepinephrine and elevated levels of the hormone cortisol in individuals with PTSD (Baker et al., 1999). It has also been found that enduring heightened arousal over time may alter the hippocampus (portion of the brain that regulates stress hormones) and impair the ability to respond to stressful situations in the future (Bremner, 1999). Reduction of brain volume has also been associated with early onset of PTSD. At least one study has found reductions in brain volume (smaller intracranial and cerebral volume) in children with early onset and/or type II PTSD (De Bellis, Keshavan, & Clark, 1999).

Behavioral Model

Using a paradigm similar to the one that was previously discussed in the behaviorist explanations of the acquisition of phobias, models of classical conditioning can also be used to explain how PTSD develops. Although it is highly unlikely that severe trauma (e.g., plane crash, mugging) will reoccur in the future, negative thoughts are continually recycled, producing increased connections through stimulus generalization. Therefore, connections are forged that will cause the traumatic event to live on in thoughts, appearances, and images that trigger memory of the traumatic event long after the actual event is done.

Cognitive Behavioral Model

How one processes the event cognitively interacts with attributions of how future events are appraised. Relatively harmless events can trigger painful memories and thoughts resulting in linking signals to a renewed potential of threat (Foa & Kozak, 1986). At a cognitive level, traumatization may result in recursive thoughts patterns that continue to associate the trauma (objects, feelings, thoughts) with anxiety and fear. These thoughts may be so overwhelming that they result in dysfunctional beliefs about the future (Ehlers & Clark, 2000).

Parenting Style and Attachment

It is not surprising to find that one of the most stable predictors of child outcomes following exposure to trauma is the influence of the mental health status of the caregiver on the child's ability to manage and adapt to stress (Laor et al., 1997; Pynoos, Goenjian, & Steinberg, 1998). For example, one study found that parent responses to their child's PTSD at either end of the spectrum had adverse effects: overprotectiveness of children with PTSD led to worst child outcomes, while maternal avoidance of child PTSD symptoms resulted in an escalation in symptoms (McFarlane, 1987). On the other hand, studies that have focused on improving parent/child communication and coping surrounding stressful events have yielded significant increases in positive child outcomes (Olds et al., 1998).

In order to better understand the role of caregivers in mediating the expression of PTSD symptoms in young children, Scheeringa and Zeanah (2001) have formulated a theory of **Relational PTSD** to demonstrate how adult responses can influence child expression of symptoms in an adverse way. The authors propose three patterns of parent responses and likely child reactions: withdrawn/unresponsive parent and/or overprotective parent patterns resulting in worsening of PTSD symptoms in child; and fearful pattern resulting in increased avoidance in the child. With respect to the latter response pattern, we are reminded of the disorganized attachment patterns of infants who simultaneously seek comfort and yet fear their caregivers (Main & Solomon, 1986). Although normally, the need for attachment and comforting by the caregiver is elevated at times of stress, for children whose parents are themselves unable to cope with the stressful situation, little comfort is provided, and increased discomfort and stress may be the result. When trauma is revisited by a caregiver who themselves carry the burden of unresolved trauma in the past, disorganized attachment patterns may resurface, setting the stage for increased child stress.

Lyons-Ruth and Jacobvitz (1999) discuss this recurring disorganizational pattern in caregivers, who themselves were victims of early maternal deprivation, as part of a stress–relational–diathesis model. The authors suggest that early disorganizational patterns may be latent and only reappear when the caregiver is again rendered vulnerable by an overwhelming situation, resulting in activation of dysfunctional, atypical, and maladaptive behaviors.

The influence of caregiver's response to trauma gains increasing importance in the light of recent investigations of responses to terrorist attacks on the World Trade Center (9/11). Stuber, Fairbrother, and Galea (2002) found that symptoms of PTSD were evident in twice as many parents compared to nonparents. Devoe, Bannon, and Klein (2006) studied help-seeking behaviors in a highly exposed sample of 180 New York City parents of children under age 5. Researchers found only 15% sought counseling for their young children with the most salient predictors of help seeking being the development of new fears in children, and parent depressive symptoms.

Treatment

Cognitive behavioral therapy (CBT).   In their recent meta-analysis of treatments for youth with PTSD, Feeny, Foa, Treadwell, and March (2004) found several approaches that demonstrate successful outcomes. (The review follows Feeney et al., 2004.) Although empirical support for CBT is strong for adults as well as youth, there is far less research on other forms of treatment that might be available. The authors found several categories of treatment programs within the CBT framework, including imaginal and in vivo exposure, **eye-movement desensitization and reprocessing (EMDR)**, **anxiety-management training (AMT)**, group treatments, and child-parent treatments.

Imaginal and *in vivo* exposure.   As was previously discussed in treatment responses to phobias, exposure therapy techniques can also apply to PTSD related fears (situations, objects, memories). Although prolonged exposure (PE) to traumatic fears, using either *imagined* (in memory) or *in vivo* (confrontation of actual object or situation) techniques, has been successful in the treatment of adults with PTSD (Foa & Rothbaum, 1998), only a handful of studies have evaluated the technique with children. In a series of related studies, Saigh, (1986, 1989) found the technique helpful in reducing anxiety, depression, and avoidance symptoms in Lebanese children with war-related trauma.

Eye-movement desensitization and reprocessing (EMDR).   The EMDR technique (Shapiro, 1995) involves invoking a traumatic memory in the client and then engaging them in rapid eye movement task (tracking the therapists finger as it moves laterally back and for across the eyes). At least one study found this method to be effective in the long-term reduction of PTSD symptoms (6 months postdisaster) for children exposed to Hurricane Iniki (Chemtob, Nakashima, & Carlson, 2002).

Anxiety-management training (AMT).   AMT (Meichenbaun, 1974) is a program that relies upon cognitive restructuring (CR) in order to reframe maladaptive thinking into more adaptive thought patterns. A preliminary investigation of this technique with a small sample of sexually abused children has found encouraging results (Farrell, Hains, & Davies, 1998).

Group treatment.   A number of studies have evaluated the use of CBT techniques in schools. March, Amaya-Jackson, Murray, and Shulte (1998) provided a manualized program that was comprised of several components, including awareness, exposure to trauma stories, anxiety management, anger control, and positive self–talk (stress innoculation). After 18 weekly sessions in the school, a majority of the group of 14 student participants who had experienced different types of traumas reported significant reduction in PTSD symptoms. CBT has also been used school-based interventions for children exposed natural disasters. To combat PTSD symptoms in response to an earthquake, Goenjian, Armen, Karayan, and Pynoos (1997), developed a program that modeled several techniques based on crisis intervention (discussion, relaxation, desensitization, grief work, and normalization). Children who participated in this program had greater reduction in PTSD symptoms compared to children who received no treatment. In a third study, Hamada, Kameoka, and Yanagida (2003) compared individual and group treatments for PTSD symptoms following Hurricane Iniki. Both treatments involved a 4-session manualized program that was developed to assist children going through recovery stages: safety and helplessness, loss, regaining competence, issues of anger, and going forward. Both the individual and group versions of the program were successful in significantly reducing symptoms of PTSD.

Memory Bank

Steps in Crisis Management. Mental health workers often receive some form of training in **critical incident stress debriefing** in order to help those in crisis to express their feelings and responses to traumatic events. Often discussions will follow a 4-step approach (Michaelson, 1993):

1. Normalize: educate that these are normal responses to abnormal situation.
2. Express: talking about feelings can reduce anxiety, fears, and anger.
3. Cope: teach skills of meditation, relaxation to assist coping.
4. Refer: refer to appropriate source if further help is needed.

Intervention for complex trauma.   Cook and colleagues. (2005) stress the need to target deficits in core competencies of self-regulation and interpersonal relatedness that exist in children and adolescents exposed to prolonged complex trauma. The authors suggest six core components in an intervention program for complex trauma. The components are viewed as building blocks, such that each step incorporates values and skills learned in the previous stage:

1. Safety (addressing issues of child protection);
2. Self-regulation (capacity to regulate emotions, behaviors, states of arousal, cognition);
3. Self-reflection (executive functions: problem solving, self monitoring, planning);
4. Integration of traumatic experiences (healthy management of traumatic memories and development of coping skills);
5. Interpersonal relationships (trust, assertiveness, boundaries and limit setting, reciprocity); and
6. Positive affect (enhances self-appraisals and attributions, future orientation, and increased mastery).

CHAPTER REVIEW AND SUMMARY

This chapter focused on anxiety disorders with onset in later childhood and adolescence: obsessive-compulsive disorder, social phobia, and panic disorder with and without agoraphobia. Consistent with earlier onset anxiety disorders discussed in chapter 6 (specific phobias, SAD, and

GAD), later onset anxiety disorders share similar features of uncontrollable and pervasive fears resulting from the *perception of threat*. However, unlike the anxiety disorders, stress disorders (acute and posttraumatic stress disorder), represent physiological, cognitive, and emotional responses to horrific and catastrophic events that cluster around three central themes: *reexperiencing, avoidance/numbing, and hyperarousal*. Children and youth can experience stress disorders, although there is significant controversy whether *DSM* criteria are appropriate for children of younger ages.

1. **Obsessive-Compulsive Disorder (OCD)**
   Although young children commonly engage in rituals, OCD represents an extreme variant of intrusive and persistent thoughts (obsessions) followed by compulsive and uncontrollable behaviors. The most common types of OCD among children and youth involve fears of contamination (compulsive handwashing/cleaning) and perfectionism/symmetry (ordering, straightening). A high percentage of adults (30%–50%) with OCD report childhood onset. Children can be secretive about their behaviors due to embarrassment and may go undetected for some time. Etiology has been linked to genetics, overactivity in particular areas of the brain, and low levels of serotonin. Treatment can involve SSRI medications, behavioral therapy (Rachman's procedure), and CBT.

2. **Social Phobia**
   Onset of social phobia in adolescence is marked by extreme fears of embarrassment that potentially might result from errors in performance or socially (e.g., fears of eating or writing in public). In order to avoid the possibility of embarrassment, feared situations are avoided and can compromise normal development. The type of social phobia that generalizes across situations is more serious and disabling than social phobias linked to more specific situations (e.g., public speaking). Increased risk for social phobia has been found in individuals with an inhibited temperament, those with a bias to interpret threat, individuals who experience negative affectivity. A diagnosis of social phobia requires that the symptoms be present for at least 6 months. Treatments previously discussed for specific phobia can also be successful for social phobia, with the additional emphasis on conjoint social skills training.

3. **Panic Disorder With and Without Agoraphobia**
   Based on the intensity and severity of physiological symptoms (heart palpitations, sweating, chest pain, shortness of breath), adults experiencing a panic attack may initially fear they are having a heart attack. There is an accompanying sense of loss of control, fear of going crazy, and depersonalization. Symptoms usually peak within about 10 minutes. Less is known about panic attacks in children and youth, although they can occur in response to feeling vulnerable, a specific phobia, or being forced to leave home in a child with SAD. Repeated panic attacks can result in a panic disorder (fear of having a panic attack), while avoidance of threatening situations can result in individuals becoming homebound (panic disorder with agoraphobia). Panic attacks in younger children seem to be more event related. Irregular neurotransmitter activity, and interactions between temperament, behavioral inhibition, and behavioral conditioning have been suggested as precipitating causes. Antidepressant medications and CBT are the treatments of choice.

4. **The Stress Disorders and Posttraumatic Stress Disorder (PTSD)**
   Most individuals encounter a wide variety of daily stressors and young children are no exception. The impact of stress can be moderated by age (developmental level), gender and individual characteristics (temperament). Poverty is one of the leading mediators of

stress and predicts increased risk for negative outcomes. When an extreme stress response occurs in relation to a catastrophic and life-altering event or series of events, a stress disorder may be the result. Unlike the other anxiety disorders that represent uncontrollable and pervasive fears resulting from the *perception of threat*, acute and posttraumatic stress disorders represent responses to a horrific and catastrophic event that cluster around three central themes: *reexperiencing, avoidance/numbing, and hyperarousal.* The diagnosis of PTSD in young children can be problematic, since over half the diagnostic criteria on the *DSM* require verbal responses. Explanations for the development of PTSD have included biological, neurological, behavioral, and family environment factors. Treatments have mainly focused on methods that incorporate CBT into the process.

Consolidate and Communicate

1. Studies of obsessive-compulsive disorder (OCD) in young children reveal a number of commonly occurring associated thoughts and behaviors. Name six common OCD obsessive themes and the types of behaviors that result. Discuss how OCD can impact the child's functioning at school and at home.

2. Is selective mutism an early precursor to social phobia? Based on your understanding of selective mutism, what are the arguments for and against the association with social phobia?

3. What is the difference between panic attacks and panic disorder? What are the two subtypes of panic disorder, and how are they distinguished?

4. Wanda is a teenager who develops a panic attack while standing in line at the supermarket. All of a sudden she feels trapped and frightened that she cannot escape. Describe what symptoms Wanda is likely to exhibit and how these might be different from symptoms evident in a younger child. Based on her psychologist's theoretical framework, how would he or she describe why the panic attack occurred?

5. According to Grant, Compass, and Thurm (2006), what is the difference between mediator and moderator variables, and what does the research predict regarding moderator effects and stress?

6. The *DSM* (2000) outlines three clusters of symptoms found in PTSD. Describe the three clusters, the symptoms related to each, and the appropriateness of these criteria for the diagnosis of PTSD in young children.

7. Fran had to work late. As a result she has to walk to her apartment from the bus stop alone and in the dark—a 10-minute walk through a desolated area. When she finally arrives, her heart is pounding, and she quickly locks the door behind her as she feels an immediate sense of relief that begins to calm her racing heart. However, as soon as she turns the hall light on, she is faced with an uninvited guest: a huge raccoon is sitting in the dark on her kitchen table, having let himself in from an open window near the roof. Once again, her body is immediately called to action, as two important systems are activated. Fran screams and the raccoon quickly exits. Quickly, she slams the window shut and sits down trying to calm herself down for the final time. Describe the two systems that are at work in this stressful situation and how the different pathways have relayed messages that have served to put Fran on alert, begin to calm her and then send her back into high alert, and will eventually work to set her at ease.

Chapter Review Questions

1. A contamination obsession might include all the following behaviors, except:
   a. excessive cleaning
   b. aligning
   c. handwashing
   d. teeth brushing

2. Individuals who recognize that OCD thoughts and behaviors are ego–dystonic believe that:
   a. others can share their feelings by proxy
   b. an alien has planted a thought in their head
   c. their thoughts and behaviors are illogical but are the result of their own doing
   d. their thoughts are the result of mind/body dualism

3. In the study by Piacentini et al. (2003), the two most common areas of school-related problems in children with OCD were:
   a. social relationships with peers
   b engaging in extracurricular activities
   c. eating with others
   d. concentration and homework

4. PANDAS is a:
   a. pandemic anxiety reaction that mimics OCD
   b. a streptococcal infection that can produce acute OCD
   c. a streptococcal infection that can produce acute tic disorders
   d. both b and c are correct

5. In order to diagnose social phobia in young children, the *DSM* (2000) requires two criteria beyond symptoms of refusal to engage in social situations. These criteria are:
   a. refusal to eat in public
   b. demonstrate normal social responses with familiar people
   c. social phobic response must occur in peer interaction situations only
   d. social phobic response must occur primarily in adult situations

6. The Behavioral Inhibition System (BIS) has been implicated in the potential etiology of a number of anxiety disorders in children. The BIS is:
   a. a quality of life characteristic describing one's tempo
   b. a brain system that serves to alert individuals of possible threat
   c. a personality dynamic that dulls one's sensitivity to threat
   d. an emotional response system that serves to redirect impulses to safe channels

7. Agoraphobia is a fear of:
   a. ants
   b. the market place
   c. spiders
   d. sports

8. There is some research support for the notion that a certain level of physical/cognitive maturity is required for panic attacks to occur. In one study of sixth- and seventh-grade girls (Hayward et al., 1992), researchers found that panic attacks were most severe for"
   a. younger girls, who reported the least amount of panic attacks
   b. younger boys, who reported the least amount of panic attacks
   c. older girls, who reported the most amount of panic attacks
   d. older boys, who reported the most amount of panic attacks

9. I am trying to cure my friend's obsession with dirt and cleanliness. I am studying psychology and I have read about a program that I think will cure him. I blindfold my friend, tie his hand behind his back, and lead him into the kitchen where I have dumped an entire bag of potting soil for plants in the middle of the kitchen floor. When the blindfold is removed, I immediately tell my friend that he cannot clean the floor for two days. This procedure is referred to as:
   a. systematic desensitization
   b. imagined desensitization
   c. exposure and response prevention
   d. behavioral inhibition

10. Which of the following is FALSE regarding the moderator effects of stress?
   a. Girls are more likely to respond to stress with internalizing symptoms and boys with externalizing symptoms.
   b. If race was identified as a factor, it was most common for Black youth.
   c. Older youth with negative self-thoughts were at greater risk for depression in response to stressors.
   d. Boys were more likely to respond to stress negatively if the stressor involved property, divorce, or abuse.

Glossary of New Terms

obsessive-compulsive disorder
obsessions
compulsions
ego-dystonic
serotonin
basal ganglia
orbital region/frontal cortex
caudate nuclei
thalamus
pediatric autoimmune neuropsychiatric disorder (PANDAS)
expressed emotion
exposure and response prevention therapy (ERP)
family based CBT (CBTFT)
focus program
social phobia
generalized social phobia
specific social phobia
selective mutism
behavioral inhibition system (BIS)
social skills training
panic attack
panic disorder
panic disorder with or without agoraphobia
norepinephrine
locus ceruleus
amygdale

panic control treatment for adolescents (PCT-A)
stress moderators
stress mediators
acute stress disorder
posttraumatic stress disorder (PTSD)
survivor guilt
traumatic event
recurrent images and re-experiencing
avoidant behaviors
emotional numbing
agitation and arousal
hypervigilence and startle response
time skew
repetitive trauma play
magical powers and omen formation
earlier onset PTSD
later onset PTSD
type I trauma and type II trauma
developmental trauma disorder
hypothalamus
autonomic nervous system (ANS)
endocrine system
sympathetic nervous system pathway
hypothalamic-pituitary-adrenal (HPA) pathway
epinephrine (adrenaline)
norepinephrine (noradrenaline)
parasympathetic system
adrenocorticotropic hormone (ACTH)
corticosteroids
cortisol
hippocampus
fight or flight
relational PTSD
imaginal and *in vivo* exposure
eye-movement desensitization and preprocessing (EMDR)
critical incident stress debriefing

Multiple Choice Answers:
1. b; 2. c; 3. d; 4. d; 5. b; 6. b; 7. b; 8. c; 9. c; 10. b.

8

The Mood Disorders

Depression, Bipolar Disorder, and Suicide

CHAPTER PREVIEW

Despite reports of childhood depression dating as far back as the 1930s, there was early skepticism whether children were capable of experiencing depression. In the 1960s it was thought that depression in children manifested as delinquent behaviors whereas the 1970's ushered in the belief that children could experience depressed feelings, but only on a temporary basis (e.g., adjustment reaction). Today, it is recognized that children can experience the entire gamut of depressed feelings from depressed mood to depressed syndromes to depressive disorders; although there is controversy whether children and adolescents express the same symptoms as adults, and how to best categorize, assess, and treat the disorder in children and youth. The *DSM–IV–TR* (APA, 2000) does not include depressive disorders under disorders with child or adolescent onset, but includes child features in the most recent text revision. Mood disorders can be classified as unipolar disorders (major depressive disorder, dysthymic disorder) if negative affect is predominant and there is no evidence of a manic episode. Bipolar disorder is diagnosed if an individual meets criteria for one of the depressive disorders and also experiences a manic episode. Youth with depression and bipolar disorder are at increased risk for suicide. Suicide increases dramatically after 14 years of age and rates have increased significantly in the past 10 years.

1. Unipolar Depression

Individuals who experience *unipolar depression* experience negative feelings of being sad or blue that can range from very mild to very severe. In addition, while some depressed feelings can be linked to an identifiable source (e.g., loss of job, break-up of romance), other feelings may be vague and seem unrelated to any particular situation or event. Based on the system of classification used, depression can be conceptualized as *depressed/withdrawn syndrome* (AESBA, 2001), or as *major depressive disorder* or *dysthymic disorder* (*DSM–IV–TR*, 2000).

   a. Major Depressive Disorder (MDD): The defining feature of MDD is either a pervasive "depressed mood state" or a loss of pleasure in daily activities (defined as *anhedonia*), an acute condition lasting at least 2 weeks (*DSM–IV–TR*: APA, 2000). Irritability may replace depressed mood state in children. *Four* additional symptoms are required from a total list of seven, including *vegetative* (e.g., physical responses such as loss of appetite, somatic complaints, sleep problems), *behavioral/psychomotor*, and *cognitive/affective* responses.

b. Dysthymic Disorder (DD): This is a less intense form of depression and represents a pervasive depressed mood (loss of interest or *anhedonia*), accompanied by two additional symptoms from the MDD list, lasting for at least 2 years (1 year in children) without relief for more than 2 months.

c. Developmental Characteristics and Course: Symptoms of depression can be expressed in different forms depending on the type of depression (*hedonic depression* or *anhedonic depression*), the cause and severity of the depression, and the child's developmental level. Research suggests that the majority of younger children develop depression in response to situational events, whereas depression in adolescence may be attributed more to genetic causes. There are higher rates of suicide attempts and fatalities in teens compared to prepubertal children.

d. Risks and Protective Factors: There are many factors across all levels of influence that can increase a child's vulnerability to depression: *individual* (difficult temperament, low self-esteem, low positive mood); *family* (conflict, level of expressed emotion, parenting style, maternal depression); *peer and school* (peer rejection, aggression); and *socioeconomic* (poverty, stressful life events). Children and youth who have other comorbid disorders (ADHD, conduct or learning disorders), suffer from a chronic illness (like diabetes), or experience trauma (post traumatic stress disorder, abuse) are at increased risk for depression. Some protective factors that can buffer children from depression include increased attentional control (ability to shift attention to other nondepressive areas), high academic achievement, school connectedness, family cohesion, and a supportive peer group.

e. Etiology, Assessment, and Treatment: *Biological models* of depression include specific risk genes and low levels of the neurotransmitter serotonin. The hypothalamic–pituitary–adrenal system (HPA) can also produce a neuroendocrine imbalance when excess levels of the hormone cortisol are produced in response to stress making some children more vulnerable to depression. The *cognitive behavioral perspective* (CBT) focuses on the *negative triad* (helpless, hopeless, worthless) generated by maladaptive thinking. *Family and peer influence models* have linked an adversarial climate and poor interpersonal skills with increased depressive responses in children and youth. An *ecological transactional model* has also been proposed to address the complex and on-going interaction among different levels of influence. There are a number of assessment instruments developed specifically to assess depression in children and adolescents. An important component of assessment of depression involves screening for suicidal ideation. Initially, treatment had focused primarily on CBT methods that have empirical support; however, more recently combining CBT with medication has proved to be more effective. The use of medication has been controversial due to limited research regarding dosing, safety, and efficacy of medications in child and adolescent populations.

2. Bipolar Disorder

The diagnosis of bipolar disorder in children has received increasing attention. Individuals with bipolar disorder experience both the lows of depression and the highs of mania (euphoric feelings). The *DSM–IV–TR* (APA, 2000) defines a *manic episode* as a distinct period (at least 1 week) wherein an individual experiences an abnormally elevated mood that contains at least three of seven symptoms. A *hypomanic episode* is a less severe manic episode (same number of symptoms required but qualitatively less severe), lasting for at least 4 days and often causing limited dysfunction. *Mixed manic episodes* involve an overlap between manic and depressive episodes. *Bipolar I* is diagnosed when MDD and manic (or mixed) episodes are involved, while *bipolar II* includes MDD and a hypomanic episode. *Cyclothymia* refers to mood states that range from dysthymic episodes to hypomanic episodes. Rapid cycling is used to refer to the experience of cases where there is more frequent fluctuation between mood states; however, the range of emotions is less severe (hypomanic and depression not meeting criteria for MDD). The specifier *rapid cycling* is used if four or more mood episodes occur within a 12-month period.

    a. Developmental Characteristics and Course: A relatively new diagnosis for children, there is significant concern regarding how the disorder manifests in childhood relative to the *DSM* criteria which is based largely on research with adults. Additionally, manic states of bipolar can resemble other disorders (ADHD, conduct problems, anxiety) and stimulant medications prescribed for ADHD can produce severe aggressive reactions in children with bipolar disorder. There is evidence that the disorder is more severe in childhood than in adulthood and resembles the *rapid cycling* features of the more severe adult forms. There is significant controversy regarding how the disorder should be conceptualized and diagnosed in childhood since episodes (chronic, continuous, mixed, or ultradian rapid cycling rather than episodic), clinical features (irritability rather than grandiosity or euphoria), and rates of comorbidity (highly comorbid in younger populations) may be significantly different from the adult version of the disorder and hence the *DSM–IV–TR* (APA, 2000) criteria. Attempts to understand the disorder have led researchers to compare subtypes of BD along a number of dimensions, including age of onset, nature of episodes, clinical phenotypes, and comorbid associations.

    b. Risk Factors: Factors that increase the risk for BD include having a parent with BD, having certain temperament qualities (disinhibition, novelty seeling), earlier onset, and life stress.

    c. Etiology, Assessment, and Treatment: A biological model provides the most plausible explanation for the etiology of bipolar disorder, as evident in high rates of genetic transmission. How brain chemistry is involved continues to be the subject of significant investigation; however, low levels of serotonin and high norepinephrine levels are one possible explanation, as is low levels of glutamate and/or glutamine. Abnormalities in the cortico-limbic neural circuitry have also been implicated. Neuropsychological findings include deficits in executive functions, sustained attention, verbal learning, and memory.

    Recommended treatments include medical management plus psychotherapeutic intervention that includes a relapse prevention component. The FDA, who previously approved lithium for use with adolescents who have BD, recently approved (August 2007) the use of Risperdal for biopolar disorder in children and youth ages 10 to 17.

3. Suicide

The rate of suicide among children and youth has increased dramatically in the past 10 years. Knowing the symptoms that can predict suicide attempts in children and adolescents can be instrumental in increasing awareness of peers, mentors, and family with the intention of averting potential suicide attempts.

    a. Risks and Protective Factors: Low self-esteem and engaging in high risk taking have both been associated with increased suicidal risk. Family history of suicide, association with deviant peers, substance use, and number of life stressors can all be contributing factors in increasing the risk of suicide. Protective factors can be found in family cohesion, absence of family history for suicide, and positive peer support.

b. Etiology: Biological factors can interact with environmental risk factors to increase the risk for suicide attempts. Risk increases for youth whose family history includes a relative who committed suicide. In addition, low levels of serotonin have been linked to depression and aggression, which may serve to mobilize energy into self-destructive tendencies.

c. Assessment, Intervention, and Prevention: Children and youth who are depressed or have BD should be continually monitored for suicidal risk. School-based suicide prevention programs are widely used, but until recently have been poorly supported empirically. In addition, there has been growing concern that programs might have an iatrogenic effect on an already vulnerable population. The *Signs of Suicide SOS Program* has been the first suicide prevention program that has empirically demonstrated a significant reduction in suicidal behavior in a randomized study of high school students. The program is currently being used in over 675 schools across the United States.

Historical Background

Although Bleuler published his review of case studies of childhood depression in 1934 and Spitz (1946) followed 10 years later with a description of **anaclitic depression** in institutionalized infants (a depressive condition appearing between 6 and 12 months of age), many theorists continued to question whether depression could exist in children.

Memory Bank

According to Freudian theorists, adult depression could not exist in children because young children lacked a well-defined superego and, as such, could not direct aggression towards the self.

Historically, there have been several debates regarding how depression should be conceptualized in children and youth. In the 1960s, the tendency was to think of child depression as **"masked depression,"** a term used to imply that children and youth manifest symptoms of depression in ways that are different from adults, e.g., acting out behaviors, delinquency, truancy, lying, etc. (Carlson & Cantwell, 1980). On the positive side, this direction in thinking recognized that symptoms of depression might present differently in children and adults. On the negative side, regarding these behaviors as extensions of the child's depressive psychopathology could conceivably rule out the presence of comorbid disorders (e.g., depression plus conduct disorder).

Development in Focus

Concepts of masked depression inferred a cause and effect relationship between the behavior and the underlying pathology. For example, a child's misbehavior would be attributed to the depression in the following manner of explanation: The child was "acting in this way" (lying, stealing, etc.) because the child was depressed. Viewing the "acting out" behaviors within this framework would make it less likely to think of two separate but co-occurring disorders: conduct problems and depression.

In the early 1980s mounting evidence provided support for the existence of depression syndrome in children and adolescents (Cantwell & Carlson, 1983). In addition, at this time, it was recognized that children could experience **"mixed disorders,"** having both features of neurotic and conduct disorders (Rutter, Tizard, & Whitmore, 1981). This paradigm shift opened the door for an overwhelming number of studies in the late 1980s that investigated the potential existence of multiple co-occurring (comorbid) disorders in children.

In their longitudinal study of major depressive disorder (MDD), dysthymic disorder, and adjustment disorder with depressed mood, Kovacs and colleagues (1988) investigated the role of comorbid conduct disorder (CD) on symptom presentation and child outcomes. Results indicated that 16% of their population with MDD had comorbid CD initially, while that percentage rose to 23% for the study duration. One significant finding of this study was that long-term outcomes for depressed children who also had CD were worse than outcomes for those who had MDD alone.

Depressive Symptoms, Syndromes, and Disorders

Depression can be conceptualized as **depressed mood**, **depressive syndromes**, or **depressive disorders** (Angold, 1988). In the opening *Case in Point*, you are introduced to three children who experience symptoms of depression that range from mild and transitory to severe and incapacitating.

Case in Point: A Trilogy of Depression

Darla is upset and unhappy. Her mother is worried because Darla has just not been herself since the family moved from Chicago 2 months ago. Darla misses her friends, cries herself to sleep at night, and repeatedly says that she is angry with her parents for making her leave her friends. Darla's mother invites some neighbors and their children over to enjoy the pool and to help celebrate Darla's 10th birthday. At the party, Darla meets some girls her age who are excited to have a new friend and can't wait to introduce her to the other kids when school starts in a few weeks. As a result, Darla is her old self again.

At the party, Darla meets Rachel, whose parents divorced 18 months ago. Rachel is not very friendly and she does not have a welcoming smile. She looks angry all the time. Darla and the other girls do not include Rachel in their game, because she looks mean. Rachel's mother is concerned because Rachel is upset and irritable most of the time. Rachel can't concentrate at school and her grades have been slipping this past year. Her mother is very concerned about the upcoming school year. Rachel keeps trying to think of ways to get her parents back together again, but nothing works. She hates the fact that she can only see her dad once a week. Rachel's mother is concerned because Rachel has been irritable and very hard to live with for over a year now. Rachel's mother is beginning to think that this is more than just a phase.

Eric is Darla's teenage brother. Eric refuses to come out of his room and he has lost the energy he once had. He says that he does not feel like eating, even when his mother makes his favorite dish. For the past 2 weeks, he has been sleeping most of the day. He feels as if his feet are in cement. He cannot get up. He has not even attempted to visit his new high school to register for the fall term. He talks about quitting school altogether. His mood has spiraled again. He was severely depressed a year ago but responded to therapy and antidepressants. The move has triggered another bout of major depression for Eric.

In the above scenario, Darla, Rachel, and Eric all demonstrate symptoms of depression. Most people who experience a *depressed mood* will not meet clinical criteria for a depressive disorder.

RECURRENT THEMES The above *Case in Point* illustrates several of the recurring themes emphasized in this text. Most children will normally feel sad, or distressed, on occasion, due to difficult circumstances, at the time. In most cases, depressed mood will represent a transitory response to a specific situational event. (*Theme 1: Normal development follows a predictable path.*) However, for some children, feelings of sadness or irritability can last for a long time (possibly years) or become overwhelming and intense in a short period of time (2 weeks). The *Case in Point* illustrates how depressed mood can represent a deviation from the normal path of emotions and the degree to which depressed feelings can vary along a continuum of severity from mild to severe. (*Themes 2 and 3: Maladaptive behaviors represent deviations from the norm, and are represented by a continuum of severity.*) While Rachel's depression seems to be related to her parent's divorce, Eric seems to be struggling with recurrent episodes of major depressive disorder. Although this latest bout may have been triggered by a stressor (moving to a new home at a vulnerable age), it is not known whether there is a family history of depression and if underlying genetic factors are also operative. (*Theme 4: Factors, at all levels, individual, interpersonal, contextual, can influence deviations in development.*) Fortunately for Darla, her symptoms of depression are most likely related to the adjustment of relocating and may finally abate due to her positive contact with a new peer group. Darla will likely overcome her negative feelings and readjust to a more positive lifestyle.

Symptoms of Depressed Mood

Children who are irritable and upset in response to a distressing situation may be experiencing a *depressed mood* as a transitory emotional state that occurs in response to a particular stressor. Often these feelings subside when the stressors diminish. At other times, feelings of nostalgia or melancholy can bring on feelings of sadness. Our mood can also be influence by physiological (hormonal) changes or changes that are substance induced (e.g., alcohol, which is a depressant). Children can demonstrate many symptoms of depression. The National Institute of Mental Health (NIMH, 2000) suggests a number of potential symptoms of depression that children and adolescents may experience. Some children may feign illness or refuse to go to school. Others may become very clingy and want to remain close to their parents. Others may be more irritated, and may sulk or withdraw from social contacts. Depression can also be associated with getting into trouble at school, having a negative attitude, or feeling misunderstood. Parents may have difficulty deciding if these moods are part of a phase the child is going through or if the mood suggests something more serious (NIMH Web site: http://www.nimh.nih.gov).

The nature of depressive symptoms may also change with different developmental ages and stages. Some young children may complain of physical symptoms (malaise, headaches, or stomach pains), and be more subdued in their play, while others may become more aggressive and agitated. Older children may withdraw from social contacts, spend more time in isolation, and pay less attention to their personal appearance than normal.

Depressed Syndrome

When a number of symptoms of depression cluster together and share similar features, they can be classified as a *syndrome*. Examples of depressed syndromes include *depressive/withdrawn syndrome* (e.g., prefers to be alone, shy) and *anxious/depressed syndrome* (fearful, worried, feels worthless, guilty).

Recall and Rewind

The Achenbach scales (ASEBA, 2001) provide a measure of two symptom clusters *(syndromes)* for depression: *anxious/depressed syndrome* (anxious aspects of negative affectivity) and *depressed/withdrawn syndrome* (the negative aspects of negative affectivity or low positive affect). These syndromes provide an index of depression along a continuum from mild to clinically significant levels. As part of their newly revised format, the ASEBA scales (2001) also provide *DSM–oriented scales* which will be discussed shortly.

Through instruments like the Achenbach scales, clinicians can obtain ratings of a child's depressive symptoms from parents, teachers, and self-reports (if the child is at least 11 years of age). The Achenbach scale includes 13 potential symptoms for the anxious/depressed syndrome (cries, fears, feels need to be perfect, feel guilty, worries, etc.) and 8 symptoms for the withdrawn/depressed syndrome (prefers to be alone, secretive, sad, withdrawn, etc.). The elevation of scores on each of the syndrome scales is based on the number of items endorsed by the rater and the intensity and frequency with which the symptoms are indicated as occurring (0 = Not True, 1 = Sometimes or Somewhat True, 2 = Often True or Very True). Scores are compared to norms available for each of the syndrome scales for children at various age levels. Scores are computed for the total syndrome scale and indicate whether the child's score is in the normal, borderline, or clinical range.

Memory Bank

The Achenbach scales tabulate scores as *T* scores with a mean of 50 and a standard deviation of 10. Scores are considered to be within the normal range if they are within one standard deviation of the mean (Range 40 to 60). *T* scores that fall between 64 and 69 are considered to be in the Borderline Clinical Range (93rd to 97th percentile). *T* scores at or above 70 represent scores in the Clinical Range and are at or beyond the 98th percentile.

Depressive Disorders

Within the spectrum of depressive disorders (*DSM–IV–TR;* APA, 2000), there are currently three major diagnostic categories to consider, if a child has symptoms of depression: **adjustment disorder with depressed mood, dysthymic disorder,** and **major depressive disorder** (*DSM–IV–TR;* APA, 2000).

Adjustment disorder with depressed mood.   In the introductory *Case in Point*, Darla's depressed mood presents an example of an adjustment disorder with depressed mood. According to the *DSM–IV–TR* (APA, 2000), an adjustment disorder is a "temporary" psychological reaction (usually no longer than 6 months duration) to an *identifiable stressor* with onset within 3 months of the stressor. In the above example, Darla is responding with depressed symptoms to the family move which was very stressful for her. Depressed mood is only one of the many possible responses to distressing situations. Other normal emotional reactions to stressors can include anxiety, somatic complaints, withdrawal, or conduct problems. By their nature, adjustment disorder reactions are a response to an *identifiable stressor* and of a "*temporary*" nature and usually subside within 6 months. If the depressed response continues longer than 6 months duration, then it will be important to consider whether the child is suffering from another type of depressive disorder.

Dysthymic disorder (DD). Although the onset of Rachel's symptoms can also be linked to an identifiable stressor (her parents' divorce), the length of time that she has been distressed far exceeds that of an adjustment disorder. Rachel's symptoms are likely indicative of dysthymic disorder, a chronic and enduring form of depression (at least 1 year in children and 2 years in adults). Dysthymic disorder (DD) is similar to a low grade flu, with people never really feeling sick enough to be ill, but never really feeling well either. However, DD can also result in dysfunction evident in reduced social interaction (withdrawal), lack of concentration, and a general malaise.

Major depressive disorder (MDD). If DD can be likened to is a low grade flu, then major depressive disorder (MDD) is the more serious strain that has significant consequences; however, while the flu usually only last for 24 hours, the intensity of MDD continues for at least 2 weeks at a minimum. Eric's acute, intense, and overwhelming incapacitation due to his depression has been evident for the past 2 weeks and is indicative of a major depressive disorder.

Memory Bank

If the tendency in the 1960s was to view depression as "masked depression," there seemed to be an equally strong tendency in the 1970s and early 1980s to consider the child's depression as temporary. Within this period, it is likely that many children were diagnosed with adjustment reaction with depressed mood.

Currently, debate continues whether children and adolescents express depression in forms unique to adult depression (aggression, delinquency, acting out behaviors, and somatic complaints), or whether children essentially express the same core symptoms as adults with slight modifications (current *DSM*; APA, 2000). However, increased emphasis has been placed on how these symptoms are displayed at various developmental stages and the role of developmental pathways in establishing etiology and predicting outcomes. From a developmental perspective, Cicchetti and Toth (1998) have developed an ecological transactional model for depression in children and adolescence. This model will be discussed shortly.

Despite the significant amount of interest and research in the area of child and adolescent mood disorders, and the increasing awareness of early onset, the *DSM–IV–TR* (APA, 2000) does not recognize childhood depression under the category of disorders most likely to be diagnosed initially in childhood or adolescence. However, the *DSM–IV–TR* (APA, 2000) has updated information about how these disorders may appear in childhood or adolescence and has altered the duration of the mood disorders for the child and youth criteria.

Mood Disorders: Unipolar Depression

Depression is a mood that can vary along a continuum of severity, especially in children and youth. Children who are depressed can be fretful, irritable, distressed, and upset. At the other end of the spectrum, children can also display a wide range of emotions that denote elation, happiness, and excitement. Although depressed symptoms can be dimensional, at the extreme ends of the spectrum the mood changes are qualitatively different and become associated with an increasing number of related problems (Ruscio & Ruscio, 2000).

There are two main mood states classified under Mood Disorders in the *DSM–IV–TR* (APA, 2000): **depression**, a state of low positive affect; and **mania,** which represents the polar opposite, a state of euphoria. While those suffering from a severe depressive episode are often rendered immobile by their lack of energy, motivation, and desire, those experiencing a manic episode often display frenzied states of high activity evident in pressured speech and rapid thoughts. While the majority of individuals will experience only the dark side of depression, or **unipolar depression**, others will experience the roller coaster ride from the height of mania to the depths of depression. The latter condition is referred to as **bipolar disorder** (previously known as manic depressive disorder). We will discuss bipolar disorder at length, later in this section, and will begin our discussion of mood disorders with a look at unipolar depression and the major depressive episode.

Major Depressive Episode and Major Depressive Disorder

The diagnosis of a **major depressive disorder** (**MDD**) is made when an individual is considered to have experienced a **major depressive episode**. According to the *DSM–IV–TR* (APA, 2000) an adult is considered to have experienced a major depressive episode if the episode lasts for at least 2 weeks and the individual demonstrates at least five of a possible nine symptoms. Of the five potential symptoms, one of the symptoms must be either

- depressed mood (pervasive depressed mood state/anhedonia), or
- loss of interest or pleasure in day to day activities.

The *DSM–IV–TR* (APA, 2000) notes that in children, however, a pervasive mood of **irritability** may be evident as the "depressed mood."

Having established the existence of either, pervasive "irritable" mood (in children) or loss of interest, the *DSM* then requires *four additional symptoms* from a potential list of seven symptoms. The symptoms encompass the entire range of vegetative, behavioral/psychomotor, and cognitive/affective responses:

Recall and Rewind

Vegetative symptoms refer to physical or somatic problems such as sleeping and eating problems.

- *Vegetative Symptoms*
  1. Significant (plus or minus 5%) weight loss or gain. (In children, this is designated As failure to meet anticipated weight/height ratios.)
  2. Insomnia (inability to fall asleep or stay asleep) or hypersomnia (excessive sleep)
- *Cognitive/Affective Symptoms* (*nearly every day*)
  3. Excessive thoughts/feelings of worthlessness and/or excessive and inappropriate guilt
  4. Inability to concentrate, inattentive, indecisive
  5. Recurrent suicidal ideation (thoughts of self-harm)

- *Behavioral/ Psychomotor Symptoms* (*nearly every day*)
  6. Psychomotor agitation or retardation
  7. Fatigue, loss of energy

Depressive symptoms and depressive disorders represent one of the most significant mental health problems for children and youth. According to the World Health Organization (WHO), unipolar depression is the leading cause of disability worldwide (WHO, 1996). Although the WHO report was based on responses from those 15 to 44 years of age, there is growing concern regarding early onset of mood disorders and the increase of life long risk (Costello et al., 2002).

There are two main types of unipolar depression: **MDD**, an intense acute form of the disorder; and **DD**, a milder but chronic form of depression. Although individuals who suffer from depression often recover to normal states of mood, they may relapse into a depressed state at some future time.

Dysthymic Disorder (DD)

According to the *DSM–IV–TR* (APA, 2000), dysthymic disorder is diagnosed in adults if there is evidence of a pervasive depressed mood (loss of interest, anhedonia) for at least 2 years and the depression is accompanied by *at least two symptoms* from the list of seven symptoms of the major depressive episode:

- Problems with appetite
- Insomnia or hypersomnia
- Low energy or fatigue
- Low self-esteem
- Poor concentration/decision making
- Feelings of hopelessness (*DSM–IV–TR*, 2000, p. 380).

In children and adolescents the *duration can be 1 year*, and the depressed mood can be irritability. During the time period (2 years for adults, 1 year for children and teens), there has been no evidence of symptom relief for more than a 2-month period.

Focus on Development: Recurrent Pediatric Depression

There is growing evidence that depression can be highly recurrent in pediatric populations, possibly even more so than with adults. In one study, 72% of those with depression suffered a relapse within 5 years (Emslie et al., 1997). Other studies have reported between 30% and 50% recurrence rates in populations that have been followed from youth through to early adulthood (Angst, Merikangas, Scheidegger, & Wicki, 1990; Rao, Hammen, & Daley, 1999).

At their worse, depressed states endure for a long time causing problems with day-to-day functioning, and can seriously impair relationships. Recalling the trilogy of depressive symptoms in the three children in the opening case examples, depression (which can manifest as irritable mood in children) can take over and permeate social relationships, family relationships, and academic functioning.

Unipolar Depression: Associated Clinical Features

Growing evidence that adult depression can often be traced to childhood onset has increased investigations of how symptoms of depression might be expressed at different age levels in childhood and adolescence. With respect to symptom differences between adult and child populations, the most recent revision of the *DSM–IV–TR* (APA, 2000) includes sections on associated features of disorders across cultures, gender, and age. The recognition of *irritability* as a cardinal marker for depression in childhood is a critical turning point in acknowledging unique features of child depression. In addition, the *DSM–IV–TR* (APA, 2000) has also lowered the time requirements for symptom presentation in children (1 year for dysthymia in children vs. 2 years for adults), and included a number of associated features that are particularly geared to different developmental levels.

A list of general characteristics that might be associated with depression in children and adolescents can be found in Table 8.1.

There has been increased research emphasis on identifying symptoms of depression at different developmental levels. The following summary presents findings of the latest research in the area of developmental trends in depressive symptoms.

Development in Focus

One of the earliest accounts of infant depression was noted in institutionalized infants (Spitz, 1946). Although the infants' physical needs were tended to by custodial staff, there was minimal attention to their affective needs. In the absence of affectionate nurturing, the infants were observed to waste away (a condition referred to as *marasmus*). Depression was evident in chronic sobbing, and listlessness, a reaction that Spitz referred to as **anaclitic depression**.

Table 8.1 Characteristics Associated With Depression in Children and Adolescents

Characteristics and signs that may be associated with child and adolescent depression:

- Repeated complaints of vague physical symptoms (e.g., headaches, stomachaches, leg pains, feeling tired, weary, dizzy, feeling sick to the stomach); not feeling well
- Frequent school absences without medical support; poor school performance
- Extreme vulnerability to criticism; overly sensitive
- Reckless and impulsive behavior; heightened risk taking
- Loss of interest in social contact; withdrawal from playing with friends
- Frequent complaints of boredom
- Irritable outbursts, angry provocations; hostility towards others
- Unexplained crying; easily upset
- Talk of running away from home
- Substance or alcohol abuse
- Repeated comments that no one cares about them; or no one loves them
- Difficulty with relationships

Source: Adapted from the NIMH Fact Sheet (2000) on depression.

Toddlers and Preschool Level

> **Important Distinction**
>
> In their studies of depression in preschoolers, Luby and colleagues distinguished between two forms of depression in their sample: **hedonic depression** (a reactive form of depression), and **anhedonic depression** (melancholia characterized by a loss of pleasure or joy).

Recently, a number of studies conducted by researchers at the Washington University School of Medicine have focused on depression in preschool children (Luby et al., 2002, 2003, 2006). Initially, efforts focused on modifications to the *DSM–IV* diagnostic criteria requiring only four symptoms instead of five, and essentially eliminating the criteria of 2 weeks for a stable depressed mood which is not suitable for preschoolers (Luby et al., 2002). Subsequently, Luby and colleagues (2003) compared preschoolers with subtypes of depression (**hedonic depression** or **anhedonic depression**) to preschoolers with other psychiatric problems (ADHD or ODD) and healthy preschoolers.

The researchers found that while both hedonic and anhedonic depressed preschoolers had significantly higher depression severity scores then either the healthy or psychiatric groups, the anhedonic group was also significantly more severe than the hedonic group. The researchers found that family history of major depressive disorder, presence of neurovegetative symptoms, and greater elevations of *cortisol* in response to stress were suggestive that the anhedonic type of depression may be biologically based. On the other hand, the researchers felt that hedonic depression in preschoolers might be more environmentally linked since this group had significantly worse family income and significantly more stressful life events. Further investigation by Luby and colleagues (2006) has revealed preschoolers with anhedonic depression to be more noncompliant and avoidant and less enthusiastic than healthy preschoolers.

Other symptoms of depression in toddlers may take the form of delayed acquisition of developmental milestones (walking, talking, toilet training), regression in previously obtained milestones, and nightmares or night terrors. Other more agitated expressions might include excessive head-banging, or rocking behaviors. Investigators have also found that the analysis of themes of children's play could be a useful method of obtaining information regarding the nature of depressive symptoms at this age level (Luby et al., 2003). In their investigation of the influence of depression on play, Mol Lous, de Wit, De Bruyn, and Riksen-Walraven (2002) found that depressed preschoolers engaged in less symbolic play, less organized play, and more nonplay behaviors than their peers who were not depressed.

> **Memory Bank**
>
> Luby and colleagues (2003) found that when the *DSM–IV* (APA, 1994) criteria for MDD were strictly applied to the preschool population (especially the duration criterion), MDD was underdiagnosed at this age level. This is not unlike other child advocates who have stressed the lack of compatibility between *DSM* criteria and symptoms in young children (e.g., Scheeringa and Zeanah, 1995 concerning diagnostic criteria for PTSD in preschool populations).

Although the role of maternal loss or maternal separation was initially thought to be the predisposing factor to depression in institutionalized infants (Spitz, 1946; Bowlby, 1973), later research comparing children in foster care to institutionalized children revealed that since children in foster care were significantly less depressed, the depression was more likely a result of institutionalization rather than maternal loss (Robertson & Robertson, 1971).

Development in Focus

Often symptoms of depression can go undiagnosed in children and adolescents either because they are interpreted as normal "mood swings" of the developmental age or stage, or because of a reluctance of parents or physicians to attach a label of depression to someone at a relatively young age (NIMH, 2000).

Childhood

Although studies by Luby and colleagues have shed new light on the possibility of subtypes of depression that may be linked to genetic or environmental causes, much of the previous research concerning childhood (prepubertal) depression has stressed environmental (situational) versus genetic causes (Eley, Deater-Deckard, Fombonne, & Fulker, 1998; Thapar, Harold, & McGuffin, 1998). One of the most consistent findings is that children and youth who are exposed to stressful life events and live in stressful life conditions are at greater risk for developing depression. Examples of environmental factors that might increase the risk of depression include, interpersonal stressors, such as family conflict, parenting style, and peer rejection. In childhood, symptoms often include somatic complaints, irritability, and social withdrawal. Common comorbid clusters within this age-range include behavior disorders, ADHD, and anxiety disorders (*DSM–IV–TR*: APA, 2000).

There has been increased emphasis on evaluating how temperament might interact with environmental factors to increase or decrease risks for depression in children. For example, traits such as *positive emotionality, negative emotionality,* and *constraint-attentional control* have all been implicated in increased risk or vulnerability for depression.

Development in Focus: Spotlight on Temperament

Children who demonstrate *positive emotionality* (increased activity and social activity) are less likely to develop depression, whereas children who have traits of *negative emotionality* (fearfulness, distress, and irritability) are at greater risk for developing depression (Rothbart & Bates, 1998). A difficult temperament (Enns & Cox, 1997) or demonstrating high levels of negative affect (Caspi, Moffit, Newman, & Silva, 1996) in the early years can signal elevated rates of depressive symptoms in youth and adults.

In their study, Lengua, Wolchik, Sandler, and West (2000) found that low positive emotionality interacted with parental rejection to produce depressive symptoms in some children, while high positive emotionality served as a protective factor and buffered children from the impact of parental rejection. Furthermore, Lengua and Long (2002) found that negative emotionality predicted increased appraisals of threat, avoidant coping style, and greater internalizing and externalizing problems among children. Some researchers suggest that traits of temperament (such as *attentional control*) can work to moderate environmental stressors. An example would be the child who is able to consciously shift his or her attention away from a distressing situation, thereby reducing the potential negative impact.

At this stage of development, depression can manifest in poor academic achievement and poor social relationships. Often behaviors may vacillate between acting out (anger) and withdrawal (sadness). Low frustration tolerance is likely (Yorbik, Birmaher, Axelson, Williamson, & Ryan, 2004).

Adolescence

Based on current knowledge, it seems that rates for depression increase age-wise from approximately 2 % in childhood to roughly 4%–7% in adolescence (Costello et al., 2002). However, given the fact that depression is a relatively new focus for research in child populations, and in light of growing concerns about the appropriateness of *DSM–IV–TR* (APA, 2000) diagnostic criteria for children at younger ages, it is possible that the lower estimates for earlier ages merely reflect deficiencies in the detection of depression at younger age levels. While depression in childhood has been more frequently identified in response to situational events, at least one study has found up to 30% of the variance in depressive symptoms for adolescent girls can be attributed to genetic liability with the remainder due to environmental factors, such as negative life events (Silberg et al., 1999).

Research on depression in adolescence has revealed a higher rate of *melancholic (anhedonic) subtype* of depression in this population, compared to earlier childhood. However, findings of the melancholic/anhedonic depression subtypes in preschoolers (Luby et al., 2002) will undoubtedly spark research into the investigation of the prevalence of this subtype in childhood and increase our understanding of the trajectory of this subtype of depression, developmentally.

According to the *DSM–IV–TR* (APA, 2000), common characteristics of adolescent depression include psychomotor retardation/hypersomnia and delusions (especially auditory hallucinations). Comorbid with depression at this age level are behavior disorders, ADHD, anxiety disorders, substance disorders, and eating disorders. While rates for depressive disorders are equal among boys and girls up until late childhood, this changes dramatically in adolescence and by age 16, girls are twice as likely to experience depression as boys (Hankin & Abramson, 2001).

Risk and Protective Factors

Risks and Vulnerability

There are a number of factors that can increase the risk of depression in children and youth, such as abuse or neglect; stress; loss of a parent or loved one; comorbid disorders (ADHD, conduct or learning disorders); break-up of a romantic relationship; having a chronic illness, like diabetes; and other trauma, such as a natural disaster (NIMH Fact Sheet, 2000). Risk factors can be evident in many areas that influence a child's life, and result in increased vulnerability to depression and/or suicidal behaviors, including family, peers, and psychosocial difficulties. A summary of risks and protective factors is available in Table 8.2.

Individual risk factors. Personality factors that have been associated with increased risk for MDD and suicidal ideation include high levels of neuroticism, novelty seeking, and low self-esteem (Fergusson, Beautrais, & Horwood, 2003). Youth who had a difficult temperament at an early age (behavioral inflexibility, withdrawal, lower positive mood, poor concentration) are at increased risk of depressive symptoms later on (Windle & Davies, 1999).

Family risk factors. Having a parent who is an alcoholic (Puig-Antich, Kaufman, Ryan, & Williamson, 1993), family poverty, conflict between parents (Hammen, 2006), family illness, and strain from living with a single parent (Garrison, Addy, Jackson, McKeon, & Waller, 1992) have all been implicated in increasing the risk for depression in children. Families who engage in high levels of *expressed emotion* (Asarnow, Thompson, Hamilton, Goldstein, & Guthrie, 1994),

Table 8.2 Risk and Protective Factors for Depression and Suicide in Children and Adolescents

Characteristics	Risk Factors	Protective Factors
Individual	Having a chronic illness High levels neuroticism High levels novelty-seeking Low self-esteem Insecure attachments Difficult temperament Behavioral inflexibility Poor emotion regulation Low positive mood Poor concentration Having another comorbid disorder Previous suicide attempt Alcohol abuse	High attentional control Low levels of neuroticism Low levels of novelty seeking Higher levels self-esteem School connectedness Academic achievement Emotional well-being (females) High grade point averages (males)
Family	Loss of a parent Abuse or neglect Parent is an alcoholic Family poverty Marital conflict Family illness Stress of single parenting High levels of expressed emotion Negative, harsh, controlling parenting style Family history of suicide attempt Maternal depression	Absence of family history of suicide Family cohesion Family connectedness
Peers and School	Low peer support Peer rejection Peer neglect Deviant peer affiliations Feelings of isolation Having friends who do not get along (females)	Positive team sport involvement Having a circle of friends that are not in conflict (females) Having a support network (males)
Life Events	Romantic break-up Natural disaster Chronic stress Increased number of stressors Conflict with parents and peers Teen pregnancy Conflict in the home Exposure to suicide Relocation	Reduction in number and intensity of stressful life events Positive life events

characterized by a predominantly negative, harsh, controlling, and nonsupportive communication style also increase risk for depression in youth (Messer & Gross, 1995).

Maternal depression.   Infants and toddlers of depressed mothers are at higher risk for developing insecure attachments and having poor emotion regulation. Furthermore, females raised by depressed mothers are at increased risk for becoming depressed themselves (Cicchetti & Toth, 1998). Investigations of the parenting style of depressed mothers have revealed that mothers who are depressed are less emotionally available for their children (withdrawn), and more intrusive (controlling, irritable, and impatient), than mothers who are not depressed (Malphurs, Field, Larraine, Pickens, & Pelaez-Nogueras, 1996).

Peer and school influence.   As children grow and develop, more time is spent outside the home as peers and school begin to exert greater influence. Lack of social competence, low peer support, and rejection or peer neglect are all risk factors for child and adolescent depression (Harter & Marold, 1994). In the trilogy case presentation, it was not surprising that Rachel—who was depressed—was not approached to engage in social contact by her peers. *Irritability*, one of the cardinal markers of child depression, may actually act as a deterrent to social engagement from others, while tendencies to engage in negative/aggressive interactions provide an additional deterrent (Altmann & Gotlib, 1988). Furthermore, depressed youth tend to evoke more negative events than nondepressed youth (Fergusson et al., 2003).

Stressful life events.   Stressful events have been linked with depressive symptoms at all ages (Wagner & Compass, 1990). Chronic stress such as daily hassles, and psychosocial difficulties, can accumulate to increase risk for depression (Wagner & Compass, 1990). In one study, researchers found that the total number of stressful life events was higher in depressed youth than healthy youth, and that stressors were described as on-going, on a daily basis. Events that were dependent on the youth's own behavior (conflict with parents and peers) were also more evident in depressed versus nondepressed youth (Olsson, Nordstrom, Arinell, & von Knorring, 1999).

Protective Factors and Resiliency

Individual factors.   Youth high on attentional control are better able to divert attention from adverse conditions (Compas, Conner-Smith, & Jaser, 2004) and less likely to become vulnerable in adverse family situations. Other protective factors include lower levels of neuroticism and novelty seeking, higher levels of self-esteem (Fergusson et al., 2003), high academic achievement, school connectedness, high grade point average in boys, and emotional well-being in girls (Borowsky, Ireland, & Resnick, 2001).

Family factors.   Absence of a family history of suicide attempt (Fergusson et al., 2003), and family cohesion/connectedness (Borowsky et al., 2001), are two family factors that have been associated with reduced risk for depression in children.

Peers and school.   At least one study has demonstrated that positive team sport involvement can mediate risks for depression in early adolescent boys and girls (Boone & Leadbeater, 2006). Having a circle of friends proves to be a protective factor for boys and girls, but in slightly different ways. It is important for girls that the friendship network be cohesive and interconnected and that friends are not at odds with one another. On the other hand, boys' peer friendships did not mediate suicide risk; however, having a network of friends who participate in common activities was a protective factor for males. The investigators suggest that for males, the network may provide more of a supportive network than a few close friends (Bearman & Moody, 2004).

Prevalence

Prevalence rates for child and adolescent depression vary widely based on the population sampled (clinical vs. normal), diagnostic criteria used, and age ranges surveyed. Currently, there is no nationally derived epidemiological data for child and adolescent psychopathology; however, independent studies suggest rates for childhood onset between 1% and 2% and between 4% and 8% in adolescence (Costello et al., 2002; Fleming & Offord, 1990). Approximately 25% of youth will experience a depressive episode by their 18th birthday (Clarke, Hawkins, Murphy, & Sheeber, 1993).

Memory Bank

In a recent national survey of students in grades 9–12, more than one quarter (29%) reported feeling sad or hopeless every day for at least 2 consecutive weeks in the past year (Centers for Disease Control and Prevention, 2006). Ethnically, adolescents of Hispanic origin were the most likely to report feeling sad/hopeless (36%) compared with Black (28%) or White (26%) respondents. Responses to this survey revealed high female responses relative to males, although both Hispanic females (47%) and males (26%) were at the top of their categories, compared to overall percentages of 20% males and 37% females.

Researchers have found that in childhood there is minimal difference in male and females who have depression; however, by adolescence, females are significantly more likely to have a depressive disorder than males (Fleming & Offord, 1990).

Developmental Course

The course of depression can be long and enduring. Although only 2-weeks duration is required for a major depressive episode, the average length of MDD is approximately 4 months, while the average duration of dysthymic disorder is from 2–4 years. Kovacs, Gatsonis, Pollock, and Parrone (1994) found that recovery from adjustment disorder with depressed mood was the quickest, while recovery from dysthymic disorder took the longest time. Although children with a MDD had the highest rates of recovery, like Eric in the introductory case study (a trilogy of depressive disorders), these children also had high rates of relapse. The outlook for children—like Rachel in the trilogy, who have early onset dysthymic disorder—is even more devastating; Kovacs and colleagues (1994) found that 76% of these children went on to develop major depressive disorder, later in life.

Memory Bank

There are two very important points that should be stressed:

1. At the end of a lengthy bout of dysthymic disorder, it is possible that rather than lift, the emotional burden continues to deepen. In cases such as this, dysthymic disorder can develop into MDD. When dysthymic disorder develops into MDD, the condition is referred to as **double depression**.
2. Following a severe bout of MDD, which renders some individuals incapable of initiating activities, some individuals seem to regain their energy and initiative. Unfortunately, this may place individuals at increased risk for suicidal behavior, since regained focus and momentum can result in the initiative to implement a suicide plan that they could not implement in their state of inertia.

Etiology and Theoretical Perspectives

Both genetic and environmental factors can influence the development of MDD and dysthymic disorder in children and adolescence.

Biological Model

Children, adolescents and adults who have a family history of depression are at greater risk for depression. *Family pedigree studies* (studies that investigate the degree to which relatives share similar disorders), *twin studies,* and *adoption studies* all suggest that vulnerability to depression is increased among 1st-degree relatives. It has been estimated that that genetic transmission of depression is within the range of 20% to 45% (Rutter., Silberg, O'Connor, & Simonoff, 1999). Recently, investigators have isolated abnormalities in the 5-HTT gene (gene responsible for transporting the neurotransmitter serotonin) in individuals with depression (Caspi et al., 2003; Hecimovic & Gilliam, 2006). Discussion of this topic will resume shortly.

Science Talks

Studies of monozygotic twins (identical), dizygotic twins (fraternal), and adoption studies have provided support for theories of a genetic predisposition to depression. If a mono-zygotic twin has unipolar depression, the risk to the other twin is 46%, while a dyzygotic twin has a 20% risk if the other twin has unipolar depression (McGuffin, Katz, Watkins, & Rutherford, 1996). Adoption studies have also linked cases of severe unipolar depression to the biological parents of severely depressed adoptees (Wender et al., 1986).

Neurochemical Functions

Neurotransmitters. The neurotransmitters *serotonin* and *norepinephrine* have been linked to adult unipolar depression. Although it was initially thought that low levels of either neurotransmitter could result in depression, more recent investigations suggest more complex interactions may cause an imbalance not only in serotonin and norepinephrine but also in other neurotransmitters in the brain such as dopamine and acetycholine (Thase, Jindal, & Howland, 2002).

Recent studies of the serotonin transporter gene (5-HTT) and the serotonin transporter promoter polymorphism (5-HTTLPR) have revealed very interesting and complex associations between the gene's susceptibility to depression (5-HTT) and aggression (5-HTTLPR). Beitch-man and colleagues (2006) studied children with "extreme, persistent, and pervasive aggression" and found that children who had the "low expressing" genotypes had twice the risk of aggres-sive behavior than peers who did not have the low expressing gene. Caspi and colleagues (2003) found that children who had one or two short alleles of the 5-HTT serotonin transporter gene exhibited more depressive symptoms and suicidal ideation in response to stressful events than peers who did not have a copy of the short allele. Researchers have been aware that the serotonin nerve pathways play an integral role in controlling mood, emotions, sleep, aggression, and anxiety (National Institute on Drug Abuse, 2003). Since the serotonin pathway (especially the serotonin transporter) is so strongly linked to mood control, numerous antidepression medications target the release of serotonin.

Although treatment for adult depression has relied on selective serotonin reuptake inhibitors (SSRIs) such as *sertraline* (Zoloft) and *fluoxetine* (Prozac) that increase serotonin levels, these medications have not been all that effective in reducing symptoms of depression in young children (Fischer & Fischer, 1996). The topic of medication will be addressed further in the discussion of treatment alternatives.

Hypothalmic–pituitary–adrenal system (HPA). There is evidence of a neuroendocrine imbalance (hormone cortisol) in adult cases of depression. Theories suggest that the release of excessive amounts of cortisol during times of severe stress may cause the brain to be overly sensitive to perceived threat and place an individual at increased risk for other psychopathology, such as depression (Pliszka, 2002). The follow-up study of children with PTSD that was discussed previously in chapter 7 (McDermott & Palmer, 2002) provides support for this theory and furthermore suggests that some children may be more vulnerable to depression following a severe stressor at certain developmental levels.

Recall and Rewind

The HPA system was previously discussed in relation to posttraumatic stress disorder (PTSD) and can be reviewed in Figure 7.1. When stressful events occur, the hypothalamus sets in motion a series of reactions that trigger the release of chemicals. While the autonomic nervous system (ANS) responds to regulate activity of the organs, the endocrine system is activated to release hormones (such as cortisol) into the bloodstream. In their study of young children following a bushfire disaster, McDermott and Palmer (2002) found that the youngest children (Grades 4 to 6) and oldest children (Grades 11 and 12) with PTSD were most likely to develop *depressive symptoms* 6 months postdisaster, while the middle age children were most likely to respond with *emotional distress*.

Recent studies by Luby and colleagues (2002) found that preschoolers with the anhedonic subtype of depression revealed elevated levels of cortisol when placed in stressful situations.

Cognitive Behavioral Model

Within a cognitive framework, negative appraisals result from maladaptive thought processes, such as **negative thinking** (a bias to interpret events in negative ways; Beck, 1997), *and* **learned helplessness** (tendencies to give up in adverse situations based on previous lack of success; Seligman, 1975). According to Beck (1997), negative schemas develop as a result of negatively recurring thought patterns. Negative thinking can perpetuate the negative thought process, including minimizing the positive and magnifying or overgeneralizing the negative. Ultimately, negative thoughts result in the development of a **negative triad,** where individuals interpret their experiences, their selfhood, and their future in negative ways: hopelessness, helplessness, and worthlessness.

Seligman (1975) originally coined the term **learned helplessness** to describe reactions of experimental animals that were repeatedly shocked without an avenue of escape. When the animals were provided an opportunity to escape, the majority of dogs did not take advantage of their escape route. Seligman reasoned that the dogs had learned that the shocks were not within their control and did not engage in problem-solving behaviors as a result. Currently, **attribution theory** has expanded initial assumptions and incorporated the impact of how *global* (far reaching), *stable* (consistency of response), and *internal* (self-determined) factors add to the mix. For example, if a person considers failure to have a pervasive impact (global), be constantly occurring (stable), and be due to personal weakness (internal), the influence is far greater than if the failure was seen as situation specific, rare, and due to external causes. In the former case, the attributions would be more likely to result in feelings of depression than the latter.

Family, Parenting, and Peers

The role of family processes on depression.   Researchers suggest four key areas in family dynamics that can increase an adolescent's vulnerability to depression (Sheeber, Hops, & Davis, 2001):

1. An adversarial family climate (high stress/low support) provides a mechanism for creating on-going stress, while providing little relief or support;

2. A *negative reinforcement model* wherein a daughter's depression may actually be reinforced (bidirectionally) in family interactions, since the daughter's depression serves to as a mechanism for moderating parent support;

3. *Cognitive attributions (negative thinking)* become a self-fulfilling prophecy, as the child learns to think and behave in ways that are expected; and

4. Family climate does not foster development of skills in *emotion regulation,* leaving the adolescent bereft of coping skills to moderate distress.

Peer influences in mediating depression.   A negative family environment can also set the stage for negative interactions with peers. Patterson and Capaldi (1990) suggest that children reared in a negative family environment are disadvantaged socially. Many suffer from low self-esteem, poor interpersonal skills, tendencies to respond aggressively (verbal or physical), and interact with a negative cognitive style. These influences become the mediators, which in turn result in further peer rejection and escalated oppositional behaviors resulting in further rejection, loss of self-esteem, and increased risk for depression.

Ecological Transactional Model

In discussing their model, Cicchetti and Toth (1998) emphasize the need to consider the concepts of *multifinality* and *equifinality* in discussing the potential course and outcomes of depression in children and adolescents.

Recall and Rewind

The principle of *multifinality* refers to the fact that one influence may have several outcomes (e.g., while living with a depressed mother may place a child at greater risk for depression), not all children with depressed mothers become depressed. The principle of *equifinality* suggests that several different factors may result in the same outcome. For example, two children may be depressed, but the depression may have been caused by two very different situations: one child's depression may result from a family divorce; another child's depression may result from repeated rejection by peers.

Cicchetti and Toth (1998) present a model that integrates components across biological and psychological systems in a way that helps explain how depression evolves developmentally. Whether or not a child develops depression will ultimately be influenced, not only by their specific vulnerability or the protective factors they encounter, but the interplay between current and previous levels of adaptation to developmental demands. In other words, their current level of coping will impact how they deal with adversity, at that point in time. Influences at distal levels (macrosystem and exosystem) and proximal levels (microsystem and ontogenic development) will exert different types of influences and challenges for adaptation. An example of how the systems interact to influence future adaptation can be found in the area of *self-regulation.* While right brain systems seem to be activated under conditions of stress, left brain activity can act to inhibit negative arousal and produce a positive affect (Davidson, 1991). Chichetti and Toth suggest that a parent's ability to soothe an infant in distress can impact on the maturation of the infant's self-regulatory system. The authors cite research evidence (Zahn-Waxler, Iannotti, Cummings, & Denham, 1990) that toddlers of depressed mothers demonstrated more dysregulated and uncontrolled behaviors than toddlers of nondepressed mothers, and that poor affect regulation in preschoolers has been associated with poor social interaction and aggressive responses to conflict in boys (Hay, Zahn-Waxler, Cummings, & Iannotti, 1992).

Assessment

In addition to structured and semistructured interview schedules discussed earlier, many of the general behavioral rating scales and individual personality scales also include measures of depression. The most commonly used inventories specific to measuring depression are listed in Table 8.3.

Memory Bank

As an internalizing disorder, depression is more difficult to discern and may not be readily observed in outsider (teacher, parent) reports. Irritability is a mood that may not be recognized as a symptom of depression, and might be misinterpreted as aggression or problems of conduct. Youth may also be unaware that what they are feeling is depression.

Klein, Dougherty, and Olino (2005) highlight several controversies that exist in the diagnosis and classification of child and adolescent depression which can ultimately influence how depression is assessed, including:

Table 8.3 Common Assessment Instruments for Evaluation of Depression in Children and Adolescents

Instrument	Ages/Years	Brief Description
Child Depression Inventory (*CDI*; Kovacs, 1992).	6 to 17	27 items. Score for Total Depression, as well as 5 subscales: Negative Mood, Interpersonal Problems, Ineffectiveness, Anhedonia, and Negative Self-Esteem.
Children's Depression Rating Scale—Revised (*CDRS–R*; Poznanski & Mokros, 1999).	6 to 12	17 items. Clinician rating scale, based on information provided by child or parent. Items include cognitive, somatic, and psychomotor symptoms.
The Depression Scale of Beck Youth Inventories (Beck, Beck, & Jolly, 2005).	7 to 14	20 items. Assesses depression based on *DSM–IV* criteria. Four-choice format measures negative thoughts related to self, life, and future expectations.
Depression and Anxiety in Youth Scale (*DAYS*; Newcomer, Barenbaum, & Bryant, 1994).	6 to 18	22 items (self-report), 20 items (teacher scale), 28 items (parent scale). Identification of major depressive disorder and overanxious disorder based on the *DSM–IIIR* classification.
The Hopelessness Scale for Children (Kazdin, Rodgers, & Colbus, 1986).	6 to 13	17 items. Questions posed in true/false response format to assess "hopelessness" which correlates highly with depression and suicide ideation.
Inventory of Suicide Orientation–30 (King & Kowalchuk, 1994)	13 to 18	30 items. Self-report rating on 4-point scale. Scale measures 5 constructs: hopelessness, low self-esteem, inability to cope with emotions, social isolation and withdrawal, and suicidal ideation. The total score is compared to a cut off for risk, and a critical item list is also present.
Moods and Feelings Questionnaire (*MFQ*; Angold, Costello, Messer, & Pickles, 1995).	8 to 18	32 items. *DSM–III–R* criteria for depression and symptoms such as loneliness and feeling unloved or feeling ugly. A shorter 13-item version is also available.
Reynolds Adolescent Depression Scale (*RADS*; Reynolds, 1987).	13 to 18	30 items. Self-report measure based on 4-choice format yields a score for Total Depression.
Reynolds Child Depression Scale (*RCDS*; Reynolds, 1989).	Grades 3 to 6	30 items. Self-report measure provides graphic choice format (5 faces ranging from happy to sad) for young children. Score for Total Depression.

- the continuity between child, adolescent, and adult depression;
- whether depression is a discrete entity or a region on a continuum of behavior;
- whether it should be classified using a categorical or dimensional system; and
- what the boundaries are between depression and normal variations in mood and other forms of psychopathology. (p. 413)

All issues are crucial to the assessment of depression and an understanding of how symptoms of depression manifest in children and adolescents. Klein et al. (2005) list several general guidelines to assist the assessment of depression in children and adolescents including:

- ruling out exclusionary diagnosis, such as bipolar disorder
- assessing suicidal ideation
- investigating the areas of functional impairment (school, family, and peers)

Since depression in children and adolescents can result in significant dysfunction in relationships with family and friends and academic performance, Klein et al. emphasize the importance of assessing psychosocial functioning to determine the severity of impairment in these areas. Two instruments recommended by the authors to assess psychosocial functioning are the *Child and Adolescent Functional Assessment Scale* (CAFAS; Hodges, 1999) and the *Social Adjustment Inventory for Children and Adolescents* (SAICA; John, Gammon, Prusoff, & Warner, 1987). An evaluation of stressful life events related to "loss, disappointments, conflict, or rejection" and exploring the family history for psychopathology are two factors that should be addressed as part of the clinical assessment to assist in treatment planning (Klein et al., 2005, p. 425).

Treatment

Medication and Combined Treatment

Treatment resistance is common in childhood depression with 30%–40% failing to show a positive response to medication (Emslie et al., 1997). Schreiner (2003) outlines the problems inherent in validating prescriptive medications for children with mental health concerns. According to Schreiner, of all drugs approved for pediatric use between 1973–1997, the vast majority (between 70% and 80%) contained no information about pediatric use (pediatric labeling information). The consequences of prescribing medications without appropriate information about child dosage exposes children to increased risk of side effects due to the lack of controlled clinical trials involving children. With increased attention to the need and risks of involving children in clinical trials, hopefully, clinicians working with children will be provided with increased information about drug effects specific to child populations, while at the same time, children will receive the benefit of increased protection to their inclusion in these much needed research programs.

Researchers (Emslie et al., 1997) have found better success with fluoxetine; however, clinical trials continue to evaluate the effectiveness of this medication. Currently, fluoxetine (Prozac) is the only FDA-approved medication for use with children 8 years and older. Other SSRIs (serotonin reuptake inhibitors), when used, are currently administered on an *off-label basis* and include sertraline (Zoloft), citalopram (Celexa), escitalopram (Lexapro), or fluvoxamine (Luvox). The FDA has recommended that paroxetine (Paxil) not be used with children or adolescents in the treatment of MDD.

Memory Bank

On March 22, 2004, the FDA issued a public health advisory to closely monitor adults, children, and adolescents for a potential worsening of depression and suicidal behaviors in patients being treated with antidepressant medications. Furthermore, since antidepressants can induce manic episodes in bipolar patients, the FDA recommended particular vigilance in monitoring patients who may be at risk. Drugs included in the advisory are: Prozac, Zoloft, Paxil, Luvox, Celexa, Lexapro, Wellbutrin, Effexor, Serzone, and Remeron. An independent panel of international experts on suicide, the Suicidality Classification Project, will convene to develop guidelines for documenting what should be classified as suicidal behavior to assist in documenting these incidents for future reference. In 2006, an advisory committee to the FDA suggested that the risk be extended to include young adults up to age 25 (http://www.nimh.nih.gov; retrieved August 9, 2007).

A *black box warning* by the FDA is the most serious form of flagging a significant side effect of a prescription drug. Although the "black box" warning has increased caution in prescribing medications for depression to children and adolescents, there are those who are concerned that the rates of suicide may increase as a result of not being prescribed an antidepressant medication. This controversy is highly relevant to the findings of a 6-year investigation across 13 different sites, the *Treatments for Adolescents with Depression Study* (TADS) sponsored by the NIMH. Results revealed that the combined treatment model using antidepressants and cognitive therapy was the most effective, while cognitive therapy alone was the least effective treatment (Apter, Kronenberg, & Brent, 2005; TADS, 2004). The controversial results from this study will certainly be the focus of considerable future research efforts, since cognitive behavioral therapy has been supported empirically in past research, as will be discussed later in this chapter.

Furthermore, Bridge and colleagues (2007) recently reported results of their comprehensive review of all pediatric trials conducted in the past 18 years (1988–2006) and concluded that the benefits of antidepressant medications for children and youth with major depressive disorder outweigh any potential risks.

Other Empirically Supported Treatments

Weisz, Doss, and Hawley (2005) reviewed youth treatment research conducted between 1962 and 2002 concerning four highly prevalent disorders in children and youth: anxiety, depression, ADHD, and conduct problems. Studies not using random assignment procedures were excluded from the analysis. Concerning studies of depression, the authors found 18 acceptable studies which tested 27 treatments and involved 28 treatment–control comparisons. Compared to research in the other three cluster areas, research on depression included the oldest (13.87 years) age for participants, which the authors suggest may reflect increased base rates for depression in adolescents compared to childhood. In addition, 94% of the studies of depression relied on youth as the informant and another 55% obtained parent information, which was substantially higher than informant rates in other clusters. Overall, youth-focused treatments were far more common for all clusters compared to parent or family focused treatments. The most common youth-oriented treatments for depression involved behavioral/learning-based approaches (78%) and under this category, programs using CBT were by far the most common (67%). Group therapy (89%) was the most common form of service delivery for the treatment of depression in youth, with approximately 12 sessions as the average treatment span.

> **Important Distinction**
>
> From a historical perspective, Weisz et al. (2005) note that the first randomized trial used to study depression (Prout & DeMartino, 1986) occurred 2 decades later than the other clusters. The authors suggest that the late "acceptance" of depression as a childhood disorder likely explains the late onset of research effort in this area.

As has been noted by previous reviewers, behavioral and cognitive treatments continue to be overwhelmingly represented in the research and the need for investigation of other types of treatment modalities continues to exist. Most recently, investigations of medications and CBT (combined or alone) suggest that the use of medication and CBT may be more beneficial in treating adolescent depression than either treatment in isolation (Apter et al., 2005; TADS, 2004).

Specific Treatment Programs

Kaslow and Thompson (1998) identified two treatment programs as meeting the criteria for probably efficacious treatments: a CBT program for children (Stark, Swearer, Jurkowski, Sommer, & Bowen, 1996); and a CBT program for adolescents (Lewinsohn, Clarke, Rhode, Hops, & Seeley, 1996).

Cognitive behavioral treatment. Stark et al. (1996) initially developed their program as a school-based CBT approach. Ultimately, the program has been modified to include depressed children and their parents, and is available in individual and group formats. The program draws on the CBT technique of reframing and assists children to shift negative thought patterns into a more positive framework. Lewinsohn et al. (1996) modified an adult CBT program for use with adolescents and can also accommodate parents of depressed teens.

Interpersonal therapy for adolescents. Mufson, Weissman, and Moreau (1999) found that a once-weekly, 12-week program involving problem solving regarding important adolescent issues was successful in alleviating depressive symptoms.

Mood Disorders: Bipolar Disorders

The *DSM* defines mood disorders relative to specific criteria evident in the two predominant mood episode categories which include the **major depressive episode**, which was previously discussed, and the **bipolar episodes** of which there are three versions: **manic, mixed,** or **hypomanic**. According to the *DSM*, the episodes serve as the starting points ("building blocks") and provide information regarding, at a minimum, what is required to meet criteria for a given episode. As was already discussed, a major depressive episode provides the reference point for clinical decision making regarding whether a depressed mood should be classified as a major depressive disorder or dysthymic disorder. We will now learn how the knowledge about a major depressive episode in conjunction with information about manic episodes can inform decisions regarding the type of bipolar disorder experienced.

> **Important Distinction**
>
> In addition to symptoms of a major depressive episode, children and adolescents who have bipolar disorder also experience manic episodes. The type of manic episode experienced guides the clinician in a diagnosis of whether symptoms meet criteria for bipolar I or bipolar II.

As with the other mood disorders, such as MDD and DD, the *DSM* provides criteria for manic, mixed, and hypomanic episodes of a bipolar disorder.

Types of Manic Episodes and Bipolar Disorder

Manic Episode

In adults, a *manic episode* is a distinct period (at least 1 week) characterized by *an abnormally elevated, expansive, or irritable mood* which often causes significant impairment. At least *three* of the following seven symptoms are evident in addition to expansive mood:

- Heightened sense of self-esteem or grandiosity
- Decreased need for sleep
- Excessive need to talk/pressured speech
- Flight of ideas
- Distractibility
- Increased goal-directed activity (agitation, sexualized behaviors, socialization)
- Excessive engagement in high-risk activities (theft, sexual behavior, buying, or spending)

A close look at the symptoms reveals that manic episodes cover the same areas as the major depressive episode (affective/emotional, cognitive, behavioral, and vegetative), but in the reverse sense. Those experiencing mania, unlike their depressed peers, are in a state of excitement, heightened emotional responsiveness, and feel that they can conquer the world and do just about anything. Often energy is so pronounced that individuals are extremely active *physically* (pacing, high energy), *verbally* (pressured speech and rapid discourse), and *mentally* (flight of ideas and rapid shifting between topics).

Mixed manic episode.   A *mixed episode* (mixed mania) meets criteria for both major depressive episode and a manic episode overlapping within a 1-week period.

Hypomanic episode.   A *hypomanic episode* is less severe than a manic episode. A hypomanic episode does not cause significant impaired functioning. The mood is heightened and expansive, but is usually of shorter duration than a manic episode (lasting for at least 4 days). Similar to criteria for a manic episode, a hypomanic episode also requires the presence of *three symptoms* from the mania list; however, the symptoms are qualitatively less severe.

Bipolar I, Bipolar II, and Cyclothymic Disorder

Bipolor I disorder.   *Bipolar I disorder* is diagnosed if an individual experiences one or more **full manic episodes** and a major depressive episode. The majority of adults will demonstrate patterns of mood states that indicate a period of time where a full manic episode will be evident (usually a number of weeks), followed by a period of time that they are relatively symptom free. However, the period of relative normal functioning is not stable. Inevitably, the mood begins to deteriorate as the individual slips into the darker side of a MDD. Some individuals demonstrate a slightly different pattern in the alteration of mood states. These individuals will experience mixed mood states where they actually shift between manic to depressive episodes within the span of a short period of time (can be daily). Bipolar I disorder causes significant impairment and dysfunction.

Bipolar II disorder. Individuals with **Bipolar II disorder** do not experience the heights of a full-blown manic episode, although they do experience the full consequences of a major depressive episode. Their euphoric state is more moderate and as such is called a **hypomanic episode**. Although the criteria for bipolar II disorder requires the same number of symptoms from the manic episode as bipolar I (three from the list of manic symptoms), the symptoms are less pronounced and often the individual can actually be quite productive during a hypomanic episode.

Cyclothymic disorder. **Cyclothymic disorder** is a chronic fluctuating mood disturbance (*DSM–IV–TR*; APA, 2000) and is diagnosed when the prevailing mood for the past 2 years has involved symptoms of **hypomanic episodes** and **depressive symptoms** (not meeting criteria for MDD). The various types of bipolar disorder and their relationship to the manic and depressive episodes is presented in Table 8.4, and graphically in Figures 8.1a and 8.1b.

Table 8.4 Types of Bipolar Disorder

Types of Bipolar Disorder	Type of Depressive Episode	Type of Manic Episode
Bipolar I	Major depressive episode	Full manic episode
Bipolar II	Major depressive episode	Hypomanic episode
Cyclothymic disorder	Episode does not meet criteria for major depression Possible dysthymic episode	Hypomanic episode

Source: DSM–IV–TR, APA (2000).

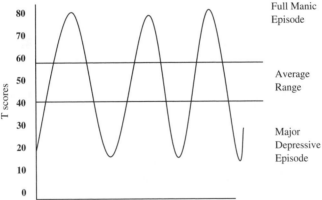

Figure 8.1a Bipolar I disorder.

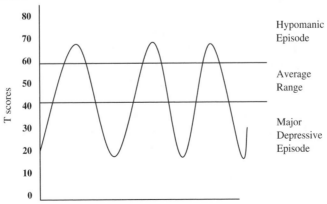

Figure 8.1b Bipolar II disorder.

> **Read All About It**
>
> "Volatile aggressive behavior is the chief complaint that most often brings children to inpatient psychiatric care…an escalation of a history of behavioral dyscontrol…in concert with…chronic impulsivity and affect dysregulation" (Blader & Carlson, 2007, p. 107). This constellation of behaviors has increasingly been diagnosed as bipolar disorder. With the increased diagnosis of bipolar disorder in children and youth has come the recognition that the symptom presentation and course may differ substantially from the more classic versions of adult bipolar disorder (Leibenluft, Charney, Towbin, Bhangoo, & Pine, 2003) as described in the *DSM–IV–TR* (APA, 2000).

Developmental Course and Associated Features

Diagnosis of early onset bipolar disorder is a controversial topic that represents a clinical challenge for professionals (Blader & Carlson, 2007; Geller, Tillman, Badner, & Cook, 2005; Masi et al., 2006b; Sanchez, Hagino, Weller, & Ronald, 1999). Difficulties exist for a variety of reasons and a number of concerns that have been voiced are listed below:

1. The application of adult-derived diagnostic criteria to children has essentially ignored how these symptoms might exist at different developmental levels (Swann et al., 2005).
2. The use of symptoms such as *hyperactivity* and *irritability* as diagnostic markers, rather than *mania*, per se, has lead to overdiagnosis of the disorder in children (Biederman & Klein, 1998).
3. Bipolar disorder (BD) may be underdiagnosed or misdiagnosed due to overlapping symptom presentations with problems of conduct, intermittent explosive disorder, or ADHD (Wilens et al., 2003).
4. "Controversies regarding pediatric BD largely center on the boundary between BD on the one hand and disruptive behavior disorders on the other" (Brotman et al., 2007, p. 995).
5. The pathology manifested by many, if not the majority of pediatric bipolar patients, conforms poorly to the *DSM–IV* classification of bipolar disorder phenotypes (Birmaher et al., 2006; Leibenluft, Charney, Towbin, Bhangoo, & Pine, 2003).
6. Unlike adult mania, BD in children seldom manifests euphoria as the predominant mood; instead, *severe irritability* and *psychomotor agitation* are often evident as 'extended aggressive temper outbursts.' Unlike the episodic and acute form of mood disturbance found in adult BD, symptoms in children and youth tend to be chronic and continuous (Biederman et al., 2005a).
7. *Severe irritability* has been suggested by many to be the predominant feature of BD in children and youth (Biederman et al., 1996; Wozniak, 2005; Wozniak et al., 1995). However, while some support the clinical relevance of irritability as a cardinal marker (Mick, Biederman, Faraone, Murray, & Wozniak, 2003; Wozniak et al., 2005), others questions the clinical utility and suggest that irritability should be excluded as a marker due to a lack of specificity (Geller et al., 2000; Leibenluft et al., 2003).
8. Children with BD, or juvenile bipolar disorder (JBD), are basically *nosologic orphans,* since they do not conform to the rules of the *DSM* diagnostic criteria (Carlson, Pine, Nottelmann, & Leibenluft, 2004).

Issues in Understanding Bipolar Disorder in Children and Youth

Until the late 1990s, experts continued to debate whether biopolar disorder existed in children or whether the symptoms reflected a more serious variation of ADHD. However, as Wozniak (2003) so aptly suggests, the debate has shifted from consideration of whether the disorder exists in young children to discussions concerning how best to diagnose and treat the disorder in its early onset form. Attempts to develop a framework for conceptualizing the disorder in children and youth have led many researchers to consider different methods of subtyping the disorder for comparative purposes. To this end, it has been suggested that perhaps dimensional criteria (e.g., symptoms continuum) may be more helpful than categorical classifications (yes/no) in deriving subtyping alternatives (Kendell & Jablensky, 2003). Several subtyping systems have been suggested, including (1) *subtyping by age of onset* (adult vs. juvenile onset; early childhood onset vs. adolescent onset; preschool vs. childhood onset); (2) *subtyping by nature of developmental episodes*; (3) *subtyping by clinical phenotypes: narrow and broad phenotypes*; and (4) *subtyping by comorbid associations*.

1. Subtyping by Age of Onset

Adult versus juvenile onset. There is growing evidence that a number of cases of adult bipolar disorder have prepubertal onset (Geller et al., 1995). In one study of 480 patients with BD, 14% reported onset prior to 13 years of age, while 36% reported onset in adolescence (Leverich et al., 2007). Compared to later onset, subjects in this study who reported the earliest onset (prior to 13 years of age) also reported a more severe life course for the disorder, evident in greater comorbidity and recurrence/chronicity (Perlis et al., 2004). Other studies comparing **juvenile bipolar disorder** (**JBD**) to adult BD have also confirmed a more severe course (Carlson, Bromet, Driessens, Mojtabai, & Schwartz, 2002), with chronic, severe (**ultradian rapid cycling**, psychosis, mixed mania), and longer duration of episodes (Geller, Tillman, Craney, & Bolhofner, 2004). Furthermore, compared to adults, children and adolescents with BD present with "higher rates of mixed episodes, rapid cycling and co-occurring ADHD than adults with BD" (DelBello, Adler, & Strakowski, 2006, p. 298).

Memory Bank

The term *ultradian rapid cycling* is used to describe polarity switching (high-to-low or low-to-high) within the same day (Kramlinger & Post, 1996).

While initial studies focused on a comparison of the symptoms and course of BD with onset in juvenile versus adult populations, there has been increasing emphasis on evaluating features of bipolar spectrum disorders across the developmental span and to investigate potential trajectories based on initial symptom presentation.

Early childhood onset versus adolescent onset. Masi and colleagues (2006a) posed two important questions about the nature of bipolar disorder in childhood and adolescence:

1. Is there research evidence to support the notion that bipolar disorder in childhood and adolescence is the same clinical entity?
2. Is there evidence of developmental variation in symptom expression? (p. 682)

In response to their inquiry, the researchers suggest that there is evidence to support both assumptions. Stability of the disorder across ages and stages supports the notion that bipolar disorder is a disorder that endures across the lifespan (Biederman et al., 2005a; Findling et al., 2001). Yet, comparing how the disorder manifests at different developmental levels suggest that symptoms may evolve across the lifespan, initially satisfying the more broad criteria, but ultimately conforming to the more narrow concepts of BD in adulthood.

Important Distinction

After considerable debate, the National Institute of Mental Health (NIMH): Roundtable on Prepubertal Bipolar Disorder (2001) recommended that researchers subtype juvenile mania into two classifications. If JBD is similar to adult onset, then a *"narrow"* phenotype might be most appropriate which conforms to *DSM–IV–TR* criteria for adult mania, including euphoria, grandiosity, and classic symptoms of a manic episode (Geller et al., 2005; Leibenluft et al., 2003). If, however, BD in children presents different from BD in adults, *"broad"* phenotypes focusing more on irritability and nonspecific labile mood shifts might be more appropriate (Wozniak et al., 2005).

However, prior to discussing these findings, it is important to note a number of inherent inconsistencies in research design that have made it difficult to generalize findings across studies.

a) Use of inconsistent age ranges to define subject sample groupings. In reviewing articles for this section, **childhood-onset** (and subsequently adolescent onset) has been defined by a number of different age ranges including 5–13 years (Blader & Carlson, 2007); prior to 13 years (Perlis et al., 2004); and younger than 12 years (Masi et al., 2006a). For example, in defining the subject population in one study, the mean age of childhood onset was 7.7 years (Masi et al., 2006a), while in another, the mean age of adolescent onset was 9.5 years (Findling et al., 2001).

b) Use of different criteria and assessment instruments to diagnose BD. Studies have adopted a wide range of criteria for establishing the existence of BD in the sample, from use of standardized interviews (K–SADS), to modification of *DSM* criteria, to strict adherence to *DSM* criteria.

c) Use of clinic versus community samples. While the majority of studies focus on patients who are referred to clinics for treatment, a select few evaluate the prevalence in community samples.

Findings of childhood versus adolescent onset. The most definitive feature that separates childhood versus adolescent onset is the greater comorbidity with ADHD in populations with earlier childhood onset (Biederman et al., 2005a). Other differences between childhood and adolescent onset reported in the literature include:

- More frequent observation of a chronic irritable subtype in child onset populations and more frequent evidence of episodic-elated moods in adolescent onset. Child onset is also associated with significantly higher rates for comorbid disorders compared to adolescent onset: ADHD (38.7% vs. 8.9%); and ODD (35.9% vs. 10.7%). No difference in conduct disorder or anxiety disorders were noted between childhood or adolescent onset (Masi et al., 2006a).
- Childhood onset is significantly more likely to report onset of symptoms of mania at 5 years of age or younger (Biederman et al., 2005a).
- Childhood onset is significantly more frequent in males than females, and often dates as

far back as preschool. The predominant symptom in childhood onset is irritability rather than euphoria. This is a severe form of irritability, which is often associated with behaviors that are persistent, highly disabling, and can often involve violent outbursts. Aggressive out-of-control behaviors that result in attacks on others are not uncommon (Wozniak et al., 1995).

- Adolescents with mania can appear predominantly irritable with mixed manic episodes that follow a chronic course. Masi et al. (2006a) found that youth in their study who met criteria for mania also met criteria for major depression, ADHD, disruptive behavior disorders, psychosis, and anxiety disorders. Although males were predominant among those with childhood onset, youth with adolescent onset were more equally distributed by gender. Moods in adolescence, compared to adults, were more chronic rather than episodic.

Preschool versus childhood onset.   Wilens and colleagues (2003) compared 44 preschoolers with BD (4–6 years of age) and 29 school-age children with BD (7 to 9 years of age). Results revealed little difference in the number of symptoms demonstrated by children with preschool onset (average 5.3 symptoms) compared to those with school age onset (average 5.1 symptoms). Within this sample, preschoolers had an average of 7.7 lifetime manic episodes, while school age children had an average of 11 manic episodes over their lifetime.

In their study, Wilens and colleagues (2003) modified *DSM–IV–TR* (APA, 2000) criteria to suit a preschool or young school-age population. Mania was described as a severely impairing episode, lasting for a week or longer, with consistent abnormally elevated symptoms for this age group of "giddy, goofy, drunk-like," or severely irritable mood involving frequent temper outbursts (p. 497).

Other symptoms were modified to suit the age, and included at least three of the following symptoms (four if irritability was one of the symptoms):

- grandiosity (feeling superior to others, evident in trying to complete tasks clearly beyond their ability)
- insomnia
- pressured speech (many times unintelligible)
- flight of ideas (resulting in confusion)
- greater distractibility than noted previously
- extreme goal-directed behavior (high risk and perseverative)
- excessive pleasurable activities (e.g., masturbation). (p. 497)

In their study of preschool and school-age onset BD, Wilens et al. (2003) also noted high levels of comorbidity that existed in their population: 95% of preschoolers and 93% of school-aged youngsters with BD also had ADHD. Evidence of ODD and conduct disorder (CD) were also at inflated rates in both groups of children with BPD.

2. Subtyping by nature of developmental episodes
In addition to subtyping BD by age of onset, researchers have also focused on the nature of the episodes of BD in children in order to determine whether features of episodes may also be developmental in nature. In the preschool and school ages sample discussed previously, Wilens et al. (2003) found that 80% of preschoolers and 76% of school-aged children had *mixed manic states*. In another study of school-aged children with BD, Geller et al. (1995) found that 87% of the young children with BD (average age 7 years) had **rapid cycling** (four episodes of mood disturbance in a 12-month period).

Although rapid cycling is seen in approximately 10–20% of adult populations, findings suggest that this may be a predominant feature of BD in children. Geller and Luby (1997) suggest that childhood-onset bipolar disorder may be more severe, chronic, and have rapid-cycling features similar to the more severe adult types of BD that are often treatment resistant.

Development in Focus

The mixed manic and rapid cycling patterns evident in young children may manifest as brief and multiple episodes, which may cycle numerous times within a single day (Geller et al., 1995).

Masi and colleagues (2006b) compared 136 youth with BD (mean age 13.5 years) and found that the nature of the episode and clinical features were associated with age of onset. Episodic mood states were found in 56.6% of children with the majority being older and having elated (51%) mood. Chronic mood states were noted by 43.4% of the study population who were younger. Irritable mood state, which was noted in 44.9% of the study population, was predominantly associated with younger BD onset and chronic mood states.

Case in Point

Jordan was very tearful and crying when his third-grade classroom returned from lunch. He was sobbing so intensely that his teacher could not determine what had set him off this time. Yet within a span of minutes, Jordan was giggling and jumping up and down, pointing a finger at his classmate because his classmate had accidentally dropped his book bag and the contents had spilled all over the floor. When reprimanded by his teacher, Jordan again developed another mood and threw his own book bag on the floor. When sent to time out, Jordan put his head down and began to sob again, only to be distracted when a class visitor (Officer Prentice) arrived to talk about school safety. When Officer Prentice asked for class volunteers for a demonstration, Jordan again became extremely giddy, jumping up and yelling "Me Me! Pick Me!" When reprimanded again by his teacher, Jordan began yelling, saying the teacher wasn't fair and didn't like him and he was going to tell his mother to send him to a school where they liked kids, not this dump! This type of scenario involving a kaleidoscope of emotions was a common occurrence for Jordan, who eventually was diagnosed with early-onset bipolar disorder.

In the above scenario, Jordan displays many of the symptoms typical of childhood-onset bipolar disorder. In their literature review, Geller and Luby (1997) provide examples from their own research and that of their colleagues to assist in better understanding how the core features of a manic episode might be evident in childhood and adolescence. The following summary is based upon their review.

Childhood episodes of BD tend to involve rapid mood shifts vacillating between elation and irritability. Grandiosity may present as inflated self-esteem. Beliefs may exceed normal expectations/logic and be fueled by aspirations that are well beyond normal age ability. Some examples in later childhood/early adolescence of grandiose expectations in manic periods may include aspirations of being a famous athlete, musician, or astronaut, when in reality, they are often failing in day-to-day school requirements. Reduced need for sleep may be evident in watching television all night in their rooms instead of sleeping; rearranging furniture at all hours; or in adolescence, late night partying. Although excessive need to talk and flight of ideas may be pervasive, the topic would be geared to developmentally appropriate themes. Excessive goal directed activity may take the form of multitasking (telephone calls while making illustrations, sorting card collections, etc.). Dangerous and risk-taking behaviors may be evident in sexual promiscuity, fast driving/skate-boarding, spending sprees, and theft.

3. Subtyping by Clinical Phenotypes: Narrow and Broad Phenotypes

Given the wide range of presentations in episodes (mixed, rapid cycling) that can be evident in children and youth with BD, there has been controversy regarding how to diagnose children with a constellation of chronic and severe symptoms of irritability, hyperactivity, and abnormal mood (often quickly shifting from sadness to anger). Some psychiatrists would give such children a diagnosis of mixed mania or rapid cycling bipolar disorder, while others would not (Biederman & Klein, 1998).

Leibenluft and colleagues (2003) suggest that in addition to the two anchor points of *narrow* and *broad* phenotypes, two intermediary types could also be helpful in bridging the two extremes. In keeping with the *DSM–IV–TR,* the distinction between hypomanic and manic episodes, referred to as (hypo) manic in their model, is based on symptom severity and duration:

1. *Narrow phenotype*: Those cases that match the full *DSM–IV–TR* (2000) criteria for elevated mood or grandiosity and evidence clear episodes lasting 4 (hypomanic) to 7 (manic) days.
2. *(Hypo) mania NOS:* Episodes that are too short to meet the narrow criteria.
3. *Irritable (hypo) mania*: For cases lacking the cardinal marker of elevated mood.
4. *Broad phenotype:* Cases of severe irritability and hyperarousal that do not demonstrate clear episodes of (hypo) mania.

In addition, Leibenluft et al. (2003) address concerns voiced by other researchers (Geller et al., 2000) regarding the use of irritability as a marker for BD in children in youth, since "episodic irritability can also be seen in depressed children, while chronic irritability is common to ODD, ADHD and some variants of PDD" (p. 434). As an alternative, the researchers suggest **severe mood dysregulation syndrome** to refer to children who experience extreme irritability.

Wozniak et al. (2005) examined the *DSM–IV–TR* (APA, 2000) cardinal markers for BD (grandiosity, euphoria, or irritability) in a clinical sample of 86 children and youth. Results revealed that irritability was a cardinal marker in 94% of the population, compared to only 51% for euphoria. Furthermore, while 48% of those with predominant irritability also demonstrated euphoria only 6% presented with primarily euphoria alone. Grandiosity was not commonly reported in this sample. As a result of this study and other similar findings (Biederman et al., 1996; Fergus et al., 2003), Wozniak and colleagues (2005) suggest that there is "significant support that severe irritability is the predominant abnormal mood in bipolar youth" (p. 586). Accordingly, Wozniak et al. suggest three levels of irritability of increasing severity can be identified:

1. Irritability associated with ODD (easily annoyed, loss of temper).
2. Irritability as mad/cranky mood associated with MDD, occurring most of the day.
3. Super angry/grouchy/cranky irritability as in mania. Examples of this severe form of irritability include irritable most of the day and explosive on a daily basis (slamming doors, kicking, screaming) from 30 to 60 minutes in response to a routine parent request such as asking the child to brush their teeth, or put away a toy. (p. 587)

As is readily apparent, there continues to be significant controversy regarding how the disorder is to be diagnosed or conceptualized in children and adolescents. In addition to subtyping of

JBD based on age of onset, episodes, and cardinal markers, some researchers have also suggested subtyping based on comorbid associations.

4. Subtyping according to comorbid associations

Bipolar disorder shares many common features with other disorders of childhood and adolescence and it is often common to find bipolar disorder comorbid with other psychiatric diagnoses. The following information provides a brief research review of the findings regarding the most common comorbid associations.

- *ADHD:* Sixty to 90% of youth with BP also have comorbid ADHD (Borchardt & Bernstein, 1995) and associated neurological deficits in such areas as attention, executive functions, processing speed, and overall cognitive ability (Willcutt, Doyle, Nigg, Faraone, & Pennington, 2005). A significant difficulty in diagnosing JBD is the number of shared features with ADHD. Staton, Volness, and Beatty (2007) note that distractibility and inattention are pervasive among those with JBD regardless of the subtype. Furthermore, symptoms of distractibility/inattention are often associated in research with symptoms of racing thoughts and with a manic psychomotor acceleration factor (racing thoughts, pressured speech, increased motor activity, and distractibility). According to Leibenluft et al. (2003), a major problem in diagnosing "juvenile (hypo)mania" stems from criterion overlap with ADHD regarding criteria of: pressure to "keep talking" (hypomania) and "often talks excessively" (ADHD); psychomotor agitation (hypomania) and "often runs about or climbs excessively" (ADHD); and "distractibility," which is used to describe both hypomania and ADHD. According to Leibenluft and colleagues, differential diagnosis can be made by emphasizing two points: 1. unlike (hypo)mania, ADHD is not episodic; and 2. the identification of (hypo) manic symptoms that are not shared by ADHD. Others in the field would disagree based on research findings already discussed regarding the "chronic and continuous" mood states of BD that seem to be more prevalent in young children and more similar to characteristics of ADHD (Biederman et al., 2003; Masi et al., 2006a).
- *Anxiety Disorders:* JBD with anxiety disorders have earlier onset and more hospitalization than JBD without anxiety disorders (Dickstein et al., 2005). BPD in adolescents is associated with higher risk for separation anxiety disorder (SAD) and obsessive compulsive associations (Lewinsohn, Klein, & Seeley, 2000). JBD with anxiety (social anxiety, general anxiety, or phobias have *higher bias-to-threat* (Brotman et al., 2007) and *fear-of-harm* associated with anxious and obsessive thoughts (Papolos, Hennan, & Cockerman, 2005). JBD children and youth with high *fear-of -harm anxieties* engaged in twice as much self-injurious behavior than low fear-of-harm JBD peers and 8 times the amount of hostile aggression towards others. In one sample of 224 youth with JBD, 22.8% had comorbid panic disorder which was more frequent in females and more often associated with BP II (Masi et al., 2006c).
- *Substance Use:* Wilens and colleagues (2004) found that childhood onset BD was associated with greater risk for substance use disorders, drug and alcohol abuse, and dependence in adolescence regardless of whether conduct disorder was a comorbid disorder. Furthermore, Wilens et al. (2007) found higher rates of BD and of substance use disorders (SUD) in parents of youth with BD. The researchers suggest that SUD and BD may share transmissible familiar risk factors (e.g., genetic risk for BD might serve to increase risk for SUD). However, they also acknowledge the possibilities that the stressful conditions of living with a substance-abusing parent may also increase the risk for BD in offspring, or that the difficulties of raising child with BD child might trigger parental SUD.

- *Child Behavior Checklist Syndromes:* Carlson and colleagues (2004) found that youth with JBD also demonstrated elevated scores on three syndromes of the Child Behavior Checklist (ASEBA; Achenbach & Rescorla, 2001): attention problems (AP), aggressive behavior (AGB), and anxious/depressed syndrome (AD). The researchers found that this phenotype cluster occurred in 1% of children at each age level assessed in their study.
- *Personality and Temperament:* Papolos, Hennen, Cockerham, and Lachman (2007) compared prominent symptom dimensions for 260 sibling pairs with JBD and matched controls in an attempt to isolate symptom dimensions of phenotypic subgroups that may have a genetic link. Results revealed six factors that evidenced the strongest concordance coefficients, including *fear-of-harm, aggression, anxiety, sensory sensitivity, sleep-wake cycle disturbance,* and *attention/executive function deficits.* The researchers pointed out that none of the above factors are currently part of the categorical definition of BD. Furthermore, symptoms of classic adult BD were relatively sparse for this sample. Papolos and colleagues (2007) conclude that in JBD the "fear-of-harm symptom dimension…may be a heritable feature that characterizes a phenotypic subgroup who are described as fearful, irritable and explosive in clinical samples…which may be subsumed under categories of commonly diagnosed comorbid anxiety and behavior disorders" (p. 34).

Studies of adults with BD and adults with ADHD have found heightened *novelty seeking behaviors* in this population (Cloninger & Svrakic, 1997).

Memory Bank: Novelty Seeking Behaviors

Heightened novelty seeking is a temperament/personality trait that involves behaviors of impulsivity, disregard for rules, and regulations and increased thrill-seeking behaviors.

While temperament/personality is relatively stable over the course of lifetime, character traits are molded through experience and are more event dependent (Cloninger & Svrakic, 1997). Tillman, Geller, and Craney (2003) studied temperament and characteristic traits in three groups of children and youth (7–16 years of age): youth diagnosed with BD; youth diagnosed with ADHD (no previous history of BD or MDD); and healthy youth. Results revealed that similar to adults, *novelty seeking* was significantly higher in groups with BD and ADHD than the healthy group. In addition, ADHD and BD groups were significantly less reward-dependent, persistent, self-directed, and cooperative than healthy youth.

Risk Factors

A number of risk factors have been isolated in the potential development of JBD, including having a parent with BD, living in conditions of increased life stress, evidence of early behavior disorders, and having certain aspects of difficult temperament, such as *behavioral disinhibition.* There has been an increased attempt to isolate risk factors relative to different developmental periods.

Having a parent with BD.   Children whose parents have BD are at significantly elevated risk for developing BD compared to peers whose parents are not diagnosed with BD (Hirshfeld-Becker et al., 2007). A 10-year follow-up of children who had a major depressive disorder between 6 and 12 years of age, found that 48.6% had a diagnosis of bipolar disorder upon follow-up, while 33% were diagnosed with major depressive disorder. In this population, a crucial marker for emergent bipolar disorder was a positive family history for the disorder (Geller et al., 2002). In one study,

78% of those who had at least one parent with BD were diagnosed with at least one *DSM–IV* diagnosis compared to only 24% of healthy controls. Furthermore, 16% met criteria for bipolar I compared to 0% of the controls (Singh et al., 2007). Initially, offspring of parents with BD are at greatest risk for diagnoses of anxiety disorders (Akiskal et al., 1985). In early and middle childhood, offspring of BD parents are at greatest risk for diagnoses as ADHD, separation anxiety, generalized anxiety disorder, and social phobia. By adolescence, risk increases for diagnoses of panic disorder and BD (Henin et al., 2005). Furthermore, children whose parents have BD are at greater risk for having elevated levels of behavioral disinhibition (heightened threshold for emotional reactivity), which may be a risk factor for the development of mood and disruptive behavior disorders (Hirshfeld-Becker et al., 2007).

Children of bipolar parents also have an increased risk for ADHD, while relatives of ADHD children have increased risk of BD. These associations support the theory that early onset BD may be a developmental subtype of BD (Faraone et al., 1997b).

Earlier onset and behavioral disinhibition. Earlier onset BD has been associated with greater frequency of mixed states, which is one of the more serious courses of the disorder. In one study, 30% of bipolar adults with mixed bipolar state reported younger age of onset. In this sample, younger age of onset was associated with increased rates of suicide, longer duration of illness, poorer outcomes, poor response to lithium, and increased risk for neuropsychiatric abnormalities suggestive of ADHD (McElroy et al., 2001).

Important Distinction

Some children react to novel situations with a sense of *wariness*, evident in avoidant behaviors that indicate distress and discomfort. This tendency, termed *behavioral inhibition*, has been linked to lowered thresholds for activation of the limbic and sympathetic systems. In essence they are highly reactive to novel stimuli (Kagan, Reznick, & Snidman, 1988; Schwartz, Wright, Shin, Kagan, & Rauch, 2003). Other children react to novel stimuli with the opposite reaction or *behavioral disinhibition,* a tendency to approach boldly and without reservation. It has been speculated that the latter tendency reflects a higher threshold of activation and that children may compensate by active sensation-seeking behaviors (Hirshfeld-Baker et al., 2007).

In their 5-year follow-up of preschoolers, Hirshfeld-Baker and colleagues (2006) found that preschoolers who demonstrated elevated levels of behavioral disinhibition were at greater risk for disruptive behavior disorders, particularly ODD. By middle childhood, risks in this population increased for comorbid mood disorders plus disruptive behavior disorders.

Adolescent onset and life stress. Those who have onset in adolescence often witness a significant deterioration in functioning in areas of academics (especially mathematics) and interpersonal relationships. While 85% of youth with unipolar depression graduate on schedule, only 58% with adolescent onset BD graduate from high school on schedule (Kutcher, 2005). The experience of chronic stress in family, romantic, and peer relationships has been associated with less improvement in mood symptoms among adolescents with bipolar disorder, with increased frequency of stressors associated with increases in mood deterioration. Kim, Miklowitz, Biukians, and Mullen (2007) suggest the importance of targeting stressors in family and relationships in psychosocial interventions.

Prevalence

Given difficulties inherent in the diagnosis of early onset BD, prevalence rates are relatively un-known in child populations; however, adolescent prevalence has been suggested to be around 1% of the population. Establishing prevalence rates for bipolar disorder in children and youth is even more difficult than most other disorders due to the overlap in symptom presentation with other disorders such as ADHD.

In childhood, symptoms of BD often include chronically volatile behavior patterns as well as low frustration tolerance; these patterns are often more likely to meet diagnostic criteria for disruptive behavior disorders, especially ODD, which is frequently accompanied by ADHD. However, the recognition that BD can and does occur in children at alarmingly young ages has resulted in increased tendencies to diagnose the disorder in children. Brotman and colleagues (2006) compared the overall psychiatric discharge rates for children (5–13 years), adolescents (14–18 years), and adults diagnosed with bipolar disorder between 1996 and 2004. Results revealed dramatic increases between 1996 in the diagnosis of BD in children and adolescents. There was a 53.2% increase in the diagnosis for children and a 58.5% increase in the diagnosis for adolescents, compared to only a 3.5% increase in the rate for adult patients. Compared to other psychiatric disorders, a diagnosis of bipolar disorder was likely in 34.11% of children referred for psychiatric services (compared to 10% in 1996) and 49.8% of adolescents (compared to previous rates of 10.24%). The authors concluded that

> Bipolar disorder was one of the least frequent diagnoses among child inpatients in 1996 but was the most common in 2004. Among adolescents in 1996, there were twice as many discharges with depressive disorder as with BD diagnosis, but by 2004 the rates were about equal. These increases significantly outpace the more moderate rise in BD among adults over the same period. (Brotman et al., 2006, p. 111)

The authors suggest several possibilities for increased growth rates including shorter inpatient stays, which may actually have increased re admission data; greater sensitivity to the possibility of BD in children and adolescents; or "rebranding" of youth with BD who would previously have been diagnosed with conduct problems. Regardless, the authors stress the importance of clarification of diagnosis and attention to differential diagnoses in comorbid cases due to the potential problems with prescribing different medication alternatives.

Read All About It

A feature article in a current edition of the *New York Times* reported results of a recent study by Mark Olfson and colleagues of a 40-fold increase in the diagnosis of children (two-thirds males) with bipolar disorder between 1994 and 2003. Half of those diagnosed also had comorbid ADHD. The most common medications prescribed were antipsychotic drugs (Risperdal or Seroquel 50%), mood stabilizers (epilepsy drug Depakote), or stimulants/antidepressants. Most children were on two or more medications (Carey, B., 2007, September 4, "Bipolar Illness Soars as a Diagnosis for the Young," Health Section, *The New York Times*. Retrieved September 4, 2007, from http://www.nytimes.com).

Etiology

Biological Model

Genetic vulnerability.   Family history of BD is one of the significant markers that can help distinguish between BD and other disorders with overlapping symptoms. It has been suggested that there is a 30%–40% risk of being diagnosed with BD, if one parent has the disorder (Levine, 1999).

Neurobiological findings.   *Brain chemistry and function.*   While low levels of serotonin have been linked to depression, there is no evidence that high serotonin activity is related to mania. Instead, low levels of serotonin have also been linked to mania. It has been suggested that when low serotonin is coupled with high levels of norepinephrine (Shastry, 2005; Sobezak, Honig, van Duinen, & Riedel, 2002), the combination may produce a manic episode. Conceptually, it has been reasoned that while low serotonin and low norepinephrine levels usher in depression, low serotonin and high norepinephrine levels may result in mania.

Glutamate and/or glutamine levels.   Atypical antipsychotic medications such as risperidone have been shown to increase serum glutamate levels (Goff et al., 2002) in subjects with schizophrenia and have also been effective in the treatment of bipolar disorder in children and youth (Biederman et al., 2005b). Furthermore, glia cell abnormalities have been found in the *frontal cortex* in major psychiatric illnesses including MDD and BD. Glia are instrumental in providing a pathway for neuronal glutamate synthesis (Cooper, Bloom, & Roth, 2003; Moore et al., 2007).

Cortico-limbic neural circuitry.   Research using neuroimaging has isolated structural and functional abnormalities in the amygdala, ventral striatum, and ventral prefrontal cortex (VPFC) in children and adults with BD that can cause disturbances in the regulation of emotions and motivated behavior (Blumberg, 2007, p. 104).

Although both increases and decreases in amygdale volume have been reported in adults with BD, only amygdala volume deficits have been identified in adolescents with BD (Blumberg et al., 2003; Chang et al., 2005). As a result, it has been speculated that one of the reasons that BD might be especially difficult to differentiate from other disorders of affect and impulse regulation in childhood, is due to the fact that the "full, prototypical adult BD phenotype might not be expressed until later adolescence or early adulthood" (Blumberg, 2007, p. 104).

Neuropsychological findings.   *Cognitive and processing defects.*   Studies have found that adults with BD demonstrate deficits in executive functions (set shifting, planning, working memory, resistance to interference), sustained attention, verbal learning, and memory (Bearden, Hoffman, & Cannon, 2001). Doyle and colleagues (2005) found that even after controlling for ADHD, youth with JBD demonstrated impairments on several tasks of *sustained attention, working memory,* and *processing speed.* Youth also experienced more problems with academics (especially mathematics) and required more tutoring and involvement in special education programs.

Researchers using functional MRI have found a link between negative mood and faulty cognition in bipolar youth 12 to 18 years of age (Pavuluri, Birmaher, & Naylor, 2005). Because children with BD can be highly reactive and sensitive to criticism, the researchers focused on how youth with BD process information—such as negative insults—compared with how they process neutral or positive words. Compared to controls, when negative words were presented, youth with BD showed increased activation of the amygdale and ventromedial prefrontal cortex, the part of the brain that controls emotions. At the same time, compared to controls, youth with BD showed less activation in the dorsolateral prefrontal cortex, the area of the brain that controls cognitive processing. Although the sample size was small (10 youth with BD and 10 healthy youth), results provide an interesting source of information regarding how youth with BD process information (especially negative information) relative to healthy peers. The authors suggest it may be possible to reduce excessive reactivity through cognitive behavioral therapy.

Assessment and Differential Diagnosis

As has already been discussed, bipolar disorder can often be misdiagnosed due to overlapping symptoms with other disorders, such as ADHD and conduct disorder. Researchers are continually adding to our information about BD in children at all age levels, and no doubt increased ability to diagnose the disorder correctly will be forthcoming. It has been recommended, in the meantime, that when children or adolescents present with symptoms of depression in addition to a severe variant of ADHD-like symptoms (excessive temper outbursts, rapid mood swings), professionals should consider the possible existence of bipolar disorder, especially if family history is positive for the disorder (NIMH Fact Sheet: Child and Adolescent Bipolar Disorder, 2001).

Memory Bank

Unlike the euphoric states of mania present in adult forms of the disorder, mania in children may look more like highly irritable, temper outbursts and aggressively de-structive behaviors. While early-onset BPD may be readily confused with ADHD and conduct problems, there is evidence that problems may be evident early and continue in a chronically repetitive manner. On the other hand, later onset in adolescence tends to have a sudden and acute onset, often starting with a manic episode and showing less cormorbidity with ADHD and conduct disorder (NIMH Fact Sheet: Child and Adolescent Bipolar Disorder, 2001).

The major difficulty in diagnosing BD in children is *"How are you going to tell a child with mania from a child with ADHD?"* (Geller, 2001, p. 4). When criteria for mania are reviewed along side criteria for ADHD, it becomes evident that almost half of the criteria (decreased need for sleep, excessive talking, distractibility, irritable mood) are shared by symptoms of ADHD. Given this situation, greater emphasis has been placed on isolating the two cardinal features of mania (*elation* and/or *grandiosity*) and combining these two features into one necessary criterion. In this way, there is greater likelihood of distinguishing between bipolar and ADHD. Another criterion which can also help with differential diagnosis is the manic symptom of *hypersexuality,* which was found in 43% of the bipolar sample in the absence of any reported history of sexual abuse (Geller, Fox, & Clark, 1994).

However, as the diagnostic boundaries have stretched and blurred in an attempt to accommodate children who are seriously impaired whose symptoms do not adhere to adult *DSM* criteria, it remains to be seen whether these children will better conform to the "adult type" of BD as they mature (Youngstrom, Findling, Youngstrom, & Calabrese, 2005). In their evaluation of empirical assessment practices for pediatric bipolar disorder, Youngstrom et al. (2005) suggest that the diagnostic interview should contain, in addition to family history, three other key sources of information:

1. *Handle symptoms:* Those symptoms that assist a clinician to get a handle on what the primary problem is

2. Evidence of cycling or distinct spontaneous changes in mood functioning
3. An interview format that goes beyond a single session interview

The authors acknowledge that the explosive rages resulting from irritability and aggressive behaviors are often the presenting complaint; however, they emphasize that these behaviors alone do not define BD. Nor are *distractibility, impulsivity, problems in concentration,* and *motor agitation* helpful in making a differential diagnosis. Instead, they support Geller in focusing on those symptoms that can assist in differentiating BD form other disorders, namely, ***elevated mood, grandiosity, hypersexuality, pressured speech,*** and ***racing thoughts*** characteristic of mania. The authors also suggest that assessment should take into account base rate estimates, and recommend that for practitioners in a nonspecialty outpatient clinic, no more that 5% of the clients should receive a diagnosis of BD. Finally, the authors recommend the use of multiple informants and rating scales such as the Achenbach (CBCL) to assist in making a diagnosis.

The Child Bipolar Questionnaire (CBQ): Papolos, Hennen, Cockerham, Thode, & Youngstrom, (2006). The CBQ is a relatively new parent report form developed to identify subgroups of children with BD. The CBQ has 65 questions, the majority of which are developed based on *DSM–IV* symptom criteria for mania and major depression, as well as symptoms of comorbid features such as anxiety and behavior disorders. Items are on a Likert scale: never (1), sometimes (2), often (3), and very often or almost always (4). The Total Score is derived from those items rated a 3 or 4.

Treatment

A multimodal treatment plan combining medications and psychotherapeutic interventions, including emphasis on relapse prevention, has been recommended by the American Academy of Child and Adolescent Psychiatry (AACAP, Practice Parameters, 1997).

Memory Bank

A manic episode might be triggered in a child with BD if an antidepressant is given in the absence of a mood stabilizer. Stimulant medication for ADHD-like symptoms given to a child with BPD can exacerbate manic symptoms. (NIMH Fact Sheet: Child and Adolescent Bipolar Disorder, 2001).

Lithium is a mood stabilizer that has been demonstrated to be well tolerated by children and adolescents (Tueth, Murphy, & Evans, 1998) in the treatment of BD. It is important to note, however, that side effects (stomach upset, nausea, overeating, weight gain, tremor, enuresis, and acne) often result in compliance issues with adolescent populations. In one study, 90% of youth who were noncompliant with lithium relapsed in an 18-month time span (Strober, Morrell, Lanpert, & Burroughs, 1990). Atypical antipsychotics (Risperidone and Olanzapine) have also proven effective in the treatment of acute mania in children and youth, 6–17 years of age (Biederman et al., 2005a) and preschoolers (Biederman et al., 2005b). In the preschool population, Risperidone and Olanzapine successfully reduced mania, and Risperidone but not Olanzapine successfully reduced the symptoms of depression as well. Side effects including increased levels of prolactin and weight gain require further consideration, especially in longer term usage. As was previously discussed in the use of medications for children with symptoms of depression, a major difficulty exists in the prescribing of medications to children without appropriate information regarding dosages due to limited research involving children and youth.

Read All About It

At 2 years of age, Rebecca was described as a rambunctious toddler and she was diagnosed with ADHD. By 3 years of age, she was diagnosed with bipolar disorder. By 4 years of age, she was dead from a drug overdose and her parents have been charged with her murder. At the time of her death, Rebecca was taking the anticonvulsant Depakote (valproate) and the anti-psychotic Seroquel (quetiapine fumarate) to stabilize her mood and clonidine—a blood pressure drug—which has been prescribed to have a calming effect on children [Carey, B., 2007, February 15, "Debate over Children and Psychiatric Drugs," National News, *New York Times*, Retrieved August 21, 2007, from http://www.nytimes.com).

The tragic case of Rebecca Riley has once again placed concern about overmedicating children at the center of controversy, previously seen when medications for ADHD skyrocketed in the early 1990s. Some clinicians blame the increase in diagnosis of BD in children and youth on the *DSM–IV* widening the definition of bipolar disorder in the 4th edition (*DSM–IV*; APA, 1994), thereby opening the door for broader interpretation and overdiagnosis of the disorder. Others cite the lack of agreement among child clinicians regarding how to best conceptualize a disorder whose predominant characteristics do not match *DSM–IV* criteria for adults and overlap with many other child-onset disorders leading to overdiagnosis or misdiagnosis. At this point in time, the diagnosis, assessment, and treatment of JBD remains one of the most controversial and challenging areas in child psychopathology.

News Flash: Adult Psychiatric Drug OK'd for Kids

On August 22, 2007, the FDA approved the use of Risperdal, an antipsychotic drug (previously sanctioned for use with adults), for the treatment of schizophrenia and bipolar disorder in children and adolescents. Up to this point, only Lithium was approved by the FDA for bipolar disorder in adolescents. Risperdal can now be used for bipolar disorder in children and youth 10 to 17 years of age (FDA, retrieved August 22, 2007, from http://www.fda.gov).

Suicide

Although suicide is rare among children, rates are now 8 times higher than they were in the 1950s (Goldman & Beardslee, 1999). Suicide rates increase dramatically, and suicidal attempts and ideation become increasingly more common after 14 years of age.

Currently, suicide rates for youth in the United States and Canada are among the highest in the industrialized world (Johnson, Krug, & Potter, 2000).

Suicide in childhood.   Approximately 500 children under 14 years of age commit suicide annually, with boys 5 times more likely to commit suicide than girls. It is estimated that 1 child out of 100 will attempt suicide in any given year through such means as stabbing, cutting, or overdosing (Cytryn & McKnew, 1996).

Suicide and Hopelessness

Yorbik et al. (2004) found that suicidal ideation in prepubertal boys and girls was associated with significantly greater severity of MDD and lifetime history of disruptive behavior than nonsuicidal peers. In their study, girls expressed more hopelessness than males or nonsuicidal youth. As a result, researchers have questioned whether hopelessness might be a gender-specific characteristic of depressed girls.

There are several behaviors that may serve as a warning to a pending suicide attempt in younger children. Studies have found that several behaviors can be predictive of suicide attempts, including:

- running away from home
- temper outbursts and tantrums
- low frustration tolerance
- social withdrawal, loneliness, and self-criticism
- preoccupation with death (drawings, stories)
- oversensitivity to criticism. (Papolos et al., 2005; Cytryn & McKnew, 1996)

Adolescence and suicide.   Studies focused on teen populations have found higher rates of suicide attempts and fatalities at this age compared with prepubertal children (Ryan et al., 1987). The rate of suicides increases after age 14, and approximately 2,000 teens commit suicide annually in the United States, while as many as 500,000 are thought to make suicide attempts (Goldman & Beardslee, 1999). Suicidal attempts are especially linked to MDD when the disorder is also accompanied by conduct disorder, and alcohol/substance abuse (Beautrais, 1999; Gould & Kramer, 2001). One study found that youth with depressive disorders account for between one third to one half of all suicide attempts (Beautrais, 1998). In another longitudinal study of 1,265 New Zealand youth, having MDD resulted in suicide ideation 5 times higher and suicide attempts 10 times greater than nondepressed peers (Fergusson, Beautrais, & Horwood, 2003).

Youth who contemplate committing suicide have suicidal thoughts or what is called **suicidal ideation**. Fortunately, not all suicide ideation will result in a *suicide attempt*, and not all attempts will result in a *completed suicide*. Studies that focus on accumulative risk models have suggested that environmental factors (such as social disadvantage and childhood adversity) can interact with personal problems (personality/temperament, heritability of mental health problems) to increase the risk of depression, suicide ideation, and suicide attempts in adolescents (Fergusson et al., 2003).

Science Talks

In 1997, suicide was the third leading cause of death in youth 10 to 19 years of age (Shaffer & Craft, 1999). From 1979 to 1997, the suicide rate for early adolescence (10 to 14 years) doubled, while the rate for late adolescence (15 to 19 years) increased by 13% (Guyer et al., 1998).

Youth who report suicidal ideation experience intense feelings of depression, anger, hopelessness, anxiety, and worthlessness. They often feel helpless and ineffective in being able to change circumstances which are causing overwhelming psychological pain. Youth who have been sexually abused are at increased risk for a suicide attempt (Fergusson & Mullen, 1999). Girls are more likely to attempt suicide than boys, but boys are more likely to succeed in completed suicides due to the different methods used by males and females. While girls often use a drug overdose, boys are more likely to employ lethal methods such as guns (60% fatality rate) or hanging (Garland & Zigler, 1993). Some adolescents who attempt suicide suffer from clinical depression, feelings of hopelessness, and low self-esteem, while others attempt suicide in response to high levels of stress, anger, and impulsivity (King & Apter, 2003; Sheras, 2001).

Read All About It: Press Release, September 6, 2007

Following a trend in declining suicide rates for 10- to 24-year-olds, the Center for Disease Control (CDC) released its report of the largest 1-year increase (2003–2004) in youth suicide rates in the past 15 years. The greatest increase (approximately 76%) was in girls aged 10–14 years with 94 suicides in that age group compared to 56 the previous year. Rates also increased for females and males in the 15–19 year bracket.

The methods used also had noted significant change. In 1990, firearms were the most reported method for boys and girls; however, in 2004, hanging/suffocation accounted for 71% of suicides among the 10- to 14-year-old girls and 49% of 15- to 19-year-old girls. Firearms remain the most common method for males. (Retrieved September 8, 2007, from http://www.cdc.gov)

Risks for Suicide

Individual risk factors.   Personality factors associated with increased risk for suicidal ideation include high levels of neuroticism, novelty seeking, and low self-esteem (Ferguson et al., 2003).

Family risk factors.   Family history of suicide attempt increases vulnerability to suicidal risk in youth (Fergusson et al., 2003).

Peer and school influence.   Increased risk for suicidal behaviors has also been linked with deviant peer affiliations (Fergusson et al., 2003). The influence of deviant peers may escalate risks of substance use and antisocial behaviors both of which have been associated with increased suicidal behaviors (Beautrais, 1999). One possible explanation for increased rates of suicide among teens may be concomitant increases in the rates of alcohol abuse (Brent, 2001). Prior suicide attempt is also a high risk indicator. In one study, risk for suicide behavior was 18 times more likely if there was a previous suicide attempt (Lewinsohn et al., 1996). Investigators have found as high as 66% of those who completed suicides shared had at least one of three main risk factors: prior suicide attempt; substance/alcohol abuse; and evidence of a mood disorder. Suicide attempt was most often precipitated by a life stressor (Shaffer et al., 1996).

Investigators have recently found that girls who feel isolated and friendless are at twice the risk of suicide ideation as their peers and as high a risk for suicide ideation, as girls who knew someone who committed suicide. Furthermore, having friends who do not get along increased the risk of suicide ideation (Bearman & Moody, 2004).

Stressful life events.   Increased risk for suicide attempts in young children have been linked to real or anticipated loss of a loved one, family stress and financial concerns, child abuse, and being diagnosed with depression (Pfeffer, 2000; Goldman & Beardsley, 1999).

Shaffer and colleagues (1996) identified the following list of common stressors that can precipitate suicide attempts in adolescence:

- teen pregnancy
- on-going physical or sexual abuse
- disciplinary crisis/trouble with school or the law
- conflict with parents or conflict in the home between parents
- exposure to suicide (e.g., contagion effect)
- a recent, unwelcomed relocation

In their study of Black, Hispanic, and White adolescents, Borowsky et al. (2001) found that experiencing a same-sex romantic attraction (homosexual orientation) predicted suicide attempts across all racial/ethnic groups for males and for Black and White females.

Science Talks

In their study of suicide risk among an ethnically diverse population of adolescents, Borowsky and colleagues (2001) found that having three protective factors reduced suicide risk by 70–80%.

Protective Factors and Resiliency

Family factors.   Family cohesion/connectedness (Borowsky et al., 2001) and absence of a family history of suicide attempt (Fergusson et al., 2003) are protective factors against suicide and depression.

Peers and school.   Gender differences have been noted in the role of friends as a protective factor. For girls, cohesion of their support network was a protective factor for depression and suicide, while for males peer friendships did not mediate suicide risk, although sharing common activities with a network of friends was a protective factor for males (Bearman & Moody, 2004).

Etiology

Genetic factors.   In addition to the risk factors noted above that can increase one's vulnerability to suicidal ideation, researchers have also studied possible biological factors that can contribute to suicide risk. Pedigree studies have suggested that suicidal rates among parents and close relatives can be predictive of increased risk. In one study, over 30% of adolescents who committed suicide had a relative who was also suicidal (Gould, Shaffer, & Davies, 1990).

Neurotransmitters.   Low levels of serotonin have been implicated, not only in depression, but also in increased risk for suicide attempts. In one study, suicide attempters who had low serotonin levels were 10 times more likely to re-attempt suicide in the future (Roy, Rylander, & Sarchiapone (1997). The link between low serotonin and suicide attempts is thought to be mediated by aggressive impulses, since aggressive men also show lower levels of serotonin than nonaggressive peers. Aggressive impulses might serve to mobilize self-destructive tendencies in depressed individuals resulting in suicide attempts (Mann, Brent, & Arango, 2001).

Assessment

As previously discussed, assessment for suicidal ideation will also likely be part of initial and on-going screenings and monitoring of depressed mood. In addition to clinical interviews directed towards establishing whether suicide thoughts are evident and if there is a suicide plan, assessment instruments are also available to provide a more objective assessment of suicidal features. A review of the assessment instruments in Table 8.3 will provide examples of assessments available specifically for suicidal ideation, such as the Inventory of Suicide Orientation-30. Also, elevations on the Hopelessness Scale for Children would also suggest increased risk for potential suicide.

Treatment, Intervention, and Prevention

Treatments and interventions for children and youth with suicidal ideation follow the same treatment paths discussed previously for depression and depressed mood. Therapeutic intervention often involves some combination of cognitive behavioral therapy and medical management.

Between 1991 and 1997, a significant increase was reported in the number of students who engaged in self-injurious behaviors related to suicide attempts. Epidemiological studies conducted in the Unites States by the CDC (Kann et al., 2000) and in Canada (Joffe, Offord, & Boyle, 1998) revealed that between 17% and 24% of youth reported having contemplated suicide in the year previous, while between 5% and 10% actually made suicide attempts. Due to the increasing rates of suicide in the United States and Canada, there has been increased effort in evaluating and promoting programs for suicide prevention. As with all programs, especially programs directed towards preventing suicide, the need to protect against possible iatrogenic effects is of paramount concern. As a result, there has been significant concern and apprehension regarding the potential negative effects that suicide prevention programs might have for youth who are potentially in a very vulnerable state (Gould et al., 2005; Shaffer et al., 1991).

Since children and adolescents spend the greater part of their day within the school setting, it is not surprising that school-based suicide prevention programs are the most common form of prevention program used throughout the United States (Kalafat & Elias, 1995). Programs can take a variety of forms, including *curriculum-based prevention programs, staff in-service programs*, and *school-wide student screening programs* (Eckert, Miller, DuPaul, & Riley-Tillman, 2003). However, despite the wide usage and variety of programs available, reviews of the efficacy of the majority of programs have produced disappointing results.

Curriculum-based programs. These programs can vary in their duration (usually a few hours) and normally focus on increasing student awareness of symptoms associated with suicidal ideation in an attempt to facilitate the recognition of these potential behaviors in peers and provide information about available resources in the community. There is some support that such programs may be successful in providing a positive attitude shift away from suicidal intentions; however, the criticism outweighs the support. Although popular (Mazza, 1997), the efficacy of this approach has been suspect due to lack of empirical support, methodological problems, and evidence that the program may be most distressing to those who are most in need (Shaffer, Garland, Vieland, Underwood, & Busner, 1991). For example, in one study, some students reported an increase in distressed feelings and hopelessness after involvement in the program (Overholser, Hemstreet, Spirito, & Vyse, 1989). After a comprehensive review, given the evidence to date, Gould and Kramer (2001) have advised caution when proceeding with curriculum-based suicide prevention programs.

Based on the knowledge that only 25% of peers would report a friend's suicidal ideation to an adult (Kalafat & Elias, 1995), researchers in Canada developed a program to increase the effectiveness of peers as first responders to suicidal ideation in adolescents. The Peer Gatekeeper Training Program (Stuart, Waalen, & Haelstromm, 2003) provided extended peer training (2 half days, 1 week apart with a 3-month follow-up session) for adolescents to increase their ability to assess and respond to suicidal ideation in peers. Preliminary findings suggest that peer training might be a valuable component to a more extensive suicide prevention program.

Faculty and staff awareness programs.   Although numerous programs focus on awareness sessions that target staff and school faculty, little is known about the empirical effectiveness of this practice. However, staff in-service was reported to be an integral part of at least one successful school-based program (Zenere & Lazarus, 1997).

School-wide screening.   Reynolds (1991) has proposed a 2-stage, school-based screening model which uses the Suicidal Ideation Questionnaire (SIQ; Reynolds, 1988). In this two-tiered process, students who score within the clinical range on the SIQ are then referred for individual risk assessment. Initial findings show this model to be potentially promising (Shaffer & Craft, 1999).

Signs of suicide (SOS) prevention program.   The SOS Program (Aseltine, 2003; Aseltine & DiMartino, 2004) is the only suicide prevention program to date that has been empirically demonstrated to reduce suicidal behavior (40% reduction in suicide attempts) in a randomized study. The program, which has been recognized by SAMHSA's National Registry of Effective Programs (NREP), had been universally adopted by 675 schools by the 2004–2005 academic year. The program's credentials have been further enhanced by a randomized trial that ruled out any evidence of possible iatrogenic effects.

The program trains high school students to recognize the warning signs of suicide and focuses on suicidal ideation as a medical emergency in need of an immediate response: **ACT** (**acknowledge, care, and tell**):

- **Acknowledge** the signs of suicide that others display and take them seriously.
- Let the person know you **Care** about him or her, and that you want to tell.
- Then **Tell** a responsible adult.

The SOS Program has been described in several publication (Aseltine, 2003; Aseltine, James, Schilling, & Glanovsky, 2007; Aseltine & DiMartino, 2004) and the following provides a brief synopsis of the program goals and procedures. The program focuses on two important suicide prevention strategies: a curriculum designed to increase student awareness of suicidal ideation; and a screening instrument to detect evidence of suicide ideation or other known risk factors (underlying mental illness such as depression and problems with alcohol). The goal of the program is to increase awareness that suicidal ideation is not a normal response to stress or disappointment, but a product of serious mental illness and as such requires a response to an emergency, as one would respond to any serious medical illness.

The curriculum involves a short film, *Friends for Life*, which provides signs of depression and suicidal ideation and a discussion guide to assist in developing appropriate ways to act and respond to someone who is depressed or suicidal. The current screening instrument is the *Brief Screen for Adolescent Depression* (BSAD; Lucas et al., 2001). The BSAD is self-administered and students are advised that anyone scoring above a given level should seek immediate help from a teacher, counselor, or appropriate adult. While the first study supported the use of the program in student populations that were economically disadvantaged (Aseltine & DiMartino, 2004), recent results from a 2-year investigation involving 9 schools confirmed the program's effectiveness in increasing knowledge, adaptive attitudes about suicide and depression, and significantly reducing the number of suicide attempts in school populations of socially, economically, and geographically diverse high school students.

CHAPTER SUMMARY AND REVIEW

Historically childhood depression was recognized as early as 1934, yet skepticism overshadowed progress, as many questioned whether children were capable of experiencing depression. In the 1960s, a popular notion of "masked depression" sought to explain delinquent behaviors as the outcome of child depression. Ten years later, *adjustment reaction* was used to explain away childhood depression as a transitory experience. Currently, evidence of depression in childhood is well documented, with more recent investigations focusing on depression in preschoolers to better understand symptoms and etiology of depression, at these early ages. Other contemporary issues include whether children and adolescents express the same symptoms as adults, and how to best categorize, assess, and treat the disorder in children and youth. Mood disorders can be *unipolar* (focus on negative affectivity) or *bipolar* (alternating between depressed and manic mood states). A major concern with the diagnosis of bipolar disorder in children and youth is differential diagnosis due to shared symptoms with other disorders such as ADHD and lack of consistency between child symptoms and current *DSM–IV–TR* (2000) criteria which was based on adult populations. Suicide among youth is a serious and significant growing concern in the past 10 years. Although school-based prevention programs have been numerous, empirical support has been poor until recently. The Signs of Suicide (SOS) Prevention Program provides the first empirically supported approach to effectively reducing suicide attempts in youth.

1. **Unipolar Depression**
   The two major systems of classification define unipolar depression in children and adolescents as *depressed syndrome*: *depressed/withdrawn syndrome or depressed/ anxious syndrome* (AESBA, 2001), or as one of two *depressive disorders*: *major depressive disorder (MDD) or dysthymic disorder (DD; DSM–TR–IV*, 2000).
   a. **Depressed Syndromes:** *Depressed/Withdrawn Syndrome*—Symptoms featured on this scale of the ASEBA (Achenbach & Rescorla, 2001) focus on characteristics of negative affectivity, such as lack of enjoyment, withdrawal, lack of communication, apathy, and lethargy. *Anxious/Depressed Syndrome* concentrates on those symptoms that are related to more agitated forms of depression, such as feelings of guilt, anxious to please, feeling unloved, need for perfection, and fears.
   b. **Major Depressive Disorder (MDD) and Dysthymic Disorder (DD):** The cardinal features of the unipolar disorders is either a pervasive "depressed mood state" or a loss of pleasure in daily activities (may be expressed as *irritability* in children). MDD is acute, lasting at least 2 weeks, and requires at least four symptoms from a list of seven (vegetative, behavioral/psychomotor, cognitive/affective). DD is longer lasting (at least 2 years, 1 year in children) and is accompanied by two additional symptoms from the MDD list.
   c. **Developmental Characteristics and Course:** Research suggests that while younger children tend to experience depression in response to situational events, adolescents seem

to demonstrate more genetic causes. Suicide is the third leading cause of death among adolescents and the number has increased dramatically in the past 20 years.

d. **Risks and Protective Factors**: There are a multitude of factors that have been demonstrated to increase the risk of depression in children and youth and risk factors can be found at all levels of influence: individual, family, peers, neighothoods, schools, and socioeconomic conditions. More recently, efforts have been directed towards uncovering protective factors which also have been identified at all levels of influence.

e. **Etiology, Assessment, and Treatment:** A family history of depression and abnormalities in serotonin function can place children at greater risk for depression. Maladaptive thinking that focuses on negative thoughts can increase risks by thoughts that include the *negative triad* (helpless, hopeless, worthless) or feelings of learned helplessness. An adversarial family climate and poor interpersonal skills can also have implications for depressive etiology. Cicchetti and Toth (1998) proposed an ecological transactional model to address the complex and on-going interaction among different levels of influence. Although CBT treatment methods have had the most empirical support for reducing depression, and the use of medication remains controversial, recent investigations suggest that the most effective treatment may be a combination of medication and CBT.

2. **Bipolar Disorder**

Individuals with bipolar disorder experience both the lows of depression and the highs of mania (euphoric feelings). The *DSM* defines a *manic episode* and *hypermanic episode* as abnormally elevated mood states that contain at least three of seven symptoms and last for a distinct period of time (at least 1 week for mania; at least 4 days for hypomania). Hypomanic episodes are qualitatively less severe causing limited dysfunction. *Mixed manic episodes* are severe mood changes involve an overlap between manic and depressive episodes. *Bipolar I* is diagnosed when MDD and manic (or mixed) episodes are involved, while *bipolar II* includes MDD and a hypomanic episode. *Cyclothymia* refers to mood states that range from dysthymic episodes to hypomanic episodes. The specifier *rapid cycling* is used if four or more mood episodes occur within a 12-month period. There is considerable controversy about childhood onset BD relative to criteria for adult versions of the disorder as noted above.

a. **Developmental Characteristics and Course:** The diagnosis continues to be controversial but has now gained greater acceptance. Considerable research effort has been devoted to understanding BD in children and adolescents and the majority of these efforts have relied on subtyping to provide a continuum of comparison. Common areas of subtyping have included age of onset, nature of episodes, clinical phenotypes, and comorbid associations. Results suggest that the disorder is more chronic, continuous, general (features of irritability), and comorbid in children with early onset. Adolescent onset tends to progress towards more episodic, euphoric, and narrow definitions of the disorder that are more congruent with the adult forms. Earliest onset seems to be more similar to the most severe form in adulthood, that of *rapid cycling*.

b. **Risk Factors:** There are several factors that can increase the risk for BD in children and youth, including genetic vulnerability (having a parent with BD) and temperament (disinhibition, novelty seeling). Increased risk for a more serious life path of BD has been related to earlier onset, and repeated life stress.

c. **Etiology, Assessment, and Treatment:** There are high rates of genetic transmission and diagnostic work-up can often be assisted by information about family history. Low levels of serotonin and high levels of norepinephrine have been suggested as an underlying chemical dynamic in this disorder, as have low levels of glutamate or glutamine. Disturbances in the regulation of emotions and motivated behavior have also been linked to abnormalities in the cortico-limbic neural circuitry. Cognitive processing deficits have also been linked to deficits in executive functions, verbal learning, sustained attention, and memory. Advances in effective medical treatment have seen the approval of Lithium for use with adolescent patients with BD and most recently Risperdal (FDA, 2007) for use with children and youth with BD (10 to 17 years). Cojoint therapy such as psychotherapeutic intervention, education and disorder awareness, and measures to include relapse prevention have all been suggested.

3. **Suicide**

Suicide is the third leading cause of death among children and youth in the United States. In addition to identifying a number of characteristics that can be associated with potential suicidal ideation, researchers have also investigated the risks that can increase the potential for suicide attempts in children and youth.

a. **Risks and Protective Factors:** Identifiable risks that have been associated with suicidal ideation and attempts include low self-esteem, high risk taking, family history of suicide, substance use and abuse, association with deviant peers, and increased number of life stressors. Family cohesion, no history for suicide in immediate relatives, and positive peer support have been identified as protective factors.

b. **Etiology:** In addition to risk by heritability (family pedigree), low levels of the neurotransmitter serotonin have been linked to depression and aggression. This association may serve to mobilize negative energy into self-destructive tendencies.

c. **Assessment, Intervention, and Prevention:** Treating children and youth with depression or BD requires continual monitoring for suicidal risk. Although school-based suicide prevention programs have been a popular way to attempt to reach suicidal youth, the vast majority have been poorly supported empirically, or provided mixed findings at best. Growing concerns about possible iatrogenic effects, in the light of poor empirical support, has increased the pressure to develop programs with strong empirical support. The *Signs of Suicide SOS Program* is the first suicide prevention program that has empirically demonstrated a significant reduction in suicidal behavior in a randomized study of high school students. The program focuses on two important facets of suicide prevention: a curriculum to teach awareness to peers with the underlying message that suicidal ideation is a medical alert calling peers to ACT (acknowledge, care, and tell), and a self-screening instrument that alert students to their own level of suicide risk.

Consolidate and Communicate

1. Historically, there have been many different ways that unipolar depression has been conceptualized in childhood. Prepare a historical graph that illustrates the different perspectives voiced from the early 1930s until now. Do these trends mimic overall historic thoughts about child psychopathology, and if not, what other factors might account for the trends (patterns in social, economic, historic, theories of child rearing, and child development)?

2. Recent investigations of depression in preschoolers (Luby et al., 2002, 2003, 2006) suggest that preschoolers express depression in complex ways and in ways that are not readily accessible to diagnosis by the *DSM*. Compare and contrast findings of Luby and colleagues regarding depression in preschoolers with Scheeringa and Zeanah's (1995) investigation of the manifestation of PTSD in preschoolers and their comments about the validity of the *DSM* for diagnosis and identification of PTSD in preschoolers.

3. One of the most consistent findings is that children and youth who live in stressful life conditions are at greater risk for developing depression. Support this statement with your knowledge of risk factors discussed in this chapter and the extensive information on risk factors presented in chapter 3. Discuss how different ethnic groups might be expected to suffer greater risk for depression based on this information. Based on your knowledge, what measures could be adopted to increase protective factors in the most vulnerable ethnic populations?

4. One study revealed that depression increases from approximately 2% in childhood to 4–7% in adolescence.
    a. What is one criticism of this reported statistic reflecting reality?
    b. If the statistic does represent an increase in reality, what are some possible explanations for why depression would be higher in adolescence (use research to support your answer)?
    c. How does adolescent depression differ from depression in childhood?

5. Develop a program to reduce depression in teens, based on your understanding of risks and protective factors. What would you want to increase, and how would you do it? What would you want to decrease and how would you integrate this into your program?

6. How is bipolar in children different from bipolar in adults? How can you distinguish bipolar from ADHD? Why do you think bipolar disorder is often misdiagnosed in childhood? Why do you think that bipolar disorder may be overdiagnosed in childhood? Support your answers with documented statements or research evidence from experts in the field.

Chapter Review Questions

1. The term "masked depression" was used to refer to:
    a. youth who were not able to experience depression
    b. youth who expressed depression in acting out or delinquent ways
    c. depressed symptoms in a child were really not true
    d. children who intentionally hid their depressive feelings from adults

2. Which of the following is true?
    a. Dysthymia is acute and lasts for 2 weeks
    b. Major depression is acute and lasts for 2 months
    c. Major depression is acute and lasts for 2 weeks
    d. Major depression is chronic and lasts for many years

3. The three versions of manic states are:
    a. manic, mixed, and hypomanic
    b. hypomanic, manic, and moderate
    c. manic, mixed, and hypermanic
    d. mild, moderate, and hypermanic

4. Which of the following would be considered a vegetative symptom?
    a. inability to concentrate
    b. suicide ideation
    c. weight loss or gain
    d. psychomotor agitation/retardation

5. In research by Luby and colleagues, preschoolers exhibit depression in all but which of the following ways?
    a. delayed acquisition of milestones
    b. nightmares

   c. excessive head-banging
   d. all were symptoms of depression
6. All of the following have been found to increase the risk for childhood depression, *except*:
   a. family conflict
   b. increased attentional control
   c. harsh parenting style
   d. peer rejection
7. Which of the following statements about suicide is incorrect?
   a. youth who are sexually abused are at increased risk of suicide attempt
   b. females are more likely to attempt suicide than males
   c. females are more likely to succeed at suicide than males
   d. females often use drug overdose
8. Children and youth who were raised by depressed mothers exhibit all of the following *except*:
   a. increased risk for developing insecure attachments
   b. increased risk for depression themselves
   c. increased emotional regulation
   d. responses to having a mother who is less emotionally available
9. Double depression refers to which of the following sequences?
   a. major depressive episode is followed by another major depressive episode
   b. major depressive episode is followed by a dysthymic episode
   c. two major depressive episodes are encountered within the same year
   d. dysthymic disorder is followed by major depressive disorder
10. Bipolar disorder in children most resembles which form of bipolar disorder in adults?
   a. Bipolar I
   b. Rapid Cycling
   c. Bipolar II
   d. None of the above

Glossary of New Terms

anaclytic depression
masked depression
mixed disorders
adjustment disorder with depressed mood
depressed mood
depressive syndrome
dysthymia
major depressive disorder
mania
unipolar depression
bipolar disorder
major depressive episode
dysthymia
dysthymic disorder
irritability
vegetative symptoms

anaclitic depression
hedonic depression
anhedonic depression
double depression
negative thinking
learned helplessness
negative triad
attribution theory
bipolar disorders
full manic episode
hypomanic episode
mixed episode/mixed manic states
bipolar I disorder
bipolar II disorder
cyclothymic disorder
rapid cycling
juvenile bipolar disorder
ultradian rapid cycling
severe mood dysregulation syndrome
behavioral inhibition/disinhibition
suicidal ideation
ACT: acknowledge, care, and tell
SOS program

Answers to Multiple Choice Questions:
1. b; 2. c; 3. a; 4. c; 5. d; 6. b; 7. c; 8. c; 9. d; 10. b.

IB

Externalizing Problems
An Introduction

The Nature of Externalizing Problems

While internalizing problems and disorders can be severely disturbing to those who suffer from them, externalizing problems and disorders can be extremely disturbing to others in their environment. Externalizing behaviors include a number of highly visible, intrusive, disruptive, and disturbing behaviors. Children with externalizing problems can be aggressive, engage in fights, and demonstrate high activity levels and impulsivity. Their behaviors can often be physically and verbally intimidating to others.

Section IB At-A-Glance
The Nature of Externalizing Problems

Classification of Externalizing and Disruptive Behaviors
    Dimensional Classification System
    Categorical Classification System: DSM–IV–TR
    Educational Classification System

Externalizing Problems:
    Prevalence Rates and Comorbidity
    Developmental Course
    Etiology, Risks, and Protective Factors

Classification of Externalizing and Disruptive Behaviors

At one time or another, most children or adolescents will engage in some form of aggressive or disruptive behavior. In order to establish whether an individual's behavior patterns are excessively outside the range of normal expectations enough to warrant concern, clinicians can use one of two classification systems. Each system has its own unique advantages and limitations (see chapter 5). The dimensional system classifies these behaviors under the umbrella of "externalizing behaviors" and views aggressive/disruptive behaviors along a continuum using deviation from the norm as a yardstick. The *DSM* categorizes youth as either having or not having a disorder based on the number of symptoms they exhibit. There are also differences in terminology, with the dimensional system referring to these behaviors as externalizing behaviors, while the categorical system classifies these behaviors primarily under the heading of **disruptive behavior disorders**.

Dimensional Classification System

Through the use of multivariate statistical analyses, such as factor analysis, investigators have identified a number of behaviors that cluster together under the umbrella of externalizing behaviors. There has been a systematic effort to come up with subscales that can further delineate subtypes of externalizing behaviors. Based on this information, a number of rating scales and models have been developed. The various rating scales differ in the specific items that are used to identify these behaviors and the individual sub-scales also differ by nomenclature, however, there are also many similarities among the different rating scales within this classification system (Achenbach & Rescorla, 2001; Conners, 1997; Quay, 1986; Quay & Patterson, 1997; Reynolds & Kamphaus, 2005). See Table IB.1 for a summary of the different subscales that have been identified under the externalizing domain and the types of behaviors represented as "externalizing" behaviors.

According to the ASEBA (Achenbach & Rescorla, 2001), the two syndrome scales that are subsumed under the externalizing behavior scale are *rule breaking* and *aggressive behavior*. On the BASC-2 (Reynolds & Kamphaus, 2004), the externalizing score is based on responses to items from scales for *aggression, conduct problems*, and *hyperactivity*. The Conners Scales (1997) include a scale for *oppositional behavior, social problems, family problems*, and *problems with anger control*, all of which may be informative regarding externalizing behaviors. The Revised Behavior Problem Checklist (Quay & Peterson, 1996) address issues of *overt conduct problems* (undersocialized aggression), *covert problems* (socialized aggression), and *impulsive, hyperactive behaviors*. The Beck Youth Inventories BYI 2nd edition (Beck, Beck, & Jolly, 2002) include a *Disruptive Behavior Inventory* and an *Anger Inventory*, and the items on these "two scales assess most symptoms associated with conduct disorder and oppositional defiant disorder in young children" (p. 20).

Based on findings from a meta-analysis of over 60 studies that used a statistical approach to classify of child psychopathology, Quay (1986) isolated three factors that clustered under the externalizing domain: **undersocialized aggressive conduct disorder**, **socialized aggressive conduct disorder**, and **attention deficit hyperactivity disorder (ADHD)**. According to Quay (1986) three pominant types of externalizing behaviors include:

Undersocialized aggressive conduct disorder. This syndrome is described by Quay as a relatively stable pattern of behaviors that share a common feature of motor overactivity and an underlying theme of aggressive, noncompliant and disruptive tendencies;

Socialized aggressive conduct disorder. The predominant feature of this syndrome is the tendency to engage in unlawful or illegal activity and deviant, rule-braking behaviors as part of a group, or gang;

Attention deficit hyperactivity disorder (ADHD). Although Quay identifies ADHD as a third cluster of behaviors, youth who have ADHD are not a homogenous group. While some children with ADHD have primarily the "*hyperactive-impulsive*" type, others with the disorder can be just the opposite, e.g., sluggish, dreamy, and inattentive (ADHD, *primarily inattentive type*).

Table IB.1 A Sample of Behaviors Considered to Be Externalizing or Disruptive Behaviors by Different Classification Sources

Classification Source/ & Assessment Instrument	Disruptive Behavior Categories / Conduct Problems	Examples of Behaviors
Achenbaach System of Empirically Based Assessment: ASEBA (Aschenbach & Rescorla, 2001)	Rule breaking	Lies, cheats Truant, uses drugs Swears, steals others/ home,
	Aggressive behavior	Argues, fights, hot temper, destructive, threatens, disobeys
Behavioral Assessment System for Children (BASC2: Reynolds & Kamphaus, 2004)	Aggression	Argues, bullies, steals, cheats, has been suspended, hits others, seeks revenge
	Conduct problems	Lies, deceptive
	Hyperactivity	Lack of turn taking, loses control
Quay's Classification (1986) Revised Behavior Problem Checklist (Quay & Patterson, 1996)	Undersocialized aggressive conduct disorder	Overt acts: hits, fights temper tantrums, uncooperative, explosive, irritable, domineering/threatening
	Socialized aggressive conduct disorder	Covert acts: associates with deviant peers, gang membership, lies & cheats, steals from others/ home
	Attention problems	Daydreaming, passivity, preoccupied
Beck Youth Inventories (BYI: Beck, Beck & Jolly, 2002)	Disruptive behavior	(CD) Aggression toward people and animals; Destruction of property, theft, rule violations
	Inventory anger	(ODD) Arguing, defying adults, annoying, blaming, spiteful
	Inventory for youth	Anger affect: get mad, stay mad, feel mad; Anger cognitions: think others are unfair, try to control me, are against me.
Conner's Rating Scales (Conners, 1997)	Oppositional scale Anger control problems scale	Being angry, hostile, losing temper
DSM–IV–TR (APA, 2000)	Opposition defiant disorder (ODD)	Loses temper, argues, defiant, angry & resentful, spiteful, deliberately annoys others,
	Conduct disorder (CD)	Violation of rights of others, rule–violations: bullies, fights, steals, destructive, lies, truant
	ADHD impulsive-hyperactive type	Restless, fidgety, excessive movement, loud, problems waiting turn intrusive

Categorical Classification: DSM–IV–TR (APA, 2000)

The *DSM–IV–TR* (APA, 2000) considers three disorders under the major category of *Attention Deficit and the Disruptive Behavior Disorders*: **Attention deficit hyperactivity disorder (ADHD)**, **oppositional defiant disorder (ODD)**, and **conduct disorder (CD)**. Two subtypes of conduct disorder are recognized based on age of onset: **childhood onset (CD)** or **adolescent-onset (CD)**.

Important Distinction

Although the *DSM–IV–TR* (APA, 2000) recognizes that "a substantial portion (approximately half) of clinic-referred children with ADHD also have ODD," the manual clarifies that "the rates of co-occurrence of ADHD with these other **disruptive behavior disorders** … is most likely in the two subtypes marked by hyperactivity—impulsivity (Hyperactive-Impulsive and Combined Types)" (p. 88).

A brief sample of associated symptoms for ODD, CD, and ADHD (hyperactive impulsive type) are available in Table IB.1.

Educational Classification System

Three laws that are of particular importance for classification purposes within the educational system are: the Americans with Disabilities Act of 1990 (ADA), Section 504 of the Rehabilitation Act of 1973, and the **Individuals with Disabilities Education Improvement Act (IDEA) of 2004**, which went into law July, 2005. From a perspective of governance, the Department of Education (DOE) is responsible for ensuring that public education complies with the laws concerning issues of civil liberties (ADA, Section 504) and **educational rights (IDEA)**. Although the IDEA provides guidelines and definitions for categories of disabilities, there continues to be wide variations between school districts regarding how the definitions are interpreted and applied.

Emotional Disturbance (previously called seriously emotionally disturbed) is defined within the educational classification system as a long-lasting condition causing significant impairment *and interferes with educational performance* in one of five areas: :

1. Inability to learn not explained by intellectual, sensory or health factors;
2. inability to develop or maintain interpersonal relationships with peers or teachers;
3. age-appropriate behaviors;
4. pervasive mood of unhappiness or depression;
5. tendency to exhibit physical symptoms or fears associated with school or personal problems.

The definition also includes the category of **schizophrenia**, a severe emotional disorder that is rarely diagnosed in children. The educational system does not distinguish between *internalizing problems* (depression, anxiety, somatic complaints) and *externalizing problems* (acting out, aggression or disruptive behavioral problems); therefore, it is highly possible that children who qualify for special education services under the category of emotional disturbance would receive services in within the same educational program. Some children may also be designated as having **severe emotional disturbance**." If the severity of the emotional disturbance results in fears of safety for either the child (self-destructive behaviors) or the peer environment (threats to others), an alternative educational placement may be required, either on a temporary (such as a 45 day program) or more intensive (residential placement) basis" (Wilmshurst & Brue, 2005, p. 97).

Within the educational system, children with emotional disturbance may be designated by a number of different labels, including: Emotionally disturbed (ED), behaviorally disordered (BD), and emotionally and behaviorally disordered (EBD). Because the disturbance interferes with the child's ability to learn (necessary component in order to qualify for **special education** and any *related services*), emotional and behavioral support systems are incorporated into the child's **individualized education program (IEP)**. The IEP will include a **functional behavioral**

assessment (FBA) outlining the specific areas of need and an appropriate **behavioral intervention plan (BIP)** to address how the needs will be met. If **related services** are required, such as individual or group counseling, anger management, or social skills training, these would also become part of the child's program and a component of the child's IEP.

Memory Bank

In the 2000 to 2001 academic year, approximately 472,000 children and youth in the U.S. were receiving special education and related services for emotional disturbance (Wilmshurst & Brue, 2005, p. 95).

Externalizing Problems

Prevalence Rates and Comorbidity

As might be anticipated, prevalence rates for externalizing problems vary widely, depending on: the population sampled (clinical versus non-clinical, age of subjects), the disorders/syndromes or symptoms included (conduct disorder, oppositional defiant disorder, aggression, delinquency, etc), and the classification system used (dimensional or categorical, educational). According to the *DSM–IV–TR* (APA, 2000), prevalence rates for CD in boys is between 6%–16%, while prevalence rates for girls ranges between 2%–9%. Prevalence rates for conduct disorder in the general population have ranged between 4 and 12% (Offord, Boyle & Racine, 1989), whereas rates for ODD have been estimated to be between 2% and 16% (*DSM–IV–TR*, APA, 2000). In the Great Smokey Mountain Study (Costello et al., 1996), 38% of those with behavior disorders had another comorbid disorder. High rates of comorbidity exist between CD, ODD, and ADHD.

Developmental Course

A growing body of research has demonstrated that early-onset externalizing problems, such as aggressive, destructive and oppositional behaviors, increase the risk of developing more severe problems (conduct problems, ADHD, delinquency) later on (Campbell, 2002). As a result, there has been increasing emphasis on the identification of problem behaviors at earlier and earlier age levels. In a recent study conducted in the Netherlands, van Zeijl and colleagues (2006) found evidence that externalizing behaviors can be identified as early as 12 months of age; a result that supported previous findings for age of onset for physical aggression at 12 months (Tremblay et al., 1999). In their study, van Zeijl and researchers reported that externalizing behaviors detected at 12 months remained stable one year later, suggesting a moderate level of prediction for future development at this very early age. In normal development, it is anticipated that externalizing behaviors will show a pattern of peaking around age two and then follow a course of increased decline throughout development (Tremblay, 2000). However, for some, early onset externalizing problems remain a stable force to be reckoned with (Campbell, 2002).

Hill, Degnam, Calkins, and Keane (2006) examined longitudinal profiles for externalizing behaviors across the preschool period for boys and girls at two, four, and five years of age. In their study 11% of girls and 9% of boys demonstrated clinical levels of externalizing behaviors that remained stable across the preschool period. Gender differences were noted. While low SES, was a predictor for boys, it was not a predictor for girls who were more seriously at risk, if they had low scores for emotion regulation at two years. Inattention at two years was a predictor for clinical-chronic externalizing behaviors for both boys and girls. Gender factors also were evident in a non-clinical sample of school aged children (9 to 12 years of age) with externalizing and internalizing problems (Roelofs, Meesters, ter Huurne, Bamelis, & Muris, 2006). In this study Roelofs, and colleagues (2006) found that rejection by the mother was related to externalizing (aggression) and internalizing (depression) behaviors in girls, while rejection by the father was related to externalizing (aggression) and internalizing (depression) behaviors in boys.

Etiology, Risks, and Protective Factors

Several theories and models have been developed to explain the origin of externalizing disorders, including: social learning, biological, family/parenting, and/or some combination thereof. Whereas isolating specific biologically based factors can be problematic (Deutsch & Kinsbourne, 1990), social learning models have demonstrated that some parenting practices can be powerful predictors of externalizing behaviors. The parent-child relationship develops over time resulting from a transactional process where behaviors (parent and child) influence behaviors (parenting and child reactions) in on-going cycles of reciprocity (Lollis & Kuczynski, 1997).

Research has demonstrated that positive child-parent relationships result in far more positive outcomes for children compared to negative child-parent interactions (Darling & Steinberg, 1993). For example, harsh and inconsistent discipline practices, weak parental monitoring and supervision, and exposure to adult aggression have all been linked to increased risk for child externalizing problems (Patterson et al., 1991). In addition, lack of family cohesion and parental warmth (Resnick et al., 1997), repeated family changes and separations (Henry, Feehan, McGee, Stanton, Moffitt, & Silva, 1993), and family conflict (Fergusson, Horwood, & Lloyd, 1992) are all implicated in elevated risk for externalizing behaviors. In one study, researchers found that lower levels of perceived parental involvement and higher levels of granting adolescents autonomy for their own decision making (13- to 14-year-olds) predicted increases in externalizing problems one year later (Reitz, Dekovic, & Meijer, 2006). Whereas in another study, researchers found that unilateral parent decision-making increased the risk for externalizing behaviors in school-aged children (Lansford, Malone, Stevens, Dodge, Bates, & Pettit, 2006). In addition to parenting practices, other external factors that can increase risk for developing externalizing behaviors include environmental factors, such as, family poverty (Widom, 1989), or living in dangerous neighborhoods (Attar, Guerra, & Tolan, 1994).

Individuals who have been physically abused as youth are at increased risk for developing later internalizing and externalizing problems. Externalizing problems linked to a history of child physical abuse include: aggression (Lansford et al., 2002), conduct disorder (Lynch & Chicchetti, 1998), and juvenile delinquency (Stouthamer-Loeber, Loeber, Homish, & Wei, 2001).

Protective factors can help to buffer children from adverse experiences. Child characteristics that can buffer adverse experiences, include: social competence (Luthar, 1991), developing positive friendships (Ladd, Kochenderfer, & Coleman, 1997) and successful social problem-solving ability (Lochman & Wells, 2002). On the other hand, children who bring a **hostile attribution bias** (the interpretation of ambiguous behaviors of others as having hostile intent) to social situations are at increased risk for developing externalizing problems (Dodge, Price, Bachorowski, & Newman, 1990).

Glossary of New Terms

Disruptive behavior disorders
Undersocialized aggressive conduct disorder
Socialized aggressive conduct disorder
Attention deficit hyperactivity disorder (ADHD)
Childhood onset CD
Adolescent onset CD
Individuals with Disabilities Education Improvement Act (IDEA,2004)
Educational rights (IDEA)
Emotional disturbance
Schizophrenia
serere emotional disturbance (SED)
Individualized education plan (IEP)
Functional behavioral assessment (FBA)
Behavioral intervention plan (BIP)
Special education
Related services
Hostile attribution bias

9

Behavioral Problems and Disruptive Disorders

CHAPTER PREVIEW

Aggression can be a normal reaction to frustration or it can be a defensive response to feeling victimized. Developmentally, overt acts of aggression (*instrumental aggression*) peak during the toddler period and give way to more socialized acts of negotiation. However, for some children, aggression can be traced to early difficulties with emotion regulation and deficits in self-control, ultimately culminating in chronic acts of physical, verbal, and psychological intimidation of others. The identification of subtypes of aggressive behaviors—proactive and reactive aggression—have provided a framework for evaluating developmental correlates, etiology, and outcomes. Children who are aggressive at an early age (*early starters*) have the most negative developmental trajectories. Often, at later ages, these youth tend to engage in deviancy training activities recruiting other high risk youth into acts of *socialized aggression*. Risk factors for negative outcomes include *child characteristics* of hyperactivity, difficult temperament, low inhibition, and insecure attachment; and *environmental characteristics* of coercive parenting practices, maternal depression/rejection, familial stressors, low socioeconomic status (SES), poverty, and neighborhood risk.

1. Developmental Trajectories

The normal developmental trajectory for aggressive behavior peaks at about 2 years of age and then follows a progressive decline with age. The nature of aggressive responses also follows a developmental pathway *with instrumental aggression* as a precursor to *hostile aggression*. Research has shown that aggression is a relatively stable characteristic and that early starters ("early aggressive onset") have the most negative long-term outcomes. Children who demonstrate primarily reactive aggressive patterns tend to have earlier onset and respond defensively in a "hot-blooded" manner to a perceived threat. Those who are proactively aggressive are described as "cold-blooded," premeditated, and motivated to aggress for gain.

2. Emotion Regulation and Self-Control

Children who demonstrate poor emotion regulation coupled with a heightened responsiveness to emotional stimuli tend to have the worst outcomes for social adaptation. For children who demonstrate externalizing behaviors, this can result in heightened responsiveness to situations that elicit negative emotions (anger, fights) or positive emotions (overly enthusiastic to the point of being disruptive). For those who are fearful, withdrawn, and defensive, attacks are possible.

3. Bullying

Aggression comes in many forms and degrees of severity. Interpersonal aggression can take the form of *relational aggression,* as is typically seen more often in females, or it can be a response to a faulty perception of threat, as in a *hostile attribution bias.* Bullying consists of repeated acts of aggression, intimidation, and victimization of others through physical, verbal, and/or psychological means. Acknowledgment of the seriousness of negative outcomes of victimization has resulted in increased efforts at early intervention and prevention.

4. Disruptive Behavior Disorders: Oppositional Defiant Disorder and Conduct Disorder

The *DSM–IV–TR* (APA, 2000) recognized two disruptive behavior disorders: oppositional defiant disorder (ODD) and conduct disorder (CD). Age of onset for ODD is typically younger than CD, and while 75% of youth with ODD do not develop CD, 90% of youth with

CD had an initial diagnosis of ODD. The cardinal feature of ODD is a persistent, hostile, and defiant attitude towards authority figures, while youth with CD engage in overt and covert behaviors (aggression, destruction of property, deceit or theft, and rule violations) that involve the violation of social norms or violate the rights of others. Researchers have isolated a number of different subtypes of CD.

5. Etiology, Assessment, and Treatment

From a biological basis, decreased activity in the frontal lobes has been associated with reduced behavioral inhibition. Genetic transmission has also linked aggressive behaviors to a history of family clinical disorders and chemical and hormonal imbalance (increased levels of testosterone and sensation seeking). The contribution of heredity versus environment in the development of aggressive behaviors is complex due to the increased risk posed by factors such as poverty, witness to violence, and living in violent neighborhoods. Youth with ODD and CD are at increased risk for developing substance use disorders in adolescence. Treatments have focused on parent training, collaborative problem solving, and multisystemic programs.

Aggressive Behavior Across the Developmental Spectrum

Aggressive behaviors can vary in both the intensity of response and the reasons for the reaction. Aggression can be **proactive** and **cold blooded** (as in planned and premeditated), requiring little provocation, or **reactive and hot blooded** (Dodge, Lochman, Harnish, Bates, & Pettit, 1997). Some children are more aggressive than others from an early age (**early starters**) and these children tend to have the most negative developmental trajectories. Children with difficult temperaments who are hyperactive and have problems inhibiting responses are at higher risk for demonstrating aggressive behaviors. Living in a family environment where coercive parenting practices are performed; having a mother who is depressed; and living in poverty all increase the risk for aggressive behaviors.

Although behaviors, such as bullying, vary in severity along the aggressive continuum, the *DSM–IV–TR* (APA, 2000) recognizes two disorders that cause severe impairment in functioning: **oppositional defiant disorder (ODD)** and **conduct disorder (CD)**. While initial thoughts were that ODD was a milder form and possible precursor to CD, empirical evidence supports the retention of two qualitatively distinct disorders.

The extent to which children develop the ability to regulate and control their emotions can often be fundamental to predictions concerning positive or negative child outcomes. Developmentally, children gain increasing ability to self-regulate their behaviors resulting in improved capacity for self-management. Emotion regulation and increasing self-control are evident in such milestones as the ability to *delay gratification* and greater *ability to inhibit impulses (behavioral inhibition)*. There are several factors involved in the development of self-control, including *socialization, cognition,* and *emotion regulation*. An overview of how these areas are affected by self-control and emotion regulation is displayed in Figure 9.1.

Two behavioral responses that are highly influenced by self-control/emotional regulation are *acts of aggression and prosocial behaviors* (DeHart, Sroufe, & Cooper, 2000). Although both behaviors are acts directed toward others, aggressive acts are forceful and negative, while prosocial acts are nurturing, empathic, and positive.

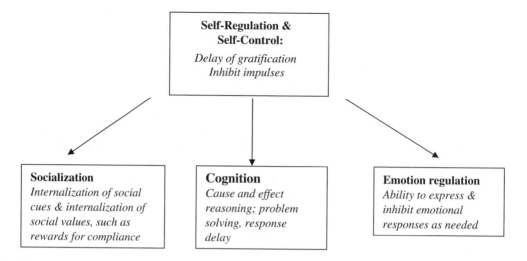

Figure 9.1 The ability to develop behavioral self-control and to increase emotion regulation influences behavior and development in many areas.

Important Distinction

In addition to emotion regulation or self-control, another essential and requisite skill for initiating an aggressive or prosocial act is the cognitive awareness of *the actor as agent*. In other words, it is the child's recognition that they can exert an influence over another for better (prosocial) or worse (aggression).

Developmentally, acts of aggression and prosocial acts change qualitatively as the child acquires greater understanding of the impact of their behaviors on others.

Developmental Focus

The developmental pathway towards increased capacity for empathic awareness and responsiveness unfolds in three stages: a primitive contagion response (crying babies elicit crying in other babies); the development of more purposeful helping behaviors; and ultimately, the ability to take the perspective of another and respond appropriately to another's needs (Zahn-Waxler, Radke-Yarrow, Wagner, & Chapman, 1992).

The study of aggression in infants as young as 5 months of age has lead researchers such as Tremblay, LeMarquand, and Vitaro (1999) to conclude that aggression is an innate rather than learned characteristic. One does not have to learn how to have a temper tantrum. However, what is learned is prosocial behavior and how to effectively control and manage aggressive impulses.

The way in which aggressive behavior is expressed also follows developmental patterns. Toddlers will often engage in aggressive acts either as a means to obtain a desired object, **instrumental aggression** (e.g., Billy shoves John off the tricycle so he can ride), or in venting of emotions, such as angry outbursts (temper tantrums) in response to frustration and/or parent limit setting. However, with increasing cognitive capacity and a developing sense of fairness or understanding of what *should* happen, preschool children can become increasingly involved in acts of **interpersonal aggression** or **hostile aggression**, evident in behaviors that are deliberately directed towards hurting someone else.

Important Distinction

The goal of *instrumental aggression* is to obtain an object (shove to remove an obstacle), while the goal of *hostile aggression* is to cause someone else distress (shove to hurt or get even).

Over the course of development, instrumental aggression gives way to more sophisticated means of "negotiation," while hostile aggression continues to increase well into middle school. In middle school, aggressive acts are often retaliatory in nature (to get even), in a response of self-vindication, or in response to feeling that "rights" have been compromised. Expressions of aggression also change developmentally as verbal insults (name calling, derogatory remarks about the person or the person's family members) replace more primitive physical responses (hitting, shoving, pushing).

Longitudinal studies (Tremblay, Japel, et al., 1999) have demonstrated that the normal trajectory for overt acts of aggression, peaks in the 2nd year and diminishes with age, as children become more socialized. However, not all children follow this preferred developmental path. For some children, overt aggression is a stable pattern of behavior from middle school, well into adolescence. This pattern or developmental trajectory of increased aggressive responses seems particularly durable for *early starters* (Aguilar, Sroufe, Egeland, & Carlson, 2000). In the first three years of development, Aguilar and colleagues found that the following family characteristics placed children at the greatest risk for developing disruptive behavior disorders:

- avoidant attachment
- caregiver depression
- stress
- low social economic status (SES)
- lack of caregiver sensitivity
- low quality of care-giving

Science Talks

Olweus (1979) reviewed 16 longitudinal studies of aggressive behavior in boys. The results were startling. Olweus found that early aggression was a significant predictor of later aggression and that among stable characteristics, aggression was as stable a characteristic as IQ.

RECURRENT THEMES Feelings of anger are a normal human response and temper tantrums are a likely occurrence for a frustrated 3-year-old. However, temper tantrums displayed by a 9 year old are not expected or appropriate. Our ability to discern what is normal or atypical aggressive behavior in children requires an understanding that normal aggressive responses typically follow an orderly and predictable path (*Theme 1*); that maladaptive aggressive behaviors represent deviations from the normal path (*Theme 2*); and that there is a continuum of severity of aggressive behaviors from less to more severe (*Theme 3*). The underlying mechanisms that precipitate and maintain maladaptive aggressive behaviors also entails an appreciation of how individual, interpersonal, contextual, and cultural factors influence deviations in aggressive behaviors (*Theme 4*).

Aggression, Emotion Regulation, and Self-Control

Proactive and Reactive Aggression

For the past 2 decades, researchers have collected data and provided increasing support for the notion that aggression is a multidetermined and heterogeneous behavior. Efforts have focused on developing a method of subtyping aggressive responses of youth with behavioral problems, especially those who have been diagnosed with ODD and CD. Conceptually, subtyping could provide increased understanding of the etiology and underlying processes which could better inform treatment efforts. In the past 20 years, significant research effort has been focused on determining the validity and correlates of **reactive aggression** and **proactive aggression** (Dodge & Coie, 1987; Dodge et al., 1997; Vitaro, Barker, Boivin, Brendgen, & Tremblay, 2006). Theoretically, reactive aggression has its basis in the frustration-aggression model (Berkowitz, 1978), whereas proactive aggression is best explained using Bandura's social learning model (1973).

Many distinct correlates, risks and outcomes have been associated with reactive and proactive aggression.

Important Distinction

Proactive aggression is an organized or premeditated aggressive act that is executed to obtain a reward (e.g., control, power, and increased status) and is influenced by *positive reinforcement*.

Reactive aggression is an aggressive response that is a defensive reaction to a threat or perceived threat or provocation. Since the aggressive act serves to remove the threat, it is under the control of *negative reinforcement* (Vitaro et al., 2006).

Proactive aggression.   This *"cold-blooded"* variant of aggressive behaviors is less emotional, and is associated with little autonomic arousal. Acts of aggression (bullying, domination, teasing, and coercive acts) are executed to obtain positive consequences and are reward driven. Onset is later than for reactive aggression. In at least one study, self-reported drug use, expressed hostility, and maladaptive parenting were associated with proactive aggression in both males and females; however, early traumatic stress and low verbal IQ were linked to proactive aggression in females (Connor, Steingard, Anderson, & Melloni, 2003).

Reactive Aggression.   Researchers have associated reactive aggression with *"hot-blooded anger,"* a response that is activated by the autonomic nervous system and exacerbated by frustration and lack of self-control. Onset is earlier than for proactive aggression. Developmental history notes maltreatment and rejection by parents or peers. Early experiences are often stressful and chaotic. Individuals prone to reactive aggression demonstrate early-onset patterns of **emotion dysregulation**, evident in somatization, depressive symptoms, sleep disorder symptoms, and personality disorders (Dodge et al., 1997). Neuropsychological deficits that impair the executive functioning capacity to activate behavioral controls have been found in early starters who evidence developmental trajectories of stable aggressive characteristics (Moffitt, 1993).

Memory Bank

Although there is significant research support for the existence of two distinct forms of aggressive behaviors, *reactive* and *proactive aggression*, there is also evidence that these two forms can be manifested by the same individual (Barker, Tremblay, Nagin, Lacourse, & Vitaro, 2006; Crick & Dodge, 1996). Approximately half of children who engage in aggressive acts vacillate between the two forms of aggression; about one third of children will only be aggressive in a reactive sense. Only about 15% of aggressive children will engage exclusively in proactive acts of aggression (Dodge et al., 1997).

Harsh parenting practices, an unpredictable environment, and abusive or cold parents have all been associated with reactive aggression, although recent researchers found the same family patterns in children who were proactively aggressive (Vitaro et al., 2006). The authors suggest that harsh parenting may have underlying mechanisms that can potentially trigger differential responses in the two groups. Children who respond with a hypervigilant sense of bias to threat may go on to develop reactive aggressive patterns, while others may learn to model these behaviors in a proactive aggressive pattern.

Differences in temperament have been found to influence developmental outcomes in a number of different ways. Vitaro and colleagues (2006) also investigated the potential links between difficult temperament and the development of reactive or proactive aggression. They found that **negative emotionality** (irritability, or low tolerance to frustration) predicted reactive aggression but not proactive aggression. Because temperament is a heritable trait (Goldsmith, 1996), the authors suggest:

> Since negative emotionality is partly heritable, the (probably direct) link between negative emotionality and reactive aggression suggests that reactive aggression may aslso be partly under genetic influence. (Vitaro et al., 2006, p. 692)

Emotion Regulation and Self-Control

There are also wide variations in individual responses to heightened levels of negative arousal; while some children are **fearful** and try to escape or avoid the stress associated with heightened arousal (Kagan, Reznick, & Gibbons, 1989), other children are **fearless** and approach novel situations or people without apprehension (Kagan, 1997). Furthermore, the extremes of fearless and fearful characteristics have been shown to be relatively stable throughout the course of development (Schwartz, Snidman, & Kagan, 1996). Studies have shown that fearless children are at greater risk for developing disruptive behavior disorders in middle childhood and adolescence (Raine, Reynolds, & Venables, 1998; Schwartz et al., 1996).

Rydell, Berlin, and Bohlin (2003) recently investigated the role of temperament (emotionality and emotion regulation) on the social adaptation of children 5 to 8 years of age. The study is highly relevant to this discussion, not only in the study findings but in the theoretical framework proposed.

Memory Bank

Individual differences in emotion regulation/self-control can produce extreme deviations from the norm noted in **overcontrolled** behaviors evident in internalizing disorders, or **undercontrolled** behaviors manifested in externalizing, or aggressive acting out behaviors.

Studies of child temperament (Kagan, 1994) have suggested that children who demonstrate withdrawal tendencies have an overactive system of behavioral inhibition, and furthermore, these "shy" and "wary" tendencies are relatively stable and persevere from infancy throughout childhood. (Information concerning the different types of temperament was discussed in chapter 2 and can be reviewed in Table 2.1.) One of the most important characteristics of temperament, particularly important to a study of emotion regulation, is the characteristic of **emotionality**, which refers to the sensory threshold required to elicit a response. Children who are high on emotionality require little stimulation to activate their physiological, cognitive, or behavioral response repertoire, and they respond with a heightened intensity of response.

Rydell and colleagues (2003) investigated the interactions between emotionality, emotion regulation, and social adaptation. Results of their study are summarized in the in Figure 9.2.

As can be seen in Figure 9.2, children who are *low on emotionality* (have high threshold for intense emotions) and *high on emotion regulation* (good ability to manage their emotions) are ultimately the most successful socially and produce strong positive outcomes in the area of **social**

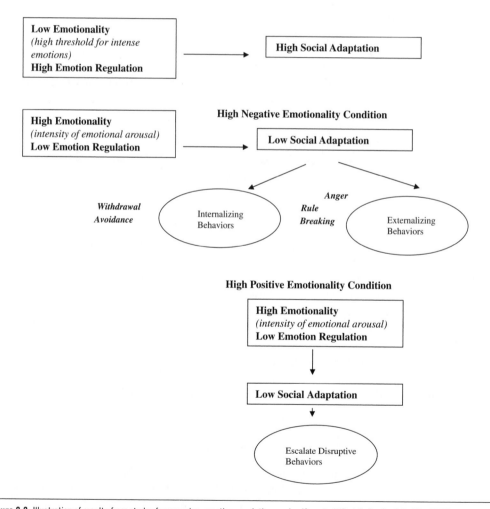

Figure 9.2 Illustration of results from study of aggression, emotion regulation, and self-control (Rydell, Berlin, & Bohlin, 2003).

adaptation (peer competence, prosocial behavior, few problem behaviors). In situations that can cause high negative emotionality (e.g., anger, frustration, feeling threatened), children with *high emotionality* (children are more intensely aroused) and *low emotion regulation* have the worse outcomes, which can manifest as internalizing behaviors (such as increased withdrawal, avoidance, and fear) or externalizing behaviors (such as increased aggression, disruptive behaviors, hyperactivity, and rule breaking).

Although the initial intent was to examine responses to situations involving high negative emotionality, in their final analysis, the authors found that children who had problems regulating their emotions and who responded with intense emotional responsiveness in externalizing behaviors also experienced significant difficulties in situations of high positive emotionality. In these situations, children who exhibited externalizing behaviors were also poor in social adaptation because their inability to regulate their emotions coupled with their highly intense reactions to the positively charged situations also resulted in escalating behaviors that were disruptive.

Memory Bank

Studies have repeatedly demonstrated that poor emotion regulation in situations eliciting negative emotions (anger, frustration, threat) result in poor social outcomes for children with externalizing behaviors. However, results from the study by Rydell and colleagues (2003) suggest that it is equally as likely that *positive situations* that are highly charged emotionally might also elicit externalizing behaviors which are equally as inappropriate, excessive, and disruptive.

From an interactionist point of view, several studies have investigation the impact of child characteristics (child temperament, emotion regulation) on the development of disruptive behaviors in conjunction with the *moderating effects* of parenting practices, such as caregiving, warmth, and monitoring. Maternal depression and depressive features, such as irritability, negativism/criticism and low positive affect can all contribute to the development of disruptive behaviors (Aguilar et al., 2000) which can be enduring and stable (Webster-Stratton, 1990). Studies of school-age children and adolescents have demonstrated that between 5% and 7% of children will demonstrate persistent aggressive and oppositional behaviors across the developmental span (Laird, Pettit, & Dodge, 1999; Newman, Moffitt, & Caspi, 1996). Recently this projection has been extended to a sample of children from 2 to 8 years replicating almost the identical percentages; 5.6% of the sample demonstrated persistent oppositional and aggressive behaviors from preschool to elementary school (Owens & Shaw, 2003). In their investigation of early risk factors for the development of persistent aggressive and oppositional behaviors, Owens and Shaw (2003) found that in the first 2 years of life, the child characteristic of fearlessness and maternal characteristics of depression/rejection placed the children at greatest risk.

Science Talks

The most proximal factors that have been identified in producing increased risk for the development of stable aggressive and/or oppositional behaviors include the child characteristic of **low inhibition** (Schwartz et al., 1996) and parenting characteristics of **maternal depression** (Zahn-Waxler et al., 1990) and rejection (Loeber & Stouthamer-Loeber, 1998).

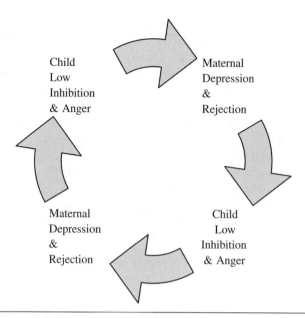

Figure 9.3 The cycle of maternal depression, rejection, and child aggresson.

It is hypothesized by Patterson and colleagues (1992) and Owens and Shaw (2003) that these three risk factors contribute to an endless coercive cycle of aggressive responses, resulting in increased maternal depression and rejection which results in increased aggressive responding (see Figure 9.3).

Recall and Rewind

Reactive aggression is most similar to descriptions of **high emotionality** (hot-blooded) and *low emotion regulation* (low threshold for autonomic arousal; increased feelings of threat).

Proactive aggression is best suited to descriptions of **low emotionality** (cold-blooded) *and high emotion regulation* (controlled and premeditated choice of aggressive behaviors).

The many faces of aggression.   Aggressive behaviors across the developmental spectrum can indicate delays or deficits in self-control and emotion regulation. However, although aggression is a common thread among the disruptive disorders, there are many faces of aggression.

Case in Point

Ely is a 3-year-old preschooler who can be very active. Ely has problems sitting in one place for very long and often when the teacher is reading a story, Ely is disturbing some-one sitting next to him. During play time, Ely wants to ride the tricycle, so he pushes Ronnie off the seat so he can get on. Ronnie, who is a very timid and shy child, imme-diately begins to sob and the teacher comes to rescue him. The teacher firmly tells Ely to return the tricycle to Ronnie. Ely reluctantly complies with the request. At home that evening, Ely's 10-year-old brother, John, shoves Ely into the wall because he has gone into his room and taken a hand held video game. John's mother, Mona, is upset with him because he could really hurt Ely due to the size difference. John has always been hard to manage at home due to his willfulness and deliberate attempts to annoy those around him. Although John's noncompliance and defiance have escalated in the past 8 months, since his father moved out of the house, the behaviors are not new. John is repeatedly in trouble at school for being aggressive towards his peers and deliberately aggravating the other students. Lately, other parents have complained that John is bullying some of the younger children. John received a bus suspension this week for pushing Eric off his seat because Eric was "looking at him." The next day, John immediately sought out Eric and threatened to beat him up after school because he told the bus driver on him. Eric tells the teacher and John is suspended from school. When Mona arrives home with John, they are greeted by a police cruiser in their driveway. Josh, the eldest boy, has been arrested for breaking into a neighbor's car and with theft of a number of CDs that were in the car. Josh is 13 years old and has not been a major problem up until the past few months. Mona recently caught Josh smoking in his bedroom and he was in a fight at school 2 weeks ago and received a 3-day suspension. Josh says that the CDs belonged to him and he was just trying to get them back.

Aggression can be physical or verbal. Aggressive acts can also be direct and overt or indirect and covert, such as females tendencies to engage in **relational aggression** (target an individual's social circle). Aggression may be reactive, as in a response to a legitimate threat, or in response to a faulty perception of threat evident in a **hostile attribution bias** (tendency to interpret ambigu-ous expressions as having a hostile intent; Dodge, Bates, & Pettit, 1990). Aggression can also be proactive and without apparent cause, as in bullying behaviors. For some children, aggression may be the first line of defense due to a restricted range of responses (learned and modeled behavior). Aggression can also be a normal response to frustration and victimization.

In the *Case in Point*, Mona is faced with the difficult task of raising three boys who demonstrate various levels of aggressive behavior. From a developmental perspective, Ely's aggressive behavior could best be classified as a relatively normal response for a 3-year-old. Ely was using force to obtain a desired object (*instrumental aggression*). Ely has learned that Ronnie is timid and force usually works because Ronnie does not put up a fight. Empirically, we know from longitudinal studies of aggressive behaviors that normally, overt acts of aggression peak in the 2nd year and diminish with age, as children become more socialized (Tremblay et al., 1999). However, some children, like John, develop a pattern of overt aggression as a stable behavioral trait that can persist through middle school and adolescence (Aguilar et al., 2000).

John's aggressive behavior represents *interpersonal aggression* or *hostile aggression* because the intent is to inflict distress on another person. At 10 years of age, typical aggressive patterns are more likely to have a *retaliatory* quality to them; however, developmentally, we know that John should be making the shift away from more physical demonstrations of anger towards increased evidence of verbal aggression (name calling, derogatory remarks). We are cautioned about the more serious nature of John's aggressive behavior and there are warning flags that signal a more chronic nature to the increasing severity of his offences. Although the family situation has had a recent traumatic change (parents' separation), which might be seen as a *precipitating factor* for John's aggression, other comments suggest that aggressive behaviors have been *maintained* for a much longer duration. John has *always been difficult to manage*; and he has a *history of noncompliant and defiant responses* at home. John is repeatedly in trouble at school for being *aggressive towards his peers* and *deliberately annoying* them. The types of symptoms, the duration and severity may be indicative of a more serious disorder called ***Oppositional Defiant Disorder*** (***ODD***; *DSM*; APA, 2000). **Coercion theory** (Patterson et al., 1991) would predict that John and his mother would likely engage in battles that escalate conflict. More serious interventions are likely necessary.

Josh's aggressive behavior is more difficult to analyze. The nature of his rule violations is serious: aggressive fighting, smoking in the house, breaking into a car, and "stealing." Given these symptoms in isolation, one might suspect a ***Conduct Disorder*** (***CD***; *DSM–IV–TR*; APA, 2000). However, given the rather acute onset of these behaviors, the fact that Josh *has not been a major problem up until the past few months,* and the fact that Josh's father has recently left the family, further consideration is required.

Science Talks

Bullying victimizes children by their exposure to repeated negative comments, gestures, physical acts, or intentional exclusion by a group. The victim is often overpowered and defenseless (Olweus, 1995). Children who are exposed to *bullying* tactics suffer significant and long-term social, emotional, physical, and academic consequences, such as lower self-esteem, decreased academic performance, fewer friendships, increased dropout rates, increased school absences, and increased illness and somatic complaints (Ballard, Argus, & Remley, 1999; Rigby & Slee, 1999).

Aggression and Bullying

Bullying can manifest in three forms:

- **physical bullying** (hitting, kicking, spitting)
- **verbal bullying** (taunting, name calling)
- **psychological bullying** (emotional abuse: spreading rumors, exclusion; intimidation)

Although bullying is not always associated with physical violence, it can lead to violent outcomes. There has been increasing research on peer victimization, especially in light of reports that school bullying might have been a contributing factor to the Columbine High School shootings in Littleton, Colorado, in 1999, and Santana High School in Santee, California, in early 2001 (OJJDP Fact Sheet, 2001).

Olweus (1995) reports that up to 40% of bullies are later convicted of multiple criminal offences. Bullying is rampant and widespread. In one recent study of more than 15,000 students in the United States, 29.9% reported engaging in moderate to frequent bullying; 13% reported being bullied; while 6.3% admitted to being both the bully and the target (Nansel, Overpeck, & Ramani, 2001). Within one 5-year period (1994–1999) more than 250 violent deaths were reported in schools as a result of bullying (Anderson & Bushman, 2001). The literature suggests that the impact of bullying can be different for males and females. Boys tend to be both the bully and the target, and experience more physical aggression than girls (Siann, Callaghan, & Glissov, 1994). Aggression is more likely to be expressed as **relational aggression** (rumor spreading, exclusion from group) in females, or more specifically in **intentional isolation** (Crick & Grotpeter, 1995). Bullying involving direct physical contact seems to peak in middle school and decline in high school, whereas verbal aggression and verbal abuse remain constant (Batsche & Knoff, 1994).

Little Known Fact

Studies show that victims have a higher percentage of overprotective parents or overprotective school personnel and as a result, do not develop adequate coping skills (Batsche & Knoff, 1994).

Intervention and Prevention

Prevention models that address the need to recognize bullying behavior have gained increasing acceptance. Research suggests that interpersonal aggression is a learned response which can be prevented if targeted early through educational programs (Hazler, 1996; Stein, Towey, & Hollander, 1995). Bullying behaviors are considered to be part of the repertoire of responses that are found in *proactive aggression* (Dodge et al., 1997). It has been revealed that approximately 75% of elementary school students either passively observe or actively support bullying (O'Connell, Pepler, & Craig, 1999). Likely because of this fact, school-wide programs have been demonstrated to be more effective than pull-out programs targeted specifically at victims or bullies (Salmivalli, 1999).

Disruptive Behavior Disorders: ODD and CD

Under the category of Disorders Usually First Diagnosed in Infancy, Childhood, or Adolescence (*DSM*; APA, 2000), there are two disorders which are listed, specifically, as disruptive behavior disorders. The two disorders share a common thread of aggressive behavior: *oppositional defiant disorder* (*ODD*) and *conduct disorder* (*CD*). In addition to sharing aggressive features, both disorders have been classified as externalizing disorders in factor analytic studies based on clusters of specific behavioral symptoms (Achenbach & Rescorla, 2001).

While the internalizing disorders may often go undiagnosed due to their covert nature, the externalizing disorders are often too visible and, as such, are often the first to be reported to clinicians because of their intrusive and disruptive natures, which are virtually impossible to ignore. By the time that parents or teachers appeal for help from professionals in managing these very difficult behaviors, the situation is often one in which the child is *"out of control ... and in control."*

Case in Point

As a toddler, Brandon was definitely more demanding than his siblings. He was not content to stay anywhere for very long. When he couldn't have his way, Brandon would often scream and have tantrums, which were relentless. Ultimately Donna would give in just to preserve her sanity and maintain the peace. Brandon was very easily frustrated, highly reactive, and almost impossible to calm down when upset. Initially, Donna was able to distract him by offering something else, but that didn't last for very long. Donna was beginning to believe that for Brandon the "terrible 2s" were part of his personality and not just a phase that he would grow out of. Now 6 years later, she is afraid that she was right.

Donna has learned not to argue with Brandon. When she tries to get him to clean his room or do his homework, Brandon either ignores her or flat out refuses, saying his little brother doesn't have to clean his room. Donna has tried to explain that Brandon is 8 and his brother is only 3, but Brandon will not listen to reason. When Donna engages in arguments with Brandon it invariably becomes a "lose–lose situation": either he wears her down and she gives in; or she loses it and "grounds him for life." Last month, Donna was so upset that she took every electronic device out of Brandon's room as a punishment and locked them in the spare room (TV, radio, electronic games). Brandon retaliated by kicking the door down, hurting his foot, and then blaming her for making him do it.

At 8 years of age, Brandon has become the "house bully." Rather than cause a disturbance, on most occasions his mother lets him have his way in order to avoid a confrontation; however, when she does get upset, she often goes overboard with punishments that are way out of proportion to the offense. Brandon's father is not concerned, because when he sees Brandon every 2nd weekend, they go fishing and hunting, and everything is fine. He blames Donna for not being able to handle Brandon.

Lately, Brandon has begun to repeatedly ignore his teacher's requests and will be adamant that he did not hear her, or stating that she is picking on him and demanding more of him than his classmates. Although his teacher has yet to catch him in the act, she suspects that he is also bossy with a few of the more passive children, since she has received complaints from some of the parents about Brandon intimidating them and calling them names. Brandon has a few "friends" but he tends to associate with two other boys who are equally as aggressive and noncomplaint. Brandon's academic performance is weak because he does not complete his assignments and homework is often not done or not handed in.

Oppositional disorder and conduct disorder: Two unique disorders or one?   Although early research argued for consideration of ODD and CD as a continuum, with ODD being a milder form or precursor to CD (Anderson, Williams, & McGee, 1987), there are several reasons which argue in support of retaining the two disorders as distinct. One reason is that age of onset for ODD (typically 4–8 years) is earlier than for CD (**childhood onset**, one symptom prior to age 10; **adolescent onset**, no conduct problem prior to age 10). Another reason is that 75% of children with ODD do not develop CD. Although ODD and CD share aggressive features, studies have revealed that these two disorders present with "qualitatively distinct" forms of aggressive behavior.

Important Distinction

Arguments in favor of retaining separate categories for ODD and CD, include age of onset (ODD earlier than CD); discontinuity rather than continuity (majority of children with ODD do not develop CD); and "qualitatively distinct" forms of aggressive behavior (ODD aggressive/nondestructive; CD destructive and rule violations).

In their meta-analysis of 60 factor analytic studies, Frick and colleagues (1993) identified 4 quadrants of behaviors aligned along 2 dimensions: overt versus covert behaviors and destructive versus non-destructive behaviors. The four resulting behavior subtypes can be viewed in Figure 9.4.

The items that clearly clustered under the ODD category were the **overt and nondestructive** types of behaviors, and aggressive behaviors of the **overt destructive** variety which were more intrusive behaviors. The covert behaviors which were either destructive (property violations), or nondestructive (status violations) seemed most indicative of behaviors associated with CD.

In addition, Frick and colleagues (1993) were also able to identify age of onset for each of the subtypes, with oppositional and aggressive behaviors being identified as early as 4 and 6 years of age, respectively. Children with ODD share behaviors common to the oppositional and aggressive subtypes, while children with CD share features more indicative of property and status violations; categories which were also associated with later ages of onset. Age of onset for property violations was approximately 7 years, 6 months of age, while status violations did not occur until at least 9 years of age.

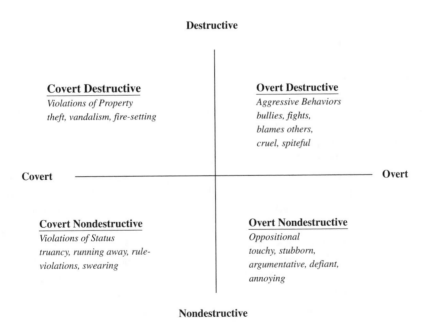

Figure 9.4 Four quadrants of aggressive behaviors resulting from the meta-analytic factor analysis of child conduct problems (Frick et al., 1993).

Memory Bank

The behavioral items in the study by Frick and colleagues (1993) map on to the two syndromes which make up the Externalizing Scale on the Achenbach scales (Achenbach & Rescorla, 2001): Aggressive Scale behaviors fitting best with ODD; and the Delinquent Scale fitting behaviors of CD.

Oppositional Defiant Disorder (ODD)

Clinical Description and Associated Features

According to the *DSM–IV–TR* (APA, 2000), the cardinal feature of ODD is a *persistent, hostile, defiant, disobedient, and negative pattern of behaviors directed towards authority figures*. Given this constellation of behaviors, there is little question as to why children with ODD create significant stress in any environment where compliance and rule-governed behavior are expected. The oppositional behavior pattern is persistent, relentless, and durable (*must be evident for at least 6 months*). Children with ODD display a number of behavioral symptoms which make them extremely difficult to manage because of their confrontational nature. A diagnosis of ODD (*DSM–IN–TR*; APA, 2000) requires *four of the following eight symptoms,* occurring on a frequent basis (often):

- loss of temper
- argumentative with adults: confrontational
- defiant; refuses to comply with requests
- deliberately annoying
- blames others for mistakes or problems
- touchy and easily irritated
- angry and resentful
- spiteful and vindictive

The behaviors must occur more frequently and in excess of what would be expected given the child's age and developmental level. As would be anticipated given the types of behaviors demonstrated and the frequency and intensity with which they are expressed, significant impairment can be evident at home (family relationships), in school (social and academic), and employment situations. In addition to the above criteria, *a diagnosis of ODD must occur before age 18*, and symptoms must not be better accounted for by either CD or Antisocial Personality Disorder. In other words, the clinician is required to make a differential diagnosis between ODD and CD. Because CD is the more severe disorder, it would take precedence over ODD in the pecking order in making a differential diagnosis, if symptoms met criteria for CD.

In the previous *Case in Point*, Brandon demonstrated many behaviors that conform to the clinical and associated features of ODD. Children with ODD are often stubborn and noncompliant. They can be very contrary and argumentative with others; however, they are quick to shift the blame to other people, defending their actions as necessary given others' *unreasonable* demands. These children may also appear to be passively aggressive, as they systematically ignore repeated requests to follow directions. They will not compromise, refusing to bend even a little, and often adhere stubbornly to a refusal to negotiate.

Developmental Focus

It is always important to consider the influence of age and developmental stage when making a diagnosis. ODD symptoms must be *more frequent and in excess of what would be expected given the child's age and developmental level.* The *DSM–IV–TR* (APA, 2000) cautions that **transient oppositional behavior** can be quite common at certain developmental ages and stages. For example, developmental stages where the task is to obtain greater independence will often be marked with increased oppositional behavior as the child attempts to flex their new found independence. Therefore, the transient oppositional behavior often demonstrated by toddlers and teenagers (the two terrible Ts) would not warrant a diagnosis of ODD, unless the intensity and duration were atypical.

ODD behaviors almost always are initiated on the homefront and often carry over to familiar adults with whom they will push the boundaries and test the limits. These children may deliberately annoy others, especially well-known peers and siblings, who may also be a constant source for intimidation and verbal aggression.

Memory Bank

ODD behaviors may not be evident in the school or community, and are not likely to be evident in the clinical interview. These children seem to be most comfortable with pushing the boundaries in *familiar* territory and seem to have a good sense of compartmentalizing their behavior accordingly. ODD behaviors may extend into the school situation, if they are very ingrained/ automatic and if reinforced by teachers or peers.

Children with ODD may present with either a low self-concept or a sense of inflated self-esteem. Often, like Brandon, children with ODD will engage parents in battles that escalate into a high level of emotional turmoil on both sides. Parents often ultimately employ a coercive and negative parenting style in response to their children's aggressive and defiant behaviors. However, it has been well documented that these negative and coercive practices often serve to perpetuate rather than alleviate the problem (Patterson et al., 1991; Snyder, Horsch, & Childs, 1997).

Science Talks

Coercion Theory (Patterson et al., 1991) would predict that parents who engage in highly charged hostile and negative interchanges with their children actually serve to escalate their child's aggressive and defiant behaviors. Patterns of hostile and negative interactions serve to actually reinforce and maintain increasing levels of aggressive and defiant behaviors. Behaviors are precipitated and maintained because they are negatively reinforced. Furthermore, parents develop a **negative schema** (anticipate the worst responses from these children) of negative expectations which continually activates the coercive parenting pattern. These patterns are called **transactional patterns** or processes because the behaviors of parents and children serve to shape and determine the other's behaviors.

Prevalence

Depending on the nature of the population sampled and methods used to determine the existence of ODD, prevalence rates have been estimated between 2% and 16% of the population (*DSM*; APA, 2000). Prior to puberty, more males than females are diagnosed with ODD, however the rates equalize in adolescence.

Comorbidity: High rates of comorbidity have been established for ODD with CD, learning disorders, and ADHD. More than 80% of children diagnosed with ODD have comorbid ADHD; while 65% of children with ADHD will have ODD.

Developmental Course

Path analysis suggests that there is a potential for developmental continuity in a developing a sequence of maladaptive behaviors which begins with ADHD, progresses to ODD, and ultimately culminates in CD (Loeber, Green, Lahey, Christ, & Frick, 1992). However, while this pattern is predictive of a poor prognosis for early onset conduct problems, there is also evidence that discontinuity can exist (behaviors dissipate with age) in the milder forms of the maladaptive behaviors (Loeber & Stouthamer-Loeber, 1998).

Conduct Disorder (CD) and Conduct Problems (CP)

There has been considerable debate and discussion regarding the use of terminology in classifying the disruptive behavior disorders (see Hinshaw & Lee, 2002, for further review). Predominant descriptors, based on symptom clusters, fall into three main categories: *oppositional, antisocial,* and *conduct-disordered*. While the *DSM* (APA, 2000) uses the term **conduct disorder** as a diagnostic classification, literature often uses the term **conduct problems** (CP) to refer to behaviors associated with the more serious end of the disruptive behavior spectrum.

Clinical Description and Associated Features

According to the *DSM* (APA, 2000), the cardinal clinical feature of CD is a repetitive and persistent behavioral pattern which involves the **violation of social norms or violation of the rights of others.**

Important Distinction

While ODD is associated with overt and nondestructive behaviors, CD is linked with overt and covert behaviors which can be destructive and violate the rights of others.

Criteria for CD are based on symptoms that fall into *four categories* of aggressive behaviors: aggressive acts towards others (including animals), destruction of property, deceit or theft, and rule violations:

- **Acts of aggression towards others and animals:**
  1. bullies, threatens
  2. initiates fights
  3. use of a weapon causing harm
  4. cruelty to others

5. cruelty to animals
6. theft while confronting (e.g., mugging)
7. forced sexual activity
- **Destruction of property**
  8. fire setting with intent to harm
  9. property destruction
- **Deceit or theft**
  10. break-in (house, car)
  11. cons others
  12. theft (shoplifting, forgery)
- **Rule violations**
  13. out all night*
  14. run away
  15. frequent truancy*

(*evidence of behaviors occurring prior to 13 years of age)

A diagnosis of CD requires at least **3** of the above 15 criteria. The criteria must be present for the past 12 months, with evidence of at least one symptom within the previous 6 months. If the youth is older than 18 years, then CD can only be diagnosed if antisocial personality disorder is not the more appropriate diagnosis.

Memory Bank

In order of severity, the most severe disorder takes precedence in diagnosis. From the least to most severe, the disorders are: ODD, CD, antisocial personality disorder. However, antisocial personality disorder cannot be given as a diagnosis to persons under 18 years of age.

Youth with CD often initiate aggressive acts and will often engage in physical altercations or threaten, bully, and intimidate others. Often these youth can manipulate others through skillful ability to con others through lying, deceit, and a failure to follow through on promises and obligations. Rule violations begin at an early age (prior to 13 years of age) and youth may stay out all night without parent permission, and be truant from school. Youth may run away from home (at least twice) or for a lengthy duration (*DSM–IV–TR*; APA, 2000).

Youth with CD may show little remorse or empathy, and demonstrate minimal concern for the feelings and thoughts of others. Aggressive tendencies may be heightened in situations which are more ambiguous, as they may have a bias towards reading hostile intent into the motives of others, and react accordingly. Often youth with CD may feign feelings of guilt/remorse in order to avert a harsher punishment, or divert blame to their companions. Despite a show of *bravado*, youth are often low in self-esteem and may overcompensate by putting on a false sense of conceit, or tough exterior. Other associated features include engaging in high risk behaviors. Consequences of recklessness and risk taking may include increased risk of accidents, substance use/ abuse, sexually transmitted diseases, and teen pregnancy (*DSM–IV–TR*; APA, 2000).

The *DSM–IV–TR* (APA, 2000) lists two subtypes of the disorder based on the onset of the disorder: ***childhood onset and adolescent onset***. There are also specifiers that can be used to distinguish the severity of the disorder from: *mild* (few criteria and minor harm); ***moderate to severe*** (many criteria causing significant harm to others).

Important Distinction

CD with *childhood-onset type* applies if at least one criterion symptom was present prior to 10 years of age, while CD with *adolescent-onset type* is the classification applied if no symptoms were evident prior to 10 years of age. Studies have demonstrated that earlier onset is associated with more negative outcomes, such as increased intensity of disruptive behaviors and longevity of impact. Many youth with the *childhood-onset type* go on to develop antisocial personality disorder (Loeber et al., 1992).

More data on subypes of CD:

Rewind and Recall

In a factor analysis of criteria associated with ODD and CD, Frick and colleagues (1993) found 4 quadrants of potential responses based on overt/covert and destructive/nondestructive behaviors (Review Figure 9.4.)

Using the clusters of overt/covert and destructive/nondestructive behaviors and information from their longitudinal study of problem behaviors in children and youth, Loeber and Keenan (1994) suggest a number of potential subtypes of CD:

- **Authority conflict pathway:** Similar to ODD, these behaviors where defiant, and involved rule violations; however, defiance did not result in harm to others (e.g., truancy, running away).
- **Covert pathway:** Violations included rule violations (shoplifting, vandalism) but did not include acts of violence towards others.
- **Overt pathway:** Youth who were aggressive as children and engaged in more serious acts of aggression and violence towards others.
- **Dual overt/covert:** Youth were engaged in rule violations and aggressive acts.
- **Triple-pathway:** Youth demonstrated all three clusters.

Results of their study revealed the following outcomes: the *triple-pathway* youth had the worst overall future outcomes; the *dual overt/covert* youth were most likely to engage in delinquent behaviors. For youth on the *overt pathways*, unless intervention was successful, aggression led to increasing violence, crimes, and increasingly poor adolescent outcomes. Those youth on an exclusive *authority conflict pathway* continued to wage battles with authority figures, however, had the best overall outcomes of all subtypes.

Science Talks

In addition to the subtypes of CD discussed thus far, investigators have also probed the potential for distinguishing subtypes based on interpersonal and affective style (Frick & Ellis, 1999). The researchers found that among the childhood-onset CD, two subgroups could be identified given the presence or absence of **callous and unemotional (CU)** traits. Children who were high on the CU factor were more likely to have parents with antisocial personality disorder, police contacts, and poorer outcomes (Christian, Frick, & Hill, 1997). Furthermore, children with elevated CU traits also had lower levels of behavioral inhibition and higher levels of behavioral dysregulation than children with CD in the absence of CU traits (Frick, Cornell, & Barry, 2003). Children with high CU traits more closely resemble characteristics of the proactive rather than reactive aggression pattern.

Developmental Course

Pathways and Progressions

Within the realm of disruptive behavior disorders, conduct problems (CP) represent the most serious, complex, and problematic behaviors. Therefore, it is crucial that assessment procedures and intervention programs address the developmental, contextual, and transactional nature of these behavior patterns (McMahon & Estes, 1997).

Considerable research focus has been placed on the major pathways delineated by the onset of conduct problems: childhood onset, also called **"early starters"**; and adolescent onset, also referred to as **"late starters."**

Early-onset/"early starters." As was noted previously, longitudinal studies suggest that overt aggression should desist in a downward progression after the age of 2 years. However, young children who evidence conduct problems at a very early age often persist and develop more serious conduct behaviors over time which generalize across situations, reaching further out into the community at large (Loeber & Farrington, 2000; Patterson & Yoerger, 2002). It has also been noted that children on this developmental path tend to have poor social relationships and tend to gravitate towards other youth with similar developmental trajectories and engage in "deviancy training" among disordered peers (Dishion, Spracklen, Andrews, & Patterson, 1996). Outcomes for children and youth in this category are poor and ingrained behaviors can be highly resistant to intervention. Risk factors associated with this pathway include *child characteristics* of hyperactivity (Moffit, 1993); difficult temperament (Loeber & Keenan, 1994; Moffit, 1993); social cognitive deficits (Coie & Dodge, 1998); *interpersonal characteristics* (insecure attachment; DeKlyen & Speltz, 2001); *parenting characteristics* (coercive parenting style; Patterson, Reid, & Dishion, 1992), and *environmental characteristics* (familial stressors, low SES, poverty, and neighborhood risk; Keenan & Wakschlag, 2000). Children who demonstrate *reactive aggressive* patterns also demonstrate early onset aggression (Dodge et al., 1997).

Late-onset pathway: "late starters." There is less research information available about this subgroup, who seem to have less deviance and end up getting into trouble by association with the more deviant peer group, often due to inadequate parental monitoring (Patterson et al., 1991). This group may be more resilient because they have developed more adequate coping skills (socially and behaviorally) at earlier levels. Youth with later aggressive onset tend to demonstrate *proactive aggression* patterns and engage in more "socialized" aggression (Dodge et al., 1997).

Prevalence

Although rates vary depending on the populations sampled and measurements used, within the population at large, prevalence rates for CD have been estimated to be between 1% and 10%. There are indications that the prevalence rate for CD has increased (*DSM–IV–TR*; APA, 2000). Conduct disorder is one of the most frequent presenting concerns of youth who are referred to mental health settings (Earls, 1994). Males outnumber females; however, gender differences have been reported for different behavioral outcomes. Males tend to exhibit symptoms of vandalism, physical altercations, theft, and have more school discipline issues. Females with CD manifest symptoms in running away, substance use, truancy, and prostitution (*DSM–IV–TR*; APA, 2000).

Comorbidity. As with ODD, high rates of comorbidity exist for CD. Attention deficit hyperactivity disorder (ADHD) and ODD are the categories most often comorbid with CD. One longitudinal study of inner city youth—mostly African Americans—found that problems with attention and concentration (in the 1st grade) predicted significantly higher levels of aggression 6 years later (Schaeffer, Petras, Ialongo, Poduska, & Kellam, 2003). Due to the increasing age of the population, in addition to those areas of comorbidity already mentioned for ODD, youth with CD also have high comorbid associations with substance abuse and depression. Approximately, half of youth with bipolar disorder share a diagnosis of CD (Kovacs & Pollock, 1995), while half of youth with CD have substance abuse problems (Reebye, Moretti, & Gulliver, 1995).

Disruptive Behavior Disorders

Etiology

As previously discussed, research supports the existence of ODD and CD as two unique disorders (Frick et al., 1993; Loeber & Keenan, 1994). However, as disruptive behavior disorders, ODD and CD share many common features, such as defiance, aggression, and rule breaking behaviors, and have much in common regarding etiology, assessment, and treatment. Furthermore, although 75% of children with ODD will not be diagnosed with CD, 90% of youth with CD had an initial diagnosis of ODD (Rey, 1993). The following sections (etiology, assessment, and treatment) will be used to apply to both ODD and CD, unless otherwise specified.

Although anger and aggression can be very normal responses to frustration, within the realm of the disruptive behavior disorders, clinical decision making often requires an analysis of the nature and extent of aggressive responses. In fact, analysis of aggressive behavior is often pivotal to a diagnosis of the disruptive behavior disorders, ODD and CD.

 The **K–3 Paradigm** highlights three important areas:

- knowledge of development
- knowledge of sources of influence (child and environmental characteristics)
- knowledge of theoretical models

These provide the framework for understanding the etiology, risks, and protective factors that can be involved in the development of maladaptive aggressive behaviors.

Biological Model

Biological, neurological, and genetic factors.   Neurological investigations have found less frontal lobe activity in the brains of youth with CD (Moffit & Henry, 1989).

Memory Bank

Decreased activity in frontal lobe functioning has been associated with poor ability to inhibit behavioral responses and weaknesses in planning ability. This association may help explain why there are such high rates of comorbidity between ADHD and the disruptive behavior disorders.

Weighing the relative contributions of heredity against environment in the development of aggressive behaviors has been difficult due to the complex nature of assessing the role of other factors such as IQ and SES. It has also been difficult to isolate specific etiological factors that might be responsible for elevated aggressive behaviors, although there are indications that some children may be more vulnerable to aggressive behaviors due to genetic transmission (Yoshikawa, 1994). Twin and adoption studies have also indicated that CD can be influenced by both genetic and environmental factors. Increased risk for disruptive behavior disorders has been noted in families where the biological or adoptive parent has antisocial personality disorder, or when biological parents suffer from alcohol dependence, mood disorders, schizophrenia, or a history of ADHD (*DSM–IV–TR*; APA, 2000).

Based on findings from studies conducted with adult populations, elevated levels of the hormone testosterone (Dabbs & Morris, 1990) may be implicated in the genetic transmission of aggressive impulses. In addition, low levels of DBH (which converts dopamine to noradrenaline) may produce higher thresholds for sensation-seeking behaviors in some children (Quay, 1986).

Potential neurodevelopmental pathways to aggression.   Sugden, Kile, and Hendren (2006) suggest that different types of aggression can be linked to different diagnosable mental disorders: *impulsivity* in individuals with ADHD can lead to increased risk for accidents and self injury; *emotional instability* (bipolar, borderline, intermittent explosive disorder) can result in emotionally charged aggression; *irritability* (depressive disorders) may lead to aggressive acting out or self-destructive acts; *excessive anxiety* may result in low frustration tolerance leading to aggression; *disordered thinking* (substance abuse or thought disorders) may result in confused aggressive acts; while the *sensation seeking* of those with CD and ODD may result in a type of predatory aggression (p. 303). Given that these disorders relate to abnormalities in brain function in different regions of the brain and different neurotransmitter activity, the authors propose a model of aggression based on clinical experience and a review of the literature. The neurodevelopmental model involves 5 symptom domains:

- impulsivity (impulsive aggression related to behavioral inhibition)
- affect instability (emotional dysregulation: exaggerated responses to negative or frustrating stimuli)
- anxiety/hyperarousal (hypervigilance and overstimulation)
- cognitive disorganization (distorted perceptions, e.g., paranoia)
- predatory aggression (premeditated aggressive acts) (pp. 303–310)

In their article, the authors link each of the symptom domains to brain structure, function, and neuromodulators, ultimately suggesting that their model could be beneficial in more effective treatment selection. Future testing of the model should provide interesting information in this regard.

Psychodynamic Model

A psychodynamically oriented therapist might interpret aggressive and defiant behaviors as a manifestation of deep-seated feelings of lack of parental love, absence of empathy, and inability to trust (Gabbard, 1990). A proponent of ego psychology might want to pursue whether negativisitic and defiant behaviors are related to unconscious conflicts regarding issues of autonomy and control.

Behavioral Model

Within a behavioral framework, noncompliant and aggressive behaviors would develop in response to a prescribed set of learning principles. A clinician from a behaviorist perspective would attempt to isolate the factors in the environment responsible for reinforcing and sustaining the behavior. Within the family context, *coercion theory* (Patterson et al., 1991) might be used to explain how patterns of noncompliance and aggression have been sustained by the parents' repeated giving in to demands, ultimately getting caught in the **reinforcement trap**. Within the realm of social learning theory, parent/child interactions sustain maladaptive behaviors through the mechanism of *negative reinforcement*. In these interactions negative behaviors are attended to (reinforced) while positive behaviors are ignored (extinguished).

Barkley (1997) suggests a 4-factor model which can be used to explain the underlying processes which serve to maintain and increase noncompliant behavior. The model is well suited to understanding the underlying processes and in developing an intervention plan.

Putting It All Together

According to Barkley, predisposing and maintaining factors may include:

1. the *temperament of the child* (temperamental, high emotional reactivity, impulsive, active, inattentive)
2. *temperament of the parents* (immature, temperamental, and impulsive)
3. *child management patterns* (inconsistent, harsh, indiscriminate, and coercive parenting and poor monitoring of child activities)
4. *distressed family environment* (financial, health, and personal stressors)

Research has repeatedly demonstrated that the nature of parent–child interactions is a strong predictor of childhood noncompliant, defiant, and aggressive behavior patterns. Poor management practices due to ineffective, inconsistent, and indiscriminate parental controls often result in overly harsh but inconsistent discipline and inadequate monitoring of activities. As a result, child noncompliance becomes an effective means of avoidance or escape from doing undesirable tasks such as in requests to comply (e.g., picking up toys or cleaning a bedroom). Coercion theory would predict that in these situations, the parent will often respond with escalating and coercive responses (yelling, screaming, hitting) likely due to their occasional success. However, within this model, the child has learned how to successfully avoid unpleasant tasks on the one hand, while learning to model negative behaviors on the other.

Cognitive Model

Viewing hostile and aggressive behaviors from the vantage point of the cognitive perspective, emphasis would be placed on determining how maladaptive thoughts influence hostile and defiant behaviors. Studies by Dodge and colleagues (Dodge, 1991; Dodge & Coie, 1987; Dodge, Lochman, Harnish, Bates, & Pettit, 1997) have revealed that aggressive children often have a hostile attribution bias and misread ambivalent cues as being inherently hostile (e.g., a half smile is interpreted as a "sneer"), or rejecting. In these instances, children may respond in a hostile and defensive manner because they attribute hostile/rejection intentions to others.

Parenting and Attachment Models

A family systems clinician might focus on the parent–child relationship and childhood aggression may be interpreted as the child's attempt to shift the balance of power due to inconsistent or extreme boundaries or limit setting imposed by parents. With respect to theories of attachment and parenting, research evidence has linked insecure attachment to aggressive preschool behaviors (Erickson, Sroufe, & Egeland, 1985). Baumrind (1991) would suggest that an authoritarian parenting style could set the stage for latent aggression giving way to expression in the adolescent years.

Risks and Protective Factors

An overview of some of the factors that can increase the risk of developing disruptive behavior disorders is presented in Table 9.1 and has been compiled from studies discussed throughout this chapter.

In their investigation of *reactive and proactive aggression*, Brendgen, Vitaro, Tremblay, and Lavoie (2001) studied the moderating influence of parent monitoring parental warmth and caregiving behavior on the development of different aggressive pathways in 525 low SES boys at 13 years of age, and again at 16 and 17 years of age.

Table 9.1 Specific Risk Factors That Have Been Identified for Conduct Problems and Aggression

Level of Influence	Risk Factor	Protective Factor
Individual	Early aggression Neuropsychological deficits (impaired behavioral control/ behavioral inhibition) High emotional reactivity Fearless Low emotion regulation High emotionality (low threshold for arousal) Biological parent has clinical disorder (antisocial personality disorder, alcoholism, schizophrenia, mood disorders, ADHD) Low levels DBH	Connectedness to school Achievement
Microcosm	Avoidant attachment Caregiver depression Caregiver rejection Caregiver irritability, negativism, and criticism Low positive affect Family Stress Low caregiver sensitivity Low quality of caregiving Coercive parenting style	Caregiver warmth Caregiver monitoring
Exosystem	Social Economic Status	

Important Distinction

Proactive aggression has been described as "cold-blooded," requiring neither provocation nor anger, while *reactive aggression* has been described as a "hot-blooded," often defensive outburst of anger in response to a perceived threat or provocation.

The authors selected the target ages for assessments based on the rationale that aggression is well established by 13 years of age, and that violent delinquent behavior is at its peak during these latter years (Loeber & Hay, 1997). Measures of physical violence (16 years) and physical violence against a dating partner (17 years) were collected. Results supported the retention of proactive aggression and reactive aggression as two distinct constructs, with unique predictive pathways for later delinquency related to violence and dating violence. Results are summarized in Table 9.2.

The study supports earlier suggestions that lack of maternal (in this case, not paternal) warmth and caregiving can be indicative of poor parent–child attachment patterns that set the stage for creating negative expectations regarding relationship issues. In the case of negative reactive boys, negative attributions about relationships might serve to fuel the fire of their "hot-blooded" angry outbursts and unleash these behaviors towards their dating partner.

ODD and CD as risk factors.   In addition to studies looking at factors that place youth at greater risk or protecting youth from developing ODD and CD, studies have also investigated long-term outcomes for children who have been diagnosed with ODD and CD. Children with CD and ODD are at greater risk for development a wide range of negative outcomes, including school failure and school drop out, criminal activity, substance use and abuse, unemployment, and becoming inadequate parents (see Asher & Coie, 1998; Dishion, French, & Patterson, 1995; Loeber & Stouthamer-Loeber, 1998). While some of the risks may take an indirect route, others are directly related. For example, Clark, Parker, and Lynch (1999) found that disruptive behavior disorders were directly related to increased risk for developing substance use disorders in adolescence.

Longitudinal studies have looked at risk factors important in predicting continued aggressive behavior resulting in later delinquency and violence. Nagin and Tremblay (1999) found that approximately 4% to 5% of boys in their study who were aggressive in Kindergarten never learned to control and mange their aggressive behaviors by 17 years of age. Of this subgroup, one third were arrested by age 17, 90% were behind academically, and 40% were sexually active by 13 years of age. *Low maternal education* and *having a teenage mother* were the two risk factors that separated the highly aggressive continuation group from those whose aggressive behaviors subsided over time. Combined, these two risk factors increased the likelihood of highly aggressive behaviors more than 9 fold.

Table 9.2 Proactive and Reactive Aggression as Two Distinct Pathways

Pattern of Aggression (% in study)	Later Violence	Moderating Influence
Proactive aggression (28.8%)	Delinquent physical violence	Low parent monitoring/supervision
Reactive aggression (41.1%)	Violence against dating partner	Low maternal warmth and caregiving
No proactive aggression, and No reactive aggression (52.6%)	No delinquent physical violence No violence against dating partner	High parental monitoring and High maternal warmth and caregiving

Source: Brendgen et al., 2001, pp. 293–304.

Assessment

In their review of evidence-based assessment measures for conduct problems, McMahon and Frick (2005) emphasize that given the heterogeneity of behaviors associated with conduct problems (CP), a primary goal of assessment should be to identify the "number, types, and severity of the CP and the level of impairment that the CP is causing for the child or adolescent (e.g., school suspensions, police contacts, peer rejections)" (p. 479). Due to the complex nature of the problem, multiple methods of assessment are recommended, including interviews with parents, youth, and teachers; completion of appropriate behavioral rating scales by multiple informants; and the observation of the youth in different settings. In addition to the general structured and semistructured interview schedules and the behavioral rating scales previously discussed in chapter 5, a number of rating scales specifically targeting disruptive behaviors are presented in Table IB.1 in the introductory comments leading up to this chapter.

With respect to the general rating scales, in addition to elevations on scales for likely comorbid disorders, the following specific scales would be anticipated to have clinical or borderline clinical elevations for ODD and CD populations. On the *ASEBA* (Achenbach & Rescorla, 2001), children with ODD and CD will likely have elevated scores on the following syndrome scales: *Social Problems, Rule-Breaking Behavior, Aggressive Behavior, Externalizing Problems,* and *Total Problems.* The *DSM Oriented Scales* of the ASEBA will likely show elevations on ODD and CD. *Conner's* parent and teacher scales (CPSR, CTSR, 1998) would have elevations on the *Oppositional* and *Social Problem Scales,* while the **Conners–Wells'** adolescent self-report scale (CASS, 1997) would likely indicate *Family Problems, Conduct Problems,* and problems with *Anger Control.* On the **Behavior Assessment System for Children** (BASC2; Reynolds & Kamphaus, 2004) the *Aggression, Conduct Problems,* and *Composite Externalizing Problems Scales* would indicate elevations in the at-risk to clinical ranges.

Treatment and Intervention

One of the problems in finding evidence-based treatments specifically for ODD or CD has been that initial tendencies were to consider ODD as a precursor to CD and for interventions to target the broad category of "disruptive behavior disorders." Brestan and Eyberg (1998) reviewed and evaluated 82 studies involving more than 5,000 youth with ODD and CD according to criteria established by the APA Task Force on evidence-based treatments. The majority of programs reviewed were based on cognitive behavioral methods, and included children alone or children and parents.

Think About It

Brestan and Eyberg (1998) conclude that parent training might be better suited for the youngest children and that cognitive behavioral techniques might be more appropriate for older children. However, it has also been suggested that including parents in the school-aged programs may be better than either treatment alone (Kazdin, Siegel, & Bass, 1992).

Brystan and Eyberg (1998) found two programs which met the criteria for *Well Established Psychosocial Interventions,* a parent-training program developed to reduce behavior problems in young children (Webster-Stratton, 1984) and a behavioral parent-training program based on a manual called *Living with Children* produced by Patterson and Guillion (1968). The manual provides lesson plans for parents directed towards improving skills in areas of prioritizing and targeting behaviors for intervention and developing reinforcement programs to reduce unwanted and increase desirable behaviors. In the *Probably Efficacious Treatment category*, Brestan and Eyberg found programs developed to improve children's problem solving skills (Kazdin, Esveldt-Dawson, French, & Unis, 1987) and targeting anger control (Lochman, Burch, Curry, & Lampron, 1984).

The *Problem Solving–Skills Training* (PSST; Kazdin, 1996) is a 20-session program (45-minute sessions) in which children are taught how to solve problems in a highly predictable and logical manner, including problem definition, goal identification, generating, evaluating and selecting the best options, and evaluating the outcome. Skills are applied and practiced in role playing and therapeutic games.

Coping power (Larson & Lochman, 2002) has been expanded from the original 12-session format to a 33-session program developed to promote anger control.

Oppositional Defiant Disorder

Intervention programs for ODD have met with significant difficulties due to the complex nature of this highly comorbid disorder, stability/persistence of the disorder, and resistance to intervention (Rey, 1993). In addition, many programs have failed to address contextual factors which impact on high risk families (Kazdin, 1995). As was noted earlier, programs specific to ODD have recently begun to attract increased attention. (This following information on intervention will follow Greene, Ablon, Goring, Fazio, & Morse, 2003, unless otherwise noted.) In their review of existing interventions for ODD, Green and colleagues (2003) emphasize the limitations of parent training (PT) and behavioral family therapy programs cited earlier by Brestan and Eyeberg (1998), namely that these programs have focused almost exclusively on changing parenting practices. Given that these families are often highly stressed, parents often have difficulty complying with training requirements and attrition rates are high. Therefore, results often present a bias picture of only the most motivated who completed the program, and even among this population, changes are statistically significant, but not necessarily clinically significant (Kazdin, 1993).

Memory Bank

Kazdin (1993) and others have argued that it is important to demonstrate clinical, as well as statistical, change. If a child improves in a statistically significant way, but remains in the clinical range, then the change is not clinically significant.

Based on the above reasoning, Green and colleagues (2003) suggest that interventions for ODD should also include alternative models, such as targeting cognitive factors like cognitive distortions and deficiencies evident in children with ODD. In this regard, the authors draw attention to the category of *Probably Efficacious Interventions* for problem solving (Kazdin et al., 1987); anger management (Ecton & Feindler, 1990; Lochman & Wells, 2002); and multisystemic therapy (MST; Henggeler et al., 1992).

Based on their belief of the need to incorporate cognitive components in the intervention program for ODD, and the underlying premise that ODD behaviors are largely a byproduct of an *incompatibility between parent and child characteristics*, the authors (Greene et al., 2003) have developed an alternative intervention program. In this program, Greene and colleagues address deficiencies in the ODD child's processing in areas of emotion regulation, frustration tolerance, problem-solving, and flexibility. The program is called *Collaborative problem solving* (CPS; Greene, 2001; Green & Ablon, 2004; Green, Ablon, & Goring, 2003). The CPS program is designed to increase parent awareness of the underlying parent/child characteristics that propel the ODD behavior through the development of three strategies to manage behaviors.

Memory Bank

The three strategies Greene and colleagues (2003) incorporate in their CPS program are:
1. Imposition of adult will;
2. Collaborative problem solving; and
3. Removal of unmet expectations.

Empirical investigations comparing the CPS program to Parent Training (PT), using Barkley's defiant youth program (Barkley, 1997), revealed superior short-term and long-term improvement for ODD children which was statistically and clinically significant.

Conduct Disorder

Children and youth with serious emotional and behavioral disorders have been serviced by a continuum of care from the least restrictive (outpatient) to most restrictive (residential treatment centers; RTC) alternatives. Until recently, the majority of empirical support for treatment effectiveness has come mainly from clinic-based analogue-type studies, and research concerning community based alternatives had been minimal (Weisz et al., 1995). Despite the extensive use of RTC placements for the most severely disordered youth, empirical evidence has been minimal and lacking in experimental controls (Blotcky et al., 1984; USDHSS, 1999).

Home-based alternatives, such as family preservation programs, also have suffered from a lack of empirical support (Littell & Schuerman, 1995), or have demonstrated inconsistent outcomes (Meezan & McCroskey, 1996). Yet studies of the effectiveness of multisystemic therapy (MST) have demonstrated that providing services in the community can be successful for juvenile offenders (Henggeler & Borduin, 1990; Schoenwald, Borduin, & Henggeler, 1998), compared to hospitalization as an alternative (Schoenwald et al., 2000). Success of the MST approach, which focuses on multiple determinants of deviant behavior, has been attributed to ecological validity (community outreach) and cognitive/behavioral methods (Schoenwald et al., 1998).

Other community-based alternatives, which have been supported empirically, include comparisons by Chamberlain and Reid (1991, 1998) of the success of juveniles placed in specialized foster care programs (SFC) using methods developed by Patterson, Reid, Jones, and Conger (1975) compared to juveniles assigned to RTCs. In another study, Wilmshurst (2002) found that youth with severe emotional and behavioral disorders (EBD) who were randomly assigned to a community-based family preservation program (using cognitive behavioral methods) made significant gains (statistically and clinically) compared to peers assigned to a 5–day residential alternative.

In their review of treatment programs for youth with conduct problems, McMahon and Kotler (2004) stress the need to include family in the assessment and intervention process due to significant influence of the family in precipitating and maintaining the conduct problems. The authors select several programs for discussion, among them, programs in Oregon designed by Patterson and colleagues, Functional Family Therapy and Multisystemic Therapy. (For a more extensive review, see McMahon & Kotler, 2004).

Oregon Social Learning Center (OSLC) parent training programs. The program developed by Gerald Patterson and colleagues (1975) was one of the *Well Established Programs* identified by

Brestan and Eyberg's (1998) extensive review. The program has been extensively researched and replicated and found to be successfully modified as an intervention for families with younger children (2.5–6.5 years), older children (6.5–12.5 years) and adolescents (Bank, Marlowe, Reid, Patterson, & Weinrott, 1991; Forgatch & Patterson, 1989) and in conditions that reduced family treatment time from 31 hours to 13 to 16 hours (Dishion & Patterson, 1992; Patterson, Cobb, & Ray, 1973; Weinrott, Bauske, & Patterson, 1979). The program focuses on assisting parents in targeting and tracking specific behaviors, and then developing reinforcement systems (point systems, contingency plans) to increase positive and decrease negative behaviors. Parents are trained to improve problem solving and negotiation strategies.

Functional family therapy (FFT).   Alexander and colleagues (Alexander & Parsons, 1982; Barton & Alexander, 1981) have developed an extensive family-based intervention plan which combines family systems and behavioral approaches. The three-stage program focuses on *engagement/motivation phase* (initiation and education regarding awareness of negative attributions); *behavior change phase* (application); and *generalization phase* (evaluation, monitoring, and disengaging of the therapeutic alliance). Recent empirical investigations have demonstrated that the program can be an effective home-based alternative to clinic treatment (Gordon, Graves, & Arbuthnot, 1995).

Multisystemic therapy (MST).   Henggeler and colleagues (1998) have developed a manualized multidimensional program for working with juveniles in their community involving family, schools, and peers. The multimodal program is a strengths-based approach to family empowerment and uses a wide variety of techniques: family therapy, cognitive, and behavioral approaches (contingency management, anger management, etc.). The MST approach has been researched extensively and there is wide empirical support for the use of MST across a wide variety of serious juvenile problems: sexual offenders, chronic offenders, violent offenders, and youth with comorbid substance use and abuse (Henggeler & Borduin, 1990; Schoenwald et al., 1998; Schoenwald, Brown, & Henggeler, 2000).

CHAPTER SUMMARY AND REVIEW

Instrumental aggression peaks at about 2 years of age and is replaced by increasing ability to negotiate verbally. Aggressive, *early starters* have the most negative developmental trajectories and tend to be those who demonstrate problems with *emotion regulation* and *self-control*. Approximately half of aggressive children vacillate between **proactive aggression**, "cold-blooded" acts of violence in the absence of provocation, and **reactive aggression**, "hot-blooded" and defensive responses to perceived threat or provocation. Children who demonstrate *proactive aggressive patterns* tend to have life persistent problems, although youth who engage primarily in *reactive aggressive patterns* have the worst long-term outcomes for dating violence. Maternal warmth, attachment, and positive caregiving can moderate the effects of reactive aggression, while parental monitoring and supervision can significantly reduce the possibility of proactive aggression. Several other risk factors for aggressive behaviors have been identified, including child characteristics (*hyperactivity, difficult temperament, low inhibition*) and environmental characteristics (*coercive parenting practices, maternal depression/rejection, familial stressors, low SES, poverty, and neighborhood risk*).

1. **Developmental Trajectories**
    Developmentally, *instrumental aggression* is a precursor to *hostile aggression*. Aggression is a relatively stable characteristic and early aggressive onset is associated with the most

negative long-term outcomes. Poor emotion regulation and heightened responsiveness to emotional stimuli are two characteristics that predict poor social adaptation. The combination results in particularly poor social outcomes for children with externalizing behaviors since they tend to overreact in a disruptive way to both negative as well as positive charged situations. Individuals who are reactively aggressive are at greater risk for internalizing disorders, depression, and suicide attempts.

2. **Bullying**

   Aggression can take the form of *relational aggression* (females tend to target a victim's personal relationships: e.g., rumor spreading, isolation), or aggression might result from a misperception of threat, as in a *hostile attribution bias.* Repeated acts of aggression or victimization (physical, verbal, or psychological abuse) are the result of bullying; a practice that is all too common.

3. **Disruptive Behavior Disorders: ODD and CD**

   Two disruptive behavior disorders are recognized by the *DSM–IV-TR* (2000): oppositional defiant disorder (ODD) and conduct disorder (CD). Of the two disorders, CD is the most serious and 90% of youth with CD had an initial diagnosis of ODD. While children with ODD can be annoying, hostile, and defiant, youth with CD engage in overt and covert behaviors (aggression, destruction of property, deceit or theft, and rule violations) that target and violate social norms or the rights of others. Researchers have isolated a number of different subtypes of CD. Age of onset for ODD is typically younger than CD and approximately one quarter of youth with ODD will develop CD.

4. **Etiology, Risks, Protective Factors, and Treatment**

   Brain-based deficits (decreased activity in frontal lobe), genetic transmission, and chemical imbalance have all been linked to increased risk for aggressive behavior, as have environmental factors, such as poverty, stress, and parenting practices. Youth with behavior disorders are at increased risk for development substance use disorders, school drop out, and delinquent behaviors. Treatments have focused on parent training, collaborative problem solving, and multisystemic programs.

Consolidate and Communicate

1. Bullying behaviors involve a bully and a victim. What are some of the main differences between males and females in their bullying behaviors and response to victimization? Do an Internet search and find out information that addresses the following questions:
   a. What are some of the current statistics on bullying in the schools today?
   b. Do these numbers represent increases or decreases from previous statistics?
   c. What are some of the most successful contemporary treatment programs for the intervention and prevention of bullying behaviors?
   d. Is bullying primarily a North American problem? If so, why do you think this is so? If not, what does that say about the phenomenon?

2. Self-control and emotion regulation are pivotal factors in the development of prosocial and aggressive behaviors. Discuss this statement and include the following terms in your discussion: empathy, instrumental aggression, actor as agent, low emotionality, high emotionality, social adaptation, internalizing and externalizing behaviors.

3. There has been a discussion as to whether ODD and CD represent a continuum of disordered behavior with ODD being a precursor to CD. Discuss ways in which the two disorders conform to a continuum theory and why they may be better represented as two distinct disorders. Be sure to include Frick's research findings in your response.

4. Research has determined a number of subtypes of CD. Discuss the various subtypes and the outcomes for these various forms of behavioral disorders.
5. Bill is a 15-year-old boy who is very aggressive. He has been this way since early preschool. John is also 15 and he has become more aggressive in the past year. Based on your understanding of the research, what would be predicted about future outcomes for Bill and John?
6. John is watching television and his mother is trying to prepare dinner in the kitchen. She calls out from the kitchen and asks John to bring her a big roasting pan from the storage room in the basement. John is intent on watching his program so he ignores her first request. In a few minutes his mother yells again. John continues to ignore her. His mother comes into the living room and begins the all too familiar scenario:

Mom: I told you to get me the pan.
John: I'm watching something.
Mom: I need the pan now.
John: I'll get it in a minute.
Mom: I want it now.
John: Go get it yourself, then.
Mom: (Stomps over and turns the TV off in the middle of the show.)
John: (Throws the remote on the floor and swears at his mother.)
Mom: Don't you use that tone with me. Go to your room.
John: You go to your room. (Gets up and turns the TV back on.)
Mom: (Turns it off, and so on and so on, until John leaves the house and slams the door behind him.)

Barkley (1997) proposes a 4-factor model for understanding the underlying process that maintains and increases noncompliant behavior. Using this model, explain how John and his mother get into very serious battles that seemingly start over nothing but escalate way out of proportion to the initial situation.

Chapter Review Questions

1. According to Zahn-Waxler and colleagues (1992), empathic awareness and responsiveness unfolds in three stages. Which of the following is not one of the stages?
   a. a primitive contagion response
   b. actor/observer bias
   c. development of purposeful helping behaviors
   d. ability to take perspective of another
2. Which of the following is FALSE regarding early starters?
   a. Early starters have increased aggressive responses that are durable throughout childhood.
   b. Early starters tend to have a history of avoidant attachment.
   c. Early starters are at greater risk for developing disruptive behavior disorders.
   d. Early starters are associated with highest levels of parent sensitivity.
3. Which of the following statements is FALSE regarding the normal trajectory of aggressive behavior?
   a. Instrumental aggression peaks at about 2 years of age.
   b. In middle school, aggressive acts are often for self-vindication or revenge.
   c. Hitting, pushing, and shoving occur developmentally prior to verbal insults.
   d. For the majority overt aggression is a stable pattern from middle school to adolescence.

4. In their study of positive and negatively charged situations, Rydell and colleagues (2003) found all of the following results, except:
   a. internalizing children reacted with avoidance to high negative situations
   b. externalizing children reacted with aggression to high negative situations
   c. internalizing children emitted disruptive behaviors to high positive situations
   d. externalizing children emitted disruptive behaviors to high positive situations
5. Sam hits Joey because he thinks that Joey is going to hit him. Joey is shocked because he just turned around to look at the clock on the wall behind Sam. Sam's behavior is likely the result of:
   a. relational aggression
   b. hostile attribution bias
   c. instrumental aggression
   d. bullying
6. Which of the following behaviors is an example of a covert destructive behavior (Frick et al., 1993)?
   a. vandalism
   b. truancy
   c. bullying
   d. stubborness
7. Loeber and Keenan (1994) suggest a number of potential subtypes of CD. Which of the following was most likely to have the best outcomes?
   a. authority conflict pathway
   b. covert pathway
   c. dual overt/covert pathway
   d. overt pathway
8. Neurological investigations have found _____ in aggressive youth.
   a. increased frontal lobe activity
   b. high levels of DBH
   c. decreased frontal lobe activity
   d. low levels of hormone testosterone
9. Green and colleagues (2003) argue that parent/child compatibility is often at the root of noncompliance and have designed an intervention program to correct for this called:
   a. Coping Power
   b. Collaborative Problem Solving
   c. Coping Cat
   d. Coercive Corrections
10. Which of the following intervention program has not been demonstrated to be effective with youth who have disruptive behavior disorders?
    a. Multisystemic Therapy
    b. Functional Family Therapy
    c. OSLC Parent Training Programs
    d. Psychodynamic Therapy for Disturbed Youth

Glossary of New Terms

proactive aggression/cold-blooded
reactive aggression/hot-blooded
early starters
oppositional defiant disorder (ODD)

conduct disorder (CD)
instrumental aggression
interpersonal aggression
hostile aggression
emotion dysregulation
negative emotionality
fearful/fearless
overcontrolled/undercontrolled
emotionality
high or low emotion regulation
social adaptation
high emotionality
low inhibition
maternal depression
relational aggression
hostile attribution bias
coercion theory
physical bullying
verbal bullying
psychological bullying
intentional isolation
overt and nondestructive
overt and destructive
transient oppositional behavior
negative schema
transactional patterns
violation of social norms
violation of the rights of others
CD: childhood onset
CD: adolescent onset
authority conflict pathway
covert pathway
overt pathway
dual overt/covert
triple pathway
callous and unemotional (CU)
reinforcement trap
insecure attachment

Answers to Multiple Choice Questions:
1. b; 2. d; 3, d; 4. c; 5. b; 6. a; 7. a; 8. c; 9. b; 10. b.

II
Problems of Attention and Learning
An Introduction

Although any decision to cluster problems together for purposes of discussion is in some sense arbitrary, the decision to discuss attention disorders within the same section as specific learning disabilities (SLD) is a conscious decision. For example while the *DSM-IV* (APA, 2000) clusters attention deficit hyperactivity disorder (ADHD) next to the disruptive behavior disorders, the manual also clarifies that the alignment between the disruptive disorders and ADHD is primarily the result of associations between these disorders and ADHD subtypes of the impulsive hyperactive type and the combined type. The argument is equally and perhaps more compelling to align ADHD with the Learning Disorders, since children and youth who have ADHD often experience significant learning problems and depending on the population sampled and measures used comorbid rates between ADHD and SLD have been reported to be as high as 45% (Dykman & Acherman, 1992; Semrud-Clikeman et al., 1992).

Another important reason for discussing ADHD and SLD in the same section is that from a developmental perspective, children with ADHD, inattentive type and SLD are not recognized as having difficulties until the onset of school-related problems. Children with ADHD and SLD do not necessarily stand out in the family context or on the playground. Since these children often demonstrate average intellect in other aspects of their life, lack of school success may be misinterpreted as laziness, immaturity or lack of motivation. Often by the time the real reason for their failure is discovered, these children have suffered significant losses in self esteem.

In addition to experiencing significant academic difficulties due to problems processing, attending to, or recalling information, these children also often encounter problems socially resulting from an inability to read or attend sufficiently to social cues. High rates of social problems are evident for children who have ADHD or SLD. In one study as many as 50% of those with ADHD (Pelham & Bender, 1982) and 70% of those with SLD (Kavale & Forness, 1996) experienced social difficulties.

10

Attention Deficit Hyperactivity Disorder (ADHD)

CHAPTER PREVIEW

Our understanding of attention deficit hyperactivity disorder (ADHD) has increased substantially over the past 30 years. Yet, there is still considerably more to learn about this disorder that occurs in between 3% and 9% of the population. Controversy has existed over the years as to whether ADHD should be considered as a single disorder consisting of a multitude of symptom presentations, or whether the disorder should be classified into subtypes based on symptom clusters of inattentive, hyperactive, or impulsive behaviors. Currently, the *DSM–IV–TR* (2000) recognizes three subtypes of ADHD: ADHD, primarily inattentive type;

ADHD, primarily hyperactive impulsive type; and ADHD, combined type (satisfies criteria for both inattentive and hyperactive/impulsive). A fourth category, ADHD NOS (not otherwise specified), is used to classify atypical cases such as those with sluggish tempo. All variants of ADHD have onset prior to 7 years of age, are pervasive across situations, and must be evident for at least 6 months. Symptom presentations differ depending on the nature of the symptoms and the child's developmental level.

1. ADHD Primarily Inattentive Type

The DSM (2000) requires six symptoms for classification in this category from a potential list of nine symptoms, including: *problems sustaining attention, poor attention to details, distractibility, poor follow through, disorganization, forgetful, loss of necessary materials, appears to not listen, poor ability to sustain focus, and disorganization.* This type of ADHD is diagnosed less than other forms, is less visible, and manifests in school-related problems. There is some research to support that females with ADHD are primarily of the inattentive type.

2. ADHD Primarily Hyperactive Impulsive Type

Six symptoms are required from a potential list of six symptoms of hyperactivity (*fidgety, problems staying seated, excess movement, loud play, on the go, incessant talking*) and three symptoms of impulsivity (*blurts out answers, problem with turn-taking, intrusive*). This type of ADHD is diagnosed earlier (3 years of age) and significantly more often (90% of all ADHD). These children experience problems socially and academically.

3. ADHD Combined Type

As might be anticipated, these children who meet the criteria for both the inattentive type and the hyperactive impulsive type are the most severe due to the number and nature of the symptoms.

4. ADHD in Developmental Context

As a diagnostic guide, the *DSM* criteria (2000) are the most appropriate for children 6–12 years of age and less appropriate for younger or older (adolescent) populations. Early predictors for ADHD include difficult temperament, excess activity, poor sleep patterns, and irritability. By school age, young children with ADHD may be misunderstood as being unmotivated or lazy, often recognized as being off task, out of their seats, or daydreaming during lessons. Work is often incomplete and homework is often lost or forgotten. Children may be accident prone and also experience problems engaging and disengaging from tasks. Teenagers are involved in more traffic accidents and experiences significant difficulties in response to increased demands academically and socially.

5. ADHD and Comorbidity

Approximately two thirds of children with ADHD have another comorbid disorder. Rates vary depending on the nature of the sample (clinic or community) and measurements. As many as 30% repeat a grade, while anywhere from 16% to 45% have specific learning disabilities. Internalizing disorders such as depression and anxiety are highly represented in this population (30%–35%), while even higher levels (50%) have been noted for comorbid conduct problems. Other comorbid associations include substance use/abuse, social problems, and sleep problems.

6. Etiology

Increased technological advances have contributed to our understanding of the different brain structures (frontal system, cingulated gyrus) and functions that are involved in individuals with ADHD and the role of the catecholamines (dopamine, norepinephrine, epinephrine) associated with attention and motor activity. Genetic transmission is also prominent in the profiles of individuals with ADHD. Investigations of the role of executive functions and arousal level have contributed significantly to understanding of deficits that reduce the efficiency of individuals with ADHD. Barkley's (1997) model provides a framework for understanding the impulsive/hyperactive type of ADHD.

7. Diagnosis, Assessment, and Treatment

Several instruments are available to assist our understanding of how symptoms of ADHD manifest behaviorally and with respect to cognitive processing. Rating scales can provide benchmarks for ADHD symptoms (inattention, impulsivity, hyperactivity), any comorbid features, and provide an inventory of executive function. Other assessment instruments can evaluate processing difficulties and problem solving skills or deficits. Treatments have primarily focused on stimulant medications or a newly added nonstimulant (strattera), behavioral therapy, or combinations of the two.

Historical Background and Clinical Description of the Disorder

Classification of ADHD: Historical Perspective

Despite the fact that **Attention Deficit Hyperactivity Disorder (ADHD)** is among the most prevalent disorders in childhood and adolescence, a complete understanding of the nature of the disorder has challenged professionals over the past 100 years. In recent years, ADHD has been a topic for much discussion, publications, controversy, and concern regarding the possible over diagnosis of the disorder and subsequently overprescribing of stimulant medications (Angier, 1994; Diller, 1996). Through advances in technology, our conceptual understanding of the disorder has evolved significantly from an initial suggestion that the disorder represented a *Morbid Defect of Moral Control* (1902) to a growing understanding of disorder subtypes and greater insight into the potential genetic and neurological basis of the disorder.

Historically, the disorder has appeared under a number of different guises, including hyperkinesis, hyperkinetic syndrome, minimal brain dysfunction (MBD), attention deficit disorder, with ADDH, with or without hyperactivity (ADD), attention deficit hyperactivity disorder (ADHD), and currently, attention-deficit/hyperactivity disorder (AD/HD), although the latter designation is often simplified to ADHD in the literature. A historical look at the changing ways in which the disorder has been conceptualized by researchers and the *DSM* can be found in Table 10.1.

Although early speculation considered ADHD-type symptoms to be the result of some form of atypical brain function or brain damage (**postencephalitic behavior disorder; minimal brain dysfunction, MBD**), given the lack of sophisticated resources, at the time, research efforts failed to find evidence for any actual brain damage. As a result, this line of reasoning was abandoned in favor of conceptualizing ADHD as an extreme form of temperament in children. By the time the *DSM* was revised, (*DSM–II*; APA, 1968), the manual included **hyperkinetic reaction of childhood**, a new diagnostic category based on symptoms of "overactivity, restlessness, distractibility, and short attention span" (p. 50). The disorder was thought to be restricted to childhood and resolved by adolescence.

Table 10.1 A Historical Look at ADHD

Year	Characteristics of ADHD
1865	German physician Heinrich Hoffman describes character of *Fidgety Phil*.
1902	Still presents a series of lectures to the Royal College of Physicians regarding a number of children in his clinical practice that displayed what he called a *"Morbid Defect of Moral Control."*
1920s	Encephalitis epidemic (1917–1918) led to linking ADHD-type symptoms of inattention and poor self-control to brain damage resulting in *postencephalitic behavior disorder*.
1930s–1940s	The concept of *Minimal Brain Dysfunction* (*MBD*) is introduced. Levin suggests inattentive and restless behaviors could result from frontal lobe lesions. Investigators research several other potential sources of *Brain Damage*, such as birth trauma, epilepsy, head injury, lead toxicity. Investigators turn to medication (amphetamines) trials for treatment.
1950s–1960s	**DSM–II:** *Hyperkinetic reaction of childhood disorder* (1968). Lack of research support for finding actual brain damage in many children with ADHD-type symptoms, and overinclusiveness of the concept of MBD, led to further refinement and conceptualization. Chess (1960) considers the symptoms as a more extreme variant of temperament in young children. DSM characterized the disorder as "overactivity, restlessness, distractibility and short attention span" (p. 50), which was usually resolved prior to adolescence.
1956	Ritalin a form of methyl-phenidate is marketed as a stimulant treatment for overactivity and short attention span.
1970s	Douglas and her research teams at McGill University (Quebec, Canada) developed a model for ADHD which included increased emphasis on attention deficits, or problems of sustained attention, in hyperactive children.
1975	Feingold promotes the theory that hyperactivity develops from food additives and the popular Feingold Diet is launched as an alternative to medications, in the wake of growing criticism regarding overprescribing for children.
1980	**DSM–III:** *Attention deficit disorder* (*ADD*), with and without hyperactivity replaces hyperkinetic reaction disorder, with a shift in emphasis from hyperactivity to core problems of sustained attention and impulse control as additional defining features of subtypes of the disorder. Three separate lists of symptoms and defining criteria were stipulated: inattention (3 of 5 symptoms); impulsivity (3 of 6 symptoms); and hyperactivity (2 of 5 symptoms).
1987	**DSM–IIIR:** *Attention deficit hyperactivity disorder* (*ADHD*): Controversy stemming from lack of research support for subtyping the disorder results in reversion to a single symptom list (prioritized based on field trials) from which 8 of 14 symptoms must be present. Fidgeting, problems remaining seated, and ease of distraction are the top 3 symptoms.
1994 (*DSM–IV*)/ 2000 (*DSM–IV–TR*)	**DSM–IV–TR:** *Attention deficit/hyperactivity disorder* (*AD/HD*): Currently, the DSM recognizes disorder subtypes (predominantly inattentive; predominantly hyperactive/impulsive; or combined) based on symptom criteria. The disorder is described as a "persistent pattern of inattention and/or hyperactivity/impulsivity that is more frequently displayed and more severe than is typically observed in individuals at a comparable level of development" (*DSM–IV–TR*, p. 84). Other criteria include: onset prior to age seven; causes impairment in at least two situations (e.g., home and school); and symptoms not better accounted for by another disorder (e.g., mental retardation).

The main conceptual challenge in the past 30 years has been how to reconcile the debate whether ADHD represents one disorder with two subtypes: inattentive or hyperactive impulsive types; whether the subtypes actually represent different disorders; or whether ADHD represents a single disorder with many variations in presentation. The *DSM–III* (1980) designated the disorder as having two variants, attention deficit disorder without hyperactivity (ADD; a disorder featuring problems in sustained attention), or attention deficit disorder with hyperactivity (ADDH) to reflect individuals who demonstrated the combined symptom cluster of problems of sustained attention and lack of impulse control. However, by the time the manual was revised 7 years later

(*DSM–III–R;*APA, 1987), ADHD was again represented as a single disorder with one symptom list. Eight of 14 symptoms were required for a diagnosis with symptoms describing various forms of impulsivity, overactivity, and inattention.

According to the most recent revision of the *DSM* (APA, 2000), ADHD is best represented by three subtypes that can be identified based on the degree to which the child demonstrates three core features of the disorder: *inattention, hyperactivity, and impulsivity.* The three subtypes are:

1. **Attention deficit disorder, primarily inattentive type**
2. **Attention deficit disorder, primarily hyperactive/impulsive type**
3. **Attention deficit disorder, combined type**

A fourth derivation, ADHD NOS (not otherwise specified), is reserved for atypical cases with prominent symptoms, but that do not conform to strict diagnostic guidelines, such as onset after 7 years of age or with inattention accompanied by *hypoactive* behavior patterns (e.g., "sluggishness and daydreaming," p. 93).

Case in Point

Reggie is not doing well in school. His teacher is convinced that he is just not trying. He doesn't listen and he rarely completes work in class time. When work is done, Reggie often misses important details. What is turned in is often incomplete. Furthermore, he is constantly losing pencils and paper, and his binder is a mess. Reggie has many symptoms of ADHD, inattentive type.

Current Classification DSM-IV-TR *(APA, 2000)*

Attention Deficit Disorder: Primarily Inattentive Type

According to the current diagnostic criteria, the *inattentive type* must have 6 of a possible 9 symptoms evident prior to 7 years of age. The symptoms must have persisted for at least 6 months, cause significant impairment, be in excess of developmental expectations, and occur in more than one setting (e.g., home and school). The 9 symptoms include:

- careless attention to details
- problems sustaining attention over time
- does not appear to listen
- poor follow through (school work, homework, chores)
- poorly organized
- poor ability to sustained mental attention (e.g., homework, independent seatwork at school)
- loses necessary materials (e.g., pencils, notebooks, assignment sheets, homework)
- easily distracted
- forgetful

Science Talks

A recent study of approximately 300 children with ADHD found that while children with the Inattentive Type of ADHD tended to have less severe overall impairments in functioning than the Combined Type, inattentive children demonstrated more: comorbid internalizing disorders, academic difficulties, learning disabilities, and were between 2 and 5 times more likely to also be referred for speech and language problems (Weiss, Worling, & Wasdell, 2003).

Attention Deficit Disorder: Primarily Hyperactive/Impulsive Type

According to the current diagnostic criteria, the *hyperactive/impulsive type* must have 6 of a possible 9 symptoms which have persisted for at least 6 months, cause significant impairment, be in excess of developmental expectations and occur in more than one setting (e.g., home and school). Once again, symptom onset must be prior to 7 years of age. The 9 symptoms include:

Hyperactivity
- fidgety or squirmy
- problems remaining seated
- excessive motion
- problems engaging in quiet play
- constantly on the go
- incessant talking

Impulsivity
- blurts out answers, comments
- impatient, problems with turn-taking
- intrusive to others

Attention Deficit Disorder: Combined Type

The *combined type* matches criteria for both the *inattentive type* and the *hyperactive/impulsive type* (the combined type diagnosis requires a total of 12 symptoms: 6 symptoms from the hyperactive/impulsive cluster and 6 symptoms from the inattentive list). However, Barkley (1998) has questioned whether the combined type shares the same nature of inattentive behaviors as the inattentive type. According to Barkley, while the inattentive type is characterized by a "sluggish" information processing style and problems with **focused/selective attention**, the combined type encounters more difficulties with **sustained attention** and **task persistence** *due to ease of distractibility*. The future diagnostic possibility of considering these 2 subtypes as distinct and separate disorders remains to be seen.

Important Distinction

Barkley (1998) cautions clinicians and researchers to use greater vigilance in the diagnosis of these separate subtypes of disorders, especially in adolescent and adult populatons where there is a decline in overt overactivity due to age.

Prevalence

> **Memory Bank**
>
> There can be wide variations in prevalence rates reported for the majority of disorders based on whether the samples are drawn from a clinical or general population, and the method used to classify the disorder. Unless otherwise stated, all prevalence data reported in this text will refer to data noted in the *DSM–IV-TR* (APA, 2000).

Prevalence rates reported in the *DSM–IV–TR* (APA, 2000) suggest a 3%–7% range for the total population of school-aged children. However, the vast majority of children (90%) who are diagnosed with ADHD will have the more obvious form of ADHD-hyperactive/impulsive type or the combined type. Children with the more subtle ADHD-inattentive type are identified at later chronological ages and at a far lesser rate. Of children identified with ADHD, 1 in 10 will be diagnosed with the inattentive type. Actual comparisons of prevalence rates for the inattentive type relative to hyperactive/impulsive and combined types are problematic, since many more children with the inattentive type can go undiagnosed because of the subtle nature of this subtype.

Prevalence and gender.   Whether there are male–female differences in the subtypes of ADHD symptoms continues to be an area of debate. The ratio of males to females has been reported anywhere from 2:1 to 9:1. There is a question of whether there are gender links to specific subtypes of ADHD, although at present this remains unclear. While one recent study revealed that females were twice as likely as males to demonstrate the inattentive type of ADHD (Biederman, Mick, & Faraone, 2002), the generalizability of these findings has been challenged on the grounds that the difference could be accounted for by the fact that this female sample was less impaired than the males overall, and demonstrated fewer behavior and learning problems (Goldstein & Gordon, 2003). However, although females with ADHD are not as likely to be referred as males, there is evidence that, as a whole, females diagnosed with ADHD may be more vulnerable on a number of levels, including self-reports of comorbid anxiety and depression (Rucklidge & Tannock, 2001).

> **Science Talks**
>
> Research findings regarding gender and ADHD subtypes continue to present conflicting results. A recent review of clinical data for 143 Inattentive and 133 combined type presentations revealed that children who had the Inattentive Type were more likely to be female (Weiss et al., 2003); a finding that could be seen to support results obtained by Biederman et al. (2002).

Development in Focus

The core symptoms of ADHD emerge within different developmental time frames. While hyperactivity/impulsivity may be evident as early as 3 years of age, problems of inattention may not be recognizable until the child is engaged in formal schooling (6 or 7 years of age, or as late as 10–11 years).

Developmental Considerations and Associated Features

In addition to variations in symptom onset, symptoms may also appear different, developmentally. Research has demonstrated that while **disinhibition** and **lack of self-control** are likely to improve with age, problems of inattention remain relatively stable across the developmental spectrum (Hart, Lahey, Loeber, Applegate, & Frick, 1995). The current *DSM* symptom criteria were based on field trials of children 5 to 16 years of age. The question has also been posed regarding the reliability and appropriateness of applying these symptoms to populations outside of this age range (e.g., preschool children or young adults). Studies by Murphy and Barkley (1996) suggest that the thresholds established for children were too high for the adult populations,and likely too low for preschool children.

Children who experience problems with *overactivity, impulsivity,* and *inattention* will encounter different types of problems relative to the nature of developmental tasks emphasized at a given stage of development.

Science Talks

Can excessive early TV viewing be linked to ADHD? Researchers have found that television exposure at ages 1 to 3 years is associated with attention problems at age 7. In fact, they found that each hour of daily viewing increased the risk of ADHD by almost 10% at age 7. As a result, the authors suggest limiting exposure to television viewing in the formative years of brain development (Christakis, Zimmerman, DiGiuseppe, & McCarty, 2004).

While a diagnosis of ADHD is very difficult prior to 3 years of age, retrospective interviews have revealed early warning signs that may indicate increased risk for ADHD in later years.

Birth to 1 year. There is wide variability in infant response to stimulation. While some infants respond to caregiver touch and physical pressure in a positive way, other infants may overreact to excessive stimulation. Some infants who have difficult temperaments may be at greater risk for developing ADHD later on, especially if the difficult behaviors include: *excessive activity, poor sleep patterns, difficult to soothe,* and *irritability* (Barkley, 1998). A greater incidence of sleep difficulties has been reported as early as infancy in children who are later diagnosed as ADHD (Trommer, Hoeppner, Rosenberg, Armstrong, & Rothstein, 1988). Infants with difficult temperaments may have greater difficulty establishing secure attachments with their caregivers.

Toddler period (1–2-1/2 years). While the toddler period is by definition a time of increased activity, parents of children who have excessive activity levels and risk-taking behaviors may require higher levels of supervision and baby proofing. Other earmarks of normal development include underregulated behavior (lack of self-control) and increased drive towards autonomy and independence, which result in greater self-assertion and the customary "No!", which has come to be associated with the terrible twos. Given that these indicators are common at this stage of development, diagnosis of ADHD at this stage is very difficult.

RECURRENT THEMES   Awareness of the recurrent themes can be very helpful in under-standing why a diagnosis of ADHD is so difficult prior to 3 years of age. In the first 3 years of development, children normally exhibit behaviors of inattention, overactivity, and impulsivity which are typical at this age, and at the same time, cardinal symptoms associated with ADHD (*Theme 1*). As a result, the ability to distinguish between normal and atypical behaviors, or whether these behaviors represent deviations from the normal path (*Theme 2*), is extremely difficult.

Development in Focus

One of the major transitions between the Toddler Stage and the Preschool Stage is the development of the young child's increased ability to **self-regulate** their behaviors evident in gaining greater *self-control.*

Preschool stage (3 to 6 years).   At this stage of development, a potential diagnosis of ADHD begins to take on greater meaning. According to Barkley (1996), this period of development represents the initial time when a diagnosis of ADHD might be possible. However, while excessive levels of overactivity and impulsivity may flag an ADHD youngster at this stage, it is highly unlikely that children who have difficulties with inattention are likely to be noticed until much later.

RECURRENT THEMES   After 3 years of age, it is possible to recognize symptoms of im-pulsivity and overactivity that are deviations from the normal path (*Theme 1*), given increases in children's ability to regulate and control their behaviors, at this time. How-ever, the ability to detect problems with attention and distractibility usually will not surface until much later, when children are exposed to the demands of an educational environment (*Theme 3*).

Some difficulties which young children with ADHD and their families face at this stage of development are: increased problems in *unsupervised situations* (Altepeter & Breen, 1992); *strained relationships with peers, parents, and preschool teachers*; and increased tendencies for parents to see these children as *more demanding*, and *more stressful* than children who do not have ADHD (Campbell & Ewing, 1990). Research has also demonstrated that children with ADHD are significantly more likely to sustain injuries resulting from accidents and are more likely to be "accident prone" (Reebye, 1997).

School-age (6–11 years)
Inattentive type.   One of the major developmental tasks of the school aged child is to develop a sense of competence, mastery, and efficacy. However, children with ADHD face significant challenges in meeting increased academic and social demands.

> **Memory Bank**
>
> Children with the *inattentive type* of ADHD can frequently be misunderstood. These children often begin to fall behind their peers academically due to problems sustaining their attention, poor organizational skills, and ease of distractibility. They often seem to be one step behind, and are prone to attentional drifts and daydreaming. They may be "off task" more often than they are "on task." These children often do poorly on tests because they have a very poor concept of time and manage time poorly, which results in an inability to finish tests or tasks within the required time frame. Often inattention is interpreted as lack of motivation.

Lack of attention to details often reduces grade scores due to careless errors. Children with ADHD inattentive type have particular difficulties completing homework assignments (sustaining attention for boring tasks) and appear unmotivated. If homework assignments are completed, often under intense parent scrutiny, the student may forget to bring them to school or lose them somewhere in the mess of papers at the bottom of the back pack. At home, these children often exhibit problems with completion of routine chores, and parent–child conflicts often ensue due to difficulties engaging and disengaging from tasks.

Hyperactive/impulsive type. Children who evidence symptoms of impulsivity and hyperactivity have considerable difficulty curbing their excessive motor activity which is evident in constant talking, moving, fidgeting, turning in their seats, or blurting out answers.

> **Memory Bank**
>
> Children with the *hyperactive/impulsive type* are at risk socially. Their inability to wait their turn does not make them very popular with their peers. Often these children have problems socially because of their intrusive and excessive behaviors. Children with ADHD often present with poor social skills and experience difficulty making and maintaining friendships. Often, these children will gravitate towards other troubled children and may engage in various forms of rule breaking and other behavioral problems.

Academically, these children tend to rush through assignments; are impulsive and often approach tasks incorrectly because they do not wait until all the directions are provided. Children with ADHD, hyperactive/impulsive type, often evidence low frustration tolerance which ultimately results in their abandoning a task that does not have an immediate solution. In this sense, giving up should not suggest lack of cognitive ability, but a lack of ability to sustain effort and persist in their effort to derive a solution. At this developmental stage, the risk of accidental injury is most prevalent in bicycle accidents, head injuries, and pedestrian injuries (Barkley, 1998).

ADHD Goes to School

The increasing recognition of the potential impact of ADHD on academic performance has resulted in the creation of two important avenues for obtaining special services and modifications in programming for these children in the United States:

1. **Section 504 of the Rehabilitation Act of 1973**

Children with ADHD are entitled to adaptations and modifications to their individual education program (IEP) under this act, which insures that disabled children receive an appropriate education. With this in mind, the school team can develops a 504 Plan to address specific problem areas resulting from the ADHD disability (e.g., provide additional time for formal test-taking; provide the student with a peer note-taker; encourage the use of books on tape; use the student agenda to involve parents in the monitoring process for assignments). Additional lists of school based accommodations can be found at: http://www.add.org

2. **Individuals with Disabilities Education Improvement Act (IDEA, 2004)**

Recent changes to the IDEA have made it possible for some children with ADHD to receive more intensive formal special education services under the exceptional category of "Other Health Impaired." The impairment in this case is defined as impairment in "vitality or alertness, including heightened altertness to environmental stimuli that results in limited alertness with respect to the educational environment" (IDEA, 2004; Federal Register C71FR 46540. Retrieved August 14, 2006 from http://www.edgov/legislation/FedRegister/finrul/2006-3/081406a.pdf).

Adolescence: The teen years. There has been increasing recognition that ADHD symptoms will continue to impact on functioning in adolescence (Barkley, 1998), even if the symptoms are not as obvious as they were earlier on. It is now known that at least half of children diagnosed with ADHD will meet criteria for the disorder throughout adolescence. The shift in focus from elementary school to middle school and high school places greater strain on children with ADHD. In addition to increased educational demands (quality and quantity of school work), there are now increased expectations that youth have the necessary maturity to managing transitions between classes and become accustomed to a rotary system where different teachers provide instruction for different subjects. Academic concerns in the teen years often focus on the ADHD child's inability to manage their increasing work load due to poorly developed independent study skills. Poor work habits, lack of organizational skills, and poor follow-through often result in significant academic difficulties at the middle and high school level.

Memory Bank

Adolescents with ADHD are often at-risk emotionally. Lack of success academically and concomitant social problems often can result in progressive development of comorbid internalizing problems, such as anxiety and depression (Biederman, Faraone, & Lapey, 1992), and externalizing problems, such as aggression, defiance, and forms of delinquent behavior (Barkley, Fischer, Edelbrock, & Smallish, 1990a). While one of the major tasks of the teen years is to develop a positive self-concept based on peer acceptance and increasing competence, teens with ADHD often experience low self-esteem, poor acceptance from peers, and bouts of depression (Hechtman, Weiss, & Perlman, 1980).

Other social/emotional concerns prevalent at this developmental stage include safety concerns, such as reckless driving accidents (Barkley, Murphy, & Kwasnick, 1996) and participation in other high risk behaviors, such as substance use (alcohol, hallucinogens), which is reported to be higher in ADHD populations.

Comorbid and Related Disorders

ADHD is a highly comorbid disorder and is often accompanied by another disorder. Approximately 66% of elementary school-aged children referred to clinics with ADHD have, at a minimum, one additional diagnosable disorder (Cantwell, 1994). A summary of some of the findings about these comorbid relationships is presented in Table 10.2.

Table 10.2 ADHD, Comorbidity, and Related Problems

Comorbid Disorders and Related Problems	Rate	Source
Specific Learning Learning Disabilities	16% Reading 21% Math 38%–45% Reading	Frick et al., 1991. Used a 20-point discrepancy between IQ and Academics Dykman & Ackerman, 1992; Semrud-Clikeman et al., 1992. Used a 10-point discrepancy between IQ and Academics
Learning Problems	Almost 30% repeat a grade; 30% drop out; 40% need special education	Barkley, 1998
Internalizing Disorders:		
Major Depression	30%	Biederman et al., 1996
Depression/dysthymia	48%	Bird, Gould, & Staghezza, 1993
Bipolar	90% with Bipolar have ADHD	Geller & Luby, 1997
Anxiety Disorders	27%–30% 36%	Biederman et al., 1991 Bird et al., 1993
Obsessive Compulsive Disorder (OCD)	10%–30% OCD	King, Leonard, & March, 1998
Somatization Disorder	24% males 35% females	Szatmari, Boyle, & Offord, 1989
Externalizing Disorders:	50% ODD or CD 25%–75% 36% community sample	Clinic population (*DSM–IV*, 2000) Barkley, 1998 Bird et al., 1993
Oppositional Defiant Disorder (ODD)	54%–67%	Barkley, DuPaul, and McMurray, 1990b; Faraone & Biederman, 1997
Conduct Disorder (CD)	44%–50%	Szatmari, Boyle, & Offord, 1989
Substance Abuse:	48% Cigarettes 41% Alcohol	Barkley et al., 1990.
Social Relationship Problems: Peers	50%	Pelham & Bender, 1982
Sleep Problems:	50% insomnia, problems waking	Barkley, 1998; Dixon, Monroe, & Jakim, 1981
Restless leg syndrome (RLD) or periodic limb movement (PLMD)	60%	Pichietti & Walters, 1999
Sleep Disordered Breathing (SDB)	30%	Chervin, Dillon, Bassetti, Ganoczy, & Pituch, 1997

Science Talks

Although it has been known for some time that the behaviors of children with ADHD can impede their own learning effectiveness (high levels of off-task behaviors, overactivity, and intrusive verbalizations (Whalen, Henker, Collins, Finck, & Dotemoto, 1979), less attention has been paid to the degree to which these behaviors may place greater stress on the teachers and the classroom environment that they are in. In a recent study, Greene, Beszterczey, Katzenstein, Park, and Goring (2002) found that children with ADHD who also had comorbid aggression, oppositional behaviors, or serious social problems were significantly more likely to cause teacher's stress than children who had ADHD without these related problems.

ADHD and learning difficulties/general academic problems. Academic problems are common in children with ADHD because the core symptom features (inattention, impulsivity, and overactivity) often directly interfere with efficient and effective learning. Although the nature and severity of academic difficulties can be moderated by the extent to which these features are present, statistics suggest that for many children, the academic consequences of having ADHD can be severe.

Science Talks

Almost one third of children with ADHD will repeat a grade and 30% will drop out before completing high school. At least 40% will require some type of special education intervention (Barkley, 1998).

ADHD and specific learning disabilities. It is very difficult to determine prevalence rates for comorbid ADHD + specific learning disabilities (SLD) because there is wide variability among published studies regarding how SLD is defined and measured.

Memory Bank

Definitions of learning disabilities can vary depending on whether one uses the *DSM* criterion for diagnosing a learning disorder or the Individuals with Disabilities Education Improvement Act (IDEA, 2004) criteria for determining the presence of a specific learning disability. Although the *DSM* recognizes a significant or substantial discrepancy between expectations and achievement, this criteria is no longer required under IDEA 2004. Under IDEA 2004, at the discretion of the school district, a **response to intervention (RTI)** model may replace the discrepancy criterion. Further discussion of some of the main issues involved in this controversy will be presented in chapter 11: Specific Learning Disabilities.

In studies that have used a **discrepancy criterion** (standard score differences between achievement scores and IQ scores), there are variations in how the criterion is established. For example, in one study when a 20-point discrepancy between IQ and achievement was used, prevalence figures for comorbid ADHD + SLD were reported to be in the 16%–21% range (Frick et al., 1991). In other studies, however, where a 10-point discrepancy between IQ and achievement was used, the prevalence rate for ADHD + SLD was 38%–45% (Dykman & Ackerman, 1992; Semrud-Clikeman, Biederman, Sprich-Buckminster, Lehman, Faraone, & Norman, 1992).

Important Distinction

Some researchers believe that children with ADHD should be distinguished by the predominant nature of their problems. This subtyping would recognize those with more cognitive/learning problems as cognitive ADHD; while those who demonstrate more behavioral problems could be subtyped as behavioral ADHD. This possibility has been suggested by different researchers (August & Garfinkel, 1989; Halperin et al., 1990).

ADHD and internalizing disorders. Research has noted high rates of comorbidity with depression, bipolar disorder, anxiety disorder, somatization, and obsessive compulsive disorder.

Caution

Diagnosis of ADHD + depression or ADHD + bipolar disorder is a complex process, since there is considerable degree of symptom overlap among these disorders. Lack of concentration occurs in both ADHD and depression, while overactivity and ease of distraction are shared by ADHD and bipolar disorders. (Difficulties with differential diagnosis among these disorders were also addressed in chapter 8.)

ADHD and depression. Child and adolescent depression is often manifested in symptoms that are different from adult depression. Symptoms of depression in children can be manifested as irritability, social withdrawal, negativistic and oppositional thinking, and somatic complaints. Many of these symptoms overlap with symptoms of ADHD.

Science Talks

Biederman, Farone, Mick, Moore, and Lelon (1996) found that approximately 30% of the children in their study had comorbid ADHD + major depression. When data were grouped to include children referred for both major and mild forms of depression, Biederman and colleagues (1995) found that 70% of these children also had comorbid ADHD.

ADHD and bipolar disorder. Adults with bipolar disorder experience mood swings that last for at least 1 week of elevated manic mood (bipolar I) or at least 4 days (bipolar II). A mixed episode is characterized by a period of time when criteria are met for both a manic episode and an episode of major depression (*DSM–IV–TR*; APA, 2000). As was discussed at length in chapter 8, one of the cardinal features of a major depressive episode, a manic episode, and a mixed episode is a prominent **irritable mood**. However, irritability in children can often be expressed as *restlessness, agitation, concentration problems, distractibility,* and *impulsivity,* all of which can look very much like ADHD. In addition, "ADHD and a mixed episode are both characterized by excessive activity, impulsive behavior, poor judgment and denial of problems" (*DSM–IV–TR*; APA, 2000, p. 364). The *DSM* suggests that differential diagnosis can be based on:

- age of onset (ADHD before age 7), and
- the chronic (ADHD) versus a more episodic presentation (mixed mood) of symptoms

However, if criteria are met for both, then a **dual diagnosis** (ADHD + bipolar disorder) is possible.

Bipolar disorder in children is often marked by **rapid cycling** with features quick mood shifts from irritability to elation, occurring in brief and multiple mood bursts, which can be demonstrated within a single day. Other symptoms of bipolar disorder—*distractibility, pressured speech,* and *overactivity*—all look very much like ADHD. Comorbidity of ADHD in children referred for BD is extremely high, especially for children referred at younger ages. Approximately 90% of the younger (prepubertal) children and 30% of the adolescent population referred for bipolar disorder have comorbid ADHD (Geller & Luby, 1997).

ADHD and anxiety.   Biederman et al. (1991) found that the comorbidity rate for ADHD and an anxiety disorder, such as overanxious disorder, was between 27%–30%. Children with comorbid anxiety + ADHD are less impulsive that ADHD without anxiety (Epstein, Goldberg, Conners, & March, 1997). Approximately 10%–30% of children with OCD, a specific anxiety disorder which features obsessions and compulsions, have comorbid ADHD (King et al., 1998).

ADHD and somatization disorders.   Children with ADHD have more somatic complaints (e.g., headaches, stomachaches) than children without ADHD (Barkley et al., 1990). Approximately 24% of boys and 35% of girls meet the diagnosis for comorbid ADHD + somatization disorder (Szatmari, Offord, & Boyle, 1989).

ADHD and externalizing disorders.   In the *DSM–IV–TR* (APA 2000), ADHD appears as one of the 10 categories of disorders classified under *Disorders Usually First Diagnosed in Infancy, Childhood, or Adolescence.* ADHD is clustered with the Disruptive Behavior Disorders: conduct disorder (CD) and oppositional defiant disorder (ODD).

Don't Forget

Although it might be assumed, given the categorical clustering, that ADHD falls under the Disruptive Behavior Disorders, it is important to recall the distinction between the inattentive type and the hyperactive/impulsive type or combined type. The Inattentive Type "tend to be socially passive, and appear to be neglected rather than rejected by peers," whereas "peer rejection" is "most salient in types marked by hyperactivity and impulsivity." Furthermore, although approximately 50% of clinic-referred children have ADHD plus ODD or CD, "this co-occurrence is in the two subtypes marked by hyperactivity and impulsivity: Hyperactive Impulsive and Combined Types" (*DSM–IV–TR;* APA, 2000, p. 88).

Outcomes for children and adolescents with ADHD plus ODD or CD are much worse than outcomes for children with ADHD alone (Barkley et al., 1990b; Weiss & Hechtman, 1993) and suggest that these children are more seriously maladjusted (Moffit, 1990). According to the *DSM* (APA, 2000), between 25% and 75% of adolescents with ADHD also meet the criteria for ODD or CD.

ADHD and ODD.   Children with ODD are oppositional, defiant, negativistic, stubborn, and can be easily annoyed and annoying. ODD children are also often aggressive, at least verbally, and often at odds and in conflict with parents, initially, and ultimately other authority figures and peers. Studies have demonstrated as high as 67% comorbidity between these two disorders (Barkley et al., 1990b; Faraone, Biederman, Jetton, & Tsuang, 1997).

ADHD and conduct disorder (CD).   Children with CD are usually older than children with ODD and display a more serious form of overt and covert aggression (Frick et al., 1992). As many as 50% of children with ADHD will develop CD (Szatmari, Boyle, & Offord, 1989).

ADHD and substance abuse.   In their 8-year follow-up of ADHD children in adolescence, Barkely and colleagues (1990a) found that hyperactive teens with ADHD were significantly more likely to use cigarettes and alcohol than their nonhyperactive peers. However, a recent study which followed ADHD children into adolescence revealed higher levels of substance use across a wide variety of subtances (alcohol, tobacco, and illicit drugs) than their non-ADHD peers (Brooke & Pelham, 2003). Furthermore, the authors suggest that a diagnosis of ADHD in childhood seems to be as strong a predictor for substance use as having a family history of substance abuse, and that this risk is not substance specific, but cuts across alcohol, tobacco, marijuana, and other drugs.

Science Talks

A remarkable finding in one study was that, it was not the severity of hyperactive/impulsive symptoms or the ODD/CD symptoms that predicted risks for substance use; it was the *severity of inattention* symptoms that predicted the vulnerable population (Brooke & Pelham, 2003).

Brooke and Pelham (2003) suggest that results may point to a developmental pathway from inattention to substance abuse mediated by academic impairment and suggest that executive functioning deficits may be at the basis of this link to substance abuse.

Important Distinction

Often parents express concern that the use of stimulant medication to treat children with ADHD may open the door to increased tendencies to use and abuse substances (alcohol, drugs) later on. However, research demonstrates that just the opposite is true. Adults with ADHD who were not treated in their youth had much higher rates of substance abuse that adults whose ADHD was successfully managed with stimulant medication. In this case, successful medical management of ADHD is protective against later substance abuse (Biederman, Wilens, Mick, Spencer, & Faraone, 1999).

Social Relationship Problems.   Approximately half of children with ADHD will experience difficulties in their relationships with peers (Pelham & Bender, 1982). According to Greene, Biederman, Faraone, Sienna, and Garcia-Jetton (1997), there is a subtype of children with ADHD that are also **socially disabled** (ADHD + SD). These children experience a significant discrepancy between their intellectual scores and their scores for social adaptation. Compared to children who have ADHD alone, children with ADHD + SD demonstrate higher levels of substance abuse, family problems, anxiety, mood problems, and conduct problems.

Science Sleep Talks

In the population at large, approximately 17% of school-aged children have sleep disturbances (Simeon, 1985). Parents report that as many as half of their children with ADHD have sleep problems (Allen, Singer, Brow, & Salam, 1992). Types of sleep disturbances reported in ADHD children include insomnia (Dixon et al., 1981), difficulty getting up in the morning, and decrease in the overall quality of sleep (Barkley, 1998). Researchers, (Picchietti, England, Walters, Willis, & Verrico, 1998; Pichietti & Walters, 1999; Walters, Mandelbaum, Lewin, Kugler, England, & Miller, 2000) have found as high as 66% of children with ADHD experienced **periodic limb movement disorder (PLMD)** and/or **restless legs syndrome (RLS)**, compared to only 5% of their non-ADHD peers with sleep complaints. Furthermore, treating the sleep disorder with levodopa (which increases dopamine activity in the brain) resulted in improvement in ADHD symptoms. The researchers suggest the possibility that **dopamine deficiency** might be a common link between sleep disorders and ADHD.

Sleep disorders/problems.   Furthermore, researchers (Chervin et al., 1997) have found that other sleep disorders, such as **sleep-disordered breathing (SDB),** were evident in as many as one third of children diagnosed with ADHD who were reported to engage in habitual snoring. Another study which compared children with ADHD to their non-ADHD siblings found that children with ADHD had significantly higher prevalence rates for single or multiple sleep disturbances, as well as initial and middle insomnia compared to their siblings (Ring et al., 1998).

Important Distinction

Can ADHD be mistaken for Sleep Deprivation? Researchers have found that children 8 to 14 years of age who do not get at least 6-1/2 hours of sleep a night (or children under 8 years who do not get at least 10 hours of sleep) simulate ADHD-like symptoms resulting from their sleep deprivation. Furthermore, hyperactivity increased in proportion to the number of nights that the children did not get adequate sleep (Chervin et al., 2002).

Comorbidity and subtypes of ADHD.   There has been increased discussion whether a number of subtypes of ADHD exist and if so, how to best measure and categorize them. Findings have often been controversial and results often inconsistent; however, researchers continue to investigate potential subtyping clusters in the hopes of refining treatment alternatives and obtaining better outcomes. With this goal in mind, many researchers suggest subtyping of ADHD by virtue of the comorbid and associated features.

Memory Bank

Significant emphasis has been placed on subtypes of ADHD + comorbid *externalizing problems*, such as CD, ODD, and aggression. Outcomes for children with ADHD + CD/ODD subtype are often poor with higher risk for delinquent and antisocial behavior (Biederman et al,1991). Overactivity is often associated with aggressive responses, while impulsivity can produce volatile and highly reactive patterns of behavior (Carlson & Rapport, 1989).

An alternative approach to subtyping would be to subtype using the **internalizing dimension**. Biederman and colleagues (1991) suggest another viable subtyping approach might be to include subtypes of ADHD with *comorbid internalizing problems*: ADHD + major depression, and ADHD + anxiety. In a recent study investigating whether internalizing disorders might distinguish subtypes, researchers found that children with ADHD/combined and ADHD/inattentive experienced similar levels of anxiety and depression, providing additional support for Biederman's subtyping approach (Power, Costigan, Eiraldi, & Leff, 2004).

Etiology: The Biological and Neurological Model

Despite its status as one of the most prevalent childhood disorders, researchers have continued to be perplexed by the exact cause of ADHD, which is now thought to involve a complex interaction between biological factors and their interaction with environmental factors (Wolraich, 2000). Increased research into the potential neurobiological basis for ADHD has focused on increased knowledge and identification of how the key features of ADHD (inattention, impulsivity, and overactivity) are linked to genetic transmission, brain structures, brain function (*neurocognitive processing*), and neurotransmitter activity.

Genetic Transmission

Fifty percent of all parents with ADHD have a child who also has the disorder (Biederman et al., 1995). Information from recent twin studies suggests that as much as 75% might be accounted for by genetic factors (Sherman, Iacono, & McGue, 1997), while increasing research has begun to focus on the implications of having a parent with ADHD on subsequent child treatment.

Caution

Research has demonstrated that parent training programs can be an important component in the treatment of children with ADHD (McKee, Harvey, & Danforth, 2004). Furthermore, enhancing parent management skills can increase the quality of parent child relationships, reduce parent stress, and serve as a protective factor for a child's mental well being (Lange et al., 2005). However, a recent study revealed that while children of mothers with low and medium symptoms of ADHD demonstrated significant posttraining reduction in symptoms, children of the high-symptom mothers showed no improvement. The authors suggest that in cases where the parent also demonstrates high symptoms of ADHD, it may be necessary to treat the parent prior to intervention (Sonuga-Barke, Daley, Thompson, Laver-Bredbury, & Weeks, 2002).

Brain Structures

The frontal system. The frontal region which houses the **executive functions** is intricately involved in connecting with other brain systems, such as the **limbic system** (motivation) and the **reticular activating system** (arousal). The executive function system is responsible for *goal-directed or problem-solving behaviors*. Studies have demonstrated that there is less activity in the frontal lobes of populations with ADHD compared to populations without ADHD (Zametkin, Liebner, & Fitgerald, 1993). Furthermore, using MRI technology, Castellanos, Giedd, Marsh, and Hamburger (1996) found significantly smaller right prefrontal lobes in children with ADHD.

> **Science Talks**
>
> Researchers have studied activity levels and brain structures (volume, asymmetry) to determine how the brains of children and adults with ADHD differ from normal brains. Studies have used a number of increasingly sophisticated technological advances: positron emission tomography (PET), magnetic resonance imaging (MRI), functional magnetic resonance imaging (fMRI), and SPECT brain scan (single photon emission computed topography). Results of these studies have generated increased interest in three main neuroanatomical sites: the **prefrontal cortex, the cingulate gyrus,** and the **basal ganglia**.

Cingulate gyrus. The cingulate gyrus (cingulate refers to encircling) can be found on the inside of the **cerebrum** (which separates the brain hemispheres). The cingulate gyrus is part of the limbic system and has been associated with control of motivation. The cingulate gyrus is involved in focusing of attention and in directing response selection. The cingulate gyrus mediates messages between the decision-making processes of the *frontal system* and the emotional world of the *limbic system*. In humans, stimulation of this region can produce positive or negative feelings. Recent research has suggested links between the emotions and the anterior cingulate cortex. In studies out of UCLA, Eisenberg, Lieberman, and Williams (2003) have found that the front or anterior part of the cingulate gyrus registers social/emotional pain (rejection, hurt feelings) much the same way that physical pain is registered in other parts of the brain.

> **Recall and Rewind**
>
> High activity levels in the cingulate gyrus have also been associated with **Tourette's syndrome** (vocal, motor, and facial tics) and OCD.

Basal ganglia. Patients with Parkinson's often demonstrate difficulties with the perception of time, a dysfunction which is thought to be associated with abnormal reduction of dopamine within the basil ganglia. The basil ganglia have nerve cells that are primarily associated with the neurotransmitter dopamine.

> **Science Talks**
>
> Using fMRI techniques, researchers have recently isolated the basal ganglia (located deeply within the brain's structures) and the parietal lobe (situated on the surface of the right side of the brain), as brain systems which have an integral role in *governing a sense of time* (Rao, Mayer, & Harrington, 2001). Defective time perception implicated in ADHD might signal the basal ganglia as an important area of dysfunction in ADHD populations.

Brain Function: Neurocognitive Processing

There has been growing interest in determining how executive functioning and arousal level contribute to cognitive, emotional, and behavioral processing deficits in children with ADHD.

> **Memory Bank**
>
> Relative to theories and research surrounding the core features of overactivity and impulsivity, significantly less information is available concerning the inattentive type of ADHD. One likely reason for this fact is the unobtrusiveness of the disorder compared to the intrusiveness of the other two components of the triad. In sharp contrast to the symptom presentations of the highly active and reactive counterparts (impulsivity and overactivity), the inattentive child is often diagnosed at a later age, prescribed medications less often, and often mistaken for a child of slower ability or lacking in motivation and effort due to the sluggish and slow tempo caused by their processing deficits.

Executive functioning. The executive functions serve as the leaders in information processing in their capacity to *manage, direct, and control the course of activity.* Although models of executive functioning have continued to emphasize problem solving as the overall goal (Stuss & Benson, 1986; Welsh & Pennington, 1988), there has been significant growth in our understanding of how the subprocesses contribute to the overall final product, and which parts of the brain may be implicated in the process.

> **Memory Bank**
>
> One key subset of regulatory and management functions includes the ability to *initiate* certain activities on demand, while being able to *inhibit* competing activities.

Another key problem-solving skill includes *flexibility* in being able to readily shift focus between tasks, when required, and to adapt strategies as needed. Also inherent in problem-solving success is the ability to *monitor, evaluate, and revise strategies.* The executive functions serve not only to organize and manage cognitive functions but pertain to the management and control of other *regulatory functions,* including *behavioral and emotional control.* Ultimately, the task of being able to hold information in memory while performing these problem-solving tasks involves the use of *working memory.*

> **Recall and Rewind**
>
> Executive functioning tasks include: initiation/inhibition; flexibility in shifting focus; monitoring, evaluating, and adapting strategies as needed.

Executive functioning from a developmental perspective. Developmentally, the initiation of executive functioning begins to emerge when the infant establishes a sense of object permanence (8 to 12 months of age) and begins to put together *goal directed and purposeful chains of behavior* (e.g., moving an object out of the way to retrieve another object). In the latter half of the next 12 months, the toddler will gain greater ability to perform tasks requiring *delayed imitation* based on increased cognitive capacity for symbolic or representational thought.

Development in Focus

The ability to form mental representations increases rapidly during the toddler period and is evident in newly developing concepts such as self-awareness, other awareness, and emotional awareness (feelings of pride and shame). There will be greater focus on attempting to regulate behaviors relative to rules and standards in order to gain parent approval versus parental criticism. At this time, the parent's role is to provide a model for *guided self-regulation* (Sroufe, 1996) by setting limits, rewarding appropriate behaviors, and providing consequences for inappropriate actions.

Increased self-regulatory functions can be evident in increased self-control based on internalizing parental models and the increased use of inner language which serves to guide and direct appropriate behavior and inhibit inappropriate responses.

RECURRENT THEMES Sroufe's (1996) focus on the role of the parent in providing models of *guided self-regulation* for their children emphasizes the need to consider the influences of environmental characteristics (parent models), as well as child characteristics (self-control) in evaluating underlying mechanisms that can ameliorate or exacerbate a child's difficulties (*Theme 4*).

Over the course of development, increased cognitive capacity (memory span, developing more effective coding and retrieval strategies, increases in working memory) and ultimately the emergence of abstract reasoning and metamemory (knowledge about memory functions) act to refine approaches to problem solving and more effective use of executive functions.

Science Talks

ADHD and Gender: A recent longitudinal investigation of the relationship between inhibition, executive functioning, and ADHD symptoms found that while inhibition was highly related to ADHD symptoms across situations (home and school) for boys, the relationship held for girls only in the school context. Furthermore, early difficulties with inhibition predicted later problems in executive functions associated with ADHD for boys, but not for girls. The authors suggest further investigation is needed to determine whether different predictors might exist for girls, or if girls with executive functioning problems are somehow buffered from ADHD symptoms (Berlin, Bohlin, & Rydell, 2003).

Barkley's model of ADHD (1997). Barkley has developed a model for **ADHD-hyperactive/Impulsive type** which is based on our current knowledge and understanding of ADHD and the executive functions. The model was developed to assist in understanding how *behavioral inhibition,* a central feature of the disorder, relates to other executive functioning deficits and problems with sustained attention. Barkley is clear in his emphasis that this model does not attempt to explain the inattentive type of ADHD.

Memory Bank

Behavioral inhibition is defined as the ability to inhibit a response (delay) or stop an active response, and to maintain the delay as a manner of interference control in order that goal-directed behavior can be initiated and maintained (Barkley, 1997).

According to Barkley, behavioral inhibition is at the hub of ADHD and is highly influential in determining the outcome of four central executive functioning tasks: **working memory, self-regulation** *(affect, motivation, and arousal)*, **internal speech,** and **reconstitution**. Since behavioral inhibition precedes the development of executive functions in the four areas cited, then delays in the development of behavioral inhibition not only can be observed in such overt behaviors as lack of self-control (emotional, behavioral), but immaturity in this area will also serve to undermine the processing of key executive tasks at a covert level.

Recall and Rewind

For Barkley, the ability to delay a response (**behavioral inhibition**) is an essential step towards higher order functioning, because the delay allows sufficient time to develop skills in the four major areas, which are in turn focal points for the development and refining of other essential skills.

Working memory permits the development of such tasks as sequential ordering and planning based on the anticipation of future consequences. *Self-regulation* is necessary to the development of skills which modulate activity states in order to initiate goal-directed behavior and sustain effort. *Internalization of speech* provides yet another mechanism which serves to slow down reactivity and promote inner reflection (*analysis*). Finally, it is necessary to coordinate the information (*synthesis*) in order to select the best appropriate response, given the situation, a process which Barkley refers to as *reconsititution*. Ultimately, given sufficient delay in responding, the problem-solving strategy is developed which culminates in the final goal-directed response which is subject to objectivity, cognitive control, and further monitoring and evaluation (see Figure 10.1).

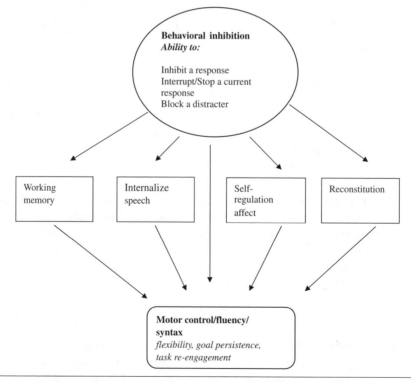

Figure 10.1 Barkley's (1997) model of the four executive functions and how these relate to behavioral inhibition.

Case in Point

Gloria is perplexed. Her son Billy has recently been diagnosed with ADHD, which she understands to mean that he has problems focusing his attention. Gloria is the first to agree with the psychologist, since getting Billy to stay on task is a very difficult chore. Each night, Gloria and Billy engage in on-going battles regarding homework completion. However, if Billy has such problems with **sustained attention**, Gloria does not understand how Billy can remain riveted to the computer playing video games for hours on end. Gloria calls the psychologist, who gives Gloria the following explanation, which is based on Barkley's concept of **contingency based attention**. Yes, Billy does have significant problems sustaining his attention in tasks requiring goal-directed behavior, especially for low interest tasks like homework or other tasks which are not inherently self-rewarding. The reasons for Billy's problems in this area are well explained by Barkley's model of behavioral inhibition. However, video games are high interest, novel, and provide immediate gratification. Under these conditions, attention remains focused (which Barkley refers to as contingency-based or self-rewarding attention) due to the nature of the task.

The *Case in Point* illustrates another important distinction addressed by Barkley (1997) regarding qualitative differences evident in two different forms of attention: **contingency-shaped attention** and **goal-directed persistence**. Circumstances that can serve to increase or decrease contingent attention include novelty of the task, inherent interest in the task, reinforcing properties of the task, alertness-versus-fatigue of the participant and the presence or absence of a monitor (e.g., adult supervision/ monitoring system). Barkley contends that this form of sustained attention is not problematic for children with ADHD because it is *intrinsically rewarding* and virtually *effortless*. On the other hand, *goal-directed persistence* requires tasks that are extremely difficult for children with ADHD to accomplish or sustain, such as sustained persistence of attention and effort when conditions are not highly reinforcing or inherently interesting. In the latter circumstance, attention is *effortful,* and *rewards are virtually nonexistent.*

Neurotransmitters. The **catecholamines** (*dopamine, norepinephrine, epinephrine*) have been associated with attention and motor activity. Medications such as Dexedrine (dextrpamphetamine), Ritalin (methylphenidate), and Cylert (pemoline) increase the number of catecholamines in the brain (Barkley, 1998). Dopamine research is especially fruitful, since both the prefrontal cortex and limbic system have an abundance of dopamine pathways (Barkley, 1998).

Subtyping based on brain region activity. A third method of subtyping has resulted from the use of SPECT scans of brain activity. Based on his investigations of ADHD brains, using SPECT scans of localized brain activity, Amen (1998, 2001) and Amen and Carmichael (1997) suggest the possibility of 6 subtypes of ADHD based on different brain patterns involving the prefrontal cortex, anterior cingulate gyrus, basal ganglia, temporal lobes, or deep limbic system. The 6 types include classic (hyperactive/impulsive), inattentive, overfocused, temporal lobe, limbic, and ring of fire. However, because there are dangers in exposing children to low doses of radiation during SPECT scans, and because neuroimaging is used primarily for research rather than diagnosis, the utility of this method remains suspect. In their review of neuroimaging research, Leo and Cohen (2003) criticize the lack of published research to support the use of SPECT scans to differentiate between the brains of those with and without ADHD, or to demonstrate the six different types of ADHD that Amen has described (p. 42).

Assessment

While an exhaustive review of materials available for ADHD assessment is beyond the scope and intention of this text, it is imperative that clinicians obtain an accurate clinical picture of ADHD. Therefore, several strategies will be suggested to assess whether the child or adolescent adequately meets the diagnostic criteria stipulated in the *DSM* (APA, 2000); whether differential diagnosis can rule out competing diagnostic categories with similar features; and to verify whether other co-occuring or comorbid features exist. It is also essential that assessment strategies be appropriately selected based on the child's or adolescent's developmental level.

In their review of evidence-based assessment of ADHD in children and adolescents, Pelham, Fabiano, and Massetti (2005) emphasize the need to focus on:

- the *reliability and validity* of methods used to identify the symptoms and associated impairments of ADHD; and
- *treatment utility* or how to best integrate information from a variety of assessment instruments to best inform treatment planning (p. 450).

Pelham and colleagues (2005) also point out that assessment of ADHD is driven by our definition of ADHD, which at this point is primarily a *behavioral definition* that considers the manifestation of ADHD based on the extent to which the child or youth demonstrates symptoms of *inattention, hyperactivity,* and *impulsivity.* Until recently, there has been far less emphasis placed on the *cognitive aspects* of ADHD that exist in impairments of executive dysfunction and frontal lobe dysfunction (Castellanos et al., 2003).

The Assessment Process

Detailed clinical and developmental history. There are several interview formats available (structured, semistructured) that can be used to gather pertinent information about the child's psychosocial, developmental, and medical history. These interview instruments were discussed in chapter 5, and will not be discussed again at this time.

Family dynamics (including family stressors) are also important and especially relevant information about any family or extended family members who may have symptoms of ADHD.

Accessing information from multiple sources across multiple settings. Important information, in addition to that already mentioned, is a review of the educational history, and social/emotional history, since many of these children experience academic- and peer-related problems. Since one of the defining features of the disorder is that it be pervasive across situations, it is most important that information be collected from teachers as well as parents. Although pediatric guidelines for diagnosing ADHD are available (American Academy of Child and Adolescent Psychiatry, 1997), it is important to note that current guidelines in the *DSM* (APA, 2000) are most appropriate for children in the 6–12 year old range. Recently, increased emphasis has been placed on how to best assess ADHD in teenage populations (Barkley, 2003). A list of some of the most common instruments that can assist in the assessment of ADHD are available in Table 10.3.

Table 10.3 ADHD: A Comprehensive Look at Domains of Assessment

Assessment Domain	Assessment Instruments	Examples of Areas Assessed
General Behavior General Rating Scales Internalizing and Externalizing Behaviors: inattention, hyperactivity, impulsivity	ASEBA (2002); BASC2 (2004);	Aggression, depression, anxiety, social problems, thought problems; inattention; impulsivity/ hyperactivity
ADHD Behaviors ADHD Specific Rating Scales	Conners Scales (Conners, 1998) Adolescent Self-Report (Conners & Wells, 1997)	Attentive type hyperactive/impulsive type *DSM* ADHD
Behavioral Observation	Structured or informal	On-task/off-task behavior; In seat/out of seat Interrupts/Blurts out answers
General Cognitive Functioning Intellectual and Problem Solving; Memory; Processing Speed	Wechsler Scales (WISC–IV; Wechsler, 2003; WPSSI–III; Wechsler, 2002)	Verbal/Visual intelligence, Working Memory, Processing Speed
	Stanford Binet 5 (SB; Roid, 2003)	Verbal/Nonverbal; Intelligence/Working Memory
	Woodcock Johnson III (WJIII COG; Woodcock, McGrew, & Mather, 2001).	Twenty tests: verbal comprehension, Visual/auditory learning, auditory working memory,
Specific Areas of Function Executive Functions	BRIEF (Gioia, Isquith, Guy, & Kenworthy, 2000) BRIEF Self-Report (Guy, Isquith, & Gioia, 2004)	Behavior Regulation (inhibit, shift, emotion control) Meta Cognition (initiate, working memory, plan, organize)
	Brown ADD Scales (Brown, 2001).	Cognitive flexibility, problem solving, fluency and impulsivity
Neuropsychological development	Delis–Kaplan Executive Function System (D–KEFS; Delis, Kaplan, & Kramer, 2001)	Memory and learning and executive function: inhibition, regulation, flexibility, fluency, and vigilance
	NESPY (Korkman, Kirk, & Kemp, 1997)	Attention, language, sensorimotor, visuospatial, learning, memory
Cognitive Flexibility (Visual)	Category Test—Child Version (Boll, 1993)	Ability to shift cognitive set for visual patterns and themes
Processing and Attention Sustained Visual Attention	Conner's Continuous Performance Test (Conners, 2000)	Ability to attend to low interest visual task and execute performance demands
	Test of Variables of Attention (TOVA: Leark, Dupuy, Greenberg, Corman, & Kindescki, 1996)	Fixed interval responding to rapid and spaced stimuli
Sustained Auditory Attention	California Verbal Learning Test—Children's version (CVLT–C; Delis, Kramer, Kaplan, & Ober, 1994)	Verbal learning and recall over a series of trials with an interference task interspersed.

Important Distinction

Wolraich and colleagues (2005) suggest that the assessment of adolescents represents an increased challenge, compared to assessments involving younger children. Ideally, assessment should involve multiple methods, from multiple sources, to obtain information across multiple situations. Although parents are often astute observers of their younger children at home and at play, they often are not as accurate in their information regarding their younger child's day to day functioning at school. In adolescence, school and home information becomes even more difficult to access, due to youth's increasing demands for privacy and increased time spent with peers, engaged in activities outside the home. Academically, secondary school students have multiple teachers who are primarily aware of the student's performance in their own subject area only. Often they have little information about a youth's functioning in less structured activities (transitions between classes, cafeteria, etc.). In addition, research suggests that secondary school teacher behavioral ratings as a whole do not demonstrate a high level of interrater consensus (Molina, Pelham, Blumenthal, & Galiszewski 1998).

Assessment Instruments

Parent, Teacher, and Youth Rating Scales
ADHD and general behavior.   One important area of investigation for the clinician is whether symptoms may manifest differently in different situations (e.g., home, school). Another key area of concern is whether the child has comorbid features, since rates of comorbidity are very high for ADHD. General, broad band rating scales provide an excellent way of amassing information for both areas of concern noted above; they provide a comprehensive look at other major dimensions of child and adolescent psychopathology and provide multiple perspectives. Behavioral rating scales such as the Achenbach System of Empirically Based Assessment (ASEBA; Achenbach & Rescorla, 2001), and the Conner's Revised Scales (Conners, 1997) provide information from both a dimensional and categorical approach to DSM–IV classification of ADHD, as well as, evaluating several other major problem areas. Similar to the ASEBA and CRS, the Behavior Assessment System for Children (BASC2; Reynolds & Kamphaus, 2004), also provides parallel rating forms for parents, teachers, and youth. These scales have been reviewed extensively in other chapters and will not be repeated here.

Developmental impact on rating scale accuracy.   Developmentally, elementary school teachers spend the majority of the academic year with the same set of children and, as such, their ratings can provide an in-depth assessment of how the child compares to peers academically, behaviorally, and socially. However, in middle school and high school, teachers spend proportionally less time with individual students due to increased class sizes and academic rotation. Clinical practice suggests that these teachers are less valid observers of clinical symptoms, unless these symptoms are severe or highly visible, and this assumption has been backed by research support (Molina et al., 1998). In addition, the tendencies for visible signs of hyperactive behaviors to subside with increasing age suggest that ratings for hyperactive/impulsive behaviors may be underestimated in the teen years.

Youth self-ratings.   Two of the most popular ADHD self-rating scales for youth are the ***Brown ADD Scales for Adolescents*** (Brown, 2001) and the ***Conners-Wells Adolescent Self-Report Scale***

(Conners & Wells, 1997). Although these questionnaires have been developed to provide youth with the opportunity of reporting their perceptions of the severity of the disorder and reporting symptoms that they experience, and as such are an integral part of the total assessment process, a cautionary note is in order. Studies have found that youth tend to significantly underreport the severity and the number of symptoms experienced (Kramer, Phillips, & Hargis, 2004; Smith, Pelham, & Gnagy, 2000).

ADHD and executive functioning. The *Brown ADD Scales for Children and Adolescents* (Brown, 2001) are available as parent and teacher questionnaires (3–12 years) and a self-report form, as noted above for those from 8 years to adult. The scales measure executive functioning in six areas: organization, attention, sustained effort, modulating emotions, working memory, and monitoring/evaluation. A comprehensive diagnostic form is also available to assist clinicians in integrating information from clinical history and to provide guidance in screening for comorbid disorders.

The *Behavior Rating Inventory of Executive Function* (BRIEF; Gioia, Isquith, Guy, & Kenworthy, 2000) is available in parent and teacher rating forms, and a newly developed youth self-rating form (Guy, Isquity, & Gioia, 2004). The scale provides a rating of executive functions in two broad areas: *Behavioral Regulation* (inhibit, shift, emotional control) and *Meta-Cognition* (initiate, working memory, plan/organize, organize materials, monitor). The instrument is available in school-age (5–18) and preschool versions.

Direct Observations (classroom, playground, etc.)

In addition to parent, teacher, and youth self-report rating scales, direct observation can also provide significant information regarding inattention, hyperactivity, and impulsivity.

Because of the subtle nature of the disorder, however, inattention (daydreaming, staring into space) may be more difficult to detect than hyperactive (turning in chair, fidgeting, getting out of seat, verbalizing, and social chattering) or impulsive behaviors (blurting out answers, butting in, etc.). Systems of observation that have demonstrated adequate discriminant validity between children with and without ADHD include Classroom Observation of Conduct and Attention Deficit Disorders (COCADD; Atkins et al., 1985); Classroom behavior code (Klein & Abikoff, 1997); and Response Class Matrix (Barkley & Cunningham, 1979). An example of an observational recording form used to measure on-task and off-task behaviors was presented in Table 2.3. Observational recordings can also be a valuable pre–post instrument to evaluate the degree to which medication might be effective.

Individual Assessment: Cognitive and Iintelligence Testing

Children with ADHD can often also experience academic concerns and comorbid learning disabilities. Therefore, individual intellectual assessment may be an important part of the assessment process in order to rule out other potential diagnostic categories (e.g., mental retardation), or to provide patterns of cognitive reasoning associated with ADHD, such as deficits in working memory. Although the intent of this chapter is not to provide an in-depth analysis of intellectual and cognitive assessment, there are a number of common response patterns and trends that may be helpful in assisting to identify protocols of youth with ADHD.

Memory Bank

When assessing children and teens with ADHD, it is important to remember that the testing situation, like the analogue experiment, may be lacking in ecological validity for several reasons. Unlike the classroom environment, the testing situation can be an ideal environment for stimulating "contingent attention" (Barkley, 1998) by providing one to one monitoring/attention, novel tasks and is usually free from distractions. Furthermore, although intellectual assessment measures problem-solving abilities for novel tasks, the examiner performs many of the frontal lobe functions by directing the child to task specific demands and monitoring performance.

The Wechsler Intelligence Scale for Children—fourth edition (WISC–IV; Weschler, 2003).   Research has indicated that although children with ADHD score within the average range for overall intellectual functioning, they are more likely to exhibit deficits in processing speed and working memory, relative to the norm and relative to their own scores for perceptual organization (Barkley, Murphy, & Bush, 2001; Hinshaw, Carte, & Sami, 2002). The *WISC–IV* technical and interpretive manual reports that significant differences were obtained when scores for the ADHD sample were compared to normative samples for the Processing Speed Index, Working Memory Index, and Full Scale IQ. Compared to non-ADHD populations, children with ADHD are most likely to experience difficulty with subtests involving *coding, vocabulary, comprehension, general information,* and *mental arithmetic* (*WISC–IV*; Weschler, 2003).

Stanford Binet, fifth edition (SB5; Roid, 2003).   The examiner's manual of the *SB5* cautions that many children with ADHD may be especially vulnerable to lowered scores on the Working Memory factor which measures verbal and nonverbal working memory.

Woodcock-Johnson Cognitive–III (WJ Cog–III; Woodcock, McGrew, & Mather, 2001).   The *WJ Cog–III* assesses cognitive ability in several areas of functioning and provides cluster scores in many areas that may be associated with processing deficits in children with ADHD (working memory, executive functions, processing speed, etc).

Individual Assessments: Executive Functions
The Delis–Kaplan Executive Function System (D–KEFS; Delis, Kaplan, & Kramer, 2001) assesses higher level cognitive functioning in children and adults (8 years to 89 years). The D–KEFS measures executive functioning in several areas, including: cognitive flexibility, problem solving, fluency, and planning/impulsivity.

The NEPSY (Korkman, Kirk, & Kemp, 1997) measures neuropsychological development in children ages 3 to 12 years. The *NEPSY* evaluates memory and learning in addition to attention/executive functioning in several areas including: inhibition, self-regulation, flexibility in thinking, fluency, vigilance, as well as sustained and selective attention.

The Category Test—Children's Version (Boll, 1993) provides an evaluation of a child's problem-solving ability using visual spatial tasks and the ability to shift set from one set of rules to determining a new rule for a new set of configurations. Cognitive flexibility and frustration tolerance are required to succeed.

Individual Assessments: Attention and Processing

Measures of sustained visual attention. The *Conner's Continuous Performance Test, Second Edition* (*CPT–II*; 2000) is a measure of sustained attention, response inhibition, and impulsivity to visual stimuli in children from 4 years of age upwards. In this measure, letters are flashed on a visual screen, at various speeds, in order to measure a child's ability to respond or inhibit responses to task requires and modulate responses to variable speeds. Scores are evaluated based on peer measures of accuracy (accurate hits, omissions, and errors) and speed.

The *Test of Variables of Attention* (*TOVA*; Leark, Dupuy, Greenberg, Corman, & Kindescki, 1996) measures similar areas to the *CPT* above; however the *TOVA* uses a fixed interval for stimulus presentation (2 seconds) throughout the test and varies the frequency of target presentation between the first half of the test (infrequent) and the second half of the test (frequent).

Measures of a sustained auditory attention/auditory learning and auditory memory. There is less research information available for tests of sustained auditory information. Available measures in this category include the auditory versions of previous visual measures, the *TOVA* and *CPT*. The *California Verbal Learning Test—Children's Version* (*CVLT–C*; Delis, Kramer, Kaplan, & Ober, 1994) measures children's (5 to 16–11 years) verbal learning and memory prior to and after an interference task under free recall and cued recall conditions. Children with ADHD often show less consistency in recall than children without ADHD on this task (Delis et al., 1994).

Assessment: A brief summary. Significant emphasis in this chapter has focused on the assessment of ADHD in children and adolescents. Although psychological assessment is not a prerequisite to making a diagnosis of ADHD, information from the assessment process can make a significant contribution to treatment planning and effectiveness. In addition to providing significant direction for intervention strategies, information from a comprehensive assessment can assist in ruling out differential diagnoses, as well as identifying existing comorbid associations. Each part of the assessment process can assist in providing pieces of the puzzle that, in the end, will provide a clinical picture of the unique way in which ADHD manifests in this individual child or adolescent. Interviews, rating scales, and measures of cognitive processing and executive functioning can all provide insight into the severity of the disorder and the pervasiveness of the impairment. The discussion of assessment procedures in this text is not exhaustive and is meant to provide a representational sample of what is currently available. It is imperative that clinicians keep up to date with current assessment instruments, revisions of existing instruments, and empirical support for the instruments used.

Case in Point

Ryan has been referred to school psychologist because he is struggling academically, and his parents want to know what can be done to help him. The psychologist visits Ryan's Grade 3 classroom and observes him for a half-hour period. It is not hard to find Ryan because he walks up to the psychologist, and welcomes her into the classroom. Ryan's desk is turned towards the wall and he is seated at the back of the classroom. Apparently, this is an intervention to minimize Ryan's behaviors from distracting the other students. Ryan gets out of his seat, stands by his desk and talks to himself as he tries to complete his seatwork. He searches for a pencil in his desk, which is crammed with paper balls and test papers. The papers fall on the floor and Ryan is instructed to pick them up and place them in his desk. Doing this, he finds a plastic airplane lodged in the back of the desk and begins playing with it. Ryan is cued to get back to his seatwork. Unsure of his answer, Ryan calls out to the teacher for help, and is readily admonished for inappropriate behavior and not raising his hand before speaking. The teaching assistant does come to his aid, but as soon as she turns around, he is calling out again with another question (this time while raising his hand). Again, he is told that he has to raise his hand first and then wait till he is called. Ryan sits with his hand raised, but the teacher is engaged with another student, and Ryan calls out to the aid. It is clear to the psychologist that it is not a case of Ryan *not knowing what to do* (raise hand and wait), *but not being able to do what he knows*. This type of behavior is often observed in children who have the hyperactive/impulsive type of ADHD.

In the *Case in Point*, although Ryan demonstrates obvious symptoms of overactivity and impulsivity, when a comprehensive assessment is conducted, the results reveal that Ryan's problems were more complex than immediately perceived. In addition to ADHD, Ryan also can be diagnosed with a *specific learning disability* (*SLD*). Based on the assessment information, the psychologist would be better able to work with Ryan's parents and the school to provide modifications to his academic programming that would help Ryan become more successful. In addition to increased parental awareness of the problem and discussions of potential ways to help Ryan at home (home school reporting agenda), a visit to the family pediatrician was also recommended to discuss medical alternatives to help Ryan focus more clearly on his tasks and curb his impulsivity.

Treatment

Treatment alternatives for ADHD will vary depending upon associated targets (comorbid features), symptoms, and the nature and extent of functional impairment. Interventions have focused on ameliorating conditions often affected by the ADHD disorder at home (parent training and family interventions); at school (behavior management and increasing on-task behaviors); and in interactions with peers (social skills training). Evidence-based research has for the most part focused on the effects of stimulant medications.

Medical Management
There are three main classes of stimulants currently in use for ADHD:

- **amphetamines** (Dexedrine, Adderall, Dextrostat)
- **methylphenidates** (Ritalin, Focalin, Concerta, Metadate, Methylin)
- **pemoline** (Cylert)

Important Distinction

Although stimulant medications have primarily been the medications of choice for ADHD, a nonstimulant medication recently met with FDA approval for use with ADHD populations. The drug, **Strattera**, is a selective norepinephrine reuptake inhibitor (SSRI).

In addition to different types of **stimulant medications**, many of the medications are available in *short acting* (Dexedrine and Ritalin) and *slow release forms* (Ritalin–SR), and *longer acting* forms (Ritalin–LA). Investigators have demonstrated that stimulant medication can provide performance enhancing effects for those with ADHD by increasing attention and reducing impulsive/hyperactive behaviors (Elia & Rapoport, 1991; Pelham & Milich, 1991). Furthermore, studies have provided support for stimulant medications in reducing aggressive behaviors (Hinshaw, Heller, & McHale, 1992) and enhancing parent-child interactions (Barkley & Cunningham, 1978).

Science Talks

Although numerous studies have demonstrated the positive effects of stimulant medications in reducing aggressive and impulsive behaviors in children and youth, at least one study found that some children responded to stimulant medication with increased social passivity, and social withdrawal, resulting in decreased popularity with peers (Buhrmester, Whalen, & Henker, 1992).

There has been less success in the use of stimulant medication for children who have ADHD and comorbid anxiety or depression. In an review of studies involving ADHD + anxiety or depression, Spencer and colleagues (1996) report that the majority of studies found less success for stimulant medications in these comorbid populations relative to ADHD children without comorbid internalizing features. Furthermore, in a large scale study, anxious youth with ADHD receiving behavior therapy responded as well as anxious youth who received medication alone (MTA Cooperative Group, 1999).

Recent empirical investigations. A multimodal treatment study of ADHD (MTA) has been the focus of the MTA cooperative group (six independent research teams) in collaboration with the National Institute of Mental Health (NIMH). Treatment alternatives investigated in the studies included: medication management alone (MedMgt), behavioral modification (Beh), combined treatment (Comb), and community comparision (CC). At the conclusion of the treatment phase (Swanson, Kraemer, & Hinshaw, 2001), the two groups of ADHD youth who received medication either alone or in combination with behavioral treatment (MedMgt, Comb) exhibited less severe symptoms than comparison groups who did not have medication (Beh and CC).

However, since there has been little long-term follow up of ADHD treatment effects (*DSM–IV–TR*; APA, 2000), the MTA cooperative group intended to follow-up the treatment groups over time. At first follow up (14 months), the effect size was reduced by 50%. A subsequent follow up and analysis of data at 24 months posttreatment revealed continued deterioration of effects for the MedMgt and Comb groups. Further within group analysis revealed that changes in medication usage mediated the deterioration in ADHD symptoms. The largest deterioration in symptom presentation was found in the subgroup that reported that they stopped taking medication (Med/No Med), while the group showing improvement was the subgroup that reported starting medication post treatment (No Med/Med). Also important in the findings was that the group that reported taking the medication throughout the treatment and follow ups (Med/Med) had reduced height gain relative to peers in the group that had never taken medication (NoMed/NoMed; MTA Cooperative Group, 2004). As a result of the MTA study and follow up, increased understanding is beginning to unfold regarding subtypes of ADHD and the implications that different comorbid clusters may have regarding treatment alternatives.

Important Distinction

Additional analysis of the MTA findings (Jensen, 2002) revealed differential treatment effects for different comorbid clusters. Using behavior therapy (BT), medication management (Med Mgt), and combined behavior therapy and medication managements (BT + Med Mgt) alternatives, results suggest that children with ADHD and anxiety are likely to respond positively to all forms of treatment, while those with ADHD alone or ADHD + conduct problems are more likely to require treatments involving medication and that behavior therapy alone is less likely to be effective. Children who present with ADHD + anxiety + conduct problems are likely to need a combined treatment approach.

Alternative Treatment Methods

Although medical treatment is often the treatment of choice for ADHD (Abikoff, Gittelman-Klein, & Klein, 1977), there are cases where parents or children refuse medical treatment, or unpleasant side effects result in discontinuing medication. In addition, it has been argued that while stimulant medication provides short-term symptom relief, that long-term and life-long changes also require behavior management programs to develop skills in many of the deficit areas (organizational skills, social skills, time management, etc.).

Behavior management programs and functional behavioral assessments.   Although it was once thought that cognitive behavioral (CBT) programs would be the answer to working with ADHD children and getting them to slow down and think, unfortunately CBT programs have not been proven to be an effective approach to working with ADHD populations (Abikoff, Ganeles, & Reiter, 1988). Results of the MTA studies (MTA Cooperative Group, 1999) revealed medication to be the most consistent treatment in the reduction of the core symptoms of ADHD; however, behavioral treatment did provide benefits in improving symptoms in other key areas, e.g., social skills, aggressive responses, and parent/child interactions.

Interventions in the home and school environments.   Interventions for children with ADHD that can be used in the home and school environments to increase positive behaviors often involve plans that use a contingency management approach. Through the use of a functional behavioral assessment, therapists can obtain information necessary to develop a behavioral intervention program. Several treatment manuals exist that can assist clinicians in developing programs for parents of children with oppositional behaviors, social problems, and parent/child conflict (Barkley, 1997; Bloomquist, 1996).

Two Parent Training (PT) programs that have empirical support include those developed by Barkley (1997) and Forehand and McMahon (1981). These programs place emphasis on increasing parent understanding and practice in using behavior management skills to effectively reinforce positive behavior. The programs target increasing parent awareness and skills in areas such as, recognizing and responding to good behavior; strategies for effective communication; and how to reduce inappropriate behaviors through such techniques as time out and response cost. PT programs generally run for 8 to 12 sessions. Empirically, studies have demonstrated PT programs to be effective in improved parenting skills, reduction of parent stress, reduction of core symptoms of ADHD, and noncompliance (Anastopoulos, Shelton, & DuPaul, 1993; Sonuga-Barke et al., 2001). Including teacher consultation in the PT program can assist in generalization of behaviors from the home to school environment, especially when communication between home and school is monitored through the use of daily communication. One mechanism that can work to provide this information is the student agenda. Linking parent and teacher communication can result in significant improvementin home and school behaviors (Pelham, Wheeler, & Chronis, 1988).

Contingency management programs evolve around specific systems of positive and negative consequences that are developed to insure behavioral change. Children with ADHD respond best to programs that have immediate reinforcers for good behavior and to programs that have clearly defined goals and specific target behaviors. Successful programs involve opportunities for the behavior to generalize to different settings and to include measures to avoid response relapse. Children with ADHD are highly responsive to visual charts which can be used to display their improved behaviors graphically.

Memory Bank

Studies have found that positive reinforcement for good behavior alone is not as effective as having some form of consequence for negative behaviors. The use of response cost or penalty is often an effective approach to emphasizing the need to reduce inappropriate behaviors (loses a token or privilege), as well as strengthen positive behaviors (Pfiffner & O'Leary, 1993).

Successful classroom interventions for ADHD children have been demonstrated in a wide variety of studies and include peer tutoring, the use of functional behavioral interventions (outlining antecedent and consequent conditions), and the use of computer assisted instruction (DuPaul & Eckert, 1998; Hoffman & DuPaul, 2000).

CHAPTER REVIEW

Historically, accounts of hyperactivity have dated back as far as 1865 in the story of "fidgety Phil." Yet some hundred years later, we are still searching for pieces of the puzzle to add to our understanding of ADHD. The *DSM* has recognized the disorder since the 1960s when hyperkinetic reaction of childhood disorder first appeared in the *DSM–II* (1968). Since that time, the disorder has evolved based on increased research findings. Currently, the *DSM–IV–TR* (2000) recognizes three subtypes of ADHD: ADHD primarily inattentive type; ADHD, primarily hyperactive impulsive type; and ADHD combined type (satisfies criteria for both inattentive and hyperactive/impulsive). A fourth category, ADHD NOS (not otherwise specified) is used to classify atypical cases. Three criteria are common to all types of ADHD: disorder is pervasive across situations; must be evident for at least 6 months; and must have been evident prior to 7 years of age.

1. **ADHD Primarily Inattentive Type**
   The inattentive type of ADHD is diagnosed less than other forms, which is likely due to its less obvious features. Often the disorder is not suspected until the student meets with lack of school success. There is some research support that females with ADHD are primarily of the inattentive type. Criteria (*DSM*, 2000) requires the presence of 6 symptoms from a list of 9. Symptoms describe behaviors that are inattentive, distractible, dreamy, and off task. Lack of attention to details, disorganization, forgetfulness, and poor follow through result

in many school-related difficulties and are often misunderstood as being unmotivated or lazy.

2. **ADHD Primarily Hyperactive Impulsive Type**

   Individuals in this category demonstrate at least 6 of 9 symptoms of hyperactivity and impulsivity, including excessive need to be on the go, driven, and fidgety. Excess need for motion is evident in problems remaining seated, excessive talking, and problems with quiet play. Their impulsivity is evident in the classroom, where they may blurt out answers and socially where they can be intrusive and inpatient. The high visibility and excess nature of their symptoms results in earlier (3 years of age), more prevalent (90% of all ADHD) diagnosis.

3. **ADHD Combined Type**

   Children who meet criteria for both the inattentive type and the hyperactive impulsive type are classified as the combined type. As a result, these individuals have significant difficulties in all areas of functioning: socially, emotionally, behaviorally, and academically.

4. **ADHD in Developmental Context**

   At present, *DSM* (APA, 2000) criteria are the least appropriate for diagnosing adolescents and adults with ADHD, due to the nature of the symptoms which were developed based on younger children (6 to 12 years). Children diagnosed with ADHD were often described as having a difficult temperament, excess activity, poor sleep patterns, and irritability in early childhood. Due to the nature of their symptoms, children with ADHD can be vulnerable to a multitude of school-related problems and peer-related problems. By adolescence, problems can escalate due to several factors, including lack of previous success, increased work load, and social pressures.

5. **ADHD and Comorbidity**

   Sixty percent of children who are diagnosed with ADHD have at least one other disorder. Rates of comorbidity are high for specific learning disabilities, internalizing disorders, externalizing disorders, social problems, sleep disorders, and substance use/abuse.

6. **Etiology**

   Brain structures (*frontal system, cingulated gyrus*), functions (*executive functions*), and neurotransmitters (*catecholamines, dopamine, norepinephrine, epinephrine*) associated with attention and motor activity have all been implicated in the etiology and maintenance of ADHD symptoms. Fifty percent of those with ADHD have a relative with the disorder. Our understanding of the contribution of arousal level and executive functions has been aided by models such as the one proposed by Barkley's (1997) for the impulsive/hyperactive type of ADHD. Less is known about the inattentive type.

7. **Diagnosis, Assessment, and Treatment**

   Although there is no single assessment for the identification of ADHD, several instruments provide information concerning how the symptoms of ADHD manifest behaviorally and with respect to cognitive processing. Since there is no "homogenous ADHD profile," an assessment battery using a multitude of informants and a wide range of instruments can provide valuable information concerning how ADHD is manifested that can serve to guide treatment and interventions. Treatments have primarily focused on medications (primarily stimulant medications), behavioral therapy, or combinations of the two. Research from the latest MTA follow up suggests that different comorbid clusters of ADHD (ADHD, ADHD + anxiety or conduct problems or anxiety and conduct problems) might respond differentially to different combinations of medication and behavioral therapy.

Consolidate and Communicate

1. Historically, ADHD has evolved from early thoughts of the disorder being a morbid defect of moral control to thoughts that inattentive and restless behaviors resulted from damage to the frontal lobes (during the 1930s to 1940s). Discuss how the interpretation of symptoms of inattention, hyperactivity, and impulsivity have changed over time, and what you anticipate might be the future of ADHD when *DSM–V* is released.

2. Ninety percent of diagnosed cases of ADHD are the hyperactive/impulsive type, including the combined type. Females seem to be diagnosed more with the inattentive type. Discuss these statements and the potential implications that they might have for young girls in elementary school.

3. There a number of issues with the *DSM* criteria for the diagnosis of ADHD, especially with respect to older youth. What are some of the challenges facing teens with ADHD and what are some of the challenges facing psychologists who attempt to diagnose ADHD in adolescence?

4. Desmond's mother is very confused and is having a very difficult time trying to understand how Desmond can be so involved in video games and yet not able to concentrate on school work. She is not so sure that she buys into this whole "attention deficit" problem when she observes to very contradictory situations. Explain to Desmond's mother why he is able to focus on video games and not school work. Be sure to incorporate Barkley's discussions of contingency-shaped and goal-directed persistence in your response.

5. Tony is a highly impulsive, hyperactive, and oppositional child. He is having problems academically and in his relationships with peers. He never seems to consider others' feelings and is very impatient with peers. In school, he rushes through assignments and blurts out answers to questions before the teacher has even finished the question. Using Barkley's model (1997) of behavioral inhibition, compare Tony's approach to tasks with the ways that his classmate Sammy might respond, given that Sammy is a straight-A student who is very popular with peers.

6. Discuss the types of services that students identified with ADHD might receive to assist with school-related problems. Be sure to address how these children would be identified under IDEA 2004 and Section 504 of the Rehabilitation Act of 1973.

Chapter Review Questions

1. What percentage of the school-aged population can be expected to have ADHD?
   a. 20%–25%
   b. 12%–15%
   c. 1%–2%
   d. 3%–7%

2. Which of the following is a likely consequence of having the hyperactive/impulsive type of ADHD as a teenager?
   a. increased risk of car accidents as teenagers
   b. increased risk of drop out before graduation
   c. increased risk of having conduct problems
   d. all of the above

3. Parents report that children who are diagnosed with ADHD demonstrated all of the following in early childhood except:
   a. excessive sleep
   b. difficult temperament
   c. irritability
   d. establishing secure attachments with caregivers

4. Which of the following is FALSE regarding children with ADHD?
   a. Excessive TV viewing at ages 1–3 years places children at increased risk for ADHD.
   b. Thirty percent of children with ADHD will repeat a grade.
   c. Ten percent will require special education attention.
   d. Thirty percent will drop out and not graduate.

5. According to the *DSM*, which type of ADHD is least likely to result in developing a disruptive behavior disorder?
   a. Combined type
   b. Inattentive type
   c. Hyperactive/impulsive type
   d. All are equally as likely

6. Which of the following sleep disorders were not associated with increased risk for ADHD?
   a. restless leg syndrome
   b. periodic limb movement
   c. night terrors
   d. sleep disordered breathing

7. In their study of risks for substance abuse, Brooke & Pelham (2003) found which of the following predicted the most vulnerability to later substance use?
   a. severity of inattention
   b. severity of hyperactivity
   c. severity of impulsivity
   d. all were equally as likely to predict vulnerability for substance use

8. What percentage of children with ADHD experience problems with peer relationships?
   a. 10%
   b. 70%
   c. 35%
   d. 50%

9. High activity levels in the cingulated gyrus have been associated with all of the following except:
   a. Tourettes's syndrome
   b. motivational control
   c. sense of time
   d. obsessive compulsive disorder

10. Which of the following is not a stimulant medication?
    a. Ritalin
    b. Dexadrine
    c. Adderal
    d. Strattera

Glossary of New Terms

attention deficit hyperactivity disorder (ADHD)
postencephalitic behavior disorder
minimal brain dysfunction
hyperkinetic reaction of childhood
ADHD primarily inattentive type
ADHD primarily hyperactive/impulsive type
ADHD combined type
ADHD NOS
focused/selective attention
sustained attention
task persistence
disinhibition
lack of self-control
self-regulate
section 504 of rehabilitation act of 1973
Individuals with Disabilities in Education Improvement Act (IDEA 2004)
response to intervention
discrepancy criterion
irritable mood
dual diagnosis
rapid cycling
socially disabled
periodic limb movement disorder (PLMD)
restless legs syndrome (RLS)
dopamine deficiency
sleep-disordered breathing (SDB)
frontal cortex system
cingulated gyrus
basal ganglia
executive functions
limbic system
reticular activating system
cerebrum
Tourette's syndrome
behavioral inhibition
working memory
self-regulation
internal speech
reconstitution
contingency based attention
sustained attention
goal-directed persistence
catecholamines
amphetamines
methlphenidates

pemoline
strattera
stimulant medications

Multiple Choice Answers:
1. d; 2. d; 3. a; 4. c; 5. b; 6. c; 7. a; 8. d; 9. c; 10. d.

11
Specific Learning Disabilities (SLD)

CHAPTER PREVIEW

Although the term "learning disability" was first used by Kirk in 1963, learning disabilities were not recognized formally until 1975 with the passing of Public Law 94–142. Since 1985, the learning disability movement has been in a "turbulent period," plagued with controversy over how to best define, assess, identify, and treat individuals with specific learning disabilities (SLD). With the most recent reauthorization of IDEA (Individuals with Disabilities Education Improvement Act, 2004) *response to intervention* (RTI) was introduced as a possible method of identifying students with SLD; a concept that has caused significant controversy and debate, especially from proponents in favor of retention of the discrepancy model which has been used for the past 30 years.

Although the *DSM* and the educational system both classify SLD from a categorical perspective, the systems differ in the nature of how the disorder is defined.

1. SLD and *DSM*

The *DSM* (APA, 2000) recognizes three primary learning disorders: Reading, Mathematics, and Written Expression. The *DSM* applies the discrepancy model for diagnostic purposes. A disorder is present if there is a *substantial* difference (2 standard deviations) between expected and actual performance based on intelligence, ruling out other potential contributing factors (e.g., poor teaching, second language, etc).

2. SLD and Educational System

SLD is a disorder in one of more of the basic *psychological processes* resulting in an imperfect ability to perform in one of eight areas of academic performance, including: *expression* (oral, listening, written); *reading* (basic skill, fluency, comprehension); and *mathematics* (calculation, problem solving). Prior to IDEA (2004), the discrepancy model was the only means available for identification. Currently, districts are allowed the use of RTI to identify SLD.

3. Other Definitions and Controversial Debates

Major interest groups *Learning Disability Association* (LDA, 1986), the *Interagency Committee on Learning Disabilities* (ICLD, 1987), and the National Joint Committee for Learning Disabilities (NJCLD, 1988) differ in their definitions of SLD and debate regarding which definition is the most appropriate has been on-going. The major debate in the field currently concerns the use of RTI versus the discrepancy model for the identification of SLD.

4. Prevalence and SLD Subtypes

Wide variations in prevalence rates exist due to differences in definitions. The *DSM* (2000) suggests 2%–10% and currently about 6% of school-aged children are labeled as SLD. Schools are concerned that identification of SLD has doubled since 1979, and there are debates concerning potential overidentification which led to change in identification criteria (introduction of RTI). Different subtypes of SLD have been recognized, including dyscalculia (mathematics), dysgraphia (written expression), dyslexia (reading, spelling), dyspraxia (fine motor function), and nonverbal learning disability (mathematics and spatial awareness).

5. Dyslexia

The most prevalent type of SLD (80%). Etiology has been linked to genetic transmission (DCDC2 gene) and brain function. Normal readers access the left hemisphere and develop neural pathways that mature from back to the front of the brain and from the right to left hemisphere. Dyslexics activate the right side of brain more than left and back (posterior systems) instead of frontal systems. Current interventions are attempting to "rewire" neural pathways in poor readers.

6. Dyscalculia

Less is known about dyscalculia. Associated deficits in visual/spatial processing may also be evident. Problems are more difficult to assess, since composite scores on mathematical tests often mask particular gaps in understanding. Cardinal markers of dyscalculia include deficits in calculation fluency and acquisition of number sense. Working memory deficits have been associated with use of fingers in counting, while semantic memory deficits may result in poor recall for number facts.

7. Nonverbal Learning Disability (NLD)

Children with NLD exhibit normal to superior reading (decoding) ability, although comprehension is compromised. Performance is poor in arithmetic with associated deficits in tactile and visual perception and visual spatial processing. NLD has been linked to right hemisphere dysfunction. Intellectual profiles often reveal significantly higher verbal skills compared to performance, which is the reverse pattern to more traditional types of SLD. Poor social skills result from nonverbal weaknesses associated with poor ability to read subtle social cues.

8. Social Skills Deficits

While it has been argued by many that the prevalence of social skills deficits among those with SLD signifies the need to consider the existence of a social learning disability, only the LDA (1986) recognizes social skills deficits as a type of SLD. However, some studies have demonstrated as high as 75% of students with SLD are rejected by peers. Intervention programs to improve social skills have been plentiful, but recently have come under scrutiny for lack of effectiveness. Suggestions for improved social skills interventions include improved assessment to better target behaviors and the use of empirically validated programs.

SLD: Historical Perspectives in Definition and Classification

In their quest to understand the nature and complexities of specific learning disabilities, researchers have probed the brain, sensory systems, and the unknown in their search for answers. Hallahan and Mercer (2001) suggest five important periods in the historical evolution of learning disabilities: Foundation Period in Europe (1800–1920); Foundation Period in the United States (1920–1960);

Emergent Period in the United States (1960–1975); Solidification Period (1975–1985); and Turbulent Period (1985–present). The summary follows from Hallahan and Mercer (2001) unless otherwise noted. Highlights from the first four periods are available in Table 11.1.

Historical Perspectives: An Overview

Foundation period: Europe (1800–1920). Gall's work on the relationship between brain injury and mental impairment led others to ponder where functions such as speech and language were located in the brain. Later, Kussmaul coined the phrase **word blindness** to describe inability to recognize text. Later, Hinshelwood developed theories of congenital word blindness, heritability, and a preponderance of males afflicted with the phenomenon. By 1920, a growing number of articles and case studies could be found in medical journals in Europe describing cases of adults and children with specific disabilities in reading.

Foundation periods: United States (1920–1960). Samuel Orton (1925) found that approximately 15% of children who scored within the average range on the Stanford Binet experienced severe reading problems due to letter reversals or mirror reading. Problems were thought to originate from mixed cerebral dominance and emphasis was placed on multisensory training as a correction. At this time, Fernald's multisensory program called the VAKT approach (visual/auditory/kinesthetic/tactual) was also very popular. Another important figure during this period was Marion Monroe (research associate with Orton), who developed diagnostic instruments to guide remediation. Monroe introduced the controversial concept of the **discrepancy criterion** to identify children with reading disabilities by comparing expected achievement (based on mental age) to actual achievement. Samuel Kirk met Marion Monroe when he was a graduate student. Kirk later developed the Illinois Test of Psycholinguistic Abilities (ITPA; Kirk, McCarthy, & Kirk, 1968), an instrument designed to discriminate between different types of learning disabilities.

Other researchers were focusing on learning problems specific to brain-injured (brain damaged or brain disordered) children, many of who had problems of attention, distractibility, and hyperactivity. According to Hallahan and Mercer (2001), it is likely that these children were similar to what is known today as having a specific learning disability with comorbid ADHD. William Cruickshank suggested important instructional accommodations that are still used today, including reducing distractions, increasing relevant stimuli, and increasing structure in the learning environment.

Emergent period (1960–1975). In 1963, Kirk announced the term **learning disability** to a group of parents of children with perceptual handicaps (reading problems). On the heels of this announcement, parent advocates founded the Association for Children with Learning Disabilities (ACLD), which in its current form is known as the **Learning Disability Association (LDA)**. However, it was not until 1975, with the passing of Public Law 94–142, that learning disabilities were formally accepted as a category to receive funding for direct services. Although the definition for learning disabilities in the Act was similar to Kirks' definition (1962), when the federal regulations were released, the discrepancy criteria was added as part of the selection process. The discrepancy model is controversial and continues to be an area of significant debate today.

Table 11.1 Perspectives on Learning Disabilities: The Early Years

Year	Learning Disabilities: Milestones and Historical Perspectives
1802	Franz Joseph Gall writes of the relationship between the brain and mental impairment based on his observations of soldiers.
1860s	Pierre Paul Broca locates speech in the left frontal lobe. Impaired speech production (aphasia) located in Broca's area (inferior left frontal lobe).
1874	Carl Wernicke discovers problems with recognition and comprehension of words (sensory aphasia) located in the left temporal lobe.
1877	Adolph Kussmaul identifies a severe reading deficit in an otherwise intact adult. Names the condition "word blindness."
1896	W. Pringle Morgan reports the first case of word blindness in a child (14-year-old boy).
1903	Hinshelwood identifies the angular gyrus as the location of reading process in the brain.
1917	Hinshelwood publishes *Congenital Word Blindness* in which he identifies a preponderance of males in the literature, and the possible heredity of word blindness in cross-generation studies.
1921	Fernald and Keller introduce VATK approach.
1925	Samuel Orton sets up a mobile clinic to identify children with learning problems and finds approximately 15% with severe reading problems score average on the Binet Simon IQ test.
1932	Marion Monroe publishes *Children who Cannot Read*. Uses diagnostic assessment instruments and error analysis to guide remediation. Introduces concept of discrepancy between mental expectation and academic achievement to identify reading disabilities.
1937	Orton publishes *Reading, Writing and Speech Problems in Children* in which he describes reading problems resulting from mixed cerebral dominance. Estimates over 10% of school population have word blindness. Recommends multisensory training.
1947	*Psychopathology and Education of the Brain Injured Child* (Werner & Strauss) is published based on studies of children with exogenous and endogenous brain damage.
1961	William Cruikshank coauthors *A Teaching Method for Brain Injured and Hyperactive Children*.
1961	The Illinois Test of Psycholinguistic Abilities (ITPA) is published to identify specific learning disabilities in children.
1962	Kirk publishes *Educating Exceptional Children* and provides a definition for learning disabilities.
1963	Kirk talks of learning disabilities to a group of parents of children with perceptual handicap in Chicago.
1964	Association for Children with Learning Disabilities (ACLD), now known as LDA, formed.
1965	Barbara Bateman, a student of Kirk's, reintroduces discrepancy criterion in LD definition.
1960s	Federal Involvement: Two task forces work at defining learning disabilities.
1966	Education of the Handicapped Act (EHA) excludes category of learning disabilities.
1968	Division for Children with Learning Disabilities (DCLD) of the Council for Exceptional Children (CEC) was founded.
1968	National Advisory Committee on Handicapped Children (NACHC) adopts definition similar to Kirk (1962).
1969	Children with Specific Learning Disabilities Act of 1969 adopts the NACHC definition of SLD.
1970	Public Law 91–230 several acts for funding children with disabilities are consolidated. SLD is not recognized as a formal category. Discretionary funds applied to research and training in SLD.
1975	Congress passes Public Law 94–142, the Education for All Handicapped Children Act. Learning disabilities recognized as an eligible category for funding. (Adopts NACHC definition used).
1978	National Joint Committee for Learning Disabilities (NJCLD) formed from major professional organizations and ACLD.
1977	PL 94–142 is implemented. SLD required determination of severe discrepancy between expectation and IQ.
1981	NJCLD announces its own definition of learning disabilities, omitting "psychological processes" from the definition.
1982	DCLD splits from CED and founds Council for Learning Disabilities (CLD), an organization separate from CEC. CEC restructures with a new division the Division for Learning Disabilities (DLD) of CEC.

> **Memory Bank**
>
> The multiple definitions generated for *specific learning disabilities* by different organizations and classification systems continue to be problematic today. How these systems differ and the implications of having multiple definitions will be addressed later.

Solidification period (1975–1985). This period represents a time of relative affluence for funding and grant-writing opportunities related to learning disabilities in areas of research and training. As a result, a multitude of research programs were initiated as researchers carved out niches of expertise in their field.

Turbulent period (1985–Present). Hallahan and Mercer (2001) conclude their historical review in the turbulent present with its controversial debates concerning how specific learning disabilities should best be conceptualized; how children with learning disabilities should best be identified (discrepancy criterion versus response to intervention); and whether current practices are responsible for identifying too many children, especially minority children, as learning disabled.

Current Issues: Definition and Systems of Classification

It is not surprising that there is such debate concerning how children with specific learning disabilities (SLD) should be identified, since there is still significant controversy regarding how SLD should best be defined and/or classified. At present, there are a number of different definitions of SLD offered by various organizations and systems in the United States that have evolved over the years: Diagnostic and Statistical Manual of Mental Disorders (*DSM–IV–TR*; APA, 2000); Individuals with Disabilities Education Improvement Act (IDEA, 2004); the National Joint Committee for Learning Disabilities (NJCLD, 1988), Association for Children with Learning Disabilities/Learning Disabilities Association (ACLD/LDA, 1986), and Interagency Committe on Learning Disabilities (ICLD, 1987).

> **Recall and Rewind**
>
> Why classify? As was discussed at length in chapter 5, systems of classification are purposefully developed to assist those in the field to organize information into meaningful clusters based on common identifiable features. Good systems of classification clearly articulate:
>
> - *defining features* (in operational terms)
> - *composition* (what is included and what is not included)
> - *exceptions* (what might be allowable, under specified conditions)
>
> Having a common classification system among those working in the field eases dialogue between professionals who are using the same terminology and conceptual basis for comparisons.

Two Systems of Classification: The DSM–IV–TR *(APA, 2000) and IDEA (2004)*

The *DSM–IV–TR* (APA, 2000) is a categorical classification system. Clinicians are able to determine whether individuals should be diagnosed with a specific type of disorder based on the match between an individual's symptoms and symptom criteria established in the manual. The categorical system is a binary system that produces a match (diagnosis) or no match (no diagnosis) outcome.

The classification model used by the educational system (currently **IDEA, 2004**) also fits the categorical model (Power & Eiraldi, 2000). Thus, from a categorical perspective, the two classification systems can be viewed as parallel processes. Within a mental health setting, the clinician performs a diagnostic evaluation using the *DSM* as a guide, while in the educational setting, the Child Study Team must assess and evaluate whether the child meets the criteria necessary for determination as 1 of the 13 categories of disorders eligible for special education and related services under IDEA (2004).

However, while the systems reflect parallel processes, the goals and procedures differ. It is the *clinician's goal* to determine:

1. whether the child meets criteria for diagnosis of a *mental disorder* according to *DSM criteria*, and
2. whether the disorder causes *serious dysfunction.*

However, it is the *Child Study Team goal* to determine:

1. whether the child meets *eligibility criteria* for having a disability *under IDEA (2004),* and
2. whether the disability significantly *interferes* with a child's *ability to learn.*

With this initial set of parallel processes in mind, the following discussion will compare the similarities and differences between IDEA (2004) and the *DSM* (APA, 2000) regarding the determination of specific learning disabilities (SLD).

The *DSM–IV–TR* (APA, 2000): Clinical Classification and Diagnostic Criteria

The *DSM–IV–TR* (APA, 2000) clusters specific learning disabilities under the category of **Learning Disorders**, formerly called Academic Skills Disorders. The disorders appear in the subsection under the larger category of: *Disorders Usually First Diagnosed in Infancy, Childhood, or Adolescence.* The *DSM* recognizes four different types of learning disorders:

- Reading disorder
- Mathematics disorder
- Disorder of written expression, and
- Learning disorder NOS (Not otherwise specified, for atypical variations)

Memory Bank

The presentation of information on disorders in the *DSM* follows the same format for all disorders presented in the manual. After a discussion of the diagnostic features (and criteria), information is presented concerning associated features and disorders (comobidity), specific culture features, prevalence, and differential diagnosis.

Reading disorder, mathematics disorder, and disorder of written expression.   Initially, the *DSM* presents the generic features of **learning disorders** and outlines the three general criteria that must be met in order to diagnose all of the learning disorders:

1. The individual's achievement on individually administered, standardized tests in reading, mathematics, or written expression, is *substantially below* that expected for age, schooling, and level of intelligence.
2. Learning problems significantly interfere with academic achievement or activities of daily living that require reading, mathematic, or writing skills.
3. If a sensory deficit is present, then the learning disabilities must be in excess of those usually associated with the deficit (p. 49–50).

Important Distinction

The *DSM* clarifies "substantially below" to be a **discrepancy between achievement and intelligence** that is in excess of 2 standard deviations between IQ and achievement. However, if in the clinical judgment of the examiner there is reason to believe that the IQ score has been lowered or compromised, a smaller discrepancy (between 1 and 2 standard deviations) may be used.

The *DSM* outlines several possible conditions that might result in compromising and serving to lower an IQ score, including associated disorders in cognitive processing, comorbid disorders such as emotional disorders, a general medical condition, or ethnic or cultural background. All of these conditions should be considered if the IQ score seems lower than anticipated given other assessment findings. If the child has a sensory deficit, such as a vision or hearing problem, then the processing problem (e.g., visual memory) must not be a result of the vision problem, but the underlying processing difficulty. Children who have vision and hearing problems can also have specific learning disabilities.

Associated Features

Consistent with the diagnostic criteria, the *DSM* recognizes that learning disabilities may impact activities of daily living (associated with poor reading, mathematics, or writing skills) and children may present with feelings of *demoralization* and *low self-esteem*. Educational outcomes for many with learning disabilities are poor with as high as a 40% drop out rate in high school which is 1.5 times greater than the average high school drop out rate (*DSM–IV–TR*; APA, 2000). Learning disorders may persist into adulthood, and may be exhibited in difficult personal and professional relationships.

Cognitive processing problems may also be evident and appear as deficits in visual perception, linguistic process, attention, memory, or any combination of these (*DSM-IV-TR*, APA, 2000, p. 50).

Differential diagnosis. A diagnosis of a learning disorder requires that the disorder be differentiated from academic difficulties that might exist as a result of normal variations in academic performance or from academic difficulties due to lack of opportunity, cultural factors, or poor teaching. It is also noted that some children who may attend classes in schools that have poor instructional quality may also suffer from more absenteeism due to illness or impoverished and chaotic living environments (*DSM–IV–TR*; APA, 2000, p. 51).

Important Distinction

As part of the differential diagnoses, the *DSM–IV–TR* (APA, 2000) notes that a key defining feature in making a differential diagnosis between mental retardation and a learning disorder is that in mental retardation, academic achievement is low, but commensurate with expected IQ. However, in those with a learning disorder, academic achievement is substantially below measured intelligence.

Reading Disorder

In addition to meeting the criteria B and C, as set out in the *DSM* for all learning disorders, the diagnosis of a **reading disorder** requires that reading achievement is specifically measured by individually administered standardized tests that evaluate reading accuracy, speed, or comprehension and that the outcome is significantly below the expected level, given the child's chronological age, measured intelligence, and age-appropriate educational background (Criterion A). The *DSM–IV–TR* notes that reading disorder has also been called **dyslexia**. Common reading problems evident in oral reading are distortions, substitutions, or omissions. Whether reading is done orally or silently, problems will be evident in the length of time required to complete the task (slow reading pace) and in faulty comprehension (*DSM-IV-TR*, 2000, p. 52).

Mathematics Disorder

In addition to evidence of criteria B and C required for a diagnosis of a learning disorder, a **mathematics disorder** requires that mathematics ability (calculation or math reasoning) is substantially below the expected level, as determined by individually administered standard tests of mathematical ability.

Mathematics ability may be impaired due to skill deficits in a number of areas, such as linguistic problems (naming or understanding mathematical concepts, terms, and operations), or memory/attention (misreading mathematical signs, forgetting to add carried numbers, etc.). Problems with underlying mathematical skills such as one-to-one correspondence for counting, remembering the sequence of mathematical steps, or being able to recall multiplication tables can all contribute to a mathematics disorder. Generally, mathematics disorders are not as prevalent as the other learning disorders and are seen in approximately 1% of the population.

Disorders of Written Expression

Of all the learning disorders, written expression is the most difficult to measure, since there are few standardized instruments available. As a result, the *DSM* criteria require individually administered standardized tests or *functional assessments* of writing skills to determine whether an individual is functioning substantially below the expected level, given the individual's chronological age, measured intelligence, and age-appropriate education (Criterion A). Criteria B and C are consistent with criteria listed for the other disorders.

The most common types of expressive writing problems that are encountered include errors in grammar, punctuation, poor paragraph organization, spelling errors, and poor handwriting. The diagnosis is not considered complete if only spelling or handwriting exist, in the absence of other expressive problems. Due to limitations in existing assessment instruments for written expression (the majority of those that exist are often very tedious to score and can still be quite subjective), the *DSM–IV–TR* has suggested alternative methods (comparison of multiple samples of written work with age-expected samples; use of tasks where the child is ask to copy, transcribe dictation, or to spontaneously compose in response to a prompt, all of which may be necessary to evaluate the extent of impairment). Additional complications in evaluating written expression result due to age limitations. Often a disorder of written expression will not be detected until at least the second grade, when greater emphasis is placed on the development of written performance.

Differential diagnosis. Similar to spelling, poor handwriting in the absence of other problems of written expression would be unlikely to be diagnosed as a **disorder of written expression**. However, the *DSM* does suggest that poor handwriting may be the result of poor motor coordination and recommends that further evaluation to determine whether a diagnosis of *developmental coordination disorder* might be appropriate.

Learning Disorder Not Otherwise Specified (NOS)

Throughout the *DSM–IV–TR* (APA, 2000), the category of NOS is available for those disorders (in this case learning) that do not meet all the criteria in the prescribed manner, yet clinical judgment suggests high probability of a learning disorder. The *DSM* gives the example of an individual who might not qualify as having a learning disorder in reading, or mathematics, or written expression, individually, but who is nevertheless substantially below overall achievement expectations due to the combined effect of impairments in all three areas.

Developmental Coordination Disorders and Communication Disorders

Although developmental coordination disorders and language disorders do not fall under the category of learning disorders, a brief mention of these disorders will be provided at this time, since the information can be helpful for purposes of differential diagnosis.

Developmental coordination disorders. Developmental coordination disorders occur in approximately 6% of children between 5 and 11 years of age and can cause significant impairment in academic and daily living skills. Coordination is substantially below what is expected given age and intelligence, and may be seen as delays in motor milestones, "clumsiness," and poor performance in gross motor (sports) and fine motor (handwriting) activities. The diagnosis is not made if poor coordination is due to a medical condition (e.g., cerebral palsy) or pervasive developmental disorder, and only in those with MR if it exceeds what would be expected given the MR diagnosis.

Communication disorders. There area four disorders included in this category: *Expressive language disorder, mixed expressive-receptive disorder, phonological disorder, and stuttering.*

Expressive language disorder. There are a wide variety of language-based skills that fall under the rubric of expressive language disorder, including limitations in vocabulary, production errors (tense, word retrieval problems, shortened sentences, and unusual word order in sentences), and problems with fluency. As with other disorders in the *DSM*, expressive language disorder requires functioning substantially below expectations, based on standardized measures. Although language delay is quite common in children under 3 years of age (10%–15%), prevalence rates for school age children are approximately 3%–7%. There are two main types of expressive language disorders: *developmental* (associated with delayed language development), and *acquired* (neurological or other condition after a period of normal development, e.g., encephalitis, head injury).

Memory Bank

According to the *DSM*, expressive language disorders may occur in communication regardless of whether the communication is oral or sign language.

Mixed receptive–expressive language disorder. In addition to having expressive language problems, as outlined above, children in this category also experience receptive language difficulties (understanding words, sentences, or types of words, e.g., spatial, quantity, and so forth). Similar to expressive language disorder, the mixed disorder may also be developmental or applied. Prevalence rates are estimated to be approximately 3% of school aged children.

Phonological disorder. *(Formerly Developmental Articulation Disorder)* Approximately 2% of 6- and 7-year-old children exhibit a failure to develop speech sounds appropriate for age and dialect, resulting in impaired academic, social, or occupational communication. Sound production is poor involving errors in sound sequencing, sound substitutions, or sound distortions. Some children are not diagnosed until formal school entrance (preschool, Kindergarten) because they are considered unintelligible outside the immediate family.

Stuttering. Onset of stuttering is typically between 2 and 7 years of age (peaking around 5 years), and is evident in about 1% of school-age children. Stuttering is a disturbance of expressive fluency more prevalent in males than females, and usually starts gradually with repetition of initial consonants (e.g., "C-c-c-c-can I go?"), first words in a phrase, or lengthy words. Recovery can be spontaneous.

IDEA (2004): Educational Definition and Eligibility Criteria

Definition

The newly reauthorized IDEA (Individuals with Disabilities Education Improvement Act, 2004) was signed into law by President Bush December 2004, and went into effect July 2005. After a period of time reserved for public comments regarding the proposed regulations, and after having considered the comments, the U.S. Department of Education published the final set of federal rules and regulations (August 14, 2006). IDEA (2004) maintains the definition for SLD, as originally set out in IDEA (1997), and as such the definition of specific learning disability remains as follows:

Specific learning disability. *(i) means a disorder in one or more of the basic psychological processes involved in understanding or in using language, spoken or written, that may manifest itself in the imperfect ability to listen, think, speak, read, write, spell or to do mathematical calculations, including conditions such as perceptual disabilities, brain injury, minimal brain dysfunction, dyslexia, and developmental aphasia.*

   (ii) Disorders not included: Specific learning disability does not include learning problems that are primarily the result of visual, hearing or motor disabilities, of mental retardation, of emotional disturbance, or of environmental, cultural or economic disadvantage (Federal Register, 2006: 300.8 (10), p. 46757).

   The definition continues to pose difficulties for some due to the vague references to basic psychological processes inherent in the disorder and the resulting imperfect ability in a number of areas. The Register has published some of the comments generated about the definition and why they have not changed it. For example, with respect to "imperfect ability," the Register did not see fit to change the wording because they did not agree that the term implied a minor problem.

Memory Bank

The definition of SLD as it appears under IDEA (2004) refers to basic psychological processes; however, there is no further clarification of what these processes refer to. Historically, Kirk, McCarthy, and Kirk (1968) developed the Illinois Test of Psycholinguistic Abilities (ITPA) in an attempt to evaluate psycholinguistic processes. Although the instrument gained initial popularity, it soon fell out of favor.

Identification Procedures and Criteria

Although both IDEA (2004), effective July 2005, and the accompanying federal regulations, effective October 13, 2006, maintain the same definition for SLD noted in previous versions of the law and regulations, significant changes were made to the *identification procedures and criteria* concerning the discrepancy formula. In the recent guidelines, it is clearly stated that:

A State must adopt, consistent with 300.309 (*determining the existence of a specific learning disability*), criteria for determining whether a child has a specific learning disability as defined in 300.8 (see above). In addition, the criteria adopted by the State—

1. *Must not require* the use of a severe discrepancy between intellectual ability and achievement for determining whether a child has a specific learning disability;
2. *Must permit the use* of a process based on the child's response to scientific, research-based intervention;
3. *May permit the use* of other alternative research-based procedures for determining whether a child has a specific learning disability. (Federal Register, 300.307(a), p. 46786)

As part of the child's educational team, according to the regulations, the determination of whether a child has SLD is to be made by child's parents and a team of qualified professionals, which must include a teacher (child's teacher or teacher qualified to teach students of the child's age), and at least one person qualified to conduct diagnostic examinations (school psychologist, speech pathologist, remedial reading teacher).

4. Determination that lack of achievement is not primarily due to: a disability (visual, motor, hearing), mental retardation, emotional disturbance, cultural factors, economic disadvantage, limited English proficiency, or inappropriate instruction. To insure that underachievement is not due to inadequate teaching, documentation (data) of appropriate instruction (observations, and repeated assessments) and monitoring of progress during instruction are required. Ultimately, children who do not make adequate progress and continue to demonstrate a need for special education and related services will require parental permission for further (comprehensive) evaluation.

IDEA (2004): Additional procedures. In addition to the requirements already discussed above, the federal regulations have included additional procedures for determining the existence of SLD.

1. *Underachievement.* Evidence that the child does not achieve adequately and meet State-approved grade-level standards in one or more of the following eight areas:
   oral expression
   listening comprehension
   written expression
   basic reading skill
   reading fluency skill
   reading comprehension
   mathematics calculation
   mathematics problem solving
2. *Response to intervention (RTI).* Evidence that the child does not improve in the identified academic areas when using a process (*a series of interventions*) based on the child's response to scientific, research-based intervention; *or*
3. *Pattern of strengths and weaknesses.* The child exhibits a pattern of strengths and weaknesses in performance, achievement, or both relative to age (using grade level standards or intellectual information). This profile analysis (intra-individual differences in standard achievement scores or intellectual functioning (IQ) often results in a comparison of response profiles within and between assessment instruments. This procedure has typically been used to determine a discrepancy between IQ and achievement in the past, and could still be used in this capacity.
4. *Determination of appropriate instruction.* Prior to identification as SLD, the district must provide evidence of appropriate instruction in the area of underachievement (as defined in the No Child Left Behind Act of 2001).
5. *Rule out underachievement due to other factors.* Prior to identification as SLD, the district must also rule out other factors (e.g., limited English proficiency, economic disadvantage).

Memory Bank

The steps required to determine if a student has SLD under current regulations involve, determining:
1. Underachievement
2. Response to intervention (RTI) *or*
3. Pattern of strengths and weaknesses
4. Appropriate instruction
5. Other factors are not accountable

The Discrepancy Approach: What the Critics Say

Historical background.   For the past 20 years concerns have been expressed regarding the over-reliance on the ability–achievement model. Criticisms have been levied against most aspects of this model from its theoretical foundation (Kavale, 1987) to its developmental application (Parrill, 1987) and its statistical basis (Wilson, 1987). The on-going controversy and debate among professionals regarding the definition and classification of SLD has for the most part focused on the question of *how to identify children with SLD.* One of the most controversial issues has been whether children with SLD should continue to be identified using the IQ-achievement discrepancy criterion.

Recall and Rewind

The IQ-achievement discrepancy was initially introduced by the U.S. Department of Education in 1977 as part of the federal regulations that were developed to accompany the Education for All Handicapped Children Act of 1975 (P.L. 94-142), now known as the Individuals with Disabilities Education Improvement Act (IDEA 2004). The discrepancy formula was included as the process and criteria for identification of students with a specific learning disability (SLD) and was the primary method of differentiating between students with low achievement due to low mental ability (low IQ), and those whose low achievement was unexpected (normal or above-normal IQ) and could not be accounted for by other factors (e.g., limited English proficiency, inadequate teaching, etc.).

Criticisms of the discrepancy model.   The discrepancy approach has been used by both educational and clinical communities to determine whether a significant discrepancy exists between intellectual ability and academic achievement. Recent changes to special education law have resulted from growing discontent with the discrepancy approach on several levels:

1. *Lack of consistency among states in determining what is a significant discrepancy*: Wide variations exist, with some states using 1SD difference (15 points between IQ and achievement), while others are using 1.5 (22 points) or 2 SD (30 points) differentials.
2. *Questionable research support for the discrepancy formula* (Stanovich, 1991).
3. *Failure mentality and age bias*: Older aged children are more likely to have significant discrepancy than younger aged children.
4. *IQ bias for students with lower IQs*: Children who score in the borderline range (IQ in the 70s) or lower limits of the average range (IQ 80–85) typically are not eligible for services because they do not qualify under the discrepancy approach.
5. *Matthew effects*: Phrase coined by Stanovich (1986) to described poor readers who suffer from increasingly detrimental effects of poor vocabulary development, which in turn may lower IQ scores and hence nullify any potential for a discrepancy between IQ and achievement.

Response to Intervention (RTI): What the Critics Say
Despite the many criticisms levied against the use of the discrepancy approach, the response to intervention (RTI) approach that has been adopted as an alternative method for identification has also met with considerable controversy and debate. Mather and Gregg (2006) discuss the struggle that exists between attempting to achieve consensus on a conceptual definition for SLD and the operational diagnostic criteria that will be used for the identification of SLD. The authors caution that any sole criteria can be problematic and call for increased need for clinical judgment in the diagnosis of SLD.

The Debate Heats Up

The controversy surrounding SLD has lead one prominent spokesman in the field to conclude: "The present SLD definition is too broad to be wrong and too vague to be complete" (Kavale, 2005). Furthermore, Kavale contends that "changes to the operational definition (RTI) without changes to the formal definition are "indefensible" and result in a "disconnect between the formal definition and the operational definition" (p. 553).

What is the response to intervention (RTI) approach   Use of the RTI approach as a diagnostic or identification approach would determine whether a child would be classified as SLD based on failure to respond to an intervention (academic remediation). Typically, as described in the literature, RTI would use a **curriculum-based assessment (CBA)**. Use of a CBA might typically involve direct observation and data collection concerning a child's performance in the curriculum currently being used for the student's academic program, and making informed decisions based on that information. There are three common characteristics that can be found in the majority of CBA programs (Shapiro & Derr, 1990):

1. student's performance in curriculum as a baseline measure
2. progressive monitoring of instructional-intervention success
3. use of the data to inform the intervention strategies

Memory Bank

Placed within a behavioral framework, CBA can be seen as a three stage approach to academic change (Dombrowski, Kamphaus, & Reynolds, 2004):
1. baseline data
2. application of intervention program
3. post-intervention data collection
At the third stage, students who do not respond to intervention would likely be classified as SLD, if they meet with the additional criteria as set out in the regulations.

Some of the more notable criticisms of the RTI approach include:

*   Generally, RTI has been described as a multitiered process for academic and behavioral screening that would include a valid measure and monitoring. However, there is currently no explanation of either the screening tool, or how it would be used (Semrud-Clikeman, 2005).
*   The system as proposed is too vague, and does not allow for uniformity of diagnosis and communication of basic processes across school districts and professionals (Dombrowski, Kamphaus, & Reynolds, 2004).
*   RTI suffers from the same criticism levied against the discrepancy model; namely for some children, identification would not occur until repeated failures which would not only support a failure based model, but also seriously delay the onset of the comprehensive assessment (Semrud-Clikeman, 2005).
*   Students may not respond to intervention for a number of potential reasons, including SLD, emotional problems, motivation, etc. "If RTI cannot discriminate, how can it classify" (Mastropieri & Scurggs, 2005, p. 528).
*   Critical developmental periods for learning brain based connections (between 5 and 8 years, or between 12–15 years for higher level thinking skills) may be passed by without appropriate intervention due the implementation of an RTI intervention (Teeter & Semurd-Clikeman, 1997).
*   RTI as the new "operational definition of SLD," radically alters how SLD is conceptualized (responsiveness vs. nonresponsiveness; Kavale, 2005).
*   RTI is a skill-focused evaluation/intervention and does not provide any information about the child's ability (intelligence), which could drastically alter the intervention required (Semrud-Clikeman, 2005).

- RTI can only document low achievement compared to a discrepancy approach, which was able to provide data on both low achievement and unexpected low achievement, given ability (Kavale, 2005).
- Current conceptualizations of RTI are vague, especially concerning the potential role of teachers and diagnosticians and how SLD will be differentiated from other disabilities (Mastropieri & Scruggs, 2005).

Although the primary goal of the Response to Intervention (RTI) Symposium hosted by the National Research Center on Learning Disabilities (NRCLD: Kansas, December, 2003) was to evaluate the usefulness of RTI for the identification of SLD, it also provided a forum for critiques of the RTI approach (as seen above) and presentation of alternative perspectives.

Johnson, Mellard, and Byrd (2005) reviewed a number of salient discussions and alternate viewpoints presented during the NRCLD symposium have reported features common to the alternative models presented, namely:

- retention of the multifaceted nature of the SLD construct
- support for the basic credo that students with SLD are fundamentally different from other students with low achievement due to inherent difficulties evident in disorders of psychological processes

Within this framework, key components of the identification process should include *evaluation of* psychological processes, and intraindividual discrepancies, and the *application of exclusionary criteria* to rule out factors other than SLD that might be contributing to low achievement (p. 571). Within this model, RTI would be considered as an initial step, or a "prereferral writ large" (Kavale, Holdnack, Mostert, & Schmied, 2003) which could serve to enhance quality control in the regular classroom concerning appropriate instruction, but which is, in isolation, insufficient as an identification system for SLD.

Within a similar mind set, Semrud-Clikeman (2005) also suggests that if RTI would acknowledge the potential contribution that could be made by neurpsychology, then screenings could focus on **predictor variables** (e.g., *working memory, attention and executive functions*) that would not only allow for monitoring of progress in these crucial areas, but also provide access to those students who are at higher risk in these areas.

The Discrepancy Approach: A Supportive View

In addition to criticisms levied against the use of RTI in isolation, and proposed alternative models, there have also been several arguments made in defense of retaining the discrepancy approach. For example, Mastropieri, and Scruggs (2005) caution others to be cognizant of the strong bond that exists between the IQ-achievement discrepancy criteria and the category of LD itself, while Kavale et al. (2003) argue for more rigorous methods in implementing the discrepancy approach rather than adopting a new model. Furthermore, Kavale and colleagues suggest that the "vilification" of the IQ concept has occurred partly in response to positive or negative connotations, which may be associated with the bearer (e.g., SLD is a preferred designation to MR in some households). However, as clinical judgment and empirical evidence support, the difficulty with the discrepancy formula may be more a problem of inconsistency in application, than deficits in the model itself (MacMillan, Gresham, & Bocian, 1998).

Other Definitions of Specific Learning Disabilities

While the educational definition for specific learning disabilities used today has virtually remained unchanged since its inception in Public Law 94–142 (1977), by the mid-1980s prominent organizations in the field were revising their definitions to reflect information available from research and to address contemporary issues (Hallahan & Mercer, 2001).

Three other prominent and vocal organizations have developed definitions of learning disabilities that have both subtle and major variations on a theme. All three definitions recognize the presumed neurological or central nervous system dysfunction that underlies the disorder and compromises the acquisition and development of skills in areas such as listening, thinking, speaking, reading, writing, reasoning, and calculating numbers. The **Learning Disability Association (LDA**, 1986) stresses the *chronic nature* of the condition and emphasizes SLD as a handicapping condition that impacts *adaptation* on all levels of daily functioning, including self-esteem, vocation, socialization, and education. In their definition, the **Interagency Committee on Learning Disabilities** (**ICLD**, 1987) specifically excludes any reference to psychological processes and includes *social skills deficits* as an area of learning disability. The ICLD definition is also unique due to its recognition of the existence of other *comorbid associations*, such as attention deficit disorder, that can accompany SLD. In 1988, the **National Joint Committee for Learning Disabilities (NJCLD)** revised their definition in response to the revisions by LDA and ICLD. In this revision, NJCLD added that the disorder may occur across the life span (similar to LDA); however, unlike ICLD, the NJCLD is clear in stating that although associated social problems may occur, they do not support the existence of a social learning disability. The NJCLD definition is concordant with the two other definitions acknowledging that although other handicapping conditions (sensory, mental retardation, serious emotional disturbance) or environmental influences (cultural, inappropriate instruction) may exist comorbidly, they cannot account for the disability; however, unlike ICLD, there is no specific mention of attention deficit disorder.

Prevalence of Specific Learning Disabilities

In the *DSM–IV–TR* (APA, 2000), prevalence rates for learning disorders range from approximately 2% to 10% of the population. Given the wide variation in definitions of SLD, it is not surprising to find an equally wide range of prevalence rates quoted in the literature, depending on how SLD is defined and measured.

Important Distinction

One criticism of the discrepancy approach focuses on the lack of guidelines regarding the "optimum" standard deviation differential that should be used, and the resulting inconsistency in the application of the procedure. For example, in one study, using a 20-point discrepancy between intelligence (IQ) and achievement, Frick and colleagues (1991) reported a comorbidity rate between 16%–21% for ADHD and SLD. However, in other studies, using a 10-point discrepancy between the standard reading scores and the IQ, researchers reported prevalence rates for comorbid ADHD and SLD as high as 38%–45% (Dykman & Ackerman, 1992; Semrud-Clikeman et al., 1992).

Concerns Regarding Growing Prevalence Rates and Overidentification in Education

One major concern has been the implication that the discrepancy model has been instrumental in the over-identification of students with specific LD, resulting in inflated numbers of identified

Table 11.2 Children 3 to 21 Years of Age Served in Federally Funded Programs by Type of Disability

Type of Disability	Year 1976–1977	Year 1980–1981	Year 1989–1990	Year 1990–1991	Year 1995–1996	Year 1999–2000	Year 2000–2001	Year 2001–2002
Specific Learning Disability	a. 21.5	a. 35.3	a. 44.6	a. 45.2	a. 46.3	a. 45.7	a. 45.2	a. 44.4
	b. 1.8	b. 3.6	b. 5.0	b. 5.2	b. 5.8	b. 6.0	b. 6.0	b. 6.0
Speech and Language	a. 35.2	a. 28.2	a. 21.1	a. 20.9	a. 18.3	a. 17.4	a. 17.2	a. 16.9
	b. 2.9	b. 2.9	b. 2.4	b. 2.3	b. 2.3	b. 2.3	b. 2.3	b. 2.3
Mental Retardation	a. 26.0	a. 20.0	a. 11.9	a. 11.4	a. 10.2	a. 9.7	a. 9.5	a. 9.2
	b. 2.2	b. 2.0	b. 1.3	b. 1.3	b. 1.3	b. 1.3	b. 1.3	b. 1.2
Emotional Disturbance	a. 7.7	a. 8.4	a. 8.3	a. 8.3	a. 7.9	a. 7.8	a. 7.5	a. 7.4
	b. 0.6	b. 0.8	b. 0.9	b. 0.9	b. 1.0	b. 1.0	b. 1.0	b. 1.0
Autism and Traumatic Brain Injury	a. -	a. -	a. -	a. -	a. 0.7	a. 1.3	a. 1.5	a. 1.8
	b. -	b. -	b. -	b. -	b. 0.1	b. 0.1	b. 0.2	b. 0.2
Other Health Impaired	a. 3.8	a. 2.4	a. 1.1	a. 1.2	a. 2.4	a. 4.1	a. 4.6	a. 5.3
	b. 0.3	b. 0.2	b. 0.1	b. 0.1	b. 0.3	b. 0.5	b. 0.6	b. 0.7

* Federally funded programs (chapter 1 and IDEA).
a. Percentage distribution of children served in federally supported programs
b. Percentage served in program based on total school population
- Not available
Source: U.S. Department of Education, Office of Special Education and Rehabilitative Services, Annual Report to Congress on the Implementation of the Individuals with Disabilties Act, various years, and unpublished tabulations; and National Center for Education Statistics, Statistics of Public Elementary and Secondary School Systems, various years, and the NCES Common core of Data (CCD), "State Nonfiscal Survey of Public Elementary/Secondary Education," 1989–90 through 2001–02. (This table was prepared July 2003.) Retrieved January 29, 2007 from http://nces.ed.gov/programs/digest/d02/dt052.asp

students, and more specifically, the overrepresentation of minorities classified as learning disabled (Kavale, Holdnack, & Mostert, 2005). The percentages of children in federally supported programs for children with disabilities (3 to 21 years of age) for selected years, is presented in Table 11.2.

Currently, children with specific learning disabilities represent 6% of the school-aged population, compared with only 1.8% in 1976–1977. Recall, however, that SLD was not formally recognized until the passing of Public Law 94–142 in 1977. Shortly afterward (1980–1981), the number of students identified as SLD doubled (1.8% to 3.6%), while the number of students identified as having mental retardation decreased by 0.7% (2.0% to 1.3%). In the past 10 years, the percentage increase in students identified as SLD has been 1 percent (1990–1991: 5%; 2001–2002: 6%). However, increased numbers of student identified for special education services is not unique to children with SLD. In the 26th annual report to Congress on the implementation of IDEA (2004), the disability distribution was reviewed for prevalence rates reported in 1992 and 10 years later (2002). The target population served under IDEA was children and youth ages 6 to 21 years. Results of that report are summarized in Table 11.3.

In 2002, the category of SLD accounted for almost half (48.3%) of all students receiving special education and related services, followed by speech or language (18.7%), mental retardation (9.9%), emotional disturbance (8.1%), and other health impaired (6.6%). The category of SLD is noted as the most prevalent disability across all ethnic and racial groups. There has been an increase in the identification of younger students with SLD in the 10-year interim. Other categories that noted an increase in identified students included, other health impaired (0.1% to 0 .6%) which is most noted in the White (non-Hispanic) population. Explanations for the rise in this category are inclusions of ADD and ADHD in this category. Autism has also noted an increase in identification during the 10-year span across all age levels. A likely explanation is an increased awareness and inclusion of other pervasive developmental disorders within this category.

Table 11.3 Percentage of Students Receiving Special Education and Related Services for Students 6 Through 21 Years of Age Under IDEA, 1992 and 2002 and Ethnic Distribution by Disability for 2002

Type of Disability	Year 1992	Year 2002	*American/ Indian Alaska Native	Asian/ Pacific Islander	Black *not Hispanic*	Hispanic	White *not Hispanic*
Specific Learning Disability	a. 4.5 b. 6.0	a. 4.0 b. 6.9	55.3%	40.8%	45.1%	58.3%	46.8%
Other Health Impaired	c. 0 .1	c. 0.6	5.0%	4.8%	5.1%	3.6%	8.0%
Autism	a. 0.04 c. 0.03	a. 0.3 c. 0.18	0.9%	4.9%	1.6%	1.3%	2.2%
SeriousEmotional Disturbance	—	—	7.9%	4.7%	11.3%	4.9%	7.9%
Mental Retardation	—	—	7.8%	9.1%	16.8%	7.8%	8.3%
**Dev. Delay	1997 d. 0.02	2002 d. 0.36	2.2%	1.4%	1.1%	0.5%	1.0%

a. % of students aged 6 through 11
b. % of students aged 12 through 17
c. % of students aged 6 through 21 years
d. % of students aged 6 though 9 years
— minimal change
* Percentages of ethnic distribution, by category, receiving special education Fall 2002
**Developmental Delay
Source: US Department of Education, Office of Special Education and Rehabilitative Services, Office of Special Education Programs, 26th Annual (2004) Report to Congress on the Implementation of the Individuals with Disabilities Education Act, Vol.1, Washington, D.C., 2005. Retrieved January 28, 2007, from http://www.ed.gov/about/reports/annual/osep/2004/26th-vol-1.pdf

Specific Types of Learning Disabilities

There are many reasons why children and youth may perform poorly in school and learning problems can result from a host of problems not related to learning disabilities, such as emotional or family problems, lack of motivation, living conditions that are not conducive to learning (unsafe/violent neighborhood or living in poverty), or lower mental capacity. A subset of children with learning problems will experience learning difficulties due to a SLD, a neurologically based disorder. In order to distinguish children with SLD from students whose learning suffers from other factors, definitions of SLD have exclusionary clauses to rule out learning problems related to intellectual factors, emotional disturbance, social or cultural conditions, or due to primary visual, hearing, or motor disability. Many children with SLD also have other comorbid disorders, such as ADHD, which can exacerbate problems and pose increased challenges regarding identification and intervention. Children who experience SLD are a heterogeneous group with wide variations in symptom presentation. As a result, researchers have attempted to identify subtypes of the disorder based on symptom clusters.

Consider This

Children with SLD can be identified via the nature of processing difficulties, intraindividual profile analysis, discrepancy between aptitude and achievement, or by the nature of their academic problems. Lyon, Fletcher, and Barnes (2003) suggest that SLD can be represented by six major types of achievement problems: word recognition, reading fluency, reading comprehension, mathematics computations, reading and math, and written expression.

Learning disabilities and subtypes.   Specific reading disability (SRD) or dyslexia is by far the most well-known and well-researched type of SLD. The effects of having SLD can manifest differently for different individuals and can range from mild to severe impairment.

Five specific subtypes of learning disabilities (and the subject area influenced) have been identified: **dyscalculia, dysgraphia, dyslexia, dyspraxia,** and **nonverbal learning disability.**

Each of the five subtypes is summarized briefly in Table 11.4. The following discussion will focus on three of the specific types of learning disabilities: Dyslexia, dyscalculia, and nonverbal learning disabilities.

Table 11.4 Specific Types of Learning Disabilities

Type of Learning Disability	Primary Area Affected	Description of Difficulties
Dyscalculia	Mathematics	Problems understanding and using math concepts and symbols, recalling math facts and understanding concepts such as time and money. At its most basic level, problems may exist in simple counting due to problems with one to one correspondence. Student may not be able to count by 3s or 5s . Math word problems are difficult because the student does not have a sense of what information is relevant and what is irrelevant to solving the problem.
Dysgraphia	Written Expression	Handwriting can be illegible due to poor letter formation and poor letter spacing. Academic problems may include spelling and excessive time required to execute written notes and assignments. Often experience difficulty organizing information and in starting written assignments.
Dyslexia	Reading, Spelling	Problems in recalling letter sequences ("gril" for "girl"), sound to symbol association (recall the sound that goes with the letter b), and word forms (was vs. saw). Student may mix up letters within words and words within sentences while reading. Letter reversals (b and d), inversions (p and d) are common, and can also extend to numbers (9 for 6). Often there are problems with directionality and spatial orientation (left and right).
Dyspraxia	Tasks requiring fine motor skills	May demonstrate a specific disorder in the area of motor skill development. May experience problems planning and completing fine motor tasks. Approximately 2% of the general population is afflicted and about 70% are male. Simple tasks such as buttoning a shirt or more complex tasks such as using scissors to cut straight lines or brushing teeth may be a challenge.
Nonverbal Learning Disability	Mathematics and Spatial Awareness	Impaired functioning evident in nonlanguage areas, such as mathematics, visual/spatial organization and motor coordination. Social skills are also impaired due to problems with interpreting subtle social cues.

Specific Learning Disability in Reading/Developmental Dyslexia

Definition and Associated Features

Memory Bank

There is a common misperception that all people with dyslexia see words backwards (e.g., was for saw). However, only about 30% of dyslexics have trouble with reversing letters and numbers.

Children who experience specific reading disabilities (SRD), often referred to as dyslexia or developmental dyslexia, are of average intelligence, and similar to other types of SLD, their disability is not related to other factors (inappropriate instruction, socioeconomic disadvantage, or sensory deficits). The disability impacts the acquisition of basic reading skills from simple phonological processing (sound symbol association), to word identification, reading fluency, and passage comprehension.

In a recent paper produced by the *International Dyslexia Association*, Lyon and Shaywitz (2003) discuss a definition of developmental dyslexia, which expands on the original working definition developed in 1994. The current definition differs from that derived in 1994 by specifying the disability as *neurobiological in origin* and conceptualizing the reading disability as a *specific type of disability rather than one of several general disabilities*:

> Dyslexia is a specific learning disability that is neurobiological in origin. It is characterized by difficulties with accurate and/or fluent word recognition and by poor spelling and decoding abilities. These difficulties typically result from a deficit in the phonological component of language that is often unexpected in relation to other cognitive abilities and the provision of effective classroom instruction. Secondary consequences may include problems in reading comprehension, and reduced reading experience that can impede growth of vocabulary and background knowledge. (Lyon & Shaywitz, 2003, p. 2)

The current definition proposed by the Dyslexia Association is clear in its recognition of "fluency" as a major and long-term outcome of dyslexia. Although many readers with dyslexia will increase their reading accuracy as a result of intervention, lack of fluency will produce long-term problems resulting in effortful, slow, and laborious reading (Shaywitz, 2003), and the side effects of arrested development in areas of vocabulary and impoverished background knowledge.

Memory Bank

Stanovich (1986) used the phrase **Matthew effects** to refer the rich-get-richer/poor-get-poorer consequences that result from the ever-widening gap between good and poor readers.

Prevalence

Dyslexia is the most prevalent type (80%) of specific learning disability, occurring in an estimated 5% to 17.5% of school-age children (Shaywitz, 1998). The range in prevalence is due to differences in definitions proposed by different classification systems. Although the major definitions all share an exclusionary framework, debate regarding identification of the disorder will no doubt be influenced by the controversial procedures of response to intervention versus discrepancy approach discussed earlier.

Etiology

Biological Model

Genetic transmission.   In one longitudinal study, it was reported that family members of dyslexic children had significantly lower reading levels than a matched set of controls (DeFries, Singer, Foch, & Lewitter, 1978). Studies of monozygotic twins with dyslexia have reported concordance rates as high as 84%–100%, while studies comparing dizygotic twins report rates between 20%–38% (Bakwin, 1973; DeFries & Alercon, 1996). Genetic effects seem most pronounced in children with high IQs compared to those with lower IQs (Demonet, Taylor, & Chaix, 2004). As many as 50% of children of dyslexic parents also have dyslexia (Knopik et al., 2002). Recent reports have implicated a gene called DCDC2 (doublecortin domain containing 2) that may be responsible for disrupting the formation of normal brain circuits that influence fluent reading (Meng et al., 2005; Schumacher et al., 2006).

Brain structure and function.   The revised definition of dyslexia proposed by Lyon and Shaywitz (2003) recognizes the neurological basis of the disorder which has been confirmed through the use of functional magnetic resonance brain imaging (fMRI) and magnetoencephalography (MEG). Neuroimaging studies of adults and children with dyslexia have reported underlying variations in the way that dyslexics and nondyslexics process information. In their article, Shaywitz et al. (2003) report localized reading function within three brain regions located within the left hemisphere: phoneme recognition (**left frontal gyrus**); mapping of phonemes to letters (**left parietal/temporal**); and long-term storage of sight vocabulary (**left temporal/occipital**). The activation of the left hemisphere is important to reading because it is the region of the brain that is specialized for language functions.

Normal adult readers use the frontal regions of the brain to a greater extent than children who are just beginning to read (Schlaggar, 2003). Developmentally, children move from activation of the posterior systems associated with visual perceptual processes and letter and word naming, to increased activation of the frontal systems involved in reading comprehension. As a result, *neural pathways mature from the back to front of the brain and from the right to the left hemisphere* (Shaywitz, 2003). However, children with dyslexia activate the right side of the brain more than the left and posterior systems.

Individuals with reading problems do not access the readily available storage of words as do their high-reading peers. Poor readers engage in the more laborious exercises of phonetic recognition and mapping, as if they are experiencing the word for the first time, each time. In adults with dyslexia compared to nondyslexic controls, there is reduced activation in the left posterior pathways that are involved in the reading process (Frith & Frith, 1999).

There are two different brain systems that have been implicated in reading in nondyslexic individuals: the *left parietal/temporal region* is involved and activated during **phonetic tasks** (letter pronunciation), while the **left inferior temporal/occipital area** is activated during **sight decoding tasks** (letter and word perception). The phonetic task draws upon the more intense and initial laborious system of phonetic awareness, while the sight task is often the more rapid decoding process used by skilled readers. In a study of 144 children with dyslexia and controls, Shaywitz et al. (2002) found that there was increased activity in the in the *right hemisphere,* **frontal gyrus** (right-sided region involved in letter to sound decoding), likely to compensate for poor ability to utilize the back and left systems adequately. It is this system that carries the entire load for the dyslexic population.

Memory Bank

Cognitively, the linguistic and visual coding processes should work together to provide links between the written and spoken word. From a cognitive perspective, both permanent memory and working memory are involved in learning to read.

Increased research effort and technological advances have also confirmed that deficits in the phonological components of language are at the basis of dyslexia. In their revised definition, Lyon and Shaywitz (2003) incorporated the identification of two key processes entailed in reading: *accurate word recognition* (identification of real words) and *the ability to decode* (pronouncing pseudowords). Children with dyslexia are slower at decoding (naming) words, pseudowords and numbers then their nondyslexic peers (Aaron et al., 1999).

At the core of dyslexia is the problem with phonemic awareness necessary to break the reading code. This deficit in phonology is the most specific factor in predicting dyslexia to date (Morris et al., 1998). Phonemic awareness, the laborious part of attaching sound to symbol, is so difficult for those with dyslexia that they experience lifetime problems with reading fluency (Lyon & Shaywitz, 2003).

Assessment

The assessment of learning disabilities is integrally related to issues of definition and identification. In their review of evidence-based assessment of learning disabilities, Fletcher, Francis, Morris, and Lyon (2005) identify four assessment models based on:

1. the discrepancy between aptitude and achievement,
2. low achievement,
3. intraindividual differences, and
4. response to intervention (RTI).

The authors note that any "valid classification and measurement system for LD must identify a unique group of underachievers that is clearly differentiated from groups with other forms of underachievement" (p. 507). The authors emphasize that in any assessment of SLD, the tests selected will be based on the underlying model of identification that drives the process of assessment (e.g., discrepancy model will result in administration of intellectual and norm based academic measures; low achievement models will focus on achievement tests and exclude aptitude; cognitive or neuropsychological processing instruments will be used to measure intraindividual profiles; and RTI models will include measures of the integrity of the intervention used and the progress made).

Fletcher et al. (2005) conclude that of the four models evaluated, a hybrid model that focuses on low achievement, and RTI should be used for the identification of children with SLD. The authors base their decision on their inability to find empirical support for the use of assessments of cognitive neuropsychological or intellectual ability to identify children with SLD. In their opinion, intellectual assessments should only be used in the rare cases of suspected mental retardation. Furthermore, they suggest that this model is applicable to all identification procedures regardless of whether a child is being assessed by a psychologist in a school, hospital, or private practice

(p. 519). The authors also suggest that intervention is warranted for anyone with achievement scores below the 25th percentile and that only those that do not respond to intervention executed through the RTI approach be considered as possible SLD. Two norm referenced achievement instruments that are identified by Fletcher and colleagues that are capable of identifying academic difficulties in all six areas outlined by Lyon et al. (2003) are the Weschler Individual Achievement Test (*WIAT–2*) and the Woodcock Johnson Achievement Test (*WJ–III*). The authors also suggest that CBAs may also be a way that the school can evaluate intervention progress.

Important Distinction

Failure to learn or failure to teach? Lyon and Shaywitz (2003) emphasize the need to document educational/instructional history, especially formal schooling in the essential linguistic and prereading skills required for effective reading. The authors believe that for many children with reading problems, targeting early prereading skills can alleviate the problem in many cases. In at least one study, a reduction in reading failure from 18% to less than 6% was due to effective early intervention (Torgesen, 2000).

Although Fletcher et al. (2005) outline their concerns regarding what they consider to be limited value or information obtained from neuropsychological or cognitive input; it is important to recall the importance that neuropsychology places on the identification of underlying processes in order to develop appropriate interventions targeting these processing deficits. In addition, interventions aimed at areas of the brain have in essence served to "rewire" some responses in poor readers (Simos, Mouzaki, & Papanicolauo, 2004). It is also important to consider the comments of Fletcher and colleagues (2005) in the light of some of the problems cited earlier regarding the RTI approach.

Memory Bank

Identification of executive functions such as working memory, response inhibition, self-monitoring, and metacognitive skills—such as the child's ability to understand their own thinking processes—is crucial not only to the identification of underlying processes that influence reading problems, but also in their remediation as well (Semrud-Clikeman, 2005, p. 565).

Semrud-Clikeman (2005) suggests that identification of problems in executive functions can be important in providing information to guide intervention. In chapter 10, several assessment instruments were discussed that are particularly helpful in this regard (see Table 10.3 for a review).

Assessments of brain functioning using neuroimaging techniques suggest that developmentally, reading may progress from the use of the right hemisphere to more sophisticated use of the left hemisphere (Rourke, 1982; Simos et al., 2001). If this is true, then it is likely that as the nervous system matures reading skills become more localized in the left hemisphere, and that this developmental shift is somehow compromised children with dyslexia (Collins & Rourke, 2003). Longitudinal studies currently in process hope to identify and map brain features identifying how distinct profiles can predict neuropsychological functioning or dysfunction.

Dyslexia: Intervention

The cumulative effect of poor reading skills is self-evident. Poor readers lack the exposure to information presented in print and have less opportunity to develop their vocabularies, general knowledge, and language skills. Interventions can take the form of direct instruction targeting weak reading skill areas, or targeting areas of the brain for remediation in an attempt to "rewire" faulty circuits.

Remedial reading instruction.   Aaron and Joshi (1992) suggest that poor readers can be grouped into one of three categories:

- category 1: deficient decoding but adequate comprehension (fluency problem)
- category 2: adequate decoding but poor comprehension
- category 3: poor decoding and comprehension

It is most likely that children with dyslexia will fall into either categories 1 or 3.

Reading fluency and repeated readings.   One reading intervention that has been successful in increasing reading fluency is the technique of repeated readings (O'Shea, Sindelar, & O'Shea, 1985). The task includes selection of a reading passage (curriculum based) which the student reads to determine a baseline for improved performance. Students then determine their reading rate (words per minute) for repeated readings of the same passage. Comprehension questions inserted at the end of the reading passage can provide an index of rate/comprehension. The exercise is well suited to individual graphing of reading rate as a visual reinforcer for improved fluency.

Reading comprehension and graphic organizers.   Graphic organizers (Ausubel, 1963) are visual and/or spatial headings that highlight important information to be presented. Graphic organizers can draw on a reader's previous knowledge-base and provide a framework for facilitating and incorporating information. Since children with SLD often have difficulty transferring information between tasks, graphic organizers can be particularly effective. Kim, Vaughn, Wanzek, and Wei (2004) conducted a meta-analysis of more than 21 studies concerning the use of graphic organizers to improve comprehension in students with SLD. Results revealed that graphic organizers are most effective when they are created by the students, positioned after the text, and used for a longer period of time (Dunston, 1992). Graphic organizers assist students with SLD with organizing and recalling verbal information (Wong, 1978). Despite some methodological difficulties in addressing the numerous types of organizers used in the studies, Kim and colleagues (2004) suggest the use of graphic organizers seemed to have a beneficial effect for students with dyslexia in enhancing reading comprehension through the use of semantic organizers. Although the authors suggest that graphic organizers might be very beneficial for those with dyslexia, they emphasize the scarcity of recent research (three studies) concerning graphic organizers for SLD students in the past 10 years.

Recently, fMRI scans of children's brains before and after intensive instruction in reading have revealed that as children overcome their reading disability, they demonstrate increased activity in the area of the brain that is responsible for visual recognition (Shaywitz, 2004). However, Simos and colleagues (2000) found that even when children with dyslexia accessed the same brain regions as their nondyslexic peers, there were marked differences between the two groups in the time it took for different areas to actually be activated and the order in which they were activated. However, results of their latest study indicate that these differences can be minimized, even eliminated in some cases, with intensive intervention. The researchers provided 16 weeks of intensive training, with 2 hours of daily practice in phonological awareness (awareness of speech sounds) for the first 8 weeks, followed by daily, 1-hour exercises in word recognition, comprehension, and fluency for the final 8 weeks. Posttest results revealed improved reading in all areas. In addition, there was evidence of increased shift of activity into parts of the brain associated with normal reading as well as improved timing of activity. Some children, however—especially those that use their own compensatory strategies (right side of the brain)—may not benefit from attempts at "rewiring" their brain circuits (Simos et al., 2000).

Specific Learning Disability in Mathematics: Dyscalculia

Definition and Associated Features

Memory Bank

Dyscalculia is a term used to refer to "a severe or complete inability to calculate" (Hallahan, Lloyd, Kauffman, Weiss, & Martinez, 2005). The *DSM–IV–TR* (APA, 2000) refers to the disorder as a mathematics disorder, while IDEA (2004) classifies the disorder under the general class of specific learning disabilities with identified problems in calculation (arithmetic) or problem solving in mathematics.

The two primary conditions associated with primary mathematics learning disabilities (MLD) are underachievement in math that may be related to deficits due to other verbal learning disabilities, and/or dyscalculia. As part of the general source of learning problems that influence other learning disabilities, deficits can be found in any of the stages of information processing discussed earlier, including: input, integration, memory, or expression. In addition, particular deficits in visual/spatial processing may influence a child's ability to align numbers properly, understand place value systems, and cause poor performance in map related functions or geometry (Geary, 2003).

Identification of children and youth with MLD is complicated for several reasons. For one, lower than unexpected mathematics achievement in and of itself does not verify the presence of MLD. Children may score poorly in mathematics in one grade and then score better in another. By contrast, students who have persistent low scores across assessment periods and who also have memory or cognitive deficits are likely candidates for MLD (Geary, 2004). Geary also suggests that assessment of math abilities using composite scores may be misleading, since overall scores may mask severe weaknesses in specific areas. Another complication in the identification of MLD is overlap in symptoms with nonverbal learning disability, or right hemisphere disability, wherein the primary academic impairment is evident in an inability to perform in mathematics (Rourke, 1985, 1989; Rourke & Conway, 1997).

A cardinal marker of mathematics difficulties, specific or otherwise, can be found in deficits in **calculation fluency** (Gersten, Jordan, & Flojo, 2005). However, one characteristic that may distinguish children with MLD from children with other problems is treatment resistance (e.g., difficulties that persist in automatic recall for math facts, or number combinations, such as 5×4 or $5 + 8$), despite intensive direct instruction and remediation in the area (Howell, Sidorenko, & Jurica, 1987). A second area of difficulty appears to be early acquisition of **number sense**, which includes such concepts as estimating and judging magnitude, ability to detect erroneous conclusions, sequential counting, and quantity discrimination (Gersten et al., 2005).

Science Talks

In one study, researchers found that Kindergarten children differed in their ability to answer the question: "Which number is bigger—4 or 3?" Despite controlling for student ability to count and produce simple calculations, students with higher socioeconomic status (SES) answered the question correctly 96% of the time compared to only 18% accuracy for children from lower SES backgrounds. The researchers suggest that number sense development may be linked to informal learning in some home environments and that early intervention (pre-K or K) may be beneficial in allowing some students to catch up (Griffin, Case, & Siegler, 1994)

Other common characteristics of children with MLD include the use of immature strategies (counting on their fingers) and procedures (counting instead of using number facts). Children with MLD also make more counting errors, such as double counting on the first item. Other common mathematical errors include poor alignment of number columns and errors of carrying or borrowing numbers across columns.

Prevalence

It has been suggested that some form of specific math learning disability (MLD) is evident in approximately 5% to 8% of the school aged population (Geary & Hoard, 2002).

Etiology

Biological Model
Genetic transmission. Shalev and colleagues (2001) report that family members (parents, siblings) of children with MLD have a 10 times greater risk for having MLD than individuals in the population at large.

Brain structure and function. Although reading disabilities (dyslexia) have attracted volumes of research, there has been much less attention paid to students who exhibit early problems with basic mathematical concepts (Robinson, Menchetti, & Torgesen, 2002). Although research concerning MLD is lagging far behind that of dyslexia, studies of dyslexia that have included comorbid dyslexic/MLD populations have identified some potential neural systems, such as memory retrieval deficits associated with left hemisphere subcortical regions (Ashcraft, Yamashita, & Aram, 1992). Furthermore, central executive functions, such as the attentional and inhibitory processes that are necessary to engage in problem-solving activities, often require integration of both the language and visuopatial systems to execute math tasks (Baddeley, 1986). The language systems may be important in forming number words when counting, while visuopatial systems may be necessary in tasks such as estimating magnitude or having a sense of spatial form (Geary, 2004). Working memory deficits have also been associated with MLD, suggesting that reliance on finger counting may be a strategy that helps reduce the load on working memory (Geary, 2000). Semantic memory deficits have also been postulated to help explain the severe problems often encountered by individuals with MLD in retrieving number facts from long term memory (Bull & Johnston, 1997; Geary & Brown, 1991).

Assessment and Intervention

In addition to the traditional assessment protocol outlined for other learning disabilities, assessment of mathematical understanding is of course crucial to identification of students with a learning disability in mathematics. In a recent issue of the *Journal of Learning Disabilities* (Vol. 38, 2005), several articles are devoted to issues of early identification and intervention of students with MLD. While Gersten, Jordan, and Flojo (2005) note that "research on valid early screening measures of subsequent mathematics proficiency is in its infancy" (p. 293), they suggest that enough data has been accumulated to isolate areas that require intensive support and intervention.

Ultimately, the authors suggest the *Number Knowledge Test* (Okamoto & Case, 1996) is the strongest screening measure that provides good predictive validity from several levels of knowledge of basic arithmetic concepts, operations, number sense (magnitude), and counting strategies. Based on their research review, Gersten et al. (2005) suggest three brief measures that can be linked to instructional objectives, including quantity discrimination (magnitude), identification of missing numbers, and number identification. Other valid predictors noted include rapid automatic number identification and working memory for mathematical information (Gersten et al., p. 300).

The Syndrome of Nonverbal Learning Disabilities

In addition to subtyping of learning disabilities into areas of academic deficit, Rourke and colleagues have identified two subtypes of SLD based on their differential patterns of neuropsychological strengths and weaknesses (Rourke, 1982, 1985, 1993, 1999; Rourke, Hayman-Abello, & Collins, 2003). The subgroups consist of children with **basic phonological processing disorder (BPPD)** and those with **nonverbal learning disabilities (NLD)**. Children with BPPD (dyslexia) demonstrate poor ability to decode single words and spell, but have adequate performance in math. However, children with NLD exhibit the opposite pattern: normal to superior decoding ability, but poor performance in arithmetic. While those with BPPD have deficits in phonological processing, children with NLD show deficits in "tactile and visual perception, complex psychomotor skills and in dealing with novelty" (Collins & Rourke, 2003). Mattson, Sheer, and Fletcher (1992) compared hemisphere activity in children with BPPD and NLD and found that while children with BPPD demonstrated less activity in the left hemisphere while doing verbal tasks, children with NLD demonstrated less activity in the right hemisphere on nonverbal tasks.

Science Talks

Based on EEG patterns of brain activity, it has been suggested that children with dyslexia have left hemisphere dysfunction, while children with NLD experience dysfunction in the right hemisphere (Mattson et al., 1992). In another comparative study, children with dyslexia exhibited deficits in processing auditory/verbal information, while children with NLD experienced problems processing visual/spatial information (Miles & Stelmack, 1994).

There have been difficulties in establishing legitimacy for the NLD subtype within the educational system, which tends to conform to the more traditional concept of learning disabilities as language based disorders (Thompson, 1997). Whereas the more traditional type of SLD often reveals an elevated Performance IQ relative to lower Verbal IQ, the profile of NLD is the reverse, with Verbal IQ often significantly higher than Performance IQ.

Although research on learning disabilities has for the most part focused on children with neuropsychological deficits related to linguistic abilities (Eden, Stein, Wood, & Wood, 1995), in recent years, NLD has developed growing interest clinically and in research endeavors. However, one major obstacle to integrating findings from research efforts concerning NLD relates to the variety of different nomenclatures used to refer to individuals with this symptom cluster. In the literature, in addition to **nonverbal learning disability (NLD)**, it is also possible to find information on NLD syndrome under the name of **developmental right-hemisphere syndrome (DRHS), nonverbal learning disorder** (Strang & Casey, 1994; Gross-Tsur, Shalev, Manor, & Amir, 1995), and/or **visiospatial learning disability** (Carnoldi, Vnneri, Marconato, Molin, & Montinari, 2003).

NLD: Definition and Associated Features

Understanding the neurodevelopmental dynamics of NLD has evolved over the past 30 years and since the late 1980s, Rourke and colleagues have developed and refined the **white matter model** to explain the syndrome of NLD and the role it plays in other types of pediatric neurological dysfunction. Rourke et al. (2002) define the syndrome of NLD as:

> characterized by significant primary deficits in some dimensions of tactile perception, visual perception, complex psychomotor skills, and in dealing with novel circumstances. These primary deficits lead to secondary deficits in tactile and visual attention and to significant limitations in exploratory behavior. In turn, there are tertiary deficits in tactile and visual memory and in concept-formation, problem-solving and hypothesis-testing skills. Finally these deficits lead to significant difficulties in the content (meaning) and function (pragmatics) of language. (p. 311)

According to Rourke and colleagues (2002), the degree to which the effects of the phenotype of NLD may be manifest in any individual is dependent upon the degree to which an individual's **right cerebral hemisphere** is compromised by white matter (long myelinated fibers) abnormalities due to being underdeveloped, damaged, or dysfunctional (Rourke, 1995). Brain scans of individuals with NLD often reveal mild abnormalities of the right cerebral hemisphere, while many of the developmental histories are positive for some form of neurological insult to the brain resulting from either acquired or congenital brain injury.

What Is the White Matter Model?

The **white matter model** suggests that due to injury to the right hemisphere, there is a reduction in the white matter (myelinated fibers) connections in the right hemisphere thereby causing a disconnect between the left and right hemispheres. As a result, the left hemisphere primarily functions on its own and does not communicate with the right hemisphere (Thompson, 1997).

There are three broad areas of symptom clusters that evidence impairments in children with NLD: motor skills, the analysis and synthesis of visual spatial information, and social/pragmatic development.

Motor skills deficits. Although capable of simple motor tasks, motor clumsiness is common and children often appear poorly coordinated. This, in conjunction with poor spatial awareness, can lead to poor ability to judge one's body position in space and poor understanding of social and personal space. Balance is also poor and injuries may be evident in frequent falls related to faulty visual motor judgment. Slow speed of executing motor tasks and weak fine motor skills may result in the need for extended time to complete paper and pencil tasks. In their investigation of clinical characteristics associated with NLD, Gross-Tsur et al. (1995) found that slow cognitive and motor performance was evident in 80% of children with NLD; 90% demonstrated graphomotor impairment; and 67% had dyscalculia. Soft neurological signs on the left side of the body were evident in some of the children with NLD.

Visual/spatial organization. Individuals with NLD exhibit processing deficits in their ability to organize the visual/spatial field, adapt to novel situations and attend to, or interpret, nonverbal cues. Visual/spatial deficits are evident in several areas including the organization, discrimination, and interpretation of visual information. In one study, Liddell and Rasmussen (2005) found that despite average performance on tasks of verbal memory, children with NLD revealed significant deficits on measures of visual memory. In particular, immediate memory for faces was significantly below average and more impaired than delayed memory for faces. The researchers suggest several possible explanations for these findings, including encoding of facial features without attention to the gestalt, or the lack of emotional salience for facial expressions. The authors also suggest that impairments in parts of the right hemisphere responsible for processing faces (right temporal lobe and fusiform gyrus) may also be responsible. The fact that delayed recall was less impaired than immediate recall also suggests the possibility that children with NLD may require more time to consolidate the information, or that additional repetitions (third time they were exposed to the faces in this experiment) may have resulted in a practice effect on the delayed task.

Science Talks

Children with autistic spectrum disorders, especially Asperger's syndrome or higher functioning autism, have often been compared to children with NLD. Interestingly, children with autistic spectrum disorders also demonstrate deficits on tasks of memory for faces but not on tasks involving memory for words (Gunter, Ghaziuddin, & Ellis, 2002).

Social and pragmatic deficits. In their investigation of children with NLD, Gross-Tsur et al. (1995) found that all children in their study had evidence of poor social skills (inappropriate facial expressions, eye contact, weak pragmatic language, and poor ability to understand social rules). Nonverbal problem solving was a particular area of weakness. Harnadek and Rourke (1994) suggest that children with NLD suffer from very poor ability to transfer information from previous experiences, including social experiences, and as a result evidence deficits in concept formation and hypothesis testing. They are poorly equipped to adapt to changes in their environment and may appear scripted or inappropriate in their responses. Children with NLD often show extreme deficits in social perception, judgment, and interaction. As a result, they are often ostracized by peers become withdrawn and socially isolated. The inability to deal with novel situations results in extreme anxiety, which may even culminate in a panic attack. According to Rourke and colleagues (Rourke, 1989; Rourke et al., 2002) long-term prognosis for NLD without intervention reveals an increased risk for internalizing disorders, depression, suicide ideation, and increased isolation as adults. There are increased rates for depression (Rourke, 1995) and risk for suicide in children with NLD compared to those with dyslexia (Rourke, Young, & Leenaars, 1989).

Although language skills are the primary means of communication, commentary is often repetitive and verbose with poor understanding of the underlying **social pragmatics** (interpersonal communication skills) and subtle nuances often inherent in language (bound by literal interpretations). In addition, interpretation of body language, facial expressions, and other nonverbal information is impaired, resulting in significant difficulties understanding and interpreting social situations (Matte & Bolaski, 1998).

Furthermore, excessive verbosity in children with NLD may also be another factor that causes peer rejection and an alternate pathway to depression (Tsatsanis, Fuerst, & Rourke, 1997). In other subtypes of SLD, poor language skills may result in poor social communication, ultimately leading to social rejection.

Associated features and symptoms shared with other developmental disorders. As with many other disorders discussed in this text, symptom overlap between disorders is not uncommon. A recent literature review of studies over the past 12 years revealed that all of the 26 studies reported concerns with differential diagnoses with similar disorders, such as semantic pragmatic disorder and Asperger's syndrome (Thompson, 1997). For example, in one study, the entire sample of children with NLD (20 children) met the diagnosis for ADHD and all children were socially impaired (Gross-Tsur et al., 1995).

Science Talks

NLD or Asperger's syndrome? A recent comparison of children with Asperger's syndrome (AS) and children with NLD revealed that while both groups demonstrated nonverbal weaknesses, children with NLD were significantly better on several language-based academic tasks, while those with AS preformed significantly better than those with NLD on visual spatial tasks (Dumitrescu, 2006).

Rourke and colleagues (2002) recently reviewed the manner in which the syndrome of NLD might be manifested in several types of pediatric neurological disorders. For example, the relationship of NLD to Asperger's syndrome (AS) and high-functioning autism (HFA) was discussed. Rourke and colleagues (2002) ranked the disorders from the highest level of overlap (Level 1: virtually all of the NLD assets and deficits are manifest) to the lowest level (similar, but basically different). They found considerable overlap in the cardinal symptoms of AS (impaired motor skills, pragmatics and understanding of language, social understanding and interaction, visual/spatial deficits) and NLD. As a result of their review, the authors concluded that AS contained virtually all of the NLD assets and deficits. However, despite sharing the symptom of "verbosity," those with HFA have primarily left rather than right cerebral dysfunction. As a result, HFA was ranked at the lowest level being similar to but basically different from NLD.

Prevalence

It has been estimated that only 0.1% of the population would be diagnosed with NLD, although this might be an underestimate, since children may not be identified due to lack of understanding of the subtype. Unlike language based SLD that is more common in males than females, males and females are equally vulnerable to having NLD (Rourke, 1989).

Etiology

Biological Model

While language-based SLDs (dyslexia, dysgraphia) have a prominent history of genetic transmission, the genetic link to NLD is not clear. Research would suggest that NLD is more closely linked to brain structure and function, primarily impairment in the right cerebral hemisphere which specializes in nonverbal processing.

Brain structure and function. Brain scans of children with NLD have linked right cerebral hemisphere dysfunction with accompanying problems with visuospatial tasks (Semrud-Clikeman & Hynd, 1990). Brain trauma, such as neurological insult or injury, may also be responsible for damage to right hemisphere connections needed to integrate information between the left and right hemispheres. Rourke (1982, 1995) has suggested that deficits (destruction or dysfunction) in the white matter (white matter model) may interfere with accessing the right hemisphere, causing an inability to integrate information in a cross modal way.

Assessment and Intervention

Assessment. Asssessment of NLD can involve a number of psychological and neuropsychological instruments. On his Web site (www.nld-bprourke.ca), Byron Rourke outlines the protocols that he uses to make a determination of whether a child has NLD. He cautions that tests should only be administered under the supervision of a neuropsychologist with expertise in the assessment of children. There are two assessment protocols: one for children from 9 to 15 years of age, and another for younger children (5 to 8 years). The protocol for older children contains assessment instruments ranging from measures of motor and psychomotor functions, such as grip strength and static steadiness, to more complex functions measured by the mazes and the grooved pegboard. Visual/spatial/organization is measured by tests such as the Trail Making Test (Halstead-Reitan Neuropsychological Test Battery; Reitan, 1993) and the Block Design and Object Assembly subtests from the Wechsler Intelligence Scales for Children. Problem solving and ability to shift set are measured by such instruments as the Children's Category Test (Boll, 1993) and Wisconsin Card Sorting Tests (Heaton, Chelune, Talley, Kay, & Glenn, 1993). Psychosocial functioning is addressed thought the Vineland Adaptive Behavior Scale (Sparrow, Balla, & Cicchetti, 1984) and the Personality Inventory for Children (PIC; Lachar & Gruber, 2001). Additional information on this protocol and instruments used in the assessment of younger children can be found on the Web site (www.nld-bprourke.ca).

Cornoldi, Venneri, Marconato, Molin, and Montinari (2003) acknowledge that "although there is a large and well-established pool of evaluation procedures available for linguistic LD that usually lead to the early and reliable detection of affected children, no straightforward instrument is available to teachers for a preliminary identification of nonverbal learning difficulties in the classroom" (p. 305). To this end, the researchers have recently developed a rapid screening measure to assist in the identification of children with visuospatial learning disability (VSLD) in the schools. In their studies, the Shortened Visuospatial Questionnaire (SVS)—containing 18 of the original 37 items—was found to be a reliable predictor of those children who were identified as having VSLD through psychometric testing. Given the extent of visuospatial difficulties encountered by children with NLD, the instrument may have considerable value for use in the schools to screen children with NLD for further psychological and neuropsychological assessment.

Intervention.   Interventions for children with NLD target the many *academic* and *social challenges* that these children face. Academic deficits involve reading comprehension, graphomotor coordination, mathematics, and science (Matte & Bolaski,1998). Although intitially, verbal skills can even seem advanced to some, often these skills are acquired through rote memory; although the child may sound very intelligent, they often are lacking in comprehension.

Poor graphomotor skills can be improved considerably, but extensive practice is required (Rourke, 1995). Math skills remain a significant area of weakness and computational skills may not go beyond the fifth grade. Although it was initially thought that mechanical math was main source of difficulty, more recently math deficits have been found to affect the majority of math functions (Rourke, 1995). Although a prominent symptom, not all children with NLD have deficiencies in math (Pennington, 1991; Semrud-Clikeman & Hynd, 1990). According to Rourke (2000), 72% of children with NLD demonstrate deficits in math functioning.

There are limited formal and empirically driven intervention programs for children with NLD, although numerous resources and suggestions for parents and teachers are available on the NLD Web site (http://www.nldontheweb.org).

Foss (1991) suggests a number of areas that can be targeted when developing remedial interventions for children with NLD that focus on deficits in processing and production, including:

- clarification of language concepts,
- enhancing verbal reasoning,
- increasing comprehension and written output,
- improving social cognition, and
- enhancing self-esteem and feelings of self-efficacy.

Because these children experience problems making connections, often interventions would require direct instruction, not only in clarifying the subtleties in language but also in illustrating the different body and facial cues that can be interpreted in different ways.

In a preliminary case study investigation, Brodeur (2006) found that a 15-year-old female student with NLD who participated in a class that taught social pragmatics evidenced gains on all measures (self-report, teacher report, and parent report) of adaptive skills, social skills, and leadership. Future recommendations for social pragmatic instruction included emphasis on forming and maintaining friendships, while younger children could benefit from instruction in maintaining eye contact, and refraining from interrupting others.

Learning Disabilities and Social Skills Deficits

Whether definitions for SLD should include social deficits as specific types of learning disability has been a point of controversy for almost 3 decades. The association between learning disabilities and social difficulties is so prevalent that it has been suggested that social disability should be included in the definition proper (Rourke, Young, & Leenaars, 1989). It has been argued that since "specific patterns of central processing abilities and deficits" result in different types of SLD, as well as deficits in social competence, then academic learning deficits and psychosocial disturbances can both be conceptualized as emanating from patterns of neurological processing deficits (Rourke & Fuerst, 1991).

Stone and La Greca (1990) investigated the specific types of social difficulties encountered by children with SLD through the use of sociometric procedures in a sample of children in the 4th through 6th grades. Results revealed that in addition to significantly lower sociometric scores relative to their nondisabled peers, children with SLD were overly represented in the *rejected* and *neglected* sociometric categories and underrepresented in the popular and average groups. More than half of the children with SLD were classified into one of the low status groups by their peers (28% in the *rejected* category; 26% in the *neglected* category). The authors also found that social skills deficits impacted not only on social competence but academic achievement as well.

Science Talks

In their investigations of children's social status groups, Coie, Dodge, and Coppotelli (1982) found five distinct social classification subgroups: **popular, rejected, neglected, average,** and **controversial**. Children who were *rejected* by their peers demonstrated more loneliness, aggressive and disruptive behaviors (Asher & Wheeler, 1985), and were at greater risk for long-term negative outcomes than their nonrejected peers (Coie, 1985). *Neglected* children were shy and withdrawn (Coie & Kupersmidt, 1983), had higher levels of social anxiety, and were at greater risk for internalizing problems than their nonneglected peers. Neglected children are considered to have *low social impact* scores (low social visibility), while those that are rejected score high on social impact, but low on social preference (likeability).

Kavale and Forness (1996) conducted a meta-analysis of 152 studies involving more than 6,000 children. The authors reported that approximately 75% of students with SLD obtained negative assessments of their social skills, regardless of who was reporting the information (teachers, peers, self-ratings). Teachers saw children with SLD as less competent academically and less engaged socially. Children without SLD rejected 80% of their peers with SLD, placed them in categories of low social acceptance (not a friend), and described peers with SLD as less communicative and cooperative than their non-SLD peers. The majority of children and youth with SLD (70%) report that they have fewer social skills than their peers, while 80% expressed significant concern about their academic competence.

A number of studies have probed nonverbal communication through the use of the **Profile of Nonverbal Sensitivity** (PONS: Rosenthal, Hall, DiMatteo, Rogers, & Archer, 1979). Results from the PONS suggest that students with SLD function at about the 16th percentile compared to their non-SLD peers in their ability to interpret events, messages, and feelings in social situations. Other areas of social deficit included social problem solving, resolving social conflict, and overall social competence. Low levels of self-concept and self-esteem were evident in 70% of children with SLD, indicating a negative self (Coie, 1985) view relative to their non-SLD peers.

Important Distinction

SLD and Attributions Information from their meta-analysis (Kavale & Forness, 1996) revealed that the majority of SLD students were most likely to attribute successes to outside influences (e.g., luck), rather than their own effort. Unfortunately, these same children attributed their failures to internal (stable) causes, such as lack of ability, rather than situational or less stable influence, such as a lack of effort. While external forces are changeable, internal forces are seen as less amenable to change (e.g., ability).

Overall, the meta-analysis conducted by Kavale and Forness (1996) revealed that the majority of students with SLD exhibit social skills deficits. However, the authors report that although studies demonstrated deficits, the underlying causes have not been clearly identified. They suggest that future effort should be directed towards greater understanding of how academic and social deficits are related, and how processing problems (language, memory, perception, and cognition) influence social competence and/or social dysfunction. The authors conclude that although social deficits constitute an associated feature of many SLD profiles, inclusion of social deficit as a criterion for SLD is not recommended at this time.

Can Stable Friendships Impact Academic Performance?

Ladd, Kochenderfer, and Coleman (1996) found that Kindergarten children who made and retained friendships from the beginning of the school year had better academic outcomes than children who were rejected. Berndt and Keefe (1995) reported similar findings for children transitioning from middle school to junior high school.

Social Skills Intervention Programs

Since the 1960s, countless social skills training (SST) programs have been developed for a wide variety of problem populations. However, there has been increasing concern about the effectiveness of these programs in improving child social outcomes (Bullis, Walker, & Sprague, 2001; Gresham, Sugai, & Horner, 2001).

Maag (2005) reports that meta-analyses of SST programs have revealed three major shortfalls of SST programs:

1. targeting behaviors that are not socially valid
2. failing to pinpoint specific skills that are deficient (e.g., nonverbal miscue, sequencing errors, etc.)
3. failing, for the most part, to demonstrate increased peer acceptance as a result of involvement in the SST program

---

Science Talks

SST may be more successful for some types of problems. For children who are neglected by peers, SST programs have been successful in treating depression, anxiety, fears, and social withdrawal (Barrios & O'Dell, 1998; Ladd, 1981). However, rejected children have been less successful in achieving peer acceptance following SST. It is suggested that rejecting peers may require a longer time frame to change their impressions of these students following SST (Bierman, Miller, & Stabb, 1987).

Suggestions for improved SST interventions.   Success of SST interventions may have been compromised by lack of consensus regarding what constitutes social skills (e.g., social problem solving, making and keeping friendships, peer group entry, communication skills), and how these skill sets are to be measured and defined (Gresham, 1986). Another area of contention is how to conceptualize the relationship between *social skills* and *social competence*. Vaughn and Hogan (1994) suggest that social competence requires adequate functioning in four areas:

1. effective social behaviors (skills)
2. social relationships
3. social cognition
4. adaptive behaviors (absence of maladaptive behaviors)

The following suggestions have been recommended in order to enhance SST programs and improve social outcomes:

- *Base SST programs on functional behavioral assessments (FBA) that include* **replacement behavior training** (**RBT**). Although Maag (2005) acknowledges that traditionally, FBA runs contrary to SST by focusing on inappropriate behaviors versus appropriate behaviors, FBA can be integrated into SST programs by teaching appropriate (*RBT*) as part of the behavioral intervention plan. In this way, children will learn how to obtain reinforcements in a positive way, which will serve to better link treatment to outcomes and also provide appropriate measures of change.
- Increase reliance on using SST intervention programs that are empirically validated; insure sufficient length of training; and increase use of norm-referenced measures (Kavale & Mostert, 2004). For example, the authors suggest that the *Social Skills Rating System* (*SSRS*; Gresham & Elliot, 1990) and the *Walker–McConnell Scale of Social Competence and Adjustment* (Walker & McConnell, 1988) are well-researched instruments that are under utilized in research. Kavale and Mostert (2004) call for greater focus on *increased construct validity* concerning such distinctions as social skills versus social competence, skill deficits versus performance deficits, social validity and identification of underlying processes that contribute to social deficits.

The need to identify underlying processes of social competence has resulted in Weiner (2003) considering the appropriateness of single- and multiple-risk models. Ultimately, Weiner suggests the need to consider *multiple risk factors* in children with SLD (e.g., comorbid ADHD, poverty, inappropriate parenting) in order to understand how these influences can put children with SLD at increased risk for social relationship difficulties, which in turn can result in internalizing or externalizing problems causing further damage to social relationships.

CHAPTER REVIEW

Historically, the concept of learning disabilities has witnessed several changes in how the disorder is conceptualized and defined. Once described as "word blindness," and believed to be the result of mixed cerebral dominance, multisensory programs such as Fernald's VATK approach were very popular, as a result. Currently, the field is immersed in debate over issues of identification of SLD for educational purposes. Concerns regarding the overidentification of SLD has ushered in changes to the identification process and in the newly reauthorized IDEA (2004), *response to intervention* (RTI) was added as a possible method of identifying students with SLD. Those who support retention of the discrepancy model have levied several criticisms against RTI due to the vagueness of the concept and the failure to address original concerns, such the use of a failure-based model.

Although the *DSM* and the educational system both classify SLD from a categorical perspective, the systems differ in the nature of how the disorder is defined.

1. **SLD and *DSM* (APA, 2000)**
   Three learning disorders are recognized by the *DSM* (APA, 2000), including reading, mathematics, and written expression. The *DSM* applies the discrepancy model as a criterion for determining whether the disorder has resulted in *substantial* difference (2 standard deviations) between expected academic performance and based on intelligence.

2. **SLD and Educational System**

   SLD is a disorder in one of more of the basic *psychological processes* resulting in an imperfect ability in *expression* (oral, listening, written), *reading* (basic skill, fluency, comprehension), or *mathematics* (calculation, problem solving). Prior to IDEA (2004), the discrepancy model (IQ/academic discrepancy similar to *DSM*) was the only means available for identification. Currently, districts are allowed to use a response to intervention model (RTI) to determine SLD based on poor response to intervention.

3. **Other Definitions and Controversial Debates**

   Other major interest groups have opted for different definitions of SLD depending on the focus of the defining body and have continued to debate which definition is best. The most recent all-consuming debate is over RTI versus retention of the discrepancy model. Those in favor of RTI criticize the discrepancy model on several grounds including lack of consistency in application, questionable research support, failure model, and having age and IQ bias. The RTI model has been criticized for being too vague, a failure model and lacking identification as to why a child is having problems (only documents low achievement).

4. **Prevalence and SLD Subtypes**

   Currently between 2% and 10% of school-aged children meet criteria for SLD (*DSM*, 2000) and approximately 6% of school-aged children are labeled as SLD. Schools are concerned because the percentage of identified students has doubled since 1979, and SLD represent about half of all special education students. As a result, identification criteria have been modified. Different subtypes of SLD have been recognized, including: dyscalculia (mathematics), dysgraphia (written expression), dyslexia (reading, spelling), dyspraxia (fine motor function), and donverbal learning disability (mathematics and spatial awareness).

5. **Dyslexia**

   Genetic transmission and neurological processing have been identified in the etiology. While mature readers predominantly use the left side of the brain for processing reading, dyslexic children use the right side and continue to process using posterior regions compared to good readers who progress to the more frontal regions. Current interventions are attempting to "rewire" neural pathways in poor readers.

6. **Dyscalculia**

   Less is known about dyscalculia and problems are more difficult to assess. Deficits usually involve calculation fluency and the acquisition of number sense. Working memory deficits have been associated with use of fingers in counting, while semantic memory deficits may result in poor recall for number facts.

7. **Nonverbal Learning Disability (NLD)**

   Children with NLD have IQ profiles the reverse of those with more tradition SLD, demonstrating strengths in verbal and weaknesses in performance functioning. They are good readers, but poor at arithmetic. Deficits in tactile and visual perception and visual/spatial processing often result in poor social skills due to their inability to process social cues. NLD has been linked to right hemisphere dysfunction.

8. **Social Skills Deficits**

   Many individuals with SLD and NLD experience social skills deficits. As a result, numerous social skills training (SST) programs have been developed over the years. Recently, SST programs have come under scrutiny for lack of effectiveness. Suggestions for improved social skills interventions include improved assessment to better target behaviors and use of empirically validated programs.

Consolidate and Communicate

1. Historically, the concept of SLD has changed over time and continues to be an area of high debate regarding how SLD is defined and what causes SLD. Have different groups that advocate for SLD children actually done more harm than good by the number of different definitions that currently exist? Discuss. Should social disability be considered as a subtype of SLD? Debate.

2. The *DSM* and the Educational System both use a categorical approach to the identification of SLD. Compare and contrast how the *DSM* and Educational Classification Systems are alike and how they are different.

3. The Educational System definition for SLD has not changed, but the identification process is in a state of current flux with the introduction of RTI alongside existing models of the discrepancy criteria. There is heated debate regarding these two models of identification. Debate the pros and cons of both systems of identification. Is there any way that both these models can be integrated into one more comprehensive approach? Some argue that getting rid of the discrepancy model would represent "throwing the baby out with the bath water." What does this mean and how does it relate to the debate?

4. You have a child who is currently 7 years old and is struggling with reading. Despite hiring a tutor and providing after-school sessions, your child's reading is still very poor. She cannot remember sounds and approaches each word as if it were the first time she has ever seen it, despite having seen the word only minutes ago. Unfortunately, she reminds you of an uncle who never learned to read and remains illiterate, despite being a smart man in many other ways. Your daughter is getting frustrated, but her teacher thinks she will catch up eventually and is recommending that she repeat the second grade. Based on your understanding of SLD, why do you think your daughter cannot read? Discuss how Shaywitz and Lyon (2003) would consider your daughter's problem in the light of their definition. What might be a possible neurological explanation for what is happening when your daughter tries to read?

5. Nonverbal learning disabilities (NLD) have been described as almost the reverse of more traditional SLD profiles. Describe what is meant by this and how this might impact identification within the educational system.

6. Social skills training (SST) programs have come under recent criticisms for a number of reasons. Describe some flaws and suggestions for improvement.

Chapter Review Questions

1. Kussmaul coined the phrase _____ to refer to reading problems.
    a. mirror reading
    b. reading disability
    c. word blindness
    d. reading blindness

2. The discrepancy formula was first used to identify children with reading disabilities by:
    a. Monroe
    b. Kirk
    c. Public Law 94–142
    d. Cruickshank

3. Which of the following definitions for SLD advocates for inclusion of social skills as a disability category?

    a. Learning Disability Association (LDA)

    b. Interagency Committee on Learning Disabilities (ICLD)

    c. *DSM*

    d. National Joint Committee for Learning Disabilities (NJCLD)

4. Identify which is false. According to IDEA (2004), identification procedures adopted by the State:

    a. must permit the use of a process based on the child's response to scientific research-based identification.

    b. may permit the use of other alternative research-based procedures.

    c. must require the use of a severe discrepancy between intellectual ability and achievement.

    d. must include determination of whether a child has SLD to be made by child's parents and a team of qualified professionals.

5. According to the *DSM*, the likely prevalence rate for SLD in a school-aged population is:

    a. 5%–15%

    b. 8%–15%

    c. 1%–3%

    d. 2%–10%

6. Currently, children with SLD represent what percent of the school aged population?

    a. 48%

    b. 6%

    c. 20%

    d. 10%

7. The SLD subtype that involves problems with fine motor skills is referred to as:

    a. dysgraphia

    b. dyscalculia

    c. dyspraxia

    d. dystonia

8. Stanovich (1986) used this phrase to describe the process whereby good readers continue to gain vocabulary skills and general knowledge, while poor readers gain less information and vocabulary:

    a. Jonathan effects

    b. Poor reader, rich reader effects

    c. Widening gap effects

    d. Matthew effects

9. Shaywitz and colleagues have localized normal reading in three parts of the brain. Which is not one of the regions?

    a. left frontal gyrus

    b. left temporal/occipital

    c. right posterior region

    d. left parietal/temporal region

10. Which is true of children with SLD, according to Kavale's and Forness's meta-analysis?

    a. 75% of students with SLD received negative social ratings from all rating sources.

    b. 70% reported they have fewer social skills than their peers.

    c. 80% expressed significant concern about their academic ability.

    d. All are true.

Glossary of New Terms

word blindness
discrepancy criterion
learning disability
Learning Disabilities Association (LDA)
learning disorders
reading disorder
mathematics disorder
disorder of written expression
learning disorder not otherwise specified (NOS)
discrepancy between achievement and intelligence
dyslexia
functional assessments
developmental coordination disorder
response to intervention (RTI)
curriculum-based assessment (CBA)
predictor variables
Interagency Committee on Learning Disabilities (ICLD)
National Joint Committee for Learning Disabilities (NJCLD)
Individuals with Disabilities Education Improvement Act, 2004
dyscalculia
dysgraphia
dyslexia
dyspraxia
nonverbal learning disability
Matthew effects
left frontal gyrus
left parietal/temporal
left temporal/occipital
phonetic tasks
left inferior temporal/occipital area
sight decoding task
calculation fluency
number sense
basic phonological processing disorder (BPPD)
nonverbal learning disabilities (NLD)
developmental right-hemisphere syndrome (DRHS)
visiospatial learning disability
right cerebral hemisphere
white matter model
social pragmatics
semantic pragmatic disorder
Asperger's syndrome
rejected, neglected, popular, controversial
profile of nonverbal sensitivity (PONS)
replacement behavior training (RBT)

Multiple Choice Answers:
1. c; 2. a; 3. a; 4. c; 5. d; 6. b; 7. c; 8. d; 9. c; 10. d.

III

Problems With Onset in Late Childhood or Adolescence

An Introduction

Eating Disorders, Body Dissatisfaction, and Substance Use and Abuse

Adolescence is a transition period marked by significant developmental changes in biological, psychological and social systems (Cicchetti & Rogosh, 2002). During this period of "storm and stress," adolescents face numerous challenges in their attempts to negotiate increased autonomy in the face of escalating mood disruptions, risk behaviors, and conflict with parents (Arnett, 1999). While the majority of adolescents will manage to navigate a course that is relatively well-adjusted by maneuvering around bumps in the road, for some, the trajectory will be marked with increases in risk taking behaviors that result in elevated negative outcomes. Resilient youth who live in adverse conditions have a better sense of psychological well-being, have had the benefit of better parenting, and score higher on IQ tests than their less resilient peers (Masten, Hubbard, Gest, Tellegen, Garmezy, & Ramirez, 1999). On the other hand, youth who are at higher risk for negative outcomes have experienced school failure, and increased opportunities for unstructured free time, as well as, association with peers who were involved in high risk activities (Blum et al., 2000).

Some children may be less well equipped to cope with the stress inherent in the adolescent transition period, while others may be less ready to cope. Early maturing adolescents may be particularly vulnerable to making poorer life choices. The onset of puberty produces increased weight in young girls and is accompanied by a dramatic increase in body dissatisfaction. As a result, in the wake of media messages and pursuit of the "thin ideal", early maturing girls are at greater risk for developing eating disorders (Swarr & Richards, 1996). In adolescent girls, increased risk for substance use has been linked to elevated levels of mood disturbance. In addition, initial eating pathology and/or antisocial behavior both predicted increased risk for substance use in adolescent females. Since females tend to use stimulants as their substance of choice (Chasin, Ritter, Trim, & King, 2003), it has been suggested that this choice might be motivated by increased opportunity for weight loss.

Among youth, cigarettes, alcohol, and marijuana are the most commonly used substances. The majority of youth experiment with substances and do not develop long-term addictions and dependence. Trends show that, overall, substance use has declined in recent years. However, disturbing findings from the latest survey (Monitoring the Future, 2005) revealed a significant increase in inhalant use among eighth graders and in the use of prescription medication (Oxy-Contin) by high school seniors. Peer drug use remains the single most powerful predictor for drug use in youth.

12
Eating Disorders

CHAPTER PREVIEW

Eating disorders represent one of the most common and chronic psychiatric problems facing young women today. Eating disorders can result in serous medical complications and are often complex and difficult to treat due to their comorbid association with other types of psychopathology, such as mood disorders, affective disorders, and substance abuse (Keller, Herzog, Lavori, Bradburn, & Mahoney, 1992). There is increasing evidence that body dissatisfaction is also becoming more common in males (Jones, 2004; Presnell, Bearman, & Stice, 2004). Although most readers will be familiar with severe disturbances in eating behaviors often associated with female adolescents and young adults, few may realize that developmentally, onset of eating disorders can actually begin in infancy or early childhood and present as persistent eating and feeding disturbances.

1. Contemporary Issues in Body Image and Weight Control

Many who may not meet full criteria for eating disorders (*DSM*, 2000), nonetheless demonstrate many symptoms of disordered eating. Athletes in "aesthetic" sports or "elite sports" may be particularly vulnerable to disordered eating patterns due to perfectionistic tendencies, drive to excel, and emphasis on body control. At the other end of the spectrum, one third of the children in the United States are either obese or at risk for being obese and a host of associated medical problems. Rates of overweight youth have been steadily increasing.

2. Body Dissatisfaction and Contemporary Youth

According to the Youth Risk Behavior Surveillance Summaries (YRBS, 2005), approximately 30% of youth expressed body image concerns, with males voicing increased concern over the last 10 years. Female rates for body image dissatisfaction increase with age during secondary school. More than 60% of teens are currently dieting. While 38% report feeling overweight, in reality only 10% actually meet criteria for being overweight. The *Tripartite Influence Model* suggests three significant influences in body dissatisfaction: peers, parents, and media.

3. Feeding and Eating Disorders First Diagnosed in Infancy or Early Childhood

The *DSM* (APA, 2000): recognizes three early eating disorders: *pica, rumination disorder, and feeding disorder*. Pica (eating of odd substances such as paint, string, clay, sand, insects, etc.) and rumination disorder (regurgitation and rechewing of food) are most prevalent among individuals with mental retardation. Feeding disorder, or failure to thrive (FTT), is characterized by food refusal and occurs in 3% to 4% of the population. Although parent neglect was initially thought to be a cause of FTT, more recent research suggests several other factors that may be implicated.

4. Eating Disorders (ED)

The *DSM* (APA, 2000) recognizes three categories of eating disorders: *anorexia nervosa (AN), bulimia nervosa (BN), and eating disorders not otherwise specified (EDNOS)*.

5. Historical Background of ED

Extreme eating habits have been documented, historically, ranging from acts of gluttony (early Roman empire) to self-starvation (Roman Catholic saints). Although anorexia was initially thought of as an adjunct to other disorders (such as schizophrenia), Hilde Bruch's (1973) book on eating disorders established anorexia nervosa (AN) as a disorder in its own right. Similarly, while bulimia was initially thought of as a symptom of anorexia, bulimia nervosa (BN) was later described as *an ominous variant of AN* by Gerald Russell (1979) in his account of over 30 women with the disorder.

6. Anorexia Nervosa (AN)

The characteristic feature of AN is a refusal to maintain a body weight within 85% of what is normal. Other criteria include an intense fear of gaining weight, distorted body perception, and absence of thee consecutive menstrual cycles (amenorrhea). Anorexics—of which 90% are female—are often preoccupied with food and demonstrate one of two eating patterns: *restricting subtype* (fasting, excess exercise) or *binge-eating/purging subtype* (eating followed by compensatory behaviors).

7. Bulimia Nervosa (BN)

The bulimic cycle starts with feelings of built-up tension that result in the consumption of large quantities of food in a short period of time. Post-binge feelings include guilt, depression, and a need to restore a sense of control which is accomplished by one of two types of compensatory behaviors: *purging type* (self-induced vomiting enemas, laxatives, diuretics); or *nonpurging type* (excessive exercise or fasting).

8. A Comparison of AN and BN

AN and BN often occur after a period of intense dieting and share several characteristics, including intense fear of obesity, preoccupation with thinness, and distorted sense of body image. The major difference between AN and BN is that individuals with AN maintain a body weight less than 85% of what is considered normal. AN binge/purge type is most similar to BN purge type and both disorders have poorer outcomes than the other subtypes (suicide attempts, depression, substance abuse). Onset for AN is usually earlier than onset for BN.

9. Etiology, Treatment, and Prevention of Eating Disorders

Risk factors for developing eating disorders include genetic transmission, family dynamics, media, and peer pressure and maladaptive thinking/perceptions of body image. Treatment for AN is a three stage process: restore weight loss, reframe disturbances in body perception, and long-term recovery (awareness, education, and family therapy). Treatment for BN can include antidepressant medication, cognitive behavioral therapy, and family interventions. Successful contemporary prevention programs have targeted media messages concerning body image.

Disordered Eating, Body Dissatisfaction, Obesity, and Weight Control

---

Science Talks

After puberty, there is a dramatic increase in body image dissatisfaction among young girls (Rosenblum & Lewis, 1999). The time when most young girls become increasingly weight conscious and most vulnerable to dieting (11 to 13 years of age) coincides with that period of time where increases in weight are normal due to changes brought on by puberty. Swarr and Richards (1996) found that early maturing girls are at greater risk for developing eating disorders than later maturing girls.

Studies of community populations report that few adolescents (between .04% and 2.8%) meet the diagnostic criteria for a full-syndrome eating disorder (Lewinsohn, Striegel-Moore, & Seeley, 2000; Stice, Presnell, & Bearman, 2001). Yet, rates for binge-eating behaviors among high school students have been reported as high as 45% in females and 16% in males (Greenfield, Quinlan, Harding, Glass, & Bliss, 1987). One study found that 16% of 6th graders reported engaging in binge eating behaviors (Maloney, McGuire, Daniels, & Specker, 1989), while in another study, 9% of a sample of 6–13 year olds reported binge behaviors in the past 28 days (Tanofsky-Kraff et al., 2004). In the latter study, compared to normal-weight peers, overweight children engaged in significantly more loss-of-control eating episodes, experienced eating-disordered cognitions, and were rated by their parents as experiencing more internalizing and externalizing problems.

Obesity Rates Among Youth in the United States

While *obesity* is not recognized as an eating disorder by the *DSM–IV–TR* (APA, 2000), approximately one third of children in the United States are either obese or at-risk for becoming obese. Childhood rates for obesity in 2004 were 4 times what they were in 1963, while adolescent rates for obesity tripled within that time frame (Institute of Medicine, 2005).

The growing problem of obesity.   Adolescents and children are considered overweight if their **body mass index (BMI)** is at or above the 95th percentile, or they are considered at-risk to be overweight if they are between the 85th and 95th percentile (Centers for Disease Control and Prevention; CDC: Youth Risk Behavior Surveillance Summaries [YSBS], 2005; MMWR 2006, June).

Memory Bank

Body Mass Index (BMI) is a ratio that is calculated by dividing your weight (lbs) by your height^2 (squared) and multiplying the result by 703. For example, Sally weighs 90 pounds, and she is 4 feet and 9 inches tall (57 inches). Sally's BMI would be calculated as follows: divide 90 by 3249 (57^2) = .0277, then multiply that number (.0277) by 703 to derive a final BMI score of = 19.47. Sally is of normal weight for her height. Normal range for the BMI is 18.5 to 25. A score of 25+ would be overweight, while a score above 29.9 would be considered obese. Scores below 18.5 are considered underweight, while a score 15 or below might signal an eating disorder.

Sixty percent of obese children are at-risk for cardiovascular disease (CVD), while 30% of obese boys and 40% of obese girls will develop Type 2 diabetes over their lifetime (IOM, 2005). Although there can be a genetic link to weight gain, the majority of obesity has been attributed to overeating and taking in more calories than can be utilized (Koplan, Liverman, & Kraak, 2005). In addition to medical and health complications, psychosocial consequences of obesity have also been reported (IOM, 2005). Outcomes such as depression and poor self-esteem have been found in overweight girls as young as 5 years of age (Davison & Birch, 2001). Children who are overweight are also often targets for discrimination, bullying, teasing, and stereotyping (IOM, 2005). The IOM lists a number of factors that contribute to increased rates of obesity, including:

- lack of physical activity (lack of sidewalks and other measures to encourage walking, lack of physical activities at schools)
- overreliance on high-caloric convenience foods (lack of access to nutritious alternatives)
- increased time in sedentary activity (watching television, playing video games)

Consider This

Children spend an average of 4 hours a day sitting in front of a screen (television/computer). Ninety-nine percent of youth have access to a television set in their home, while 65% have a television set in their bedroom, providing on-going access to commercials advertising food (Harper, 2006). Children (9–14 years old) who reported more screen time, caloric intake, and less physical activity revealed a 1-year increase in BMI (Berkey, Rockett, & Field, 2000).

The Youth Risk Behavior Survey (YRBS): Questions and Answers

The National Center for Disease Control (CDC) has disseminated a national survey, the Youth Risk Behavior Survey (YRBS) since 1991. The survey monitors high risk behaviors among youth including substance use, injuries, tobacco use, sexual behaviors, and unhealthy dietary behaviors. Results from this survey will be presented in a series of tables that have been developed to answer specific questions regarding eating habits among youth based on YRBS data.

Q: *Overall, what was the reported prevalence rate for being overweight among high school students in 2005, and how does this rate compare to reports generated from data collected in 1999?* (See Table 12.1.)

A: Since 1999, height and weight for survey respondents have been recorded to allow for tabulation of BMI scores. A BMI at or above the 95th percentile is considered overweight, while BMI scores between the 85th and 95th percentiles are considered at-risk for being overweight. In 1999, 9.9% of youth in high school were overweight, compared to 13.1% in 2005. Youth in the at-risk categories also increased from 14.4% in 1999 to 15.7% in 2005. Currently, more than one quarter (28.8%) of high school students are at-risk or overweight.

Q: *Overall, are there gender differences?*

A: In the 2005 survey, 16% of males were overweight, compared to 10% of females. There was very little differentiation between males and females in the at-risk categories. Since 1999, the number of overweight males has increased by 4.5 %, and females by 2.1%.

Table 12.1 Prevalence Rates: Percentage of High School Students Who Were Overweight or At-Risk for Being Overweight in 1999 and 2005

Behaviors/ Descriptions	1999			2005		
	Total	Female	Male	Total	Female	Male
Total Overweight	9.9	7.9	11.5	13.1	10.0	16.0
At Risk	14.4	13.9	14.8	15.7	15.5	15.8
White Overweight	9.2	6.8	11.1	11.8	8.2	15.2
At Risk	12.9	12.3	13.5	14.5	13.8	15.2
Black Overweight	11.9	12.8	11.0	16.0	16.1	15.9
At Risk	21.1	22.1	20.1	19.8	22.6	17.7
Hispanic Overweight	12.4	9.7	15.0	16.8	12.1	21.3
At Risk	16.4	17.1	15.7	16.7	16.8	16.5

Source: Centers for Disease Control and Prevention (CDC): National Youth Risk Behavioar Surveillance (YRBS): 1999 and 2005

Q: *Overall, are there different ethnic trends?*

A: Compared to 1999, all ethnic groups reported increases in the number of overweight youth. The greatest increases were reported among Hispanic youth (1999: 12.4%; 2005: 16.8%) and Black youth (1999: 11.9%; 2005: 16%), compared to White youth (1999: 9.2%; 2005: 11.8%).

The YRBS survey also asked youth whether they thought they were overweight and if they were currently engaged in weight loss activities. Prevalence rates for responses to those questions are available in Table 12.3, for three rating periods; 1991, 1999, and 2005.

Q: *Overall, have high school student concerns about body image and weight loss changed in the past 14 years?* (See Table 12.2.)

A: Overall total prevalence rates for body image concern (rated self as overweight) reveal that the rate has remained relatively stable over the 14-year period: 31.8% in 1991 to 31.5% in 2005.

Q: *Overall, what are the body dissatisfaction trends for females and males over the 14-year period?*

A: Females show an uneven profile, but current rates of body dissatisfaction (38.1%) are lower than those reported in 1991 (42.3%). For males, the trend has been for increasing body dissatisfaction across the period reported, from 21.7% in 1991 to 25.1% in 2005.

Comparing grade-level responses for body dissatisfaction (described selves as overweight) for males and females in 2005, reveals that female reports of body dissatisfaction, increased steadily from Grade 9 (36.2%) through Grade 12 (41.8%), while males showed only a marginal increase from Grade 9 (24.3%) to Grade 12 (25.6%). These results support research findings that by 14 years of age, females are significantly more dissatisfied with their body image than males, and that girls become increasingly dissatisfied over the course of adolescence (Bearman, Presnell, Martinez, & Stice, 2006).

Q: *Overall, are there different ethnic trends for body dissatisfaction during this time frame?*

A: Although overall scores for White students showed a decline in 1999 (29.2%) from the initial prevalence rate reported in 1991 (32.8%), the rate for 2005 (31.5%) has edged closer to levels noted in 1991. Trends for Blacks and Hispanics have shown a steady increase in body dissatisfaction across these reported dates: Blacks—23.6%, 24.9%, 27.2%; Hispanics—34.9%, 36.7%, 37.1%.

Q: *Overall, what percentage of youth are dieting?*

Table 12.2 Body Image Concerns and Dieting Among High School Students: A Comparison of Responses on the Youth Risk Behavior Surveillance, 1991, 1999, and 2005

	1991			1999			2005		
Behaviors/ Descriptions	Total	Female	Male	Total	Female	Male	Total	Female	Male
Describe Selves as Overweight Total	31.8	42.3	21.7	30.0	36.4	23.7	31.5	38.1	25.1
White	32.8	44.1	22.5	29.2	35.7	23.0	31.1	37.7	24.7
Black	23.6	29.7	16.4	24.9	32.3	17.1	27.2	36.3	17.6
Hispanic	34.9	46.9	21.8	36.7	42.3	32.0	37.1	42.2	32.0
Were Trying to Lose Weight Total	41.8	61.7	22.7	42.7	59.4	26.1	45.6	61.7	29.9
White	43.4	65.9	22.9	42.6	61.4	24.9	45.9	63.5	28.8
Black	30.3	42.2	16.4	36.3	48.3	23.6	38.9	52.7	24.4
Hispanic	46.6	61.7	29.9	50.6	63.6	37.3	51.2	64.1	38.6

A: The number of students who are actively trying to lose weight has steadily increased from 41.8% (1991) to 42.7% (1999) to a current high of 45.6%.

Q: Overall, what are the dieting trends for females and males?

A: In 1999, more than half of females were dieting (59.4%). Although this represented a decrease from 1991 (61.7%), current rates for 2005 (61.7%) are equal to those noted in the original survey. For males, the trend mirrors the pattern noted for body dissatisfaction, increasing across the period reported, from 22.7% in 1991 to 29.9% in 2005.

Q: Are there different ethnic/gender trends regarding the overweight/versus describes self as overweight categories?

A: Scores for females in all ethnic groups indicated a greater percentage who perceived themselves as being overweight, compared to those who actually scored overweight by BMI standards. Ethnically, in 2005, while 10% of White females actually scored in the overweight category, 38.1% reported that they see themselves as overweight; that is, approximately 28% of White females reported a distorted sense of body image (rates selves as overweight when they were not). Approximately 17% of Hispanic females and 13% of Black females reported perceptions of being overweight, relative to actually being overweight. For males, the largest discrepancy between feeling overweight and actually being overweight occurred for Hispanic males (10.7% rated poorer body perception than reality), followed by White males (9.5%). Black males had the most accurate score and least distorted perception of body image versus body weight of all ethnic groups (1.7% difference between perceived versus actual body weight).

Consider This

Although there are concerns that youth may engage in excessive dieting behaviors to their own detriment, it has also been suggested that eating-disordered cognitions, particularly body dissatisfaction and weight concerns, may actually have an adaptive value and serve a needed function in motivating a healthier lifestyle (Heinberg, Thompson, & Matzon, 2001).

Healthy versus unhealthy dieting behaviors. Dieting practices can be healthy (exercise, reduced fat diet) or unhealthy (fasting, pills/powders, laxatives/vomiting). Results from the YRBS (CDC, 2005) report on healthy versus unhealthy dieting practices are available in Table 12.3.

Table 12.3 Prevalence of Healthy Versus Unhealthy Dieting Practices for Weight Loss Among High School Students

Weight Loss Practices	Total 1999	Female	Male	Total 2005	Female	Male
Use of Healthy Weight Loss:						
Exercise	58.4	67.4	49.5	60.0	67.4	52.9
Ate less; low fat	40.4	56.1	25.0	40.7	54.8	26.8
Unhealthy Weight Loss:						
Fasting	12.6	18.8	6.4	12.5	17.6	7.5
Pills or powder	7.6	10.9	4.4	6.3	8.1	4.6
Laxatives or vomited	4.8	7.5	2.2	4.5	6.2	2.8

Exercising to lose weight was the most frequently reported healthy activity for females (67.4%) and males (52.9%). However, females also engaged in significantly more unhealthy weight loss methods than males. More than 17% of females reported fasting (going without food for 24 hours) within the 30 days prior to the survey. In 2005, females were most likely to engage in fasting in Grade 9 (18.4%), taking pills or powders in Grade 12 (10.2%), and vomiting or using laxatives in Grade 10 (7.2%). The number of female students who were trying to lose weight increased with each grade level, beginning with 60.1% in Grade 9 and culminating in 64% in Grade 12.

Body Dissatisfaction: Risks and Protective Factors

Understanding the dynamics of body dissatisfaction can contribute to greater comprehension of eating pathology.

Risk factors. Body dissatisfaction and weight concerns can exacerbate bulimic symptoms, leading to dieting and negative affect (Heatherton & Polivy, 1992; Stice & Agras, 1998), be predictive of increased dieting (Stice, Mazotti, Krebs, & Martin, 1998), eating pathology (Attie & Brooks-Gunn, 1989), and the onset of major depression (Stice, Hayward, Cameron, Killen, & Taylor, 2000). According to Stice (2001), "body dissatisfaction has emerged as one of the most robust risk factors for eating disturbances" (p. 55). Many influences have been identified that can increase the risk of body dissatisfaction. The *Tripartite Influence Model* (Thompson, Heinberg, Altabe, & Tantleff-Dunn, 1999) suggests three significant influences (peers, parents, and media) that can impact body image perceptions through processes of internalization of the "thin ideal" and social "appearance" comparisons.

RECURRENT THEMES   The **Tripartite Influence Model** emphasizes many of the themes stressed in this text. Developmentally, adolescence is a vulnerable period for youth with body image concerns (*Theme 1*). The extent to which disordered eating becomes an eating disorder (*Themes 2 and 3*) will depend on three significant influences, at this time: peers, parents, and the media (*Theme 4*).

Several potential risk factors have been suggested to account for increased body dissatisfaction in emerging adolescence. Bearman et al. (2006) suggest six domains that can influence body dissatisfaction, including internalization of an ideal body image, adiposity in females, social influence, attitudes towards dieting, negative affect, and age. Risk and protective factors are summarized in Table 12.4.

Body image ideal. During adolescence, males and females inherently strive to identify with their gender stereotypes (Hill & Lynch, 1983). However, while stereotypes for females have been linked to increased emphasis on physical attractiveness (Stice et al., 2000) and a drive for thinness (Smolak, Levine, & Thompson, 2001), males may be more inclined to "bulk up" in an attempt to appear more masculine (McCabe & Ricciardelli, 2004).

Puberty and body mass. From approximately 8 years of age on, girls start to add fat (adiposity) to their arms, legs, and trunk, a process that accelerates between 11 and 16 years of age. By contrast, fat in males decreases during this period, as muscle strength continues to increase. The sharp rise in body weight and fat in females that occurs at this time relates to the threshold level of body fat that is necessary for the initiation of puberty and for maintenance of fertility in women (Brandao, Lombardi, Nishida, Hauache, & Vieira, 2003). As body mass increases, girls' body dissatisfaction also increases (Stice & Whitenton, 2002). Although increases in muscle may

Table 12.4 Risks and Protective Factors: Research Findings Concerning Factors Related to Adolescent Body Dissatisfaction (BD)

Risk Factors for Body Dissatisfaction (BD)	Study	Outcomes
Ideal Body Internalization	Jones (2004);	Predicted BD in males and females
	Stice and Whitenton (2002)	Predicted BD in females
BMI	Bearman et al. (2006);	Did not predict BD in males or females
	Barker and Galambos (2003);	
	Presnell et al. (2004);	Predicted BD in females
	Field et al. (2001)	Predicted BD in males
Negative affect	Bearman et al. (2006);	Predicted BD in males and females
	Presnell et al. (2004);	
	Stice and Whitenton (2002)	Predicted BD in females
Social support deficits:		
Lack of Parent support	Bearman et al. (2006);	Predicted BD in females and males
	Stice and Whitenton (2002)	Predicted BD in females
Negative **or** Encouraging maternal comments	Wertheim et al. (2002)	Predicted BD, drive for thinness, and disordered eating in females
Lack of Peer support	Jones (2004)	Predicted BD in females
Peer weight teasing	Weirtheim et al. (2002)	Predicted bulimic behaviors and drive for thinness in females
	van den Berg et al. (2002)	Predicted BD and disturbed eating
Increased restriction of food intake and dieting	Bearman et al. (2006);	Predicted BD in females and males
	Barker and Galambos (2003)	Predicted BD in females
Early versus late maturation	McCabe and Ricciardelli (2004)	Early maturation predicted BD in females
Protective factors for Body Satisfaction		
Supportive maternal relationship	Barker and Galambos (2003)	Increased body satisfaction in females
Early versus late maturation	McCabe and Ricciardelli (2004)	Early maturation predicted increased satisfaction in males

increase body satisfaction for some males (McCabe, Ricciardelli, & Banfield, 2001), results have not been consistent (Bearman et al., 2006).

Social influence: Family and peer pressure. Lack of having a social support system in adolescence has been linked to lowered self-esteem and increased body dissatisfaction (Wichstrom, 1999). Criticism from peers concerning body appearance has been associated with higher scores on eating disordered profiles (Cattarin & Thompson, 1994). Adolescent girls who perceive that their body image does not match up to social comparison are more likely to have disordered eating symptoms, while weight-related teasing by peers has been associated with increased body dissatisfaction, disturbed eating habits (Thompson, Coovert, Richards, Johnson, & Cattarin, 1995), and found to be predictive of bulimic behaviors and drive for thinness.

One study found that about one quarter of middle school girls are subjected to appearance-related teasing by a parent and one third are teased by at least one sibling. Girls were especially sensitive to teasing by fathers. Compared to girls who were not teased, girls in family teasing situations demonstrated lower levels of self-esteem, had higher levels of body dissatisfaction, depression, and engaged in greater levels of social comparison, internalization of a thin ideal, and restrictive and bulimic eating behaviors (Keery, Boutelle, van den Berg, & Thompson, 2005).

Individuals with BN report that their families are high in anger and conflict and low in cohesion and caring (Kent & Clopton, 1992). While positive maternal support has been identified as a protective factor for girls in at least one study (Barker & Galambos, 2003), other findings suggest that even supportive maternal comments can be misconstrued as critical (Hanna & Bond, 2006). Other factors that have been identified as predictive of increased body dissatisfaction include early separation anxiety and insecure or preoccupied attachment (Troisi et al., 2006).

Important Distinction

What did you mean by that? Gross and Nelson (2000) suggest that perceived negative messages about eating, food, weight, or shape, whether intentional or unintentional, may serve to overemphasize the importance of weight and shape. Maternal criticism was found to compromise self-esteem (Sherwood & Neumark-Szatainer, 2001) and increase disordered eating symptomatology (Gross & Nelson, 2000). Furthermore, in one study, maternal *encouragement* was also related to disordered eating, drive for thinness, and higher body dissatisfaction (Hanna & Bond, 2006). In discussing this result, the researchers suggest that in their attempt to be supportive, mothers' comments about food or weight may inadvertently be misinterpreted by their sensitive daughters.

Dieting. Reducing calorie intake without increasing physical activity can be a self-defeating process, and actually result in weight gain rather than weight loss. According to **weight set point** theory (Garner, Garfinkel, & O'Shaughnessy, 1985), individuals have their own weight regulator that stabilizes weight based on genetic inheritance and early eating practices. If dieting results in a weight loss below that established by the weight set point, the metabolism slows and a message of food preoccupation is sent to the brain which increases the desire to binge in an effort to restore the original weight set point. In young girls, gaining weight while dieting can result in further damage to their vulnerable self-concept, sense of self-efficacy, and increase their body dissatisfaction (Barker & Galambos, 2003). Less is known about the impact of dieting on males. In at least one study, self-reports of dietary restraint were related to increased body dissatisfaction in adolescent males and females (Bearman et al., 2006).

Dieting Facts

Some reports have indicated that as many as 20% of 7-years-old girls (Edlund, Halvarsson, & Sjoden, 1996) and as high as 40% to 80% of adolescent girls (Rosenvinge, Sundgot Borgen, & Borresen, 1999) engage in dieting behaviors and express eating disordered attitudes.

Negative affect. It may be difficult to determine whether negative affect causes body dissatisfaction or whether body dissatisfaction results in negative affect. The relationship between these two variables is not clear. One study found that negative affect predicted body dissatisfaction for boys only (Presnell et al. 2004), while another found consistent associations of negative affect and body dissatisfaction for both boys and girls (Bearman et al., 2006).

In their study of adolescent girls, Measlle, Stice, and Hogansen (2006) found that depression was predictive of eating pathology, substance abuse, and antisocial behavior, while in another study, Stice, Burton, and Shaw (2004) found that depression and bulimia were reciprocal influences, each exacerbating the other.

Age.   Results of the YRBS (CDC, 2005) revealed that greater percentages of females reported body dissatisfaction compared to males and that dissatisfaction progressively increased from Grade 9 to Grade 12. Bearman et al. (2006) report that body dissatisfaction was comparable for boys and girls at 13 years of age; however, by age 14, girls were significantly more dissatisfied with their bodies than males.

Gender and risk.   Bearman and colleagues (2006) investigated risk factors for body dissatisfaction in a longitudinal community-based sample of 428 adolescent males and females. Although rates were higher for females, the actual risk factors for body dissatisfaction were very similar for males and females, and included all six of the domains just discussed. However, while body dissatisfaction in females can be predicted by a linear path from increased body mass to increased body dissatisfaction, trajectories for males may be more complex, since BMI does not distinguish between weight gain due to increased muscle mass (likely positive association) and weight gain due to increased fat (likely viewed more negatively).

Self-esteem and perfectionism.   Low self-esteem has been found to correlate significantly with disordered eating attitudes in high school students (Fisher, Pastore, Schneider, Pegler, & Napolitano, 1994). Perfectionism (excessive worry about making mistakes and striving to match an ideal) is also an identifiable risk factor for bulimic behavior (Hewitt, Flett, & Ediger, 1995).

Protective factors.   Considerably more information is available concerning risks for ED compared to protective factors. Fifteen years ago, Rodin, Striegel-Moore, and Silberstein (1990) reported that research concerning protective factors for ED was virtually nonexistent. Currently, there continues to be a dearth of information available, relative to risks.

Social influence: Sports participation.   Although the potential risk of participation in the elite athletics has already been discussed, there is research evidence that participation in sports can serve to protect against ED. In their meta-analysis of 34 sports-related studies, Smolak, Murnen, and Roble (2000) reported that contrary to peers participating in elite sports that emphasize thinness (e.g., divers, gymnastics, figure skaters), those who participated in nonelite sports in high school had fewer eating problems then peers who were not involved in athletic programs. Furthermore, female athletes also reported higher levels of self-efficacy and less negative life view than nonparticipating peers (Fulkerson, Keel, Leon, & Dorr, 1999).

   In the absence of other information, based on what is known about risk factors, it also can be suggested that likely protective factors might include enhanced self-esteem, cohesive family units, and improved body image ideals.

Feeding and Eating Disorders First Diagnosed in Infancy or Early Childhood

Currently, the *DSM–IV–TR* (APA, 2000) recognizes three eating and feeding disorders as *Disorders First Diagnosed in Infancy, Childhood, or Adolescence:* **pica, rumination disorder, and feeding disorder**.

Pica.   While it is common for infants to mouth objects, children with pica will repeatedly crave nonnutritive substances on a regular and persistent basis, for at least a month's duration. Infants and younger children commonly consume paint, hair, cloth, plaster, and string. Older children typically may eat animal droppings, sand, insects, pebbles, or leaves, while adolescents or adults will eat clay and soil. The disorder is most often associated with mental retardation or one of the pervasive developmental disorders. The prevalence rate for adults with severe mental retardation can be as high as 15% (*DSM–IV–TR*; APA, 2000). The DSM reports that it is important to rule out cultural practices in making a diagnosis of pica, since some cultures sanction ingesting nonnutritive substances, such as soil.

Rumination disorder. The disorder is common in infants and individuals with mental retardation and consists of the repeated regurgitation and rechewing of food. Common outcomes include weight loss and failure to thrive. Death may be imminent in as many as 25% of cases. Onset is between 3 and 12 months, with stressful conditions, lack of stimulation/neglect, and strained parent/child relationship associated with onset of the disorder. Mental retardation is associated with onset in older children and adults (*DSM–IV–TR,* APA, 2000).

Feeding disorder of infancy or early childhood. While "food refusal" refers to the child's behavior, **failure to thrive** (**FTT**) is the outcome (Douglas, 2002). Children with FTT account for between 1% to 5% of all infant hospital admissions. It is not uncommon for infants or young children to refuse food due to poor appetite or dislike of certain tastes or textures. However, while a "picky eater" often compensates by consuming more foods from preferred categories, children who exhibit FTT become malnourished and fail to gain weight at the expected rate. Prevalence rates have been estimated between 3%–4% (Wilensky et al., 1996). The cause of FTT is unclear. Although initial studies focused on parent neglect as a primary factor for FTT, more recent research suggests that this may have been overstated. Wright and Birks (2000) studied 97 children with FTT and controls matched for levels of economic deprivation. Only four children with FTT showed evidence of major neglect. Compared to controls, parents of children with FTT reported significantly more feeding problems, introduced solid foods later in their diet, and described the children as more passive with low appetites. Children with FTT were described as "variable eaters, undemanding and shy and less often as hungry" as their healthy peers (Wright & Birks, 1999, p. 5). Boddy, Skuse, and Andrews (2000) found differences in cognitive functioning at 15 months in their sample of infants with FTT relative to controls. However, by school age (6 years), although smaller in stature than the controls, little evidence remained of any cognitive disadvantage of children who had FTT relative to their normal peers.

According to the *DSM–IV–TR* (APA, 2000), onset for feeding disorder must be prior to 6 years of age. The disorder is diagnosed when failure to eat adequately results in inability to maintain proper weight or in substantial weight loss. Often the infant or child presents with symptoms of irritability, withdrawal, and developmental delays. The *DSM* states that child abuse and neglect may be a predisposing factor, although more recent research has questioned the degree to which this is evident.

A Case for Multiple Causality (*Equifinality*)

Douglas (2002) suggests that food refusal behaviors can develop in response to a multitude of factors, including parent characteristics (available resources, mental health), child characteristics (temperament, health), and family characteristics (stressors, resources, relationships).

RECURRENT THEMES   Douglas' findings underscore the importance of *Theme 4,* which emphasizes the importance of individual and environmental influences on deviations in development.

As a first step in addressing feeding problems, it is important to address any potential underlying organic cause (Douglas, 2000). Once medical causes are ruled out, Douglas (2000) discusses three theoretical models that can provide a framework for understanding how eating and feeding disorders (FTT) can develop.

Following the principles of *learning theory*, eating can become an aversive activity through prior associations with being forced to eat, gagging on food, pain associated with eating (acid reflux), becoming ill after eating, or using food as a power struggle.

According to the *developmental model,* the child's developmental stage will determine whether the necessary oral motor coordination is available to shift from liquids to solids, as well as maturity of taste and food preferences.

The *attachment theory model* can also be helpful for understanding feeding and eating disorders, since children with feeding disorders often evidence more attachment problems, and impaired parent/child relationships than their healthy peers (Drotar, Stein, & Perrin, 1995).

Based on the different theoretical perspectives, Douglas (2000) suggests that targeting areas inherent in the models can provide guidelines for intervention and treatment of FTT. As an example, with respect to the *attachment theory model*, Chatoor (1997) has suggested that feeding disorders may actually represent three different subtypes of feeding/eating disorders relative to different types of attachment problems based on poor reciprocity between mother and child resulting from difficulties both experience with emotion regulation; lack of mutual engagement due to the child's lack of social responsiveness or mother 's lack of emotional availability (e.g., substance abuse, emotional disorder); and separation resulting from difficulties in limit setting, resulting in conflict and negotiations at meal times.

 The K–3 Paradigm: Douglas' (2000) research provides another example of how knowledge from normal expectations, sources of influence, and theoretical models can provide guidelines for increased understanding of the disorder and inform decisions regarding intervention.

Eating Disorders in Later Childhood and Adolescence

The *DSM–IV–TR* (APA, 2000) currently recognizes three categories of eating disorders characterized by severe disturbances in eating behaviors: **anorexia nervosa (AN)**, **bulimia nervosa (BN)**, and **eating disorder not otherwise specified (EDNOS)**. The characteristic feature of AN is restriction in food intake, while BN patterns evidence an episode of binge eating, followed by maladaptive compensatory behaviors such as vomiting, laxatives use, excessive exercise, or fasting to inhibit weight gain. Both AN and BN are considered to be part of the typical diagnostic patterns of eating disorders and share a common concern with body weight and fear of obesity. The EDNOS category was created to house atypical eating disorders that do not satisfy all the criteria for AN or BN. Examples of EDNOS include AN without loss of menstrual cycles, or weight loss 15% below normal; BN with less frequent episodes, purging after not binging and chewing and spitting of food but not swallowing. **Binge-eating disorder,** characterized by binges without the compensatory behaviors noted in BN, is listed as an example of EDNOS, although the full description for *binge-eating disorder* appears in the Appendix of the *DSM–IV–TR* (APA, 2000) among a host of other disorders that have been proposed for inclusion, but have not yet officially been approved as a formal psychiatric diagnosis.

Binge-Eating Disorder

The suggested criteria for binge-eating disorder include impaired ability to control excessive eating episodes that cause significant distress, with overindulgence followed by guilt, embarrassment, disgust, and depression. There has been a lack of consensus regarding whether any compensatory behaviors (e.g., purge on occasion) would be allowed or excluded. Binging without purging would likely result in being overweight or obese. Onset is suggested in adolescence or early adulthood, with depression a comorbid feature.

Although the majority of research has focused on eating disorders that develop during adolescence or early adulthood, some reports suggest that onset can occur during childhood, later in adulthood, and even in the elderly (Becker, Grinspoon, Klibanski, & Herzog, 1999). Although the *International Classification of Diseases* (*ICD–10*) includes obesity as a general medical condition, it is not considered a disorder in the *DSM–IV–TR*.

And the Survey Says…

In 2005, 38.1% of females and 25.1% of males in high school described themselves as overweight (Youth Risk Behavior Survey; CDC, 2005). Furthermore, 61.7% of all female high school students, and 29.9% of male students stated that they were trying to lose weight. Females tried to lose weight by fasting for 24 hours (17%), taking diet pills or powders (8.1%), or by inducing vomiting or taking laxatives (6.2%). Although male rates lagged behind female rates across all categories, there is increasing evidence that body dissatisfaction is also a substantial concern for adolescent males (Jones, 2004; Presnell, Bearman, & Stice, 2004).

Eating Disorders (ED): A Historical Perspective

Historically, the word *bulimia* is derived from the Greek words *bous* (ox) and *limos* (hunger). Together bous/limos can be literally translated to refer to someone who has an appetite as large as an ox, or who is hungry enough to consume an ox (Parry-Jones & Parry-Jones, 1991).

When in Rome…

Crichton (1996) traced reports of bulimia dating back to the early Roman Empire, in accounts of the binging and vomiting behaviors of the Roman Emperors Claudius and Vitellius. Regarding Claudius, Crichton cites reports that after one enormous feast, Claudius fell asleep with his mouth open and a "feather was inserted into his throat to induce vomiting" (p. 204) to empty his stomach to allow him to partake in more ravenous pleasures.

At the other extreme end of the eating disordered spectrum, self-starvation and food abstinence were practiced by female Roman Catholic saints as early as 1200 AD with fasting as a tribute to religious discipline (Garfinkel & Dorian, 2001). In the late 1600s, Richard Morton, an English physician, recognized and reported the medical significance of weight loss due to food refusal brought on by nervous causes in a young adolescent girl (Bisaga & Walsh, 2005). Case studies provide descriptions of bulimia occurring in anorexic patients as early as the mid 1800s. For example, Gull (1873) described one anorexic patient who on occasion would demonstrate a voracious appetite, and another who would induce vomiting by thinking of nauseating images.

In the mid 1940s, psychoanalytic theorists attempted to unravel how unconscious conflicts, fears, and drives perpetuated the refusal to eat which was associated with giving way to oral fantasies. While in Germany, the case of Ellen West (Binswanger, 1944) captured the interest of many who were intrigued by Ellen's reports in her diary of her episodes of binge eating, vomiting, and the emotions that consumed her struggle over weight gain for years. In 1959, Stunkard described characteristics of two overeating syndromes that he had observed in women who tended to respond to stressful situations by bouts of overeating. He used the terms *night eating syndrome* and *binge eating syndrome* to identify these two eating patterns.

By the mid-1960s, outside the realm of the psychoanalytic framework, the concept of AN began to take on a more generic role and was considered as a condition of weight loss that accompanied another psychiatric disorder (e.g., weight loss and depression, or weight loss and schizophrenia). It wasn't until 1973 that AN regained status as a disorder in its own right with its own symptoms and pathology. In a seminal work that took on the challenge of describing the pathology of eating disorders, Hilde Bruch (1973) published her work, *Eating Disorders: Obesity, Anorexia Nervosa and the Person Within*. In her book, Bruch described bulimic symptoms among her AN cases who demonstrated disturbances in body perceptions and maladaptive thinking (delusions of being overweight while skeletal), disturbances of sensations (lack of awareness of hunger), and feelings of ineffectiveness. Although bulimia was initially thought of as a symptom of AN, Bosking-Lodahl and White (1978) introduced the term **bulimiarexia,** to refer to a cyclical pattern of binge eating followed by purging evident in college women with a distorted sense of body image, poor self-esteem, feelings of inadequacy, and helplessness.

Gerald Russell (1979) proposed the original criteria for AN and what he called Bulimia Nervosa (BN), "an ominous variant of anorexia nervosa" based on an eating pattern he had observed in 30 women who satisfied two primary criteria: "an irresistible urge to over-eat, followed by self induced vomiting, or purging; and a morbid fear of becoming fat" (p. 429). Although the majority of women initially seemed anorexic, and were preoccupied with weight gain, unlike those with true AN, the women with BN tended to be heavier, more active sexually, and more likely to have regular menses (Russell, 1979). Very soon afterwards, Pyle, Mitchell, and Eckert (1981) published their report of 34 patients with binge-eating episodes, followed by vomiting who shared common characteristics of depression, excessive fear of weight gain, and problems with impulse control (theft and substance abuse). By the mid-1980s there was considerable controversy concerning whether bulimia nervosa, bulimarexia, and binge-eating were separate eating disorders or all variations on the same theme (Cullari & Redmon, 1983; Nagelberg, 1984).

In 1980, the *DSM* (*DSM–III*; APA, 1980) recognized four eating disorders—AN, bulimia, pica and rumination disorder of infancy—which were placed under the category of *disorders usually first evident in infancy, childhood, and adolescence*. In response to the growing body of research and reported cases of anorexia and bulimia, the *DSM–IIIR* (APA, 1987) included a new category called "Eating Disorders," which contained anorexia nervosa (AN) and bulimia nervosa (BN).

Anorexia Nervosa (AN): *DSM–IV–TR* (APA, 2000)

Description and Associated Developmental Features

The cardinal diagnostic feature of AN is the refusal to maintain a minimally acceptable weight, at least 15% less than expected (based on one of several available versions of the Metropolitan Life Insurance tables or pediatric growth chart). The *ICD–10* diagnostic criteria define this minimum in terms of a body mass index (BMI) equal to or lower than 17.5 kg/m^2. Individuals with AN have an intense fear of obesity that drives their motivation to monitor their food intake to an extreme extent. Although the term "anorexia" literally means "loss of appetite," in reality, individuals with AN are preoccupied with food. The path to self–starvation is driven by a distorted sense of body size and shape and perpetual fear of gaining weight. Weight loss is usually initiated by excluding higher calorie foods, but over time increasing restrictions are added until few "low calorie" foods remain in their diet. According to the *DSM–IV–TR*, criteria for AN include:

- maintaining of weight less than 85% of minimum expected
- intense fear of gaining weight or becoming fat
- distorted sense of body shape
- absence of three consecutive menstrual cycles (a condition referred to as **amenorrhea**)

Associated characteristics that often accompany AN include feelings of ineffectiveness, perfectionism, inhibited emotional expression, lack of spontaneity, rigid thinking patterns, and a strong need to control environmental influences, especially their desire to eat (*DSM–IV–TR*; APA, 2000).

Case in Point

It all started when Jessica got the flu. She was very sick and could not keep any food down for about 4 days. But, a strange thing happened: when she was well, she still did not eat. When she was sick, she didn't eat, and now she realizes that she has the power within her to not eat if she wants to. She can have control and she will exercise her right to refuse to eat. The road is a difficult one because she thinks of food all the time. But, for every thought that comes into her head, her inner voice shouts a powerful message, saying: "NO! You can do it. Don't give in." Then there is the deceit and trickery. She has to wear bulky clothes to hide the weight loss and get rid of the food off her plate when no one is looking. She tells her mother she has eaten at school and tells her coach that she has eaten at home. Jessica is 5'2' and weighs only 90 pounds when she should weigh 105. Jessica has not had a menstrual cycle in the past 3 months. Jessica has AN.

Preoccupation with body image results in self-concept being equated with physical appearance. Distorted perceptions and perfectionistic tendencies often result in self-starvation to the extent that they become an emaciated and skeletal remnant of what they once were. Individuals with AN view weight loss as an achievement and self-starvation as the ultimate test of control and strength of character. Physiologically, highly restricted diets can deplete the body's resources and cause significant health problems. Medical interventions, such as hospitalization and tube feeding, may be necessary in order to prevent a fatality.

Subtypes of AN

The *DSM–IV–TR* (APA, 2000) recognizes two subtypes of Anorexia Nervosa: *AN restricting subtype* and *AN binge-eating/purging subtype.*

1. The **restricting subtype** occurs in approximately half of those with AN who maintain their low weight by practicing restraint and self-deprivation. Restrictions are placed on the types and amount of foods to be eaten, and can include fasting or excess exercise to reduce the amount of caloric intake. Individuals with this subtype do not normally engage in the binge and purge process.

2. The **binge-eating/purging subtype** engage in a pattern of eating more than they normally would consume (binge) followed by a process of purging (self-induced vomiting, laxatives). Although the majority would not engage in a binge to the extent that those with BN would, the act of eating, even a small amount, relative to what they usually consume, triggers the need to engage in purging behaviors to rid the body of the excess calories. Usually binge and purge activities likely take place on a regular (weekly) basis. One longitudinal study reported that individuals with the binge/purge subtype of AN reported less overall life satisfaction and less improvement in global functioning over time than those in the restricting group (Herzog et al., 1999).

Memory Bank

Individuals with AN develop eating patterns that can become self-perpetuating and self-defeating cycles of disordered thoughts and behaviors. Fear of being obese and a distorted body image are the thoughts and perceptions that begin the **anorexic cycle** (See Figure 12.1). Thoughts of being obese trigger self-starvation which results in a preoccupation with food. Ultimately, anxiety and depression are woven into the cycle at each stage.

Clinical Course

Individuals with the *restricting type* of AN who engage in chronic starvation and weight loss run the risk of succumbing to severe dehydration and electrolyte imbalance that may necessitate

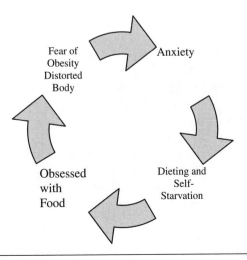

Figure 12.1 The anorexic cycle: Restricting subtype.

hospitalization. Unfortunately, 1 out of 10 individuals with AN who are hospitalized will die either due to complications from AN (e.g., starvation, electrolyte imbalance) or suicide (*DSM–IV–TR*; APA, 2000). However, within the first 5 years, many individuals with the restricting type of AN gradually develop an eating pattern which conforms more to the typical *binge-eating/purging subtype*. Depending on the amount of weight gained due to the binges, the shift from the *restricting type* to the *binge-eating/ purging subtype* of AN, may also signal a shift in diagnosis from AN to BN.

Symptoms of AN may present somewhat differently in children than adults. Features that might typically be present in a 10–11 year old girl or a 13–14 year old boy (which includes the typical 2-year pubertal gap between genders at this age level) might include restricted food intake, restraint around eating, excessive exercise, self-induced vomiting, preoccupation with food and food preparation, concern about eating in front of others, and low self-esteem. It is also common for children to restrict fluid intake, as well as solids, which may result in more serious medical complications (Nicholls, 2005).

Developmentally, at least one study found that premenstrual girls with AN scored lower on the drive for thinness than their postmenstrual peers, although no difference between groups was evident on measures of body dissatisfaction or perfectionism. Compared to the older girls, younger girls exhibited more disordered eating behaviors and scored higher on measures of internal locus of control and social desirability (Arnow, Sanders, & Steiner, 1999). The authors suggest that early onset AN may be indicative of individuals who have a purer form of the disorder that does not require bodily changes at puberty to trigger symptoms.

Comorbidity.   Characteristics often associated with AN include depression, irritability, anxiety, social withdrawal, and insomnia. Obsessive-compulsive characteristics are also common and are manifested in preoccupations with food (*DSM–IV–TR*). Obsessive-compulsive disorder (OCD) is more prevalent in AN than other eating disorders (Blinder, Cumella, & Sanathara, 2006). Individuals who have the binge/purge subtype of AN often are low on impulse control and are at greater risk for substance abuse. Almost three quarters of individuals with AN also experience anxiety (75%), depression (73%), and personality disorders (74%; Deep, Nagy, Weltzin, Rao, & Kaye, 1995; Herzog, Schellberg, & Deter, 1997).

Prevalence

Currently, the lifetime prevalence for AN is thought to be about 1% of the population, and predominantly present in Western, developed countries (Crisp, Palmer, & Kalucy, 1976) and industrialized societies (*DSM–IV–TR*, APA, 2000). Countries where the disorder is most frequent include United States, Canada, Europe, Australia, Japan, New Zealand, and South Africa. The incidence of eating disorders is considerably lower in countries where women have fewer decision-making roles (Miller & Pumariega, 1999).

The disorder is found primarily in females (approximately 90%) and is most pronounced in female adolescents from middle-to-upper class Caucasian families (Pate, Pumariega, Hester, & Garner, 1992). Age of onset for AN is typically between 14 to 18 years of age, with a more positive prognosis associated with earlier adolescent onset. Unfortunately, only 1 in 10 individuals with AN will experience a complete recovery from the disorder, while almost 50% achieve partial recovery (Herzog et al., 1993). Approximately 50% of females with AN will develop bulimia at some later stage (Clinton & Glant, 1992).

Important Distinction

Individuals with BN and those with AN share feelings of anxiety and tension resulting from an obsessive preoccupation with food and an overwhelming fear of obesity. However, the thoughts and feelings that develop as a result of the anxiety and the methods used to cope are very different in these two populations. While those with AN, restricting subtype, are prompted to respond to these anxious feelings by increased control (self-induced starvation), those with BN (binge/purge type) succumb to the anxiety when they impulsively consume major quantities of food (binge).

Bulimia Nervosa (BN)

Description and Associated Developmental Features

The **bulimic cycle** may begin with a feeling of tension or irritability that is accompanied by a strong urge to eat. Lacking in self-control, individuals with BN eventually give in and engage in binge eating, consuming mass quantities of food. Although binging provides an immediate sense of relief from pent up anxiety, feelings of guilt soon take their place accompanied by feeling uncomfortably full and depressed. Acts of purging (vomiting, laxatives, excessive exercise) dispel food and guilt, and restore a sense of control (see Figure 12.2).

Case in Point

On the surface, Susan looks like your typical 15 year old. Susan is 5'2" and weighs 120 pounds—at least that's what the scales report this morning. Susan weighs herself daily and sometimes more than once. Last week she was beginning to edge up the scale and was approaching 130. That's when she stopped eating altogether. For the next 4 days, Susan's diet consisted of sunflower seeds and diet soda. Susan is disgusted with her appearance feeling like she is a "bloated cow." As she flips through pages in the magazines, she is constantly reminded of what she "should" look like. She is hungry and irritable and has refused to go out with her friends because she is too fat. The more she sees the pictures of those models, the worse she feels. She is alone, trapped within her ugly body. She feels so badly that she heads for the refrigerator. Once the binge begins, there is no turning back. Susan loses complete control. In a 2-hour period, Susan will consume an entire cheese cake, large soda, cheeseburger, large fries, box of chocolate chip cookies, and a half-quart of ice cream. After the binge, Susan will feel guilty, depressed, upset, and angry with herself. That's when she will remove all the food from her body through self-induced vomiting. Finally, she is back in control…until the next time. Tension, irritability, binge, guilt, purge, until the whole cycle begins again. Susan has bulimia nervosa.

The *DSM–IV–TR* (APA, 2000) requires the following criteria for a diagnosis of BN:

- Recurrent episodes of *binge eating*: Consume more than normal amount of food in a given period of time (e.g., 2 hours); and eating is accompanied by a sense of loss of control (can't stop eating).
- Recurrent bouts of compensatory behaviors to prevent weight gain (e.g.,self-induced vomiting, excessive use of laxatives, diuretics, enemas, fasting, or excessive exercise).

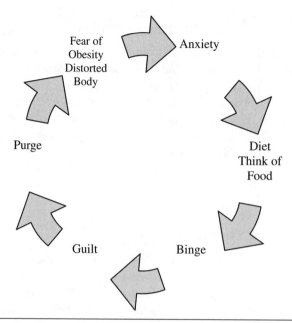

Figure 12.2 The bulimic cycle: Binge/purge type.

- Binge and compensatory behaviors occur at least twice weekly for at least 3 months.
- Self-perception and evaluation are unduly attributed to body shape and weight. (p. 594)

If an individual demonstrates AN and binge/purge behaviors, then a diagnosis of AN is preferred, since it is the more serious of the two disorders.

There are two types of BN that can be distinguished based on the types of compensatory behaviors used:

1. The **purging type of BN** involves compensatory acts that are immediate and driven to remove the food from the body, such as self-induced vomiting, enemas, laxatives, or diuretics. A large epidemiological study revealed that individuals with the purging type, compared to the nonpurging type, demonstrated earlier onset and increased risk for anxiety and affective disorders, alcoholism, sexual abuse, and parental discord (Garfinkel et al., 1996).
2. The **nonpurging type of BN** engage in other forms of compensatory behaviors, such as excessive exercise or fasting.

Memory Bank

Subtypes of AN and BN are presented in Figure 12.3. The binge-eating/purging type of AN and the purging type of BN have both been associated with loss of control and impulsivity, with increased risk for substance abuses as high as 55% for those with BN purge and 23% for AN binge-purge (Holderness, Brooks-Gunn, & Warren, 1994). The restricting type of anorexia and nonpurging type of bulimia both share tendencies to use fasting and excessive exercise to control weight gain.

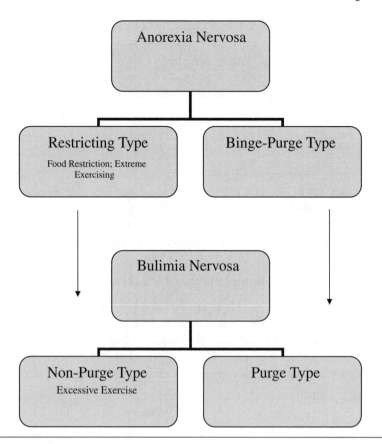

Figure 12.3 Subtype of anorexia nervosa and bulimia nervosa.

Repeated vomiting can produce several physical side effects due to strong stomach acids, such as deterioration of the esophagus and erosion of teeth enamel. In addition, vomiting actually can result in increased feelings of hunger which increases the risk for repeat binge/purge episodes (Wooley & Wooley, 1985). A sense of guilt and shame surround disordered and ritualistic binging and purging behaviors. As a result, binges can be spread over a number of different settings (eating large quantities of food in several different restaurants in succession to avoid detection) or in the privacy or secrecy of their own room. Food is often consumed at a rapid pace, often followed by feelings of physical and emotional discomfort, self-loathing, guilt, and lack of self-worth.

Clinical Course

Both BN and binge eating disorder are associated with comorbid alcohol and drug use/abuse. Among high school students with BN, substance use is associated with other high risk behaviors, including suicide attempts, sexual activity, and theft (Conason & Sher, 2006). Disordered eating patterns (binging, dieting, and purging) in middle and high school students have been associated with tobacco smoking, alcohol drinking, and marijuana use (Field et al., 2002; Lock, Reisel, & Steiner, 2001). Binge eating has been associated with alcohol and illicit drug use and body dissatisfaction (Ross and Ivis, 1999; von Ranson, Iacono, & McGue, 2002). Piran and Robinson (2006) suggest that use of illicit drugs (stimulants/amphetamines, cocaine) by those trying to lose weight may be related to the welcomed side effects of appetite suppression.

Bulimic pathology in adolescence has consistently been linked with major depression and substance abuse (Johnson, Cohen, Kasen, & Brook, 2002). In their study of 496 adolescents in the community, Stice, Burton, and Shaw (2004) found that while substance abuse and bulimic pathology were not directly related, the association between depression and bulimic pathology was bidirectional in nature, in that each promoted increased risk for the onset of the other disorder.

Prevalence

Lifetime prevalence for BN is approximately 1%–3% with a male-to-female ratio of 1 male for 10 females. The typical age of onset for BN is in later adolescence or early adulthood. Individuals with BN can experience disturbed eating behaviors for years and often go undiagnosed. Rates of relapse are high. Most individuals with BN have fluctuating weight loss, but primarily remain within the average weight range for their height (*DSM–IV–TR*, APA, 2000).

A Comparison of AN and BN: Bulimic Versus Restrictive Subtypes

There are several similarities that exist between AN and BN, including onset after a period of intense dieting, preoccupation with food, fear of obesity, and distorted perception of body image. In their clinical sample of females with ED, Blinder, Cumella, and Sanathara (2006) found that individuals with all types of ED (AN, BN, EDNOS) shared high prevalence rates for comorbid mood disorders (94%), mostly unipolar depression and anxiety disorders (56%).

Memory Bank

Similarities between AN and BN
Features shared by both AN and BN include:
- Onset after a period of intense dieting
- Fear of obesity
- Preoccupation with thinness, food
- Distorted sense of body shape and weight

It has been reported that women with AN who have bulimic symptoms (binge/purge type of AN), compared to those with the restricting type of AN, demonstrate greater psychopathology (Garner, Garner, & Rosen, 1993) and have poorer overall outcomes (Garfinkel, Modolfsky, & Garner, 1980), evident in poorer impulse control, greater tendencies to abuse substances, experience emotional distress (DaCosta & Halmi, 1992; Garner et al., 1993), exhibit symptoms of posttraumatic stress disorder (Blinder et al., 2006), and have elevated rates of suicide attempts (Milos, Spindler, Hepp, & Schnyder, 2004). On a similar note, the purging subtype of BN also has poorer outcomes compared to the nonpurging subtype of BN, noted in higher rates of alcoholism, sexual abuse, and parental discord (Garfinkel et al., 1996). Substance abuse/dependence has been reported in more than half (55%) of individuals with BN and almost one quarter (23%) of those with the binge/purge type of AN (Holderness, Brooks-Gunn, & Warren, 1994). Remember that although eating patterns share similarities between AN (binge/purge) and BN (purge), the major distinction will be that those with AN will weight less than 85% of normal expectations.

Science Talks: Eating Disorders and Suicide Attempts

In their study of 288 women with ED, Milos and colleagues (2004) found that the lifetime prevalence of suicide attempts was 26%, a rate 4 times that in the normal population. Suicide attempts were lowest for AN restrictive (10.5%) and BN nonpurge (14.3%) and highest for AN binge/purge (34.7%) and BN purge (29.9%). The investigators concluded that the subtype of eating disorder (purging versus nonpurging type) was more inform- ing that the general category (AN versus BN), since these behaviors are associated with disturbances in impulse control.

Greater differences are found when comparisons are made between the restricting type of AN and the binge/purge type of BN. A summary of the important distinctions can be found in Table 12.5.

In summary, onset of anorexia occurs earlier than bulimia and studies have shown that family characteristics, personality characteristics, and comorbid associations seem to differ in females with AN (restricting subtype) and BN (binge/purge type). While anorexics are more likely to be sexually immature, bulimics tend to have greater difficulties with impulse control and can be more sexually active (Halmi, 1995).

Table 12.5 Differences Between Anorexia Nervosa (AN) and Bulimia Nervosa (BN)

Anorexia Nervosa (Restricting Type)	Bulimia Nervosa
Age of onset: 14 to 18 years	Age of onset: 15 to 21 years
Amenhorrhea (menstrual cycles cease for at least 3 months in response to low body weight)	Menstrual cycles may be irregular, but do not stop unless body weight is very low
Refusal to maintain body weight within 85% of norm	Body weight fluctuates from underweight to overweight
More severe outcome and greater medical risk. Some possible medical complications: Low body temperature, low blood pressure Reduced bone mineral density Slow heart rate Body swelling Metabolic and electrolyte imbalance Dry, parched skin; hair loss Lanugo (fine down-like covering on face, extremities, and trunk)	Less severe outcome and less medical risk. Some possible medical complications: Damage to esophagus and teeth (loss of teeth enamel and dental problems) due to increased acid (vomiting) Chronic diarrhea (overuse of laxatives) Potassium deficiencies, intestinal disorders Kidney disease
Anorexic families: enmeshed, overprotective, rigid, and denial of conflict	Bulimic families: more psychopathology, open hostility, par- ent/child conflict, confrontation, and relational aggression
Personality: withdrawn, rigid, perfectionistic, obsessive	Personality: outgoing and social
Comorbidity: Compared to other EDs, obsessive-compulsive Disorder (OCD) twice as likely and schizophrenia/other psychoses three times more likely (Blinder et al., 2006); Com- pared to controls, increased use of amphetamines (Wieder- man & Pryor, 1996) and drug use (Holderness et al., 1994)	Comorbidity: Compared to other EDs, Alcohol abuse/dependence twice as likely; polysubstance abuse/dependence three times as likely (Blinder et al., 2006); Cluster B personality disorders significantly more likely (dra- matic/ emotional/ borderline personality disorder; Milos et al., 2004); greater tendency to self-prescribe psycho- tropic medications (tranqilizers, hynotics, antidepressants) than AN (Corcos et al., 2001) Compared to controls, increased nicotine dependence and alcohol use (Garfinkel et al., 1995)

Eating Disorders: Contemporary Issues

Contemporary Issues in Etiology

In their paper, *The Mass Marketing of Disordered Eating and Eating Disorders*, Hesse-Biber, Leavy, Quinn, and Zoino (2006) stress the importance of considering how eating problems are driven by the media promotion of a "cult of thinness." From a social psychology perspective, the authors discuss how contemporary mass marketing of body image ideals can influence some vulnerable women and produce what they refer to as "culturally induced" manifestations of the disorders (p. 4).

The Media and the Message

The tabloids often feature stories of celebrities who suffer from eating disorders, such as Princess Diana. In the early 1980s when eating disorders were less visible, many were shocked to hear of the death of Karen Carpenter, a famous singer and entertainer who died from medical complications resulting from anorexia nervosa.

Messages concerning body image and the culturally thin ideal are available through television, movies, the Internet, and magazines (Stice & Shaw, 1994). Concerns about weight and body dissatisfaction have increasingly become the norm in Westernized countries obsessed with dieting (Rodin, Silberstein, & Striegel-Moore, 1985), as the line between pathological and normal eating behaviors becomes more difficult to distinguish (Herzog & Delinsky, 2001). Although eating problems have primarily been thought of as a "white woman's problem" in the past, indications are that there is a narrowing of the gap regarding eating concerns between different ethnic groups (Botta, 2000). For example, one study found that both White and Latina women associate economic success with being thin (Goodman, 2002).

Important Distinction

In their discussion of "culturally induced eating" behaviors, Hesse-Biber, Leavy, Quinn, and Zoino (2006) make an important distinction between disordered eating patterns that define clinical eating disorders (*DSM*), and disordered patterns of eating that do not meet full-blown criteria for an ED. Many women who would not meet the *DSM* criteria for ED nevertheless continue to engage in maladaptive eating patterns that resemble AN and BN in an attempt to minimize weight gain and match body image ideals.

There has been an increased awareness of the pressures that female athletes face that can lead to eating disorders. For example, Rosen, McKeag, Hough, and Curley (1986) surveyed female gymnasts in college and found that 62% were engaged in self-destructive weight control techniques: diet pills (24%), self-induced vomiting (26%), laxatives (7%), and diuretics (12%). Athletes participating in activities that emphasize leanness for performance and appearance seem to be at greater risk for eating disorders. Rosen and Hough (1988) found that the prevalence of eating disorders was significantly higher among athletes in what they called "aesthetic" sports, which include sports such as diving, figure skating, and gymnastics.

The onset of ED can be triggered by a stressful event. Female athletes may be particularly vulnerable to ED given the stress inherent in athletic performance and encouragement to maintain an ideal body size and shape. Underlying anxiety about performance coupled with negative self-appraisals may be the factors that serve to maintain the anorexic cycle over time (Williamson et al., 1995). Furthermore, living in a highly competitive environment that demands discipline and reinforces obsessive characteristics, such as intense motivation to achieve, a drive for perfectionism, emphasis on body control, and attention to detail (Ludwig, 1996), can provide the ideal climate for the development and maintenance of eating disordered behaviors.

Science Talks

Sundgot-Borgen (1994) found prevalence rates of 1.3% for AN and 8.2% for BN among Norwegian elite athletes. In a more recent study, Sundgot-Borgen and Torstveit (2004) compared more than 1,500 Norwegian elite athletes with controls and found that 10.5% of the athletes had an ED compared with 3.2% of the controls. Among the athletes, 20% of females and 8% of males were either at risk or within clinical range of having an ED. Prevalence of disorders among female athletes with an ED was 45% for EDNOS, 36% for BN, and 11% for AN.

Etiology and Theoretical Models

Body dissatisfaction and drive for thinness have been related to increased attempts at dieting that may result in individuals engaging in a variety of unhealthy weight loss techniques. However, not all individuals who are dissatisfied with their body image will develop an ED.

Recall and Rewind: *Disordered Eating Versus Eating Disorder*

Remember that one way to help distinguish pathological from nonpathological behavior is to consider the behavior according to the Four Ds: *distress, deviance, dysfunction,* and *danger.* Individuals with eating disorders are *distressed* and anxious about their distorted perceptions of their body image and their intense fear of becoming obese. They are *deviant* in their preoccupation with food and in their eating habits which can involve restricting weight to 85% of the ideal (AN) or binging and purging at least twice a week for 3 months (BN). Food and eating habits can take on a life of their own and render an individual *dysfunctional* in their employment, schooling, and/or relationships. Finally, restrictive eating habits can pose a *danger* to the physical and mental health of those with eating disorders. Eating disorders and self-starvation can be fatal.

There are several possible explanations regarding how and why eating disorders develop, although it is highly likely that etiology is a complex interaction between biological, psychological, and environmental (family and peer stressors) factors. The following discussion will review some of the more common theories regarding the etiology of ED.

Biological Model
Biological, genetic, and neurotransmitter functions.   Genetic background remains one of the most robust predictors for the development of ED. Risk for developing ED is 6 times as great if the person has a relative with ED (Strober, Freeman, Lampert, Diamond, & Kaye, 2000). Research with twin populations have found that if one monozygotic twin has bulimia, then there is a 23% chance that the other twin will develop the disorder (Walters & Kendler, 1995). The neurotransmitter *serotonin* has also been implicated (Carrasco, Diaz-Marsa, Hollander, Cesar, & Saiz-Ruiz, 2000), which is not surprising given the high rates of comorbidity with depression. Heredity and early eating patterns are thought to establish the *weight set point* (Garner et al., 1985), which

serves to modulate eating patterns. Genetically, there seems to be a history of maternal obesity in families of bulimics.

Temperament and personality. Increasingly, researchers are exploring the relationship between impulsivity and increased self-control in the development of different types of eating disorders.

ED Spectrum

Some theorists believe that AN–R (restrictive type), AN–BP (binge/purge type), and BN represent a spectrum of ED with respect to different degrees of self-control versus impulsivity and obsessive–compulsive personality traits (McElroy, Phillips, & Keck, 1994).

Approximately half of anorexics will be restrictive while the other half will demonstrate characteristics of the binge purge type. Personalities among these two types differ, with the AN–BP sharing many feature of BN evident in a more outgoing and impulsive nature, compared to AN–R with increased obsessive traits, self-control, and being more inhibited, perfectionistic, insecure, and conforming (Casper, Hedeker, & McClough, 1992). Although in one study, Claes, Nederkoorn, Vandereycken, Guerrieri, and Vertommen (2006), found that one component of perfectionism (elevated concern about making mistakes, when mistakes were interpreted as failures) was significantly related to both AN and BN.

 The K–3 Paradigm is an important concept to assist in understanding the development of eating disorders through the relationship between theories, contexts, and developmental course. Body dissatisfaction, especially for females, coincides with a time, developmentally, that they are naturally gaining weight due to puberty and is exacerbated by media images that stress "thin is in."

Family Influence Models

Mothers of females with eating disorders tend to be perfectionistic and also prone to dieting themselves (Pike & Rodin, 1991).

Hilde Bruch (1991): Effective Versus Ineffective Parenting

Bruch integrates psychodynamic and cognitive behavioral perspectives to illustrate how different parenting practices can protect children from ED or to increase the risk of children developing ED. Within this model, *effective parents* are sensitive to their child's needs and respond appropriately to signals of the child's biological (*hunger*) and emotional (*nurturing*) needs. On the other hand, *ineffective parents* respond inappropriately by providing "comfort" food at times when their children are distressed, but not hungry. While *effective parents* assist their children to better understand their own physiological and emotional needs, *ineffective parents* essentially block their children from becoming attune to their biological needs, while at the same time increase their association of eating with emotional nourishment.

Structured family therapy. Minuchin, Rosman, and Baker (1978) applied structured family therapy to the dynamics of families with eating-disordered individuals. Within this context, **anorexic families** demonstrate rigid boundaries that enmesh family members within an overprotective environment driven to preserve outward appearances and deny any underlying conflict. Individuals with AN living in such an environment remain under the control of the family, and are denied any opportunity to develop independence. Within this context, the anorexic's refusal to eat serves two contradictory purposes: exert independence by controlling their own food intake, while at the same time, ensuring their continued dependence by delaying or reversing maturation (lack of onset of "womanhood" and absence of menstruation). While the emphasis in anorexic families is on "control," **bulimic families** are more notorious for their lack of control, and increased psychopathology (depression and substance abuse; Fairburn, Welch, Doll, Davies & O'Conner, 1997). Rather than avoid confrontation, families of bulimics engage in more open hostility, parent/child conflict, and confrontation (Fairburn et al., 1997). Families of bulimics also engage in more relational aggression intent on blaming and attempting to control each other (Humphrey, 1986).

Sociocultural Models

The incidence of eating disorders among adolescent youth has increased steadily in the past 30 years (Raphael & Lacey, 1994). Significant increases in body dissatisfaction have been reported as weights for the ideal woman have decreased in the media (Spitzer, Henderson, & Zivian, 1999) and young males have demonstrated increased concern with their physical appearance (Pope, Olivardi, Gurber, & Borowiecki, 1999). While 25% of women expressed concern over body image when interviewed in 1972, 25 years later, twice the number (56%) expressed concern over body image. Although women were less content than men about their body image, male rates for body dissatisfaction almost tripled from 15% in 1972 to 43% in 1997 (Garner,Cooke, & Morano, 1997). In one study of 9- and 10-year-old girls, researchers found that between 31% and 81% of 9-year-old girls and between 46% and 81% of 10-year-old girls expressed fear of being fat, and had engaged in dieting and binge eating episodes (Mellin, Irwin, & Scully, 1992).

According to the sociocultural model, influences from peers, family, and media have increased body dissatisfaction among youth who try to match their body type to ideals that have been internalized based on cultural ideals (Ricciardelli & McCabe, 2001). As a result of dissatisfaction with their body image, relative to idealized standards, many youth engage in disordered eating behaviors (Stice, 1994; Stice & Whitenton, 2002). In addition to sociocultural risk factors for increased body dissatisfaction outlined earlier (Bearman et al., 2006), the tendency to make social comparisons has also been associated with increased dissatisfaction of body image in prepubescent girls (Vander Wal & Thelen, 2000), as well as, female and male adolescents (Jones, 2001). In a recent study, Halliwell and Harvey (2006) found support for Stice's (1994) sociocultural model with adolescent girls, and boys and expanded the model to include influences from appearance related social comparisons which they found mediated between perceived pressure and internalization. In this model, perceived pressure to lose weight predicted eating behaviors through social comparison, internalization, and body dissatisfaction. Recently, Keery, van den Berg, and Thompson (2004) also demonstrated that the *Tripartite Influence Model* (Thompson et al., 1999), concerning influences of peers, parents, and media provides a useful framework for understanding the underlying dynamics of how body dissatisfaction and eating disturbances develop in adolescent girls.

Cognitive and Behavioral Models

Cognitive distortions are evident in the thought processes of individuals with eating disorders. Tendencies towards negative self-appraisals and obsessional preoccupation with food are prominent features of this pattern of maladaptive thinking. Behaviorally, the anorexic cycle and the bulimic cycle are negatively reinforcing and self-perpetuating. The role of negative affect on thought processes and self-evaluations has been addressed in the section on risks and protective factors.

Assessment

Many of the broad assessment instruments discussed previously are helpful in assessments of comorbid disorders that often can accompany ED. Domain specific assessment instruments which are suitable for use with children and adolescents are summarized briefly.

The eating disorder inventory–2 (EDI–2; Garner, 1991). This self-report instrument assesses common psychological and behavioral traits associated with bulimia and anorexia. The scale comprises eight subscales: *Drive for Thinness, Bulimia, Body Dissatisfaction, Ineffectiveness Scale, Perfectionism, Interpersonal Distrust, Interoceptive Awareness, and Maturity Fears.*

Eating attitudes test (EAT; Garner & Garfinkel, 1979). The EAT is a 40-item questionnaire that provides an overall score, as well as three subscale scores: *Dieting, Bulimia/Food Preoccupation,* and *Oral Control.* Adolescents with AN elevate all subscales, while those with binge/purge features elevate many of the Bulimia items.

Children's eating attitude test (ChEAT; Maloney, McGuire, Daniels, & Specker, 1988). The ChEAT is the children's version of the EAT and is suitable for preadolescent children in Grade 3 and older. The ChEAT is a screening tool that can be used to identify children at risk for developing eating disorders. Children respond to questions with a 5-point range from never (1) to all the time (5).

Body rating scales for adolescents (BRS; Sherman, Iacono, & Donnelly, 1995). Based on a series of figures of different body shapes and sizes. Youth are asked to select figures that best match how they look, and how they would like to look.

McKnight risk factor survey (MRFS–III; Shisslak et al., 1999). The survey provides information about risk and protective factors that have been associated with disordered eating in preadolescent and adolescent girls.

Kids eating disorders survey (KEDS; Childress, Jarrell, & Brewerton, 1993). A screening instrument to detect eating disorder symptoms on two scales: weight dissatisfaction and purging/restricting.

Intervention, Treatment, and Prevention

Although relatively rare among youth, BN and AN continue to be serious disorders that can lead to significant impairments in physical, social, and emotional well- being (Becker, Grinspoon, Klibanski, & Herzog, 1999). Although there has been increased effort to develop evidence-based treatments and preventative programs for ED, one of the major stumbling blocks to treatment is that many of those with ED do not willingly seek treatment or are referred for treatment (Hoek, 1991). Garvin and Striegel-Moore (2001) suggest that epidemiological information is missing about minorities and youth that would help to better understand treatment needs, especially for those who do not meet the full diagnostic criteria for BN or AN and may not qualify for services as a result. Children with eating problems may be an especially vulnerable population due to reliance on adults for referrals, and because they often do not meet diagnostic criteria that have been based on field trials (*DSM*) for older youth and adult populations. Likely due to greater visibility, one study of more than 5,500 high school students revealed that 83.3% of youth with AN were receiving treatment, compared to only 27.8% of those with BN (Whitaker, 1992).

Treatment of Anorexia Nervosa

Specific programs designed for the treatment of AN include three main stages:

1. restoration of weight loss
2. treatment of disturbances in perceptions about body image, low self-esteem, and interpersonal conflicts
3. achievement of long-term remission and rehabilitation or recovery (National Institute of Mental Health-National Institute of Health; NIMH–I, 2001).

Medical interventions.   Prior to any other interventions, attention must be directed to restoring severe weight loss. Close contact with the primary care physician is very important in cases of eating disorders due to the seriousness of the physical complications that can develop. Medical attention might be provided in a hospital setting and could necessitate the use of feeding tubes to stabilize weight and restore electrolyte balance. Increasingly, medical attention is provided in outpatient settings (Pyle, 1999).

Behavioral interventions.   Behavioral interventions can be used to restore weight and to target positive behaviors to replace and intervene in the anorexic cycle. Individuals with AN can be placed on behavioral plans that offer tangible rewards (access to telephone, television, make-up, etc.) for eating properly and restriction of privileges for lack of compliance.

Cognitive behavioral therapy.   Several cognitive behavior programs have been developed to assist individuals with AN. Clinical researchers have recognized the need to address underlying psychological problems and disturbed patterns of thinking in individuals with AN. Programs typically combine individual and family therapies (especially in the case of children and adolescents) and include components to provide educational awareness about the disorder (King, 2001). Robin, Bedway, Diegel, and Gilroy (1996) investigated the impact of a combined cognitive therapy and family therapy program for adolescent girls with AN. Results revealed a 64% success rate (reached ideal weight) at the end of a 16-month treatment program. Follow-up, 1 year later, revealed that 82% maintained gains. Cognitive based programs often address the individual's need for greater independence and alternate methods of gaining control over their lives beyond attempts to control their eating habits (Robin, Siegel, & Moye, 1995). Individuals also need to become better connected to their internal sensations and feelings (Kaplan & Garfinkel, 1999). Awareness of maladaptive thought patterns (perfectionism, negative thinking) is a major focus of cognitive-based treatments. In addition, individual therapeutic sessions would address psychosocial stressors (family, peers) and therapy directed towards any comorbid problems (e.g., anxiety and depression). Cognitive/behavioral programs can be provided on an individual or group basis and frequently involve the family. Other important components of cognitive treatment programs include:

- educational awareness of eating disorder awareness
- developing appropriate weight goals and attitudes

- linking privileges to goal attainment
- monitoring of eating behaviors by an adult (to avoid purging)
- techniques to reduce tension, such as relaxation techniques, can be an important sustaining method and assist in relapse prevention

Family interventions. Minuchin and colleagues (1978) pioneered several techniques for working with anorexic families, including observations of family dynamics during meal times. Today family therapy continues to play a major role in the treatment of AN to address family attitudes towards eating, communication patterns, and direct as well as indirect messages that are sent or perceived. Family systems interventions focus on issues of enmeshment and the family's tendencies to avoid issues of marital or family conflict by diverting energy on the "anorexic" child. There is growing empirical support of the role of family therapy or parent counseling in the treatment of individuals with AN (Robin, 2003).

Treatment of Bulimia Nervosa

Medical interventions. Individuals with BN rarely pose the severity of medical threat evident in those with AN. However, depending on the frequency and intensity of binge and purge episodes, medical side effects can result and require intervention (damage to esophagus, teeth; gastrointestinal problems; etc.). There is increasing evidence that antidepressants (SSRIs) such as fluoxetine (Prozac) may be an effective adjunct to the treatment of bulimia in reducing depressive symptoms, elevating mood, and decreasing the need to engage in binge episodes (Fairburn, 1985). Studies have demonstrated that antidepressants can assist 25% to 40% of individuals with BN (Mitchell et al., 2002)

Cognitive behavioral therapy. The most widely researched approach to the treatment of BN is cognitive behavioral therapy (CBT). Studies have demonstrated the effectiveness of CBT and maintenance of effects on follow-up a year later (e.g., Agras et al., 1994). CBT approaches frequently attempt to modify maladaptive thinking such as linking self-esteem to dissatisfaction with body image and engaging in dieting behaviors, as a result. In this model, dieting (food deprivation) ultimately precipitates binge eating to restore caloric deprivation, and ultimately results in feelings of guilt, shame, and loss of self-esteem. In another derivation of the model, it has been proposed that individuals may engage in bulimic behaviors in an attempt to escape from negative mood states (Meyer, Waller, & Waters, 1998). Consideration of negative mood states as the precipitating factor to binge eating, rather than caloric deprivation, has resulted in the development of an alternate model of BN proposed by Wonderlich, Peterson, Mitchell, and Crow (2000). The proposed integrative model differs from previous models in its "greater emphasis on cultural factors, self-oriented cognition, interpersonal schemas, interpersonal patterns and emotional experiences and integrates interpersonal, cognitive-affective, cultural and biological factors" (Wonderlich, Mitchell, Peterson, & Crow, 2001, p. 176). In this model, it is proposed that individuals with BN have a propensity to avoid harm (avoid change and situations that threaten self-esteem) and negative moods. Yet due to a history of negative experiences (family conflict, anxious attachments) and tendencies to engage in negative self-evaluations (self-ideal discrepancy), they are ill prepared for interpersonal relationships. Faced with a fear of abandonment and rejection, individuals with BN either submit or withdraw. In this case, the more impulsive type of BN may go on the offensive and attack the relationship. Wonderlich et al. (2001) suggest three extreme cognitive styles used by those with BN to regulate negative moods and negative self-evaluations (self-discrepancy): *self-control, self-attack,* and *self-neglect.*

Ultimately, interpersonal patterns (submission, withdrawal, attack) result in increased interpersonal distress, which in conjunction with extreme and maladaptive cognitive styles propels the individual to extreme dieting to reduce body image discrepancy, and avoid negative states by focusing on food. Although in the preliminary stages, Wonderlich et al. (2001) have developed a 4-stage treatment program, *Integrative Cognitive Therapy* (*ICT*) that addresses the underlying issues faced by individuals with BN:

Phase I: Enhancing motivation and psychoeducation (sessions 1–3)
Phase II: Normalization of eating and associated coping skills (sessions 4–8)
Phase III: Interpersonal patterns and schemas (sessions 9–18)
Phase IV: Relapse prevention and lifestyle management (sessions 19–20)

Family interventions.   Due to the fact that bulimic families are much more volatile than anorexic families, therapy would likely be directed at more appropriate methods of communication, appropriate conflict resolution, and re-establishing appropriate boundaries.

Prevention of ED

With the average age of onset for ED in early to midadolescence (Striegel-Moore, Jacobson, & Rees, 1997), it is not surprising that many of the prevention programs that have been developed target young females.

Science Talks

In one study of more than 1900 Australian girls between 14 and 15 years of age, dieting was the single most important predictor of ED (Patton, Selzer, Coffey, Carlin, & Wolfe, 1999). Females who were seriously involved in dieting were 18 times more likely to develop ED within 6 months compared to peers who did not diet. Even girls who dieted at a moderate level increased their risk for ED 5 times higher than peers who did not diet. According to the latest YRBS (CDC, 2005), currently 59.6% of high school girls in the United States are engaged in dieting practices.

In general, prevention programs for ED can target *primary prevention* (focus on reducing risks and increasing protective factors) or *secondary prevention* (programs focusing on early identification) for youth at risk of developing ED (Piran, 2005). Carter, Stewart, Dunn, and Fairburn (1997) reviewed six school-based programs that were developed to address the primary prevention of eating disorders by targeting dieting behaviors that have been identified to increase the risk for ED in youth. All six programs were similar in content and targeted educational awareness concerning the seriousness of ED, the adverse effects of dieting and increasing resistance to social pressures to diet. Although the programs were successful in increasing awareness, there was no significant change in dieting behaviors as a result of participation in any of the programs. As a result, Carter and colleagues (1997) developed their own 8-week program embedded in the school curriculum and targeted girls 13–14 years of age. In addition to educational awareness in a number of areas and assertiveness training to resist social pressures, the researchers also included cognitive (changing maladaptive thinking) and behavioral (self-monitoring of eating habits) interventions. Initial results of the pilot study were extremely encouraging and the girls demonstrated a significant increase in their awareness of ED and actually altered their eating disordered patterns as a result of their participation. However, follow-up 6 months later revealed that although awareness remained intact, dieting had returned and was actually higher than recorded prior to intervention. As a result, the researchers posed the important question of whether primary prevention of eating disorders might do more harm than good (Carter et al., 1997).

Science Talks About Iatrogenic Effects

The first principle in the APA ethical guidelines for psychologist is *Beneficence and Non-maleficence, or "do not harm."* Sometimes, intervention or prevention programs can have surface validity, yet may produce the reverse effect of what was intended. Some examples of iatrogenic effects (when treatments harm) for youth in the past include increased delinquency and substance use resulting from aggregating youth with conduct problems for treatment (Dishion, & McCord, & Poulin, 1999) and increased substance use by suburban students who had participated in a Drug Abuse Resistance Education (DARE) relative to students who did not participate in DARE (Rosenbaum & Gordon, 1998).

Pratt and Woofenden (2006) evaluated 12 prevention studies that matched strict inclusion criteria including: randomization, use of a control group, and having at least 85 participants. The studies involved more than 3,000 children, and all but 3 of the 12 studies were school-based. From their analysis, the researchers found only one statistically significant pooled effect that was successful in reducing the risk of ED. The successful programs focused on discussions and critical evaluation of media messages concerning body image (Kusel, 1999; Neumark-Sztainer, Sherwood, Coller, & Hannon, 2000). Additionally, in response to concerns voiced by Carter and colleagues (1997), Pratt and Woolfenden (2006) addressed the increasingly awareness of the need to strike a balance between delivering preventive *interventions* for *eating disorders* and fears about the potential to cause harm. An important practical implication of the findings of this systematic review concerns the lack of evidence for harm being caused as a result of any of the *interventions* included in their the review.

Kusel (1999) conducted a 2-day program for 172 young girls (Grades 4–6). Girls watched videos, learned how to critically analyze deceptive media techniques, and discussed alternatives other than appearance to evaluate others. Girls in the control group engaged in discussions of the pros and cons of fame, looked at a video and photos of music stars, and participated in stress management techniques. At the end of the intervention program, girls significantly decreased their dieting, body dissatisfaction, internalization of body stereotypes, and increased their self-esteem relative to controls. Three months later, perceptions of body distortion remained significantly lower, and awareness of stereotypes significantly higher than controls. However, at follow-up, controls unexpectedly demonstrated a significant reduction in restricting and purging relative to girls in the intervention groups. As a result, Kusel (1999) has suggested that stress management techniques may be a more effective intervention for targeting signs of ED than focusing on weight or body shape.

Whether successful prevention programs can meet the challenge of dispelling cultural myths about the ideal body image remains to be seen. As a result of findings from their review, Pratt and Woofenden (2006) stress the need for future prevention programs to address the strong influence of media and peers in reinforcing growing body dissatisfaction among youth and urge greater awareness that developing belief systems in youth may be very resistant to change.

CHAPTER REVIEW

Although only about 1%–3% of the population will meet criteria for a full-blown eating disorder (ED), as outlined in the *DSM-IV-TR* (APA, 2000), 90% of these will be women. Furthermore, although many may not meet diagnostic criteria ED, there are high percentages of adolescent females and an increasing number of adolescent males who are voicing concern about body dissatisfaction and engaging in unhealthy practices to lose weight. Developmentally, onset of eating disorders can actually begin in infancy or early childhood and present as persistent eating and feeding disturbances.

1. **Contemporary Issues in Body Image and Weight Control**
   Athletes in sports that focus on body image and control, such as the "aesthetic" sports or "elite sports," may be particularly vulnerable to disordered eating behaviors due to perfectionistic tendencies and focus on body control. On the other hand, overeating in the absence of exercise can be equally problematic. One third of the children in the United States are either obese or at risk for being obese and indications are that the numbers are steadily increasing.

2. **Body Dissatisfaction and Contemporary Youth**
   Youth responses to risk surveys indicate that approximately 30% report body image concerns, and that males are voicing increased concerns over body image in the last 10 years. While 38% of females report feeling overweight, in reality only 10% actually meet criteria for being overweight. The *Tripartite Influence Model* suggests three significant influences in body dissatisfaction including: peers, parents, and media.

3. **Feeding and Eating Disorders First Diagnosed in Infancy or Early Childhood**
   Three early eating disorders listed in the *DSM* (APA, 2000) include *pica, rumination disorder,* and *feeding Ddisorder*. Individuals with mental retardation are most likely to be candidates for pica (eating of odd substances such as, paint, string, clay, sand, insects, etc) and rumination disorder (regurgitation and rechewing of food). Although feeding disorder (food refusal), or failure to thrive (FTT) was initially thought to be related to parental neglect, more recent research suggests several other factors that may be implicated.

4. **Eating Disorders (ED)**
   The *DSM* (APA, 2000) recognizes three categories of eating disorders: *anorexia nervosa (AN), bulimia nervosa (BN), and eating disorders not otherwise specified (EDNOS)* or atypical ED. Onset for AN is typically between 14–18 years of age, while onset for BN is later adolescence to early adulthood.

5. **Historical Background of Eating Disorders (ED)**
   Early accounts of anorexia linked symptoms to the expressions of other disorders (such as schizophrenia). In 1973, Hilde Bruch's book on eating disorders established anorexia nervosa (AN) as a disorder in its own right, while in 1979, George Russell established credibility for bulimia nervosa (BN) in his research account of more than 30 women who demonstrated symptoms of the disorder.

6. **Anorexia Nervosa (AN)**
   Refusal to maintain at least 85% of normal weight is the cardinal marker of AN. Intense fear of gaining weight, distorted body perception, and absence of three consecutive menstrual cycles (amenorrhea) are other *DSM* criteria (APA, 2000). Ninety percent of those with AN are females who exhibit one of two eating patterns: *restricting subtype* (fasting, excess exercise) or *binge-eating/purging subtype* (eating followed by compensatory behaviors).

7. **Bulimia Nervosa (BN)**

   Pent-up tension can trigger a bulimic cycle that results in an intense overeating binge, followed by feelings of guilt and depression. Compensatory behaviors attempt to restore a sense of control. Two compensatory patterns include: *purging type* (self-induced vomiting enemas, laxatives, diuretics); or *nonpurging type* (excessive exercise or fasting).

8. **A Comparison of AN and BN**

   AN and BN share several characteristics, including intense fear of obesity, preoccupation with thinness, and distorted sense of body image. Both often occur after a period of intense dieting. However, while those with AN are successful in maintaining a body weight less than 85% of what is considered normal, those with BN are often normal to slightly above normal weight. Also, onset for AN is usually earlier than onset for BN. The AN binge/purge type is most similar to BN purge type and both disorders have poorer outcomes than the other subtypes (suicide attempts, depression, substance abuse).

9. **Etiology, Treatment, and Prevention of Eating Disorders**

   Genetics, family dynamics, media, peer pressure, and maladaptive thinking/perceptions of body image can all contribute to disordered eating habits. Treatment focus depends on severity with restoring normal weight for those with AN a primary concern. Other areas of intervention include targeting comorbid associations through antidepressants, cognitive behavioral therapy, substance abuse counseling, and family interventions. Training in critical thinking and awareness of media messages concerning body image has been a successful component in prevention programs with youth.

Consolidate and Communicate

1. Obesity or risk for being overweight is evident in approximately 30% of children and youth. What are the major factors that contribute to increases in obesity among youth and what are some suggestions for improving health among this overexpanding population?

   Based on results posted in Table 12.1, what are some of the more important trends in obesity that were revealed in the Youth Risk Behavior Surveillance Summaries (YRBS, 2005) survey?

2. Despite the fact that a significant proportion of youth are obese or at risk for being obese, body dissatisfaction can be inflated in some youth who consider themselves to be overweight when, in fact, they are not. Based on the information from the YRBS (2005; Table 12.2), discuss body dissatisfaction trends as they relate to race and gender over the past 10–15 years. What can we conclude from these statistics?

3. There are healthy (moderate exercise, lowering intake of fatty foods) and unhealthy methods of attempting weight reduction. Referring to Table 12.3, and the chapter discussion, comment on trends that are evident in types of methods used and gender differences. Why do you think that different methods are more likely at different age levels (Grades 9–12), and can you think of why this might be so?

4. Based on your knowledge of trends in disordered eating and body dissatisfaction, suggest a prevention program that might target young girls or boys at risk of developing eating problems. Be sure to identify the age and gender that your program will target and support why you have identified these areas in your program. Discuss how concepts from the *Tripartite Influence Model* (Thompson et al., 1999) might be incorporated in your prevention program.

5   As a mother of an adolescent with significant body dissatisfaction problems research has demonstrated that you might be in a lose–lose situation. Discuss.

6. Athletes may be particularly vulnerable to eating disorders. What does the research suggest that might support or oppose this statement?

7. What is weight set point, and why is yo-yo dieting often the result?

Chapter Review Questions

1. Rumination disorder involves:
    a. thinking about eating
    b. eating of nonnutritive substances
    c. regurgitation and rechewing of food
    d. food refusal

2. Which of the following is not a category of eating disorder formally recognized by *DSM–IV–TR* (APA, 2000)?
    a. Eating disorder not otherwise specified (EDNOS)
    b. Anorexia nervosa (AN)
    c. Bulimia nervosa (BN)
    d. Binge eating disorder (BED)

3. Ellen West was a German woman who:
    a. caused herself to vomit using a feather
    b. wrote a diary about her struggles with binge eating and vomiting
    c. became famous for self-starvation
    d. was the first woman to be identified with night eating syndrome

4. Bulimiarexia was a term that was used to describe:
    a. a pattern of binge eating followed by purging in college women
    b. anorexia that was not followed by purging
    c. a laboratory condition that occurred in mice that were stressed
    d. an eating disorder characterized by pica

5. The cardinal feature of anorexia (AN) that distinguishes it from bulimia (BN) is:
    a. intense preoccupation with food
    b. onset after an intense period of dieting
    c. distorted sense of body image
    d. weight at 15% less than normal

6. Amenorrhea refers to:
    a. cessation of at least three menstrual cycles
    b. down-like hair growth
    c. disintegration of the esophagus
    d. loss of enamel on teeth

7. All of the following are examples of the purging type of bulimia nervosa (BN) except:
    a. self-induced vomiting
    b. excessive exercise
    c. enemas
    d. diuretics

8. Research has found that the most common comorbid disorder among all eating disorders is:
    a. anxiety disorders
    b. substance use disorders

    c. mood disorders

    d. personality disorders

9. Although many youth would not meet criteria for eating disorders (*DSM*, APA, 2000), as many as _____% of females demonstrate many binge-eating symptoms.

    a. 20%

    b. 5%

    c. 45%

    d. 80%

10. In their study of body dissatisfaction, Bearman et al. (2006) found that while body dissatisfaction was comparable for boys and girls at younger ages, by age _____ girls were significantly more dissatisfied with their bodies than males.

    a. 8

    b. 10

    c. 11

    d. 14

Glossary

body mass index (BMI)
obesity
tripartite influence model
weight set point
pica
rumination disorder
feeding disorder
failure to thrive (FTT)
anorexia nervosa (AN)
bulimia nervosa (BN)
eating disorder not otherwise specified (EDNOS)
binge-eating disorder
night eating syndrome
binge eating syndrome
bulimiarexia
amenorrhea
anorexia nervosa restricting subtype
anorexia nervosa binge-eating/purging subtype
anorexic cycle
bulimic cycle
binge eating
bulimia nervosa purging type
bulimia nervosa nonpurging type
anorexic families
bulimic families

Answers to Multiple Choice Questions:
1. c; 2. d; 3. b; 4. a; 5. d; 6. a; 7. b; 8. c; 9. c; 10. d.

13
Substance Use and Abuse Among Youth

Youth Substance Use: Developmental Trends
> *Developmental Trends*
> > The Gateway Hypothesis
> > Risks and Protective Factors
> > Comorbid Associations
> *Youth Prevalence Rates*
> *Etiology of Substance Use/Abuse*
> > The Biological Model
> > The Behavioral Model
> > The Sociocultural Model
> > The Diathesis-Stress Model
> *Issues in the Treatment of Substance Related Disorders*
> > Group Versus Individual Treatment
> > Treatment Challenges
> > Treatment Programs
> *Prevention*

CHAPTER PREVIEW

The lifetime prevalence rate of drug use in adolescent 10th and 12th graders is currently 50%, while approximately 20% of eighth graders admit to having used an illicit drug. The *DSM–IV–TR* (APA, 2000) currently recognizes two broad categories of substance disorders: *substance use disorders* (including substance dependence and substance abuse) and *substance-induced disorders* (substance intoxication and withdrawal). There are 11 substance categories listed in the *DSM*, and each category has a unique cluster of symptoms for intoxication and withdrawal. There is considerable concern regarding the degree to which *DSM* diagnostic criteria derived from adult populations are appropriate for use with adolescents and youth. There is also controversy concerning whether drugs have a prescribed sequence of initiation (*gateway hypothesis:* do alcohol/cigarettes precede other illicit drugs, such as marijuana).

1. Substance Use Disorders (SUD)
SUD can have a detrimental effect on health and performance at work, school, and in relationships, involving either substance dependence (repetitive pattern of compulsive substance use, tolerance, and withdrawal) or substance abuse, harmful consequences resulting from excessive use that compromises fulfilling major life roles, and increases risks for engaging in high risk behaviors, legal problems, and causing relationship problems.

2. Substance-Induced Disorders
Substance intoxication is the reversible clusters of thoughts and behaviors that result from taking a substance resulting from changes in central nervous system (CNS). Substance withdrawal refers to the syndrome specific set of behaviors associated with taking decreased amounts or no amounts of a substance after repeatedly engaging in substance use over a prolonged period of time.

3. Substances Commonly Used by Youth: Cigarettes, Alcohol, Marijuana
Survey reports on 15 different substances used by youth in Grades 8, 10, and 12 reveal that approximately 20% of youth (12 to 17) used cigarettes during 2004, while usage in middle school was reported to be almost 12%. More than 68% of 12th graders (2005)

reported alcohol consumption, while 28% reported binge drinking (more than 5 drinks in a row within the past 2 weeks). In one study, prior tobacco use was significantly related to increased risk for alcohol use. Approximately one third of high school sophomores and seniors report using marijuana in 2005. Among eighth graders, approximately 12% reported marijuana use in 2000.

4. Trends in Substance Use Among Youth

Although overall rates for substance use have declined compared to rates in the late 1990s, there have been significant increases in the use of specific substances at the extreme ends of those surveyed: eighth graders have increased inhalant usage, while 12th graders have substantially increased the use of prescription medications for nonmedicinal purposes. In 2005, 9% of youth (12–17 years of age) reported use of a prescription medication (OxyContin, Vicodin, tranquilizers) for nonmedical reasons in the past year. Inhalants represent a wide range of chemicals found in household products and cleaners and can cause hallucinations, delusions, and "sudden sniffing death." Inhalants can cause damage to the central nervous system and brain atrophy.

5. Etiology, Comorbidity, Risks, Protective Factors, and Treatment

Increased risk for drug use can be related to genetics, or depletion of normally occurring chemicals (GABA) through repeated drug usage. Increased dopamine activity associated with substance use supports behavioral theories of increased usage due to self-induced rewards. The diathesis stress model suggests that individual vulnerabilities placed within stressful circumstances may activate otherwise latent tendencies to use drugs. Numerous disorders increase the risk for developing substance abuse, including conduct disorder, depression, posttraumatic stress disorder, anxiety disorder, bulimia nervosa, and ADHD. Although group treatment can be successful for adults, concerns about aggregating youth with similar problems have flagged inherent risks in this approach for youth. Twelve-step models, CBT approaches, and family-based treatment (MST) all have promise for therapeutic intervention. The use of empirically supported prevention programs, such as the Life Skills Training (LST), can reduce the risk for substance use.

Youth Substance Use and Abuse: History and Trends

Since 1975, a series of annual national surveys have been distributed to a representative sample of 12th graders to obtain information concerning drug usage, perceived risk, disapproval, and perceived availability of drugs. In 1991, the survey expanded to include 8th and 10th graders. The survey, *Monitoring the Future (MTF)*, is administered by the University of Michigan, and the latest press releases, listings of all publications, and reports are available online at http://www.monitoringthefuture.org.

Recall and Rewind

In chapter 4, the influence of *cohort effects* on research findings was introduced. Recall that cohort effects refer to the generational influence on research findings. Surveys for *Monitoring the Future* dramatically portray how drug usage and drug approval shifts from generation to generation as 8th graders progress to 10th and 12th graders, and how responses from new generations of 8th graders demonstrate a new wave of result patterns.

In one of the most recent publications of *Monitoring the Future: Overview of Key Findings 2005* (Johnston, O'Malley, Bachman, & Schulenberg, 2005), the researchers discuss the potential role of **cohort effects** on trends emerging over the years.

For example, usage of the drug **Ecstasy (MDMA)** demonstrated a rapid gain from 1998 through 2001; however, increased awareness of the dangers associated with the drug resulted in a steep decline after 2002. Yet, in 2005, only the 12th graders demonstrated further decline. The authors suggest that in addition to cohort effects, a phenomenon of **generational forgetting** might also act to spur new waves of drug interest that serve to sustain drug resilience. Not only are new drugs being introduced to youth, but old drugs tend to be "rediscovered" by young people. The researchers suggest that the rediscovery of LSD and methamphetamine are examples of how drugs that were once popular in the 1960s have made their way back into the current drug scene. Another roadblock to prevention is the decision-making process regarding whether to use or abstain from drugs. Decision making often involves weighing benefits versus risks. However, as the authors suggest, "benefits of using a drug usually spread much faster than information about adverse consequences" with the result that youth are enticed to sample the benefits long before any evidence is forthcoming about potential adverse consequences, such as risks of brain damage, death, or addictive potential (Johnston et al., 2005, p. 7).

The University of Michigan studies (Monitoring the Future: MTF) have reported drug behaviors and attitudes among high school seniors for the past 30 years which provides an opportunity to review trends in drug usage over that time span. From the inception of the study in 1975, percentage rates for youth admitting to having used an illicit drug have risen from 55% the first year to 66% in 1981. After years of progressive decline, the percentage of usage in 1992 had dropped to 41%. However, lifetime usage again rose to a recent high of 55% in 1999 and is currently at a lifetime percentage of 50% in 2005. Drug usage by grade level has revealed a continuing decline in usage among 10th and 12th graders since 2001; however, 8th graders have remained constant since 2003 (approximately 20% indicating they have participated in illicit drug usage). Other trends noted in the research reports are that males tend to have somewhat higher rates of illicit drug usage than females, while non-college-bound students are at greater risk for illicit drug usage. Additional information from the MTF study (Johnston et al., 2005) will be reviewed as specific drugs are introduced and discussed throughout this chapter.

Youth and Risk Taking Behaviors

Tendencies for youth to engage in risky behaviors is not a new phenomenon; however, the manner in which youth demonstrate these risks can shift over time. In one recent survey of more than 10,000 adolescents (Grades 7 through 12) living in the United States, 9% of youth surveyed admitted to using a weapon in the past year (Blum et al., 2000). In the same survey, 25% had smoked cigarettes in the past 30 days, while one out of seven students in 7th and 8th grades reported that they had already experienced sexual relations. The researchers found that the tendency to engage in high-risk behaviors increased significantly if youth experienced school failure, had increased opportunities for unstructured free time, and associated with peers who were involved in high-risk activities.

DSM–IV–TR (APA, 2000): Classification of Substance Related Disorders

The *DSM–IV–TR* (APA, 2000) uses the term **substance** to refer to *a drug of abuse, a medication, or a toxin*. There are 11 reported substance categories found in the *DSM–IV–TR* (APA, 2000), including alcohol; amphetamines; caffeine; cannabis; cocaine; hallucinogens; inhalants; nicotine; opioids; phencyclidine (PCP); sedatives; hypnotics; or anxiolytics. Increasingly, many over- the-counter medications and prescription medications are also being used by youth that can result in substance use, abuse and related disorders.

Important Distinction

The concept of substance use or abuse often triggers visions of alcohol, tobacco, and illicit drugs such as marijuana or amphetamines. However, in their report of drug use in 2005, prescription drugs such as **sedatives** and **OxyContin** were the two drugs that showed increased use among 12th graders. In 2005, the annual prevalence rate for sedatives was 7.2% (the highest rate since 1980), while the annual prevalence rate for OxyContin rose by 40% and is now at 5.5% (Johnston et al., 2005). This situation is of grave concern because of the highly addictive nature of OxyContin.

The *DSM–IV–TR* (APA, 2000) distinguishes between substance related disorders that are **substance use disorders** (**substance dependence** and **substance abuse**) and those that are considered to be **substance-induced disorders** (**substance intoxication** and **substance withdrawal**). The relationship between these categories is depicted in Table 13.1.

Currently, the *DSM–IV–TR* (APA, 2000) criteria are the only established criteria for diagnosing substance related disorders. There has been concern regarding the degree to which these criteria are appropriate for use with adolescent populations, since the criteria have been developed for use primarily with adults. At present, there is no clear agreement regarding specific criteria that might be used to more appropriately define abuse and dependence in adolescents and youth (Winters, Latimer, & Stinchfield, 2001).

Substance Use Disorders

Substance use disorders refer to patterns of substance use that result in impairment in everyday living in a wide variety of areas, including work, school, and relationships. Substance use can have a detrimental effect on general health and performance, as well as increase tendencies to be impulsive and/or aggressive. Increased rates of accidents, fatalities, and suicide have all been associated with substance use. Substance use in pregnancy can cause serious consequences for the unborn baby, such as fetal alcohol syndrome, or result in the baby born addicted to a substance such as cocaine.

The *DSM* distinguishes two types of substance use disorders: *substance dependence* and *substance abuse.*

Table 13.1 Classification of Substance-Related Disorders

Substance Use	
Substance Dependence	**Substance Abuse**
With Physiological Dependence	
Without Physiological Dependence	
Substance-Induced Disorders	
Substance Intoxication	**Substance Withdrawal**

Source: DSM–IV–TR, APA (2000).

> **Memory Bank**
>
> The nature of the **withdrawal symptoms** varies depending on the nature of the substance. For example, withdrawal from alcohol can produce symptoms of insomnia, anxiety, and psychomotor agitation, while withdrawal from amphetamines can cause fatigue, increased appetite, and vivid, unpleasant dreams.

Substance Dependence

In essence, the nature of dependence is defined by a cluster of cognitive, behavioral, and physiological symptoms that develop and sustain the individual's need to continue to use the substance despite increases in substance-related problems. Often a self-perpetuating cycle develops where repeated self-administration results in increased tolerance, withdrawal, and the compulsive need to continue taking the substance. The core feature of substance dependence, according to the *DSM–IV–TR* (APA, 2000), is a *compulsive reliance on a substance*, on a repeated basis, despite experiencing adverse effects as a result of taking the substance. In addition to satisfying this criteria, <u>three</u> other conditions must also be met within a 12-month period:

1. *Tolerance*
   Tolerance refers to the need to increase the amount of a substance used to achieve the same effect, or conversely, experiencing less of an effect than previous from taking the same amount.

2. *Withdrawal Symptoms*
   A reduction in the amount of substance used or in abstinence from the substance results in the development of behavioral, physiological, or cognitive changes, causing clinically significant distress or impairments in functioning. Although not a necessary part of the withdrawal criterion, many individuals in withdrawal develop a craving for the substance to relieve the symptoms of withdrawal.

3. *Increased use and increased amounts*
   The substance may be taken in greater amounts and over a longer period of time than initially anticipated. For example, the individual may decide to have only one cigarette, but by the end of the night has finished the entire pack.

4. *Unsuccessful attempts to control the use*
   Despite frequent efforts to quit or cut down on usage, the attempts remain unsuccessful.

5. *Extensive time involved in obtaining or maintaining the use*
   The substance eventually begins to take control as more time is spent using the substance, procuring the substance or recovering from the substance.

6. *Forgoing important activities (social, work, etc.)*
   The substance dominates the individual's life and he or she may withdraw from activities or hobbies in order to partake of the substance, or spend more time with others who are also involved in taking the substance.

7. *Continued use despite adverse physical or psychological consequences*
   The continued use of the substance continues to prevail regardless of the physical, social, or emotional consequences that may result. The individual is powerless and not able to abstain despite the adverse consequences.

The template for substance dependence can be applied to each of the 11 substances discussed in the *DSM–IV–TR* (APA, 2000) with the exception of caffeine.

What the *DSM–IV–TR* (APA, 2000) Says About Caffeine

Currently, the *DSM–IV–TR* recognizes **caffeine intoxication**, which may result after consuming more than 2–3 cups of coffee. The symptoms, which cause significant distress or impairment, include *five or more* of the following: restlessness, nervousness, excitement, insomnia, flushed face, diuresis, gastrointestinal disturbance, muscle twitching, rambling speech, rapid heart rate, and psychomotor agitation (APA, 2000, p. 232).

However, the *DSM* states that there is presently insufficient evidence to warrant classification of disorders of dependence, abuse, or withdrawal for the substance of caffeine.

It is important to note that individuals can vary in their tolerance levels for different substances, depending on the substance used, the degree to which the central nervous system is affected, and individual differences in sensitivity to the substance. For example, some people may be able to tolerate some substances better than other individuals, and it is also possible to have variations in one's own tolerance level given different physiological or mental conditions that are salient at that point in time. Based on the *DSM* criteria, it is possible for an individual to meet criteria for substance dependence without exhibiting either tolerance or withdrawal (as part of the three symptoms). It is highly likely, however, that individuals who do demonstrate tolerance and withdrawal are at greater risk for relapse rates and the development of associated medical problems.

Important Distinction

In order to provide additional diagnostic information as to whether tolerance and withdrawal are part of the symptom constellation, clinicians may use two different specifiers:

1. **Substance dependence with physiological dependence** (tolerance and withdrawal are part of the symptom presentation).
2. **Substance dependence without physiological dependence** (an absence of tolerance and withdrawal).

Substance Abuse

While substance dependence refers to the tolerance, withdrawal, and compulsive reliance on the substance, substance abuse refers to the **recurrent and adverse consequences** caused by the substance. The cardinal feature of substance abuse is a *maladaptive pattern of impairment* due to substance abuse, resulting in *one or more* of the following situations occurring within *a 12-month period*:

- *Failure to fulfill a major obligation*
  Substance abuse results in irresponsible behaviors that seriously impair the ability to fulfill obligations. These behaviors may result in school problems (truancy, suspension, expulsion, school failure); work-related problems (repeated absences from work, poor work performance, inappropriate behaviors); and neglecting parenting responsibilities (child care, household chores).
- *Engaging in physically high-risk behaviors*
  Such behaviors as driving or operating machinery while impaired may pose a danger to oneself or others.

- *Legal problems*
  Individuals may have repeated arrests for driving while impaired, or becoming involved in conduct-related problems.
- *Relationship problems*
  Continued substance abuse leads to problems with significant others (spouse, children, employers, friends) and may result in severing relationship ties through substance induced fights or arguments.

Memory Bank

According to the *DSM*, **substance dependence** and **substance abuse** are two mutually exclusive categories. One of the criteria for substance abuse is that the criteria have never been met for substance dependence. While substance dependence involves a pattern of tolerance, withdrawal, and compulsive substance use, substance abuse refers to the harmful consequences that excessive and abusive substance use can have for the individual and the potential danger that this abuse can also pose for others.

Classification of substance use/abuse disorders among youth. There is concern that the *DSM–IV–TR* (APA, 2000) criteria for *substance use disorders* and *substance abuse disorders* may not adequately describe how these disorders present in children and youth, since the criteria have been derived from field studies involving primarily adult populations. The fact that experimental use of substances is anticipated to some extent in youth, it is important to be able to discern the seriousness of the substance use in order to provide an effective and appropriate level of treatment (Burrow-Sanchez, 2006). With this goal in mind, Winters (2001) has suggested the use of a dimensional or continuum approach to gauge severity, as an alternative to the categorical (*DSM*) approach. According to Winters (2001), classification of the severity of substance use should provide a range of drug involvement from abstinence to heavy usage, including:

- abstinence
- experimental use
- early abuse
- abuse
- dependence
- recovery

The final category of recovery encompasses those who have relapsed and who may have retraced their steps through the initial stages a number of times.

Substance-Induced Disorders

The *DMS–IV–TR* (APA, 2000) currently includes two disorders under the category of substance-induced disorders: **substance intoxication** and **substance withdrawal**.

Substance Intoxication

Intoxication occurs when enough of a substance is taken to produce a specific set of symptoms (**substance-specific syndrome**). Although the *DSM* refers to 11 different classes of substances, and each substance has its own set of syndrome specific symptoms, some substances can be grouped by similar features. Different substances can produce similar effects. For example, alcohol shares features with sedatives, hypnotics, and anxiolytics, while cocaine shares features with the amphetamines (e.g., grandiosity and hyperactivity). The three categories of substance clusters include: **depressants** (alcohol, sedative-hypnotic drugs, opioids); **stimulants** (cocaine, anphetamines, caffeine, nicotine); and **hallucinogens** (LSD, MDMA, mescaline, psilocybin, and Cannabis). The categories and a brief description of the shared symptom features of intoxication within these category clusters is presented in Table 13.2.

Intoxication is considered **"reversible"** because once the effect of the substance wears off, behavior reverts to preintoxication levels. Some examples of intoxicated behaviors include:

- belligerence
- labile mood
- grandiosity

Table 13.2 Categories of Substances and Symptoms of Substance Intoxication

Category	Substances	Symptoms of Intoxication
Depressants Slows down the activity of the CNS	Alcohol	Bind to the **GABA** receptor sites; Tension reduction and decreased inhibition Impaired concentration Impaired balance and motor control
	Sedative-Hypnotic Drugs Barbiturates	Anxiolytics (anxiety reducing drugs) Drowsiness, excess amounts can depress the **reticular formation** brain's arousal center. Overdoes can result in coma and death. Agonist causing increase GABA activity (Valium, Xanax)
	Benzodiazepines	Include opium from opium poppy Medically used to relieve pain Addictive

	Opioids
	  Morphine
	  Codeine
	  Heroin
		Illicit drug, highly addictive

Stimulants Increase activity of the CNS	Cocaine	Coca plant Increase in blood pressure, heart rate, impulsivity, and motor responses; **Dopamine** agonist "rush " euphoria Stimulates **serotonin** and **norepinephrine** Individual "*crashes*" when stimulation subsides. *Crack* form of *free-based* cocaine (vaporized by heat and inhaled) Highly addictive
	Amphetamines	Manufactured in laboratories (benzedine, dexedrine, methedrine). Historically used to medically treat asthma. Also used to aid in weight loss, sustained wakefulness. Manufactured in illicit "meth labs" and sold illegally. Agonist for dopamine, serotonin, and norepinephrine. Tolerance builds quickly resulting in dependence on drug.
	Caffeine and Nicotine	Increase activity of CNS
Hallucinogens and Cannabis Alter sensations and perceptions	LSD (lysergic acid diethylamide) Cannabis	Alter sensory perceptions. Can cause hallucinations and delusions. Other drugs in this category, include: MDMA (Ecstacy), mescaline, and psilocybin. (See Table 13.3 for detailed information about the Hallucinogens and Cannabis.)

Source: DSM–IV–TR, APA (2000).

- withdrawal
- cognitive impairment
- impaired judgment

The effects of intoxication can be anticipated somewhat, however, the substance's effect on **central nervous system** (**CNS**) functioning may not always be predictable. Different substances influence the CNS in different ways, in different individuals and may also have different effects at different times within the same individual due to the interaction of other factors (mood, fatigue, etc.). In addition, taking more than one substance at the same time, referred to as **polysubstance use**, can result in multiplying the overall effect.

Synergistic Effect: When the whole is greater than the sum of its parts

A **synergistic effect** can occur when two substances that have similar effects are taken at the same time. For example, combining alcohol and a barbiturate or opioid (all within the depressive cluster) can produce a drug overdose resulting in coma or even death.

Intoxication can cause changes in a number of sensory functions, including disturbances of perception; wakefulness; psychomotor behavior (reflexes); concentration and attention; cognitive processing, as well as influence personality and interpersonal behaviors (*DSM–IV–TR*; APA, 2000, p. 200). Although initially, alcohol may be used to provide a sense of social ease in releasing less inhibited social behaviors, repeated usage may actually result in increased withdrawal from social contact and depression.

Substance Withdrawal

After having taken a substance repeatedly over a prolonged time period, abstinence from the substance or marked reduction in the amount of substance taken can result in a set of withdrawal behaviors (*substance-specific syndrome*) specifically related to that substance. The resulting syndrome can be distressing enough to cause significant impairment in day-to-day functioning in school, work, and/or relationships. Due to the high level of physiological and psychological discomfort associated with these symptoms, individuals often crave the substance to reduce the impact of the symptoms of withdrawal. Substances which are likely to cause withdrawal symptoms include alcohol, cocaine, nicotine, opioids, and sedatives. Most symptoms of withdrawal are the opposite of symptoms noted for intoxication.

Youth Substance Use: Nature and Course

Monitoring the Future (*MTF*) generates annual reports of drug usage among adolescents in the United States concerning 15 of the most commonly used drugs in adolescence. The current list includes the following drugs:

- tobacco
- alcohol, sedatives (barbiturates), methaqualone, tranquilizers rohypnol
- marijuana/hashish
- inhalants and nitrites
- LSD, PCP, MDMA (Ecstacy)
- steroids
- cocaine, crack, heroin, amphetamines, methamphetamine, ice

Table 13.3 Drug Usage and Symptoms of Intoxication

Drug Name	Street Names	Side Effects	Symptoms of Intoxication
Marijuana: Most prevalent illicit drug Active ingredient: THC (delta-9-tetrahydrocannabinol)	Weed, Pot, Bud, Herb, Grass, Reefer, Ganja, Green, Mary Jane, Hash, Cheeba, Dope, Smoke	Depression, anxiety, or irritability seen in 1/3 of regular users; Possible paranoid ideation Short-term memory problems. Dizziness, perceptual disturbance	The high generally wears off in about 2–3 hours, mood elevation, increased awareness of senses, increased appetite, sleepiness
Club Drugs: MDMA (pill)	MDMA: Ecstacy	MDMA: can result in liver, kidney, and cardiovascular system failure, and death	MDMA chemically similar to the stimulant methamphetamine: sense of euphoria
GHB: Clear odorless substance that can be mixed with drinks	**"date rape" drugs** GHB: "liquid ecstasy," "soap"	GHB: Coma and seizures can occur; insomnia, anxiety, tremors, and	GHB: euphoric, sedative, and anabolic (body building) effects
Ketamine It can be injected or snorted	Ketamine: "special K" or "vitamin K"	Ketamine delirium, amnesia, impaired motor function, high blood pressure, depression, and potentially fatal respiratory problems	Ketamine: dream-like states and hallucinations
Rohypnol	Rohypnol: "rophies," "roofies," "roach," and "rope"	Rohypnol: can produce "anterograde amnesia," (loss memory) events they experienced while under the effects of the drug. Also, Rohypnol may be lethal when mixed with alcohol and/or other depressants.	Used to overpower victims Disinhibition, disorientation, and confusion
LSD synthetic Hallucinogen	Acid, dots, hits, blotter, sugar cube, Elvis, blue cheer, electric Kool-Aid	Negative "bad trip" effects: paranoia, delusions, anxiety, and mood swings	Dilated pupils, tremors, flushing, chills. (Distorted sense of time)
PCP synthetic dissociated drug; Snorted, ingested orally, smoked or injected	*PCP*: Angel dust, amoeba, sherms, STP, *embalming fluid: PCP + Marijuana*	Low dose: drowsy, constricted pupils, impaired; unpredictable	Often used to "lace" other drugs, e.g., sold as many other drugs; motor skills Higher dose: erratic behavior

*Information adapted from http://www.justfacts.org, a Web site provided by The Center for Substance Abuse Research (CESAR), University of Maryland, College Park, MD.

A brief summary of some of the side effects and symptoms of intoxication for a sample of drugs used by adolescents in presented in Table 13.3.

Over the past 25 years, research concerning adolescent drug use in the United States has consistently pointed to a developmental pathway for substance use. In the initial stages of substance use, tobacco or alcohol (legal drugs) is used, followed by marijuana, which is used prior to involvement with other illicit drugs, such as hallucinogens, other pills, and lastly heroin and cocaine (Kandel, 2002). The exact nature of the progression of drug use has led some to speculate about which drugs are potential **gateway drugs** (function to initiate users to other drugs) and question why some individuals only experiment while others follow a more serious drug use trajectory. Theories surrounding the gateway hypothesis will be revisited later in the chapter.

The most prevalent drugs used by youth include **alcohol, tobacco (including smokeless cigarettes)**, and **marijuana**. Among eighth graders, inhalant use increased from 8.7% (annual prevalence rate) in 2003 to a high of 9.5% in 2005. The use of prescription drugs such as *OxyContin* by 12th graders increased from 4.5% in 2003 to 5.5% in 2005 (Johnston et al., 2005). The following section provides information concerning the prevalence rates, nature, and course of substance use for some of the most commonly used drugs by contemporary youth.

Tobacco

Prevalence and Trends

The prevalence rates for tobacco usage are available from several national surveys conducted concerning smoking habits in youth. The Monitoring the Future (MFT) studies (Table 13.4 and Table 13.5) reveal that in 2005, more than 25% of youth in the eighth grade had smoked a cigarette, while 10 % had tried *smokeless tobacco* (chewing tobacco or snuff). Compared to surveys conducted in 2001 and 2003, these rates represent declines in smoking over the three intervals. In 2005, heavy smoking (at least a half pack of cigarettes a day) was reported by 1.7 % of 8th graders, 3.1 % of 10th graders, and 6.9 % of 12th graders. All rates noted a decline since 2001.

Table 13.4 Monitoring the Future: A Comparison of Lifetime* Prevalence Rates for Substance Use in Adolescent 8th, 10th, and 12th Graders in 2001, 2003, and 2005

Drug	8th Grade 2001	8th Grade 2003	8th Grade 2005	10th Grade 2001	10th Grade 2003	10th Grade 2005	12th Grade 2001	12th Grade 2003	12th Grade 2005
Any Illicit Drug	26.8	22.8	21.4	45.6	41.4	38.2	53.9	51.1	50.4
Marijuana	20.4	17.5	16.5	40.1	36.4	34.1	49.0	46.1	44.8
Inhalants	17.1	15.8	17.1	15.2	12.7	13.1	13.0	11.2	11.4
LSD	3.4	2.1	1.9	6.3	3.5	2.5	10.9	5.9	3.5
Cocaine	4.3	3.6	3.7	5.7	5.1	5.2	8.2	7.7	8.0
Crack	3.0	2.5	2.4	3.1	2.7	2.5	3.7	3.6	3.5
Heroin	1.7	1.6	1.5	1.7	1.5	1.5	1.8	1.5	1.5
Tranquilizer	5.0	4.4	4.1	9.2	7.8	7.1	10.3	10.2	9.9
Amphetamine	10.2	8.4	7.5	15.7	13.1	11.1	16.2	14.4	13.1
Meth	4.4	3.9	3.1	6.4	5.2	4.1	6.9	6.2	4.5
Steroids	2.8	2.5	1.7	3.5	3.0	2.0	3.7	3.5	2.6
MDMA	5.2	3.2	2.8	8.0	5.4	4.0	11.7	8.3	5.4
Smokeless Tobacco	11.7	11.3	10.1	19.5	14.6	14.5	19.7	17.0	17.5
Alcohol Any Use	50.5	45.6	41.0	70.1	66.0	63.2	79.7	76.6	75.1
Been Drunk	23.4	20.3	19.5	48.2	42.4	42.1	63.9	58.1	57.5
Cigarettes Any Use	36.6	28.4	25.9	52.8	43.0	38.9	61.0	53.7	50.0

Source: Johnson et al., 2006.
*"Lifetime Prevalence" refers to use at least once during a respondent's lifetime.

Table 13.5 Monitoring the Future: A Comparison of Annual* Prevalence Rates and 30-Day Daily Prevalence for Substance Use in Adolescent 8th, 10th, and 12th Graders in 2001, 2003, and 2005

Drug	8th Grade 2001	8th Grade 2003	8th Grade 2005	10th Grade 2001	10th Grade 2003	10th Grade 2005	12th Grade 2001	12th Grade 2003	12th Grade 2005
Any Illicit Drug	19.5	16.1	15.5	37.2	32.0	29.8	41.4	39.3	38.4
Marijuana	15.4	12.8	12.2	32.7	33.5	31.7	37.0	34.9	33.6
Inhalants	9.1	8.7	9.5	6.6	5.4	6.0	4.5	3.9	5.0
LSD	2.2	1.3	1.2	4.1	1.7	1.5	6.6	1.9	1.8
Cocaine	2.5	2.2	2.2	3.6	3.3	3.5	4.8	4.8	5.1.
Crack	1.7	1.6	1.4	1.8	1.6	1.7	2.1	2.2	1.9.
Heroin	1.0	0.9	0.8	0.9	0.7	0.9	0.9	0.8	0.8
OxyContin	-	1.7	1.8	-	3.6	3.2	-	4.5	5.5
Vicodin	-	2.8	2.6	-	7.2	5.9	-	10.5	9.5
Tranquilizers	2.8	2.7	2.8	7.3	5.3	4.8	6.9	6.7	6.8
Steroids	1.6	1.4	1.1	2.1	1.7	1.3	2.4	2.1	1.5
MDMA	3.5	2.1	1.7	6.2	3.0	2.6	9.2	4.5	3.0
Amphetamines	6.7	5.5	4.9	11.7	9.0	7.8	10.9	9.9	8.6
Meth	2.8	2.5	1.8	3.7	3.3	2.9	3.9	3.2	2.5
Alcohol Any Use	41.9	37.2	33.9	63.5	59.3	56.7	73.3	70.1	68.6
Been Drunk	16.6	14.5	14.1	39.9	34.7	34.2	53.2	48.0	47.7
**30 Day: **									
Marijuana Daily	1.3	1.0	1.0	4.5	3.6	3.1	5.8	6.0	5.0
30 Day:									
Alcohol Daily	0.9	0.8	0.5	1.9	1.5	1.3	3.6	3.2	3.1
5+ drinks in row last 2 weeks**	13.2	11.9	10.5	24.9	22.2	21.0	29.7	27.9	28.1.
Cigarettes 1/2 pack+/ day**	2.3	1.8	1.7	5.5	4.1	3.1	10.3	8.4	6.9

Source: Johnson et al., 2006.
*"Annual" refers to use at least once during the year preceding an individual's response to the survey.
**"30-day" refers to use at least once during the 30 days preceding an individual's response to the survey.

Surveys conducted in both 2003 and 2004 by the *National Survey on Drug Use and Health* (NSDUH, 2004) revealed that among youth 12 to 17 years of age, 14% reported use of tobacco products (including cigarettes and smokeless tobacco) in the past month . The rate was consistent in the 2 years surveyed. In 2004, 22.7 % of males and 21.4% of females, 12 to 17 years of age, reported use of a tobacco product in the past year.

Based on 27, 933 responses from middle school (Grades 6–8) and high school students (Grades 9–12), the *National Youth Tobacco Survey* (*NYTS*), conducted by CDC, in 2004, revealed that 11.7% of middle school students and 28% of high school students reported current use of a tobacco product (within the past 30 days). No significant changes in overall percentages were noted from 2002 to 2004.

Nature and Characteristics of Tobacco Use

Bidis and Kreteks.   In the MTF school survey of 8th, 10th, and 12th graders, Johnston and colleagues (2005) revealed that in 2005, 1.6 % of 8th and 10th graders and 3.3 % of 12th graders reported the use of **Bidis** (pronounced "bee-dees") in the past year, while 1.4% of 8th graders, 2.8% of 10th graders, and 7.1% of 12th graders have used **Kreteks** (pronounced "cree-techs").

Bidis and Kreteks

Bidis are small, thin, hand-rolled cigarettes imported to the United States primarily from India and other Southeast Asian countries (CDC, 2004). They consist of tobacco wrapped in a tendu or temburni leaf (plants native to Asia). Bidis can be flavored (e.g., chocolate, cherry, and mango) or unflavored. They have higher concentrations of nicotine, tar, and carbon monoxide than conventional cigarettes sold in the United States (Watson, Polzin, Calafat, & Ashley, 2003).

   Kreteks, also called *clove cigarettes*, are imported from Indonesia, and typically contain a mixture consisting of tobacco, cloves, and other additives (Malson, Lee, Murty, Moolchan, & Pickworth, 2003). Similar to bidis, kreteks also deliver higher concentrations of nicotine, carbon monoxide, and tar than conventional cigarettes.

No research studies on the health effects of bidis have been conducted in the United States; however, studies from India have linked bidi smoking with increased risk of cancer of the mouth, lungs, stomach, and esophagus (Rahman & Fukui, 2000).

   According to the *National Youth Tobacco Survey* (*NYTS; CDC, 2004*), an estimated 3% of high school students are current bidi smokers, with prevalent rates among males (4 percent) twice that compared to females (2 percent). Approximately 2% of middle school students smoke bidis, which is also more common among males. Kretek smoking is currently practiced by 3% of high school students and 2% of middle school students and is more popular among males (CDC, 2005).

Smokeless tobacco.   Chewing tobacco and snuff are considered to be smokeless tobacco products. In 2005, the lifetime prevalence for smokeless tobacco usage among 8th, 10th, and 12th graders was reported as 17.5% of 12th graders, 14.6 % of 10th graders, and 10.1% of 8th graders (MTF; Johnston et al., 2005).

Tobacco Use: Developmental Course

A review of the statistics from the *National Survey on Drug Use and Health* (*SAMSHA*, 2004) reveals that lifetime prevalence for tobacco usage increases dramatically among youth between 12 (8.5%) and 19 (68.7%) years of age. The developmental trajectory for tobacco use is steep during the early middle school years; usage doubles between 12 (8.5%) and 13 (17.2%), and continues to rise sharply at yearly intervals: 14 years (28.1%), 15 years (38.5%), 16 years (47.7), 17 years (56.7%), and 18 years (65.8%) of age. The lifetime prevalence for youth can be viewed graphically in Figure 13.1.

   As part of their survey, the National Youth Tobacco Survey (NYTS) questioned the ease of access to tobacco for youth. The results were surprising:

- 70.6% of the current smokers in middle school reported that they were not asked to show proof of age when purchasing cigarettes
- 66.4% stated that they had never been refused a purchase based on their age

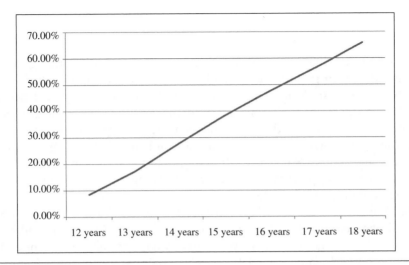

Figure 13.1 Tobacco use during 2004 by age of user.

In their study of protective factors, Hawkins, Hill, Guo, and Battin-Pearson (2002) found that stronger bonding to mothers was associated with lower risk of tobacco initiation. However, peer influence and social norms of smoking acceptance were predictive of adverse effects. Ultimately, the more favorable the youth's attitude (norms) was to tobacco, the more likely she or he would be to initiate tobacco use, even after controlling for all other predictors.

Dependence on tobacco products, **nicotine dependence**, is often sustained by the use of nicotine to fend off symptoms of **nicotine withdrawal**, which cause significant distress and impairment in important areas of functioning, and include at least four from a list of eight potential symptoms:

- Depressed mood
- Insomnia
- Irritability, frustration
- Anxiety
- Problems concentrating
- Restlessness
- Decreased heart rate
- Increased appetite or weight gain (*DSM–IV–TR*; APA, 2000, p. 266)

Withdrawal symptoms are most intense among those who smoke cigarettes, since nicotine is more rapidly absorbed into the system. Physical dependence can be a significant deterrent to smoking cessation. Among adults, 80% of smokers express a desire to quit; however, although 35% attempt to quit annually, less than 5% are able to quit without assistance (DSM–IV–TR; APA, 2000). Complications resulting from chronic use include risk of respiratory conditions such as bronchitis and increased potential for developing lung disease.

Alcohol

Prevalence

Cohen and colleagues (1993) interviewed 500 adolescents and youth regarding substance use and abuse. Based on their information, alcohol abuse was reported by 4% of males and 3% of females in the 14 to 16 year old age range. Older youth (17 to 20 years) reported increased rates for girls (9%) and significant increases among older males (20%). Rates for drug abuse were much lower in this study, with less than 2% of the younger group reporting drug abuse. However, within the older group, rates again noted an increase for males with up to 5% disclosing drug abuse, compared to less than 3% of females. In 2005, two thirds (68.6%) of 12th graders reported alcohol consumption in the past year, while 28% reported **binge drinking** (consumed more than 5 drinks in a row in the past 2 weeks).

Prevalence rates in 2005 for alcohol consumption (56.7%) and binge drinking (21%) by 10th graders and alcohol consumption (33.9%) and binge drinking (10.5%) by 8th graders were also reported. Lifetime prevalence rate among youth for consuming alcohol was reported as 75% by senior year, 70% for sophomores, and 41% by eighth grade. By the time they had reached the eighth grade, almost one in five students had at least one episode of being drunk (19.5%).

Nature and Characteristics

Alcohol intoxication produces different symptoms depending on the amount of alcohol consumed. Initially, symptoms of talkativeness, sense of well-being, and expansive mood result in response to increase blood alcohol levels. Later, depression, cognitive impairment, and withdrawal are associated with reduced blood alcohol levels. At very high alcohol blood levels, sleep may be induced. At dangerously high levels (e.g., in excess of 300–400 mg/dL), respiratory arrest is possible and can be fatal (*DSM–IV–TR;* APA, 2000, p. 221).

Risks for alcohol use and binge drinking.   Bahr, Hoffman, and Yang (2005) investigated peer and parental influences on alcohol consumption and binge drinking in a sample of 4,230 adolescents from Grades 7–12. In their sample, the frequency of alcohol use was 25% higher for boys than girls, with 11% of youth reporting binge drinking within the past 2 weeks. Risks for increased alcohol consumption was related to parental tolerance (80% more likely) and sibling alcohol use (71% more likely) and peer alcohol use. Peer alcohol use was the strongest single predictor for adolescent binge drinking. As the number of close friends who were drinkers increased, the risk of binge drinking doubled.

Memory Bank

In the MTF survey of adolescent drug habits, Johnston and colleagues (2005) included questions regarding binge drinking. The term *binge drinking* is used to refer to heavy consumption on a single occasion (e.g., 5 or more drinks during the same drinking session). Since most prevalence rates for drug usage often refer to frequency of taking drugs rather than quantity of drug consumed, this question provided a new source of information about drinking habits of youth. In a different survey, approximately 33% of high school seniors and 25% of sophomores reported that they engaged in *binge drinking* at least twice a month (Johnston & Pandina, 2000).

Developmental Course

In their study of norms and transition in substance use, Hawkins et al. (2002) found that prior tobacco use was significantly related to increased risk for the initiation of alcohol use in the following year. Consequences of alcohol use have been noted in poor school performance, severe family conflicts, truancy, and delinquent and criminal behaviors (Miller, Alberts, Hecht, Trost, & Krizek, 2000).

In a longitudinal study of teens, substance abuse, and driving, Shope (2001) found that positive parental influences (monitoring, nurturing, and family connectedness) reported by fifth and sixth graders predicted lower rates for substance abuse and subsequent rates of serious driving offenses and crashes in their mid-20s.

According to the *DSM–IV–TR* (APA, 2000), as many as 90% of adults have had alcohol at some point in their life, with a large portion (60% males; 30% females) having experienced an alcohol-related adverse incident (absent from school or work, driving while impaired). **Alcohol dependence** develops after a period of chronic use with physiological dependence evident in **alcohol withdrawal symptoms** that can include sleep problems (insomnia), nausea, anxiety, increased hand tremors, autonomic hyperactivity, and psychomotor agitation. Symptoms of alcohol withdrawal are relieved by alcohol consumption or use of another brain depressant. Symptoms usually peak in intensity after the 2nd day of abstinence. However, in particularly chronic cases, symptoms of anxiety, insomnia, and autonomic dysfunction may persist as long as 3–6 months (*DSM*, p. 216).

Alcohol Related Injuries

Alcohol use is associated with increased risk for accidents, violence, and suicide. In one survey of alcohol-related injuries, Spirito, Jelalian, Rasile, Rohrbeck, and Vinnick (2000) interviewed 643 males and 782 females in grades 9–12 regarding alcohol usage, risk taking behavior, and injury. Results revealed that 21% of males and 15% of females reported at least one alcohol-related injury. Rates were highest among Caucasian (19.6%) relative to African American (14.8%), Asian (7.4%), and Hispanic (5%) youth.

Alcohol abuse and dependence are often associated with other substances (e.g., cannabis, amphetamines, nicotine) and are accompanied by symptoms of depression, anxiety, and insomnia. Among adolescents, those with conduct disorder and antisocial behaviors are at high risk for the development of comorbid alcohol abuse or dependence, and/or other substance-related disorders. Male-to-female ratio for alcohol abuse and dependence can be as high as 5:1 for males, but varies with different age groups (*DSM–IV–TR*; APA, 2000).

Cannabis (Marijuana)

Prevalence

Approximately one third of 12th graders and 10th graders reported using marijuana in 2005, while 5% of 12th graders and 3.1% of 10th graders admitted to daily usage in the past 30 days (see Table 13.4). Among eighth graders, 12.2% reported using marijuana in the past year, with 1% admitting to daily usage. These rates represent a slight drop from those reported in 2001. Marijuana is the most prevalent illicit psychoactive drug used across all age levels, and second only to alcohol use among youth. In 2003, marijuana was the third most commonly abused drug responsible for drug-related admissions to emergency departments in the United States, at 12.6%, following cocaine (20%) and alcohol (48.7 %).

Nature and Characteristics

Cannabis is derived from the cannabis plant (cannabinoids), which is cultivated from the upper leaves, tops, and stems, which are dried and rolled into cigarettes, called marijuana. Hashish oil is a more concentrated form. The main active chemical in marijuana is *THC* (delta-9-tetrahydrocannabinol). The membranes of certain nerve cells in the brain contain protein receptors that bind to THC, resulting in a series of cellular reactions leading to a "high" that users experience when they smoke marijuana. The THC content of marijuana has increased significantly since the 1960s, going from approximately 1%–5% to current levels as high as 10%–15% (*DSM–IV–TR*; APA, 2000, p. 235).

Cannabis dependence may involve persistent use despite adverse physical (chronic cough) or psychological effects (loss of goal-directed activities, excess sedation). **Cannabis abuse** potentially includes such adverse consequences as relationship problems, dangerous driving while impaired, and poor school and work performance.

Cannabis intoxication usually lasts for about 3–4 hours and is described as a "high" feeling including symptoms of *euphoria, inappropriate laughter, grandiosity, sedation,* and *lethargy.* Information processing is impaired with respect to short-term memory, judgment, distortion of sensory perceptions, and impaired sense of time. Motor performance is also compromised. The magnitude of symptoms will depend on the strength of the dosage, and may persist longer or reoccur due to the slow release of some of the psychoactive substances. Adverse side effects might include anxiety, dysphoria, and social withdrawal. Cannabis intoxication also includes *at least two of the following* occurring within 2 hours of use: *conjunctival injection, increased appetite, dry mouth,* or *tachycardia.* The specifier **with perceptual disturbances** is used to account for hallucinations or illusions that result within the context of intact reality testing (individual is aware that these are substance induced).

In approximately one third of regular cannabis users, symptoms of mild depression, anxiety, and irritability are present. High dosages can result in "bad trips" similar to those experienced by LSD, heightened anxiety (resembling panic attacks), paranoid delusions, and hallucinations. Episodes of depersonalization are also possible (*DSM–IV–TR*; APA; 2000, p. 239).

Cannabis: Developmental Course

As with the majority of substances, dependence and abuse develop over a course of chronic use, although the process may be accelerated in some individuals. The *DSM–IV–TR* notes that a history of conduct disorder in childhood or adolescence and antisocial personality disorder in adults have been associated as risk factors for the development of many substance related disorders, including cannabis-related disorders. Cannabis, alcohol, caffeine, and nicotine use often appear early in the course of substance use in those who go on to develop dependence on other substances. The pathway has led some to speculate that cannabis may be a *gateway drug* for the use of other illicit drugs (Hall & Lynskey, 2005).

Is Cannabis a Gateway Drug?

Hall and Lynskey (2005) suggest that there are multiple, complex, and interacting factors surrounding the question. Part of the reason may be attributed to the *selective recruitment* of socially deviant youth (nonconformist and antisocial conduct) to early cannabis use. Youth may tend to aggregate with other like-minded peers who are more likely to use cannabis and other drugs. Frequency of cannabis use has also been suggested as another factor that contributes to the gateway phenomenon. For example, Fergusson and Horwood (2000) found a dose response association between frequency of cannabis use and use of other illicit drugs. Youth who had used cannabis once or twice were 3.5 times more likely to use illicit drugs.

Inhalants

Prevalence

Between 2002 and 2005, eighth graders reported a significant increase in the annual abuse rates of inhalants, from 7.7 % to 9.5%. In 2004, the lifetime abuse of inhalants had increased significantly among eighth graders, from 15.8% (2003) to 17.1% in 2005, continuing an upward trend after several years of decline (see Table 13.3). According to the NSDUH survey (2002), rates for inhalant use among 12–17 years of age were reported as the following percentages: lifetime (10.5%), past year (4.4%), and past month (1.2%).

Nature and Characteristics

Inhalants are a broad range of chemicals found in countless products such as cleaning fluids, gasoline, glue, correction fluids, and felt-tip marker fluids. Vapors are inhaled to induce a psychoactive mind-altering effect. (Information on inhalants has been obtained from the National Institute on Drug Abuse [NIDA]; Research Report Series, Inhalant Abuse, 2004). Because of their ease of availability, inhalants are often the first drugs that children experience. Inhalants can be classified into four general categories:

1. **volatile solvents** (liquids that vaporize at room temperature)
2. **aerosols** (sprays)
3. **gases** (nitrous oxide found in whipped cream dispensers)
4. **nitrites** (room odorizers)

Most inhalants act directly on the central nervous system (CNS) and are used to alter mood. *Texas shoe-shine* and silver/gold spray paints are popular inhalants containing the chemical **toluene**. Nitrates act primarily to dilate blood vessels and relax muscles and are used as sexual enhancers. Nitrites are often sold on the street as **poppers** or **snappers**. The most common types of inhalants reported by 12 and 13 year olds in 2003 (NSDUH, 2003) included glue, or toluene (4.3%); gasoline or lighter fluid (3.3%); spray paints (2.9%); and correction fluid, degreaser or cleaning fluid (2.1%).

Inhalants can be sniffed, sprayed directly into the mouth, or inhaled through **bagging** (breathing fumes from a bag) or **huffing** (soaked rag). The effects of **inhalant intoxication** are similar to alcohol (slurred speech, poor coordination, euphoria, dizziness); however, unlike alcohol, the intoxication last only a few minutes, resulting in abusers continuing to inhale over the course of longer and longer periods of time. Hallucinations and delusions are possible, as well as loss of consciousness, which can be fatal. Brain imaging studies have shown that chronic use of inhalants, such as toluene, can result in **brain atrophy** (shrinkage).

Developmental Course

There are dire consequences of chronic usage of inhalants, although in cases, immediate damage can also be devastating. Damage to the central nervous system can result in spasticity, cognitive impairments, and loss of feeling, hearing, or vision. **Sudden sniffing death** has also been associated with the abuse of butane, propane, and chemicals found in aerosols. Risks to nitrate abusers include engaging in unsafe sex and the risk of contracting HIV/AIDS and hepatitis. Increased inhalant use has been associated with poverty, a history of child abuse, poor academic performance, and dropping out of school.

Recall and Rewind

The recent significant increase in the use of inhalants by eighth graders may reflect what Johnston and colleagues (2005) referred to as *cohort effects* or generational influences, such as, *generational forgetting*. This phenomenon is evident in a new wave of drug users who have *rediscovered* the "positive" aspects of the drug without recall for its powerful adverse side effects. Ease of access and availability of inhalants will continue to pose a threat to potential drug usage of inhalants among the very young.

There is evidence to support that the earlier the onset of inhalant abuse, the more damaging the long-term consequences. For example, compared to those who initiated inhalant use at 14 years of age, those who used inhalants at 13 years of age or younger were more likely to not complete high school, and reported more dependence on or abuse of other drugs and engage in more illegal activity (MFT; Johnston et al., 2005).

Nonmedical Use of Prescription Psychotherapeutics: OxyContin

Prevalence Rates

Annual abuse of **OxyContin** by youth was first surveyed in 2002, and since that time has continued to demonstrate levels of increased concern. Nonmedical use of prescription-type medications was surveyed in 12–17 year-olds as part of the National Survey on Drug Use and Health (NS-DUH; SAMHSA, Office of Applied Studies [OAS], 2004). Results of the NSDUH survey indicate that 9.1% of youth in that age group (9.9% females; 8.2 % males) had used a **prescription-type psychotherapeutic drug** without a prescription in the past year. There was a significant increase in the use of OxyContin in this age group from 2002 (.9%) to 2004 (1.2%), with 305,000 youth (12–17 years of age) reporting the use of OxyContin.

Results from the MFT study (Johnston et al., 2005) indicated that despite overall trends that showed a continuing general decline in drug use, the nonmedical use of some prescription drugs by youth continued to show relatively high rates or long-term increases in 2005 (see Table 13.4 and Table 13.5).

> **Declining Trends Reverse**
>
> In 2005, 9.5 % of 12th graders reported using Vicodin in the past year, and 5.5 % of students in this grade reported using OxyContin in the past year (Johnston et al., 2005). In 2005, the rate of nonmedical use of OxyContin among 12th graders (5.5%) was significantly higher than the reported nonmedical use of this drug (4.5%) among 12th graders in 2002. In addition, the nonmedical use of sedatives in the past year (2005) among 12th graders was the highest since 1991. Since 2001, there has been a 25% increase in the annual abuse of sedatives/barbituates among 12th graders.

Nature and Characteristics

OxyContin is a time-release formula of oxycondone, semisynthetic opiate prescribed for pain relief. Dosage ranges from 10mg to 80 mg, although the medications Percocet, Percodan, and Tylox contain smaller doses (2.5mg to 10mg) combined with other ingredients such as aspirin or acetaminophen. OxyContin is known as a **Schedule II controlled substance** with high additive and abuse potential. OxyContin acts similar to heroin by elevating the neurotransmitter dopamine, producing a euphoric high. Although OxyContin comes in a pill form, it can be crushed, snorted, or dissolved in water and injected in order to defeat the time-release mechanism. When it is chewed or mashed and snorted, OxyContin produces a sudden, powerful high similar to heroin. Some street names for OxyContin include *Oxy, OC, Kickers, Blue, Hillbilly Heroin,* and *Killers.* Adverse side effects include impaired mental functioning, respiratory depression, headaches, nausea, and dizziness. Seizures and heart failure are possible. Prolonged use results in increased tolerance and the need for greater quantities to obtain the same effect. **OxyContin withdrawal** symptoms include *anxiety, nausea, insomnia, muscle pain,* and *other flu-like symptoms* (Center for Substance Abuse Research [CESAR]; http://www.justfacts.org).

Developmental Course

According to the NSDUH survey conducted in 2004 (NSDUH; SAMSHA, 2004), there was a significant increase in the use of OxyContin in youth 12 to 17 years of age from 2002 to 2004. In 2004, pain killer usage more than doubled from 2.5% at 12 years of age, to 6.4 % at 14 years of age. The use of painkillers peaked at 19 years of age with a reported usage of 13.9%. The MTF survey (Johnston et al., 2005) revealed a reported increase in lifetime prevalence for OxyContin use among 12th graders from 4.5 % in 2003 to 5.5% in 2005. **Vicodin** (hydrocodone) another opioid used as a pain killer is derived from two naturally occurring opiates (codeine and thebaine). Vicodin is another addictive narcotic that binds to opiate receptors in the central nervous system (CNS). Usage rates for Oxycontin and Vicodin were significantly higher among 12th graders in 2005 (5.5% Oxycontin; 9.5% Vicodin), compared to 10th graders (3.2% Oxycontin; 5.9% Vicodin). Although there has been no definitive statement on why the increase has been significant, speculation is that increased use is related to ease of availability (teens can buy the pills on the street, or from friends whose parents have the medications legitimately through prescriptions; or ease of purchasing and obtaining the drugs on the Internet from Web sites that do not require doctor's prescriptions or offer free online "consultations" with physicians).

Youth Substance Use: Developmental Trends

Developmental Trends

The developmental course of substance use and abuse has been investigated by a number of researchers. Studies of age of onset and comorbid associations with drug use have revealed:

- earlier *substance use* (prior to age 15) is more likely to result in later *substance abuse*
- the number of conduct problems reported increases the corresponding risk for substance abuse (Robins & McEvoy, 1990)

Science Talks

According to the latest Youth Risk Behavior Surveillance Survey (YRBSS, 2005), 18.6% of ninth graders reported having used drugs for the first time before age 13.

The Gateway Hypothesis

According to Kandel, there are two underlying assumptions inherent in the controversial *Gateway Hypothesis*:

1. An individual who participates in one drug behavior is at risk for progressing to another drug.
2. There is a *"progressive and hierarchical sequence of stages of drug use"* (Kandel, 2002, p. 3).

Important Distinction

Kandel (2002) makes an important distinction between the **Stepping-Stone Theory** of the 1930s that posited a *direct causal link* from marijuana to heroin and the *Gateway Hypothesis* which suggests that certain drugs pose an *increased risk* for the use of other drugs. In the Gateway Hypothesis, this pathway is not inevitable.

Heavy users versus experimenters and the Gateway Hypothesis. The Gateway Hypothesis is controversial because it implies that the sequence of onset for drug use is universal, and that individual differences will determine the eventual end stage of drug use progression. However, while a number of studies have provided support for a universal sequence of drug use (alcohol/cigarettes precede marijuana and other illicit drugs) in the United States as well as in other countries (Kandel & Yamaguchi, 1999), other researchers have emphasized that the model does not address differences between heavy drug users and those who merely experiment. Golub and Johnson (1994) have emphasized the fact that the Gateway Hypothesis does not address why the vast majority of drug users remain experimental users, nor has it addressed different patterns of usage in heavy users. As a result of their investigations, Golub and Johnson (1994) have questioned the validity of the Gateway Hypothesis based on the results that:

- only one third of heavy drug users reported the expected drug sequence (with alcohol or tobacco onset)
- 91% of heavy users reported marijuana drug onset

- 75% of heavy users reported alcohol as the initial drug

Based on these findings, Golub and Johnson (1994) suggest for heavy drug users, marijuana might more appropriately be considered as the gateway drug.

The majority of drug experimentation in adolescence does not amount to a significant and life-long addiction, with the vast majority abandoning the practice once they enter young adulthood (Kouzis & Labouvie, 1992). Yet, for some, the developmental pathway is not so positive. Youth who rely on heavy and repeated substance use over time develop poorer outcomes and are at higher risk for teen pregnancy, juvenile delinquency, and academic failure (Newcomb & Felix-Ortiz, 1992).

Although information concerning usage is readily available through Web sites sponsored by the National Institute on Drug Abuse (NIDA) and MTF Web site, there is far less information available concerning *substance abuse*, and the underlying dynamics that lead from onset to abuse.

Social attitudes, supply and demand, and the Gateway Hypothesis.   Another point of argument or discussion is the fact that principles of supply and demand and prevailing social attitudes may be more predictive of the ***drug du jour*** than any prescribed order of drug usage (e.g., tobacco → alcohol → marijuana). In support of this argument is the fact that history predicts that attitudes and availability have been highly influential in drug usage patterns. Historically, whether a drug is more socially acceptable, viewed as less harmful, and easy to procure, have often been very instrumental in shifting drug preferences (Hawkins et al., 2002).

Inhalant use and Gateway Hypothesis.   Although the majority of researchers agree that the most common progression in drug-taking begins with alcohol and cigarettes and then progresses to marijuana, this progression does not include inhalant use. Recent information regarding inhalant use may influence how this progression is perceived in the future. Increases in inhalant abuse and the ease of availability of inhalants may signal that inhalant use may be one of the first drugs available to young children. Support for this suggestion can be found in the lifetime prevalence rate for inhalants published in the most recent MFT report which states that by the eighth grade, 17.1% of children had already used inhalants, suggesting a much younger age of onset than previously thought (Johnston et al., 2005).

Another Trend in the Wrong Direction

In the recent MTF report, lifetime use for inhalants among eighth graders (17.1%) was higher than for marijuana (16.5%). In another recent survey, NSDUH (2003), 718,000 (8.6%) of youth 12 or 13 years of age reported using inhalants in their lifetime. Males had a higher prevalence (9%) than females (8%) in this age group.

Since early onset of substance use has been linked to a variety of substance use disorders, delinquent behaviors, and other adjustment problems (Anthony & Petronis, 1995), the early and increased use of inhalants is of significant concern. Youth who had reported a lifetime prevalence for inhalants at 12 and 13 years of age were twice as likely to have been in a serious fight at school, than youth who had never used inhalants and six times more likely to have stolen an article worth more than $50. Furthermore, 35.4% of youth in the early onset inhalant category had used another illicit drug, compared to only 7.5% of those who had never used inhalants.

Risks and Protective Factors

Although risks and protective factors were discussed at length in chapter 3, some of the factors that are particularly relevant to increasing or reducing risks of substance use and abuse will be addressed briefly in this section. Bronfenbrenner's (1979) levels of influence are particularly helpful in organizing information concerning risks and protective factors.

Recall and Rewind

Bronfenbrenner's system of classification (1979) evolves around four levels of influence on development, beginning with the child at the central core:
1. *individual* (*individual* traits, dispositions and genetic factors)
2. *immediate environment* (*microsystem*: including family, peers, schooling/education, and neighborhood surroundings)
3. *social and economic context* (*exosystem*: including health care systems and community/social institutions relative to such areas as poverty and child welfare);
4. *cultural values and laws* (*macrosystem*: relevant laws or changes in laws relevant to education, employment/immigration, and cultural values).

Individual characteristics.   Genetic links to an alcoholic parent may increase vulnerability to self-medicate with drugs as environmental pressures increase (Blum et al., 2000; Finckh, 2001). There is also evidence for genetic transmission of other drugs, such as marijuana and cocaine (Morral, McCaffery, & Paddock, 2002). Issues with self-esteem, depression, anxiety, and attentional problems have all been linked to increased risk for substance use, as has a history of child abuse. One of the most powerful risk factors for substance abuse is early substance use. One study found that while African American youth are more likely to be exposed to risks of substance use by contextual risk factors, such as poverty and academic failure, White youth are more likely to be exposed to individual and interpersonal risk factors, such as sensation seeking and the influence of peer drug use (Wallace & Muroff, 2002).

Although all early users do not develop substance abuse problems, those who do are more likely to be described as deviant, nonconformist, rebellious, and isolated in high school (Newcomb, 1997).

Temperament.   Researchers (Colder & Chassin, 1997;Hawkins, Catalano, & Miller, 1992) have found a number of character traits, or temperament characteristics that are associated with increased risk for substance use, including:

- sensation seeking
- low harm avoidance
- poor impulse control
- negative emotionality
- novelty seeking

Protective factors that can reduce the risk of substance use include good school achievement, good mental health, connectivity with a sense of belonging to the community (schools, youth, or church groups), and good problem-solving skills (Burrow-Sanchez, 2006).

Immediate environment (microsystem).   The *Immediate Family/Microsystem* can also exert powerful influences on drug related activity. Social Learning theory can be used to address how attitudes and behaviors are learned and subsequently influence drug-taking behaviors. Youth whose parent or older sibling used drugs are at increased risk for substance use (Brook, Whiteman, Gordon, & Brook, 1990). Exposure opportunities (e.g., youth who are exposed to substances at an earlier age) can significantly increase the risk for substance use. Wagner and Anthony (2002) found that youth who used alcohol or tobacco reported 3 times the incidence of cannabis initiation when the opportunity arouse, and also experienced exposure opportunities at younger ages than those not exposed to alcohol and tobacco. Other environmental influences include social approval by peers.

Science Talks

Fergusson and Horwood (1997) followed 990 New Zealand children from birth to 21 years of age. Early and frequent cannabis use (use by age 16) was associated with low SES, and a home life that had a history of parent conflict, parent criminality, alcohol and drug use, and low parental attachment. Individuals had lower self-esteem, a history of conduct problems, high novelty seeking, and associations with delinquent peers.

While the majority of studies have focused on peer influences on youth drug activities, Bahr et al. (2005) included a number of family variables across five different categories: parental tolerance of drug use, sibling use, adult use, attachment, and parental monitoring of drug activity. Findings revealed that although peer drug use had the stronger effects, several family variables resulted in significant effects independent of peer influences. Two of the strongest risk factors from the family cluster included parental tolerance for drug usage and sibling drug use. Parental monitoring had the greatest effect for reduction in marijuana use and illicit drug use, but the least effect for reducing tobacco use.

Risks and protective factors can impact on individuals in different ways depending on other factors, such as age, ethnicity, gender, and culture (Hawkins et al., 1992). Protective factors can serve to decrease the probability of developing problems with substance use and abuse. Although peer group influence can be a strong predictor in adolescence, parent monitoring and parent attitudes about drugs may be a strong protective factor against earlier use. Having a supportive family, exposure to effective parenting practices (including monitoring of activities and supervision, limit setting), association with positive peers, and connections to positive community youth groups have all been associated with decreased risk of involvement in substance related activities (Glantz & Sloboda, 1999; Hawkins et al., 1992). Another protective factor that can decrease the risk of substance use involves parental attitudes against drug use behavior (Hawkins et al., 1992). According to the National Survey on Drug Use and Health (NSDUH; SAMHSA, 2003), of the 89% of youth who reported that their parents would strongly disapprove of their using marijuana, only 5.5% admitted to the use of marijuana within the past month. Parenting practices that have been influential in protecting against drug use include the use of effective parenting practices, such as giving clear guidelines, limits, consistency, and high monitoring of youth activities (Burrow-Sanchez, 2006).

Social and financial context (exosystem). Social and economic conditions can have a profound effect on the growing child. Communities that have highly concentrated levels of poverty are often disorganized and chaotic because residents are either too fearful or unwilling to intervene or mobilize defenses in response to antisocial behaviors of youth in the community (Sampson et al., 1997). Children living in impoverished environments may also be socialized into the street role at an early age because parents may be involved in addiction problems themselves, or because the youth are looking for support from an alternative family support system (Vigil, 2002).

Culture and political environment (macrosystem). Two important contextual influences on adolescent substance abuse are drug laws and availability of substances (Hawkins et al., 1992). For example, it has been reported that when legal drinking age is increased, fewer alcohol-related traffic accidents occur (Saffer & Grossman, 1987). However, when drugs are highly visible and available, rates of drug use increase. According to a recent survey of the CDC (2005), a significant increase in the use of tobacco products was observed between 2002–2004, which coincides with the time when tobacco products began appearing on the Internet.

Recall and Rewind

Middle school students (Grades 6–8) report ease of availability of tobacco products, with 70.6% of smokers revealing that they were not asked to show proof of age when purchasing cigarettes, and less than one third reporting ever having been refused a purchase because of their age.

Among adolescents 12 to 17 years of age, more than half consider marijuana relatively easy to obtain in their communities (NSDUH; SAMHSA, 2003).

Risks for substance abuse and dependence. The majority of studies concerning risks and protective factors have focused on risk for experimentation and initial substance use, or the trajectories that lead form initial to subsequent substance use. Far less is known about the risks for substance abuse, dependence, and addiction. However, there is increasing research support that a genetic component might mediate the trajectory from experimentation to dependence for tobacco, alcohol, and illicit drug use in some youth (Kendler et al., 2000; McGrue et al, 2001). In essence, while the majority of youth may experiment and then discontinue use of the substance, for some youth who are genetically vulnerable, initiation may lead to a more seriously addictive and substance-dependent trajectory.

Comorbid Associations

Youth who are at risk for progressing from drug experimentation to the chronic use and abuse of drugs often have other comorbid disorders and associated risk factors.

In adolescence, frequent use of drugs and alcohol is often associated with the onset or presence of a comorbid disorder (Ferdinand, Blum, & Verhulst, 2001). When two or more disorders are present (sometimes called dual diagnosis), it is often difficult to determine the direction of effects or pathway.

A Question of Direction of Effects

Do youth who are depressed take drugs to **self-medicate** (Khantzian, 1997), or does increased drug use among youth lead to depression (Weissman et al., 1999)? Clinical studies suggest that in cases of comorbid substance abuse, psychiatric problems precede substance abuse (Ellickson & Hays, 1991; Elliott, Huizinga, & Menard, 1988). In pediatric populations, that seems to be true for disorders such as conduct disorder which is associated with earlier onset of substance use and abuse (Armstrong & Costello, 2002).

However, the pathway is less clear for other disorders associated with substance abuse, such as depression and bipolar disorder (Kessler et al., 2001). Pathways for anxiety disorders, on the other hand, vary with the disorder, such as the increased risk for substance use following the onset of posttraumatic stress disorder (PTSD).

Several disorders have been linked to substance use and abuse, including depression, anxiety, disruptive behavior disorders, eating disorders, and attention deficit disorder. Multiple disorders may be present, such as ADHD and depression, in addition to substance abuse (Loeber, Farrington, Southamer-Loeber, & Van Kammen, 1998). Results for anxiety disorders may be masked when different anxiety disorders are aggregated in one category. In one study, it was reported that those with anxiety disorders are 2 to 3 times more likely to engage in substance use compared to their nonanxious peers (Kendler, Gallagher, Abelson, & Kessler, 1996).

Barkley et al. (1990) conducted a follow up of children diagnosed with ADHD and found that the hyperactive teens were significantly more likely to use cigarettes and alcohol than their non-ADHD peers. In fact, Molina and Pelhan (2003) suggest that a diagnosis of ADHD in childhood seems to be as strong a predictor for substance use as having a family history of substance abuse. The authors report that the risk is not substance specific, but cuts across alcohol, tobacco, marijuana, and other drugs. In their study, the researchers found higher levels of substance use in many areas (alcohol, tobacco, and illicit drug use) in adolescents with ADHD than their non-ADHD peers. However, it is important to note that contrary to findings of substance link to hyperactive ADHD youth in the study by Barkley and colleagues (1990); ADHD youth in the Molina and Pelhan (2003) study were of the inattentive type. In their study, it was not the severity of hyperactivity, ODD, or CD that predicted substance use, but the severity of the problems with *inattention*. The possibility exists that there is a developmental pathway from inattention to substance abuse that is mediated by academic impairment. The authors suggest that executive functioning deficits may be at the basis of the association to substance abuse.

Important Distinction

A common misperception is that the use of stimulant medication to treat ADHD may act as a gateway drug to later substance use. In reality, research findings are just the opposite. Successful treatment of ADHD acts as a protective factor for later substance abuse. Research shows that adults with ADHD who were not treated successfully have much higher rates of substance abuse compared to adults who received successful treatment as a child (Biederman et al., 1999).

Several research reviews have been published recently concerning substance use and comorbid psychopathology in adolescence. Because prevalence rates vary widely based on the population sampled (e.g., community vs. clinical populations), findings will be discussed within the context of the different populations sampled by different studies. Results are available in Table 13.6.

Table 13.6 Substance Use Disorders (SUD) and Comorbid Associations in Youth from Community, Clinical, and Juvenile Justice Populations

Population	Substance Use/Abuse	Primary Comorbid Disorder	
Community (Armstrong & Costello, 2002)	Youth withoug SUD	Any Psychiatric Disorder	20%*
		Disruptive Behavior Disorders	0–12%
		ADHD	3%–7%**
		Depression	5%–11%
		Anxiety	3%–16%
	Youth with SUD including use, abuse, or dependence	Any Psychiatric Disorder (Lewinsohn et al., 1993)	60%
		Disruptive Behavior Disorders	46%
		Conduct Disorder (median)	52%
		ADHD (Chong et al., 1999)	12.3%
		Depression (Median)	18.8%
		Anxiety (Median)	17%
		PTSD	11%
Clinical (Couwenbergh et al., 2006)	Youth in treatment for SUD (Median rates and weighted means)	Any Comorbid Disorder	74%
		CD	64 %
		ADHD	22%
		Depression	26%
		Anxiety	7%
		PTSD	11%
Juvenile Justice (Abram et al., 2003; Vreugdenhil et al., 2003)	Comorbidity with substance use disorders (Median or weighted ratings)	Externalizing (CD,ODD ADHD)	74%
		Internalizing	24%
		Mood	19%

* Surgeon General's Report
** *DSM–IV–TR* (APA, 2000)

Community populations. Armstrong and Costello (2002) reviewed 15 community studies that examined psychiatric comorbidity in youth with substance use disorders (SUD), including substance use, abuse, or dependence. Sixty percent of youth with SUD also had a comorbid disruptive behavior disorder (CD, ODD), compared to a high of 12% for youth without SUD. Depression was the next most prevalent comorbid disorder with estimates ranging from 11.1% to 32%, with a median of 18.8%. Results for "anxiety" as a generic disorder provided the most inconsistent results ranging from 7% in one study (Brook, Cohen, & Brook, 1998) to 40.4% in another (Feehan, McGee, Raja, & Williams, 1994). However, "anxiety" is a very broad concept that includes at least 10 different subtypes (*DSM–IV–TR*, 2000) which might explain the diversity in responses. It is possible that while individuals with some types of anxiety disorder might be driven to SUD behaviors in an attempt to self-medicate, others might fear the consequences of engaging in SUD behaviors and be more predisposed to withdraw. As a result, in studies that have evaluated the role of generic anxiety in SUD, differential effects could possibly have cancelled each other out.

Different Strokes for Anxious Folks

Kaplow, Curran, Angold, and Costello (2001) reported that children with *separation anxiety disorder* (*SAD*) were least likely than their peers to engage in SUD, while those with *generalized anxiety disorder* (*GAD*) were more likely than peers to use alcohol at an early age and more frequently than their peers.

In one study (Chong, Chan, & Cheng, 1999), 12.3% of those with ADHD also reported a SUD. Lewinsohn, Hops, Roberts, Seeley, and Andrews (1993) found that 60% of youth with SUD had at least one other diagnosable psychiatric disorder, a rate that was twice the rate for non-SUD peers.

Science Talks

Measelle, Stice, and Hogansen (2006) investigated the relationship among comorbid depressive disorders, eating disorders, antisocial behaviors, and substance abuse problems in adolescent girls. Researchers found that increased risk for substance use was associated with elevated levels of mood disturbance. In addition, initial eating pathology and/or antisocial behavior both predicted increased risk for substance use in adolescent females. Since females tend to use stimulants as their substance of choice (Chasin, Ritter, Trim, & King, 2003), it is suggested that this selection might be motivated by eating pathology and weight loss concerns.

Clinical populations.   As might be anticipated, prevalence rates for clinical populations are much higher than those for nonclinical populations. One recent study found that 89% of youth who were in treatment for alcohol and other drug related problems also had a diagnosis of conduct disorder (Clark & Bukstein, 1998). In their study of youth in treatment for SUD, Couwenbergh and colleagues (2006) found that 74% also met the diagnostic criteria for another clinical disorder, while 64% had comorbid conduct disorder.

Juvenile justice populations.   In their study of youth in the juvenile justice system, Abram, Teplin, McClelland, and Dulcan (2003) investigated the rates of comorbidy for SUD and other psychiatric disorders. Almost half (48%) of incarcerated youth had a SUD of which 64% had another comorbid externalizing disorder. In another study of incarcerated Dutch youth, Vreugdenhil, van den Brink, Wouters, and Doreleijers (2003) reported that the prevalence rate for SUD was 55% of which 90% had at least one other psychiatric disorder.

Youth Prevalence Rates

Prevalence rates for drug usage by 8th, 10th, and 12th graders, collected over a 3-year period (2001, 2003, and 2005), can be found in Table 13.4 and Table 13.5.

Important Distinction

Lifetime prevalence refers to the percentage of respondents who indicate that they have experienced a given situation (in this case, substance usage) at least once over the course of their lifetime. *Annual prevalence* refers to the number of respondents who indicated that they had experienced a given situation during the preceding year.

Based on recent data from the MTF study (Johnston et al., 2005), approximately 50% of 12th graders report having used an illicit drug at least once in their lifetime. The rates for 10th graders (38.2%) and 8th graders (21.4%) are understandably lower. Although these rates appear to be higher than ideal, a review of all available survey information reveals that peak years for illicit drug use occurred in 1996 for 8th graders and in 1997 for 10th and 12th graders. Compared to those levels, current levels represent drops of 35% for 8th graders, 23% among 10th graders, and 10% among 12th graders. However, as was revealed in the previous discussions, recent increases in inhalant abuse among eighth graders and the use of prescription drugs, such as OxyContin, in high school students is cause for increased concern.

Age of onset has been declining according to research reports. It was estimated in 1994 that indoctrination into drug use begins around 11–12 years of age (Fitzgerald, Davies, Zucker, & Klinger, 1994). However, the fact that most surveys do not include children younger than 12 years of age may be one reason why even younger-aged users have not been identified. In the one tobacco survey conducted by the Center for Chronic Disease Prevention and Health Promotion (CDC, 2005), surveys completed by a national sample of middle and high school students revealed that there was a lack of significant decreases in the use of almost all tobacco products among U.S. middle and high school students from 2002 to 2004. In 2004, 11.8% of middle school children (Grades 6 to 8) reported that they were current users of a tobacco product.

Ethnic differences in prevalence of substance use/abuse. Investigations of ethnic differences in drug use have found that abuse of alcohol, barbiturates, amphetamines, and hallucinogens is reported as more prominent among Caucasian males, while abuse of heroin, crack, and cocaine seems to be more prevalent among Hispanic youth. Native American youth tend to abuse alcohol (Vik, Brown, & Myers, 1997).

Etiology of Substance Use/Abuse

The Biological Model

Biological, genetic, and neurotransmitter function. Studies of alcohol abuse have found that if one twin abuses alcohol, the likelihood for the other twin is 54% (Kaij, 1960). In addition, adoption studies have shown that children of alcoholics adopted at birth show a higher rate of alcohol abuse than children who did not have biological parents that were alcoholics (Cadoret, Yates, Troughton, Woodworth, & Stewart, 1993). An abnormal dopamine receptor (D2) has been found in the majority of individuals with alcohol dependence and in at least half of those addicted to cocaine (Lawford et al., 1997).

How Do We Become Addicted to Substances?

The biological model might predict that that recurrent substance use mimics the effect of naturally occurring neurotransmitters and, as a result, the body reduces production (Goldstein, 1994). For example, repeated use of alcohol, which mimics GABA, sends a message to the brain that there is less need to produce GABA. As tolerance is increased, the person becomes dependent on alcohol to produce the GABA substance that is no longer produced naturally.

The Behavioral Model

Because many drugs impact dopamine and produce a pleasurable effect, behaviorists would explain drug usage as a system of self-reward. In addition, reduction of tension—an initial side effect of a number of drugs, including alcohol and marijuana—is also rewarding. Given a high level of stress and tension, many people may *self-medicate* to reduce tension. Support for this suggestion can be found in studies that have found high levels of depression and anxiety among those who abuse substances.

> ## Peer Group Influences
>
> Peers can be one of the most powerful influences on substance use among both majority and minority youth (Beauvais, 1998). Identity formation can also provide a framework for peer associations based on engaging in similar activities and sharing similar goals and predict different group outcomes.

The Sociocultural Model

Eccles and Barber (1999) identified three different outcomes among different group associations. For example, youth who participate in organized school athletics may engage in high alcohol use, but may continue to do well academically and go on to college. A second group may consume similar amounts of alcohol, but do poorly in school and engage in high risk behaviors. A third group—highly anxious youth—consumed alcohol to relieve their anxiety, a practice which increased from the sixth grade to high school. Eccles and Barber (1999) suggest that based on the differences found between the three groups, it is unlikely that there is one intervention program that would fulfill three very different needs.

Information from the MTF recent surveys (Johnston et al., 2005) have revealed that alcohol consumption among high school students is the norm rather than the exception; it has become increasingly evident that the majority of adolescents will experiment with substances. Within this "normative" perspective, it is important to recognize that it has been statistically demonstrated that the majority of youth engage in experimentation and that "maturing out" of the process and defying gateway theory predictions is the norm rather than the exception (Kaplow, Curran, & Dodge, 2002). In their longitudinal study of 100 youth, Shedler and Block (1990) found that youth who *experimented with marijuana* actually had better outcomes (psychological well-being and adjustment) than *abstainers* or *frequent users*. Yet, for some, peer associations and family tolerance of substance use can contribute to long-term negative outcomes.

A year-long investigation of 6th, 8th, and 10th graders (Urberg, Degirmencioglu, & Pilgrim, 1997) revealed that if a close friend had started drinking or smoking cigarettes, the youth was more likely to initiate alcohol and cigarette use. In another study concerning youth (aged 12–18 years), Maxwell (2002) reports that onset of a friend's use of cigarettes, marijuana, and alcohol predicted subsequent substance use in the other friend.

> ## Science Talks
>
> In their study of peer influence among 10- to 15-year-olds, D'Amico and McCarthy (2006) found that perceived alcohol use by peers was associated with the initiation of alcohol use. Youth who believed that their peers were using alcohol were more likely to use both alcohol and marijuana. Furthermore, those youth who believed their peers were smoking marijuana were more likely to increase their alcohol use.
>
> These results suggest the importance of peer influence on the subsequent onset and escalation of substance use across multiple substances, and at younger ages than previously studied.

The Diathesis–Stress Model

Given the nature of drug use and abuse, it is highly likely that etiology results from a combination of multiple factors. Social influences, such as peer pressure, media portrayals of drug use, and individual vulnerability can all play a role in whether or not drugs are used and abused. One model that attempts to incorporate several factors into an explanation of the development of drug abuse is the **diathesis–stress model** (Windle & Tubman, 1999). The model looks at how some individuals might be more vulnerable to drug related attempts to cope with stress based on individual characteristics (familial alcoholism, genetic transmission, personality/temperament). At the best of times, coping skills might be adequate; however, when environmental factors (family, school, peers, and economics) are adverse, resulting stress may make some individuals more likely to respond using drugs to self-medicate and buffer stress.

 The K–3 Paradigm stresses the need to integrate information from our knowledge of theories, development, and contexts of influence. The *diathesis–stress model* states that some individuals may be more vulnerable at this time in adolescence (familial alcoholism, temperament) and respond to social influences (peer pressure, media) by taking drugs in response to stress.

Case in Point

The influence of peer group activities has long been recognized as a highly influential source in shaping future behaviors. This influence was dramatically revealed in 12-week intervention program called the Adolescent Transitions Program (APT), developed by colleagues at the University of Oregon (Dishion, McCord, & Poulin, 1999). The intervention program targeted 158 middle school youth (11 to 14 years of age: 83 boys and 75 girls) who were considered high risk for drug abuse and increasingly more serious delinquent behaviors. There study included four groups: peer group; peer plus parent; parent only; and the control (no intervention). Youth in the program focused on skill building (emotion management, relationship building) and limit setting (saying no to drugs), while parents focused on communication skills and problem management. Short-term results were encouraging with gains noted for all groups but the control. However, long term follow up (3 years later) revealed that youth who were aggregated with other problem peers during the 12-week period reported twice the tobacco use compared to nongrouped peers and 75% more delinquent behaviors. Furthermore, those youth who had the least amount of delinquent behaviors initially showed the greatest amount of negative change.

Issues in the Treatment of Substance Disorders

Group Versus Individual Treatment

In their paper, "When interventions harm: Peer groups and problem behavior," Dishion, McCord, and Poulin (1999) attribute the negative treatment effects (termed **iatrogenic effects**) to a form of "deviancy training" that occurred as a result of grouping peers together who had similar types of problems . The study provided a dramatic demonstration of how negative peer influences can encourage rule breaking behaviors and drug use in a vulnerable population. The intervention program then was instrumental in providing exposure to a deviant peer group, at a time when peer influence is at a peak and the likelihood of experimentation with drugs the most pronounced. Past research has demonstrated that this type of context provides furtive ground for recruitment of adolescents with low self-esteem or those who are alienated who are likely the most vulnerable to drug use as a way to enhance acceptability and peer status (Maggs & Galambos, 1993).

Group treatment approaches are among the most common treatments for alcohol and other drug problems (Khantzian, 2001). The popularity of group treatment for adolescents with drug related problems is also understandable for several reasons, including the importance of peer group affiliations during this stage of development; preference of adolescents for group versus individual therapy (O'Leary et al., 2002), and cost effectiveness (French et al., 2002). However, despite the benefits, Macgowan and Wagner (2005) emphasize that previous studies have demonstrated the risk of iatrogenic effects when youth with conduct problems are grouped together (see the *Case in Point*), and since there is a high correspondence between conduct problems and drug use, it is important to consider the potential negative consequences that group therapy can have on adolescents who are in treatment for drug use and abuse. With this consideration in mind, Macgowan and Wagner (2005) reviewed existing research to provide information on three factors that might be instrumental in undermining the effectiveness of group treatment for adolescents who use drugs and are most likely conduct disordered:

1. **Group composition:** Grouping of juvenile offenders with students at risk for school drop out (Catterall, 1987) and aggregating teens with conduct problems for the purposes of skills training (Ang & Hughes, 2002) are examples of studies where "within-group factors" (e.g., deviancy training, leadership behaviors) resulted in negative outcomes. "Therefore, group composition is an important component that can set the stage for expression of antisocial behavior and deviancy training leading to poor outcomes" (Macgowan & Wagner, 2005, p. 83).
2. **Antisocial behavior and deviance training in group:** Dishion and colleagues (1999) noted that rule-breaking talk reinforced by laughter increased the risk of later smoking and delinquency (e.g., deviancy training) in group members.
3. **Group leader behaviors:** Drawing on information from the classic studies by Lewin, Lippitt, and White (1939), Macgowan and Wagner (2005) emphasize that authoritarian group leadership serves to promote significantly more negatively cohesive behaviors, such as aggression and scapegoating among group members (e.g., "united we stand"). Also, negative group leadership behaviors (as identified by Feldman, Caplinger, & Wodarski, 1983, such as criticism, threats, or negative attention), also served to increase negative outcomes.

Based on their analysis, Macgowan and Wagner (2005) suggest that the three factors, as outlined above, work together to influence adolescent outcomes concerning the efficacy of group treatment. The authors note that there is no existing research that considers the iatrogenic effects of group therapy for adolescents with drug-related problems and recommend research in the area to determine how to best address these potential issues in the development of future prevention programs for youth with substance use and abuse problems.

Treatment Challenges

Youth with SUD can present a challenge to professionals involved in treatment for several reasons. Youth may often underreport the extent and nature of their SUD (Winters, Stinchfield, Henly, & Schwartz, 1992). In addition, the majority of youth are not likely to self-refer for treatment and will come to treatment that is either mandated or required by parents or schools after a history of problem behavior. Burrow-Sanchez (2006) describes four key clinical issues that need to be addressed when providing therapeutic services for adolescents who abuse substances: "establishing a working relationship, assessing the severity of the problem, identifying a treatment approach and acknowledging the potential for relapse" (p. 285).

Treatment resistance.   One suggestion for lowering resistance to substance abuse counseling is the use of *Motivational Interviewing* (*MI*; Miller & Rollnick, 2002) to determine the adolescent's current stage of motivation to change.

Severity of use/abuse.   According to Winters (2001), recognition of the severity of substance use or abuse can be aided through the use of a hierarchical system composed of six categories of use/ abuse: recovery, abstinence, experimental use, early abuse, abuse, and dependence. Other important issues to consider that will influence the nature of the treatment include types of substances used, frequency of use, durations of use (early vs. late onset), reason for use, and any other comorbid disorders.

Treatment approach.   In addition to individual and group therapy approaches already discussed, depending on the severity of the abuse, treatment can also occur on an outpatient, residential (highly structured and controlled environment), and inpatient (hospital) basis. Currently in the United States, 37% of all treatment facilities for substance abuse offer adolescent services (NSDUH; SAMHSA, 2003).

Potential for relapse.   Of all youth who enroll in treatment programs, approximately half will re-lapse within the first 3 months after treatment is concluded (Pagliaro & Pagliaro, 1996). Although several options are available to provide aftercare and support (e.g., self-help groups, follow-up appointments), research regarding the efficacy of any particular approach is still limited. How-ever, adult programs often include skill building to incorporate cognitive behavioral methods into the program that include such topics as recognizing and responding to high risk situations that might result in a relapse.

Treatment Programs

There has been an increasing recognition that drug abuse in youth has many unique features com-pared to drug abuse in adults. One important consideration is the need to incorporate protective factors in these programs, while guarding against *deviance training* (Deas, Riggs, Langenbuncher, Goldman, & Brown, 2000). Research has demonstrated that drug activity is influenced by risks from the individual and environment and that prevention programs should attempt to influence how youth perceive drug use and how to deal with social pressures to use.

Twelve-step models.   The 12-step models have as their origin the 12-step orientation developed by Alcoholics Anonymous (AA) and Narcotics Anonymous (NA), founded on the beliefs that addiction is a progressive disease and that treatment requires abstinence (Kassel & Jackson, 2001). Traditionally, the programs have involved community-based meetings attended by recovering members who support each others' abstinence through confessions, sharing stories, and often provide opportunities for connecting with a life-line buddy for crisis purposes. Because ano-nymity of the individuals involved remains a high priority in the programs, empirical evidence has been difficult to accumulate. What evidence there is, however, indicates that 12-step groups (Alcoholics Anonymous, Cocaine Anonymous, and Narcotics Anonymous) are well attended by youth in recovery (Brown, 1993). Kassel and Jackson (2001) reported that youth who attended the 12-Step Minnesota Model had better outcomes than untreated youth.

Cognitive behavioral therapy (CBT).   Therapeutic approaches that focus on substance abuse from a cognitive behavioral perspective incorporate principles of learning into their programs. By recognizing environmental triggers that can cue substance activity, individuals are taught coping skills required to change maladaptive thought patterns. Individuals learn how to reframe thoughts into more positive thought patterns that serve to alter behaviors. The underlying premise is based on learning theory and hypothesizes that substance abuse develops as a response to environmental cues or triggers and consequences (socially reinforcing events, physiological arousal) that precipitate and maintain abusive habits. Waldron and Kern-Jones (2004) suggest that often, multiple factors are involved in the acquisition and maintenance of substance abuse through such mechanisms as observational and imitative learning (parents and peers). Behaviors can be learned and reinforced through social reinforcement, feelings of self-efficacy, and can result in the development of belief systems which serve to perpetuate substance use activities.

Inherent in the development of CBT programs is the inclusion of components, such as self-monitoring, assertiveness/refusal skills, avoidance of specific triggers, problem solving, relaxation training, and other approaches to adaptive coping (Monti, Kadden, Rohsenhow, Cooney, & Abrams, 2002). One key component that is incorporated into the CBT program is the element of **relapse prevention**. Programs can be flexible and delivered individually, in groups, or with family. Liddle and Hogue (2001) found that youth demonstrated declines in drug use, as well as internalizing and externalizing behaviors, regardless of whether they attended individual CBT or family-based programs. However studies have also demonstrated a delay in achieving results when programs were delivered on an individual-versus-family basis (Liddle & Hogue, 2001; Waldron & Kern-Jones, 2004). It has also been suggested that positive trends noted on follow up that were not evident at the conclusion of treatment likely represent time required to consolidate the CBT skills after the program is completed (Liddle & Hogue, 2001). Although it is possible to present CBT programs in group format, it is important to be aware of potential iatrogenic effects (Waldron & Jones, 2004) found in other studies that have aggregated high-risk youth (Azrin, Donohue, Bedalel, Kogan, & Acierno, 1994; Dishion et al., 1999). Ultimately, a greater understanding will be obtained regarding how to best deliver treatment that is supportive and not detrimental.

Family-based treatment. Investigations that include the family in treatment alternatives for substance use and abuse have used a variety of theoretical frameworks, including CBT (see above), multisystemic therapy (Henggeler, Schoenwald, Borduin, Rowland, & Cunningham, 1998), functional behavioral family therapy (Emery, 2001) and family systems approaches. From the family systems framework, substance abuse is considered within the context of the immediate family (parents and siblings), extended family (grandparents, aunts, uncles, cousins), and any subsystems that may exist within the family (Ozechowski & Liddle, 2000).

Inclusion of a family component in the treatment program can increase participant engagement in the process (Stanton & Shadish, 1997) and increase program effectiveness (Waldron, 1997). Azrin and colleagues (1994) found that behavioral family therapy resulted in a 50% success rate in the reduction of alcohol and drug use, compared to a an increase in drug related activity for youth involved in a process oriented treatment. In another comparison study, Donohue and Azrin (2001) found family behavioral therapy superior to a program using a problem-solving method. In their review of treatment outcomes for youth with substance use disorders, Williams and Chang (2000) found outpatient family therapy to be superior to other forms of outpatient treatment, while Deas and Thomas (2001) remain more cautious regarding the results of their review of controlled studies of adolescent substance treatment programs. According to Deas and Thomas (2001), although family based and CBT programs seem promising, more evidence is needed from controlled studies before claims can be made regarding the superiority of either one of these programs to the other.

Recall and Rewind

The Youth Risk Behavior Surveillance Survey (YRBSS; Centers for Disease Control and Prevention, Youth Risk Behavior Surveillance, 2005) revealed that prior to 13 years of age, 16% of youth have smoked a cigarette, 25.6% have had alcohol, and 8.7% have tried marijuana. According to the National Youth Tobacco Survey (NYTS; MMWR, 2005), 11.8% of those in middle school (Grades 6–8) have already tried a tobacco product.

Prevention

Federal funds have been available since 1994 to aid in the development of prevention programs. Since 1998, access to funds has been contingent on the use of empirically based programs (evidence-based curriculum). To this end, several programs exist that incorporate features that have been proven effective, through research, to reduce drug use and abuse, including: awareness of the harmful effects of illicit drugs, nicotine, and alcohol; and information regarding how to be more assertive and effective in refusing drugs, when offered. Empirically based drug abuse prevention programs targeted at middle school students have been successful in significantly reducing early use of tobacco, alcohol, and other drugs. Yet, in 2002, a survey conducted by Ringwalt and colleagues (2002) reported that 75% of middle schools were using programs that were not supported by research. The most common program used by the majority of middle schools, the *Drug Abuse Resistance Education program* (*DARE*) has been researched extensively and found to be ineffective in the prevention of drug use and abuse. Other than DARE, the two most popular programs used in public and private schools that have research support are *Project Alert* and *Life Skills Training*.

Life skills training (LST). LST has been demonstrated effective in significantly reducing drug use and abuse in minority students at risk for drug use due to poor academic performance and association with substance-abusing peers. (Botvin, Griffin, Diaz, & Iffil-Williams, 2001; Griffin, Botvin, Nichols, & Doyle, 2003). The program's effectiveness has been demonstrated in 29 different inner-city schools in New York schools. The program consists of 15 lessons (45 minutes) targeted at seventh graders and can be incorporated into the regular curriculum. The focus is on the development of social skills, drug refusal, and personal management. Relative to the standard New York drug education program, the LST program was more successful in lowering rates of alcohol, cigarette, and inhalant abuse.

The National Institute on Drug Abuse (NIDA) has recently published the second edition of *Preventing drug use among children and adolescents: A research-based guide* (2003). The prevention guidelines (NIDA, 2003) are available on the NIDA Web site, http://www.drugabuse.gov, and list areas to target in family programs (drug awareness; parent skills training; increased monitoring and supervision; and the need for consistent discipline and limit-setting). The importance of developmental considerations is highlighted in the report and school-based programs should focus on increasing age-appropriate behaviors and reducing maladaptive behaviors. In preschool populations, reduction of aggression and increases in self-control are emphasized. For elementary school populations, programs should focus on increased emotional awareness, social problem solving, communication, and academic support. In middle and high school populations, emphasis should be placed on improved study habits, academic support, drug resistance skills, self-efficacy, and the development of antidrug attitudes. The report notes that combined family and school programs enhance a community's efficacy in promoting cohesiveness and a sense of belonging.

Montoya, Atkinson, and McFaden (2003) surveyed the literature over the past 20 years with the goal of identifying best practices in adolescent prevention programs for gateway drugs (tobacco, alcohol, marijuana). The authors reviewed school-based programs, family-based programs, and community-based programs, and found six factors that were key to successful drug prevention programs. The first characteristic was *good parenting* which included the development of strong family bonds; and parental involvement in school-based drug prevention program. Next, programs included *skill development* (resistance skills, social skills) and *normative education* (awareness of faulty beliefs that drug use is acceptable and prevalent). Counteracting peer influence to engage in substance-related activities has also been a crucial factor in the successful prevention of drug use. *Retention of program participants* and *prevention of drop out* from the program were also seen as highly important to program success. The final two factors important in contributing to the success of prevention of drug use were antidrug media campaigns and support of laws and policies for a drug-free environment. The authors stress the importance of tailoring the program to best meet the needs of the youth in question (e.g., inclusion of family-based programs to counteract a chaotic family environment). Ultimately, the authors suggest three important steps in prevention program development:

Step 1: Identify the relevant risk factors
Step 2: Choose the necessary characteristics to overcome the risks
Step 3: Select the best environment (home, school, community) for conducting the program (Montoya, Atkinson, & McFaden, 2003, p. 81)

CHAPTER REVIEW

Rates for illicit substance use among youth increases incrementally with age as 15.5% of 8th graders, 29.8% of 10th graders, and 38.4% of 12th graders reported illicit drug use within the past year (2005). Although these rates represent a decline from previous annual reports, there have been significant increases in some types of usage at the extreme ends of those surveyed: 8th graders have increased inhalant usage, while 12th graders have substantially increased the use of prescription medications for non medicine purposes.

The *DSM* (APA, 2000) recognizes two broad categories of substance disorders: substance use disorders (including substance dependence and substance abuse) and substance-induced disorders (substance intoxication and withdrawal). The applicability of *DSM* criteria to adolescent populations remains controversial, as does the gateway hypothesis that suggests a prescribed sequence for drug initiation (e.g., the use of alcohol/ cigarettes precedes other illicit drugs, such as marijuana).

1. **DSM classification: Substance Use Disorders (SUD) and Substance-Induced Disorders (SID).**

   SUD can involve *substance dependence* (repetitive pattern of compulsive substance use, tolerance, and withdrawal) and *substance abuse* (harmful consequences of repeated over-indulgence, including failure to fulfill major roles, engaging in high risk behaviors, legal problems, and relationship problems).

   SIDs are unique to the substance used. Substance intoxication is the reversible clusters of thoughts and behaviors that result from the substance's impact on the central nervous system (CNS). Substance withdrawal refers to the syndrome specific set behaviors associated with taking decreased amounts or no amounts of a substance after repeatedly engaging in substance use over a prolonged period of time.

2. **Substances Commonly Used by Youth.**
   Annual surveys of drug use by youth (Monitoring the Future) report on 15 different substances used by youth in grades 8, 10, and 12. Cigarettes, alcohol, and marijuana are the most commonly used substances and by the 12th grade, 75% of youth have used alcohol, 50% have used cigarettes and 44.8% report marijuana use (2005). Lifetime prevalence for tobacco use doubles between 12 (8.5%) and 13 (17.2%) years of age and continues to increase with age. In one study, prior tobacco use was significantly related to increased risk for alcohol use. In 2005, 28% of 12th graders reported binge drinking within the past 2 weeks, while 5% reported marijuana use in the past 30 days. Alcohol usage has been reported to be higher in youth whose parents have higher tolerance for alcohol, and in youth whose siblings or peers use alcohol.

3. **Nonmedical Use of Prescription Medications (OxyContin) and Inhalants.**
   Results from one survey revealed that 9% of youth (12–17 years of age) had used a prescription medication for nonmedical reasons in the past year, such as OxyContin, a highly addictive pain killer, Vicodin, and tranquilizers. OxyContin use by high school seniors increased significantly from 2003 (4.5%) to 2005.

   Inhalants are easily accessible and found in many household products. Inhalants can cause hallucinations, delusions and can cause damage to the central nervous system and brain atrophy. Inhalant use in eighth graders increased significantly from 8.7% in 2003 to 9.5% in 2005.

4. **Etiology, Comorbidity, Risks, and Protective Factors and Treatment**
   It is possible to inherit a genetic predisposition to use some substances. Repeated use of some substances that mimic neurotransmitters (e.g., GABA) may deplete natural resources and create dependencies. Drug associations with dopamine and pleasure effects can reinforce future drug use, while associations with drug using peers can send the message that drug use is acceptable. The diathesis–stress model suggests that individual vulnerabilities placed within stressful circumstances may activate otherwise latent tendencies. Numerous disorders increase the risk for developing substance abuse, including conduct disorder, depression, posttraumatic stress disorder, anxiety disorder, bulimia nervosa, and ADHD.

   Twelve-step models, CBT approaches, and family-based treatment (MST) all have promise for therapeutic intervention. Prevention programs that are empirically based, such as the Life Skills Training (LST) program can target youth at vulnerable ages and can reduce the risk for future substance use.

Consolidate and Communicate

1. In their description of substance usage over the age span and across generations of drug usage, Johnson and colleagues (2005) discuss the potential role of *cohort effects* and *generational forgetting* on patterns of drug usage. Describe what is meant by these terms and how they impact our understanding of trends in drug usage. What impact can this have on future prevention programs?

2. How do tolerance and withdrawal work together to create substance dependence? What is the difference between dependence with and without physiological dependence?

3. The *gateway hypothesis* is controversial in many respects. What are some of the main arguments in support and what are some of the main arguments opposed to this theory?

   How is the gateway hypothesis different from the *stepping-stone theory* of the 1930s?

4. You have been asked to develop a prevention program to target cigarette use among youth.

What would be the ideal target age for such a program and what are some of the main features you would want to include in this program? What would you be most concerned about guarding against?

5. Binge drinking is an increasing concern, especially among college students. What does the research say about prevention of binge drinking on campus? Are there any effective programs that have made a difference? Based on results of the Monitoring the Future survey, when, ideally, should prevention programs begin to target binge drinking in youth?

6. Is cannabis a gateway drug? Respond and discuss.

7. Both inhalant use among eighth graders and the use of prescription medications for non-medical reasons, such as OxyContin, among high school seniors have increased significantly in the 2005 compared to 2003 report. What are some potential reasons why usage in these areas has increased and is there any way to prevent further increases in usage?

8. Discuss the different risk and protective factors that can influence substance use in youth. Be sure to identify which populations these risks apply to (community, clinical, or juvenile justice).

Chapter Review Questions

1. In 2005, which two substances showed increased usage among high school seniors?
   a. marijuana and alcohol
   b. prescription medications and inhalants
   c. inhalants and sedatives
   d. prescription medications and sedatives

2. In 2005, which substance showed increased usage among eighth graders?
   a. marijuana
   b. inhalants
   c. prescription medications
   d. alcohol

3. Tolerance refers to:
   a. the need to increase the amount of a substance used to achieve the same effect
   b. experiencing less of an effect than previous from taking the same amount
   c. behavioral, physiological, or cognitive changes causing clinically significant distress
   d. both a and b are correct

4. According to the gateway hypothesis
   a. there is a direct causal link from marijuana to heroin
   b. alcohol/cigarettes precede marijuana use
   c. there is no predictable sequence of drug initiation
   d. only a minority of drug users are experimenters

5. Kreteks and bidis are:
   a. high nicotine cigarettes imported from India and Asia
   b. smokeless tobacco
   c. cigarettes that contain THC
   d. not used by youth in the United States

6. According to the National Survey on Drug Use and Health (2004), cigarette usage doubled between which ages:
   a. 16 and 17
   b. 14 and 15

    c. 12 and 13

    d. 10 and 11

7. Bahr, Hoffman, and Yang (2005) found that as the number of close friends who are drinkers increases, the risk of binge drinking:

    a. increases by 10%

    b. triples

    c. increases by 20%

    d. doubles

8. While marijuana in the 1960s contained approximately _____% THC, today the amount is closer to _____.

    a. 1%–5%, 10%–15%

    b. 10%–15%, 1%–5%

    c. 5%–10%, 20%–25%

    d. 1%–5%, 15%–20%

9. A clear, odorless substance that can be mixed with drinks ("date rape drug") is:

    a. MDMA

    b. PCP

    c. GHB

    d. LSD

10. What percent of youth in juvenile justice and clinical settings with subsance use disorders (SUD) will have at least one other comorbid disorder?

    a. 50%

    b. 74%

    c. 34%

    d. 61%

Glossary

cohort effects

Ecstacy (MDMA)

generational forgetting

substance

sedatives

OxyContin

substance use disorders

substance-induced disorders

substance dependence

substance abuse

substance withdrawal symptoms

caffeine intoxication

substance dependence, with physiological dependence

substance dependence, without physiological dependence

recurrent and adverse consequences

substance intoxication, substance withdrawal

substance-specific syndrome

depressants

stimulants

hallucinogens
intoxication and reversible effects
central nervous system (CNS)
polysubstance use
synergistic effect
gateway drugs
alcohol
tobacco (including smokeless cigarettes)
bidis
kreteks (clove cigarettes)
nicotine dependence, nicotine withdrawal
binge drinking
alcohol intoxication, alcohol dependence, alcohol withdrawal
cannabis abuse, cannabis intoxication, with perceptual disturbances
volatile solvents
aerosols
gases
nitrates
tolunene
poppers/snappers
bagging, huffing
inhalant intoxication
brain atrophy
sudden sniffing death
prescription-type psychotherapeutic drug
schedule II controlled substance
OxyContin withdrawal
Vicodin
Stepping-stone theory
self-medicate
Diathesis–stress model
iatrogenic effects
relapse prevention

Multiple Choice Answers:
1. d; 2. b; 3. d; 4. b; 5. a; 6. c; 7. d; 8. a; 9. c; 10. b.

IV

Intellectual and Developmental Disabilities and Pervasive Developmental Disorders

An Introduction

Introduction

The final section of the volume examines Intellectual and Developmental Disabilities (IDD), or Mental Retardation (MR), and the Pervasive Developmental Disorders (PDD). The decision to cluster these two disorders in the same section may be somewhat controversial given the recent debate concerning the association between MR and autism. While the *DSM-IV-TR* (APA, 2000) suggests that the majority of cases with autism will have an associated diagnoses of mental retardation (from mild to profound), this comment has recently come under significant scrutiny. Fombonne (2003) conducted a meta-analysis of 20 studies and found support for the *DSM*, since at least 70% of children with autism had at least a mild form of mental retardation, with approximately 30% of those cases in the mild to moderate range. However, in another meta-analysis, Edelson (2006) criticized findings of high MR rates among children with autism stating that those claims were based on outdated research and reports that were not empirically based. The debate is even more contentious as prevalence rates fluctuate depending on the definitions used, the populations sampled (clinical vs. community based), and the instruments used to measure intelligence. In addition, validity issues are also a problem when assessing intelligence in children with such severe disorders who are especially compromised in language, and social interaction. Regardless of the above concerns, children with MR and those with PDD share many difficulties including being diagnosed with a disorder that has life long implications for learning and adjustment.

Although the concept of intelligence can appear different in different cultures, the core theme recognized universally is that intelligence is functional and involves problem solving in novel situations. Although individuals with MR do not demonstrate the regressive nature of intellectual deterioration that can occur in some forms of PDD, individuals with MR are often compromised by intellectual limitations that frame their world within the boundaries of concrete thinking. Although some individuals with PDD are capable of higher level reasoning (higher functioning autism or Asperger's disorder), they are often compromised in their adaptive ability due to limitations in areas of reciprocity required to engage in social interactions, and their need to adhere to restricted, repetitive, and stereotypical patterns of behavior.

Effective, January 1, 2007, "the American Association on Mental Retardation (AAMR), a 130-year-old association representing disability professionals, worldwide, changed its name to the American Association on Intellectual and Developmental Disabilities (AAIDD), establishing a new standard in disability terminology and making way for a more socially-acceptable way of addressing people with intellectual disabilities" (AAMR News, November, 2006). According to Hank Bersani, current president of AAIDD, "*Intellectual Disability*," provides closer alignment with terminology currently used throughout Europe and in Canada and also better represents the mission of AAIDD which is to serve the needs of those with various developmental disabilities, such as autism, that often co-exist with an intellectual disability. Whether or not the future revision of the *DSM* will also incorporate this shift in terminology remains to be seen.

14

Intellectual and Developmental Disabilities (IDD)

> Assessment
>
> **Intervention and Prevention**
>   *Intervention Programs*
>   *Prevention and Early Intervention*

CHAPTER PREVIEW

It is virtually impossible to understand intellectual and developmental disabilities (IDD) without an appreciation of intelligence and what intelligence means in terms of mental age versus chronological age. Also inherent in our understanding of IDD is the ability to distinguish between delays in development and life-long deficits in learning and reasoning. Recently, the American Association on Mental Retardation (AAMR) changed its name to the American Association on Intellectual and Developmental Disabilities (AAIDD, 2007) to effectively replace "Mental Retardation" with the term "Intellectual Disability" in keeping with terminology currently in use throughout Europe and Canada and to better reflect the mission of the organization to serve individuals with various developmental disabilities. Historically, AAMR, founded by Sequin in 1876, has been the major source for initiating and advocating changes in how mental retardation (MR) has been conceptualized and defined. In 1973, the IQ cut-off score for MR suggested by AAMR was 85. The decisions to include adaptive behavior deficits, child onset, and a reduction in the IQ score criteria from 85 to70 have all resulted from movements initiated by AAMR. The most recent AAMR (2002) definition for MR has witnessed a paradigm shift moving away from the *DSM* classification of severity of MR based on ranges of IQ scores to focusing on the individual needs and intensity of service required to meet those needs. With the reauthorization of IDEA (2004), educational classification continues to remain in-line with definitions proposed by *DSM–IV–TR* (APA, 2000). Educational classification has continued to place significant emphasis on targeting developmental delay at the earliest possible time with a set of early regulations now supporting interventions from birth to 3 years of age.

1. Classification of MR: *DSM–IV–TR* (APA, 2000)

With the exception of personality disorders, MR is the only other disorder to be coded on Axis II due to the life long nature of MR. The *DSM* requires three criteria for a diagnosis of MR: significantly subnormal intelligence (IQ 70 or less); impaired adaptive functioning (at least two of 10 areas); and onset before age 18. The *DSM* does not provide guidance on the degree of impairment for adaptive functioning. Four levels of severity are diagnosed depending on IQ ranges: Mild, Moderate, Severe, and Profound.

2. Classification of MR: AAMR (2002)

The AAMR definition includes: IQ score of approximately 70 (75 allowing for measurement error); deficits in one of three broad adaptive skill areas (2 standard deviations below mean); and onset prior to 18 years. The Supports Intensity Scale (SIS; AAMR, 2003) is used to assess the intensity and nature of service required. AAMR recently changed its name to the American Association on Intellectual and Developmental Disabilities (AAIDD, 2007) to usher in a shift in terminology from MR to Intellectual and Developmental Disabilities (IDD).

3. Classification of MR: Educational System (IDEA, 2004)

Initially, education used the 85IQ for MR recommended by AAMR (1973) but the majority of districts have changed to an IQ of 70, following AAMR's lead. IDEA (2004) defines MR as significantly subaverage IQ, with deficits in adaptive behavior and developmental onset. While Parts A and B of the law pertain to children 3 to 21 years of age; Part C addresses services for infants and toddlers. Developmental delay (DD) in any of five global areas is interpreted as 25% delay in two areas or 35% delay in one area. While the DD category can be used up to 9 years of age, there are several debates concerning the optimum time to utilize this category.

4. Associated Characteristics
The majority of children have mild IDD and continue to be served in local schools. Associated delays may be evident in motor skills (fine, gross) communication, social skills, and learning. Children with IDD are 3 to 4 times more likely to have a comorbid disorder than their non-MR peers. Children with more severe forms of IDD have more neurological and multiple problems.

5. Etiology, Assessment, and Treatment
IDD can be the result of genetic conditions, problems during pregnancy, or postdelivery complications. Some genetic conditions that are associated with IDD include: Down syndrome, Prader–Willi syndrome, Angelman syndrome, and Fragile X syndrome. MR resulting from toxins either in utero or environmental, include substance use/abuse (fetal alcohol syndrome, cocaine use), exposure to lead-based paint, and complications from rubella. Assessment of IDD involves, at a minimum, a developmental history, intellectual assessment, and adaptive inventory. Intervention and prevention programs have been developed to address prenatal health and awareness and early intervention, such as the High/Scope Perry Preschool Program.

Historical Perspectives in Definition and Classification

Individuals with IDD have limitations in mental functioning and adaptive skills. Mental functioning is measured by an individual intelligence test, while adaptive skills are often evaluated through the use of structured interviews which assess capacity in such areas as self-care, communication, and social skills. Limitations in these global areas often result in problems in learning (both the quality and quantity of information learned) and a slower pace of development compared to children who do not have these limitations. Children with IDD may be delayed in the acquisition of developmental milestones (talking, walking, self-helping skills). There is a wide range of functioning in these children and while some are only moderately delayed, others have severe adaptive and learning problems.

Early Period

The concept of IDD has changed over the course of time, as has the terminology used to classify the condition or syndrome. However, most definitions have included some reference to characteristic problems in learning, difficulties in everyday functioning (adaptive and social skills), and age of onset in childhood. The first clear indication that there was a distinction between mental capacity and mental illness came in 1838 when the scientist Jean Esquirol (1772–1840) published a book on mental health with a large section devoted to **Idiocy**, in which he declared that there was a difference between "idiots" who never developed their mental capacity and "mentally-deranged persons" who once had intellectual capacity but had lost it (Sattler, 2001, p. 129). In his chapter on Idiocy, Esquirol describes features of a particular category of patient who clearly fits the description of what we now know as Down syndrome (Roubertouz & Kerdelhue, 2006).

One of the first educators to work diligently to develop a program for teaching children with IDD was Edouard Seguin (Sheerenberger, 1983). Seguin's program, the *Physiological Method*, incorporated a sensory training component and was based on the assumption that increased acuity and coordination of the senses (vision, hearing, taste, smell, touch) would increase cognitive capacity. The program later expanded to include emphasis on memory, imitation, reinforcement, and vocational training. When Seguin moved to North America from Europe in 1850, he revolutionized education for individuals with mental retardation (MR) in the United States. Twenty-five years later, (1876), he became the founding father of the **American Association on Mental Retardation (AAMR)**. Since that time, sensory training continues to be an integral part of many programs that have been developed for working with children who have IDD.

Although Esquirol worked hard to find measures to distinguish mentally incompetent from mentally deranged individuals, his focus on physical measures and speech patterns did not successfully discriminate between these two groups. Fifty years later, fascinated with his cousin's, Charles Darwin, theories on the *Origins of the Species* (1859), Sir Francis Galton (1883) developed a battery of tests that he administered out of his laboratory in London. It was Galton's belief that individual's with higher intelligence would also have keen sensory capacities and motor coordination. However, results did not support his theory (Nietzel et al., 1994).

Period: 1900–1950

At the turn of the century, Alfred Binet (1857–1911), a French lawyer and scientist, and Theodore Simon (1873–1961) were commissioned by the French government to develop measures that would help to identify school-aged children with mental retardation. Binet and Simon believed that measuring mental capacity required a shift in focus from concentrating on primitive sensory capacities to incorporating an emphasis on higher mental processes. The resulting 30 item survey, the **Binet Simon Scales** (1905) became the first instrument to discriminate degrees of mental retardation through the use of a series of age-based cognitive probes (Sattler, 2001). The scales were brought to the United States in 1908 by Henry Goddard, Director of Research at the training school in Vineland, New Jersey.

At this time in the United States, terms such as **feeblemindedness** and **mental deficiency** were used to refer to those who had MR. It was Goddard's intent to use the scales to measure intelligence of the "feeble-minded" children who attended the clinic he had set up 2 years previous. Goddard published an American version of the test in 1910, after standardizing the test on 2,000 children in America. Unfortunately, while Binet envisioned that the identification of children with mental retardation would ultimately lead to special education interventions that would increase their capacity to learn, Goddard's views were firmly entrenched in beliefs that intelligence was primarily inherited, and the main purpose of the test was to identify those who were feeble minded (Nietzel et al., 1994). At this time (1910), the American Association on Mental Deficiency (later, AAMR), suggested that feeblemindedness resulted from arrested development, and identified three levels of functioning in this population: **idiot** (development equivalent to a 2 year old); **imbecile** (development equivalent to a 2 to 7 year old); and **moron** (those individuals who could attain a mental age between 7 and 12 years of age at maturity; Biasini et al.,1999).

In 1916, Terman revised and renamed the intelligence test the Stanford-Binet. Terman was also responsible for the development of the **intelligence quotient (IQ)** which was part of this revision. Terman did not believe that just knowing a child's mental age provided enough information. The intelligence quotient would be a ratio of the child's mental age to their chronological age and thus could provide a means of comparing the relative performance of two children of different age levels. The scales were revised a number of times and in 1972 **the ratio IQ** was replaced with a more sophisticated mathematical computation of the **deviation IQ** (Sattler, 2001).

Memory Bank

Terman's idea of the intelligence quotient (IQ) would allow for comparing the mental functioning of children of different ages. The formula was to divide mental age by chronological age (multiply by 100). For example, Sally is 8 years old (chronologically), but she functions like a 6 year old. Her IQ would be 6/8 x 100 = 75. Wanda is 6 years old, but she functions more like a 9 year old. Wanda's IQ would be 9/6 x 100 = 150.

Over the next 50 years, intelligence testing was rampant and as a result, residential training schools for the mentally retarded were widely established. In 1935, Edgar Doll produced the **Vineland Social Maturity Scale**, an adaptive measure of daily living skills for those with mental retardation. Equipped with the necessary instruments to assess intelligence and adaptive behaviors, psychologists and educators looked at the residential training schools as facilities that could provide "cures" for mental retardation. Discouraged by a lack of successful cures for MR and overcrowding, residential training schools began to fall out of favor. With changes in education, many of the students were moved back into the community into special education classes. As a result, only the most severe remained at the residential training schools which provided mostly custodial care, by this point.

Period: Late-1950s–1970s

One of the main arguments of AAMR in the late 1950s was that determination of MR on the sole basis of IQ score was inappropriate because it did not consider social adaptive factors.

Six-Hour Retardates

In support of including social adaptive functioning were proponents who argued that many individuals, although unable to perform to required academic standards, were quite capable of independent functioning outside of the classroom. They referred to this group of individuals with acceptable social adaptive functioning and low academic skills as **6-hour retardates**, because their limitations were only noted in the 6-hour period when they attended school.

By the end of the 1950s, the AAMR officially proclaimed its full support of expanding criteria to determine MR to include measures of social adaptive functioning in addition to IQ.

At this time, mental retardation was defined as having *three components*, including:

1. low IQ (less than 85)
2. impaired adaptive behavior
3. origination before age 16

However, although the Vineland Scales had been developed by this time, as a rule, only IQ was measured psychometrically. Adaptive behavior deficits usually were based on subjective interview data. At this time, a classification scheme was introduced that outlined *five levels of retardation*:

1. borderline retardation (IQ 67–83)
2. mild retardation (IQ 50–66)
3. moderate retardation (IQ 33–49)
4. severe retardation (IQ 16–32)
5. profound retardation (IQ < 16; Heber, 1961)

Issues of advocacy and changes in definition of MR.   In the 20 year span between the 1950s and 1970s, advocacy groups such as the National Association of Retarded Citizens and the President's Commission on Mental Retardation were established. In the 1970s, the landmark class-action suit in Alabama, the Wyatt-Stickney federal court action, established the right to treatment of individuals living in residential facilities. As a result, purely custodial care was no longer acceptable (Biasini et al., 1999). Also at this time, there was growing concerns about the overrepresentation of minority children in special education, which lead to a change in the definition of mental retardation in the early 1970s (Grossman, 1973). The upper IQ boundary was shifted from an IQ of 85 to an IQ of 70.

Mental retardation and education law.   Given the change in definition in the 1970s, the number of individuals who would be identified as mentally retarded was significantly reduced, thereby lessening the number of children who would qualify for special education assistance and the federal funding that accompanied these services. Many children who might have qualified for special assistance previously would no longer be deemed ineligible.

Recall and Rewind

The average IQ score of 100 is at the 50th percentile in the standard distribution which has a standard deviation of 15. Sixty-eight percent of the population will have an IQ within one standard deviation of the mean (e.g., between 85 and 115). Dropping the IQ score threshold for MR from an IQ of 85 to an IQ of 70 established the criteria for MR intellectual functioning as two standard deviations below the norm instead of the previous difference of one standard deviation below the norm. Approximately 2% of the population would be expected to have an IQ score below 70, whereas 16% would be expected to have an IQ score below 85. In 1977, the upper boundary for MR was extended to 75 to account for 5% error in measurement (Grossman, 1977). Today, the *DSM–IV–TR* (APA, 2000) defines intellectual functioning in MR as "an IQ of about 70 or below" to account for this measurement error.

During this time period, concerns over the number of minority children in special education programs came to a head in California with the case of **Larry P. v. Riles.** The California Circuit Court issued an injunction to prevent the San Francisco school district from using IQ scores to place Black children in special classes designed for the educable mentally retarded. The plaintiffs claimed that the IQ tests were culturally biased, and as such, use of the tests for placement purposes represented a violation of their 14th amendment rights. As a result, the determination was that IQ tests could not be the sole determinant for placement in special education programs.

Contemporary Issues and Trends

Growing discontent and lobbying in support of the rights of all children with disabilities to have a free and appropriate education resulted in the passing of bill **Public Law 94–142** in 1975. The bill focused on the need to protect the rights of the handicapped and supported the AAMR initiatives to include adaptive, as well as, intellectual measures in determining MR in children. The law, then called the **Education of All Handicapped Children Act (EHA)**, legislated grants to states specifically for the education of children with disabilities.

The law has been amended several times since then and was renamed the **Individuals with Disabilities Education Act (IDEA)** in 1990. The law was reauthorized in 1997, and after considerable debate, Congress passed the most recent reauthorization, titled the **Individuals with Disabilities Education Improvement Act of 2004**, in November 2004 (Wilmshurst & Brue, 2005, p. 3).

Today, there continues to be considerable controversy regarding the role that intellectual assessment should have in the identification of children with special needs. Based on results of a recent survey, the *School Civil Right Compliance Report* (1992), Oswald, Coutinho, Best, and Nguyen (2001) found that African Americans continue to be identified at rates well in excess of their Caucasian peers. According to the authors, African American children were identified as mentally retarded 2.5 times more and seriously emotionally disturbed, 1-1/2 times more than their non-African American peers.

Rewind and Recall

In chapter 11 (Specific Learning Disabilities), the ethnic distribution by disability of children receiving special education and related services under IDEA in 2002 was presented in Table 11.3. Data from this table revealed that in 2002, the rate for Black children identified as MR by the educational system (16.8%) was double the percentage identified in any other ethnic group: American Indian/Alaskan Native (7.8%); Asian/Pacific Islander (9.1%); Hispanic (7.8%); and White (8.3%).

Furthermore, Skiba, Poloni-Staudinger, Gallini, Simmons, and Feggins-Azziz (2006) found that, regardless of type of disability, African American students were overrepresented in the more restrictive educational environments and underrepresented in the less restrictive environments compared to all other students with the same disability.

Memory Bank

Often ethnic minority groups also are associated with poverty, which has led many researchers to question whether ethnicity or poverty or an interaction between the two should be used when discussing differences in IQ scores. Although Oswald and associates (2001) found that African Americans who were living in poverty were more likely to be identified as mentally retarded, they also found that African Americans living in the more affluent areas were more likely to be identified as having severe emotional problems relative to their white peers.

Current Issues: Definition and Systems of Classification

There are currently three existing systems for the classification of MR in North America: the *DSM–IV–TR* (APA, 2000); AAMR (2002); and Educational System (IDEA, 2004).

The DSM–IV–TR *(APA, 2000): Mental Retardation (MR)*

Clinical Classification and Diagnostic Criteria

Mental retardation (MR) is the first disorder to appear under the major category of *Disorders Usually First Diagnosed in Childhood or Adolescence.* Unlike other disorders—except personality disorders—MR is the only other disorder that is coded on Axis II, instead of Axis I. The rationale behind coding MR and personality disorders on Axis II is due to their lifetime impact The *DSM–IV–TR* (APA, 2000) presents three main criteria for a diagnosis of MR:

1. significantly subnormal intellectual functioning
2. impairment in adaptive functioning
3. onset before the age of 18

Significantly subnormal intellectual functioning. According to the *DSM*, subnormal intellectual functioning is an IQ of approximately 70 or less obtained on a standard and well recognized instrument that has been developed specifically to assess intelligence (e.g., *Wechsler Intelligence Scale for Children: WISC–IV; Stanford-Binet 5th Edition; SB5*).

Recall and Rewind

An IQ score of 70 is 2 standard deviations below the mean. This is the approximate level selected to determine mental retardation. Two deviations above the mean (an IQ of 130), is usually the threshold for identifying the gifted population. Both of these extremes are approximately at the 2nd percentile (IQ 70) and the 98th percentile (IQ 130).

There is a confidence interval of 5% for the intellectual assessment instruments, which means that the score is likely to be accurate within a 5% error margin. Given this, the IQ determination for MR has been set at "approximately 70" to allow for the standard error of measurement. Given this 5-point margin of error, on either side of the obtained IQ score, the approximate range would be IQ range of 65–75.

Memory Bank

How valid are IQ scores? Although the current IQ instruments are highly valid and reliable measures, a child may obtain a lower IQ score due to disadvantages such as a lack of exposure to stimulation in their environment or lack of opportunities to develop their existing cognitive skills. With proper stimulation and early intervention (e.g., Perry Preschool Project; Head Start Programs), these children may increase their cognitive skills and IQ scores, as a result.

Impairment in adaptive functioning. The ability to function independently is a highly valued characteristic. Adaptive functioning refers to a wide variety of life skills that determine the extent to which an individual is capable of functioning independently in a number of important areas. When making a diagnosis of MR, in addition to subnormal IQ, the *DSM* requires that adaptive functioning deficits be identified that are significantly below age and cultural expectations, *in at least two areas* of the following areas:

- communication skills
- self-care
- home living
- social/interpersonal skills
- use of community resources
- self-direction
- functional academic skills
- work
- leisure
- health and safety

It is important to note, however, that level of adaptive functioning may be influenced by many factors other than intellectual ability, including motivation, comorbid conditions, deprivation, opportunities to access supportive services, and family support.

How Do You Measure Adaptive Behavior?

Although the *DSM* suggests that deficits are required in 2 areas of adaptive functioning from approximately 10 areas, there is little direction given as to how this deficit should be measured or the extent of "deficit" required to meet the criteria for MR.

Although the *DSM* does not specify the extent of deficit required, there are several scales that can be used to measure adaptive functioning. A number of the most popular instruments are presented in Table 14.1.

The instruments have been developed to provide normative information concerning the individual's level of adaptive functioning in the areas mentioned above relative to developmental expectations. Although information is obtained through structured interview format, results provide standard scores that can be used to directly compare standard scores for adaptive levels with standard scores for intellectual functioning. The instruments also provide age equivalent scores to assist in determining current developmental level. When obtaining information regarding a child's performance through interviews or rating scales, it is always advisable to obtain information from different informants who can provide different perspectives on behavior demonstrated in different environments (*DSM–IV–TR*; APA, 2000).

Levels of Severity

The *DSM* also distinguishes levels of severity of MR based on IQ levels as the criteria in distinguishing ranges of impairment. There are four levels of MR: **mild MR, moderate, MR, severe MR, and profound MR.**

Memory Bank

The four ranges of MR, according to the *DSM-IV-TR* (APA, 2000) are:

Mild MR: 50–55 to approximately 70 IQ
Moderate MR: 35–40 to 50–55
Severe MR: 20–25 to 35–40
Profound MR: Below IQ of 20–25

Table 14.1 Assessment Instruments for Intelligence and Adaptive Behaviors

Some Common Individually Administered Intellectual Assessment Instruments	
Instrument/Age Level	**Measures**
The Wechsler Preschool and Primary Intelligence Test: WPPSI–III (Wechsler, 2002) Ages: 2 years, 6 months to 7 years, 3 months	Full Scale IQ, Verbal IQ, Performance IQ
The Wechsler Intelligence Scale for Children WISC–IV (Wechsler, 2002). Ages: 6 years to 16 years, 11 months	Full Scale IQ: Verbal Comprehension Perceptual Reasoning, Processing Speed and Working Memory Indexes.
The Stanford Binet, 5th edition (Roid, 2003) Ages: 2 years to 85 years	Full Scale IQ, Verbal IQ, Performance IQ
The Differential Abilities Test, 2nd edition DAS II (Elliott, 2007) *Preschool Level* 2 years, 6 months to 5 years, 11 months *School Age Level* 6 years to 17 years, 11 months	Verbal Ability, Nonverbal Ability, Spatial Ability, and General Conceptual Ability
Leiter International Performance Scales—Revised (Roid & Miller, 1997). Ages: 2 to 20 years	Nonverbal Assessment includes two test batteries: Visualization and Reasoning; and Attention and Memory.
Mullen Scales of Early Learning (Mullen, 1995) Birth to 68 Months	Five scales assessing Verbal and Nonverbal Ability
Bayley Scales of Infant Development–II (Bayley, 1993) Ages: 1 month to 42 months	Three Scales: Mental, Motor, Behavior

Some Common Adaptive Behavior Instruments		
Instrument/Age Level	**Assessment**	**Measures**
Vineland Adaptive Behavior Scales (Sparrow, Balla, & Cicchetti, 1984) Ages: Birth to 18 –11	Interview Survey Interview Expanded Classroom Edition	Adaptive Behavior in Four Domains: Communication, Daily Living Skills; Socialization and Motor Skills
AAMR Adaptive Behavior Scales— School (2nd ed.): ABS–S:2 (Lambert, Nihira, & Leland, 1993). **Ages:** 3 years through 18-11	Behavior Rating Scale	Five factor scales: personal self-sufficiency, community self-sufficiency, personal/social responsibility, social adjustment, and personal adjustment
Adaptive Behavior Assessment System: ABAS II (Harrison & Oakland, 2003) Ages: Birth to 21	Parent and Teacher Rating Scales	Assesses 10 specific adaptive skills (*DSM*), plus three general areas (AAMR).

Mild mental retardation. Children in this category make up approximately 85% of the population of mentally retarded. Prior to entrance into school, these children may appear as delayed but generally develop social skills, motor skills, and communication skills not unlike their preschool peers. Academic expectations for children and adolescents in this category likely peak at the Grade 6 level. Adolescents and adults can usually be successful in vocational settings with minimal support and supervision. However, if under stressful conditions or if the rules change appreciably, these individuals may not be able to successfully adapt without assistance.

Moderate mental retardation. Approximately 10% of individuals with MR fall within this category. Academic expectations are equivalent to about a Grade 2 level. Those with a moderate level of retardation will be able to function under supervision, in sheltered workshops, or with minimal supervision in highly structured tasks. Training in social and vocational skills can be achieved using behavioral methods and structured programmed instruction.

Severe mental retardation.   As the degree of retardation increases, so do the number of medical, neurological, and motor problems. Approximately 3%–4% of the population have severe MR. Learning is limited to very basic pre-academic skills, although with significant repetition, a limited survival vocabulary of sight words can be mastered. Long-range planning often involves living within group home facilities where needs can be monitored at a close level.

Profound mental retardation.   The profoundly mentally retarded are the most handicapped and MR is often the result of an underlying neurological condition. About 1%–2% of the mentally retarded population fall within this category. Close monitoring is required, as are alternative systems of care for sensorimotor impediments and neurological deficits. **Augmentative communication systems** (individuals may carry picture boards to help them communicate their needs by pointing to an item such as food) and technical aids can often be very helpful in assisting communication and independent skills. Long-term placement would most likely involve sheltered settings where they can learn to perform basic tasks and benefit from close monitoring.

American Association of Mental Retardation Definition (AAMR, 2002)

Current Definition and Criteria
In 1992, the AAMR made a landmark decision to shift emphasis from the DSM focus on severity of disorder (mild, moderate, severe, and profound) to a focus on intensity of intervention required (intermittent, limited, extensive, or pervasive). In the 1992 definition of MR, the emphasis also noted a more applied focus, especially with its emphasis on "functional academics." This new definition stated that MR resulted in

> substantial limitations in present functioning…characterized by significantly subaverage intellectual functioning, existing concurrently with related limitations in two or more of the following applicable adaptive skill areas: communication, self-care, home living, social skills, community use, self-direction, health and safety, functional academics, leisure, and work. Mental retardation manifests before age 18. (AAMR, 1992)

Doing away with levels of dysfunction also placed greater emphasis on the **intensity of intervention** required in order to assist individual to have greater functioning ability. The levels of intensity of intervention were listed as:

- intermittent
- limited
- extensive
- pervasive

At this time, the upper level for onset was also increased from 16 to 18 years of age.

Current definition.   Beginning with definitions of MR that date back to 1908, the AAMR is currently in its 10th revision of *MR: Definition, Classification and Systems of Support (2002)*. This is the most current definition supported by AAMR, recently renamed as the American Association of Intellectual and Developmental Disabilities (AAIDD, 2007). The current revision reinforces and builds upon the 1992 revision. Although the *DSM* contains the disorder in its manual of mental disorders, the most recent definition of MR (AAMR, 2002), emphasizes that MR is *not* a mental disorder or a medical disorder. Instead, AAMR defines MR as a *state of functioning beginning in* *childhood that is characterized by limitations in intellectual and adaptive skills.* The definition (2002) recognizes and emphasizes the need to consider the role of multidimensional and ecological influences that can provide increased insight into interventions through the recognition of strengths and weaknesses in the conceptual, social, and practical adaptive areas. Therefore, the current definition (2002) reinforces that AAMR/AAIDD is strongly supportive of interventions aimed at individualized supports to enhance productivity.

Current criteria for mental retardation

Comparisons of DSM-IV-TR *(APA, 2000) and the AAMR (2002).* There is agreement between definitions by AAMR (2002) and *DSM-IV-TR* (APA, 2000) that a diagnosis of MR should involve an individual IQ score of approximately 70 or below and the recognition that given the error of measurement (5 points), that the ceiling can reach a standard score of 75. Furthermore, there is agreement that IQ score alone is unacceptable and must be accompanied by evidence of deficits in adaptive functioning and must have onset prior to 18 years of age. However, fundamental differences exist between the *DSM* and AAMR regarding how adaptive behavior is defined; how deficits are determined; and the subclassification of MR into levels of severity based on IQ.

While the *DSM* (APA, 2000) provides little guidance as to how to measure a "significant deficit" in adaptive functioning, the AAMR (2002) is specific in its operational definition of adaptive limitations meeting a threshold of two standard deviations below the norm on a standardized measure. Furthermore, The AAMR definition requires a deficit (2SD below the mean) on one of *three* broad adaptive skill areas: *conceptual, social, or practical skills.*

Rewind and Recall

In 1992, the AAMR revamped its definition of MR based on the decision that optimum functioning required individualized support systems designed to match unique needs. This framework was developed in direct opposition to the *DSM* diagnostic criteria that provide specific IQ ranges for the classification of the severity of MR based on IQ score ranges (mild, moderate, severe, and profound). The AAMR system moved away from categorical classification based on IQ level to a more individualized approach of classification based on intensity of services required.

Current definition of MR. The current definition (AAMR, 2002) expands upon this foundation and currently recognizes nine areas where supports should be evaluated, including *human development, life-long learning, home living, community living, employment, health, and safety behavior, social and protection/advocacy issues.* The most recent initiation by AAMR is the development of the **Supports Intensity Scale (SIS**; AAMR, 2003) developed to evaluate level of support intensity needed to assist in more effective treatment planning. The SIS provides a structured assessment instrument to evaluate:

- the frequency of support required
- amount of daily support time (0 to in excess of 4 hours)
- type of support required (monitoring, verbal prompts, partial physical, and full physical)

The SIS evaluates the frequency, amount, and type of support required for each of the following areas:

- home living
- community living
- life-long learning
- employment
- health and safety
- social activities

In addition, the SIS also provides evaluation and monitoring of protection and advocacy issues, medical needs, and behavioral supports.

IDEA (2004): Educational Definition and Eligibility Criteria

There has been considerable change in the way that disabilities have been defined over the years and the education system is no exception in this regard. Historically, IDEA has modified its definition of MR and the recommended levels of IQ functioning to align with definitions and IQ levels suggested by AAMR. Initially, criteria for MR within the educational system involved an IQ range of 55 to 80 for classification as either **educable mentally retarded** (EMR) or **educable mentally handicapped** (EMH). The EMR and EMH labels are the two most common labels used by school districts to depict the MR category, although other derivations are possible. Students with IQs in the 25–55 range traditionally have been most commonly classified by the educational system as **trainable mentally retarded** (TMR) or **trainable mentally handicapped** (TMH).

However, the suggested IQ level to serve as threshold for MR has changed over the years and has dropped from an initial consideration of 85, (AAMR, 1973) to its current cut-off score of an IQ of 70 (+ 5) in most states. Although IDEA provides the general driving force for educational determination, funds for special education programs are allocated by state codes that also set cut-off scores that determine eligibility for programs. As a result, actual IQ ranges for MR may vary from state to state.

Memory Bank

While the majority of states conform to the most common MR cutoff at an IQ between 70 and 75, some states, like Iowa, have retained earlier cutoff levels (IQ 85: MacMillan & Forness, 1998).

Studies that have looked at classification and placement procedures have found considerable disparity in their results. For example, MacMillan and Forness (1998) suggest that placement decisions may be made more on compliance issues (allotted placements per category) than on predetermined criteria. In one sample in their California study, they found that of 43 children scoring below 75 on their IQ test, only 6 of the 43 were designated as MR. Fifty percent of children with IQ scores at this level were classified as Learning Disabled (LD).

When IDEA was reauthorized in 1990, the definition of MR used by IDEA (1990) was in agreement with definitions of MR set by AAMR at that time. As a result, three key areas were deemed necessary for identification of having MR:

1. significant limitations in intellectual functioning
2. significant limitations in adaptive functioning
3. onset prior to 18 years of age

IDEA (2004): Definition of MR.   The latest version of IDEA, the Individuals with Disabilities Education Improvement Act (2004) became effective as of July 2005. IDEA 2004 lists 13 specific categories of disabilities that can potentially receive special education and related services under the law. Mental retardation is 1 of the 13 categories. Children between the ages of 3 and 21 are entitled to special education and related services, as part of their **individualized education program** (**IEP**) provided that it can be demonstrated that they require these services to assist educational performance as a result of their disability.

Currently, IDEA (2004) defines mental retardation as

…significantly subaverage general intellectual functioning, existing concurrently with deficits in adaptive behavior and manifested during the developmental period, that adversely affects a child's educational performance. [34 *Code of Federal Regulations* §300.7(c)(6)]

Important Distinction

While the *DSM-IV-TR* (APA, 2000) includes criteria for disorders that at a minimum cause significant distress and dysfunction in major life areas such as relationships and employment, under IDEA designation, 1 of the 13 categories of disabilities requires—at a minimum—that the disability interferes with *educational performance*.

Goals of IDEA 2004.   The major goal of IDEA 2004 is to improve educational outcomes for children who have disabilities by ensuring that they have the same opportunities for participation, independent living, and economic self-sufficiency as their nondisabled peers. At its core, the legislation strives to ensure that children with disabilities have access to a **free appropriate public education** (**FAPE**) that includes special education and **related services**, when these services are required to address the child's individual learning needs. Additionally, the legislation seeks to ensure that funds are available to support states and local school districts in the provision of services, as well as monitor the effectiveness of educational programs in meeting the needs of children with disabilities.

What Are Related Services?

Under IDEA (2004) any child who is eligible for special education is also eligible for related services. Some examples of related services include physical therapy, occupational therapy, speech therapy, counseling, etc.

Since the majority of children and youth with MR (85%) fall within the mild level of retardation with intellectual scores ranging somewhere between 55 and 70 (*DSM*; APA, 2000), the vast majority of children will likely reside and attend schools in their local community. Therefore, the need to understand how MR is conceptualized by the educational system and the resources that are available through this system has gained increasing importance for child clinicians. As a result, the following discussion will include several references from the most recent educational law that is particularly relevant to children with MR.

The law has four main parts: *Parts A and B*, which cover eligibility procedures, regulations, and required services for children between the ages of 3 years and 21 years of age; *Part C,* which deals with services for infants and toddlers with disabilities, under 3 years of age; and *Part D,* which addresses national activities that have been promoted to enhance educational services for children with disabilities. Familiarity with IDEA (2004) is particularly important for those who are involved with children and/or families of children with mental retardation and developmental delays, since the majority of these children will receive their education and related services through public education programs.

Early Identification Procedures and Developmental Delay

Sections of IDEA (2004) that are concerned with early identification of children at the beginning of the process (infants and toddlers) are covered under Part C. In Part C, Section 635, IDEA (2004) defines **developmental delay** as "a delay of 35% or more in one of the developmental areas or 25% or more delayed in two or more of the developmental areas."

There are *five global areas of potential delay* outlined in IDEA (2004; Sec. 632):

- Cognitive development
- Motor skills
- Communication skills
- Social or emotional development
- Adaptive functioning

Included under adaptive functioning are those skills involved in daily living, such as self-help, being able to dress or feed oneself, etc. IDEA (2004) also mandates services for infants and toddlers who *have a diagnosed physical or mental condition which has a high likelihood of resulting in a developmental delay.*

Infants and toddlers.   Under IDEA (2004), infants and toddlers who have disabilities or suspected developmental delays can also receive intervention services through an **Individualized Family Service Plan (IFSP**; Wilmshurst & Brue, 2005). Congress has allocated funds to help states develop early intervention services. If the state chooses, it can also use these funds to develop programs for children who are **at risk of developing disabilities**. For children under 3 years of age, services are provided by a number of different agencies. While in some states, the department of education may be responsible for programs for children of all ages, in other states, other agencies, such as the department of health, may be responsible for these programs.

Memory Bank

IDEA (2004) uses the term *at-risk infant or toddler* to refer to anyone under 3 years of age who is suspected of being at considerable risk for being delayed, if intervention services are not provided.

Eligibility for services.   In order to determine whether a child is eligible for intervention services, according to IDEA (2004), an evaluation will be provided at no cost to parents to determine whether a child meets eligibility criteria for services. Information will be collected by the intervention team, a multidisciplinary team that might include a social worker, school psychologist, speech and language pathologist, physical therapist, and/or occupational therapist.

Based on information collected by professionals familiar with the child, infants and toddlers with disabilities and delays who are eligible for services can receive intervention programs designed to target specific areas of delay (as outlined above). The service coordinator will provide assistance to the family until the child either no longer requires services or the child turns 3 years of age. At this time, the coordinator will assist the family in the transition to appropriate services for children 3 years and older. Within this model, the family is seen as the focal point and services are built around a plan that has family at the core: the individualized family service plan (IFSP).

Under Part C of IDEA (2004; Sec. 636), each infant or toddler with a disability, and the infant's or toddler's family, are entitled to a multidisciplinary assessment of the child's strengths and individual needs; the identification of services appropriate to meet such needs; a family-based assessment to determine the family needs (resources, concerns); and available community resources and services to assist the family in meeting the child's developmental needs.

IDEA (2004) stresses the importance of *developing an effective* **transition plan** to assist in providing a smooth and effective transition from services covered under Part C (Infants and Toddlers) to services covered in Part B. IDEA (2004) mandates that by the child's 3rd birthday, an individualized education program (IEP) or an individualized family service plan (IFSP) must be developed and implemented.

Children Between Ages 3 and 21 years

Preschool-aged child.   With the introduction of IDEA, special education preschool programs became mandated for eligible children with disabilities who were between 3 and 5 years of age. Children can become eligible for special education services if they:

- have received an individual evaluation (as set out in the regulations)
- the evaluation has confirmed the existence of a disability (in 1 of 13 specified areas)
- the disability interferes with the child's ability to learn

Children at risk of developing disabilities: Children with developmental delays.   Prior to the 1997 reauthorization of IDEA, the law stipulated that preschool-aged children (3 to 5 years of age) who demonstrated *developmental delays* could be eligible for special education services, if the child demonstrated significant developmental delays determined through a comprehensive initial evaluation. However, the "developmental delay" classification was to be removed prior to the child's 6th birthday. At that time, further evaluation would be conducted to determine whether the child would continue to receive services under 1 or more of the 13 categories of disabilities, or whether the child was no longer eligible to receive services under IDEA.

With the 1997 reauthorization of IDEA, the age range for consideration of developmental delay was expanded from "3 to 5 years," to the age range of "3 through 9 years." Under IDEA (2004), this expanded age range of 3 through 9 is retained and now the terms, "including the subset of ages 3 through 5" have been added to age description. For children with identified delays in one of the five developmental areas (*physical development, cognitive development, communication development, social or emotional development, or adaptive development) may be granted* access to special education and related services, at the discretion of the state, if these services are deemed necessary.

Discretionary Services

IDEA (2004) did not change the discretionary nature of this service, and states are not mandated to provide special education and related services for children with developmental delays.

The controversy regarding whether the expanded age should be adopted has resulted in wide variations in age criteria for the developmental delay category among the states. Proponents in favor of extending the age of classification believe that standardized tests are not as reliable in early childhood and could possibly lead to misdiagnosis. Furthermore, the need to have children meet criteria for 1 of the 13 disability categories might also lead to inappropriate diagnoses or ineligibility for services at a time when increased services might have the most impact.

Those who are not in favor of increasing the age span are concerned with the overidentification of children eligible for special education services.

School-aged children.   According to IDEA (2004), if a child (ages 3–21) has a disability that interferes with his ability to learn, then he is legally entitled to a *free appropriate public education* (FAPE) in the *least restrictive environment* (LRE). Special education and related services (such as special transportation, speech and language, assistive technology) must be available from the child's 3rd birthday until receipt of a high school diploma or the end of the school year of the student's 21st birthday, whichever is earlier. However, under IDEA (2004), it has been more clearly noted that schools are not required to conduct an exit evaluation in order to terminate special education services when the child graduates with a standard diploma or is no longer eligible for services due to age (22 years of age).

A child who is suspected of having a disability that is interfering with his or her ability to learn can be identified by either the child's teacher or the child's parent. Under IDEA (2004) Sec. 614, the school district shall conduct a full and individual initial evaluation to determine whether a child meets eligibility criteria for special education and related services. IDEA (2004) notes that requests for an initial evaluation can be made by a parent of a child, a state department of education or other state agency, or the school district.

Transition services must be included in all IEPs once a child reaches 16 years of age. The term "transition services" means a coordinated set of activities for a child with a disability that is focused on facilitating the child's movement from school to postschool activities, including postsecondary education; vocational education; integrated employment (including supported employment); continuing and adult education; adult services; independent living; or community participation. If appropriate, daily living skills and functional vocational evaluation may also be included.

Section 504 of the Rehabilitation Act of 1973

A child with a disability that does not qualify for services under IDEA (2004), can still receive modifications to their educational program through **Section 504 of the Rehabilitation Act of 1973**. Section 504 is a civil rights law that was developed to protect individuals with disabilities by prohibiting discrimination. Special accommodations to the educational program can be obtained if there is a substantial mental or physical impairment that limits a major life activity, such as self-care, performing manual tasks, walking, seeing, hearing, speaking, breathing, learning, or working. One of the mental impairments that are referred to is mental retardation. Determining eligibility under Section 504 is a school-team decision and may result in the development of a 504 plan, a legal document, designed to create a program of instructional services for implementation in the regular education program. Examples of 504 plan accommodations include homework journals, extra time to complete tasks, and a behavioral contract (Wilmshurst & Brue, 2005).

Developmental and Associated Features

Today the majority of children and youth with IDD would fall within the mild level of retardation (according to the *DSM* classification system). As such, these children will most likely reside and attend schools in their local community, unless they are transported to different schools for special programs that are not available in their home schools. The features of IDD vary widely depending on the severity, associated personality, and behavioral characteristics and the developmental level. While some children may experience developmental delays and in a sense, catch up with increased maturity and stimulation/enrichment, others with diagnosable mental retardation may vary only within a limited range of development. As was noted earlier, some individuals with IDD live a relatively normal life despite cognitive limitations due to their adequate adaptive skills.

Associated features that may become more obvious over time are delays in achieving milestones in areas that are key to developmental progress. Examples include delays in the following global areas:

- *gross motor skills* (sitting independently, crawling, walking);
- *fine motor skills* (drawing, printing, coloring);
- *communication skills* (late speech development, trouble talking);
- *cognitive skill development* (problems understanding, problem-solving, remembering and transferring information from one situation to another); and
- *social skills* (problems understanding social rules or subtle social cues).

Similar to all children, children with IDD may have behavior problems or aggressive features; however, occurring together with IDD, these comorbid features can restrict the range of positive outcomes and further reduce the child's ability to adjust and adapt successfully. Some characteristic features that can carry a particularly high risk of negative outcomes include self-injurious behaviors, aggression, stereotypical movements, communication problems, and overactivity (Aman, Hammer, & Rohahn, 1993).

Depending on the level of severity, some individuals with mild IDD (such as upper level Down syndrome), can function quite adequately, at a slower and more deliberate pace, as long as goals are modified, appropriately. As might be anticipated, cognitive limitations are less noticeable in environments that are predictable and structured, and most noticeable in novel or unpredictable situations, or when abrupt changes in routine occur unexpectedly.

Science Talks

There are two schools of thought regarding the nature of cognitive functioning in individuals with MR compared to their normal peers. Some theorists believe that cognitive development in individuals with MR proceeds in a similar, but *slower pace* than normal with expectations set to an overall *lower level* of attainment than would be anticipated in peers (Hodapp & Zigler, 1995). Other theorists believe that organic deficits in information processing in individuals with MR result in cognitive functioning which is *deficient* and distinctively *different* than the norm.

There is support for both sides of the discussion. While advocates of the *slower and lower* theory use Piagetian tasks to confirm that these children follow the same sequence of development,advocates of the *deficient and different* position cite research on how attention, memory and problem solving are different in individuals with MR.

Prevalence Rates

According to the *DSM* (APA, 2000) approximately 1%–3% of the population has mental retardation, with males more highly represented in this population. It has been reported that as high as 3 out of every 100 people in the country may have mental retardation (The Arc, 2001). Considering school-aged children (6–21 years of age), approximately 613,000 have some degree of mental retardation, and require special education assistance in school (24th Annual Report to Congress, U.S. Department of Education, 2002). In fact, 1 out of every 10 children who need special education has some form of mental retardation. As was note previously, the vast majority of the MR population (85%) is in the category of mild mental retardation. By definition, onset is before 18 years of age, but the earliest diagnoses are often associated with the more severe degrees of MR, while those with milder delays may not be identified until they experience learning problems related to academic subjects in school.

Comorbidity. Individuals with MR are 3 to 4 times more likely to have a comorbid disorder than individuals in the population at large. In addition, comorbid disorders associated with MR are often more complex and more difficult to diagnose and treat, since disorder features may be modified by the presence of MR (*DSM*; APA, 2000)). According to the DSM (APA, 2000) the most common comorbid disorders associated with MR, include ADHD, mood disorders, pervasive developmental disorders (PDD), stereotypic movement disorder, and mental disorders due to a medical condition (e.g., head trauma). Furthermore, different disorders that fall under the umbrella of MR (such as Fragile X, Prader–Willi) have different features, etiology, and different types of comorbid associations. For example, while children with Fragile X often have high rates of comorbid ADHD and social phobia, Prader–Willi syndrome is often accompanied by anxiety and ADHD.

Memory Bank

It is very difficult to diagnose ADHD in the presence of MR. When contemplating a dual diagnosis of MR plus ADHD, it is important to remember that many children with MR are often inattentive and active. An important distinction regarding MR populations is that a diagnosis of ADHD is only made if these symptoms are excessive for the child's *mental age, not chronological age.*

Etiology and Subtypes: The Biopsychosocial Model

There are many causes of IDD and MR. The most common are those which relate to the biomedical and genetic domain, and include genetic conditions, problems during pregnancy (toxins); problems during delivery; or health related problems.

IDD due to Genetic Conditions and Chromosome Abnormalities

Sometimes IDD is caused by genetic defects that can be inherited from parents, or result from chromosomal abnormalities when genes combine, or other genetic reasons. Examples of genetic conditions are *Down syndrome, Prader–Willi syndrome, Angleman syndrome, Williams Syndrome, Fragile X syndrome,* and *phenylketonuria (PKU).*

Down Syndrome

In their review of the history of Down's syndrome, Roubertoux and Kerdelhue (2006) present the landmark events in understanding the disorder/syndrome and argue for renaming the disorder Trisomy 21. (The following historic account follows from Roubertoux & Kerdelhue, 2006.) In 1862, John Langdon Haydon Down described characteristic features of a "Mongolian type of idiocy; a congenital condition characterized by speech problems (thick and indistinct) and having a relatively short life span." Down also reported that despite their limitations, children with the syndrome seemed to have a "considerable power of imitation" (as cited in Roubertoux & Kerdelhue, 2006, p. 347). The term "mongolism" was eventually replaced by Down syndrome (1961), to honor Down's pioneering work in the field, although Roubertoux and Kerdelhue (2006) suggest that Down only added to work that had been pioneered by Esquirol (1838) and Sequin (1846) .

Down syndrome (DS) is a chromosomal abnormality involving chromosome 21 (incorrect number of chromosomes or damaged chromosomes). There are variations within the disorder and not all features are present in every one with DS. Some of the more classic features include, short stature, short broad hands and feet, round face, almond-shaped eyes (oblique eye fissures), flat facial features (protruding tongue), and low muscle tone. Language and motor skills are the most impaired in children with DS.

The majority of children with (DS) demonstrate significant problems with language, including linguistic grammar, expressive language, and articulation. Grammatically, most children with DS are equivalent to a child of approximately 3 years of age in their grammatical abilities and fall well below their overall mental age levels in this area (Fowler, 1990). Expressive language disabilities have been reported in as many as 83% to 100% of children with DS (Miller, 1999). Kumin (1994) reports that 95% of parents disclose that articulation problems result in outsiders having difficulty understanding the speech of their child with DS. Yet despite deficits in grammar, expressive language, and articulation, children with DS demonstrate relative strengths in visual short-term memory tasks (Hodapp et al., 1992).

Personality often is socially engaging and affectionate, but, people with DS can also show a dominant will and stand their ground. Speech problems are common, as are health problems, especially with the heart. Other problems that may be evident in children with Down syndrome include: delayed motor development and lack of control over muscle stiffness (Davis & Kelso, 1982); visual–spatial deficits (Vicari, Bellucci, & Carlesimo, 2005); and memory deficits, especially short-term or working memory (Baddeley, 1986), relative to normal developing peers.

The cardinal feature of Down syndrome is a limitation in intellectual functioning. It is possible for some children with Down syndrome to have an IQ score in the upper limits of the low average range (IQ 85–89: referred to as upper level Down syndrome), in which case they would not be considered to fall under the diagnostic category of MR (Epstein, 1989). However, the average score for an individual with Down syndrome is approximately an IQ of 50, and a functioning range for the majority between IQ levels of 30 to 70 (Chapman & Hesketh, 2000; Vicari, 2006). Mental age in individuals with Down syndrome is typically 8 years of age or lower (Gibson, 1978). Although wide variations in IQ level have been reported for individuals with Down syndrome, it has become recognized that IQ progressively declines with age (Pennington, Moon, Edgin, Stedron, & Nadel, 2003). There is increased risk for having a child with Down syndrome with increases in maternal and paternal age. Although normally approximately 1 in 800 births will be a Down syndrome infant, the risk for women over 45 years of age is 1 in 25 births.

Prader–Willi Syndrome

Chromosome 15 is implicated in Prader–Willi syndrome and the disorder is inherited from the father, unlike Angelman syndrome, also involving chromosome 15, but which is inherited from the mother. It was one of the first examples of gene imprinting, where the expression of genes is imprinted by the parent and in this case the male (Milner et al., 2005). The disorder is often recognized soon after birth due to associated features of delay noted low muscle tone and low reflex responses. In school-aged children, Prader–Willi is recognizable physically (short stature, small hands and feet), and behaviorally (impulsivity, temper tantrums, compulsive eating, mood fluctuations, stubbornness, and aggression; Dykens & Cassidy, 1995). The disorder is characterized by a triad of behavioral symptoms that include in addition to the maladaptive behaviors noted above, obsessive-compulsive traits and skin picking (Wigren & Hansen, 2005). Compulsive eating results in progressive obesity. Intellectually, there is some degree of mental retardation that accompanies the syndrome, which is typically in the IQ range of 60–80 (Milner et al., 2005).

Angelman Syndrome

Originally labeled as "Happy Puppet" syndrome (Horsler & Oliver, 2006), Angelman syndrome also involves chromosome 15 but in this case gene imprinting is inherited from the mother. There are four characteristics that have been identified consistently in individuals with Angelman syndrome: developmental delay, speech impairment, movement disorder, and frequent and often inappropriate laughing/smiling. Easily excitable and overaroused, they have short attention span and hyperactivity. Other characteristics often evident include: microcephaly, seizures, and a flattened head. Prevalence is thought to be approximately 1 in 10,000 births (Horsler & Oliver, 2006).

Williams Syndrome

Williams syndrome (WS) was identified in 1961 by a New Zealand cardiologist, Dr. J. C. Williams. The genetic neurodevelopmental disorder is rare, occurring in approximately 1 in 7,500 births. Dr. Ursula Bellugi has been researching Williams syndrome for the past 20 years and has amassed considerable information concerning the rare disorder. The following information summarizes one of the latest publications available concerning Williams syndrome reported by Bellugi and colleagues (2007). The disorder develops as a result of a deletion on chromosome 7 (part of the chromosome is missing). Although the deletion occurs as a random genetic mutation, individuals with WS have a 50% likelihood of passing the mutation on to offspring. One function of the missing component is the gene ELN which is involved in making blood vessels, heart valves, and other tissue elastic. As a result, individuals with WS often suffer from cardiovascular problems at an early age and may have premature death (average lifespan of 50 years). Other features of WS include hypersensitivity to sound and a distinctive facial appearance with puffiness around the eyes, a short nose with a broad tip, wide mouth, full cheeks and lips, and small chin. As infants, they are usually colicy and irritable and often experience feeding problems. Chronic abdominal problems are characteristic of adolescence, while the majority develop diabetes or prediabetes in their 30s. The auditory nerve is compromised and as a result, mild to moderate *sensorineural hearing loss* may be evident as early as late childhood (National Institute of Neurological Disorders: NINDS; Williams syndrome Information Page; retrieved September 23, 2007 from http://www.ninds.nih.giv/disorders/williams/williams.htm).

Most individuals with WS have mild to moderate intellectual impairments and have relatively well-developed verbal skills (verbal IQ) compared with very poor performance skills (performance IQ). Those with WS demonstrate strengths in language (concrete and practical language rather than abstract) and significant weaknesses in areas of visual cognition and visual–spatial functioning, with the exception of facial recognition which remains intact. Rourke and colleagues (2002) consider Williams syndrome to share many of the same processing deficits as those with Nonverbal Learning Disabilities (NLD), especially in their language skills (strength, yet obvious weakness in pragmatics) and deficits in visual spatial functioning. According to the NINDS Web site, approximately 50% of children with WS have ADHD and about 50% have specific phobias (especially fear of loud noises); most of the majority are highly anxious and worry excessively.

The personality of those with WS is remarkable in that they are highly gregarious and driven to social engagement. Bellugi and colleagues (2007) describe the personality of those with WS as having a characteristic "hypersociability, including overfriendliness and heightened approachability toward others, combined with anxiety relating to new situations and objects and a difficulty forming and maintaining friendships with peers" (p. 99). Despite anxiety for novel situations and objects, children with WS demonstrate significantly less fear than typically developing children in response to threatening faces. In one study (Meyer-Lindenberg et al., 2005) using functional magnetic resonance imaging (fMRI), exposure to threatening faces elicited abnormally low levels of activation in areas regulated by the amygdale (which also regulates the fear response) in individuals with WS compared to controls. Such underlying dynamics may help explain why children with WS can be overly friendly and approach strangers without fear.

In their most recent investigations, Bellugi and colleagues (2007) found significantly more social references in the language of children and teens with WS compared to their typically developing peers. Although they attempted to elicit anger and frustration in toddlers with WS by placing an attractive toy behind a plastic barrier, the researchers were unable to collect data on many of the WS toddlers who were more interested in gazing and engaging in social interaction with the experimenter. Intense gazing behaviors are another characteristic feature of toddlers with WS.

Three Wishes and Sentence Completion

In their study of responses to projective measures (If you could have three wishes…and the Sentence Completion Test), Dykens, Schwenk, Maxwell, and Myatt (2007) found that compared to individuals with Prader–Willi syndrome, those with Williams syndrome or Down syndrome provided more socially oriented responses (responses that included references to friends, dating) when responding to wishes and in completing their sentences. However, individuals with Williams syndrome also gave more responses involving negative affect. The researchers suggest that these responses likely reflect generalized anxiety, fears, and phobias often evident in individuals with WS. An unexpected finding was that food was not mentioned more frequently by those with Prader–Willi syndrome (those with Down syndrome offered the most food-related responses).

Bellugi and colleagues (2007) address the issue that despite being driven to engage socially, children with WS often exhibit problems maintaining relationships with peers. They speculate that the disconnectedness between social–perceptual abilities and social–expressive behaviors may be found in the fact that although children with WS are socially fearless, they are also endowed with nonsocial anxiety that may undermine their ability to relate to others.

Fragile X. This is the most common inherited cause of mental retardation in the mild to moderate levels and occurs when there is a change or mutation in a gene called the Fragile X Mental Retardation 1 (FMR1) gene which is responsible for producing a protein necessary for normal brain development. If only mild changes in the gene are present, there may be few symptoms;

however, greater change in the gene produces increased symptoms of Fragile X syndrome (Reiss & Dant, 2003). The symptoms of Fragile X, which can vary relative to the degree of change in the gene, include intellectual deficits, and possible physical characteristics (longer ears, faces, and jaws). There may also be challenging behaviors (fearfulness, anxiety) and males may tend to be inattentive or aggressive, while females may appear withdrawn and shy. In one study of social escape behavior, Hall, De Bernardis, and Reiss (2006) found that males exhibited higher levels of fidgeting and lower levels of eye contact in response to stressful circumstances (higher levels of salivary cortisol). Language problems are also often evident and children may exhibit heightened sensitivity to sound, touch, and bright light (National Institute of Child Health & Development: NICHD). A number of children with Fragile X will also have comorbid autism.

Phenylketonuria PKU

A number of disabilities can be caused by recessive genes. One of the most commonly occurring recessive disorders that can cause serious mental retardation is **phenylketonuria**, or *PKU*. Infants born with two recessive genes lack a necessary enzyme which is responsible for converting one of the basic amino acids that make up proteins into a product (phenylalanine) that is essential to body functioning (tyrosine). If the enzyme is not present, phenylalanine will continue to build, reaching toxic levels that can damage the central nervous system (CNS). Unchecked, the infant will develop progressive MR and if not found prior to 1 year of age, the infant will become permanently retarded. All infants in the United States and Canada are tested for PKU at birth and placed on a low phenylalanine diet. Detected early, children with PKU can develop normally and reach a normal level of intelligence.

IDD due to Environmental Toxins (Taratogens)

Mental retardation can result when the fetus is exposed to environmental toxins (called **teratogens**) that can cause damage to the unborn fetus when they cross the placenta during pregnancy when vital organs and the nervous system are in the process of being developed.

Maternal Substance Use/Abuse

Babies born to mothers who use cocaine can suffer a wide range of side effects after birth, including physical defects and brain dysfunction in hemorrhages and seizures (Espy, Kaufmann, & Glisky, 1999). Mothers who are addicted to crack often give birth to infants who suffer from low birth weight and damage to the CNS (Richardson, Hamel, & Goldschmidt, 1996).

Fetal alcohol syndrome (FAS).   Approximately 33% of all babies born to mothers who are heavy consumers of alcohol will be born with **fetal alcohol syndrome** (**FAS**). Clinical features of FAS include CNS dysfunction (mental retardation, hyperactivity, irritability); impaired motor coordination; and overactivity (Connor, Sampson, & Bookstein, 2001). Physically, these children often evidence slow growth and unusual facial features, including underdeveloped upper lip, flattened nose, or short and upturned, widely spaced eyes, and small head. Although facial features become less pronounced with age, cognitive deficits remain (Schonfeld, Mattson, & Lang, 2001). If a child has a milder set of symptoms, often associated with less maternal alcohol consumption during pregnancy, the resulting syndrome is referred to as **fetal alcohol effects** (**FAE**; Streissguth, Bookstein, & Barr, 2004).

Case in Point

I met Casey when I was doing my internship in a residential treatment center. Casey was 13 years old but very tiny for her age. Her appearance was rather odd, with small eyes and a pointed noise. Despite the small size of her face, her eyes seemed to be spaced further apart than one would expect. Casey was also a very hyperactive girl who was constantly in motion, fidgeting, and moving her hands and feet, at all times. Casey's IQ was in the MR range (IQ 65). The problem at this point was how to deal with Casey's increasingly provocative behaviors towards male students, teachers, and support staff. I had been asked to meet with the social worker and nurse to discuss how we could develop a plan to assist Casey to curtail her newly found promiscuous behaviors in a way that she could comprehend, and that would be effective given her limitations. This type of case scenario represents a common problem for those working with youth who have intellectual disabilities. Although their minds remain at a much younger age level (mental age), their physical bodies continue to develop as they encounter the same hormonal changes that accompany normal adolescence.

Exposure to Toxins, Infectious Diseases, or Birth Trauma

Exposure to lead-based paint.   **Lead-based paint** has been implicated in many complications regarding pregnancy, birth, and infant/child outcomes. As was discussed in the introductory chapters, lead-based paint can be consumed by infants from paint chips that fall off the walls of older residences, or pregnant women can be exposed to these conditions. Prenatal exposure to lead-based paint has been linked to brain damage and a host of physical side effects (Davis, Chang, Burns, Robinson, & Dossett, 2004). Studies have demonstrated IQ differences between children exposed to lead and children who have not been exposed, even at relatively low levels (Boivin & Giordani, 1995). In one study, Coppens, Hunter and Bain (1990) found elevated levels of lead in children who were enrolled in special education programs relative to their nonspecial education peers. A number of studies have demonstrated the harmful effects of lead exposure to human and animals in addition to IQ in areas of attention, learning, memory, school performance, and behavior (Davis et al., 2004; Minder, Das-Smaal, Brand, & Orlebeke, 1994).

Memory Bank

Did you ever wonder why toddlers would be tempted to eat paint chips, especially paint chips laced in lead-based paint? Apparently, lead acetate—lead sugar—has a very sweet taste. It has been speculated that the Romans use of lead to sweeten and produce wine may have ultimately been responsible for the recorded insanity and death of several prominent figures in ancient Rome (Hernberg, 2000; Nriagu, 1983).

Rubella.   The extent of impairment of the unborn child depends upon when the mother is exposed to **rubella** relative to fetal development. The greatest impairments in the fetus occur if exposure coincides with the embryonic period (3 to 8 weeks gestation). Mothers who contract rubella during this time frame expose the unborn embryo to a 50% chance of impairments in the formation of eye, ear, heart, inner organs, and mental capacity (Eberhart-Phillips, Frederick, & Baron, 1993). As a result of exposure to rubella in utero, children born with congenital rubella syndrome often have multiple handicaps including low IQ, sensory impairments (vision, hearing loss), and demonstrate self-injurious behaviors (SIB) or aggression (Carvill & Marston, 2002).

Problems at Birth.   A lack of oxygen at birth (**anoxia**) can result due to several reasons including having the cord wrapped around the babies' neck, or the baby presenting in a difficult position for birth (e.g., breech position requiring delivery to be feet first). A lack of oxygen supply to the brain could result in higher risk for intellectual deficits.

Health Problems.   Contracting diseases like **encephalitis** or **meningitis** can result in reduced mental capacity and adaptive functioning. Mental retardation can also be caused by extreme malnutrition and lack of medical care. Risk factors for MR may also be related to having another medical condition at birth, such as cerebral palsy, or a seizure disorder such as epilepsy.

Risks and Protective Factors

Knowing the possible causes of mental retardation is one of the most valuable protective factors, since many of the causes are risks that are preventable. Ensuring that you are inoculated against contracting rubella prior to contemplating pregnancy is an important step in protecting the unborn child. Eating properly and ensuring that housing is free of lead-based paint will also reduce the risk of mental impairments. Refraining from substances during pregnancy that are known contributors to mental impairments is another protective factor.

Assessment

There are several steps in the assessment of possible MR:

1. A full developmental and medical history is essential in order to determine the potential etiology, onset (prior to 18), and to rule out other competing diagnoses. As the severity of MR increases, there will likely also be existing medical complications which may be added to Axis III of the *DSM*. Developmental milestones provide valuable information concerning which aspects of development might be most affected (for example, delays in sitting or walking may indicate motor problems; while delays in language acquisition might signal language problems). The degree of delay can also be helpful in determining extent of problem (e.g., 1 month delay compared to 2 year delay). Information about a child's strengths can also be very helpful for future intervention. Some children with MR have excellent ability to imitate others and in this case, modeling can be an effective intervention strategy.

2. An individual intellectual assessment is also crucial to determine whether the IQ score falls within the ranges associated with MR. Although an IQ score of 70 is normally associated as the upper limit of the MR range, in recognition of measurement error in any test administration (e.g., performance many fluctuate due to fatigue, illness, etc), an additional 5 points (reflecting 5% variance) can be added to raise the score to 75. The AAMR (2002) has emphasized that it is crucial that intelligence be evaluated using the most up-to-date norms possible to control for the **Flynn effect** (see Science Talks for a description of what the Flynn effect is and why it is important to consider when evaluating individuals for potential MR.)

Science Talks

Intelligence testing and the Flynn effect. The *Flynn effect* is named after James R. Flynn, who published the first systematic study of IQ gains in America (Flynn, 1984). The effect refers to change over time in IQ scores based on when particular tests were normed. According to Flynn (2006), IQ tests can vary between administrations at the rate of .3 IQ points per year between norming years. Flynn (2006) cites the following example based on results from a study by Kanaya, Scullin, and Ceci (2003). Following the release of the revised *Wechsler Intelligence Scale for Children (WISC–III)* in 1991, there was an unprecedented rise in the number of children who were classified as mentally retarded. The *WISC–III* was normed on a 1989 sample, compared to the previous version (*WISC–R*) which was normed in 1972. Due to IQ gains over time, students were scoring, on average, approximately 5 IQ points (17 years x .3 = 5.1) lower on the new version compared to the previous version of the *WISC*.

---

3. In addition to a low IQ (approximately 2 standard deviations below the mean), a diagnosis of MR also requires identification of significant deficits in adaptive behaviors, which were discussed earlier in the chapter.

Common instruments used for individual intellectual assessments and adaptive behavior interviews are available in Table 14.1.

Intervention and Prevention

Intervention Programs

Interventions for children with MR vary widely depending on the specific area targeted for improvement. The majority of interventions focus on the reduction of behavioral/emotional issues, or increasing social, educational, or adaptive functions.

Behavioral interventions. Behavioral programs have been very successful in targeting and altering problematic social, emotional, and behavioral concerns. The reason for the success of the behavioral programs can be linked to the programs focus on breaking down problem behaviors into component parts (simplicity) and to systematically shape behaviors into more socially adaptive behaviors through contingency management.

There is a wealth of empirical support for the use of behavioral methods with MR populations (Handen, 1998). Within the behavioral framework, there are many different techniques that can be adapted to suit programs across the developmental spectrum and can be applicable to a wide range of problem behaviors (behavior chaining, secondary rewards, token economies). Behavioral programs that use **contingency management** techniques (such as *consequences* for good behavior, e.g., rewards; or *consequences* for inappropriate behaviors, such as removal of privileges) can be developed to address problem behaviors whether these involve a decrease of inappropriate behaviors (aggression, noncompliance) or an increase in deficit behaviors (compliance, social skills) at school and in the home (Wielkiewicz, 1995).

Parent training programs. Including parents in the intervention process (whether academic, behavioral, or social) is extremely important. Research has demonstrated that parents can be effective monitors of their child's progress and improve overall success by helping children to transferring skills from one situation to the next (Handen, 1998). There are many ways that parents can increase their child's success, such as helping in transferring skills learned at school to the home environment or skills learned in leisure activities to social activities (generalizabilty). Remember that transferring information across situations is one of the more difficult tasks for children with MR.

Educational programs. There is continual and at times, heated, debate over whether children with MR are better served within special education programs or the regular class (a practice referred to as mainstreaming or inclusion). It is possible to find support for either side of the debate in research studies. Hocutt (1996) reviewed more than 100 studies from the past 25 years comparing special education to regular class placement for children with mild MR and found that there was considerable variability in results. However, Hocutt concluded that much of the research is flawed methodologically or is outdated relative to current educational systems. Based on his findings, Hocutt suggests that it is the type of intervention program (intensive instruction, individual attention, monitoring of progress) rather than the type of class placement that ultimately predicts the level of success. However, how likely is monitoring to occur in classrooms that have higher numbers of students? At least one study found that mainstreaming did not have a positive impact on academic performance of students with mild MR (Gottlieb, Alter, & Gotlieb, 1991) and another looking at social skills found that children (Grades 3–6) with mild MR who were mainstreamed reported more feelings of loneliness and dissatisfaction in their social relationships than their non-MR peers (Taylor, 1986). There is additional support that children with MR may demonstrate deficits in social awareness and exhibit inappropriate social behaviors that actually result in their rejection by normative peers (Farmer & Rodkin, 1996)

Prevention and Early Intervention

The importance of prevention and early intervention cannot be overemphasized. Prevention programs have been launched at all levels of intervention from prenatal awareness campaigns (effects of drug abuse and alcohol; genetic counseling) to early intervention programs targeting parenting skills and early stimulation programs (**The High/Scope Perry Preschool Project**). The impact of early intervention programs within the first 5 years of life has been clearly documented in the prevention of increasing cognitive declines (Guralnick, 1998).

Early Intervention

The High/Scope Perry Preschool Project followed the lives of 123 high-risk African Americans born in poverty and at high risk of failing in school. Between 1962 and 1967, 58 of the preschool children, at ages 3 and 4, were randomly assigned to a high quality preschool program, and 65 were assigned to the control group and did not have the benefit of the program. The initial IQ (Stanford-Binet) ranged from 70–85.

Children attended the program Monday through Friday for 2.5 hours per day. The program lasted for 2 years. In addition, teachers made family home visits for 1.5 hours per week.

The high/scope Perry preschool project. Outcomes of the High /Scope Perry Preschool Progam have been evaluated on three levels: social responsibility, scholastic success, and socioeconomic success (Schweinhart, Berrueta-Clement, Barnett, Epstein, & Weikart, 1985):

Social responsibility. Delinquency rates were significantly lower for children who attended the program relative to the control group. At 19 years of age, children in the program had significantly fewer arrests and fewer visits to juvenile court (Schweinhart, Barnes, & Weikart, 1993). At 27 years of age, adults who had been in the control group had been arrested twice as many times as adults who had attended the program as preschoolers. Among female participants, 40% of those who attended the program were married compared to only 8 % of those in the control group.

Scholastic success. Thirty-four percent of the control group received special education, compared to only 15% of those who attended the program. Children who had attended the program had higher achievement scores, higher grade-point averages in secondary school, and had a 71% success rate for graduation from high school, compared to only a 54% graduation rate for the control group.

Socioeconomic success. Fifteen percent of the program group required social assistance, compared to 32% of the control group. Monthly earnings for the control group were significantly higher. While 29% earned $2,000 or more, only 7% of the control group earned that much. Those who attended the program were also significantly better represented among homeowners and automobile owners.

A cost-benefit analysis conducted on the project (Barnett, 1993) revealed that the public benefits from the program amounted to $105,324 per participant, which represents a benefit of approximately $7.16 for every dollar spent.

Early childhood and prenatal care. Programs such as the Prenatal and Early Childhood Nurse Home Visitation Program supported by the Office of Juvenile Justice and Delinquency Prevention (OJJDD) have demonstrated that early prenatal and postnatal prevention can reduce the risk factors that contribute to delinquency and later school drop out (Olds, Hill, & Rumsey, 1998). One factor that has been identified as an early risk factor that can compromise mental development is language functions. Language can predict later intellectual advancement and can be a critical mediator between intelligence and delinquency (Stattin & Klackenberg-Larsson, 1993). Early intervention in language based learning can contribute to greater school success and involvement.

CHAPTER REVIEW

Since 1876, the American Association for Mental Retardation (AAMR) has been instrumental in shaping how MR is defined and conceptualized. In 1973, the predominant method of determining MR was the IQ score, which at that time was determined by AAMR to be an IQ of 85 (1 standard deviation below the mean). Decisions to include adaptive behavior deficits as part of the determination, as well as child onset, and to reduce the IQ score criteria to 70 (2 standard deviations below the mean) have all resulted from movements initiated by AAMR. Although AAMR (2002) continues to use an IQ score of 70 (up to 75 accounting for testing error), the new definition no longer recognizes the ranges of severity found in the DSM. Instead, AAMR addresses intensity of services based on individual need. AAMR has recently been renamed as the American Association on Intellectual and Developmental Disabilities (AAIDD, 2007) to better reflect the various developmental disabilities served by the organization, and to better conform to terminology of "intellectual disability" used throughout Europe and Canada. Educational classification, IDEA (2004), follows the *DSM* guidelines and has continued to address early intervention for developmental delay, now from birth to 3 years of age.

1. **Classification of MR:** *DSM-IV-TR* **(APA, 2000)**

    MR is coded on Axis II, due to its lifelong nature. The three criteria for diagnosis include: significantly subnormal intelligence (IQ 70 or less); impaired adaptive functioning (at least two of 10 areas); and onset before age 18. The *DSM* recognizes four levels of severity of MR: Mild (IQ 50–55 to 70), Moderate (IQ 35–40 to 50–55), Severe (20–25 to 35–40), and Profound (IQ below 20–25).

2. **Classification of MR: AAMR (2002)**

    Three criteria for MR include: IQ range of 70–75 (allowing for measurement error); deficiencies (2 standard deviations below mean) in one of three global adaptive areas (conceptual, social, or practical skills); and onset prior to 18 years. Intensity and nature of support is determined using the SIS (AAMR, 2003). AAMR has recently been renamed the American Association of Intellectual and Developmental Disabilities (AAIDD, 2007) to reflect changing trends in terminology from mental retardation to intellectual disability.

3. **Classification of MR: Educational System (IDEA, 2004)**

    The majority of school districts currently use an IQ of 70 in their classification of MR. Other criteria include deficits in adaptive functioning and developmental onset. States decide how and what adaptive functions are used in the determination. Increasing emphasis in contemporary IDEA reauthorizations has been to address early intervention (now birth to 3 years of age) for global delays and address transition services at the upper end for students with MR as they leave the school system. Children with MR in the school system will often require related services for associated problems, such as delays in motor skills (fine, gross), communication, social skills, and learning.

4. **Etiology, Assessment, and Treatment**

    Down syndrome, Prader–Willi syndrome, Angelman syndrome, Williams syndrome, and Fragile X syndrome are all examples of MR/IDD due to genetic causes, while prenatal substance use/abuse can result in conditions with MR, such as fetal alcohol syndrome (FAS). Environmental toxins such as exposure to lead-based paint or rubella while in utero can also result in MR. Conducting a developmental history, intellectual assessment and adaptive inventory are three important components of assessment for MR. Longitudinal follow up of children who attended the High/Scope Perry Preschool Program suggests that early intervention can have dramatic and long-term positive outcomes.

Consolidate and Communicate

1. Historically, AAMR has been instrumental in taking the lead and championing changes for individuals with MR, the most recent of which has seen a shift in terminology from mental retardation to intellectual disability. The role of intellectual assessment in determining MR has undergone several changes and currently, there continues to be concerns regarding the number of minority children in special education programs. Discuss the role of the IQ in positively and negatively impacting how children are labeled and subsequently how they receive services in education.

2. Discuss the concept of 6-hour retardates and how this can impact an individual's ability to function.

3. In the movie *I am Sam*, Sean Penn plays the role of a man who is on the borderline of mental retardation. What are some concerns that the court was faced with concerning his ability to raise his daughter and how well are his rights defended in court? Discuss whether Sean

Penn's role in the movie was an accurate portrayal and what parts of the role assist you in better understanding the challenges faced by individuals with MR in their adult life.

4. Educational law (IDEA, 2004) has made several changes over the years to address early identification of developmental delays. However, while some districts take advantage of this category for service for the entire range from 3 through 9 years of age, other districts require that a child must be identified with 1 of the 13 categories under IDEA by their 6th birthday. What are some of the pros and cons of providing services under the category of developmental delay for the entire range available (3 through 9 years), and what are some of the pros and cons of cutting this range short (say, 3 to 5 years)?

5. There are several different types of MR that can result due to genetic conditions. Provide some examples and find out more about these different types of MR.

6. Some states have laws that require testing to determine children's levels of lead-based paint. Do some research to find out whether your state tests for lead levels. Should this be mandatory? Discuss.

7. What is the Flynn effect, and how can this influence impressions regarding the numbers of children who qualify for programs based on IQ scores given at different times?

8. Some have criticized programs like the High/Scope Perry Preschool Program, saying these programs cost too much money and results are only temporary. Based on what you have read, how would you defend programs like the Perry Preschool Project?

Chapter Review Questions

1. In 1910, the American Association on Mental Deficiency identified three levels of feeble-mindedness. Which of the following was not one of the levels?
   a. moron
   b. imbecile
   c. idiot
   d. mentally-deranged

2. Terman's idea of the intelligence quotient (IQ) was a formula based on a ratio of mental age to chronological age. Based on this formula, what would Sally's IQ be if she were functioning like a 10 year old, but she was really 15 years of age?
   a. 67
   b. 150
   c. 80
   d. 55

3. Oswald and colleagues (2001) found that:
   a. African Americans living in poverty were more likely to be identified as MR.
   b. African Americans living in affluent areas were more likely to be identified as having severe emotional problems.
   c. identification of African Americans was not related to living conditions.
   d. Both a and b are true.

4. According to the *DSM–IV–TR*, which of the following children would be considered to have a moderate degree of MR?
   a. Wanda, who has an IQ of 48 and has three adaptive deficits.
   b. Orlin, who has an IQ of 56 and has two adaptive deficits.
   c. George, who has an IQ of 30 and has four adaptive deficits.
   d. Horace, who has an IQ of 34 and has three adaptive deficits.

5. Given the moderate level of retardation, academic expectations would be equivalent to:
   a. Grade 6 level.
   b. pre-academic skills.
   c. about a Grade 2 level.
   d. Grade 5 level.
6. Down syndrome was initially classified as:
   a. Warren's syndrome.
   b. mongolism.
   c. Fragile X syndrome.
   d. moronic syndrome.
7. Happy puppet was the initial name given to which disorder?
   a. Prader–Willi syndrome
   b. Williams syndrome
   c. Angelman syndrome
   d. Fetal alcohol syndrome
8. hich of the following is not a teratogen?
   a. alcohol
   b. anoxia
   c. lead-based paint
   d. rubella
9. Which of the following is not an intelligence test?
   a. Bayley Scales of Infant Development
   b. Leiter International Performance Scales
   c. Vineland Adaptive Behavoir Scales
   d. The Stanford Binet
10. As a result of attending the High/Scope Perry Preschool Project, those who were involved had significantly better measured outcomes in all areas, except:
    a. social responsibility
    b. health and diet
    c. scholastic success
    d. socioeconomic success

Glossary of New Terms

idiocy
American Association on Mental Retardation (AAMR)
Binet Simon Scales
feeblemindedness
mental deficiency
idiot, imbecile, moron
intelligence quotient
ratio IQ
deviation IQ
Vineland Social Maturity Scale
six-hour retardates
Larry P v. Riles
Public Law 94–142

Education of All Handicapped Children Act (EHA)
Disabilities Education Act (IDEA)
Individuals with Disabilities Education Improvement Act of 2004
mild, moderate, severe, profound
augmentative communication system
intensity of intervention
supports intensity scale
educable mentally retarded (EMR)
educable mentally handicapped (EMH)
trainable mentally retarded (TMR)
trainable mentally handicapped (TMH)
individualized educational program (IEP)
free appropriate public education (FAPE)
related services
developmental delay
at-risk of developing disabilities
individualized family service plan (IFSP)
transition plan
section 504 of Rehabilitation Act of 1973
Down syndrome
Mongolism
Prader–Willi syndrome
Angelman syndrome
Williams syndrome
fragile x syndrome
Phenyulketonuria (PKU)
sensorineural hearing loss
teratogens
fetal alcohol syndrome (FAS)
fetal alcohol effects (FAE)
lead-based paint
rubella
anoxia
encephalitis
meningitis
Flynn effect
Contingency management
High/Scope Perry Preschool Project

Answers to Multiple Choice Questions:
1. d; 2. a; 3. d; 4. a; 5. c; 6. b; 7. c; 8. b; 9. c; 10. b.

CHAPTER PREVIEW

The *DSM–IV–TR* (APA, 2000) recognizes five disorders under the category of Pervasive Developmental Disorders (PDD). The disorders are marked by pervasive neurological problems that have onset in childhood and persist throughout the lifespan: Rett's disorder, childhood disintegration disorder (CDD), autistic disorder, Asperger's disorder (also referred to as Asperger's syndrome), and PDDNOS (not otherwise specified). Disorders share features of qualitative impairments in social interaction, verbal and/or nonverbal communication and a restricted range of activities. Rett's Disorder and CDD evidence a rapid deterioration in functions after a period of "apparently" normal development. Children with autism also demonstrate a pattern of regression that occurs after 3 years of "apparently" normal development. There has been debate whether autistic disorder (AD) and Asperger's syndrome (AS) represent two distinct disorders or whether the disorders represent different end-points along a continuum of autistic spectrum disorders (ASD). The situation is further complicated when higher functioning autism (HFA) is thrown into the mix. The *DSM–IV–TR* (APA, 2000) distinguishes autism from AS primarily on the basis of language. While both autism and AS share features of impaired social interaction and engagement in restricted, repetitive, and stereotypical patterns of behavior, only autism (not AS) has a third criteria of qualitative impairment in communication. The category of PDDNOS is reserved for those cases that are atypical.

1. Rett's Disorder

Normal development is replaced by progressive deterioration, as purposeful hand movement is replaced by hand wringing, while brain development and head growth decelerate. The disorder progresses through four stages, including: 1) early symptom onset (6–18 months); 2) rapid deterioration (1–4 years) and ataxia (unsteady gait); 3) plateau and less deterioration in some areas with improved behavior in others, e.g., social alertness (2–10 years); and 4) late deterioration (10 years and beyond). While most will remain at stage 3, some will continue to deteriorate. Only females survive Rett's disorder at birth, which involves a genetic mutation (MeCP2) responsible for synthesizing protein located on the X chromosome.

2. Childhood Disintegration Disorder (CDD)

CDD is a rare disorder that occurs primarily in males between 2 and 10 years of age, after at least 2 years of normal development, and is characterized by a marked regression in two of the following areas: expressive or receptive language, social or adaptive skills, bowel or bladder function, play or motor skills. Loss of function is also accompanied by qualitative impairment in two of the three areas associated with PDD, including social interaction, communication, and restricted range of activities (stereotypical patterns). Differential diagnosis between CDD and autism is possible based on the deterioration of function in multiple areas not seen in autism. Severe mental retardation is not uncommon.

3. Autistic Disorder (AD)

A *DSM* diagnosis of autism requires onset prior to 3 years of age and 6 symptoms from a list of 12 from three categories: qualitative impairment in social interaction (2 symptoms); qualitative impairment in communication (1 symptom); and restricted stereotypical behavior (1 symptom). Lack of social reciprocity has been linked to limited activation of the amygdale, lack of eye contact and social smile, and deficits in social imitation. While it was once thought that the majority of children with AD also had MR, there is concern these numbers were inflated. Individuals with AD who have an IQ above 70 are said to have high functioning autism (HFA). Treatment programs often involve intense service delivery, such as Lovaas ABA Program or Schopler's TEACCH Program.

4. Asperger's Syndrome (AS)

Unlike their autistic peers, children with AS do not exhibit language delay, or significant delays in cognitive or adaptive functioning, although they do share features of qualitative impairment in social interaction (2 symptoms) and restricted, stereotypical behaviors (1 symptom). Compared to other children with PDD, children with AS tend to have intellectual functioning in the normal range. Although language is intact and children can be verbose and pedantic, they often miss the subtle nuances of the language and less often engage in reciprocal communication. Teens with AS may become depressed due to lack of social contacts. Treatment focus is often on increased social skills and social awareness.

5. Autistic Disorder and Asperger's Syndrome

Although autism and AS have been identified since the mid-1940s, controversy continues whether these disorders should be conceptualized as distinct, or part of the autistic spectrum disorders (ASD). One meta-analysis comparing high functioning autism (HFA) with AS found that although HFA had later onset of language, by the time youth were in their teens there was minimal difference between the two groups. Other studies have shown that children with AS perform better on verbal IQ and *theory of mind* tasks than children with HFA. The debate continues, although children with AS seem to have better outcomes than those with HFA. Results of recent surveys suggest that prevalence rates for autistic spectrum disorders may be much higher than initially anticipated.

6. Pervasive Developmental Disorder, Not Otherwise Specified: PDDNOS

This is a highly controversial category due to the limited explanation in the *DSM–IV–TR* (APA, 2000) and confusion with other PDD categories that often overlap symptoms, resulting in tenuous boundaries between the different subtypes. PDDNOS is reserved for "atypical" cases. The concern is that children who have a heterogeneous collection of symptoms who are diagnosed as PDDNOS are likely to have deficits in a variety of different areas and as a result, the label may provide very little direction as to appropriate treatment or prognosis.

Pervasive Developmental Disorders: An Overview

The term pervasive developmental disorders (PDD) is a relatively new classification which was first used in the 1980s to describe a class of childhood-onset brain disorders that resulted in severe and *pervasive* impairments in functioning. Disorders within this classification share common characteristics of impairments in social interaction, imaginative activity, verbal and nonverbal communication skills, and a limited number of interests and activities that tend to be repetitive. The latest revision of the *DSM–IV–TR* (APA, 2000) recognizes five disorders under the category of Pervasive Developmental Disorders:

1. Rett's Disorder
2. Childhood Disintegrative Disorder (CDD)
3. Autistic Disorder
4. Asperger's Disorder (or Asperger's syndrome [AS])
5. Pervasive Developmental Disorder Not Otherwise Specified, or PDDNOS

The PDDNOS category is reserved for individual's who meet some of the criteria, or have atypical features of PDD.

Children with PDD have a lifelong disability and often have a number of comorbid problems, including intellectual impairment, language and learning problems, seizures, and neurological dysfunction (*DSM–IV–TR*; APA, 2000). Individuals with PDD are also at risk for comorbid psychiatric problems, including internalizing disorders (anxiety and mood), ADHD and tics (Mouridsen, Rich, & Isager, 1999). The *DSM–IV–TR* (APA, 2000) criteria provided a reliable system of identification of PDD, especially for children who are 3 years of age or older; however, identification of the subtypes within PDD (autistic disorder, AS, CDD, and PDDNOS) continues to pose a challenge to clinicians (Miller & Ozonoff, 1997; Szatmari, Archer, Fisman, Streiner, & Wilson, 1995).

Two of the lesser known and less prevalent disorders which have similar types of onset are Rett's disorder and childhood disintegrative disorder (CDD). This chapter will begin with a discussion of these two disorders that share a common feature of children beginning their development in an apparently normal fashion. However, following a period of what looks like normal development, there is an onset of progressive deterioration of function. Children with autistic disorder and AS also share similar features; however, there are significant differences between these two disorders regarding degree of impairment. Some theorists prefer to discuss autistic disorder and AS as the *autistic spectrum disorders (ASD)* to reflect the possibility that these two disorders represent a continuum along a single dimension rather than two unique disorders. The debate as to whether autism and AS are two unique disorders is a controversial one. Finally, PDDNOS is a category reserved for disorders that feature many atypical characteristics compared to the norm. PDDNOS is a reminder that some children do not neatly fit into subcategories within PDD but have an atypical presentation of unique and common features.

Rett's Disorder/Rett Syndrome

Rett's disorder, also known as **Rett syndrome** (RS), was originally described by Dr. Andreas Rett of Australia in 1966; however, it was not until a second article was published in 1983 that the disorder gained increased notice. There are variations in the course of the disorder due to differences in age of onset and a range in the severity of symptoms. Initially, within the first 5 months, infants appear to be developing normally in their motor skills and mental functioning (*DSM–IV–TR*; APA, 2000). However, at some time between 6 and 18 months of age, the onset of the disorder becomes evident in a progressive deterioration in function (National Institute of Neurological Disorders and Stroke; NINDS, 2006). Deterioration is evident in loss of function (purposeful hand movement is gradually replaced by compulsive hand wringing and washing movements), deceleration of brain and head growth, abnormalities of gait, and onset of seizures and mental retardation. One of the first symptoms of Rett syndrome is **hypotonia** or a gradual loss of muscle tone (NINDS, 2006).

Description and Associated Features

The *DSM* diagnostic criteria outline features that can be identified at two periods: those occurring up to 5 months of age, and those occurring after 5 months of age. At birth, and within the first 5 months, the following features must be present in order to diagnose Rett's disorder: Apparently normal

1. prenatal and perinatal development
2. psychomotor functioning for the first 5 months
3. head circumference at birth

After 5 months of age, onset of all of the following must be evident in order to diagnose Rett's disorder or syndrome:

1. deceleration of head growth (between 5 and 48 months)
2. loss of purposeful hand function (between 5 and 30 months) and development of repetitive hand movements (wringing, hand washing)
3. deterioration in social engagement
4. onset of poor coordination, gait
5. severe psychomotor retardation
6. impairment in expressive and receptive language (*DSM–IV–TR*; APA, 2000, p. 77)

Developmental Course

Rett syndrome is a child neurodevelopmental disorder with an unpredictable onset of regression. Onset of regression can be abrupt. **Apraxia** (inability to perform motor functions) can be disabling as motor coordination problems impact body movement from gross motor tasks such as walking or crawling to more specific functions such as eye movement or speech (Unless other wise specified, information is from NINDS, 2006).

   Individuals with Rett syndrome share some features common to other PDD disorders (stereotypical movements, restricted range of activities, lack of social reciprocity, and imitative play). Other symptoms that might be expressed include toe walking, sleep difficulties, and seizures. There are four stages of symptom presentation in Rett syndrome.

Stage 1: Early onset (6–18 months).   The early symptoms of Rett syndrome may not always be noticeable due to their subtle nature and the fact that parents are just in the early stages of getting acquainted with their infant's personality. There may be less frequent eye contact and less interest in toys. However, passivity may be misinterpreted as a "good baby" who is calm and quiet. Depending on language development, what might have been the beginnings of a small vocabulary of single words may soon be lost. More obvious signs might be the replacement of purposeful hand activity with stereotypical hand wringing and the slowing of head growth which was of normal circumference at birth.

Stage II: Rapid deterioration/destructive stage (1–4 years).   The second stage may be either rapid or gradual in onset. The child loses her ability to speak and to make purposeful hand movements. There is increasing use of wringing, clapping, or tapping, and hand-to-mouth movements may also appear and intensify. There may be noticeable episodes of **apnea** (breath stopping), and hyperventilating (rapid shallow breathing). None of these motor movements or breathing problems seem evident during sleep, although sleep problems may be evident in irregular sleep patterns and agitation/irritability. If walking was present, gait may become unsteady (**ataxia**) and there may be periods of trembling or shaking.

Stage III: Plateau or pseudostationary stage (2–10 years). During this stage, while some functions continue to deteriorate, there is an improvement in other areas of function. Motor problems, apraxia, and seizures appear or continue throughout this stage. On a positive note, there is a decrease in negative behaviors such as irritability, crying, and autistic-like behaviors, and improvements in social awareness, attention, alertness, and possibly communication skills.

Stage IV: Late deterioration of motor skills (10+ years). Many of those with Rett syndrome (the vast majority of which are females) may remain at Stage III for the majority of their lives. However, others will have progressive deterioration of motor functioning which can last for years. In this stage, they will experience increased loss of their mobility; some stop walking. Others will experience muscle weakness, muscle rigidity (**spasticity**), or **scoliosis** (curvature of the spine). Despite deterioration in mobility, there is no loss of cognitive or communication skills, while repetitive hand movements may decrease.

PDD Triad

All of the disorders in the PDD category in the *DSM–IV–TR* (APA, 2000) share the criteria of atypical functioning and qualitative impairment in at least two of the following three areas:
  1. Impaired social interaction
  2. Impaired communication
  3. Restricted range of activity, noted in repetitive and stereotypical patterns

---

Etiology

Rett syndrome has been linked to a genetic mutation in the MECP2 (meck-pea-two) gene which was discovered in 1999. The gene is located on the X chromosome and is responsible for synthesizing a protein (MeCP2), which is instrumental in controlling protein production in other genes. Due to a malfunction of the MeCP2, insufficient amounts of proteins, or abnormal forms of proteins, are produced. The result is that the brain does not follow a course of normal development and sensory, motor, and emotional functions remain arrested at an infant stage of development. Research continues in an effort to pinpoint the process more specifically. Approximately 80% of females diagnosed with Rett syndrome have the **MeCP2 genetic mutation**. Although it is likely that the disorder is due to a genetic mutation, the disorder is rarely inherited. To date, there is less than 1% of recorded cases linked to heredity.

Prevalence

The prevalence for Rett syndrome is less than other PDD disorders. It is difficult to obtain prevalence rates since the disorder has only been recognized in the past 20 years. However, it is estimated that female rates for the disorder range from 1 in every 10,000 births to 1 in every 15,000 births. Because the disorder involves the X chromosome, until recently it was thought that only females were affected. However, because females have two X chromosomes, while males have an X and Y chromosome, it has been more recently suggested that when one of the X chromosomes is compromised, females have the ability to activate the other X chromosome, and only about half of the cells in the nervous system will use the defective gene. However, since males have only one X chromosome, they become vulnerable to the harmful effects of the disorder. It is not a case of males not being susceptible to the genetic mutation; rather, it is a case that they do not survive the effects. Males with such a defective gene die shortly after birth.

Prognosis/Treatment

Despite the severity of the symptoms, at this stage of data gathering, it appears that those with Rett syndrome can live until middle age (40s to 50s). However, little is known about the long-term prognosis. Presently, there is no cure for Rett syndrome, although research efforts to find treatment solutions are on-going. Currently, treatment is intended to ease the symptoms and to keep the patient mobile as long as possible. It will include most or all of the following:

- Medications for seizures, breathing problems, and difficulties with muscle control
- Physical therapy for mobility, range of motion, and preventing muscle contractures
- Hand or elbow splints may be used to reduce repetitive hand movements and increase the child's purposeful use of her dominant hand. Patients who develop **kyphosis** (humpback) or **scoliosis** (spine curvature) may be fitted for spinal braces.
- Occupational therapy
- Speech therapy, alternative communication systems (communication boards, or electronic devices)

Childhood Disintegration Disorder (CDD)

While the onset for Rett syndrome can be evident as early as 5 months of age, individuals with **childhood disintegration disorder (CDD)** sustain a normal period of development for at least *2 years* (*DSM–IV–TR*; APA, 2000). Although Rett syndrome is found only in females, children with CDD are more likely to be male.

Historical Background

Although the identification of CDD predates Kanner's description of autism, far less is known about this relatively rare disorder. (The following historical information follows Hendry, 2000, unless otherwise noted.) The disorder was initially reported in 1908 by Theodore Heller, who used the term **dementia infantilis** to identify a cluster of symptoms he observed in six cases. Ultimately, Heller tracked the symptoms of 28 children from 1905 to 1925. Heller noted that in the vast majority of cases, after a period of normal development, between the ages of 3 and 4, there was a marked deterioration and loss of function in the majority of areas, including expressive and receptive language, and motor functioning. Deterioration was such that children could require custodial care as a result.

Other terms have been used for CDD: *Heller's syndrome, progressive disintegrative psychosis of childhood, late onset autism,* and *disintegrative psychosis,* which was the term used in the *ICD–9 Codes* (WHO, 1977). In the *DSM–III* (APA, 1980) *infantile autism* and *childhood onset pervasive developmental disorder (COPDD)* were seen as two separate disorders, with distinct ages of onset. However, by the time the *DSM* was revised (*DSM–III–R*; APA, 1987) COPDD was removed as a category, replaced by *developmental disorder not otherwise specified,* while *infantile autism* was renamed as *autistic disorder.* Finally, with the 4th revision of the *DSM–IV* (APA, 1994), based on information obtained from the APA field trials (Volkmar et al., 1994), CDD was recognized as a specific disorder with its own classification criteria.

> ### Across the Pond
>
> In Europe, CDD is termed **other childhood disintegrative disorder** (to distinguish it from Rett's disorder) according to the latest *ICD Codes* (*ICD–10*; WHO, 1993). Although conceptually similar to the *DSM–IV*, the *ICD* (*International Statistical Classification of Diseases and Related Problems*) is used throughout the world and is somewhat more detailed and operationalized to the extent that there is a more explicit indication that "behavioral criteria for autism must be met" (Volkmar, Klin, Marans & Cohen, 1997, p. 49).

Description and Associated Features

According to the *DSM–IV–TR* (APA, 2000), the cardinal marker for CDD is defined by:

Criterion A, which states that there is a "marked regression in multiple areas of functioning following a period of *at least 2 years* of apparently normal development" (p. 77). Normal development is outlined as age-appropriate development in all areas of functioning (e.g., expressive and receptive skills, verbal and nonverbal communication, social skills, adaptive behavior and play).

Criterion B requires that after the first 2 years of life, a progressive loss of previous function (prior to age 10) is evident in at least *two* of the following five areas:

1. expressive or receptive language
2. social or adaptive skills
3. bowel or bladder function
4. play
5. motor skills

Criterion C states that the loss of function noted in Criterion B is accompanied by at least two areas of atypical functioning and qualitative impairment from the following three areas:

1. qualitative impairment in social interaction
2. qualitative impairment in communication
3. restricted range, repetitive, and stereotyped patterns of behavior (p. 79)

Social interaction is impaired and qualitatively different from normal development in areas of nonverbal communication, lack of reciprocity in social relationships, and an inability to develop relationships with peers. Communication deficits can be evident in a failure to develop language, lack of imaginative play, and a lack of engagement in conversation which is often replaced by a repetitive and stereotyped use of language. There is a restricted range of activities (repetitive and stereotypical patterns of behavior, such as rocking behaviors, lining up of objects, or spinning object parts).

Criterion D is an exclusionary clause which states that CDD is diagnosed if it is possible to rule out another PDD or Schizophrenia.

Developmental Course

According to the *DSM–IV–TR* (APA, 2000), CDD is usually accompanied by severe mental retardation, which, if present, should be coded on Axis II.

Recall and Rewind

The *DSM–IV–TR* (APA, 2000) is a multiaxial system of classification. All disorders are coded on Axis I with the exception of mental retardation (MR) and personality disorders which are coded on Axis II, since these are considered to be life-long and pervasive disorders. Given the explanation and rationale for coding disorders on Axis I or Axis II, it is curious that, given the pervasive nature of PDD, it is not also coded on Axis II.

Many of the reported cases of CDD have evidence of seizures or nonspecific neurological abnormalities, such as an irregular EEG. In some cases, a medical condition has also been reported (e.g., metachromatic leukodystrophy [MLD]) and if medical problems do exist, they should be coded on Axis III. MLD is one of a number of lipid storage diseases that result in a toxic buildup of fatty materials (lipids) in cells in the nervous system, liver, and kidneys, which may explain loss of bladder function in some children with CDD.

Myelin the Effective Communicator

Metachromatic leukodystrophy (MLD) is a disease that impairs the development of the *myelin sheath*, the fatty covering that acts as an insulator around nerve fibers. Myelin, which lends its color to the white matter of the brain, is implicated in the increased efficiency of the brain's ability to send messages. **Myelination** is responsible for the rapid growth of the brain in the first 2 years of life, when the brain increases from 30% of adult size at birth to 70% of adult size at 2 years of age (Thatcher et al., 1996).

Normal development is demonstrated for at least the first 2 years. However, in some cases, normal development can continue as late as 10 years of age prior to deterioration of function. Onset of deterioration is most common between 3 and 4 years of age, and onset can be sudden or be evident in a more subtle progression of deterioration. Prior to the decline in function (loss of speech and other skills), children may appear more irritable and exhibit increased levels of activity and anxiety, as well as a loss of interest in their surroundings. Often the deterioration will reach a plateau, unless accompanied by neurological complications, in which case, the deterioration may be more progressive and severe

In their review of the literature regarding CDD up to the mid 1990s, Klin and Volkmar (1997) noted that only approximately 100 cases of CDD had been reported. Attempts to conduct a meta-analysis have been frustrating due to the range of behaviors reported, developmental changes resulting in variations in symptom presentations, and confounding factors such as psychological or medical conditions precipitating the occurrence of CDD-like behaviors and subsequent deterioration. Malhotra and Gupta (2002) identified 12 cases of CDD and 21 cases of typical autism (TA), using *ICD–10 Codes* for identification of a population derived from a clinical setting in northern India. Within this sample, the average age of onset for CDD was 3.76 years with onset in this population sample ranging from 2.5–7 years of age. A comparison of the Malhotra and Gupta (2002) study with findings from a meta-analysis by Volkmar et al. (1997) and Kurita, Koyama, Setoya , Shimizu, and Osada (2004) is presented in Table 15.1.

Table 15.1 Characteristics of Childhood Disintegration Disorder (CDD): A Comparison of Results From Different Sources

Characteristics CDD	Malhotra and Gupta (2002)	Cohen and Volkmar (1997)*	Kurita et al. (2004)
Total sample size (male/female)	12 (10/2)	105 (84/21)	10 (7/3)
Average age onset	3.76	3.36	2.76*
Speech loss/deterioration	100%	100%	100%
Social disturbance	100%	99%	—
Affective/anxiety/fear	25%	74%	80%
Stereotypy	67%	91%	80%
Loss bladder/bowel skills	58%	68%	—
Epilepsy	33%		30%
Mean IQ	34		39.4
Precipitating event	50%		80%

*Includes cases from Malhorta and Singh (1993); Volkmar and Rutter (1995); and Wolgemuth et al. (1994).

A comparison of results across studies should be viewed with caution because descriptive categories were similar but not identical (e.g., *affective anxiety* in studies by Malhotra and Grupta and Vokmar, versus *fearfulness* in the study by Kurita and colleagues). Nevertheless, age of onset in all three reports confirms the *DSM–IV–TR* (APA, 2000) diagnostic criteria of normal development for the first 2 years, and speech loss surfacing as the most common and pervasive symptom of deterioration. Other common characteristics for CDD were evident in stereotypical behaviors, loss of bladder and bowel skills, and disturbance of social function. The disorder is more prevalent in males, with IQ levels in the severe range of MR and higher rates of epilepsy than in the normal population. In addition, Malhotra and Gupta (2002) also report that 75% of their sample of children with CDD demonstrated loss of play skills, while 42% demonstrated aggressive behaviors.

Results of theses studies provide further support for consistency of characteristics across a variety of studies, and evidence of the universality of the phenomenon from records obtained during *DSM–IV* field trials and subsequently to data collected in India (Malhotra & Grupta, 2002) and Japan (Kurita et al., 2004).

Important Distinction

Kurita, Osada, and Miyake (2004) suggest that variations in reported incidence of epilepsy in individuals with CDD may be a function of subject age. For example, while Malhotra and Grupta (2002) found epilepsy in 30% of children reviewed, Mouridsen et al. (1999) noted that 77% of their adult population reported epilepsy. Kurita et al. (2004) relate the higher incidence of epilepsy in CDD compared to autism supports the notion that there is more severe brain dysfunction in CDD than autism.

Differential Diagnosis

In making a differential diagnosis between CDD and autistic disorder, there could be a period in which age of onset may be a difficult criterion, since autistic disorder has an age of onset prior to 3 years of age, while CDD must have at least 2 years of normal development. In most cases of CDD, the onset is between 3 and 4 years and may be acute or progressive. According to the *DSM–IV–TR* (APA, 2000), differential diagnosis between CDD and autism can be based a number of differentials, including:

- the *deterioration of function* in multiple areas that occurs in CDD is not evident in autism
- the fact that in autism developmental abnormalities can often be detected in the 1st year, while CDD has normal development for the first 2 years

The *DSM* states that in situations where it is not possible to document early normal development (e.g., records may not be available), a diagnosis of autism is made (p. 74).

Developmental regression is evident in autism, Rett's disorder, CDD, and total blindness from birth. While Rett's disorder and total blindness are readily distinguished from CDD, the distinction between CDD and autism can be far more subtle, and has lead some theorists to question the merits of the distinction between these two disorders (e.g., Hendry, 2000; Malhotra & Gupta, 2002).

Science Talks

From what little can be generalized from the research, it appears that age of onset, being mute, and having a lower IQ are three factors that might distinguish CDD from autism (Hendry, 2000).

In one comparative study, Kurita, Kita, and Miyake (1992) reported that the only major differences between individuals with autism (196 cases) and those with CDD (18 cases) were greater prevalence of developmental delays, and higher incidence of irregular EEGs in individuals with CDD. However, more recent comparison of a number of variables between CDD and autism cases reported by Kurita et al. (2004) supports the distinction between the two populations evident in higher rates of epilepsy, fearfulness during regression, and greater stereotypy in individuals with CDD than those with autism While a diagnosis of autism requires that the symptoms be present by 30 or 36 months, criteria for CDD state that development must be normal for the first 2 years of life, with later onset of deterioration compared to autistic-like behaviors. In addition, description of cases with CDD report unique characteristics not associated with autism, including "a phase of markedly fearful, anxious behavior that accompanies the regressive period and evidence of motor involvement including loss of motor coordination, loss of physical skills (dressing, toileting, self-feeding) and development of ataxia, drooling and other neurological symptoms" (Rogers, 2004).

Important Distinction

Volkmar and colleagues (1997) point out that while deterioration in autism is more likely to involve loss of the ability to speak single words, deterioration in those with CDD appears more severe based on higher levels of initial language functioning and is accompanied by loss in multiple areas in addition to speech.

In summary. While Rett's disorder and CDD note a characteristic decline in functioning after a relatively normal period of initial development, individuals with autism demonstrate arrested development, after an apparent "normal" beginning.

Prognosis/Treatment

Children with CDD who have moderate-to-severe mental retardation and lack of communicative language have a worse prognosis than those who are less impaired. The disorder is lifelong with impaired functioning throughout the course of life. Risk of seizures increases with age and peaks at adolescence (Vernstein, 2006). The etiology is unknown and treatments have focused on medication for seizures and behavioral programs that have been developed for children with autism. There have been minimal outcome studies due to the rarity of the disorder; however, a follow-up study over 22 years concerning 39 cases of CDD matched to autistic controls revealed that outcomes for CDD were poorer than for autism, with greater incidence of epilepsy and lower overall functioning (Mouridsen et al., 1998).

Autistic Spectrum Disorders

Austistic Disorder

Description and Associated Features

The first diagnostic criterion for autistic disorder (*DSM–IV–TR*; APA, 2000) involves <u>Criterion A</u>, which requires 6 or more symptoms from a list of 12 symptoms. The symptoms must come from 3 symptom clusters with at least 2 symptoms from cluster 1 and at least 1 symptom from each of clusters 2 and 3. The symptom clusters represent the three core features of autism.

Criterion A:

1. Qualitative impairment in social interaction (*at least 2 symptoms*)
   - impaired nonverbal behavior (lack of social gestures, eye contact, facial expression)
   - failure to develop appropriate peer relationships
   - lack of social referencing (spontaneous desire to share objects, activities of interest)
   - failure to engage in social or emotional reciprocity
2. Qualitative impairment in communication (*at least 1 symptom*)
   - delay or lack of spoken language or compensatory gestures
   - if speech is present, lack of initiation or sustaining of conversation
   - stereotyped, repetitive use of language (robotic, echolalic, use of third person)
   - lack of spontaneous make-believe play, or imitative play
3. Restricted, repetitive, and stereotyped patterns of behavior, interests, activities (*at least 1 symptom*)
   - preoccupation with restricted interest
   - adherence (not flexible) to nonfunctional routines
   - repetitive, stereotyped mannerisms (hand flapping)
   - preoccupation with parts of objects (spinning a car wheel)

In addition to the 6 symptoms from the above 3 categories, two other criteria exist:

Criteria B: Onset prior to 3 years of age, with delays or abnormal functioning in one of the following areas:

1. social interaction
2. communicative language
3. symbolic or imaginative play

Criteria C: The disturbance is not better accounted for by Rett's disorder or CDD (*DSM–IV–TR*; APA, 2000, p. 75).

Memory Bank

The 3 core features of autism include:
1. Qualitative Impairment in Social Interaction (2 symptoms)
2. Qualitative Impairment in Communication (1 symptoms)
3. Restricted Range of Activities (1 symptom)

Impairment in social interaction: Developmental considerations. Children with autism are often lacking in those behaviors that are evident in normal social interactions, such as maintaining eye contact, producing a range facial expressions, and use of appropriate nonverbal communication (gestures, postures, etc.). While younger children may have no interest in appropriate social contact with peers, at older age levels, even if interest for peer contact does increase, it is usually not possible due limited understanding of social conventions.

➡️ **RECURRENT THEMES** The study of autistic behaviors requires an understanding that normal development typically follows an orderly and predictable path (*Theme 1*) and that maladaptive behaviors represent deviations from the normal path (*Theme 2*). Awareness of the continuum of severity of maladaptive behaviors (*Theme 3*) provides increased ability to understand the degree of impairment and differences that exist between normal children and those with autism, high functioning autism, and AS.

Normal Development and Socialized Communication

In normally developing infants, **joint attention behavior** is evident at about 6 to 9 months and is the process whereby infants attempt to engage and share their attention with the caregiver. The process of **referential looking** (shifting gaze between caregiver and object of interest) is often followed by gestures (pointing, pulling) to actively engage the caregiver in the area of interest. Later, **social referencing** occurs, which involves looking to the caregiver for reinforcement and verification of behaviors or engagement in activities.

Studies have determined deficits in *joint attention behavior* in autistic populations (Mundy, 1995). Children with autism do not engage in social referencing, nor do they spontaneously seek to share their interests or attempt to engage others or share activities with others either by physical proximity or pointing, gesturing, etc. Studies of brain activation have demonstrated that there is limited or no activation of the **amygdale** (center for processing emotional memories and motivations) in individuals with autism during social cognitive tasks. Rather, parts of the brain are activated that are more typically associated with processing of objects, rather than people (Pierce, Muller, Ambrose, Allen, & Courchesne, 2001). This may help to explain why individuals with autism often involve others only as needed and as objects, without attention to social or emotional reciprocity and often are unaware of other's feelings or apparent distress. Unlike their peers with mental retardation, who often have strength in the area of imitative behavior, children with autism fail to engage in imitative play or social behaviors. When they do prescribe to routines, it is in a mechanical way that preempts any emotional engagement in the task.

In addition to information processing difficulties resulting from atypical brain-based activation, studies have also documented several deficits that can contribute to underlying difficulties in social reciprocity, including:

- lack of use of normal eye contact to establish reciprocal exchange (Volkmar & Mayes, 1990)
- lack of social smile (Dawson, Spencer, Galpert, & Watson, 1990)
- deficiencies in social imitation (Klinger & Dawson, 1996).

In early childhood, children appear socially aloof (Wing & Attwood, 1987). School-aged children with autism show little social interest in peers. In adolescence and adulthood, social interest increases; however, social skills are poorly developed, as is the understanding of social rules and reciprocal interchanges (Rutter, 1983).

Impaired language and communication. The degree of communication impairment can be wide ranging in individuals with autistic disorder. If speech is evident, it is often delayed and there is much difficulty initiating or sustaining a conversation. Impairment is evident in verbal and non-verbal communication. Speech often may have a stilted, robotic quality to it with a tendency to raise pitch at the end of a statement, as if asking a question. They can be highly imitative vocally, with tendencies to repeat what is said to them (**echolalia**), rather than provide an appropriate response. There are frequent pronoun reversals and use of literal rather than figurative interpretations. Also included within this category is the lack of spontaneous make-believe or socially initiated play. Children with **higher functioning autism (HFA)** compared to those with Asperger's syndrome (AS) tend to have a greater tendency to use inappropriate intonation in conversation (Gillberg, 1989), as well as increased use of echolalia and pronoun reversal.

Several researchers have investigated why difficulties exist in language development and imaginative play. In one study, it was found that even if children were capable of making gestures, they do not use gestures spontaneously to communicate (Prior & Werry, 1986). Studies have shown that children with autism develop **syntax** (understanding of sentence production) comparable to other children of the same mental age (Tager-Fusberg et al., 1990). However, difficulties become more evident as the tasks become more abstract. While vocabulary for concrete objects may be available, these children experience problems understanding **relational concepts**, such as *short–tall* and in comprehending the concept of **desire or intention** (*want, believe*). Children who have autism and are verbal will often talk at someone (monologue) rather than engage in a reciprocal verbal exchange, demonstrating significant problems with the **social pragmatics** of language (Volkmar, 1987). An inability to comprehend another's mental state (**theory of mind**) is likely a prominent factor in undermining their ability to engage in social communication (Perner, Wheeler, & Chronis, 1989).

Restricted, repetitive, behaviors, and interests. In children with autism, preoccupation can be with

- symmetry and sameness (doing the same thing at the same time)
- refusing to adapt to change in routine (inflexibility)
- preoccupation with nonfunctional routines

For example, a nonfunctional routine might be to continually line up objects, spin tops, or engage in some other form of **self-stimulation**. Often there is a preoccupation with parts of objects, as in spinning a wheel on a toy car, or opening and closing a box. In higher functioning autism, preoccupation can be a fixation with numbers, timetables, schedules, or other odd obsessions (recalling every name in a telephone book, or every television program in the TV

Guide). One of the most popular screen portrayals of this rigidity is seen in the movie *Rainman,* cited in the *Case in Point.*

Case in Point

One of the best portrayals of autism on the screen has been depicted by Dustin Hoffman, who played Charlie Babbit, an autistic adult locked into a structured world of rigid routines (in Charlie's case, watching Judge Wapner on television or reciting the "Who's on first" Abbot and Costello routine). Any attempts to alter Charlie's rigid schedule by his misguided brother resulted in Charlie being overwhelmed and extremely distraught.

Research investigations have suggested several possible reasons for the need for repetition and sameness. Children with autism have been described by parents as being either **hyper-responsive** (low threshold for sensory stimulation; easily overwhelmed by external input) or **hypo-sensitive** (high threshold for stimulation; unresponsive to external input). When their senses are overwhelmed, these children may find solace in hyper-focusing on a repetitive nonfunctional task (spinning wheels on a truck; lining up toys) or in the rigid adherence to the familiar. Deficits in organizing and filtering information may also contribute to information or **sensory overload** (Frith & Baron-Cohen, 1987).

In a recent investigation of the *restricted, repetitive behaviors, and interests* (RRBIs) domain, Szatmari and colleagues (2006) isolated two underlying factors or dimensions, **insistence on sameness (IS)** and **repetitive, sensory, and motor behaviors (RSMB)**. Factor analysis revealed three items which loaded on the *IS factor,* including:

- difficulties with change in personal routine
- difficulties with change in environment
- compulsions/rituals

Items that loaded on the *RSMB factor* included:

- unusual sensory interests
- hand and finger mannerisms
- rocking
- repetitive use of objects
- complex mannerisms

Furthermore, the *RSMB factor* was negatively correlated with level of adaptive functioning with those children who were most delayed demonstrating more repetitive motor behaviors. On the other hand, the *IS factor,* which was more closely related to lack of flexibility, was positively associated with higher intellectual functioning and rigidity in communication skills. The authors suggest that further investigation of these two factors might be helping in distinguishing autism and AS or HFA.

Intellectual Functioning: Autism and Mental Retardation

As part of the associated features of autism, the *DSM–IV–TR* (APA, 2000) notes that "in most cases there is an associated diagnosis of mental retardation which can range from mild to profound" (p. 71). As part of a major review of studies concerning autism, Fombonne (2003) reported findings from 20 studies that addressed intellectual functioning in children with autism. Although caution is advised due to the different rates and ranges for cognitive impairment used in the studies, Frombonne found that the median proportion of subjects without intellectual impairment in these studies was 30% (ranging from a low of 0% to a high of 60%). That would suggest that 70% of children with autism have at least a mild form of MR. Within cases falling within the range of mental retardation, mild-to-moderate mental retardation was reported in 30%, of the cases, while severe-to-profound mental retardation was found in 40% of cases. In another epidemiological look at preschool children, Chakrabarti & Fombonne (2001) found between 40% and 55% of children with autism also had MR.

In another review of the literature, Edelson (2006) reviewed 215 studies published between 1937 and 2003, of which 53 were empirical reports. Edelson cautions that many of the claims of high MR rates among those with autism come from nonempirical reports or those that cite research that is outdated (25 to 45 years ago). As a reply to Edelson's research paper, Freeman and Van Dyke (2006) provide further support for the notion of overidentifying children with autism as MR, citing the fact that children with autism are penalized on intellectual assessments due to their poor language skills and their deficits in motivation. Freeman and Van Dyke also emphasize that treatment may be compromised if cognitive capacity is underestimated.

High Functioning Autism (HFA)

Although the majority of those with autism will score below average on intellectual assessments, 20%–30% will score above an IQ score of 70 (Klin, Volkmar, & Sparrow, 2000). Children with autism, who score above an IQ of 70, are referred to as having *high functioning autism (HFA)*. Among those diagnosed with autism, males are 9 times more likely than females to be designated as HFA (Volkmar, Szatmari, & Sparrow, 1993).

Developmental Issues and Concerns

One of the most striking features of autism is the nature of developmental regression associated with the disorder. Rogers (2004) recently reviewed the literature concerning developmental regression in autism which has an onset in the 2nd or 3rd year of life, after an apparently normal beginning. While some believe that loss of skills is the pattern most typically associated with autism, in large population samples, only about 25% of children with autism experience this form of regression (Taylor et al., 2002). The number is higher (a third to a half) in smaller samples (Davidovich, Glick, Holtzman, Tirosh, & Safir, 2000; Goldberg & Osann, 2003).

Rogers and DiLalla (1990) outline *three different patterns of autism onset*, including:

1. Congenital group: atypical behaviors are present from birth
2. Failure to develop skills: early milestones followed by developmental plateau
3. Period of normal development, followed by regression and loss of previous skills

Depending on the population, it has been estimated that between 33% and 65% of those with autism fall within the congential group (Short & Schopler, 1988), while approximately one third to one half experience a regression of some degree. However, based on improved observational techniques, it is now thought that the social skills that autistic infants posses demonstrate social/developmental delays associated with autism and that approximately 15% of those with autism experience developmental regression after a "normal" period of development.

Prevalence

Based on the incidence of autism appearing in published studies, it has been demonstrated that autism has increased dramatically in the 1990s. In California, a reported increase in autism rose from 44/100,000 in 1980 to 208/100,000 in 1994 (Dales, Hammer, & Smith, 2001), while in Georgia, rates increased from 4/10,000 to 34/10,000 in 1996 (Yeargin-Allsopp et al., 2003). In the United Kingdom, the cumulative incidence reportedly rose from 7/10,000 in 1988 to 28/10,000 in 1993 and 33/10,000 in 1996 (Jick & Kaye, 2003; Kaye, Melero-Montes, & Jick, 2001). These rates are much higher than rates found in the *DSM–IV–TR* (APA, 2000) which suggests prevalence rates as low as 5 cases per 10,000 or as high as 20–25 per 10,000.

It is estimated that males receive a diagnosis of autism 4 to 5 times more frequently than females, although females who do have the disorder are likely to be more severe and exhibit comorbid mental retardation (*DSM–IV–TR*; APA, 2000, p. 73).

Important Distinction

Because of the dramatic increase in reports of autism, there has been significant controversy and debate regarding whether autism can be caused by a childhood vaccine (particularly the **MMR vaccine**: measles/mumps/rubella), or a mercury-containing compound **thimerosal** used as a preservative in some childhood vaccines since 1930. A recent report published by the Institute of Medicine (IOM) summarized in *Infection Control Today* (5, 2004) revealed results of the IOM review of 19 studies on autism and vaccines. The IOM panel found: 1. No evidence of thimerosal causing autism; 2. no evidence that the MMR vaccine causes autism; and 3. no support for the theory that vaccines may trigger an immune response that damages the brain. In their analysis, Jick and Kaye (2003) found no relationship between immunizations or vaccines and incidence. The authors suggest that increased incidence of autism is a reflection of improved diagnostic practices in the identification of autistic disorder.

Etiology: The Biological Model

Genetics, Brain Structure, and Brain Function. Nicholson and Szatmari (2003) reviewed the findings of genetic and brain-imaging studies of autism for the past 15 years. (The following information is reported in Nicholson and Szatmari, 2003, unless otherwise noted.) Current prevalence rates suggest that autism occurs in approximately 1 in 300 children. Genetic information has revealed that the risk to siblings of children with autism is approximately 3% to 6%, which is about 50 to 100 times greater than risk appearing in the population at large. Nicholson and Szatmari suggest that autism is "the most heritable psychiatric disorder" (p. 527).

The neurotransmitter serotonin has been implicated. However, unlike other disorders which were linked to a low level of serotonin (depression, obsessive-compulsive disorder), studies have demonstrated elevated levels of **serotonin** in approximately 25% of those with autistic disorder (Klinger & Dawson, 1996). At present, in addition to elevated levels of peripheral **serotonin** (**5-HT**), there is also the possibility that GABA genes associated with chromosome 15 might also be implicated. Curran et al. (2006) conducted a study involving 148 families using a varied and heterogeneous sample with respect to PDD disorders (55% met criteria for autism; 45% met criteria for atypical autism, AS, or other PDD). Results indicated a genetic association with GABARB3, despite the wide range of PDD subjects. The researchers suggest that these results support previous findings that "genetic liability to autism confers a risk for a broader range of autistic-like impairments" (p. 712).

Other factors that have been reported in the research include increased head circumference (exaggerated brain volume), likely associated with accelerated brain growth in early development. Yet, despite the increased size of the brain, the **corpus callosum**, which allows lateralization of function, is reduced in the brains of those with autism, suggesting important considerations for understanding impaired language functioning in this population. Other important areas of the brain that seem to be compromised in autism are the areas of the **amygdale** (emotion) and the **fusiform gyrus** (**face processing**). Functional MRI studies have noted limited or no activation of the amygdale in individuals with autism during social cognitive tasks, with compensatory activation of parts of the brain that are more typically associated with processing objects.

Assessment

The assessment of children with autism can be a complex and on-going process that will likely involve an investigation of sensory and medical concerns prior to the administration of other more formal assessment instruments. Children with autism, HFA, and AS can represent a complex challenge to even the most experienced practitioners and clinicians. Specific assessment parameters for ASD have been generated by the American Academy of Neurology (Filipek et al., 2000) and the American Academy of Child and Adolescent Psychiatry (Volkmar, Cook, Pomeroy, Realmuto, & Tanguay, 1999). Two levels of screening have been recommended:

- Level I, a general developmental screening most likely conducted by a pediatrician
- Level II, a comprehensive and in-depth assessment conducted by a clinician familiar with PDD for children identified at Level I

In their review of the evidence-based criteria for the assessment of children with ASD, Ozonoff, Goodlin-Jones, and Solomon (2005) outline the major issues and parameters that should be part of the evaluation process. (The following description is based on the article by Ozonoff et al., 2005, unless otherwise stated.) Ozonoff and colleagues highlight three important features necessary to an appropriate assessment of individuals with ASD:

1. Since autism is a lifelong disorder, it is understandable that the form and nature of symptoms will change with age, necessitating the integration of a developmental perspective into the on-going evaluation and monitoring.
2. Another major consideration is the need to include multiple informants, since an individual's behaviors may be viewed quite differently by different individuals in different situations (e.g., parent vs. teacher; home vs. school; playground vs. classroom; special classroom vs. regular classroom).
3. Finally, it is essential to incorporate individuals from multiple disciplines in the assessment process (speech pathology, psychologists, psychiatrists, educators, etc.).

The K–3 Paradigm is an important reminder of the need to integrate knowledge from development, contexts of influence, and different theoretical perspectives in order to appreciate the complex nature of children's disorders. Ozonoff et al. (2005) have captured the essence of this integration in their guidelines for the assessment of autism, as outlined above.

The assessment of autism or AS has benefited from a number of interviews, observational schedules, and rating systems that have been developed in recent years. A summary of some of the most commonly used instruments is presented in Table 15.2.

Table 15.2 Some Assessment Instruments for Autistic Spectrum Disorders

Instrument/Age Level	Assessment	Measures
Gilliam Autism Rating Scale (**GARS**; Gilliam, 1995): 3 years through 22	Behavior Rating Scale	Autism Quotient, 4 scales: Stereotyped behaviors, social interaction, communication, and developmental disturbance
Childhood Autism Rating Scale (**CARS**; Schopler, Reichler, & Renner, 1988): 2+ years	Behavior Rating Scale	Classifies autistic symptoms into mild-moderate-severe range
Asperger Syndrome Diagnostic Scale (**ASDS**; Myles, Bock & Simpson, 2001): 5 through 18 years	Behavior Rating Scale	Asperger Quotient, 5 scales: Cognitive, maladaptive, language, social, and sensorimotor
Gilliam Asperger's Disorder Scale (**GADS**; Gilliam, 2001): 3 through 22 years	Behavior Rating Scale	Four scales: social interaction, restricted patterns of behavior, cognitive patterns, pragmatic skills
Autism Diagnostic Interview—Revised (**ADI–R**; Rutter, LeCouteur, & Lord, 2003): 18 months to adult	Parent Interview	Semistructured interview format. Long Version (3 hours); Short Version (90 minutes)
Autism Diagnostic Observation Schedule (**ADOS**; Lord, Rutter, Di-Lavore, & Risi, 2002): 2 years to adult	Interactive Assessment	Play, interaction, and social communication

The *Childhood Autism Rating Scale* (*CARS*; Schopler et al., 1988) is one of the most commonly used instruments by clinicians in the field due to its ease of administration, while school psychologists are most likely to use the *Gilliam Autism Rating Scale* (*GARS*; Gilliam, 1995) and the *Gilliam Asperger's Disorder Scale* (*GADS*; Gilliam, 2001) since both scales have available forms for teachers, as well, as parents. The *Autism Diagnostic Interview—Revised* (*ADI–R*; Rutter, LeCouteur & Lord, 2003) and the *Autism Diagnostic Observation Schedule* (*ADOS*; Lord et al., 2002) are instruments which have been used increasingly in research; however, their administration and scoring is complex and time consuming. In addition to instruments specific to autism, given the nature of the disorder, a comprehensive psychological assessment would also include measures of intelligence and cognitive functioning, adaptive behavior, and academic achievement.

Treatment and Intervention

Ozonoff and colleagues (2005) address the important contribution that assessment instruments should provide in the evaluation of treatment effectiveness. However, the measurement of behavior change can be problematic for several reasons, including lack of agreement on what constitutes clinical significance and what behaviors are most in need of change. However, few would take issue with those intervention goals which targeted such areas as adaptive behavior, comorbid symptoms, quality of life, and family functioning (Wolery & Garfinkle, 2002).

Given the range of individual differences in the presentation of symptoms among individuals with **autistic spectrum disorder** (**ASD**), the prospects concerning treatment and intervention can present a confusing array of choices for parents who may diligently search the internet with little guidance regarding quality control. To this end, it has been emphasized that professionals should counsel parents in their independent search for treatments (Jacobson, 2000).

In their review of programs that have been developed for individuals with autistic spectrum disorders (ASD), Hurth, Shaw, Izeman, Whaley, and Rogers (1999) report a number of features identified as priorities in intervention goals, including:

- intervene as early as possible
- need for intensive interventions
- inclusion of parent training components
- focus on enhancing social and communication skills
- incorporate individual goals in systematic instruction
- provide significant opportunities for generalizing skills across situations

Rogers (1998) identified 8 comprehensive programs that obtained positive and empirically supported outcomes. The programs were intensive (involving anywhere from 15 to 40 hours a week), focused on early intervention (5 years or younger), and used behavioral methods. Significant gains were noted in decreased symptoms of autism, enhanced language skills, achievement of developmental goals, and social relations.

Approximately half of the children who participated in programs that were empirically sound and conformed to the parameters outlined above were able to bypass special education and enroll in the regular elementary school classroom (Dawson & Osterling, 1996). In their research review, Dawson and Osterling suggested several characteristics common to successful programs, including:

- targeting specific deficits (attention, compliance, appropriate play)
- use of a highly structured and predictable program with low pupil-to-staff ratio
- integration of programs across situations (clinic, home, school)
- engagement of parents as cotherapists
- careful monitoring of transitions between programs

Intensity of intervention is a particularly salient feature to program success (Hurth et al., 1999). Two programs that have demonstrated successful outcomes for children with ASD are outlined below.

Lovaas and the UCLA ABA program.   Ivar Lovaas (1987) developed his program for children with ASD modeled on principles of **applied behavioral analysis (ABA)**. The program was intensive (3 year duration; 40 hours a week), pervasive (home and clinic), and relied heavily upon behavioral methods of operant conditioning, imitation, and reinforcement. The average age on entrance to the program was approximately 2.5 years of age, and the program spanned 3 years of intense intervention:

1. *Year One*: Intense focus on appropriate behavior (reducing disruptive behavior and increasing compliance and imitation)
2. *Year Two*: Focus on language training (increased use of appropriate expressive and receptive responses and social play)
3. *Year Three:* Opportunities for fine-tuning skills to assist with integration into the school system (emotional expression; pre-academic skills, etc.)

At 7 years of age, outcomes for the 19 children who participated in the intensive intervention were compared to results obtained for two other groups of children with autism: less intensive group (19 children who received 10 hours of ABA per week, plus regular special education programs) and a control group (21 children who were not involved in the program and received only special education services). Almost half (47%) of the children in the intensive group increased their IQ scores an average of 37 points (placing them in the average range) and were promoted to the regular second grade. Unfortunately, children who received less intensive services, or only special education, demonstrated minimal gains overall. A follow up 6 years later revealed that gains made were maintained and children were successful in the normal education stream.

Schopler and the treatment and education for autistic and related communication handicapped children: TEACCH program. Another program which has gained increasing popularity is the **TEACCH program** (Schopler, 1994), a structured teaching system that focuses on the person with autism and the development of a program around the person's skills, interests, and needs. The program differs from the ABA approach in that the program is based on the idea that the environment should be adapted to the individual with autism, rather than trying to fit the child to the environment. The program focuses on the individual, and instead of focusing on a specific behavior, the focus is on teaching children to communicate their needs. Children who throw tantrums would be seen as frustrated because they cannot make their needs known to others. The focus would then be on teaching the child how to signal frustration through communication skills.

The child's learning abilities are assessed using the Psycho Educational Profile (PEP) and teaching strategies are mapped to enhance needed communication skills, social skills, and coping skills. The program focuses on incorporating visual supports into structured classroom activities (e.g., visual schedules, etc.) to increase understanding. The underlying premise is that children are motivated to learn language as **intentional communication**, in a means–end association. For example, a child will be motivated to learn the words *candy* or *eat*, if the end result is that the child will be able to obtain the candy from the dish. In this way, it is felt that learning has a practical and contextual basis and becomes better integrated into the child's daily repertoire as a result.

Future treatment initiatives. In their paper concerning the challenges that exist in evaluating interventions for individuals with ASD, Lord and colleagues (2005) review the focus of presentations and discussions that took place at the meeting sponsored by the National Institutes of Health in 2002. One important point that was discussed was the fact that most group-design research concerning ASD has involved comprehensive curricula with the end result that it has been difficult to identify specific components of these programs. Another important point of discussion was that although the majority of treatments for ASD involve similar methods, such as behavioral techniques (such as Lovaas, 1987), attention to developmental sequences and communication intent (TEACCH), the variation between programs is often in the content, fidelity, and intensity with which the programs are delivered. The authors conclude their paper with a number of broad recommendations for future research (e.g., study designs that could be pooled for greater documentation, improved measurement of parent–child interactions, inclusion of randomized clinical trials). Significant areas of "uncharted territory" are also highlighted, and include closer attention to documenting the number of hours of intervention required to produce significant change, and evaluations that compare the relative effectiveness of common treatments, such as the TEACCH program, with models based on Applied Behavioral Analysis ABA, in enhancing social and cognitive development (Lord et al., 2005, p. 703).

Asperger's Disorder/Asperger's Syndrome

Description and Associated Features
Compared to children with autistic disorder, individuals with Asperger's syndrome (AS) do not demonstrate language delays. In fact, the *DSM–IV–TR* (APA, 2000) criteria specifically state that there can be no significant language delay, either in general language acquisition or

communication. Children with AS would be expected to have achieved normal language developmental milestones, using single words by 2 years of age and producing phrases by 3 years of age. Although individuals with autism and AS share difficulties in social interaction and emotional relatedness, individuals with AS present with "fewer symptoms and have a different presentation" (Volkmar et al., 1994, p. 1365). Similarly, although they share features of an unusual or restricted pattern of interests and preoccupation, the way these symptoms are manifested in those with autism and AS differ qualitatively. While those with AS may be focused on a particular topic of interest (e.g., maps, dinosaurs), those with autism may be preoccupied with a part of an object (e.g., spinning a wheel on a car). The *DSM–IV–TR* (APA, 2000) criteria for AS requires the following core features.

Qualitative impairment in social interaction.   Criterion A requires that *2* of 4 items be present. The 4 items are identical to those outlined for autism:

- impairment in nonverbal behaviors
- failure to develop appropriate peer relationships
- lack of spontaneous sharing
- lack of social reciprocity

In children with AS, verbal skills are often much better developed than their autistic peers. Lack of social reciprocity, however, often results in social conversations becoming a "one way communication system," as these children can talk endlessly about a specific preoccupation, in monologue, without any interest in, or attention to, their audience's reaction. As noted by Van Krevelen (1971), while children with autism will disregard others entirely, children with AS may approach others, especially as they get older; however, they will do so in odd or eccentric ways.

Children with AS are more likely than their autistic peers to want to establish peer friendships as they become older; however, they have few social skills and little understanding of the process involved. Their lack of social skills often may be interpreted as insensitivity to the feelings of others, which in turn will only add to the frustration of not being accepted by peers. While those with HFA may appear more withdrawn and less interested in others, individuals with AS are often painfully aware of their lack of social success (Klin & Volkmar, 1997).

Important Comparison

Rourke and colleagues (2002) note that children with AS share many symptoms of children with nonverbal learning disabilities (NLD), especially in their very limited understanding of the use of nonverbal communication and limited ability to read and use nonverbal cues which often leads to difficulties maintaining social relationships. Visual–spatial deficits are also a common bond between these two disorders.

Restricted, repetitive, and stereotyped patterns of behavior or interests.   Criterion B requires at least 1 symptom from a list of 4 items. The items are also identical to those cited for autism:

- preoccupation with a restricted range of focus
- inflexible adherence to nonfunctional routines
- stereotyped and repetitive motor movements
- preoccupation with parts of objects

From this category, while individuals with autism would be most likely to engage in object manipulation, visual–spatial abilities, and possess **"savant skills,"** children with AS are more likely to accumulate a wealth of information on a particular topic or area of interest (Klin & Volkmar, 1997).

Savant Skills

In the movie *Rainman*, the main character Charlie Babbit suffers from autism, albeit the HFA type. Despite his ability to mentally calculate square roots of numbers without effort, he has no idea of the value of money. Savant skills have sometimes been referred to as *"islands of intelligence"* because they are unrelated to other areas of functioning. Another example of savant skills is the ability to name the day of the week for any day selected at random, e.g., able to know that Friday was the 1st of the month in March and November of 1940, yet be unable to figure out the amount of change you would get back if you bought a shirt for $4 with a $10 bill.

Some individuals with AS can amass a wealth of information in specific areas due to an obsessive preoccupation with such topics as naming capitals of the world; identifying of flags of the world; programming computers; studying dinosaurs, the weather, etc. Although normally children will pursue areas of specific interest developmentally, (e.g., collecting hockey cards, baseball cards, stamps, coins, etc), children with AS often are more narrow in their interests and will amass enormous amounts of information without understanding the broader concepts that may be involved (Klin & Volkmar, 1997).

Case in Point

The school psychologist was attempting to obtain an IQ score for an unmotivated and uncooperative 9 year old, referred for very odd social behaviors and emotional outbursts. One of the odd preoccupations noted about this child was that he knew every flag and every capital city for every country in the world. Eventually, the psychologist was able to obtain an IQ score for the child by bringing a world globe into the examining room and using the globe as a reinforcer, for every question on the IQ test responded to by the child, the psychologist would spin the globe, point to a country, and say "Name that capital."

While individuals with autism have a greater tendency to engage in repetitive motor movements (e.g., hand flapping), and indicate relative strengths in visual motor functioning, individuals with AS are more likely to demonstrate atypical motor development by their clumsy or awkward motor movements. Clinical observation or parental reports may indicate poor coordination, awkward or odd gait, and other deficits in visual motor function (Gillberg, 1990).

Other *DSM* criteria. In addition to satisfying the criteria noted above, a diagnosis of AS also requires:

- significant dysfunction (cause significant impairment in employment/school)
- no significant language delay
- no clinically significant delay in cognitive or adaptive functioning
- ruling out other PDD or schizophrenia

Other associated features.   Onset of AS may be diagnosed later than that of autism, due to the lack of significant delays in language acquisition, cognitive development or adaptive skills. Although autism, even HFA, must have onset prior to 3 years, the *DSM–IV–TR* (APA, 2000) does not specify an age of onset for AS. There are two common characteristics that are often evident in the early development of children with AS, which may also be helpful in distinguishing children with AS from those with autism. There can be preoccupation with numbers and letters. As a result, the child may be **hyperlexic** and able to decode words with ease at a very young age. Second, young children with AS often establish attachments to parents, siblings, and other family members. However, they do not generalize these attachments to peers and can often be unpredictable in social situations in their attempts to initiate social contact, by either approaching too closely (staring into their eyes, hugging inappropriately) or screaming at the child.

Although children with AS will have access to language, often they are lacking in the subtle nuances of the language and in the reciprocity involved in social communication. Older children with AS may carry on conversations much like a monologue with very little interest in the listener's response. Cognitively, children with AS possess intellectual functioning within the normative range, compared to other children with PDD who often have some degree of mental retardation.

Compared to children with autism, even HFA, children with AS were less likely to use echolalia, but were inclined to use more repetitive speech. Parents also described these children as "highly verbal," tending to go into long pedantic conversations, using idiosyncratic speech and unusual voice tone (Eisenmajer et al., 1996). Although children with AS have a better developed vocabulary than those with HFA, they share problems in areas of pragmatics, comprehension, and intonation with their higher functioning autistic peers (Ramberg, Ehlers, Nyden, Johansson & Gillberg, 1996). Despite language differences noted between children with higher functioning autism and those with AS concerning language, studies suggest that by the time these children are in middle school, there language skills will look far more similar (Ghaziuddin & Gerstein, 1996).

Prevalence

Although the *DSM–IV–TR* (APA, 2000) does not report a prevalence rate for AS, Fombonne (2003) suggests that the ratio of autism to AS can be estimated to be 4 to 1, based on a review of epidemiological surveys. If so, it would mean that "the rate for AS disorder would be one fourth that of autism" (p. 373). In another study, Bertrand and colleagues (2001) included AS and PDDNOS in a category separate from autism and found that 4.0 cases per 1,000 children met full criteria for autism, compared with 2.7 cases per 1,000 for the combined category (PDDNOS and AS). AS is significantly more prevalent in males than females and the diagnosis is made at least 5 times more frequently in males than females (*DSM–IV–TR*; APA, 2000, p. 82).

AS and comorbid disorders.   Children with AS disorder often demonstrate symptoms of ADHD and a variety of anxiety disorders. Szatmari (1991) notes that elective mutism (now termed **selective mutism**) may be evident in the preschool years, and may later develop into specific phobias and generalized anxiety.

Selective Mutism

The *DSM–IV–TR* (APA, 2000) defines selective mutism as a failure to speak in specific social situations (such as school) despite speaking in other situations (such as home). Often associated with some form of anxiety, children will not speak in selective situations (e.g., to strangers or in a novel environment). The onset is usually prior to 5 years and often dissipates within a few years.

Szatmari (1991) also notes that in adolescence the desire to be part of the "teen" group is accompanied by overwhelming stress because their lack of social awareness and poorly developed social skills result in an inability to develop social relationships and subsequent rejection by peers. As a result, the adolescent may become depressed and require antidepressant medication.

There is increasing evidence that individuals with AS demonstrate a number of comorbid disorders. In one study, as many as 20% of those with AS demonstrated clinical levels of depression and anxiety (Kim, Szatmari, Bryson, Streiner, & Wilson, 2000). Other comorbid associations that commonly occur with AS include learning disabilities and academic problems, resulting from difficulties making inferences and tendencies to inappropriately apply literal translations. On a more positive note, one study comparing executive function in children with AS disorder to those with ADHD found that the profile and developmental course were unique to AS. As children with AS mature, problems with executive functions subside, possibly due to applied educational interventions or individual coping strategies (Happe, Booth, Charlton, & Hughes, 2006)

Differential Diagnosis
In addition to issues and concerns already discussed regarding a diagnosis of AS relative to other PDD, such as autism and HFA, there are also concerns noted due to similarities with other childhood disorders, namely, *nonverbal learning disability (NLD), developmental right hemisphere syndrome (DRHS),* and *semantic-pragmatic disorder*. For an in-depth discussion of NLD and DRHS, the reader is referred to chapter 11. It has been suggested that similarities between AS and NLD (DRHS) might be an important way of distinguishing AS **(right hemisphere dysfunction)** from autism, which typically has been linked to a **left hemisphere dysfunction** (Klin & Volkmar, 1997).

Recall and Rewind

Despite obvious strengths in the verbal areas, children with NLD/ DRHS demonstrate poor social awareness, poor visual–motor performance, and lack of understanding of the subtle nuances of language, such as idioms and humor. Inability to process social/emotional information has been linked to deficits in the right hemisphere.

The term **semantic–pragmatic disorder** was initiated by Rapin and Allen (1983) to describe a language disorder concerning the semantic and pragmatic aspects of language and communication. Although articulation skills, and the formal and structural (e.g., syntax) aspects of language remain intact, children with the disorder suffer from poor ability to engage in conversation and demonstrate an inappropriate use of language (stereotyped utterances, incessant questioning). Children who have semantic–pragmatic disorder share many similarities of language dysfunction and behaviors with their AS peers (Bishop, 1989, 1995). So much so that Bishop (1989) suggested placing autism, Asperger syndrome, and semantic-pragmatic syndrome on a 2-dimensional continuum from abnormal to normal behaviors, with meaningful verbal communication on the horizontal axis and interests and social relationships on the vertical axis. The resulting profile (envisioned by three intersecting circles) reflects semantic-pragmatic syndrome with a marked and isolated deficit in the verbal communication sphere with preserved social abilities and an absence of marked restricted interests; an opposite profile for AS (deficits in the social interaction area, restricted interests, and a mildly atypical communication); and autism closest to the abnormal/abnormal axis for both areas with compromises and deficits in both areas.

Etiology: The Biological Model

Genetics, brain structure, and brain function. Although the cause of autism is poorly understood, information concerning the cause of AS is even less known. There are a number of reasons why this is the case, including the fact that although AS was first reported in 1944, official criteria did not enter the *DSM* until the 4th edition in 1994. Another reason is that many of the studies conducted have included a wide range of subjects including those with autism, HFA, and AS in their investigations. Two recent studies that have focused specifically on AS populations can provide insight into the specificity of cause, although both studies involved the use of adults with AS and may not apply to atypical activity in the brains of children.

Gaigg and Bowler (2007) conducted a study of fear conditioning in a population of 15 adults with AS relative to typical peers. Results revealed that individuals with AS demonstrated an attenuated fear response and although they were able to acquire the fear response (fear acquisition), they demonstrated an impaired ability to discriminate between nonconditioned and conditioned stimuli (fear discrimination). As a result Gaigg and Bowler (2007) suggest that atypical amygdale function, especially poor connectivity with associated cortical areas may be implicated in atypical responses to emotional stimuli in individuals with AS.

In another study, Murphy et al. (2006) found that the cortical 5-HT$_{2A}$ receptors were significantly reduced in adults with AS. The serotonergic (5-HT) system is responsible for "modulating social behavior, amygdale response to facial emotion, and repetitive behaviors" (p. 934). Furthermore, results revealed that reduced 5-HT$_{2A}$ receptors in the cingulate, frontal, and temporal cortex was associated with qualitative abnormalities in reciprocal social interaction. Due to differences in brain anatomy found in individuals with AS (abnormal neuronal integrity in the frontal region), it was inconclusive whether the differences in serotonergic system activity and/or anatomy may influence brain development in AS.

Treatment

Impairment in social interaction impacts social friendships through a lack of understanding of emotion and the nuances of social exchange. Lindner and Rosen (2006) found that children with AS had more difficulty decoding emotions in all forms presented in the study, including static pictures, dynamic expressions, and tone of voice, compared to normal controls. The authors reasoned that overreliance on verbal content can inhibit the ability to focus on facial expressions and the tone used in conversation. Integrating these two components into a direct instructional intervention might help train those with Asperger's to obtain increased levels of social awareness. Sansosti and Powell-Smith (2006) investigated the use of social stories (brief, individualized stories about a social situation to teach new prosocial behaviors) in a small sample of school-aged children. Although the intervention met with marked improvements in social behavior for two of the three children, behaviors were not maintained over time. However, the authors recommend further research into the effectiveness of this intervention which can readily be integrated into the child's educational program.

One important consideration in the use of stories as an intervention technique is how individuals with autism process linguistic content. Functional MRI studies of brain activation in individuals with and without autism reveal that those with autism tend to think in pictures, activating the parts of the brain that use mental imagery regardless of sentence content and are more reliant on visualization to support their language comprehension (Kana, Keller, Cherkassky, Minshew, & Just, 2006). Therefore, the use of highly visual supports to aid in the recall and consolidation of story information may be highly relevant to increased success over time.

Autistic Disorder and Asperger's Syndrome: Two Disorders or One?

Historical Background: Issues and Controversies

Kanner first documented accounts of autism in 1943, when he described seemingly incompatible and atypical characteristics shared in a number of case studies. On one hand, the children seemed noncommunicative, aloof, and engaged in nonproductive and meaningless activity (obsessive need for sameness, inability to relate to people, failure to communicate). Yet on the other hand, the children demonstrated what Kanner felt was good cognitive potential demonstrated in their remarkable rote memory and performance on the Seguin form board test. Kanner labeled the syndrome **infantile autism**. For the next 30 years, controversy and confusion surrounded how to best conceptualize these atypical children. Similar to the historical accounts of other childhood disorders, a variety of different diagnostic labels have been used over the course of time to refer to this population who demonstrate atypical and often times puzzling features, including **infantile autism, childhood psychosis,** and **childhood schizophrenia** (Rutter, 1978).

In 1944, one year after Kanner published his report on what is now known as autism, Hans Asperger, an Austrian pediatrician, described a syndrome which he called **autistic psychopathy** to describe a cluster of symptoms, involving stereotypical speech, clumsiness, impaired social skills, and an obsession with sameness. Asperger's account remained relatively unheard of until Wing (1981) and later Szatmari (1989) published papers about AS. Since that time, there has been considerable debate regarding whether AS and autism (particularly high functioning autism) are distinct entities, or whether AS is a subcategory of autism. Although autism has been recognized by both the *DSM–IV–TR* (APA, 2000) and the ICD–10 (WHO, 1993) for quite some time, AS is a relatively new diagnostic category, having only recently been added to both the *DSM* (1994) and ICD–10 (1993).

Autism and AS share a number of common features (qualitative social impairment, restricted range of activities/interests), yet, there is a significant difference in the criteria that distinguish these two disorders. Recall that, in order to be diagnosed with autism, the individual must have language delay and/or qualitative impairment in language, while a diagnosis of AS requires no significant language delay. According to the *DSM–IV–TR* (APA, 2000), AS is not diagnosed if the criteria are met for autistic disorder (p. 74). However, several studies do not support the current diagnostic criteria.

Important Question: Do individuals with AS and autism represent two distinct disorders or do they represent more or less severe forms of the same disorder along the autistic spectrum?

This question has been at the core of the controversy surrounding the autism/AS debate. It has been argued that AS represents a less severe type of autism (Schopler, 1985). On the other hand, it has been recommended that separate categories be retained, specifically due to the language-based differences noted in the criteria (Howlin, 1987; Wing, 1981).

Researchers have found children who meet the criteria for AS, but who also encounter language problems (Eisenmajet et al., 1996, Prior et al., 1998), while others have found autistic children who do not demonstrate significant language delay (Eisenmajer et al., 1996; Miller & Ozonoff, 2000). Prevalence rates for the two disorders also seem to differ. Based on a review of epidemiological surveys, Fombonne's (2003) suggests that the ratio of autism to AS can be estimated to be 4 to 1. In other words, "the rate for AS disorder would be one fourth that of autism" (p. 373).

The most recent prevalence rates released by the Center for Disease Control (CDC, Fact Sheet, February 2007) are based on results from six communities assessed as part of the autism spectrum disorder (ASD) surveillance project (data collected in 2000 and 2002). All children in the studies were 8 years of age. Included in the study were children with autistic disorder, PDDNOS (including atypical autism), and Asperger's disorder. Results revealed that 6.7 children out of 1,000 had ASD in 2000, and an average of 6.6 out of 1,000 had ASD in the 2002 study. Although the numbers don't represent a national estimate, the numbers do point to an increase in rates in the areas surveyed compared to earlier estimates. Whether these numbers represent actual increases or increased awareness of the disorder remains to be seen.

A Comparison of High Functioning Autism (HFA) and AS

High Functioning Autism (HFA)

Recall and Rewind

Children with autism who score above an IQ of 70 are referred to as having *high functioning autism (HFA)*. Within the diagnosis of autism, males are 9 times more likely than females to be labeled as HFA (Volkmar, Szatmari, & Sparrow, 1993).

There is a wide range in functioning among those diagnosed with autism, resulting in varied patterns of abilities depending on the level of severity and the nature of the disorder. However, among those with HFA, patterns of behaviors and cognitive abilities and disabilities have been found. For example, although mechanical language skills (word knowledge, grammar) may evidence delayed development, with time, these skills become more normalized and ultimately are reported to be within the average range (Klin, Volkmar, Sparrow, Cicchetti, & Rourke, 1995). However, while those with HFA may produce verbose conversations, these monologues are often one-sided, perseverative in nature, and speech may evidence problems in articulation (Klin et al., 1995). Their understanding of language is at a literal or concrete level and is lacking in an awareness of language subtleties (humor, idioms) or *social pragmatics*. Despite having intact skills in areas of sensory-perception (Minshew & Rattan, 1992), rote verbal memory (Klin et al., 1995) visual-spatial skills and basic attention (Minshew, Goldstein, & Siegel, 1997), they experience difficulty with the nonverbal aspects of communication, such as use of eye contact and gesture.

Academically, children with HFA do not have specific problems with core academic subjects (reading, spelling, arithmetic), although they may experience problems as learning becomes more complex (Minshew, Goldstein, Taylor, & Siegel, 1994). Individuals with HFA encounter significant problems when they are required to make flexible adjustments to their surroundings or when structure is limited. For example, situations such as the following could cause someone with HFA to become readily overwhelmed and distraught:

- tasks are not accompanied by a specific set of rules
- they are forced to adapt to an unpredictable change in their environment

- they are in a situation where they have to improvise or problem solve on their own (Ciesielski & Harris, 1997)

Comparison of HFA and AS

Recently, Macintosh and Dissanayake (2004) reviewed all relevant studies on AS and autism (until 2002) in an attempt to resolve the controversy as to whether autism and AS should be considered distinct diagnostic categories, or whether both disorders should be considered along the same autistic spectrum. The authors were especially interested in studies that compared individuals diagnosed as AS with individuals diagnosed with HFA. The authors focus their comparison on areas of language development and cognitive functioning.

Language development. In their review, Macintosh and Dissanayake (2004) found that although the HFA demonstrated later language onset, and greater communication dysfunction in preschool, with increasing age (elementary school), the two groups of children became increasingly similar (Eisenmajer et al., 1996). Language patterns did differ, however, with the HFA group demonstrating more atypical speech patterns (echolalia, noun reversals, atypical gestures), while the AS group tended to have more verbal rituals, and asked odd questions. However, by adolescence, the only distinguishing feature between these two groups was the tendencies for teens with AS disorder to engage in more pedantic dialogues (Howlin, 2003).

However, other studies have noted subtle differences in linguistic style between those with AS and those with HFA. Language skills in those with AS seem superior to those with HFA and while those with AS will engage others in conversation, those with HFA are much less likely to do so (Siegel, 1998).

Cognitive and neuropsychological functioning. Studies have also investigated cognitive patterns on intellectual test scores and results are mixed. Some studies have found children with AS have strengths in Verbal IQ, while those with HFA have strengths in Performance IQ (Ehlers et al., 1997; Klin et al., 1995). Other studies have supported findings of strengths for children with AS in the Verbal and Full Scale IQ, but have failed to substantiate any differences between the two groups on Performance IQ (Gilchrist et al., 2001; Iwanaga, Kawasaki, & Tsuchida, 2000). Other studies have investigated capabilities for **Theory of Mind** in children with autism and AS. Theory of Mind is the study of an individual's ability to comprehend that others have a "mental set" or belief system which may influence their actions. An example of a theory of mind scenario is presented in the Case in Point.

Case in Point

The examiner provides a child with the following scenario: John is very happy with his new box of crayons. When John leaves the room, I take the crayons out of his crayon box and put bubble gum in the box instead. When John comes back into the room what will he say is in the crayon box?

When faced with the scenario presented above, studies have shown that those with autism (even HFA) have significantly more difficulty with predicting the correct response than normal children or children with AS (Ozonoff, Rogers, & Pennington, 1991). As a result, children with HFA would respond to the above scenario by saying that John would think the crayon box contained bubble gum, because that is what they know. However, it has been suggested that children with AS perform better on theory of the mind tasks due to their verbal capacity which is much higher than those with autistic disorder (Volkmar & Klin, 2000).

Klin and Volkmar (1997) suggest that differential diagnosis between AS and HFA may be increased through consideration of:

- onset (AS is usually later and with more positive outcome than HFA)
- severity (deficits in social skills, communication, and motor mannerisms are usually less severe in AS)
- preoccupation of interest is usually more prominent in AS than HFA

Similarly, Rourke and colleagues (2002) address a number of similarities that exist between AS, HFA, and nonverbal learning disabilities (NLD), including "strengths in simple verbal and auditory memory, and word reading, weaknesses in social interaction, complex reasoning and in both the use and comprehension of nonverbal communication" (p. 329). However, Rourke and colleagues suggest that there are important differences as well, especially neuropsychological differences that have surfaced when comparing profiles of those with HFA, AS, and NLD. In one study, while 18 out of 22 children with AS also met criteria for NLD, only 1 out of 19 with HFA met criteria for NLD (Klin et al., 1995). Results have increasingly pointed to "shared difficulties between AS and NLD in areas of tactile and visual perception, visual–spatial organization and psychomotor coordination" in contrast to HFA who demonstrate none of the above deficits in a consistent manner. As a result, Rourke and colleagues have concluded that despite some similarities, HFA and AS should remain distinct disorders (Rourke et al., 2002, p. 329). Furthermore, Rourke and colleagues suggest that there seems to be greater left than right hemisphere dysfunction in HFA compared to NLD or AS.

Comparative Evaluation of Autism (HFA) and AS: A Summation

Based on the findings of their very extensive review, Macintosh and Dissanayake (2004) suggest that there is neither sufficient evidence of either "qualitatively different or unique patterns of key behaviors, symptoms, developmental course or etiology to support the claim that these are distinct diagnostic entities," nor is there "reliable evidence of an absence of differences...required to support the notion that HFA and AS are manifestations of the same syndrome" (p. 431). However, the authors caution that methodological problems and different criteria for initial group selection variables made comparisons between studies difficult. Yet, given the fact that differences noted between these two groups at early ages tended to dissipate with increasing age, the authors suggest that results favor conceptualizing AS on a continuum with autism, rather than a unique disorder. Within this framework, the authors suggest that best clinical practice might be to consider both disorders as part of the *autism spectrum disorder* and then to specify the subtype of the disorder as either autistic disorder or AS. On the other hand, Rourke and colleagues (2002) suggest that from a neuropsychological perspective, AS shares far more features with NLD than HFA which they consider to be a similar but different disorder. The controversy continues.

Pervasive Developmental Disorder Not Otherwise Specified (Including Atypical Autism): PDDNOS

Description and Associated Features

The fifth and final type of PDD is called PDDNOS, and this classification is reserved for those children who

1. either do not fully meet the criteria of symptoms to be diagnosed with any of the four other types of PDD described previously, and/or
2. do not have the degree of impairment outlined in the previous criteria for PDD.

The *DSM* devotes very little space to this disorder which basically is summed up in one paragraph. According to the *DSM–IV–TR* (APA, 2000), this category should be used

> when there is a severe and pervasive impairment in the development of social interaction or verbal and nonverbal communication skills, or when stereotyped behavior, interests, and activities are present, but the criteria are not met for a specific Pervasive Developmental Disorder, Schizophrenia, Schizotypal Personality Disorder, or Avoidant Personality Disorder. (p. 84)

This category includes **atypical autism**, which includes symptom presentations that do not meet the criteria for autism due to "late age at onset, atypical symptomatology, or subthreshold symptomatology, or all of these" (p. 84).

In response to the growing concern regarding PDD, the National Dissemination Center for Children with Disabilities (NICHY) has developed a Briefing Paper in response to numerous questions which have been posited about disorders under PDD. (Unless otherwise stated, the following summary of PDD follows the Briefing Paper produced by NICHCY.)

Currently, there is considerable confusion regarding which children should be identified using which of the PDD labels. In part, this confusion has developed because the *DSM–IV–TR* (APA, 2000) criteria are primarily diagnostic guidelines and do not address how to measure the severity of a person's symptoms. As has been discussed throughout this chapter, there is considerable overlap between the types of PDD and the boundaries between different types of PDD are often not clear; nowhere is this more evident than for the category of PDDNOS. The PDDNOS category is vague, and an individual can be diagnosed as having PDDNOS if he or she has *some* behaviors that are seen in autism. There is also the distinct possibility that autistic disorder and PDDNOS are on a continuum (ADS) and as such an individual with autistic disorder can improve to the extent that they can be reclassified as PDDNOS; the converse could also be true (a child could regress from PDDNOS to a full-blown autistic disorder).

The situation becomes even more complex in the light of a new classification system (*Diagnostic Classification of Mental Health and Developmental Disorders of Infancy and Early Childhood*) that was developed to address diagnostic concerns of very young children by ZERO TO THREE: National Center for Infants, Toddlers, and Families (1994). Under this system, PDD is referred to as **Multisystem Developmental Disorder, or MSDD**.

Because the criteria are so vague, generally, children who are diagnosed with PDDNOS may have varying degrees of deficits in social behavior, impairments in verbal or nonverbal communication, and demonstrate unusual patterns of behavior (resistance to change, ritualistic and compulsive behaviors, and abnormal attachments). Some children may exhibit atypical responses to sensory information (touch, smell, taste) and may be readily overwhelmed (overresponsive) or virtually nonresponsive. Disturbances of movement may be evident in problems with imitation skills, or repetitive and odd motor responses such as hand flapping, toe walking, or body rocking.

Although the PDDNOS category was created to acknowledge that some presentations will have atypical or inconsistent features, the generic criteria that currently exist for this category in the *DSM* allows for diagnosis of a child with PDDNOS even if they have impairments in only two of the three autistic domains. One prominent spokesperson in the field has stated that "The lack of specificity of the definition has added little to understanding these children, has not stimulated fruitful research, and the validity and usefulness of the diagnosis remain to be demonstrated" (Scheeringa, 2001). In addition, likely due to the wide range of behaviors that can be subsumed under PDDNOS, the category seems to be the most common of the autistic spectrum disorders (Volkmar et al., 1994).

CHAPTER REVIEW

There are five different categories of Pervasive Developmental Disorders (PDD) that are currently recognized by the *DSM–IV–TR* (APA, 2000), including: Rett's disorder, childhood disintegration disorder, autism, Asperger's disorder, and PDDNOS. The disorders are marked by varying degrees of neurological problems that have onset in childhood and are pervasive throughout the lifespan. Although all the disorders share features of qualitative impairments in social interaction, verbal, and/or nonverbal communication and a restricted range of activities, each disorder presents with a different cluster of symptoms within these three areas. After a period of normal development, children with Rett's disorder and CDD experience a rapid deterioration in functions. Prior to 3 years of age, children with autism appear normal; however, a pattern of regression sets in that compromises language, social, and behavioral functioning. Boundaries between disorders are often blurred and there may be problems distinguishing between variants, such as higher functioning autism (HFA), AS, and PDDNOS. The *DSM–IV–TR* (2000) distinguishes autism from AS primarily on the basis of language. While both autism and AS share features of impaired social interaction and engagement in restricted, repetitive, and stereotypical patterns of behavior, only autism (not AS) also exhibits qualitative impairment in communication. PDDNOS is a vague category providing little direction for the diagnosis of cases that are atypical.

1. **Rett's Disorder (Rett Syndrome)**
   Loss of function, progressive deterioration, and the replacement of purposeful hand movements with hand wringing, all follow an initial period of normal development. There are four stages of deterioration: 1. *6–18 months*—brain development and head growth decelerate, motor function declines; 2. *1–4 years*—rapid deterioration and ataxia (unsteady gait); 3. *2–10 years*—less deterioration in some areas and some social improvement; and 4. *10+ years*—late deterioration. Many reach a plateau in remain in stage 3, although for some deterioration continues. Only females with the disorder survive.

2. **Childhood Disintegration Disorder (CDD)**
   Primarily found in males, CDD is a rare disorder with onset between 2 and 10 years of age, after at least 2 years of normal development. In addition to qualitative impairment in at least two of the three areas associated with PDD, (*social interaction, communication,* and *restricted stereotypical behaviors*), marked regression occurs in two areas of functioning: expressive or receptive language; social or adaptive skills; bowel or bladder function; play or motor skills. Severe mental retardation is often comorbid.

3. **Autistic Disorder (AD)**
   Onset for AD is prior to 3 years of age and includes evidence of qualitative impairment in three areas of functioning: social, communication, and restricted range of activities. There is evidence that minimal activation of the amygdale during social situations, poor eye contact, lack of a social smile, and poor imitative behavior all contribute to lack of social reciprocity. Engagement in ritualistic and nonfunctional activities also interfere with functional

behaviors. Previous reports of high levels of MR comorbid with AD have recently come under criticism.

4. **Asperger's Disorder/Asperger's Syndrome (AS)**

   Lack of language delay, and lack of any significant delays in cognitive (usually normal intelligence), or adaptive functioning set children with AS apart from those with AD. Children with AS do exhibit qualitative impairment in social interaction and restricted, stereotypical behaviors, although these behaviors are often less severe than those with AD. Language often lacks a sense of reciprocity and subtle nuances are often interpreted at a concrete level. Social awareness and social skills development are often the targets of intervention.

5. **Autistic Disorder (HFA) and Asperger's Syndrome (AS)**

   Whether autism (particularly HFA) and AS are distinct disorders or represent varying degrees of severity among the spectrum of autistic disorders continues to be debated. Boundaries are less clear when comparisons are made among children with AS and high functioning autism (HFA). Results of studies are mixed with some finding very little difference, especially at older ages (adolescence) and other studies reporting differences in Verbal IQ and *Theory of Mind* tasks. Recent surveys report that prevalence rates for autistic spectrum disorders (ASD) may be as high as 6.7 per 1,000.

6. **Pervasive Developmental Disorder, Not Otherwise Specified: PDDNOS**

   Due to the minimal information provided for this category by the *DSM* (APA, 2000), there is much confusion as to what types of cases would actually receive a PDDNOS label. PDD categories often exhibit symptom overlap and it is questionable what new information this category could potentially provide regarding treatment and prognosis, in its current capacity as a home for "atypical" cases.

Consolidate and Communicate

1. A parent brings her 2-year-old child to your clinic because the child, although seemingly normal for the first 2 years, has just begun to demonstrate deterioration on a number of levels. Although speech was developing normally, Alex now remains mostly mute with very little attempt at communication verbally or nonverbally. Prior to this, Alex seemed to go through a restless period and was irritable and difficult to get along with. Other skills such as playfully engaging with toys, has been replaced by being fixated on parts of the toys, like spinning a wheel on the truck for hours. Although almost potty trained, now Alex soils and has forgotten any potty routines that were established.

   a. Given the above description, what are the types of PDD that seem most likely for this diagnosis?

   b. Which diagnostic category is most likely the best fit and why would you rule out other PDD subtypes (what is the nature of your differential diagnosis)?

   c. What are some of the theoretical issues that have been discussed regarding a differential diagnosis between this category and other PDD categories?

   d. Based on your knowledge, what are some of the other associated features that might be anticipated given the disorder?

   e. What is the treatment and prognosis for the disorder?

   f. Is Alex more likely a girl or boy and why?

2. Should autism and Asperger's syndrome (AS) be considered as two distinct disorders, or should they be considered as a more severe and less severe form of the same disorder, autistic

spectrum disorder (ASD)? Support your arguments with information from researchers who have investigated this question.

3. Develop an experiment to test the concept of *Theory of Mind* for children with autism, higher functioning autism, Asperger's syndrome and their nondisordered peers. Predict the outcomes of the experiment for each group of children represented above. How would responses differ qualitatively among the groups? Don't forget to include the age of the children that will be included in your study and address how this might also influence the results.

4. A number of possible explanations have been postulated to describe why children with autism and AS have impairments in social interaction. Discuss at least five different reasons that have been suggested.

5. Rogers and DiLalla (1990) suggest that there are three patterns of autism onset. What are the patterns and how do they differ?

6. Differential diagnosis of Asperger's syndrome from several other disorders is discussed in the text. Which disorders are most problematic for decision making, and why?

Chapter Review Questions

1. The term pervasive developmental disorders (PDD) is a relatively new category of classification. The term was first used in the:
   a. 1960s
   b. 1940s
   c. 1980s
   d. 1990s

2. Which of the following is **not** true regarding Rett's disorder?
   a. functional hand use is replaced by hand wringing movements
   b. deceleration of head growth
   c. onset of poor coordination, gait
   d. loss of speech function

3. Which of the following is true regarding Rett's disorder?
   a. Males who have the mutated gene die shortly after birth
   b. Males cannot inherit the disorder because it is on an X chromosome
   c. Only females are affected by the mutated gene
   d. Males are not susceptible to the genetic mutation

4. In their study of children with CDD, Malhotra, Grupta (2002), and Vokmar et al. (1994) found that the most common and pervasive symptom of deterioration in the first 2 years was:
   a. bladder control
   b. hand wringing and washing
   c. ataxia
   d. speech loss

5. Which of the following is **false** regarding prevalence rates for PDD?
   a. The ratio of autism to Asperger's disorder has been reported as 4 to 1.
   b. Males are more likely to be diagnosed with autism than females.
   c. Females have less severe forms of autism than males.
   d. Males are 5 times more likely to be diagnosed with Asperger's syndrome than females.

6. The intervention program for autistic children labeled TEACCH differs from the majority of other intervention programs for autistic children. Which of the following is unique to the TEACCH program?
   a. Language is taught as an isolated skill
   b. Words are taught as rewards
   c. Words are taught to develop intentional and relevant communication skills by integrating language into ongoing activities
   d. Language is taught through the use of music and listening to recordings

7. The need for repetition and sameness in children with autism has been which of the following?
   a. Children are hyperresponsive (low threshold for sensory information)
   b. Children are hyposensitive (high threshold for stimulation)
   c. Children are unresponsive to external output
   d. all of the above

8. Which of the following was **not** one of the three different patterns of autism onset, according to Rogers and DiLalla (1990)?
   a. congential group (atypical behaviors present at birth)
   b. normal onset, followed by regression and loss
   c. start, stop, restart and stop group: early start, failure to develop, burst of growth, plateau, and decline
   d. failure to develop skills (early milestones followed by plateau)

9. Research support is available for all of the following concerning brain structure and function associated with autism, except
   a. lower levels of serotonin than normal
   b. possible implication of GABA genes with chromosome 15
   c. limited or no activation of the amygdale during social cognitive tasks
   d. increased head circumference and likely accelerated brain growth in early development

10. Which of the following is **false** regarding comparisons of children with high functioning autism (HFA) and children with Asperger's syndrome (AS)?
    a. By adolescence, language skills of those with HFA and AS are only minimally different.
    b. Adolescents with HFA tend to engage in more verbose and pedantic discourse on topics of interest that teens with AS.
    c. Adolescents with AS are more painfully aware of their lack of social success as adolescents than youth with HFA and may become depressed as a result.
    d. Children with AS are less likely to use echolalia than those with HFA.

Glossary of New Terms

Rett's disorder/Rett syndrome
childhood disintegrative disorder (CDD)
autistic disorder
Asperger's disorder/Asperger's syndrome (AS)
pervasive developmental disorder not otherwise specified (PDDNOS)
autistic spectrum disorders (ASD)
hypotonia

apraxia
apnea
hyperventilating
ataxia
spasticity
scoliosis
MECP2 gene
kyphosis
dementia infantilis
other childhood disintegrative disorder
metachromatic leukodystrophy (MLD)
myelin sheath
myelination
affective anxiety
fearfulness
koint attention behavior
referential looking
social referencing
amygdale
echolalia
syntax
relational concepts
desire or intention
social pragmatics
hyperresponsive
hyporesponsive
sensory overload
insistence on sameness (IS)
repetitive, sensory and motor behaviors (RSMB)
high functioning autism (HFA)
MMR vaccine
thimerosal
serotonin (5-HT)
corpus callosum
amygdale
fusiform gyrus
applied behavioral analysis (ABA)
TEACCH program
intentional communication
hyperlexic
selective mutism
semantic-pragmatic disorder
right hemisphere dysfunction
left hemisphere dysfunction
infantile autism
childhood psychosis
childhood schizophrenia

autistic psychopathy
social pragmatics
theory of Mind
autistic spectrum disorder
atypical autism
multisystem developmental disorder (MSDD)

Answers to Multiple Choice Questions:
1. c; 2. d; 3. a; 4. d; 5. c; 6. c; 7. d; 8. c; 9. a; 10. b

References

Aalsma, M. C., Lapsley, D. K., & Flannery, D. J. (2006). Personal fables, narcissism, and adolescent adjustment. *Psychology in the Schools, 43*, 481–491.

Aaron, P. G., & Joshi, R. M. (1992). *Reading problems: Consultation and remediation.* New York: Guilford.

Aaron, P. G., Joshi, R. M., Ayotollah, M., Ellsberry, A., Henderson, J., & Lindsey, K. (1999). Decoding and single-word naming: Are they two independent components of word-recognition skills? *Reading and Writing: An Interdisciplinary Journal, 14*, 89–127.

Abram, K., Teplin, L., McClelland, G., & Dulcan, M. (2003). Comorbid psychiatric disorders in youth in juvenile detention. *Archives of General Psychiatry, 60*, 1097–1108.

Abikoff, H., Ganeles, D., & Reiter, G. (1988). Cognitive training in academically deficient ADDH boys receiving stimulant medication. *Journal of Abnormal Child Psychology, 16*, 411–432.

Abikoff, H. Gittelman-Klein, R., & Klein, D. (1977). Validation of a classroom observation code for hyperactive children. *Journal of Consulting and Clinical Psychology, 45*, 772–783.

Abramovitch, R., Freedman, J., Henry, K., & Van Brunschot, M. (1995). Children's capacity to agree to psychological research: Knowledge of risks and benefits and voluntariness. *Ethics & Behavior, 5*, 25–48.

Abramovitch, R., Freedman, J., Thoden, K., & Nikolich, C. (1991). Children's capacity to consent to participation in psychological research: Empirical findings. *Child Development, 62*, 1100–1109.

Achenbach. T. M. (1991). *Manual for the child behavior checklist/4-18 and 1991 profile.* Burlington, VT: University of Vermont, Department of Psychiatry.

Achenbach, T. M. (1995). Developmental issues in assessment, taxonomy, and diagnosis of child and adolescent psychopathology. In D. Cicchetti & D. J. Cohen (Eds.), *Developmental psychopathology: Vol. 1. Theory and methods* (pp. 57–80). New York: Wiley.

Achenbach, T. M., & Edelbrock, C. (1978). The classification of child psychopathology: A review and analysis of empirical efforts. *Psychological Bulletin, 85*, 1275–1301.

Achenbach, T. M., Howell, C. T., McConaughy, S., & Stanger, C. (1995). Six-year predictors of problems in a national sample: III. Transitions to young adult syndromes. *Journal of the American Academy of Child & Adolescent Psychiatry, 34*(5), 658–669.

Achenbach, T. M., McConaughy, S., & Howell, C. T. (1987). Child and adolescent behavioral and emotional problems: Implications of cross-informant correlations for situational specificity. *Psychological Bulletin, 101*, 213–232.

Achenbach, T. M., & Rescorla, L. A. (2001). *Manual for the ASEBA School-Age Forms & Profiles.* Burlington, VT: University of Vermont, Research Center for Children, Youth & Families.

Agras, W. S., Rossiter, E. M., Arnow, B., Telch, C. F., Raeburn, S. D., Bruce, B., & Koran, L. (1994). One-year follow-up of psychosocial and pharmacologic treatments for bulimia nervosa, *Journal of Clinical Psychiatry, 55*, 179–183.

Aguilar, B., Sroufe, L. A., Egeland, B., & Carlson, E. (2000). Distinguishing the early-onset/persistent and adolescent-onset antisocial behavior types. From birth to 16 years. *Development and Psychopathology, 12*, 109–132.

Ahadi, S. A., Rothbart, M. K., & Ye, R. (1993). Children's temperament in the US and China: Similarities and differences. *European Journal of Personality, 7*, 359–377.

Akiskal, H. S., Downs, J., Jordan, P., Watson, S., Daugherty, D., & Pruitt, D. B. (1985). Affective disorders in referred children and younger siblings of Manic-depressives. Mode of onset and prospective course. *Archives of General Psychiatry, 42*, 996–1003.

Albano, A. M., Chorpita, B. F., & Barlow, D. (1996). Childhood anxiety disorders. In E. J. Mash & R. A. Barkley (Eds.), *Child psychopathology.* New York: Guilford.

Albertini, R. S., Phillips, K. A., & Guevremont, D. (1996). Body dysmorphic disorder. *Journal of the American Academy of Child and Adolescent Psychiatry, 35*, 1425–1426.

Alexander, J. F., & Parsons, B. (1982). *Functional family therapy.* Monterey, CA: Brooks/Cole.

Allen, R. P., Singer, H. S., Brow, J. E., & Salam, M. (1992). Sleep disorders in Tourette syndrome: A primary or unrelated problem? *Pediatric Neurology, 8*, 275–280.

Allport, G. W. (1961). *Pattern and growth in personality.* New York: Holt.

Altepeter, T. A., & Breen, M. J. (1999). Situational variation in problem behavior at home and school in attention deficit disorder with hyperactivity: A factor analytic study. *Journal of Child Psychology and Psychiatry, 33*, 741–748.

Altmann, E., & Gotlib, I. H. (1988). The social behavior of depressed children: An observational study. *Journal of Abnormal Child Psychology, 16,* 29–44.

Aman, M. G. (1993). Efficacy of psychotropic drugs for reducing self-injurious behavior in the developmental disabilities. *Annals of Clinical Psychiatry, 5,* 171–188.

Aman, M. G., Hammer, D., & Rohahn, J. (1993). Mental Retardation. In T. H. Ollendick & M. Hersen (Eds.), *Handbook of child and adolescent assessment* (pp. 321–45). Needham Heights, MA: Allyn & Bacon.

Amaya-Jackson, L., & March, J. (1995a). Posttraumatic stress disorder in adolescents: Risk factors, diagnosis and intervention. *Adolescent Medicine, 6,* 251–269.

Amaya-Jackson, L., & March, J. (1995a). Posttraumatic Stress Disorder. In J. S. March (Ed.), *Anxiety disorders in children and adolescents* (pp. 276–3000). New York: Guilford.

Ambrosini, P. J. (2000). Historical development and present status of the Schedule for Affective Disorders and Schizophrenia for School-Age Children (K–SADS). *Journal of the American Academy of Child and Adolescent Psychiatry, 39,* 49–58.

Amen, D. G. (1998). Attention Deficit Disorder: A guide for primary care physicians. *Primary Psychiatry 5,* 76–85.

Amen, D. G. (2001, February 26). Attention doctors. *Newsweek, 137,* 72–73.

Amen, D. G., & Carmichael, B. D. (1997). High-resolution brain SPECT imaging in ADHD. *Annals of Clinical Psychiatry, 9,* 81–86.

American Academy of Child and Adolescent Psychiatry Work Group on Quality Issues. (1997). Practice parameters for the assessment and treatment of children, adolescents, and adults with attention-deficit/hyperactivity disorder. *Journal of the American Academy of Child & Adolescent Psychiatry, 36*(Suppl.), 85S–121S.

American Counseling Association (ACA). (2002). The American Counseling Association code of ethics. Retrieved July, 2007 from http://www.counselling.org.

American Psychiatric Association (APA). (1980). *Diagnostic and statistical manual of mental disorders* (3rd ed.). Washington, DC: American Psychiatric Press.

American Psychiatric Association. (APA). (1987). *Diagnostic and statistical manual of mental disorders* (3rd rev ed.). Washington, DC: American Psychiatric Press.

American Psychiatric Association (APA). (1994). *Diagnostic and statistical manual of mental disorders* (4th ed.). Washington, DC: American Psychiatric Press.

American Psychiatric Association (APA). (2000). *Diagnostic and statistical manual of mental disorders* (4th ed., Text Revision). Washington, DC: American Psychiatric Press.

American Psychological Association (APA). (2002). *Ethical principles of psychologists and code of conduct.* Retrieved July, 2007 from http://www.apa.org/ethics

American School Counselors Association (ACSA). (1998). *Ethical standards for school counselors.* Retrieved July, 2007 from http://www.schoolcounselor.com

Anastopoulos, A. D., Shelton, T. L., & DuPaul, G. J. (1993). Parent training for attention-deficit hyperactivity disorder: Its impact on parent functioning. *Journal of Abnormal Child Psychology 21,* 581–596.

Anderson, C. A., & Bushman, B. J. (2001). Effects of violent video games on aggressive behavior, aggressive cognition, aggressive affect, physiological arousal, and prosocial behavior: A meta-analytic review of the scientific literature. *Psychological Science, 12*(5), 353–359.

Anderson, J. C., Williams, S. M., & McGee, R. (1987). *DSM–III* disorders in preadolescent children: Prevalence in a large sample from the general population. *Archives of General Psychiatry, 44*(1), 69–76.

Angier, N. (1994, July 24). The debilitating malady called boyhood. *New York Times,* section 4:14.

Angold, A. (1988). Childhood and adolescent depression. I. Epidemiological and etiological aspects. *British Journal of Psychiatry, 152,* 601–617.

Angold, A., Costello, E. J., & Erkanli, A. (1999). Comorbidity. *Journal of Child Psychology and Psychiatry, 40,* 57–87.

Angold, A., Costello, E. J., Messer, S. C., & Pickles, A. (1995). Development of a short questionnaire for use in epidemiological studies of depression in children and adolescents. *International Journal of Methods in Psychiatric Research, 5,* 237–249.

Angold, A., Erkanli, A., Farmer, E. M. Z., Fairbank, J. A., Burns, B. A., Keeler, G. S., et al. (2002). Psychiatric disorder, impairment, and service use in rural African American and white youth. *Archives of General Psychiatry, 59,* 893–901.

Ang., R. P. & Hughes, J. N. (2002). Differential benefits of skills training with antisocial youth based on group composition: A meta-analytic investigation. *School Psychology Review, 31,* 164–185.

Angst, J., Merikangas, K. M. Scheidegger, P., & Wicki, W. (1990). Recurrent brief depression: A new subtype of affective disorder. *Journal of Affective Disorders, 19,* 87–98.

Anthony, J., & Petronis, K. (1995). Early-onset drug use and risk of later drug problems. *Drug and Alcohol dependence, 40,* 9–15.

Anthony, J. L., Lonigan, C. J., Hooe, E. S., & Phillips, B. M. (2002). An affect-based, hierarchical model of temperament and its relations with internalizing symptomatology. *Journal of Clinical Child and Adolescent Psychology, 31,* 480–490.

Appleyard, K., Egeland, B., van Dulmen, M. H. M., & Sroufe, L. A. (2005). When more is not better: The role of cumulative risk in child behaviour outcomes. *Journal of Child Psychology and Psychiatry, 46,* 235–245.

Apter, A., Kronenberg, S., & Brent, D. (2005). Turning darkness into light: A new landmark study on the treatment of adolescent depression. Comments on the TADS study. *European Child and Adolescent Psychiatry, 14,* 113–116.

Armstrong, T. D., & Costello, E. J. (2002). Community studies on adolescent substance use abuse or dependence and psychiatric comorbidity. *Journal of Consulting and Clinical Psychology, 70,* 1224–1239

Arnett, J. (1992). Reckless behavior in adolescence: A developmental perspective. *Developmental Review, 12,* 339–373.

Arnow, B., Sanders, M. J., & Steiner, H. (1999). Premenarcheal versus postmenarcheal anorexia nervosa: A comparitive study. *Clinical Child Psychology and Psychiatry, 4,* 403–414.

Asarnow, J. R., Thompson, M., Hamilton, E. B., Goldstein, M. J., & Guthrie, D. (1994). Family expressed emotion, childhood-onset depression, and childhood-onset schizophrenia spectrum disorders: Is expressed emotion a non-specific correlate of child psychopathology or a specific risk factor for depression. *Journal of Abnormal Child Psychology, 20,* 129–146.

Aseltine, R. H. (2003). Evaluation of a school based suicide prevention program. *Adolescent and Family Health, 3,* 81–88.

Aseltine, R. H., & di Martino, R. (2004). An outcome evaluation of the SOS suicide prevention program. *American Journal of Public Health, 94,* 446–451.

Aseltine, R. H., James, A., Schilling, E. A., & Glanovsky, J. (2007). Evaluating the SOS suicide prevention program: A replicatin and extension. *BMC Public Health.* Retrieved August 15, 2007, from http://www. biomedcentral. com/1471-2458/7/161

Ashcraft, M. H., Yamashita, T. S., & Aram, D. M. (1992). Mathematics performance in left and right brain-lesioned children. *Brain and Cognition, 19,* 208–252.

Asher, S. R., & Wheeler, V. A. (1985). Children's loneliness: A comparison of rejected and neglected peer status. *Journal of Consulting and Clinical Psychology, 53,* 500–505.

Atkins, M., Pelham, W. E., & Licht, M. H. (1985). A comparison of objective classroom measures and teacher ratings of attention deficit disorder. *Journal of Abnormal Child Psychology, 13,* 155–167.

Attie, I., & Brooks-Gunn, J. (1989). Development of eating problems in adolescent girls: A longitudinal study. *Developmental Psychology, 25,* 70–79.

Atzaba-Poria, N., Pike, A., & Deater-Deckard, K. (2004) . Do risk factors for problem behaviour act in a cumulative manner? An examination of ethnic minority and majority children through an ecological perspective. *Journal of Child Psychology and Psychiatry, 45,* 707–718.

August, G. J., & Garfinkel, B. D. (1989). Behavioral and cognitive subtypes of ADHD. *Journal of the American Academy of Child and Adolescent Psychiatry, 28,* 739–748.

Ausubel, D. P. (1963). *The psychology of meaningful verbal learning.* New York: Grune & Stratton.

Axline, V. (1964). *Dibbs in search of self.* New York: Ballantine Books.

Azar, B. (1997, May). Nature, nurture: not mutually exclusive. *The Monitor,* American Psychological Association.

Azrin, N. H., Donohue, B., Besalel, V. A., Kogan, E. S., & Acierno, R. (1994). Youth drug abuse treatment: A controlled outcome study. *Journal of Child and Adolescent Substance Abuse, 3,* 1–16.

Baca Zinn, M., & Pok, A. Y. K. (2002). Tradition and transition in Mexican-origin families. In R. L. Taylor (Ed.), *Minority families in the United States: A multicultural perspective* (pp. 79–100). Saddle River, NJ: Prentice Hall.

Baddeley, A. D. (1986). *Working memory.* Oxford, England: Oxford University Press.

Bahr, S. J., Hoffmann, J. P. & Yang, X. (2005). Parental and peer influences on the risk of adolescent drug use. *The Journrnal of Primary Prevention, 26,* 529–551.

Baker, D. G., West, S. A., Nicholson, W. E., Ekhator, N., Kasckow, J., Hill, K. K., et al. (1999). Serial CSF corticotropin-releasing hormone levels and adrnocortical activity in combat veterans with posttraumatic stress disorder. *American Journal of Psychiatry, 156,* 585–588.

Baker, F. M., & Bell, C. (1999). Issues in psychiatric treatment of African Americans. *Psychiatric Services, 50*(3), 362–368.

Bakwin, H. (1973). Reading disability in twins. *Developmental Medicine and Child Neurology, 15,* 184–187.

Ballard, M., Argus, T., & Remley, T. P. (1999). Bullying and school violence: A proposed intervention program. *NASSP Bulletin, 83,* 38–47.

Bandura, A. (1973). *Aggression: A social learning theory analysis.* New York: Prentice Hall.

Bandura, A. (1977). *Social learning theory.* Englewood Cliffs, NJ: Prentice Hall.

Bandura, A. (1985). A model of causality in social learning theory. In M. Mahony & A. Freeman (Eds.), *Cognition and therapy.* New York: Plenum Press.

Bandura, A. (1986). *Social foundations of thought and action: A social cognitive theory.* Englewood Cliffs, NJ: Prentice Hall.

Bandura, A. (1994). Self-efficacy. In V. S. Ramachaudran (Ed.), *Encyclopedia of human behavior* (Vol. 4, pp. 71–81). New York: Academic Press.

Bandura, A. (1995). *Self-efficacy in changing societies.* New York: Cambridge University Press.

Barker, E. D., Tremblay, R. E., Nagin, D. S., Lacourse, E., & Vitaro, F. (2006). Development of male proactive and reactive aggression during adolescence. *Journal of Child Psychology and Psychiatry, 47,* 783–790.

Barker, E. T., & Galambos, N. L. (2003). Body dissatisfaction of adolescent girls and boys: Risk and resource factors. *Journal of Early Adolescence, 23,* 141–165.

Barkley, R. A. (1997). Behavior inhibition, sustained attention and executive function. *Psychological Bulletin, 121,* 65–94.

Barkley, R. A. (1998). *Attention Deficit Hyperactivity Disorder: A handbook for diagnosis and treatment, 2nd edition.* New York: Guilford.

Barkley, R. A. (2003). Attention-deficit/hyperactivity disorder. In E. J. Mash & R. A. Barkley (Eds.), *Child psychopathology* (2nd ed., pp. 75–143). New York: Guilford.

Barkley, R. A., DuPaul, G. J., & McMurray, M. D. (1990). A comprehensive evaluation of attention deficit disorder with and without hyperactivity.

Barkley, R. A., & Cunninghan, C. E. (1978). Do stimulant drugs improve the academic performance of hyperkinetic children? A review of outcome research. *Clinical Pediatrics, 17,* 85–92.

Barkley, R. A., Fischer, M., Edelbrock, C. S., & Smallish, L. (1990). The adolescent outcome of hyperactive children diagnosed by research criteria: 1. An 8 year perspective follow-up study. *Journal of the American Academy of Child and Adolescent Psychiatry, 32,* 233–256.

Barkley, R. A., Murphy, K. R. & Bush, T. (2001). Time perception and reproduction in young adults with attention deficit hyperactivity disorder. *Neuropsychology, 15,* 351–360.

Barkley, R. A., Murphy, K. R., & Kwasnick, D. (1996). Psychological adjustment and adaptive impairments in young adults with ADHD. *Journal of Attention Disorders, 1,* 41–54.

Barlow, D. (2002). *Anxiety and its disorders: The nature and treatment of anxiety and panic* (2nd ed.). New York: Guilford.

Barnett, W. (1993). Benefit-cost analysis of preschool education: Findings from a 25-year follow-up. *American Journal of Orthopsychiatry, 63*, 25–50.

Barnett, W. (1996). Lives in the balance: Age-27 benefit-cost analysis of the High/Scope Perry Preschool Program. *Monographs of the High/Scope Educational Research Foundation, 11*. Ypsilanti, MI: High/Scope Press.

Barrett, P. M. (1998). Evaluation of cognitive-behavioral group treatments for childhood anxiety disorders. *Journal of Clinical Child Psychology, 27*, 459–468.

Barrett, P. M., Dadds, M., & Rapee, R. (1996). Family treatment of childhood anxiety: A controlled trial. *Journal of Consulting and Clinical Psychology, 64*(2), 333–342.

Barrett, P. M., Healy-Farrell, L., & March, J. S. (2004). Cognitive-behavioral family treatment of childhood obsessive-compulsive disorder: A controlled trial. *Journal of the American Academy of Child & Adolescent Psychiatry, 43*(1), 46–62.

Barrett, P. M., Johnson, S., & Turner, C. (2004). Examination of developmental differences in school-based prevention of anxiety and depressive symptoms and disorders. *Clinical Child Psychology and Psychiatry, 27*, 459–468.

Barrett, P. M., Rappee, R. M., Dadds, M. M., & Ryan, S. M. (1996). Family enhancement of cognitive style in anxious and aggressive children. *Journal of the American Academy of Child and Adolescent Psychiatry, 24*, 187–203.

Barrett, P. M., & Turner, C. M. (2004). Prevention of childhood depression. In P. M. Barrett & T. H. Ollendick (Eds.), *Handbook of interventions that work with children and adolescents* (pp. 429–474). West Sussex, UK: Wiley.

Barrios, B. A., & O'Dell, S. L. (1998). Fears and anxieties. In E. J. Mash & R. A. Barkley (Eds.), *Treatment of childhood disorders* (pp. 249–337). New York: Guilford.

Barton, C., & Alexander, J. F. Functional family therapy. In A. S. Gurman & D. P. Kniskern (Eds.), *Handbook of family therapy* (pp. 403-443). New York: Brunne/Mazel.

Bates, J. E., Pettit, G. S., Dodge, K. A., & Ridge, B. (1998). The interaction of temperamental resistance to control and parental discipline in the prediction of children's externalizing problems. *Developmental Psychology, 34*, 982–995.

Batsche, G. M., & Knoff, H. M. (1994). Bullies and their victims: Understanding a pervasive problem in the schools. *School Psychology Review 23*(2), 165–174.

Baumrind, D. (1991). The influences of parenting style on adolescent competence and substance use. *Journal of Early Adolescence, 11*, 56–95.

Bayley, N. (1993). *The Bayley Scales of Infant Development* (2nd ed.). San Antonio, TX: The Psychological Corporation.

Bearden, C. E., Hoffman, K. M., & Cannon, T. D. (2001). The neuropsychology and neuroanatomy of bipolar affective disorder: A critical review. *Bipolar Disorder, 3*, 106–153.

Beardslee, W. R., Versage, E. M., Wright, E., Salt, P., Rothberg, P. C., Drezner, K., & Gladstone, T. G. (1997). Examination of preventive interventions for families with depression: Evidence of change. *Developmental Psychopathology, 9*, 109–130.

Bearman, P. S., & Moody, J. (2004). Suicide and friendships among American adolescents. *American Journal of Public Health, 94*, 89–95.

Bearman, S., Presnell, K., Martinez, E., & Stice, E. (2006). The skinny on body dissatisfaction: A longitudinal study of adolescent girls and boys. *Journal of Youth and Adolescence, 35*, 229–241.

Beautrais, A. L. (1998). Risk factors for serious suicide and attempted suicide among young people: A case-control study. In R. J. Klosky, H. S. Eshkevari, R. D. Godney, & R. Hassan (Eds.), *Suicide prevention: The global context* (pp. 167–181). New York: Plenum.

Beautrais, A. L. (1999). Risk factors for suicide and attempted suicide and among young people. In *Commonwealth Department of Health and Aged Care, National Youth Suicide Prevention Strategy-Setting the Evidence-based Research Agenda for Australia (A Literature Review*; pp. 113–278). Commonwealth of Australia: Canberra.

Beauvais, F., Wayman, J. C., Jumper-Thurman, P., Plested, B., & Helm, H. (2002). Inhalant abuse among American Indian, Mexican American and non-Latino White adolescents. *American Journal of Drug and Alcohol Abuse, 28*, 171–187.

Beck, A. T. (1997). Cognitive therapy: Reflections. In J. K. Zeig (Ed.), *The evolution of psychotherapy: The third conference*. New York: Brunner/Mazel.

Beck A., Beck, J., & Jolly, J. (2005). *The Beck Youth Inventories of Emotional & Social Impairment* (2nd ed.). San Antonio, TX: The Psychological Corporation.

Beck, A. T., Emery, G., & Greenberg, R. (1996). Cognitive therapy for evaluation anxieties. In C. Lindermann (Ed.), *Handbook of the treatment of the anxiety disorders* (2nd ed., pp. 235–260). Lanham, MD: Jason Aronson.

Becker, A. E., Grinspoon, S. K., Klibanski, A., & Herzog, D. B. (1999). Eating disorders. *New England Journal of Medicine, 340*, 1092–1098.

Beers, S. R., & DeBellis, M. (2002). Neuropsychological function in children with maltreatment-related posttraumatic stress disorder. *American Journal of Psychiatry, 159*, 483–486.

Behnke, S. H., & Kinscherff, R. T. (May 2002). An ethics rounds: Must a psychologist report past child abuse? *Monitor on Psychology.* American Psychological Association, Vol. 33, no. 5 (pp. 56–57).

Beidel, D., Turner, S. M., & Morris, E. L. (1995). A new inventory to assess childhood social anxiety and phobia: The Social Phobia and Anxiety Inventory for Children. *Psychological Assessment, 7*, 73–79.

Beidel, D., Turner, S. M., & Morris, E. L. (1999). Psychopathology of childhood social phobia. *Journal of the American Academy of Child & Adolescent Psychiatry, 38*, 643–650.

Beitchman, J. H., Baldassarra, L., Mik, H., De Luca, V., King, N., Bender, D., et al. (2006). Serotonin transporter polymorphisms and persistent pervasive childhood aggression. *American Journal of Psychiatry, 6*, 1103–1105.

Bellodi, L., Sciuto, G., Diaferia, G., Ronchi, P., & Smeraldi, E. (1992). Psychiatric disorders in the families of patients with obsessive-compulsive disorder. *Psychiatry Research, 42*, 111–120.

Belluge, U., Jarvinen-Pasley, A., Doyle, T., Reilly, J., Reiss, A., & Korenberg, J. (2007). Affect, social behavior and the brain in Williams syndrome. *Current Directions in Psychological Science, 10*, 99–104.

Berkey, C. S., Rockett, H. R., & Field, A. E. (2000). Activity, dietary intake, and weight changes in a longitudinal study of preadolescent and adolescent boys and girls. *Pediatrics, 105*, 56–68.

Berkowitz, L. (1978) Whatever happened to the frustration-aggression hypothesis? *American Behavioral Scientist, 32,* 691–708.

Berlin, L., Bohlin, G., & Rydell, A. (2003). Relations between inhibition, executive functioning, and ADHD symptoms: A longitudinal study from age 5 to 8-1/2 years. *Child Neuropsychology, 9,* 255–266.

Berndt, T. J., & Keefe, K. (1995). Friends' influence on adolescents' adjustment to school. *Child Development, 66,* 1312–1329.

Bernstein, G. A. (1990) Anxiety disorders. In B. D. Garfinkel, G. A. Carlson, & E. B. Weller (Eds.), *Psychiatric disorders in children and adolescents* (pp. 64–83). Philadelphia: W. B. Saunders.

Bernstein, G. A., & Borchardt, C. M. (1991). Anxiety disorders of childhood and adolescence: A critical review. *Journal of the American Academy of Child and Adolescent Psychiatry, 30,* 519–532.

Biasini, F., Grupe, L., Juffman, L., & Bray, N. W. (1999). Mental retardation: A symptom and a syndrome. In S. D. Netherton, D. Holmes, & E. C. Walker (Eds.), *Child and adolescent psychological disorders: A comprehensive textbook* (pp. 6–23). New York: Oxford University Press.

Biederman, J., Faraone, S., & Lapey, K. (1992). Comorbidity of diagnosis in attention-deficit hyperactivity disorder. In G. Weiss (Ed.), *Child and adolescent psychiatry clinics in North America: Attention deficit disorder* (pp. 335–360). Philadelphia: W. B. Saunders.

Biederman, J., Faraone, S. V., Mick, E., Moore, P., & Lelon, E. (1996). Child Behavior Checklist findings further support co-morbidity between ADHD and major depression in a referred sample. *Journal of the American Academy of Child and Adolescent Psychiatry, 35,* 734–742.

Biederman, J., Faraone, S., Mick, E., Wozniak, J., Chen, L., Oullette, C., et al. (1996). Attention deficit hyperactivity disorder and juvenile mania: An overlooked comorbidity? *Journal of the American Academy of Child and Adolescent Psychiatry, 35,* 997–1008.

Biederman, J., Faraone, S., Wozniak, J., Mick, E., Kwon, A., Cayton, G., et al. (2005a). Clinical correlates of bipolar disorder in a large, referred sample of children and adolescents. *Journal of Psychiatric Research, 39,* 611–622.

Biederman, J., & Klein, R. G. (1998). Resolved: Mania is mistaken for ADHD in prepubertal children. *Journal of the American Academy of Child & Adolescent Psychiatry, 37*(10), 1091–1099.

Biederman, J., Mick, E., & Faraone, S. V. (2002). Influence of gender on attention deficit hyperactivity disorder in children referred to a psychiatric clinic. *American Journal of Psychiatry, 159,* 36–42.

Biederman, J., Mick, E., Wozniak, J., Aleardi, M., Spencer, T., & Faraone, S. (2005). An open-label trial of risperidone in children and adolescents with bipolar disorder. *Journal of Child and Adolescent Psychopharmacology, 15,* 113–117.

Biederman, J., Newcorn, J., & Sprich, S. (1991). Comorbidity of attention deficit hyperactivity disorder with conduct, depres-sive, anxiety, and other disorders. *American Journal of Psychiatry, 148*(5), 564–577.

Biederman, J., Rosenbaum, J. F., Bolduc-Murphy, E. A., Faraone, S. V., Chaloff, J., Hirshfeld, D. R., et al. (1993). A 3-year fol-low-up of children with and without behavioral inhibition. *Journal of the American Academy of Child and Adolescent Psychiatry, 32,* 814–821.

Biederman, J., Wilens, T., Mick, E., Spencer, T., & Faraone, S. V. (1999). Pharmacotherapy of attention-deficit/hyperactivity disorder reduces risk for substance use disorder. *Pediatrics, 104,* 20.

Biederman, J., Wozniak, J., Kiely, K., Ablon, S., Faraone, S., Mick, E., et al. (1995). CBCL clinical scales discriminate prepubertal children with structured-interview-derived diagnosis of mania from those with ADHD. *Journal of the American Academy of Child and Adolescent Psychiatry, 34,* 464–471.

Bierman, K. L., Miller, C. L., & Stabb, S. D. (1987). Improving the social behavior and peer acceptance of rejected boys: Effects of social skill training with instructions and prohibitions. *Journal of Consulting and Clinical Psychology, 55,* 194–200.

Billingsley, A. (1992). *Climbing Jacob's Ladder.* New York: Simon & Schuster.

Binder, R. (1999). Are the mentally ill dangerous? *Journal of the American Academy of Psychiatry and the Law, 27,* 189–201.

Binswanger, L. (1944). Der Fall Ellen West. In Binswanger, L. (1956). *Schizophrenie.* Pfuhlingen:Neske.

Bird, H. R (2002). The diagnostic classification, epidemiology, and cross-cultural validity of ADHD. In P. Jensen & J. Cooper (Eds.), *Attention deficit hyperactivity disorder: State of the science-best practices* (pp. 2–16). Kingston, NJ: Civic Research Institute.

Bird, H. R., Gould, M. S., & Staghezza, B. (1992). Aggregating data from multiple informants in child psychiatry epidemiologi-cal research, *Journal of the American Academy of Child and Adolescent Psychiatry, 31,* 78–85.

Bird, H. R., Gould, M. S., & Staghezza, B. M. (1993). Patterns of diagnostic comorbidity in a community sample of children aged 9 through 16 years of age. *Journal of the American Academy of Child and Adolescent Psychiatry, 32,* 361–368.

Birmaher, B., Axelson, D., Strober, M., Gill, M. K., Valeri, S., Chiappetta, L., et al. (2006). Clinical course of children and ado-lescents with bipolar spectrum disorders. *Archives of General Psychiatry, 63,* 175–183.

Bisaga, K., & Walsh, T. (2005). History of the classification of eating disorders. In C. Norring & B. Palmer (Eds.), *EDNOS: Eating Disorders Not Otherwise Specified* (pp. 10–40). Hove, UK: Routledge.

Bishop, D. V. M. (1989). Autism, Asperger's syndrome and semantic-pragmatic disorder: Where are the boundaries? *British Journal of Disorders of Communications, 24,* 107–121.

Bishop, D. V. M. (1995, October). *Semantic-pragmatic disorder and Asperger syndrome.* Paper presented at the *42nd* annual meeting of the American Academy of Child and Adolescent Psychiatry, New Orleans, LA.

Black, B. (1995). Separation anxiety disorder and panic disorder, In J. S. March (Ed.), *Anxiety disorders in children and ado-lescents.* New York: Guilford.

Blader, J. C., & Carlson, G. A. (2007). Increased rates of bipolar disorder diagnoses among U. S. child, adolescent and adult inpatients, 1996–2004. *Biological Psychiatry, 62,* 107–114.

Blatt, B., & Kaplan, F. (1966). *Christmas in purgatory: A photographic essay on mental retardation.* Boston: Allyn & Bacon.

Bleuler, E. (1934). *Textbook of psychiatry.* New York: Macmillan.

Blinder, B. J., & Cadenhead, K. (1989). Bulimia: A historical overview. In S. C. Feinstein, A. H. Esman, J. G. Looney, A. Z.

Schwartzberg, A. Sorosky, et al. (Eds). *Adolescent psychiatry: Developmental and clinical studies, Vol. 13* (pp. 231–240). Chicago, IL: University of Chicago Press.

Blinder, B. J. & Chao, K. H. (1994). Eating disorders: A historical perspective. In L. Alexander-Mott, & D. B. Lumsden (Eds). *Understanding eating disorders: Anorexia nervosa, bulimia nervosa, and obesity* (pp. 3–35). Philadelphia: Taylor & Francis.

Blinder, B. J., Cumella, E. J., & Sanathara, V. A. (2006). Psychiatric comorbidities of female inpatients with eating disorders. *Psychosomatic Medicine, 68*, 454–462.

Bloomquist, M. L. (1996). *Skills training for children with behavior disorders: A parent and therapist guidebook.* New York: Guilford.

Blotcky, M. J., Dimperio, T. L., & Gossett, J. T. (1984). Follow-up of children treated in psychiatric hospitals. *American Journal of Psychiatry, 141*, 1499–1507.

Blum, R. W., Beuhring, T., Shew, M., Bearinger, L., Sieving, R., & Resnick, T. (2000). The effects of race/ethnicity, income and family structure on adolescent risk behaviors. *American Journal of Public Health, 90*, 1885–1891.

Blumberg, H. P. (2007). Dimensions in the development of bipolar disorder. *Biological Psychiatry, 62,* 104–106.

Blumberg, H. P., Kaufman, J., Martin, A., Witeman, R., Zhang, J. H., Gore, J. C., et al. (2003). Amygdala and hippocampal volumes in adolescents and adults with bipolar disorder. *Archives of General Psychiatry, 60*, 1201–1208.

Boddy, J., Skuse, D., & Andrews, B. (2000). The developmental sequelae of nonorganic failure to thrive. *Journal of Child Psychology and Psychiatry, 41*, 1003–1014.

Bogels, S., & Zigterman, D. (2000). Dysfunctional cognitions in children with social phobia, separation anxiety disorder, and generalized anxiety disorder. *Journal of Abnormal Child Psychology, 28*, 205–211.

Boll, T. (1993). *Children's category test.* San Antonio, TX: The Psychological Corporation.

Boone, E. M., & Leadbeater, B. J. (2006). Game on: Diminishing risks for depressive symptoms in early adolescence through positive involvement in team sports. *Journal of Research on Adolescence, 16*, 79–90.

Borchardt, C. M., & Bernstein, G. A. (1995). Comorbid disorders in hospitalized bipolar adolescents compared with unipolar depressed adolescents. *Child Psychiatry and Human Development, 26*, 11–23.

Boris, N., Seanah, C., Larrieu, J. A., Scheeringa, M. S., & Heller, S. (1998). Attachment disorders in infancy and early childhood: A preliminary investigation of diagnostic criteria. *American Journal of Psychiatry, 155*, 295–297.

Borowsky, I., Ireland, M., & Resnick, M. D. (2001). Adolescent suicide attempts: Risks and protectors. *Pediatrics, 107*, 485–493.

Bosking-Lodahl, M., & White, W. (1978). The definition and treatment of bulimarexia in college women: A pilot study. *Journal of the American College Health Association, 27*, 84–86.

Botta, R. (2000). The mirror of television: A comparison of Black and White adolescents' body image. *Journal of Communication*, 144–159.

Botvin, G. J., Griffin, K. W., Diaz, T. M., & Ifill-Williams, M. (2001). Preventing binge drinking during early adolescence: One- and two-year followup of a school-based prevention intervention. *Psychology of Addictive Behaviors, 15*, 360–365.

Bowd, A. D. (1983). Children's fears of animals. *The Journal of Genetic Psychology, 142*, 313–314.

Bowlby, J. (1973). *Attachment and loss: Vol. 2. Separation: Anxiety and anger.* New York: Basic Books.

Bradley, R. C. (1998). Child rearing in African American families: A study of the disciplinary practices of African American parents. *Journal of Multicultural Counseling and Development, 26*, 273–281.

Brandao, C. M., Lombardi M. T., Nishida, S. K., Jauache, O. M., & Vieira, J. G. (2003). Serum leptin concentration during puberty in healthy nonobese adolescents. *Brazilian Journal of Medical & Biological Research, 36*, 1293–1296.

Brando, D. M., Lombardi, M. T., Nishida, S. K., Hauache, O. M., & Vieriera, J. G. (2003). *Brazilian Journal of Medical and Biological Research, 36*, 1293–1296.

Bratton, S. C., Ray, D., Rhine, T., & Jones, L. (2005). The efficacy of play therapy with children: A meta-analytic review of treatment outcomes. *Professional Psychology: Research and Practice, 36*(4), 376–390.

Bremner, J. D. (1999). Does stress damage the brain? *Biological Psychiatry, 45*, 797–805.

Brendgen, M., Vitaro, F., & Tremblay, R. E. (2001). Reactive and proactive aggression: Predictions to physical violence in different contexts and moderating effects of parental monitoring and caregiving behavior. *Journal of Abnormal Child Psychology, 29*, 293–304.

Brent, D. A. (2001). Assessment and treatment of the youthful suicidal patient. In H. Hendin & J. J. Mann (Eds.), *The clinical science of suicide prevention* (Vol. 932, pp. 106–131). New York: Annals of the New York Academy of Sciences.

Breslau, N., Davis, G., Andreski, P., & Peterson, E. (1991). Traumatic events and post-traumatic stress disorder in an urban population of young adults. *Archives of General Psychiatry, 48*, 218–222.

Breslau, N., Paneth, N. S., & Lucia, V. C. (2004). The lingering effects of low birth weight children. *Pediatrics, 114*(4), 1035–1040.

Brestan, E. V., & Eyberg, S. M. (1998). Effective psychosocial treatments of conduct-disordered children and adolescents: 29 years, 82 studies and 5,272 kids. *Journal of Clinical Child Psychology, 27*, 180–189.

Bricklin, P. (2001). Being ethical: More than obeying the law and avoiding harm. *Journal of Personality Assessment, 77*(2), 195–202.

Bridge, J. A., Iyengar, S., Salary, C. B., Barbe, R. P., Birmaher, B., Pincus, H. A., et al. (2007). Clinical response and risk for reported suicidal ideation and suicide attempts in pediatric antidepressant treatment: A meta-analysis of randomized controlled trials. *Journal of the American Medical Association, 297*, 1683–1696.

Briere, J. (1996). *Trauma symptom checklist for children: Professional manual.* Lutz, FL: Psychological Assessment Resources.

Brodeur, C. (2006). Building social competence in children with nonverbal learning disabilities; A preliminary study. *Dissertation Abstracts International: B. The Sciences and Engineering, 67*, 531.

Brody, G., Flor, D., & Nuebaum, E. (1998). Coparenting processes and child competence among rural African American families. In M. Lewis & C. Feiring (Eds.), *Families, risk, and competence* (pp. 227–243). Mahwah, NJ: Erlbaum.

Bronfenbrenner, U. (1979). *The ecology of human development.* Cambridge, MA: Harvard University Press.

Bronfenbrenner, U. (1989). Ecological systems theory. *Annals of Child Development, 6,* 187–249.

Brook, J. S., Whiteman, M., Gordon, A. S., & Brook, D. W. (1990). The role of older brothers' drug use viewed in the context of parent and peer influences. *Journal of Genetic Psychology, 151,* 59–75.

Brook, J. S., Cohen, P., & Brook, D. S. (1998). Longitudinal study of co-occurring psychiatric disorders and substance use. *Journal of the American Academy of Child and Adolescent Psychiatry, 37,* 322–330.

Brooke, M., & Pelham, W. E. (2003). Childhood predictors of adolescent substance use in a longitudinal study of children with ADHD. *Journal of Abnormal Psychology, 112,* 497–508.

Brooks-Gunn, J., & Duncan, G. J. (1997). The effects of poverty on children. *The Future of Children, 7,* 55–71.

Brotman, M. A., Rich, B. A., Schmajuk, M., Reising, M., Monk, C. S., Dickstein, D. P., et al. (2007). Attention bias to threat faces in children with bipolar disorder and comorbid lifetime anxiety disorders. *Biological Psychiatry, 61,* 819–821.

Brotman, M. A., Schmajuk, M., Rich, B. A., Dickstein, D. P., Guyer, A. E., Costello, E. J., et. al. (2006). Prevalence, clinical correlates and longitudinal course of severe mood dysregulation in children. *Biological Psychiatry, 60,* 991–997.

Brown, S. A. (1993). Recovery patterns in adolescent substance abusers. In J. S. Baer, G. A. Marlatt, & R. J. McMahon (Eds.), *Addictive behaviors across the lifespan: Prevention, treatment and policy issues* (pp. 161–183). Newbury Park, CA: Sage.

Brown, T. A., Chorpita, B., F., & Barlow, D. H. (1998). Structural relationships among dimensions of the *DSM-IV* anxiety and mood disorders and dimensions of negative affect, positive affect, and autonomic arousal. *Journal of Abnormal Psychology, 107*(2), 179–192.

Brown, T. E. (2001). *Brown ADD Scales for Children and Adolescents.* San Antonio, TX: Psychological Corporation.

Bruch, H. (1973). *Eating disorders: Obesity, anorexia and the person within.* New York: Basic Books.

Buchanan, A. (1997). The investigation of acting on delusions as a tool for risk assessment in the mentally disordered. *British Journal of Psychiatry, 170,* 12–14.

Buchanan, A. (1999). Risk and dangerousness. *Psychology and Medicine, 29,* 465–473.

Buhrmester, D., Whalen, C., & Henker, B. (1992). Prosocial behavior in hyperactive boys: Effects of stimulant medication and comparison with normal boys. 103–121.

Buka, S. L., Stichick, T. L., Birdthistle, I., & Earls, F. (2001). Youth exposure to violence: Prevalence, risks and consequences. *American Journal of Orthopsychiatry, 71,* 298–310.

Bull, R., & Johnston, R. S. (1997). Children's arithmetical difficulties: Contributions from processing speed, item identification and short-term memory. *Journal of Experimental Child Psychology, 65,* 1–24.

Bullis, M., Walker, H. M., & Sprague, J. R. (2001). A promise unfulfilled: Social skills training with at-risk and antisocial children and youth. *Exceptionality, 9,* 67–90.

Burrow-Sanchez, J. (2006). Understanding adolescent substance abuse: Prevalence, risk factors and clinical implications. *Journal of Counseling & Development, 84,* 283–290.

Buss, A. H., & Plomin, R. (1975). *A temperament theory of personality development.* New York: Wiley.

Byrne, M., Barry, M., & Sheridan, A. (2004). Implementation of a school-based mental health promotion program in Ireland. *International Journal of Mental Health Promotion, 6,* 17–25.

Cadoret, R., Yates, W. R., Troughton, E., Woodworth, G., & Stewart, M. A. (1995). Adoption study demonstrating two genetic pathways to drug abuse. *Archives of General Psychiatry, 52,* 42–52.

Cain, D. S., & Combs-Orme, T. (2005). Family structure effects on parenting stress and practices in the African American family. *Journal of Sociology and Social Welfare, 32*(2), 19–40.

Campbell, S. B., & Ewing, L. J. (1990). Follow-up of hard to mange preschoolers: Adjustment at age 9 and predictors of continuing symptoms. *Journal of Child Psychology and Psychiatry, 31,* 871–889.

Cantwell, D. P. (1996). Attention Deficit Disorder: A review of the past 10 years. *Journal of American Academy of child and Adolescent Psychiatry, 35,* 978–987.

Cantwell, D., & Carlson, G. (1983). Issues in classification. In I. D. Cantwell & G. Carlson, (Eds.), *Affective disorders in childhood and adolescence: An up-date* (pp. 19–38). New York: Spectrum.

Carlson, G., Bromet, E., Driessens, J., Mojtabai, R., & Schwartz, J. (2002). Age at onset, childhood psychopathology and 2-year outcome in psychotic bipolar disorder. *American Journal of Psychiatry, 159,* 307–309.

Carlson, G., & Cantwell. D. (1980). Unmasking masked depression in children and adolescents. *American Journal of Psychiatry, 137,* 445–449.

Carlson, G., Pine, D., Nottelmann, J., & Leibenluft, E. (2004). Defining subtypes of childhood bipolar illness. *Journal of the American Academy of Child and Adolescent Psychiatry, 43,* 3–4.

Carlson, G., & Rapport, M. D. (1989). Diagnostic classification issues in attention-deficit hyperactivity disorder. *Psychiatric Annals, 19,* 576–583.

Carlson, V., Cicchetti, D., Barnett, D., & Braunwald, K (1989). Disorganized/disoriented attachment relationships in maltreated infants. *Developmental Psychology, 25,* 525–531.

Carrasco, J., Diaz-Marsa, M., Hollander, E., Cesar, J., & Salz-Ruiz. (2000). Decreased platlet monoamine oxidase activity in female bulimia nervosa. *European Neuropsychoparmacology, 10,* 113–117.

Carrion, V. G., Weems, C. F., Ray, R., & Reiss, A. L. (2002). Towards an empirical definition of pediatric PTSD: The phenomenology of PTSD symptoms in youth. *Journal of the American Academy of Child & Adolescent Psychiatry, 41,* 166–173.

Carter, J., Stewart, D., Dunn, V., & Fairburn, C. (1997). Primary prevention of eating disorders: Might it do more harm than good? *International Journal of Eating Disorders, 22,* 167–172.

Carvill, S., & Marston, G. (2002). People with intellectual disability, sensory impairments and behavior disorder: A case series. *Journal of Intellectual Disability Research, 26,* 264–272.

Cashel, M. L. (2002). Child and adolescent psychological assessment: Current clinical practices and the impact of managed care. *Professional Psychology: Research and Practice, 33*(5), 446–453.

Casper, R. C., Hedeker, D., & McClough, J. F. (1992). Personality dimensions in eating disorders and their relevance for subtyping. *Journal of the American Academy of Child and Adolescent Psychiatry, 31*, 830–840.

Caspi, A., Henry, B., McGee, R., Moffitt, T., & Silva. P. A. (1995). Temperamental origins of child and adolescent behavior problems: From age three to age fifteen. *Child Development, 66*, 55–68.

Caspi, A., McClay, J., Moffitt, E. E., Mill, J., Martin, J., Craig, I., Taylor, A., & Poulton, R. (2002). Role of genotype in the cycle of violence in maltreated children. *Science, 297*, 851–854.

Caspi, A., Moffitt, T. E., Newman D. L., & Silva, P. A. (1996). Behavioral observations at age 3 predict adult psychiatric disorders: Longitudinal evidence from a birth cohort. *Archives of General Psychiatry, 53*, 1033–1039.

Caspi, A., Sugden, K., Moffit, T. E., Taylor, A., Craig, I., Harrington, H., et al. (2003). Influence of life stress on depression moderation by a polymorphism in the 5-HTT gene. *Science, 18*, 386–389.

Cassidy, J., & Mohr, J. (2001). Unsolvable fear, trauma, and psychopathology: Theory, research and clinical considerations related to disorganized attachment across the life span. *Clinical Psychology: Science and Practice, 8*, 275–298.

Castellanos, F. X., Giedd, J., Marsh, W., & Hamburger, S. (1966). Quantitative brain magnetic resonance imaging in attention-feficit hyperactivity disorder. *Archives of General Psychiatry, 53*, 607–616.

Castellanos, F. X., Sharp, W. S., Gottesman, R. F., Giedd, J. N., & Rapoport, J. L. (2003). Anatomic brain abnormalities in monozygotic twins discordant for attention-deficit/hyperactivity disorder. *American Journal of Psychiatry, 160*, 1693–1696.

Cattarin, J. A., Thompson, J. K. (1944). A three-year longitudinal study of body image, eating disturbance, and general psychological functioning in adolescent females. *Eating Disorders: Journal of Treatment and Prevention, 2*, 114–125.

Catterall, J. S. (1987). An intensive group counseling dropout prevention intervention: Some cautions on isolating at-risk adolescents within high schools. *American Education Research Journal, 24*, 521–540.

Cauce, A. M., & Domenech-Rodriguez, M. (2002). Latino families: Myths and realities. In J. M. Contreras, K. A. Kerns, & A. M. Neal-Barnett (Eds.), *Latino children and families in the United States* (pp. 3–25). Westport, CT: Praeger.

Centers for Disease Control (CDC, 1999) Bidi use among urban youth—Massachusetts, March–April 1999. *Morbidity and Mortality Weekly Report, 48*(36), 796–799.

Centers for Disease Control and Prevention (CDC, 2005). Tobacco Use, Access, and Exposure to Tobacco in Media Among Middle and High School Students—United States, 2004. *Morbidity and Mortality Weekly Report, 54*(12), 297–301.

Centers for Disease Control and Prevention (CDC, 2005). Youth Risk Behavior Surveillance (YRBS, 2005). *Morbidity and Mortality Weekly Report, 55*(SS55).

Chakrabarti, S., & Fombonne, E. (2001). Pervasive developmental disorders in preschool children. *Journal of the American Medical Association, 285*(24), 3093–3099.

Chamberlain, P., & Reid, J. (1998). Comparison of two community alternatives to incarceration for chronic juvenile offenders. *Journal of Consulting and Clinical Psychology, 66*, 624–633.

Chambless, D., & Hollon, S. (1998). Defining empirically supported therapies. *Journal of Consulting and Clinical Psychology, 66*(1), 7–18.

Chan, S. Families with Asian roots. In E. W. Lynch & M. J. Hanson (Eds.), *Developing cross-cultural competence* (2nd ed., pp. 251–354). Baltimore: Paul H. Brookes.

Chang, K., Karchemskly, R., Barnea-Goraly, A., Garrett, A., Simeonova, D., Reiss, A., et al. (2005). Reduced amygdalar gray matter volume in familiar pediatric bipolar disorder. *Journal of the American Academy of Child & Adolescent Psychiatry, 44*, 565–573.

Chapman, R. S., & Hesketh, L. J. (2000). Behavioral phenotype of individuals with Down syndrome. *Mental Retardation and Developmental Disabilities Research Review, 6*, 84–95.

Chassin, L., Ritter, J., Trim, R., & King, K. M. (2003). Adolescent substance abuse disorders. In E. L. Mash & R,A. Barkley (Eds.), *Child psychopathology* (2nd ed., pp. 199–230). New York: Guilford.

Chatoor, I. (1997). Feeding disorders of infants and toddlers. In S. Greenspan, S. Wieder, & J. Osofsky (Eds.), *Handbook of child and adolescent psychiatry. Vol. 1. Infants and preschoolers: Development and syndromes* (pp. 367–386). New York: Wiley.

Chemtob, C. M., Nakashima, J., & Carlson, J. (2002). Brief treatment for elementary school children with disaster-related posttraumatic stress disorder: A field study. *Journal of Clinical Psychology, 58*(1), 99–112.

Chen, X., Rubin, K., & Li, B. (1995). Depressed mood in Chinese children: Relations with school performance and family environment. *Journal of Consulting and Clinical Psychology, 63*, 938–947.

Chervin R. D., Archbold, K. H., Dillon, J. E., Panahi, P., Pituch, K. J., Dahl, R. E., et al. (2002). Inattention, hyperactivity, and symptoms of sleep-disordered breathing. *Pediatrics, 109*, 449–456.

Chervin, R. D., Dillon, J. E., Bassetti, C., Ganoczy, D. A., & Pituch, K. J. (1997). Symptoms of sleep disorders, inattention, and hyperactivity in children. *Sleep, 20*, 1185–1192.

Children's Defense Fund. (2005). *The state of American's children, 2005*. Washington, DC: Children's Defense Fund.

Childress, A., Brewerton, T., Hodges, E., & Jarrell, M. (1993). The Kids' Eating Disorders Survey (KEDS): a study of middle school students. *Journal of the American Academy of Child & Adolescent Psychiatry, 32*, 843–850.

Christakis, S. A., Zimmerman, F. J., DiGiuseppe, D. L., & McCarty, C. A. (2004). Early television exposure and subsequent attentional problems in children. *Pediatrics, 113*, 708–713.

Christian, R. E., Frick, P. J., & Hill, N. L. (1997). Psychopathy and conduct problems in children: II. Implications for subtyping children with conduct problems. *Journal of the American Academy of Child & Adolescent Psychiatry 36*(2), 233–241.

Chong, M. Y., Chan, K. W., & Cheng, A. T. (1999). Substance sue disorders among adolescents in Taiwan: Prevalence, sociodemographic correlates, and psychiatric comorbidity. *Psychological Medicine, 29*, 1387–1396.

Chorpita, B. F. (2002). The tripartite model and dimensions of anxiety and depression: An examination of structure in a large school sample. *Journal of Abnormal Child Psychology, 30*, 177–190.

Chorpita, B. F., Plummer, C. P., & Moffitt, C. (2000). Relations of tripartite dimensions of emotion to childhood anxiety and mood disorders. *Journal of Abnormal Child Psychology, 28*, 299–310.

Cicchetti, D., & Rogosh, F. A. (1996). Editorial: Equifinality and multifinality in developmental psychopathology. *Development and Psychopathology, 8,* 597–600.

Cicchetti, D., & Toth, S. L. (1991). A developmental perspective on internalizing and externalizing psychopathology. *Development and Psychopathology, 8,* 597–600.

Cicchetti, D., & Toth, S. L. (1998). The development of depression in children and adolescents. *American Psychologist, 53*(2), 221–241.

Cicchetti, D., & Rogosh, F. A. (1996). Editorial: Equifinality and multifinality in developmetal psychopathology. *Development and Psychopathology, 8,* 597–600.

Cicchetti, D., & Rogosch, F. A. (2002). A developmental psychopathology perspective on adolescence. *Journal of Consulting and Clinical Psychology, 70,* 6–20.

Cicchetti, S., & White, J. (1990). Emotion and developmental psychopathology. In N. Stein, B. Leventhal, & T. Trabasso (Eds.), *Psychological and biological approaches to emotion* (pp. 359–382). Hillsdale, NJ: Erlbaum.

Claes, L., Nederkoorn, C., Vandereycken, W., Guerrieri, R., & Vertommen, H. (2006). Impulsiveness and lack of inhibitory control in eating disorders. *Eating Behaviors, 7,* 196–203.

Clarizio, H. F. (1994). *Assessment and treatment of depression in children and adolescents* (2nd ed.). Brandon, VT: Wiley.

Clark, L. A., & Watson, D. (1991). Tripartite model of anxiety and depression: Psychometric evidence and taxonomic implications. *Journal of Abnormal Psychology, 100,* 316–336.

Clark, L. A., Watson, D., & Mineka, S. (1994). Temperament, personality, and the mood and anxiety disorders. *Journal of Abnormal Psychology, 103,* 103–116.

Clarke, G., Hawkins, W., Murphy, M. & Sheeber (1993). School-based primary prevention of depressive symptomatology in adolescents: Findings from two studies. *Journal of Adolescent Research, 8,* 183–204.

Clifford, C. A., & Mills, P. A. (2002). *I am a living prayer of my ancestors: Youth transition issues and practices in Casey Family Program's Native American sites.* Unpublished Manuscript.

Clinton, D. N., & Glant, R. (1992). The eating disorders spectrum of *DSM-III-R:* Clinical features and psychosocial concomitants of 86 consecutive cases from a Swedish urban catchment area*, Journal of Nervous and Mental Disease, 180,* 244–250.

Cloninger, C. F., & Svrakic, D. M. (1997). A multidimensional psychobiological model of violence. In A. Raine, B. Brennan, D. Farrington, & S. Mednick (Eds.), *Biosocial bases of violence* (pp. 39–54). New York: Plenum.

Cobham, V. E., Dadds, M. R., & Spence, S. H. (1998). The role of parental anxiety in the treatment of childhood anxiety. *Journal of Consulting and Clinical Psychology, 66,* 893–905.

Cohen, P., Cohen, J. Kasen, S., Velez, C. N. Hartmark, C., Johnson, J., Rojas, M., Brook, J., & Streuning, E. L. (1993). An epidemiological study of disorders in late childhood and adolescence: I. Age-and gender-specific prevalence. *Journal of Child Psychology and Psychiatry, 34,* 851–867.

Coie, J. D. (1985). Fitting social skills interventions to the target group. In B. Schneider, K. Rubin, & J. Ledingham (Eds.), *Peer relationships and social skills in childhood* (Vol. 2). New York: Springer.

Coie, J. D., & Dodge, K. A. (1983). Continuity of children's social status: A five-year longitudinal study. *Merrill-Palmer Quarterly, 29,* 261–282.

Coie, J. D., & Dodge, K. A. (1998). Aggression and antisocial behavior. In W. Damon & N. Eisenberg (Eds.), *Handbook of child psychology, 5th ed., Vol. 3. Social, emotional, and personality development* (pp. 779–862). Hoboken, NJ: Wiley.

Coie, J. D., Dodge, K., & Coppotelli, H. (1982). Dimensions and types of social status: A cross-age perspective. *Developmental Psychology, 18,* 557–570.

Coie, J. D., & Kupersmidt, J. B. (1983). A behavioral analysis of emerging social status in boys' groups. *Child Development, 54,* 1400–1416.

Colder, C., & Chassin, L. (1997). Affectivity and impulsivity: Temperament risk for adolescent alcohol involvement. *Psychology of Addictive Behaviors, 11,* 83–97.

Collins, D. W., & Rourke, B. P. (2003). Learning-disabled brains: A review of the literature. *Journal of Clinical and Experimental Neuropsychology, 25,* 1101–1034.

Comer, R. J. (2001). *Abnormal psychology* (4th ed.). New York: Worth Publishers.

Conason, A. H., & Sher, L. (2006). Alcohol use in adolescents with eating disorders. *International Journal of Adolescent Medicine and Health, 18,* 31–36.

Conduct Problems Prevention Research Group. (1992). A developmental and clinical model for the prevention of conduct disorder: The FAST Track Program. *Development and Psychopathology, 4,* 509–528.

Conners, C. K. (1998). *Conners Rating Scales—Revised technical manual.* North Tonawanda, NY: Multi-Health Systems.

Conners, C. K. (2000). *Continuous Performance Test-II.*

Conners, C. K., & Wells, K. (1997). *Conners-Wells Adolescent Self-Report Scale.* North Tonawanda, NY: Multi-Health Systems.

Connor, D. F., Steingard, R. J., Cunningham, J., Anderson, J., & Melloni, R. H. (2004). Proactive and reactive aggression in referred children and adolescents. *American Journal of Orthopsychiatry, 74,* 129–136.

Connor, P. D., Sampson, P., & Bookstein, F. L. (2001) Direct and indirect effects of prenatal alcohol damage on executive function. *Developmental Neuropsychology, 18,* 331–354.

Constantine, M., Alleyne, V. L., Wallace, B. C., & Franklin-Jackson, D. C. (2006). Africentric cultural values: Their relation to positive mental health in African American adolescent girls. *Journal of Black Psychology, 32,* 141–154.

Cook, A., Spinazzola, J., Ford, J., Lanktree, C., Blaustein, M., Cloitre, M., et al. (2005). Complex trauma in children and adolescents. *Psychiatric Annals, 35,* 390–439.

Cooper, J., Bloom, F., & Roth, R. (2003). *Amino acid transmitters (8th ed.). The Biochemical Basis of Neuropharmacolgy.* New York: Oxford University Press.

Cooper, M. (1996). Obsessive compulsive disorder: Effects on family members. *American Journal of Orthopsychiatry, 66,* 296–304.

Coppens, N. M., Hunter, P. N., & Bain, J. A. (1990). The relationship between elevated lead levels and enrollment in special education. *Family & Community Health, 12*, 39–46.

Corey, G., Corey, M., & Callanan, P. (1998). *Issues and ethics in the helping professions.* Belmont, CA: Thomson Brooks/Cole.

Cornoldi, C., Venneri, A., Marconato, R., Molin, A., & Montinari, C. (2003). A rapid screening measure for the identification of visuospatial learning disability in schools. *Journal of Learning Disabilities, 36*, 299–306.

Costello, J., Pine, D., Hammen, C., March, J., Plotsky, P. M., Weissman, M., et al. (2002). Development and natural history of mood disorders. *Biological Psychiatry, 52*(6), 529–542.

Couwenbergh, C., van den Brick, W., Zwart, K., Vreugdenhil, C., van Wijngaarden-Cremers, P., & van der Gaag, R. (2006). Comorbid psychopathology in adolescents and young adults treated fro substance use disorders. *European Child and Adolescent Psychiatry, 15*, 319–328.

Cowen, E. L., Wyman, P., Work, W. C., & Parker, G. R. (1990). The Rochester Child Resilience Project: Overview and summary of first year findings. *Development and Psychopathology, 2*, 193–212.

Creswell, J. W. (2003). *Research design: Qualitative methods, quantitative methods and mixed methods approaches.* Thousand Oaks, CA: Sage.

Crichton, P. (1996). Were the Roman emperors, Claudius and Vitellius Bulimic? *International Journal of Eating Disorders, 19*, 203–207.

Crick, N. R., & Dodge, K. A. (1996). Social information–processing mechanisms in reactive and proactive aggression. *Child Development, 67*, 993–1002.

Crick, N. R., & Grotpeter, J. K. (1995). Relational aggression, gender, and social-psychological adjustment. *Child Development, 66*, 710–722.

Crisp, A. H., Palmer, R. L., Kalucy, R. S. (1976). How common is anorexia nervosa? A prevalence study. *British Journal of Psychiatry, 128*, 549–554.

Criss, M., Pettit, G. S., Bates, J. D., Dodge, K. A., & Lapp, A. L. (2002). Family adversity, positive peer relationships and children's externalizing behavior: A longitudinal perspective on risk and resilience. *Child Development, 73*(4), 1220–1237.

Cuffe, S. P., McCullough, E. L., & Pumariega, A. J. (1994). Comorbidity of attention deficit hyperactivity disorder and post-traumatic stress disorder. *Journal of Child and Family Studies, 3*, 327–336.

Cullari, S., & Redmon, W. K. (1983). Bulimarexia, bulimia and binge eating: A bibliography. *Professional Psychology: Research and Practice, 14*, 400–405.

Cummins, J. (1984). *Bilingual special education: Issues in assessment and pedagogy.* San Diego, CA: College-Hill.

Cunninghan, E. G., Brandon, C. M., & Frydenberg, E. (1999). Building resilience in early adolescence through a universal school-based prevention program. *Australian Journal of Guidance and Counseling, 9*, 15–23.

Curran, S., Powell, J., Neale, B., Dworzynski, K., Li, T., Murphy, D., et al. (2006). An association analysis of candidate genes on chromosome 15 q11-13 and autism spectrum disorder. *Molecular Psychiatry, 11*, 709–713.

Cytryn, L., & McKnew, D. H. Jr. (1996). *Growing up sad: Childhood depression and its treatment.* New York: Norton.

Dabbs, J., & Morris, R. (1990). Testosterone, social class and antisocial behavior in a sample of 4,462 men. *Psychological Science, 1*, 209–211.

DaCosta, M., & Halmi, K. (1992). Classifications of anorexia nervosa: Question of subtypes. *International Journal of Eating Disorders, 11*, 305–313.

Dadds, M., Barrett, P. M., Rapee, R. M., & Ryan, S. (1996). Family process and child anxiety and aggression: An observational analysis. *Journal of Abnormal Child Psychology, 24*, 715–734.

Dales, L., Hammer, S. J., & Smith, N. J. (2001). Time trends in autism and MMR immunization coverage in California. *Journal of the American Medical Association, 285*, 1183–1185.

Dasen, P. R., Ngini, L., & Lavallee, M. (1979). Cross-cultural training studies of concrete operations. In L. Eckensberger, Y. Poortinga, & W. Lonner (Eds.), *Cross-cultural contributions to psychology* (pp. 94–104). Amsterdam: Swets & Zeitlinger.

Davidovitch, M., Glick, L., Holtzman, G., Tirosh, E., & Safir, M. P. (2000). Developmental regression in autism: Maternal perception. *Journal of Autism and Developmental Disorders, 30*(2), 113–119.

Davidson, J. (1993). Issues in the diagnosis of post-traumatic stress disorder. In R. S. Pynoos (Ed.), *Posttraumatic stress disorder. A Clinical Review* (pp. 1–15). Lutherville, MD: The Sidran Press.

Davies, P. T., & Cicchetti, D. (2004). Toward and integration of family systems and developmental psychopathology approaches. *Development and Psychopathology, 16*, 477–481.

Davis, D. W., Chang, F., Burns, B., Robinson, J., & Dossett, D. (2004). Lead exposure and attention regulation in children living in poverty. *Developmental Medicine & Child Neurology, 46*, 825–831.

Davis, W. E., & Kelso, J. A. (1982). Analysis of "invariant characteristics" in motor control of Down's syndrome and normal subjects. *Journal of Motor Behavior, 14*, 194–212.

Davison, K. K., & Birch, L. L. (2001). Weight status, parent reation and self-concept in five-year-old girls. *Pediatrics, 107*, 46–53.

Deas, D., Riggs, P., Langenbuncher, J., Goldman, M., & Brown, S. (2000). Adolescents are not adults: Developmental considerations in alcohol users. *Alcoholism: Clinical and Experimental Research, 24*, 232–237.

Deas, D., & Thomas, S. E. (2001). An overview of controlled studies of adolescent substance abuse treatment. *The American Journal on Addictions, 10*, 178–189.

Deater-Deckard, K., Dodge, K., Bates, K. A., & Pettit, G. S. (1996). Physical discipline among African-American and European-American mothers: Links to children's externalizing behaviors. *Developmental Psychology, 32*, 1065–1072.

DeBellis, M., Keshavan, M. S., Clark, D. B. (1999). Developmental traumatology: II. Brain development. *Biological Psychiatry, 45*(10), 1271–1284.

Deep, A. L., Nagy, L. M., Weltzin, T. E., Rao, R., & Kaye, W. H. (1995). Premorbid onset of psychopathology in long-term recovered anorexia nervosa. *International Journal of Eating Disorders, 17*, 291–297.

DeFries, J. C., & Alarcon, M. (1996). Genetics of specific reading disability. *Mental Retardation & Developmental Disabilities Research Reviews, 2,* 39–48.

DeFries, J. C., Singer, S. M., Foch, T. T., & & Lewitter, F. L. (1978). Familial nature of reading disability. *British Journal of Psychiatry, 132,* 361–367.

DeHann, E., Hoogduin, K., Buitelaar, J., & Keijser, S. (1998). Behavior therapy versus clomipramine for the treatment of obsessive-compulsive disorder. *Journal of the American Academy of Child & Adolescent Psychiatry, 37,* 1022–1029.

DeHart, G. B., Sroufe, L. A., & Cooper, R. (2000). Child development: Its nature and course (4th ed.). New York: McGraw-Hill.

DeKlyen, M., & Speltz, M. (2001). Attachment and conduct disorder. In J. Hill & B. Maughan (Eds.), *Conduct disorders in childhood and adolescence* (pp. 320–345). New York: Cambridge University Press.

DelBello, M., Adler, C., & Strakowski, S. (2006). The neurophysiology of childhood and adolescent bipolar disorder. *CNS Spectrums, 11,* 298–311.

Delis, D. C., Kaplan, E., & Kramer, J. H. (2001). *Delis-Kaplan Executive Function System (D-KEFS): Examiner's manual.* San Antonio, TX: The Psychological Corporation.

Delis, D. C., Kramer, J. H., Kaplan, E., & Ober, B. A. (1994). *California Verbal Learning Test—Children's version.* San Antonio, TX: The Psychological Corporation.

DeLos Reyes, A., & Kazdin, A. E. (2005). Informant discrepancies in the assessment of childhood psychopathology: A critical review, theoretical framework, and recommendations for further study. *Psychological Bulletin, 131*(4), 483–509.

Demonet, J-F., Taylor, M. J. & Chaix, Y. (2004). Developmental dyslexia. *The Lancet, 363,* 1451–1460.

Deykin, E. Y., & Buka, S. L. (1997). Prevalence and risk factors for posttraumatic stress disorder among chemically dependent adolescents. *American Journal of Psychiatry, 154,* 752–757.

Dickstein, D. P., Rich, B. A., Binstock, A., Pradella, A., Towbin, K., Pine, D. S., et al. (2005). Comorbid anxiety in phenotypes of pediatric bipolar disorder. *Journal of Child and Adolescent Psychopharmacology, 15,* 534–548.

DiLalla, L. F., & Gottesman, I. (1991). Biological and genetic contributions to violence: Wisdom's untold tale. *Psychological Bulletin, 109,* 125–129.

Diller, L. H. (1996). The run on Ritalin: Attention deficit disorder and stimulant treatments in the 1990s. *Hastings Center Report, 26,* 12–18.

Dishion, T. J., & Kavanagh, K. (2000). A multilevel approach to family-centered prevention in schools: Process and outcome. *Addictive Behaviors, 25,* 899–911.

Dishion, T. J., McCord, J., & Poulin, F. (1999). When interventions harm. Peer groups and problem behavior. *American Psychologist, 54,* 755–764.

Dishion, T. J., & Patterson, G. R. (1992). Age effects in parent training outcome. *Behavior Therapy, 23,* 719–729.

Dishion T. J., Spracklen, K. M., Andrews, D . W., & Patterson, G. R. (1996). Deviancy training in male adolescent friendships. *Behavior Therapy, 27,* 373–390.

Dixon, K., Monroe, L., & Jakim, S. (1981). Insomniac children. *Sleep, 4,* 313–318.

Dodge, K. A. (1991). The structure and function of reactive and proactive aggression. In D. J. Pepler & K. H. Rubin (Eds.), *The development and treatment of childhood aggression* (pp. 201–218). Hillsdale, NJ: Erlbaum.

Dodge, K. A., Bates, J., & Pettit, G. (1990). Mechanisms in the cycle of violence. *Science, 250,* 1678–1683.

Dodge, K. A., & Coie, J. D. (1987). Social–information—Processing factors in reactive and proactive aggression in children's peer groups. *Journal of Personality and Social Psychology, 53,* 1146–1158.

Dodge, K. A., Lochman, J. E. & Harnish, J. D., Bates, J., & Pettit, G. (1997). Reactive and proactive aggression in school children and psychiatrically impaired chronically assaultive youth. *Journal of Abnormal Psychology, 106,* 37–51.

Dodge, K. A., Pettit, G., & Bates, J. (1994). Effects of physical maltreatment on the development of peer relations. *Development and Psychopathology, 6,* 43–56.

Dodge, K. A., Price, J. M., Bachorowski, J. & Newman, J. P. (1990). Hostile attributional biases in severely aggressive adolescents. *Journal of Abnormal Psychology, 99,* 385–392.

Dombrowski, S. C., Kamphaus, R. W., & Reynolds, C. R. (2004). After the demise of the discrepancy: Proposed learning disabilities diagnostic criteria. *Professional Psychology: Research and Practice, 35,* 364–372.

Donohue, B., & Azrin, N. (2001). Family behavior therapy. In E. F. Wagner & H. B. Waldron (Eds.), *Innovations in adolescent substance abuse interventions* (pp. 205–227). Oxford: Elsevier Science.

Douglas, J. (2002). Psychological treatment of food refusal in young children. *Child and Adolescent Mental Health, 7*(4), 173–180.

Doyle, A. E., Wilens, T. E., Kwon, A., Seidman, L. J., Faraone, S., Fried, R., et al. (2005). Neuropsychological functioning in youth with bipolar disorder. *Biological Psychiatry, 58,* 540–548.

Drell, M. J., Siegel, C. H., & Gaensbauer, T. (1993). Post-traumatic stress disorder. In C. H. Zeanah (Ed.), *Handbook of infant mental health* (pp. 291–304). New York: Guilford.

Drotar, D., Stein, R., & Perrin, E. (1995). Methodological issues in using the Child Behavior Checklist and its related instruments in clinical child psychology research. *Journal of Clinical Child Psychology, 21*(2), 184–192.

Dumitrescu, C. (2006). Neuropsychological profile differences between children with Asperger's Syndrome and Nonvera Learning Disability. (2006). *Dissertation Abstracts International: Section B: The Sciences and Engineering, 66,* 39–45.

Duncan, G., Brooks-Gunn, J., & Klebanov, P. (1994). Economic deprivation and early childhood development. *Child Development, 65,* 296–318.

Dunston, P. J. (1992). A critique of graphic organizer research. *Reading Research and Instruction, 31,* 57–65.

DuPaul, G., & Eckert, T. L. (1998) Academic interventions for students with attention-deficit/hyperactivity disorder: A review of the literature. *Reading & Writing Quarterly: Overcoming Learning Difficulties, 14,* 59–82.

Durlak, J. (1998). Common risk and protective factors in successful prevention programs. *American Journal of Orthopsychiatry, 68*, 512–520.

Dykman, B., Horowitz, L. M., Abramson, L., & Usher, M. (1991). Schematic and situational determinants of depressed and nondepressed students' interpretation of feedback. *Journal of Abnormal Psychology, 100*, 45–55.

Dykman, R. A., & Ackerman, P. T. (1992). Attention deficit disorder and specific eating disability: Separate but often overlapping disorders. In S. Shaywitz, & B. Shaywitz, (Eds.), *Attention deficit disorder comes of age: Toward the twenty-first century* (pp. 165–184). Austin, TX: Pro-Ed.

Dykens, E. M., & Cassidy, S. B. (1995). Correlates of maladaptive behavior in children and adults with Prader–Willi syndrome. *Neuropsychiatric Genetics, 60*, 546–549.

Earls, F. (1994). Violence and today's youth. *The Future of Children, 14*(3), 4–23.

Eckert, T. L., Miller, D. N., DuPaul, G., & Riley-Tillman, T. C. (2003). Adolescent suicide prevention: School psychologists' acceptability of school-based programs. *School Psychology Review, 32*, 57–76.

Ecton, R. B., & Feindler, E. (1990). Anger control training for temper control disorders. In E. L. Feindler & G. R. Kalfus (Eds.), *Adolescent behavior therapy handbook* (pp. 351–371). New York: Springer.

Edelson, M. G. (2006). Are the majority of children with autism mentally retarded? A systematic evaluation of the data. *Focus on Autism and other Developmental Disabilities, 21*, 66–83.

Eden, G. G., Stein, J. F., Wood, M. H., & Wood, F. B. (1995). Verbal and visual problems in reading disability. *Journal of Learning Disabilities, 28*, 48–57.

Edlund, B., Halvarsson, K., & Sjoden, P. O. (1996). Eating behaviors and attitudes to leating, dieting and body image in 7-year-old Swedish girls. *European Eating Disorders Review,4*, 40–53.

Egeland, B., & Sroufe, L. A. (1981). Developmental sequelae of maltreatment in infancy. In D. Cicchetti & R. Rizley (Eds.), *New directions in child development: Developmental approaches to child maltreatment.* San Francisco: Jossey-Bass.

Ehlers, A., & Clark, D. M. (2000). A cognitive model of posttraumatic stress disorder. *Behavior Research and Therapy, 38*, 319–345.

Ehlers, S., Nyden, A., Gillberg, C., Dahlgren, S. A., Dahlgren, S. O., Hjelmquist, E., et al. (1997). Asperger syndrome, autism and attention disorders: A comparative study of the cognitive profiles of 120 children. *Journal of Child Psychology and Psychiatry, 38*, 207–217.

Eisenberg, N., Pidada, S., & Liew, J. (2001). The relations of regulation and negative emotionality to Indonesian children's social functioning. *Child Development, 72*, 1747–1763.

Eisenberg, N., Zhou, Q., Spinrad, T. L., Valiente, C. Fabes, R. A., & Liew, J. (2005). Relations among positive parenting, children's effortful control, and externalizing problems: A three-wave longitudinal study. *Child Development, 76*, 1055–1071.

Eisenberger, N. I., Lieberman, M. D., & Williams, K. D. (2003). Does rejection hurt? An fMRI study of social exclusion, *Science, 302*, 290–292.

Eley, T. C. (1999). Behavioral genetics as a tool for developmental psychology: Anxiety and depression in children and adolescents. *Clinical Child and Family Psychology Review, 2*, 21–36.

Eley, T. C., Deater-Deckard, K., Fombonne, E., & Fulker, D. W. (1998). An adoption study of depressive symptoms in middle childhood. *Journal of Child Psychology and Psychiatry and Allied Disciplines, 39*, 337–345.

Elia, J., & Rapoport, J. L. (1991). Ritalin versus dextroamphetamine in ADHD: Both should be tried. In L. L. Greenhill & B. B. Osmon (Eds.), *Ritalin: Theory and patient management* (pp. 69–74). New York: Mary Ann Liebert.

Elkind, D. (1967). Egocentrism in adolescence. *Child Development, 38*, 1025–1034.

Elkind, D., & Bowen, R. (1979). Imaginary audience behavior in children and adolescents. *Developmental Psychology, 15*, 38–44.

Ellickson, P. L., & Hays, R. D. (1988). Antecedents of drinking among young adolescents with different alcohol use histories. *Journal of Studies on Alcohol, 52*, 398–408.

Elliott, C. D. (2007). *Differential Ability Scales* (2nd ed.). San Antonio, TX: The Psychological Corporation.

Elliott, D. S., Huizinga, D., & Menard, S. (1988). *Multiple problem youth: Delinquency, substance use and mental health problems.* New York: Springer-Verlag.

Emery, R. E. (2001). Behavioral family intervention: Less "behavior" and more "family. " In A. Booth, A. C. Crouter, & M. Clements (Eds.), *Couples in conflict* (pp. 241–249). Mahwah, NJ: Erlbaum.

Emery, R. E., Fincham, F. D., & Cummings, E. M. (1992). Parenting in context: Systemic thinking about parental conflict and its influence on children. *Journal of Consulting and Clinical Psychology, 60*(6), 909–912.

Emslie, G. J., Rush, A. J., Weinberg, W. A., Kowatch, R. A., Hughes, C., Carmody, T., et al. (1997). A double-blind, randomized, placebo-controlled trial of fluoxetine in children and adolescents with depression. *Archives of General Psychiatry, 54*, 1031–1037.

Ennett, S. T., Tobler, N. S., Ringwalt, C. L., & Flewelling, R. L. (1994). How effective is Drug Abuse Resistance Education? A meta-analysis of project DARE outcome evaluations. *American Journal of Public Health, 84*, 1394–1404.

Enns, M. W., & Cox, B. (1997). Personality dimensions and depression: Review and commentary. *Canadian Journal of Psychiatry, 42*, 274–284.

Epstein, C. J. (1989). Down syndrome. In C. R. Scriver, A. L. Beaudet, W. S. Sly, & P. Valle (Eds.), *The metabolic basis of inherited disease* (pp. 291–396). New York: McGraw-Hill.

Epstein, J. N., Goldberg, N. A., Conners, C. K., & March, J. S. (1997). The effects of anxiety on continuous performance test functioning in an ADHD clinic sample. *Journal of Attention Disorders, 2*, 45–52.

Epsy, K. A., Kaufmann, P. M., & Glisky, M. L. (1999). Neuropsychologic function in toddlers exposed to cocaine in utero: A preliminary study. Developmental Neuropsychology, 15, 447–460.

Erickson, M. F., Sroufe, L. A., & Egeland, B. (1985). The relationship between quality of attachment and behavior problems in preschool in a high-risk sample. *Monographs of the Society for Research in Child Development, 50*(1–2), 147–166.

Essau, C. A., Contradt, J., & Petermann, F. (1999). Prevalence, comorbidity and psychosocial impairment of somatoform disorders in adolescents. *Psychology, Health, and Medicine, 4*, 169–180.

Essau, C. A., Conradt, J., & Petermann, F. (2000). Frequency, comorbidity and psychosocial impairment of specific phobia in adolescents. *Journal of Clinical Child Psychology, 29*, 221–232.

Everett, F., Proctor, N., & Carmell, B. (1983). Providing psycholocial services to American Indian children and families. *Professional Psychology: Research and Practice, 14*, 588–603.

Fabrega, H. (1990). Hispanic mental health research: A case for cultural psychiatry. *Hispanic Journal of Behavioral Science, 12*, 339–365.

Fairburn, C. G., Welch, S. l., Doll, H. A., Davies, B. A., & O'Connor, M. E. (1997). Risk factors for bulimia nervosa: A community-based case-control study. *Archives of General Psychiatry, 54*, 509–517.

Faraone, S. V., Biederman, J., Jetton, J. G., & Tsuang, M. T. (1997a). Attention deficit disorder and conduct disorder: Longitudinal evidence for a familial subtype. *Psychological Medicine, 27*, 291–300.

Faraone, S., Biederman, J., Wozniak, J., Mundy, E., Mennin, D., O'Donnell, D. (1997b). Is comorbidity with ADHD a marker for junvenil-onset mania? *Journal of the American Academy of Child and Adolescent Psychiatry, 36*, 1046-1055.

Farmer, T. W., & Rodkin, P. C. (1996). Antisocial and prosocial correlates of classroom social positions: The social network centrality perspective. *Social Development, 5*, 174–188.

Farrell, S. P., Hains, A., & Davies, W. H. (1998). Cognitive behavioral interventions for sexually abused children exhibiting PTSD symptomatology. *Behavior Therapy, 29*(2), 241–255.

Fas, P. S. (2003). Children and globalization. *Journal of Social History*, 963–977.

Feehan, M., McGee, R., Raja, S. N., & Williams, S. M. (1994). *DSM-III-R* Disorders in New Zealand 18-year-olds. *Australian and New Zealand Journal of Psychiatry, 28*, 87–99.

Feldman, R. A., Caplinger, T. E., & Wodarski, J. S. (1983). *The St. Louis conundrum: The effective treatment of antisocial youths.* Englewood Cliffs, NJ: Prentice-Hall.

Ferdinand, R. F., Blum, M., & Verhulst, F. C. (2001). Psychopathology in adolescence predicts substance use in young adulthood. *Addiction, 96*, 861–870.

Fergus, E. L., Miller, R. B., Luckenbaugh, D. A., Leverich, G. S., Findling, R. L., Speer, A. M., et al. (2003). Is there progression from irritability/dyscontrol to major depressive and manic symptoms? A retrospective community survey of parents of bipolar children. *Journal of Affective Disorders, 77*, 71–78.

Fergusson, D. M., Beautrais, A. L., & Horwood, L. J. (2003). Vulnerability and resiliency to suicidal behaviors in young people. *Psychological Medicine, 33*, 61–73.

Fergusson, D. M., & Horwood, L. J. (1997). Early onset cannabis use and psychosocial adjustment in young adults. *Addiction, 92*, 279–296.

Fergusson, D. M., & Mullen, P. E. (1999). *Childhood sexual abuse: An evidence based perspective.* Thousand Oaks, CA: Sage.

Field, A. E., Austin, S. B., Frazier, A. L., Gillman, M. W., Comargo, C. A., & Colditz, G. A. (2002). Smoking, getting drunk and engaging in bulimic behaviors: In which order are the behaviors adopted? *Journal of the American Academy of Child and Adolescent Psychiatry, 41*, 846–853.

Filipek, P. A., Accardo, P. J., Ashwal, S., Barnanek, G. T., Cook, E. H. Jr., Dawson, G., et al. (2000). Practice parameter: Screening and diagnosis of autism. *Neurology, 55*, 468–479.

Finckh, U. (2001). The dopamine D2 receptor gene and alcoholism: Association studies. *Alcohol in health and disease* (151–176). New York: Marcel Dekker.

Findling, R., Gracious, B., McNamara, N. K., Youngstrom, E. A., Demeter, C., & Calabrese, J. R. (2001). Rapid, continuous cycling and psychiatric comorbidity in pediatric bipolar disorder. *Bipolar Disorder, 3*, 202–210.

Fisher, C. (2004). Informed consent and clinical research involving children and adolescents: Implications of the Revised APA Ethics Code and HIPPA. *Journal of Clinical Child and Adolescent Psychology, 33*(4), 832–839.

Fisher, C., Hoagwood., K., Boyce, C., Duster, T., Frank, D. A., Grisso, T., et al. (2002). Research ethics for mental health science involving ethnic minority children and youth. *American Psychologist, 57*, 1027–1040.

Fisher, M., Pastore, D., Schneider, M., Pegler, C., & Napolitano (1994). Eating attitudes in urban and suburban adolescents. *International Journal of Eating Disorders, 16*, 67–74.

Fitsgibbon, M. L., Spring, B., Avellone, M. E., Blackman, L. R., Pingitore, R., & Stolley, M. R. (1998). Correlates of binge eating among Hispanic, Black and White women. *International Journal of Eating Disorders, 24*, 43–52.

Fitzpatrick, K. M., & Boldizar, J. P. (1993). The prevalence and consequences of exposure to violence among African American youth. *Journal of the American Academy of Adolescent Psychiatry, 32*, 424–430.

Flannery-Schroeder, E., & Kendall, P. C. (2000). Group and individual cognitive-behavioral treatments for youth with anxiety disorders: A randomized clinical trial. *Cognitive Therapy and Research, 24*, 251–278.

Fletcher, J. M., Francis, D. J., Morris, R. D., & Lyon, G. R. (2005). Evidence-based assessment of learning disabilities in children and adolescents. *Journal of Clinical Child and Adolescent Psychology, 34*, 506–522.

Fleming, J., & Offord, D. R. (1990). Epidemiology of childhood depressive disorders: A critical review. *Journal of the American Academy of Child & Adolescent Psychiatry, 29*, 571–580.

Flynn, J. R. (2006). Tethering the elephant: Capital cases, IQ, and the Flynn Effect. *Psychology, Public Policy and Law, 12*, 170–189.

Foa, E. B. (2000). "The expert consensus guideline series: Treatment of posttraumatic stress disorder" reply. *Journal of Clinical Psychiatry, 61*(10), 786–797.

Foa, E. B., & Kozak, M. J. (1986). Emotional processing of fear: Exposure to corrective information. *Psychological Bulletin, 99*, 220–235.

Foa, E. B., & Rothbaum, B. (1998). *Treating the trauma of rape: Cognitive-behavioral therapy for PTSD.* New York: Guilford.

Fombonne, E. (2003). Epidemiological surveys of autism and other pervasive developmental disorders: An update. *Journal of Autism and Developmental Disorders, 33*, 365–382.

Fonagy, P., & Target, M. (1996). A contemporary psychoanalytical perspective: Psychodynamic developmental therapy. In E. D. Hibbs & P. S. Jensen (Eds.), *Psychosocial treatments for child and adolescent disorders: Empirically based strategies for clinical practice* (pp. 619–638). Washington, DC: APA.

Forehand, R., & Kotchick, B. (1996). Cultural diversity: A wake-up call for parent training. *Behavior Therapy, 27*, 187–206.

Forehand, R., & McMahon, R. J. (1981). Predictors of cross setting behavior change in the treatment of child problems. *Journal of Behavior Therapy and Experimental Psychiatry, 12*, 311–313.

Forgatch, M., & Patterson, G. R. (1989). *Parents and adolescents living together. Part 2: Family problem solving*. Eugene, OR: Castalia.

Foss, J. M. (1991). Nonverbal learning disabilities and remedial interventions. *Annals of Dyslexia, 41*, 128–140.

Fowler, A. (1990). Language abilities in children with Down syndrome: Evidence for a specific syntactic delay. In D. Cicchetti & M. Beeghly (Eds.), Children with Down syndrome: A developmental perspective (pp. 302–328). Cambridge, UK: Cambridge University Press.

Fox, K., Becker-Green, J., Gault, J., & Simmons, D. (2005). Native American youth in transition: The path from adolescence to adulthood in two Native American communities. Portland, OR: National Indian Child Welfare Association.

Francis, G., & Ollendick. T. H. (1988). Social withdrawal. In M. Hersen & C. G. Last (Eds.), *Child behavior therapy casebook* (pp. 31–41). New York: Plenum.

Freedman, D. (1974). *Human infancy: An evolutionary perspective*. Hillsdale, NJ: Erlbaum.

Freeman, B. J., & Van Dyke, M. (2006). Are the majority of children with autism mentally retarded? Invited commentary. *Focus on Autism and Other Developmental Disabilities, 21*, 86–88.

French, M., Roebuck, M., Dennis, M., Diamond, G., Godley, S., Tims, F., et al. (2002). The economic cost of outpatient marijuana treatment for adolescents: Findings from a multi-site field experiement. *Addiction, 97*, 84–97.

Frick, P. J., Cornell, A., & Barry, C. T. (2003). Callous–unemotional traits and conduct problems in the prediction of conduct problem severity, aggression, and self-report of delinquency. *Journal of Abnormal Child Psychology, 31*(4), 457–470.

Frick, P. J. & Ellis, M. (1999). Callous–unemotional traits and subtypes of conduct disorder. *Clinical Child and Family Psychology Review, 2*(3), 149–168.

Frick, P. J., Kamphaus, R. W., Lahey, B. B., Loeber, R., Christ, M. A. G., Hart, E. L., & Tannenbaum, L. E. (1991). Academic underachievement and the disruptive behavior disorders. *Journal of Consulting and Clinical Psychology, 59*, 289–294.

Frick, P. J., Lahey, B. B., Loeber, R., Stouthamer-Loeber, M., Christ, T., & Hanson, K. (1992). Familial risk factor to oppositional defiant disorder and conduct disorder: Parental psychopathology and maternal parenting. *Journal of Consulting and Clinical Psychology, 60*, 49–55.

Frick, P. J., Lahey, B. B., Loeber, R., Tannenbaum, L., Van Horn, Y., Christ, M. A. G., et al. (1993). Oppositional defiant disorder and conduct disorder: A meta-analytic review of factor analyses and cross validation in a clinical sample. *Clinical Psychology Review, 13*, 319–340.

Frith, C. D., & Frith, U. (1999). Interacting Minds- A biological basis. *Science, 286*, 1692–1696.

Fritz, G. K., Fritsch, S., & Hagino, O. (1997). Somatoform disorders in children and adolescents: A review of the past 10 years. *Journal of the American Academy of Child and Adolescent Psychiatry, 36*, 1329–1338.

Fryer, A. J., Mannuzza, S., Chapman, R. F., Liebowitz, M. R., & Klein, D. F. (1993). A direct interview family study of social phobia. *Archives of General Psychiatry, 50*, 286–293.

Fulkerson, J. A., Keel, P., Leon, G. R., & Dorr, T. (1999). Eating-disordered behaviors and personality characteristics of high school athletes and nonathletes. *International Journal of Eating Disorders, 26*, 73–79.

Furstenberg, R. F. Jr. (1993). How families manage risk and opportunity in dangerous neighborhoods. In W. J. Wilson (Ed.), *Sociology and the Public Agenda* (pp. 231–258). Newbury Park, CA: Sage.

Gabbard, G. O. (Winter, 2005). Genes-Environment Interactions: Developmental and Psychotherapeutic Implications. *American Psychoanalytic Association Winter Meeting, New York*. Retrieved August 26, 2006, from http://psychiatrictimes. com/article/showAarticle. jhtml?articleId=167100516

Gaigg, S., & Bowler, D. (2007). Differential fear conditioning in Asperger's syndrome: Implications for an amygdale theory of autism. *Neuropsychologia, 45*, 2125–2134.

Garber, J., Walker, L. S., & Seman, J. (1991). Somatization symptoms in a community sample of children and adolescents. Further validation of the Children's Somatization Inventory. *Journal of Consulting and Clinical Psychology, 199*, 588–595.

Garber, J., Zeman, J., & Walker, L. S. (1990). Recurrent abdominal pain in children: psychiatric diagnoses and parental psychopathology. *Journal of the American Academy of Child and Adolescent Psychiatry, 29*, 648–656.

Garcia Coll, C. T., Lamberty, G., Jenkins, R., McAdoo, H. P., Crnic, K., Wasik, B. H., et al. (1996). An integrative model for the study of developmental competencies in minority children. *Child Development, 67*, 1891–1914.

Garfinkel, P., & Dorian, B. (2001). Improving understanding and care for the eating disorders. *Eating disorders: Innovative directions in research and practice* (pp. 9–26). Wasington, DC: APA.

Garfinkel, P. E., Lin, E., Goering, P., Spegg. C., Goldbloom, D., Kennedy, et al. (1996). Purging and nonpurging forms of bulimia nervosa in a community sample. *International Journal of Eating Disorders, 20*, 231–238.

Garland, A. F., & Zigler, E. (1993). Adolescent suicide prevention: Current research and social policy implications. *American Psychologist, 48*, 169–182.

Garmezy, N., Masten, A., & Tellegen, A. (1984). The study of stress and competence in children. *Child Development, 55*, 97–111.

Garner, D. M., Cooke, A. K., & Marano, H. E. (1997). The 1997 body image survey results. *Psychology Today*, 30–44.

Garner, D. M., Garfinkel, P. E., & O'Shaughnessy, M. (1985). The validity of the distinction between bulimia with and without anorexia nervosa. *American Journal of Psychiatry, 142*, 581–587.

Garner, D. M., Garner, M., & Rosen, L. (1993). Anorexia nervosa "restricters" who purge: Implications for subtyping anorexia nervosa. *International Journal of Eating Disorders, 12*, 171–185.

Garrison, C. Z., Addy, C., Jackson, K . L., McKeon, R., & Waller, J. L. Major depressive disorder and dysthymia in young adolescents. *American Journal of Epidemiology, 135*, 792–802.

Garvin, V., & Striegel-Moore, R. H. (2001). Health services research for eating disorders in the United States: A status report and a call to action. In R. H. Striegel-Moore & L. Smolak (Eds.), *Eating Disorders: Innovative Directions in Research and Practice* (pp. 135–152). Washington, DC:APA.

Geary, D. C. (2000). Mathematical disorders: An overview for educators. *Perspectives, 26*, 6–9.

Geary, D. C. (2003). Learning disabilities in arithmetic. In H. L. Swanson, K. R. Harris, & S. Graham (Eds.), *Handbook of learning disabilities* (pp. 199–212). New York: Guilford.

Geary, D. C. (2004). Mathematics and learning disabilities. *Journal of Learning Disabilities, 37*, 4–15.

Geary, D. C., & Brown, S. C. (1991). Cognitive addition: Strategy choice and speed-of-processing differences in gifted, normal, and mathematically disabled children. *Developmental Psychology, 27*, 398–406.

Geary, D. C., & Hoard, M. K. (2002). Learning disabilities in basic mathematics: Deficits in memory and cognition. In J. M. Royer (Ed.), *Mathematical cognition* (pp. 93–115). Greenwich, CT: Information Age Publishing.

Geller, B. (2001). A prepubertal and early adolescent bipolar disorder phenotype has poor one-year outcome. *The Brown University Child and Adolescent Psychopharmacology Update, 3*, 1–5.

Geller, B., Fox, L., & Clark, K. (1994). Rate and predictions of prepubertal bipolarity during follow-up of 6- to 12-year-old depressed children. *Journal of the American Academy of Child and Adolescent Psychiatry, 33*, 461–468.

Geller, B., Luby, J., (1997). Child and Adolescent Bipolar Disorder: A Review of the Past 10 Years. *Journal of the American Academy of Child and Adolescent Psychiatry, 36*,1168–1176.

Geller, B., Tillman, R., Badner, J., & Cook, E. (2005). Are the arginine vasopressin V1a receptor cirosatellites related to hypersexuality in children with prepubertal and early adolescent bipolar disorder phenotype? *Bipolar disorders, 7*, 610–616.

Geller B., Tillman, R., Craney, J. L., & Bolhofner, K. (2004). Four-year prospective outcome and natural history of mania in children with a prepubertal and early adolescent bipolar disorder phenotype. *Archives of General Psychiatry, 61*, 459–467.

Geller, B., Zimerman, B., Williams, M., Bolhofner, K., & Craney, J. L. (2001). Bipolar disorder at prospective follow-up of adults who had prepubertal major depressive disorder. *American Journal of Psychiatry, 158*(1), 125–127.

Geller, B., Zimerman, B., Williams, M., Bolhofner, K. Craney, J. L., Delbello, M. P., et al. (2000). Diagnostic characteristics of 93 cases of prepubertal and early adolescent bipolar disorder phenotype by gender, puberty, and comorbid attention deficit hyperactivity disorder. *Journal of Child and Adolescent Psychopharmacology, 10*, 157–164.

Geller, B., Zimerman, B., Williams, M., DelBello, R., Bolhofner, J., Craney, J., et al. (2002). *DSM–IV* mania symptoms in a prepubertal and early adolescent bipolar disorder phenotype compared to attention-deficit hyperactive and normal controls. *Journal of Child and Adolescent Psychopharmacology, 12*, 11–25.

Geller, D. A., Biederman, J., Farapine. S., Agranat, A., Cradlock, K., Hagermoser, L., et al. (2001). Disentangling chronological age from age of onset in children and adolescents with obsessive-compulsive disorder. *International Journal of Neuropsychopharmacology, 4*, 169–178.

Geller, D. A., Biederman, J., Jones, J., Park, K., Schwartz, S., Shapiro, S., & Cofey, B. (1998). Is juvenile obsessive-compulsive disorder a developmental subtype of disorder? A review of the pediatric literature. *Journal of the American Academy of Child and Adolescent Psychiatry, 37*, 420–427.

Geller, D. A., Biederman, J., & Stewart, S. E. (2003). Impact of comorbidity on treatment response to paroxetine in pediatric obsessive-compulsive disorder: Is the use of exclusion criteria empirically supported in randomized clinical trials? *Journal of Child and Adolescent Psychopharmacology, 13*(2, Suppl.), S19–S29.

Gersten, R., Jordan, N., & Flojo, J. R. (2005). Early identification and interventions for students with mathematics difficulties. *Journal of Learning Disabilities, 38*, 293–304.

Ghaziuddin, M., & Gerstein, L. (1996). Pedantic speaking style differentiates Asperger syndrome from high-functioning autism. *Journal of Autism and Developmental Disorders, 26*, 585–595.

Gibbs, J. T. (2001). African American adolescents. In J. T. Gibbs & L. N. Huang (Eds.), *Children of color* (pp. 171–214). San Francisco: Wiley.

Gibbs, J. T., & Huang, L. (2001) A conceptual framework for the psychological assessment and treatment of minority youth. In J. T. Gibbs & L. A. Huang (Eds.), *Children of color* (pp. 1–32). San Francisco: Jossey-Bass.

Gibson, D. (1978). Down Syndrome: The psychology of mongolism. London: Cambridge University Press.

Gilchrist, A., Green, J., Cox, A., Burton, D., Rutter, M., & LeCouteur, A. (2001). Development and current functioning in adolescents with Asperger syndrome: A comparative study. *Journal of Child Psychology and Psychiatry, 42*, 227–240.

Gilgun, J. F. (2002). Completing the circle: American Indian medicine wheels and the promotion of resilience of children and youth in care. *Journal of Human Behavior in the Social Environment, 6*, 65–84.

Gillberg, C. (1998). Asperger syndrome and high-functioning autism. *British Journal of Psychiatry, 172*, 200–209.

Gilliam, J. E. (1995). *Gilliam autism rating scale*. Austin, TX: PRO–ED.

Gilliam, J. E. (2001). *Gilliam Asperger disorder scale*, Austin, TX: PRO–ED.

Gilliam, W. S. (2005). Prekindergarteners left behind: Expulsion rates in state pre-Kindergarten systems. Retrieved June 16, 2007, from http://www. fcd-us. org/resources/resources_show. htm?doc_id=464280

Gillig, S. & Cingel, P. (2004). The United States. In M. P. Duffy & S. Gillig (Eds.), *Teen gangs: A global view* (pp. 215–223). Westport, CT: Greenwood Press.

Gillispie, Z. (2006). Mindfulness theory and cultural identity: Predicting positive mental health outcomes among Latino students. *Dissertation Abstracts International, B. The Physical Sciences and Engineering, 67*, 34–49.

Gioia, G. A., Isquith, P. K., Guy, S. C., & Kenworthy, L. (2000). *Behavior rating inventory of executive function (BRIEF) professional manual*. Odessa, FL: Psychological Assessment Resources.

Gladstone, T. G., & Beardslee, W. R. (2000). The prevention of depression in at-risk adolescents: Current status and future directions. *Journal of Cognitive Psychotherapy: An International Quarterly, 14*, 9–23.

Glantz, M., & Slobada, Z. (1999). Analysis and reconceptualization of resilience. *Resilience and development: Positive life adaptations* (pp. 109–126). Dordrecht, Netherlands: Kluwer.

Goff, D. C., Hennen, J., Lyoo, I. K., Tsai, G., Wald, L., Evins, A., et al. (2002). Modulation of brain and serum glutamatergic concentrations following a switch from conventional neuroleptics to olanzapine. *Biological Psychiatry, 51,* 493–497.

Goldberg, W. A., & Osann, K. (2003). Language and other regression: Assessment and timing. *Journal of Autism and Developmental Disorders, 33,* 607–615.

Goldman, S., & Beardslee, W. R. (1999). Suicide in children and Adolescents. In D. G. Jacobs (Ed.), *The Harvard Medical School guide to suicide assessment and intervention.* San Francisco: Jossey-Bass.

Goldsmith, H. H. (1996). Studying temperament via construction of the Toddler Behavior Assessment Questionnaire. *Child Development, 67,* 218–235.

Goldstein, A. (1994). *Addiction: From biology to drug policy.* New York: W. H. Freeman.

Goldstein, S., & Gordon, M. (2003, August). Gender issues & ADHD: Sorting fact from fiction. *The ADHD Report, 11*(4), 7–16.

Golub, A., & Johnson, B. D. (1994). The shifting importance of alcohol and marijuana as gateway substances among serious drug abusers. *Journal of Studies on Alcohol, 55,* 607–614.

Gonzales, N. A., Knight, G. P., Morgan-Lopez, A. A., Saenz, D., & Sirolle, A. (2002). Acculturation and the mental health of Latino youths: An integration of critique of the literature. In J. M. Contreras, K. A. Kerns, & A. M. Neal-Barnett, (Eds.), *Latino Children and Families in the United States* (pp. 45–74). Westport, CT: Praeger.

Goodman, R. (2002). Flabless is fabulous: How Latina and Anglo women read and incorporate the excessively thin body ideal into every experience. *Journalism and Mass Communication Quarterly, 79,* 712–727.

Goodman, W. K., Price, L. H., Rasmussen, S., Mazure, C., Fleischmann, R., Hill, C. L., et al. (1989). The Yale-Brown Obsessive-Compulsive Scale: I. Development, use and reliability. *Archives of General Psychiatry, 46,* 1006–1011.

Gordon, D. A., Graves, K., & Arbuthnot, J. (1995). The effect of functional family therapy for delinquents on adult criminal behavior. *Criminal Justice and Behavior, 22,* 60–73.

Gottesman, I., & Gould, T. D. (2003). The endophenotype concept in psychiatry: Etymology and strategic intentions. *American Journal of Psychiatry,160,* 636–645.

Gottlieb, J., Alter, M., & Gottlieb, B. W. (1991) Mainstreaming mentally retarded children. In J. Matson, J. A. Mulick, & A. Elmsford (Eds.), *Handbook of mental retardation* (2nd ed.; pp. 63–73). New York: Pergamon Press.

Gould, M. S., & Kramer, R. A. (2001). Youth suicide prevention. *Suicide and Life-Threatening Behavior, 31*(Suppl.), 6–31.

Gould, M. S., Marrrocco, F., Kleinman, M., Thomas, J., Mostkoff, K., Cote, J, et al. (2005). Evaluating iatrogenic risk of youth suicide screening programs. *Journal of the American Medical Association, 293,* 1635–1643.

Gould, M. S., Shaffer, D., & Davies. (1990). Truncated pathways from childhood to adulthood: Attrition in follow-up studies due to death. In L. Robins & M. Rutter (Eds.), *Straight and devious pathways from childhood to adulthood.* Cambridge, UK: Cambridge University Press.

Grados, M., Labuda, M. C., Riddle, M. A., & Walkup, J. T. (1997). Obsessive-compulsive disorder in children and adolescents. *International Review of Psychiatry, 9,* 83–98.

Grant, K., Compas, B. E., & Thurm, A. (2006). Stressors and child and adolescent psychopathology: Evidence of moderating and mediating effects. *Clinical Psychology Review, 26*(3), 257–283.

Gray, J. A. (1987). *The psychology of fear and stress.* New York: Cambridge University Press.

Gray, J. A. (1991). The neuropsychology of temperament. In J. Strelau & A. Angleiter (Eds.), *Explorations in temperament: International perspectives in theory and measurement* (pp. 105–128). New York: Plenum.

Gray, J. A. (1995). Neural systems, emotion and personality. In J. Madden, S, Matthysse, & J. Barchas (Eds.), *Adaptation, learning and affect.* New York: Raven Press.

Green, B. L. (1996). Traumatic stress and disaster: Mental health effects and factors influencing adaptation. In F. L. Mak & C. C. Nadelson (Eds.), *International Review of Psychiatry* (Vol. 2; pp. 177–210). Washington, DC: APA.

Green, R. W., & Ablon, J. S. (2004). *The Collaborative Problem-Solving approach: Cognitive-behavioral treatment of oppositional defiant disorder.* New York: Guilford.

Greenberg, M. A., Domitrovich, C., & Bumbarger, B. (2001). The prevention of mental disorders in school-aged children: Current state of the field. *Prevention and Treatment, 4,* 189–206.

Greene, R. W. (2001). *The explosive child: Understanding and parenting easily frustrated, chronically inflexible children.* New York: Harper Collins.

Greene, R. W., Ablon, J. S., & Goring, J. C. (2003). A transactional model of oppositional behavior: Underpinnings of the Collaborative Problem Solving approach. *Journal of Psychosomatic Research, 55,* 67–75.

Greene, R. W., Ablon, J. S., Goring, J. C., Fazio, V., & Morse, L. R. (2003). Treatment of oppositional defiant disorder in children and adolescence. In P. M. Barrett & T. H. Ollendick (Eds.), *Handbook of interventions that work with children and adolescents* (pp. 369–393). Chichester, UK: Wiley.

Greene, R. W., Beszterczey, S. K., Katzenstein, T., Park, K., & Goring, J. (2002). Are students with ADHD more stressful to teach? *Journal of Emotional & Behavioral Disorders, 10,* 79–90.

Greene, R. W., Biederman, J., Faraone, S. V., Sienna, M., & Garcia-Jetton, J. (1997). Adolescent outcome of boys with attention-deficit/hyperactivity disorder and social disability: Results from a 4-year longitudinal follow-up study. *Journal of Consulting and Clinical Psychology, 65,* 758–787.

Greenfield, D., Quinlan, D., Harding, P., Glass, E., & Bliss, A. (1987). Eating behavior in an adolescent population. *International Journal of Eating Disorders, 6,* 99–111.

Gresham, F. M. (1986). Conceptual and definitional issues in the assessment of social skills: Implications for classification and training. *Journal of Clinical Child Psychology, 15,* 16–25.

Gresham, F. M., & Elliot, S. N. (1990). *Social Skills Rating System.* Circle Pines, MN: American Guidance Service.

Gresham, F. M., Sugai, G., & Horner, R. H. (2001). Interpreting outcomes of social skills training for students with high-incidence disabilities. *Exceptional Children, 67*, 331–344.

Griffin, K. W., Botvin, G. J., Nichols, T. R., & Doyle, M. M. (2003). Effectiveness of a universal drug abuse prevention approach for you at high risk for substance use initiation. *Prevention Medicine, 36*, 1–7.

Griffin, S. A., Case, R., & Siegler, R. S. (1994). Rightstart: Providing the central conceptual prerequisites for first formal learning of arithmetic to students at risk for school failure. In K. McGilly (Ed.), *Classroom lessons: Integrating cognitive theory and classroom practice* (pp. 24–49). Cambridge, MA: MIT Press.

Grisso, T., & Steinberg, L. (2005). Between a rock and a soft place: Developmental research and the child advocacy process. *Journal of Clinical Child and Adolescent Psychology, 34*, 619–627.

Grisso, T., & Steinberg, L. (2006). Developmental research and the child advocacy process. *Child and Family Policy and Practice Review, 2*, 3–7.

Grisso, T., Steinberg, L., Woolard, J., Cauffman, E., Scott, E., Graham, S., et al. (2003). Juveniles' competence to stand trial: A comparison of adolescents' and adults' capacities as trial defendants. *Law and Human Behavior, 27*, 333–363.

Gross, R. M., & Nelson, E. S. (2000). Perceptions of parental messages regarding eating and weight and their impact on disordered eating. *Journal of College Student* Psychotherapy, *15*, 57–78.

Grossman, H. J. (Ed.). (1973). *Manual on the terminology in mental retardation* (Rev. ed.). Washington, DC: American Association on Mental Deficiency.

Grossman, H. J. (Ed.). (1977). *Manual on the terminology in mental retardation* (Rev. ed.) Washington, DC: American Association on Mental Deficiency.

Grossmann, K., Grossmann, K. E., Spangler, S., Suess, G., & Unzer, L. (1985). Maternal sensitivity and newborn attachment orientation responses as related to quality of attachment in northern Germany. In I. Bretherton & E. Waters (Eds.), *Growing points of attachment theory. Monographs of the Society of Research in Child Development, 50*(1–2 Serial No. 209).

Gross-Tsur, V., Shalev, R. S., Manor, O., & Amir, N. (1995). Developmental right hemisphere syndrome: Clinical spectrum of the nonverbal learning disability. *Journal of Learning Disabilities, 28*, 80–86.

Guilmet, G. M., Whited, D. L., Dorpat, N., & Pijanowski, C. (1998). The safe futures initiative at Chief Leschi schools: A school-based tribal response to alcohol-drug abuse, violence, and crime on an urban reservation. *American Indian Culture and Research Journal, 22*, 407–440.

Gull. W. W. (1874). Anorexia nervosa (apepsia hysterica, anorexia hysterica). *Transactions of the Clinical Society of London, 7*, 22–28.

Gunter, H., Ghaziuddin, M, & Ellis, H. (2002). Asperger syndrome: Tests of right hemisphere functioning and interhemispheric communication. *Journal of Autism and Developmental Disorders, 32*, 263–281.

Gustavsson, N. S., & Balgopal, P. R. (1990). Violence and minority youth: An ecological perspective. In A. R. Stiffman & L. E. (Eds), *Ethnic issues in adolescent mental health* (pp. 115–130). Thousand Oaks, CA: Sage.

Guy, S. C., Isquith, P. K., & Gioia, G. A. (2004). *The BRIEF Self Report professional manual.* Odessa, FL: Psychological Assessment Resources.

Guyer, B., MacDorman, M. F., Martin, J. A. Peters, K. D., & Strobino, D. M. (1998) Annual summary of vital statistics—1997. *Pediatrics, 102*, 1333–1349.

Hall, S., De Bernardis, M., & Reiss, A. (2006). Social escape behaviors in children with fragile X syndrome. *Journal of Autism and Developmental Disorders, 36*, 935–947.

Hall, W. D., & Lynskey, M. (2005). Is cannabis a gateway drug? Testing hypotheses about the relationship between cannabis use and the use of other illicit drugs. *Drug and Alcohol Review,24*, 39–48.

Hallahan, D. P., Lloyd, J. W., Kauffman, J. M., Weiss, M., & Martinez, E. A. (2005). *Learning disabilities: Foundations, characteristics, and effective teaching.* Boston: Allyn & Bacon.

Hallahan, D. P., & Mercer, C. D. (2001, August). *Learning disabilities: Historical perspectives.* Paper presented at the Learning Disabilities Summit: Building a Foundation for the Future. Washington, DC.

Halliwell, E., & Harvey, M. (2006). Examination of a sociocultural model of disordered eating among male and female adolescents. *British Journal of Health Psychology, 11*, 235–248.

Halmi, K. A. (1995). Current concepts and definitions. In G. Szmukler, C. Dare, & J. Treasure (Eds.), *Handbook of eating disorders: Theory, treatment and research* (pp. 29–42). Chichester, UK: Wiley.

Halperin, J. M., Newcorn, J. H., Sharma, V., Healey, J. M., Wolf, L. E., Pascualvaca, D. M., & Schaartz, S. (1990). Inattentive and noninattentive ADHD children: Do they constitute a unitary group? *Journal of Abnormal Child Psychology, 18*, 437–449.

Hamada, R. S., Kameoka, V., & Yanagida, E. (2003). Assessment of elementary school children for disaster-related posttraumatic stress disorder symptoms: The Kauai recovery index. *Journal of Nervous and Mental Disease, 191*(4), 268–272.

Hammen, C. (2006). Stress generation in depression: Reflections on origins, research and future directions. *Journal of Clinical Psychology, 62*, 1065–1082.

Hammen, C., Burge, D., & Stansbury, K. (1990). Relationship of mother and child variables to child outcomes in a high-risk sample: A causal modeling analysis. *Developmental Psychology, 26*, 34–30.

Hammen, C., & Rudolph, K. D. (1996). Childhood depression. In E. J. Mash & R. A. Barkley (Eds.), *Child psychopathology* (pp. 153–195). New York: Guilford.

Hankin, B. L., & Abramson, L. Y. (2001). Development of gender differences in depression: An elaborated cognitive vulnerability–transactional stress theory. *Psychological Bulletin, 127*, 773–796.

Hanna, A. C., & Bond, M. (2006). Relationships between family conflict, perceived maternal verbal messages and daughters' disturbed eating symptomatology. *Appetite, 47*, 205–211.

Hanna, G., Piacentini, J., Cantwell, D., Fischer, D., Himle, J., & Van Etten, M. (2002). Obsessive-compulsive disorder with and without tics in a clinical sample of children and adolescents. *Depression and Anxiety, 16*, 59–63.

Happe, F., Booth, R., Charlton, R., & Hughes, C. (2006). Executive function deficits in autism spectrum disorders and attention-deficit/hyperactivity disorder: Examining profiles across domains and ages. *Brain and Cognition, 61*(1), 25–39.

Harlow, C. W. (2002). *Educational and correctional populations.* Washington, DC: Bureau of Justice Statistics: Office of Justice Programs.

Harlow, H. F., & Harlow, M. K. (1969). Effects of various mother–infant relationships on rhesus monkey behaviors. In B. M. Foss (Ed.), *Determinants of infant behavior* (Vol. 4; pp. 252–261). London: Methuen.

Harnadek, M. C. & Rourke, B. P. (1994). Principal identifying features of the syndrome of nonverbal learning disabilities in children . *Journal of Learning Disabilities, 27*, 144–153.

Harper, M. G. (2006). Childhood obesity: Strategies for prevention. *Family Community Health, 29*, 288–298.

Harris, M., & Greco, D. (1990). Weight control and weight concern in competitive female gymnasts. *Journal of Sport and Psychology, 12*, 427–433.

Harrison, P., & Oakland, T. (2003). *Adaptive Behavior Assessment System (ABAS) and the ABAS—Second edition with downward extension.* San Antonio, TX: The Psychological Corporation.

Hart, E., Lahey, B. B., Loeber, R., Applegate, B., & Frick, P. J. (1995). Developmental changes in attention deficit hyperactivity disorder in boys: A four-year longitudinal study. *Journal of Abnormal Child Psychology, 2*, 729–750.

Hartup, W., & Laursen, B. (1993). Conflict and context in peer relations. In C. Hart (Ed.), *Children on playgrounds: Research perspectives and applications.* Ithaca, NY: SUNY.

Hawkins, J. D., Catalano, R. F., & Miller, J. Y. (1992). Risk and protective factors for alcohol and other drug problems in adolescence and early adulthood: Implications for substance abuse prevention. *Psychological Bulletin, 112*, 64–105.

Hawkins, F. D., Hill, K. G, Guo, F., & Battin–Pearson, S. R (2002). Substance use norms and transitions in substance use. In D. B. Kandel (Ed.), *Stages and pathways of drug involvement* (pp. 42–64). Cambridge, UK: Cambridge University Press.

Hay, D., Zahn-Waxler, C., Cummings, E. M., & Iannotti, R. (1992). Young children's views about conflict with peers: A comparison of the daughters and sons of depressed and well women. *Journal of Child Psychology and Psychiatry, 33*, 669–693.

Hayward, C., Killen, J. D., & Hammer, L. D. (1992). Pubertal stage and panic attack history in sixth- and seventh-grade girls. *American Journal of Psychiatry, 149*(9), 1239–1243.

Hayward, C., Killen, J. D., & Taylor, C. B. (1989). Panic attacks in young adolescents. *American Journal of Psychiatry, 146*(8), 1061–1062.

Hazler, R. J. (1996). *Breaking the cycle of violence: Interventions for bullying and victimization.* Washington, DC: Accelerated Development.

Heatherton, T. F., & Polivy, J. (1992). Chronic dieting and eating disorders: A spiral model. In J. H. Crowther, D. L. Tennenbaum, S. E. Hobfold & M. A. Parris-Stephens (Eds.). *The etiology of bulimia nervosa: The individual and familial context* (pp. 133-155). Washington, DC: Hemisphere.

Heaton, R., Chelune, G., Talley, J., Kay, G., & Glenn, C. (1993). Wisconsin Card Sorting Test: Revised and expanded. Odessa, FL: Psychological Assessment Resources.

Heber, R. A. (1961). A manual on terminology and classification in mental retardation (2nd ed.). *Monograph Supplement to the American Journal of Mental Deficiency.*

Hechtman, L., Weiss, G., & Perlman, T. (1980) Hyperactives as young adults: Self-esteem and social skills. *Canadian Journal of Psychiatry, 125*. 478–483.

Hecimovic, H., & Gilliam, F. G. (2006). Neurobiology of depression and new opportunities for treatment. In F. G. Gilliam, A. M. Kanner, & Y. I. Sheline (Eds.), *Depression and brain dysfunction* (pp. 51–84). New York: Taylor & Francis.

Heinberg, L. J., Thompson, J. K., & Matzon, J. L. (2001). Body image dissatisfaction as a motivator for healthy lifestyle change: Is some distress beneficial? In R. H. Striegel-Moore & L. Smolak (Eds.). *Eating disorders, Innovative directions in research and practice* (pp 215–232). Washington, DC: APA.

Hendry, C. N. (2000). Childhood disintegrative disorder: Should it be considered a distinct diagnosis? *Clinical Psychology Review, 20*(1), 77–90.

Henggeler, S. W., & Borduin, C. M. (1990). *Family therapy and beyond: A multisystemic approach to treating the behavior problems of children and adolescents.* Pacific Grove, CA: Brooks/Cole.

Henggeler, S. W., Melton, G. B., & Smith, L. A. (1992). Family preservation using multisystemic therapy: An effective alternative to incarcerating serous juvenile offenders. *Journal of Consulting and Clinical Psychology, 60*, 953–961.

Henggeler, S. W., Schoenwald, S. K., Borduin, C. M., Rowland, M. D., & Cunningham, P. B. (1998). *Multisystemic treatment of antisocial behavior in youth.* New York: Guilford.

Henin, A., Biederman, J., Mick, E., Sachs, G. S., Hirshfeld-Becker, D., Siegel, R., et al. (2005). Psychopathology in the offspring of parents with bipolar disorder: A controlled study. *Biological Psychiatry, 58*, 554–561.

Herrenkohl, T. I., Maguin, E., & Hill, K. G. (2000). Developmental risk factors for youth violence. *Journal of Adolescent Health, 26*(7), 176–186.

Herzog,, D., & Delinsky, S. (2001). Classification of eating disorders. In R. H. Striegel-Moore & L. Smolak (Eds.), *Eating Disorders: Innovative directions in research and practice* (pp. 32-50). Washington, DC: APA.

Herzog, D., Dorer, D., Keele, P. K., Selwyn, S. D., Ekeblad, E., Flores, A. T., et al., (1999). Recovery and relapse in anorexia and bulimia nervosa. *Journal of the American Academy of Child and Adolescent Psychiatry, 38*, 829–837.

Hesse-Biber, S., Leavy, P. Quinn, C. E., Zoino, J. (2006). The mass marketing of disordered eating and Eating Disorders: The social psychology of women, thinness and culture. *Women's Studies International Forum, 29*, 208–224.

Hewitt, P. L., Flett, G. L., & Ediger, E. (1995). Perfectionism traits and perfectionistic self-presentation in eating disorder attitudes, characteristics and symptoms. *International Journal of Eating Disorders, 18*, 317–326.

Hibbs, E. D., Hamburger, S., Lenane, M., Rapoport, J. L., Kruesi, M. J., Keysor, C. S., & Goldstein, M. (1991). Determinants of expressed emotion in families of disturbed and normal children. *Journal of Child Psychology and Psychiatry, 32*, 757–770.

Hill, J. P., & Lynch, M. E. (1983). The intensification of gener-related role expectations during early adolescence. In J. Brooks-

Gunn, & A. C. Peterson (Eds.), *Girls at Puberty: Biological and psychosocial perspectives* (pp. 201–228). New York: Plenum.

Hill, R. B. (1998). Understanding Black family functioning: A holistic perspective. *Journal of Comparative Family Studies, 29*(1), 15–25.

Hinshaw, S. P., Carte, E. T. & Sami, N. (2002). Preadolescent girls with attention-deficit/hyperactivity disorder: II. Neuropsychological performance in relation to subtypes and individual classification. *Journal of Consulting and Clinical Psychology, 70*, 1099–1111.

Hinshaw, S. P., Heller, T., & McHale, J. P. (1992). Covert antisocial behavior in boys with attention deficit hyperactivity disorder: External validation and effects of methylphenidate. *Journal of Consulting and Clinical Psychology, 60*, 274–281.

Hinshaw, S. P., & Lee, S. S. (2003). Conduct and oppositional defiant disorders. In E. Mash & R. A. Barkley (Eds.), *Child psychopathology* (2nd ed., pp. 144–198). New York: Guilford.

Hirshfeld-Becker, D., Biederman, J., Henin, A., Faraone, S., Micco, J., van Grondelle, A., et al. (2007). Clinical outcomes of laboratory-observed preschool behavioral disinhibition at five-year follow-up. *Biological Psychiatry*. Retrieved August 15, 2007.

Hodapp, R. M., Leckman, J. F., Dykens, E. M., Sparrow, S. S., Zelinsky, D., & Ort, S. I. (1992). K–ABC profiles in children with Fragile X syndrome, Down syndrome, and non-specific mental retardation. American Journal on Mental Retardation, 97, 39–46.

Hodapp, R. M., & Zigler, E. P. (1995). Past, present and future issues in the developmental approach to mental retardation and developmental disabilities. In D. Cicchetti & D. J. Cohen (Eds.), *Developmental psychopathology, Vol. 2: Risk, disorder and adaptation* (pp. 299–331). Oxford, UK: Wiley.

Hodges, K. (1999). Child and Adolescent Functional Assessment Scale (CAFAS). In M. E. Maruish (Ed.), *The use of psychological testing for treatment planning and outcomes assessment* (2nd ed., pp. 631–664). Mahwah, NJ: Erlbaum.

Hoek, H. (1991). The incidence and prevalence of anorexia and bulimia nervosa in primary care. *Psychological Medicine, 21*, 455–460.

Hoffman, E. C., & Mattis, S. G. (2000). A developmental adaptation of panic control treatment for panic disorder in adolescence. *Cognitive and Behavioral Practice, 7*, 253–261.

Hoffman, J., &DuPaul, G. J. (2000). Psychoeducational interventions for children and adolescents with attention-deficit/hyperactivity disorder. *Child and Adolescent Psychiatric Clinics of North America, 9*, 647–661.

Hojnoski, R., Morrison, R., Brown, M., & Matthews, W. (2006). Projective test use among school psychologists: A survey and critique. *Journal of Psychoeducational Assessment, 24*(2), 145–159.

Holderness, C. C., Brooks-Gunn, J., & Warren, M. P. (1994). Co-morbidity of eating disorders and substance abuse: Review of the literature. *International Journal of Eating Disorders, 16*, 1–34.

Holmbeck, G. N, Greenley, R. N., & Franks, E. A. (2004). Developmental issues in evidence-based practice. In P. M. Barrett & E. H. Ollendick (Eds.), *Handbook of interventions that work with children and adolescents: Prevention and treatment* (pp. 27–48). London: Wiley.

Horn, M. (1984). The moral message of child guidance 1925–1945. *Journal of Social History, 18*, 25–36.

Horn, M. (1989). Before it's too late. The child guidance movement in the United States, 1922–1945.

Horowitz, K., Weine, S., & Jekel. J. (1995). PTSD symptoms in urban adolescent girls: Compounded community trauma. *Journal of the American Academy of Child and Adolescent Psychiatry, 34*, 1353–1361.

Horsler, K., & Oliver, C. (2006). The behavioral phenotype of Angelman syndrome. *Journal of Intellectual Disability Research, 50*, 33–53.

Howell, R., Sidorenko, E., & Jurica, J. (1987). The effects of computer use on the acquisition of multiplication facts by a student with learning disabilities. *Journal of Learning Disabilities, 20*, 336–341.

Hudson, J. L., & Rapee, R. M. (2000). The origins of social phobia. *Behavior Modification, 24*, 102–129.

Huesmann, L. R., Moise-Titus, J., & Podolski, C. (2003). Longitudinal relations between children's exposure to TV violence and their aggressive and violent behavior in young adulthood: 1977–1992. (2) 201–221.

Huey, S, Henggeler, S. W., Brondino, M., & Pickrel, S. G (2000). Mechanisms of change in multisystemic therapy: Reducing delinquent behavior through therapist adherence and improved family and peer functioning. *Journal of Consulting and Clinical Psychology, 68*, 451–467.

Humphrey, L. L. (1986). Family dynamics in bulimia. In S. C. Feinstein, A. H. Esman, J. C. Looney, A. Z. Schwartzberg, A. D. Sorosky, & M. Sugar (Eds.), *Adolescent psychiatry: Developmental and clinical studies* (pp. 315–332). Chicago: University of Chicago Press.

Hunsley, J., Lee, C. M., & Wood, J. (2003). Controversial and questionable assessment techniques. In S. O. Lilenfield, J. M. Lohr, & S. J. Lynn (Eds.), *Science and pseudoscience in contemporary clinical psychology* (pp. 39–76). New York: Guilford.

Hurth, J., Shaw, E., Izeman, S. G., Whaley, K., & Rogers, S. J. (1999). Areas of agreement about effective practices among programs serving young children with autism spectrum disorders. *Infants and Young Children, 12*(2), 17–26.

Hutton, J. B., Dubes, R., & Muir, S. (1992). Assessment practices of school psychologists: Ten years later. *School Psychology Review, 21*(2), 271–284.

Institute of Medicine. (2005). *Progress in Preventing Childhood Obesity: Focus on Schools. Brief Summary: Institute of Medicine Regional Symposium.* Committee on Progress in Preventing Childhood Obesity. Retrieved June 15, from http://www.nap. edu/catalog/ 11461. html

Ishii-Kuntz, M. (2000). Diversity within Asian American families. In D. H. Demo, K. R. Allen, & M. A. Fine (Eds.), *Handbook of family diversity* (pp. 345–363). New York: Oxford University Press.

Iwanaga, R., Kawasake, C., & Tsuchida, R. (2000). Brief report: Comparison of sensory-motor and cognitive function between autism and Asperger syndrome in preschool children. *Journal of Autism and Developmental Disorders, 30*, 169–174.

Jacobson, J. W. (2000). Early intensive behavioral intervention: Emergence of a consumer-driven service model. *The Behavior Analyst, 23*, 149–171.

Jacobson, N. S., Roberts, L. J., Berns, S. B., & McGlinchey, J. G. (1999). Methods for determining the clinical significance of treatment effects: description, application, and alternatives. *Journal of Consulting and Clinical Psychology, 67*, 300–307.

Jarrett, R. L. (1992). A family case study: An examination of the underclass debate. In J. Gilgun, G. Handel, & K. Daley (Eds.), *Qualitative methods in family research* (pp 172–197). Newbury Park, CA: Sage.

Jarrett, R. L. (1998). African American children, families, and neighborhoods: Qualitative contributions to understanding developmental pathways. *Applied Developmental Science, 2*, 2–16.

Jensen, B. J., & Haynes, S. N. (1986). Self-report questionnaires and inventories. In A. R. Ciminero, K. S. Calhoun, & H. E. Adams (Eds.), *Handbook of behavioral assessment* (pp. 150–175). New York: Wiley.

Jensen, P. S. (2002) ADHD comorbidity findings from the MTA Study: New diagnostic subtypes and their optimal treatments. In J. E. Helzer & J. J. Hudziak (Eds.), *Defining psychopathology in the 21st Century: DSM–V and beyond* (pp. 169–192). Washington, DC: APA.

Jick, H., & Kaye, J. (2003). Epidemiology and possible causes of autism. *Pharmacotherapy, 23*, 1524–1530.

Joffe, R. T., Offord, D. R., & Boyle, M. H. (1998). Ontario child health study: Suicidal behavior in youth age 12–16 years. *American Journal of Psychiatry, 145*, 1420–1423.

John, K., Gammon, G. D., Prusoff, B. A., & Warner, V. (1987). The Social Adjustment Inventory for children and adolescents (SAICA): Testing of a new semistructured interview. *Journal of the American Academy of Child & Adolescent Psychiatry, 26*, 898–911.

Johnson, E., Mellard, D. F., & Byrd, S. E. (2005). *Journal of Learning Disabilities, 38*, 569–572.

Johnson, G. R., Krug, E. G., & Potter, L. B. (2000). Suicide among adolescents and young adults: A cross national comparison of 34 countries. *Suicide & Life Threatening-Behavior, 30*, 74–82.

Johnson, J. G., Cohen, P., Kasen, S., & Brook, J. S. (2002). Eating disorders during adolescence and the risk for physical and mental disorders during early adulhthood.*Archives of General Psychiatry, 59*, 545–552.

Johnson, L., O'Malley, P. M., Bachman, J. G., & Schulenberg, J. E. (2006). Monitoring the Future national results on adolescent drug use: Overview of key findings, 2005. (NIH Publication No. 06-5882). Bethesda, MD: National Institute on Drug Abuse. Retrieved July 2008 from http://www.drugabuse.gov/PDF/overview2005.pdf

Johnson, V., & Pandina, R. (2000). Alcohol problems among a community sample: Longitudinal influences of stress, coping and gender. *Substance use and Misuse, 35*, 669–686

Jones, D. C. (2001). Social comparisons and body image: Attractiveness comparisons to models and peers among adolescent girls and boys. *Sex Roles, 45*, 645–664.

Jones, D. C. (2004). Body image among adolescent girls and boys: A longitudinal study. *Developmental Psychology, 40*, 823–835.

Jones, E. E., & Nisbett, R. E. (1972). The actor and the observer: Divergent perspectives in the causes of behavior. In E. E. Jones, D. E. Kanouse, J. H. Kelley, R. E. Nisbett, S. Valins, & B. Weiner (Eds.), *Attribution: Perceiving the causes of behavior* (pp. 79–94). Morristown, NJ: General Learning.

Jones, M. B., & Offord, D. R. (1989). Reduction of antisocial behavior in poor children in nonschool skill development. *Journal of Child Psychology and Psychiatry, 30*, 737–750.

Kagan, A. E. (1992). Yesterday's promises, tomorrow's promises. *Developmental Psychology, 28*, 990–997.

Kagan, J. (1994). *Galen's prophecy: Temperament in human nature.* New York: Basic Books.

Kagan, J. (1997). Temperament and the reactions to unfamiliarity. *Child Development, 68*, 139–143.

Kagan, J., Reznick, J. S., & Gibbons, J. (1989). Inhibited and uninhibited types of children. *Child Development, 60*, 838–845.

Kagan, J., Reznick, J. S., & Snidman, N. (1988). Biological bases of childhood shyness. *Science, 240*, 167–171.

Kagan, J., & Snidman, N. (1999). Early childhood predictors of adult anxiety disorders. *Biological Psychiatry, 46*, 1536–1541.

Kaij, L. (1960). *Alcoholism in twins: Studies on the etiology and sequels of abuse of alcohol.* Stockholm: Almquist & Wiksell.

Kalafat, J., & Elias, M. J. (1995). Suicide prevention in an educational context: Broad and narrow foci. *Suicide and Life-Threatening Behavior, 25*, 123–133.

Kana, R., Keller, T., Cherkassky, V., Minshew, N., & Just, M. (2006). Sentence comprehension in autism: Thinking in pictures with decreased functional connectivity. *Brain, 129*, 2484–2493.

Kanaya, T. Scullin, M. H., & Ceci, S. J. (2003). The Flynn Effect and U. S. Policies: The impact of rising IQ scores on American society via mental retardation diagnoses. *American Psychologist, 58*, 778–790.

Kandel, D. B. (2002). Examining the gateway hypothesis. In D. B. Kandel (Ed.), *Stages and pathways of drug involvement* (pp. 3–15). Cambridge, UK: Cambridge University Press.

Kandel., D. B., & Yamaguchi, K. (1999). Developmental stages of involvement in substance use. In R. E. Tarter,R. J. Ammerman, & P. J. Ott (Eds.), *Sourcebook on substance abuse: Etiology, assessment and treatment* (pp. 50–74). Boston: Allyn & Bacon.

Kann, L., Kinchen, S. A., Williams, B., Ross, J., Lowry, R., Grunbaum, J., et al. (2000). Centers for Disease Control and Prevention: Youth risk behaviors surveillance—United States. *CDC Surveillance Summaries, 49*, 22–25.

Kaplan, A. S., & Garfinkel, P. E. (12999). Difficulties in treating patients with eating disorders: A review of patient and clinician variables. *Canadian Journal of Psychiatry, 44*, 665–670.

Kaplow, J. B., Curran, P. J., Angold, A., & Costello, E. J. (2001). The prospective relation between dimensions of anxiety and the initiation of adolescent alcohol use. *Journal of Clinical Child & Adolescent Psychology, 30*, 316–326.

Kashani, H. H., & Orvaschel, H. (1988). Anxiety disorders in midadolescence: A community sample. *American Journal of Psychiatry, 145*, 960–964.

Kassel, J. D., & Jackson, S. I. (2001). Twelve-step-based interventions for adolescents. In E. F. Wagner & H. B. Waldron (Eds), *Innovations in adolescent substance abuse interventions* (pp. 329–342). Oxford, UK: Elsevier Science.

Kavale, K. A. (1987). Theoretical issues surrounding severe discrepancy. *Learning Disabilities Research, 3*, 12–20.

Kavale, K. A. (2005). Identifying specific learning disability: Is response to intervention the answer. *Journal of Learning Disabilities, 38*, 553–562.

Kavale, K. A., & Forness, S. R. (1996). Social skill deficits and learning disabilities: A meta-analysis. *Journal of Learning disabilities, 29*, 226–237.

Kavale, K. A., Holdnack, J. A., & Mostert, M. P. (2005). Responsiveness to intervention and the identification of specific learning disability: A critique and alternative proposal. *Learning Disability Quarterly, 28*, 2–16.

Kavale, K. A., Holdnack, J., Mostert, M. P., & Schmied, C. M. (2003, December). *The feasibility of a responsiveness to intervention approach for the identification of specific learning disability: A psychometric alternative.* Paper presented at the National Research Center on Learning Disabilities Responsiveness-to-Intervention Symposium, Kansas City, MO.

Kavale, K. A., & Mostert, M. P. (2004). Social skills interventions for individuals with learning disabilities. *Learning Disability Quarterly, 27*, 31–41.

Kaye, J., Melero-Montes, M., & Jick, H. (2001). Mumps, measles and rubella vaccine and the incidence of autism recorded by general practitioners: A time-trend analysis. *British Medical Journal, 322*, 460–463.

Kazdin, A. E. (1993). Research issues in child psychotherapy. In T. Kratochwill & R. J. Morris (Eds.), *Handbook of psychotherapy with children and adolescents* (pp. 541–565). Needham Heights, MA: Allyn & Bacon.

Kazdin, A. E. (1995). Child, parent and family dysfunction as predictors of outcome in cognitive-behavioral treatment of antisocial children. *Behaviour Research and Therapy, 33*, 271–281.

Kazdin, A. E. (1996). Problem solving and parent management in treating aggressive and antisocial behavior. In E. D. Hibbs & P. S. Jensen (Eds.), *Psychosocial treatments for child and adolescent disorders* (pp. 377–408). Washington, DC: APA.

Kazdin, A. E. (1997). A model for developing effective treatments: Progression and interplay of theory, research, and practice. *Journal of Clinical Child Psychology, 26*, 114–129.

Kazdin, A. E., Esveldt-Dawson, K., French, N. H., & Unis, A. S (1987). Problem-solving skills training and parent management training in the treatment of antisocial behavior in children. *Journal of Consulting and Clinical Psychology, 55*, 76–85.

Kazdin, A. E., & Kagan, J. (1994). Models of dysfunction in developmental psychopathology. *Clinical Psychology: Science and Practice, 1*, 35–52.

Kazdin, A. E., Rodgers, A., & Colbus, D. (1986). The Hopelessness Scale for Children: Psychometric characteristics and concurrent validity. *Journal of Consulting and Clinical Psychology, 54*, 241–245.

Kazdin, A. E., Siegel, T., & Bass, D. (1992). Cognitive problem-solving skills training and parent management training in the treatment of antisocial behavior in children. *Journal of Consulting and Clinical Psychology, 60*, 733–747.

Kearney, C. A., Albano, A. M., Eisen, A. R., Allan, E. D., & Barlow, D. H. (1997). The phenomenology of panic disorder in youngsters: An empirical study of a clinical sample. *Journal of Anxiety Disorders, 11*, 49–62.

Kearney, C. A., Eisen, A. R., & Silverman, W. K. (1995). The legend and myth of school phobia. *School Psychology Quarterly, 10*(1), 65–85.

Keenan, K., & Wakschlag, L. S. (2000). More than the terrible twos: The nature and severity of behavior problems in clinic-referred preschool children. *Journal of Abnormal Child Psychology, 28*(1), 33–46.

Keery, H., Boutelle, K., van den Berg, P., & Thompson, J. K. (2005). The impact of appearance-related teasing by family members. *Journal of Adolescent Health, 37*, 120–127..

Keery, H., van den Berg, P., & Thompson, J. K. (2004). An evaluation of the Tripartite Influence Model of body dissatisfaction and eating disturbance with adolescent girls. *Body Image, 1*, 237–251.

Keller, M. B., Herzog, D. B., Lavori, P. W., Bradburn, I. S., & Mahoney, E. M. (1992). The natural history of bulimia nervosa: Extraordinarily high rates of chronicity, relapse, recurrence, and psychosocial morbidity. *International Journal of Eating Disorders, 12*, 1–9.

Kelley, M., Power, T. G., & Wimbush, D. D. (1992). Determinants of disciplinary practices in low-income black mothers. *Child Development, 63*, 573–582.

Kendall, P. C. (1994). Treating anxiety disorders in children: Results of a randomized clinical trial. *Journal of Consulting and Clinical Psychology, 62*, 100–110.

Kendall, P. C. (2000). *Cognitive behavioral therapy for anxious children: Treatment manual* (2nd ed.). Aramore, PA: Workbook.

Kendall, P. C., Brady, E. U., & Verduin, T. L. (2001). Comorbidity in childhood anxiety disorders and treatment outcome. *Journal of the American Academy of Child and Adolescent Psychiatry, 40*, 787–794.

Kendall, P. C., Chanskyu, T. E., Kane, M. T., Kim, R., Kortlander, E., Ronan, K. R., et al. (1992). *Anxiety disorders in youth: Cognitive-behavioral interventions.* Needham Heights, MA: Allyn & Bacon.

Kendall, P. C., & Ronan, K. R. (1990). Assessment of children's anxieties, fears, and phobias: Cognitive-behavioral models and methods. In C. R. Reynolds & R. W. Kamphaus (Eds.), *Handbook of psychological and educational assessment of children* (Vol. 2, pp. 223–244). New York: Guilford.

Kendall, P. C., & Southam-Gerow, M. (1996). Long-term Follow-up of a cognitive-behavioral therapy for anxiety disordered youths. *Journal of Consulting and Clinical Psychology, 64*, 724–730.

Kendell, R., & Jablensky, A. (2003). Distinguishing between the validity and utility of psychiatric diagnoses. *American Journal of Psychiatry, 160*, 4–12.

Kendler, K. S., Gallagher, T. J., Abelson, J. M., & Kessler, R. C. (1996) Lifetime revalence, demographic risk factors and diagnostic validity of nonaffective psychosis as assessed in a US community sample. The National Comorbidity Survey. *Archives of General Psychiatry, 53*, 1022–1031.

Kent, J. S., & Clopton, J. R. (1992). Bulimic women's perceptions of their family relationships. *Journal of Clinical Psychology, 48*, 281–292.

Kershaw, R., Songua-Barke, E. (1998). Emotional and behavioral difficulties: Is this a useful category? The implications of clustering and comorbidity, the relevance of a taxonomic approach. *Educational and Child Psychology, 15*, 45–55.

Kessler, R., Aguilar-Gaxiola, S., Berglund, P/. Caraveo-Anduaga, J., DeWit, D., Greenfield, S., et al. (2001). Patterns and predictors of treatment seeking after onset of substance us disorder. *Archives of General Psychiatry, 58*, 1065–1071.

Keyes, C. (2006). Mental health in adolescence: Is America's youth flourishing? *American Journal of Orthopsychiatry, 76*, 395–402.

Khantzian, E. (1997). The self-medication hypothesis of substance use disorders: A reconsideration and recent applications. *Harvard Review of Psychiatry, 4*, 241– 244.

Khantzian, E. (2001). Reflections on group treatments as corrective experiences for addictive vulnerability. *International Journal of Group Psychotherapy, 51*, 11–20.

Kibria, N. (1993). *Family tightrope: The changing lives of Vietnamese Americans.* Princeton, NJ: Princeton University Press.

Kihlstrom, J. F. (2002). To Honor Kraepelin: From symptoms to pathology in the diagnosis of mental illness. In L. E. Beutler & M. L. Malik (Eds.), *Rethinking the DSM: A psychological perspective. Decade of behavior* (pp. 279–303). Washington, DC: APA.

Kim, A., Vaughn, S., Wanzek, J., & Wei. S. (2004). Graphic organizers and their effects on reading comprehension of students with LD: A synthesis of research. *Journal of Learning Disabilities, 37*, 105–118.

Kim, E. Y., Miklowitz, D., Biukians, A., & Mullen, K. (2007). Life stress and the course of early-onset bipolar disorder. *Journal of Affective Disorders, 99*, 37–44.

Kim, J., Szatmari, P., Bryson, S. E., Streiner, D. L., & Wilson, F. J. (2000). The prevalence of anxiety and mood problems among children with autism and Asperger syndrome. *Autism, 4*, 117–132.

King, J. D., & Kowalchuk, B. (1994). *Inventory of Suicide Orientation–30 (ISO–30).* Minneapolis, MN: NCS.

King, N. (2001). Young adult women: Reflections on recurring themes and a discussion of the treatment process and setting. In B. Kinoy (Ed.), *Eating disorders: New directions in treatment and recovery* (2nd ed., pp. 148–158). New York: Columbia University Press.

King, N. J., Ollendick, T. H., Mattis, S. G., Yang, B., & Tonge, B. (1997). Nonclinical panic attacks in adolescents: Prevalence symptomatology, and associated features. *Behaviour Change, 13*, 171–183.

King, R. A., & Apter, A. (Eds.). (2003). *Suicide in children and adolescents.* New York: Cambridge University Press.

King, R. A., Leonard, H., & March, J. (1998). Practice parameters for the assessment and treatment of children and adolescents with obsessive-compulsive disorder. *Journal of the American Academy of Child & Adolescent Psychiatry, 37*, 27S–45S.

Kirk, S. A., McCarthy, J. J., & Kirk, W. D. (1968). *The Illinois Test of Psycholinguistic Abilities.* Urbana: University of Illinois Press.

Klein, D. N., Dougherty, L. R., & Olino, T. M. (2005). Toward guidelines for evidence-based assessment of depression in children and adolescents. *Journal of Clinical Child and Adolescent Psychology, 34*, 412–432.

Klein, R. G., & Abikoff, H. (1997). Behavior therapy and methylphenidate treatment of children with ADHD. *Journal of Attention Disorders, 2*, 89–114.

Klin, A., & Volkmar, F. R. (1997). Asperger's syndrome. In D. Cohen & F. R. Volkmar (Eds.), *Handbook of autism and pervasive developmental disorders* (2nd ed., pp. 94–122). New York: Wiley.

Klin, A., Volkmar, F. R., Sparrow, S. S., Cicchetti, D. V., & Rourke, B. P. (1995). Validity and neuropsychological characterization of Asperger syndrome: Convergence with nonverbal learning disabilities syndrome. *Journal of Child Psychology and Psychiatry, 36*, 1127–1140.

Knoff, H. M. (2002). Best practices in personality assessment. In A. Thomas & J. Grimes (Eds.), *Best practices in school psychology IV* (pp. 1281–1302). Bethesda, MD: NASP.

Knopik, V. S., Smith, S. D., Cardon, L., et al. (2002). Differential genetic etiology of reading component processes as a function of IQ. *Behavior Genetics, 32*, 181–198.

Kockanek, K. D., Murphy, S. L., & Anderson, R. N. (2004). Deaths: Final data for 2002. *National Vital Statistics Reports 53, 5*, 1–116.

Kodish, E. (2003). Informed consent for pediatric research: Is it really possible? *Journal of Pediatrics, 142*, 89–90.

Koenen, K. C. (2005). Nature-nurture interplay: Genetically informative designs contribute to understanding the effects of trauma and interpersonal violence. *Journal of Interpersonal Violence, 20*, 507–512.

Koplan, J. P., Liverman, C. T., & Kraak, V. (2005) *Prevention childhood obesity: Health in the balance.* Washington, DC: National Academics Press.

Korkman, M., Kirk, U., & Kemp, S. (1998). *NEPSY: A developmental neurological assessment.* San Antonio TX: The Psychological Corporation.

Kovacs, M. (1992). *The Child Depression Inventory.* North Tonawanda, NY: Multi-Health Systems.

Kovacs, M., Gatsonis, C., Pollock. M., & Parrone, P. (1994). A controlled prospective study of DSM–III adjustment disorder in childhood: Short-term prognosis and long- term predictive validity. *Archives of General Psychiatry, 51*, 535–541.

Kovacs, M., Paulauskas, S., Gatsonis, C., & Richards, C. (1988). Depressive disorders in childhood: III. A longitudinal study of comorbidity with and risk for conduct disorders. *Journal of Affective Disorders, 15*(3), 205–217.

Kovacs, M., & Pollock, M. (1995). Bipolar disorder and comorbid conduct disorder in childhood and adolescence. *Journal of the American Academy of Child & Adolescent Psychiatry, 34*, 715–723.

Krahn, G. L., & Eisert, D. (2000) Qualitative methods in clinical psychology. In D. Drotar (Ed), *Handbook of research methods in pediatric and clinical child psychology* (pp. 145–164). New York: Plenum.

Kramer, T. L., Phillips, S. D., & Hargis, M. B. (2004). Disagreement between parent and adolescent reports of functional impairment. *Journal of Child Psychology and Psychiatry, 45*, 248–259.

Kramlinger, K., & Post, R. M. (1996). Ultra-rapid and ultradian cycling in bipolar affective illness. *British Journal of Psychiatry, 168*, 314–323.

Kronenberger, W. G., & Meyer, R. G. (2001). *The child clinician's handbook* (2nd ed.). Needham Heights, MA: Allyn & Bacon.

Krysanski, V. L. (2003). A brief review of selective mutism literature. *Journal of Psychology: Interdisciplinary and Applied, 137*(1), 29–40.

Kumaabe, K. T., Nishida, C., & Hepworth, D. H. (1985). *Bridging ethnocultural diversities in social work and health.* Honolulu: University of Hawaii.

Kumin, L. (1994). Intelligibility of speech in children with Down syndrome in natural settings: Parents' perspective. Perceptual and Motor Skills, 78, 307–313.

Kurita, H., Kita, M., & Miyake, Y. (1992). A comparative study of development and symptoms among disintegrative psychosis and infantile autism with and without speech loss. *Journal of Autism and Developmental Disorders, 22,* 175–188.

Kurita, H., Koyama, T., Setoya, Y., Shimizu, K., & Osada, H. (2004). Validity of childhood disintegrative disorder apart from autistic disorder with speech loss. *European Child & Adolescent Psychiatry, 13,* 221–226.

Kurita, H., Osada, H., & Miyake, Y. (2004). External validity of childhood disintegrative disorder in comparison with autistic disorder. *Journal of Autism &Developmental Disorders, 34,* 355–362.

Kurrien, R., & Vo, E. D. (2001). Who's in charge? Coparenting in South and Southeast Asian families. *Journal of Adult Development, 11,* 207–219.

Kusel A. B. (1999). Primary prevention of eating disorders through media literacy training of girls. *Dissertation Abstracts International B: The Sciences & Engineering, 60*(4–B),1859.

Kutcher, S. (2005). ADHD/bipolar children and academic outcomes. *Directions in Psychiatry, 25,* 111–117.

Lachar, D., & Gruber, C. P. (1995). *Personality Inventory for Youth (PIY) manual.* Los Angeles: Western Psychological Services.

Lachar, D., & Gruber, C. (2001). *Personality Inventory for Children* (2nd ed.). Los Angeles, CA: Western Psychological Services.

Ladd, G. W. (1981). Effectiveness of a social learning method for enhancing children's social interactions and peer acceptance. *Child Development, 52,* 171–178.

Ladd, G. W., Kochenderfer, B. J., & Coleman, C. C. (1996). Friendship quality as a predictor of young children's early school adjustment. *Child Development, 67,* 103–1118.

LaFromboise, T. D., & Graff Low, K. (2001). American Indian Children and Adolescents. In J. T. Gibbs & L. N. Huang (Eds.), *Children of Color* (pp. 112–142). San Francisco: Jossey-Bass.

La Greca, A. M., Silverman, W. K., Vernberg, E. M., & Prinstein, M. (1996). Symptoms of posttraumatic stress in children after hurricane Andrew: A prospective study. *Journal of Consulting and Clinical Psychology, 64,* 712–723.

Lahey, B., Moffitt, E. E., & Caspi, A. (Eds.). (2003). *Causes of conduct disorder and juvenile delinquency.* New York: Guilford.

Lambert, N., Nihira, K., & Leland, H. (1993). *ABS-S:2: The Adaptive Behavior Scale School* (2nd ed.). Austin, TX: PRO-ED.

Lange, G., Sheerin, D., Carr, A., Dooley, B., Barton, V. Marshall, D., et al. (2005). Family factors associated with attention deficit hyperactivity disorder and emotional disorders in children. *Journal of Family Therapy, 27.* 76–96.

Lansford, J. E., Change, L., Dodge, K. A., Malone, P. S., Oburu, P., Palmerus, K., et al. (2005). Physical discipline and children's adjustment: Cultural normativeness as a moderator. *Child Development, 76,* 1234–1246.

Lansford, J. E., Deater-Deckard, K., Dodge, K. A., Bates, J. E., & Pettit, G. S. (2004). Ethnic differences in the link between physical discipline and later adolescent externalizing behaviors. *Journal of Child Psychology and Psychiatry, 45,* 801–812.

Laor, N., Wolmer, L., & Cohen, D. (2001). Mothers' functioning and children's symptoms 5 years after a SCUD missile attack. *American Journal of Psychiatry, 158*(7), 1020–1026.

Lapsley, D. K. (1993). Toward an integrated theory of adolescent ego development: The "new look" at adolescent egocentrism. *American Journal of Orthopsychiatry, 63,* 562–571.

Larson, J., & Lochman, J. E. (2002). *Helping school children cope with anger: A cognitive-behavioral intervention.* New York: Guilford.

Last, C. (1991). Somatic complaints in anxiety disordered children. *Journal of Anxiety Disorders, 5*(2), 125–138.

Last, C. G., Hersen, M., Kazdin, A. E., Finkelstein, R., & Strauss, C. C. (1987). Comparison of DSM–III separation anxiety and overanxious disorder: Demographic characteristics and patterns of comorbidity. *Journal of the American Academy of Child and Adolescent Psychiatry, 26,* 527–531.

Last, C. G., Hersen, M., Kazdin, A. E., Orvaschel, H., & Perrin, S. (1991). Anxiety disorders in children and their families. *Archives of General Psychiatry, 48*(10), 928–934.

Last, C. G., Perrin, S., Hersen, M., & Kazdin, A. E. (1992). DSM–III–R anxiety disorders in children. Sociodemographic and clinical characteristics. *Journal of the American Academy of Child and Adolescent Psychiatry, 31,* 1070–1076.

Last, C. G., Perrin, S., Hersen, M., & Kazdin, A. E. (1996). A prospective study of child anxiety disorders. *Journal of the American Academy of Child and Adolescent Psychiatry, 35,* 1502–1510.

Lau, L. A., Jernewall, N. M., Zane, N., & Myers, H. F. (2002). Correlates of suicidal behaviors among Asian American outpatient youths. *Cultural Diversity & Ethnic Minority Psychology, 8,* 199–213.

Lawford, B. R., Young, R., Rowell, J. A., Gibson, J. N, et al. (1997). Association of the D2 dopamine receptor A1 allele with alcoholism: Medical severity of alcoholism and type of controls. *Biology and Psychiatry, 41,* 386–393.

Lazarus, A. A., & Abramowitz, A. (1962). The use of emotive imagery in the treatment of children's phobias. *Journal of Mental Science, 108,* 191–195.

Lazear, K., Doan, J., & Roggenbaum, S. (2003). *Youth suicide prevention school-based guide—Issue brief 9: Culturally and linguistically diverse populations.* Tampa, FL: Department of Child and Family Studies, Division of State and Local Support, Louis de la Parte Florida Mental Health Institute, University of South Florida. (FMHI Series Publication #218–9).

Leark, R. A., Dupuy, L. M., Greenberg, L. M., Corman, C. L., & Kindescki, C. L. (1996). *Test of Variables of Attention (TOVA) manual.* Los Alamitos, CA: TOVA Company.

LeCroy, C. W. (1994). Social skills training. In. C. W. LeCroy (Ed.), *Handbook of child and adolescent treatment manuals.* New York: Lexington.

Lee, J. P., & Kirkpatrick, S. (2005). Social meanings of marijuana use for Southeast Asian Youth. *Journal of Ethnicity in Substance Abuse, 4*, 135–152.

Lefebre-Mcgevna, J. A. (2007). A developmental attachment-based play therapy (adapt™: A new treatment for children diagnosed with reactive attachment and developmental trauma disorders. *Dissertation Abstracts International. B: The Sciences and Engineering, 67*, 4715.

Leibenluft, E., Charney, D. S., Towbin, K. E., Bhangoo, R. K., & Pine, D. S. (2003). Defining clinical phenotypes of juvenile mania. *American Journal of Psychiatry, 160*, 430–437.

Leo, J., & Cohen, D. (2003). Broken brains or flawed studies? A critical review of ADHD neuroimaging research. *The Journal of Mind and Behavior, 24*, 29–56.

Leonard, H., Goldberger, E., & Rapoport, J. L. (1990). Childhood rituals: Normal development or obsessive compulsive symptoms? *Journal of the American Academy of Child & Adolescent Psychiatry, 21*, 17–23.

Lengua, L. J., & Long, A. C. (2002). The role of emotionality and self-regulation in the appraisal-coping process: Tests of direct and moderating effects. *Journal of Applied Developmental Psychology, 23*, 471–493.

Lengua, L. J., Wolchik, S. A., Sandler, I. N., & West, S. G. (2000). The additive and interactive effects of parenting and temperament in predicting adjustment problems of children of divorce. *Journal of Clinical Child Psychology, 29*, 232–244.

Levine, M., & Levine, A. *Helping children: A social history*. New York: Oxford University Press.

Lewin, K., Lippitt, R., & White, R. K. (1939). Patterns of aggressive behavior in experimentally created "social climates." *Journal of Social Psychology, 10*, 271–299.

Lewinsohn, P. M., Clarke, G., Hops, H., & Andrews, J. A. (1990). Cognitive-behavioral Treatment for depressed adolescents. *Behavior Therapy, 21*, 385–401.

Lewinsohn, P. M., Clarke, G. N., Rhode, P., Hops, H., & Seeley, J. (1996). A course in coping: A cognitive-behavioral approach to the treatment of adolescent depression. In E. D. Hibbs & P. S. Jensen (Eds.), *Psychosocial treatments for child and adolescent disorders: Empirically based strategies for clinical practice* (pp. 109–135). Washington, DC: APA.

Lewinsohn, P. M., Hops, H., Roberts, R. E., Seeley, J. R., & Andrews, J. A. (1993). Adolescent Psychopathology: I: Prevalence and incidence of depression and other *DSM-III-R* disorders in high school students. *Journal of Abnormal Psychology, 102*, 133–144.

Lewinsohn, P. M., Klein, D. N., & Seeley, J. R. (2000). Bipolar disorder during adolescence and young adulthood in a community sample. *Bipolar Disorder, 3*, 281–293.

Lewinsohn. P. M., Striegel-Moore, R. H., & Seeley, J. R. (2000). Epidemiology and natural course of eating disorders in young women from adolescence to adulthood. *Journal of the American Academcy of Child and Adolescent Psychiatry, 39*, 1284–1292.

Lichter, D., Qian, Z., & Crowley, M. (2005). Child poverty among racial minorities and immigrants: Explaining trends and differentials. *Social Science Quarterly, Special Issue, 86*(5), 1037–1059.

Liddell, G., & Rasmussen, C. (2005). Memory profile of children with nonverbal learning disability. *Learning Disabilities Research & Practice, 20*, 137–141.

Liddle, H. A., & Hogue, A. (2001). Multidimensional family therapy for adolescent substance abuse. In E. F. Wagner & H. B. Waldron (Eds.), *Innovations in adolescent substance abuse interventions* (pp. 229-261). Oxford, UK: Elsevier Science.

Lindner, J. L., & Rosen, L. A. (2006). Decoding of emotion through facial expression, prosody and verbal content in children and adolescents with Asperger's syndrome. *Journal of Autism and Developmental Disorders, 36*, 769–777.

Littell, J. H., & Schuerman, J. R. (1995). *A synthesis of research on family preservation and family reunification programs.* Part of the National Evaluation of Family Preservation Services for the Office of the Assistant Secretary for Planning and Evaluation, Department of Health and Human Services, Westat, Inc. in association with James Bell Associates, and the Chaplin Hall Center for Children at the University of Chicago.

Lloyd, G. K., Fletcher, A., & Minuchin, M. C. W. (1992). GABA agonists as potential anxiolytics. In C. D. Burows, S. M. Roth, & R. Noyes, Jr. (Eds.), *Handbook of anxiety* (Vol. 5). Oxford, UK: Elsevier.

Lochman, J. E., Burch, P. R., Curry, J., & Lampron, L. (1984). Treatment and generalization effects of cognitive-behavioral and goal-setting interventions with aggressive boys. *Journal of Consulting and Clinical Psychology, 53*, 915–926.

Lochman, J. E., & Wells, K. C. (2002). Contextual social-cognitive mediators and child outcome: A test of the theoretical model in the coping power program. *Development and Psychopathology, 14*, 945–967.

Lock, J., Reisel, B., & Steiner, H. (2001). Associated health risks of adolescents with disordered eating: How different are they from their peers? Results from a high school survey. *Child Psychiatry and Human Development, 31*, 249–265.

Loeber, R., & Farrington, D. P. (2000). Young children who commit crime: Epidemiology, developmental origins, risk factors, early interventions, and policy implications. *Development and Psychopathology, 12*(4), 737–762.

Loeber, R., Farrington, D. P., Stouthamer-Loeber, M., & Van Kammen, W. B. (1998). Multiple risk factors for multiproblem boys: Co-occurrence of delinquency, substance use, attention deficit, conduct problems, psychical aggression, covert behavior, depressed mood and shy/withdrawn behavior. In R. Jessor (Ed.), *New perspectives on adolescent risk behavior* (pp. 90–149). New York: Cambridge University Press.

Loeber, R., Green, S. M., Lahey, B. B., Christ, M. A., & Frick, P. J. (1992). Developmental sequences in the age of onset of disruptive child behaviors. *Journal of Child and Family Studies, 1*, 21–41.

Loeber, R., & Hay, D. (1997). Key issues in the development of aggression and violence from childhood to early adulthood. *Annual Review of Psychology, 48*, 371–410.

Loeber, R., & Keenan, K. (1994). Interaction between conduct disorder and its comorbid conditions: Effects of age and gender. *Clinical Psychology Review, 14*, 497–523.

Loeber, R., & Stouthamer-Loeber, M. (1998). Development of juvenile aggression and violence: Some common misconceptions and controversies. *American Psychologist, 53*, 242–259.

Lonigan, C. J., Carey, M. P., & Finch, A. J. (1994). Anxiety and depression in children and adolescents: Negative affectivity and the utility of self reports. *Journal of Consulting and Clinical Psychology, 62*, 1000–1008.

Lonigan, C. J., Shannon, M. P., Saylor, C. M., Finch, A. J. & Sallee, F. R. (1994). Children exposed to disaster: II. Risk factors for the development of post-traumatic symptomatology. *Journal of the American Academy of Child and Adolescent Psychiatry, 33*, 94–105.

Lonigan, C. J., Vasey, M. W., Phillips, B., & Hazen, R. (2004). Temperament, anxiety, and the processing of threat-relevant stimuli. *Journal of Clinical Child and Adolescent Psychology, 33*, 8–20.

Lord, C., Rutter, M., DiLavore, P. C., & Risi, S. (2002). *Autism diagnostic observation schedule manual.* Los Angeles: Western Psychological Services.

Lord, C., Wagner, A., Rogers, S., Szatmari, P., Aman, M., Dawson, G., et al. (2005). Challenges in evaluating psychosocial interventions for autistic spectrum disorders. *Journal of Autism and Developmental Disorders, 35*(6), 695–708.

Luby, J. L., Heffelfinger, A., Mrakotsky, C., Hessler, M., Brown, K., & Hildebrand, T. (2002). Preschool major depressive disorder: Preliminary validation for developmentally modified *DSM–IV* criteria. *Journal of the American Academy of Child and Adolescent Psychiatry, 41*, 928–937.

Luby, J. L., Mrakotsky, C., Heffelfinger, A., Brown, K., & Spitznagel, E. (2004). Characteristics of depressed preschoolers with and without anhedonia: Evidence for a melancholic depressive subtype in young children. *American Journal of Psychiatry, 161*, 1998–2005.

Luby, J. L., Sullivan, J., Belden, A., Stalets, M., Blankenship, S., & Spitznagel, E. (2006). An observational analysis of behavior in depressed preschoolers: Further validation of early onset depression,. *Journal of the American Academy of Child and Adolescent Psychiatry, 45*, 203–212.

Lucas, A., Beard, C. M., O'Fallon, W., & Kurland, L. T. (1988). Anorexia nervosa in Rochester, Minnesota: A 45-year study. *Mayo Clinic Proceedings, 63*, 433–442.

Lucas, C. P., Zhang, H., Fisher, P., Shaffer, D., Regier, D. A., Narrow, W. E., et al. (2001). The DISC Predictive Scales (DPS): efficiently screening for diagnoses. *Journal of the American Academy of Child & Adolescent Psychiatry, 40*, 443–449.

Ludwig, M. (1996). A sport psychology perspective. *Journal of Physical Education Recreation & Dance, 67*, 31–35.

Luther, S. S., Cicchetti, D., & Becker, B. (2000). The construct of resilience: A critical evaluation and guidelines for future work. *Child Development, 71*, 543–562.

Lynch, E. W. (1998). Developing Cross-Cultural Competence. In E. W. Lynch & M. J. Hanson (Eds.), *Developing Cross-Cultural Competence* (2nd ed., pp. 47–90). Baltimore: Paul H. Brookes.

Lyon, G. R., Fletcher, J. M., & Barnes, M. C. (2003). Learning disabilities. In E. J. Mash & R. A. Barkley (Eds.), *Child psychopathology* (2nd ed., pp. 520–586). New York: Guilford.

Lyon, G. R. & Shaywitz, S. E. (2003). Part I: Defining dyslexia, comoridity, teachers' knowledge of language and reading. *Annals of Dyslexia, 53*, 1–14.

Lyons-Ruth, K., & Jacobvitz, D. (1999). Attachment Disorganization: Unresolved loss, relational violence and lapses in behavioral and attentional strategies. In J. Cassidy & P. R. Shaver (Eds.), *Handbook of attachment: Theory, research, and Clinical Applications* (pp. 520–554). New York: Guilford.

Maag, J. (2005). Social skills training for youth with emotional and behavioral disorders and learning disabilities: Problems, conclusions and suggestions. *Exceptionality, 13*, 155–172.

Macgowan, M. J., & Wagner, E. F. (2005). Iatrogenic effects of group treatment on adolescents with conduct and substance use problems: A review of the literature and a presentation of a model. In C. Hilarski, (Ed.), *Addiction, assessment and treatment with adolescents, adults and families* (pp. 79-90). Birmingham, NY: Haworth Social Work Practice Press.

MacMillan, D. L., & Forness, S. R. (1998). The role of IQ in special education placement decisions: Primary and determinative or peripheral inconsequential? *Remedial and Special Education, 19*, 239–253.

MacMillan, D. L., Gresham, F. M., & Bocian, K. M. (1998). Discrepancy between definitions of learning disabilities and school practices: An empirical investigation. *Journal of Learning Disabilities, 31*, 314–326.

Mail, P. D., & Heurtin-Roberts, S. (2002). Where do we go from here? Unmet research needs in American Indian alcohol use. In P. D. Mail, S. Huertin-Roberts, S. E. Martin, & J. Howard (Eds.), *Alcohol use among American Indian and Alaska Natives: Multiple perspectives on a complex problem* (pp. 459–786). (NIAA Research monograph No. 37.) Bethesda, MD: U. S. Department of Health and Human Services.

Main, M., & Hesse, E. (1990). Parents' unresolved traumatic experiences are related to infant disorganized attachment status: Is frightened and/or frightening parental behavior the linking mechanism? In M. T. Greenberg, D. Cicchetti, & E. M. Cummings (Eds.), *Attachment in the preschool years: Theory, research, and intervention* (pp. 161–182). Chicago: University of Chicago Press.

Mak, W., & Rosenblatt, A. (2002). Demographic influences on psychiatric diagnoses among youth served in California systems of care. *Journal of Child and Family Studies, 11*, 165–178.

Malhotra, S., & Gupta, N. (2002). Childhood disintegrative disorder: Re-examination of the current concept. *European Child & Adolescent Psychiatry, 11*, 108–114.

Malmquist, C. P. (1986). Children who witness parental murder: Posttraumatic aspects. *Journal of the American Academy of Child & Adolescent Psychiatry, 25*, 320–325.

Maloney, M., McGuire, J. B., Danierls, S., & Specker, B. (1989). Dieting behavior and attitudes in children, *Pediatrics, 84*, 482–489.

Malphurs, J., Field, T., Larraine, C., Pickens J., & Pelaez-Nogueras, M. (1996). Altering withdrawn and intrusive interaction behaviors of depressed mothers. *Infant Mental Health Journal, 17*, 152–160.

Malson, J. L., Lee, E. M., Murty, R., Moolchan, E. T., & Pickworth, W. B. (2003). Clove cigarette smoking: Biochemical, physiological, and subjective effects. *Pharmacology Biochemistry and Behavior, 74*, 739–745.

Manassis, K., & Hood, J. (1998). Individual and familial predictors of impairment in childhood anxiety disorders. *Journal of the American Academy of Child and Adolescent Psychiatry, 37*, 428–434.

Manassis, K., Mendlowitz, S. L., Scapillato, D., Avery, D., Fiksenbaum, L., Freire, M., et al. (2002). Group and individual cognitive-behavioral therapy for childhood anxiety disorders. A randomized trail. *Journal of the American Academy of Child & Adolescent Psychiatry, 41*, 1423–1430.

Mann, J. J., Brent, D., & Arango, V. (2001). The neurobiology and genetics of suicide and attempted suicide: A focus on the serotonergic system. *Neuropsychopharmacology, 24*, 467–477.

March, J., Amaya-Jackson, L., & Pynoos, R. S. (1994). Pediatric posttraumatic stress disorder. In J. W. Weiner (Ed.), *Textbook of child & adolescent psychiatry* (pp. 507–527). Washington, DC: American Psychiatric Press.

March, J., Frances, A., Carpenter, D., & Kahn, D. (1997). Expert consensus guidelines: Treatment of obsessive-compulsive disorder. *Journal of Clinical Psychology, 58*, 1.

Martini, D. R. (1995). Common anxiety disorders in children and adolescents. *Current Problems in Pediatrics, 25*, 271–280.

Mash, E. J., & Hunsley, J. (2005). Evidence-based assessment of child and adolescent disorders: Issues and challenges. *Journal of Clinical Child and Adolescent Psychology, 34*(3), 362–379.

Mash, E. J., & Wolfe, D. A. (2002). *Abnormal child psychology* (2nd ed.). Belmont, CA: Wadsworth.

Masi, G. Perugi, G., Millepiedi, S., Mucci, Toni, C., Bertini, N., et al. (2006a). Developmental differences according to age at onset in juvenile bipolar disorder. *Journal of Child and Adolescent Psychopharmacology, 16*, 679–685.

Masi, G., Perugi, G., Toni, C., Millepiedi, S., Mucci, M., Bertini, N., et al. (2006b). The clinical phenotypes of juvenile bipolar disorder: Toward a validation of the episodic-chronic-distinction. *Biological Psychiatry, 59*, 603–610.

Masi, G., Perugi, G., Millepiedi, S., Toni, C., Mucci, M., Bertini, N., et al. (2006c). Clinical and research implications of panic bipolar comorbidity in children and adolescents. *Psychiatry Research.* Retrieved August 15, 2007.

Masten, A. S., Hubbard, J. J., Gest, S. D., Tellegen, A., Garmezy, N., & Ramirez, M. (1999). Competence in the context of adversity: Pathways to resilience and maladaptation from childhood to later adolescence. *Development and Psychopathology, 11*, 143–169.

Mastropieri, M. A., & Scruggs, T. E. (2005). Feasibility and consequences of response to intervention: Examination of the issues and scientific evidence as a model for the identification of individuals with learning disabilities. *Journal of Learning Disabilities, 38*, 525–531.

Mather, N., & Gregg, N. (2006). Specific learning disabilities: Clarifying, not eliminating a construct. *Professional Psychology: Research and Practice, 37*, 99–106.

Matte, R. R., & Bolaski, J. (1998). Nonverbal learning disabilities: An overview. *Intervention in School & Clinic, 34*, 1–5.

Mattson, A. J., Sheer, D. E., & Fletcher, J. M. (1992). Electrophysiological evidence of lateralized disturbances in children with learning disabilities. *Journal of Clinical and Experimental Neuropsychology, 14*, 707–716.

Matsumoto, D. (2000). *Culture and psychology* (2nd ed.) Belmont, CA: Wadsworth.

Maxfield, M. G., & Widom, C. S. (1996). The cycle of violence: Revisited six years later. *Archives of Pediatric and Adolescent Medicine, 150*, 390–395.

Mazza, J. J. (1997). School-based suicide prevention programs: Are they effective? *School Psychology Review, 26*, 382–396.

McAdoo, H. P. (1997). *Black families* (3rd ed.). Beverly Hills, CA: Sage.

McCabe, K., Yeh, M., Hough, R. L., Lansverk, J., Hurlburt, M., Culver, S., et al. (1999). Racial/ethnic representation across five public sectors of care for youth. *Journal of Emotional and Behavioral Disorders, 7*, 72–82.

McCabe, M. P., & Ricciardelli, L. A. (2004). A longitudinal study of pubertal timing and extremebody change behaviors among adolescent boys and girls. *Adolescence, 39*, 145–166.

McCabe, M. P., Ricciardelli, L. A., & Banfield, S. (2001). Body image, strategies to change muscles and weight, and puberty: Do they impact on positive and negative affect among adolescent boys and girls? *Eating Behavior, 2*, 129–149.

McClellan, J. M., & Werry, J. (2003). Evidence-based treatments in Child and adolescent Psychiatry: An inventory. *Journal of the American Academy of Child & Adolescent Psychiatry, 42*(12), 1388–1400.

McClure, E. B., Kubiszyn, T., & Kaslow, N. (2002). Advances in the diagnosis and treatment of childhood disorders. *Professional Psychology: Research and Practice, 33*(2), 125–134.

McConaughy, S. H., & Achenbach, T. M. (1993). Comorbidity of externalizing and internalizing problems. *School Psychology Review, 22*, 421–436.

McConaughy, S. H., & Achenbach, T. M. (2001). *Manual for the semistructured clinical interview for children and adolescents* (2nd ed.). Burlington: University of Vermont, Research Center for Children, Youth and Families.

McConaughy, S. H., & Skiba, R. (1993). Comorbidity of externalizing and internalizing problems. *School Psychology Review, 22*(3), 421–436.

McCord, J., Tremblay, R. E., Vitaro, F., & Desmarais-Gervais, L. (1994). Boys' disruptive behavior, school adjustment and delinquency: The Montreal prevention experiment. *International Journal of Behavioral Development, 17*, 739–752.

McCreary, L. L., & Dancy, B. L. (2004). Dimensions of family functioning: Perspectives of low-income African American single-parent families. *Journal of Marriage and Family, 66*, 690–701.

McDermott, B. M., & Palmer, L. J. (2002). Postdisaster emotional distress, depression and event-related variables: findings across child and adolescent developmental stages. *Australian and New Zealand Journal of Psychiatry, 36*, 754–761.

McElroy, S., Altshuler, L., Suppes, T., Keck, P., Frye, M., Denicoff, K. D., et al. (2001). Axis I psychiatric comorbidity and its relationship to historical illness variables in 288 patients with bipolar disorder. *American Journal of Psychiatry, 158*, 420–426.

McElroy, W. L., Phillips, K. A., & Keck, P. E. (1994). Obsessive compulsive spectrum disorders. *Journal of Clincial Psychiatry, 55*, 33–51.

McFarlane, A. (1987). Post-traumatic phenomena in a longitudinal study of children following a natural disaster. *Journal of the American Academy of Child and Adolescent Psychiatry, 26*, 764–769.

McGrue, M., Iacono, W. G., Legrand, L. N. & Elkins, I. (2001). Origins and consequences of age at first drink. 1. Associations with substance-use disorders, disinhibitory behavior, psychopathology and P3 amplitude. *Alcoholism, Clinical and Experimental Research, 25*, 1156–1165.

McGuffin, P., Katz, R., Watkins, S., & Rutherford, J. (1996). A hospital-based twin register of the heritability of DSM–IV unipolar depression. *Archives of General Psychiatry, 53*, 129–136.

McKee, T. E., Harvey, E., & Danforth, J. S. (2004). The relation between parental coping styles and parent-child interactions before and after treatment for children with ADHD and oppositional behavior. *Journal of Clinical Child and Adolescent Psychology 33*, 158–168.

McLeer, S., Callaghan, M., & Henry, D. (1994). Psychiatric disorders in sexually abused children. *Journal of the American Academy of Child & Adolescent Psychiatry, 33*(3), 313–319.

McLeer, S., Deblinger, E., Henry, D., & Orvaschel, H. (1992). Sexually abused children at high risk for post-traumatic stress disorder. *Journal of the American Academy of Child and Adolescent Psychiatry, 32*, 875–879.

McLeod, J., & Shanahan, M. J. (1993). Poverty, parenting and children's mental health. *American Sociological Review, 58*, 351–366.

McLoyd, C. V. (1990). The impact of economic hardship on black families and children: Psychological distress, parenting, and socioemotional development. *Child Development, 61*, 311–346.

McLoyd, C. V. (1998). Children in poverty: Development, public policy and practice. In W. Damon (Series Ed.) & E. E. Siegel & K. A. Renniger (Vol. Eds.), *Handbook of child psychology: Vol. 4, Child psychology in practice* (5th ed., pp. 135–208). New York: Wiley.

McMahon, R. J., & Estes, A. M. (1997). Conduct problems. In E. Mash & L. G. Terdal (Eds.), *Assessment of childhood disorders* (3rd ed., pp. 130–193). New York: Guilford.

McMahon, R. J., & Frick, P. J. (2005). Evidence-based assessment of conduct problems in children and adolescents. *Journal of Clinical Child and Adolescent Psychology, 34*, 477–505.

McMahon, R. J., & Kotler, J. S. (2004). Treatment of conduct problems in children and adolescents. In P. M. Barrett & T. H. Ollendick (Eds.), *Handbook of interventions that work with children and adolescents* (pp. 395–425). Chichester, UK: Wiley.

Meaney, M. (2001). Maternal care, gene expression and the transmission of individual differences in stress reactivity across generations. *Annual Review of Neuroscience, 24*, 1161–1192.

Measelle, J. R., Stice, E., & Hogansen, J. M. (2006). Developmental trajectories of co-occurring depressive, eating, antisocial and substance abuse problems in female adolescents. *Journal of Abnormal Psychology, 115*, 524–538.

Meezan, W., & McCroskey, J. (1996). Improving family functioning through family perseveration services: Results of the Los Angeles experiment. *Family Preservation Journal, 46*, 21–32.

Mendlowitz., S., Manassis, K., Bradley, S., Scapillato, D., Miezitis, S., & Shaw, B. F. (1999). Cognitive-behavioral group treatments in childhood anxiety disorders: The role of parental involvement. *Journal of the American Academy of Child and Adolescent Psychiatry, 38*, 1223–1229.

Meng, H., Smith, S., Hager, K., Held, M., Liu, J., Olson, R., et al. (2005, November). DCDC2 is associated with reading disability and modulates neuronal development in the brain. *Proceedings of the National Academy of Sciences, 102*, 17053–17058.

Messer, S., & Gross, A. (1995). Childhood depression and family interactions: A naturalistic observation study. *Journal of Clinical Child Psychology, 24*, 77–88.

Meyer, C., Waller, G., & Waters, A. (1998). Emotional states and bulimic psychopathology. In J. W. Hoek, J. L. Treassure, & M. A. Katzman (Eds.), *Neurobiology in the treatment of eating disorders* (pp. 271–289). New York: Wiley.

Meyer-Lindenberg, A., Hariri, A., Munoz, K., Mervin, C., Mattay, V., Morris, C. A., et al. (2005). Neural correlates of genetically abnormal social cognition in Williams syndrome. *Nature Neuroscience, 8*, 991–993.

Michaelson, R. (1993). Flood volunteers build emotional levees. *APA Monitor, 24*, 30.

Mick, E., Biederman, J., Faraone, S., Murray, K., & Wozniak, J. (2003). Defining a developmental subtype of bipolar disorder in a sample of nonreferred adults by age of onset. *Journal of Child and Adolescent Psychopharmacology, 13*, 453–462.

Miles, J., & Stelmack, R. M. (1994). Learning disability subtypes and the effects of auditory and visual priming on visual event-related potentials to words. *Journal of Clinical and Experimental Neuropsychology, 16*, 43–64.

Miller, D. L. (1979). *Mother's perception of Indian child development.* Unpublished research report, Institute for Scientific Analysis, San Francisco.

Miller, J. F. (1999). Profiles of language development in children with Down syndrome. In J. F. Miller, M. Leddy, & L. A. Leavitt (Eds.), Improving the communication of people with Down syndrome (pp. 11–39). Baltimore: Brookes.

Miller, J. N., & Ozonoff, S. (1997). Did Asperger's cases have Asperger disorder? A research note. *Journal of Child Psychology and Psychiatry, 38*, 247–251.

Miller, M. A., Alberts, J. K., Hecht, M. L., Trost, M. R., & Krizek, R. L. (2000). *Adolescent relationships and drug use.* Mahwah, NJ: Erlbaum.

Miller, M. N., & Pumariega, B. (1999). Culture and eating disorders. *Psychiatric Times*, XVI (2). Retrieved October, 2004, from http://www. psychiatrictimes. com/p990238. html

Miller, W. R., & Rollnick, S. (2002). *Motivational Interviewing: Preparing people for change* (2nd ed.). New York: Guilford.

Miller, V. A., Drotar, D., & Kodish, E. (2004). Children's competence for assent and consent: A review of empirical findings. *Ethics & Behavior, 14*(3), 255–295.

Milner, K. M., Craig, E. E., Thompson, R., Veltman, W. M., Thomas, N. S., Roberts, S., et al. (2005). Prader-Willi syndrome: Intellectual abilities and behavioral features by genetic subtype. Journal of Child Psychology and Psychiatry, 46, 1089–1096.

Milos, G., Spindler, A., Hepp, U., & Schnyder, U. (2004). Suicide attempts and suicidal ideation: Links with psychiatric comorbidity in eating disorder subjects. *General Hospital Psychiatry, 26*, 129–135.

Minuchin, P. (1985). Families and individual development: Provocations from the field of family therapy. *Child Development, 56*, 289–302.

Minuchin, S., Rosman, B. L., & Baker, L. (1978). *Psychosomatic families: Anorexia nervosa in context.* Cambridge, MA: Harvard University Press.

Mirande, A. (1991). Ethnicity and fatherhood. In F. W. Bozett & S. Hanson (Eds.), *Fatherhood and families in cultural context* (pp. 53–82). New York: Springer.

Mitchell, J. E., Halmi, K., Wilson, G. T., Agras, W., Kraemer, H., & Crow, S. (2002). A randomized secondary treatment study of women with bulimia nervosa who fail to respond to CBT. *International Journal of Eating Disorders, 32*, 271–281.

Miyake, K. (1993). Temperament, mother-infant interaction and early emotional development. *The Japanese Journal of Research on Emotions, 1*(1), 48–55.

Moffitt, T. E. (1990). Juvenile delinquency and attention deficit disorder: Boys' developmental trajectories from age 3 to 15. *Child Development, 61*, 893–910.

Moffitt, T. E (1993). The neuropsychology of conduct disorder. *Development and Psychopathology, 5*(1–2), 135–151.

Moffitt, T. E. (2005). The new look of behavioral genetics in developmental psychopathology: Gene-environment interplay n antisocial behaviors. *Psychological Bulletin, 131*(4), 533–554.

Moffitt, T. E., & Henry, B. (1989). Neuropsychological assessment of executive functions in self-reported delinquents. *Development and Psychopathology, 1*,105–118.

Molina, B., & Pelham, W. E. (2003). Childhood predictors of adolescent substance use in a longitudinal study of children with ADHD. *Journal of Abnormal Psychology, 112*, 497–507.

Molina, B., Pelham, W. E., Blumenthal, J., & Galiszewski, E. G. (1998). Agreement among teachers' behavior ratings of adolescents with childhood history of attention deficit hyperactivity disorder. *Journal of Clinical Child Psychology, 27*, 330–339.

Mol Lous, A., de Wit, C., De Bruyn, D., & Riuksen-Walraven, J. M. (2002). Depression markers in young children's play: A comparison between depressed and nondepressed 3-to-6-year-olds in various play situations. *Journal of Child Psychology and Psychiatry, 43*, 1029–1038.

Monti, P. M., Kadden, R., Rohsenow, D., Cooney, N., & Abrams, D. (2002). *Treating alcohol dependence: A coping skills training guide* (2nd ed.). New York: Guilford.

Montoya, I. D., Atkinson, J., & McFaden, W. C. (2003). Best characteristics of adolescent gateway drug prevention programs. *Journal of Addictions Nursing, 14*, 75–83.

Moore, C. A., Biederman, J., Wozniak, J., Mick, E., Aleardi, M., Wardrop, M., et al. (2007). Mania, glutamate/glutamine and risperidone in pediatric bipolar disorder: A proton magnetic resonance spectroscopy study of the anterior cingulate cortex. *Journal of Affective Disorders, 99*, 19–25.

Moore, M. R., & Brooks-Gunn, J. (2002). Adolescent parenthood. In M. Bornstein (Ed), *Handbook of parenting* (Vol. 3; pp. 173–214).

Moore, W., Jr. (1969). *The vertical ghetto: Everyday life in an urban project.* New York: Random House.

Morral, A., McCaffrey, D., & Paddock, S. (2002). Reassessing the marijuana gateway effect. *Addiction, 97*, 1493–1504.

Morris, R. D., Stuebing, K. K., Fletcher, J. M., Shaywitz, S. E., Lyon, G. R., Shankweiler, D. P., et al. (1998). Subtypes of reading disability: Variability around a phonological core. *Journal of Educational Psychology, 90*, 347–373.

Mosher, C., Rotolo, T., Phillips, D., Krupski, A., & Stark, K. D. (2004). Minority adolescents and substance use risk/protective factors: A focus on inhalant use. *Adolescence, 39*, 489–502.

Mouridsen, S., Rich, B & Isager, T. (1998). Validity of childhood disintegrative psychosis. General findings of a long-term follow-up study. *British Journal of Psychiatry, 172*, 263–267.

Mouridsen, S., Rich, B., & Isager, T. (1999). Epilepsy in disintegrative psychosis and infantile autism: A long-term validation study. *Developmental Medicine & Child Neurology, 41*, 110–114.

MTA Cooperative Group (1999). A 14-month randomized clinical trial of treatment strategies for attention-deficit-/hyperactivity disorder. *Archives of General Psychiatry, 56*, 1073–1086.

MTA Cooperative Group (2004). National Institute of Mental Health Treatment Study of ADHD (NIMH: MTA) follow up: 24 month outcomes of treatment strategies for attention-deficit/hyperactivity disorder. *Pediatrics, 113*, 754–761.

Mullen, E. M. (1995). *Mullen Scales of Early Learning.* Circle Pines, MN: American Guidance Service.

Muris, P., Luermans, J., Merckelbach, E., & Mayer, R. (2000). "Danger is lurking everywhere": The relation between anxiety and threat perception abnormalities in normal children. *Journal of Behavior Therapy and Experimental Psychiatry, 31*, 123–136.

Muris, P., Meesters, C., & van Melick, M. (2002). Treatment of childhood anxiety disorders: A preliminary comparison between cognitive-behavioral group therapy and a psychological placebo intervention. *Journal of Behavior Therapy and Experimental Psychiatry, 33*, 143–158.

Muris, P., Merckelbach, H., Meesters, C., & Van Lier, P. (1997). What do children fear most often? *Journal of Behavior Therapy and Experimental Psychiatry, 28*(4), 263 –267.

Muris, P., & Ollendick, T. H. (2005). The role of temperament in the etiology of child psychopathology. *Clinical Child and Family Psychology Review, 8*(4), 271–289.

Murphy, D., Daly, E., Schmitz, N., Toal, F., Murphy, K., Curran, S., et al. (2006). Cortical serotonin 5-HT$_{24}$ receptor binding and social communication in adults with Asperger's syndrome: An in vivo SPECT study. *American Journal of Psychiatry, 163*, 934–936.

Murphy, K., & Barkley, R. A. (1996). Attention deficit hyperactivity disorder in adults. *Comprehensive Psychiatry, 37*, 393–401.

Murphy, M. L., & Pinchinero, M. E. (2002). Prospective identification and treatment of children with pediatric autoimmune neuropsychiatric disorder associate with Group A streptococcal infection (PANDAS). *Archives of Pediatric and Adolescent Medicine, 156*, 356–361.

Myles, B. S., Bock, S. J., & Simpson, R. (2001). *Asperger Syndrome Diagnostic Scale.* Austin TX: PRO-ED.

Nachmias, M., Gunnar, M., Mangelsdorf, S., Parritz, R., & Buss, K. (1996). Behavioral inhibition and stress reactivity: The moderating role of attachment security. *Child Development, 67*, 508–522.

Nagata, D. K. (2001). The Assessment and Treatment of Japanese American Children and Adolescents. In J. T. Gibbs & L. N. Huang (Eds.), *Children of color* (pp 68–111). San Francisco: Jossey-Bass.

Nagelberg, D. (1984). Bulimia = bulimarexia = bulimia nervosa. *Professional Psychology: Research and Practice, 15*, 475–476.

Nagin, D., & Tremblay, R. E. (1999). Trajectories of boys' physical aggression, opposition and hyperactivity on the path to physically violent and non-violent juvenile delinquency. *Child Development, 70*, 1181–1196.

National Association of School Psychologists (NASP). (2000). Professional conduct manual and principles for professional ethics: Guidelines for the provision of school psychological services. Retrieved July 2007 from http://www.naspweb.org

National Institute on Drug Abuse (NIDA, 2003). The Neurobiology of Ecstasy. Retrieved August 15, 2007, from http://www.drugabuse. gov/pubs/teachcing/teaching4/Teaching3. html

National Institute of Mental Health (NIMH) Fact Sheet. (2000). Depression in children and adolescents: A fact sheet for physicians. Retrieved July 2008 from http://www.mental-healthmatters.com/articles/article.php?artID=320

Neumark-Sztainer, D., Sherwood, N., Coller, T., & Hannan, P. (2000). Primary prevention of disordered eating among preadolescent girls: Feasibility and short-term effect of a community-based intervention. *Journal of the American Dietetic Association, 100,*1466–1473.

Newacheck, P. E., & Halfon, N . (2000). Prevalence, impact and trends in childhood disability due to asthma. *Archives of Pediatric and Adolescent Medicine, 154*(3), 287–293.

Newcomb, M. (1997). Psychosocial predictors and consequences of drug use: A developmental perspective within a prospective study. *Journal of Addictive Diseases, 16*, 51–89.

Newman, D. L., Moffitt, T. E., & Caspi, A. (1996). Psychiatric disorder in a birth cohort of young adults: Prevalence, comorbidity, clinical significance, and new case incidence from ages 11-21. *Journal of Consulting and Clinical Psychology, 64*(3), 552–562.

New York Times (1926, Jan. 14). Editorial.

Ngo, H., & Le, T. (2007). Stressful life events, culture and violence. *Journal of Immigrant & Minority Health, 9*, 75–84.

Nicholls, D. (2005). Eating disorders in children. In C. Norring & B. Palmer (Eds.), *EDNOS: Eating disorders Not Otherwise Specified* (pp. 241–265). Hove, East Sussex, UK: Routledge.

Nicholson, R., & Szatmari, P. (2003). Genetic and neurodevelopmental influences in autistic disorder. *Canadian Journal of Psychiatry, 48*, 526–537.

Nietzel, M., Bernstein, D., & Milich, R. (1994). *Introduction to Clinical Psychology* (4th ed). Englewood Cliffs, NJ: Prentice Hall.

Nriagu, J. O. (1983). Saturnine gout among Roman aristocrats: Did lead poisoning contribute to the fall of the empire? *New England Journal of Medicine, 308*, 660–663.

O'Connell, P., Pepler, D., & Craig, W. (1999). Peer involvement in bullying: Insights and challenges for intervention. *Journal of Adolescence, 22*(4), 437–452.

Office of Juvenile Justice and Delinquency Prevention. (OJJDP; 2001). Fact Sheet: Mental Health Initiatives. August #30. U. S. Department of Justice, Office of Justice Programs. Retrieved August 21, 2007, from http://www. ncjrs. gov/pdffiles l/ojjdprfs200130. pdf

Offord, D. R., Boyle, M., & Racine, Y. (1989). Ontario Child Health Study: Correlates of disorder. *Journal of the American Academy of Child & Adolescent Psychiatry, 28*, 855–860.

Ogbu, J. U. (1981). Origins of human competence: A cultural-ecological perspective. *Child Development, 52*, 413–429.

Ogunwole, S. U. (February 2006). *We the People: American Indians and Alaska Natives in the United States.* U. S. Census Bureau, 2000. Washington DC: U. S. Census Bureau.

Ohman, A., Erixon, G., & Lofberg, I. (1975). Phobias and preparedness: Phobic versus neutral stimuli for human autonomic responses. *Journal of Abnormal Psychology, 84*(1), 41–45.

Okamoto, Y., & Case, R. (1996). Exploring the microstructure of children's central conceptual structures in the domain of number. *Monographs of the Society for Research in Child Development, 61*, 27–59.

Olds, D., Hill, P., & Rumsey, E. (1998*). Prenatal and early childhood nurse home visitation* [Bulletin]. Washington, DC: U. S. Department of Justice, Office of Justice Programs, Office of Juvenile Justice and Delinquency Prevention.

O'Leary, T. A., Brown, S. A., Colby, S. M., Cronce, J. M., D'Amico, E,. G., Fader, J. S., et al. (2002). Treating adolescents together or individually? Issues in adolescent substance abuse interventions. *Alcoholism, Clinical, and Experimental Research,26*, 890–899.

Ollendick, T. H. (1983). Reliability and validity of the Revised Fear Survey Schedule for Children (FSSC–R). *Behavior Research and Therapy, 21*, 395–399.

Ollendick, T. H. (1998). Panic disorder in children and adolescents: New developments, new directions. *Journal of Clinical Child Psychology, 27*, 234–245.

Ollendick, T. H., & King, N. J. (1998). Empirically supported treatment for children with phobic and anxiety disorders: Current status. *Journal of Clinical Child Psychology, 27*, 156–167.

Ollendick, T. H., & King, N. J. (2004). Empirically supported treatments for children and adolescents: Advances toward evidence-based practice. In P. M. Barrett & T. H. Ollendick (Eds.), *Handbook of interventions that work with children and Adolescents* (pp. 3–26). West Sussex, UK: Wiley.

Olsson, G., Nordstrom, M. L., Arinell, H., & Von Knorring, A. L. (1999). Adolescent depression and stressful life events: A case-control study within diagnostic subgroups. *Nordic Journal of Psychiatry, 53*, 339–346.

Olweus, D. (1979). Stability of aggressive reaction patterns in males: A review. *Psychological Bulletin, 86*, 852–875.

Olweus, D. (1993). *Bullying at school: What we know and what we can do.* Oxford, UK: Blackwell.

Olweus, D. (1994). Bullying at school: Basic facts and effects of a school-based intervention program. *Journal of Child Psychology and Psychiatry, 33*, 1171–1190.

Olweus, D. (1995). Bullying or peer abuse at school: Facts and interventions. *Current Directions in Psychological Science, 4*(6), 196–200.

Olweus, D. (1996). Bullying at school: Knowledge base and an effective intervention program. In C. F. Ferris & T. Grisso (Eds.), *Understanding aggressive behavior in children* (Vol. 794, pp. 265–276). New York: New York Academy of Sciences.

O'Shea, L. J., Sindelar, P. T., & O'Shea, D. J. (1985). The effects of repeated readings and attentional cues on reading fluency and comprehension. *Journal of Reading Behavior, 17,* 129–142.

Ostrov, E., Offer, D., & Howard, K. I. (1989). Gender differences in adolescent symptomatology: A normative study. *Journal of the American Academy of Child and Adolescent Psychiatry, 28,* 394–398.

Oswald, D. P., Coutinho, M. J., Best, A. M., & Nguyen, M. (2001). Impact of sociodemographic characteristics on the identification rates of minority students as having mental retardation. *Mental Retardation, 39,* 351–367.

Overholser, J., Hemstreet, A. H., Spirito, A., & Vyse, S. (1989). Suicide awareness programs in the schools: Effects of gender and personal experience. *Journal of the American Academy of Child and Adolescent Psychiatry, 28,* 925–930.

Owens, E. B., & Shaw, D. S. (2003). Predicting growth curves of externalizing behavior across the preschool years. *Journal of Abnormal Child Psychology, 31*(6), 575–590.

Ozechowski, T. J., & Liddle, H. A. (2000). Family-based therapy for adolescent drug use: Knowns and unknowns. *Clinical and Family Psychology Review,3,* 269–298.

Ozonoff, S., Goodlin-Jones, B., & Solomon, M. (2005). Evidence-based assessment of autism spectrum disorders in childhood and adolescents. *Journal of Clinical Child and Adolescent Psychology, 34,* 523–540.

Ozonoff, S., Rogers, S. J., & Pennington, B. F. (1991). Asperger's syndrome: Evidence of an empirical distinction from high-functioning autism. *Journal of Child Psychology and Psychiatry, 32,* 1107–1112.

Pagliaro, A. M., & Pagliaro, L. A. (1996*). Substance use among children and adolescents.* New York: Wiley.

Papolos, D., Hennen, J., & Cockerham, M. S. (2005). Factors associated with parent-reported suicide threats by children and adolescents with community-diagnosed bipolar disorder. *Journal of Affective Disorders, 86,* 267–275.

Papolos, D., Hennen, J., & Cockerham, M. S., & Lachman, H. (2007). A strategy for identifying phenotypic subtypes: Concordance of symptom dimensions between sibling pairs who met screening criteria for a genetic linkage study of childhood- onset bipolar disorder using the child bipolar questionnaire. *Affective Disorders, 99,* 27–36.

Papolos, D., Hennen, J., Cockerham, M. S., Thode, H. C., Jr., & Youngstrom, E. A. (2006). The child bipolar questionnaire: A dimensional approach to screening for pediatric bipolar disorder. *Journal of Affect Disorders, 95,* 149–158.

Parke, R. D. (2004) Development in the family. *Annual Review of Psychology, 55,* 365–399.

Parker, J., & Asher, S. R. (1987). Peer relations and later personal adjustment: Are low-accepted children at risk? *Psychological Bulletin, 102,* 357–389.

Parrill, M. (1987). Developmental issues surrounding severe discrepancy. *Learning Disabilities Research, 3,* 32–41.

Parry-Jones, B. A., & Parry-Jones, W. (1991). Bulimia: An archival review of its history in psychosomatic medicine. *International Journal of Eating Disorders, 10,* 129–143.

Pate, J. E., Pumariega, A. J., Hester, C., & Garner,D. M. (1992). Cross-cultural patterns in eating disorders: A review. *Journal of the American Academy of Child and Adolescent Psychiatry, 31,* 802–808.

Patterson, C., Kupersmidt, J., & Vaden, N. (1990). Income level, gender, ethnicity, and household composition as predictors of children's school-based competence. *Child Development, 61,* 485–494.

Patterson, G. R. (1982). *Coercive family process.* Eugene, OR: Castalia.

Patterson, G. R., & Capaldi, D. M. (1990). A mediational model for boys' depressed mood. In J. Rolf, A. S. Masten, D. Cicchetti, K. H. Nuechterlein, & S. Weintraub (Eds.), *Risk and protective factors in the development of psychopathology* (pp. 141–163). Cambridge, UK: Cambridge University Press

Patterson, G. R., Capaldi, D., & Bank, L. (1991). An early starter model for predicting delinquency. In D. Pepler & K. H. Rubin (Eds.), *The development and treatment of childhood aggression* (pp. 139–168). Hillsdale, NJ: Erlbaum.

Patterson, G. R., Cobb, J. A., & Ray, R. S. (1973). A social engineering technology for retraining the families of aggressive boys. In H. E. Adams & I. P. Unikel (Eds.), *Issues and trends in behavior therapy* (pp. 139–210). Springfield, IL: Charles C. Thomas.

Patterson, G. R., DeBaryshe, B. D., & Ramsey, E. (1989). A developmental perspective on antisocial behavior. *American Psychologist, 44,* 329–335.

Patterson, G. R., & Gullion, M. E. (1968). *Living with children: New methods for parents and teachers.* Champaign, IL: Research Press.

Patterson, G. R., Reid, J., & Dishion, T. J. (1992). *A social learning approach* (Vol. 4). *Antisocial boys.* Eugene, OR: Castaglia.

Patterson, G. R., Reid, J. B., Jones, R. R., & Conger, R. E. (1975). *A social learning approach to family intervention. Vol. 1: Families with aggressive children.* Eugene, OR: Castalia.

Patterson, G. R., & Yoerger, K. (2002). A developmental model for early and late onset delinquency. In J. B. Reid, G. R. Patterson, & J. Snyder (Eds.), *Antisocial behavior in children and adolescents: A developmental analysis and model for intervention* (pp. 147–172). Washington, DC: APA.

Pattison, C., & Lynd-Stevenson, R. M. (2001). The prevention of depressive symptoms in children: The immediate and long-term outcomes of a school-based program. *Behavior Change, 18,* 92–102.

Patton, G. C., Selzer, R., Coffey, C., Carlin, J. B., & Wolfe, R. (1999). Onset of adolescent eating disorders: Population based cohort study over 3 years. *British Medical Journal, 318*(7186), 765–768.

Pavuluri, M. N., Birmaher, B., & Naylor, M. W. (2005). Pediatric bipolar disorder: A review of the past 10 years. *Journal of the American Academy of Child and Adolescent Psychiatry, 44,* 846–871.

Pelham, E. E., & Milich, R. (1991). Individual differences in response to Ritalin in classwork and social behavior. In L. L. Grennhill & B. B. Osmon (Eds.). *Ritalin: Theory and patient management* (pp. 203–221). New York: Mary Ann Liebert.

Pelham, W. E., & Bender, M. E. (1982). Peer relationships in hyperactive children: Description and treatment. In K. D. Gadow & I. Bialer (Eds.), *Advances in learning and behavioral disabilities* (Vol. 1, pp. 365–436). Greenwich, CT: JAI Press.

Pelham, W. E., Fabiano, G. A., & Massetti, G. M. (2005). Evidence-based assessment of attention deficit hyperactivity disorder in children and adolescents. *Journal of Clinical Child and Adolescent Psychology, 34,* 449–476.

Pelham, W. E., Jr., Wheeler, T., & Chronis, A. (1998). Empirically supported psychosocial treatments for attention deficit hyperactivity disorder. *Journal of Clinical Child Psychology, 27*, 190–205.

Pennington, B. *Diagnosing learning disorders: A neuropsychological framework.* New York: Guilford.

Pennington, B., Moon, J., Edgin, J., Stedron, J., & Nadel, L. (2003). The neuropsychology of Down syndrome: Evidence of hippocampal dysfunction. *Child Development, 74*, 74–93.

Perlis, R. H., Miyahara, S., Marangell, L., Wisniewski, S. R., Ostacher, M., DelBello, M., et al. (2004). Long-term implications of early onset in bipolar disorder: Data from the first 1000 participants in the systematic treatment enhancement program for bipolar disorder (STEP:BD). *Biological Psychiatry, 55*, 875–881.

Peterson, C., Maier, S. F., & Seligman, M. (1993). *Learned helplessness: A theory for the age of personal control.* New York: Oxford University Press.

Peterson, L., & Roberts, M. C. (1991). Treatment of children's problems. In C. E. Walker (Ed.), *Clinical psychology: Historical and research foundations.* New York: Plenum.

Petri, T., & Stoever S. (1993). The incidence of Bulimia Nervosa and pathogenic weight control behaviors in female college gymnasts. *Research Quarterly in Exercise and Sport, 56*, 245–250.

Pfeffer, C. R. (2000). Suicidal behavior in prepubertal children: From 1980s to the new millennium. In R. W. Maris, S. S. Canetto, J. L. McIntosh, & M. M. Silverman (Eds.), *Review of suicidology, 2000* (pp. 259–273). New York: Guilford.

Pfefferbaum, B. (1997). Posttraumatic stress disorder in children: A review of the past 10 years. *Journal of the American Academy of Child & Adolescent Psychiatry, 36*, 1503–1511.

Pfiffner, L. J., & O'Leary, S. G. (1993). School-based psychological treatments. In J. Matson (Ed.), *Handbook of hyperactivity in children* (pp. 234–255). Needham Heights, MA: Allyn & Bacon.

Piacentini, J., Bergman, R. I., Keller, M., & McCracken, J. (2003). Functional impairment in children and adolescents with obsessive-compulsive disorder. *Journal of Child and Adolescent Psychopharmacology, 13*, 61–70.

Picchietti, D. L., England, S. J., Walters, A. S., Willis, K., & Verrico, T. (1998). Periodic limb movement disorder and restless legs syndrome in children with attention-deficit-hyperactivity disorder. *Journal of Child Neurology, 13,* 588–594.

Picchietti, D. L, & Walters A. S. (1999). Moderate to severe periodic limb movement disorder in childhood and adolescence. *Sleep, 22,* 297–300.

Pickersgill, M. J., Valentine, J. D., Pincus, T., & Foustok, H. (1999). Girls fearfulness as a product of mothers' fearfulness and fathers' authoritarianism. *Psychological Reports, 85*, 759–760.

Pierce, K., Muller, R. A., Ambrose, J., Allen, G., & Courchesne, E. (2001). Face processing occurs outside the fusiform "face area" in autism: Evidence from functional MRI. *Brain, 124*, 2059–2073.

Pike, K. M., & Rodin, J. (1991). Mothers, daughters, and disordered eating. *Journal of Abnormal Psychology, 100*, 198–201.

Pimentel, S. S., & Kendall, P. C. (2003). On the physiological symptom constellation in youth with Generalized Anxiety Disorder (GAD). *Journal of Anxiety Disorders, 17*, 211–221.

Piran, N. (2005). Prevention of eating disorders: A review of outcome evaluation research. *Israel Journal of Psychiatry and Related Sciences, 42*, 171–177.

Piran, N. & Robinson, S. R. (2006). Associations between disordered eating behaviors and licit and illicit substance use and abuse in a university sample. *Addictive Behaviors, 31*, 1761–1775.

Pliszka, S. R. (2002). *Neuroscience for the mental health clinician.* New York: Guilford.

Plomin, R. (1994). *Genetics and experience: The interplay between nature and nurture.* Thousand Oaks, CA: Sage.

Poe-Yamagata, E., & Jones, M. (2000). *And justice for some.* National Council on Crime and Delinquency (NCCD).

Pope, J. G., Olivardia, R., Gruber, A., & Borowiecki, J. (1999). Evolving ideals of male body image as seen through action toys. *International Journal of Eating Disorders, 26*, 65–72.

Pope, K. S., & Vetter, V. A. (1992). Ethical dilemmas encountered by members of the American Psychological Association. *American Psychologist, 47*(2), 397–411.

Power, T. J., Costigan, T., Eiraldi, R., & Leff, S. (2004). Variations in anxiety and depression as a function of ADHD subtypes defined by DSM–IV: Do subtype differences exist or not? *Journal of Abnormal Child Psychology 32*, 27–37.

Power, T. J., & Eiraldi, R. B. (2000). Educational and psychiatric classification systems. In E. S. Shapiro & T. R. Kratochwill (Eds.), *Behavioral assessment in schools: Theory, research, and clinical foundations* (pp. 464–488). New York: Guilford.

Poznanski, E. O., & Mokros, H. B. (1999). *Children Depression Rating Scale-Revised (CDRS–R).* Los Angeles: Western Psychological Services.

Pratt, B. M, & Woolfenden, S. R. (2006). Interventions for preventing eating disorders in children and adolescents. In *The Cochrane Library* (Issue 1). Oxford, UK: Update Software.

Presnell, K., Bearman, S. K., & Stice, E. (2004). Risk factors for body dissatisfaction in adolescent boys and girls: A prospective study. *International Journal of Eating Disorders, 36*, 389–401.

Puig-Antich, J., Kaufman, J., Ryan, N. D., & Williamson, D. E. (1993). The psychosocial functioning and family environment of depressed adolescents. *Journal of the American Academy of Child & Adolescent Psychiatry, 32*, 244–253.

Pyle, R. L. (1999). Dynamic psychotherapy. In M. Hersen, & A. S. Bellack (Eds.), *Handbook of comparative interventions for adult disorders* (2nd ed.). New York: Wiley.

Pyle, R., Mitchell, J., & Eckert, E. (1981). Bulimia: A report of 34 cases. *Journal of Clinical Psychiatry, 42*, 60–64.

Pynoos, R. S. (1990). Post-traumatic stress disorder in children and adolescence. In B. Grafinkel, G. Carlson, & E. Weller (Eds.), *Psychiatric disorders in children and adolescents* (pp. 48–63). Philadelphia: W. B. Saunders.

Pynoos, R. S. (1994). Traumatic stress and developmental psychopathology in children and adolescents. In R. S. Pynoos (Ed.), *Posttraumatic stress disorder: A clinical review* (pp. 64–98). Lutherville, MD: The Sidran Press.

Pynoos, R. S., Goenjian, A. K., & Steinberg, A. (1998). A public mental health approach to the postdisaster treatment of children and adolescents. *Child and Adolescent Psychiatric Clinics of North America, 7*(1), 195–210.

Pynoos, R. S., & Nader, K. (1993). Issues in the treatment of posttraumatic stress in children and adolescents. In J. P. Wilson & B. Raphael (Eds.), *International handbook of traumatic stress syndromes* (pp. 535–549). New York: Plenum.

Quay, H. C. (1986). Conduct disorders. In H. C. Quay & J. S. Werry (Eds), *Psychopathological disorders of childhood* (3rd ed., pp. 1–34). New York: Wiley.

Rachman, S. (1993). Obsessions, responsibility, and guilt. *Behaviour Research and Therapy, 31*, 149–154.

Rae-Grant, N., Thomas, B. H., Offord, D. R., & Boyle, M. H. (1989). *Journal of the American Academy of Child and Adolescent Psychiatry, 28*, 262–268.

Rahman M, Fukui T. (2000). Bidi smoking and health. *Public Health 2000, 114*, 123–127.

Raine, A., Reynolds, C., & Venables, P. (1998). Fearlessness, stimulation-seeking, and large body size at age 3 years as early predispositions to childhood aggression at age 11 years. *Archives of General Psychiatry, 55*(8), 745–751.

Ramirez, O. (2001). Mexican American children and adolescents. In J. T. Gibbs & L. N. Huang (Eds.), *Children of color* (pp. 215–239). San Francisco: Jossey-Bass.

Rao, U., Hammen, C., & Daley, S. (1999). Continuity of depression during the transition to adulthood: A 5-year longitudinal study of young women. *Journal of the American Academy of Child and Adolescent Psychiatry, 38*, 908–915.

Rao, S. M., Mayer, A., & Harrington, D. L. (2001). The evolution of brain activation during temporal processing. *Nature Neuroscience, 4*(3), 317–323.

Rapee, R. M. (1997). Potential role of childrearing practices in the development of anxiety and depression. *Clinical Psychology Review, 17*, 47–67.

Rapee, R. M. (2002). The development and modification of temperamental risk for anxiety disorders: Prevention of a lifetime of anxiety. *Biological Psychiatry. 52*, 947–957.

Raphael, F. J., & Lacey, J. H. (1994). The aetiology of eating disorders: A hypothesis of the interplay between social, cultural and biological factors. *European Eating Disorders Review, 2*, 143–154.

Rapin, I., & Allen, D. (1983). Developmental language disorders. In U. Kirk (Ed.), *Neuropsychology of language, reading and spelling* (pp. 96–112). New York: Academic Press.

Raymond, J. H., Jones, F., & Cooke, V. (1998). African American scholars and parents cannot blame current harsh physical punishment of black males on slavery: A response to "cultural interpretations of child ellipsis." *The Family Journal, 6*, 279–286.

Redmond, D. E. (1981). Clonidine and the primate locus coeruleus: Evidence suggesting anxiolytic and anti-withdrawal effects. In H. Lal & S. Fielding (Eds.), *Psychopharmacology of clonidine*. New York: Alan R. Liss.

Reebye, P. N. (1997, October). *Diagnosis and treatment of ADHD in preschoolers.* Paper presented at the annual meeting of the American Academy of Child and Adolescent Psychiatry, Toronto, Canada.

Reebye, P. N., Moretti, M. M., & Gulliver, L. (1995). Conduct disorder and substance use disorder. Comorbidity in a clinical sample of preadolescents and adolescents. *Canadian Journal of Psychiatry, 40*, 313–319.

Reiboldt, W. (2001). Adolescent interactions with gangs, family and neighborhoods. *Journal of Family Issues, 22*, 211–242.

Reitan, R. (1993). *Halstead-Reitan Neuropsychological Test Battery.* Tucson, AZ: Reitan Neuropsychology Laboratory/Press.

Renaud, J., Birmaher, B., Wassick, C. C., & Bridge, J. (1999). Use of selective serotonin reuptake inhibitors for the treatment of childhood panic disorder: A pilot study. *Journal of Child and Adolescent Psychopharmacology, 9*, 73–83.

Reschly. D. J., & Wilson, M. (1995). School psychology practitioners and faculty: 1986 to 1991–92 trends in demographics, roles, satisfaction and system reform. *School Psychology Review, 24*, 62–80.

Rey, J. M. (1993). Oppositional defiant disorder. *American Journal of Psychiatry, 150*, 1769–1777.

Reynolds, C. R., & Kamphaus, R. W. (2004). *BASC2: Behavior Assessment System for Children manual.* Circle Pines, MN: American Guidance Service.

Reynolds, C. R., & Richmond, B. O. (1985). *Revised Children's Manifest Anxiety Scale: Manual.* Los Angeles: Western Psychological Services.

Reynolds, W. M. (1987). Reynolds Adolescent Depression Scale (RADS). Odessa, FL: Psychological Assessment Resources.

Reynolds, W. M. (1988). *Suicidal ideation questionnaire: Professional manual.* Odessa, FL: Psychological Assessment Resources.

Reynolds, W. M. (1989). Reynolds Child Depression Scale (RCDS). Odessa, FL: Psychological Assessment Resources.

Reynolds, W. M. (1991). A school-based procedure for the identification of adolescents at risk for suicidal behaviors. *Family Community Health, 14*, 64–75.

Reynolds, W. M. (1998). *Adolescent psychopathology scale: Administration and interpretive manual.* Odessa, FL: Psychological Assessment Resources.

Reynolds, W. M. (2000). *Adolescent psychopathology scale—short form: Professional manual.* Odessa, FL: Psychological Assessment Resources.

Reynolds, W. M. (2001). *Reynolds adolescent adjustment screening inventory: Professional manual.* Odessa, FL: Psychological Assessment Resources.

Ricciardelli, L. A., & McCabe, M. P. (2001). Self-esteem and negative affect as moderators of sociocultural influences on body dissatisfaction, strategies to decrease weight and strategies to increase muscles among adolescent boys and girls. *Sex Roles, 44*, 189–207.

Rice, K. G., Herman, M. A., & Petersen, A. C. (1993). Coping with challenge in adolescence: A conceptual model and psycho-educational intervention. *Journal of Adolescence, 16*, 235–251.

Rice, K. G., & Meyer, A. L. (1994). Preventing depression among young adolescents: Preliminary process results of a psycho-educational intervention program. *Journal of Counseling and Development, 73*, 145–156.

Richardson, G., Hamel, S. C., & Goldschmidt, L. (1996). The effects of prenatal cocaine use on neonatal neurobehavioral status. *Neurotoxicology and Teratology, 18*, 519–528.

Richters, J. E. (1993). The NIMH community violence project: I. Children as victims of and witnesses to violence. *Psychiatry, 56*, 7–21.

Rickels, K., Downing, R., & Schweizer, E. (1993). Antidepressants for the treatment of generalized anxiety disorder: A placebo-controlled comparison of imipramine, trazodone, and diazepam. *Archives of General Psychiatry, 50*(11), 884–895.

Riddle, M. A., Scahill, L., King, R., Hardin, M. T., Toublin, K. E., Ort, S. I., et al. (1990). Obsessive-compulsive disorder in children and adolescents. Phenomenology and family history. *Journal of the American Academy of Child and Adolescent Psychiatry, 29*, 766–772.

Ring, A., Stein, D., Barak, Y., Teicher, A., Hadjez, J., Elizur, A., et al. (1998). Sleep disturbances in children with attention deficit hyperactivity disorder: A comparative study with healthy siblings. *Journal of Learning Disabilities, 31*, 572–578.

Robertson, J., & Robertson, J. (1971). Young children in brief separation. *Psychoanalytic Study of the Child, 26*, 264–315.

Robin, A. L. (2003). Behavioral family systems: Therapy for adolescents with anorexia nervosa. In A. Kazdin, & J. R. Weisz (Eds.), *Evidence-based therapies for children and adolescents* (pp. 358–373). New York: Guilford.

Robin, A. L., Bedway, M., Diegel, P. T., & Gilroy, M. (1996). Therapy for adolescent anorexia nervosa. Addressing cognitions, feelings, and the family's role. In E. D. Hibbs & P. S. Jensen (Eds.), *Psychosocial treatments for child and adolescent disorders: Empirically-based strategies for clinical practice*. Washington, DC: APA.

Robin, A. L., Siegel, P. T., & Moye, A. (1995). Family versus individual therapy for anorexia: Impact on family conflict. Topical Section: Treatment and therapeutic processes. *International Journal of Eating Disorders, 17*, 313–322.

Robinson, C., Menchetti, B., & Torgesen, J. (2002). Toward a two-factor theory of one type of mathematics disabilities. *Learning Disabilities Research & Practice, 17*, 81–89.

Robinson, D. J. (2000). *The Mental Status Exam–explained*. Port Huron, MI: Rapid Psychier Press.

Robinson, D. P., Greene, J. W., & Walker, L. S. (1988). Functional somatic complaints in adolescents: Relationship to negative life events, self concept, and family characteristics. *The Journal of Pediatrics, 113*, 588–593.

Robinson, T., & Anderson, A. (1985). Anorexia nervosa in American Blacks. *Journal of Psychiatry Research, 19*, 183–188.

Rodin, J., Silberstein, L. R., & Striegel-Moore, R. (1985). Women and weight: A normative discontent. In T. B. Sonderegger (Ed.), *Nebraska symposium on motivation* (pp. 267–307). Lincoln: University of Nebraska Press.

Rodin, J., Striegel-Moore, R. H., & Silberstein, L. R. (1990). Vulnerability and resilience in the age of eating disorders: Risk and protective factors for bulimia nervosa. In J. Rolf, A. S. Masten, D. Cicchetti, K. H. Neucherlein, & S. Weintraub (Eds.), *Risk and protective factors the development of psychopathology* (pp. 361–383). New York: Cambridge University Press.

Rogers, H. R. (1986). *Poor women, poor families*. Armonk, NY: Sharpe.

Rogers, M. R., Ingraham, C. L., Bursztyn, A., Cajigas-Segredo, N., Esquivel, G., Hess, R. S., et al. (1999). Best practices in providing psychological services to racially, ethnically, culturally, and linguistically diverse individuals in the schools. *School Psychology International, 20*, 243–264.

Rogers, S. J. (2004). Developmental regression in autism spectrum disorders. *Mental Retardation and Developmental Disabilities Research Reviews, 10*, 139–143.

Rogers, S. J., & DiLalla, D. (1990). Age of symptom onset in young children with pervasive developmental disorders. *Journal of the American Academy of Child and Adolescent Psychiatry, 239*, 863–872.

Rogler, L. H. (1999). Methodological sources of cultural insensitivity in mental health research. *American Psychologist, 54*(6), 424–433.

Roid, G. H. (2003). *Manual for the Stanford Binet Intelligence Scales* (5th ed.). Itasca, IL: Riverside Publishing Company.

Roid, G. H., & Miller, L. (1997). *Leiter International Test of Intelligence—Revised*. Chicago: Stoelting.

Rolf, J. E. (1972). The academic and social competency of children vulnerable to schizophrenia and other behavior pathologies. *Journal of Abnormal Psychology, 80*, 225–243.

Rosen, L., & Hough, D. (1988). Pathogenic weight control behaviors in female college gymnasts. *Physician and Sportsmedicine, 16*, 141–146.

Rosen, L., McKeag, D., Hough, D., & Curley, V. (1986). Pathogenic weight control behavior in female athletes. *Physician and Sportsmedicine, 14*, 79–95.

Rosenbaum, D. P. & Gordon S. H. (1998). Assessing the effects of school-based drug education: A six-year multilevel analysis of project D. A. R. E. *Journal of Research in Crime and Delinquency, 35*,, 381–412.

Rosenblatt, J. A., & Furlong, M. J. (1998). Outcomes in a system of care for youths with emotional and behavioral disorders: An examination of differential change across clinical profile. *Journal of Child and Family Studies, 7*, 217–232.

Rosenblum, G., & Lewis, M. (1999). The relations among body image, physical attractiveness and body mass in adolescence. *Child Development, 70*, 50–64.

Rosenheim, M. K., & Testa, M. F. (1992). *Early parenthood and coming of age in the 1990s*. New Brunswick, N. J: Rutgers University Press.

Rosenvinge, J. H., Sundgot Borgen, J., & Borresen, R. (1999). The prevalence and psychological correlates of anorexia nervosa, bulimia nervosa and binge eating among 15-year-old students: A controlled epidemiological study. *European Eating Disorders Review, 7*, 382–391.

Rosenthal, R., Hall, J. A., DiMatteo, M. R., Royers, P. I., & Archer, D. (1979). *Sensitivity to nonverbal communication—The PONS test*. London: John Hopkins University Press.

Ross, H. E., & Ivis, F. (1999). Binge eating and substance use among male and female adolescents. *International Journal of Eating Disorders, 26*, 245–260.

Rossman, B., Bingham, R., & Emde, R. N. (1997). Symptomatology and adaptive functioning for children exposed to normative stressors, dog attack, and parental violence. *Journal of the American Academy of Child & Adolescent Psychiatry, 36*(8), 1089–1097.

Rothbart, M. K. (1981). Measurement of temperament in infancy. *Child Development, 52*, 569–578.

Rothbart, M. K., Ahadi, S. A., & Evans, D. E. (2000). Temperament and personality: Origins and outcomes. *Journal of Personality and Social Psychology, 78*(1), 122–135.

Rothbart, M. K., & Bates, J. E. (1998). Temperament. In N. Eisenberg (Ed.) & W. Damon (Series Ed), *Handbook of child psychology: Vol. 3. Social, emotional and personality development* (5th ed., pp. 105–176). New York: Wiley.

Roubertoux, P. L., & Kerdelhue, B. (2006). Trisomy 21: From chromosomes to mental retardation. *Behavior Genetics, 36,* 346–354.

Rourke, B. P. (1982). Central processing deficiencies n children: Toward a developmental neuropsychological model. *Journal of Clinical Neuropsychology, 4,* 1–18.

Rourke, B. P. (1985). *Neuropsychology of learning disabilities: Essentials of subtype analysis.* New York: Guilford.

Rourke, B. P. (1989). *Nonverbal learning disabilities: the syndrome and the model.* New York: Guilford.

Rourke, B. P. (1993). Arithmetic disabilities, specific or otherwise: A neuropsychological perspective. *Journal of Learning Disabilities, 26,* 214–226.

Rourke, B. P. (1995). *Syndrome of nonverbal learning disabilities.* New York: Guilford.

Rourke, B. P. (2000). Neuropsychological and psycho-social subtyping: A review of investigations within the University of Windsor laboratory. *Canadian Psychology, 41,* 34–51.

Rourke, B. P., Ahmad, S., Collins, D., Jayman-Abello, B., Hayman-Abello, S., & Warriner, E. M. (2002). Child clinical/pediatric neuropsychology: Some recent advances. *Annual Review of Psychology, 53,* 309–339.

Rourke, B. P., & Conway, J. A. (1997). Disabilities of arithmetic and mathematical reasoning: Perspectives from neurology and neuropsychology. *Journal of Learning Disabilities, 30,* 34–46.

Rourke, B. P. & Fuerst, D. R. (1991). *Learning disabilities and psychosocial functioning: A neuropsychological perspective.* New York: Guilford.

Rourke, B. P., Hayman-Abello, B. A., & Collins, D. W. (2003). Learning disabilities: A neuropsychological perspective. In B. S. Fogel, R. B. Schiffer, & S. M. Rao (Eds.), *Neuropsychiatry* (2nd ed., pp. 630–659). New York: Lippincott, Williams, & Wilkins.

Rourke, B. P., Young, G. C., & Leenaars, A. A. (1989). A childhood learning disability that predisposes those afflicted to adolescent and adult depression and suicide risk. *Journal of Learning Disabilities, 22,* 169–175.

Routh, D. K., Patton, L., & Sanfilippo, M. D. (1991). Celebrating 20 years of the Journal of Clinical Child Psychology: From child advocacy to scientific research and back again. *Journal of Clinical Child Psychology, 20,* 2–6.

Roy, A., Rylander, G., & Sarchiapone, M. (1997). Genetics of suicide. Family studies and molecular genetics. *Annals of the New York Academy of Sciences, 836,* 135–157.

Rubio-Stipec, M., Walker, R., & Murphy, J. (2002). Dimensional measures of psychopathology: The probability of being classified with a psychiatric disorder using empirically derived symptoms scales. *Social Psychiatry and Psychiatric Epidemiology, 37,* 553–560.

Rucklidge, J. J., & Tannock, R. (2001). Psychiatric, psychosocial, and cognitive functioning of female adolescents with ADHD. *Journal of the American Academy of Child & Adolescent Psychiatry, 40,* 530–540.

Russell, G. (1979). Bulimia nervosa: An ominous variant of anorexia nervosa. *Psychological Medicine, 9,* 429–448.

Russell, G. (1985). The changing nature of anorexia nervosa: An introduction to the conference, *Journal of Psychiatric Research, 19,* 101–109.

Rutter, M. (1979). Protective factors in children's responses to stress and disadvantage. In M. Whalen & J. E. Rolf (Eds.), *Primary Prevention of Psychopathology: Vol. 3. Social competence in children* (pp. 49–79). Hanover, NH: University Press of New England.

Rutter, M. (1983). Cognitive deficits in the pathogenesis of autism. *Journal of Child Psychology and Psychiatry, 24,* 513–531.

Rutter, M. (1985). Resilience in the face of adversity. *British Journal of Psychiatry, 147,* 598–611.

Rutter, M. (1989). Isle of Wight revisited: Twenty-five years of child psychiatric epidemiology, *Journal of the American Academy of Child & Adolescent Psychiatry, 28*(5), 633–653.

Rutter, M. (1990). Changing patters of psychiatric disorders during adolescence. In J. Bancroft & J. Reinisch (Eds.), *Adolescence and puberty* (pp. 124–145). New York: Oxford University Press.

Rutter, M., Cox, A., Tupling, C., Berger, M., & Yule, W. (1975). Attainment and adjustment in two geographical areas: I. *British Journal of Psychiatry, 126,* 493–509.

Rutter, M., LeCouteur, A., & Lord, C. (2003). *Autism diagnostic interview—Revised manual.* Los Angeles: Western Psychological Services.

Rutter, M., Silberg, J., O'Connor, T., & Simonoff, E. (1999). Genetics and child psychiatry II: Empirical research findings. *Journal of Child Psychology and Psychiatry and Allied Disciplines, 40,* 19–55.

Rutter M., & Sroufe, L. A. (2000). Developmental psychopathology: Concepts and challenges. *Development and Psychopathology, Special Issue: Reflecting on the Past and Planning for the Future of Developmental Psychopathology, 12*(3) 265–296.

Rutter, M., Tizard, J., & Whitmore, K. (1981). *Education health and behavior.* Huntington, NY: Krieger.

Ryan, N. D., Puig-Antich, J., Ambrosini, P., Rabinovich, H. M., Nelson, B., Iyengar, S., et al. (1987). The clinical picture of major depression in children and adolescents. *Archives of General Psychiatry, 44,* 854–861.

Rydell, A., Berlin, L., & Bohlin, G. (2001). Emotionality, emotion regulation and adaptation among 5-to 8-year old children. *Emotion, 3,* 30–47.

Saavedra, L. M, & Silverman, W. K. (2002). Classification of anxiety disorders in children: What a difference two decades make. *International Review of Psychiatry, 14,* 87–101.

Saffer, H., & Grossman, M. (1987). Beer taxes, the legal drinking age, and youth motor vehicle fatalities. *Journal of Legal Studies, 16,* 351–374.

Saigh, P. (1986). In vitro flooding in the treatment of a 6-year-old boy's posttraumatic stress disorder. *Behaviour Research and Therapy, 24*(6), 685–688.

Saigh, P. (1989). A comparative analysis of the affective and behavioral symptomology of traumatized and nontraumatized children. *Journal of School Psychology, 27*(3), 247–255.

Saint-Cyr, Jean A., Taylor, A. E., & Nicholson, K. (1995). Behavior and the basal ganglia. In W. J. Weiner & A. E. Lang (Eds.), *Behavioral neurology of movement disorders* (pp. 1–28). New York: Raven Press.

Salkovskis, P. M. (1989). Cognitive behavioral factors and the persistence of intrusive thoughts in obsessional problems. *Behavior Research and Therapy, 27,* 677–682.

Salmivalli, C. (1999). Participant role approach to school bullying: Implications for intervention. *Journal of Adolescence, 22*(4), 453–459.

Sameroff, A., & Chandler, M. (1975). Reproductive risk and the continuum of caretaking casualty. In F. D. Horowitz (Ed.), *Child development research* (Vol. 4, 117–120). Chicago: University of Chicago Press.

Sameroff, A., & Fiese, B. H. (2000). Transactional regulation: The developmental ecology of early intervention. In J. P. Shonkoff & S. J. Meisels (Eds.), *Handbook of early childhood intervention* (2nd ed., pp. 135–159). SAMHSA's National Mental Health Information Center: Cultural Competence in Serving Children Adolescents with Mental Health Problems. Retrieved September 15, 2006, from http://mentalhealth. samhsa. gov/publications/allpubs/CA-0015/default. asp

Sampson, R. J., Raudenbush, S. W., & Earls, F. (1997). Neighborhoods and violent crime: A multilevel study of collective efficacy. *Science, 277,* 918–924.

Sanchez, L., Hagino, O., Weller, E., & Ronald, W. (1999). Bipolarity in children. *Psychiatric Clinics of North America, 22*(3), 629–648.

Sanders, M. R., Markie-Dadds, C., Turner, K. M., & Ralph, A. (2004). Using the triple P System of intervention to prevent behavioral problems in children and adolescents. In P. M. Barrett & T. H. Ollendick (Eds.), *Handbook of interventions that work with children and adolescents* (pp. 489–616). West Sussex, UK: Wiley.

Sansosti, F. J., & Powell-Smith, K. A. (2006). Using social stories to improve the social behaviour of children with Asperger syndrome. *Journal of Positive Behavior Interventions, 8,* 43–57.

Sattler, J. M. (2001). *Assessment of children: Cognitive applications* (2nd ed.). San Diego, CA: Jerome M Sattler.

Sattler, J. M. (2002). *Assessment of children: Behavioral and clinical applications* (4th ed.). LaMesa, CA: Jerome M. Sattler.

Saxena, S., Brody, A. L., & Maidment, K. M. (1999). Localized orbitofrontal and subcortical metabolic changes and predictors of response to paroxetine treatment in obsessive-compulsive disorder. *Neuropsychopharmacology, 21*(6), 683–693.

Scarr, S., & McCartney, K. (1984). How people make their own environments. *Child Development, 54,* 424–435.

Schaeffer, C., Petras, H., Ialongo, N., Poduska, J., & Kellam, S. (2003). Modeling growth in boys' aggressive behavior across elementary school: Links to later criminal involvement, conduct disorder and antisocial personality disorder. *Developmental Psychology, 39,* 1020–1035.

Schaie, K. W., Willis, S. L., Jayu, G., & Chipuer, H. (1989). Structural invariance of cognitive abilities across the adult life span: A cross-sectional study. *Developmental Psychology, 25,* 652–662.

Scheeringa, M. S. (2001). The differential diagnosis of impaired reciprocal social interaction in children: A review of disorders. *Child Psychiatry and Human Development, 32*(1), 71–89.

Scheeringa, M. S., Wright, M., & Hunt, J. P. (2006). Factors affecting the diagnosis and prediction of PTSD symptomatology in children and adolescents. *American Journal of Psychiatry, 163*(4), 644–651.

Scheeringa, M. S., & Zeanah, C. H. (1995). Symptom expression and trauma variables in children under 48 months of age. *Infant Mental Health Journal, 16,* 259–270.

Scheeringa, M. S., & Zeanah, C. H. (2001). A relational perspective on PTSD in early childhood. *Journal of Traumatic Stress, 14,* 799–815.

Schlaggar, B. L. (2003, November). *FMRI and the development of single word reading.* Paper presented at the International Dyslexia Association conference, San Diego, CA.

Schoenwald, S., Borduin, C. H., & Henggeler, S. W. (1998). Multisystemic therapy: Changing the natural and service ecologies of adolescents and families. In M. Epstein, K. Kutash, & A. Duchnowski (Eds), *Outcomes for children and youth with emotional and behavioral disorders and their families: Programs and evaluation best practices* (pp. 485–511). Austin, TX: PRO-ED.

Schoenwald, S. K., Brown, T. L., & Henggeler, S. (2000). Inside Multisystemic Therapy: Therapist, supervisory, and program practices. *Journal of Emotional and Behavioral Disorders, 8,* 113–127.

Schoenwald, S. K., Ward, D. M., Henggeler, S. W., & Rowland, M. D. (2000). Multisystemic therapy versus hospitalization for crisis stabilization of youth: Placement outcomes 4 months postreferral. *Mental Health Services Research, 2,* 3–12.

Schonfeld, A., Mattson, S. N., & Lang, A. (2001). Verbal and nonverbal fluency in children with heavy prenatal alcohol exposure. *Journal of Studies on Alcohol, 62,* 239–246.

Schopler, E., Reichler, R., & Renner, B. (1988). *The Childhood Autism Rating Scale (CARS).* Los Angeles: Western Psychological Services.

Schumacher, J., Anthoni, J., Dahdouh, F., Konig, I., Hillmer, A., Kluck, N., et al. (2006). Strong genetic evidence of DCDC2 as a susceptibility gene for dyslexia. *The American Journal of Human Genetics, 78,* 52–62.

Schwartz, C., Wright, C. I., Shin, L., Kagan, J., & Rauch, S. L. (2003). Inhibited and uninhibited infants "grow up." Adult amygdalar response to novelty. *Science, 300,* 1952–1953.

Schwartz, D., Dodge, K., & Coie, J. (1993). The emergence of chronic peer victimization in boys' play groups. *Child Development, 64,* 1755–1772.

Schweinhart, L. J., Barnes, H. V., & Weikart, D. P. (1993). Significant benefits: The High/Scope Perry Preschool Study Though Age 27. *Monographs of the High/Scope Educational Research Foundation, No. 10.* Ypsilanti, MI: High/Scope Press.

Schweinhart, L. J., Berueta-Clement, J. R., Barnett, W. S., Epstein, A. S., & Weikart, D. P. (1985). Effects of the Perry Preschool program on youth through age 19: A summary. *Topics in Early Childhood Special Education, 5,* 26–35.

Scott, S., Spender, Q., Doolan, M., Jacobs, B., & Aspland, H. (2001). Multicentre controlled trial of parenting groups for childhood antisocial behaviour in clinical practice. *British Medical Journal, 323,* 1–6.

Seligman, M. E. P. (1975). *Helplessness.* San Francisco: W. H. Freeman.

Seligman, M., & Peterson, C. (1986). A learned helpless perspective on childhood depression: Theory and research. In M. Rutter, C. E. Izard, & P. B. Read (Eds.), *Depression in young people* (pp. 223–249). New York: Guilford.

Semrud-Clikeman, M. (2005). Neuropsychological aspects for evaluating learning disabilities. *Journal of Learning Disabilities, 38*, 563–568.

Semrud-Clikeman, M., Biederman, J., Sprich-Buckminster, S., Lehman, B. K., Faraone, S. V., & Norman, D. (1992). Comorbidity between ADDH and learning disability: A review and report in a clinically referred sample. *Journal of the American Academy of Child and Adolescent Psychiatry, 31*, 439–448.

Semrud-Clikeman, M. & Hynd, G. W. (1990). Right hemisphere dysfunction in nonverbal learning disabilities: Social, academic, and adaptive functioning in adults and children. *Psychological Bulletin, 107*, 196–209.

Shaffer, D., & Craft, L. (1999). Methods of adolescent suicide prevention. *Journal of Clinical Psychiatry, 60*, 70–74.

Shaffer, D., Garland, A., Vieland, V., Underwood, M., & Busner, C. (1991). The impact of curriculum-based suicide prevention programs for teenagers. *Journal of the American Academy of Child and Adolescent Psychiatry, 30*, 588–596.

Shaffer, D., Gould, M. S., Fisher, P., Trautment, P., Moreau, D., Kleinman, M., et al. (1996). Psychiatric diagnoses in child and adolescent suicide. *Archives of General Psychiatry, 53*, 339–348.

Shaffer, D., Fisher, P., Lucas, C., Dulcan, M. K., & Schwab-Stone, M. E. (2000). NIMH diagnostic interview schedule for children version IV (NIMH DISC–IV): description, differences from previous versions, and reliability of some common diagnoses. *Journal of the American Academy of Child and Adolescent Psychiatry, 39*, 28–38.

Shalev, R. S., Manor, O., Kerem, B., Ayali, M., Badichi, N., Friedlander, Y., et al. (2001). Developmental dyscalculia is a familial learning disability. *Journal of Learning Disabilities, 34*, 59–65.

Shapiro, E. S., & Derr, T. F. (1900). Curriculum-based assessment. In T. B. Gutkin & C. R. Reynolds (Eds.), *The handbook of school psychology* (2nd ed.; 365-387). Oxford, UK: Wiley.

Shapiro, E. S., & Heick, P. (2004). School psychologist assessment practices in the evaluation of students referred for social/behavioral/emotional problems. *Psychology in the Schools, 41*(5), 551–561.

Shapiro, F. (1995). *Eye movement desensitization and reprocessing: Basic principles, protocols, and procedures.* New York: Guilford.

Shastry, B. S. (2005). Bipolar disorder: An update. *Neurochemistry International, 46*, 273–279.

Shaw, D. S., Owens, E. B., Vondra, J. I., Keenan, K., & Winslow, E. G. (1996). Early risk factors and pathways in the development of early disruptive behaviour problems. *Development and Psychopathology, 8*, 679–699.

Shayer, M., Demetriou, A., & Perez, M. (1986). The structure and scaling of concrete operational thought: Three studies in four countries and only one story. *Genetic Psychology Monographs, 114*, 307–376.

Shaywitz, S. E. (1998). Current concepts: Dyslexia. *New England Journal of Medicine, 338*(5), 307–312.

Shaywitz, B. A., Shaywitz, S. E., Pugh, K. R., Menci, W. E., Fulbright, R. K., Skudlarski, P., et al. (2002). Disruption of posterior brain systems for reading in children with developmental dyslexia. *Biological Psychiatry, 52*, 101–110.

Shaywitz, B. A., Shaywitz, S. E., Blachman, B. A., Pugh, K. R., Fulbright, R. K., Skudlarski, P., et al. (2004). Development of left occipitotemporal systems for skilled reading in children after phonologically-based intervention. *Biological Psychiatry, 55*, 926–933.

Shaywitz, B. A., Shaywitz, S. E., Pugh, K. R., Menci, W. E., Fulbright, R. K., Skudlarski, P., et al. (2002). Disruption of posterior brain systems for reading in children with developmental dyslexia. *Biological Psychiatry, 52*, 101–110.

Shaywitz, S. E. (1998). CurentCurrent concepts: Dyslexia. *New England Journal of Medicine 338*(5), 307–312.

Shaywitz, S. E., Shaywitz, B. A., Fulbright, R. K., Skudlarski, P., Menci, W. E., Constable, R. T., et al. (2003). Neural systems of compensation and persistence: Young adult outcomes of childhood reading disability. *Biological Psychiatry, 54*, 25–33.

Sheeber, L., Hops, H., & Davis, B. (2001). Family processes in adolescent depression. *Clinical Child & Family Psychology Review, 4*, 19–35.

Sheerenberger, R. C. (1983). *A history of mental retardation.* Baltimore: Brookes.

Sheras, P. L. (2001). Problems of adolescence. In C. E. Walker & M. C. Roberts (Eds.), *Handbook of clinical child psychology* (3rd ed., pp. 619–803). New York: Wiley.

Sherman, D. K., Iacono, W., & Donnelly, J. (1995). Development and validation of body rating scales for adolescent females. *International Journal of Eating disorders, 18*, 327–333.

Sherman, D. K., Iacono, W. G., & McGue, M. K. (1997). Attention-deficit hyperactivity disorder dimensions: A twin study of inattention and impulsivity-hyperactivity. *Journal of the American Academy of Child & Adolescent Psychiatry, 36*(6), 745–753.

Sherwood, N. E., & Neumark-Sztainer, D. (2001). Internalization of the sociocultural ideal: Weight-related attitudes and dieting behaviors among young adolescent girls. *American Journal of Health Promotion, 15*, 228–231.

Shirk, S. R., & Russell, R. L. (1996). *Change processes in child psychotherapy: Revitalizing treatment and research.* New York: Guilford.

Shisslak, C., Renger, R., Sharpe, T., Crago, M., McKnight, K., Gray, N., et al. (1999). Development and evaluation of the McKnight Risk Factor Survey for assessing potential risk and protective factors for disordered eating in preadolescent and adolescent girls. *International Journal of Eating Disorders, 25*, 195–214.

Shor, E. (1986). Use of health care services by children and diagnoses received during presumably stressful life transitions. *Pediatrics, 77*, 834–841.

Short, A. B., & Schopler, E. (1988). Factors relating to age of onset in autism. *Journal of Autism and Developmental Disorders, 18*, 207–215.

Shope, J. (2001). Teens, substance abuse and driving. *UMTRI Research Review, 32*, 6–9.

Siann, G., Callaghan, M., & Glissov, P. (1994). Who gets bullied? The effect of school, gender and ethnic group. *Educational Research, 36*(2), 123–134.

Siegel, M., & Barthel, R. P. (1986). Conversion disorders on a child psychiatry consultation service. *Psychosomatics, 27*, 201–204.

Silberg, J., Pickles, A., Rutter, M., Hewitt, J., Simonoff, E., Maes, H., et al. (1999). The influence of genetic factors and life stress on depression among adolescent girls. *Archives of General Psychiatry, 56*, 225–232.

Silverman, W. K., & Albano, A. M. (1996). *Anxiety disorders interview schedule for children for DSM–IV (child and parent versions)*. San Antonio, TX: The Psychological Corporation.

Silverman, W. K., & Ginsburg, G. (1995). Specific phobias and generalized anxiety disorder. In J. March (Ed.), *Anxiety disorders in children and adolescents*. New York: Guilford.

Silverman, W. K., & Nelles, W. B. (2001). The influence of gender on children's ratings of fear in self and same-aged peers. *The Journal of Genetic Psychology, 148*, 17–21.

Silverman, W. K., & Ollendick, T. H. (2005). Evidence-based assessment of anxiety and its disorders in children and adolescents. *Journal of Clinical Child and Adolescent Psychology, 34*(3), 381–411.

Silverman, W. K., Saavedra, L. M., & Pina, A. A. (2001). Test-retest reliability of anxiety symptoms an diagnoses using the Anxiety Disorders Interview Schedule for *DSM–IV*: Child and parent versions (ADIS for *DSM–IV*: C/P). *Journal of the American Academy of Child and Adolescent Psychiatry, 40*, 937–944.

Simeon, J. G. (1985). Sleep in children: Recent advances. In J. D. Noshpitz (Ed.), *Basic handbook of child psychiatry* (Vol. 5, pp. 327–337). New York: Basic Books.

Simos, P. G., Breier, J. L., Fletcher, J. M., Foorman, B. R., Mouzaki, A., & Papanicolaou, C. C. (2001). Age-related changes in regional brain activation during phonological decoding and printed word recognition. *Developmental Neuropsychology, 19*, 191–210.

Simos, P. G., Mouzaki, A., & Papanicolaou, C. C. (2004). A. Reading and reading disability: The contribution of functional brain imaging methods. *Hellenic Journal of Psychology, 1*, 56–79.

Singh, M. K., DelBello, M., Soutullo, C., Stanford, K. E., McDonough-Ryan, P., & Strakowski, S. (2007). Obstetrical complications in children at high risk for bipolar disorder. *Journal of Psychiatric Research, 41*, 680–685.

Skiba, R. J., Poloni-Staudinger, L., Gallini, S., Simmons, A. D., & Feggins-Azziz, R. (2006). Disparate access: The disproportionality of African American students with disabilities across educational environments. *Exceptional Children, 72*, 411–424.

Smets, A. C., & Hartup, W. W. (1988). Systems and symptoms: Family cohesion/adaptability and childhood behaviour problems. *Journal of Abnormal Psychology, 16*, 233–246.

Smith, B., Pelham, W. E., &, Gnagy, E. (2000). The reliability, validity and unique contributions of self-report by adolescents receiving treatment for attention-deficit/hyperactivity disorder. *Journal of Consulting and Clinical Psychology, 68*, 489–499.

Smith, P. K., & Drew, L. M. (2002). Grandparenthood. In M. Bornstein (Ed.), *Handbook of parenting* (Vol. 3, pp. 141–172). Mahwah, NJ: Erlbaum.

Smolak, L., Levine, M., & Thompson, J. K. (2001). The use of the Sociocultural Attitudes Towards Appearance Questionnaire with middle school boys and girls. *International Journal of Eating Disorders, 29*, 216–223.

Smolak, K., Murnen, S. K., & Ruble, A. E. (2000). Female athletes and eating problems: A meta-analysis. International Journal of Eating Disorders, 27, 371–380.

Snyder, J., Horsch, E., & Childs, J. (1997). Peer relationships of young children: Affiliative choices and the shaping of aggressive behavior. *Journal of Clinical Child Psychology, 26*(2), 145–156.

Sobczak, S., Honig, A., van Duinen, M. A., & Riedel, W. J. (2002). Sertonergic dysregulation in bipolar disorders: A literature review of serotonergic challenge studies. *Bipolar Disorders, 4*, 347–356.

Sonuga-Barke, E. J., Daley, D., Thompson, M., Laver-Bredbury, C., & Weeks, A. (2001). Parent-based therapies for preschool attention-deficit/hyperactivity disorder: A randomized, controlled trial with a community sample. *Journal of the American Academy of Child and Adolescent Psychiatry, 40*, 402–408.

Spaccarelli, S., Cotler, S., & Penman, D. (1992). Problem-solving skills training as a supplement to behavioral parent training. *Cognitive Therapy and Research, 27*, 171–186.

Sparrow, S. S., Balla, D. A., & Cicchetti, D. V. (1984). *Vineland Adaptive Behavior Scales*. Circle Pines, MN: American Guidance Service.

Spence, S. H. (1997). Structure of anxiety symptoms among children: A confirmatory factor-analytic study. *Journal of Abnormal Psychology, 106*(2), 280–297.

Spence, S. H. (1998). A measure of anxiety symptoms among children. *Behavior Research and Therapy, 36*, 545–566.

Spence, S. H., Donovan, C., & Brechman-Toussaint, M. (1999). Social skills, social outcomes, and cognitive features of childhood social phobia. *Journal of Abnormal Psychology, 108*(2), 211–221.

Spencer, J. H., & Le, T. (2006). Parent refugee status, immigration stressors and Southeast Asian youth violence. *Journal of Immigrant and Minority Health, 8*, 359–368.

Spencer, M. B. (1990). Development of minority children: An introduction, *Child Development, 61*, 267–279.

Spencer, T. J., Biederman, J., & Harding, M. (1996). Growth deficits in ADHD children revisited: Evidence for disorder-associated growth delays? *Journal of the American Academy of Child & Adolescent Psychiatry, 35*, 1460–1469.

Spielberger, C. S. (1973). *Manual for the State-Trait Anxiety Inventory for children*. Palo Alto, CA: Consulting Psychologists Press.

Spinazzola, J., Ford, J., Zucker, M., van der Kolk, B., Silva, S., Smith, S., et al. (2005). Survey evaluates complex trauma exposure, outcome and intervention among children an adolescents. *Psychiatric Annals, 35*, 433–439.

Spirito, A., Jelalian, E., Rasile, D., Rohrbeck, C. & Vinnick, L. (2000). Adolescent risk taking and self-reported injuries associated with substance use. *American Journal of Drug and Alcohol Abuse, 26*(1), 113–123.

Spitz, R. A. (1946). Anaclitic depression. *Psychoanalytic Study of the Child, 2*, 313–342.

Spitzer, R. L., Davies, M., & Barkley, R. A. (1990). The DSM–III–R field trial of disruptive behavior disorders. *Journal of the American Academy of Child & Adolescent Psychiatry, 29*(5), 690–697.

Spitzer, B. L., Henderson, K. A., & Zivian, M. T. (1999). Gender differences in population versus media body sizes: A comparison over four decades. *Sex Roles, 40*, 545–565.

Sroufe, L. A. (1990). Considering normal and abnormal together: The essence of developmental psychopathology. *Development and Psychopathology, 2*, 335–347.

Sroufe, L. A. (1996). *Emotional development: The organization of emotional life in the early years.* New York: Cambridge University Press.

Sroufe, L. A., Egeland, B., & Kreutzer, T. (1990). The fate of early experience following developmental change: Longitudinal approaches to individual adaptation in childhood.

Sroufe, L. A., & Rutter, M. (1984). The domain of developmental psychopathology. *Child Development, 55*, 17–29.

Stanovich, K. E. (1986). Matthew effects in reading: Some consequences of individual differences in the acquisition of literacy. *Reading Research Quarterly, 21*, 360–407.

Stanovich, K. E. (1991). Discrepancy definitions of reading disability: Has intelligence led us astray? *Reading Research Quarterly, 26*, 7–29.

Stanovich, K. E. (2000). *Progress in understanding reading: Scientific foundations and new frontiers.* New York: Guilford.

Stanton, M. D., & Shadish, W. R. (1997). Outcome, attrition and family/couples treatment for drug abuse: A review of the controlled, comparative studies. *PsychologicalBulletin, 122*, 170–191.

Stark, K. D., Reynolds, W. M., & Kaslow, N. J. (1987). A comparison of the relative efficacy of self-control therapy and a behavioral problem-solving therapy for depression in children. *Journal of Abnormal Child Psychology, 15*, 91–113.

Stark, K. D., Rouse, K. L., & Livingston, R. (1991). Treatment of depression during childhood and adolescence: Cognitive-behavioral procedures for the individual and family. In P. Kendall (Ed.), *Child and adolescent therapy* (pp. 165–206). New York: Guilford.

Staton, D., Volness, J., & Beatty, W. (2007). Diagnosis and classification of pediatric bipolar disorder. *Journal of Affective Disorders.* Retrieved August 15, 2007.

Stattin, H., & Klackenberg-Larsson, I. (1993). Early language and intelligence development and their relationship to future criminal behavior. *Journal of Abnormal Psychology, 102*, 369–378.

Stein, D. J., Towey, J., & Hollander, E. (1995). The neuropsychiatry of impulsive aggression. In E. Hollander & D. Stein (Eds.), *Impulsivity and aggression* (pp. 137–158). Oxford, UK: Wiley.

Stice, E. (1994). Review of the evidence for a sociocultural model of bulimia nervosa: An explanation of the mechanisms of action. *Clinical Psychology Review, 14*, 633–661.

Stice, E. (2001). Risk factors for eating pathology: Recent advances and future directions. In R. H. Striegel-Moore & L. Smolak (Eds), *Eating Disorders: Innovative directions in research and practice* (pp. 51-73). Washington, DC: APA.

Stice, E., & Agras, W. S. (1998). Predicting onset and cessation of bulimic behaviors during adolescence: A longitudinal grouping analyses. *Behavior Therapy,29*, 257–276.

Stice, E., Burton, E. M., & Shaw, H. (2004). Prospective relations between bulimic pathology, depression and substance abuse: Unpacking comorbidity in adolescent girls. *Journal of Consulting and Clinical Psychology, 72*, 61–72.

Stice, E., Hayward, C., Cameron, R., Killen, J. D., & Taylor, C. B. (2000). Body image and eating related factors predict onset of depression in female adolescents: A longitudinal study. *Journal of Abnormal Psychology, 109*, 438–444.

Stice, E., Mazotti, L., Krebs, M., & Martin, S. (1998). Predictors of adolescent dieting behaviors: A longitudinal study. *Psychology of Addictive Behaviors, 12*, 195–205.

Stice, E., Presnell, K., & Bearman, S. K. (2001). Relation of early menarche to depression, eating disorders, substance abuse, and comorbid psychopathology among adolescent girls. *Developmental Psychology, 37*, 608–619.

Stice, E., & Shaw, H. (1994). Adverse effects of the media portraed thin-ideal on women and linkages to bulimic symptomatology. *Journal of Socialand Clinical Psychology, 13*, 288–308.

Stice, E., & Whitenton, K. (2002). Risk factors for body dissatisfaction in adolescent girls: A longitudinal investigation. *Developmental Psychology, 38*, 669–678.

Stone, W. L. & La Greca, A. M (1990). The social status of children with learning disabilities: A reexamination. *Journal of Learning Disabilities, 23*, 32–37.

Strang, J. D., & Casey, J. E. (1994). The psychological impact of learning disabilities: A developmental neurological perspective. In L. F. Koziol & E. E. Scott (Eds.), *The neuropsychology of mental disorders: A practical guide* (pp. 171–186). Springfield, IL: Charles C Thomas.

Strauss, C. C., Lease, C. A., Last, C. G., & Francis, G. (1988). Overanxious disorder: An examination of developmental differences. *Journal of Abnormal Child Psychology, 16*, 433–443.

Streissguth, A. P., Bookstein, F. L., & Barr, H. M. (2004) Risk factors for adverse life outcomes in fetal alcohol syndrome and fetal alcohol effects. *Journal of Developmental & Behavioral Pediatrics, 25*, 228–238.

Striegel-Moore, R. H., Jacobson, M. S., & Rees, J. M. (1997). Risk factors for eating disorders. *Adolescent nutritional disorders: Prevention and treatment* (pp. 98–109). New York: Academy of Sciences.

Striegel-Moore, R., H., & Smolak, L. (1997). The role of race in the development of eating disorders. In L. Smolak, M. P. Levine, & R. Striegel-Moore (Eds.), *Developmental psychopathology of eating disorders* (pp. 259–284). Mahwah, NJ: Erlbaum.

Strober, M., Freeman, R., Lampert, C., Diamond, J., & Kaye, W. (2000). Controlled family study of anorexia nervosa and bulimia nervosa. Evidence of shared liability and transmission of partial syndromes. *American Journal of Psychiatry, 157*(3), 393–401.

Strober, M., Morrell, W., Lampert, C., Burroughs, J. (1990). Relapse following discontinuation of lithium maintenance therapy in adolescents with bipolar illness: A naturalistic study. *American Journal of Psychiatry, 147*, 457–461.

Strupp, H. (1989). Psychotherapy: Can the practitioner learn from the researcher? *American Psychologist, 44*(4), 717–724.

Strupp, H. (1996). Some salient lessons from research and practice. *Psychotherapy: Theory, Research, Practice, Training, 33*(1), 135–138.

Stuart, C., Waalen, J. K., & Haelstromm, E. (2003). Many helping hearts: An evaluation of peer gatekeeper training in suicide risk assessment. *Death Studies, 27*, 321–333.

Stuart, R. (2004). Twelve practical suggestions for achieving multicultural competence. *Professional Psychology: Research and Practice, 35*, 3–9.

Stuber, J., Fairbrother, G., & Galea, S. (2002). Determinants of counseling for children in Manhattan after the September 11 attacks. *Psychiatric Services, 53*(7), 815–822. *Child Development, 61*, 1363–1373.

Stunkard, A. (1959). Eating patterns and obesity. *Psychiatric Quarterly, 33*, 248–295.

Stuss, D. T., & Benson, D. F. (1986). *The frontal lobes*. New York: Raven.

Sue, S. (2006). Cultural competency: From philosophy to research and practice. *Journal of Community Psychology, 34*(2), 237–245.

Sugarman, A., & Kanner, K. (2000). The contribution of psychoanalytic theory to psychological testing. *Psychoanalytic Psychology, 17*(1), 3–23.

Sugden, S. G., Kile, S., & Hendren, D. (2006). Neurodevelopmental pathways to aggression: A model to understand and target treatment in youth. *Journal of Neuropsychiatry and Clinical Neuroscience, 18*, 302–317.

Sundgot-Borgen, J. (1994) Risk and trigger factors for the development of eating disorders in female elite athletes. *Medicine and Science in Sports and Exercise, 26*, 414–419.

Sungot-Borgen, J. & Torstveit, M. (2004). Prevalence of eating disorders in elite athletes is higher than in the general population. *Clinical Journal of Sport Medicine, 14*, 25–32.

Swann, A. C., Dougherty, D., Pazzaglia, P., Phan, M., Steinberg, J. L., & Moeller, F. G. (2005). Increased impulsivity associated with severity of suicide attempt history in patients with bipolar disorder. *American Journal of Psychiatry, 162*, 1680–1687.

Swanson, J. M., Kraemer, H., & Hinshaw, S. P. (2001). Clinical relevance of the primary findings of the MTA: Success rates based on severity of ADHD and ODD symptoms at the end of treatment. *Journal of the American Academy of Child & Adolescent Psychiatry, 40*, 168–179.

Swarr, A. E., & Richards, M. H. (1996). Longitudinal effects of adolescent girls'pubertal development, perceptions of pubertal timing, and parental relations on eating problems. *Developmental Psychology, 32*, 636–646.

Swedo, S. E., Rapoport, J. L., Leonard, H., Leanane, M., & Cheslow, D. (1989). Obsessive-compulsive disorder in children an adolescents: Clinical phenomenology of 70 consecutive cases. *Archives of General Psychiatry, 46*, 335–341.

Szatmari, P. (1991). Asperger's syndrome: Diagnosis, treatment, and outcome. *Pervasive Developmental Disorders, 14*(1), 81–93.

Szatmari, P., Archer, L., Fisman, S., Streiner, D. L., & Wilson, F. J. (1995). Asperger's syndrome and autism: Differences in behaviour, cognition and adaptive functioning. *Journal of the American Academy of Child and Adolescent Psychiatry, 34*, 1662–1671.

Szatmari, P., Boyle, M., & Offord, D. R. (1989). ADDH and conduct disorder: Degree of diagnostic overlap and differences among correlates. *Journal of the American Academy of Child and Adolescent Psychiatry, 28*, 865–872.

Szatmari, P., Offord, D. R., & Boyle, M. (1989). Ontario Child Health Study: Prevalence of attention deficit disorder with hyperactivity. *Journal of Child Psychology and Psychiatry, 30*, 219–230.

Szatmari, P., Stelios, G., Bryson, S., Zwaigenbaum, L., Roberts, W., Mahoney, W., et al. (2006). Investigating the structure of the restricted, repetitive behaviors and interests domain of autism. *Journal of Child Psychology and Psychiatry, 47*, 582–590.

TADS (Treatment for Adolescents with Depression Study Team, US). (2004). Fluoxeting, cognitive behavioral therapy, and their combination for adolescents with depression: Treatment for Adolescents with Depression Study (TADS) randomized controlled trial. *Journal of American Medical Association, 292*, 807–820.

Tanofsky-Krafft, M., Yanovski, S., Wilfley, D. E., Marmarosh, C., Morgan, C., & Yanovski, J. (2004). Eating-disordered behaviors, body fat, and psychopathology in overweight and normal-weight children. *Journal of Consulting and Clinical Psychology, 72*, 53–61.

Taylor, B., Miller, E., Lingam, R., et al. (2002). Measles, mumps, and rubella vaccination and bowel problems or developmental regression in children with autism: Population study. *British Medical Journal, 324*, 393–396.

Taylor, M. J. (2000). The influence of self-efficacy on alcohol use among American Indians. *Cultural Diversity and Ethnic Minority Psychology, 6*, 152–167.

Taylor, T. K., Schmidt, S., Pepler, D., & Hodgins, H. (1998). A comparison of eclectic treatment with Webster–Stratton's Parents and Children Series in a children's mental health center: A randomized control trial. *Behavior Therapy, 29*, 221–240.

Teeter, P. A., & Semrud-Clikeman, M. (1997). *Child Neuropsychological Assessment and Intervention*. Boston: Allyn & Bacon.

Teplin, L. A., Abram, K. M., McClelland, G. M., Dulcan, M. K., & Meride, A. A (2002). Psychiatric disorders in youth in juvenile detention. *Archives of General Psychiatry, 59*, 1133–1143.

Thapar, A., Harold, G., & McGuffin, P. (1998). Life events and depressive symptoms in childhood—shared genes or shared adversity? A research note. *Journal of Child Psychology & Psychiatry, 39*, 1153–1158.

Thase, M. E., Jindal, R., & Howland, R. H. (2002). Biological aspects of depression. In I. H. Gotlib & C. L. Hammen (Eds.), *Handbook of depression* (pp. 192–218). New York: Guilford.

Thatcher, R., Lyon. G., Rumsey, J., & Krasnegor, J. (1996). *Developmental neuroimaging*. San Diego, CA: Academic Press.

Thomas, A., & Chess, S. (1977). *Temperament and development*. New York: Brunner/Mazel.

Thompson, J. K., Coovert, M. D., Richards, K. J., & Johnson, S., Cattarin, J. (1995). Development of body image, eating disturbance, and general psychological functioning in female adolescence: Covariance structure modeling and longitudinal investigations. *International Journal of Eating Disorders, 18*, 221–236.

Thompson, J. K., Heinberg,L. J., Altabe, M., & Tanteleff-Dunn, S. (1999). *Exacting beauty: Theory, assessment, and treatment of body image disturbance*. Washington, DC: APA.

Thompson, S. (1997). *Nonverbal learning disorders*. Retrieved September 12, 2007, from http://www. nldontheweb. org

Tillman, R., Geller, B., & Craney, J. L. (2003). Temperament and character factors in a prepubertal and early adolescent bipolar disorder phenotype compared to attention deficit hyperactive and normal controls. *Journal of Child and Adolescent Psychopharmacology, 13*, 5231–5243.

Torgesen, J. K. (2000). Individual differences in response to early interventions in reading: The lingering problem of treatment resisters. *Learning Disabilities Research & Practice, 1*, 55–64.

Tremblay, R. E., Japel, C., Perusse, D., McDuff, P., Boivin, M., Zoccolillo, M., et al. (1999). The search for the age of "onset" of physical aggression: Rousseau and Bandura revisited. *Criminal Behavior and Mental Health, 9*, 8–23.

Tremblay, R. E., LeMarquand, D., & Vitaro, F. (1999). The prevention of oppositional defiant disorder and conduct disorder. In H. C. Quay & A. E. Hogan (Eds.), *Handbook of disruptive behavior disorders* (pp. 525–558). New York: Kluwer.

Tremblay, R. E., Vitaro, F., Bertrand, L., LeBlanc, M., Beauchesne, H., Boileau, H., et al. (1992). Parent and child training to prevent early onset of delinquency: The Montreal Longitudinal-Experimental Study. In J. McCord & R. E. Tremblay (Eds.), *Preventing antisocial behavior: Interventions from birth through adolescence* (pp. 117–138). New York: Guilford.

Trommer, B. L., Hoeppner, J. B., Rosenberg, R. S., Armstrong, K. J., & Rothstein, J. A. (1988). Sleep disturbances in children with attention deficit disorder. *Annals of Neurology, 4*, 35.

Troisi, A., DiLorenzo, G., Alcini, S., Nanni, R. C., DiPasquale, C., & Siracusano, A. (2006). Body dissatisfaction in women with eating disorders: Relationship to early separation anxiety and insecure attachment. *Psychosomatic Medicine, 68*, 449 September 12, 2007453.

Tsatsanis, K. D., Fuerst, D. R., & Rourke, B. P. (1997). Psychosocial dimensions of learning disabilities: External validation and relationships with age and academic functioning. *Journal of Learning Disabilities, 30*, 490–502.

Tsunokai, G. (2005). Beyond the lenses of the model minority myth: A descriptive portrait of Asian gang members. *Journal of Gang Research, 12*, 37–58.

Tucker, D. M., Leckman, J. F., & Scahill, L. A. (1996). A putative poststreptococcal case of OCD with chronic tic disorder, not otherwise specified. *Journal of the American Academy of Child & Adolescent Psychiatry, 35*(12), 1684–1691.

Tueth, M., Murphy, T. K., & Evans, D. L. (1998). Special considerations: Use of lithium in children, adolescents and elderly populations. *Journal of Clinical Psychiatry, 59*, 66–73.

Urberg, K. A., Degirmencioglu, S. M., & Pilgrim, C. (1997). Close friend and group influence on adolescent cigarette smoking and alcohol use, *Developmental Psychology 33*, 834–844

Valiente, C., Eisenberg, N., Smith, C. L., Reiser, M., Fabes, R., Losoya, S., et al. (2003). The relations of effortful control and reactive control to children's externalizing problems : A longitudinal assessment. *Journal of Personality, 71*, 1171–1196.

Valleni-Basile, L. A., Garrison, C. Z., Jackson, K. I., Waller, J. L., McKeown, R. E., Addy, C. L., et al. (1995). Family and psychosocial predictors of obsessive-compulsive disorder in a community sample of young adolescents. *Journal of Child and Family Studies, 4*, 193–206.

van der Kolk, B. (2005). Developmental trauma disorder: Toward a rational diagnosis for children with complex trauma histories. *Psychiatric Annals, 35*, 401–408.

van der Kolk, B., Rothe, S., Pelcovitz, D., Sunday, S., & Spinazzola, J. (2005). Disorders of extreme stress: The empirical foundation of a complex adaptation to trauma. *Journal of Traumatic Stress, 18*, 389–399.

Vander Wal, J. S., & Thelen, M. H. (2000). Predictors of body image dissatisfaction in elementary-age school girls. *Eating Behaviors, 1*, 105 –122.

Van Krevelen, D. A. (1971). Early infantile autism and autistic psychopathy. *Journal of Autism and Child Schizophrenia, 1*(1), 82–86.

Vasey, M. W. (1993). Development and cognition in childhood anxiety: The example of worry. *Advances in Clinical Child Psychology, 15*, 1–39.

Vasey, M. W., & Dadds, M. R. (2001). *The developmental psychopathology of anxiety*. New York: Oxford University Press.

Vaughn, S., & Hogan, A. (1994). The social competence of students with learning disabilities over time: A within-individual examination. *Journal of Learning Disabilities, 27*, 292–303.

Vendlinski, M., Silk, J. S., Shaw, D. S. & Lane, T. J. (2006). Ethnic differences in relations between family process and child internalizing problems. *Journal of Child Psychology and Psychiatry, 47* (9). 960–969.

Versi, M. (1995). Differential effects of cognitive behavior modification on seriously emotionally disturbed adolescents exhibiting internalizing or externalizing problems. *Journal of Child and Family Studies, 4*, 279–292.

Vicari, S. (2006). Motor development and neuropsychological patterns in persons with Down syndrome. *Behavior Genetics, 36*, 355–364.

Vicari, S., Bellucci, S., & Carlesimo, G. A. (2005). Differential pattern of impairments in Williams and Down syndromes. *Developmental Medicine & Child Neurology, 47*. 305–311.

Vigil, J. D. (2002). *A rainbow of gangs: Street cultures in a mega-city*. Austin TX: University of Texas Press.

Vigil, J. D., & Yun, S. C. (1990). Vietnamese youth gangs in southern California . In T. Huff (Ed.), *Gangs in California*. Beverly Hills, CA: Sage.

Vik, P. W., Brown, S. A., & Myers, M. G. (1997). Adolescent substance abuse problems. In E. J. Mash & L. G. Terdal (Eds), *Assessment of childhood disorders* (pp. 717–748). New York: Guilford.

Vitaro, F., Barker, E. D., Boivin, M., Brendgen, M., & Tremblay, R. E. (2006). Do early difficult temperament and harsh parenting differentially predict reactive and proactive aggression? *Journal of Abnormal Child Psychology, 34*, 685–695.

Vohra, S. (2006). Sowing seeds of happiness through value inculcation in adolescents. *Psychological Studies, Special Issue: Psychology of Health and Well-Being, 51*, 183–186.

Volkmar, F. R., Cook, E. H., Jr., Pomeroy, J., Realmuto, G., & Tanguay, P. (1999). Practice parameters for the assessment and treatment of children, adolescents, and adults with autism and other pervasive developmental disorders. *Journal of the American Academy of Child & Adolescent Psychiatry, 38*, 32S–54S.

Volkmar, F. R., & Klin, A. (2000). Diagnostic issues in Asperger syndrome. In A. Klin, F. R. Volkmar, & S. S. Sparrow (Eds.), *Asperger syndrome* (pp. 25–71). New York: Guilford.

Volkmar, F. R., Klin, A., Marans, W. & Cohen, D. (1997). Childhood disintegrative disorder. In D. Cohen & F. R. Volkmar (Eds.). *Handbook of autism and pervasive developmental disorders* (2nd ed.; pp. 47–59). New York: Wiley.

Volkmar, F. R., Klin, A., Siegel, B., Szatmari, P., Lord. C., Campbell, M., et al. (1994). Field trial for autistic disorder in DSM–IV. *American Journal of Psychiatry, 151*(9), 1361–1367.

Von Bergen, C. W., Soper, B., Rosenthal, G. T., Cox, S. J., & Fullerton, R. (1999). When helping hurts: Negative effects of benevolent care. *Journal of the American Psychiatric Nurses Association, 5*(4), 134–136.

von Ranson, K. M., Iacono, W. G., & McGue, M. (2002). Disordered eating and substance use in an epidemiological sample: I. Associations within individuals. *International Journal of Eating Disorders, 31*, 389–403.

Vreugdenhil, C., Van Den Brink, W., Wouters, L. F. & Doreleijers, D. (2003). Substance use, substance use disorders, and comorbidity patterns in a representatiave sample of incarcerated male Dutch adolescents. *Journal of Nervous Mental Disorders, 91*, 372–378.

Wagner, B. M., & Compas, B. E. (1990). Gender, instrumentality and expressivity: Moderators of the relation between stress and psychological symptoms during adolescence. *American Journal of Community Psychology, 18*, 383–406.

Waldron, H. B. (1997). Adolescent substance abuse and family therapy outcome: A review of randomized trials. In T. H. Ollendick & R. J. Prinz (Eds.), *Advances in clinical child psychology* (vol. 19; pp. 199–234). New York: Plenum.

Waldron, H. B., & Kern-Jones, S. (2004). Treatment of substance abuse disorders in children and adolescents. In P. M. Barrett & T. H. Ollendick (Eds.), *Handbook of interventions that work with children and adolescents: Prevention and treatment* (pp. 329–342). Chichester, UK: Wiley.

Walker, H. M., & McConnell, S. (1988). *Walker-McConnell Scale of Social Competence and School Adjustment.* Austin, TX: PRO-ED.

Walker, L. S., Garber, J., & Greene, J. W. (1991). Psychosocial correlates of recurrent childhood pain: a comparison of pediatric patients with recurrent abdominal pain, organic illness and psychiatric disorders. *Journal of Abnormal Child Psychology, 102*, 248–258.

Wallace, J., & Muroff, J. (2002). Preventing substance abuse among African American children and hyouth: Race differences in risk factor exposure and vulnerability. *Journal of Primary Prevention, 22*, 235–261.

Walls, M. L., Whitbeck, L. B., Hoyt, D. R., & Johnson, K. D. (2007). Early-onset alcohol use among Native American youth: Examining female caretaker influence. *Journal of Marriage and Family, 69*, 451–464.

Walrath, C., Nicherson, K., Crowel, R., & Leaf, P. (1998). Serving children with serious emotional disturbance in a system of care. Do mental health and non-mental health agency referrals look the same? *Journal of Emotional and Behavioral Disorders, 6*, 205–213.

Walters, A. S, Mandelbaum, D. E., Lewin, D. S, Kugler, S., England, S. J., & Miller, M. (2000). Dopaminergic therapy in children with restless legs/periodic limb movements in sleep and ADHD. *Pediatric Neurology, 22*, 182–186.

Walters, E. E., & Kendler, K. S. (1995). Anorexia nervosa and anorexia-like syndromes in a population based female twin sample. *American Journal of Psychiatry, 152*, 64–71.

Warren, S. L., Huston, L., Egeland, B., & Sroufe, L. A. (1997). Child and adolescent anxiety disorders and early attachment. *Journal of the American Academy of Child and Adolescent Psychiatry, 36*, 637–644.

Waters, T., Barrett, P., & March, J. (2001). Cognitive-behavioral family treatment of childhood obsessive-compulsive disorder: An open clinical trial. *American Journal of Psychotherapy, 55*, 372–387.

Watkins, C. E., Campbell, V., Nieberding, R., & Hallmark, R. (1995). Contemporary practice of psychological assessment by clinical psychologists. *Professional Psychology: Research and Practice, 26*(1), 54–60.

Watson C. H, Polzin, G. M, Calafat A. M, & Ashley D. L. (2003). Determination of the tar, nicotine, and carbon monoxide yields in the smoke of bidi cigarettes. *Nicotine & Tobacco Research, 5*(5), 747–753.

Watson, D., & Clark, L. A. (1984). Negative affectivity: The disposition to experience negative emotional states. *Psychological Bulletin, 96*, 465–490.

Webster-Stratton, C. (1981). Modification of mothers' behaviors and attitudes through video-tape modeling group discussion program. *Behavior Therapy, 12*, 634–642.

Webster-Stratton, C. (1984). Randomized trial of two parent-training programs for families with conduct-disordered children. *Journal of Consulting and Clinical Psychology, 52*, 666–678.

Webster-Stratton, C. (1990). Long-term follow-up of families with young conduct problem children: From preschool to grade school. *Journal of Clinical Child Psychology, 19*(2), 144–149.

Webster-Stratton, C., Kolpacoff, M., & Hollinsworth, T. (1988). Self-administered videotape therapy for families with conduct-problem children: Comparison with two cost-effective treatments and a control group. *Journal of Consulting and Clinical Psychology, 56*, 558–566.

Wechsler, D. (2002). *Manual for the Wechsler Preschool and Primary Scale of Intelligence, 3rd ed. (WPPSI–III).* San Antonio, TX: The Psychological Corporation.

Wechsler, D. (2003). *Manual for the Wechsler Intelligence Scale for Children, 4th ed. (WISC–IV).* San Antonio, TX: The Psychological Corporation.

Weddle, K. D., & McKenry, P. C. (1995). Self-destructive behaviors among Black youth: Suicide and homicide. In R. L. Taylor (Ed.), *African American youth: Their social and economic status in the United States* (pp. 271–286). New York: Praeger.

Weems, C. F., Saltzman, K. M., Reiss, A., & Carrion, V. G. (2003). A prospective test of the association between hyperarousal and emotional numbing in youth with a history of traumatic stress. *Journal of Clinical Child and Adolescent Psychology, 32*, 166–171.

Weinrott, M. R., Bauske, B. W., & Patterson, G. R., (1979). Systematic replication of a social learning approach to parent training. In P. P. O. Sjoden (Ed.), *Trends in behavior therapy* (pp. 331–351). New York: Academic Press.

Weiss, G., & Hechtman, L. (1993). *Hyperactive children grow up* (2nd ed.). New York: Guilford.

Weiss, M. D., Worling, D. E., & Wasdell, M. B. (2003). A chart review study of the Inattentive and Combined Types of ADHD. *Journal of Attention Disorders, 7*(1), 1–9.

Weissman, M. M., Wolk, S., Wickramaratne, P., Goldstein, R. B., Adams, P., & Greenwald, S., et al. (1999). Children with prepubertal-onset major depressive disorder and anxiety grown up. *Archives of General Psychiatry, 56*, 794–801.

Weisz, J. R., & Weiss, B. (1993). *Effects of psychotherapy with children and adolescents*. Thousand Oaks, CA: Sage.

Weisz, J. R., Weiss, B. B., Han, S. S., Granger, D. A., & Morton, E. (1995). Effects of psychotherapy with children and adolescents revisited: A meta-analysis of treatment outcome studies. *Psychological Bulletin, 117*, 450–468.

Weithorn, L. (1987). Informed consent for prevention research involving children: Legal and ethical issues. In J. A. Steinberg & M. M. Silverman (Eds.), *Preventing mental disorders: A research perspective* (pp. 226–242). Rockville, MD: NIMH.

Welsh, M., & Pennington, B. F. (1988). Assessing frontal lobe functioning in children: Views from developmental psychology. *Developmental Neuropsychology, 4*, 199–230.

Wender, P. H., Kety, S. S., Rosenthal, D., Schulsinger, F., Ortmann, J., & Lunde, I. (1986). Psychiatric disorders in the biological and adoptive families of adopted individuals with affective disorders. *Archives of General Psychiatry, 43*, 923–929.

Werner, E., & Smith, R. (1992*). Overcoming the odds*. Ithaca, NY: Cornell University Press.

Wever, C., & Phillips, N. (1994). *The secret problem*. Sydney, Australia: Shrink-Rap Press.

Whalen, C. K., Henker, B., Collins, B., Finck, D., & Dotemoto, S. (1979). A social ecology of hyperactive boys: Medication effects in systematically structured classroom environments. *Journal of Applied Behavior Analysis, 1*, 65–81.

Whitaker, A. (1992). An epidemiological study of anorectic and bulimic symptoms in adolescent girls: Implications ofr pediatricians. *Pediatric Annals 21*, 752–759.

Wichstrom, L. (1999). The emergence of gender difference in depressed mood during adolescence: The role of intensified gender socialization. *Developmental Psychology, 35*, 232–245.

Wiener, J. (2003). Resilience and Multiple Risks: A Response to Bernice Wong. *Learning Disabilities Research & Practice, 18* (2), 77–81.

Wigren, M., & Hansen, S. (2005). ADHD symptoms and insistence on sameness in Prader-Willi syndrome. *Journal of Intellectual Disability Research, 49*, 449–456.

Wilens, T., Biederman, J., Adamson, J., Monuteaux, M., Henin, A., Sgambati, S., et al. (2007). Association of bipolar substance use disorders in parents of adolescents with bipolar disorder. *Biological Psychiatry, 62*, 129–134.

Wilens, T., Biederman, J., Forkner, P., Ditterline, J., Morris, M., Moore, H., et al. (2003). Patterns of comorbidity and dysfunction in clinically referred preschool and school-age children with bipolar disorder. *Journal of Child and Adolescent Psychopharmacology, 13*, 495–505.

Wilens, T. Biederman, J., Kwon, A., Ditterline, J., Forkner, P., Chase, R., et al. (2004). Risk for substance use disorders in adolescents with bipolar disorder. *Journal of the American Academy of Child and Adolescent Psychiatry, 43*, 1380–1286.

Wilensky, D. S., Ginsberg, G., Altman, M., Tulchinsky, T. H., Yishay, F. S., & Auerbach, J. (1996). A community based study of failure to thrive in Isreal. *Archives of Disease in Childhood, 75*, 145–148.

Willcutt, E. G., Doyle, A. E., Nigg, J. T., Faraone, S., & Pennington, B. F. (2005). Validity of the executive function theory of ADHD: A meta-analytic review. *Biological Psychiatry, 57*, 774–803.

Williams, R. J., & Chang, S. Y. (2000). A comprehensive and comparative review of adolescent substance abuse treatment outcomes. *Clinical Psychology: Science and Practice, 7*, 138–166.

Williams, S., Anderson, J., McGee, R., & Silva, P. A. (1990). Risk factors for behavioral and emotional disorder in preadolescent children. *Journal of the American Academy of Child and Adolescent Psychiatry, 29*, 413–419.

Williams, T., & Kornblum, W. (1985). *Growing up poor*. Lexington MA: Lexington.

Williamson, D. et al. (1995). Structural equation modeling of risk factors for the development of eating disorder symptoms in female athletes. *International Journal of Eating Disorders, 17*, 387–393.

Wilmshurst, L. (2002). Treatment programs for youth with emotional and behavioral disorders: An outcomes study of two alternate approaches. *Mental Health Services Research, 4*, 85–96.

Wilmshurst, L. (2003). *Child and adolescent psychopathology: A casebook*. Thousand Oaks, CA: Sage.

Wilmshurst, L., & Brue, A. (2005). *A parents guide to special education*. New York: AMACOM.

Wilson, V. L. (1987). Statistical and psychometric issues surrounding severe discrepancy. *Learning Disabilities, 3*, 21–23.

Wilson, W. J., & Aponte, R. (1985). Urban poverty. *Annual Review of Sociology, 11*, 231–258.

Windle, M., & Davies, P. T. (1999). Depression and heavy alcohol use among adolescents: Concurrent and prospective relations. *Development and Psychopathology, Special issue: Developmental approaches to substance use and abuse, 11*, 823–855.

Windle, M., & Tubman, J. G. (1999). Children of alcoholics. In W. K. Silverman & T. H.Ollendick (Eds.), *Developmental issues in the clinical treatment of children* (pp. 393–414). Boston: Allyn & Bacon.

Wing, L., & Attwood, A. (1987). Syndrome of autism and atypical development. In D. Cohen & A. Donnellan (Eds.), *Handbook of autism and pervasive developmental disorders* (pp. 3–19). New York: Wiley.

Winters, K. C. (2001). Assessing adolescent substance use problems and other areas of functioning: State of the art. In P. M. Monti, S. M. Colby, & T. A. O'Leary, (Eds.), *Adolescents, alcohol, and substance abuse: Reaching teens through brief interventions* (pp. 80–108). New York: Guilford.

Winters, K. C., Latimer, W. W., & Stinchfield, R. (2001). Assessing adolescent substance use. In E. F. Wagner & H. B. Waldron (Eds.), *Innovations in adolescent substance abuse interventions* (pp. 1–29). Oxford: Elsevier Science.

Winters, K. C., Stinchfield, R. D., Henly, G. A., & Schwartz, R. H. (1992). Validity of adolescent self-report of alcohol and other drug involvement. *International Journal of the Addictions, 25*, 1379–1395.

Wirt, R. D., Lachar, D., Seat, P. D., & Broen, W. (2001). *Personality inventory for children* (2nd ed.). Los Angeles: Western Psychological Services.

Wolery, M., & Garfinkle, A. N. (2002). Measures in intervention research with young children who have autism. *Journal of Autism and Developmental Disorders, 32*, 463–478.

Wolpe, J. (1958). *Psychotherapy by reciprocal inhibition.* Stanford, CA: Stanford University Press.

Wolraich, M. L. (2000). *Attention deficit hyperactivity disorder: Current diagnosis and treatment.* Paper presented at the American Academy of Pediatrics annual meeting. Retrieved October 2004 from http://www. medscape. com/viewarticle/420198

Wolraich, M. L., Wibbelsman, C., Brown, E. E., Evans, S. W., Gotlieb, E. M., Knight, R. R., et al. (2005). Attention deficit hyperactivity disorder among adolescents: A review of the diagnosis, treatment, and clinical implications. *Pediatrics, 115*, 1734–1746.

Wonderlich, S. A., Mitchell, J. E., Peterson, C. B., & Crow, S. (2001). Integrative cognitive therapy for bulimic behavior. In R. H. Striegel-Moore & L. Smolak (Eds.), *Eating Disorders: Innovative Directions in Research and Practice*, 173–195. Washington, DC: APA.

Wonderlich, S. A., Peterson, C. B., Mitchell, J. E., & Crow, S. (2000). Integrative cognitive therapy for bulimic behavior. *Comparative treatments for eating disorders* (pp. 258–282). New York: Springer.

Wong, B. (1978). The effects of directive cues on the organization of memory and recall in good and poor readers. *Journal of Educational Research, 72*, 32–38.

Wong, M. G. (1995). Chinese Americans. In P. G. Min (Ed.), *Asian Americans: Contemporary trends and issues* (pp. 58–94). Beverly Hills, CA: Sage.

Woodcock, R. W., McGrew, K. S., & Mather, N. (2001). *The Woodcock-Johnson Cognitive III.* Itasca, IL: Riverside

Wooley, S. C., & Wooley, O. W. (1985). Intense outpatient and residential treatment for bulimia. In D. M. Garner & P. E., Garfinkel (Eds.), *Handbook of psychotherapy for anorexia nervosa and bulimia* (pp. 303–320). New York: Guilford.

World Health Organization. (1993). The *ICD–10* classification of mental and behavioral disorders. Clinical descriptions and diagnostic guidelines. Geneva, Switzerland: WHO.

Wozniak, J. (2003). Pediatric bipolar disorder: The new perspective on severe mood dysfunction in children. *Journal of Child and Adolescent Psychopharmacology, 13*, 449–451.

Wozniak, J. (2005). Recognizing and managing bipolar disorder in children. *Journal of Clinical Psychiatry, 66*(Suppl.1), 18–21.

Wozniak, J., Biederman, J., Kiely, K., Ablon, S., Faraone, S., Mundy, E., et al. (1995). Mania-like symptoms suggestive of childhood onset bipolar disorder in clinically referred children. *Journal of the American Academy of Child and Adolescent Psychiatry, 34*, 867–876.

Wozniak, J., Biederman, J., Kwon, A., Mick, E., Faraone, S., Orlovsky, K., et al. (2005). How cardinal are cardinal symptoms in pediatric bipolar disorder? An examination of clinical correlates. *Biological Psychiatry, 58*, 583–588.

Wright, C., & Birks, E. (2000). Risk factors for failure to thrive: A population-based survey. *Child: Care, Health and Development, 26*, 5–16.

Yeargin-Allsopp, M., Rice, C., Karapurkar, T., Doembberg, J., Boyle, C., & Murphy, C. (2003). Prevalence of autism in a U. S. metropolitan area. *Journal of the American Medical Association, 289*, 49–55.

Yeh, C. J., & Huang, K. (2000). Interdependence in ethnic identity and self: Implications for theory and practice. *Journal of Counseling and Development, 78*, 420–429.

Yeh, M., Eastman, K., & Cheung, M. K. (1994). Children and adolescents in community health centers: Does the ethnicity or the language of the counselor matter? *Journal of Community Psychology, 22*, 153–163.

Yeh, M., McCabe, K., Hurlburt, M., Hough, R., Hazen, A., Culver, S., et al. (2002). Referral sources, diagnoses and service types of youth in public outpatient mental health care: A focus on ethnic minorities. *Journal of Behavioral Health Services & Research, 29*(1), 45–60.

Yeh, M., Takeuchi, D. T., & Sue, D. (1994). Asian-American children treated in the mental health system: A comparison of parallel and mainstream outpatient service centers. *Journal of Clinical Child Psychology, 23*, 5–12.

Yellowbird, M., & Snipp, C. M. (2002). American Indian families. In R. L. Taylor (Ed.), *Minority families in the United States: A multicultural perspective* (pp. 227–249). Upper Saddle River, NJ: Prentice Hall.

Yorbik, O., Birmaher, B., Axelson, D., Williamson, D., & Ryan, N. (2004). Clinical characteristics of depressive symptoms in children and adolescents with major depressive disorder. *Journal of Clinical Psychiatry, 65*, 1654–1659.

Yoshikawa, H. (1994). Prevention as cumulative protection: Effects of early family support and education on chronic delinquency and its risks. *Psychological Bulletin, 115*, 28–54.

Youngstrom, E. A., Findling, R., Youngstrom, J. K., & Calabrese, J. R. (2005). Toward an evidence-based assessment of pediatric bipolar disorder. *Journal of Clinical Child and Adolescent Psychology, 34*, 433–448.

Yule, W. (1998). Posttraumatic stress disorder in children and its treatment. In T. W. Miller (Ed.), *Children of trauma: Stressful life events and their effects on children and adolescents* (pp. 219–243). Madison, CT: International Universities Press.

Zahn-Waxler, C., Iannotti, R., Cummings, E. M., & Denham, S. (1990). Antecedents of problem behaviors in children of depressed mothers. *Development and Psychopathology, 2*, 271–291.

Zahn-Waxler, C., Radke-Yarrow, M., Wagner, E., & Chapman, M. (1992). Development of concern for others. *Developmental Psychology, 28*, 126–136.

Zametkin, A., Liebner, L. L., Fitzgerald, G. A. (1993). Brain metabolism in teenagers with attention deficit hyperactivity disorder. *Archives of General Psychiatry, 50*, 333–340.

Zaubler, T., & Katon, W. (1998). Panic disorder in the general medical setting. *Journal of Psychosomatic Research, 44*(1), 25–42.

Zeanah, C. H., Boris, N. W., & Larrieu, J. A. (1997). Infant development and developmental risk: A review of the past 10 years. *Journal of the American Academy of Child and Adolescent Psychiatry, 36*, 165–178.

Zinn, M. B., & Wells, B. (2000). Diversity within Latino families: New lessons for family social science. In D. H. Demo, K. R. Allen, & M. A. Fine (Eds.), *Handbook of family diversity* (pp. 252–273). New York: Oxford.

Zoccolillo, M. (1992). Co-occurrence of conduct disorder and its adult outcomes with depressive and anxiety disorders: A review. *Journal of the American Academy of Child & Adolescent Psychiatry, 31*(3), 547–556.

Zohar, A. H., & Bruno, R. (1997). Normative and pathological obsessive-compulsive behavior and ideation in childhood: A question of timing. *Journal of Child Psychology and Psychiatry, 38,* 993–999.

Zwaanswijk, M., van der Ende, J., & Verhaak, P. F. M. (2003). Factors associated with adolescent mental health service need and utilization. *Journal of the American Academy of Child and Adolescent Psychiatry, 42,* 692–700.

Index

Page numbers in italics refer to figures or tables.